Development Across the Life Span

Ninth Edition

Robert S. Feldman
University of Massachusetts Amherst

Senior Producer and Strategy Manager: Kelli Strieby
Content Producer: Lisa Mafrici
Content Developer: Cathy Murphy
Portfolio Manager Assistant: Caroline Fassett
Senior Executive Product Marketing Manager: Christopher Brown
Senior Field Marketing Manager: Debi Henion
Content Producer Manager: Amber Mackey
Content Development Manager: Marita Sermolins Bley
Art/Designer: Integra-Chicago
Digital Studio Course Producer: Lindsay Verge
Full-Service Project Manager: Integra-Chicago
Compositor: Integra-Chicago
Printer/Binder: LSC Communications, Inc.
Cover Printer: LSC Communications, Inc.
Cover Art Director: Cate Rickard Barr
Cover Designer: Gary Pikovsky/Piko Design LLC
Cover Images: A-Digit/Getty Images

Library of Congress Cataloging-in-Publication data

Names: Feldman, Robert S. (Robert Stephen), author.
Title: Development across the life span / by Robert S. Feldman.
Description: Ninth Edition. | New York, NY : Pearson, [2019] | Revised edition of the author's Development across the life span, [2017] | Includes bibliographical references and index.
Identifiers: LCCN 2018050234 | ISBN 9780135188026 (pbk. : alk. paper)
Subjects: LCSH: Developmental psychology—Textbooks. | Human Development. | Psychology.
Classification: LCC BF713 .F45 2019 | DDC 155—dc23
LC record available at https://lccn.loc.gov/2018050234

Access Code Card
ISBN 10: 0-13-519804-6
ISBN 13: 978-0-13-519804-9

Revel Combo Card
ISBN 10: 0-13-544770-4
ISBN 13: 978-0-13-544770-3

Rental Edition
ISBN 10: 0-13-518802-4
ISBN 13: 978-0-13-518802-6

Loose-Leaf Edition
ISBN 10: 0-13-517357-4
ISBN 13: 978-0-13-517357-2

Instructor's Review Copy
ISBN 10: 0-13-517354-X
ISBN 13: 978-0-13-517354-1

Brief Contents

Contents

PART FOUR The Middle Childhood Years

PART FIVE Adolescence

18 Social and Personality Development in Late Adulthood 581

19 Death and Dying 610

Preface

This book tells a story: the story of our lives, and our parents' lives, and the lives of our children. It is the story of human beings and how they get to be the way they are.

Unlike any other area of study, lifespan development speaks to us in a very personal sense. It covers the range of human existence from its beginnings at conception to its inevitable ending at death. It is a discipline that deals with ideas and concepts and theories, but one that above all has at its heart people—our fathers and mothers, our friends and acquaintances, our very selves.

Development Across the Life Span seeks to capture the discipline in a way that sparks, nurtures, and shapes readers' interest. It is meant to excite students about the field, draw them into its way of looking at the world, and build their understanding of developmental issues. By exposing readers to both the current content and the promise inherent in lifespan development, the text is designed to keep interest in the discipline alive long after students' formal study of the field has ended.

Overview of the Ninth Edition

Development Across the Life Span, Ninth Edition—like its predecessors—provides a broad overview of the field of human development. It covers the entire range of the human life, from the moment of conception through death. The text furnishes a broad, comprehensive introduction to the field, covering basic theories and research findings as well as highlighting current applications outside the laboratory. It covers the life span chronologically, encompassing the prenatal period, infancy and toddlerhood, the preschool years, middle childhood, adolescence, early and middle adulthood, and late adulthood. Within these periods, it focuses on physical, cognitive, and social and personality development.

The book seeks to accomplish the following four major goals:

- First and foremost, the book is designed to provide a broad, balanced overview of the field of lifespan development. It introduces readers to the theories, research, and applications that constitute the discipline, examining both the traditional areas of the field and more recent innovations. It pays particular attention to the applications developed by lifespan development specialists, demonstrating how lifespan developmentalists use theory, research, and applications to help solve significant social problems.
- The second goal of the text is to explicitly tie development to students' lives. Findings from the study of lifespan development have a significant degree of relevance to students, and this text illustrates how these findings can be applied in a meaningful, practical sense. Applications are presented in a contemporaneous framework, including current news items, timely world events, and contemporary uses of lifespan development that draw readers into the field. Numerous descriptive scenarios and vignettes reflect everyday situations in people's lives, explaining how they relate to the field.
- The third goal is to highlight both the commonalities and the diversities of today's multicultural society. Consequently, the book incorporates material relevant to diversity in all its forms—racial, ethnic, gender, sexual orientation, religion, and cultural—throughout every chapter. In addition, every chapter has at least one *Developmental Diversity and Your Life* box. These features explicitly consider how cultural factors relevant to development both unite and diversify our contemporary global society.
- Finally, the fourth goal is one that is implicit in the other three: making the field of lifespan development engaging, accessible, and interesting to students. Lifespan development is a joy both to study and to teach because so much of it has direct, immediate meaning to our lives. Because all of us are involved in our own developmental paths, we are tied in very personal ways to the content areas covered by the book. *Development Across the Life Span*, then, is meant to engage and nurture this interest, planting a seed that will develop and flourish throughout readers' lifetimes.

In accomplishing these goals, the book strives to be user friendly. Written in a direct, conversational voice, it duplicates as much as possible a dialogue between author and student. The text is meant to be understood and mastered on its own by students of every level of interest and motivation. To that end, it includes a variety of pedagogical features that promote mastery of the material and encourage critical thinking.

In short, the book blends and integrates theory, research, and applications, focusing on the breadth of human development. Furthermore, rather than attempting to provide a detailed historical record of the field, it focuses on the here and now, drawing on the past where appropriate, but with a view toward delineating the field as it now stands and the directions toward which it is evolving. Similarly, while providing descriptions of classic studies, the emphasis is more on current research findings and trends.

Development Across the Life Span is meant to be a book that readers will want to keep in their own personal libraries, one that they will take off the shelf when considering problems related to that most intriguing of questions: How do people come to be the way they are?

Special Features

- **Chapter-Opening Prologues.** Each chapter begins with a short vignette, describing an individual or a situation that is relevant to the basic developmental issues being discussed in the chapter.
- **Looking Ahead Sections.** These opening sections orient readers to the topics to be covered, bridging the opening prologue with the remainder of the chapter.
- **Learning Objectives.** Each major section includes explicit learning objectives. These numbered learning objectives provide a means for instructors to evaluate student mastery of specific content. They also anchor the module reviews and chapter summary.
- **From Research to Practice.** Each chapter includes a section that describes current developmental research applied to everyday problems, helping students to see the impact of developmental research throughout society. Many are new in this edition. Each *From Research to Practice* box concludes with a Shared Writing prompt, which students can respond to, as well as respond to peers' responses, and instructors can moderate.
- **Developmental Diversity and Your Life.** Every chapter has at least one *Developmental Diversity and Your Life* section incorporated into the text. These sections highlight issues relevant to today's multicultural society.
- **Running Glossary.** Key terms are defined in the margins of the page on which the term is presented.
- **Development in Your Life.** Every chapter includes information on specific uses that can be derived from research conducted by developmental investigators. These boxes, formerly titled *Are You an Informed Consumer of Development?*, are now titled *Development and Your Life.*
- **Review and Journal Prompt Sections.** Interspersed throughout each chapter are three module reviews—short recaps of the chapter's main points keyed to learning objectives—as well as Journal Prompts designed to elicit critical thinking about the subject matter through written responses.
- **End-of-Chapter Material.** Each chapter ends with a summary and an epilogue that refers back to the opening prologue and that ties the chapter together. The Looking Back summary is keyed to the chapter's learning objectives.
- **Career Prompts.** Students will encounter frequent questions throughout the text designed to show the applicability of the material to a variety of professions, including those in the education, nursing, social work, and health care sectors.
- **Putting It All Together.** In end-of-part integrative concept maps, a short vignette is presented, and students are asked to consider the vignette from both their point of view and the points of view of parents, educators, health care workers, social workers, and so on.

What's New in the Ninth Edition?

The revision includes a number of significant changes and additions.

One figure in each chapter now includes a *Thinking About the Data* prompt, which encourages the reader to think about what is behind the data they see in graphs and tables. This critical thinking question in the figure caption is a jumping-off point to a data-driven Social Explorer activity in Revel.

Furthermore, almost all *From Research to Practice* boxes—which describe a contemporary developmental research topic and its applied implications—are new to this edition. Boxes formerly called *Are You an Informed Consumer of Development* are now titled *Development in Your Life.*

In addition, module reviews are now tied to learning objectives to help students organize section reviewing around the objectives.

Finally, the ninth edition of *Development Across the Life Span* incorporates a significant amount of new and updated information. For instance, advances in such areas as behavioral genetics, brain development, evolutionary perspectives, and cross-cultural approaches to development receive expanded and new coverage. Dozens of figures and photos have been revised or replaced, and hundreds of new citations have been added, with most of those from articles and books published in the last few years.

New topics were added to every chapter. The following sample of new and revised topics featured in this edition provides a good indication of the currency of the revision:

Chapter 1, Introduction to Lifespan Development

- Revised prologue on in vitro fertilization
- Additional material on Vygotsky and scaffolding
- Revised material on culture, ethnicity, and race, including two new *Developmental Diversity and Your Life* boxes:
    - "How Culture, Ethnicity, and Race Influence Development" discusses cultural, ethnic, racial, socioeconomic, and gender considerations in the study of development.

- "Choosing Research Participants Who Represent the Diversity of Humanity" emphasizes the importance of truly representing the general population when studying development.
- Table 1-1, Approaches to Lifespan Development, now includes sex and gender topics in the questions asked by development researchers
- Refined explanation of critical period
- Figure 1-1 on brain differences in a person with autism
- Refined explanation of cognitive neuroscience approaches
- Updated Figure 1-6 on longitudinal vs. cross-sectional research
- Figure 1-13 on the scientific method
- Using lifespan development research for public policy

Chapter 2, The Start of Life: Prenatal Development

- Prologue on genetic testing
- *From Research to Practice* box on transgenerational epigenetic inheritance
- Updated Table 2-1 on the genetic basis of various disorders
- Updated Table 2-3 on DNA-based genetic tests
- Cultural and religious concerns about reproductive technologies
- Abortion statistics
- Cross-cultural differences in abortion
- Statistics on percentage of women facing physical abuse during pregnancy
- Smoking as the single most preventable cause of death of infants and mothers
- Rate of twins by geographical region
- Miscarriage aftermaths
- Opioid use during pregnancy
- Revised art in Figures 2-3, 2-4, 2-6

Chapter 3, Birth and the Newborn Infant

- Prologue on premature infants
- *From Research to Practice* box on pre- and postpartum depression effects on child
- *Developmental Diversity and Your Life* box on the cultural differences in perception of pain of childbirth
- Statistics on length of hospital stay
- Statistics on survival rates for very preterm babies
- Figure 3-2 on cross-country comparison of length of hospital stay following delivery
- Figure 3-3 on international rates of infant mortality
- Figure 3-5 on rates of cesarean deliveries worldwide
- Figure 3-6 on rates of infant mortality in the United States by race
- Statistics on epidural use
- Revised Table 3-3 on childbirth-related parental leave policies

Chapter 4, Physical Development in Infancy

- Prologue on early first steps
- *From Research to Practice* box on SIDS prevention
- Cardboard box as the best place for an infant to sleep
- Statistics on shaken baby syndrome, with new Figure 4-5 showing damage to the brain of a shaken baby
- Introduction of SUID, along with the discussion of SIDS
- Figure 4-7 on reduction in instances of SIDS and SUID
- Benefits of co-sleeping
- Clarification of timing of breastfeeding and introduction of solid foods
- Causes of cultural differences in sleep patterns in infants
- Figure 4-9, world hunger map
- Updated terminology uses "intellectual disability" in place of "mental retardation"
- Abilities to distinguish rhythms of languages prenatally
- Brain plasticity in infancy

Chapter 5, Cognitive Development in Infancy

- Prologue on early language use
- *Developmental Diversity and Your Life* box on infants' first words
- *From Research to Practice* box on efficacy of accelerating infants' cognitive development
- Infant attention and representational competence related to later intelligence
- Babbling following the prelinguistic stage of cooing
- Infants' use of general cognitive abilities underlying development of language competence
- Brain growth and infantile amnesia
- Change in key term from scheme to schema
- Memory and hippocampus
- Supplemented description of the learning theory approach to language development

Chapter 6, Social and Personality Development in Infancy

- Prologue on observational learning in infants
- *From Research to Practice* box on evidence for racial prejudice in infants
- Motor neurons and goal-directed behavior
- Updated statistics on poverty and race
- Updated statistics on unwed mothers
- Update on parental demographics
- More on choosing an appropriate daycare situation
- *Developmental Diversity and Your Life* box on brain lateralization
- Figure 6-6 on child care choices
- Infants' understanding of morality
- Data on child care delivery modalities
- Mirror-and-rouge technique
- Clarified and expanded explanation of mirror neurons

Chapter 7, Physical and Cognitive Development in the Preschool Years

- Prologue on active toddler
- *From Research to Practice* box on the value of writing words by hand
- *Developmental Diversity and Your Life* box on brain lateralization, gender, and culture
- Figure 7-6 showing myelin development over time
- Revised growth charts
- Media and children, including:
  - Statistics on media use: Figure 7-14
  - Learning objective on media use
  - The influence of *Sesame Street*
  - Recommendations on media use by the American Academy of Pediatrics
  - New content on reducing media exposure prior to bedtime to help sleep
- Statistics on perceived health of children
- Just-right phenomenon in nutrition
- Weight, including:
  - Distinction between overweight and obese
  - Introduction of key term: BMI
  - Statistics on obesity
- Clarified distinction between syntax and grammar
- Distinction between Vygotsky and Piaget, including a new Table 7-1 comparing their theories
- Effects of lead poisoning, including the lead poisoning that occurred in Flint, Michigan
- New data on child abuse and neglect
- Additional signs of child abuse
- Change blindness

Chapter 8, Social and Personality Development in the Preschool Years

- Prologue on sibling personality differences
- *From Research to Practice* box on play and brain development
- More on development of socioeconomic awareness
- Trans-racial families
- Value of rough-and-tumble play on brain development
- Transgender preschoolers
- Hispanic parental values
- Warning signs of sexual abuse

Chapter 9, Physical and Cognitive Development in Middle Childhood

- Prologue on cognitive development and math
- *From Research to Practice* box on the value of counting with fingers in learning math
- *Developmental Diversity and Your Life* box, "The Impact of Culture on Growth"
- Causes of racial differences in asthma rates
- Online safety
- Updated statistics on prevalence of obesity, including new Figure 9-2
- Figure 9-10 on languages spoken at home
- Accomplishments of profoundly gifted children
- Auditory processing disorder
- Dyscalculia
- Dysgraphia
- Nonverbal learning disabilities
- Long-term treatment effects for ADHD
- Updated definition of obesity
- Clarified definition of specific learning disorders
- Increase over time of prevalence in psychological disorders
- Incidence of psychological disorders in children
- Clarified definition of bilingualism

Chapter 10, Social and Personality Development in Middle Childhood

- Prologue on bullied child
- *From Research to Practice* box on children of gay, lesbian, and transsexual parents
- Increase in multigenerational families

- Social intelligence curricula
- Self-esteem and social media use
- Relaxation of the one-child policy in China
- *Developmental Diversity and Your Life* box on Asians and the "model minority" stereotype
- Children and number of parents, including a new Figure 10-4 on two-parent and single-parent families
- New statistics and Figure 10-5 on children in foster care
- Update on the U.S. Supreme Court ruling on same-sex marriage
- Categories of bullying
- Upward social comparison
- Self-care drawbacks

Chapter 11, Physical and Cognitive Development in Adolescence

- Prologue on body image
- New recommendations on HPV vaccine
- *Developmental Diversity and Your Life* box on academic disidentification and stereotype threat
- Figure 11-4 on physical activity among adolescent females
- Figure 11-5 on pruning of gray matter
- Learning objective on use of social media
- Figure 11-8 on social media use by adolescents
- Social media use and social competence
- Benefits of social media use
- Grade inflation
- *From Research to Practice* box on vaping and dripping
- Brain effects of binge drinking
- Opioid epidemic
- Marijuana use
- STIs among adolescents
- Statistics on incidence of AIDS

Chapter 12, Social and Personality Development in Adolescence

- Prologue on a teen inventor
- *From Research to Practice* box on sexting and social media
- Updated Figure 12-8 on age at which adolescents have sex for the first time
- Transgender individuals
- Supreme Court legalizing same-sex marriage
- Updated statistics and Figure 12-9 on teenage pregnancy rates
- Clarified description of Marcia's theory
- Suicide attempts in adolescents
- Differential rates of suicide in gays, lesbians, and transsexuals
- Native American suicide rates
- Suicide lifeline chat information
- Benefits of cross-race friendships
- New statistics on violent deaths in adolescence
- Online dating, flirting, and sexting
- Adolescent anxiety disorders
- Emerging adulthood

Chapter 13, Physical and Cognitive Development in Early Adulthood

- Prologue on college enrollment
- Figure 13-3 on obesity rates in early adulthood (United States)
- Figure 13-4 on obesity rates worldwide
- Revised Figure 13-6 on Schaie's stages
- Relationship between age and creativity
- *From Research to Practice* box on cognitive benefits of diversity
- Statistics on gender gap in college attendance
- Explanations for the high rate of dropping out of college
- Figure 13-9 on college attendance rates, by race
- Figure 13-10, income disparity between those with and without a college degree
- Figure 13-11 on mental illness in college students
- How psychological disorders are viewed cross-culturally

Chapter 14, Social and Personality Development in Early Adulthood

- Prologue on gay couple
- *From Research to Practice* box on the relationship between having children and being happy
- More on emerging adulthood
- Updated fertility data
- Figure 14-2, marriage choice funnel
- Updated divorce statistics
- Use of LinkedIn and Monster.com by job seekers
- Millennial generation and work
- Figure 14-10 on women's earnings as a proportion of men's earnings
- Figure 14-11 on job participation by gender
- Figure 14-12, occupational prestige—perceptions by age

Chapter 15, Physical and Cognitive Development in Middle Adulthood

- Prologue on middle-age runner
- Figure 15-3, Reported Frequency of Sexual Intercourse (by age)
- *From Research to Practice* box on mammogram guidelines
- *Developmental Diversity and Your Life* box on the experience of menopause symptoms across cultures
- Figure 15-5 on life expectancy and income
- Updated statistics on life expectancy for upper and lower 1 percent of income level
- Figure 15-7 on deaths worldwide from cardiovascular disease

Chapter 16, Social and Personality Development in Middle Adulthood

- Prologue on career changes
- *From Research to Practice* box on personality changes in adulthood
- Updates to causes of divorce
- Figure 16-4 on divorce rate for adults 50 and older
- Figure 16-5 on remarriage rates
- Multigenerational families
- How to avoid career burnout
- Table 16-2 on professions prone to burnout
- Figure 16-10 on women's participation in workforce
- Figure 16-11 on rates of immigration into the United States

Chapter 17, Physical and Cognitive Development in Late Adulthood

- Prologue on inventor
- *From Research to Practice* box on cognitive skills training in late adulthood
- Figure 17-1 on growing size of the late adulthood population
- Figure 17-4 on metabolism in older adults vs. younger adults
- Figure 17-5, data on vehicular crashes involving older adults vs. teens
- Lengthening telomeres
- New drug therapies for extending life
- Figure 17-10 on world's growing centenarian population
- Figure 17-15 on technology adoption in late adulthood

Chapter 18, Social and Personality Development in Late Adulthood

- Prologue on coupling in late adulthood
- *From Research to Practice* box on retirement approaches
- Socioemotional selectivity theory
- Figure 18-2 on poverty in late adulthood
- Figure 18-4 on living arrangements in late adulthood
- Figure 18-6 on perceived benefits of growing older

Chapter 19, Death and Dying

- Prologue on a good death
- *From Research to Practice* box on grief after spouse death
- Professional mourners in China
- Displays of grief in Egypt
- Additional ways of helping children deal with grief
- New statistics on assisted suicides and jurisdictions
- Treatment of dying across cultures
- Updated statistics on infant mortality in the United States and other countries
- Figure 19-4 on predictions of life span versus reality

Revel™

Revel is an interactive learning environment that deeply engages students and prepares them for class. Media and assessment integrated directly within the authors' narrative lets students read, explore interactive content, and practice in one continuous learning path. Thanks to the dynamic reading experience in Revel, students come to class prepared to discuss, apply, and learn from instructors and from each other.

Learn more about Revel:
www.pearson.com/revel

The ninth edition includes integrated videos and media content throughout, allowing students to explore topics more deeply at the point of relevancy. Revel makes the content come alive as students respond to "Myth or Truth" and "Fun Facts and a Lie" interactives. Each chapter also includes at least one "Trending Topic" feature, which explores cutting-edge research or current events.

Highly engaging interactives encourage student participation. Interactive scenarios invite students into "choose your own path"–type activities. Other interactives lead them through how a health care professional, counselor, teacher, or parent might react to a specific developmental situation or solve a problem. Students can also explore interactive figures using drag-and-drop and predictive graphing tools, as well as hotspot images.

Each chapter includes a *Thinking About the Data* prompt, which encourages the student to think about what is behind the data they see in graphs and tables using a data-driven Social Explorer activity in Revel.

Finally, a set of carefully curated videos builds on text content, exploring developmental psychology from a variety of perspectives, including a deeper look at diversity and the latest in neuroscience.

Revel also offers the ability for students to assess their content mastery by taking multiple-choice quizzes that offer instant feedback and by participating in a variety of writing assignments, such as peer-reviewed questions and auto-graded assignments.

MyVirtualLife integration enables students to apply developmental concepts in a simulated environment within their Revel™ course. MyVirtualLife is an interactive simulation that allows students to parent a child from birth to age 18, making decisions on the child's behalf. Once the virtual child turns 18, the student user's perspective flips for the second half of the program, which enables students to live a simulated life and see the impact of their first-person decisions over the course of a lifetime.

Revel Combo Card

The Revel Combo Card provides an all-in-one access code and loose-leaf print reference (delivered by mail).

Ancillaries

Development Across the Life Span, Ninth Edition, is accompanied by a superb set of teaching and learning material.

- **Instructor's Resource Manual** (ISBN: 0135173523). The Instructor's Resource Manual has been thoroughly reviewed and revised for the ninth edition. It includes learning objectives, key terms and concepts, self-contained lecture suggestions, and class activities for each chapter. The Instructor's Resource Manual is available for download via the Pearson Instructor's Resource Center (www.pearsonhighered.com) and Revel.
- **Video Enhanced PowerPoint Slides** (ISBN: 0135192471). These slides bring the Feldman design right into the classroom, drawing students into the lecture and providing wonderful interactive activities, visuals, and videos.
- **PowerPoint Lecture Slides** (ISBN: 0135173531). The lecture slides provide an active format for presenting concepts from each chapter and feature prominent figures and tables from the text. The PowerPoint Lecture Slides are available for download via the Pearson Instructor's Resource Center (www.pearsonhighered.com) or Revel.
- **Test Bank** (ISBN: 0135173566). For the ninth edition, each question was checked for accuracy to ensure that the correct answer was marked and the page reference was accurate. The test bank contains over 1,600 multiple-choice, true/false, and essay questions, each correlated to chapter topic and learning objective. The test bank features the identification of each question as factual, conceptual, applied, or analytical. Finally, each item is also identified in terms of difficulty level to allow professors to customize their tests and ensure a balance of question types. Each chapter of the test item file begins with the Total Assessment Guide: an easy-to-reference grid that makes creating tests easier by organizing the test questions by text section, question type, and whether it is factual, conceptual, applied, or analytical. Each chapter ends by listing the Revel assessment questions featured in the digital Revel textbook product.
- **MyTest** (ISBN: 0135173558). The test bank comes with the Pearson MyTest, a powerful assessment generation program that helps instructors easily create and print quizzes and exams. Questions and tests can be authored online, allowing instructors ultimate flexibility and the ability to efficiently manage assessments anytime, anywhere. For more information, go to www.PearsonMyTest.com.
- **Pearson Teaching Films Lifespan Development Video (ISBN: 0205656021)** engages students and brings to life a wide range of topics spanning the prenatal period through the end of the life span. International videos shot on location allow students to observe similarities and differences in human development across various cultures.
- **Supplementary Texts.** Contact your Pearson representative to package any of these supplementary texts with *Development Across the Life Span*, Ninth Edition.
  - ***Current Directions in Developmental Psychology*** (ISBN: 0205597505). Readings from the American Psychological Society. This exciting reader includes over 20 articles that have been carefully selected for the undergraduate audience and taken from the very accessible *Current Directions in Psychological Science* journal. These timely, cutting-edge articles allow instructors to bring their students a real-world perspective about today's most current and pressing issues in psychology. The journal is discounted when packaged with this text for college adoptions.
  - ***Twenty Studies That Revolutionized Child Psychology* by Wallace E. Dixon, Jr.** (ISBN: 0130415723). Presenting the seminal research studies that have shaped modern developmental psychology, this brief text provides an overview of the environment that gave rise to each study, its experimental design, its findings, and its impact on current thinking in the discipline.
  - ***Human Development in Multicultural Contexts: A Book of Readings*** (ISBN: 0130195235). Written by Michele A. Paludi, this compilation of readings highlights cultural influences in developmental psychology.
  - ***The Psychology Major: Careers and Strategies for Success*** (ISBN: 0205684688). Written by Eric Landrum (Idaho State University), Stephen Davis (Emporia State University), and Terri Landrum (Idaho State University), this 160-page paperback provides valuable information on career options available to psychology majors, tips for improving academic performance, and a guide to the APA style of research reporting.

Acknowledgments

I am grateful to the following reviewers who have provided a wealth of comments, constructive criticism, and encouragement:

Mary Beth Ahlum, Nebraska Wesleyan College; Marisa Beeble, the Sage Colleges; Kimberly Brown, Ball State University; Shakiera Causey, Guilford Technical Community College; Kimberly Cherry, Edgecombe Community College; Ann Cramer, Technical College of the Lowcountry; Drew Curtis, Angelo State University; Lisa Hager, Spring Hill College; Gregory Harris, Polk State College; Peter Marino, SUNY Rockland Community College; Kristie Morris, SUNY Rockland Community College; Mary Prescott, Harrisburg Area Community College; Wanda Clark, South Plains College; Ariana Durando, Queens College; Dawn Kriebel, Immaculata University; Yvonne Larrier, Indiana University South Bend; Meghan Novy, Palomar College; Laura Pirazzi, San Jose State University.

Kristine Anthis, Southern Connecticut State University; Jo Ann Armstrong, Patrick Henry Community College; Sindy Armstrong, Ozarks Technical College; Stephanie Babb, University of Houston-Downtown; Verneda Hamm Baugh, Kean University; Laura Brandt, Adlai E. Stevenson High School; Jennifer Brennom, Kirkwood Community College; Lisa Brown, Frederick Community College; Cynthia Calhoun, Southwest Tennessee Community College; Cara Cashon, University of Louisville; William Elmhorst, Marshfield High School; Donnell Griffin, Davidson County Community College; Sandra Hellyer, Ball State University; Dr. Nancy Kalish, California State University, Sacramento; Barb Ramos, Simpson College; Linda Tobin, Austin Community College; Scott Young, Iowa State University.

Amy Boland, Columbus State Community College; Ginny Boyum, Rochester Community and Technical College; Krista Forrest, University of Nebraska at Kearney; John Gambon, Ozarks Technical College; Tim Killian, University of Arkansas; Peter Matsos, Riverside City College; Troy Schiedenhelm, Rowan-Cabarrus Community College; Charles Shairs, Bunker Hill Community College; Deirdre Slavik, NorthWest Arkansas Community College; Cassandra George Sturges, Washtenaw Community College; Rachelle Tannenbaum, Anne Arundel Community College; Lois Willoughby, Miami Dade College.

Nancy Ashton, R. Stockton College; Dana Davidson, University of Hawaii at Manoa; Margaret Dombrowski, Harrisburg Area Community College; Bailey Drechsler, Cuesta College; Jennifer Farell, University of North Carolina—Greensboro; Carol Flaugher, University at Buffalo; Rebecca Glover, University of North Texas; R. J. Grisham, Indian River Community College; Martha Kuehn, Central Lakes College; Heather Nash, University of Alaska Southeast; Sadie Oates, Pitt Community College; Patricia Sawyer, Middlesex Community College; Barbara Simon, Midlands Technical College; Archana Singh, Utah State University; Joan Thomas-Spiegel, Los Angeles Harbor College; Linda Veltri, University of Portland.

Libby Balter Blume, University of Detroit Mercy; Bobby Carlsen, Averett College; Ingrid Cominsky, Onondaga Community College; Amanda Cunningham, Emporia State University; Felice J. Green, University of North Alabama; Mark Hartlaub, Texas A&M University—Corpus Christi; Kathleen Hulbert, University of Massachusetts—Lowell; Susan Jacob, Central Michigan University; Laura Levine, Central Connecticut State University; Pamelyn M. MacDonald, Washburn University; Jessica Miller, Mesa State College; Shirley Albertson Owens, Vanguard University of Southern California; Stephanie Weyers, Emporia State University; Karen L. Yanowitz, Arkansas State University.

Many others deserve a great deal of thanks. I am indebted to the numerous people who provided me with a superb education, first at Wesleyan University and later at the University of Wisconsin. Specifically, Karl Scheibe played a pivotal role in my undergraduate education, and Vernon Allen acted as mentor and guide through my graduate years. It was in graduate school that I learned about development, being exposed to such experts as Ross Parke, John Balling, Joel Levin, Herb Klausmeier, and many others. My education continued when I became a professor. I am especially grateful to my colleagues at the University of Massachusetts, who make the university such a wonderful place in which to teach and do research.

Several people played central roles in the development of this book. The thoughtful and creative Stephen Hupp and Jeremy Jewell of Southern Illinois University–Edwardsville were partners in developing the Revel materials, and their input was critical. John Bickford of the University of Massachusetts Amherst provided important research and editorial support, and I am thankful for his help and superb writing skills. I am also grateful to Christopher Poirier of Stonehill College, who produced the wonderful Instructor Resource Manual and Test Bank that accompany *Development Across the Life Span*. Finally, John Graiff and Michelle Goncalves were essential in juggling and coordinating the multiple aspects of working on a project such as this, and I am very grateful for the substantial role they played.

I also am grateful to the superb Pearson team that was instrumental in the inception and development of this book. Kelli Streiby, senior producer and strategy manager, was an enthusiastic and thoughtful advocate for the book. Managing Editor Marita Sermolins Bley went beyond the call of duty to provide guidance as this book became a reality. I am grateful for their support. Most of all, I want to thank the always thoughtful, creative, responsive, and extremely organized

Cathy Murphy, who played a critical role in bringing this book to fruition.

On the production end of things, Program Manager Jane Lee Kaddu and Project Manager Valerie Iglar-Mobley helped in bringing all the aspects of the text together. I am also perennially grateful to Jeff Marshall, whose many ideas permeate this book. Finally, I'd like to thank (in advance) marketing manager Chris Brown, on whose skills I'm counting.

I also wish to acknowledge the members of my family, who play such an essential role in my life. My brother, Michael, my sisters-in-law and brother-in-law, my nieces and nephews—all make up an important part of my life. In addition, I am always indebted to the older generation of my family, who led the way in a manner I can only hope to emulate. I will always be obligated to Harry Brochstein, Mary Vorwerk, and Ethel Radler. Most of all, the list is headed by my father, Saul Feldman, and my mother, Leah Brochstein.

In the end, it is my immediate family who deserve the greatest thanks. My terrific kids, Jonathan and wife Leigh; Joshua and wife Julie; and Sarah and husband Jeff not only are nice, smart, and good-looking, but my pride and joy. My wonderful grandchildren, Alex, Miles, Naomi, and Lilia, have brought immense happiness from the moment of their births. And ultimately my wife, Katherine Vorwerk, provides the love and grounding that make everything worthwhile. I thank them, with all my love.

Robert S. Feldman
University of Massachusetts Amherst

About the Author

Robert S. Feldman is Professor of Psychological and Brain Sciences and Senior Advisor to the Chancellor at the University of Massachusetts Amherst. A recipient of the College Distinguished Teacher Award, he teaches psychology classes ranging in size from 10 to nearly 500 students. During the course of more than three decades as a college instructor, he has taught both undergraduate and graduate courses at Mount Holyoke College, Wesleyan University, and Virginia Commonwealth University in addition to the University of Massachusetts.

Professor Feldman, who initiated the Minority Mentoring Program at the University of Massachusetts, also has served as a Hewlett Teaching Fellow and Senior Online Teaching Fellow. He initiated distance learning courses in psychology at the University of Massachusetts.

A Fellow of the American Psychological Association, the Association for Psychological Science, and the American Association for the Advancement of Science, Professor Feldman received a B.A. with High Honors from Wesleyan University (from which he received the Distinguished Alumni Award). He has an M.S. and a Ph.D. from the University of Wisconsin-Madison. He is a winner of a Fulbright Senior Research Scholar and Lecturer award, and he has written more than 100 books, book chapters, and scientific articles. He has edited *Development of Nonverbal Behavior in Children* (Springer-Verlag) and *Applications of Nonverbal Behavioral Theory and Research* (Erlbaum), and co-edited *Fundamentals of Nonverbal Behavior* (Cambridge University Press). He is also author of *Child Development, Understanding Psychology*, and *P.O.W.E.R. Learning: Strategies for Success in College and Life*. His books have been translated into many languages, including Spanish, French, Portuguese, Dutch, Chinese, Korean, German, Arabic, and Japanese. His research interests include honesty and deception in everyday life, work that he described in *The Liar in Your Life*, a trade book published in 2009. His research has been supported by grants from the National Institute of Mental Health and the National Institute on Disabilities and Rehabilitation Research.

Professor Feldman is past president of the Federation of Associations of Behavioral and Brain Sciences Foundation, a consortium of societies that benefit the social sciences. In addition, he is on the board of New England Public Radio. Professor Feldman loves music, is an enthusiastic pianist, and enjoys cooking and traveling. He has three children and four grandchildren, and he and his wife, a psychologist, live in western Massachusetts in a home overlooking the Holyoke Mountain Range.

Development Across the Life Span

Chapter 1

An Introduction to Lifespan Development

Blend Images/Getty Images

Learning Objectives

LO 1.1 Define the field of lifespan development and describe what it encompasses.

LO 1.2 Describe the areas that lifespan development specialists cover.

LO 1.3 Describe some of the basic influences on human development.

LO 1.4 Summarize four key issues in the field of lifespan development.

LO 1.5 Describe how the psychodynamic perspective explains lifespan development.

LO 1.6 Describe how the behavioral perspective explains lifespan development.

LO 1.7 Describe how the cognitive perspective explains lifespan development.

LO 1.8 Describe how the humanistic perspective explains lifespan development.

LO 1.9 Describe how the contextual perspective explains lifespan development.

LO 1.10 Describe how the evolutionary perspective explains lifespan development.

LO 1.11 Discuss the value of applying multiple perspectives to lifespan development.

LO 1.12 Describe the role that theories and hypotheses play in the study of development.

LO 1.13 Compare the two major categories of lifespan development research.

LO 1.14 Identify different types of correlational studies and their relationship to cause and effect.

LO 1.15 Explain the main features of an experiment.

LO 1.16 Distinguish between theoretical research and applied research.

LO 1.17 Compare longitudinal research, cross-sectional research, and sequential research.

LO 1.18 Describe some ethical issues that affect psychological research.

Chapter Overview

Prologue: New Conceptions

In many ways, the first meeting of Louise Brown and Elizabeth Carr was unremarkable: just two women, one in her thirties, the other in her forties, chatting about their lives and their own children.

But in another sense the meeting was extraordinary. Louise Brown was the world's first "test-tube baby," born by *in vitro fertilization (IVF)*, a procedure in which fertilization of a mother's egg by a father's sperm takes place outside of the mother's body. And Elizabeth Carr was the first baby born by IVF in the United States.

Louise was a preschooler when her parents told her how she was conceived, and throughout her childhood she was bombarded with questions. It became routine to explain to her classmates that she, in fact, was not born in a laboratory. At times, she felt completely alone. For Elizabeth, too, growing up was not easy, as she experienced bouts of insecurity.

Today, however, Louise and Elizabeth are hardly unique. They are among the more than 5 million babies that have been born using the procedure, one that has almost become routine. And both became mothers themselves, giving birth to babies who were conceived, incidentally, the old-fashioned way (Falco, 2012; Gagneux, 2016; Simpson, 2017).

Looking Ahead

Louise Brown's and Elizabeth Carr's conceptions may have been novel, but their development, from infancy onward, has followed predictable patterns. While the specifics of our own development vary—some of us encounter economic deprivation or live in war-torn territories; others contend with family issues like divorce and stepparents—the broad strokes of the development that is set in motion the moment we are conceived are remarkably similar for all of us. Like LeBron James, Bill Gates, and, yes, Louise Brown and Elizabeth Carr, each and every one of us has traversed the territory known as child development.

IVF is just one of the brave new worlds of the 21st century. Issues ranging from cloning and the consequences of poverty on development to the effects of culture and race raise significant developmental concerns. Underlying these are even more fundamental issues. How do children develop physically? How does their understanding of the world grow and change over time? And how do our personalities and our social world develop as we move from birth through adolescence?

Each of these questions, and many others we'll encounter throughout this book, are central to the field of lifespan development. As a field, lifespan development encompasses not only a broad span of time—from before birth to death—but also a wide range of areas of development. Consider, for example, the range of interests that different specialists in lifespan development focus on when considering the lives of Louise Brown and Elizabeth Carr:

- Lifespan development researchers who investigate behavior at the level of biological processes might determine if Louise and Elizabeth's functioning prior to birth was affected by their conception outside the womb.
- Specialists in lifespan development who study genetics might examine how the genetic endowment from their parents has affected their later behavior.
- For lifespan development specialists who investigate the ways thinking changes over the course of life, their lives might be examined in terms of how each woman's understanding of the nature of her conception changed as she grew older.
- Researchers in lifespan development who focus on physical growth might consider whether their growth rates differed from children conceived more traditionally.
- Lifespan development experts who specialize in the social world and social relationships might look at the ways that Louise and Elizabeth interacted with others and the kinds of friendships they developed.

Although their interests take many forms, these specialists in lifespan development share one concern: understanding the growth and change that occur during the course of life. Taking many differing approaches, developmentalists study how both the biological inheritance from our parents and the environment in which we live jointly affect our behavior.

Some developmentalists focus on explaining how our genetic background can determine not only how we look but also how we behave and relate to others in a consistent manner—that is, matters of personality. They explore ways to identify how much of our potential as human beings is provided—or limited—by heredity. Other lifespan development specialists look to the environment, exploring ways in which our lives are shaped by the world that we encounter. They investigate the extent to which we are shaped by our early environments, and how our current circumstances influence our behavior in both subtle and obvious ways.

Whether they focus on heredity or environment, all developmental specialists acknowledge that neither heredity nor environment alone can account for the full range of human development and change. Instead, our understanding of people's development requires that we look at the interaction of heredity and environment, attempting to grasp how both, in the end, contribute to human behavior.

In this chapter, we orient ourselves to the field of lifespan development. We begin with a discussion of the scope of the discipline, illustrating the wide array of topics it covers and the full range of ages, from conception to death, that it examines. We also survey the

AP Images/Alamy Stock Photo

Julie Malakie/Associated Press

Louise Brown (at left) and Elizabeth Carr (right), who were both born by in vitro fertilization.

key issues and controversies of the field and consider the broad perspectives that developmentalists take. Finally, we discuss the ways developmentalists use research to ask and answer questions.

An Orientation to Lifespan Development

Have you ever wondered how it is possible that an infant tightly grips your finger with tiny, perfectly formed hands? Or marveled at the way an adolescent can make involved decisions about whom to invite to a party? Or wondered what it is that makes a grandfather at 80 so similar to the father he was when he was 40?

If you've ever contemplated such things, you are asking the kinds of questions that scientists in the field of *lifespan development* pose. In this section, we'll examine how the field of lifespan development is defined, the scope of the field, as well as some basic influences on human development.

Defining Lifespan Development

LO 1.1 Define the field of lifespan development and describe what it encompasses.

lifespan development
the field of study that examines patterns of growth, change, and stability in behavior that occur throughout the entire life span

Lifespan development is the field of study that examines patterns of growth, change, and stability in behavior that occur throughout the entire life span. Although the definition of the field seems straightforward, the simplicity is somewhat misleading. In order to understand what development is actually about, we need to look underneath the various parts of the definition.

In its study of growth, change, and stability, lifespan development takes a *scientific* approach. Like members of other scientific disciplines, researchers in lifespan development test their assumptions about the nature and course of human development by applying scientific methods. As we'll see later in the chapter, they develop theories about development, and they use methodical, scientific techniques to validate the accuracy of their assumptions systematically.

Lifespan development focuses on *human* development. Although there are developmentalists who study the course of development in nonhuman species, the vast majority examine growth and change in people. Some seek to understand universal principles of development, whereas others focus on how cultural, racial, and ethnic differences affect the course of development. Still others aim to understand the unique aspects of individuals, looking at the traits and characteristics that differentiate one person from another. Regardless of approach, however, all developmentalists view development as a continuing process throughout the life span.

Monkey Business/Fotolia

How people grow and change over the course of their lives is the focus of lifespan development.

As developmental specialists focus on the ways people change and grow during their lives, they also consider stability in people's lives. They ask in which areas, and in what periods, people show change and growth, and when and how their behavior reveals consistency and continuity with prior behavior.

Finally, developmentalists assume that the process of development persists throughout every part of people's lives, beginning with the moment of conception and continuing until death. Developmental specialists assume that in some ways people continue to grow and change right up to the end of their lives, while in other respects their behavior remains stable. At the same time, developmentalists believe that no particular, single period of life governs all development. Instead, they believe that every period of life contains the potential for both growth and decline in abilities and that individuals maintain the capacity for substantial growth and change throughout their lives.

The Scope of the Field of Lifespan Development

LO 1.2 Describe the areas that lifespan development specialists cover.

Clearly, the definition of lifespan development is broad, and the scope of the field is extensive. Consequently, lifespan development specialists cover several quite diverse areas, and a typical developmentalist will choose to specialize in both a topical area and an age range.

TOPICAL AREAS IN LIFESPAN DEVELOPMENT. Some developmentalists focus on **physical development**, examining the ways in which the body's makeup—the brain, nervous system, muscles, and senses, and the need for food, drink, and sleep—helps determine behavior. For example, one specialist in physical development might examine the effects of malnutrition on the pace of growth in children, while another might look at how athletes' physical performance declines during adulthood (Fell & Williams, 2008; Muiños & Ballesteros, 2014).

physical development
development involving the body's physical makeup, including the brain, nervous system, muscles, and senses, and the need for food, drink, and sleep

Other developmental specialists examine **cognitive development**, seeking to understand how growth and change in intellectual capabilities influence a person's behavior. Cognitive developmentalists examine learning, memory, problem-solving skills, and intelligence. For example, specialists in cognitive development might want to see how problem-solving skills change over the course of life, or whether cultural differences exist in the way people explain their academic successes and failures (Dumka et al., 2009; Penido et al., 2012; Coates, 2016).

cognitive development
development involving the ways that growth and change in intellectual capabilities influence a person's behavior

Finally, some developmental specialists focus on personality and social development. **Personality development** is the study of stability and change in the enduring characteristics that differentiate one person from another over the life span. **Social development** is the way in which individuals' interactions with others and their social relationships grow, change, and remain stable over the course of life. A developmentalist interested in personality development might ask whether there are stable, enduring personality traits throughout the life span, whereas a specialist in social development might examine the effects of racism or poverty or divorce on development (Lansford, 2009; Tine, 2014; Manning et al., 2017). These four major topic areas—physical, cognitive, social, and personality development—are summarized in Table 1-1.

personality development
development involving the ways that the enduring characteristics that differentiate one person from another change over the life span

social development
the way in which individuals' interactions with others and their social relationships grow, change, and remain stable over the course of life

AGE RANGES AND INDIVIDUAL DIFFERENCES. In addition to choosing to specialize in a particular topical area, developmentalists also typically look at a particular age range. The life span is usually divided into broad age ranges: the prenatal period (the period from conception to birth), infancy and toddlerhood (birth to age 3), the preschool period (ages 3 to 6), middle childhood (ages 6 to 12), adolescence (ages 12 to 20), young adulthood (ages 20 to 40), middle adulthood (ages 40 to 65), and late adulthood (age 65 to death).

It's important to keep in mind that these broad periods—which are largely accepted by lifespan developmentalists—are social constructions. A *social construction* is a shared notion of reality, one that is widely accepted but is a function of society and culture at a given time. Consequently, the age ranges within a period—and even the periods themselves—are in many ways arbitrary and are often culturally derived. For example, later in the book we'll discuss how the concept of childhood as a separate period did not even exist during the 17th century; at that time, children and adults were seen as little different from one another except in terms of size. Furthermore, while some periods have a clear-cut boundary (infancy begins with birth, the preschool period ends with entry into elementary school, and adolescence starts with sexual maturity), others don't.

For instance, consider the period of young adulthood, which at least in Western cultures is typically assumed to begin at age 20. That age, however, is notable only because

Table 1-1 Approaches to Lifespan Development

Orientation	Defining Characteristics	Examples of Question Asked*
Physical development	Emphasizes how the brain, nervous system, muscles, sensory capabilities, and needs for food, drink, and sleep affect behavior	• What determines the sex of a child? (2) • What are the long-term results of premature birth? (3) • What are the benefits of breast milk? (4) • What are the consequences of early or late sexual maturation? (11) • What leads to obesity in adulthood? (13) • How do adults cope with stress? (15) • What are the outward and internal signs of aging? (17) • How do we define death? (19)
Cognitive development	Emphasizes intellectual abilities, including learning, memory, problem solving, and intelligence	• What are the earliest memories that can be recalled from infancy? (5) • What are the intellectual consequences of watching television? (7) • Do spatial reasoning skills relate to music practice? (7) • Are there benefits to bilingualism? (9) • How does an adolescent's egocentrism affect his or her view of the world? (11) • Are there ethnic and racial differences in intelligence? (9) • How does creativity relate to intelligence? (13) • Does intelligence decline in late adulthood? (17)
Personality and social development	Emphasizes enduring characteristics that differentiate one person from another, and how interactions with others and social relationships grow and change over the life span	• Do newborns respond differently to their mothers than to others? (3) • What is the best procedure for disciplining children? (8) • When does a sense of gender identity develop, and how do sex and gender provide a context for development? (8) • How can we promote cross-race friendships? (10) • What are the causes of adolescent suicide? (12) • How do we choose a romantic partner? (14) • Do the effects of parental divorce last into old age? (18) • Do people withdraw from others in late adulthood? (18) • What are the emotions involved in confronting death? (19)

*Numbers in parentheses indicate in which chapter the question is addressed.

it marks the end of the teenage period. In fact, for many people, such as those enrolled in higher education, the age change from 19 to 20 has little special significance, coming as it does in the middle of the college years. For them, more substantial changes may occur when they leave college and enter the workforce, which is more likely to happen around age 22. Furthermore, in some non-Western cultures, adulthood may be considered to start much earlier, when children whose educational opportunities are limited begin full-time work.

DPA/The Image Works

This wedding of two children in India is an example of how environmental factors can play a significant role in determining the age when a particular event is likely to occur.

In fact, some developmentalists have proposed entirely new developmental periods. For instance, psychologist Jeffrey Arnett argues that adolescence extends into *emerging adulthood*, a period beginning in the late teenage years and continuing into the mid-twenties. During emerging adulthood, people are no longer adolescents, but they haven't fully taken on the responsibilities of adulthood. Instead, they are still trying out different identities and engaging in self-focused exploration (de Dios, 2012; Sumner, Burrow, & Hill, 2015; Arnett, 2011, 2016).

In short, there are substantial *individual differences* in the timing of events in people's lives. In part, this is a biological fact of life: People mature at different rates and reach developmental milestones at different points. However, environmental factors also play a significant role in determining the age at which a particular event is likely to occur. For example, the typical age of marriage varies substantially from one culture to another, depending in part on the functions that marriage plays in a given culture.

It is important to keep in mind, then, that when developmental specialists discuss age ranges, they are talking about averages—the times when people, on average, reach particular milestones. Some people will reach the milestone earlier, some later, and many will reach it around the time of the average. Such variation becomes noteworthy only when children show substantial deviation from the average. For example, parents whose child begins to speak at a much later age than average might decide to have their son or daughter evaluated by a speech therapist.

THE LINKS BETWEEN TOPICS AND AGES. Each of the broad topical areas of lifespan development—physical, cognitive, social, and personality development—plays a role throughout the life span. Consequently, some developmental experts focus on physical development during the prenatal period, and others during adolescence. Some might specialize in social development during the preschool years, while others look at social relationships in late adulthood. Still others might take a broader approach, looking at cognitive development through every period of life.

In this book, we'll take a comprehensive approach, proceeding chronologically from the prenatal period through late adulthood and death. Within each period, we'll look at different topical areas: physical, cognitive, social, and personality development. Furthermore, we'll also be considering the impact of culture on development, as we discuss next.

Influences on Development

LO 1.3 Describe some of the basic influences on human development.

Bob, born in 1947, is a baby boomer; he was born soon after the end of World War II (1939–1945), when an enormous surge in the birth rate occurred as soldiers returned to the United States from overseas. He was an adolescent at the height of the civil rights movement and the beginning of protests against the Vietnam War. His mother, Leah, was born in 1922; still alive at 96, she is part of the generation that passed its childhood and teenage years in the shadow of the Great Depression. Bob's son, Jon, was born in 1975. Now established in a career after graduating from college and starting his own family, he is a member of what has been called Generation X. Jon's younger sister, Sarah, who was born in 1982, is part of the next generation, which sociologists have called the Millennial Generation. She now is raising a preschooler of her own after finishing graduate school and starting her career. She sees post-Millennials, the generation that followed her, as being engrossed in social media and their iPhones.

These people are, in part, products of the social times in which they live. Each belongs to a particular **cohort**, a group of people born at around the same time in the same place. Such major social events as wars, economic upturns and depressions, famines, and epidemics (like the one due to the AIDS virus) work similar influences on members of a particular cohort (Dittmann, 2005; Twenge, Gentile, & Campbell, 2015).

cohort
a group of people born at around the same time in the same place

Cohort effects provide an example of *history-graded influences*, which are biological and environmental influences associated with a particular historical moment. For instance, people who lived in New York City during the 9/11 terrorist attack on the World Trade Center experienced shared biological and environmental challenges due to the attack. Their development is going to be affected by this normative history-graded event (Laugharne, Janca, & Widiger, 2007; Park, Riley, & Snyder, 2012; Kim, Bushway, & Tsao, 2016).

In contrast, *age-graded influences* are biological and environmental influences that are similar for individuals in a particular age group, regardless of when or where they are raised. For example, biological events such as puberty and menopause are universal events that occur at relatively the same time throughout all societies. Similarly, a sociocultural event such as entry into formal education can be considered an age-graded influence because it occurs in most cultures around age 6.

From *an educator's* perspective

How would a student's cohort membership affect his or her readiness for school? For example, what would be the benefits and drawbacks of coming from a cohort in which Internet use was routine, compared with earlier cohorts prior to the appearance of the Internet?

Development is also affected by *sociocultural-graded influences*, the social and cultural factors present at a particular time for a particular individual, depending on such variables as ethnicity, social class, and subcultural membership. For example, sociocultural-graded influences will be considerably different for children who are white and affluent than for children who are members of a minority group and living in poverty (Rose et al., 2003).

Developmental Diversity and Your Life

How Culture, Ethnicity, and Race Influence Development

In the United States, parents praise young children who ask a lot of questions for being "intelligent" and "inquisitive." The Dutch consider such children "too dependent on others." Italian parents judge inquisitiveness as a sign of social and emotional competence, not intelligence. Spanish parents praise character far more than intelligence, and Swedes value security and happiness above all.

What are we to make of the diverse parental expectations cited above? Is one way of looking at children's inquisitiveness right and the others wrong? Probably not, if we take into consideration the cultural contexts in which parents operate. In fact, different cultures and subcultures have their own views of appropriate and inappropriate methods and interpretations of childrearing, just as they have different developmental goals for children (Feldman & Masalha, 2007; Huijbregts et al., 2009; Chen, Chen & Zhen, 2012).

Specialists in child development must take into consideration broad cultural factors. For example, as we'll discuss further in Chapter 8, children growing up in Asian societies tend to have a *collectivistic orientation*, focusing on the interdependence among members of society. In contrast, children in Western societies are more likely to have an *individualistic orientation*, in which they concentrate on the uniqueness of the individual.

Similarly, child developmentalists must also consider ethnic, racial, socioeconomic, and gender differences if they are to achieve an understanding of how people change and grow throughout the life span. If these specialists succeed in doing so, not only can they attain a better understanding of human development, but they may also be able to derive more precise applications for improving the human social condition. To complicate the study of diverse populations, the terms *race* and *ethnic group* are often used inappropriately. *Race* originated as a biological concept, and initially referred to classifications based on physical and structural characteristics of species. But such a definition has little validity in terms of humans, and research shows that it is not a meaningful way to differentiate people.

For example, depending on how race is defined, there are between 3 and 300 races, and no race is genetically distinct. The fact that 99.9 percent of genetic makeup is identical in all humans makes the question of race seem insignificant. Thus, race today is generally thought of as a *social construction*, something defined by people and their beliefs (Helms, Jernigan, & Mascher, 2005; Smedley & Smedley, 2005; Alfred & Chlup, 2010).

In contrast, *ethnic group* and *ethnicity* are broader terms for which there is greater agreement. They relate to cultural background, nationality, religion, and language. Members of ethnic groups share a common cultural background and group history.

In addition, there is little agreement about which names best reflect different races and ethnic groups. Should the term *African American*—which has geographical and cultural implications—be preferred over *black*, which focuses primarily on race and skin color? Is *Native American* preferable to *Indian*? Is *Hispanic* more appropriate than *Latino*? And how can researchers accurately categorize people with multiracial backgrounds?

In order to fully understand development, then, we need to take the complex issues associated with human diversity into account. It is only by looking for similarities and differences among various ethnic, cultural, and racial groups that developmental researchers can distinguish principles of development that are universal from principles that are culturally determined. In the years ahead, then, it is likely that lifespan development will move from a discipline that focuses primarily on North American and European development to one that encompasses development around the globe (Matsumoto & Yoo, 2006; Kloep et al., 2009).

Finally, *non-normative life events* are specific, atypical events that occur in a person's life at a time when such events do not happen to most people. For example, a child whose parents die in an automobile accident when she is 6 years old has experienced a significant non-normative life event.

Key Issues and Questions: Determining the Nature—and Nurture—of Lifespan Development

LO 1.4 Summarize four key issues in the field of lifespan development.

Today, several key issues and questions dominate the field. Among the major issues (summarized in Table 1-2) are the nature of change, the importance of critical and sensitive periods, lifespan approaches versus more focused approaches, and the nature–nurture issue.

Table 1-2 Major Issues in Lifespan Development

Continuous Change	*Discontinuous Change*
• Change is gradual. • Achievements at one level build on previous levels. • Underlying developmental processes remain the same over the life span.	• Change occurs in distinct steps or stages. • Behavior and processes are qualitatively different at different stages.
Critical Periods	***Sensitive Periods***
• Certain environmental stimuli are necessary for normal development. • Emphasized by early developmentalists.	• People are susceptible to certain environmental stimuli, but consequences of absent stimuli are reversible. • Current emphasis in lifespan development.
Lifespan Approach	***Focus on Particular Periods***
• Current theories emphasize growth and change throughout life; relatedness of different periods.	• Infancy and adolescence are emphasized by early developmentalists as most important periods.
Nature (Genetic Factors)	***Nurture (Environmental Factors)***
• Emphasis is on discovering inherited genetic traits and abilities.	• Emphasis is on environmental influences that affect a person's development.

Most developmentalists agree that taking an either/or position on the continuous–discontinuous issue is inappropriate. While many types of developmental change are continuous, others are clearly discontinuous.

CONTINUOUS CHANGE VERSUS DISCONTINUOUS CHANGE. One of the primary issues challenging developmentalists is whether development proceeds in a continuous or discontinuous fashion. In **continuous change**, development is gradual, with achievements at one level building on those of previous levels. Continuous change is quantitative in nature; the basic underlying developmental processes that drive change remain the same over the course of the life span. Continuous change, then, produces changes that are a matter of degree, not of kind. Changes in height prior to adulthood, for example, are continuous. Similarly, as we'll see later in the chapter, some theorists suggest that changes in people's thinking capabilities are also continuous, showing gradual quantitative improvements rather than developing entirely new cognitive processing capabilities.

continuous change
gradual development in which achievements at one level build on those of previous levels

In contrast, one can view development as being made up of primarily **discontinuous change**, occurring in distinct stages. Each stage or change brings about behavior that is assumed to be qualitatively different from behavior at earlier stages. Consider the example of cognitive development again. We'll see later in the chapter that some cognitive developmentalists suggest that as we develop, our thinking changes in fundamental ways, and that such development is not just a matter of quantitative change but of qualitative change.

discontinuous change
development that occurs in distinct steps or stages, with each stage bringing about behavior that is assumed to be qualitatively different from behavior at earlier stages

CRITICAL AND SENSITIVE PERIODS: GAUGING THE IMPACT OF ENVIRONMENTAL EVENTS. If a woman comes down with a case of rubella (German measles) in the first 20 weeks of pregnancy, the consequences for the child she is carrying are likely to be devastating: They include the potential for blindness, deafness, and heart defects. However, if she comes down with the exact same strain of rubella in week 30 of pregnancy, damage to the child is unlikely.

The differing outcomes of the disease in the two periods demonstrate the concept of critical periods. A **critical period** is a specific time during development when a particular event has its greatest consequences. Critical periods occur when the presence of certain kinds of environmental stimuli enable development to proceed normally, or when exposure to certain stimuli results in abnormal development. For example, mothers who take drugs at particular times during pregnancy may cause permanent harm to their developing child (Mølgaard-Nielsen, Pasternak, & Hviid, 2013; Nygaard et al., 2017).

critical period
a specific time during development when a particular event has its greatest consequences and the presence of certain kinds of environmental stimuli is necessary for development to proceed normally

Although early specialists in lifespan development placed great emphasis on the importance of critical periods, more recent thinking suggests that in many realms, individuals are more malleable than was first thought, particularly in the domain of personality and social development. For instance, rather than suffering permanent damage from a lack of certain kinds of early social experiences, there is increasing evidence that people can use later experiences to their benefit, to help them overcome earlier deficits.

Consequently, developmentalists are now more likely to speak of sensitive periods rather than critical periods. In a **sensitive period**, organisms are particularly susceptible to certain kinds of stimuli in their environment. A sensitive period represents the optimal period for particular capacities to emerge, and children are particularly sensitive to environmental influences.

sensitive period
a point in development when organisms are particularly susceptible to certain kinds of stimuli in their environments, but the absence of those stimuli does not always produce irreversible consequences

It is important to understand the difference between the concepts of critical periods and sensitive periods. In critical periods, it is assumed that the absence of certain kinds of environmental influences is likely to produce permanent, irreversible consequences for the developing individual. In contrast, although the absence of particular environmental influences during a sensitive period may hinder development, it is possible for later experiences to overcome the earlier deficits. In other words, the concept of sensitive periods recognizes the plasticity of developing humans (Hooks & Chen, 2008; Hartley & Lee, 2015; Piekarski et al., 2017).

LIFESPAN APPROACHES VERSUS A FOCUS ON PARTICULAR PERIODS. On which part of the life span should developmentalists focus their attention? For early developmentalists, the answers tended to be infancy and adolescence. Most attention was clearly concentrated on those two periods, largely to the exclusion of other parts of the life span.

Today, the story is different. Developmentalists now believe that the entire life span is important, for several reasons. One is the discovery that developmental growth and change continue during every part of life—as we'll discuss throughout this book.

Furthermore, an important part of every person's environment is the presence of other people around him or her—the person's social environment. To fully understand the social influences on people of a given age, we need to understand the people who are in large measure providing those influences. For instance, to understand development in infants, we need to unravel the effects of their parents' ages on their social environments. A 15-year-old first-time mother will provide parental influences of a very different sort from those provided by an experienced 37-year-old mother. Consequently, infant development is in part an outgrowth consequence of adult development.

In addition, as lifespan developmentalist Paul Baltes points out, development across the life span involves both gains and losses. With age, certain capabilities become more refined and sophisticated, while others involve loss of skill and capacity. For example, vocabulary tends to grow throughout childhood, and this growth continues through most of adulthood. At the same time, certain physical abilities, like reaction time, improve until early and middle adulthood, when they begin to decline (Baltes, 2003; Ghisletta et al., 2010).

People also shift in how they invest their resources (in terms of motivation, energy, and time) at different points during the life span. Early in life, more of one's personal resources are devoted to activities involving growth, such as studying or learning new skills. As one grows older, more resources are devoted to dealing with the losses people face during late adulthood (Staudinger & Leipold, 2003).

THE RELATIVE INFLUENCE OF NATURE AND NURTURE ON DEVELOPMENT. One of the enduring questions of development involves how much of people's behavior is due to their genetically determined nature and how much is due to nurture, the influences of the physical and social environment in which a child is raised. This issue, which has deep philosophical and historical roots, has dominated much work in lifespan development (Wexler, 2006).

In this context, *nature* refers to traits, abilities, and capacities that are inherited from one's parents. It encompasses any factor that is produced by the predetermined unfolding of genetic information—a process known as **maturation**. These genetic, inherited influences are at work as we move from the one-cell organism that is created at the moment of conception to the billions of cells that make up a fully formed human. Nature

maturation
the predetermined unfolding of genetic information

influences whether our eyes are blue or brown, whether we have thick hair throughout life or eventually go bald, and how good we are at athletics. Nature allows our brains to develop in such a way that we can read the words on this page.

In contrast, *nurture* refers to the environmental influences that shape behavior. Some of these influences may be biological, such as the impact of a pregnant mother's use of cocaine on her unborn child or the amount and kind of food available to children. Other environmental influences are more social, such as the ways parents discipline their children and the effects of peer pressure on an adolescent. Finally, some influences are a result of larger, societal-level factors, such as the socioeconomic circumstances in which people find themselves.

THE LATER ACTION OF NATURE AND NURTURE. If our traits and behavior were determined solely by either nature or nurture, there would probably be little debate regarding the issue. However, for most critical behaviors this is hardly the case. Take, for instance, one of the most controversial areas: intelligence. As we'll consider in detail in Chapter 9, the question of whether intelligence is determined primarily by inherited, genetic factors—nature—or is shaped by environmental factors—nurture—has caused lively and often bitter arguments that have spilled out of the scientific arena and into the realm of politics and social policy.

Consider the implications of the issue: If the extent of one's intelligence is primarily determined by heredity and consequently is largely fixed at birth, then efforts to improve intellectual performance later in life may be doomed to failure. In contrast, if intelligence is primarily a result of environmental factors, such as the amount and quality of schooling and stimulation to which one is exposed, then we would expect that an improvement in social conditions could bring about an increase in intelligence.

The extent of social policy affected by ideas about the origins of intelligence illustrates the significance of issues that involve the nature–nurture question. As we address this question in relation to several topical areas throughout this book, we should keep in mind that developmentalists reject the notion that behavior is the result solely of either nature *or* nurture. Instead, the question is one of degree—and the specifics of that, too, are hotly debated.

Furthermore, the interaction of genetic and environmental factors is complex, in part because certain genetically determined traits have not only a direct influence on children's behavior, but an indirect influence in shaping children's *environments* as well. For example, a child who is consistently cranky and who cries a great deal—a trait that may be produced by genetic factors—may influence his or her environment by making his or her parents so highly responsive to the insistent crying that they rush to comfort the child whenever he or she cries. Their responsivity to the child's genetically determined behavior consequently becomes an environmental influence on his or her subsequent development (Bradley & Corwyn, 2008; Stright, Gallagher, & Kelley, 2008; Barnes & Boutwell, 2012).

Similarly, although our genetic background orients us toward particular behaviors, those behaviors will not necessarily occur in the absence of an appropriate environment. People with similar genetic backgrounds (such as identical twins) may behave in very different ways, and people with highly dissimilar genetic backgrounds can behave quite similarly to one another in certain areas (Kato & Pedersen, 2005; Segal et al., 2015; Sudharsanan, Behrman, & Kohler, 2016).

In sum, the question of how much of a given behavior is due to nature, and how much to nurture, is a challenging one. Ultimately, we should consider the two sides of the nature–nurture issue as opposite ends of a continuum, with particular behaviors falling somewhere between the two ends. We can say something similar about the other controversies that we have considered. For instance, continuous versus discontinuous development is not an either/or proposition; some forms of development fall toward the continuous end of the continuum, whereas others lie closer to the discontinuous end. In short, few statements about development involve either/or absolutes (Rutter, 2006; Deater-Deckard & Cahill, 2007).

Module 1.1 Review

LO 1.1 Define the field of lifespan development and describe what it encompasses.

Lifespan development, a scientific approach to understanding human growth and change throughout life, encompasses physical, cognitive, social, and personality development.

LO 1.2 Describe the areas that lifespan development specialists cover.

Developmentalists focus on physical development, on cognitive development, and on personality and social development. In addition to choosing to specialize in a particular topical area, developmentalists also typically look at a particular age range.

LO 1.3 Describe some of the basic influences on human development.

Membership in a cohort, based on age and place of birth, subjects people to influences based on historical events (history-graded influences). People are also subject to age-graded influences, sociocultural-graded influences, and non-normative life events. Culture and ethnicity also play an important role in development—both broad culture and aspects of culture, such as race, ethnicity, and socioeconomic status.

LO 1.4 Summarize four key issues in the field of lifespan development.

Four important issues in lifespan development are continuity versus discontinuity in development, the importance of critical periods, whether to focus on certain periods or on the entire life span, and the nature–nurture controversy.

Journal Writing Prompt

Applying Lifespan Development: What are some examples of the ways culture (either broad culture or aspects of culture) affects human development?

Theoretical Perspectives on Lifespan Development

In Europe, there was no concept of "childhood" until the 17th century. Instead, children were simply thought of as miniature adults. They were assumed to be subject to the same needs and desires as adults, to have the same vices and virtues as adults, and to warrant no more privileges than adults. They were dressed the same as adults, and their work hours were the same as adults. Children also received the same punishments for misdeeds. If they stole, they were hanged; if they did well, they could achieve prosperity, at least so far as their station in life or social class would allow.

This view of childhood seems wrong-headed now, but at the time it was what passed for lifespan development. From this perspective, there were no differences due to age; except for size, people were assumed to be virtually unchanging, at least on a psychological level, throughout most of the life span (Ariès, 1962; Hutton, 2004; Wines, 2006).

North Wind Picture Archives/Alamy Stock Photo

Society's view of childhood, and what is appropriate to ask of children, has changed through the ages. These children worked full time in mines in the early 1900s.

Although, looking back over several centuries, it is easy to reject the medieval view of childhood, it is less clear how to formulate a contemporary substitute. Should our view of development focus on the biological aspects of change, growth, and stability over the life span? The cognitive or social aspects? Or some other factors?

People who study lifespan development approach the field from a number of different perspectives. Each general perspective encompasses one or more *theories*—broad, organized explanations and predictions concerning phenomena of interest. A theory provides a framework for understanding the relationships among a seemingly unorganized set of facts or principles.

We all develop theories about development, based on our experience, folklore, and articles in magazines and newspapers. However, theories in lifespan development are different. Whereas our own personal theories are built on unverified observations that are developed haphazardly, developmentalists' theories are more formal, based on a systematic integration of prior findings and theorizing. These theories allow developmentalists to summarize and organize prior observations, and they also permit them to move beyond existing observations to draw deductions that may not be immediately apparent. In addition, these theories are then subject to rigorous testing in the form of research. By contrast, the developmental theories of individuals are not subject to such testing and may never be questioned at all (Thomas, 2001).

We will consider six major theoretical perspectives used in lifespan development: the psychodynamic, behavioral, cognitive, humanistic, contextual, and evolutionary perspectives. Each emphasizes somewhat different aspects of development and steers developmentalists in particular directions. Furthermore, each perspective continues to evolve and change, as befits a growing and dynamic discipline.

The Psychodynamic Perspective: Focusing on the Inner Person

LO 1.5 Describe how the psychodynamic perspective explains lifespan development.

When Marisol was 6 months old, she was involved in a bloody automobile accident—or so her parents tell her, since she has no conscious recollection of it. Now, however, at age 24, she is having difficulty maintaining relationships, and her therapist is seeking to determine whether her current problems are a result of the earlier accident.

Looking for such a link might seem a bit far-fetched, but to proponents of the **psychodynamic perspective**, it is not so improbable. Advocates of the psychodynamic perspective believe that much of behavior is motivated by inner forces, memories, and conflicts of which a person has little awareness or control. The inner forces, which may stem from one's childhood, continually influence behavior throughout the life span.

psychodynamic perspective
the approach stating that behavior is motivated by inner forces, memories, and conflicts that are generally beyond people's awareness and control

psychoanalytic theory
the theory proposed by Sigmund Freud that suggests that unconscious forces act to determine personality and behavior

psychosexual development
according to Sigmund Freud, a series of stages that children pass through in which pleasure, or gratification, focuses on a particular biological function and body part

FREUD'S PSYCHOANALYTIC THEORY. The psychodynamic perspective is most closely associated with a single person and theory: Sigmund Freud and his psychoanalytic theory. Freud, who lived from 1856 to 1939, was a Viennese physician whose revolutionary ideas ultimately had a profound effect not only on the fields of psychology and psychiatry but also on Western thought in general (Greenberg, 2012; Roth, 2016).

Freud's **psychoanalytic theory** suggests that unconscious forces act to determine personality and behavior. To Freud, the *unconscious* is a part of the personality about which a person is unaware. It contains infantile wishes, desires, demands, and needs that, because of their disturbing nature, are hidden from conscious awareness. Freud suggested that the unconscious is responsible for a good part of our everyday behavior.

According to Freud, everyone's personality has three aspects: id, ego, and superego. The *id* is the raw, unorganized, inborn part of personality that is present at birth. It represents primitive drives related to hunger, sex, aggression, and irrational impulses. The *ego* is the part of personality that is rational and reasonable. The ego acts as a buffer between the real world outside of us and the primitive id. Finally, the *superego* represents a person's conscience, incorporating distinctions between right and wrong. It begins to develop around age 5 or 6 and is learned from an individual's parents, teachers, and other significant figures.

In addition to providing an account of the various parts of the personality, Freud also suggested the ways in which personality developed during childhood. He argued that **psychosexual development** occurs as children pass through a series of stages in which pleasure, or gratification, is focused on a particular biological function and body part. As illustrated in Table 1-3, he suggested that pleasure shifts from the mouth (the *oral stage*) to the anus (the *anal stage*) and eventually to the genitals (the *phallic stage* and the *genital stage*).

AISA - Everett/Shutterstock

Sigmund Freud.

According to Freud, if children are unable to gratify themselves sufficiently during a particular stage—or conversely, if they receive too much gratification—fixation may

Table 1-3 Freud's and Erikson's Theories

Approximate Age	Freud's Stages of Psychosexual Development	Major Characteristics of Freud's Stages	Erikson's Stages of Psychosocial Development	Positive and Negative Outcomes of Erikson's Stages
Birth to 12–18 months	Oral	Interest in oral gratification from sucking, eating, mouthing, biting	Trust vs. mistrust	*Positive:* Feelings of trust from environmental support *Negative:* Fear and concern regarding others
12–18 months to 3 years	Anal	Gratification from expelling and withholding feces; coming to terms with society's controls relating to toilet training	Autonomy vs. shame and doubt	*Positive:* Self-sufficiency if exploration is encouraged *Negative:* Doubts about self, lack of independence
3 to 5–6 years	Phallic	Interest in the genitals; coming to terms with Oedipal conflict, leading to identification with same-sex parent	Initiative vs. guilt	*Positive:* Discovery of ways to initiate actions *Negative:* Guilt from actions and thoughts
5–6 years to adolescence	Latency	Sexual concerns largely unimportant	Industry vs. inferiority	*Positive:* Development of sense of competence *Negative:* Feelings of inferiority, no sense of mastery
Adolescence to adulthood (Freud) Adolescence (Erikson)	Genital	Reemergence of sexual interests and establishment of mature sexual relationships	Identity vs. role diffusion	*Positive:* Awareness of uniqueness of self, knowledge of role to be followed *Negative:* Inability to identify appropriate roles in life
Early adulthood (Erikson)			Intimacy vs. isolation	*Positive:* Development of loving, sexual relationships and close friendships *Negative:* Fear of relationships with others
Middle adulthood (Erikson)			Generativity vs. stagnation	*Positive:* Sense of contribution to continuity of life *Negative:* Trivialization of one's activities
Late adulthood (Erikson)			Ego integrity vs. despair	*Positive:* Sense of unity in life's accomplishments *Negative:* Regret over lost opportunities of life

occur. *Fixation* is behavior reflecting an earlier stage of development due to an unresolved conflict. For instance, fixation at the oral stage might produce an adult who is unusually absorbed in oral activities—eating, talking, or chewing gum.

psychosocial development
the approach that encompasses changes in our interactions with and understandings of one another, as well as in our knowledge and understanding of ourselves as members of society

ERIKSON'S PSYCHOSOCIAL THEORY. Psychoanalyst Erik Erikson, who lived from 1902 to 1994, provided an alternative psychodynamic view in his theory of psychosocial development, which emphasizes our social interaction with other people. In Erikson's view, both society and culture challenge and shape us. **Psychosocial development** encompasses changes in our interactions with and understandings of one another as well as in our knowledge and understanding of ourselves as members of society (Erikson, 1963; Dunkel, Kim, Papini, 2012; Jones et al., 2014; Malone et al., 2016; Knight, 2017).

Erikson's theory suggests that developmental change occurs throughout our lives in eight distinct stages (see Table 1-3). The stages emerge in a fixed pattern and are similar for all people. Erikson argued that each stage presents a crisis or conflict that the individual must resolve. Although no crisis is ever fully resolved, making life increasingly complicated, the individual must at least address the crisis of each stage sufficiently to deal with demands made during the next stage of development.

Jon Erikson/The Image Works

Erik Erikson.

Unlike Freud, who regarded development as relatively complete by adolescence, Erikson suggested that growth and change continue throughout the life span. For instance, as we'll discuss further in Chapter 16, Erikson suggested that during middle adulthood, people pass through the *generativity versus stagnation stage*, in which their contributions to family, community, and society can produce either positive feelings about the continuity of life or a sense of stagnation and disappointment about what they are passing on to future generations (de St. Aubin, McAdams, & Kim, 2004).

ASSESSING THE PSYCHODYNAMIC PERSPECTIVE. It is hard for us to grasp the full significance of psychodynamic theories represented by Freud's psychoanalytic theory and Erikson's theory of psychosocial development. Freud's introduction of the notion that unconscious influences affect behavior was a monumental accomplishment, and that it seems at all reasonable to us shows how extensively the idea of the unconscious has pervaded thinking in Western cultures. In fact, work by contemporary researchers studying memory and learning suggests that we carry with us memories—of which we are not consciously aware—that have a significant impact on our behavior.

However, many of the most basic principles of Freud's psychoanalytic theory have been called into question because they have not been validated by subsequent research. In particular, the notion that people pass through various stages in childhood that determine their adult personalities has little definitive research support. In addition, because much of Freud's theory was based on a limited population of upper-middle-class Austrians living during a strict, puritanical era, its application to broad, multicultural populations is questionable. Finally, because Freud's theory focuses primarily on male development, it has been criticized as sexist and may be interpreted as devaluing women. For such reasons, many developmentalists question Freud's theory (Schachter, 2005; Gillham, Law, & Hickey, 2010; O'Neil & Denke, 2016).

Erikson's view that development continues throughout the life span is highly important—and has received considerable support. However, the theory also has its drawbacks. Like Freud's theory, it focuses more on men's than women's development. It is also vague in some respects, making it difficult for researchers to test rigorously. And, as is the case with psychodynamic theories in general, it is difficult to make definitive predictions about a given individual's behavior using the theory. In sum, then, the psychodynamic perspective provides good descriptions of past behavior, but imprecise predictions of future behavior (Zauszniewski & Martin, 1999; de St. Aubin & McAdams, 2004).

The Behavioral Perspective: Focusing on Observable Behavior

LO 1.6 Describe how the behavioral perspective explains lifespan development.

When Elissa Sheehan was 3, a large brown dog bit her, and she needed dozens of stitches and several operations. From the time she was bitten, she broke into a sweat whenever she saw a dog, and in fact never enjoyed being around any pet.

To a lifespan development specialist using the behavioral perspective, the explanation for Elissa's behavior is straightforward: She has a learned fear of dogs. Rather than looking inside the organism at unconscious processes, the **behavioral perspective** suggests that the keys to understanding development are observable behavior and outside stimuli in the environment. If we know the stimuli, we can predict the behavior. In this respect, the behavioral perspective reflects the view that nurture is more important to development than nature.

behavioral perspective
the approach suggesting that the keys to understanding development are observable behavior and outside stimuli in the environment

Behavioral theories reject the notion that people universally pass through a series of stages. Instead, people are assumed to be affected by the environmental stimuli to which they happen to be exposed. Developmental patterns, then, are personal, reflecting a particular set of environmental stimuli, and behavior is the result of continuing exposure to specific factors in the environment. Furthermore, developmental change is viewed in quantitative, rather than qualitative, terms. For instance, behavioral theories hold that advances in problem-solving capabilities as children age are largely a result of greater mental *capacities* rather than changes in the *kind* of thinking that children are able to bring to bear on a problem.

CLASSICAL CONDITIONING: STIMULUS SUBSTITUTION.

> *Give me a dozen healthy infants, well-formed, and my own specified world to bring them up in and I'll guarantee to take any one at random and train him to become any type of specialist I might select—doctor, lawyer, artist, merchant-chief, and yes, even beggar-man and thief, regardless of his talents, penchants, tendencies, abilities. (Watson, J. B. [1925]. Behaviorism. New York: Norton.)*

With these words, John B. Watson, one of the first American psychologists to advocate a behavioral approach, summed up the behavioral perspective. Watson, who lived

Hulton Archive/Getty Images
John B. Watson.

from 1878 to 1958, believed strongly that we could gain a full understanding of development by carefully studying the stimuli that composed the environment. In fact, he argued that by effectively controlling a person's environment, it was possible to produce virtually any behavior.

classical conditioning
a type of learning in which an organism responds in a particular way to a neutral stimulus that normally does not bring about that type of response

As we'll consider further in Chapter 5, **Classical conditioning** occurs when an organism learns to respond in a particular way to a neutral stimulus that normally does not evoke that type of response. For instance, if a dog is repeatedly exposed to the pairing of the sound of a bell and the presentation of meat, it may learn to react to the bell alone in the same way it reacts to the meat—by salivating and wagging its tail with excitement. Dogs don't typically respond to bells in this way; the behavior is a result of conditioning, a form of learning in which the response associated with one stimulus (food) comes to be connected to another—in this case, the bell.

The same process of classical conditioning explains how we learn emotional responses. In the case of dog-bite victim Elissa Sheehan, for instance, Watson would say that one stimulus has been substituted for another: Elissa's unpleasant experience with a particular dog (the initial stimulus) has been transferred to other dogs and to pets in general.

OPERANT CONDITIONING. In addition to classical conditioning, other types of learning also derive from the behavioral perspective. The learning approach that probably has had the greatest influence is operant conditioning. **Operant conditioning** is a form of learning in which a voluntary response is strengthened or weakened by its association with positive or negative consequences. It differs from classical conditioning in that the response being conditioned is voluntary and purposeful rather than automatic (such as salivating).

operant conditioning
a form of learning in which a voluntary response is strengthened or weakened by its association with positive or negative consequences

In operant conditioning, formulated and championed by psychologist B. F. Skinner (1904–1990), individuals learn to act deliberately on their environment in order to bring about desired consequences (Skinner, 1975). In a sense, then, people *operate* on their environment to bring about a desired state of affairs.

Whether children and adults will seek to repeat a behavior depends on whether it is followed by reinforcement. *Reinforcement* is the process by which a stimulus is provided that increases the probability that a preceding behavior will be repeated. Hence, a student is apt to work harder in school if he or she receives good grades; workers are likely to labor harder at their jobs if their efforts are tied to pay increases; and people are more apt to buy lottery tickets if they are reinforced by winning occasionally. In addition, *punishment*, the introduction of an unpleasant or a painful stimulus or the removal of a desirable stimulus, will decrease the probability that a preceding behavior will occur in the future.

Behavior that is reinforced, then, is more likely to be repeated in the future, while behavior that receives no reinforcement or is punished is likely to be discontinued, or in the language of operant conditioning, *extinguished*. Principles of operant conditioning are used in **behavior modification**, a formal technique for promoting the frequency of desirable behaviors and decreasing the incidence of unwanted ones. Behavior modification has been used in a variety of situations, ranging from teaching severely intellectually disabled people the rudiments of language to helping people stick to diets (Wupperman et al., 2012; Wirth, Wabitsch & Hauner, 2014; Miltenberger, 2016).

behavior modification
a formal technique for promoting the frequency of desirable behaviors and decreasing the incidence of unwanted ones

SOCIAL-COGNITIVE LEARNING THEORY: LEARNING THROUGH IMITATION. A 5-year-old boy seriously injures his 22-month-old cousin while imitating a violent wrestling move he had seen on television. Although the infant sustained spinal cord injuries, he improved and was discharged five weeks after his hospital admission (Reuters Health eLine, 2002; Ray & Heyes, 2011).

Cause and effect? We can't know for sure, but it certainly seems possible, especially looking at the situation from the perspective of social-cognitive learning theory. According to developmental psychologist Albert Bandura and colleagues, a significant amount of learning is explained by **social-cognitive learning theory**, an approach that emphasizes learning by observing the behavior of another person, called a *model* (Bandura, 1994, 2002).

social-cognitive learning theory
learning by observing the behavior of another person, called a model

According to social-cognitive learning theory, behavior is learned primarily through observation and not through trial and error, as it is with operant conditioning. We don't need to experience the consequences of a behavior ourselves to learn it. Social-cognitive learning theory holds that when we see the behavior of a model being rewarded, we are likely to imitate that behavior. For instance, in one classic experiment, children who were afraid of dogs were exposed to a model, nicknamed the "Fearless Peer," who was seen playing happily with a dog (Bandura, Grusec, & Menlove, 1967). After exposure, the children who previously had been afraid were more likely to approach a strange dog than children who had not seen the model.

Bandura suggests that social-cognitive learning proceeds in four steps (Bandura, 1986). First, an observer must pay attention and perceive the most critical features of a model's behavior. Second, the observer must successfully recall the behavior. Third, the observer must reproduce the behavior accurately. Finally, the observer must be motivated to learn and carry out the behavior.

Jutta Klee/Getty Images

What form of learning is being demonstrated in this picture?

From a *social worker's* perspective

How do the concepts of social learning and modeling relate to the mass media, and how might exposure to mass media influence a child's family life?

ASSESSING THE BEHAVIORAL PERSPECTIVE. Research using the behavioral perspective has made significant contributions, ranging from techniques for educating children with severe intellectual disabilities to identifying procedures for curbing aggression. At the same time, some controversies surround the behavioral perspective. For example, although they are part of the same general behavioral perspective, classical and operant conditioning and social learning theory diverge in some basic ways. Both classical and operant conditioning present learning in terms of external stimuli and responses, in which the only important factors are the observable features of the environment. In such an analysis, people and other organisms are like inanimate "black boxes." Nothing that occurs inside the box is understood—nor much cared about, for that matter.

To social learning theorists, such an analysis is an oversimplification. They argue that what makes people different from rats and pigeons is the occurrence of mental activity, in the form of thoughts and expectations. A full understanding of people's development, they maintain, cannot occur without moving beyond external stimuli and responses.

In many ways, social learning theory has come to predominate in recent decades over classical and operant conditioning theories. In fact, another perspective that focuses explicitly on internal mental activity has become enormously influential. This is the cognitive approach, which we consider next.

The Cognitive Perspective: Examining the Roots of Understanding

LO 1.7 Describe how the cognitive perspective explains lifespan development.

When 3-year-old Jake is asked why it sometimes rains, he answers "so the flowers can grow." When his 11-year-old sister Lila is asked the same question, she responds "because of evaporation from the surface of the earth." And when their cousin Ajima, who is studying meteorology in graduate school, considers the same question, her extended answer includes a discussion of cumulonimbus clouds, the Coriolis effect, and synoptic charts.

To a developmental theorist using the cognitive perspective, the difference in the sophistication of the answers is evidence of a different degree of knowledge and understanding, or cognition. The **cognitive perspective** focuses on the processes that allow people to know, understand, and think about the world.

cognitive perspective
the approach that focuses on the processes that allow people to know, understand, and think about the world

The cognitive perspective emphasizes how people internally represent and think about the world. By using this perspective, developmental researchers hope to understand how children and adults process information and how their ways of thinking and understanding affect their behavior. They also seek to learn how cognitive abilities change as people develop, the degree to which cognitive development represents quantitative and qualitative growth in intellectual abilities, and how different cognitive abilities are related to one another.

PIAGET'S THEORY OF COGNITIVE DEVELOPMENT. No single person has had a greater impact on the study of cognitive development than Jean Piaget, who lived from 1896 to 1980. A Swiss psychologist, Piaget proposed that all people pass in a fixed sequence through a series of universal stages of cognitive development. He suggested that not only does the quantity of information increase in each stage, but the quality of knowledge and understanding changes as well. His focus was on the change in cognition that occurs as children move from one stage to the next (Piaget, 1962, 1983).

Although we'll consider Piaget's theory in detail beginning in Chapter 5, we can get a broad sense of it now. Piaget suggested that human thinking is arranged into *schemes*, that is, organized mental patterns that represent behaviors and actions. In infants, such schemes represent concrete behavior—a scheme for sucking, for reaching, and for each separate behavior. In older children, the schemes become more sophisticated and abstract, such as the set of skills involved in riding a bike or playing an interactive video game. Schemes are like intellectual computer software programs that direct and determine how data from the world are looked at and handled (Parker, 2005).

Piaget suggests that the growth in children's understanding of the world can be explained by the two basic principles of assimilation and accommodation. *Assimilation* is the process through which people understand an experience in terms of their current stage of cognitive development and way of thinking. Assimilation occurs when people use their current ways of thinking about and understanding the world to perceive and understand a new experience. In contrast, *accommodation* refers to changes in existing ways of thinking in response to encounters with new stimuli or events. Assimilation and accommodation work in tandem to bring about cognitive development.

Assessing Piaget's Theory. Piaget has profoundly influenced our understanding of cognitive development and is one of the towering figures in lifespan development. He provided masterful descriptions of how intellectual growth proceeds during childhood—descriptions that have stood the test of literally thousands of investigations. By and large, then, Piaget's broad view of the sequence of cognitive development is accurate.

However, the specifics of the theory, particularly in terms of change in cognitive capabilities over time, have been called into question. For instance, some cognitive skills clearly emerge earlier than Piaget suggested. Furthermore, the universality of Piaget's stages has been disputed. A growing amount of evidence suggests that the emergence of particular cognitive skills occurs according to a different timetable in non-Western cultures. And in every culture, some people never seem to reach Piaget's highest level of cognitive sophistication: formal, logical thought (Genovese, 2006; De Jesus-Zayas, Buigas, & Denney, 2012; Siegler, 2016).

Ultimately, the greatest criticism leveled at the Piagetian perspective is that cognitive development is not necessarily as discontinuous as Piaget's stage theory suggests. Remember that Piaget argued that growth proceeds in four distinct stages in which the quality of cognition differs from one stage to the next. However, many developmental researchers argue that growth is considerably more continuous. These critics have suggested an alternative perspective, known as the information processing approach, which focuses on the processes that underlie learning, memory, and thinking throughout the life span.

information processing approaches
models that seek to identify the ways individuals take in, use, and store information

INFORMATION PROCESSING APPROACHES. Information processing approaches have become an important alternative to Piagetian approaches. **Information processing approaches** to cognitive development seek to identify the ways individuals take in, use, and store information.

Information processing approaches grew out of developments in the electronic processing of information, particularly as carried out by computers. They assume that even complex behavior such as learning, remembering, categorizing, and thinking can be broken down into a series of individual, specific steps.

Like computers, children are assumed by information processing approaches to have limited capacity for processing information. As they develop, however, they employ increasingly sophisticated strategies that allow them to process information more efficiently.

In stark contrast to Piaget's view that thinking undergoes qualitative advances as children age, information processing approaches assume that development is marked more by quantitative advances. Our capacity to handle information changes with age, as does our processing speed and efficiency. Furthermore, information processing approaches suggest that as we age, we are better able to control the nature of processing and that we can change the strategies we use to process information.

An information processing approach that builds on Piaget's research is known as neo-Piagetian theory. In contrast to Piaget's original work, which viewed cognition as a single system of increasingly sophisticated general cognitive abilities, *neo-Piagetian theory* considers cognition as being made up of different types of individual skills. Using the terminology of information processing approaches, neo-Piagetian theory suggests that cognitive development proceeds quickly in certain areas and more slowly in others. For example, reading ability and the skills needed to recall stories may progress sooner than the sorts of abstract computational abilities used in algebra or trigonometry. Furthermore, neo-Piagetian theorists believe that experience plays a greater role in advancing cognitive development than traditional Piagetian approaches claim (Case, Demetriou, & Platsidou, 2001; Loewen, 2006; Barrouillet & Gaillard, 2011).

Assessing Information Processing Approaches. As we'll see in future chapters, information processing approaches have become a central part of our understanding of development. At the same time, they do not offer a complete explanation for behavior. For example, information processing approaches have paid little attention to behavior such as creativity, in which the most profound ideas often are developed in a seemingly nonlogical, nonlinear manner. In addition, they do not take into account the social context in which development takes place. That's one of the reasons that theories emphasizing the social and cultural aspects of development have become increasingly popular—as we'll discuss next.

COGNITIVE NEUROSCIENCE APPROACHES. One of the most recent additions to the array of approaches taken by lifespan developmentalists, **cognitive neuroscience approaches** look at cognitive development through the lens of brain processes. Like other cognitive perspectives, cognitive neuroscience approaches consider internal mental processes, but they focus specifically on the neurological activity that underlies thinking, problem solving, and other cognitive behavior.

cognitive neuroscience approaches
approaches that examine cognitive development through the lens of brain processes

Cognitive neuroscientists seek to identify actual locations and functions within the brain that are related to different types of cognitive activity rather than simply assuming that there are hypothetical or theoretical cognitive structures related to thinking. For example, using sophisticated brain scanning techniques, cognitive neuroscientists have demonstrated that thinking about the meaning of a word activates different areas of the brain than thinking about how the word sounds when spoken.

The work of cognitive neuroscientists is also providing clues to the cause of *autism spectrum disorder*, a major developmental disability that can produce profound language deficits and self-injurious behavior in young children. For example, neuroscientists have found that the brains of children with the disorder sometimes show explosive, dramatic growth in the first year of life, making their heads significantly larger than those of children without the disorder. Furthermore, brain scans show structural differences in the brains of children (see Figure 1-1). By identifying children with the disorder very early in their lives, health-care practitioners can provide crucial early intervention (Lewis & Elman, 2008; Howard et al., 2014; Grant, 2017).

Figure 1-1 The Autistic Brain.

Researchers have found abnormalities in the temporal lobe of the brain in some children diagnosed with autism spectrum disorder.

(**Source:** Boddaert, N. et al. [2009]. MRI Findings in 77 Children with Non-Syndromic Autistic Disorder, PLoS ONE. 2009; 4[2]: e4415.)

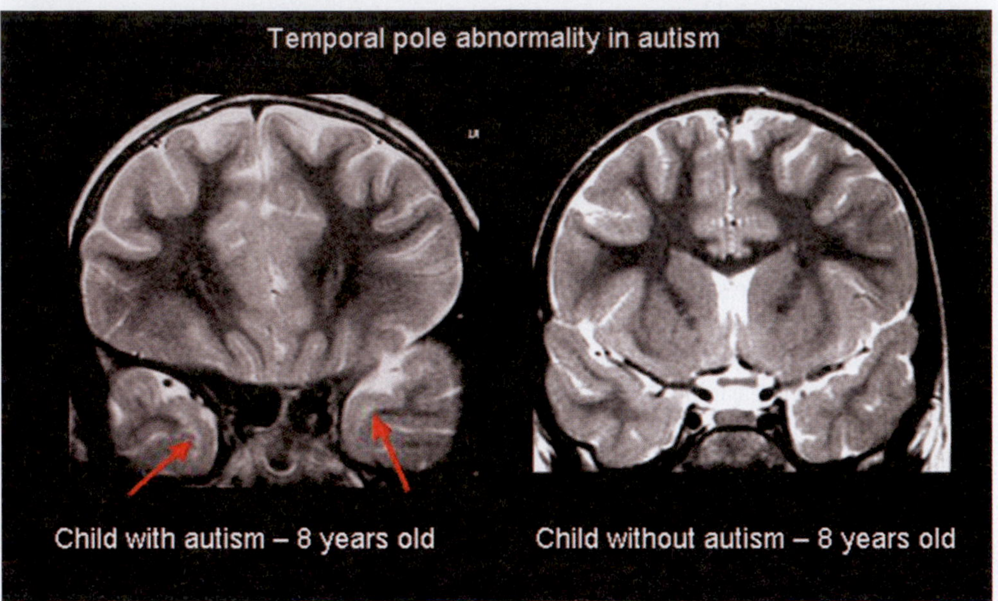

Cognitive neuroscience approaches are also on the forefront of cutting-edge research that has identified specific genes associated with disorders ranging from physical problems such as breast cancer to psychological disorders such as schizophrenia. Identifying the genes that make one vulnerable to such disorders is the first step in genetic engineering in which gene therapy can reduce or even prevent the disorder from occurring (Strobel et al., 2007; Ranganath, Minzenberg, & Ragland, 2008; Rodnitzky, 2012).

Assessing Cognitive Neuroscience Approaches. Cognitive neuroscience approaches represent a new frontier in child and adolescent development. Using sophisticated measurement techniques that many of them developed only in the past few years, cognitive neuroscientists are able to peer into the inner functioning of the brain. Advances in our understanding of genetics also has opened a new window into both normal and abnormal development and has suggested a variety of treatments for abnormalities.

Critics of the cognitive neuroscience approach have suggested that it sometimes provides a better *description* than *explanation* of developmental phenomena. For instance, the finding that children with autism spectrum disorder have larger brains than those without the disorder does not explain why their brains became larger—that's a question that remains to be answered. Still, such work not only offers important clues to appropriate treatments but ultimately can also lead to a full understanding of a range of developmental phenomena.

The Humanistic Perspective: Concentrating on the Unique Qualities of Human Beings

LO 1.8 Describe how the humanistic perspective explains lifespan development.

The unique qualities of humans are the central focus of the humanistic perspective, the fourth of the major theories used by lifespan developmentalists. Rejecting the notion that our behavior is largely determined by unconscious processes, by learning from our environment, or by rational cognitive processing, the **humanistic perspective** contends that people have a natural capacity to make decisions about their lives and to control their behavior. According to this approach, each individual has the ability and motivation to reach more advanced levels of maturity, and people naturally seek to reach their full potential.

humanistic perspective
the theory contending that people have a natural capacity to make decisions about their lives and control their behavior

The humanistic perspective emphasizes *free will*, the ability of humans to make choices and come to decisions about their lives. Instead of relying on societal standards, then, people are assumed to be motivated to make their own decisions about what they do with their lives.

Carl Rogers, who lived from 1902 to 1987, one of the major proponents of the humanistic perspective, suggested that all people have a need for positive regard that results from an underlying wish to be loved and respected. Because it is other people who provide this positive regard, we become dependent on them. Consequently, our view of ourselves and our self-worth is a reflection of how we think others view us (Rogers, 1971; Motschnig & Nykl, 2003; Malchiodi, 2012).

Rogers, along with another key figure in the humanistic perspective, Abraham Maslow (1908–1970), suggests that self-actualization is a primary goal in life. *Self-actualization* is a state of self-fulfillment in which people achieve their highest potential in their own unique way. Although the concept initially was deemed to apply to only a few select famous people, such as Eleanor Roosevelt, Abraham Lincoln, and Albert Einstein, later theorists expanded the concept to apply to any person who realizes his or her own potential and possibilities (Maslow, 1970; Sheldon, Joiner, & Pettit, 2003; Malchiodi, 2012).

ASSESSING THE HUMANISTIC PERSPECTIVE. Despite its emphasis on important and unique human qualities, the humanistic perspective has not had a major impact on the field of lifespan development. Its lack of influence is primarily due to its inability to identify any sort of broad developmental change that is the result of increasing age or experience. Still, some of the concepts drawn from the humanistic perspective, such as self-actualization, have helped describe important aspects of human behavior and are widely discussed in areas ranging from health care to business (Zalenski & Raspa, 2006; Elkins, 2009; Beitel et al., 2014).

The Contextual Perspective: Taking a Broad Approach to Development

LO 1.9 Describe how the contextual perspective explains lifespan development.

Although lifespan developmentalists often consider the course of development separately in terms of physical, cognitive, personality, and social factors, such a categorization has one serious drawback: In the real world, none of these broad influences occurs in isolation from any other. Instead, there is a constant, ongoing interaction between the different types of influence.

The **contextual perspective** considers the relationship between individuals and their physical, cognitive, personality, and social worlds. It suggests that a person's unique development cannot be properly viewed without seeing how that person is enmeshed within a rich social and cultural context. We'll consider two major theories that fall under this category: Bronfenbrenner's bioecological approach and Vygotsky's sociocultural theory.

contextual perspective
the theory that considers the relationship between individuals and their physical, cognitive, personality, and social worlds

THE BIOECOLOGICAL APPROACH TO DEVELOPMENT. In acknowledging the problem with traditional approaches to lifespan development, psychologist Urie Bronfenbrenner (1989, 2000, 2002), who lived from 1917 to 2005, proposed an alternative perspective, called the bioecological approach. The **bioecological approach** suggests that five levels of the environment simultaneously influence individuals. Bronfenbrenner noted that we cannot fully understand development without considering how a person is influenced by each of these levels (illustrated in Figure 1-2).

bioecological perspective
the perspective suggesting that different levels of the environment simultaneously influence individuals

- The *microsystem* is the everyday, immediate environment in which children lead their daily lives. Homes, caregivers, friends, and teachers all are influences that are part of the microsystem. But the child is not just a passive recipient of these influences. Instead, children actively help construct the microsystem, shaping the immediate world in which they live. The microsystem is the level at which most traditional work in child development has been directed.

Figure 1-2 Bronfenbrenner's Approach to Development.

Urie Bronfenbrenner's bioecological approach to development offers five levels of the environment that simultaneously influence individuals: the macrosystem, exosystem, mesosystem, microsystem, and chronosystem.

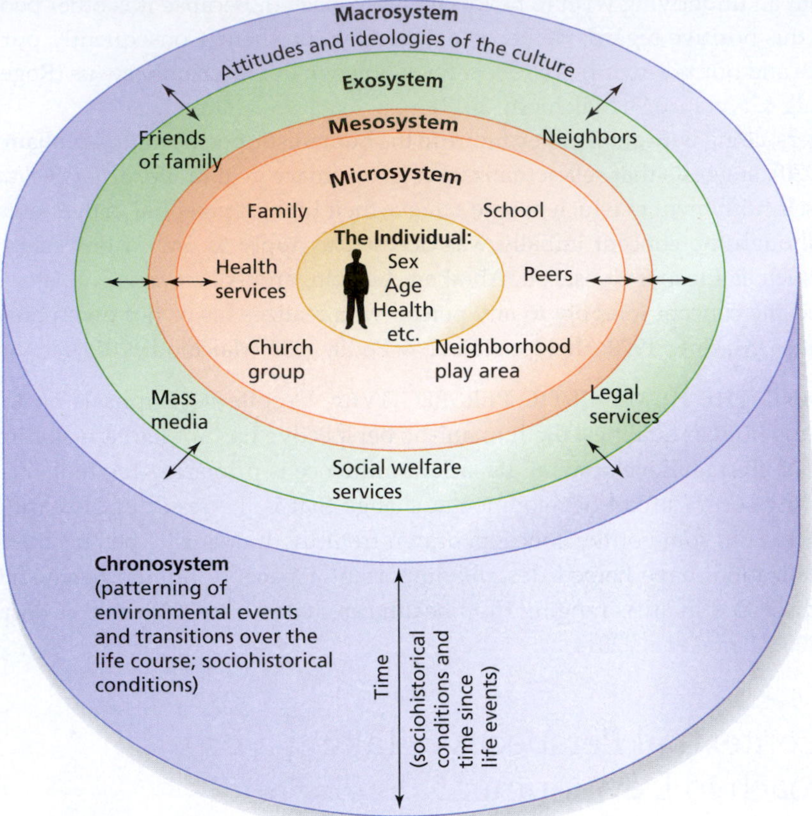

- The *mesosystem* provides connections between the various aspects of the microsystem. Like links in a chain, the mesosystem binds children to parents, students to teachers, employees to bosses, and friends to friends. It acknowledges the direct and indirect influences that bind us to one another, such as those that affect a mother or father who has a bad day at the office and then is short-tempered with her or his son or daughter at home.
- The *exosystem* represents broader influences, encompassing societal institutions such as local government, the community, schools, places of worship, and the local media. Each of these larger institutions of society can have an immediate, and major, impact on personal development, and each affects how the microsystem and mesosystem operate. For example, the quality of a school will affect a child's cognitive development and potentially can have long-term consequences.
- The *macrosystem* represents the larger cultural influences on an individual. Society in general, types of governments, religious and political value systems, and other broad, encompassing factors are parts of the macrosystem. For example, the value a culture or society places on education or the family will affect the values of the people who live in that society. Children are part of a broader culture (such as Western culture) and are influenced by their membership in a particular subculture (for instance, being part of the Mexican American subculture).
- Finally, the *chronosystem* underlies each of the previous systems. It involves the way the passage of time, including historical events (such as the terrorist attacks in September 2001) and more gradual historical changes (such as changes in the number of women who work outside of the home), affect children's development.

The bioecological approach emphasizes the *interconnectedness of the influences on development*. Because the various levels are related to one another, a change in one part of the system affects other parts of the system. For instance, a parent's loss of a job (involving the mesosystem) has an impact on a child's microsystem.

Conversely, changes on one environmental level may make little difference if other levels are not also changed. For instance, improving the school environment may have a negligible effect on academic performance if children receive little support for academic success at home. Similarly, the bioecological approach illustrates that the influences among different family members are multidirectional. Parents don't just influence their child's behavior—children also influence their parents' behavior.

Finally, the bioecological approach stresses the importance of broad cultural factors that affect development. Researchers in lifespan development increasingly look at how membership in cultural and subcultural groups influences behavior.

Consider, for instance, whether you agree that children should be taught that their classmates' assistance is indispensable to getting good grades in school, or that they should definitely plan to continue their fathers' businesses, or that children should follow their parents' advice in determining their career plans. If you have been raised in the most widespread North American culture, you would likely disagree with all three statements, since they violate the premises of *individualism*, the dominant Western philosophy that emphasizes personal identity, uniqueness, freedom, and the worth of the individual.

By contrast, if you were raised in a traditional Asian culture, your agreement with the three statements would be considerably more likely. The reason? The statements reflect the value orientation known as *collectivism*—the notion that the well-being of the group is more important than that of the individual. People raised in collectivistic cultures tend to emphasize the welfare of the groups to which they belong, sometimes even at the expense of their own personal well-being.

The individualism–collectivism spectrum is one of several dimensions along which cultures differ. Similarly, the roles played by men and women also vary across cultures in significant ways. Such broad cultural values play an important role in shaping the ways people view the world and behave (Yu & Stiffman, 2007; Cheung et al., 2016; Sparrow, 2016).

Assessing the Bioecological Approach. Although Bronfenbrenner considered biological influences as an important component of the bioecological approach, ecological influences are central to the theory. Some critics argue that the perspective pays insufficient attention to biological factors. Still, the bioecological approach is of considerable importance to child development, suggesting as it does the multiple levels at which the environment affects children's development.

Denis Pogostin/Shutterstock

Pavel Losevsky/Fotolia

The bioecological approach to development focuses on the vast differences in environments in which children develop.

Ami Parikh/Shutterstock

According to Vygotsky, children can develop cognitively in their understanding of the world, and learn what is important in society, through play and cooperation with others.

VYGOTSKY'S SOCIOCULTURAL THEORY. To Russian developmentalist Lev Semenovich Vygotsky, who lived from 1896 to 1934, a full understanding of development was impossible without taking into account the culture in which people develop. Vygotsky's **sociocultural theory** emphasizes how cognitive development proceeds as a result of social interactions between members of a culture (Vygotsky, 1926/1997; Göncü & Gauvain, 2012; Fleer, González Rey, & Veresov, 2017).

Vygotsky argued that children's understanding of the world is acquired through their problem-solving interactions with adults and other children. As children play and cooperate with others, they learn what is important in their society and, at the same time, advance cognitively in their understanding of the world. Consequently, to understand the course of development, we must consider what is meaningful to members of a given culture.

sociocultural theory
the approach that emphasizes how cognitive development proceeds as a result of social interactions between members of a culture

More than most other theories, sociocultural theory emphasizes that development is a *reciprocal transaction* between the people in a child's environment and the child. Vygotsky believed that people and settings influence the child, who in turn influences the people and settings. This pattern continues in an endless loop, with children being both recipients of socialization influences and sources of influence. For example, a child raised with his or her extended family nearby will grow up with a different sense of family life than a child whose relatives live a considerable distance away. Those relatives, too, are affected by that situation and that child, depending on how close and frequent their contact is with the child.

Theorists who built on Vygotsky's work have used the example of *scaffolds*, the temporary platforms used by construction workers when building a structure, to describe how children learn. Scaffolding is the temporary support that teachers, parents, and others provide children as they are learning a task. As children become increasingly competent and master a task, the scaffolding can be withdrawn, allowing children to carry out the task on their own (Lowe et al., 2013; Peralta et al., 2013; Dahl et al., 2017).

Assessing Vygotsky's Theory. Sociocultural theory has become increasingly influential in the decades since Vygotsky's death. The reason is the growing acknowledgment of the central importance of cultural factors in development. Children do not develop in a cultural vacuum. Instead, their attention is directed by society to certain areas, and as a consequence, they develop particular kinds of skills that are an outcome of their cultural environment. Vygotsky was one of the first developmentalists to recognize and acknowledge the importance of culture, and—as today's society becomes increasingly multicultural—sociocultural theory is helping us to understand the rich and varied influences that shape development (Rogan, 2007; Frie, 2014; van der Veer & Yasnitsky, 2016).

Sociocultural theory is not without its critics, however. Some suggest that Vygotsky's strong emphasis on the role of culture and social experience led him to ignore the effects of biological factors on development. In addition, his perspective seems to minimize the role that individuals can play in shaping their own environment.

Evolutionary Perspectives: Our Ancestors' Contributions to Behavior

LO 1.10 Describe how the evolutionary perspective explains lifespan development.

evolutionary perspective
the theory that seeks to identify behavior that is a result of our genetic inheritance from our ancestors

One increasingly influential approach is the evolutionary perspective, the sixth and final developmental perspective that we will consider. The **evolutionary perspective** seeks to identify behavior that is the result of our genetic inheritance from our ancestors (Bjorklund, 2005; Goetz & Shackelford, 2006; Tomasello, 2011).

Evolutionary approaches have grown out of the groundbreaking work of Charles Darwin (1809–1882). In 1859, Darwin argued in his book *On the Origin of Species* that a process of natural selection creates traits in a species that are adaptive to its environment. Using Darwin's arguments, evolutionary approaches contend that our genetic inheritance determines not only such physical traits as skin and eye color, but certain personality traits and social behaviors as well. For instance, some evolutionary developmentalists suggest that traits such as shyness and jealousy are produced in part by genetic causes, presumably because they helped increase the survival rates of humans' ancient relatives (Easton, Schipper, & Shackelford, 2007; Buss, 2012; Geary & Berch, 2016).

Nina Leen/GettyImages

Konrad Lorenz, seen here with geese who from their birth have followed him, considered the ways in which behavior reflects inborn genetic patterns.

The evolutionary perspective draws heavily on the field of *ethology*, which examines the ways in which our biological makeup influences our behavior. A primary proponent of ethology was Konrad Lorenz (1903–1989), who discovered that newborn geese are genetically preprogrammed to become attached to the first moving object they see after birth. His work, which demonstrated the importance of biological determinants in influencing behavior patterns, ultimately led developmentalists to consider the ways in which human behavior might reflect inborn genetic patterns.

As we'll consider further in Chapter 2, the evolutionary perspective encompasses one of the fastest-growing areas within the field of lifespan development: behavioral genetics. *Behavioral genetics* studies the effects of heredity on behavior. Behavioral geneticists seek to understand how we might inherit certain behavioral traits and how the environment influences whether we actually display such traits. It also considers how genetic factors may produce psychological disorders such as schizophrenia (Bjorklund & Ellis, 2005; Rembis, 2009; Plomin et al., 2016).

ASSESSING THE EVOLUTIONARY PERSPECTIVE. There is little argument among lifespan developmentalists that Darwin's evolutionary theory provides an accurate description of basic genetic processes, and the evolutionary perspective is increasingly visible in the field of lifespan development. However, applications of the evolutionary perspective have been subjected to considerable criticism.

Some developmentalists are concerned that because of its focus on genetic and biological aspects of behavior, the evolutionary perspective pays insufficient attention to the environmental and social factors involved in producing children's and adults' behavior. Other critics argue that there is no good way to experimentally test theories derived from the evolutionary approach because they all happened so long ago. For example, it is one thing to say that jealousy helped individuals to survive more effectively and another thing to prove it. Still, the evolutionary approach has stimulated a significant amount of research on how our biological inheritance at least partially influences our traits and behaviors (Baptista et al., 2008; Del Giudice, 2015; Barbaro et al., 2017).

Why "Which Approach Is Right?" Is the Wrong Question

LO 1.11 Discuss the value of applying multiple perspectives to lifespan development.

We have considered the six major perspectives used in lifespan development—psychodynamic, behavioral, cognitive, humanistic, contextual, and evolutionary. These

Table 1-4 Major Perspectives on Lifespan Development

Perspective	Key Ideas About Human Behavior and Development	Major Proponents	Example
Psychodynamic	Behavior throughout life is motivated by inner, unconscious forces, stemming from childhood, over which we have little control.	Sigmund Freud, Erik Erikson	This view might suggest that a young adult who is overweight has a fixation in the oral stage of development.
Behavioral	Development can be understood through studying observable behavior and environmental stimuli.	John B. Watson, B. F. Skinner, Albert Bandura	In this perspective, a young adult who is overweight might be seen as not being rewarded for good nutritional and exercise habits.
Cognitive	Emphasis on how changes or growth in the ways people know, understand, and think about the world affect behavior.	Jean Piaget	This view might suggest that a young adult who is overweight hasn't learned effective ways to stay at a healthy weight and doesn't value good nutrition.
Humanistic	Behavior is chosen through free will and motivated by our natural capacity to strive to reach our full potential.	Carl Rogers, Abraham Maslow	In this view, a young adult who is overweight may eventually choose to seek an optimal weight as part of an overall pattern of individual growth.
Contextual	Development should be viewed in terms of the interrelationship of a person's physical, cognitive, personality, and social worlds.	Urie Bronfenbrenner, Lev Vygotsky	In this perspective, being overweight is caused by a number of interrelated factors in that person's physical, cognitive, personality, and social worlds.
Evolutionary	Behavior is the result of genetic inheritance from our ancestors; traits and behavior that are adaptive for promoting the survival of our species have been inherited through natural selection.	Influenced by early work of Charles Darwin, Konrad Lorenz	This view might suggest that a young adult might have a genetic tendency toward obesity because extra fat helped his or her ancestors to survive in times of famine.

perspectives are summarized in Table 1-4 and are applied to the case of a young adult who is overweight. It would be natural to wonder which of the six perspectives provides the most accurate account of human development.

For several reasons, this question is not entirely appropriate. For one thing, each perspective emphasizes somewhat different aspects of development. For instance, the psychodynamic approach emphasizes emotions, motivational conflicts, and unconscious determinants of behavior. In contrast, behavioral perspectives emphasize overt behavior, paying far more attention to what people *do* than to what goes on inside their heads, which is deemed largely irrelevant. The cognitive and humanistic perspectives take quite the opposite tack, looking more at what people *think* than at what they do. Finally, the evolutionary perspective focuses on how inherited biological factors underlie development.

Clearly, each perspective is based on its own premises and focuses on different aspects of development. Furthermore, the same developmental phenomenon can be looked at from a number of perspectives simultaneously. In fact, some lifespan developmentalists use an *eclectic* approach, drawing on several perspectives simultaneously.

We can think of the different perspectives as analogous to a set of maps of the same general geographical area. One map may contain detailed depictions of roads; another map may show geographical features; another may show political subdivisions, such as cities, towns, and counties; and still another may highlight particular points of interest, such as scenic areas and historical landmarks. Each of the maps is accurate, but each provides a different point of view and way of thinking. Although no one map is "complete," by considering them together, we can come to a fuller understanding of the area.

The various theoretical perspectives provide different ways of looking at development. Considering them together paints a fuller portrait of the myriad ways human beings change and grow over the course of their lives. However, not all theories and claims derived from the various perspectives are accurate. How do we choose among competing explanations? The answer is *research*, which we consider in the final part of this chapter.

Module 1.2 Review

LO 1.5 Describe how the psychodynamic perspective explains lifespan development.

The psychodynamic perspective looks primarily at the influence of internal, unconscious forces on development.

LO 1.6 Describe how the behavioral perspective explains lifespan development.

The behavioral perspective focuses on external, observable behaviors as the key to development.

LO 1.7 Describe how the cognitive perspective explains lifespan development.

The cognitive perspective focuses on the processes that allow people to know, understand, and think about the world.

LO 1.8 Describe how the humanistic perspective explains lifespan development.

The humanistic perspective concentrates on the theory that each individual has the ability and motivation to reach more advanced levels of maturity and that people naturally seek to reach their full potential.

LO 1.9 Describe how the contextual perspective explains lifespan development.

The contextual perspective focuses on the relationship between individuals and the social context in which they lead their lives.

LO 1.10 Describe how the evolutionary perspective explains lifespan development.

The evolutionary perspective seeks to identify behavior that is a result of our genetic inheritance from our ancestors.

LO 1.11 Discuss the value of applying multiple perspectives to lifespan development.

The various theoretical perspectives provide different ways of looking at development. An eclectic approach paints a more complete picture of the ways humans change over the life span.

Journal Writing Prompt

Applying Lifespan Development: What examples of human behavior have you seen that seem to have been inherited from our ancestors because they helped individuals survive and adapt more effectively? Why do you think they are inherited?

Research Methods

The Greek historian Herodotus wrote of an experiment conducted by Psamtik, the king of Egypt, in the seventh century B.C. Psamtik was eager to prove a cherished Egyptian belief, that his people were the oldest race on Earth. To test this notion, he developed a hypothesis: If a child was never exposed to the language of his elders, he would instinctively adopt the primal language of humanity—the original language of the first people. Psamtik was certain this language would be Egyptian.

For his experiment, Psamtik entrusted two Egyptian infants to the care of a herdsman in an isolated area. They were to be well looked after but not allowed to leave their cottage. And they were never to hear anyone speak a single word.

When Herodotus investigated the story, he learned that Psamtik sought to learn the first word the children would say. Herodotus claims the experiment worked, but not as Psamtik had hoped. One day, when the children were 2 years old, they greeted the herdsman with the word "Becos!" The herdsman didn't know this word but when the children continued to use it, he contacted Psamtik. The king sent for the children, who repeated the strange word to him. Psamtik did some research. Becos, it turned out, was "bread" in Phrygian. Psamtik had to conclude the Phrygians had preceded the Egyptians.

With the perspective of several thousand years, we can easily see the shortcomings—both scientific and ethical—in Psamtik's approach. Yet his procedure represents an improvement over mere speculation and as such is sometimes seen as the first developmental experiment in recorded history (Hunt, 1993).

Theories and Hypotheses: Posing Developmental Questions

LO 1.12 Describe the role that theories and hypotheses play in the study of development.

Questions such as those raised by Psamtik drive the study of development. In fact, developmentalists are still studying how children learn language. Others are trying to find answers to such questions as: What are the effects of malnutrition on later intellectual

Figure 1-3 The Scientific Method.

A cornerstone of research, the scientific method is used by psychologists as well as researchers from all other scientific disciplines.

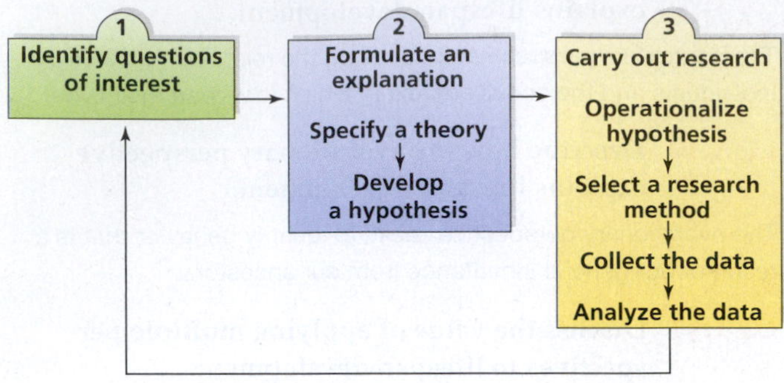

performance? How do infants form relationships with their parents, and does participation in day care disrupt such relationships? Why are adolescents particularly susceptible to peer pressure? Can mentally challenging activities reduce the declines in intellectual abilities related to aging? Do any mental faculties improve with age?

To answer such questions, developmentalists, like all psychologists and other scientists, rely on the scientific method. The **scientific method** is the process of posing and answering questions using careful, controlled techniques that include systematic, orderly observation and the collection of data. The scientific method involves three major steps: (1) identifying questions of interest, (2) formulating an explanation, and (3) carrying out research that either lends support to the explanation or refutes it (see Figure 1-3).

scientific method
the process of posing and answering questions using careful, controlled techniques that include systematic, orderly observation and the collection of data

The scientific method involves the formulation of **theories**, the broad explanations and predictions about phenomena of interest that scientists create. For instance, many people theorize that a crucial bonding period between parent and child takes place immediately after birth and is a necessary ingredient in forming a lasting parent–child relationship. Without such a bonding period, they assume, the parent–child relationship will be forever compromised (Furnham & Weir, 1996).

theories
explanations and predictions concerning phenomena of interest, providing a framework for understanding the relationships among an organized set of facts or principles

hypothesis
a prediction stated in a way that permits it to be tested

Developmental researchers use theories to form hypotheses. A **hypothesis** is a prediction stated in a way that permits it to be tested. For instance, someone who subscribes to the general theory that bonding is a crucial ingredient in the parent–child relationship might derive the more specific hypothesis that adopted children whose adoptive parents never had the chance to bond with them immediately after birth may ultimately have less secure relationships with their adoptive parents. Others might derive other hypotheses, such as that effective bonding occurs only if it lasts for a certain length of time, or that bonding affects the mother–child relationship but not the father–child relationship. (In case you're wondering: As we'll discuss in Chapter 3, these particular hypotheses have *not* been upheld; there are no long-term reactions to the separation of parent and child immediately after birth, even if the separation lasts several days.)

Choosing a Research Strategy: Answering Questions

LO 1.13 Compare the two major categories of lifespan development research.

correlational research
research that seeks to identify whether an association or relationship between two factors exists

Once researchers have formed a hypothesis, they must develop a research strategy for testing its validity. There are two major categories of research: correlational research and experimental research. **Correlational research** seeks to identify whether an association or relationship between two factors exists. As we'll see, correlational research cannot be used to determine whether one factor *causes* changes in the other. For instance, correlational research could tell us if there is an association between the number of minutes a mother and her newborn child are together immediately after birth and the quality of the mother–child relationship when the child reaches 2 years of age. Such correlational research indicates whether the two factors are *associated* or *related* to one another, but not whether the initial contact caused the relationship to develop in a particular way (Schutt, 2001).

experimental research
research designed to discover causal relationships between various factors

In contrast, **experimental research** is designed to discover *causal* relationships between various factors. In experimental research, researchers deliberately introduce a change in a carefully structured situation in order to see the consequences of that change. For instance, a researcher conducting an experiment might vary the number of minutes that mothers and children interact immediately following birth, in an attempt to see whether the amount of bonding time affects the mother–child relationship.

Because experimental research is able to answer questions of causality, it is fundamental to finding answers to various developmental hypotheses. However, some research questions cannot be answered through experiments, for either technical or ethical reasons (for example, it would be unethical to design an experiment in which a group of infants was offered no chance to bond with a caregiver at all). In fact, a great deal of pioneering developmental research—such as that conducted by Piaget and Vygotsky—employed correlational techniques. Consequently, correlational research remains an important tool in the developmental researcher's toolbox.

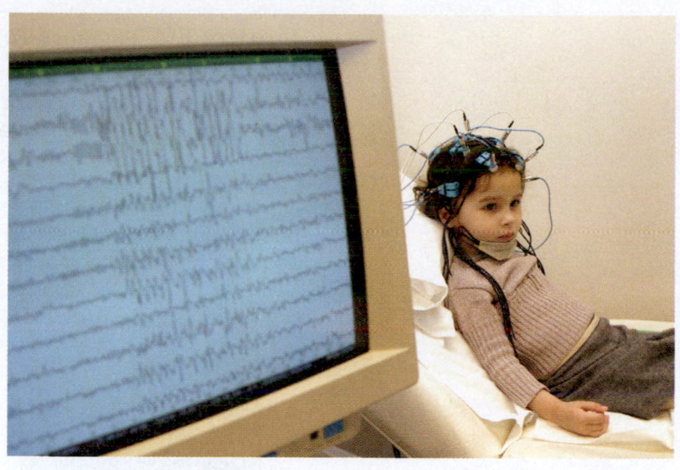

AJ Photo/BSIP/Getty Images

In experimental research, one uses controlled conditions to attempt to discover causal relationships between various factors.

Correlational Studies

LO 1.14 Identify different types of correlational studies and their relationship to cause and effect.

As we've noted, correlational research examines the relationship between two variables to determine whether they are associated, or *correlated*. For instance, researchers interested in the relationship between televised aggression and subsequent behavior have found that children who watch a good deal of aggression on television—murders, crime shows, shootings, and the like—tend to be more aggressive than those who watch only a little. In other words, as we'll discuss in greater detail in Chapter 15, viewing of aggression and actual aggression are strongly associated, or correlated, with one another (Singer & Singer, 2000; Feshbach & Tangney, 2008; Qian, Zhang, & Wang, 2013; Coyne, 2016).

But does this mean we can conclude that the viewing of televised aggression *causes* the more aggressive behavior of the viewers? Not at all. Consider some of the other possibilities: It might be that being aggressive in the first place makes children more likely to choose to watch violent programs. In such a case, then, it is the aggressive tendency that causes the viewing behavior, and not the other way around.

Or consider another possibility. Suppose that children who are raised in poverty are more likely to behave aggressively *and* to watch higher levels of aggressive television than those raised in more affluent settings. In this case, a third variable—low socioeconomic status—leads to *both* the aggressive behavior and the television viewing. The various possibilities are illustrated in Figure 1-4.

In short, finding that two variables are correlated proves nothing about causality. Although the variables may be linked causally, this is not necessarily the case.

Correlational studies do provide important information, however. For instance, as we'll see in later chapters, we know from correlational studies that the closer the genetic link between two people, the more highly associated is their intelligence. We have learned that the more parents speak to their young children, the more extensive are the children's vocabularies. And we know from correlational studies that the better the nutrition that infants receive, the fewer the cognitive and social problems they experience later (Hart, 2004; Colom, Lluis-Font, & Andrès-Pueyo, 2005; Robb, Richert, & Wartella, 2009).

THE CORRELATION COEFFICIENT. The strength and direction of a relationship between two factors is represented by a mathematical score, called a *correlation coefficient*, that ranges from +1.0 to −1.0. A positive correlation indicates that as the value of one factor increases, it can be predicted that the value of the other will also increase. For instance, if we find that people who make more money in their first job after college have higher scores on a survey of job satisfaction, and that people who make less money have lower scores when surveyed about their job satisfaction, we have found a positive correlation. (Higher values of the factor "salary" are associated with higher values of the factor "job satisfaction," and lower values of "salary" are associated with lower values of "job satisfaction.") The correlation coefficient, then, would be indicated by a positive number, and

Figure 1-4 Finding a Correlation.

Finding a correlation between two factors does not imply that one factor causes the other factor to vary. For instance, suppose a study found that viewing television shows with high levels of aggression is correlated with actual aggression in children. The correlation may reflect at least three possibilities: (1) watching television programs containing high levels of aggression causes aggression in viewers; (2) children who behave aggressively choose to watch TV programs with high levels of aggression; or (3) some third factor, such as a child's socioeconomic status, leads both to high viewer aggression and to choosing to watch television programs with high levels of aggression. What other factors, besides socioeconomic status, might be plausible third factors?

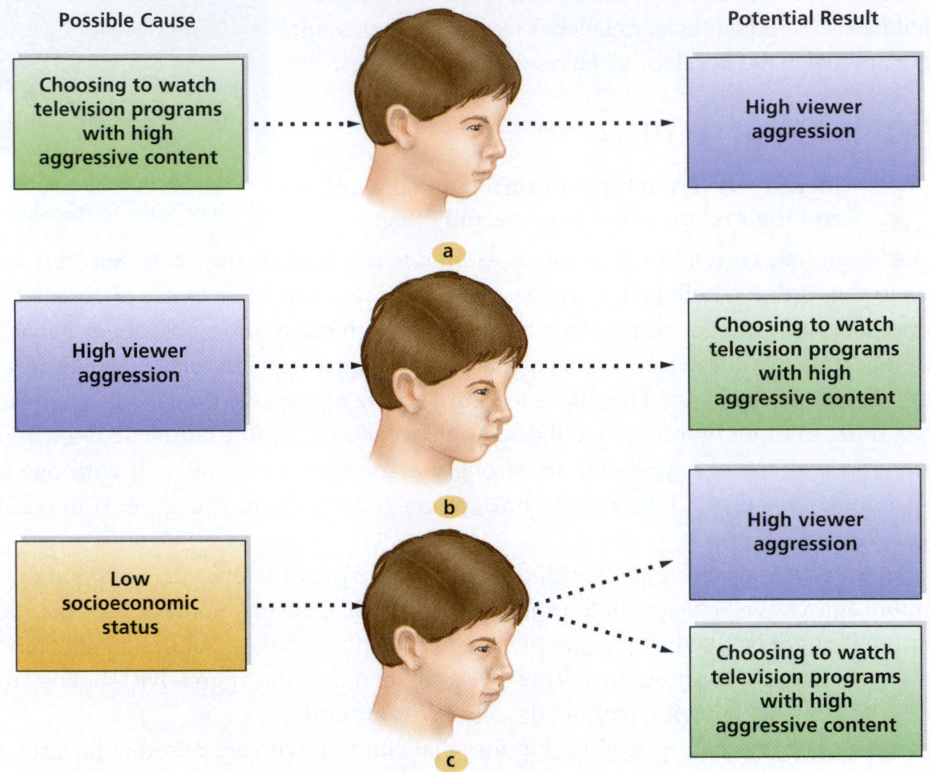

the stronger the association between salary and job satisfaction, the closer the number would be to +1.0.

In contrast, a correlation coefficient with a negative value informs us that as the value of one factor increases, the value of the other factor declines. For example, suppose we found that the greater the number of hours adolescents spend texting, the worse their academic performance is. Such a finding would result in a negative correlation, ranging between 0 and −1.0. More texting would be associated with lower performance, and less texting would be associated with better performance. The stronger the association between texting and school performance, the closer the correlation coefficient would be to −1.0.

Finally, it is possible that two factors are unrelated to one another. For example, it is unlikely that we would find a correlation between school performance and shoe size. In this case, the lack of a relationship would be indicated by a correlation coefficient close to 0.

It is important to reiterate what we noted earlier: Even if the correlation coefficient involving two variables is very strong, there is no way we can know whether one factor *causes* another factor to vary. It simply means that the two factors are associated with one another in a predictable way.

naturalistic observation
a type of correlational study in which some naturally occurring behavior is observed without intervention in the situation

TYPES OF CORRELATIONAL STUDIES. There are several types of correlational studies. **Naturalistic observation** is the observation of a naturally occurring behavior without intervention in the situation. For instance, an investigator who wishes to learn how often preschool children share toys with one another might observe a classroom over a three-week period, recording how often the preschoolers spontaneously share with one another. The key point about naturalistic observation is that the investigator simply observes the children, without interfering with the situation whatsoever (e.g., Fanger, Frankel, & Hazen, 2012; Graham et al., 2014; Snowdon & Burghardt, 2017).

Though naturalistic observation has the advantage of identifying what children do in their "natural habitat," there is an important drawback to the method: Researchers are unable to exert control over factors of interest. For instance, in some cases researchers might find so few naturally occurring instances of the behavior of interest that they are unable to draw any conclusions at all. In addition, children who know they are being watched may modify their behavior as a result of the observation. Consequently, their behavior may not be representative of how they would behave if they were not being watched.

Increasingly, naturalistic observation employs *ethnography*, a method borrowed from the field of anthropology and used to investigate cultural questions. In ethnography, a researcher's goal is to understand a culture's values and attitudes through careful, extended examination. Typically, researchers using ethnography act as participant observers, living for a period of weeks, months, or even years in another culture. By carefully observing everyday life and conducting in-depth interviews, researchers are able to obtain a deep understanding of the nature of life within another culture (Dyson, 2003).

Ethnographic studies are an example of a broader category of research known as qualitative research. In *qualitative research*, researchers choose particular settings of interest and seek to carefully describe, in narrative fashion, what is occurring and why. Qualitative research can be used to generate hypotheses that can later be tested using more objective, quantitative methods.

Although ethnographic and qualitative studies provide a fine-grained view of behavior in particular settings, they suffer from several drawbacks. As mentioned, the presence of a participant observer may influence the behavior of the individuals being studied. Furthermore, because only a small number of individuals are studied, it may be hard to generalize the findings to other settings. Finally, ethnographers carrying out cross-cultural research may misinterpret and misconstrue what they are observing, particularly in cultures that are very different from their own (Polkinghorne, 2005; Hallett & Barber, 2014).

Case studies involve extensive, in-depth interviews with a particular individual or small group of individuals. They often are used not just to learn about the individual being interviewed but to derive broader principles or draw tentative conclusions that might apply to others. For example, case studies have been conducted on children who display unusual genius and on children who have spent their early years in the wild, apparently without human contact. These case studies have provided important information to researchers and have suggested hypotheses for future investigation (Cohen & Cashon, 2003; Wilson, 2003; Ng & Nicholas, 2010; Halkier, 2013).

case study
study that involves extensive, in-depth interviews with a particular individual or small group of individuals

Using *diaries*, participants are asked to keep a record of their behavior on a regular basis. For example, a group of adolescents may be asked to record each time they interact with friends for more than 5 minutes, thereby providing a way to track their social behavior.

Surveys represent another sort of correlational research. In **survey research**, a group of people chosen to represent some larger population is asked questions about their attitudes, behavior, or thinking on a given topic. For instance, surveys have been conducted about parents' use of punishment on their children and on attitudes toward breastfeeding. From the responses, inferences are drawn regarding the larger population represented by the individuals being surveyed.

survey research
a type of study where a group of people chosen to represent some larger population is asked questions about their attitudes, behavior, or thinking on a given topic

PSYCHOPHYSIOLOGICAL METHODS. Some developmental researchers, particularly those using a cognitive neuroscience approach, make use of psychophysiological methods. **Psychophysiological methods** focus on the relationship between physiological processes and behavior. For instance, a researcher might examine the relationship between blood flow within the brain and problem-solving capabilities. Similarly, some

psychophysiological methods
research that focuses on the relationship between physiological processes and behavior

Rebecca Emery/Getty Images

Naturalistic observation is utilized to examine a situation in its natural habitat without interference of any sort. What are some disadvantages of naturalistic observation?

studies use infants' heart rate as a measure of their interest in stimuli to which they are exposed (Field, Diego, & Hernandez-Reif, 2009; Mazoyer et al., 2009; Jones & Mize, 2016).

Among the most frequently used psychophysiological measures are the following:

- ***Electroencephalogram (EEG).*** The EEG reports electrical activity within the brain recorded by electrodes placed on the outside of the skull. That brain activity is transformed into a pictorial representation of the brain, permitting the representation of brain wave patterns and diagnosis of disorders such as epilepsy and learning disabilities.
- ***Computerized axial tomography (CAT) scan.*** In a CAT scan, a computer constructs an image of the brain by combining thousands of individual X-rays taken at slightly different angles. Although it does not show brain activity, a CAT scan does illuminate the structure of the brain.
- ***Functional magnetic resonance imaging (fMRI) scan.*** An fMRI provides a detailed, three-dimensional computer-generated image of brain activity by aiming a powerful magnetic field at the brain. It offers one of the best ways of learning about the operation of the brain, down to the level of individual nerves.

Experiments: Determining Cause and Effect

LO 1.15 Explain the main features of an experiment.

experiment
a process in which an investigator, called an experimenter, devises two different experiences for participants and then studies and compares the outcomes

In an **experiment**, an investigator or experimenter typically devises two different conditions (or *treatments*) and then studies and compares the outcomes of the participants exposed to those two different conditions in order to see how behavior is affected. One group, the *treatment* or *experimental group*, is exposed to the treatment variable being studied; the other, the *control group*, is not.

Although the terminology may seem daunting at first, there is an underlying logic that helps sort it out. Think in terms of a medical experiment in which the aim is to test the effectiveness of a new drug. In testing the drug, we wish to see if the drug successfully *treats* the disease. Consequently, the group that receives the drug would be called the *treatment* group. In comparison, another group of participants would not receive the drug treatment. Instead, they would be part of the no-treatment *control* group.

Similarly, suppose you want to see if exposure to movie violence makes viewers more aggressive. You might take a group of adolescents and show them a series of movies that contain a great deal of violent imagery. You would then measure their subsequent aggression. This group would constitute the treatment group. For the control group, you might take a second group of adolescents, show them movies that contain no aggressive imagery, and then measure their subsequent aggression. By comparing the amount of aggression displayed to members of the treatment and control groups, you would be able to determine whether exposure to violent imagery produces aggression in viewers. And this is just what a group of researchers in Belgium found: Running an experiment of this very sort, psychologist Jacques-Philippe Leyens and colleagues (Leyens et al., 1975) found that the level of aggression rose significantly for the adolescents who had seen the movies containing violence.

The central feature of this experiment—and all experiments—is the comparison of the consequences of different treatments. The use of both treatment and control groups allows researchers to rule out the possibility that something other than the experimental manipulation produced the results found in the experiment. For instance, if a control group was not used, experimenters could not be certain that some other factor, such as the time of day the movies were shown, the need to sit still during the movie, or even the mere passage of time, produced the changes that were observed. By using a control group, then, experimenters can draw accurate conclusions about causes and effects.

INDEPENDENT AND DEPENDENT VARIABLES. The **independent variable** is the variable that researchers manipulate in the experiment (in our example, it is the type of movie participants saw—violent or nonviolent). In contrast, the **dependent variable** is the variable that researchers measure in an experiment and expect to change as a result of the experimental manipulation. In our example, the degree of aggressive behavior shown by the participants after viewing violent or nonviolent films is the dependent variable. (One way to remember the difference: A hypothesis predicts how a dependent variable *depends* on the manipulation of the independent variable.) In an experiment studying the effects of taking a drug, for instance, manipulating whether participants receive or don't receive a drug is the independent variable. Measurement of the effectiveness of the drug or no-drug treatment is the dependent variable. Every experiment has an independent and a dependent variable.

independent variable
the variable that researchers manipulate in an experiment

dependent variable
the variable that researchers measure in an experiment and expect to change as a result of the experimental manipulation

Experimenters need to make sure their studies are not influenced by factors other than those they are manipulating. For this reason, they take great care to make sure that the participants in both the treatment and control groups are not aware of the purpose of the experiment (which could affect their responses or behavior) and that the experimenters do not have any influence over who is chosen for the control and treatment groups. The procedure that is used is known as random assignment. In *random assignment*, participants are assigned to different experimental groups or "conditions" on the basis of chance and chance alone. By using this technique, the laws of statistics ensure that personal characteristics that might affect the outcome of the experiment are divided proportionally among the participants in the different groups, making groups equivalent. Equivalent groups achieved by random assignment allow an experimenter to draw conclusions with confidence.

Figure 1-5 illustrates the Belgian experiment on adolescents exposed to films containing violent or nonviolent imagery and its effects on subsequent aggressive behavior. As you can see, it contains each of the elements of an experiment:

- An independent variable (the assignment to a film condition)
- A dependent variable (measurement of the adolescents' aggressive behavior)
- Random assignment to condition (viewing a film with aggressive imagery versus a film with nonaggressive imagery)
- A hypothesis that predicts the effect the independent variable will have on the dependent variable (that viewing a film with aggressive imagery will produce subsequent aggression)

Given the advantage of experimental research—that it provides a means of determining causality—why aren't experiments always used? The answer is that there are some situations that a researcher, no matter how ingenious, simply cannot control. And there are some situations in which control would be unethical, even if it were possible. For instance, no researcher would be able to assign different groups of infants to parents of high and low socioeconomic status in order to learn the effects of such status on subsequent development. Similarly, we cannot control what a group of children watch on television throughout their childhood years in order to learn if childhood exposure to televised aggression leads to aggressive behavior later in life. Consequently, in situations in which experiments are logistically or ethically impossible, developmentalists employ correlational research.

Furthermore, it's also important to keep in mind that a single experiment is insufficient to answer a research question definitively. Before complete confidence can be placed in a conclusion, research must be *replicated*, or repeated, sometimes using other procedures and techniques with other participants. Sometimes developmentalists use a

Figure 1-5 Elements of an Experiment.

In this experiment, researchers randomly assigned a group of adolescents to one of two conditions: viewing a film that contained violent imagery or viewing a film that lacked violent imagery (manipulation of the independent variable). Participants were observed later to determine how much aggression they showed (the dependent variable). Analysis of the findings showed that adolescents exposed to aggressive imagery showed more aggression later. **THINKING ABOUT THE DATA:** In this experiment and others like it, why is random assignment important?

(Based on an experiment by Leyens et al., 1975.)

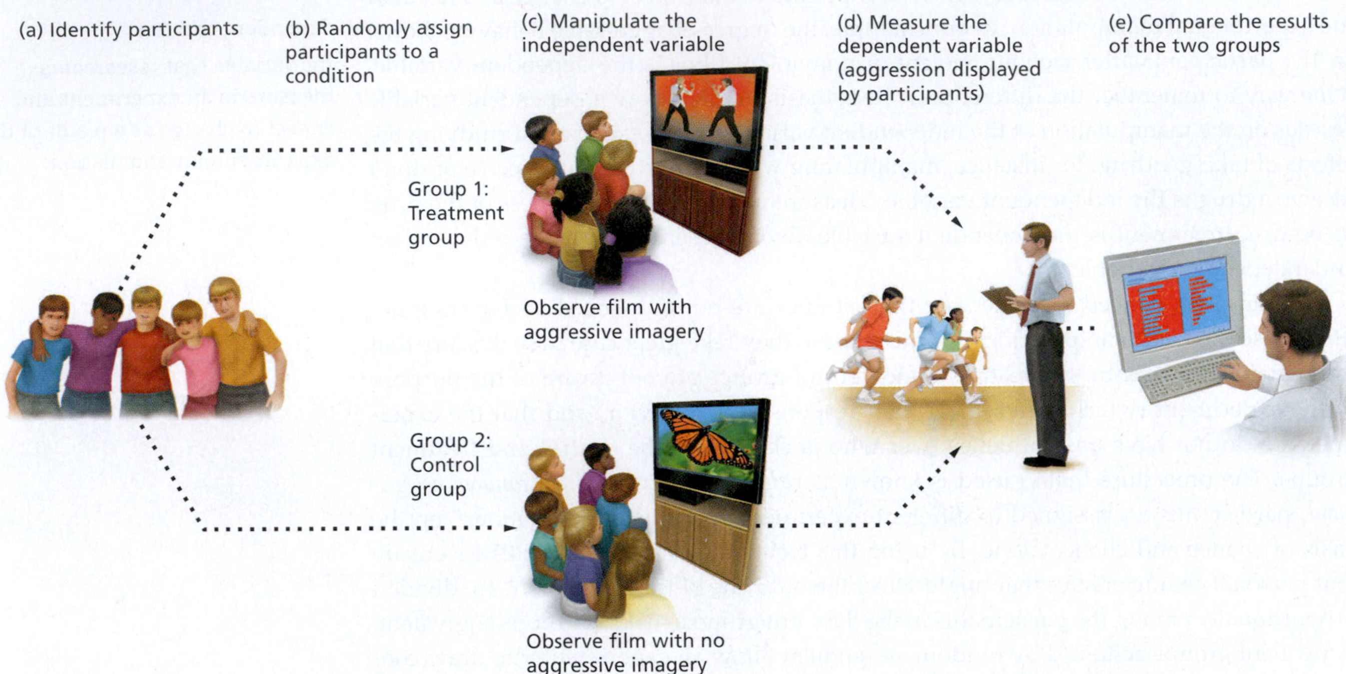

procedure called *meta-analysis*, which permits them to combine the results of many studies into one overall conclusion (Peterson & Brown, 2005; Le et al., 2010).

CHOOSING A RESEARCH SETTING. Deciding *where* to conduct a study may be as important as determining *what* to do in the experiment. In the Belgian experiment on the influence of exposure to media aggression, the researchers used a real-world setting—a group home for boys who had been convicted of juvenile delinquency. They chose this **sample**, the group of participants selected for the experiment, because it was useful to have adolescents whose normal level of aggression was relatively high and because they could incorporate showing the films into the everyday life of the home with minimal disruption.

sample
the group of participants chosen for the experiment

Using a real-world setting like the one in the aggression experiment is the hallmark of a field study. A **field study** is a research investigation carried out in a naturally occurring setting. Field studies may be carried out in preschool classrooms, at community playgrounds, on school buses, or on street corners. Field studies capture behavior in real-life settings, where research participants may behave more naturally than they would if they were brought into a laboratory.

field study
a research investigation carried out in a naturally occurring setting

Field studies may be used in both correlational studies and experiments. Field studies typically employ naturalistic observation, the technique we discussed earlier in which researchers observe some naturally occurring behavior without intervening or making changes in the situation. For instance, a researcher might examine behavior in a child-care center, view the groupings of adolescents in high school corridors, or observe elderly adults in a senior center.

However, it is often difficult to run an experiment in real-world settings, where it is hard to exert control over the situation and environment. Consequently, field studies are more typical of correlational designs than experimental designs, and most developmental

Developmental Diversity and Your Life

Choosing Research Participants Who Represent the Diversity of Humanity

In order for lifespan development to represent the full range of the human condition, its research must incorporate individuals of different races, ethnicities, cultures, genders, and other categories. The field of lifespan development is increasingly concerned with issues of human diversity, but its actual progress in this domain has been slow. For instance, although our understanding of the development of non-white children has grown substantially over the past few decades, it is still not as complete as our understanding of the development of nonminority children (McLoyd, 2006; Cabera, 2013).

Even when members of minority groups are included in research, the particular participants may not represent the full range of variation that actually exists within the group. For example, African American infants used in a research study might well be disproportionally upper and middle class, because parents in higher socioeconomic groups may be more likely to have the time and transportation capabilities to bring their infants into a research center. In contrast, African Americans (as well as members of other groups) who are relatively poor will face more hurdles when it comes to participating in research.

Something is amiss when a science that seeks to explain people's behavior—as is the case with lifespan development—disregards significant groups of individuals. Lifespan developmentalists are aware of this issue, and they have become increasingly sensitive to the importance of using participants who are fully representative of the general population (Fitzgerald, 2006; Nypaver & Shambley-Ebron, 2016).

research experiments are conducted in laboratory settings. A **laboratory study** is a research investigation conducted in a controlled setting explicitly designed to hold events constant. The laboratory may be a room or building designed for research, as in a university's psychology department. Their ability to control the settings in laboratory studies enables researchers to learn more clearly how their treatments affect participants.

laboratory study
a research investigation conducted in a controlled setting explicitly designed to hold events constant

Theoretical and Applied Research: Complementary Approaches

LO 1.16 Distinguish between theoretical research and applied research.

Developmental researchers typically focus on one of two approaches to research, carrying out either theoretical research or applied research. **Theoretical research** is designed specifically to test some developmental explanation and expand scientific knowledge, whereas **applied research** is meant to provide practical solutions to immediate problems. For instance, if we were interested in the processes of cognitive change during childhood, we might carry out a study of how many digits children of various ages can remember after one exposure to multidigit numbers—a theoretical approach. Alternatively, we might focus on how children learn by examining ways in which elementary school instructors can teach children to remember information more easily. Such a study would represent applied research, because the findings are applied to a particular setting and problem.

theoretical research
research designed specifically to test some developmental explanation and expand scientific knowledge

applied research
research meant to provide practical solutions to immediate problems

There is not always a clear-cut distinction between theoretical and applied research. For instance, is a study that examines the effects of ear infections in infancy on later hearing loss theoretical or applied research? Because such a study may help illuminate the basic processes involved in hearing, it can be considered theoretical. But to the extent that the study helps us to understand how to prevent hearing loss in children and how various medicines may ease the consequences of the infection, it may be considered applied research (Lerner, Fisher, & Weinberg, 2000).

In short, even applied research can help advance our theoretical understanding of a particular topical area, and theoretical research can provide concrete solutions to a range of practical problems. In fact, as we discuss in the *From Research to Practice* box, research of both a theoretical and an applied nature has played a significant role in shaping and resolving a variety of public policy questions.

From Research to Practice

Using Lifespan Developmental Research to Improve Public Policy

Does the Head Start preschool program enhance children's cognitive and social development?

How does the use of social media affect the self-esteem of adolescents?

How are soldiers and their families affected when they return from war?

What are some effective ways to bolster school-girls' confidence in their math and science aptitude?

Should children with developmental disabilities be schooled in regular classrooms, or are they better off in special classrooms with other children who are similarly disabled?

How should society best address the opioid epidemic affecting adolescents and adults in the United States?

Each of these questions represents a national policy issue that can be answered only by considering the results of relevant research studies. By conducting controlled studies, developmental researchers have made a number of important contributions affecting education, family life, and health on a national scale. Consider, for instance, the variety of ways that public policy issues have been informed by various types of research findings (Cramer, Song, & Drent, 2016; Crupi & Brondolo, 2017; Kennedy-Hendricks et al., 2017):

- *Research findings can provide policymakers a means of determining what questions to ask in the first place.* For example, the winding down of the wars in Iraq and Afghanistan has prompted questions about the impact on returning U.S. service members, with research showing that war has a lasting impact not only on them but also on their partners, children, and other family members whose needs should be considered in any interventions supporting the health and adjustment of veterans. Research has also disconfirmed the widespread belief that childhood vaccinations are linked to autism spectrum disorder, contributing invaluable evidence to the controversy over the risks and benefits of mandatory child immunization (Price et al., 2010; Lester et al., 2013; Young, Elliston, & Ruble, 2016).
- *Research findings and the testimony of researchers are often part of the process by which laws are drafted.* A good deal of legislation has been passed based on findings from developmental researchers. For example, research revealed that children with developmental disabilities benefit from exposure to children without special needs, ultimately leading to passage of national legislation mandating that children with disabilities be placed in regular school classes as often as possible. Research showing that children raised by same-sex couples fare just as well as children raised by a mother and father has undermined an often-used but baseless argument that same-sex marriage is harmful to children (Gartrell & Bos, 2010; Bos et al., 2016).
- *Policymakers and other professionals use research findings to determine how best to implement programs.* Research has shaped programs designed to reduce the incidence of unsafe sex among teenagers, to increase the level of prenatal care for pregnant mothers, to encourage and support women in the pursuit of math and science, and to promote flu shots for older adults. The common thread among such programs is that many of the details of the programs are built on basic research findings.
- *Research techniques are used to evaluate the effectiveness of existing programs and policies.* Once a public policy has been implemented, it is necessary to determine whether it has been effective and successful in accomplishing its goals. To do this, researchers employ formal evaluation techniques, developed from basic research procedures. For instance, careful studies of DARE, a popular program meant to reduce children's use of drugs, began to find that it was ineffective. Using the research findings of developmentalists, DARE instituted new techniques, and preliminary findings suggest that the revised program is more effective (Phillips, Gormley, & Anderson, 2016; Barlett, Chamberlin, & Witkower, 2017; Cline & Edwards, 2017).

Shared Writing Prompt

Despite the existence of research data that might inform policy about development, politicians rarely discuss such data in their speeches. Why do you think that is the case?

Measuring Developmental Change

LO 1.17 Compare longitudinal research, cross-sectional research, and sequential research.

How people grow and change through their life spans is central to the work of all developmental researchers. Consequently, one of the thorniest research issues they face concerns the measurement of change and differences over age and time. To solve this problem, researchers have developed three major research strategies: longitudinal research, cross-sectional research, and sequential research.

LONGITUDINAL STUDIES: MEASURING INDIVIDUAL CHANGE. If you were interested in learning how a child's moral development changes between the ages of 3 and 5, the most direct approach would be to take a group of 3-year-olds and follow them until they were 5, testing them periodically.

Such a strategy illustrates longitudinal research. In **longitudinal research**, the behavior of one or more study participants is measured as they age. Longitudinal research measures change over time. By following many individuals over time, researchers can understand the general course of change across some period of life.

longitudinal research
research in which the behavior of one or more participants in a study is measured as they age

The granddaddy of longitudinal studies, which has become a classic, is a study of gifted children begun by Lewis Terman (1877–1956) in 1921. In the study, a group of 1,500 children with high IQs were tested about every five years. The participants provided information on everything from intellectual accomplishment to personality and longevity (Feldhusen, 2003; McCullough, Tsang, & Brion, 2003; Subotnik, 2006; Warne & Liu, 2017).

Longitudinal research has also provided great insight into language development. For instance, by tracing how children's vocabularies increase on a day-by-day basis, researchers have been able to understand the processes that underlie the human ability to become competent in using language (Oliver & Plomin, 2007; Childers, 2009; Fagan, 2009; Kelloway & Francis, 2013).

Assessing Longitudinal Studies. Longitudinal studies can provide a wealth of information about change over time. However, they have several drawbacks. For one thing, they require a tremendous investment of time, because researchers must wait for participants to age. Furthermore, participants often drop out over the course of the research, move away, or become ill or even die as the research proceeds.

Finally, participants who are observed or tested repeatedly may become "test-wise" and perform better each time they are assessed as they become more familiar with the procedure. Even if the observations of participants in a study are not terribly intrusive (such as simply recording, over a lengthy period of time, increases in vocabulary among infants and preschoolers), experimental participants may be affected by the repeated presence of an experimenter or observer.

Consequently, despite the benefits of longitudinal research, particularly its ability to look at change within individuals, developmental researchers often turn to other methods in conducting research. The alternative they choose most often is the cross-sectional study.

cross-sectional research
research in which people of different ages are compared at the same point in time

CROSS-SECTIONAL STUDIES. Suppose again that you want to consider how children's moral development, their sense of right and wrong, changes from ages 3 to 5. Instead of using a longitudinal approach and following the same children over several years, we might conduct the study by simultaneously looking at three groups of children—3-year-olds, 4-year-olds, and 5-year-olds—perhaps presenting each group with the same problem, and then seeing how they respond to it and explain their choices.

Such an approach typifies cross-sectional research. In **cross-sectional research**, people of different ages are compared at the same point in time. Cross-sectional studies provide information about differences in development between different age groups.

Cross-sectional research allows researchers to compare representatives of different age groups at the same time.

Figure 1-6 Research Techniques for Studying Development.

In a *cross-sectional study*, 3-, 4-, and 5-year-olds are compared at a similar point in time (in the year 2019). In a *longitudinal study*, a set of participants who are 3 years old in 2019 are studied when they are 4 years old (in 2020) and when they are 5 years old (in 2021). Finally, a *sequential study* combines cross-sectional and longitudinal techniques; here, a group of 3-year-olds would be compared initially in 2019 with 4- and 5-year-olds but would also be studied one and two years later, when they themselves were 4 and 5 years old. Although the graph does not illustrate this, researchers carrying out this sequential study might also choose to retest the children who were 4 and 5 in 2019 for the next two years. What advantages do the three kinds of studies offer?

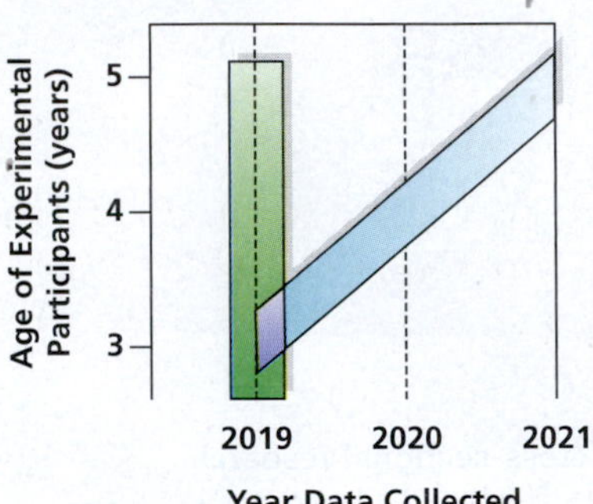

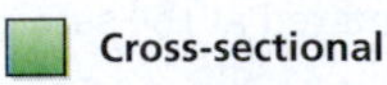

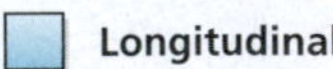

Assessing Cross-Sectional Studies. Cross-sectional research is considerably more economical in terms of time than longitudinal research: Participants are tested at just one point in time. For instance, Terman's study conceivably might have been completed decades ago if Terman had simply looked at a group of gifted 15-year-olds, 20-year-olds, 25-year-olds, and so forth, all the way through a group of 80-year-olds. Because the participants would not be periodically tested, there would be no chance that they would become test-wise, and problems of participant attrition would not occur. Why, then, would anyone choose to use a procedure other than cross-sectional research?

The answer is that cross-sectional research brings its own set of difficulties. Recall that every person belongs to a particular *cohort*, the group of people born at around the same time in the same place. If we find that people of different ages vary along some dimension, it may be due to differences in cohort membership, not age per se.

Consider a concrete example: If we find in a correlational study that people who are 25 years old perform better on a test of intelligence than those who are 75 years old, there are several alternative explanations. Although the finding may be due to decreased intelligence in older people, it may also be attributable to cohort differences. The group of 75-year-olds may have had less formal education than the 25-year-olds because members of the older cohort were less likely to finish high school than members of the younger one. Or perhaps the older group performed less well because as infants they received less adequate nutrition than members of the younger group. In short, we cannot fully rule out the possibility that the differences we find between people of different age groups in cross-sectional studies are due to cohort differences.

Cross-sectional studies also may suffer from *selective dropout*, in which participants in some age groups are more likely to quit participating in a study than others. For example, suppose a study of cognitive development in preschoolers includes a lengthy assessment of cognitive abilities. It is possible that young preschoolers would find the task more difficult and demanding than older preschoolers. As a result, the younger children would be more likely to discontinue participation in the study than the older preschoolers.

Finally, cross-sectional studies have an additional, and more basic, disadvantage: They are unable to inform us about changes in individuals or groups. If longitudinal studies are like videos taken of a person at various ages, cross-sectional studies are like snapshots of entirely different groups. Although we can establish differences related to age, we cannot fully determine whether such differences are related to change over time.

SEQUENTIAL STUDIES. Because both longitudinal and cross-sectional studies have drawbacks, researchers have turned to some compromise techniques. Among the most frequently employed are sequential studies, which are essentially a combination of longitudinal and cross-sectional studies.

sequential studies
research in which researchers examine a number of different age groups over several points in time

In **sequential studies**, researchers examine a number of different age groups at several points in time. For instance, an investigator interested in children's moral behavior might begin a sequential study by examining the behavior of three groups of children who are 3 years old, 4 years old, or 5 years old at the time the study begins. (This is no different from the way a cross-sectional study would be done.)

However, the study wouldn't stop there but would continue for the next several years. During this period, each of the research participants would be tested annually. Thus, the 3-year-olds would be tested at ages 3, 4, and 5; the 4-year-olds at ages 4, 5, and 6; and the 5-year-olds at ages 5, 6, and 7. Such an approach combines the advantages of longitudinal and cross-sectional research, and it permits developmental researchers to tease out the consequences of age *change* versus age *difference*. The major research techniques for studying development are summarized in Figure 1-6.

Ethics and Research

LO 1.18 Describe some ethical issues that affect psychological research.

In the "research study" conducted by Egyptian King Psamtik, two children were removed from their mothers and held in isolation in an effort to learn about the roots of language. If you found yourself thinking this was extraordinarily cruel, you are in good company. Clearly, such an experiment raises blatant ethical concerns, and nothing like it would ever be done today.

In order to help researchers avoid ethical problems, the major organizations of developmentalists, including the Society for Research in Child Development and the American Psychological Association, have developed comprehensive ethical guidelines for researchers. Among the basic principles that must be followed are those involving freedom from harm, informed consent, the use of deception, and maintenance of participants' privacy (American Psychological Association, 2002; Toporek, Kwan, & Williams, 2012; Joireman & Van Lange, 2015):

- ***Researchers must protect participants from physical and psychological harm.*** Their welfare, interests, and rights come before those of researchers. In research, participants' rights always come first (Sieber, 2000; Fisher, 2004).
- ***Researchers must obtain informed consent from participants before their involvement in a study.*** If they are over the age of 7, participants must voluntarily agree to be in a study. For those under 18, their parents or guardians must also provide consent.

The requirement for informed consent raises some difficult issues. Suppose, for instance, researchers want to study the psychological effects of abortion on adolescents. Although they may be able to obtain the consent of an adolescent who has had an abortion, the researchers may need to get her parents' permission as well because she is a minor. But if the adolescent hasn't told her parents about the abortion, the mere request for permission from the parents would violate her privacy—leading to a breach of ethics.

From the perspective of *a health-care provider*

Do you think there are some special circumstances involving adolescents, who are not legally adults, that would justify allowing them to participate in a study without obtaining their parents' permission? What might such circumstances involve?

- ***The use of deception in research must be justified and cause no harm.*** Although deception to disguise the true purpose of an experiment is permissible, any experiment that uses deception must undergo careful scrutiny by an independent panel before it is conducted. Suppose, for example, we want to know the reaction of participants to success and failure. It is ethical to tell participants that they will be playing a game when the true purpose is actually to observe how they respond to doing well or poorly on the task. However, such a procedure is ethical only if it causes no harm to participants, has been approved by a review panel, and ultimately includes a full debriefing, or explanation, for participants when the study is over (Underwood, 2005).
- ***Participants' privacy must be maintained.*** If participants are videotaped during the course of a study, for example, they must give their permission for the videotapes to be viewed. Furthermore, access to the tapes must be carefully restricted.

Development in Your Life

Thinking Critically About "Expert" Advice

If you immediately comfort crying babies, you'll spoil them.

If you let babies cry without comforting them, they'll be untrusting and clingy as adults.

Spanking is one of the best ways to discipline your child.

Never hit your child.

If a marriage is unhappy, children are better off if their parents divorce than if they stay together.

No matter how difficult a marriage is, parents should avoid divorce for the sake of their children.

There is no lack of advice on the best way to raise a child or, more generally, to lead one's life. From best-sellers such as *Chicken Soup for the Soul: On Being a Parent* to magazine and newspaper columns that provide advice on every imaginable topic, each of us is exposed to tremendous amounts of information.

Yet not all advice is equally valid. The mere fact that something is in print or on television or the Internet does not make it legitimate or accurate. Fortunately, some guidelines can help distinguish when recommendations and suggestions are reasonable and when they are not:

- **Consider the source of the advice.** Information from established, respected organizations such as the American Medical Association, the American Psychological Association, and the American Academy of Pediatrics is likely to be the result of years of study, and its accuracy is probably high. If you don't know the organization, investigate further to find out more about its goals and philosophy.
- **Evaluate the credentials of the person providing advice.** Information coming from established, acknowledged researchers and experts in a field is likely to be more accurate than that coming from a person whose credentials are obscure. Consider where the author is employed and whether he or she has a particular political or personal agenda.
- **Understand the difference between anecdotal evidence and scientific evidence.** Anecdotal evidence is based on one or two instances of a phenomenon, haphazardly discovered or encountered; scientific evidence is based on careful, systematic procedures. If an aunt tells you that all her children slept through the night by 2 months of age and therefore so can your child, that is quite different from reading a report that 75 percent of children sleep through the night by 9 months. Of course, even with such a report, it would be a good idea to find out how large the study was or how this number was arrived at.
- **If advice is based on research findings, there should be a clear, transparent description of the studies on which the conclusion is based.** Who were the participants in the study? What were the methods used? What do the results show? Think critically about the way in which the findings were obtained before accepting them.
- **Do not overlook the cultural context of the information.** Although an assertion may be valid in some contexts, it may not be true in all situations. For example, it is typically assumed that providing infants the freedom to move about and exercise their limbs facilitates their muscular development and mobility. Yet in some cultures, infants spend most of their time closely bound to their mothers—with no apparent long-term damage (Tronick, 1995).
- **Don't assume that because many people believe something, it is necessarily true.** Scientific evaluation has often proved that some of the most basic presumptions about the effectiveness of various techniques are invalid.

In short, the key to evaluating information relating to human development is to maintain a healthy dose of skepticism. No source of information is invariably, unfailingly accurate. By keeping a critical eye on the statements you encounter, you'll be in a better position to determine the very real contributions made by developmentalists to understanding how humans develop over the course of their life spans.

Module 1.3 Review

LO 1.12 Describe the role that theories and hypotheses play in the study of development.

Theories in development are systematically derived explanations of facts or phenomena. Theories suggest hypotheses, which are predictions that can be tested.

LO 1.13 Compare the two major categories of lifespan development research.

Correlational research seeks to identify whether an association or relationship between two factors exists. Experimental research is designed to discover *causal* relationships between various factors.

LO 1.14 Identify different types of correlational studies and their relationship to cause and effect.

Naturalistic observation, case studies, and survey research are types of correlational studies. Some developmental researchers also make use of psychophysiological methods.

LO 1.15 Explain the main features of an experiment.

Experimental research seeks to discover cause-and-effect relationships through the use of a treatment group and a control group. By manipulating the independent variable and observing changes in the dependent variable, researchers find evidence of causal links between variables. Research studies may be conducted in field settings, where participants are subject to natural conditions, or in laboratories, where conditions can be controlled.

LO 1.16 Distinguish between theoretical research and applied research.

Theoretical research is designed specifically to test some developmental explanation and expand scientific knowledge, whereas applied research is meant to provide practical solutions to immediate problems.

LO 1.17 Compare longitudinal research, cross-sectional research, and sequential research.

Researchers measure age-related change through longitudinal studies, cross-sectional studies, and sequential studies.

LO 1.18 Describe some ethical issues that affect psychological research.

Developmental researchers must follow ethical standards for conducting research. Ethical guidelines for researchers cover freedom from harm, informed consent, the use of deception, and preservation of participant privacy.

Journal Writing Prompt

Applying Lifespan Development: Formulate a theory about one aspect of human development and a hypothesis that relates to it.

Epilogue

As we've seen, the scope of lifespan development is broad, touching on a wide range of topics that address how people grow and change through the course of life. We've also found that there are a variety of techniques by which developmentalists seek to answer questions of interest.

Before proceeding to the next chapter, take a few minutes to reconsider the prologue of this chapter—about the case of Louise Brown and Elizabeth Carr, among the first children to be born through in vitro fertilization. Based on what you now know about child development, answer the following questions:

1. What are some of the potential benefits, and the costs, of the type of conception—in vitro fertilization—that was carried out for Louise's and Elizabeth's parents?
2. What are some questions that developmentalists who study either physical, cognitive, or personality and social development might ask about the effects on Louise and Elizabeth of being conceived via in vitro fertilization?
3. The creation of complete human clones—exact genetic replicas of an individual—is still in the realm of science fiction, but the theoretical possibility does raise some important questions. For example, what would be the psychological consequences of being a clone?
4. If clones could actually be produced, how might they help scientists understand the relative impact of heredity and environment on development?

Looking Back

LO 1.1 Define the field of lifespan development and describe what it encompasses.

Lifespan development is a scientific approach to questions about growth, change, and stability in the physical, cognitive, social, and personality characteristics at all ages from conception to death.

LO 1.2 Describe the areas that lifespan development specialists cover.

Some developmentalists focus on physical development, examining the ways in which the body's makeup helps determine behavior. Other developmental specialists examine cognitive development, seeking to understand how growth and change in intellectual capabilities influence a person's behavior. Still other developmental specialists focus on personality and social development. In addition to choosing to specialize in a particular topical area, developmentalists also typically look at a particular age range.

LO 1.3 Describe some of the basic influences on human development.

Each individual is subject to normative history-graded influences, normative age-graded influences, normative sociocultural-graded influences, and non-normative life events. Culture—both broad and narrow—is an important issue in lifespan development. Many aspects of development are influenced not only by broad cultural differences but also by ethnic, racial, and socioeconomic differences within a particular culture.

LO 1.4 Summarize four key issues in the field of lifespan development.

Four key issues in lifespan development are (1) whether developmental change is continuous or discontinuous; (2) whether development is largely governed by critical periods during which certain influences or experiences must occur for development to be normal; (3) whether to focus on certain particularly important periods in human development or on the entire life span; and (4) the nature–nurture controversy, which focuses on the relative importance of genetic versus environmental influences.

LO 1.5 Describe how the psychodynamic perspective explains lifespan development.

The psychodynamic perspective is exemplified by the psychoanalytic theory of Sigmund Freud and the psychosocial theory of Erik Erikson. Freud focused attention on the unconscious and on stages through which children must pass successfully to avoid harmful fixations. Erikson identified eight distinct stages of development, each characterized by a conflict, or crisis, to work out.

LO 1.6 Describe how the behavioral perspective explains lifespan development.

The behavioral perspective typically concerns stimulus–response learning, exemplified by classical conditioning, the operant conditioning of B. F. Skinner, and Albert Bandura's social-cognitive learning theory.

LO 1.7 Describe how the cognitive perspective explains lifespan development.

Within the cognitive perspective, the most notable theorist is Jean Piaget, who identified developmental stages through which all children are assumed to pass. Each stage involves qualitative differences in thinking. In contrast, information processing approaches attribute cognitive growth to quantitative changes in mental processes and capacities, and cognitive neuroscience approaches focus on biological brain processes.

LO 1.8 Describe how the humanistic perspective explains lifespan development.

The humanistic perspective contends that people have a natural capacity to make decisions about their lives and control their behavior. The humanistic perspective emphasizes free will and the natural desire of humans to reach their full potential.

LO 1.9 Describe how the contextual perspective explains lifespan development.

The contextual perspective considers the relationship between individuals and their physical, cognitive, personality, and social worlds. The bioecological approach stresses the interrelatedness of developmental areas and the importance of broad cultural factors in human development. Lev Vygotsky's sociocultural theory emphasizes the central influence on cognitive development exerted by social interactions between members of a culture.

LO 1.10 Describe how the evolutionary perspective explains lifespan development.

The evolutionary perspective attributes behavior to genetic inheritance from our ancestors, contending that genes determine not only traits such as skin and eye color, but certain personality traits and social behaviors as well.

LO 1.11 Discuss the value of applying multiple perspectives to lifespan development.

The various theoretical perspectives provide different ways of looking at development. An eclectic approach paints a more complete picture of the ways humans change over the life span.

LO 1.12 Describe the role that theories and hypotheses play in the study of development.

Theories are broad explanations of facts or phenomena of interest, based on a systematic integration of prior findings and theories. Hypotheses are theory-based predictions that can be tested. The process of posing and answering questions systematically is called the scientific method.

LO 1.13 Describe the two major categories of lifespan development research.

Researchers test hypotheses using correlational research (to determine whether two factors are associated) and experimental research (to discover cause-and-effect relationships).

LO 1.14 Identify different types of correlational studies and their relationship to cause and effect.

Correlational studies use naturalistic observation, case studies, and survey research to investigate whether certain characteristics of interest are associated with other characteristics. Some developmental researchers also make use of psychophysiological methods. Correlational studies lead to no direct conclusions about cause and effect.

LO 1.15 Explain the main features of an experiment.

Typically, experimental research studies are conducted on participants in a treatment group who receive the experimental treatment and participants in a control group who do not. Following the treatment, differences between the two groups can help the experimenter to determine the effects of the treatment. The independent variable is the variable that researchers manipulate in the experiment, whereas the dependent variable is the variable that researchers measure in an experiment and expect to change as a result of the experimental manipulation. Experiments may be conducted in a laboratory or in a real-world setting.

LO 1.16 Distinguish between theoretical research and applied research.

Theoretical research is designed specifically to test some developmental explanation and expand scientific knowledge, while applied research is meant to provide practical solutions to immediate problems.

LO 1.17 Compare longitudinal research, cross-sectional research, and sequential research.

To measure change across human ages, researchers use longitudinal studies of the same participants over time, cross-sectional studies of different-age participants conducted at one time, and sequential studies of different-age participants at several points in time.

LO 1.18 Describe some ethical issues that affect psychological research.

Ethical issues that affect psychological research include the protection of participants from harm, informed consent of participants, limits on the use of deception, and the maintenance of privacy.

Key Terms and Concepts

lifespan development 4
physical development 5
cognitive development 5
personality development 5
social development 5
cohort 7
continuous change 9
discontinuous change 9
critical period 9
sensitive period 10
maturation 10
psychodynamic perspective 13
psychoanalytic theory 13
psychosexual development 13
psychosocial development 14
behavioral perspective 15
classical conditioning 16
operant conditioning 16
behavior modification 16
social-cognitive learning theory 16
cognitive perspective 17
information processing approaches 18
cognitive neuroscience approaches 19
humanistic perspective 20
contextual perspective 21
bioecological perspective 21
sociocultural theory 24
evolutionary perspective 24
scientific method 28
theories 28
hypothesis 28
correlational research 28
experimental research 28
naturalistic observation 30
case study 31
survey research 31
psychophysiological methods 31
experiment 32
independent variable 33
dependent variable 33
sample 34
field study 34
laboratory study 35
theoretical research 35
applied research 35
longitudinal research 37
cross-sectional research 37
sequential studies 38

Chapter 2

The Start of Life: Prenatal Development

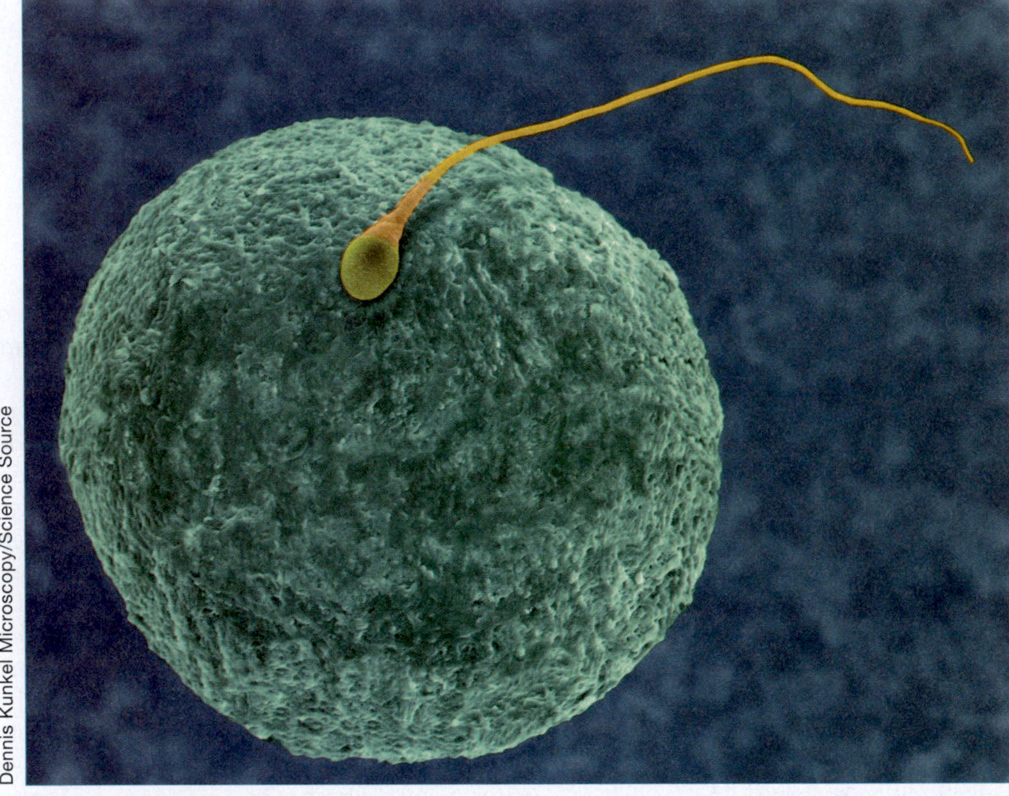

Dennis Kunkel Microscopy/Science Source

Learning Objectives

LO 2.1 Describe how genes and chromosomes provide our basic genetic endowment.

LO 2.2 Compare monozygotic twins with dizygotic twins.

LO 2.3 Describe how the sex of a child is determined.

LO 2.4 Explain the mechanisms by which genes transmit information.

LO 2.5 Describe the field of behavioral genetics.

LO 2.6 Describe the major inherited disorders.

LO 2.7 Describe the role of genetic counselors and differentiate between different forms of prenatal testing.

LO 2.8 Explain how the environment and genetics work together to determine human characteristics.

LO 2.9 Summarize how researchers study the interaction of genetic and environmental factors in development.

LO 2.10 Explain how genetics and the environment jointly influence physical traits, intelligence, and personality.

LO 2.11 Explain the role genetics and the environment play in the development of psychological disorders.

LO 2.12 Describe ways in which genes influence the environment.

LO 2.13 Explain the process of fertilization.

LO 2.14 Summarize the three stages of prenatal development.

LO 2.15 Describe some of the physical and ethical challenges that relate to pregnancy.

LO 2.16 Describe the threats to the fetal environment and what can be done about them.

Chapter Overview

Prologue: The Future Is Now

In every respect, Stephen Monaco seemed to be a healthy and normal 3-year-old. Yet one day, he developed a stomach virus that led to severe brain damage and the terrible diagnosis of a rare disease called isovaleric acidemia (IVA). IVA makes the body unable to metabolize a common amino acid found in protein. Unbeknownst to them, Stephen's parents were carriers of the disease, which struck Stephen without warning. Stephen became permanently disabled.

The case was different when Stephen's mother, Jana, became pregnant again. Her daughter, Caroline, received prenatal testing before birth. After learning that she carried the mutation that led to Stephen's illness, doctors were able to give her medication the day she was born, and immediately put her on a special diet. Although Stephen will never be able to talk, walk, or feed himself, Caroline is an active, normal child. Genetic testing, says Jana, "gave Caroline the future that Stephen didn't get to have." (Kalb, 2006; Spinelli, 2015)

Looking Ahead

A hidden genetic disorder robbed Jana and Tom Monaco's first child of a normal, healthy life. Their second child was spared the same fate by advances in genetic testing, which gave the Monacos a chance to intervene before the damage was done. They were able to stop Caroline's inherited disorder from doing the same damage by controlling aspects of her environment.

In this chapter, we'll examine what developmental researchers and other scientists have learned about ways that heredity and the environment work in tandem to create and shape human beings, and how that knowledge is being used to improve people's lives. We begin with the basics of heredity, the genetic transmission of characteristics from biological parents to their children, by examining how we receive our genetic endowment. We'll consider an area of study, behavioral genetics, that specializes in the consequences of heredity on behavior. We'll also discuss what happens when genetic factors cause development to go off track, and how such problems

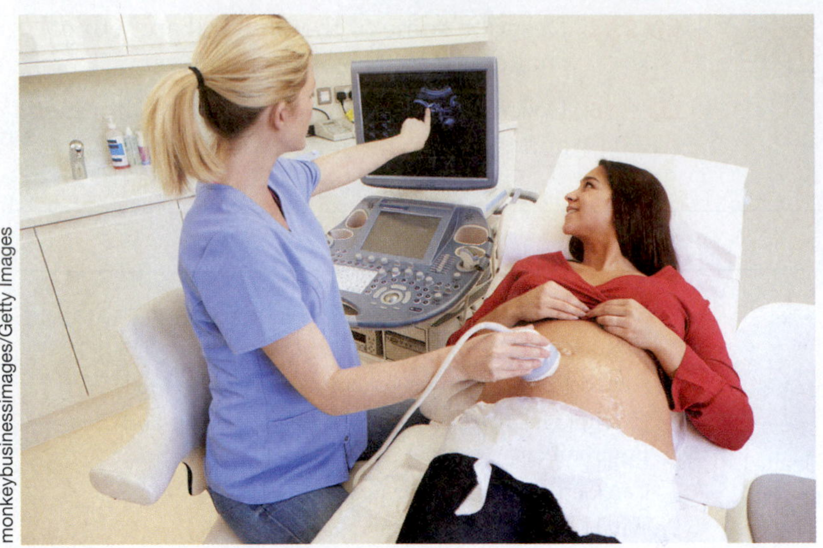
monkeybusinessimages/Getty Images

Prenatal tests have become increasingly sophisticated.

are dealt with through genetic counseling and, in some cases, manipulation of a child's genes.

But genes are only one part of the story of prenatal development. We'll also consider the ways in which a child's genetic heritage interacts with the environment in which he or she grows up—how one's family, socioeconomic status, and life events can affect a variety of characteristics, including physical traits, intelligence, and even personality.

Finally, we'll focus on the very first stage of development, tracing prenatal growth and change. We'll review some of the alternatives available to couples who find it difficult to conceive. We'll also talk about the stages of the prenatal period and how the prenatal environment offers both threats to—and the promise of—future growth.

zygote
the new cell formed by the process of fertilization

genes
the basic units of genetic information

DNA (deoxyribonucleic acid) molecules
the substance that genes are composed of, which determines the nature of every cell in the body and how it will function

chromosomes
rod-shaped portions of DNA that are organized in 23 pairs

Earliest Development

We humans begin the course of our lives simply. Like individuals from tens of thousands of other species, we start as a single cell, a tiny speck probably weighing no more than a 20-millionth of an ounce. But, as we'll see in this section, from this humble beginning, in a matter of just several months, if all goes well, a living, breathing individual infant is born.

Genes and Chromosomes: The Code of Life

LO 2.1 Describe how genes and chromosomes provide our basic genetic endowment.

The single cell we described above is created when a male reproductive cell, a *sperm*, pushes through the membrane of an *ovum*, a female reproductive cell. These *gametes*, as the male and female reproductive cells also are known, each contain huge amounts of genetic information. About an hour or so after the sperm enters the ovum, the two gametes suddenly fuse, becoming one cell, a **zygote**. The resulting combination of their genetic instructions—over 2 billion chemically coded messages—is sufficient to begin creating a whole person. The blueprints for creating a person are stored and communicated in our **genes**, the basic units of genetic information. The roughly 25,000 human genes are the biological equivalent of "software" that programs the future development of all parts of the body's "hardware."

All genes are composed of specific sequences of **DNA (deoxyribonucleic acid) molecules**. The genes are arranged in specific locations and in a specific order along 46 **chromosomes**, rod-shaped portions of DNA that are organized in 23 pairs. Only sex cells—the ova and the sperm—contain half this number, so that a child's mother and father each provide one of the two chromosomes in each of the 23 pairs. The 46 chromosomes (in 23 pairs) in the new zygote contain the genetic blueprint that will guide cell activity for the rest of the individual's life (Pennisi, 2000; International Human Genome Sequencing Consortium, 2001; see Figure 2-1). Through a process called *mitosis*, which accounts for the replication of most types of cells, nearly all the cells of the body will contain the same 46 chromosomes as the zygote.

Specific genes in precise locations on the chain of chromosomes determine the nature and function of every cell in the body. For instance, genes determine which cells will ultimately become part of the heart and which will become part of the muscles of the leg. Genes also establish how different parts of the body will function—how rapidly the heart will beat, for example, or how much strength a muscle will have.

Figure 2-1 The Contents of a Single Human Cell

At the moment of conception, humans receive about 25,000 genes, contained on 46 chromosomes in 23 pairs.

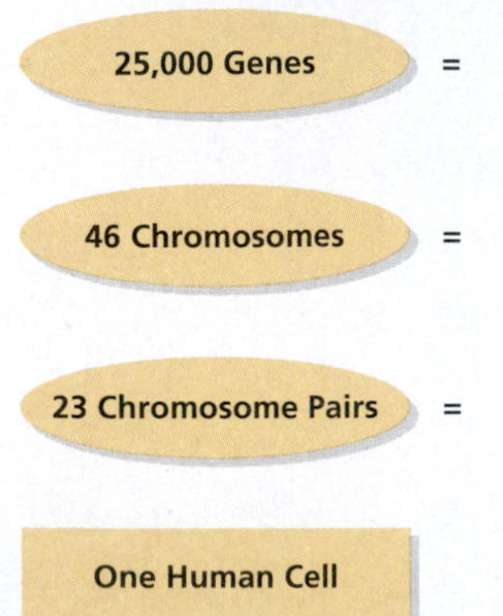

If each parent provides just 23 chromosomes, where does the potential for the vast diversity of human beings come from? The answer resides primarily in the nature of the processes that underlie the cell division of the gametes. When gametes—the sex cells, sperm and ova—are formed in the adult human body in a process called *meiosis*, each gamete receives one of the two chromosomes that make up each of the 23 pairs. Because for each of the 23 pairs it is largely a matter of chance which member of the pair is contributed, there are some 8 million different combinations possible. Furthermore, other processes, such as random transformations of particular genes, add to the variability of the genetic brew. The ultimate outcome: tens of *trillions* of possible genetic combinations.

With so many possible genetic mixtures provided by heredity, there is no likelihood that someday you'll bump into a genetic duplicate of yourself—with one exception: an identical twin.

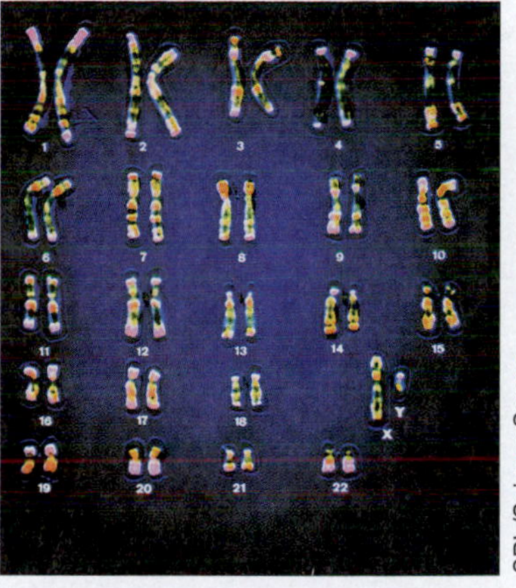
SPL/ScienceSource

At the moment of conception, humans receive 23 pairs of chromosomes, half from the mother and half from the father. These chromosomes contain thousands of genes.

Multiple Births: Two—or More—for the Genetic Price of One

LO 2.2 Compare monozygotic twins with dizygotic twins.

Although it doesn't seem surprising when dogs and cats give birth to several offspring at one time, in humans, multiple births are cause for comment. They should be: Less than 3 percent of all pregnancies produce twins, and the odds are even slimmer for triplets or higher-order multiples.

Why do multiple births occur? Some occur when a cluster of cells in the ovum split off within the first 2 weeks after fertilization. The result is two genetically identical zygotes, which, because they come from the same original zygote, are called monozygotic. **Monozygotic twins** are twins who are genetically identical. Any differences in their future development can be attributed only to environmental factors, since genetically they are exactly the same.

monozygotic twins
twins who are genetically identical

There is a second, and actually more common, mechanism that produces multiple births. In these cases, two separate ova are fertilized by two separate sperm at roughly the same time. Twins produced in this fashion are known as **dizygotic twins**. Because they are the result of two separate ovum–sperm combinations, they are no more genetically similar than two siblings born at different times.

dizygotic twins
twins who are produced when two separate ova are fertilized by two separate sperm at roughly the same time

Of course, not all multiple births produce only two babies. Triplets, quadruplets, and even higher-order multiples are produced by either (or both) of the mechanisms that yield twins. Thus, triplets may be some combination of monozygotic, dizygotic, or trizygotic.

Although the chances of having a multiple birth are typically slim, the odds rise considerably when couples use fertility drugs to improve the probability they will conceive a child. For Caucasian couples in the United States, for example, 1 in 10 couples using fertility drugs have dizygotic twins, compared to an overall figure of 1 in 86. Older women, too, are more likely to have multiple births, and multiple births are also more common in some families than in others. The increased use of fertility drugs and rising average age of mothers giving birth have meant that multiple births have increased since the 1990s (see Figure 2-2; Martin et al., 2005).

There are also racial, ethnic, and national differences in the rate of multiple births, probably due to inherited differences in the likelihood that more than one ovum will be released at a time. One out of 70 African American couples have dizygotic births, compared with 1 out of 86 for white American couples. Furthermore, in some areas of central Africa, the rate of dizygotic births is among the highest in the world (Choi, 2017).

Mothers carrying multiple children run a higher-than-average risk of premature delivery and birth complications. Consequently, these mothers must be particularly concerned about their prenatal care.

Figure 2-2 Rising Multiples

The number and rate of twin births has risen considerably over the past three decades.

(**Source:** CDC/NCHS, National Vital Statistics System, 2012.)

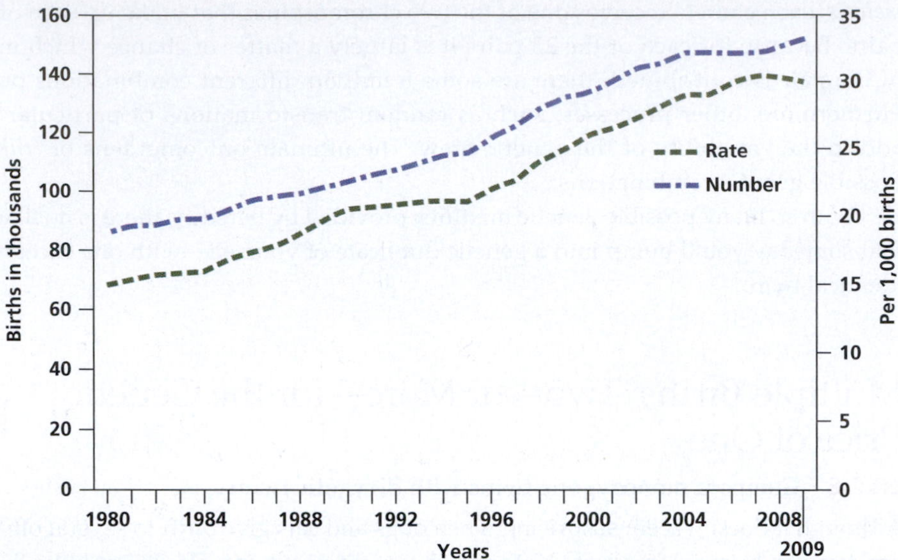

Figure 2-3 Determining Sex

When an ovum and a sperm meet at the moment of fertilization, the ovum is certain to provide an X chromosome, while the sperm will provide either an X or a Y chromosome. If the sperm contributes its X chromosome, the child will have an XX pairing on the twenty-third chromosome—a girl. If the sperm contributes a Y chromosome, the result will be an XY pairing—a boy. Does this mean that girls are more likely to be conceived than boys?

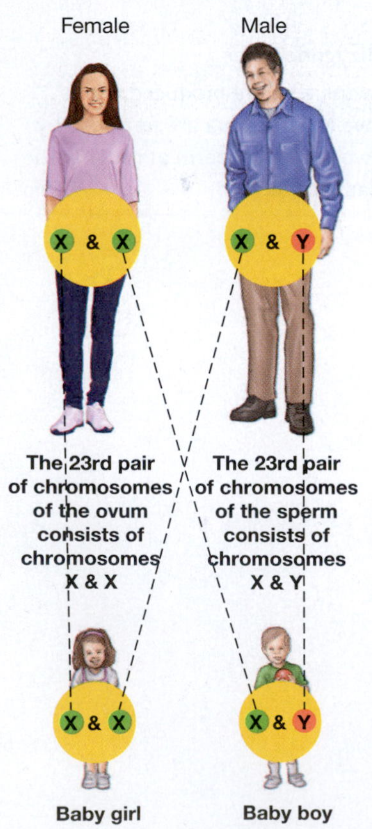

Boy or Girl? Establishing the Sex of the Child

LO 2.3 Describe how the sex of a child is determined.

Recall that there are 23 matched pairs of chromosomes. In 22 of these pairs, each chromosome is similar to the other member of its pair. The one exception is the twenty-third pair, which is the one that determines the sex of the child. In females, the twenty-third pair consists of two matching, relatively large, X-shaped chromosomes, appropriately identified as XX. In males, however, the members of the pair are dissimilar. One consists of an X-shaped chromosome, but the other is a shorter, smaller, Y-shaped chromosome. This pair is identified as XY.

As we discussed earlier, each gamete carries one chromosome from each of the parent's 23 pairs of chromosomes. Since a female's twenty-third pair of chromosomes are both Xs, an ovum will always carry an X chromosome, no matter which chromosome of the twenty-third pair it gets. A male's twenty-third pair is XY, so each sperm could carry either an X or a Y chromosome.

If the sperm contributes an X chromosome when it meets an ovum (which, remember, will always contribute an X chromosome), the child will have an XX pairing on the twenty-third chromosome—a female. If the sperm contributes a Y chromosome, the result will be an XY pairing—a male (see Figure 2-3).

It is clear from this process that the father's sperm determines the sex of the child. This fact is leading to the development of techniques that will allow parents to increase the chances of specifying the sex of their child. In one new technique, lasers measure the DNA in sperm. By discarding sperm that harbor the unwanted sex chromosome, the chances of having a child of the desired sex increase dramatically (Hayden, 1998; Belkin, 1999; Van Balen, 2005).

Of course, procedures for choosing a child's sex raise ethical and practical issues. For example, in cultures that value one sex over the other, might there be a kind of sex discrimination prior to birth? Furthermore, a shortage of children of the less preferred sex might ultimately emerge. Many questions remain, then, before sex selection becomes routine (Sharma, 2008; Bhagat, Ananya, & Sharma, 2012).

The Basics of Genetics: The Mixing and Matching of Traits

LO 2.4 Explain the mechanisms by which genes transmit information.

What determined the color of your hair? Why are you tall or short? What made you susceptible to hay fever? And why do you have so many freckles? To answer these questions, we need to consider the basic mechanisms involved in the way that the genes we inherit from our parents transmit information.

We can start by examining the discoveries of an Austrian monk, Gregor Mendel (1822–1884), in the mid-1800s. In a series of simple yet convincing experiments, Mendel cross-pollinated pea plants that always produced yellow seeds with pea plants that always produced green seeds. The result was not, as one might guess, a plant with a combination of yellow and green seeds. Instead, all of the resulting plants had yellow seeds. At first it appeared that the green-seeded plants had had no influence.

However, Mendel's additional research proved this was not true. He bred together plants from the new, yellow-seeded generation that had resulted from his original cross-breeding of the green-seeded and yellow-seeded plants. The consistent result was a ratio of three-fourths yellow seeds to one-fourth green seeds. Why did this 2-to-1 ratio of yellow to green seeds appear so consistently? It took Mendel's genius to provide an answer. Based on his experiments with pea plants, he argued that when two competing traits, such as a green or yellow coloring of seeds, were both present, only one could be expressed. The one that was expressed was called a **dominant trait**. Meanwhile, the other trait remained present in the organism, although it was not expressed (displayed). This was called a **recessive trait**. In the case of Mendel's original pea plants, the offspring plants received genetic information from both the green-seeded and yellow-seeded parents. However, the yellow trait was dominant, and consequently the recessive green trait did not assert itself.

dominant trait
the one trait that is expressed when two competing traits are present

recessive trait
a trait within an organism that is present, but is not expressed

Keep in mind, however, that genetic material relating to both parent plants is present in the offspring, even though it cannot be seen. The genetic information is known as the organism's genotype. A **genotype** is the underlying combination of genetic material present (but outwardly invisible) in an organism. In contrast, a **phenotype** is the observable trait, the trait that is actually seen.

genotype
the underlying combination of genetic material present (but not outwardly visible) in an organism

phenotype
an observable trait; the trait that is actually seen

Although the offspring of the yellow-seeded and green-seeded pea plants all have yellow seeds (i.e., they have a yellow-seeded phenotype), the genotype consists of genetic information relating to both parents.

And what is the nature of the information in the genotype? To answer that question, let's turn from peas to people. In fact, the principles are the same not just for plants and humans but for the majority of species.

Recall that parents transmit genetic information to their offspring via the chromosomes they contribute through the gamete they provide during fertilization. Some of the genes form pairs called *alleles*, genes governing traits that may take alternate forms, such as hair or eye color. For example, brown eye color is a dominant trait (B); blue eyes are recessive (b). A child's allele may contain similar or dissimilar genes from each parent. If, on the one hand, the child receives similar genes, he or she is said to be **homozygous** for the trait. On the other hand, if the child receives different forms of the gene from its parents, he or she is said to be **heterozygous**. In the case of heterozygous alleles (Bb), the dominant characteristic, brown eyes, is expressed. However, if the child happens to receive a recessive allele from each of its parents, and therefore lacks a dominant characteristic (bb), he or she will display the recessive characteristic, such as blue eyes.

homozygous
inheriting from parents similar genes for a given trait

heterozygous
inheriting from parents different forms of a gene for a given trait

EXAMPLE OF TRANSMISSION OF GENETIC INFORMATION. We can see this process at work in humans by considering the transmission of *phenylketonuria (PKU)*, an inherited disorder in which a child is unable to make use of phenylalanine, an essential

Figure 2-4 PKU Probabilities

PKU, a disease that causes brain damage and intellectual disabilities, is produced by a single pair of genes inherited from one's mother and father. (a) If neither parent carries a gene for the disease, a child cannot develop PKU. (b) Even if one parent carries the recessive gene, but the other doesn't, the child cannot inherit the disease. (c) However, if both parents carry the recessive gene, there is a one in four chance that the child will have PKU.

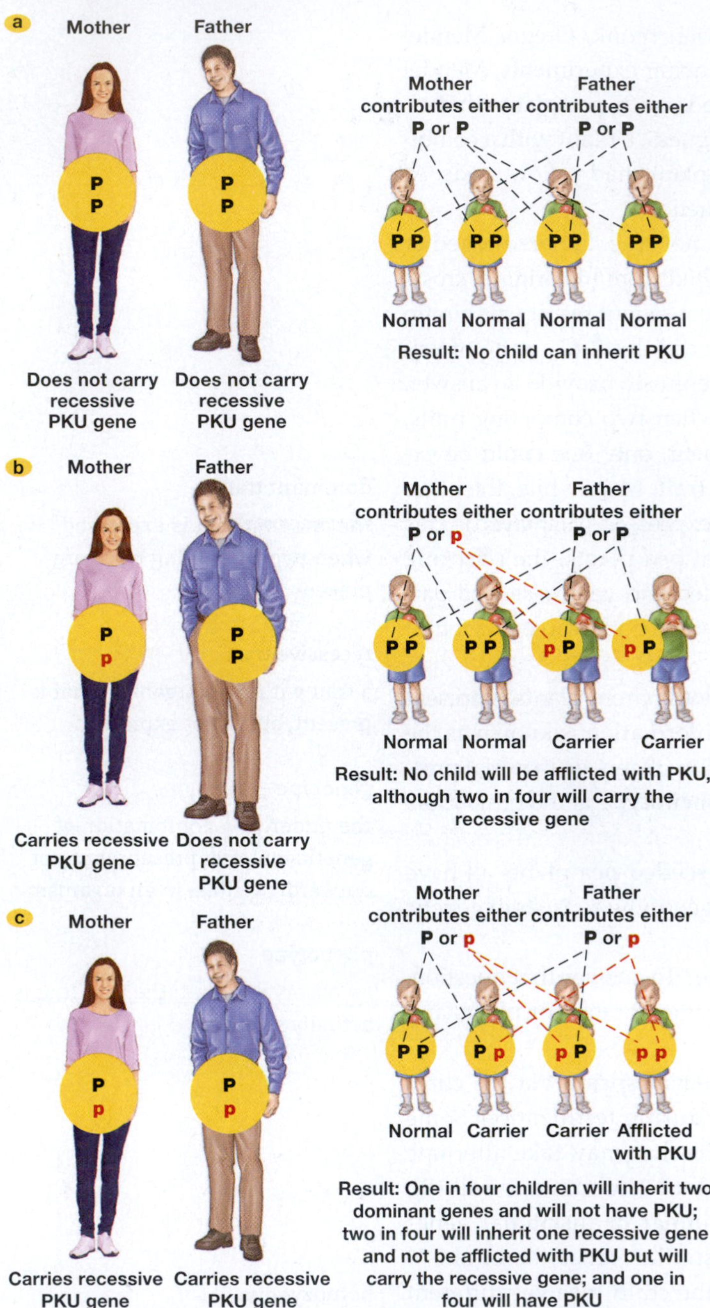

amino acid present in proteins found in milk and other foods. If left untreated, PKU allows phenylalanine to build up to toxic levels, causing brain damage and intellectual disabilities (Moyle et al., 2007; Widaman, 2009; Deon et al., 2015; Palermo et al., 2017).

PKU is produced by a single allele, or pair of genes. As shown in Figure 2-4, we can label each gene of the pair with a *P* if it carries a dominant gene, which causes the normal production of phenylalanine, or a *p* if it carries the recessive gene that produces PKU. In cases in which neither parent is a PKU carrier, both the mother's and the father's pairs of genes are the dominant form, symbolized as *PP* (Figure 2-4a). Consequently, no matter which member of the pair is contributed by the mother and father, the resulting pair of genes in the child will be *PP*, and the child will not have PKU.

Consider, however, what happens if one of the parents has a recessive *p* gene. In this case, which we can symbolize as *Pp*, the parent will not have PKU, since the normal *P* gene is dominant. But the recessive gene can be passed down to the child (Figure 2-4b). This is not so bad: If the child has only one recessive gene, it will not suffer from PKU. But what if both parents carry a recessive *p* gene (Figure 2-4c)? In this case, although neither parent has the disorder, it is possible for the child to receive a recessive gene from both parents. The child's genotype for PKU then will be *pp*, and he or she will have the disorder.

Remember, though, that even children whose parents both have the recessive gene for PKU have only a 25 percent chance of inheriting the disorder. Due to the laws of probability, 25 percent of children with *Pp* parents will receive the dominant gene from each parent (these children's genotype would be *PP*) and 50 percent will receive the dominant gene from one parent and the recessive gene from the other (their genotypes would be either *Pp* or *pP*). Only the unlucky 25 percent who receive the recessive gene from each parent and end up with the genotype *pp* will suffer from PKU.

POLYGENIC TRAITS. The transmission of PKU is a good way of illustrating the basic principles of how genetic information passes from parent to child, although the case of PKU is simpler than most cases of genetic transmission. Relatively few traits are governed by a single pair of genes. Instead, most traits are the result of polygenic inheritance. In **polygenic inheritance**, a combination of multiple gene pairs is responsible for the production of a particular trait.

polygenic inheritance
inheritance in which a combination of multiple gene pairs is responsible for the production of a particular trait

Furthermore, some genes come in several alternate forms, and still others act to modify the way that particular genetic traits (produced by other alleles) are displayed. Genes also vary in terms of their *reaction range*, the potential degree of variability in the actual expression of a trait due to environmental conditions. And some traits, such as blood type, are produced by genes in which neither member of a pair of genes can be classified

Figure 2-5 Inheriting Hemophilia

Hemophilia, a blood-clotting disorder, has been an inherited disorder throughout the royal families of Europe, as illustrated by the descendants of Queen Victoria of Great Britain.

(**Source:** Kimball, John W., *Biology*, 5th Ed., © 1983. Reprinted and electronically reproduced by permission of Pearson Education, Inc., Upper Saddle River, New Jersey.)

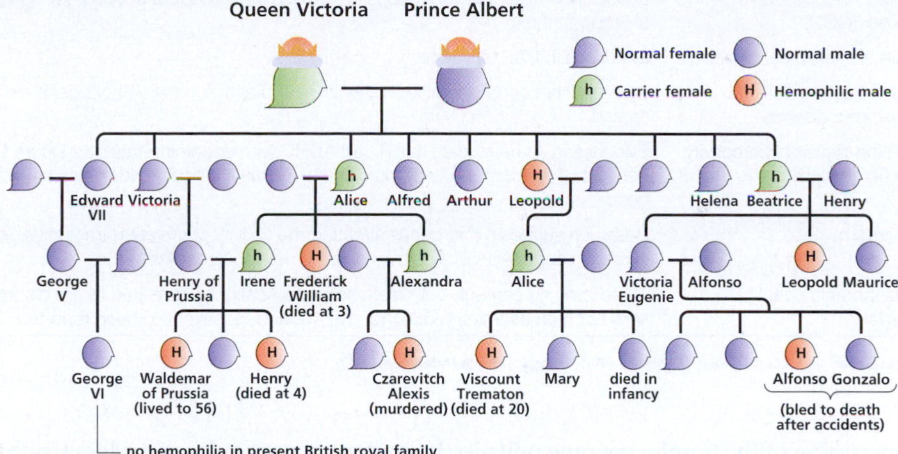

as purely dominant or recessive. Instead, the trait is expressed in terms of a combination of the two genes—such as type AB blood.

A number of recessive genes, called **X-linked genes**, are located only on the X chromosome. Recall that in females, the twenty-third pair of chromosomes is an XX pair, while in males it is an XY pair. One result is that males have a higher risk for a variety of X-linked disorders, since males lack a second X chromosome that can counteract the genetic information that produces the disorder. For example, males are significantly more apt to have red–green color blindness, a disorder produced by a set of genes on the X chromosome.

X-linked genes
genes that are considered recessive and are located only on the X chromosome

Similarly, *hemophilia*, a blood disorder, is produced by X-linked genes. Hemophilia has been a recurrent problem in the royal families of Europe, as illustrated in Figure 2-5, which shows the inheritance of hemophilia in the descendants of Queen Victoria of Great Britain.

The Human Genome and Behavioral Genetics: Cracking the Genetic Code

LO 2.5 Describe the field of behavioral genetics.

Mendel's achievements in recognizing the basics of genetic transmission of traits were trailblazing. However, they mark only the beginning of our understanding of how those particular characteristics are passed on from one generation to the next.

The most recent milestone in understanding genetics was reached in early 2001, when molecular geneticists succeeded in mapping the specific sequence of genes on each chromosome. This accomplishment stands as one of the most important moments in the history of genetics, and, for that matter, all of biology (International Human Genome Sequencing Consortium, 2001).

Already, the mapping of the gene sequence has provided important advances in our understanding of genetics. For instance, the number of human genes, long thought to be 100,000, has been revised downward to 25,000—not many more than for organisms that are far less complex than the human (see Figure 2-6). Furthermore, scientists have discovered that all humans share 99.9 percent of the gene sequence. What this means is that we humans are far more similar to one another than we are different. It also indicates that many of the differences that seemingly separate people—such as race—are, literally, only skin-deep.

Figure 2-6 Uniquely Human?

Humans have about 25,000 genes, making them not much more genetically complex than some primitive species.

(**Source:** Celera Genomics: International Human Genome Sequencing Consortium, 2001.)

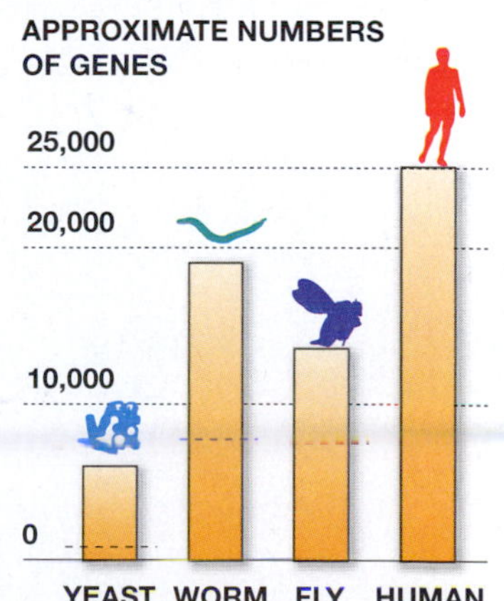

Table 2-1 Current Understanding of the Genetic Basis of Selected Behavioral Disorders and Traits

Behavioral Trait	Current Beliefs about Genetic Basis
Huntington's disease	Mutations in HTT gene
Obsessive-compulsive disorder (OCD)	Several potentially relevant genes have been identified, but environment plays an important role
Fragile X intellectual disability	Mutations in the FMR gene
Early onset (familial) Alzheimer's disease	Three distinct genes identified; at least 11 mutations in the PSEN2 gene are related
Attention-deficit/hyperactivity disorder (ADHD)	Evidence in some studies has linked ADHD with dopamine-receptor D4 and D5 genes, but the complexity of the disease makes it difficult to identify a specific gene
Alcoholism	Research suggests that genes affecting the activity of the neurotransmitters serotonin and GABA likely are involved in risk for alcoholism
Schizophrenia spectrum disorder	There is no agreement, but deletions or duplications are related to the disorder; links to chromosomes 1, 5, 6, 10, 13, 15, and 22 have also been reported

(**Source:** Based on McGuffin, Riley, & Plomin, 2001; Genetics Home Reference, 2017).

The mapping of the human genome will also help identify particular disorders to which a given individual is susceptible (Levenson, 2012; Goldman & Domschke, 2014).

behavioral genetics

the study of the effects of heredity on behavior and psychological characteristics

The mapping of the human gene sequence is supporting the field of behavioral genetics. As the name implies, **behavioral genetics** studies the effects of heredity on behavior and psychological characteristics. Rather than simply examining stable, unchanging characteristics such as hair or eye color, behavioral genetics takes a broader approach, considering how our personality and behavioral habits are affected by genetic factors (Li, 2003; Judge, Ilies, & Zhang, 2012; Krüger, Korsten & Hoffman, 2017).

Personality traits such as shyness or sociability, moodiness, and assertiveness are among the areas being studied. Other behavior geneticists study psychological disorders, such as major depressive disorder, attention-deficit/hyperactivity disorder, and schizophrenia spectrum disorder, looking for possible genetic links (Haeffel et al., 2008; Wang et al., 2012; Plomin et al., 2016; see Table 2-1).

Behavioral genetics holds substantial promise. For one thing, researchers working within the field have gained a better understanding of the specifics of the genetic code that underlies human behavior and development.

Even more important, researchers are seeking to identify how genetic defects may be remedied (Peltonen & McKusick, 2001; Bleidorn, Kandler, & Caspi, 2014). To understand how a remedial possibility might come about, we need to consider the ways in which genetic factors, which normally cause development to proceed so smoothly, may falter.

Inherited and Genetic Disorders: When Development Deviates from the Norm

LO 2.6 Describe the major inherited disorders.

PKU is just one of several disorders that may be inherited. Like a bomb that is harmless until its fuse is lit, a recessive gene responsible for a disorder may be passed on unknowingly from one generation to the next, revealing itself only when, by chance, it is paired with another recessive gene. It is only when two recessive genes come together like a match and a fuse that the gene will express itself and a child will inherit the genetic disorder.

But there is another way that genes are a source of concern: In some cases, genes become physically damaged. For instance, genes may break down due to wear and tear or chance events occurring during the cell division processes of meiosis and mitosis. Sometimes genes, for no known reason, spontaneously change their form, a process called *spontaneous mutation*.

Figure 2-7 Inhaled Air and Genetic Mutations

Inhalation of unhealthy, polluted air may lead to mutations in genetic material in sperm. These mutations may be passed on, damaging the fetus and affecting future generations.

(**Source:** Based on Samet, De Marini, & Malling, 2004, p. 971.)

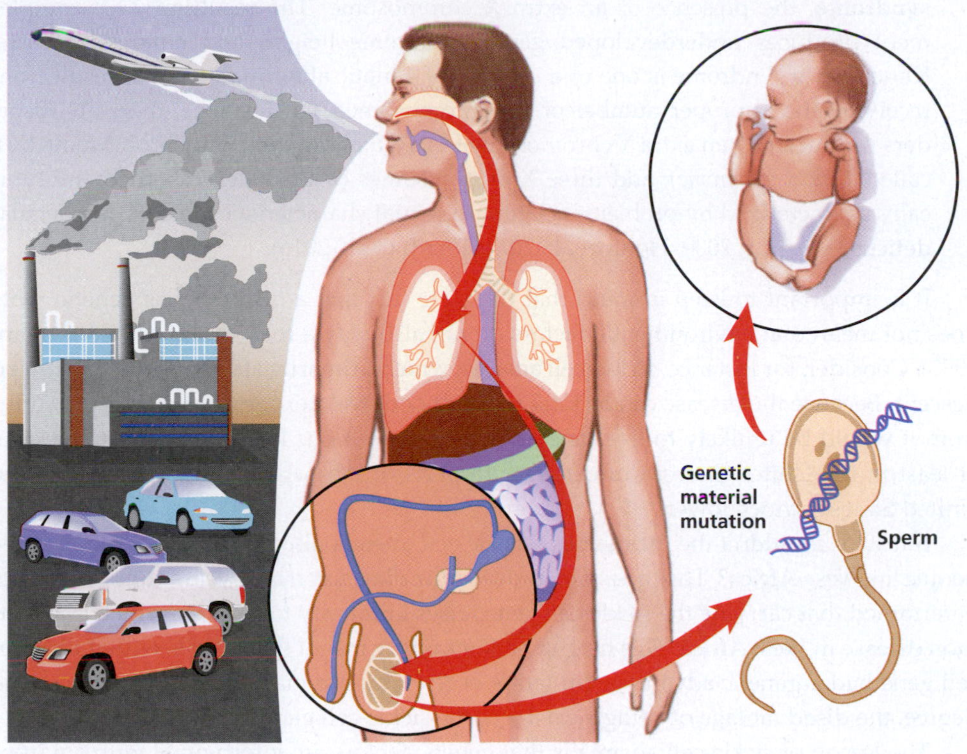

Alternatively, certain environmental factors, such as exposure to X-rays or even highly polluted air, may produce a malformation of genetic material (see Figure 2-7). When such damaged genes are passed on to a child, the results can be disastrous in terms of future physical and cognitive development (Samet, DeMarini, & Malling, 2004; Tucker-Drob, & Briley, 2014).

In addition to PKU, which occurs once in 10,000 to 20,000 births, other inherited and genetic disorders include:

- **Down syndrome.** As noted earlier, most people have 46 chromosomes, arranged in 23 pairs. One exception is individuals with **Down syndrome**, a disorder produced by the presence of an extra chromosome on the twenty-first pair. Once referred to as mongolism, Down syndrome is the most frequent cause of intellectual disabilities. It occurs in about 1 out of 700 births, although the risk is much greater in mothers who are unusually young or old (Davis, 2008; Channell et al., 2014; Glasson et al., 2016).
- **Fragile X syndrome.** **Fragile X syndrome** occurs when a particular gene is injured on the X chromosome. The result is mild to moderate intellectual disability (Cornish, Turk, & Hagerman, 2008; Hocking, Kogan, & Cornish, 2012; Shelton et al., 2017).
- **Sickle-cell anemia.** Around one-tenth of people of African descent carry genes that produce sickle-cell anemia, and 1 in 400 actually has the disease. **Sickle-cell anemia** is a blood disorder that gets its name from the shape of the red blood cells in those who have it. Symptoms include poor appetite, stunted growth, a swollen stomach, and yellowish eyes. People afflicted with the most severe form of the disease rarely live beyond childhood. However, for those with less severe cases, medical advances have produced significant increases in life expectancy.

Down syndrome
a disorder produced by the presence of an extra chromosome on the twenty-first pair; once referred to as mongolism

fragile X syndrome
a disorder produced by injury to a gene on the X chromosome, producing mild to moderate intellectual disability

sickle-cell anemia
a blood disorder that gets its name from the shape of the red blood cells in those who have it

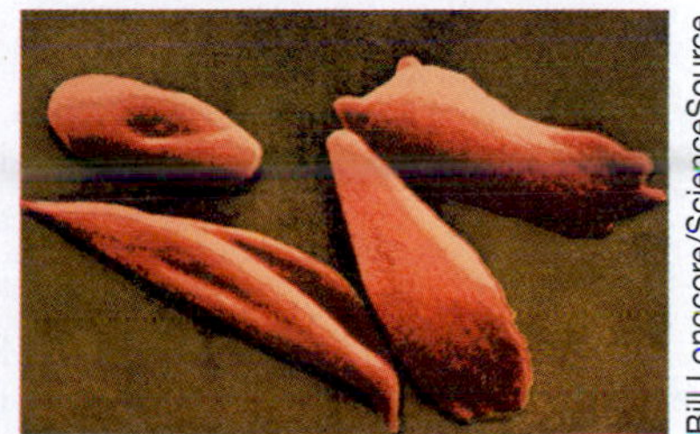
Bill Longcore/ScienceSource

Sickle-cell anemia, named for the presence of misshapen red blood cells, is carried in the genes of 1 in 10 African Americans.

Tay-Sachs disease
a disorder that produces blindness and muscle degeneration prior to death; there is no treatment

Klinefelter's syndrome
a disorder resulting from the presence of an extra X chromosome that produces underdeveloped genitals, extreme height, and enlarged breasts

- **Tay-Sachs disease.** Occurring mainly in Jews of Eastern European ancestry and in French-Canadians, **Tay-Sachs disease** usually causes death before its victims reach school age. There is no treatment for the disorder, which produces blindness and muscle degeneration prior to death.
- **Klinefelter's syndrome.** One male out of every 500 is born with **Klinefelter's syndrome**, the presence of an extra X chromosome. The resulting XXY complement produces underdeveloped genitals, extreme height, and enlarged breasts. Klinefelter's syndrome is one of a number of genetic abnormalities that result from receiving the improper number of sex chromosomes. For instance, there are disorders produced by an extra Y chromosome (XYY), a missing second chromosome (X0, called *Turner syndrome*), and three X chromosomes (XXX). Such disorders are typically characterized by problems relating to sexual characteristics and by intellectual deficits (Murphy, 2009; Hong et al., 2014; Turriff et al., 2016).

It is important to keep in mind that the mere fact that a disorder has genetic roots does not mean that environmental factors do not also play a role (Moldin & Gottesman, 1997). Consider, for instance, sickle-cell anemia, which primarily afflicts people of African descent. Because the disease can be fatal in childhood, we'd expect that those who suffer from it would be unlikely to live long enough to pass it on. This does seem to be true, at least in the United States: Compared with parts of West Africa, the incidence in the United States is much lower.

But why shouldn't the incidence of sickle-cell anemia also be gradually reduced for people in West Africa? This question proved puzzling for many years, until scientists determined that carrying the sickle-cell gene raises immunity to malaria, which is a common disease in West Africa. This heightened immunity meant that people with the sickle-cell gene had a genetic advantage (in terms of resistance to malaria) that offset, to some degree, the disadvantage of being a carrier of the sickle-cell gene.

The lesson of sickle-cell anemia is that genetic factors are intertwined with environmental considerations and can't be looked at in isolation. Furthermore, we need to remember that although we've been focusing on inherited factors that can go awry, in the vast majority of cases the genetic mechanisms with which we are endowed work quite well. Overall, 95 percent of children born in the United States are healthy and normal. For the some 250,000 who are born each year with some sort of physical or mental disorder, appropriate intervention often can help treat and, in some cases, cure the problem.

Moreover, due to advances in behavioral genetics, genetic difficulties increasingly can be forecast, anticipated, and planned for before a child's birth, enabling parents to take steps before the child is born to reduce the severity of certain genetic conditions. In fact, as scientists' knowledge regarding the specific location of particular genes expands, predictions of what the genetic future may hold are becoming increasingly exact, as we discuss next.

Genetic Counseling: Predicting the Future from the Genes of the Present

LO 2.7 Describe the role of genetic counselors and differentiate between different forms of prenatal testing.

If you knew that your mother and grandmother had died of Huntington's disease—a devastating, always fatal inherited disorder marked by tremors and intellectual deterioration—to whom could you turn to learn your own chances of developing the disease? The best person to turn to would be a member of a field that, just a few decades ago, was nonexistent: genetic counseling. **Genetic counseling** focuses on helping people deal with issues relating to inherited disorders.

genetic counseling
the discipline that focuses on helping people deal with issues relating to inherited disorders

Genetic counselors use a variety of data in their work. For instance, couples contemplating having a child may seek to determine the risks involved in a future pregnancy. In such a case, a counselor will take a thorough family history, seeking any familial

Table 2-2 Fetal Development Monitoring Techniques

Technique	Description
Amniocentesis	Done between the fifteenth and twentieth week of pregnancy, this procedure examines a sample of the amniotic fluid, which contains fetal cells. Recommended if either parent carries Tay-Sachs, spina bifida, sickle-cell, Down syndrome, muscular dystrophy, or Rh disease.
Chorionic villus sampling (CVS)	Done at 8 to 11 weeks, either transabdominally or transcervically, depending on where the placenta is located. Involves inserting a needle (abdominally) or a catheter (cervically) into the substance of the placenta but staying outside the amniotic sac and removing 10 to 15 milligrams of tissue. This tissue is manually cleaned of maternal uterine tissue and then grown in culture, and a karyotype is made, as with amniocentesis.
Embryoscopy	Examines the embryo or fetus during the first 12 weeks of pregnancy by means of a fiber-optic endoscope inserted through the cervix. Can be performed as early as week 5. Access to the fetal circulation may be obtained through the instrument, and direct visualization of the embryo permits the diagnosis of malformations.
Fetal blood sampling (FBS)	Performed after 18 weeks of pregnancy by collecting a small amount of blood from the umbilical cord for testing. Used to detect Down syndrome and most other chromosome abnormalities in the fetuses of couples who are at increased risk of having an affected child. Many other diseases can be diagnosed using this technique.
Sonoembryology	Used to detect abnormalities in the first trimester of pregnancy. Involves high-frequency transvaginal probes and digital image processing. In combination with ultrasound, it can detect more than 80 percent of all malformations during the second trimester.
Ultrasound (sonogram)	Uses very high frequency sound waves to detect structural abnormalities or multiple pregnancies, measure fetal growth, judge gestational age, and evaluate uterine abnormalities. Also used as an adjunct to other procedures, such as amniocentesis.

incidence of birth defects that might indicate a pattern of recessive or X-linked genes. In addition, the counselor will take into account factors such as the age of the mother and father and any previous abnormalities in other children they may have already had (Lyon, 2012; O'Doherty, 2014; Austin, 2016; Madlensky et al., 2017).

Typically, genetic counselors suggest a thorough physical examination. Such an exam may identify physical abnormalities that potential parents may have and not be aware of. In addition, samples of blood, skin, and urine may be used to isolate and examine specific chromosomes. Possible genetic defects, such as the presence of an extra sex chromosome, can be identified by assembling a *karyotype*, a chart containing enlarged photos of each of the chromosomes.

PRENATAL TESTING. A variety of techniques can be used to assess the health of an unborn child if a woman is already pregnant (see Table 2-2 for a list of currently available tests). The earliest test is a *first-trimester screen*, which combines a blood test and ultrasound sonography in the eleventh to thirteenth week of pregnancy and can identify chromosomal abnormalities and other disorders, such as heart problems. In **ultrasound sonography**, high-frequency sound waves bombard the mother's womb. These waves produce a rather indistinct, but useful, image of the unborn baby, whose size and shape can then be assessed. Repeated use of ultrasound sonography can reveal developmental patterns. Although the accuracy of blood tests and ultrasound in identifying abnormalities is not high early in pregnancy, it becomes more accurate later on.

ultrasound sonography
a process in which high-frequency sound waves scan the mother's womb to produce an image of the unborn baby, whose size and shape can then be assessed

A more invasive test, **chorionic villus sampling (CVS)**, can be employed if blood tests and ultrasound have identified a potential problem or if there is a family history of inherited disorders. CVS involves inserting a thin needle into the fetus and taking small samples of hair-like material that surrounds the embryo. The test can be done between the eighth and eleventh week of pregnancy. However, it produces a risk of miscarriage of 1 in 100 to 1 in 200. Because of the risk, its use is relatively infrequent.

chorionic villus sampling (CVS)
a test used to find genetic defects that involves taking samples of hair-like material that surrounds the embryo

In **amniocentesis**, a small sample of fetal cells is drawn by a tiny needle inserted into the amniotic fluid surrounding the unborn fetus. Carried out 15 to 20 weeks into the pregnancy, amniocentesis allows analysis of the fetal cells that can identify a variety of genetic defects with nearly 100 percent accuracy. In addition, the sex of the child can be determined. Although there is always a danger to the fetus in an invasive procedure

amniocentesis
the process of identifying genetic defects by examining a small sample of fetal cells drawn by a needle inserted into the amniotic fluid surrounding the fetus

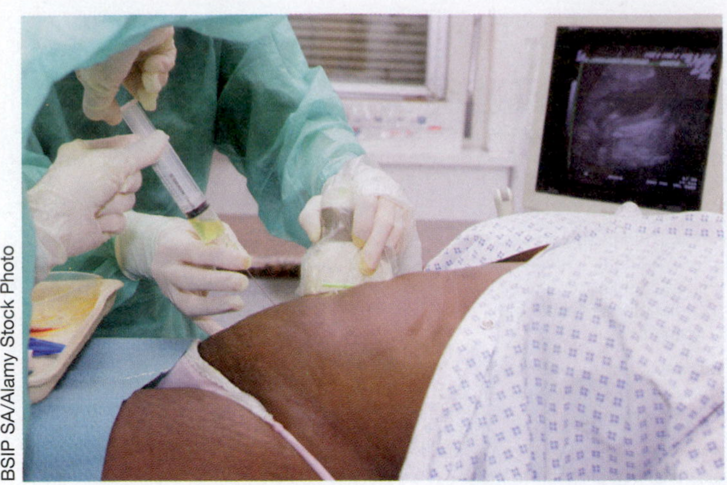
BSIP SA/Alamy Stock Photo

In amniocentesis, a sample of fetal cells is withdrawn from the amniotic sac and used to identify a number of genetic defects.

such as amniocentesis, it is generally safe, with the risk of miscarriage 1 in 200 to 1 in 400.

After the various tests are complete and all possible information is available, the couple will meet with the genetic counselor again. Typically, counselors avoid giving specific recommendations. Instead, they lay out the facts and present various options, ranging from doing nothing to taking more drastic steps, such as terminating the pregnancy through abortion. Ultimately, the parents must decide what course of action to follow.

SCREENING FOR FUTURE PROBLEMS. The newest role of genetic counselors involves testing people to identify whether they themselves, rather than their children, are susceptible to future disorders because of genetic abnormalities. For instance, Huntington's disease typically does not manifest until people reach their 40s. However, genetic testing can identify much earlier whether a person carries the flawed gene that produces Huntington's disease. Presumably, people's knowledge that they carry the gene can help them prepare themselves for the future (Cina & Fellmann, 2006; Tibben, 2007; Sánchez-Castañeda et al., 2015).

From *a health-care provider's* perspective

What are some ethical and philosophical questions that surround the issue of genetic counseling? Might it sometimes be unwise to know ahead of time about possible genetically linked disorders that might afflict your child or yourself?

In addition to Huntington's disease, more than a thousand disorders can be predicted on the basis of genetic testing (see Table 2-3). Although such testing may bring welcome relief from future worries if the results are negative, positive results may produce just the opposite effect. In fact, genetic testing raises difficult practical and ethical questions (Human Genome Project, 2006; Twomey, 2006; Wilfond & Ross, 2009; Klitzman, 2012).

Suppose, for instance, a woman who thought she was susceptible to Huntington's disease was tested in her 20s and found that she did not carry the defective gene. Obviously, she would experience tremendous relief. But suppose she found that she did carry the flawed gene and was therefore going to get the disease. In this case, she might well experience depression or anger. In fact, some studies show that 10 percent of people who find they have the flawed gene that leads to Huntington's disease never recover fully on an emotional level (Hamilton, 1998; Myers, 2004; Wahlin, 2007).

Genetic testing clearly is a complicated issue. It rarely provides a simple yes or no answer as to whether an individual will be susceptible to a disorder. Instead, typically it presents a range of probabilities. In some cases, the likelihood of actually becoming ill depends on the type of environmental stressors to which a person is exposed. Personal differences also affect a given person's susceptibility to a disorder (Bonke et al., 2005; Lucassen, 2012; Crozier, Robertson, & Dale, 2015; Djurdjinovic & Peters, 2017).

As our understanding of genetics continues to grow, researchers and medical practitioners have moved beyond testing and counseling to actively working to change flawed genes. The possibilities for genetic intervention and manipulation increasingly border on what once was science fiction—as we consider next.

ARE "DESIGNER BABIES" IN OUR FUTURE?

Adam Nash was born to save his older sister Molly's life—literally. Molly was suffering from a rare disorder called Fanconi anemia, which meant that her bone marrow was failing to produce blood cells. This disease can have devastating effects on young children, including birth defects and certain cancers. Many don't survive to adulthood. Molly's best hope

Table 2-3 Some Currently Available DNA-Based Genetic Tests

Disease	Description
Alzheimer's disease	Late-onset variety of senile dementia
Amyotrophic lateral sclerosis (Lou Gehrig's disease)	Progressive motor function loss leading to paralysis and death
Breast and ovarian cancer (inherited)	Early onset tumors of breasts and ovaries
Congenital hypothyroidism	Thyroid gland disorder
Cystic fibrosis	Thick mucus accumulations in lungs and chronic infections in lungs and pancreas
Duchenne muscular dystrophy (Becker muscular dystrophy)	Severe to mild muscle wasting, deterioration, weakness
Fragile X syndrome	Intellectual disability
Hemophilia A and B	Bleeding disorders
Hereditary nonpolyposis colon cancer[a]	Early onset tumors of colon and sometimes other organs
Huntington's disease	Progressive neurological degeneration, usually beginning in midlife
Neurofibromatosis, type 1	Multiple benign nervous system tumors that can be disfiguring; cancers
Phenylketonuria	Progressive intellectual disability due to missing enzyme; correctable by diet
Sickle-cell disease	Blood cell disorder, chronic pain and infections
Spinal muscular atrophy	Severe, usually lethal progressive muscle-wasting disorder in children
Tay-Sachs disease	Seizures, paralysis, fatal neurological disease of early childhood

[a] These are susceptibility tests that provide only an estimated risk for developing the disorder.

(**Sources:** Human Genome Project, 2010, http://www.ornl.gov/sci/techresources/Human_Genome/medicine/genetest.shtml; Genetics Home Reference, 2017, https://ghr.nlm.nih.gov/primer/testing/uses.)

for overcoming this disease was to grow healthy bone marrow by receiving a transplant of immature blood cells from the placenta of a newborn sibling. But not just any sibling would do—it had to be one with compatible cells that would not be rejected by Molly's immune system. So Molly's parents turned to a new and risky technique that had the potential to save Molly by using cells from her unborn brother.

Molly's parents were the first to use a genetic screening technique called *preimplantation genetic diagnosis* (*PGD*) to ensure that their next child would be free of Fanconi anemia. With PGD, a newly fertilized embryo can be screened for a variety of genetic diseases before it is implanted in the mother's uterus to develop. Doctors fertilized several of Molly's mother's eggs with her husband's sperm in a test tube. They then examined the embryos to ensure that they would only implant the embryo that PGD revealed to be both genetically healthy and a match for Molly. When Adam was born 9 months later, Molly got a new lease on life, too: The transplant was a success, and Molly was cured of her disease.

Molly's parents and their doctors also opened a controversial new chapter in genetic engineering involving the use of advances in reproductive medicine that give parents a degree of prenatal control over the traits of their children. Another procedure that makes this level of genetic control possible is *germ line therapy*, in which cells are taken from an embryo and then replaced after the defective genes they contain have been repaired.

While PGD and germ line therapy have important uses in the prevention and treatment of serious genetic disorders, concerns have been raised over whether such scientific advances can lead to the development of "designer babies"—infants that have been genetically manipulated to have traits their parents wish for. The question is whether these procedures can and should be used not only to correct undesirable genetic defects, but also to breed infants for specific purposes or to "improve" future generations on a genetic level.

The ethical concerns are numerous: Is it right to tailor babies to serve a specific purpose, however noble? Does this kind of genetic control pose any dangers to the human gene pool? Would unfair advantages be conferred on the offspring of those who are wealthy or privileged enough to have access to these procedures (Sheldon & Wilkinson, 2004; Landau, 2008; Drmanac, 2012)?

Designer babies aren't with us yet; scientists do not yet understand enough about the human genome to identify the genes that control most traits, much less to make genetic modifications to control how those traits will be expressed. Still, as Adam Nash's case reveals, we are inching closer to a day when it is possible for parents to decide what genes their children will and will not have.

Module 2.1 Review

LO 2.1 Describe how genes and chromosomes provide our basic genetic endowment.

In humans, the male sex cell (the sperm) and the female sex cell (the ovum) provide the developing baby with 23 chromosomes each.

LO 2.2 Compare monozygotic twins with dizygotic twins.

Monozygotic twins are twins who are genetically identical. Dizygotic twins result from two separate ova that are fertilized by two separate sperm at roughly the same time.

LO 2.3 Describe how the sex of a child is determined.

When an ovum and sperm meet at the moment of fertilization, the ovum provides an X chromosome, while the sperm provides either an X or a Y chromosome. If the sperm contributes an X chromosome, the child will have an XX pairing—a girl. If the sperm contributes a Y chromosome, the result will be an XY pairing—a boy.

LO 2.4 Explain the mechanisms by which genes transmit information.

A genotype is the underlying combination of genetic material present in an organism, but invisible; a phenotype is the visible trait, the expression of the genotype.

LO 2.5 Describe the field of behavioral genetics.

The field of behavioral genetics, a combination of psychology and genetics, studies the effects of genetics on behavior and psychological characteristics.

LO 2.6 Describe the major inherited disorders.

Several inherited and genetic disorders are caused by damaged or mutated genes.

LO 2.7 Describe the role of genetic counselors and differentiate between different forms of prenatal testing.

Genetic counselors use a variety of data and techniques to advise future parents of possible genetic risks to their unborn children. A variety of techniques can be used to assess the health of an unborn child if a woman is already pregnant, including ultrasound, CVS, and amniocentesis.

Journal Writing Prompt

Applying Lifespan Development: How can the field of behavioral genetics help researchers understand human development?

The Interaction of Heredity and Environment

Like many other parents, Jared's mother, Leesha, and his father, Jamal, tried to figure out which one of them their new baby resembled the most. He seemed to have Leesha's big, wide eyes and Jamal's generous smile. As he grew, Jared grew to resemble his mother and father even more. His hair grew in with a hairline just like Leesha's, and his teeth, when they came, made his smile resemble Jamal's even more. He also seemed to act like his parents. For example, he was a charming little baby, always ready to smile at people who visited the house—just like his friendly, jovial dad. He seemed to sleep like his mom, which was lucky since Jamal was an extremely light sleeper who could do with as little as 4 hours a night, while Leesha liked a regular 7 or 8 hours.

Were Jared's ready smile and regular sleeping habits something he just luckily inherited from his parents? Or did Jamal and Leesha provide a happy and stable home that encouraged these welcome traits? What causes our behavior? Nature or nurture? Is behavior produced by inherited, genetic influences, or is it triggered by factors in the environment?

The simple answer is: There is no simple answer.

The Role of the Environment in Determining the Expression of Genes: From Genotypes to Phenotypes

LO 2.8 Explain how the environment and genetics work together to determine human characteristics.

As developmental research accumulates, it is becoming increasingly clear that to view behavior as due to *either* genetic *or* environmental factors is inappropriate. A given behavior is not caused just by genetic factors, nor is it caused solely by environmental forces. Instead, as we first discussed in Chapter 1, the behavior is the product of some combination of the two.

For instance, consider **temperament**, patterns of arousal and emotionality that represent consistent and enduring characteristics in an individual. Suppose we found—as increasing evidence suggests is the case—that a small percentage of children are born with temperaments that produce an unusual degree of physiological reactivity. Having a tendency to shrink from anything unusual, such infants react to novel stimuli with a rapid increase in heartbeat and unusual excitability of the limbic system of the brain. Such heightened reactivity to stimuli at the start of life, which seems to be linked to inherited factors, is also likely to cause children, by the time they are 4 or 5, to be considered shy by their parents and teachers. But not always: some of them behave indistinguishably from their peers at the same age (De Pauw & Mervielde, 2011; Pickles et al., 2013; Smiley et al., 2016).

temperament
patterns of arousal and emotionality that represent consistent and enduring characteristics in an individual

What makes the difference? The answer seems to be the environment in which the children are raised. Children whose parents encourage them to be outgoing by arranging new opportunities for them may overcome their shyness. In contrast, children raised in a stressful environment marked by marital discord or a prolonged illness may be more likely to retain their shyness later in life (Kagan, 2010; Casalin et al., 2012; Merwin et al., 2017). Jared, described earlier, may have been born with an easy temperament, which was easily reinforced by his caring parents.

INTERACTION OF FACTORS. Such findings illustrate that many traits reflect **multifactorial transmission**, meaning that they are determined by a combination of both genetic and environmental factors. In multifactorial transmission, a genotype provides a particular range within which a phenotype may achieve expression. For instance, people with a genotype that permits them to gain weight easily may never be slim, no matter how much they diet. They may be *relatively* slim, given their genetic heritage, but they may never be able to get beyond a certain degree of thinness. In many cases, then, it is the environment that determines the way in which a particular genotype will be expressed as a phenotype (Plomin, 2016).

multifactorial transmission
the determination of traits by a combination of both genetic and environmental factors in which a genotype provides a range within which a phenotype may be expressed

By contrast, certain genotypes are relatively unaffected by environmental factors. In such cases, development follows a preordained pattern, relatively independent of the specific environment in which a person is raised. For instance, research on pregnant women who were severely malnourished during famines caused by World War II found that their children were, on average, unaffected physically or intellectually as adults (Stein et al., 1975). Similarly, no matter how much health food people eat, they are not going to grow beyond certain genetically imposed limitations in height. Little Jared's hairline was probably affected very little by any actions on the part of his parents.

Ultimately, of course, the unique interaction of inherited and environmental factors determines people's patterns of development.

The more appropriate question, then, is *how much* of the behavior is caused by genetic factors, and *how much* by environmental factors? (See, for example, the range of possibilities for the determinants of intelligence, illustrated in Figure 2-8.) At one extreme is the idea that opportunities in the environment are solely responsible for intelligence; on the other, that intelligence is purely genetic—you either have it or you don't. The usefulness of such extremes seems to be that they point us toward the middle ground—that intelligence is the result of some combination of natural mental ability and environmental opportunity (Asbury & Plomin, 2014).

Figure 2-8 Possible Sources of Intelligence

Intelligence may be explained by a range of differing possible sources, spanning the nature–nurture continuum. Which of these explanations do you find most convincing, given the evidence discussed in the chapter?

Nature				Nurture
Intelligence is provided entirely by genetic factors; environment plays no role. Even a highly enriched environment and excellent education make no difference.	Although largely inherited, intelligence is affected by an extremely enriched or deprived environment.	Intelligence is affected both by a person's genetic endowment and environment. A person genetically predisposed to low intelligence may perform better if raised in an enriched environment or worse in a deprived environment. Similarly, a person genetically predisposed to higher intelligence may perform worse in a deprived environment or better in an enriched environment.	Although intelligence is largely a result of environment, genetic abnormalities may produce mental retardation.	Intelligence depends entirely on the environment. Genetics plays no role in determining intellectual success.

Possible Causes

Studying Development: How Much Is Nature? How Much Is Nurture?

LO 2.9 Summarize how researchers study the interaction of genetic and environmental factors in development.

Developmental researchers use several strategies to try to resolve the question of the degree to which traits, characteristics, and behavior are produced by genetic or environmental factors. Their studies involve both nonhuman species and humans.

NONHUMAN ANIMAL STUDIES: CONTROLLING BOTH GENETICS AND ENVIRONMENT. It is relatively simple to develop breeds of animals that are genetically similar to one another in terms of specific traits. The people who raise Butterball turkeys for Thanksgiving do it all the time, producing turkeys that grow especially rapidly so that they can be brought to market inexpensively. Likewise, strains of laboratory animals can be bred to share similar genetic backgrounds.

By observing animals with similar genetic backgrounds in different environments, scientists can determine, with reasonable precision, the effects of specific kinds of environmental stimulation. For example, animals can be raised in unusually stimulating environments, with lots of items to climb over or through, or they can be raised in relatively barren environments, to determine the results of living in such different settings. Conversely, researchers can examine groups of animals that have been bred to have significantly *different* genetic backgrounds on particular traits. Then, by exposing such animals to identical environments, they can determine the role of genetic background.

Of course, the drawback to using nonhumans as research subjects is that we can't be sure how well the findings we obtain can be generalized to people. Still, animal research offers substantial opportunities. (Also see *From Research to Practice.*)

CONTRASTING RELATEDNESS AND BEHAVIOR: ADOPTION, TWIN, AND FAMILY STUDIES. Clearly, researchers can't control either the genetic backgrounds or the environments of humans in the way they can with nonhumans. However, nature conveniently has provided the potential to carry out various kinds of "natural experiments"—in the form of twins.

From Research to Practice

When Nurture Becomes Nature

A fundamental assumption about genetic inheritance has long been that environmental alterations of an organism's health cannot be passed down to future generations; if we cut off a mouse's tail, we do not expect its offspring to be tailless. Only genetic mutations—not lifestyle choices such as poor diet nor environmental insults such as exposure to toxins—were thought to be heritable. But recent research finds that an individual's life experiences can be passed down to children, grandchildren, and subsequent generations.

It's a phenomenon called *transgenerational epigenetic inheritance*, and it works a bit differently from usual inheritance. Instead of changing the genetic code itself, life experiences change the parts of DNA that switch individual genes on or off. Not every gene is active everywhere in the body; the DNA that is responsible for making insulin, for example, is only "switched on" in certain cells of the pancreas. When an event such as malnourishment or drug use affects the DNA "switches" in sperm or eggs, the alterations can be passed on to future generations (Daxinger & Whitelaw, 2012; Bahenko, Kovaklchuk, & Metz, 2016; Nestler, 2016).

In one study, healthy male rats were fed a high-fat diet that caused them to put on weight and develop symptoms consistent with type 2 diabetes, such as insulin resistance. Although these rats did not have a preexisting genetic tendency to be diabetic, their daughters also developed symptoms of type 2 diabetes as adults—even though they ate normal diets. Some researchers think that transgenerational epigenetic inheritance could partly explain the epidemic of childhood obesity: our high-fat diets may not only put us at risk, but perhaps our children as well (Skinner, 2010; Crews et al., 2012).

Happily, it's not just harmful effects that can be passed on this way. One study showed that mice developed better memory after being exposed to an enriched and stimulating environment, as previous research showed would be the case, and that the mice's offspring also showed the beneficial memory effect even though they didn't experience the same enriched environment.

The implications of this research are astounding—it may well be the case that the poor life choices we make in our youth have consequences for our progeny as well as ourselves (Arai, et al., 2009; Nestler, 2011; Heard & Martienssen, 2014).

Shared Writing Prompt:

Why would the poor life choices we make in our youth, rather than those we might make later in life, have possible consequences for our children?

Recall that monozygotic twins are identical genetically. Because their inherited backgrounds are precisely the same, any variations in their behavior must be due entirely to environmental factors.

It would be rather simple for researchers to make use of identical twins to draw unequivocal conclusions about the roles of nature and nurture. For instance, by separating identical twins at birth and placing them in totally different environments, researchers could assess the impact of environment unambiguously. Of course, ethical considerations make this impossible. What researchers can—and do—study, however, are cases in which identical twins have been put up for adoption at birth and are raised in substantially different environments. Such instances allow us to draw fairly confident conclusions about the relative contributions of genetics and environment (Agrawal & Lynskey, 2008; Nikolas, Klump, & Burt, 2012; Strachan et al., 2017).

The data from such studies of identical twins raised in different environments are not always without bias. Adoption agencies typically take the characteristics (and wishes) of birth mothers into account when they place babies in adoptive homes. For instance, children tend to be placed with families of the same race and religion. Consequently, even when monozygotic twins are placed in different adoptive homes, there are often similarities between the two home environments. As a result, researchers cannot always be certain that differences in behavior are due to differences in the environment.

Studies of dizygotic twins also present opportunities to learn about the relative contributions of nature and nurture. Recall that dizygotic twins are genetically no more similar than siblings in a family born at different times. By comparing behavior within pairs of dizygotic twins with that of pairs of monozygotic twins (who are genetically identical), researchers can determine whether monozygotic twins are more similar in a particular trait, on average, than dizygotic twins. If so, they can assume that genetics plays an important role in determining the expression of that trait.

Monozygotic and dizygotic twins present opportunities to learn about the relative contributions of heredity and situational factors. What can psychologists learn from studying twins?

Still another approach is to study people who are totally unrelated to one another and who therefore have dissimilar genetic backgrounds, but who share an environmental background. For instance, a family that adopts, at the same time, two very young unrelated children probably will provide them with quite similar environments throughout their childhood. In this case, similarities in the children's characteristics and behavior can be attributed with some confidence to environmental influences (Segal, 2000).

Finally, developmental researchers have examined groups of people in light of their degree of genetic similarity. For instance, on the one hand, if we find a high association on a particular trait between biological parents and their children, but a weaker association between adoptive parents and their children, we have evidence for the importance of genetics in determining the expression of that trait. On the other hand, if there is a stronger association on a trait between adoptive parents and their children than between biological parents and their children, we have evidence for the importance of the environment in determining that trait. If a particular trait tends to occur at similar levels among genetically similar individuals but occurs at different levels among genetically more distant individuals, signs point to the fact that genetics plays an important role in the development of that trait.

Developmental researchers have used all these approaches, and more, to study the relative impact of genetic and environmental factors. What have they found?

Before turning to specific findings, here's the general conclusion resulting from decades of research. Virtually all traits, characteristics, and behaviors are the joint result of the combination and interaction of nature and nurture. Genetic and environmental factors work in tandem, each affecting and being affected by the other, creating the unique individual that each of us is and will become (Robinson, 2004; Waterland & Jirtle, 2004; Kendler et al., 2017).

Genetics and the Environment: Working Together

LO 2.10 Explain how genetics and the environment jointly influence physical traits, intelligence, and personality.

Let's look at ways in which genetics and the environment influence our physical traits, intelligence, and personality.

PHYSICAL TRAITS: FAMILY RESEMBLANCES. When patients entered the examining room of Dr. Cyril Marcus, they didn't realize that sometimes they were actually being treated by his identical twin brother, Dr. Stewart Marcus. So similar in appearance and manner were the twins that even longtime patients were fooled by this admittedly unethical behavior, which occurred in a bizarre case made famous in the film *Dead Ringers*.

Monozygotic twins are merely the most extreme example of the fact that the more genetically similar two people are, the more likely they are to share physical characteristics. Tall parents tend to have tall children, and short ones tend to have short children. Obesity, which is defined as being more than 20 percent above the average weight for a given height, also has a strong genetic component. For example, in one study, pairs of identical twins were put on diets that contained an extra 1,000 calories a day—and ordered not to exercise. Over a 3-month period, the twins gained almost identical amounts of weight. Moreover, different pairs of twins varied substantially in how much weight they gained, with some pairs gaining almost three times as much weight as other pairs (Bouchard et al., 1990).

Other, less obvious physical characteristics also show strong genetic influences. For instance, blood pressure, respiration rates, and even the age at which life ends are more similar in closely related individuals than in those who are less genetically alike (Price & Gottesman, 1991; Melzer, Hurst, & Frayling, 2007; Wu, Treiber, & Snieder, 2013).

INTELLIGENCE: MORE RESEARCH, MORE CONTROVERSY. No other issue involving the relative influence of heredity and environment has generated more research than the topic of intelligence. Why? The main reason is that intelligence, generally measured in terms of an IQ score, is a central characteristic that differentiates humans from other species. In addition, intelligence is strongly related to success in scholastic endeavors and, somewhat less strongly, to other types of achievement.

Genetics plays a significant role in intelligence. In studies of both overall or general intelligence and of specific subcomponents of intelligence (such as spatial skills, verbal skills, and memory), as can be seen in Figure 2-9, the closer the genetic link between two individuals, the greater the correspondence of their overall IQ scores.

Not only is genetics an important influence on intelligence, but the impact increases with age. For instance, as fraternal (i.e., dizygotic) twins move from infancy to adolescence, their IQ scores become less similar. In contrast, the IQ scores of identical (monozygotic) twins become increasingly similar over the course of time. These opposite patterns suggest the intensifying influence of inherited factors with increasing age (Brody, 1993; McGue et al., 1993; Silventoinen et al., 2012; Madison et al., 2016).

Although it is clear that heredity plays an important role in intelligence, investigators are much more divided on the question of the degree to which it is inherited. Perhaps the most extreme view is held by psychologist Arthur Jensen (2003), who argued that as much as 80 percent of intelligence is a result of heredity. Others have suggested more modest figures, ranging from 50 percent to 70 percent. It is critical to keep in mind that such figures are averages across large groups of people, and any particular individual

Figure 2-9 Genetics and IQ

The closer the genetic link between two individuals, the greater the correspondence between their IQ scores. **THINKING ABOUT THE DATA:** Why is there a difference in the median correlation of IQ's between children reared together and siblings reared together? Alternatively, why is there a difference in the median correlation of IQ's between children reared together and siblings reared apart? How would you characterize the influence of genetics and environment on IQ?

(**Source:** Based on Bouchard & McGue, 1981.)

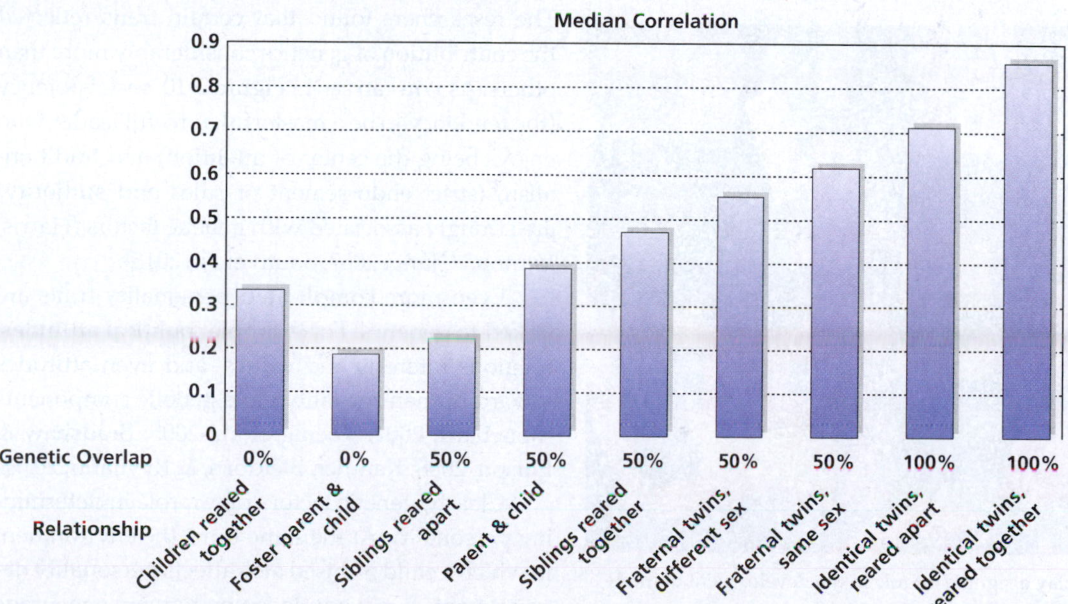

degree of inheritance cannot be predicted from these averages (e.g., Herrnstein & Murray, 1994; Brouwer et al., 2014; Schmiedek, 2017).

It is important to keep in mind that although heredity clearly plays an important role in intelligence, environmental factors such as exposure to books, good educational experiences, and intelligent peers are profoundly influential. Even those like Jensen who make the most extreme estimates of the role of genetics still allow for environmental factors to play a significant role. In terms of public policy, environmental influences are the focus of efforts geared toward maximizing people's intellectual success. As developmental psychologist Sandra Scarr suggests, we should be asking what can be done to maximize the intellectual development of each individual (Scarr & Carter-Saltzman, 1982; Storfer, 1990; Bouchard, 1997).

From *an educator's* perspective

Some people have used the proven genetic basis of intelligence to argue against strenuous educational efforts on behalf of individuals with below-average IQs. Does this viewpoint make sense based on what you have learned about heredity and environment? Why or why not?

GENETIC AND ENVIRONMENTAL INFLUENCES ON PERSONALITY: BORN TO BE OUTGOING? Do we inherit our personality? At least in part. There's increasing research evidence suggesting that some of our most basic personality traits have genetic roots. For example, two of the key "Big Five" personality traits, neuroticism and extroversion, have been linked to genetic factors. *Neuroticism,* as used by personality researchers, is the degree of emotional stability an individual characteristically displays. *Extroversion* is the degree to which a person seeks to be with others, to behave in an outgoing manner, and generally to be sociable. For instance, Jared, the baby described earlier in this chapter, may have inherited a tendency to be outgoing from his extroverted father, Jamal (Horwitz, Luong, & Charles, 2008; Zyphur et al., 2013; Briley & Tucker-Drob, 2017).

How do we know which personality traits reflect genetics? Some evidence comes from direct examination of genes themselves. For instance, a specific gene is very influential in determining risk-taking behavior. This novelty-seeking gene affects the production of the brain chemical dopamine, making some people more prone than others to seek out novel situations and to take risks (Serretti et al., 2007; Ray et al., 2009; Veselka et al., 2012).

Other evidence for the role of genetics in determining personality traits comes from studies of twins. For instance, in one major study, researchers looked at the personality traits of hundreds of pairs of twins. Because a good number of the twins were genetically identical but had been raised apart, it was possible to determine with some confidence the influence of genetic factors (Tellegen et al., 1988). The researchers found that certain traits reflected the contribution of genetics considerably more than others. As you can see in Figure 2-10, social potency (the tendency to be a masterful, forceful leader who enjoys being the center of attention) and traditionalism (strict endorsement of rules and authority) are strongly associated with genetic factors (Harris, Vernon, & Jang, 2007; South et al., 2015).

Even more complicated personality traits are linked to genetics. For example, political attitudes, religious interests and values, and even attitudes toward human sexuality have genetic components (Bouchard, 2004; Koenig et al., 2005; Bradshaw & Ellison, 2008; Kandler, Bleidorn, & Riemann, 2012).

Clearly, genetic factors play a role in determining personality. At the same time, the environment in which a child is raised also affects personality development. For example, some parents encourage

dotshock/Shutterstock

Although genetic factors clearly play a significant role in the development of intelligence, the level of environmental enrichment is also crucial.

Figure 2-10 Inheriting Traits

These traits are among the personality factors that are related most closely to genetic factors. The higher the percentage, the greater the degree to which the trait reflects the influence of heredity. Do these figures mean that "leaders are born, not made"? Why or why not?

(**Source:** Adapted from Tellegen et al., 1988.)

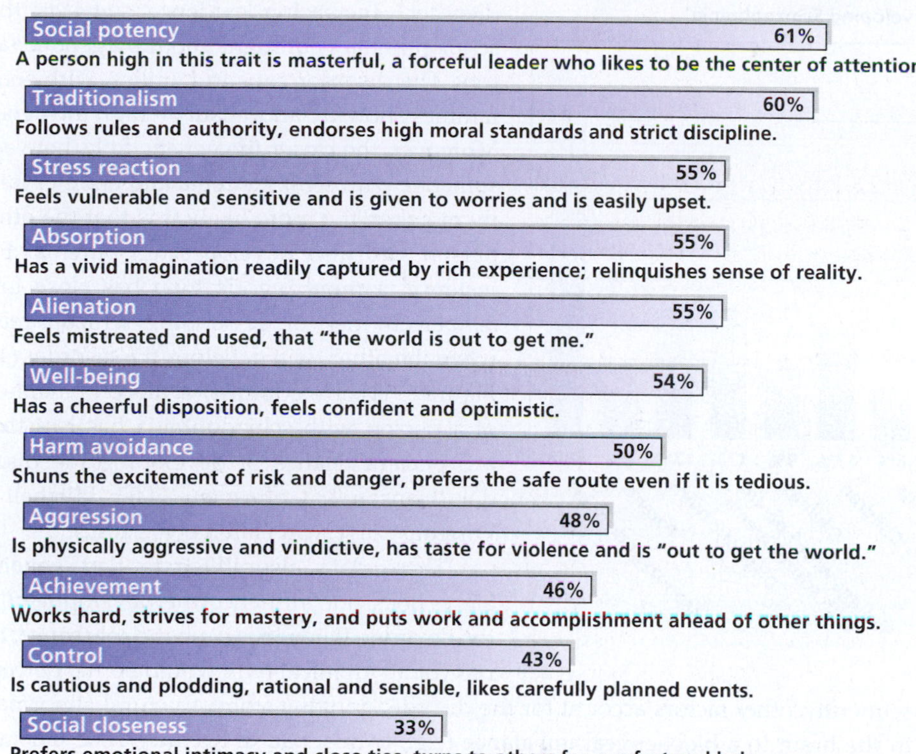

high activity levels, seeing activity as a manifestation of independence and intelligence. Other parents may encourage lower levels of activity in their children, feeling that more passive children will get along better in society. These parental attitudes are in part culturally determined; parents in the United States may encourage higher activity levels, while parents in Asian cultures may encourage greater passivity. In both cases, children's personalities will be shaped in part by their parents' attitudes (Cauce, 2008; Luo et al., 2017).

Because both genetic and environmental factors have consequences for a child's personality, personality development is a perfect example of a central fact of child development: Nature and nurture are closely intertwined. Furthermore, the way in which nature and nurture interact can be reflected not just in the behavior of individuals, but in the very foundations of a culture, as we see next.

Psychological Disorders: The Role of Genetics and Environment

LO 2.11 Explain the role genetics and the environment play in the development of psychological disorders.

When Elani Dimitrios turned 13, her cat, Mefisto, began to give her orders. At first the orders were harmless: "Wear two different socks to school" or "Eat out of a bowl on the floor." Her parents dismissed these events as signs of a vivid imagination, but when Elani approached her little brother with a hammer, her mother intervened forcibly. Elani later recalled, "I heard the order very clearly: Kill him, kill him. It was as if I was possessed."

In a sense, she *was* possessed: possessed with *schizophrenia spectrum disorder*, one of the most severe types of psychological disorders (typically referred to more simply as *schizophrenia*).

Figure 2-11 The Genetics of Schizophrenia

The psychological disorder schizophrenia has clear genetic components. The closer the genetic links between someone with schizophrenia and another family member, the more likely it is that the other person will also develop schizophrenia.

(**Source:** Based on Gottesman, 1991.)

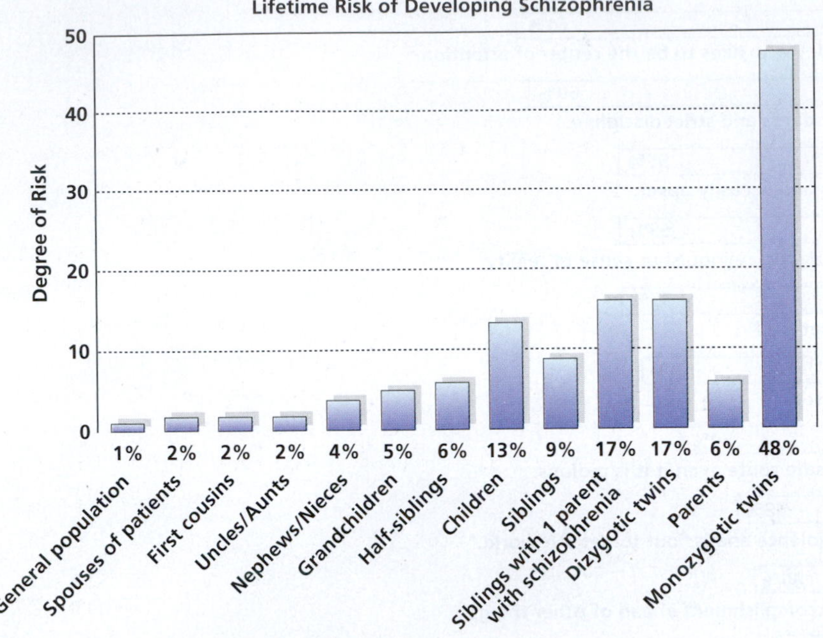

Normal and happy through childhood, Elani increasingly lost her hold on reality as she entered adolescence. For the next two decades, she would be in and out of institutions, struggling to ward off the ravages of the disorder.

What was the cause of Elani's mental disorder? Increasing evidence suggests that schizophrenia is brought about by genetic factors. The disorder runs in families, with some families showing an unusually high incidence. Moreover, the closer the genetic links between someone with schizophrenia and another family member, the more likely it is that the other person will also develop schizophrenia. For instance, a monozygotic twin has close to a 50 percent risk of developing schizophrenia when the other twin develops the disorder (see Figure 2-11). By contrast, a niece or nephew of a person with schizophrenia has less than a 5 percent chance of developing the disorder (Hanson & Gottesman, 2005; Mitchell & Porteous, 2011; van Haren et al., 2012).

These data also illustrate that genetics alone does not influence the development of the disorder. If genetics were the sole cause, the risk for an identical twin would be 100 percent. Consequently, other factors account for the disorder, ranging from structural abnormalities in the brain to a biochemical imbalance (e.g., Lyons, Bar, & Kremen, 2002; Hietala, Cannon, & van Erp, 2003; Howes & Kapur, 2009; Wada et al., 2012).

It also seems that even if individuals harbor a genetic predisposition toward schizophrenia, they are not destined to develop the disorder. Instead, they may inherit an unusual sensitivity to stress in the environment. If stress is low, schizophrenia will not occur. But if stress is sufficiently strong, it will lead to schizophrenia. At the same time, for someone with a strong genetic predisposition toward the disorder, even relatively weak environmental stressors may lead to schizophrenia (Norman & Malla, 2001; Mittal, Ellman, & Cannon, 2008; Walder et al., 2014).

Several other psychological disorders have been shown to be related, at least in part, to genetic factors. For instance, major depressive disorders, alcoholism, autism spectrum disorder, and attention-deficit/hyperactivity disorder have significant inherited components (Monastra, 2008; Burbach & van der Zwaag, 2009; Cho et al., 2017).

The example of schizophrenia spectrum disorder and other genetically related psychological disorders also illustrates a fundamental principle regarding the relationship between heredity and environment, a principle that underlies much of our previous discussion. Specifically, the role of genetics is often to produce a tendency toward a future course of development. When and whether a certain behavioral characteristic will actually be displayed depends on the nature of the environment. Thus, although a predisposition for schizophrenia may be present at birth, typically people do not show the disorder until adolescence—if at all.

Similarly, certain other kinds of traits are more likely to be displayed as the influence of parents and other socializing factors declines. For example, adopted children may, early in their lives, display traits that are relatively similar to their adoptive parents' traits, given the overwhelming influence of the environment on young children. As they get older and their parents' day-to-day influence declines, genetically influenced traits may begin to manifest themselves as unseen genetic factors begin to play a greater role (Arseneault et al., 2003; Poulton & Caspi, 2005).

Developmental Diversity and Your Life

Cultural Differences in Physical Arousal: Might a Culture's Philosophical Outlook Be Determined by Genetics?

Buddhist philosophy, an inherent part of many Asian cultures, emphasizes harmony and peacefulness. In contrast, some traditional Western philosophies, such as those of Martin Luther and John Calvin, accentuate the importance of controlling the anxiety, fear, and guilt that they assume to be basic parts of the human condition.

Could such philosophical approaches reflect, in part, genetic factors? That is the controversial suggestion made by developmental psychologist Jerome Kagan and his colleagues. They speculate that the underlying temperament of a given society, determined genetically, may predispose people in that society toward a particular philosophy (Kagan, 2003, 2010).

Kagan bases his admittedly speculative suggestion on well-confirmed findings that show clear differences in temperament between Caucasian and Asian children. For instance, one study that compared 4-month-old infants in China, Ireland, and the United States found several relevant differences. In comparison to the Caucasian American babies and the Irish babies, the Chinese babies had significantly lower motor activity, irritability, and vocalization (see Table 2-4).

Kagan suggests that the Chinese, who enter the world temperamentally calmer, may find Buddhist philosophical notions of serenity more in tune with their natural inclinations. In contrast, Westerners, who are emotionally more volatile and tense, and who report higher levels of guilt, are more likely to be attracted to philosophies that articulate the necessity of controlling the unpleasant feelings that they are more apt to encounter in their everyday experience (Kagan, 2003, 2010).

It is important to note that this does not mean that one philosophical approach is necessarily better or worse than the other. Nor does it mean that either of the temperaments from which the philosophies are thought to spring is superior or inferior to the other. Similarly, we must remember that any single individual within a culture can be more or less temperamentally volatile and that the range of temperaments found even within a particular culture is vast. Finally, as noted in our initial discussion of temperament, environmental conditions can have a significant effect on the portion of a person's temperament that is not genetically determined. But what Kagan and his colleagues' speculation does attempt to address is the back-and-forth-interchange between culture and temperament. As religion may help mold temperament, so may temperament make certain religious ideals more attractive.

The notion that the very basis of culture—its philosophical traditions—may be affected by genetic factors is intriguing. More research is necessary to determine just how the unique interaction of heredity and environment within a given culture may produce a framework for viewing and understanding the world.

Ingram Publishing/Newscom

Buddhist philosophy emphasizes harmony and peacefulness. Could this decidedly non-Western philosophy be caused, in part, by genetics?

Table 2-4 Mean Behavioral Scores for Caucasian American, Irish, and Chinese 4-Month-Old Infants

Behavior	American	Irish	Chinese
Motor activity	48.6	36.7	11.2
Crying (in seconds)	7.0	2.9	1.1
Fretting (% trials)	10.0	6.0	1.9
Vocalizing (% trials)	31.4	31.1	8.1
Smiling (% trials)	4.1	2.6	3.6

(**Source:** Kagan, Arcus, & Snidman, 1993.)

Can Genes Influence the Environment?

LO 2.12 Describe ways in which genes influence the environment.

According to developmental psychologist Sandra Scarr (1993, 1998), the genetic endowment provided to children by their parents not only determines their genetic characteristics but also actively influences their environment. Scarr suggests three ways a child's genetic predisposition might influence his or her environment.

Children tend to actively focus on those aspects of their environment that are most connected with their genetically determined abilities. For example, an active, more aggressive child will gravitate toward sports, while a more reserved child will be more engaged by academics or solitary pursuits such as computer games or drawing. Children also pay less attention to those aspects of the environment that are less compatible with their genetic endowment. For instance, two girls may be reading the same school bulletin board. One may notice the sign advertising tryouts for Little League baseball, while her less coordinated but more musically endowed friend might be more apt to spot the notice recruiting students for an after-school chorus. In each case, the child is attending to those aspects of the environment in which her genetically determined abilities can flourish.

In some cases, the gene–environment influence is more passive and less direct. For example, a particularly sports-oriented parent, who has genes that promote good physical coordination, may provide many opportunities for a child to play sports.

Finally, the genetically driven temperament of a child may *evoke* certain environmental influences. For instance, an infant's demanding behavior may cause parents to be more attentive to the infant's needs than they would be if the infant were less demanding. Or, for instance, a child who is genetically inclined to be well coordinated may play ball with anything in the house so often that her parents notice. They may then decide that she should have some sports equipment.

In sum, determining whether behavior is primarily attributable to nature or nurture is a bit like shooting at a moving target. Not only are behaviors and traits a joint outcome of genetic and environmental factors, but the relative influence of genes and environment for specific characteristics shifts over the course of people's lives. Although the pool of genes we inherit at birth sets the stage for our future development, the constantly shifting scenery and the other characters in our lives determine just how our development eventually plays out. The environment both influences our experiences and is molded by the choices we are temperamentally inclined to make.

Module 2.2 Review

LO 2.8 Explain how the environment and genetics work together to determine human characteristics.

Human characteristics and behavior often reflect multifactorial transmission, meaning that they are a joint outcome of genetic and environmental factors.

LO 2.9 Summarize how researchers study the interaction of genetic and environmental factors in development.

Developmental researchers use a number of strategies to examine the extent to which traits and behavior are due to genetic factors or environmental factors. Strategies include animal studies and research on twins, adopted siblings, and families.

LO 2.10 Explain how genetics and the environment jointly influence physical traits, intelligence, and personality.

Genetic influences have been identified in physical characteristics, intelligence, and personality traits and behaviors. Environmental factors, such as family dispositions and habits, also play a role in such traits as intelligence and personality.

LO 2.11 Explain the role genetics and the environment play in the development of psychological disorders.

Schizophrenia spectrum disorder has strong genetic roots. Other disorders, including major depressive disorder, alcoholism, autism spectrum disorder, and attention-deficit/hyperactivity disorder, have genetic components as well, but environmental influences also contribute.

LO 2.12 Describe ways in which genes influence the environment.

Children may influence their environment through genetic traits that cause them to construct—or influence their parents to construct—an environment that matches their inherited dispositions and preferences.

Journal Writing Prompt

Applying Lifespan Development: How might an environment different from the one you experienced have affected the development of personality characteristics that you believe you inherited from one or both of your parents?

Prenatal Growth and Change

Robert accompanied Lisa to her first appointment with the midwife. The midwife checked the results of tests done to confirm the couple's own positive home pregnancy test. "Yep, you're going to have a baby," she confirmed, speaking to Lisa. "You'll need to set up monthly visits for the next 6 months, then more frequently as your due date approaches. You can get this prescription for prenatal vitamins filled at any pharmacy, and here are some guidelines about diet and exercise. You don't smoke, do you? That's good." Then she turned to Robert. "How about you? Do you smoke?" After giving lots of instructions and advice, she left the couple feeling slightly dazed but ready to do whatever they could to have a healthy baby.

From the moment of conception, development proceeds relentlessly. As we've seen, many aspects are guided by the complex set of genetic guidelines inherited from the parents. Of course, prenatal growth, like all development, is also influenced from the start by environmental factors (Leavitt & Goldson, 1996). As we'll see, both parents, like Lisa and Robert, can take part in providing a good prenatal environment.

Fertilization: The Moment of Conception

LO 2.13 Explain the process of fertilization.

When most of us think about the facts of life, we tend to focus on the events that cause a male's sperm cells to begin their journey toward a female's ovum. Yet the act of sex that brings about the potential for conception is both the consequence and the start of a long string of events that precede and follow **fertilization**, or conception: the joining of sperm and ovum to create the single-celled zygote from which life begins.

fertilization
the process by which a sperm and an ovum—the male and female gametes, respectively—join to form a single new cell

Both the male's sperm and the female's ovum come with a history of their own. Females are born with around 400,000 ova located in the two ovaries (see Figure 2-12 for the basic anatomy of the female reproductive organs). However, the ova do not mature until the female reaches puberty. From that point until she reaches menopause, the female will ovulate about every 28 days. During ovulation, an egg is released from one of the ovaries and pushed by minute hair cells through the fallopian tube toward the uterus. If the ovum meets a sperm in the fallopian tube, fertilization takes place (Aitken, 1995).

Sperm, which look a little like microscopic tadpoles, have a shorter life span than ova. They are created by the testicles at a rapid rate: An adult male typically produces several hundred million sperm a day. Consequently, the sperm ejaculated during sexual intercourse are of considerably more recent origin than the ovum to which they are heading.

When sperm enter the vagina, they begin a winding journey that takes them through the cervix, the opening of the uterus, and into the fallopian tube, where fertilization may take place. However, only a tiny fraction of the 300 million cells that are typically ejaculated during sexual intercourse ultimately survive the arduous journey. That's usually okay, though: It takes only one sperm to fertilize an ovum, and each sperm and ovum contains all the genetic data necessary to produce a new human.

Figure 2-12 Anatomy of the Female Reproductive Organs

The basic anatomy of the female reproductive organs is illustrated in this cutaway view.

(**Source:** Based on Moore & Persaud, 2003.)

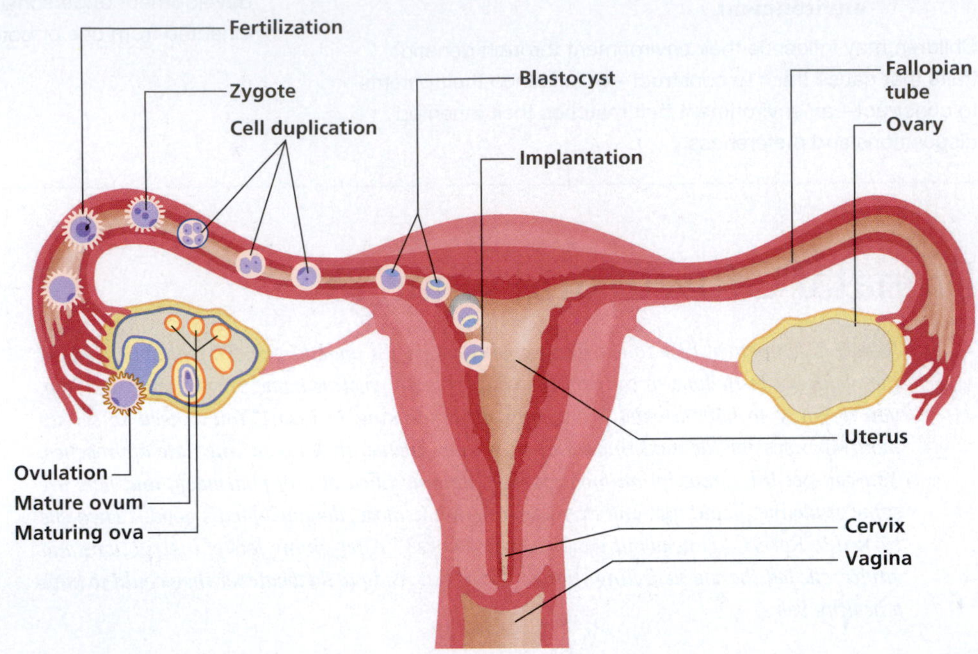

The Stages of the Prenatal Period: The Onset of Development

LO 2.14 Summarize the three stages of prenatal development.

The prenatal period consists of three stages: the germinal, embryonic, and fetal stages. They are summarized in Table 2-5.

germinal stage
the first—and shortest—stage of the prenatal period, which takes place during the first 2 weeks following conception

THE GERMINAL STAGE: FERTILIZATION TO 2 WEEKS. In the **germinal stage**, the first—and shortest—stage of the prenatal period, the zygote begins to divide and grow in complexity during the first 2 weeks following conception. During the germinal stage, the fertilized egg (now called a *blastocyst*) travels toward the *uterus*, where it becomes implanted in the uterus's wall, which is rich in nutrients. The germinal stage is characterized by methodical cell division, which gets off to a quick start: Three days after fertilization, the organism consists of some 32 cells, and by the next day the number doubles. Within a week, it is made up of 100 to 150 cells, and the number rises with increasing rapidity.

In addition to increasing in number, the cells of the organism become increasingly specialized. For instance, some cells form a protective layer around the mass of cells, while others begin to establish the rudiments of a placenta and an umbilical cord. When fully developed, the **placenta** serves as a conduit between the mother and the fetus, providing nourishment and oxygen via the *umbilical cord*, which also removes waste materials from the developing child. The placenta also plays a role in fetal brain development (Kalb, 2012).

placenta
a conduit between the mother and the fetus, providing nourishment and oxygen via the umbilical cord

embryonic stage
the period from 2 to 8 weeks following fertilization during which significant growth occurs in the major organs and body systems

THE EMBRYONIC STAGE: 2 WEEKS TO 8 WEEKS. By the end of the germinal period—just 2 weeks after conception—the organism is firmly secured to the wall of the mother's uterus. At this point, the child is called an *embryo*. The **embryonic stage** is the period from 2 to 8 weeks following fertilization. One of the highlights of this stage is the development of the major organs and basic anatomy.

Table 2-5 Stages of the Prenatal Period

Germinal Fertilization to 2 Weeks	Embryonic 2 Weeks to 8 Weeks	Fetal 8 Weeks to Birth
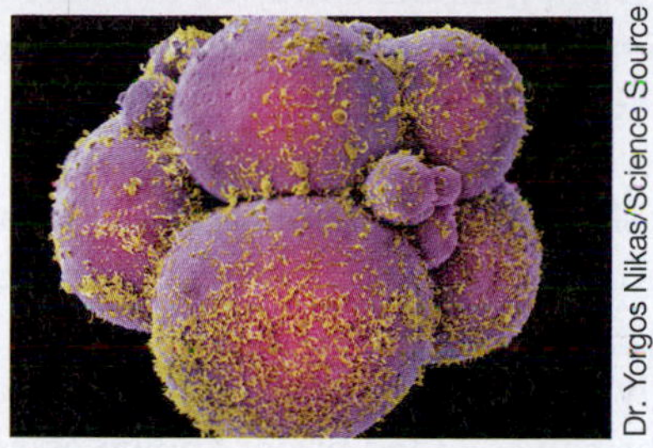 Dr. Yorgos Nikas/Science Source	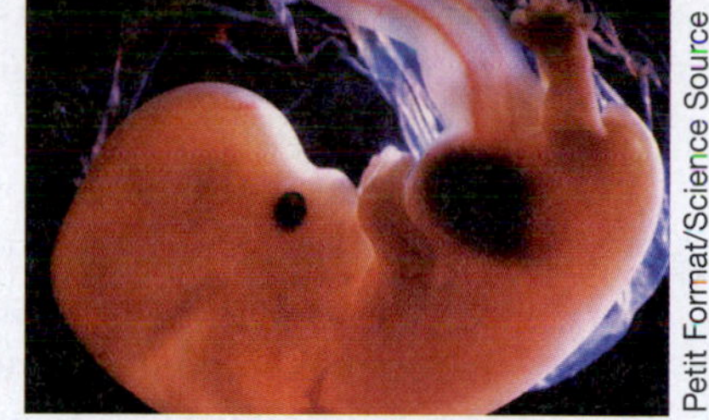 Petit Format/Science Source	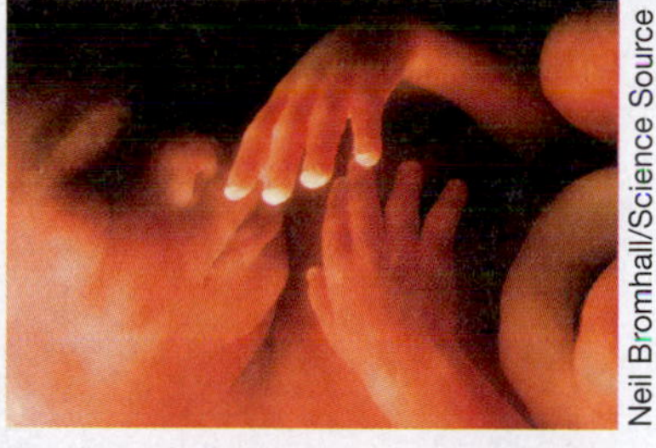 Neil Bromhall/Science Source
The germinal stage is the first and shortest, characterized by methodical cell division and the attachment of the organism to the wall of the uterus. Three days after fertilization, the zygote consists of 32 cells, a number that doubles by the next day. Within a week, the zygote multiplies to 100 to 150 cells. The cells become specialized, with some forming a protective layer around the zygote.	The zygote is now designated an embryo. The embryo develops three layers, which ultimately form a different set of structures as development proceeds. The layers are as follows: Ectoderm: skin, hair, teeth, sense organs, brain, spinal cord Endoderm: digestive system, liver, pancreas, respiratory system Mesoderm: muscles, bones, blood, circulatory system At 8 weeks, the embryo is 1 inch long.	The fetal stage formally starts when the differentiation of the major organs has occurred. Now called a fetus, the individual grows rapidly as length increases 20 times. At 4 months, the fetus weighs an average of 4 ounces; at 7 months, 3 pounds; and at the time of birth, the average child weighs just over 7 pounds.

At the beginning of the embryonic stage, the developing child has three distinct layers, each of which will ultimately form a different set of structures as development proceeds. The outer layer of the embryo, the *ectoderm*, will form skin, hair, teeth, sense organs, and the brain and spinal cord. The *endoderm*, the inner layer, produces the digestive system, liver, pancreas, and respiratory system. Sandwiched between the ectoderm and endoderm is the *mesoderm*, from which the muscles, bones, blood, and circulatory system are forged. Every part of the body is formed from these three layers.

If you were looking at an embryo at the end of the embryonic stage, you might be hard-pressed to identify it as human. Only an inch long, an 8-week-old embryo has what appear to be gills and a tail-like structure. However, a closer look reveals several familiar features. Rudimentary eyes, nose, lips, and even teeth can be recognized, and the embryo has stubby bulges that will form arms and legs.

The head and brain undergo rapid growth during the embryonic period. The head begins to represent a significant proportion of the embryo's size, encompassing about 50 percent of its total length. The growth of nerve cells, called *neurons*, is astonishing: As many as 100,000 neurons are produced every minute during the second month of life! The nervous system begins to function around the fifth week, and weak brain waves begin to be produced as the nervous system starts to function (Lauter, 1998; Nelson & Bosquet, 2000).

THE FETAL STAGE: 8 WEEKS TO BIRTH. It is not until the final period of prenatal development, the fetal stage, that the developing child becomes easily recognizable. The **fetal stage** starts at about 8 weeks after conception and continues until birth. The fetal stage formally starts when the differentiation of the major organs has occurred.

fetal stage
the stage that begins at about 8 weeks after conception, and continues until birth

Now called a **fetus**, the developing child undergoes astoundingly rapid change during the fetal stage. For instance, it increases in length some 20 times, and its proportions change dramatically. At 2 months, around half the fetus is what will ultimately be its head; by 5 months, the head accounts for just over a quarter of its total size (see Figure 2-13). The fetus also substantially increases in weight. At 4 months, the fetus weighs an average of about 4 ounces; at 7 months, it weighs about 3 pounds; and at the time of birth, the average child weighs just over 7 pounds.

fetus
a developing child, from 8 weeks after conception until birth

At the same time, the developing child is rapidly becoming more complex. Organs become more differentiated and start to work. By 3 months, for example, the fetus

Figure 2-13 Body Proportions

During the fetal stage, the proportions of the body change dramatically. At 2 months, the head represents about half the fetus, but by the time of birth, it is one-quarter of its total size.

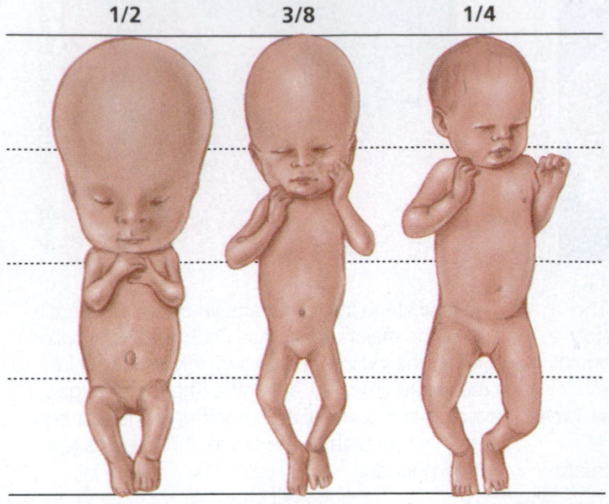

swallows and urinates. In addition, the interconnections between the different parts of the body become more complex and integrated. For example, arms develop hands; hands develop fingers; fingers develop nails.

As this is happening, the fetus makes itself known to the outside world. In the earliest stages of pregnancy, mothers may be unaware that they are, in fact, pregnant. As the fetus becomes increasingly active, however, most mothers certainly take notice. By 4 months, a mother can feel the movement of her child, and several months later, others can feel the baby's kicks through the mother's skin. In addition to the kicks that alert its mother to its presence, the fetus can turn, do somersaults, cry, hiccup, clench its fist, open and close its eyes, and suck its thumb.

The brain becomes increasingly sophisticated during the fetal stage. The two symmetrical left and right halves of the brain, known as *hemispheres*, grow rapidly, and the interconnections between neurons become more complex. The neurons become coated with an insulating material called *myelin* that helps speed the transmission of messages from the brain to the rest of the body.

By the end of the fetal period, brain waves are produced that indicate the fetus passes through different stages of sleep and wakefulness. The fetus is also able to hear (and feel the vibrations of) sounds to which it is exposed. For instance, researchers Anthony DeCasper and Melanie Spence (1986) asked a group of pregnant mothers to read aloud the Dr. Seuss story *The Cat in the Hat* two times a day during the later months of pregnancy. Three days after the babies were born, they appeared to recognize the story they had heard, responding more to it than to another story that had a different rhythm.

In weeks 8 to 24 following conception, hormones are released that lead to the increasing differentiation of male and female fetuses. For example, in males, high levels of androgen are produced that affect the size of brain cells and the growth of neural connections, which, some scientists speculate, ultimately may lead to differences in male and female brain structure and even later variations in gender-related behavior (Reiner & Gearhart, 2004; Knickmeyer & Baron-Cohen, 2006; Burton et al., 2009; Jordan-Young, 2012).

Just as no two adults are alike, no two fetuses are the same. Although development during the prenatal period follows the broad patterns outlined here, there are significant differences in the specific nature of individual fetuses' behavior. Some fetuses are exceedingly active, while others are more sedentary. (The more active fetuses will probably be more active after birth.) Some have relatively quick heart rates, while others' heart rates are slower, with the typical range varying between 120 and 160 beats per minute (DiPietro et al., 2002; Niederhofer, 2004; Tongsong et al., 2005).

Such differences in fetal behavior are due in part to genetic characteristics inherited at the moment of fertilization. Other kinds of differences, though, are brought about by the nature of the environment in which the child spends its first 9 months of life. As we will see, there are numerous ways in which the prenatal environment of infants affects their development—in good ways and bad.

Pregnancy Problems

LO 2.15 Describe some of the physical and ethical challenges that relate to pregnancy.

For some couples, conception presents a major challenge. Let's consider some of the challenges—both physical and ethical—that relate to pregnancy.

infertility
the inability to conceive after 12 to 18 months of trying to become pregnant

INFERTILITY. Some 15 percent of couples suffer from **infertility**, the inability to conceive after 12 to 18 months of trying to become pregnant. Infertility is negatively correlated with age. The older the parents, the more likely infertility will occur (see Figure 2-14).

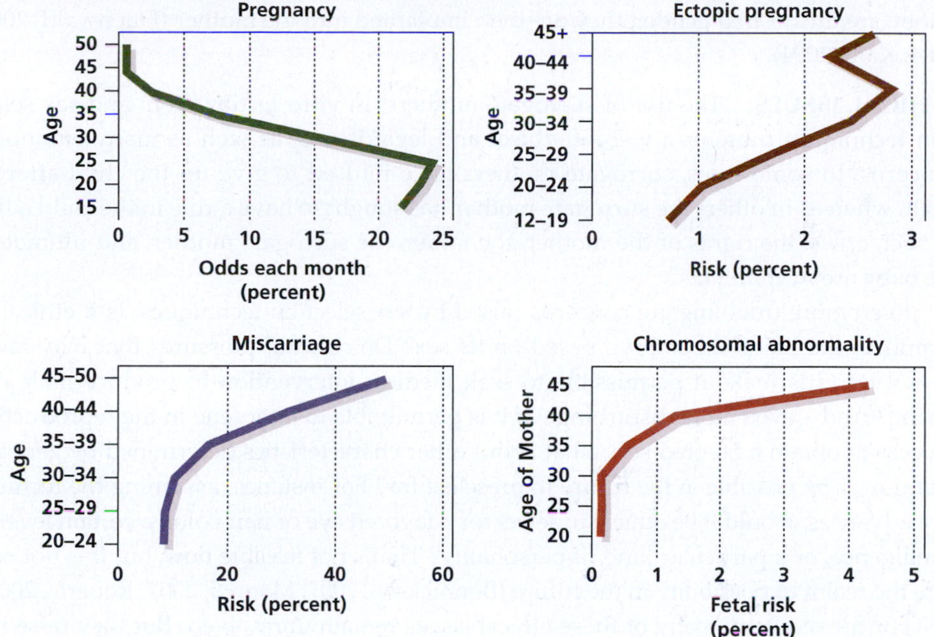

Figure 2-14 Older Women and Risks of Pregnancy

Not only does the rate of infertility increase as women get older, but the risk of chromosomal abnormality increases as well.

(**Source:** Reproductive Medicine Associates of New Jersey, 2002.)

In men, infertility is typically a result of producing too few sperm. Use of illicit drugs or cigarettes and previous bouts of sexually transmitted diseases also increase infertility. For women, the most common cause of infertility is failure to release an egg through ovulation. This may occur because of a hormone imbalance, a damaged fallopian tube or uterus, stress, or abuse of alcohol or drugs (Lewis, Legato, & Fisch, 2006; Kelly-Weeder & Cox, 2007; Wilkes et al., 2009).

Several treatments for infertility exist. Some difficulties can be corrected through the use of drugs or surgery. Another option may be **artificial insemination**, a procedure in which a man's sperm is placed directly into a woman's vagina by a physician. In some situations, the woman's husband provides the sperm, while in others it is an anonymous donor from a sperm bank.

artificial insemination
a process of fertilization in which a man's sperm is placed directly into a woman's vagina by a physician

In other cases, fertilization takes place outside of the mother's body. **In vitro fertilization (IVF)** is a procedure in which a woman's ova are removed from her ovaries, and a man's sperm are used to fertilize the ova in a laboratory. The fertilized egg is then implanted in a woman's uterus. Similarly, *gamete intrafallopian transfer* (*GIFT*) and *zygote intrafallopian transfer* (*ZIFT*) are procedures in which an egg and sperm or fertilized egg are implanted in a woman's fallopian tubes. In IVF, GIFT, and ZIFT, implantation is done either in the woman who provided the donor eggs or, in rarer instances, in a *surrogate mother*, a woman who agrees to carry the child to term. Surrogate mothers may also be used in cases in which the mother is unable to conceive; the surrogate mother is artificially inseminated by the biological father, and she agrees to give up rights to the infant (Frazier et al., 2004; Kolata, 2004; Hertz & Nelson, 2015).

in vitro fertilization (IVF)
a procedure in which a woman's ova are removed from her ovaries and a man's sperm are used to fertilize the ova in a laboratory

IVF is increasingly successful, with pregnancy rates as high as 48 percent for women under 35 (but with lower rates for older women). (Actual live birth rates are lower, since not all pregnancies ultimately result in birth.) It is also becoming more commonplace, with the procedure being used and publicized by women such as actresses Mariah Carey and Nicole Kidman. Worldwide, more than 3 million babies have been created through IVF (SART, 2012).

Furthermore, reproductive technologies are increasingly sophisticated, permitting parents to choose the sex of their baby. One technique is to separate sperm carrying the X and Y chromosomes and later implant the desired type into a woman's uterus. In another technique, eggs are removed from a woman and fertilized with sperm using in vitro fertilization. Three days after fertilization, the embryos are tested to determine their sex. If they are the desired gender, they are then implanted into the mother (Duenwald, 2003, 2004; Kalb, 2004).

ETHICAL ISSUES. The use of surrogate mothers, in vitro fertilization, and sex selection techniques presents a web of ethical and legal issues, as well as many emotional concerns. In some cases, surrogate mothers have refused to give up the child after its birth, whereas in others the surrogate mother has sought to have a role in the child's life. In such cases, the rights of the mother, the father, the surrogate mother, and ultimately the baby are in conflict.

Even more troubling are concerns raised by sex selection techniques. Is it ethical to terminate the life of an embryo based on its sex? Do cultural pressures that may favor boys over girls make it permissible to seek medical intervention to produce male offspring? And—even more disturbing—if it is permissible to intervene in the reproductive process to obtain a favored sex, what about other characteristics determined by genetics that it may be possible in the future to preselect for? For instance, assuming the technology advances, would it be ethical to select for a favored eye or hair color, a certain level of intelligence, or a particular kind of personality? That's not feasible now, but it is not outside the realm of possibility in the future (Bonnicksen, 2007; Mameli, 2007; Roberts, 2007).

For the moment, many of these ethical issues remain unresolved. But they raise important philosophical questions. Moreover, they involve cultural and religious issues. For example, in some religions, such as Catholicism, the use of some reproductive technologies such as IVF and surrogate mothers are prohibited because they are seen as violating the dignity of the child and marriage.

But the answer to one question is clear: How do children conceived using emerging reproductive technologies such as in vitro fertilization fare?

Research shows that they do quite well. In fact, some studies find that the quality of family life for those who have used such techniques may be superior to that in families with naturally conceived children. Furthermore, the later psychological adjustment of children conceived using IVF and artificial insemination is no different from that of children conceived using natural techniques (DiPietro, Costigan, & Gurewitsch, 2005; Hjelmstedt, Widström, & Collins, 2006; Siegel, Dittrich, & Vollmann, 2008).

However, the increasing use of IVF techniques by older individuals (who might be quite elderly when their children reach adolescence) may change these positive findings. Because widespread use of IVF is still a recent development, we just don't know yet what will happen with aging parents (Colpin & Soenen, 2004).

MISCARRIAGE AND ABORTION. A *miscarriage*—medically known as a spontaneous abortion—occurs when pregnancy ends before the developing child is able to survive outside the mother's womb. The embryo detaches from the wall of the uterus and is expelled.

Some 15 percent to 20 percent of all pregnancies end in miscarriage, usually in the first several months of pregnancy. (The term *stillbirth* is used to describe the death of a developing child 20 weeks or more after conception.) Many miscarriages occur so early that the mother is not even aware she was pregnant and may not even know she has suffered a miscarriage. However, as women are able to learn they are pregnant earlier than ever before due to the advent of home pregnancy tests, the number of women who know they have suffered a miscarriage has increased.

Typically, miscarriages are attributable to some sort of genetic abnormality in the fetus. In addition, hormonal problems, infections, or maternal health problems can lead to miscarriage.

Whatever the cause, women who suffer miscarriage frequently experience anxiety, depression, and grief. Because a woman's body may continue to look pregnant for a period of several weeks before it goes back to its pre-pregnant state, grief over the loss may be intensified and prolonged (Zucker & Alexander-Tanner, 2017).

Even after subsequently having a healthy child, women who have had a miscarriage in the past have a higher risk for depression. In addition, the aftereffects may linger, sometimes for years, and they may have difficulty caring for their healthy child (Leis-Newman, 2012; Murphy, Lipp, & Powles, 2012; Sawicka, 2016).

Each year, over 56 million pregnancies worldwide end in *abortion*, in which a mother voluntarily chooses to terminate pregnancy. Women in developing countries are more likely to have abortions than women in more developed countries, and the number of abortions in developed countries has declined significantly over the past several decades (Guttmacher, 2017).

Involving a complex set of physical, psychological, legal, and ethical issues, abortion is a difficult choice for every woman. A task force of the American Psychological Association (APA), which looked at the aftereffects of abortion, found that following an abortion most women experienced a combination of relief over terminating an unwanted pregnancy and regret and guilt. In most cases, for adult women with an unplanned pregnancy who had an elective, first-trimester abortion, the risk of mental health problems was not higher than for women who actually deliver that pregnancy (APA Reproductive Choice Working Group, 2000; Sedgh et al., 2012). By contrast, other research finds that abortion may be associated with an increased risk of future psychological problems. Clearly, there are significant individual differences in how women respond to the experience of abortion, and in all cases, abortion is a complicated and difficult decision (Cockrill & Gould, 2012; van Ditzhuijzen et al., 2013; Guttmacher, 2017).

The Prenatal Environment: Threats to Development

LO 2.16 Describe the threats to the fetal environment and what can be done about them.

According to the Sirionó people of South America, if a pregnant woman eats the meat of certain kinds of animals, she runs the risk of having a child who may act and look like those animals. According to opinions offered on daytime talk shows, a pregnant mother should avoid getting angry in order to spare her child from entering the world with anger (Cole, 1992).

Such views are largely the stuff of folklore, although there is some evidence that a mother's anxiety during pregnancy may affect the sleeping patterns of the fetus prior to birth. However, there are certain aspects of a mother's and father's behavior, both before and after conception, that can produce lifelong consequences for the child. Some consequences show up immediately, but half the possible problems aren't apparent before birth. Other problems, more insidious ones, may not manifest until years after birth (Couzin, 2002; Tiesler & Heinrich, 2014).

Some of the most profound consequences are brought about by teratogenic agents. A **teratogen** is an environmental agent such as a drug, chemical, virus, or other factor that produces a birth defect. Although it is the job of the placenta to keep teratogens from reaching the fetus, the placenta is not entirely successful at this, and probably every fetus is exposed to some teratogens.

teratogen
an environmental agent that produces a birth defect

The timing and quantity of exposure to a teratogen are crucial. At some phases of prenatal development, a certain teratogen may have only a minimal impact. At other periods, however, the same teratogen may have significant consequences. Generally, teratogens have their largest effects during periods of especially rapid prenatal development. Sensitivity to specific teratogens is also related to racial and cultural background. For example, Native American fetuses are more susceptible to the effects of alcohol than those of European American descent (Kinney et al., 2003; Winger & Woods, 2004; Rentner, Dixon, & Lengel, 2012).

Figure 2-15 Teratogen Sensitivity

Depending on their state of development, some parts of the body vary in their sensitivity to teratogens.

(**Source:** Moore, 1974.)

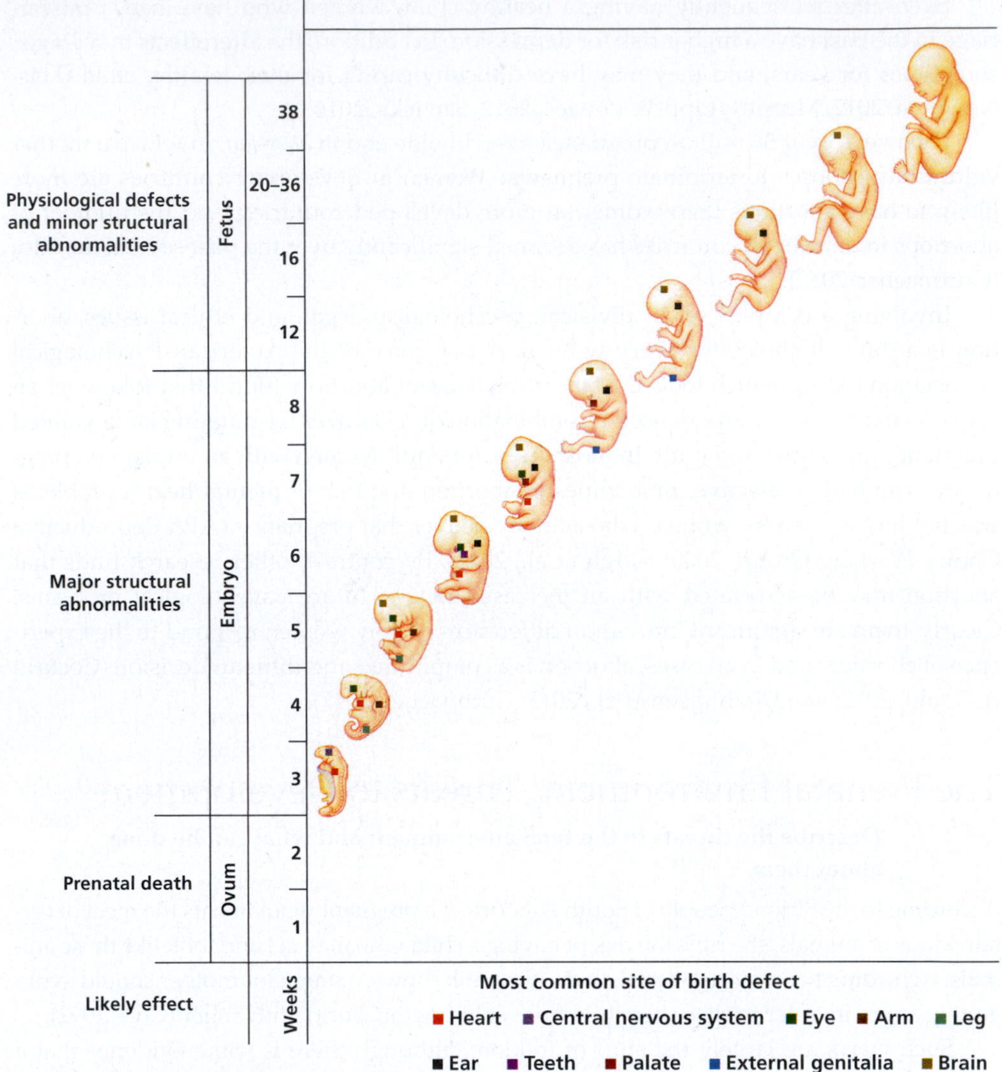

Furthermore, different organ systems are vulnerable to teratogens at different times during development. For example, the brain is most susceptible 15 to 25 days after conception, while the heart is most vulnerable 20 to 40 days following conception (see Figure 2-15; Bookstein et al., 1996; Pajkrt et al., 2004).

When considering the findings relating to specific teratogens, as we'll do next, we need to keep in mind the broader social and cultural context in which teratogen exposure occurs. For example, living in poverty increases the chances of exposure to teratogens. Mothers who are poor may not be able to afford adequate nutrition, and they may not be able to afford adequate medical care, making them more susceptible to illnesses that can damage a developing fetus. They are also more likely to be exposed to pollution. Consequently, it is important to consider the social factors that permit exposure to teratogens.

MOTHER'S DIET. Most of our knowledge of the environmental factors that affect the developing fetus comes from study of the mother. For instance, as the midwife pointed out in the example of Lisa and Robert, a mother's diet clearly plays an important role in bolstering the development of the fetus. A mother who eats a varied diet high in nutrients is apt to have fewer complications during pregnancy, an easier labor, and a generally healthier baby than a mother whose diet is restricted in nutrients (Guerrini, Thomson, & Gurling, 2007; Marques et al., 2014).

With 800 million hungry people in the world, the problem of diet is of immense global concern. Even worse, the number of people vulnerable to hunger is close to 1 *billion*. Clearly, restrictions in diet that bring about hunger on such a massive scale affect millions of children born to women living in those conditions (World Food Programme, 2016).

Fortunately, there are ways to counteract the types of maternal malnourishment that affect prenatal development. Dietary supplements given to mothers can reverse some of the problems produced by a poor diet. Furthermore, research shows that babies who were malnourished as fetuses, but who are subsequently raised in enriched environments, can overcome some of the effects of their early malnourishment. However, the reality is that few of the world's children whose mothers were malnourished *before* their birth are apt to find themselves in enriched environments after birth (Kramer, 2003; Olness, 2003).

MOTHER'S AGE. More women are giving birth later in life than was true just two or three decades ago. The cause for this change is largely transformations in society, as more women choose to continue their education with advanced degrees and to start careers prior to giving birth to their first child (Gibbs, 2002; Wildberger, 2003; Bornstein et al., 2006).

Consequently, the number of women who give birth in their 30s and 40s has grown considerably since the 1970s. However, this delay in childbirth has potential consequences for both mothers' and children's health. Women who give birth when over the age of 30 are at greater risk for a variety of pregnancy and birth complications than younger ones. For instance, they are more apt to give birth prematurely, and their children are more likely to have low birthweights. This occurs in part because of a decline in the condition of a woman's eggs. For example, by the time they are 42 years old, 90 percent of a woman's eggs are no longer normal (Cnattingius, Berendes, & Forman, 1993; Gibbs, 2002; Moore & de Costa, 2006).

Older mothers are also considerably more likely to give birth to children with Down syndrome, a form of intellectual disability. About 1 out of 100 babies born to mothers over 40 has Down syndrome; for mothers over 50, the incidence increases to 25 percent, or one in four (Gaulden, 1992). However, some research shows that older mothers are not automatically at risk for more pregnancy problems. For instance, one study found that when women in their 40s who had not experienced health difficulties were considered, they were no more likely to have prenatal problems than those in their 20s (Kirchengast & Hartmann, 2003; Carson et al., 2016).

The risks involved in pregnancy are greater not only for older mothers but for atypically young women as well. Women who become pregnant during adolescence—and such pregnancies actually encompass 20 percent of all pregnancies—are more likely to have premature deliveries. Furthermore, the mortality rate of infants born to adolescent mothers is double that for mothers in their 20s (Kirchengast & Hartmann, 2003).

MOTHER'S PRENATAL SUPPORT. Keep in mind, though, that the higher mortality rate for babies of adolescent mothers reflects more than just physiological problems related to the mothers' young age. Young mothers often face adverse social and economic factors that can affect infant health. Many teenage mothers do not have enough money or social support, a situation that prevents them from getting good prenatal care and parenting support after the baby is born. Poverty or social circumstances, such as a lack of parental involvement or supervision, may even have set the stage for the adolescent to become pregnant in the first place (Huizink, Mulder, & Buitelaar, 2004; Langille, 2007; Meade, Kershaw, & Ickovics, 2008).

MOTHER'S HEALTH. Mothers who eat the right foods, maintain an appropriate weight, and exercise appropriately maximize the chances of having a healthy baby. Furthermore, they can reduce the lifetime risk of obesity, high blood pressure, and heart disease in their children by maintaining a healthy lifestyle (Walker & Humphries, 2005, 2007).

In contrast, illness in a pregnant woman can have devastating consequences. For instance, the onset of *rubella* (German measles) in the mother prior to the eleventh week of pregnancy is likely to cause serious consequences in the baby, including blindness, deafness, heart defects, or brain damage. In later stages of a pregnancy, however, adverse consequences of rubella become increasingly less likely.

Several other diseases may affect a developing fetus, again depending on when the illness is contracted. For instance, *chicken pox* may produce birth defects, while *mumps* may increase the risk of miscarriage.

Some sexually transmitted diseases, such as *syphilis*, can be transmitted directly to the fetus, who will be born suffering from the disease. In some cases, sexually transmitted diseases such as *gonorrhea* are transmitted to the child as it passes through the birth canal to be born.

AIDS (*acquired immune deficiency syndrome*) may also affect a newborn. Mothers who have the disease or who merely are carriers of the virus may pass it on to their fetuses through the blood that reaches the placenta. However, if mothers with AIDS are treated with antiviral drugs such as AZT during pregnancy, less than 5 percent of infants are born with the disease. Those infants who are born with AIDS must remain on antiviral drugs their entire lives (Nesheim et al., 2004).

MOTHER'S DRUG USE. A mother's use of many kinds of drugs—both legal and illegal—poses serious risks to the unborn child. Even over-the-counter remedies for common ailments can have surprisingly injurious consequences. For instance, aspirin taken for a headache can lead to fetal bleeding and growth impairments (Tsantefski, Humphreys, & Jackson, 2014).

Even drugs prescribed by medical professionals have sometimes had disastrous consequences. In the 1950s, many women who were told to take *thalidomide* for morning sickness during their pregnancies gave birth to children with stumps instead of arms and legs. Although the physicians who prescribed the drug did not know it, thalidomide inhibited the growth of limbs that normally would have occurred during the first 3 months of pregnancy.

Some drugs taken by mothers cause difficulties in their children literally decades after they are taken. As recently as the 1970s, the artificial hormone *DES* (*diethylstilbestrol*) was frequently prescribed to prevent miscarriage. Only later was it found that the daughters of mothers who took DES stood a much higher-than-normal chance of developing a rare form of vaginal or cervical cancer and had more difficulties during their pregnancies. Sons of the mothers who had taken DES had their own problems, including a higher-than-average rate of reproductive difficulties (Schecter, Finkelstein, & Koren, 2005).

Birth control or fertility pills taken by pregnant women before they are aware of their pregnancy can also cause fetal damage. Such medicines contain sex hormones that affect developing brain structures in the fetus and can cause significant damage (Miller, 1998; Brown, Hines, & Fane, 2002).

Illicit drugs may pose equally great, and sometimes even greater, risks for the environments of prenatal children. For one thing, the purity of drugs purchased illegally varies significantly, so drug users can never be quite sure what specifically they are ingesting. Furthermore, the effects of some commonly used illicit drugs can be particularly devastating (Jones, 2006; Mayes et al., 2007).

Consider, for instance, the use of *marijuana*. Marijuana is one of the most commonly used drugs; millions of people in the United States have admitted trying it, and its use is now legal in many jurisdictions. However, marijuana used during pregnancy can restrict the oxygen that reaches the fetus. Its use can lead to infants who are irritable, nervous, and easily disturbed. Children exposed to marijuana prenatally show learning and memory deficits at the age of 10 (Goldschmidt et al., 2008; Willford, Richardson, & Day, 2012; Richardson, Hester, & McLemore, 2016).

During the early 1990s, *cocaine* use by pregnant women led to an epidemic of thousands of so-called crack babies. Cocaine produces an intense restriction of the arteries leading to the fetus, causing a significant reduction in the flow of blood and oxygen, increasing the risks of fetal death and a number of birth defects and disabilities (Schuetze, Eiden, & Coles, 2007).

Children whose mothers were addicted to cocaine may themselves be born addicted to the drug and may have to suffer through the pain of withdrawal. Even if not addicted, they may be born with significant problems. They are often shorter and weigh less than average, and they may have serious respiratory problems, visible birth defects, or seizures. They behave quite differently from other infants: Their reactions to stimulation are muted, but once they start to cry, it may be hard to soothe them (Eiden, Foote, & Schuetze, 2007; Richardson, Goldschmidt, & Willford, 2009).

The most recent drug problem involving pregnant mothers is the opioid epidemic in the United States. Opioids are highly addictive, and some are relatively inexpensive to obtain. Many pregnant women who are addicted to opioids such as heroin or oxycodone face barriers when they seek treatment, because the kinds of drug treatments that would normally be used to help recovery may be dangerous to the unborn child. In fact, some drug treatment facilities turn pregnant mothers away. It is a health crisis of growing proportions (Ockerman, 2017).

MOTHER'S USE OF ALCOHOL AND TOBACCO. A pregnant woman who reasons that having a drink every once in a while or smoking an occasional cigarette has no appreciable effect on her unborn child is kidding herself: Increasing evidence suggests that even small amounts of alcohol and nicotine can disrupt the development of the fetus.

Mothers' use of alcohol can have profound consequences for the unborn child. The children of alcoholics, who consume substantial quantities of alcohol during pregnancy, are at the greatest risk. Approximately 1 out of every 750 infants is born with **fetal alcohol spectrum disorder (FASD)**, a disorder that may include below-average intelligence and sometimes intellectual disability, delayed growth, and facial deformities. FASD is now the primary preventable cause of intellectual disability (Calhoun & Warren, 2007; Bakoyiannis et al., 2014; Wilhoit, Scott & Simecka, 2017).

fetal alcohol spectrum disorder (FASD)

a disorder caused by the pregnant mother consuming substantial quantities of alcohol during pregnancy, potentially resulting in intellectual disability and delayed growth in the child

Even mothers who use smaller amounts of alcohol during pregnancy place their children at risk. **Fetal alcohol effects (FAE)** is a condition in which children display some, although not all, of the problems of FASD due to their mother's consumption of alcohol during pregnancy (Baer, Sampson, & Barr, 2003; Molina et al., 2007).

fetal alcohol effects (FAE)

a condition in which children display some, though not all, of the problems of fetal alcohol syndrome due to the mother's consumption of alcohol during pregnancy

Children who do not have FAE may still be affected by their mothers' use of alcohol. Studies have found that maternal consumption of an average of just two alcoholic drinks a day during pregnancy is associated with lower intelligence in their offspring at age 7. Other research concurs, suggesting that relatively small quantities of alcohol taken during pregnancy can have future adverse effects on children's behavior and psychological functioning. Furthermore, the consequences of alcohol ingestion during pregnancy are long lasting. For example, one study found that 14-year-olds' success on a test involving spatial and visual reasoning was related to their mothers' alcohol consumption during pregnancy. The more the mothers reported drinking, the less accurately their children responded (Mattson, Calarco, & Lang, 2006; Streissguth, 2007; Chiodo et al., 2012).

Because of the risks associated with alcohol, physicians today counsel pregnant women (and even those who are trying to become pregnant) to avoid drinking any alcoholic beverages. In addition, they caution against another practice proven to have an adverse effect on an unborn child—smoking.

Smoking produces several consequences, none of which are good. For starters, smoking reduces the oxygen content and increases the carbon monoxide in the mother's blood, which quickly reduces the oxygen available to the fetus. In addition, the

Monkey Business Images/Shutterstock

Pregnant women who drink alcohol place their unborn children at risk.

nicotine and other toxins in cigarettes slow the respiration rate of the fetus and speed up its heart.

The ultimate result is an increased possibility of miscarriage and a higher likelihood of death during infancy. In fact, estimates suggest that smoking by pregnant women leads to more than 100,000 miscarriages and the deaths of 5,600 babies in the United States alone each year (Haslam & Lawrence, 2004; Triche & Hossain, 2007).

Smokers are two times as likely as nonsmokers to have babies with an abnormally low birthweight, and smokers' babies are shorter, on average, than those of nonsmokers. Furthermore, women who smoke during pregnancy are 50 percent more likely to have children with intellectual disabilities. Finally, mothers who smoke are more likely to have children who exhibit disruptive behavior during childhood (McCowan et al., 2009; Alshaarawy & Anthony, 2014).

The consequences of smoking are so profound that smoking may affect not only a mother's children but her grandchildren. For example, children whose *grandmothers* smoked during pregnancy are more than twice as likely to develop childhood asthma than children of grandmothers who did not smoke (Li et al., 2005).

DO FATHERS AFFECT THE PRENATAL ENVIRONMENT? It would be easy to reason that once the father has done his part in the sequence of events leading to conception, he would have no role in the *prenatal* environment of the fetus. Developmental researchers have in the past generally shared this view, and there is relatively little research investigating fathers' influence on the prenatal environment.

It is becoming increasingly clear, however, that fathers' behavior may well influence the prenatal environment. Consequently, health practitioners are applying the research to suggest ways fathers can support healthy prenatal development (Martin et al., 2007; Vreeswijk et al., 2013).

For instance, fathers-to-be should avoid smoking. Secondhand smoke from a father's cigarettes may affect the mother's health, which in turn influences her unborn child. The greater the level of a father's smoking, the lower the birthweight of his children (Hyssaelae, Rautava, & Helenius, 1995; Tomblin, Hammer, & Zhang, 1998).

From a *health-care provider's* perspective

In addition to avoiding smoking, what else might fathers-to-be do to help their unborn children develop normally in the womb?

Similarly, a father's use of alcohol and illegal drugs can have significant effects on the fetus. Alcohol and drug use impairs sperm and may lead to chromosomal damage that may affect the fetus at conception. In addition, alcohol and drug use during pregnancy may also affect the prenatal environment by creating stress in the mother and generally producing an unhealthy environment. A father's exposure to environmental toxins, such as lead or mercury, in the workplace may cause the toxins to bind themselves to sperm and cause birth defects (Dare et al., 2002; Choy et al., 2002; Guttmannova et al., 2016).

Finally, fathers who are physically or emotionally abusive to their pregnant partners can damage their unborn children. By increasing the level of maternal stress, or actually causing physical damage, abusive fathers increase the risk of harm to their unborn children. In fact, around 5 percent of women face physical abuse during pregnancy (Gazmararian et al., 2000; Bacchus, Mezey, & Bewley, 2006; Martin et al., 2006).

Development in Your Life

Optimizing the Prenatal Environment

If you are contemplating ever having a child, you may be overwhelmed, at this point in the chapter, by the number of things that can go wrong. Don't be. Although both genetics and the environment pose their share of risks, in the vast majority of cases, pregnancy and birth proceed without mishap. Moreover, women can do several things—both before and during pregnancy—to optimize the probability that pregnancy will progress smoothly (Centers for Disease Control and Prevention, 2017):

- **For women who are planning to become pregnant, several precautions are in order.** First, women should have nonemergency X-rays only during the first 2 weeks after their menstrual periods. Second, women should be vaccinated against rubella (German measles) at least 3, and preferably 6, months before getting pregnant. Finally, women who are planning to become pregnant should avoid the use of birth control pills for at least 3 months before trying to conceive, because of disruptions to hormonal production caused by the pills.
- **Eat well, both before and during (and after, for that matter!) pregnancy.** Pregnant mothers are, as the old saying goes, eating for two. This means that it is more essential than ever to eat regular, well-balanced meals. In addition, physicians typically recommend taking prenatal vitamins that include folic acid, which can decrease the likelihood of birth defects (Amitai et al., 2004).
- **Don't use alcohol and other drugs.** The evidence is clear that many drugs pass directly to the fetus and may cause birth defects. It is also clear that the more one drinks, the greater the risk to the fetus.
- **Don't use *any* drug unless directed by a physician.** This is the best advice, whether you are already pregnant or planning to have a child. If you are planning to get pregnant, encourage your partner to avoid using alcohol or other drugs too (O'Connor & Whaley, 2006).
- **Monitor caffeine intake.** Although it is still unclear whether caffeine produces birth defects, it is known that the caffeine found in coffee, tea, and chocolate can pass to the fetus, acting as a stimulant. Because of this, you probably shouldn't drink more than a few cups of coffee a day (Wisborg et al., 2003; Diego et al., 2007).
- **Whether you are pregnant or not, don't smoke.** This holds true for mothers, fathers, and anyone else in the vicinity of the pregnant mother, since research suggests that smoke in the fetal environment can affect birthweight. Smoking is the single most preventable cause of illness and death among infants and their mothers.
- **Exercise regularly.** In most cases, women can continue to exercise during pregnancy, particularly doing exercises involving low-impact routines. However, extreme exercise should be avoided, especially on very hot or very cold days (Evenson, 2011; DiNallo, Downs, & Le Masurier, 2012; Centers for Disease Control and Prevention, 2017).

Module 2.3 Review

LO 2.13 Explain the process of fertilization.

When sperm enter the vagina, they begin a journey that takes them through the cervix, the opening of the uterus, and into the fallopian tubes, where fertilization may take place. Fertilization joins the sperm and ovum to start prenatal development.

LO 2.14 Summarize the three stages of prenatal development.

The prenatal period consists of three stages: germinal, embryonic, and fetal.

LO 2.15 Describe some of the physical and ethical challenges that relate to pregnancy.

Some couples need medical aid to help them conceive. Among the alternate routes to conception are artificial insemination and in vitro fertilization (IVF). Some women may also experience miscarriage or opt for an abortion.

LO 2.16 Describe the threats to the fetal environment and what can be done about them.

A teratogen is an environmental agent such as a drug, chemical, virus, or other factor that produces a birth defect. The diet, age, prenatal support, and illnesses of mothers can affect their babies' health and growth.

Mothers' use of drugs, alcohol, tobacco, and caffeine can adversely affect the health and development of the unborn child. Fathers' and others' behaviors (e.g., smoking) can also affect the health of the unborn child.

Journal Writing Prompt

Applying Lifespan Development: Studies show that "crack babies" who are entering school have significant difficulty dealing with multiple stimuli and forming close attachments. How might both genetic and environmental influences have combined to produce these results?

Epilogue

In this chapter, we have discussed the basics of heredity and genetics, including the way in which the code of life is transmitted across generations through DNA. We have also seen how genetic transmission can go wrong, and we have discussed ways in which genetic disorders can be treated—and perhaps prevented—through new interventions such as genetic counseling.

One important theme in this chapter has been the interaction between hereditary and environmental factors in determining a number of human traits. While we have encountered a number of surprising instances in which heredity plays a part—including in the development of personality traits and even personal preferences and tastes—we have also seen that heredity is virtually never the sole factor in any complex trait. Environment nearly always plays an important role.

Finally, we reviewed the main stages of prenatal growth—germinal, embryonic, and fetal—and examined threats to the prenatal environment and ways to optimize that environment for the fetus.

Before moving on, return to the prologue of this chapter—about the Monaco children with IVA—and answer the following questions based on your understanding of genetics and prenatal development.

1. How could Jana and Tom Monaco have passed on a rare genetic disease to their children without knowing that they were carriers of it?
2. From the Monacos' story, would you guess that IVA is an X-linked trait or not?
3. What evidence is there in the story of the Monacos' children that the debilitating effects of IVA are determined by a combination of both genetic and environmental factors?
4. Could the Monacos have learned that they were carriers of IVA before their son Stephen was born? How?

Looking Back

LO 2.1 Describe how genes and chromosomes provide our basic genetic endowment.

A child receives 23 chromosomes from each parent. These 46 chromosomes provide the genetic blueprint that will guide cell activity for the rest of the individual's life.

LO 2.2 Compare monozygotic twins with dizygotic twins.

Monozygotic twins are twins who are genetically identical. Dizygotic twins result from two separate ova fertilized by two separate sperm at roughly the same time.

LO 2.3 Describe how the sex of a child is determined.

When an ovum and a sperm meet at the moment of fertilization, the ovum provides an X chromosome, while the sperm provides either an X or a Y chromosome. If the sperm contributes its X chromosome, the child will have an XX pairing—a girl. If the sperm contributes a Y chromosome, the result will be an XY pairing—a boy.

LO 2.4 Explain the mechanisms by which genes transmit information.

A genotype is the underlying combination of genetic material present in an organism, but invisible; a phenotype is the visible trait, the expression of the genotype.

LO 2.5 Describe the field of behavioral genetics.

The field of behavioral genetics, a combination of psychology and genetics, studies the effects of genetics on behavior and psychological characteristics.

LO 2.6 Describe the major inherited disorders.

Genes may become physically damaged or may spontaneously mutate. If damaged genes are passed on to the child, the result can be a genetic disorder.

LO 2.7 Describe the role of genetic counselors and differentiate between different forms of prenatal testing.

Genetic counselors use a variety of data and techniques to advise future parents of possible genetic risks to their unborn children. A variety of techniques can be used to assess the health of an unborn child if a woman is already pregnant, including ultrasound, CVS, and amniocentesis.

LO 2.8 Explain how the environment and genetics work together to determine human characteristics.

Behavioral characteristics are often determined by a combination of genetics and environment. Genetically based traits represent a potential, called the genotype, which may be affected by the environment and is ultimately expressed in the phenotype.

LO 2.9 Summarize how researchers study the interaction of genetic and environmental factors in development.

To work out the different influences of heredity and environment, researchers use nonhuman studies and human studies, particularly of twins.

LO 2.10 Explain how genetics and the environment jointly influence physical traits, intelligence, and personality.

Virtually all human traits, characteristics, and behaviors are the result of the combination and interaction of nature and nurture. Many physical characteristics show strong genetic influences. Intelligence contains a strong genetic component but can be significantly influenced by environmental factors. Some personality traits, including neuroticism and extroversion, have been linked to genetic factors, and even attitudes, values, and interests have a genetic component. Some personal behaviors may be genetically influenced through the mediation of inherited personality traits.

LO 2.11 Explain the role genetics and the environment play in the development of psychological disorders.

Certain psychological disorders, such as schizophrenia, are largely caused by genetics. Other disorders, including alcoholism and major depressive disorder, have both genetic and environmental causes.

LO 2.12 Describe ways in which genes influence the environment.

Children may influence their environment through genetic traits that cause them to construct—or influence their parents to construct—an environment that matches their inherited dispositions and preferences.

LO 2.13 Explain the process of fertilization.

When sperm enter the vagina, they begin a journey that takes them through the cervix, the opening of the uterus, and into the fallopian tubes, where fertilization may take place. Fertilization joins the sperm and ovum to start prenatal development.

LO 2.14 Summarize the three stages of prenatal development.

The germinal stage (fertilization to 2 weeks) is marked by rapid cell division and specialization, and the attachment of the zygote to the wall of the uterus. During the embryonic stage (2 to 8 weeks), the ectoderm, the mesoderm, and the endoderm begin to grow and specialize. The fetal stage (8 weeks to birth) is characterized by a rapid increase in complexity and differentiation of the organs. The fetus becomes active, and most of its systems become operational.

LO 2.15 Describe some of the physical and ethical challenges that relate to pregnancy.

Some couples need medical aid to help them conceive. Among the alternate routes to conception are artificial insemination and in vitro fertilization (IVF). Some women may also experience miscarriage or opt for an abortion.

LO 2.16 Describe the threats to the fetal environment and what can be done about them.

A teratogen is an environmental agent such as a drug, chemical, virus, or other factor that produces a birth defect. Factors in the mother that may affect the unborn child include diet, age, illnesses, and drug, alcohol, and tobacco use. The behaviors of fathers and others in the environment may also affect the health and development of the unborn child.

Key Terms and Concepts

Chapter 3
Birth and the Newborn Infant

karen roach/Shutterstock

Learning Objectives

LO 3.1 Describe the normal process of labor.

LO 3.2 Explain the events that occur in the first few hours of a newborn's life.

LO 3.3 Describe some of the current approaches to childbirth.

LO 3.4 Describe some of the causes of, effects of, and treatments for preterm births.

LO 3.5 Identify the risks that postmature babies face.

LO 3.6 Describe the process of cesarean delivery and the reasons for its increase in use.

LO 3.7 Describe rates of infant mortality and what factors affect these statistics.

LO 3.8 Describe the causes and effects of postpartum depression.

LO 3.9 Describe the physical capabilities of the newborn.

LO 3.10 Describe the sensory capabilities of the newborn.

LO 3.11 Describe the learning capabilities of the newborn.

LO 3.12 Describe the social competencies of newborns.

Chapter Overview

Prologue: Smaller Than a Soda Can

Doctors gave infant Tamera Dixon at best a 15 percent chance of survival. The tiny girl entered the world after only 25 weeks of gestation—months earlier than normal. When she was born, she was 10 inches, and weighed a mere 11 ounces—less than a can of soda.

Tamera was born by Caesarean section after her mother, Andrea Haws, experienced health problems during the pregnancy. "To see an 11-ounce baby, you wouldn't believe what it looked like," Andrea said. "It was just skin and bones."

But Tamera beat the odds. She gained weight and began to breathe on her own. After nearly 4 months in the hospital, she was released to the care of her parents. At the time she went home, she weighed over 4 pounds. She would have been about a week old had she been carried to term.

"It is a miracle," Andrea said. "She is a miracle."

Looking Ahead

Infants were not meant to be born as early as Tamera was. Yet, for a variety of reasons, more than 10 percent of all babies are born early, and the outlook for them to lead normal lives is improving dramatically.

All births are tinged with a combination of excitement and some degree of anxiety. In the vast majority of cases, however, delivery goes smoothly, and it is an amazing and joyous moment when a new being enters the world. The excitement of birth is soon replaced by wonder at the extraordinary nature of newborns themselves. Babies enter the world with a surprising array of capabilities, ready from the first moments of life outside the womb to respond to the world and the people in it.

In this chapter, we'll examine the events that lead to the delivery and birth of a child and take an initial look at the newborn. We first consider labor and delivery, exploring how the process usually proceeds, as well as several alternative approaches.

We next examine some of the possible complications of birth. The problems that can occur range from premature births to infant mortality. Finally, we consider the extraordinary range of capabilities of newborns. We'll look not only at their physical and perceptual abilities, but at the way they enter the world with the ability to learn and with skills that help form the foundations of their future relationships with others.

Monkey Business Images/Shutterstock

Birth

I wasn't completely naïve. I mean, I knew that it was only in movies that babies come out of the womb all pink, dry, and beautiful. But still, I was initially taken aback by my son's appearance. Because of his passage through the birth canal, his head was cone-shaped, a bit like a wet, partly deflated football. The nurse must have noticed my reaction because she hastened to assure me that all this would change in a matter of days. She then moved quickly to wipe off the whitish sticky substance all over his body, informing me as she did so that the fuzzy hair on his ears was only temporary. I leaned in and put my finger into my boy's hand. He rewarded me by closing his hand around it. I interrupted the nurse's assurances. "Don't worry," I stammered, tears suddenly filling my eyes. "He's absolutely the most beautiful thing I've ever seen."

For those of us accustomed to thinking of newborns in the images of baby food commercials, this portrait of a typical newborn may be surprising. Yet most babies come out of the womb resembling this one. Make no mistake, however: Despite their temporary blemishes, babies are a welcome sight to their parents from the moment of their birth.

The newborn's outward appearance is caused by a variety of factors in its journey from the mother's uterus, down the birth canal, and out into the world. We can trace its passage, beginning with the release of the chemicals that initiate the process of labor.

Labor: The Process of Birth Begins

LO 3.1 Describe the normal process of labor.

About 266 days after conception, a protein called *corticotropin-releasing hormone* (CRH) triggers (for some still unknown reason) the release of various hormones, and the process that leads to birth begins. One critical hormone is *oxytocin*, which is released by the mother's pituitary gland. When the concentration of oxytocin becomes high enough, the mother's uterus begins periodic contractions (Terzidou, 2007; Tattersall et al., 2012; Gordon et al., 2017).

During the prenatal period, the uterus, which is composed of muscle tissue, slowly expands as the fetus grows. Although for most of the pregnancy it is inactive, after the fourth month it occasionally contracts in order to ready itself for the eventual delivery. These *Braxton–Hicks contractions* are sometimes called "false labor," because while they can fool eager and anxious expectant parents, they do not signify that the baby will be born soon.

neonates
the term used for newborns

When birth is actually imminent, the uterus begins to contract intermittently. The increasingly intense contractions make the uterus act like a vise, opening and closing to force the head of the fetus against the *cervix*, the neck of the uterus that separates it from the vagina. Eventually, the force of the contractions becomes strong enough to propel the fetus slowly down the birth canal until it enters the world as a **neonate**—the term used for a newborn. It is this exertion and the narrow birth passage that often give newborns the battered, cone-head appearance described earlier.

KidStock/Getty Images

Labor can be exhausting and seems never-ending, but support, communication, and a willingness to try different techniques can all be helpful.

Labor proceeds in three stages (see Figure 3-1). In the *first stage of labor*, the uterine contractions initially occur around every 8 to 10 minutes and last about 30 seconds. As labor proceeds, the contractions occur more frequently and last longer. Toward the end of labor, the contractions may occur every 2 minutes and last almost 2 minutes. During the final part of the first stage of labor, a period known as *transition*, the contractions increase to their greatest intensity. The mother's cervix fully opens, eventually expanding

Figure 3-1 The Three Stages of Labor

Stage 1

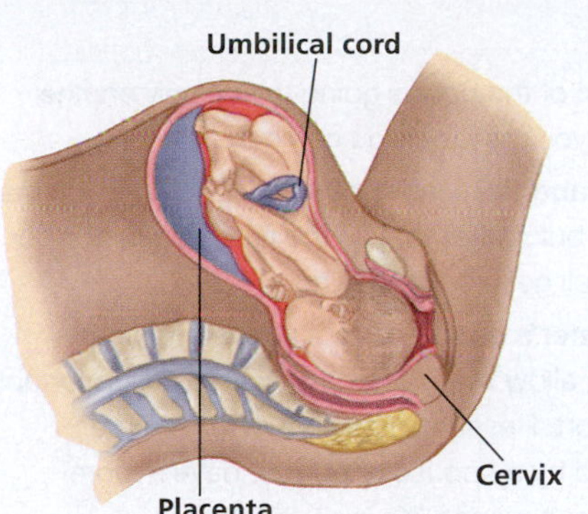

Uterine contractions initially occur every 8 to 10 minutes and last 30 seconds. Toward the end of labor, contractions may occur every 2 minutes and last as long as 2 minutes. As the contractions increase, the cervix, which separates the uterus from the vagina, becomes wider, eventually expanding to allow the baby's head to pass through.

Stage 2

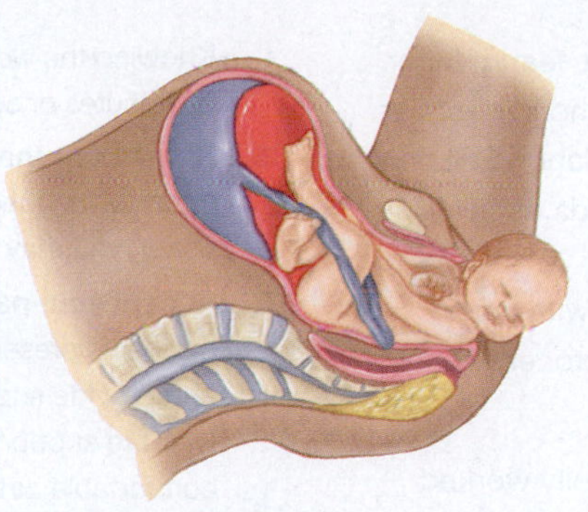

The baby's head starts to move through the cervix and birth canal. Typically lasting around 90 minutes, the second stage ends when the baby has completely left the mother's body.

Stage 3

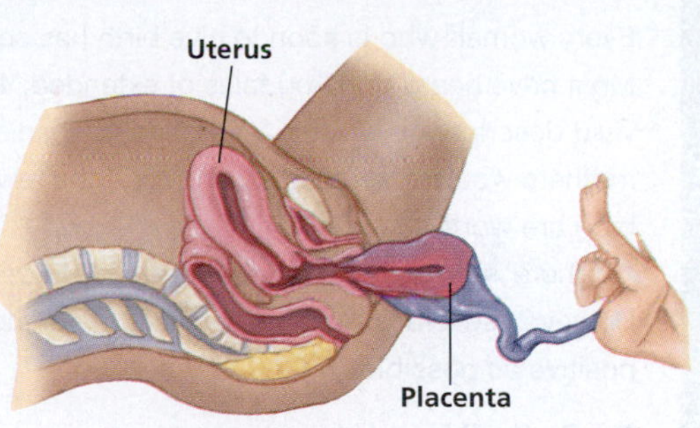

The child's umbilical cord (still attached to the neonate) and the placenta are expelled from the mother. This stage is the quickest and easiest, taking just a few minutes.

enough (usually to around 10 centimeters) to allow the baby's head (the widest part of the body) to pass through.

This first stage of labor is the longest. Its duration varies significantly, depending on the mother's age, race, ethnicity, number of prior pregnancies, and a variety of other factors involving both the fetus and the mother. Typically, labor takes 16 to 24 hours for firstborn children, but there are wide variations. Births of subsequent children usually involve shorter periods of labor.

During the *second stage of labor*, which typically lasts around 90 minutes, the baby's head emerges further from the mother with each contraction, increasing the size of the vaginal opening. Because the area between the vagina and rectum must stretch a good deal, an incision called an **episiotomy** is sometimes made to increase the size of the opening of the vagina. However, this practice has been increasingly criticized in recent years as potentially causing more harm than good, and the number of episiotomies has fallen drastically in the past decade (Dudding, Vaizey, & Kamm, 2008; Manzanares et al., 2013; Ballesteros-Meseguer, 2016). The second stage of labor ends when the baby has completely left the mother's body.

episiotomy
an incision sometimes made to increase the size of the opening of the vagina to allow the baby to pass

Finally, the *third stage of labor* occurs when the child's umbilical cord (still attached to the neonate) and the placenta are expelled from the mother. This stage is the quickest and easiest, taking just a few minutes.

There is a kernel of truth to popular stories of pregnant women in certain societies putting down the tools with which they are tilling their fields, stepping aside and giving birth, and immediately returning to work with their neonates wrapped and bundled on their backs. Accounts of the !Kung people in Africa describe the woman in labor sitting calmly beside a tree and without much ado—or assistance—giving birth to a child and quickly recovering. Furthermore, in some Asian cultures, the way in which a woman handles labor reflects on her family's honor; an inability to accept labor and childbirth stoically can be seen as bringing shame, so it is to be avoided (Callister et al., 2003; Christiaens, Verhaeghe, & Bracke, 2010).

By contrast, many societies regard childbirth as dangerous, and some even view it in terms befitting an illness. Such cultural perspectives color the way that people in a given society view the experience and expectations about dealing with childbirth, as we discuss in the *Development in Your Life* section.

Development in Your Life

Dealing with Labor

Every woman who is soon to give birth has some fear of labor. Most have heard gripping tales of extended, 48-hour labors or vivid descriptions of the pain that accompanies labor. Still, few mothers would dispute the notion that the rewards of giving birth are worth the effort.

There is no single right or wrong way to deal with labor. However, several strategies can help make the process as positive as possible:

- **Be flexible.** Although you may have carefully worked out what to do during labor, don't feel an obligation to follow through exactly. If a strategy is ineffective, turn to another one.
- **Communicate with your health-care providers.** Let them know what you are experiencing. They may be able to suggest ways to deal with what you are encountering. As your labor progresses, they may also be able to give you a fairly clear idea of how much longer you will be in labor. Knowing the worst of the pain is going to last only another 20 minutes or so, you may feel you can handle it.
- **Remember that labor is...laborious.** Expect that you may become fatigued, but realize that as the final stages of labor occur, you may well get a second wind.
- **Accept your partner's support.** If a spouse or other partner is present, allow that person to make you comfortable and provide support. Research has shown that women who are supported by a spouse or partner have a more comfortable birth experience (Kennell, 2002).
- **Be realistic and honest about your reactions to pain.** Even if you had planned an unmedicated delivery, realize that you may find the pain difficult to tolerate. At that point, consider the use of drugs. Above all, don't feel that asking for pain medication is a sign of failure. It isn't.
- **Focus on the big picture.** Keep in mind that labor is part of a process that ultimately leads to an event unmatched in the joy it can bring.

Birth: From Fetus to Neonate

LO 3.2 Explain the events that occur in the first few hours of a newborn's life.

The exact moment of birth occurs when the fetus, having left the uterus through the cervix, passes through the vagina to emerge fully from its mother's body. In most cases, babies automatically make the transition from taking in oxygen via the placenta to using their lungs to breathe air. Consequently, as soon as they are outside the mother's body, most newborns spontaneously cry. This helps them clear their lungs and breathe on their own.

What happens next varies from situation to situation and from culture to culture. In Western cultures, health-care workers are almost always on hand to assist with the birth. In the United States, 99 percent of births are attended by professional health-care workers, but in many less-developed countries less than half of births have professional health care-workers in attendance (United Nations Statistics Division, 2012).

Apgar scale

a standard measurement system that looks for a variety of indications of good health in newborns

THE APGAR SCALE. In most cases, the newborn infant first undergoes a quick visual inspection. Parents may be counting fingers and toes, but trained health-care workers look for something more. Typically, they employ the **Apgar scale**, a standard measurement system that looks for a variety of indications of good health (see Table 3-1). Developed by physician

Table 3-1 Apgar Scale

A score is given for each sign at 1 minute and 5 minutes after the birth. If there are problems with the baby, an additional score is given at 10 minutes. A score of 7 to 10 is considered normal, whereas 4 to 7 might require some resuscitative measures, and a baby with an Apgar score under 4 requires immediate resuscitation.

	Sign	0 Points	1 Point	2 Points
A	Appearance (skin color)	Blue-gray, pale all over	Normal, except for extremities	Normal over entire body
P	Pulse	Absent	Below 100 bpm	Above 100 bpm
G	Grimace (reflex irritability)	No response	Grimaces	Sneezes, coughs, pulls away
A	Activity (muscle tone)	Absent	Arms and legs flex	Active movement
R	Respiration	Absent	Slow, irregular	Good, crying

(**Source:** Apgar, 1953.)

Virginia Apgar (1909–1974), the scale directs attention to five basic qualities, recalled most easily by using Apgar's name as a guide: *a*ppearance (color), *p*ulse (heart rate), *g*rimace (reflex irritability), *a*ctivity (muscle tone), and *r*espiration (respiratory effort).

Using the Apgar scale, health-care workers assign the newborn a score ranging from 0 to 2 on each of the five qualities, producing an overall score that can range from 0 to 10. The vast majority of children score 7 or above. The 10 percent of neonates who score under 7 require help to start breathing. Newborns who score under 4 need immediate, lifesaving intervention.

Low Apgar scores (or low scores on other neonatal assessments, such as the *Brazelton Neonatal Behavioral Assessment Scale*, which we discuss in Chapter 4) may indicate problems or birth defects that were already present in the fetus. However, the process of birth itself may sometimes cause difficulties. Among the most profound are those relating to a temporary deprivation of oxygen.

At various junctures during labor, the fetus may lack sufficient oxygen. This can happen for any of a number of reasons. For instance, the umbilical cord may get wrapped around the neck of the fetus. The cord can also be pinched during a prolonged contraction, thereby cutting off the supply of oxygen that flows through it.

Lack of oxygen for a few seconds is not harmful to the fetus, but deprivation for any longer may cause serious harm. A restriction of oxygen, or **anoxia**, lasting a few minutes can produce cognitive deficits such as language delays and even mental retardation due to brain cell death (Stecker, Wolfe, & Stevenson, 2013; Hynes, Fish, & Manly, 2014; Tazopoulou et al., 2017).

anoxia
a restriction of oxygen to the baby, lasting a few minutes during the birth process, that can produce brain damage

NEWBORN MEDICAL SCREENING. Just after birth, newborns typically are tested for a variety of diseases and genetic conditions. The American College of Medical Genetics and Genomics recommends that all newborns be screened for 29 disorders, ranging from hearing difficulties and sickle-cell anemia to extremely rare conditions such as isovaleric acidemia, a disorder involving metabolism. These disorders can be detected from a tiny quantity of blood drawn from an infant's heel (American College of Medical Genetics, 2006).

The advantage of newborn screening is that it permits early treatment of problems that might otherwise go undetected for years. In some cases, devastating conditions can be prevented through early treatment of the disorder, such as the implementation of a particular kind of diet (Kayton, 2007; Timmermans & Buchbinder, 2012; Rentmeester, Pringle, & Hogue, 2017).

The exact number of tests that a newborn experiences varies drastically from state to state. In some states, only three tests are mandated, while in others over 30 are required. In jurisdictions with only a few tests, many disorders go undiagnosed. In fact, each year around 1,000 infants in the United States suffer from disorders that could have been detected at birth if appropriate screening had been conducted (American Academy of Pediatrics, 2005; Sudia-Robinson, 2011; McClain et al., 2017).

bonding
close physical and emotional contact between parent and child during the period immediately following birth, argued by some to affect later relationship strength

PHYSICAL APPEARANCE AND INITIAL ENCOUNTERS. In addition to assessing the newborn's health, health-care workers deal with the remnants of the child's passage through the birth canal. You'll recall the description of the thick, greasy substance (like cottage cheese) that covers the newborn. This material, called *vernix*, smoothes the passage through the birth canal; it is no longer needed once the child is born and is quickly cleaned away. Newborns' bodies are sometimes covered with a fine, dark fuzz known as *lanugo*, which soon disappears. The newborn's eyelids may be puffy due to an accumulation of fluids during labor, and the newborn may have blood or other fluids on parts of its body.

After being cleansed, the newborn is usually returned to the mother and, if he is present, the father. The significance of this initial encounter between parent and child has become a matter of considerable controversy. Some psychologists and physicians argued that **bonding**, the close physical and emotional contact between parent and child during the period immediately following birth, was a crucial ingredient for forming a lasting relationship between parent and child (Lorenz, 1957). Their arguments were based in part

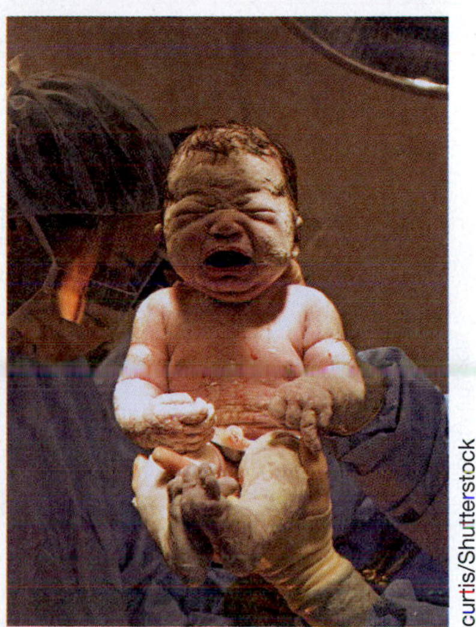

curtis/Shutterstock

The perfect image of newborns portrayed in commercials, television programs, and movies differs dramatically from reality.

on research conducted on nonhuman species such as ducklings. This work showed that there was a critical period just after birth when organisms showed a particular readiness to learn, or imprint, from other members of their species who happened to be present.

According to the concept of bonding applied to humans, a critical period begins just after birth and lasts only a few hours. During this period, skin-to-skin contact between mother and child supposedly leads to deep, emotional bonding. The corollary to this assumption is that if circumstances prevent such contact, the bond between mother and child will forever be lacking in some way. Because so many babies were taken from their mothers and placed in incubators or in the hospital nursery, medical practices often left little opportunity for sustained mother–child physical contact immediately after birth.

When developmental researchers carefully reviewed the research, however, they found little support for the existence of a critical period for bonding at birth. Although it does appear that mothers who have early physical contact with their babies are more responsive to them than those who don't have such contact, the difference lasts only a few days. Such news is reassuring to parents whose children must receive immediate, intensive medical attention just after birth. It is also comforting to parents who adopt children and are not present at their births (Bigelow & Power, 2012; Hall et al., 2014; Schmidt et al., 2016).

Although immediate mother–child bonding does not seem critical, it is important for newborns to be gently touched and massaged soon after birth. The physical stimulation they receive leads to the production of chemicals in the brain that instigate growth. Consequently, infant massage is related to weight gain, better sleep–waking patterns, better neuromotor development, and reduced rates of infant mortality (Kulkarni et al., 2011; van Reenen & van Rensburg, 2013; Álvarez, et al., 2017).

Approaches to Childbirth: Where Medicine and Attitudes Meet

LO 3.3 Describe some of the current approaches to childbirth.

toos/Getty Images

Although the observation of nonhuman animals highlights the importance of contact between mother and offspring following birth, research on humans suggests that immediate physical contact is less critical.

Carrie Blackstone had her first baby under the supervision of medical doctors and found the experience impersonal and artificial. So for her second baby, she and her husband, Sami McClough, decided on an African method of birthing that she had read about.

"The African way is more natural. You sit on a birthing stool, which has a hole in the middle. The baby comes through the hole, no fuss, no muss. And no doctors unless they're needed."

Carrie and Sami found a nurse-midwife program at Manhattan's Maternity Center that would permit her to use the stool. When the time came, Carrie and Sami were together through the whole process. With the first contractions, Sami helped her to stand up and they began rocking, "like a slow, comfortable dance," she says. "The rocking helped me through the worst contractions.

"Then I sat on the stool and when the midwife said 'Push!' out came my Dara's head." The midwife placed Dara on Carrie's breast and examined her then and there.

Parents in the Western world have developed a variety of strategies—and some very strong opinions—to help them deal with something as natural as giving birth, which occurs apparently without much thought throughout the nonhuman animal world. Today parents need to make a number of decisions. Should the birth take place in a hospital or in the home? Should a physician, a nurse, or a midwife assist? Is the father's presence desirable? Should siblings and other family members be on hand to participate in the birth?

Most of these questions cannot be answered definitively, primarily because the choice of childbirth techniques often comes down to a matter of values and opinions. No single procedure will be effective for all mothers and fathers, and no conclusive research evidence has proven that one procedure is significantly more effective than another. As we'll see, there is a wide variety of different issues and options involved, and certainly one's culture plays a role in choices of birthing procedures.

The abundance of choices is largely due to a reaction to traditional medical practices that had been common in the United States until the early 1970s. Before that time, the typical birth went something like this: A woman in labor was placed in a room with many other women, all of whom were in various stages of childbirth and some of whom were screaming in pain. Fathers and other family members were not allowed to be present. Just before delivery, the woman was rolled into a delivery room, where the birth took place. Often she was so drugged that she was not aware of the birth at all.

At the time, physicians argued that such procedures were necessary to ensure the health of the newborn and the mother. However, critics charged that alternatives were available that not only would maximize the medical well-being of the participants in the birth but also would represent an emotional and psychological improvement (Curl et al., 2004; Hotelling & Humenick, 2005).

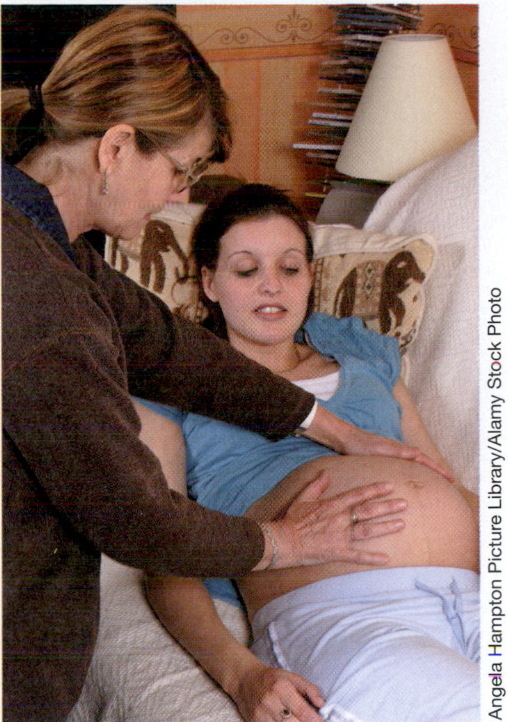
Angela Hampton Picture Library/Alamy Stock Photo

Some women choose to use a midwife to assist them in their pregnancy and delivery.

ALTERNATIVE BIRTHING PROCEDURES. Not all mothers give birth in hospitals, and not all births follow a traditional course. Among the major alternatives to traditional birthing practices are the following:

- ***Lamaze birthing techniques.*** The Lamaze method has achieved widespread popularity in the United States. Based on the writings of Dr. Fernand Lamaze (1891–1957), the method makes use of breathing techniques and relaxation training (Lamaze, 1970). Typically, mothers-to-be participate in a series of weekly training sessions in which they learn exercises that help them relax various parts of the body on command. A "coach," most typically the father or the mother's partner, is trained along with the future mother. The training allows women to cope with painful contractions by concentrating on their breathing and producing a relaxation response, rather than by tensing up, which can make the pain more acute. Women learn to focus on a relaxing stimulus, such as a tranquil scene in a picture. The goal is to learn how to deal positively with pain and to relax at the onset of a contraction (Lothian, 2005).

  Does the procedure work? Most mothers, as well as fathers, report that a Lamaze birth is a very positive experience. They enjoy the sense of mastery that they gain over the process of labor, a feeling of being able to exert some control over what can be a formidable experience. Given that, we can't be sure that parents who choose the Lamaze method aren't already more highly motivated about the experience of childbirth than parents who do not choose the technique. It is therefore possible that the accolades they express after Lamaze births are due to their initial enthusiasm and not to the Lamaze procedures themselves (Larsen et al., 2001; Zwelling, 2006).

  Participation in Lamaze procedures—as well as other natural childbirth techniques in which the emphasis is on educating the parents about the process of birth and minimizing the use of drugs—is relatively rare among members of lower-income groups, including many members of ethnic minorities. Parents in these groups may not have the transportation, time, or financial resources to attend childbirth preparation classes. The result is that women in lower income groups tend to be less prepared for the events of labor and consequently may suffer more pain during childbirth (Lu et al., 2003).

- ***Bradley method.*** The Bradley method, which is sometimes known as "husband-coached childbirth," is based on the principle that childbirth should be as natural as possible and involve no medication or medical interventions. Women are taught to "tune into" their bodies in order to deal with the pain of childbirth. To prepare for childbirth, mothers-to-be are taught muscle relaxation techniques, similar to Lamaze procedures, and good nutrition and exercise during pregnancy are seen as important to prepare for delivery. Parents are urged to take responsibility for childbirth, and the use of physicians is viewed as unnecessary and sometimes even dangerous. As you might expect, the discouragement of traditional medical interventions is quite controversial (Reed, 2005).

- ***Hypnobirthing.*** Hypnobirthing is a new, but increasingly popular, technique. It involves a form of self-hypnosis during delivery that creates a sense of peace and calm, thereby reducing pain. The basic concept is to produce a state of focused concentration in which a mother relaxes her body while focusing inward. Increasing research evidence shows the technique can be effective in reducing pain (Olson, 2006; White, 2007; Alexander, Turnball, & Cyna, 2009).
- ***Water Birthing.*** Still relatively uncommon in the United States, water birthing is a practice in which a woman enters a pool of warm water to give birth. The theory is that the warmth and buoyancy of the water is soothing, easing the length and pain of labor and childbirth, and the entry into the world is soothed for the infant, who moves from the watery environment of the womb to the birthing pool. Although there is some evidence that water birthing reduces pain and the length of labor, there is a risk of infection from the unsterile water (Thöni, Mussner, & Ploner, 2010; Jones et al., 2012).

CHILDBIRTH ATTENDANTS: WHO DELIVERS? Traditionally, *obstetricians*, physicians who specialize in delivering babies, have been the childbirth attendants of choice. In the past few decades, more mothers have chosen to use a *midwife*, a childbirth attendant who stays with the mother throughout labor and delivery. Midwives—most often nurses specializing in childbirth—are used primarily for pregnancies in which no complications are expected. The use of midwives has increased steadily in the United States—there are now 7,000 of them—and they are employed in 10 percent of births. Midwives help deliver some 80 percent of babies in other parts of the world, often at home. Home birth is common in countries at all levels of economic development. For instance, a third of all births in the Netherlands occur at home (Ayoub, 2005; Klein, 2012; Sandall, 2014).

From *a health-care worker's* perspective

While 99 percent of U.S. births are attended by professional medical workers or birthing attendants, this is the case in only about half of births worldwide. What do you think are some reasons for this, and what are the implications of this statistic?

The newest trend in childbirth assistance is also one of the oldest: the doula (pronounced doo-lah). A *doula* is trained to provide emotional, psychological, and educational support during birth. A doula does not replace an obstetrician or a midwife, and does not do medical exams. Instead, doulas, who are often well-versed in birthing alternatives, provide the mother with support and make sure the parents are aware of alternatives and possibilities regarding the birth process.

Although the use of doulas is new in the United States, they represent a return to an older tradition that has existed for centuries in other cultures. They may not be called "doulas," but supportive, experienced older women have helped mothers as they give birth in non-Western cultures for centuries.

A growing body of research indicates that the presence of a doula is beneficial to the birth process, speeding deliveries and reducing reliance on drugs. Yet concerns remain about their use. Unlike certified midwives, who are nurses and receive an additional year or two of training, doulas do not need to be certified or have any particular level of education (Humphries & Korfmacher, 2012; Simkin, 2014; Darwin et al., 2017).

Rafael Ben-Ari/Alamy Stock Photo

With water birthing, the woman enters a pool of warm water to give birth.

PAIN AND CHILDBIRTH. Any woman who has delivered a baby will agree that childbirth is painful. But exactly how painful is it?

Such a question is largely unanswerable. One reason is that pain is a subjective, psychological phenomenon, one that cannot be easily measured. No one is able to answer the question of whether their pain is "greater" or "worse" than someone else's pain, although some studies have tried to quantify it. For instance, in one survey women were asked to rate the pain they experienced during labor on a 1 to 5 scale, with 5 being the most painful (Yarrow, Scott, & Waxler 1973). Nearly half (44 percent) said "5," and an additional one-quarter said "4."

Because pain is usually a sign that something is wrong in one's body, we have learned to react to pain with fear and concern. Yet during childbirth, pain is actually a signal that the body is working appropriately—that the contractions that are meant to propel the baby through the birth canal are doing their job. Consequently, the experience of pain during labor is difficult for women in labor to interpret, thereby potentially increasing their anxiety and making the contractions seem even more painful (also see *Developmental Diversity and Your Life*).

USE OF ANESTHESIA AND PAIN-REDUCING DRUGS. Among the greatest advances of modern medicine is the ongoing discovery of drugs that reduce pain. However, the use of medication during childbirth is a practice that holds both benefits and pitfalls.

About half the women who receive anesthesia during labor do so in the form of *epidural anesthesia*, which produces numbness from the waist down. Traditional epidurals produce an inability to walk and in some cases prevent women from helping to push the baby out during delivery. However, a newer form of epidural, known as a *walking epidural* or *dual spinal–epidural*, uses smaller needles and a system for administering continuous doses of anesthetic. It permits women to move about more freely during labor and has fewer side effects than traditional epidural anesthesia (Simmons et al., 2007; Osterman & Martin, 2011).

It is clear that drugs hold the promise of greatly reducing, and even eliminating, pain associated with labor, which can be extreme and exhausting. But pain reduction comes at a cost: Drugs administered during labor reach not just the mother but the fetus as well. The stronger the drug, the greater its effects on the fetus and neonate. Because of the small size of the fetus relative to the mother, drug doses that might have only a minimal effect on the mother can have a magnified effect on the fetus.

Anesthetics may temporarily depress the flow of oxygen to the fetus and slow labor. In addition, newborns whose mothers have been anesthetized are less physiologically responsive, show poorer motor control during the first days after birth, cry more, and may have more difficulty initiating breastfeeding (Ransjö-Arvidson et al., 2001; Torvaldsen et al., 2006).

Developmental Diversity and Your Life

How the Pain of Childbirth Differs Across Cultures

Every woman's delivery depends on such factors as how much preparation and support she has before and during delivery, the specific nature of the delivery, and her culture's view of pregnancy and delivery. It also turns out that the experience of pain differs across cultures.

For example, women in India report that labor is less painful than do women in the United States. Even within Western cultures, pain is viewed differently. For example, in Belgium, women view pain as something to be avoided through the use of medication. In contrast, women living in the Netherlands see labor pain as normal and helpful to the birth process, and thus something to be embraced (Christiaens, Verhaeghe, & Bracke, 2010).

It is unlikely that the physiological reactions resulting in the perception of pain to labor differ across different cultures. Instead, it is the way the pain is perceived that makes the difference. Labor and delivery clearly depend, at least in part, on a woman's state of mind (de C. Williams et al., 2013; Karlsdottir, Halldorsdottir, & Lundgren, 2014; Steel et al., 2014; Wilsona & Simpson, 2016,).

Figure 3-2 Average Stay in Hospital After Childbirth

The length of stay after giving birth varies considerably by country.

(Source: Campbell et al., 2017)

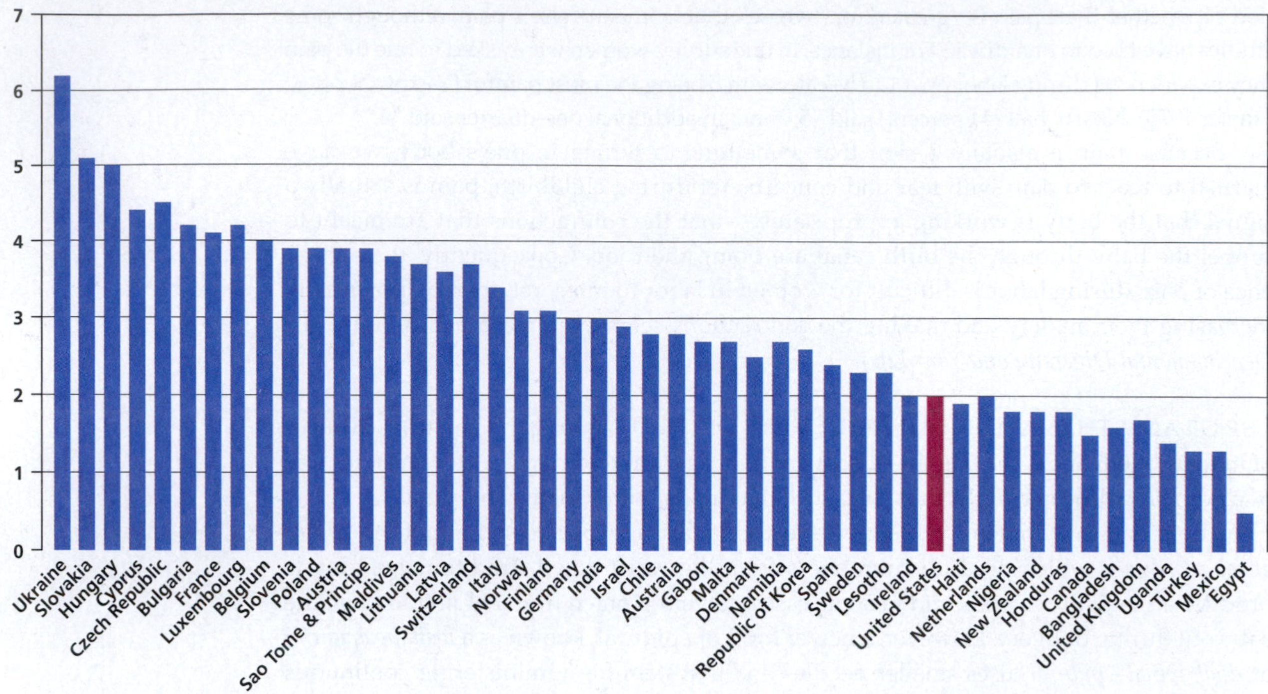

Still, most research suggests that drugs, as they are currently employed during labor, produce only minimal risks to the fetus and neonate. Guidelines issued by the American College of Obstetricians and Gynecologists suggest that a woman's request for pain relief at any stage of labor should be honored and that the proper use of minimal amounts of drugs for pain relief is reasonable and has no significant effect on a child's later well-being (ACOG, 2002; Alberts et al., 2007; Costa-Martins et al., 2014).

POSTDELIVERY HOSPITAL STAY: DELIVER, THEN DEPART? When New Jersey mother Diane Mensch was sent home from the hospital just a day after the birth of her third child, she still felt exhausted. But her insurance company insisted that 24 hours was sufficient time to recover, and it refused to pay for more. Three days later, her newborn was back in the hospital, suffering from jaundice. Mensch is convinced the problem would have been discovered and treated sooner had she and her newborn been allowed to remain in the hospital longer (Begley, 1995).

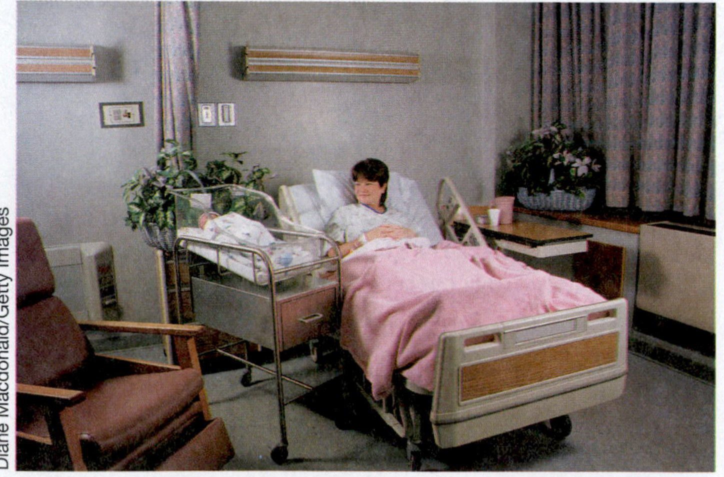

Diane Macdonald/Getty Images

Mothers who spend more time in the hospital following the birth of a child do better than those who are discharged after a shorter period.

Mensch's experience is not unusual, at least for mothers in the United States. In the 1970s, the average hospital stay for a normal birth was around 4 days. Now, it is 2 days. These changes were prompted in large part by medical insurance companies, who advocated hospital stays of only 24 hours following birth in order to reduce costs.

In other countries, mothers routinely stay longer after delivery. For example, mothers in the Ukraine and Moldova stay an average of 6 days, and 5 days is routine in Hungary and Romania. By contrast, mothers in Egypt average just half a day (Campbell et al., 2016; see Figure 3-2).

Medical care providers believe that there are definite risks involved, both for mothers and for their newborns, for too fast a departure from hospitals. For instance, mothers may begin to bleed if they tear tissue injured during childbirth. It is also riskier for newborns to be discharged prematurely from the sophisticated medical care that hospitals can provide. Furthermore, mothers are better rested and more satisfied with their medical care when they stay longer (Campbell et al., 2016).

In accordance with these views, the U.S. Congress has passed legislation mandating a minimum insurance coverage of 48 hours for childbirth. Furthermore, the American Academy of Pediatrics has issued comprehensive guidelines detailing how long women (and their infants) should stay in the hospital based on various health criteria relating to the infant and mother (Bentz, 2015).

Module 3.1 Review

LO 3.1 Describe the normal process of labor.

In the first stage of labor, contractions increase in frequency, duration, and intensity until the baby's head is able to pass through the cervix. In the second stage, the baby moves through the cervix and birth canal and leaves the mother's body. In the third stage, the umbilical cord and placenta emerge.

LO 3.2 Explain the events that occur in the first few hours of a newborn's life.

Immediately after birth, birthing attendants usually examine the neonate using a measurement system such as the Apgar scale. Newborns are also typically tested for a variety of diseases and genetic conditions. The newborn is usually returned to its parents shortly after birth so that they may hold and bond with the baby.

LO 3.3 Describe some of the current approaches to childbirth.

Many birthing options are available to parents today. They may use a midwife or doula in addition to or instead of an obstetrician, and they may weigh the advantages and disadvantages of anesthetic drugs during birth. Some women choose alternatives to traditional hospital birthing, including the Lamaze method, the Bradley method, hypnobirthing, and water birthing.

Journal Writing Prompt

Applying Lifespan Development: Why might cultural differences exist in expectations and interpretations of labor?

Birth Complications

When Ivy Brown's son was stillborn, a nurse told her that sad as it was, nearly 1 percent of births in her city, Washington, D.C., ended in death. That statistic spurred Brown to become a grief counselor, specializing in infant mortality. She formed a committee of physicians and city officials to study the capital's high infant mortality rate and find solutions to lower it. "If I can spare one mother this terrible grief, my loss will not be in vain," Brown says.

The infant mortality rate in the United States, the richest country in the world, is 6.17 deaths per 1,000 live births. Some wealthy countries, such as Japan, have an infant mortality rate that is half of that in the United States. Overall, nearly 50 countries have better birth rates than the United States (Sun, Lamb, & Wong, 2012; *World Factbook*, 2016; see Figure 3-3).

Why is infant survival less likely in the United States than in quite a few less developed countries? To answer this question, we need to consider the nature of the problems that can occur during labor and delivery.

Preterm Infants: Too Soon, Too Small

LO 3.4 Describe some of the causes of, effects of, and treatments for preterm births.

Around 1 out of 10 infants are born earlier than normal. **Preterm infants**, or premature infants, are born prior to 38 weeks after conception. Because they have not had time to develop fully as fetuses, preterm infants are at high risk for illness and death.

preterm infants
infants who are born prior to 38 weeks after conception (also known as premature infants)

The extent of danger faced by preterm babies largely depends on the child's weight at birth, which has great significance as an indicator of the extent of the baby's development.

Figure 3-3 International Infant Mortality

Infant mortality rates in selected countries. Although the United States has greatly reduced its infant mortality rate since the 1990s, it still ranks behind numerous other industrialized countries. What are some of the reasons for this?

(**Source:** *World Factbook*, 2016.)

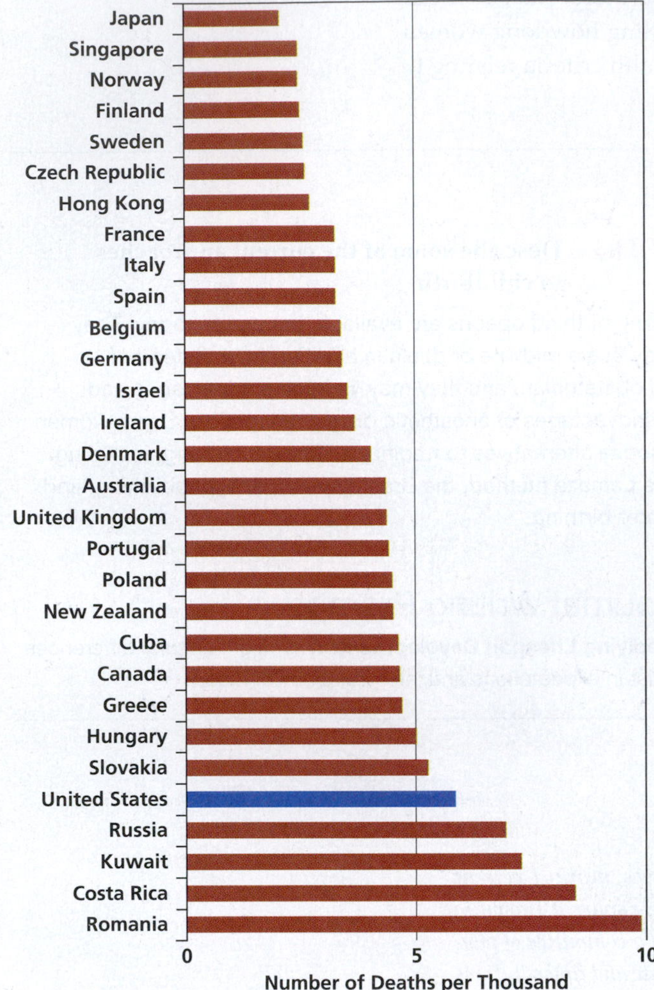

Although the average newborn weighs around 3,400 grams (about 7 1/2 pounds), **low-birthweight infants** weigh less than 2,500 grams (around 5 1/2 pounds). Only 7 percent of all newborns in the United States fall into the low-birthweight category, but they account for the majority of newborn deaths (Gross, Spiker, & Haynes, 1997; DeVader et al., 2007).

Although most low-birthweight infants are preterm, some are small-for-gestational-age babies. **Small-for-gestational-age infants** are infants who, because of delayed fetal growth, weigh 90 percent (or less) of the average weight of infants of the same gestational age. Small-for-gestational-age infants are sometimes also preterm, but may not be. The syndrome may be caused by inadequate nutrition during pregnancy (Bergmann, Bergmann, & Dudenhausen, 2008; Salihu et al., 2013).

If the degree of prematurity is not too great and weight at birth is not extremely low, the threat to the child's well-being is relatively minor. In such cases, the main treatment may be to keep the baby in the hospital to gain weight. Additional weight is critical because fat layers help prevent chilling in neonates, who are not particularly efficient at regulating body temperature.

Research also shows that preterm infants who receive more responsive, stimulating, and organized care are apt to show more positive outcomes than those children whose care is not as good. Some of these interventions are quite simple. For example, "kangaroo care," in which infants are held skin-to-skin against their parents' chests, appears to be effective in helping preterm infants develop. Massaging preterm infants several times a day triggers the release of hormones that promote weight gain, muscle development, and the ability to cope with stress (Kaffashi et al., 2013; Athanasopoulou & Fox, 2014; Nobre et al., 2017).

Newborns who are born more prematurely and who have birthweights significantly below average face a tougher road. For them, simply staying alive is a major task. For instance, low-birthweight infants are highly vulnerable to infection, and because their lungs have not had sufficient time to develop completely, they have problems taking in enough oxygen. As a consequence, they may experience *respiratory distress syndrome* (RDS), with potentially fatal consequences.

low-birthweight infants
infants who weigh less than 2,500 grams (around 5 1/2 pounds) at birth

small-for-gestational-age infants
infants who, because of delayed fetal growth, weigh 90 percent (or less) of the average weight of infants of the same gestational age

To deal with RDS, low-birthweight infants are often placed in incubators, enclosures in which temperature and oxygen content are controlled. The exact amount of oxygen is carefully monitored. Too low a concentration of oxygen will not provide relief, and too high a concentration can damage the delicate retinas of the eyes, leading to permanent blindness.

The immature development of preterm neonates makes them unusually sensitive to stimuli in their environment. They can easily be overwhelmed by the sights, sounds, and sensations they experience, and their breathing may be interrupted or their heart rates may slow. They are often unable to move smoothly; their arm and leg movements are uncoordinated, causing them to jerk about and appear startled. Such behavior is quite disconcerting to parents (Doussard-Roosevelt et al., 1997; Miles et al., 2006; Valeri et al., 2014).

Despite the difficulties they experience at birth, the majority of preterm infants eventually develop normally. However, the tempo of development often proceeds more slowly for preterm children compared to children born at full term, and more subtle problems sometimes emerge later. For example, by the end of their first year, only 10 percent of prematurely born infants display significant problems, and only 5 percent are seriously disabled. By age 6, however, approximately 38 percent have mild problems that call for special educational interventions. For instance, some preterm children show learning disabilities, behavior disorders, or lower-than-average IQ scores. They also may be at greater risk for mental illness. Others have difficulties with physical coordination. Still, around 60 percent of preterm infants are free of even minor problems (Hall et al., 2008; Nosarti et al., 2012; El Ayoubi et al., 2016).

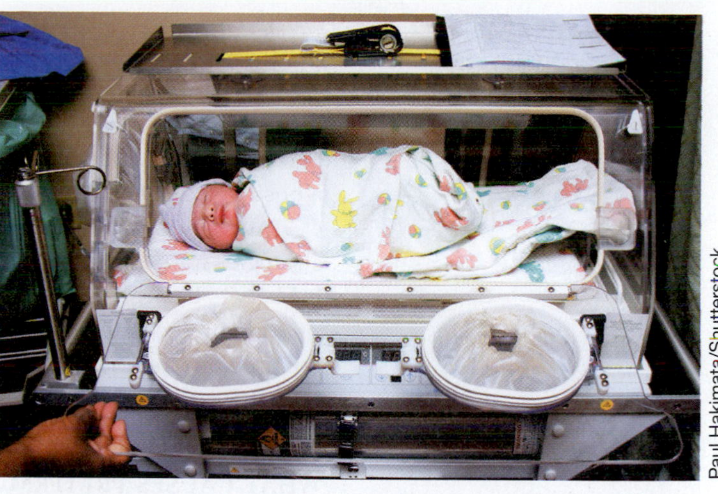

Paul Hakimata/Shutterstock

Preterm infants stand a much greater chance of survival today than they did even a decade ago.

VERY-LOW-BIRTHWEIGHT INFANTS: THE SMALLEST OF THE SMALL. The story is less positive for the most extreme cases of prematurity—very-low-birthweight infants. **Very-low-birthweight infants** weigh less than 1,250 grams (around 2 1/4 pounds) or, regardless of weight, have been in the womb less than 30 weeks.

very-low-birthweight infants
infants who weigh less than 1,250 grams (around 2 1/4 pounds) or, regardless of weight, have been in the womb less than 30 weeks

Very-low-birthweight infants not only are tiny—some fitting easily in the palm of the hand at birth—they hardly seem to belong to the same species as full-term newborns. Their eyes may be fused shut and their earlobes may look like flaps of skin on the sides of their heads. Their skin is a darkened red color, whatever their race.

Very-low-birthweight babies are in grave danger from the moment they are born, due to the immaturity of their organ systems. Before the mid-1980s, these babies would not have survived outside their mothers' wombs. However, medical advances have led to a higher chance of survival, pushing the *age of viability*, the point at which an infant can survive prematurely, to about 22 weeks—some 4 months earlier than the term of a normal delivery. Of course, the longer the period of development beyond conception, the higher are a newborn's chances of survival. A baby born earlier than 25 weeks has less than a 50–50 chance of survival (see Figure 3-4; Seaton et al., 2012).

The physical and cognitive problems experienced by low-birthweight and preterm babies are even more pronounced in very-low-birthweight infants, with astonishing financial consequences. A 3-month stay in an incubator in an intensive care unit can run hundreds of thousands of dollars, and about half of these newborns ultimately die, despite massive medical intervention (Taylor et al., 2000).

Figure 3-4 Survival and Gestational Age

Chances of a fetus surviving greatly improve after 28 to 32 weeks. Rates shown are the number per thousand of babies born after specified lengths of gestation who do not survive the first year of life. **THINKING ABOUT THE DATA:** How does the United States infant mortality rate compare with other countries at 24-27 weeks gestation? At 37 weeks gestation or later?

(**Source:** Based on MacDorman & Mathews, 2009.)

	United States	Austria	Denmark	England and Wales[2]	Finland	Northern Ireland	Norway	Poland	Scotland	Sweden
22–23 weeks[1]	707.7	888.9	947.4	880.5	900.0	1,000.0	555.6	921.1	1,000.0	515.2
24–27 weeks	236.9	319.6	301.2	298.2	315.8	268.3	220.2	530.6	377.0	197.7
28–31 weeks	45.0	43.8	42.2	52.2	58.5	54.5	56.4	147.7	60.8	41.3
32–36 weeks	8.6	5.8	10.3	10.6	9.7	13.1	7.2	23.1	8.8	12.8
37 weeks or more	2.4	1.5	2.3	1.8	1.4	1.6	1.5	2.3	1.7	1.5

1 Infant mortality rates at 22–23 weeks of gestation may be unreliable due to reporting differences.
2 England and Wales provided 2005 data.
NOTE: Infant mortality rates are per 1,000 live births in specified group.
SOURCE: NCHS linked birth/infant death data set (for U.S. data), and *European Perinatal Health Report* (for European data).

Even if a very-low-birthweight preterm infant survives, the medical costs can continue to mount. For instance, one estimate suggests that the average monthly cost of medical care for such infants during the first 3 years of life may be between 3 and 50 times higher than the medical costs for a full-term child. Such astronomical costs have raised ethical debates about the expenditure of substantial financial and human resources in cases in which a positive outcome may be unlikely (Prince, 2000; Doyle, 2004; Petrou, 2006).

As medical capabilities progress and developmental researchers come up with new strategies for dealing with preterm infants and improving their lives, the age of viability is likely to be pushed even earlier. Emerging evidence suggests that high-quality care can provide protection from some of the risks associated with prematurity, and that in fact by the time they reach adulthood, premature babies may be little different from other adults. Still, the costs of caring for preterm infants are enormous: The U.S. government estimates that caring for premature infants costs $26 billion a year (Hack et al., 2002; Saul, 2009).

WHAT CAUSES PRETERM AND LOW-BIRTHWEIGHT DELIVERIES? About half of preterm and low-birthweight births are unexplained, but several known causes account for the remainder. In some cases, premature labor results from difficulties relating to the mother's reproductive system. For instance, mothers carrying twins have unusual stress placed on them, which can lead to early labor. In fact, most multiple births are preterm to some degree (Luke & Brown, 2008; Saul, 2009; Habersaat et al., 2014).

In other cases, preterm and low-birthweight babies are a result of the immaturity of the mother's reproductive system. Young mothers—under age 15—are more prone to deliver prematurely than older ones. In addition, a woman who becomes pregnant within 6 months of a previous delivery is more likely to deliver a preterm or low-birthweight infant than a woman whose reproductive system has had a chance to recover from a prior delivery. The father's age matters, too: Pregnant women with older male partners are more likely to have preterm deliveries (Branum, 2006; Blumenshine et al., 2011; Teoli, Zullig, & Hendryx, 2015).

Finally, factors that affect the general health of the mother, such as nutrition, level of medical care, amount of stress in the environment, and economic support, all are related to prematurity and low birthweight. Rates of preterm births differ between racial groups, not because of race per se but because members of racial minorities have disproportionately lower incomes and higher stress as a result. For instance, the percentage of low-birthweight infants born to African American mothers is double that for Caucasian American mothers. (A summary of the factors associated with increased risk of low birthweight is shown in Table 3-2; Bergmann, Bergmann, & Dudenhausen, 2008; Butler, Wilson, & Johnson, 2012; Teoli, Zullig & Hendryx, 2015.)

Postmature Babies: Too Late, Too Large

LO 3.5 Identify the risks that postmature babies face.

One might imagine that a baby who spends extra time in the womb might have some advantages, given the opportunity to continue growth undisturbed by the outside world. Yet **postmature infants**—those still unborn 2 weeks after the mother's due date—face several risks.

postmature infants
infants still unborn 2 weeks after the mother's due date

For example, the blood supply from the placenta may become insufficient to nourish the still-growing fetus adequately. Consequently, the blood supply to the brain may be decreased, leading to the potential of brain damage. Similarly, labor becomes riskier (for both the child and the mother) as a fetus—who may be equivalent in size to a 1-month-old infant—has to make its way through the birth canal (Shea, Wilcox, & Little, 1998; Fok et al., 2006).

Difficulties involving postmature infants are more easily prevented than those involving preterm babies, since medical practitioners can induce labor artificially if the pregnancy continues too long. Not only can certain drugs bring on labor, but physicians also have the option of performing cesarean deliveries, a form of delivery we consider next.

Table 3-2 Birthweight

Risk Factors for Low-Birthweight Preterm Infants

• Women who have delivered preterm before, or who have experienced preterm labor
• Being pregnant with twins, triplets, or higher-order multiples
• The use of assisted reproductive technologies
• Certain medical conditions, including:
  • Urinary tract infections
  • Sexually transmitted infections
  • Certain vaginal infections
  • High blood pressure
  • Bleeding from the vagina
  • Certain developmental abnormalities in the fetus
  • Being underweight or obese before pregnancy
  • Short time period between pregnancies (less than 6 months between a birth and the beginning of the next pregnancy)
  • Placenta previa, a condition in which the placenta grows in the lowest part of the uterus and covers all or part of the opening to the cervix
  • Being at risk for rupture of the uterus
  • Diabetes
  • Blood clotting problems

Other factors that may increase risk for preterm labor and premature birth include:

• Ethnicity. Preterm labor and birth occur more often among certain racial and ethnic groups
• Age of the mother: younger than 18 and older than 35
• Certain lifestyle and environmental factors, including:
  • Late or no health care during pregnancy
  • Smoking
  • Drinking alcohol
  • Using illegal drugs
  • Domestic violence, including physical, sexual, or emotional abuse
  • Lack of social support
  • Stress
  • Long working hours with long periods of standing
  • Exposure to certain environmental pollutants

Source: U.S. Department of Health and Human Services, National Institutes of Health, Eunice Kennedy Shriver Institute of Child Health and Human Development, 2017.

Cesarean Delivery: Intervening in the Process of Birth

LO 3.6 Describe the process of cesarean delivery and the reasons for its increase in use.

As Elena entered her eighteenth hour of labor, the obstetrician who was monitoring her progress began to look concerned. She told Elena and her husband, Pablo, that the fetal monitor revealed that the fetus's heart rate had begun to repeatedly fall after each contraction. After trying some simple remedies, such as repositioning Elena on her side, the obstetrician came to the conclusion that the fetus was in distress. She told them that the baby should be delivered immediately, and to accomplish that, she would have to carry out a cesarean delivery.

Elena became one of the more than 1 million mothers in the United States who have a cesarean delivery each year. In a **cesarean delivery** (sometimes known as a *c-section*), the baby is surgically removed from the uterus rather than traveling through the birth canal.

cesarean delivery
a birth in which the baby is surgically removed from the uterus, rather than traveling through the birth canal

Cesarean deliveries occur most frequently when the fetus shows distress of some sort. For instance, if the fetus appears to be in danger, as indicated by a sudden rise in its heart rate, or if blood is seen coming from the mother's vagina during labor, a cesarean may be performed. In addition, mothers over age 40 are more likely to have cesarean deliveries than younger mothers. Overall, cesarean deliveries in the United States now make up 32 percent of all deliveries (Tang et al., 2006; Romero, Coulson, & Galvin, 2012).

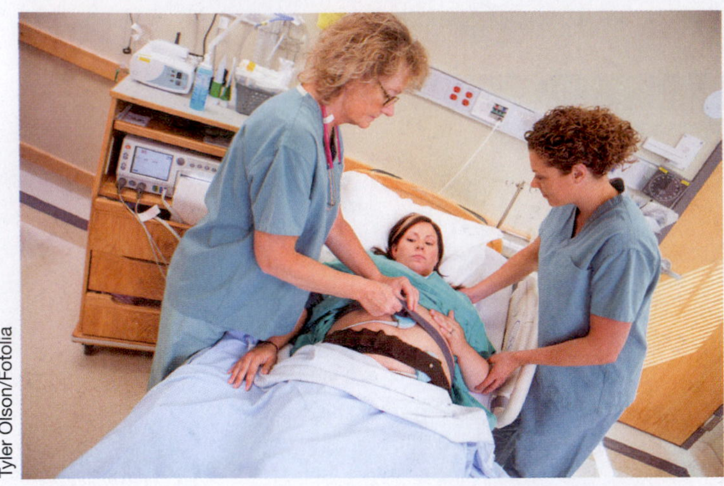

The use of fetal monitoring has contributed to a sharp increase of cesarean deliveries in spite of evidence showing few benefits from the procedure.

Cesarean deliveries are also used in some cases of *breech position*, in which the baby is positioned feet first in the birth canal. Breech position births, which occur in about 1 out of 25 births, place the baby at risk because the umbilical cord is more likely to be compressed, depriving the baby of oxygen. Cesarean deliveries are also more likely in *transverse position* births, in which the baby lies crosswise in the uterus, or when the baby's head is so large it has trouble moving through the birth canal.

The routine use of a **fetal monitor**, a device that measures the baby's heartbeat during labor, has contributed to a soaring rate of cesarean deliveries. Nearly a third of all children in the United States are born in this way, up some 500 percent from the early 1970s, when the rate stood at 5 percent (Hamilton, Martin, & Ventura, 2011; Paterno et al., 2016).

fetal monitor
a device that measures the baby's heartbeat during labor

Are cesareans an effective medical intervention? Other countries have substantially lower rates of cesarean deliveries (see Figure 3-5), and there is no association between successful birth consequences and the rate of cesarean deliveries. In addition, cesarean deliveries carry dangers. Cesarean delivery represents major surgery, and the mother's recovery can be relatively lengthy, particularly when compared to a normal delivery. In addition, the risk of maternal infection is higher with cesarean deliveries (Miesnik & Reale, 2007; Hutcheon et al., 2013; Ryding et al., 2015).

Finally, a cesarean delivery presents some risks for the baby. Because cesarean babies are spared the stresses of passing through the birth canal, their relatively easy

Figure 3-5 Cesarean Deliveries

The rate at which cesarean deliveries are performed varies substantially from one country to another. Why do you think the United States has a high rate?

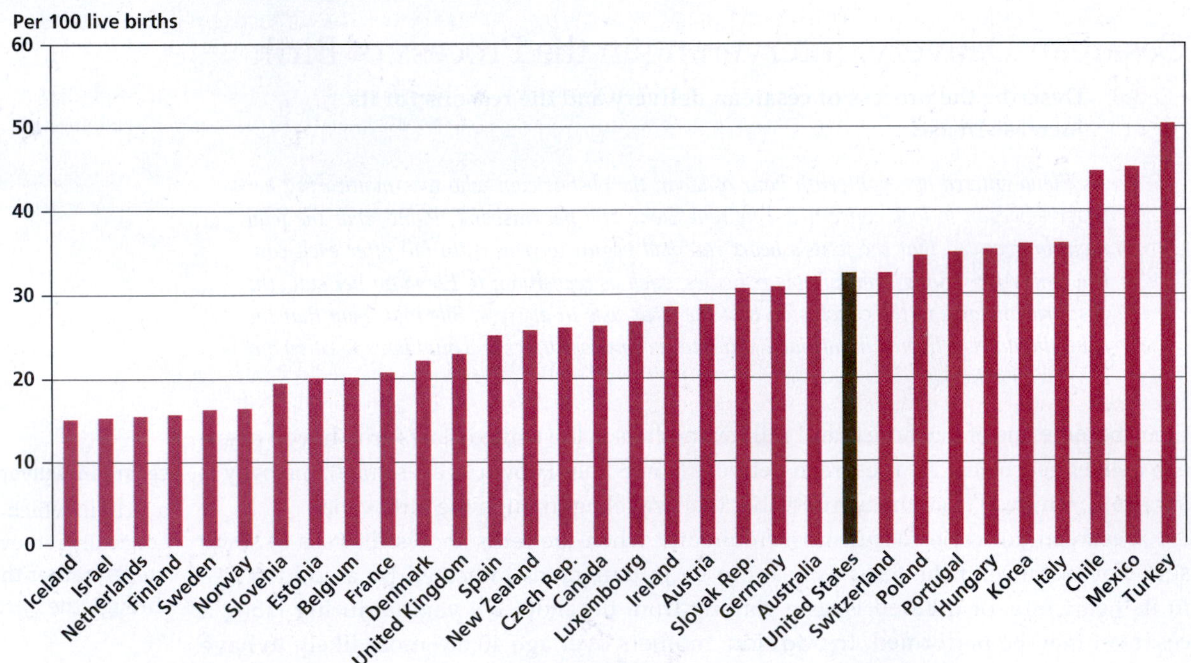

passage into the world may deter the normal release of certain stress-related hormones, such as catecholamines, into the newborn's bloodstream. These hormones help prepare the neonate to deal with the stress of the world outside the womb, and their absence may be detrimental to the newborn child. In fact, research indicates that babies born by cesarean delivery who have not experienced labor are more likely to experience breathing problems upon birth than those who experience at least some labor prior to being born via a cesarean delivery. Mothers who deliver by cesarean are often less satisfied with the birth experience, but their dissatisfaction does not influence the quality of mother–child interactions (MacDorman et al., 2008; Xie et al., 2015; Kjerulff & Brubaker, 2017).

Because the increase in cesarean deliveries is, as we have said, connected to the use of fetal monitors, medical authorities now currently recommend that fetal monitors not be used routinely. There is evidence that outcomes are no better for newborns who have been monitored than for those who have not been monitored. In addition, monitors tend to indicate fetal distress when there is none—false alarms—with disquieting regularity. Monitors do, however, play a critical role in high-risk pregnancies and in cases of preterm and postmature babies (Freeman, 2007; Sepehri & Guliani, 2017).

Studies examining what appear, in retrospect, to be unnecessary cesareans have found racial and socioeconomic differences. Specifically, black mothers are more likely to have a potentially unnecessary cesarean delivery than white mothers are. In addition, Medicare patients—who tend to be relatively poor—are more likely to have unnecessary cesarean deliveries than non-Medicare patients (Kabir et al., 2005).

Stillbirth and Infant Mortality: The Tragedy of Premature Death

LO 3.7 Describe rates of infant mortality and what factors affect these statistics.

The joy that accompanies the birth of a child is completely reversed when a newborn dies. The relative rarity of their occurrence makes infant deaths even harder for parents to bear.

Sometimes a child does not even live beyond its passage through the birth canal. **Stillbirth**, the delivery of a child who is not alive, occurs in around 1 delivery out of 100 in the United States. Sometimes the death is detected before labor begins. In this case, labor is typically induced, or physicians may carry out a cesarean delivery in order to remove the body from the mother as soon as possible. In other cases of stillbirth, the baby dies during its travels through the birth canal.

stillbirth
the delivery of a child who is not alive, occurring in 1 delivery in 100 in the United States

The overall rate of **infant mortality** (defined as death within the first year of life) is 6.17 deaths per 1,000 live births. Infant mortality generally has been declining since the 1960s, and declined 12 percent from 2005 to 2011 (McDorman, Hoyert, & Matthews, 2013; Loggins & Andrade, 2014; Prince et al., 2016).

infant mortality
death within the first year of life

Whether the death is a stillbirth or occurs after the child is born, the loss of a baby is tragic, and the impact on parents is enormous. The loss and grief parents feel, and their passage through it, is similar to that experienced when an older loved one dies (discussed in Chapter 19). The juxtaposition of the first dawning of life and an unnaturally early death may make the death particularly difficult to accept and handle. Depression is common, and it is often intensified owing to a lack of support. Some parents even experience post-traumatic stress disorder (Badenhorst et al., 2006; Cacciatore & Bushfield, 2007; Turton, Evans, & Hughes, 2009).

There are also differences related to race, socioeconomic status, and culture in infant mortality, as we discuss in the *Developmental Diversity and Your Life* section.

Developmental Diversity and Your Life

Overcoming Racial and Cultural Differences in Infant Mortality

Even though there has been a general decline in the infant mortality rate in the United States over the past several decades, African American babies are more than twice as likely to die before age 1 than white babies. This difference is largely the result of socioeconomic factors: African American women are significantly more likely to be living in poverty than Caucasian women and to receive less prenatal care. As a result, their babies are more likely to be of low birthweight—the factor most closely linked to infant mortality—than infants of mothers of other racial groups (see Figure 3-6; Duncan & Brooks-Gunn, 2000; Byrd et al., 2007; Rice et al., 2017).

But it is not just members of particular racial groups in the United States who suffer from poor mortality rates. As mentioned earlier, the rate of infant mortality in the United States is higher than the rate in many other countries. For example, the mortality rate in the United States is almost double that of Japan.

Why does the United States fare so poorly in terms of newborn survival? One answer is that the United States has a higher rate of low-birthweight and preterm deliveries than many other countries. When U.S. infants are compared to infants of the same weight who are born in other countries, the differences in mortality rates disappear (Wilcox et al., 1995; MacDorman et al., 2005; Davis & Hofferth, 2012).

Another reason for the higher U.S. mortality rate relates to economic diversity. The United States has a higher proportion of people living in poverty than many other countries. Because people in lower economic categories are less likely to have adequate medical care and tend to be less healthy, the relatively high proportion of economically deprived individuals in the United States impacts the overall mortality rate (Bremner & Fogel, 2004; MacDorman et al., 2005; Close et al., 2013).

Many countries do a significantly better job than the United States in providing prenatal care to mothers-to-be. For instance, low-cost and even free care, both before and after delivery, is often available in other countries. Furthermore, paid maternity leave is frequently provided to pregnant women, lasting in some cases as long as 51 weeks (see Table 3-3).

Figure 3-6 Race and Infant Mortality

For most groups, infant mortality fell until 2000 and then rose slightly. What could explain the rise from 2000 to 2005?

(**Source:** Child Health USA, 2009.)

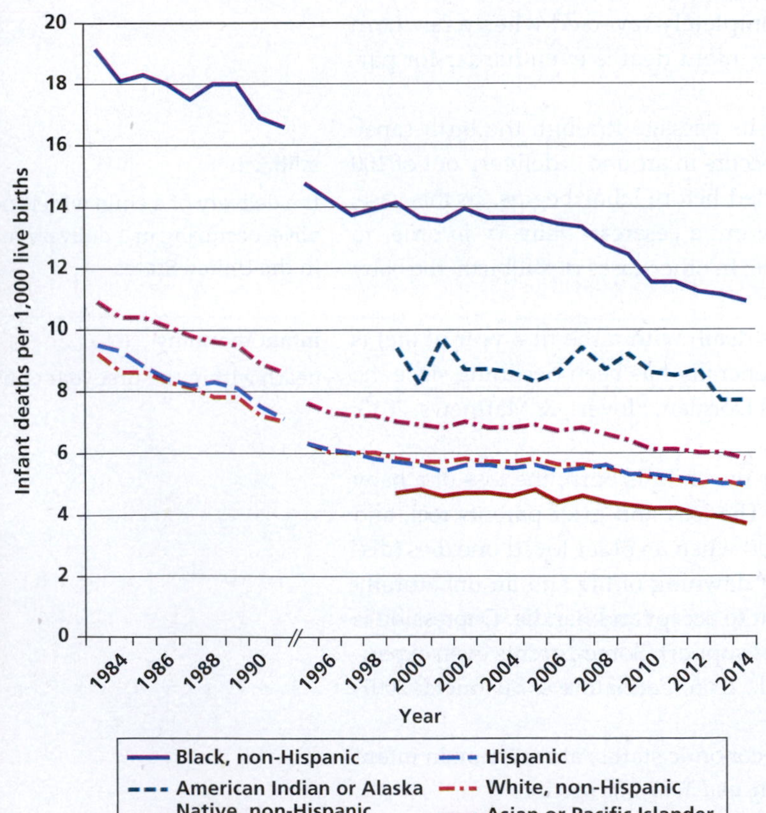

In the United States, the U.S. *Family and Medical Leave Act (FMLA)* requires most employers to give new parents up to 12 weeks of unpaid leave following the birth (or adoption or foster care placement) of a child. However, because it is unpaid leave, the lack of pay is an enormous barrier for low-income workers, who rarely are able to take advantage of the opportunity to stay home with their child.

The opportunity to take an extended maternity leave can be important: Mothers who spend more time on maternity leave may have better mental health and higher-quality interactions with their infants (Berger, Hill, & Waldfogel, 2005; Rowe-Finkbeiner et al., 2016).

Better health care is only part of the story. In certain European countries, in addition to a comprehensive package of services involving general practitioner, obstetrician, and midwife, pregnant women receive many privileges, such as transportation benefits for visits to health-care providers. In Norway, pregnant women may be given living expenses for up to 10 days so that they can be close to a hospital when it is time to give birth. And when their babies are born, new mothers receive the assistance of trained home helpers for just a small payment (DeVries, 2005).

In the United States, the story is very different. About 1 out of every 6 pregnant women has insufficient prenatal care. Some 20 percent of white women and close to 40 percent of African American women receive no prenatal care early in their pregnancies. Five percent of white mothers and

Table 3-3 Childbirth-Related Leave Policies in the United States and Selected Peer Nations

Country	Length of Leave Provided	Payment Rate
United States	12 weeks	Unpaid
Canada	54 weeks	Varies; around 55 percent
Denmark	32 weeks	100 percent
Finland	26 weeks	70 percent of prior earnings
Norway	36–46 weeks	100 percent
Sweden	60 weeks	12 months at 80 percent of prior earnings, 3 months flat rate, 3 months unpaid
France	156 weeks	Flat rate
Japan	1 year	60 percent of prior earnings
United Kingdom	18 weeks	Unpaid

(**Source:** Adapted from Addati, Cassirer, & Gilchrist, 2014.)

11 percent of African American mothers do not see a health-care provider until the last 3 months of pregnancy; some never see a health-care provider at all (Hueston, Geesey, & Diaz, 2008; Friedman, Heneghan, & Rosenthal, 2009; Cogan et al., 2012).

Ultimately, the lack of prenatal services results in a higher mortality rate. Yet this situation can be changed if greater support is provided. A start would be to ensure that all economically disadvantaged pregnant women have access to free or inexpensive high-quality medical care from the very beginning of pregnancy. Furthermore, barriers that prevent poor women from receiving such care should be reduced. For instance, programs can be developed that help pay for transportation to a health facility or for the care of older children while the mother is making a health-care visit. The cost of these programs is likely to be offset by the savings they make possible—healthy babies cost less than infants with chronic problems as a result of poor nutrition and prenatal care (Cramer et al., 2007; Edgerley et al., 2007; Barber & Gertler, 2009; Hanson, 2012).

From *an educator's* perspective

Why do you think the United States lacks educational and health-care policies that could reduce infant mortality rates overall and among poorer people? What arguments would you make to change this situation?

Postpartum Depression: Moving from the Heights of Joy to the Depths of Despair

LO 3.8 Describe the causes and effects of postpartum depression.

Renata was overjoyed when she found out that she was pregnant and had spent the months of her pregnancy happily preparing for her baby's arrival. The birth was routine, the baby a healthy, pink-cheeked boy. But a few days after her son's birth, she sank into the depths of depression. Constantly crying, confused, and feeling incapable of caring for her child, she was experiencing unshakable despair.

The diagnosis: a classic case of postpartum depression. *Postpartum depression*, a period of deep depression following the birth of a child, affects some 10 percent of all new mothers. Although it takes several forms, its main symptom is an enduring, deep feeling of sadness and unhappiness, lasting in some cases for months or even years. Mothers experiencing postpartum depression may withdraw from their family and friends, experience overwhelming fatigue or loss of energy, or feel intense irritability and anger. Furthermore, mothers may feel stigmatized by others (Mickelson et al., 2017).

In about 1 in 500 cases, the symptoms are even worse, evolving into a total break with reality. In extremely rare instances, postpartum depression may turn deadly. For example, Andrea Yates, a mother in Texas who confessed to drowning all five of her children in a bathtub, said that postpartum depression led to her actions (Yardley, 2001; Oretti et al., 2003; Misri, 2007).

From Research to Practice

From Joy to Sorrow: When Mothers Become Depressed

Imagine that you are thrilled to conceive a child after trying for many years. You have an unremarkable, normal pregnancy, labor goes smoothly, and you give birth to a beautiful and healthy baby girl. But instead of experiencing the joy of getting everything you dreamed of, you feel instead that it is the worst thing that ever happened to you, and your mood becomes one of deep sadness and depression. Suffering from a classic case of postpartum depression, you feel miserable.

But you'd probably feel worse if you knew that it's not only you who was feeling the effects of depression: Your infant might well be affected too. A growing body of research suggests that not only does postpartum depression afflict the mother, it has lasting effects on a child. For example, maternal depression is related to poor motor control and lower cognitive abilities in infancy, inadequate behavior control in childhood, and even emotional problems in adulthood. Furthermore, when depressed mothers interact with their infants, they may display little emotion and act detached and withdrawn. This lack of responsiveness leads infants to display fewer positive emotions and to withdraw from contact not only with their mothers but with other adults as well. In addition, children of depressed mothers are more prone to antisocial activities such as violence as they get older (Goodman et al., 2008; Smith-Nielsen et al., 2016; Granat et al., 2017).

In some cases, maternal depression begins during pregnancy, and the depression affects the woman's developing fetus. Maternal depression is related to such harmful effects as low birthweight, premature birth, pregnancy complications, and decreased immune function (OberlaMattes et al., 2009; Smith-Nielsen et al., 2016).

Concerns over the possible harmful effects of maternal depression make it tempting for physicians to prescribe antidepressant drugs to depressed patients. But it's unclear that this solution is any less of a concern than the original problem: While most research suggests that the effects of common antidepressant drugs on developing fetuses and nursing infants are minimal and temporary, there's just not enough research to be certain. Research on potential long-term effects is especially lacking (Ramos et al., 2008; Einarson et al., 2009; Thomson & Sharma, 2017).

Given this reality, the best option for women who experience depression during and after pregnancy may be to seek out non-drug-based psychotherapeutic interventions. Forms of talk therapy offer expectant mothers an option for treatment while posing no additional risk to the developing fetus (Oberlander and DiPietro, 2003; Ugarte et al., 2017).

Shared Writing Prompt

Should mothers routinely be screened for depression during pregnancy? Why or why not?

For mothers who suffer from postpartum depression, the symptoms are often bewildering. The onset of depression usually comes as a complete surprise. Certain mothers do seem more likely to become depressed, such as those who have been clinically depressed at some point in the past or who have depressed family members.

Furthermore, women who are unprepared for the range of emotions that follow the birth of a child—some positive, some negative—may be more prone to depression (LaCoursiere, Hirst, & Barrett-Connor, 2012; Pawluski, Lonstein & Fleming, 2017).

Postpartum depression may be triggered by the pronounced swings in hormone production that occur after birth. During pregnancy, production of the female hormones estrogen and progesterone increases significantly. However, within the first 24 hours following birth, they plunge to normal levels. This rapid change may result in depression (Klier et al., 2007; Yim et al., 2009; Engineer et al., 2013; Glynn & Sandman, 2014). (For more on depression, both pre- and post-delivery, see *From Research to Practice*.)

Module 3.2 Review

LO 3.4 Describe some of the causes of, effects of, and treatments for preterm births.

Largely because of low birthweight, preterm infants may have substantial difficulties after birth and later in life. Very-low-birthweight infants are in special danger because of the immaturity of their organ systems. Preterm and low-birthweight deliveries can be caused by health, age, and pregnancy-related factors in the mother. Income (and, because of its relationship with income, race) is also an important factor. Many preterm babies spend weeks or months in the neonatal intensive care unit receiving specialized care to help them develop.

LO 3.5 Identify the risks that postmature babies face.

Postmature infants face certain risks, including loss of blood supply and difficult births due to their size.

LO 3.6 Describe the process of cesarean delivery and the reasons for its increase in use.

Cesarean deliveries are performed with postmature babies or when the fetus is in distress, in the wrong position, or unable to progress through the birth canal. The routine use of a fetal monitor has contributed to a soaring rate of cesarean deliveries.

LO 3.7 Describe rates of infant mortality and what factors affect these statistics.

The overall rate of infant mortality is 6.05 deaths per 1,000 live births. In the United States, African American babies are more than twice as likely to die before age 1 than white babies. Infant mortality rates can be affected by the availability of inexpensive health care and good education programs for mothers-to-be.

LO 3.8 Describe the causes and effects of postpartum depression.

Postpartum depression affects about 10 percent of new mothers and may be triggered by the pronounced swings in hormone production that occur after birth.

Journal Writing Prompt

Applying Lifespan Development: Why do you think there is a higher rate of cesarean deliveries among black mothers than among white mothers?

The Competent Newborn

Relatives gathered around the infant car seat and its occupant, Kaita Castro. Born just 2 days ago, Kaita is going home from the hospital with her mother. Kaita's nearest cousin, 4-year-old Tabor, seems uninterested in the new arrival. "Babies can't do anything fun. They can't even do anything at all," he says.

Kaita's cousin Tabor is partly right. There are many things babies cannot do. Neonates arrive in the world quite incapable of successfully caring for themselves, for example. Why are human infants born so dependent, while members of other species seem to arrive much better equipped for their lives?

One reason is that, in one sense, humans are born too soon. The brain of the average newborn is just one-quarter of what it will be at adulthood. In comparison, the brain of the macaque monkey, which is born after just 24 weeks of gestation, is 65 percent of its adult size. Because of the relative puniness of the infant human brain, some observers have suggested that we are propelled out of the womb some 6 to 12 months sooner than we ought to be.

In reality, evolution probably knew what it was doing: If we stayed inside our mothers' bodies an additional half-year to a year, our heads would be so large that we'd never manage to get through the birth canal (Schultz, 1969; Gould, 1977; Kotre & Hall, 1990).

The relatively underdeveloped brain of the human newborn helps explain the infant's apparent helplessness. Because of this vulnerability, the earliest views of newborns focused on the things that they could not do, comparing them rather unfavorably to older members of the human species.

Today, however, such beliefs have taken a backseat to more favorable views of the neonate. As developmental researchers have begun to understand more about the nature of newborns, they have come to realize that infants enter this world with an astounding array of capabilities in all domains of development: physical, cognitive, and social.

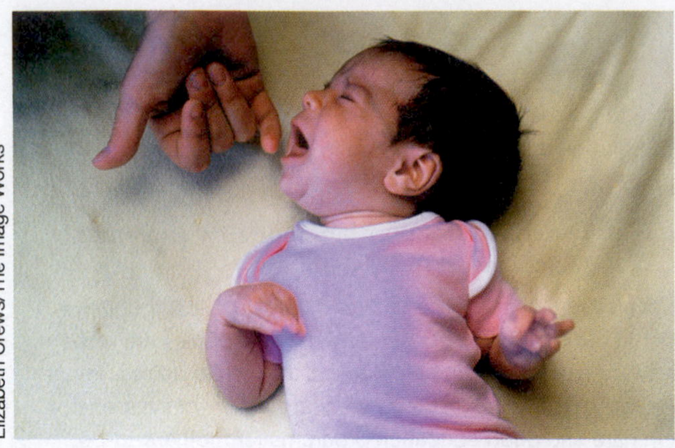
Elizabeth Crews/The Image Works

The sucking and swallowing reflexes allow newborns to begin to ingest food immediately after birth.

Physical Competence: Meeting the Demands of a New Environment

LO 3.9 Describe the physical capabilities of the newborn.

The world faced by a neonate is remarkably different from the one it experienced in the womb. Consider, for instance, the significant changes in functioning that Kaita Castro encountered as she began the first moments of life in her new environment (summarized in Table 3-4).

Kaita's most immediate task was to bring sufficient air into her body. Inside her mother, air was delivered through the umbilical cord, which also provided a means for taking away carbon dioxide. The realities of the outside world are different: Once the umbilical cord was cut, Kaita's respiratory system needed to begin its lifetime's work.

For Kaita, the task was automatic. As we noted earlier, most newborn babies begin to breathe on their own as soon as they are exposed to air. The ability to breathe immediately is a good indication that the respiratory system of the normal neonate is reasonably well developed, despite its lack of rehearsal in the womb.

reflexes
unlearned, organized, involuntary responses that occur automatically in the presence of certain stimuli

Neonates emerge from the uterus more practiced in other types of physical activities. For example, newborns such as Kaita show several **reflexes**—unlearned, organized, involuntary responses that occur automatically in the presence of certain stimuli. Some of these reflexes are well rehearsed, having been present for several months before birth. The *sucking reflex* and the *swallowing reflex* permit Kaita to begin to ingest food right away. The *rooting reflex*, which involves turning in the direction of a source of stimulation (such as a light touch) near the mouth, is also related to eating. It guides the infant toward potential sources of food that are near its mouth, such as a mother's nipple.

Not all of the reflexes that are present at birth lead the newborn to seek out desired stimuli such as food. For instance, Kaita can cough, sneeze, and blink—reflexes that help her to avoid stimuli that are potentially bothersome or hazardous.

Kaita's sucking and swallowing reflexes, which help her to consume her mother's milk, are coupled with her newfound ability to digest nutrients. The newborn's digestive system initially produces feces in the form of *meconium*, a greenish-black material that is a remnant of the neonate's days as a fetus.

Because the liver, a critical component of the digestive system, does not always work effectively at first, almost half of all newborns develop a distinctly yellowish tinge to their bodies and eyes. This change in color is a symptom of *neonatal jaundice.* It is most likely to

Table 3-4 Kaita Castro's First Encounters upon Birth

1. As soon as she is through the birth canal, Kaita automatically begins to breathe on her own despite no longer being attached to the umbilical cord that provided precious air in the womb.
2. Reflexes—unlearned, organized, involuntary responses that occur in the presence of stimuli—begin to take over. Sucking and swallowing reflexes permit Kaita to immediately ingest food.
3. The rooting reflex, which involves turning in the direction of a source of stimulation, guides Kaita toward potential sources of food that are near her mouth, such as her mother's nipple.
4. Kaita begins to cough, sneeze, and blink—reflexes that help her avoid stimuli that are potentially bothersome or hazardous.
5. Her senses of smell and taste are highly developed. Physical activities and sucking increase when she smells peppermint. Her lips pucker when a sour item is placed on her lips.
6. Objects with colors of blue and green seem to catch Kaita's attention more than other colors, and she reacts sharply to loud, sudden noises. She will also continue to cry if she hears other newborns cry but will stop if she hears a recording of her own voice crying.

occur in preterm and low-birthweight neonates, and it is typically not dangerous. Treatment most often consists of placing the baby under fluorescent lights or administering medicine.

Sensory Capabilities: Experiencing the World

LO 3.10 Describe the sensory capabilities of the newborn.

Just after Kaita was born, her father was certain that she looked directly at him. Did she, in fact, see him?

This is a hard question to answer for several reasons. For one thing, when sensory experts talk of "seeing," they mean both a sensory reaction to the stimulation of the visual sensory organs and an interpretation of that stimulation (the distinction, as you might recall from an introductory psychology class, between sensation and perception). Furthermore, as we'll discuss further when we consider sensory capabilities during infancy in Chapter 4, it is tricky, to say the least, to pinpoint the specific sensory skills of newborns who lack the ability to explain what they are experiencing.

Nyul/Fotolia

Starting at birth, infants are able to distinguish colors and even show preferences for particular hues.

Still, we do have some answers to the question of what newborns are capable of seeing and, for that matter, questions about their other sensory capabilities. For example, it is clear that neonates such as Kaita can see to some extent. Although their visual acuity is not fully developed, newborns actively pay attention to certain types of information in their environment.

For instance, neonates pay closest attention to portions of scenes in their field of vision that are highest in information, such as objects that contrast sharply with the rest of their environment. Furthermore, infants can discriminate among different levels of brightness. There is even evidence suggesting that newborns have a sense of size constancy. They seem aware that objects stay the same size, even though the size of the image on the retina varies with distance (Chien et al., 2006; Frankenhuis, Barrett, & Johnson, 2013; Wilkinson et al., 2014).

In addition, not only can newborn babies distinguish different colors, they seem to prefer particular ones. For example, they are able to distinguish between red, green, yellow, and blue, and they take more time staring at blue and green objects—suggesting a partiality for those colors (Dobson, 2000; Alexander & Hines, 2002; Zemach, Chang, & Teller, 2007).

Newborns are also clearly capable of hearing. They react to certain kinds of sounds, showing startle reactions to loud, sudden noises, for instance. They also exhibit familiarity with certain sounds. For example, a crying newborn will continue to cry when he or she hears other newborns crying. However, if the baby hears a recording of its own crying, he or she is more likely to stop crying, as if recognizing the familiar sound (Dondi, Simion, & Caltran, 1999; Fernald, 2001).

As with vision, however, the newborn's degree of auditory acuity is not as great as it will be later. The auditory system is not completely developed. Moreover, amniotic fluid, which is initially trapped in the middle ear, must drain out before the newborn can fully hear.

In addition to sight and hearing, the other senses also function quite adequately in the newborn. It is obvious that newborns are sensitive to touch. For instance, they respond to stimuli such as the brush of hair against their skin, and they are aware of puffs of air so weak that adults cannot notice them.

The senses of smell and taste are also well developed. Newborns suck and increase other physical activity when the odor of peppermint is placed near the nose. They also pucker their lips when a sour item is placed on them, and they respond with suitable facial expressions to other tastes as well. Such findings clearly indicate that the senses of touch, smell, and taste are not only present at birth, but are reasonably sophisticated (Cohen & Cashon, 2003; Armstrong et al., 2006).

In one sense, the sophistication of the sensory systems of newborns such as Kaita is not surprising. After all, the typical neonate has had 9 months to prepare for his or her encounter with the outside world, and human sensory systems begin their development well before birth. Furthermore, the passage through the birth canal may place babies in a state of heightened sensory awareness, preparing them for the world that they are about to encounter for the first time.

Early Learning Capabilities

LO 3.11 Describe the learning capabilities of the newborn.

One-month-old Michael Samedi was on a car ride with his family when a thunderstorm suddenly began. The storm rapidly became violent, and flashes of lightning were quickly followed by loud thunderclaps. Michael was clearly disturbed and began to sob. With each new thunderclap, the pitch and fervor of his crying increased. Unfortunately, before very long it wasn't just the sound of the thunder that would raise Michael's anxiety; the sight of the lightning alone was enough to make him cry out in fear. Even as an adult, Michael feels his chest tighten and his stomach churn at the mere sight of lightning.

CLASSICAL CONDITIONING. The source of Michael's fear is classical conditioning, a basic type of learning first identified by Ivan Pavlov (and discussed in Chapter 1). In **classical conditioning**, an organism learns to respond in a particular way to a neutral stimulus that normally does not bring about that type of response.

classical conditioning
a type of learning in which an organism responds in a particular way to a neutral stimulus that normally does not bring about that type of response

Pavlov discovered that by repeatedly pairing two stimuli, such as the sound of a bell and the arrival of meat, he could make hungry dogs learn to respond (in this case by salivating) not only when the meat was presented, but even when the bell was sounded without the presence of meat (Pavlov, 1927).

The key feature of classical conditioning is stimulus substitution, in which a stimulus that doesn't naturally bring about a particular response is paired with a stimulus that does evoke that response. Repeatedly presenting the two stimuli together results in the second stimulus that takes the properties of the first. In effect, the second stimulus is substituted for the first.

One of the earliest examples of the power of classical conditioning in shaping human emotions was demonstrated in the case of an 11-month-old infant known by researchers as "Little Albert" (Watson & Rayner, 1920; Fridlund et al., 2012). Although he initially adored furry animals and showed no fear of rats, Little Albert learned to fear them when, during a laboratory demonstration, a loud noise was sounded every time he played with a cute and harmless white rat. In fact, the fear generalized to other furry objects, including rabbits and even a Santa Claus mask. (By the way, such a demonstration would be considered unethical today, and it would never be conducted.)

Infants are capable of learning very early through classical conditioning. For instance, 1- and 2-day-old newborns who are stroked on the head just before being given a drop of a sweet-tasting liquid soon learn to turn their heads and suck at the head-stroking alone. Clearly, classical conditioning is in operation from the time of birth (Dominguez, Lopez, & Molina, 1999; Herbert et al., 2004; Welch, 2016).

OPERANT CONDITIONING. But classical conditioning is not the only mechanism through which infants learn; they also respond to operant conditioning. As we noted in Chapter 1, **operant conditioning** is a form of learning in which a *voluntary* response is strengthened or weakened, depending on its association with positive or negative consequences. In operant conditioning, infants learn to act deliberately on their environments in order to bring about some desired consequence. An infant who learns that crying

operant conditioning
a form of learning in which a voluntary response is strengthened or weakened, depending on its association with positive or negative consequences

in a certain way is apt to bring her parents' immediate attention is displaying operant conditioning.

Like classical conditioning, operant conditioning functions from the earliest days of life. For instance, researchers have found that even newborns readily learn through operant conditioning to keep sucking on a nipple when it permits them to continue hearing their mothers read a story or to listen to music (DeCasper & Fifer, 1980; Lipsitt, 1986).

HABITUATION. Probably the most primitive form of learning is demonstrated by the phenomenon of habituation. **Habituation** is the decrease in the response to a stimulus that occurs after repeated presentations of the same stimulus.

habituation
the decrease in the response to a stimulus that occurs after repeated presentations of the same stimulus

Habituation in infants relies on the fact that when newborns are presented with a new stimulus, they produce an *orienting response*, in which they become quiet, attentive, and experience a slowed heart rate as they take in the novel stimulus. When the novelty wears off due to repeated exposure to the stimulus, the infant no longer reacts with this orienting response. If a new and different stimulus is presented, the infant once again reacts with an orienting response. When this happens, we can say that the infant has learned to recognize the original stimulus and to distinguish it from others.

Habituation occurs in every sensory system, and researchers have studied it in several ways. One way is to examine changes in sucking, which stops temporarily when a new stimulus is presented. This reaction is not unlike that of an adult who temporarily puts down her knife and fork when a dinner companion makes an interesting statement to which she wishes to pay particular attention. Other measures of habituation include changes in heart rate, respiration rate, and the length of time an infant looks at a particular stimulus (Macchi Cassia et al., 2012; Rosburg, Weigl, & Sörös, 2014; Dumont et al., 2017).

The development of habituation is linked to physical and cognitive maturation. It is present at birth and becomes more pronounced over the first 12 weeks of infancy. Difficulties involving habituation represent a signal of developmental problems such as mental retardation (Moon, 2002). The three basic processes of learning that we've considered—classical conditioning, operant conditioning, and habituation—are summarized in Table 3-5.

Social Competence: Responding to Others

LO 3.12 Describe the social competencies of newborns.

Soon after Kaita was born, her older brother looked down at her in her crib and opened his mouth wide, pretending to be surprised. Kaita's mother, looking on, was amazed when it appeared that Kaita imitated his expression, opening her mouth as if *she* were surprised.

Table 3-5 Three Basic Processes of Learning

Type	Description	Example
Classical conditioning	A situation in which an organism learns to respond in a particular way to a neutral stimulus that normally does not bring about that type of response.	A hungry baby stops crying when her mother picks her up because she has learned to associate being picked up with subsequent feeding.
Operant conditioning	A form of learning in which a voluntary response is strengthened or weakened, depending on its positive or negative consequences.	An infant who learns that smiling at his or her parents brings positive attention may smile more often.
Habituation	The decrease in the response to a stimulus that occurs after repeated presentations of the same stimulus.	A baby who showed interest and surprise at first seeing a novel toy may show no interest after seeing the same toy several times.

wong sze yuen/Shutterstock

This infant is imitating the happy responses of his father. Why is this important?

Researchers registered surprise of their own when they first found that newborns did indeed have the capability to imitate others' behavior. Although infants were known to have all the muscles in place to produce facial expressions related to basic emotions, the actual appearance of such expressions was assumed to be largely random.

However, research beginning in the late 1970s began to suggest a different conclusion. For instance, developmental researchers found that when exposed to an adult modeling a behavior that the infant already performed spontaneously, such as opening the mouth or sticking out the tongue, the newborn appeared to imitate the behavior (Meltzoff & Moore, 1977, 2002; Nagy, 2006).

Even more exciting were findings from a series of studies conducted by developmental psychologist Tiffany Field and her colleagues (Field, 1982; Field & Walden, 1982; Field et al., 1984). They initially showed that infants could discriminate between such basic facial expressions as happiness, sadness, and surprise. They then exposed newborns to an adult model with a happy, sad, or surprised facial expression. The results suggested that newborns produced a reasonably accurate imitation of the adult's expression.

Subsequent research, however, seemed to point to a different conclusion, as other investigators found consistent evidence only for a single imitative movement: sticking out the tongue. And even that response seemed to disappear around the age of 2 months. Since it seems unlikely that imitation would be limited to a single gesture and only appear for a few months, some researchers began to question the earlier findings. Some researchers suggested that even sticking out the tongue was not imitation but merely an exploratory behavior (Jones, 2007; Tissaw, 2007; Huang, 2012).

The jury is still out on exactly when true imitation begins, although it seems clear that some forms of imitation begin very early in life. Such imitative skills are important because effective social interaction with others relies in part on the ability to react to other people in an appropriate manner and to understand the meaning of others' emotional states. Consequently, newborns' ability to imitate provides them with an important foundation for social interaction later in life (Meltzoff, 2002; Beisert et al., 2012; Nagy, Pal & Orvos, 2014).

Several other aspects of newborns' behavior also act as forerunners for more formal types of social interaction that they will develop as they grow. As shown in Table 3-6, certain characteristics of neonates mesh with parental behavior to help produce a social relationship between child and parent, as well as social relationships with others.

Table 3-6 Factors That Encourage Social Interaction between Full-Term Newborns and Their Parents

Newborn	Parent
Shows a preference for particular stimuli	Offers those stimuli more than others
Begins to show a predictable cycle of arousal states	Uses the observed cycle to achieve more regulated states
Shows some consistency in time patterns	Conforms to and shapes the newborn's patterns
Shows awareness of parent's actions	Helps newborn grasp intent of actions
Reacts and adapts to actions of parent	Acts in predictable, consistent ways
Shows evidence of a desire to communicate	Works to comprehend the newborn's communicative efforts

(**Source:** Based on Eckerman & Oehler, 1992.)

From a *child-care worker's* perspective

Developmental researchers no longer view the neonate as a helpless, incompetent creature, but rather as a remarkably competent developing human being. What do you think are some implications of this change in viewpoint for methods of childrearing and child care?

Newborns cycle through various **states of arousal**, different degrees of sleep and wakefulness that range from deep sleep to great agitation. Caregivers become involved in trying to help ease the baby through transitions from one state to another. For instance, a father who rhythmically rocks his crying daughter in an effort to calm her is engaged in a joint activity that is a prelude to future social interactions of different sorts. Similarly, newborns tend to pay particular attention to their mothers' voices, in part because they have become quite familiar after months in the womb. In turn, parents and others modify their speech when talking to infants to gain their attention and encourage interaction, using a different pitch and tempo than they use with older children and adults (Smith & Trainor, 2008; Waters et al., 2017).

states of arousal
different degrees of sleep and wakefulness through which newborns cycle, ranging from deep sleep to great agitation

The ultimate outcome of the social interactive capabilities of the newborn infant, and the responses such behavior brings about from parents, is to pave the way for future social interactions. Just as the neonate shows remarkable skills on a physical and perceptual level, then, its social capabilities are no less sophisticated.

Module 3.3 Review

LO 3.9 Describe the physical capabilities of the newborn.

Neonates are in many ways helpless, but studies of what they *can* do, rather than what they *can't* do, have revealed some surprising capabilities. For example, newborns' respiratory and digestive systems begin to function at birth. They also have an array of reflexes to help them eat, swallow, find food, and avoid unpleasant stimuli.

LO 3.10 Describe the sensory capabilities of the newborn.

Newborns' sensory competence includes the ability to distinguish among objects in the visual field and to see color differences, the ability to hear and to discern familiar sounds, and sensitivity to touch, odors, and tastes.

LO 3.11 Describe the learning capabilities of the newborn.

The processes of classical conditioning, operant conditioning, and habituation demonstrate infants' learning capabilities.

LO 3.12 Describe the social competencies of newborns.

Infants develop the foundations of social competence early in life.

Journal Writing Prompt

Applying Lifespan Development: Can you think of examples of the use of classical conditioning on infants in everyday life?

Epilogue

This chapter has covered the amazing and intense processes of labor and birth. A number of birthing options are available to parents, and these options need to be weighed in light of possible complications that can arise during the birthing process. In addition to considering the remarkable progress that has been made regarding the various treatments and interventions available for babies that are too early or too late, we examined the grim topics of stillbirth and infant mortality. We concluded with a discussion of the surprising capabilities of newborns and their early development of social competence.

Before we move on to a more detailed discussion of infants' physical development, return for a moment to the case of the premature birth of Tamera Dixon, discussed in the prologue. Using your understanding of the issues discussed in this chapter, answer the following questions.

1. Tamera was born almost 4 months early. Why was the fact that she was born alive so surprising? Can you discuss her birth in terms of "the age of viability"?
2. What procedures and activities were most likely set into motion immediately after Tamera's birth?
3. What dangers was Tamera subject to immediately after birth because of her high degree of prematurity? What dangers would be likely to continue into her childhood?
4. What ethical considerations affect the decision of whether the high costs of medical interventions for highly premature babies are justifiable? Who should pay those costs?

Looking Back

LO 3.1 Describe the normal process of labor.

In the first stage of labor, contractions occur about every 8 to 10 minutes, increasing in frequency, duration, and intensity until the mother's cervix expands. In the second stage of labor, which lasts about 90 minutes, the baby begins to move through the cervix and birth canal and ultimately leaves the mother's body. In the third stage of labor, which lasts only a few minutes, the umbilical cord and placenta are expelled from the mother.

LO 3.2 Explain the events that occur in the first few hours of a newborn's life.

After it emerges, the newborn, or neonate, is usually inspected for irregularities, cleaned, and returned to its mother and father. It also undergoes newborn screening tests.

LO 3.3 Describe some of the current approaches to childbirth.

Parents-to-be have a variety of choices regarding the setting for the birth, medical attendants, and whether to use pain-reducing medication. Sometimes, medical intervention, such as cesarean birth, becomes necessary.

LO 3.4 Describe some of the causes of, effects of, and treatments for preterm births.

Preterm, or premature, infants, born less than 38 weeks following conception, generally have low birthweight, which can cause chilling, vulnerability to infection, respiratory distress syndrome, and hypersensitivity to environmental stimuli. They may even show adverse effects later in life, including slowed development, learning disabilities, behavior disorders, below-average IQ scores, and problems with physical coordination. Very-low-birthweight infants are in special danger because of the immaturity of their organ systems. However, medical advances have pushed the age of viability of the infant back to about 24 weeks following conception.

LO 3.5 Identify the risks that postmature babies face.

Postmature babies, who spend extra time in their mothers' wombs, are also at risk. However, physicians can artificially induce labor or perform a cesarean delivery to address this situation.

LO 3.6 Describe the process of cesarean delivery and the reasons for its increase in use.

Cesarean deliveries are performed when the fetus is in distress, in the wrong position, or unable to progress through the birth canal. The routine use of a fetal monitor has contributed to a soaring rate of cesarean deliveries.

LO 3.7 Describe rates of infant mortality and what factors affect these statistics.

The infant mortality rate in the United States is higher than the rate in many other countries, and higher for low-income families than higher-income families.

LO 3.8 Describe the causes and effects of postpartum depression.

Postpartum depression, an enduring, deep feeling of sadness, affects about 10 percent of new mothers. In severe cases, its effects can be harmful to the mother and the child, and aggressive treatment may be employed.

LO 3.9 Describe the physical capabilities of the newborn.

Human newborns quickly master breathing through the lungs, and they are equipped with reflexes to help them eat, swallow, find food, and avoid unpleasant stimuli.

LO 3.10 Describe the sensory capabilities of the newborn.

Newborns' sensory competence includes the ability to distinguish among objects in the visual field and to see color differences, the ability to hear and to discern familiar sounds, and sensitivity to touch, odors, and tastes.

LO 3.11 Describe the learning capabilities of the newborn.

From birth, infants learn through habituation, classical conditioning, and operant conditioning.

LO 3.12 Describe the social competencies of newborns.

Infants develop the foundations of social competence early in life. Newborns are able to imitate the behavior of others, a capability that helps them form social relationships and facilitates the development of social competence.

Key Terms and Concepts

neonate 86
episiotomy 87
Apgar scale 88
anoxia 89
bonding 89
preterm infants 95
low-birthweight infants 96
small-for-gestational-age infants 96
very-low-birthweight infants 97
postmature infants 98
cesarean delivery 99
fetal monitor 100
stillbirth 101
infant mortality 101
reflexes 106
classical conditioning 108
operant conditioning 108
habituation 109
states of arousal 111

Summary 1

Beginnings

Andersen Ross/Getty Images

RACHEL AND JACK looked forward to the birth of their second child. They speculated—just as developmentalists do—about the role of genetics and environment in their children's development, considering issues like intelligence, resemblance, personality, schooling, and neighborhood. For the birth itself, they had many options available. Rachel and Jack chose to use a midwife rather than an obstetrician and to give birth at a traditional hospital, but in a nontraditional way. And when their baby was born, both felt pride and happiness as baby Eva reacted to the sound of her mother's voice, which she had heard from her intimate perch inside Rachel's body.

WHAT WOULD YOU DO?

- What would you tell Rachel and Jack regarding the most critical issues involved in the impending birth of their child?
- What advice would you give to Rachel and Jack about prenatal care and their decision to use a midwife?

What's your response?

Asia Images Group/Getty Images

WHAT WOULD A PARENT DO?

- What strategies would you use to prepare yourself for the upcoming birth of your child?
- How would you evaluate the different options for prenatal care and delivery?
- How would you prepare your older child for the birth of a new baby?

What's your response?

Jim Esposito Photography L.L.C./Getty Images

Introduction to Development

Blend Images/Getty Images

- Rachel and Jack considered the role of genetics (nature) versus environment (nurture) in thinking about what their child would be like.
- They also considered how their new child would develop physically, intellectually (or cognitively), and socially.

Prenatal Development

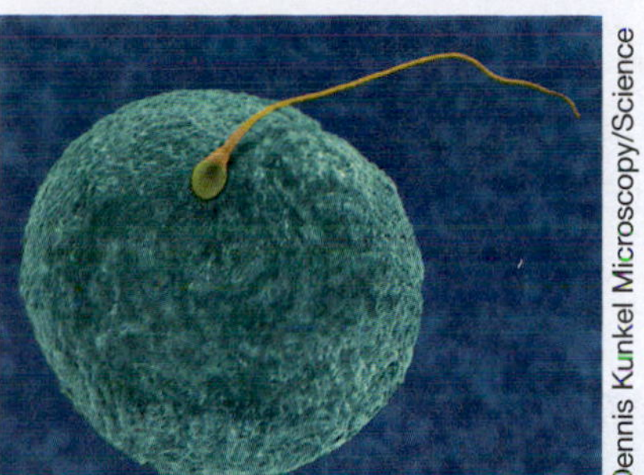
Dennis Kunkel Microscopy/Science Source

- Like all parents, Rachel and Jack contributed 23 chromosomes each at conception. Their baby's sex was determined from the particular mix of one pair of chromosomes.
- Many of Eva's characteristics will have a strong genetic component, but virtually all will represent some combination of genetics and environment.
- Eva's prenatal development started when she was a fetus and progressed through a number of stages.

Birth and the Newborn

karen roach/Shutterstock

- Rachel's labor was intense and painful, although others experience labor in different ways due to individual and cultural differences.
- Like the vast majority of births, Rachel's was completely normal and successful.
- Rachel chose to use a midwife, one of several alternative birthing methods.
- Although baby Eva seemed helpless and dependent, she actually possessed from birth an array of useful capabilities and skills.

WHAT WOULD A NURSE DO?

- How would you prepare Rachel and Jack for the upcoming birth of their baby?
- How would you respond to their concerns and anxieties?
- What would you tell them about the different options they have for giving birth?

What's your response?

Photodisc/Getty Images

WHAT WOULD AN EDUCATOR DO?

- What strategies might you use to teach Rachel and Jack about the stages of pregnancy and the process of birth?
- What might you tell them about infancy to prepare them for caring for their child?

What's your response?

Mel Yates/Getty Images

Chapter 4
Physical Development in Infancy

Ksenia Lev/Shutterstock

Learning Objectives

LO 4.1 Describe how the human body develops in the first 2 years of life, including the four principles that govern its growth.

LO 4.2 Describe how the nervous system and brain develop in the first 2 years of life and how the environment affects such development.

LO 4.3 Explain the body rhythms and states that govern an infant's behavior in the first 2 years of life.

LO 4.4 Discuss SIDS and SUID and how they can be prevented.

LO 4.5 Explain how the reflexes that infants are born with help them adapt to their surroundings and protect themselves.

LO 4.6 Summarize the landmarks of motor skill development in infancy.

LO 4.7 Summarize the role of nutrition in the physical development of infants.

LO 4.8 Summarize the benefits of breastfeeding in infancy.

LO 4.9 Describe the capabilities of infants in the realm of visual perception.

LO 4.10 Describe the capabilities of infants in the realm of auditory sensation and perception.

LO 4.11 Describe the smell and taste capacities of infants.

LO 4.12 Describe the nature of pain and touch in infants.

LO 4.13 Summarize the multimodal approach to perception.

Chapter Overview

Prologue: First Steps

We had an inkling that his first steps would not be too far in the future. Josh had previously dragged himself up, and, clutching the side of chairs and tables, managed to progress slowly around our living room. For the past few weeks, he'd even been able to stand, unmoving, for several moments without holding on.

But walking? It seemed too early: Josh was only 10 months old, and the books we read told us that most children would not take their first steps on their own until they were a year old. And our older son, Jon, hadn't walked until he was 14 months of age.

So, when Josh suddenly lurched forward, taking one awkward step after another away from the safety of the furniture and moved toward the center of the room, we were astounded. Despite the appearance that he was about to keel over at any second, he moved one, then two, then three steps forward, until our awe at his accomplishment overtook our ability to count each step.

Josh tottered all the way across the room, until he reached the other side. Not quite knowing how to stop, he toppled over, landing in a happy heap. It was moment of pure glory.

Looking Ahead

Josh's first steps at the age of 10 months marked just one of the succession of milestones that characterize the dramatic physical attainments during infancy. In this chapter, we consider physical development during infancy, a period that starts at birth and continues until the second birthday. We begin by discussing the pace of growth, noting obvious changes in height and weight as well as less apparent changes in the nervous system. We also consider how infants quickly develop increasingly stable patterns in such basic activities as sleeping, eating, and attending to the world.

Our discussion then turns to infants' thrilling gains in motor development as skills emerge that eventually allow them to roll over, take the first step, and pick up a cookie crumb from the floor—skills that ultimately form the basis of even more complex behaviors. We start with basic, genetically determined reflexes and consider how even these may be modified through experience. We also discuss the nature and timing of the development of particular physical skills, look at whether their emergence can be speeded up, and consider the importance of early nutrition to their development.

Finally, we explore how infants' senses develop. We investigate how sensory systems such as hearing and vision operate, and how infants sort through the raw data from their sense organs and transform it into meaningful information.

Growth and Stability

Average newborns weigh just over 7 pounds, which is less than the weight of the average Thanksgiving turkey. They measure about 20 inches in length, shorter than a loaf of French bread. They are helpless; if left to fend for themselves, they could not survive.

Yet after just a few years, the story is very different. Babies grow much larger, they are mobile, and they become increasingly independent. How does this growth happen? We can answer this question first by describing the changes in weight and height that occur over the first 2 years of life, and then by examining some of the principles that underlie and direct that growth.

Physical Growth: The Rapid Advances of Infancy

LO 4.1 Describe how the human body develops in the first 2 years of life, including the four principles that govern its growth.

Infants grow at a rapid pace over the first 2 years of their lives (see Figure 4-1). By the age of 5 months, the average infant's birthweight has doubled, and he or she weighs around 15 pounds. By the first birthday, the baby's weight has tripled to about 22 pounds. Although the pace of weight gain slows during the second year, by the end of his or her second year, the average child weighs around four times as much as he or she did at birth. Of course, there is a good deal of variation among infants. Height and weight measurements, which are taken regularly at physician's visits during a baby's first year, provide a way to spot problems in development.

The weight gains of infancy are matched by increased length. By the end of the first year, the typical baby grows almost a foot and is about 30 inches tall. By their second birthdays, children average a height of 3 feet.

Not all parts of an infant's body grow at the same rate. For instance, as we saw first in Chapter 2, at birth the head accounts for one-quarter of the newborn's entire body size. During the first 2 years of life, the rest of the body begins to catch up. By age 2, the baby's head is only one-fifth of body length, and by adulthood it is only one-eighth (see Figure 4-2).

Figure 4-1 Height and Weight Growth

Although the greatest increase in height and weight occurs during the first year of life, children continue to grow throughout infancy and toddlerhood.

(**Source:** Cratty, 1979.)

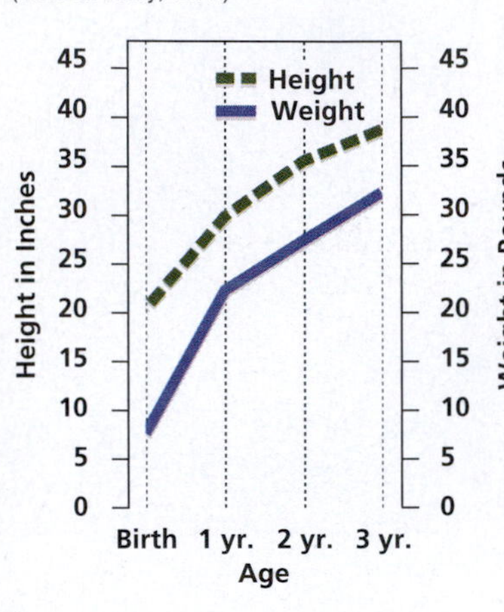

Figure 4-2 Decreasing Proportions

At birth, the head represents one-quarter of the neonate's body. By adulthood, the head is only one-eighth the size of the body. Why is the neonate's head proportionally so much larger?

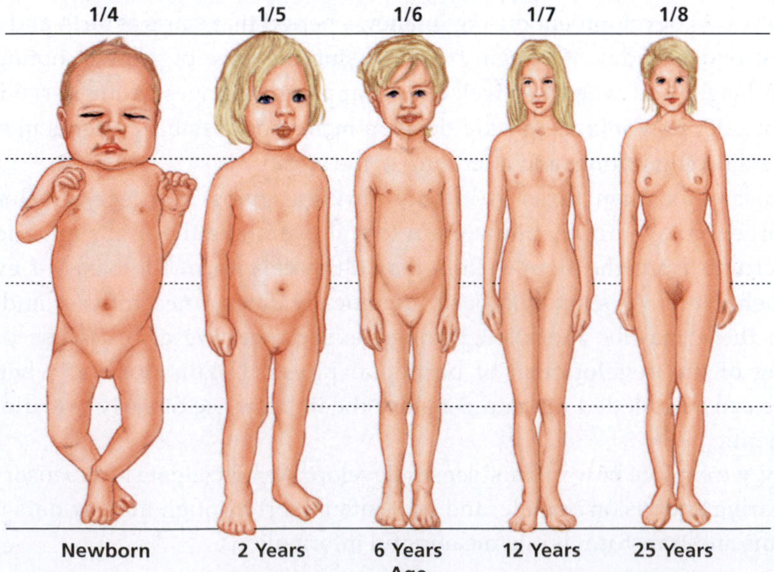

Table 4-1 The Major Principles Governing Growth

Cephalocaudal Principle	Proximodistal Principle	Principle of Hierarchical Integration	Principle of the Independence of Systems
Growth follows a pattern that begins with the head and upper body parts and then proceeds to the rest of the body. Based on Greek and Latin roots meaning "head to tail."	Development proceeds from the center of the body outward. Based on the Latin words for "near" and "far."	Simple skills typically develop separately and independently. Later they are integrated into more complex skills.	Different body systems grow at different rates.

There are also gender and ethnic differences in weight and length. Girls generally are slightly shorter and weigh slightly less than boys—differences remain throughout childhood—and, as we will see later in the book, the disparities become considerably greater during adolescence. Furthermore, Asian infants tend to be slightly smaller than North American Caucasian infants, and African American infants tend to be slightly bigger than North American Caucasian infants.

FOUR PRINCIPLES OF GROWTH. The disproportionately large size of infants' heads at birth is an example of one of four major principles (summarized in Table 4-1) that govern growth:

- The **cephalocaudal principle** states that growth follows a direction and pattern that begins with the head and upper body parts and then proceeds to the rest of the body. The cephalocaudal growth principle means that we develop visual abilities (located in the head) well before we master the ability to walk (closer to the end of the body).
- The **proximodistal principle** states that development proceeds from the center of the body outward. The proximodistal principle means that the trunk of the body grows before the extremities of the arms and legs. Furthermore, development of the ability to use various parts of the body also follows the proximodistal principle. For instance, effective use of the arms precedes the ability to use the hands.
- The **principle of hierarchical integration** states that simple skills typically develop separately and independently but that these simple skills are integrated into more complex ones. Thus, the relatively complex skill of grasping something in the hand cannot be mastered until the developing infant learns how to control—and integrate—the movements of the individual fingers.
- Finally, the **principle of the independence of systems** suggests that different body systems grow at different rates. For instance, the patterns of growth for body size, the nervous system, and sexual maturation are quite different.

cephalocaudal principle
the principle that growth follows a pattern that begins with the head and upper body parts and then proceeds down to the rest of the body

proximodistal principle
the principle that development proceeds from the center of the body outward

principle of hierarchical integration
the principle that simple skills typically develop separately and independently but are later integrated into more complex skills

principle of the independence of systems
the principle that different body systems grow at different rates

The Nervous System and Brain: The Foundations of Development

LO 4.2 Describe how the nervous system and brain develop in the first 2 years of life and how the environment affects such development.

When Rina was born, she was the first baby among her parents' circle of friends. These young adults marveled at the infant, "oohing" and "aahing" at every sneeze and smile and whimper, trying to guess at their meaning. Whatever feelings, movements, and thoughts Rina was experiencing, they were all brought about by the same complex network: the infant's nervous system. The *nervous system* is composed of the brain and the nerves that extend throughout the body.

Neurons are the basic cells of the nervous system. Figure 4-3 shows the structure of an adult neuron. Like all cells in the body, neurons have a cell body containing a nucleus.

neuron
the basic nerve cell of the nervous system

Figure 4-3 The Neuron

The basic element of the nervous system, the neuron, has a number of components.

(**Source:** Van de Graaff, 2000.)

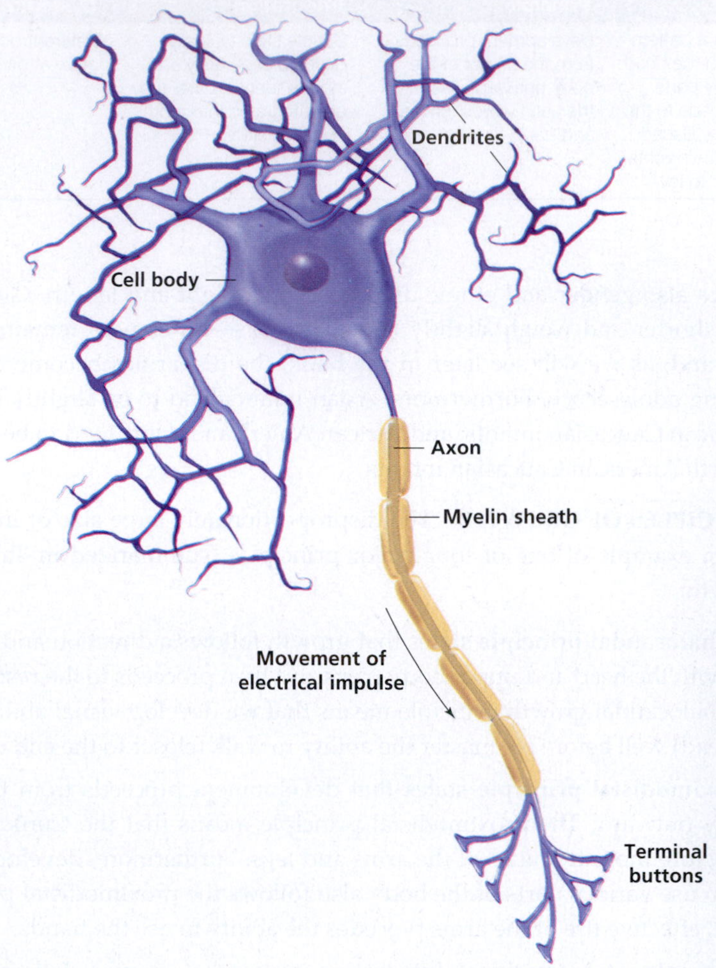

But unlike other cells, neurons have a distinctive ability: They can communicate with other cells, using a cluster of fibers called *dendrites* at one end. Dendrites receive messages from other cells. At their opposite end, neurons have a long extension called an *axon*, the part of the neuron that carries messages destined for other neurons. Neurons do not actually touch one another. Rather, they communicate with other neurons by means of chemical messengers, *neurotransmitters* that travel across the small gaps, known as **synapses**, between neurons.

synapse
the gap at the connection between neurons, through which neurons chemically communicate with one another

Although estimates vary, infants are born with between 100 billion and 200 billion neurons. In order to reach this number, neurons multiply at an amazing rate prior to birth. At some points in prenatal development, cell division creates some 250,000 additional neurons every minute.

At birth, most neurons in an infant's brain have relatively few connections to other neurons. During the first 2 years of life, however, a baby's brain will establish billions of new connections between neurons. Furthermore, the network of neurons becomes increasingly complex, as illustrated in Figure 4-4. The intricacy of neural connections continues to increase throughout life. In adulthood, a single neuron is likely to have a minimum of 5,000 connections to other neurons or other body parts.

SYNAPTIC PRUNING. Babies are actually born with many more neurons than they need. In addition, although synapses are formed throughout life based on our changing experiences, the billions of new synapses infants form during the first 2 years

Figure 4-4 Neuron Networks

Over the first 2 years of life, networks of neurons become increasingly complex and interconnected. Why are these connections important?

(Source: Conel, 1930/1963.)

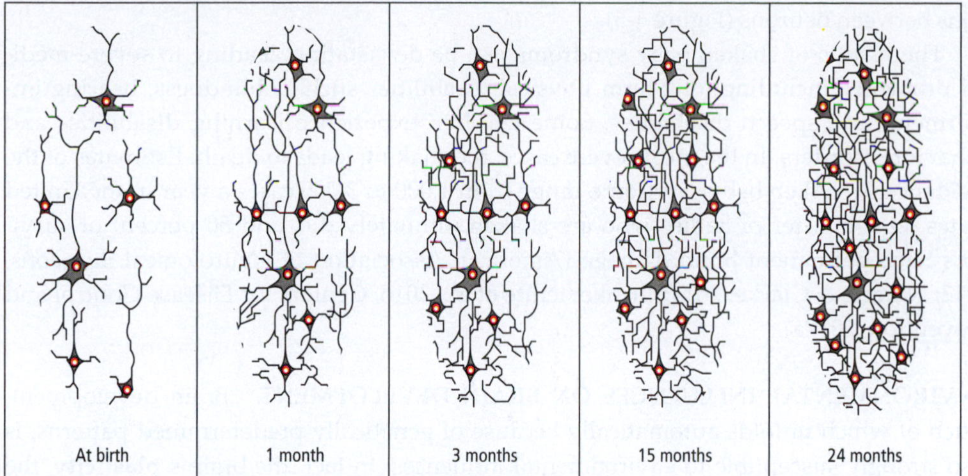

are more numerous than necessary. What happens to the extra neurons and synaptic connections?

Like a farmer who, in order to strengthen the vitality of a fruit tree, prunes away unnecessary branches, brain development enhances certain capabilities in part by a "pruning down" of unnecessary neurons. Neurons that do not become interconnected with other neurons as the infant's experience of the world increases become unnecessary. They eventually die out, increasing the efficiency of the nervous system.

As unnecessary neurons are being reduced, connections between remaining neurons are expanded or eliminated as a result of their use or disuse during the baby's experiences. If a baby's experiences do not stimulate certain nerve connections, these, like unused neurons, are eliminated—a process called **synaptic pruning**. The result of synaptic pruning is to allow established neurons to build more elaborate communication networks with other neurons. Unlike most other aspects of growth, then, the development of the nervous system proceeds most effectively through the loss of cells (Schafer & Stevens, 2013; Zong et al., 2015; Athanasiu et al., 2017).

synaptic pruning
the elimination of neurons as the result of nonuse or lack of stimulation

After birth, neurons continue to increase in size. In addition to growth in dendrites, the axons of neurons become coated with **myelin**, a fatty substance that, like the insulation on an electric wire, provides protection and speeds the transmission of nerve impulses. So, even though many neurons are lost, the increasing size and complexity of the remaining ones contribute to impressive brain growth. A baby's brain triples its weight during his or her first 2 years of life, and it reaches more than three-quarters of its adult weight and size by the age of 2.

myelin
a fatty substance that helps insulate neurons and speeds the transmission of nerve impulses

As they grow, the neurons also reposition themselves, becoming arranged by function. Some move into the **cerebral cortex**, the upper layer of the brain, while others move to *subcortical levels*, which are below the cerebral cortex. The subcortical levels, which regulate such fundamental activities as breathing and heart rate, are the most fully developed at birth. As time passes, however, the cells in the cerebral cortex, which are responsible for higher-order processes such as thinking and reasoning, become more developed and interconnected.

cerebral cortex
the upper layer of the brain

For example, synapses and myelinization experience a growth spurt at around 3 to 4 months in the area of the cortex involving auditory and visual skills (areas called the *auditory cortex* and the *visual cortex*). This growth corresponds to the rapid increase in auditory and visual skills. Similarly, areas of the cortex related to body movement grow rapidly, allowing for improvement in motor skills.

Figure 4-5 Shaken Baby

This CAT scan shows severe brain injury in an infant suspected of being abused by a caretaker.

(**Source:** Matlung et al., 2011.)

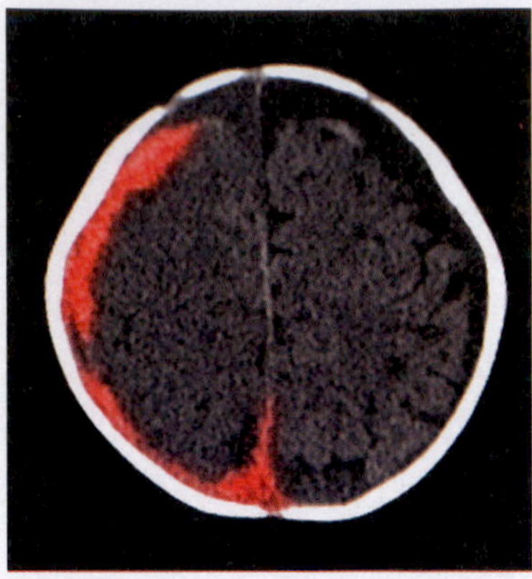

Although the brain is protected by the bones of the skull, it is highly sensitive to some forms of injury. One particularly devastating injury comes from a form of child abuse called *shaken baby syndrome* in which an infant is shaken by a caretaker or parent, usually out of frustration or anger due to a baby's crying. Shaking can lead the brain to rotate within the skull, causing blood vessels to tear and destroying the intricate connections between neurons (Figure 4-5).

The results of shaken baby syndrome can be devastating, leading to severe medical problems, including long-term physical disabilities such as blindness, hearing impairment, and speech disabilities. Some children experience learning disabilities and behavior disorders. In the most severe cases, the shaking leads to death. Estimates of the incidence of shaken baby syndrome range from 1,000 to 3,000 cases a year in the United States. One-quarter of babies who are shaken ultimately die, and 80 percent of survivors have permanent brain damage (American Association of Neurological Surgeons, 2012; Narang & Clarke, 2014; Grinkevičiūtė et al., 2016; Centers for Disease Control and Prevention, 2017a).

ENVIRONMENTAL INFLUENCES ON BRAIN DEVELOPMENT. Brain development, much of which unfolds automatically because of genetically predetermined patterns, is also strongly susceptible to environmental influences. In fact, the brain's **plasticity**, the degree to which a developing structure or behavior is modifiable due to experience, is a significant attribute of it.

plasticity

the degree to which a developing structure or behavior is modifiable due to experience

The brain's plasticity is greatest during the first several years of life. Because many areas of the brain are not yet devoted to specific tasks, if one area is injured, other areas can take over for the injured area.

For example, preterm infants who suffer damage due to bleeding in the brain can recover almost entirely by age 2. In addition, even when particular parts of infants' brains are injured due to accidents, other parts of the brain can compensate, aiding in recovery (Guzzetta et al., 2013; Rocha-Ferreira & Hristova, 2016).

Similarly, because of the high degree of plasticity in the brain, infants who suffer brain injuries typically are less affected and recover more fully than adults who have experienced similar types of brain injuries, showing the infants' high degree of plasticity. Of course, not even the brain's inherent plasticity can fully protect against severe injuries, such as those resulting from the violent shaking typical of shaken baby syndrome (Mercado, 2009; Stiles, 2012; Inguaggiato, Sgandurra, & Cioni, 2017).

Infants' sensory experiences affect both the size of individual neurons and the structure of their interconnections. Consequently, compared with those brought up in more enriched environments, infants raised in severely restricted settings are likely to show differences in brain structure and weight (Couperus & Nelson, 2006; Glaser, 2012; Musacchia et al., 2017).

Work with nonhumans has helped reveal the nature of the brain's plasticity. Studies have compared rats raised in an unusually visually stimulating environment to those raised in more typical, and less interesting, cages. Results of such research show that areas of the brain associated with vision are both thicker and heavier for the rats reared in enriched settings (Wolff & Nomikos, 2005; Axelson et al., 2013; Stephany, Frantz, & McGee, 2016).

In contrast, environments that are unusually barren or in some way restricted may impede the brain's development. Again, work with nonhumans provides some intriguing data. In one classic study, young kittens were fitted with goggles that restricted their vision so that they could view only vertical lines (Hirsch & Spinelli, 1970). When the cats grew up and had their goggles removed, they were unable to see horizontal lines, although they saw vertical lines perfectly well. Analogously, kittens whose goggles restricted their vision of vertical lines early in life were effectively blind to vertical lines during their adulthood—although their vision of horizontal lines was accurate.

In contrast, when goggles are placed on older cats that have lived relatively normal lives as kittens, such results are not seen after the goggles are removed. The conclusion is that there is a sensitive period for the development of vision. As we noted in Chapter 1, a **sensitive period** is a specific but limited time, usually early in an organism's life, during which the organism is particularly susceptible to environmental influences relating to some particular facet of development. A sensitive period may be associated with a behavior—such as the development of full vision—or with the development of a structure of the body, such as the configuration of the brain (Hartley & Lee, 2015; Opendak, Gould, & Sullivan, 2017).

sensitive period
a specific but limited time, usually early in an organism's life, during which the organism is particularly susceptible to environmental influences relating to some particular facet of development

From a *social worker's* perspective

What are some cultural or subcultural influences that might affect parents' childrearing practices?

The existence of sensitive periods raises several important issues. For one thing, it suggests that unless an infant receives a certain level of early environmental stimulation during a sensitive period, the infant may suffer damage or fail to develop capabilities, an effect that can never be fully remedied. If this is true, providing successful later intervention for such children may prove to be particularly challenging (Gottlieb & Blair, 2004; Zeanah, 2009).

The opposite question also arises: Does an unusually high level of stimulation during sensitive periods produce developmental gains beyond what a more commonplace level of stimulation would provide?

Such questions have no simple answers. Determining how unusually impoverished or enriched environments affect later development is one of the major questions addressed by developmental researchers as they try to find ways to maximize opportunities for developing children.

In the meantime, many developmentalists suggest that there are many ways parents and caregivers can provide a stimulating environment that will encourage healthy brain growth. Cuddling, talking and singing to, and playing with babies all help enrich their environment. In addition, holding children and reading to them is important, as it simultaneously engages multiple senses, including vision, hearing, and touch (Garlick, 2003; Shoemark, 2014).

Integrating the Bodily Systems: The Life Cycles of Infancy

LO 4.3 Explain the body rhythms and states that govern an infant's behavior in the first 2 years of life.

If you happen to overhear new parents discuss their newborns, chances are one or several bodily functions will be the subject. In the first days of life, infants' body rhythms—waking, eating, sleeping, and eliminating—govern the infant's behavior, often at seemingly random times.

These most basic activities are controlled by a variety of bodily systems. Although each of these individual behavioral patterns probably is functioning quite effectively, it takes some time and effort for infants to integrate the separate behaviors. One of the neonate's major missions is to make its individual behaviors work in harmony, helping the neonate, for example, to sleep through the night (Waterhouse & DeCoursey, 2004).

RHYTHMS AND STATES. One of the most important ways that behavior becomes integrated is through the development of various **rhythms**, which are repetitive, cyclical patterns of behavior. Some rhythms are immediately obvious, such as the change from wakefulness to sleep. Others are more subtle, but still easily noticeable, such as breathing and sucking patterns. Still other rhythms may require careful observation to be noticed.

rhythms
repetitive, cyclical patterns of behavior

Infants cycle through various states, including crying and alertness. These states are integrated through bodily rhythms.

For instance, newborns may go through periods in which they jerk their legs in a regular pattern every minute or so. Although some of these rhythms are apparent just after birth, others emerge slowly over the first year as the neurons of the nervous system become increasingly integrated (Thelen & Bates, 2003; Blumberg, Gall, & Todd, 2014; Xiao et al., 2017).

state
the degree of awareness an infant displays to both internal and external stimulation

One of the major body rhythms is that of an infant's **state**, the degree of awareness it displays to both internal and external stimulation. As can be seen in Table 4-2, such states include various levels of wakeful behaviors, such as alertness, fussing, and crying, and different levels of sleep. Each change in state brings about an alteration in the amount of stimulation required to get the infant's attention (Diambra & Menna-Barreto, 2004; Anzman-Frasca et al., 2013).

Some of the different states that infants experience produce changes in electrical activity in the brain. These changes are reflected in different patterns of electrical *brain waves*, which can be measured by a device called an *electroencephalogram*, or *EEG*. Starting

Table 4-2 Primary Behavioral States

States	Characteristics	Percentage of Time When in State
Awake States		
Alert	Attentive or scanning, the infant's eyes are open, bright, and shining.	6.7
Nonalert waking	Eyes are usually open but dull and unfocused. Varied, but typically high motor activity.	2.8
Fuss	Fussing is continuous or intermittent, at low levels.	1.8
Cry	Intense vocalizations occurring singly or in succession.	1.7
Transition States between Sleep and Waking		
Drowse	Infant's eyes are heavy-lidded but opening and closing slowly. Low level of motor activity.	4.4
Daze	Open but glassy and immobile eyes. State occurs between episodes of alert and drowse. Low level of activity.	1.0
Sleep–wake transition	Behaviors of both wakefulness and sleep are evident. Generalized motor activity; eyes may be closed or they open and close rapidly. State occurs when baby is awakening.	1.3
Sleep States		
Active sleep	Eyes closed; uneven respiration; intermittent rapid eye movements. Other behaviors: smiles, frowns, grimaces, mouthing, sucking, sighs, and sigh-sobs.	50.3
Quiet sleep	Eyes are closed, and respiration is slow and regular. Motor activity is limited to occasional startles, sigh-sobs, or rhythmic mouthing.	28.1
Transitional Sleep States		
Active–quiet transition sleep	During this state, which occurs between periods of active sleep and quiet sleep, the eyes are closed and there is little motor activity. Infant shows mixed behavioral signs of active sleep and quiet sleep.	1.9

(**Source:** Adapted from Thoman, E. B., & Whitney, M. P. (1990) Behavioral states in infants: Individual differences and individual analyses, In J. Colombo & J. Fagen (eds.) Individual Differences in Infancy: Reliability, Stability, Prediction. Hillsdale, N.J.: Lawrence Erlbaum Associates.)

at 3 months before birth, these brain wave patterns are relatively irregular. However, by the time an infant reaches the age of 3 months, a more mature pattern emerges and the brain waves become more regular (Thordstein et al., 2006; Cuevas et al., 2015).

SLEEP: PERCHANCE TO DREAM? At the beginning of infancy, the major state that occupies a baby's time is sleep—much to the relief of exhausted parents, who often regard sleep as a welcome respite from caregiving responsibilities. On average, newborn infants sleep some 16 to 17 hours a day. However, there are wide variations. Some sleep more than 20 hours, while others sleep as little as 10 hours a day (de Graag et al., 2012; Korotchikova et al., 2016).

Infants sleep a lot, but you probably shouldn't ever wish to "sleep like a baby." The sleep of infants comes in fits and starts. Rather than covering one long stretch, sleep initially comes in spurts of around 2 hours, followed by periods of wakefulness. Because of this, infants—and their sleep-deprived parents—are "out of sync" with the rest of the world, for whom sleep comes at night and wakefulness during the day (Burnham et al., 2002; Blomqvist et al., 2017).

In addition, most babies do not sleep through the night for several months after birth. Parents' sleep is interrupted, sometimes several times a night, by the infant's cries for food and physical contact.

Luckily for their parents, infants gradually settle into a more adult-like pattern. After a week, babies sleep a bit more at night and are awake for slightly longer periods during the day. Typically, by the age of 16 weeks, infants begin to sleep as much as 6 continuous hours at night, and daytime sleep falls into regular napping patterns. Most infants sleep through the night by the end of the first year, and the total amount of sleep they need each day is down to about 15 hours (Mao et al., 2004; Magee, Gordon, & Caputi, 2014).

Hidden beneath the supposedly tranquil sleep of infants is another cyclic pattern. During periods of sleep, infants' heart rates increase and become irregular, their blood pressure rises, and they begin to breathe more rapidly. Sometimes, though not always, their closed eyes begin to move in a back-and-forth pattern, as if they were viewing an action-packed scene. This period of active sleep is similar, though not identical, to the **rapid eye movement, or REM, sleep** that is found in older children and adults and is associated with dreaming (Blumberg et al., 2013).

rapid eye movement (REM) sleep
the period of sleep that is found in older children and adults that is associated with dreaming

At first, this active, REM-like sleep takes up around one-half of an infant's sleep, compared with just 20 percent of an adult's sleep (see Figure 4-6). However, the quantity of active sleep quickly declines, and by the age of 6 months, it amounts to just one-third of total sleep time (Burnham et al., 2002; Staunton, 2005; Ferri, Novelli &, Bruni, 2017).

The appearance of active sleep periods that are similar to REM sleep in adults raises the intriguing question of whether infants dream during those periods. No one knows the answer, although it seems unlikely. First of all, young infants do not have much to dream about, given their relatively limited experiences. Furthermore, the brain waves of sleeping infants appear to be qualitatively different from those of adults who are dreaming. It is not until the baby reaches 3 or 4 months of age that the wave patterns become similar to those of dreaming adults, suggesting that young infants are not dreaming during active sleep—or at least are not doing so in the same way as adults (Zampi, Fagidi, & Salzarulo, 2002).

What, then, is the function of REM sleep in infants? Although we don't know for certain, some researchers think it provides a means for the brain to stimulate itself—a process called *autostimulation* (Roffwarg, Muzio, & Dement, 1966). Stimulation of the nervous system would be particularly important in infants, who spend so much time sleeping and relatively little in alert states.

Infants' sleep cycles seem largely preprogrammed by genetic factors, but environmental influences also play a part. For instance, both long- and short-term stressors in infants' environments (such as a heat wave) can affect their sleep patterns. When environmental circumstances keep babies awake, sleep, when at last it comes, is apt to be less active (and quieter) than usual (Goodlin-Jones, Burnham, & Anders, 2000; Galland et al., 2012).

Figure 4-6 REM Sleep through the Life Span

As we age, the proportion of REM sleep increases as the proportion of non-REM sleep declines. In addition, the total amount of sleep falls as we get older.

(**Source:** Based on Roffwarg, Muzio, & Dement, 1966.)

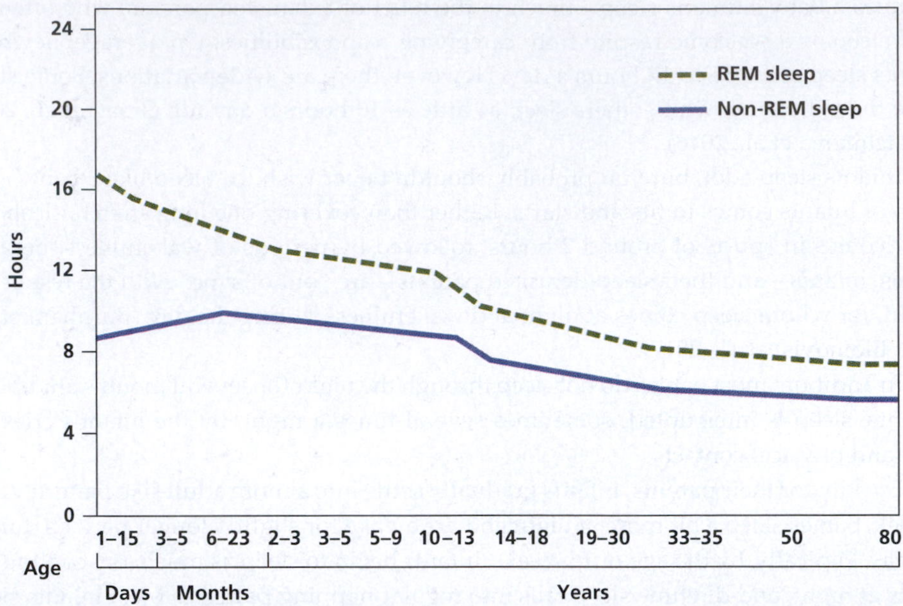

Cultural practices also affect infants' sleep patterns. For example, among the Kipsigis of Africa, infants sleep with their mothers at night and are allowed to nurse whenever they wake. In the daytime, they accompany their mothers during daily chores, often napping while strapped to their mothers' backs. Because they are often out and on the go, Kipsigis infants do not sleep through the night until much later than babies in Western societies, and for the first 8 months of life, they seldom sleep longer than 3 hours at a stretch. In comparison, 8-month-old infants in the United States may sleep as long as 8 hours at a time. One reason for these cultural differences may relate to the use of artificial light and shades used to manage natural light that varies across cultures (Super & Harkness, 1982; Anders & Taylor, 1994; Gerard, Harris, & Thach, 2002).

SIDS and SUID: The Unanticipated Killers

LO 4.4 Discuss SIDS and SUID and how they can be prevented.

sudden infant death syndrome (SIDS)
the unexplained death of a seemingly healthy baby

For a tiny percentage of infants, the rhythm of sleep is interrupted by a deadly affliction: sudden infant death syndrome. **Sudden infant death syndrome (SIDS)** is a disorder in which seemingly healthy infants die in their sleep. Put to bed for a nap or for the night, an infant simply never wakes up.

SIDS strikes about 1 in 2,500 infants in the United States each year. Although it seems to occur when the normal patterns of breathing during sleep are interrupted, scientists have been unable to discover why that might happen. It is clear that infants don't smother or choke; they die a peaceful death, simply ceasing to breathe.

While no reliable means for preventing the syndrome has been found, the American Academy of Pediatrics (AAP) suggests that babies sleep on their backs rather than on their sides or stomachs—called the *back-to-sleep* guideline. AAP guidelines also suggest that infants sleep in the same room as their parents, as we discuss in the *Research to Practice* box.

The number of deaths from SIDS has decreased significantly since these guidelines were developed. Specifically, SIDS rates fell from 130 deaths per 100,000 live births in 1990 to 39 deaths per 100,000 live births in 2015. Still, SIDS is the leading cause of death in children under the age of 1 year (Eastman, 2003; Daley, 2004; Blair et al., 2006).

Some infants are more at risk for SIDS than are others. For instance, boys and African Americans are at greater risk. In addition, low birthweight and low Apgar scores found

From Research to Practice

Preventing Sudden Infant Death Syndrome (SIDS)

There is little more tragic than situations in which parents lose a child to sudden infant death syndrome (SIDS). It is hard for them to keep from asking the question, "Is there anything we could have done to prevent this tragedy?"

The good news is that there is increasing research showing how SIDS can be avoided. In addition to the back-to-sleep guideline, the American Academy of Pediatrics suggests that infants share a bedroom (but not the same sleeping surface) with their parents until the baby turns 1 year of age, and if not than at least for the first 6 months. Sharing a room decreases the risk of SIDS by as much as 50 percent (Moon, 2016).

The guidelines also suggest avoiding the use of soft bedding, including crib bumpers, blankets, pillows, and soft toys. In other words, the crib should be bare except for a tight-fitting sheet. In fact, a simple cardboard baby box may be preferable to a crib for young infants. Such boxes have been used in Finland for decades, and that country has one of the lowest infant mortality rates in the world—half that of the United States (Ball & Volpe, 2013; Catalini, 2017; Fodaro, 2017).

Although these guidelines are unlikely to completely eradicate SIDS, they are likely to reduce the number of deaths. And for that, parents can sleep more soundly.

Shared Writing Prompt

The number of deaths of infants due to SIDS has declined since the initiation of the back-to-sleep guideline. What other reasons might account for the decline in deaths besides parents following the guideline?

at birth are associated with SIDS, as is having a mother who smokes during pregnancy. Some evidence also suggests that a brain abnormality in the hippocampus, the area of the brain that affects breathing, may produce SIDS. In a small number of cases, child abuse may be the actual cause. Other hypotheses have suggested infants who die from SIDS may have had undiagnosed sleep disorders, nutritional deficiencies, problems with reflexes, or undiagnosed illnesses. Still, there is no clear-cut factor that explains why some infants die from the syndrome. SIDS is found in children of every race and socioeconomic group and in children who have had no apparent health problems (Richardson, Walker, & Horne, 2009; Behm et al., 2012).

SIDS is part of a broader category known as **sudden unexpected infant death (SUID)**. The most common SUID is SIDS, accounting for 43 percent of infant deaths. A quarter of SUID is caused by accidental suffocation and strangulation in bed. The remainder of sudden unexpected infant death has no known cause identified (see Figure 4-7).

sudden unexpected infant death death of an infant less than 1 year old that has no immediately obvious cause

Figure 4-7 Declining Rates of SIDS

In the United States, SIDS rates have dropped dramatically as parents have become more informed and put babies to sleep on their backs instead of their stomachs. SUID: sudden unexpected infant death.

(**Source:** American SIDS Institute, based on data from the Centers for Disease Control and Prevention and the National Center for Health Statistics, 2004, National Vital Statistics System, Compressed Mortality File.)

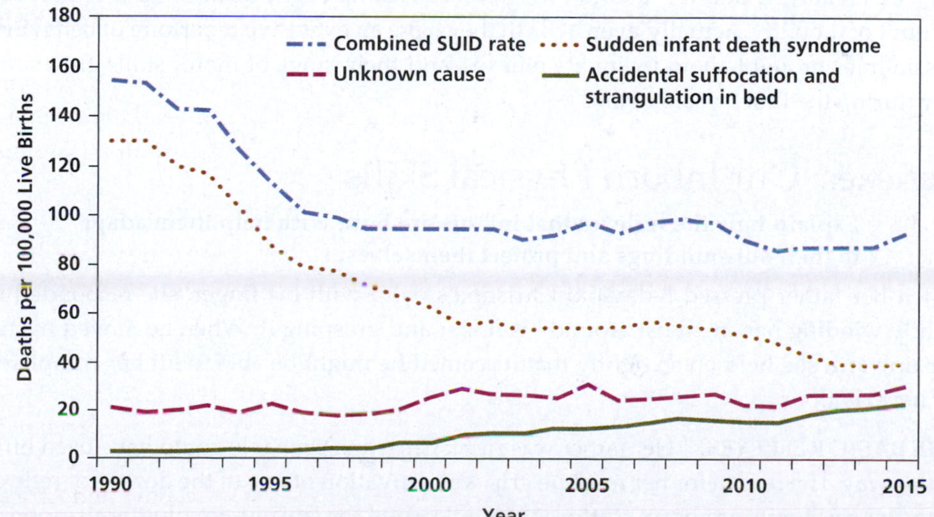

Because parents are unprepared for the death of an infant from SIDS, the event is particularly devastating. Parents often feel guilt, fearing that they were neglectful or somehow contributed to their child's death. Such guilt is unwarranted, since nothing has been identified so far that can invariably prevent SIDS (Krueger, 2006).

Module 4.1 Review

LO 4.1 Describe how the human body develops in the first 2 years of life, including the four principles that govern its growth.

The major principles of growth are the cephalocaudal principle, the proximodistal principle, the principle of hierarchical integration, and the principle of the independence of systems.

LO 4.2 Describe how the nervous system and brain develop in the first 2 years of life and how the environment affects such development.

The development of the nervous system first entails the development of billions of neurons and interconnections among them. Later, the numbers of both neurons and connections decrease as a result of the infant's experiences. Brain plasticity, the susceptibility of a developing organism to environmental influences, is relatively high. Researchers have identified sensitive periods during the development of body systems and behaviors—limited periods when the organism is particularly susceptible to environmental influences.

LO 4.3 Explain the body rhythms and states that govern an infant's behavior in the first 2 years of life.

Babies integrate their individual behaviors by developing rhythms—repetitive, cyclical patterns of behavior. A major rhythm relates to the infant's state—the awareness it displays to internal and external stimulation.

LO 4.4 Discuss SIDS and SUID and how they can be prevented.

SIDS and SUID are disorders in which seemingly healthy infants die in their sleep.

Journal Writing Prompt

Applying Lifespan Development: What evolutionary advantage could there be for infants to be born with more nerve cells than they actually need or use?

Motor Development

Suppose a genetic engineering firm hired you to redesign newborns and charged you with replacing the current version with a new, more mobile one. The first change you'd probably consider in carrying out this (luckily fictitious) job would be in the conformation and composition of the baby's body.

The shape and proportions of newborn babies are simply not conducive to easy mobility. Their heads are so large and heavy that young infants lack the strength to raise them. Because their limbs are short in relation to the rest of the body, their movements are further impeded. Furthermore, their bodies are mainly fat, with a limited amount of muscle; the result is that they lack strength.

Fortunately, it doesn't take too long before infants begin to develop a remarkable amount of mobility. Actually, even at birth they have an extensive repertoire of behavioral possibilities brought about by innate reflexes, and their range of motor skills grows rapidly during the first 2 years of life.

Reflexes: Our Inborn Physical Skills

LO 4.5 Explain how the reflexes that infants are born with help them adapt to their surroundings and protect themselves.

When her father pressed 3-day-old Christina's palm with his finger, she responded by tightly winding her small fist around his finger and grasping it. When he moved his finger upward, she held on so tightly that it seemed he might be able to lift her completely off her crib floor.

reflexes
unlearned, organized, involuntary responses that occur automatically in the presence of certain stimuli

THE BASIC REFLEXES. Her father was right: Christina probably could have been lifted in this way. The reason for her resolute grip was activation of one of the dozens of reflexes with which infants are born. **Reflexes** are unlearned, organized, involuntary responses

Table 4-3 Some Basic Reflexes in Infants

Reflex	Approximate Age of Disappearance	Description	Possible Function
Rooting reflex	3 weeks	Neonate's tendency to turn its head toward things that touch its cheek.	Food intake
Stepping reflex	2 months	Movement of legs when held upright with feet touching the floor.	Prepares infants for independent locomotion
Swimming reflex	4–6 months	Infant's tendency to paddle and kick in a sort of swimming motion when lying facedown in a body of water.	Avoidance of danger
Grasping reflex	5–6 months	Infant's fingers close around an object placed in its hands.	Provides support
Moro reflex	6 months	Activated when support for the neck and head is suddenly removed. The arms of the infant are thrust outward and then appear to grasp onto something.	Similar to primates' protection from falling
Babinski reflex	8–12 months	An infant fans out its toes in response to a stroke on the outside of its foot.	Unknown
Startle reflex	Remains in different form	An infant, in response to a sudden noise, flings out its arms, arches its back, and spreads its fingers.	Protection
Eye-blink reflex	Remains	Rapid shutting and opening of eye on exposure to direct light.	Protection of eye from direct light
Sucking reflex	Remains	Infant's tendency to suck at things that touch its lips.	Food intake
Gag reflex	Remains	An infant's reflex to clear its throat.	Prevents choking

that occur automatically in the presence of certain stimuli. Newborns enter the world with a repertoire of reflexive behavioral patterns that help them adapt to their new surroundings and serve to protect them.

As we can see from the list of reflexes in Table 4-3, many reflexes clearly represent behavior that has survival value, helping to ensure the well-being of the infant. For instance, the *swimming reflex* makes a baby who is lying facedown in a body of water paddle and kick in a sort of swimming motion. The obvious consequence of such behavior is to help the baby move from danger and survive until a caregiver can come to its rescue. Similarly, the *eye-blink reflex* seems designed to protect the eye from too much direct light, which might damage the retina.

Given the protective value of many reflexes, it might seem beneficial for them to remain with us for our entire lives. In fact, some do: The eye-blink reflex remains functional throughout the full life span. But quite a few reflexes, such as the swimming reflex, disappear after a few months. Why should this be the case?

Researchers who focus on evolutionary explanations of development attribute the gradual disappearance of reflexes to the increase in voluntary control over behavior that occurs as infants become more able to control their muscles. In addition, it may be that reflexes form the foundation for future, more complex behaviors. As these more intricate behaviors become well learned, they encompass the earlier reflexes (Myklebust & Gottlieb, 1993; Lipsitt, 2003).

It may be that reflexes stimulate parts of the brain responsible for more complex behaviors, helping them develop. For example, some researchers argue that exercise of the stepping reflex helps the brain's cortex develop the ability to walk. As evidence, developmental psychologist Philip R. Zelazo and his colleagues conducted a study in which they provided 2-week-old infants practice in walking for four sessions of 3 minutes each over a 6-week period. The results showed that the children who had the walking practice actually began to walk unaided several months earlier than those who had no such practice. Zelazo suggests that the training produced stimulation of the stepping reflex, which in

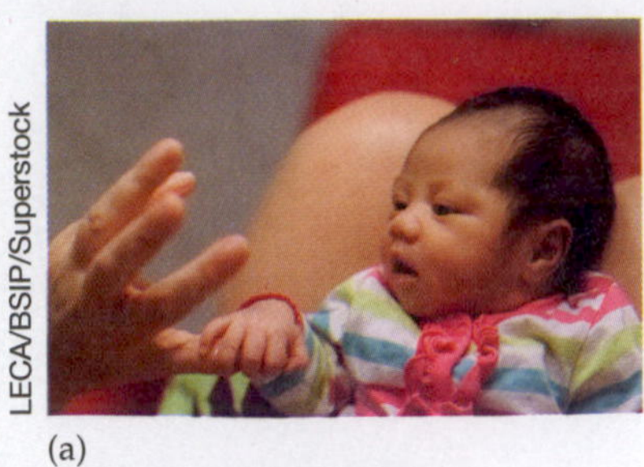
LECA/BSIP/Superstock

(a)

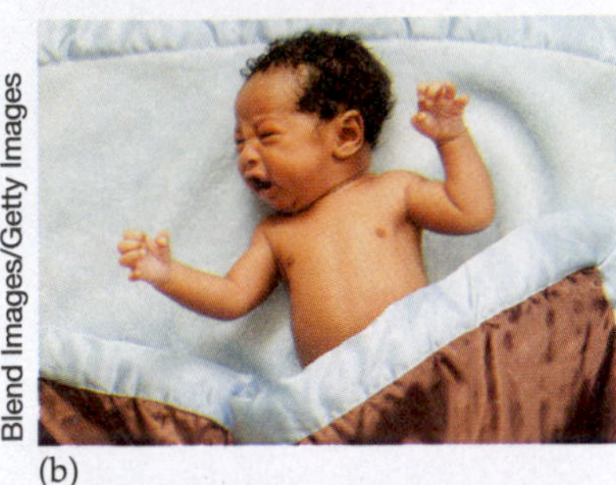
Blend Images/Getty Images

(b)

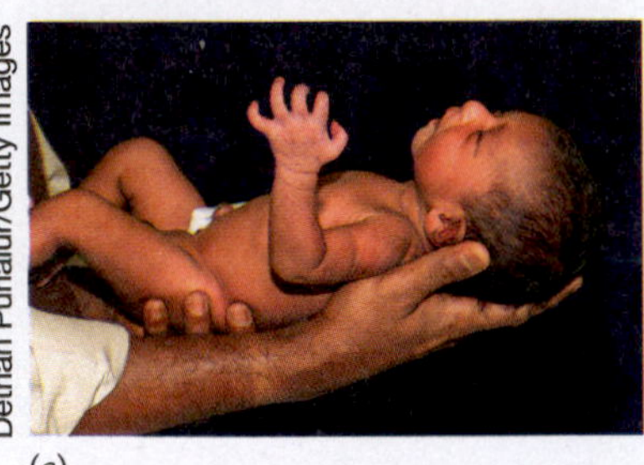
Dethan Punalur/Getty Images

(c)

Infants showing (a) the grasping reflex, (b) the startle reflex, and (c) the Moro reflex.

turn led to stimulation of the brain's cortex, readying the infant earlier for independent locomotion (Zelazo, 1998; Corbetta, Friedman & Bell, 2014).

Do these findings suggest that parents should make out-of-the-ordinary efforts to stimulate their infant's reflexes? Probably not. Although the evidence shows that intensive practice may produce an earlier appearance of certain motor activities, there is no evidence that the activities are performed qualitatively any better in practiced infants than in unpracticed infants. Furthermore, even when early gains are found, they do not seem to produce an adult who is more proficient in motor skills.

In fact, structured exercise may do more harm than good. According to the American Academy of Pediatrics, structured exercise for infants may lead to muscle strain, fractured bones, and dislocated limbs, consequences that far outweigh the unproven benefits that may come from the practice (National Association for Sport and Physical Education, 2006).

ETHNIC AND CULTURAL DIFFERENCES AND SIMILARITIES IN REFLEXES. Although reflexes are, by definition, genetically determined and universal throughout all infants, there are actually some cultural variations in the ways they are displayed. For instance, consider the *Moro reflex*, which is activated when support for the neck and head is suddenly removed. The Moro reflex consists of the infant's arms thrusting outward and then appearing to seek to grasp onto something. Most scientists feel that the Moro reflex represents a leftover response that we humans have inherited from our nonhuman ancestors. The Moro reflex is an extremely useful behavior for monkey babies, who travel about by clinging to their mothers' backs. If they lose their grip, they fall down unless they are able to grasp quickly onto their mother's fur—using a Moro-like reflex (Zafeiriou, 2004; Rousseau et al., 2017).

The Moro reflex is found in all humans, but it appears with significantly different vigor in different children. Some differences reflect cultural and ethnic variations (Freedman, 1979). For instance, Caucasian infants show a pronounced response to situations that produce the Moro reflex. Not only do they fling out their arms, but they also cry and respond in a generally agitated manner. In contrast, Navajo babies react to the same situation much more calmly. Their arms do not flail out as much, and they cry only rarely.

In some cases, reflexes can serve as helpful diagnostic tools for pediatricians. Because reflexes emerge and disappear on a regular timetable, their absence—or presence—at a given point of infancy can provide a clue that something may be amiss in an infant's development. (Even for adults, physicians include reflexes in their diagnostic bags of tricks, as anyone knows who has had his or her knee tapped with a rubber mallet to see if the lower leg jerks forward.)

Reflexes evolved because, at one point in humankind's history, they had survival value. For example, the sucking reflex automatically helps infants obtain nourishment, and the rooting reflex helps them search for the presence of a nipple. In addition, some reflexes also serve a social function, promoting caregiving and nurturance. For instance, Christina's father, who found his daughter gripping his finger tightly when he pressed her palm, probably cares little that she is simply responding with an innate reflex. Instead, he will more likely view his daughter's action as responsiveness to him, a signal perhaps of increasing interest and affection on her part. As we will see in Chapter 6, when we discuss the social and personality development of infants, such apparent responsiveness can help cement the growing social relationship between an infant and its caregivers.

Motor Development in Infancy: Landmarks of Physical Achievement

LO 4.6 Summarize the landmarks of motor skill development in infancy.

Probably no physical changes are more obvious—and more eagerly anticipated—than the increasing array of motor skills that babies acquire during infancy. Most parents can remember their child's first steps with a sense of pride and awe at how quickly she or he

Figure 4-8 Milestones of Motor Development

Fifty percent of children are able to perform each skill at the month indicated in the figure. However, the specific timing at which each skill develops varies widely. For example, one-quarter of children are able to walk well at 11.1 months; by 14.9 months, 90 percent of children are walking well. Is knowledge of such average benchmarks helpful or harmful to parents?

(**Source:** Adapted from Frankenburg et al., 1992.)

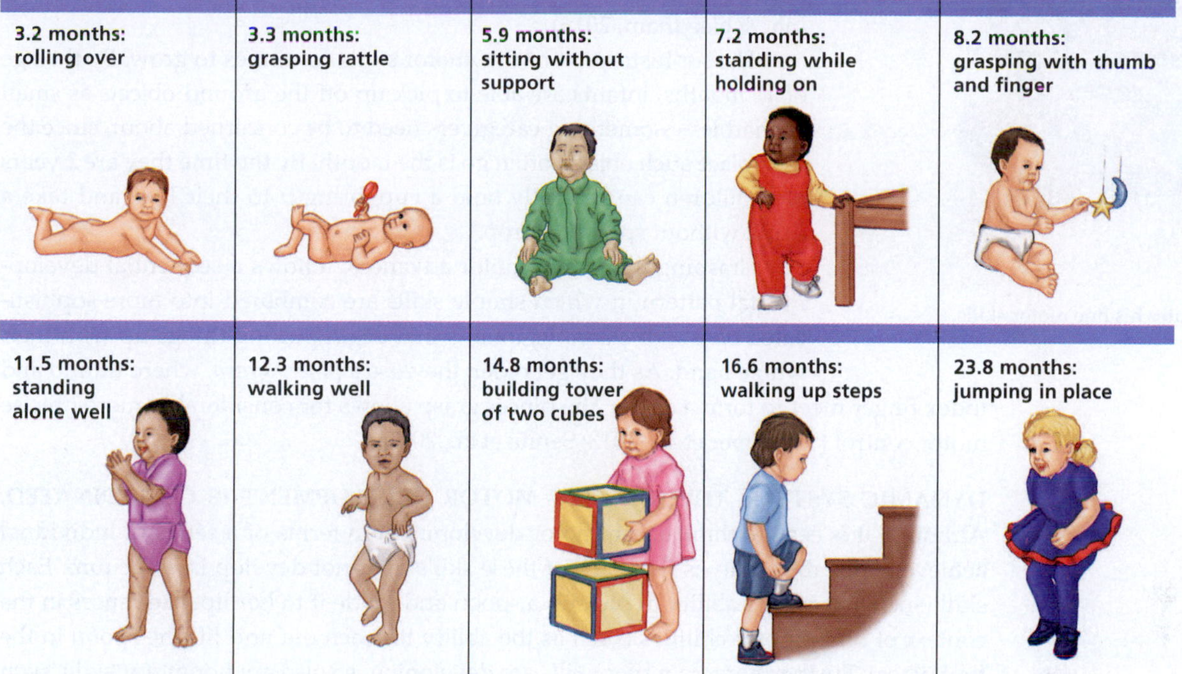

changed from a helpless infant, unable even to roll over, into a person who could navigate quite effectively in the world.

GROSS MOTOR SKILLS. Even though the motor skills of newborn infants are not terribly sophisticated, at least compared with attainments that will soon appear, young infants still are able to accomplish some kinds of movement. For instance, when placed on their stomachs, they wiggle their arms and legs and may try to lift their heavy heads. As their strength increases, they are able to push hard enough against the surface on which they are resting to propel their bodies in different directions. They often end up moving backward rather than forward, but by the age of 6 months they become rather accomplished at moving themselves in particular directions. These initial efforts are the forerunners of crawling, in which babies coordinate the motions of their arms and legs and propel themselves forward. Crawling develops typically between 8 and 10 months. Figure 4-8 provides a summary of some of the milestones of normal motor development.

Walking comes later. At around the age of 9 months, most infants are able to walk by supporting themselves on furniture, and half of all infants can walk well by the end of their first year of life.

At the same time infants are learning to move around, they are perfecting the ability to remain in a stationary sitting position. At first, babies cannot remain seated upright without support. But they quickly master this ability, and most are able to sit without support by the age of 6 months.

FINE MOTOR SKILLS. As infants are perfecting their gross motor skills, such as sitting upright and walking, they are also making advances in their fine motor skills. For instance, by the age of 3 months, infants show some ability to coordinate the movements of their limbs.

This infant demonstrates his fine motor skills.

Furthermore, although infants are born with a rudimentary ability to reach toward an object, this ability is neither very sophisticated nor very accurate, and it disappears around the age of 4 weeks. A different, more precise form of reaching reappears at 4 months. It takes some time for infants to coordinate successful grasping after they reach out, but in fairly short order they are able to reach out and hold onto an object of interest (Daum, Prinz, & Aschersleben, 2011; Foroud, & Whishaw, 2012; Libertus, Joh, & Needham, 2016).

The sophistication of fine motor skills continues to grow. By the age of 11 months, infants are able to pick up off the ground objects as small as marbles—something caregivers need to be concerned about, since the next place such objects often go is the mouth. By the time they are 2 years old, children can carefully hold a cup, bring it to their lips, and take a drink without spilling a drop.

Grasping, like other motor advances, follows a sequential developmental pattern in which simple skills are combined into more sophisticated ones. For example, infants first begin picking things up with their whole hand. As they get older, they use a *pincer grasp*, where thumb and index finger meet to form a circle. The pincer grasp allows for considerably more precise motor control (Thoermer et al., 2013; Senna et al., 2017).

DYNAMIC SYSTEMS THEORY: HOW MOTOR DEVELOPMENT IS COORDINATED. Although it is easy to think about motor development in terms of a series of individual achievements, the reality is that each of these skills does not develop in a vacuum. Each skill (such as a baby's ability to pick up a spoon and guide it to her lips) advances in the context of other motor abilities (such as the ability to reach out and lift the spoon in the first place). Furthermore, as motor skills are developing, so also are nonmotor skills such as visual capabilities.

dynamic systems theory
a theory of how motor skills develop and are coordinated

Developmentalist Esther Thelen has created an innovative theory to explain how motor skills develop and are coordinated. **Dynamic systems theory** describes how motor behaviors are assembled. By "assembled," Thelen means the coordination of a variety of skills that develop in a child, ranging from the development of an infant's muscles to its perceptual abilities and nervous system, as well as its motivation to carry out particular motor activities, and support from the environment (Gershkoff-Stowe & Thelen, 2004; Thelen & Smith, 2006; Perone & Simmering, 2017).

According to dynamic systems theory, motor development in a particular sphere, such as beginning to crawl, is not just dependent on the brain initiating a "crawling program" that permits the muscles to propel the baby forward. Instead, crawling requires the coordination of muscles, perception, cognition, and motivation. The theory emphasizes how children's exploratory activities, which produce new challenges as they interact with their environment, lead them to advancements in motor skills (Corbetta & Snapp-Childs, 2009).

Dynamic systems theory is noteworthy for its emphasis on a child's own motivation (a cognitive state) in advancing important aspects of motor development. For example, infants need to be motivated to touch something out of their reach in order to develop the skills they need to crawl to it. The theory also may help explain individual differences in the emergence of motor abilities in different children, which we consider next.

DEVELOPMENTAL NORMS: COMPARING THE INDIVIDUAL TO THE GROUP. Keep in mind that the timing of the milestones in motor development that we have been discussing is based on norms. **Norms** represent the average performance of a large sample of children of a given age. They permit comparisons between a particular child's performance on a particular behavior and the average performance of the children in the norm sample.

norm
the average performance of a large sample of children of a given age

For instance, one of the most widely used techniques to determine infants' normative standing is the **Brazelton Neonatal Behavioral Assessment Scale (NBAS)**, a measure designed to determine infants' neurological and behavioral responses to their environment.

Brazelton Neonatal Behavioral Assessment Scale (NBAS)
a measure designed to determine infants' neurological and behavioral responses to their environment

The NBAS provides a supplement to the traditional Apgar test that is given immediately following birth. Taking about 30 minutes to administer, the NBAS includes 27 separate categories of responses that constitute four general aspects of infants' behavior: interactions with others (such as alertness and cuddliness), motor behavior, physiological control (such as the ability to be soothed after being upset), and responses to stress (Brazelton, 1990; Canals, Fernandez-Ballart, & Espuro, 2003; Ohta & Ohgi, 2013).

Although the norms provided by scales such as the NBAS are useful in making broad generalizations about the timing of various behaviors and skills, they must be interpreted with caution. Because norms are averages, they mask substantial individual differences in the timing of attaining various achievements. For example, some children may be ahead of the norm. Other perfectly normal children may be a bit behind. Norms also may hide the fact that the sequence in which various behaviors are achieved may differ somewhat from one child to another (Boatella-Costa et al., 2007; Noble & Boyd, 2012).

Norms are useful only to the extent that they are based on data from a large, heterogeneous, culturally diverse sample of children. Unfortunately, many of the norms on which developmental researchers have traditionally relied have been based on groups of infants who are predominantly Caucasian and from the middle and upper socioeconomic strata. The reason: much of the research was conducted on college campuses, using the children of graduate students and faculty.

This limitation would not be critical if no differences existed in the timing of development in children from different cultural, racial, and social groups. But they do. For example, as a group, African American babies show more rapid motor development than Caucasian babies throughout infancy. Moreover, there are significant variations related to cultural factors, as we discuss in the *Developmental Diversity and Your Life* box (de Onis et al., 2007; Wu et al., 2008; Mendonça, Sargent, & Fetters, 2016).

Nutrition in Infancy: Fueling Motor Development

LO 4.7 Summarize the role of nutrition in the physical development of infants.

Rosa sighed as she sat down to nurse the baby—again. She had fed 4-week-old Juan about every hour today, and he still seemed hungry. Some days, it seemed as if all she did was breastfeed her baby. "Well, he must be going through a growth spurt," she decided, as she settled into her favorite rocking chair and put the baby to her nipple.

The rapid physical growth that occurs during infancy is fueled by the nutrients that infants receive. Without proper nutrition, infants cannot reach their physical potential, and they may suffer cognitive and social consequences as well (Tanner & Finn-Stevenson, 2002; Costello, Compton, & Keeler, 2003; Gregory, 2005).

Although there are vast individual differences in what constitutes appropriate nutrition—infants differ in terms of growth rates, body composition, metabolism, and activity levels—some broad guidelines do hold. In general, infants should consume about 50 calories per day for each pound they weigh—an allotment that is twice the suggested caloric intake for adults (Dietz & Stern, 1999; Skinner et al., 2004).

Typically, though, it's not necessary to count calories for infants. Most infants regulate their caloric intake quite effectively on their own. If they are allowed to consume as much as they seem to want, and not pressured to eat more, they will do fine.

MALNUTRITION. *Malnutrition*, the condition of having an improper amount and balance of nutrients, produces several results—none of them good. For instance, malnutrition is more common among children living in many developing countries than among children who live in more industrialized, affluent countries. Malnourished children in these countries begin to show a slower growth rate by the age of 6 months. By the time they reach the age of 2 years, their height and weight are only 95 percent of the height and

Developmental Diversity and Your Life

The Cultural Dimensions of Motor Development

Among the Ache people, *who live in the rain forest of South America, infants face an early life of physical restriction. Because the Ache lead a nomadic existence, living in a series of tiny camps in the rain forest, open space is at a premium. Consequently, for the first few years of life, infants spend nearly all their time in direct physical contact with their mothers. Even when they are not physically touching their mothers, they are permitted to venture no more than a few feet away.*

***

Infants among the Kipsigis people, *who live in a more open environment in rural Kenya, Africa, lead quite a different existence. Their lives are filled with activity and exercise. Parents seek to teach their children to sit up, stand, and walk from the earliest days of infancy. For example, very young infants are placed in shallow holes in the ground designed to keep them in an upright position. Parents begin to teach their children to walk starting at the eighth week of life. The infants are held with their feet touching the ground, and they are pushed forward.*

poco_bw/Fotolia

Cultural influences affect the rate of the development of motor skills.

Clearly, the infants in these two societies lead very different lives (Super, 1976; Kaplan & Dove, 1987). But do the relative lack of early motor stimulation for Ache infants and the efforts of the Kipsigis to encourage motor development really make a difference?

The answer is both yes and no. It's yes in that Ache infants tend to show delayed motor development relative both to Kipsigis infants and to children raised in Western societies. Although their social abilities are no different, Ache children tend to begin walking at around 23 months, about a year later than the typical child in the United States. In contrast, Kipsigis children, who are encouraged in their motor development, learn to sit up and walk several weeks earlier, on average, than U.S. children.

In the long run, however, the differences between Ache, Kipsigis, and Western children disappear. By about age 6, there is no evidence of differences in overall motor skills among Ache, Kipsigis, and Western children.

As we see with the Ache and Kipsigis babies, variations in the timing of motor skills seem to depend in part on parental expectations of what is the "appropriate" schedule for the emergence of specific skills. For instance, one study examined the motor skills of infants who lived in a single city in England but whose mothers had varied ethnic origins. In the research, English, Jamaican, and Indian mothers' expectations were first assessed regarding several markers of their infants' motor skills. The Jamaican mothers expected their infants to sit and walk significantly earlier than the English and Indian mothers, and the actual emergence of these activities was in line with their expectations. The source of the Jamaican infants' earlier mastery seemed to lie in the treatment of the children by their parents. For instance, Jamaican mothers gave their children practice in stepping quite early in infancy (Hopkins & Westra, 1989, 1990).

In sum, cultural factors help determine the time at which specific motor skills appear. Activities that are an intrinsic part of a culture are more apt to be purposely taught to infants in that culture, leading to the potential of their earlier emergence (Nugent, Lester, & Brazelton, 1989).

It is not all that surprising that children in a given culture who are expected by their parents to master a particular skill, and who are taught components of that skill from an early age, are more likely to be proficient in that skill earlier than children from other cultures with no such expectations and no such training. The larger question, however, is whether the earlier emergence of a basic motor behavior in a given culture has lasting consequences for specific motor skills and for achievements in other domains. On this issue, the jury is still out.

It is clear, however, that there are certain limitations on how early a skill can emerge. It is physically impossible for 1-month-old infants to stand and walk, regardless of the encouragement and practice they may get within their culture. Parents who are eager to accelerate their infants' motor development, then, should be cautioned not to hold overly ambitious goals. They might well ask themselves whether it matters if an infant acquires a motor skill a few weeks earlier than his or her peers.

The most reasonable answer is no. Although some parents may take pride in a child who walks earlier than other babies (just as some parents may be concerned over a delay of a few weeks), in the long run, the timing of this activity will probably make no difference.

Figure 4-9 Undernutrition by Country

Undernutrition is widespread across the globe. **THINKING ABOUT THE DATA:** What countries in Africa have higher and lower rates of underweight children? What about Asia?

(**Source:** UNICEF, May 2017).

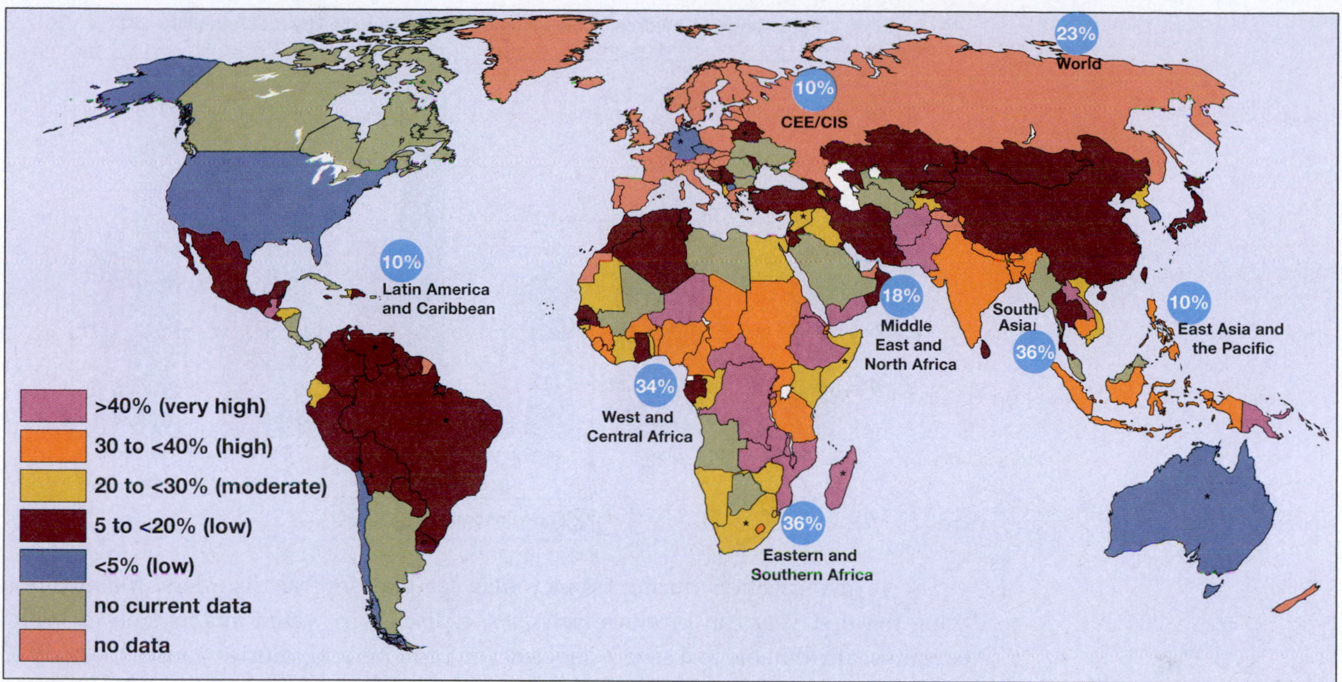

weight of children in more industrialized countries. In addition, children who have been chronically malnourished during infancy later score lower on IQ tests and tend to do less well in school. These effects may linger even after the children's diet has improved substantially (Ratanachu-Ek, 2003; Waber et al., 2014; Peter et al., 2016).

The problem of malnutrition is greatest in underdeveloped countries, where overall 10 percent of infants are severely malnourished (see Figure 4-9). In some countries, the problem is especially severe. Undernutrition is a problem across the globe, and is particularly widespread in Asia and Africa (UNICEF, 2016). For example, 25 percent of North Korean children are stunted from chronic malnutrition, and 4 percent are acutely malnourished (Chaudhary & Sharma, 2012; United Nations World Food Programme, 2013).

Problems of malnourishment are not restricted to developing countries, however. In the United States, around 20 percent of children live in poverty, which puts them at risk for malnutrition. Overall, some 26 percent of families who have children 3 years old and younger live in poverty, and 6 percent of Americans live in extreme poverty, meaning their income is $10,000 a year or less (see Figure 4-10).

From *an educator's* perspective

Think of reasons why malnourishment, which slows physical growth, also harms IQ scores and school performance. How might malnourishment affect education in developing countries?

A variety of social service programs, such as the federal Supplemental Nutrition Assistance Program (SNAP), have been created to combat this issue. These programs mean that children rarely become severely malnourished, but such children remain susceptible to *undernutrition*, in which there is some deficiency in diet. Some surveys find that as many as a quarter of 1- to 5-year-old children in the United States have diets that fall below the minimum caloric intake recommended by nutritional experts. Although the consequences are not as severe as those of malnutrition, undernutrition also has long-term costs. For instance, cognitive development later in childhood is affected by even mild to moderate undernutrition (Tanner & Finn-Stevenson, 2002; Lian et al., 2012).

Figure 4-10 Children Living in Poverty

Members of black, American Indian, and Hispanic households are more likely to live in poverty than members of white and Asian families.

(**Source:** National Center for Children in Poverty at the Joseph L. Mailman School of Public Health of Columbia University, 2013.)

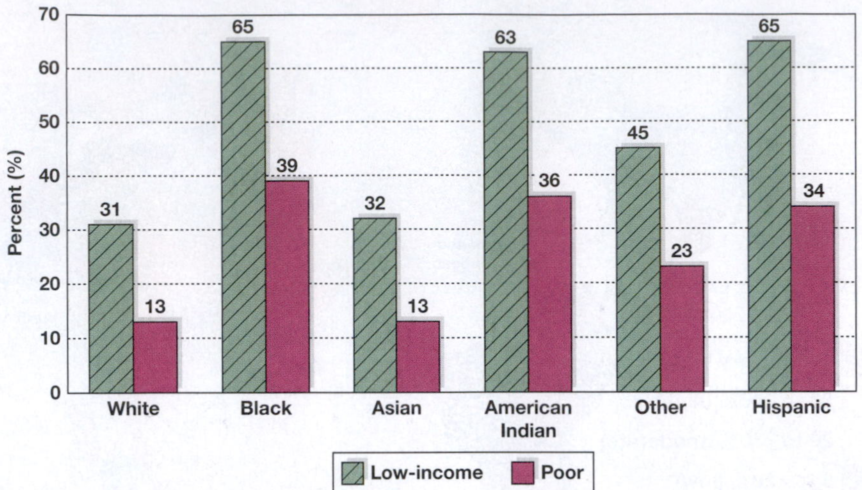

Severe malnutrition during infancy may lead to several disorders. Malnutrition during the first year can produce *marasmus*, a disease in which infants stop growing. Marasmus, attributable to a severe deficiency in proteins and calories, causes the body to waste away; it ultimately results in death. Older children are susceptible to *kwashiorkor*, a disease in which a child's stomach, limbs, and face swell with water. To a casual observer, it appears that a child with kwashiorkor is actually chubby. However, this is an illusion: The child's body is in fact struggling to make use of the few nutrients that are available (Douglass & McGadney-Douglass, 2008).

nonorganic failure to thrive
a disorder in which infants stop growing due to a lack of stimulation and attention as the result of inadequate parenting

In some cases, infants who receive sufficient nutrition act as though they have been deprived of food. Looking as though they suffer from marasmus, they are underdeveloped, listless, and apathetic. The real cause, however, is emotional: They lack sufficient love and emotional support. In such cases, known as **nonorganic failure to thrive**, children stop growing not for biological reasons but due to a lack of stimulation and attention from their parents. Usually occurring by the age of 18 months, nonorganic failure to thrive can be reversed through intensive parent training or by placing children in a foster home where they can receive emotional support.

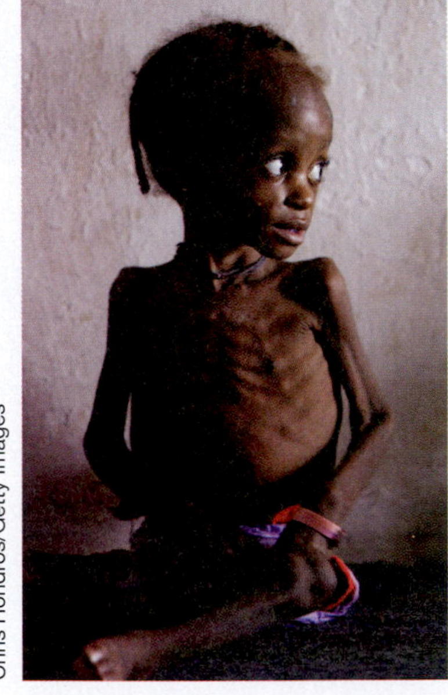

Chris Hondros/Getty Images

Malnourishment at an early age can lower IQ scores, even if diet improves later. How might this deficit be overcome?

OBESITY. It is clear that malnourishment during infancy has potentially disastrous consequences for an infant. Less clear, however, are the effects of *obesity*, defined as weight greater than 20 percent above the average for a given height.

While there is no clear association between obesity during infancy and obesity during adolescence, some research suggests that overfeeding during infancy may lead to the creation of an excess of fat cells, which remain in the body throughout life and may predispose a person to be overweight. Weight during infancy is associated with weight at age 6 and adult obesity, suggesting that obesity in babies ultimately may be found to be associated with adult weight problems. A clear link between overweight babies and overweight adults, however, has not yet been found (Taveras et al., 2009; Carnell et al., 2013; Murasko, 2015; Mallan et al., 2016).

Although the evidence linking infant obesity to adult obesity is inconclusive, it's plain that the societal view that "a fat baby is a healthy baby" is not necessarily correct. Indeed, cultural myths about food clearly lead to overfeeding. But other factors are related to obesity in infants. For example, infants delivered via cesarean section are twice as likely to become obese as infants born vaginally (Huh et al., 2011).

Given the lack of clarity regarding infant obesity, parents should concentrate less on their baby's weight and more on providing appropriate nutrition. But just what constitutes proper nutrition? Probably the biggest question revolves around whether infants should be breastfed or given a formula of commercially processed cow's milk with vitamin additives, as we consider next.

Breast or Bottle?

LO 4.8 Summarize the benefits of breastfeeding in infancy.

Fifty years ago, if a mother asked her pediatrician whether breastfeeding or bottle-feeding was better, she would have received a simple and clear-cut answer: Bottle-feeding was the preferred method. Starting around the 1940s, the general belief among child-care experts was that breastfeeding was an obsolete method that put children unnecessarily at risk.

With bottle-feeding, the argument went, parents could keep track of the amount of milk their baby was receiving and could thereby ensure that the child was taking in sufficient nutrients. In contrast, mothers who breastfed their babies could never be certain just how much milk their infants were getting. Use of the bottle was also supposed to help mothers keep their feedings to a rigid schedule of one bottle every 4 hours, the recommended procedure at that time.

Today, however, a mother would get a very different answer to the same question. Child-care authorities agree: For the first 12 months of life, there is no better food for an infant than breast milk. Breast milk not only contains all the nutrients necessary for growth, but it also seems to offer some immunity to a variety of childhood diseases, such as respiratory illnesses, ear infections, diarrhea, and allergies. Breastfeeding for as little as 4 months reduces infections by an average of 45 percent, and the reduction in infection is 65 percent lower for 6 months of breastfeeding compared to formula-fed babies. Breast milk is more easily digested than cow's milk or formula, and it is convenient for the mother to dispense. There is even some evidence that breast milk may enhance cognitive growth, leading to high adult intelligence (Duijts et al., 2010; Julvez et al., 2014; Rogers & Blissett, 2017).

Breast milk also contains complex carbohydrates called *oligosaccharides* (which are also found in such foods as asparagus, onions, wheat, and barley). Humans can't digest oligosaccharides, but bacteria can, pointing to the role of breast milk in nurturing the bacteria that normally thrive in the human gut and provide important protective functions. It turns out that these oligosaccharides are very specific: Only one species of bacterium, called *B. longum* bv. *infantis*, has all the enzymes necessary to digest them. This enables that species of bacteria to dominate any others inhabiting the infant gut, and crowding out other, potentially harmful, species of bacteria. In short, the oligosaccharides found in breast milk may provide long-term health benefits and aid in the avoidance of future problems such as diabetes and immune system difficulties (Vinukonda et al., 2016); Qiu et al., 2016).

Breastfeeding also offers significant emotional advantages for both mother and child. Most mothers report that the experience of breastfeeding brings about feelings of well-being and intimacy with their infants, perhaps because of the production of endorphins in mothers' brains. Breastfed infants are also more responsive to their mothers' touch and their mothers' gaze during feeding, and they are calmed and soothed by the experience. As we'll see in Chapter 7, this mutual responsiveness may lead to healthy social development (Gerrish & Mennella, 2000; Zanardo et al., 2001).

Breastfeeding may even be advantageous to *mothers'* health. For instance, research suggests that women who breastfeed may have lower rates of ovarian cancer and breast cancer prior to menopause. Furthermore, the hormones produced during breastfeeding help shrink the uteruses of women following birth, enabling their bodies to return more quickly to a prepregnancy state. These hormones also may inhibit ovulation, reducing

Oksana Kuzmina/Shutterstock

Photodisc/Getty Images

Breast or bottle? Although infants receive adequate nourishment from breast- or bottle-feeding, most authorities agree that "breast is best."

Infants generally start solid foods at around 4 to 6 months, gradually working their way up to a variety of different foods.

(but not eliminating!) the chance of becoming pregnant, and thereby helping to space the birth of additional children (Kim et al., 2007; Pearson, Lightman, & Evans, 2011: Kornides & Kitsantas, 2013).

Breastfeeding is not a cure-all for infant nutrition and health, and the millions of individuals who have been raised on formula should not be concerned that they have suffered irreparable harm. (Recent research suggests that infants fed enriched formula show better cognitive development than those using traditional formula.) But it does continue to be clear that the popular slogan used by groups advocating the use of breastfeeding is right on target: "Breast Is Best" (Auestad et al., 2003; Rabin, 2006; Ludlow et al., 2012).

INTRODUCING SOLID FOODS: WHEN AND WHAT? Although pediatricians agree that breast milk is the ideal initial food, at some point infants require more nutrients than breast milk alone can provide. Although the American Academy of Pediatrics and the American Academy of Family Physicians recommends exclusive breastfeeding for about 6 months, followed by continued breastfeeding for 1 year or longer, solid foods can begin to be introduced after 6 months (American Academy of Pediatrics, 2013).

Solid foods are introduced into an infant's diet gradually, one at a time, in order to identify preferences and allergies. Most often cereal comes first, followed by strained fruits. Vegetables and other foods typically are introduced next, although the order varies significantly from one infant to another.

The timing of *weaning*, the gradual cessation of breast- or bottle-feeding, varies greatly. In developed countries such as the United States, weaning frequently occurs as early as 3 or 4 months. However, some mothers continue breastfeeding for 2 or 3 years. The American Academy of Pediatrics recommends that infants be fed breast milk for the first 12 months (American Academy of Pediatrics, 2013; Lee, 2017).

Module 4.2 Review

LO 4.5 Explain how the reflexes that infants are born with help them adapt to their surroundings and protect themselves.

Reflexes are universal, genetically acquired physical behaviors.

LO 4.6 Summarize the landmarks of motor skill development in infancy.

During infancy, children reach a series of milestones in their physical development on a fairly consistent schedule, with some individual and cultural variations. Training and cultural expectations affect the timing of the development of motor skills.

LO 4.7 Summarize the role of nutrition in the physical development of infants.

Nutrition strongly affects physical development. Malnutrition can slow growth, affect intellectual performance, and cause diseases such as marasmus and kwashiorkor. The victims of undernutrition also suffer negative effects.

LO 4.8 Summarize the benefits of breastfeeding in infancy.

The advantages of breastfeeding are numerous, including nutritional, immunological, emotional, and physical benefits for the infant, and physical and emotional benefits for the mother.

Journal Writing Prompt

Applying Lifespan Development: What advice might you give a friend who is concerned that her infant is still not walking at 14 months, when every other baby she knows started walking by the first birthday?

The Development of the Senses

William James (1842–1910), one of the founding fathers of psychology, believed that the world of the infant is a "blooming, buzzing confusion" (James, 1890/1950). Was he right?

In this case, James's wisdom failed him. The newborn's sensory world does lack the clarity and stability that we can distinguish as adults, but day by day, the world grows increasingly comprehensible as the infant's ability to sense and perceive the environment develops. In fact, as we'll see in this section, babies appear to thrive in an environment enriched by pleasing sensations.

Visual Perception: Seeing the World

LO 4.9 Describe the capabilities of infants in the realm of visual perception.

The processes that underlie infants' understanding of the world around them are sensation and perception. **Sensation** is the physical stimulation of the sense organs, and **perception** is the mental process of sorting out, interpreting, analyzing, and integrating stimuli from the sense organs and the brain.

sensation
the physical stimulation of the sense organs

perception
the sorting out, interpretation, analysis, and integration of stimuli involving the sense organs and the brain

The study of infants' capabilities in the realm of sensation and perception challenges the ingenuity of investigators. And researchers have developed a number of procedures for understanding sensation and perception in different realms. Take, for instance Lee Eng, a typical infant. From the time of Lee Eng's birth, everyone who met him felt that he gazed at them intently. His eyes seemed to meet those of visitors. They seemed to bore deeply and knowingly into the faces of people who looked at him.

How good, in fact, was Lee's vision, and what, precisely, could he make out of his environment? Quite a bit, at least up close. According to some estimates, a newborn's distance vision ranges from 20/200 to 20/600, which means that an infant can see with accuracy visual material up to 20 feet that an adult with normal vision is able to see with similar accuracy from a distance of between 200 and 600 feet (Haith, 1991; Jones et al., 2015).

These figures indicate that infants' distance vision is one-tenth to one-third that of the average adult's. This isn't so bad, actually: The vision of newborns provides the same degree of distance acuity as the uncorrected vision of many adults who wear eyeglasses or contact lenses. (If you wear glasses or contact lenses, remove them to get a sense of what an infant can see of the world.) Furthermore, infants' distance vision grows increasingly acute. By 6 months of age, the average infant's vision is already 20/20—in other words, identical to that of adults (Cavallini, Fazzi, & Viviani, 2002; Corrow et al., 2012).

Other visual abilities grow rapidly. For instance, *binocular vision*, the ability to combine the images coming to each eye to see depth and motion, is achieved at around 14 weeks. Before then, infants do not integrate the information from each eye.

Depth perception is a particularly useful ability, helping babies acknowledge heights and avoid falls. In a classic study by developmental psychologists Eleanor Gibson and Richard Walk (1960), infants were placed on a sheet of heavy glass. A checkered pattern appeared under one-half of the glass sheet, making it seem that the infant was on a stable floor. However, in the middle of the glass sheet, the pattern dropped down several feet, forming an apparent "visual cliff." Gibson and Walk asked this question: Would infants willingly crawl across the cliff when called by their mothers (see Figure 4-11)?

The results were unambiguous. Most of the infants in the study, who ranged in age from 6 to 14 months, could not be coaxed over the apparent cliff. Clearly, the ability to perceive depth had already developed in most of them by that age. However, the experiment did not pinpoint when depth perception emerged, since only infants who had already learned to crawl could be tested. But other experiments, in which infants of 2 and 3 months were placed on their stomachs above the apparent floor and above the visual cliff, revealed differences in heart rate between the two positions (Campos, Langer, & Krowitz, 1970; Kretch & Adolph, 2013; Adolph, Kretch, & LoBue, 2014).

Sporrer/Getty Images

While an infant's vision is poorer than the average adult's, the vision of newborns provides the same degree of distance acuity as the uncorrected vision of many adults who wear eyeglasses or contact lenses.

Still, it is important to keep in mind that such findings do not permit us to know whether infants are responding to depth itself or merely to the *change* in visual stimuli that occurs when they are moved from a lack of depth to depth.

Infants also show clear visual preferences, preferences that are present from birth. Given a choice, infants reliably prefer to look at stimuli that include patterns than to look at simpler stimuli (see Figure 4-12). How do we know? Developmental psychologist Robert Fantz (1963) created a classic test. He built a chamber in which babies could

Figure 4-11 Visual Cliff

The "visual cliff" experiment examines the depth perception of infants. Most infants in the age range of 6 to 14 months cannot be coaxed to cross the cliff, apparently responding to the fact that the patterned area drops several feet.

Mark Richard/PhotoEdit

Figure 4-12 Preferring Complexity

In a classic experiment, researcher Robert Fantz found that 2- and 3-month-old infants preferred to look at more complex stimuli than simple ones.

(**Source:** Adapted from Fantz, 1961.)

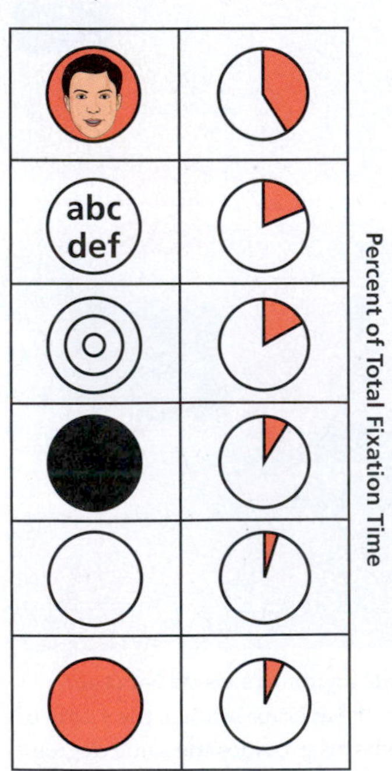

lie on their backs and see pairs of visual stimuli above them. Fantz could determine which of the stimuli the infants were looking at by observing the reflections of the stimuli in their eyes.

Fantz's work was the impetus for a great deal of research on the preferences of infants, most of which points to a critical conclusion: Infants are genetically preprogrammed to prefer particular kinds of stimuli. For instance, just minutes after birth, they show preferences for certain colors, shapes, and configurations of various stimuli. They prefer curved over straight lines, three-dimensional figures to two-dimensional ones, and human faces to nonfaces. Such capabilities may reflect the existence of highly specialized cells in the brain that react to stimuli of a particular pattern, orientation, shape, and direction of movement (Hubel & Wiesel, 2004; Kellman & Arterberry, 2006; Gliga et al., 2009).

Genetics is not the sole determinant of infant visual preferences. Just a few hours after birth, infants have already learned to prefer their own mother's face to other faces. Similarly, between the ages of 6 and 9 months, infants become more adept at distinguishing between the faces of humans, while they become less able to distinguish faces of members of other species (see Figure 4-13). They also distinguish between male and female faces. Such findings provide another clear piece of evidence of how heredity and environmental experiences are woven together to determine an infant's capabilities (Valenti, 2006; Quinn et al., 2008; Otsuka et al., 2012; Bahrick et al., 2016).

Auditory Perception: The World of Sound

LO 4.10 Describe the capabilities of infants in the realm of auditory sensation and perception.

What is it about a mother's lullaby that helps soothe a crying, fussy baby? Some clues emerge when we look at the capabilities of infants in the realm of auditory sensation and perception.

Infants hear from the time of birth—and even before. As noted in Chapter 2, the ability to hear begins prenatally. Even in the womb, the fetus responds to sounds outside of its mother. Furthermore, infants are born with preferences for particular sound combinations (Trehub, 2003; Pundir et al., 2012; Missana, Altvater-Mackensen, & Grossmann, 2017).

Because they have had some practice in hearing before birth, it is not surprising that infants have reasonably good auditory perception after they are born. Infants actually are more sensitive to certain very high and very low frequencies than adults—a sensitivity that seems to increase during the first 2 years of life. However, infants are initially less sensitive than adults to middle-range frequencies. Eventually, however, their capabilities within the middle range improve (Fernald, 2001; Lee & Kisilevsky, 2014).

It is not fully clear what, during infancy, leads to the improvement in sensitivity to middle-frequency sounds, although it may be related to the maturation of the nervous system. More puzzling is why, after infancy, children's ability to hear very high and low frequencies gradually declines. One explanation may be that exposure to high levels of noise may diminish capacities at the extreme ranges (Stewart, Scherer, & Lehman, 2003).

In addition to the ability to detect sound, infants need several other abilities in order to hear effectively. For instance, *sound localization* permits us to pinpoint the direction from which a sound is emanating. Compared to adults, infants have a slight handicap in this task because effective sound localization requires use of the slight difference in the times at which a sound reaches our two ears. Sound that we hear first in the right ear tells us that the source of the sound is to our right. Because infants' heads are smaller than those of adults, the difference in timing of the arrival of sound at the two ears is less than it is in adults, so they have difficulty determining from which direction sound is coming (Winkler et al., 2016).

Despite the potential limitation caused by their smaller heads, infants' sound localization abilities are fairly good even at birth, and they reach adult levels of success by the age of 1 year. Interestingly, their improvement is not steady: Although we don't know why, studies show that the accuracy of sound localization declines between birth and 2 months of age, but then begins to increase (Fenwick & Morrongiello, 1998; Slugocki & Trainor, 2014).

Infants can discriminate groups of different sounds, in terms of their patterns and other acoustical characteristics, quite well. For instance, infants as young as 6 months old can detect the change of a single note in a six-tone melody. They also react to changes in musical key and rhythm. In sum, they listen with a keen ear to the melodies of lullabies their mothers and fathers sing to them (Phillips-Silver & Trainor, 2005; Masataka, 2006; Trehub & Hannon, 2009).

Even more important to their ultimate success in the world, young infants are capable of making the fine discriminations that their future understanding of language will require (Bijeljac-Babic, Bertoncini, & Mehler, 1993; Gervain et al., 2008). For instance, in one classic study, a group of 1- to 4-month-old infants sucked on nipples that activated a recording of a person saying "ba" every time they sucked (Eimas et al., 1971). At first, their interest in the sound made them suck vigorously. Soon, though, they became acclimated to the sound (through a process called *habituation*, discussed in Chapter 3) and sucked with less energy. However, when the experimenters changed the sound to "pa," the infants immediately showed new interest and sucked with greater vigor once again. The clear conclusion: Infants as young as 1 month old could make the distinction between the two similar sounds (Miller & Eimas, 1995).

Even more intriguing, young infants are able to discriminate one language from another. By the age of 4½ months, infants are able to discriminate their own names from

Figure 4-13 Distinguishing Faces

Examples of faces used in a study found that 6-month-old infants distinguished human or monkey faces equally well, whereas 9-month-olds were less adept at distinguishing monkey faces as compared to human faces.

(**Source:** Pascalis, de Haan, & Nelson, 2002, p. 1322.)

other, similar-sounding words. By the age of 5 months, they can distinguish the difference between English and Spanish passages, even when the two are similar in meter, number of syllables, and speed of recitation. Some evidence suggests that even 2-day-olds show preferences for the language spoken by those around them over other languages (Chonchaiya et al., 2013; Pejovic & Molnar, 2017).

Pavel Losevsky/Fotolia

By the age of 4 months, infants are able to discriminate their own names from other, similar sounding, words. What are some ways an infant is able to discriminate his or her name from other words?

In fact, such preferences may start in the womb: Research shows that fetuses are sensitive to the rhythms of different languages and are able to discriminate between them, as evidenced by changes in heart rate depending on the kind of language they hear (Minai et al., 2017).

Given their ability to discriminate a difference in speech as slight as the difference between two consonants, it is not surprising that infants can distinguish different people on the basis of voice. From an early age they show clear preferences for some voices over others. For instance, in one experiment newborns were allowed to suck a nipple that turned on a recording of a human voice reading a story. The infants sucked significantly longer when the voice was that of their mother than when the voice was that of a stranger (DeCasper & Fifer, 1980; Fifer, 1987).

How do such preferences arise? One hypothesis is that prenatal exposure to the mother's voice is the key. As support for this conjecture, researchers point to the fact that newborns do not show a preference for their fathers' voices over other male voices. Furthermore, newborns prefer listening to melodies sung by their mothers before they were born to melodies that were not sung before birth. It seems, then, that the prenatal exposure to their mothers' voices—although muffled by the liquid environment of the womb—helps shape infants' listening preferences (DeCasper & Prescott, 1984; Jardri et al., 2012; Swingley & Humphrey, 2017).

Smell and Taste

LO 4.11 Describe the smell and taste capacities of infants.

What do infants do when they smell a rotten egg? Pretty much what adults do—crinkle their noses and generally look unhappy. By contrast, the scents of bananas and butter both produce a pleasant reaction on the part of infants (Steiner, 1979; Pomares, Schirrer, & Abadie, 2002).

The sense of smell is so well developed, even among very young infants, that at least some 12- to 18-day-old babies can distinguish their mothers on the basis of smell alone. For instance, in one experiment, infants were exposed to the smell of gauze pads worn under the arms of adults the previous evening. Infants who were being breastfed were able to distinguish their mothers' scent from those of other adults. However, not all infants could do this: Those who were being bottle-fed were unable to make the distinction. Moreover, both breastfed and bottle-fed infants were unable to distinguish their fathers on the basis of odor (Mizuno & Ueda, 2004; Allam, Marlier, & Schaal, 2006; Lipsitt & Rovee-Collier, 2012).

Shanta Giddens/Shutterstock

Infants' sense of smell is so well developed they can distinguish their mothers on the basis of smell alone.

Infants seem to have an innate sweet tooth (even before they have teeth!), and they show facial expressions of disgust when they taste something bitter. Very young infants smile when a sweet-tasting liquid is placed on their tongues. They also suck harder at a bottle if it is sweetened. Since breast milk has a sweet taste, it is possible that this preference may be part of our evolutionary heritage, retained because it offered a survival advantage. Infants who preferred sweet tastes may have been more likely to ingest sufficient nutrients and to survive than those who did not (Porges, Lipsitt, & Lewis, 1993; Blass & Camp, 2015).

Infants also develop taste preferences based on what their mothers drank while they were in the womb. For instance, one study found that women who drank carrot juice while pregnant had children who had a preference for the taste of carrots during infancy (Mennella, 2000).

Sensitivity to Pain and Touch

LO 4.12 Describe the nature of pain and touch in infants.

When Eli Rosenblatt was 8 days old, he participated in the ancient Jewish ritual of circumcision. As he lay nestled in his father's arms, the foreskin of his penis was removed. Although Eli shrieked in what seemed to his anxious parents as pain, he soon settled down and went back to sleep. Others who had watched the ceremony assured his parents that at Eli's age, babies don't really experience pain, at least not in the same way that adults do.

Were Eli's relatives accurate in saying that young infants don't experience pain? In the past, many medical practitioners would have agreed. Because they assumed that infants didn't experience pain in truly bothersome ways, many physicians routinely carried out medical procedures, and even some forms of surgery, without the use of painkillers or anesthesia. Their argument was that the risks from the use of anesthesia outweighed the potential pain that the young infants experienced.

CONTEMPORARY VIEWS ON INFANT PAIN. Today, however, it is widely acknowledged that infants are born with the capacity to experience pain. Obviously, no one can be sure if the experience of pain in children is identical to that in adults, any more than we can tell if an adult friend who complains of a headache is experiencing pain that is more or less severe than our own pain when we have a headache. What we do know is that pain produces distress in infants. Their heartbeat increases, they sweat, show facial expressions of discomfort, and they change the intensity and tone of crying when they are hurt (Kohut & Pillai Riddell, 2008; Rodkey & Riddell, 2013; Pölkki et al., 2014).

There appears to be a developmental progression in reactions to pain. For example, a newborn infant who has her heel pricked for a blood test responds with distress, but it takes her several seconds to show the response. In contrast, only a few months later, the same procedure brings a much more immediate response. It is possible that the delayed reaction in infants is produced by the relatively slower transmission of information within the newborn's less-developed nervous system (Anand & Hickey, 1992; Axia, Bonichini, & Benini, 1995; Puchalski & Hummel, 2002).

Research with rats suggests that exposure to pain in infancy may lead to a permanent rewiring of the nervous system, resulting in greater sensitivity to pain during adulthood. Such findings indicate that infants who must undergo extensive, painful medical treatments and tests may be unusually sensitive to pain when they are older (Ruda et al., 2000; Taddio et al., 2002; Ozawa et al., 2011).

In response to increasing support for the notion that infants experience pain and that its effects may be long-lasting, medical experts now endorse the use of anesthesia and painkillers during surgery for even the youngest infants. According to the American Academy of Pediatrics, painkilling drugs are appropriate in most types of surgery—including circumcision (Sato et al., 2007; Urso, 2007; Yamada et al., 2008; Lago, Allegro, & Heun, 2014).

RESPONDING TO TOUCH. It clearly does not take the sting of pain to get an infant's attention. Even the youngest infants respond to gentle touches, such as a soothing caress, which can calm a crying, fussy infant (Hertenstein, 2002; Gitto et al., 2012; Aznar & Tenenbaum, 2016).

Touch is one of the most highly developed sensory systems in a newborn, and it is also one of the first to develop; there is evidence that by 32 weeks after conception, the entire body is sensitive to touch. Furthermore, several of the basic reflexes present at birth, such as the rooting reflex, require touch sensitivity to operate: An infant must sense a touch near the mouth in order to seek automatically a nipple to suck (Haith, 1986; Field, 2014).

Infants' abilities in the realm of touch are particularly helpful in their efforts to explore the world. Several theorists have suggested that one of the ways children gain information about the world is through

Blend Images/Alamy Stock Photo

Touch is one of the most highly developed sensory systems in a newborn.

touching. As mentioned earlier, at the age of 6 months, infants are apt to place almost any object in their mouths, apparently taking in data about its configuration from their sensory responses to the feel of it in their mouths (Ruff, 1989).

In addition, as we first discussed in Chapter 3, touch plays an important role in an organism's future development, for it triggers a complex chemical reaction that assists infants in their efforts to survive. For example, gentle massage stimulates the production of certain chemicals in an infant's brain that instigate growth. Touch is also associated with social development. In fact, the brain seems primed to respond positively to slow, gentle touch (Diego, Field, & Hernandez-Reif, 2008; 2009; Gordon et al., 2013; Ludwig & Field, 2014).

Multimodal Perception: Combining Individual Sensory Inputs

LO 4.13 Summarize the multimodal approach to perception.

When Eric Pettigrew was 7 months old, his grandparents presented him with a squeaky rubber doll. As soon as he saw it, he reached out for it, grasped it in his hand, and listened as it squeaked. He seemed delighted with the gift.

One way of considering Eric's sensory reaction to the doll is to focus on each of the senses individually: what the doll looked like to Eric, how it felt in his hand, and what it sounded like. It is this approach that has dominated the study of sensation and perception in infancy.

Let's consider another approach, however: We might examine how the various sensory responses are integrated with one another. Instead of looking at each individual sensory response, we could consider how the responses work together and are combined to produce Eric's ultimate reaction. The **multimodal approach to perception** considers how information that is collected by various individual sensory systems is integrated and coordinated (Farzin, Charles, & Rivera, 2009).

multimodal approach to perception

the approach that considers how information that is collected by various individual sensory systems is integrated and coordinated

From a *health-care worker's* perspective

Persons who are born without the use of one sense often develop unusual abilities in one or more other senses. What can health-care professionals do to help infants who are lacking in a particular sense?

Although the multimodal approach is a relatively recent innovation in the study of how infants understand their sensory world, it raises some fundamental issues about the development of sensation and perception. For instance, some researchers argue that sensations are initially integrated with one another in the infant, while others maintain that the infant's sensory systems are at first separate and that brain development leads to increasing integration (Lickliter & Bahrick, 2000; Lewkowicz, 2002; Flom & Bahrick, 2007).

We do not know yet which view is correct. However, it does appear that by an early age infants are able to relate what they have learned about an object through one sensory channel to what they have learned about it through another. For instance, even 1-month-old infants are able to recognize by sight objects that they have previously held in their mouths but never seen (Steri & Spelke, 1988). Clearly, some cross-talk between various sensory channels is already possible a month after birth.

Infants' multimodal perception abilities showcase the sophisticated perceptual abilities of infants, which continue to grow throughout the period of infancy. Such perceptual growth is aided by infants' discovery of **affordances**, the options that a given situation or stimulus provides. For example, infants learn that they might potentially fall when walking down a steep ramp—that is, the ramp *affords* the possibility of falling. Such knowledge is crucial as infants make the transition from crawling to walking. Similarly, infants learn that an object shaped in a certain way can slip out of their hands if not grasped correctly. For example, Eric is learning that his toy has several affordances: He can grab it and squeeze it, listen to it squeak, and even chew comfortably on it if he is teething (Wilcox et al., 2007; Huang, 2012; Rocha et al., 2013; also see the *Development in Your Life* box).

affordances

options that a given situation or stimulus provides

Development in Your Life

Exercising Your Infant's Body and Senses

Recall how cultural expectations and environments affect the age at which various physical milestones, such as the first step, occur. While most experts feel attempts to accelerate physical and sensory perceptual development yield little advantage, parents should ensure that their infants receive sufficient physical and sensory stimulation. There are several specific ways to accomplish this goal:

- **Carry a baby in different positions.** Switching among a backpack, a frontpack, or in a football hold with the infant's head in the palm of your hand and its feet lying on your arm lets infants view the world from several perspectives.
- **Let infants explore their environment.** Don't contain them too long in a barren environment. Let them crawl or wander around—after first making the environment "childproof" by removing dangerous objects.
- **Engage in "rough-and-tumble" play that is not violent.** Wrestling, dancing, and rolling around on the floor are activities that are fun and that stimulate older infants' motor and sensory systems.
- **Let babies touch their food and even play with it.** Infancy is too early to start teaching table manners.
- **Provide toys that stimulate the senses.** Provide toys that can stimulate more than one sense at a time. For example, brightly colored, textured toys with movable parts are enjoyable and help sharpen infants' senses.

Module 4.3 Review

LO 4.9 Describe the capabilities of infants in the realm of visual perception.

Infants' sensory abilities are surprisingly well developed at or shortly after birth. Their perceptions help them explore and begin to make sense of the world. Very early, infants can see depth and motion, distinguish colors and patterns, and show clear visual preferences.

LO 4.10 Describe the capabilities of infants in the realm of auditory sensation and perception.

Infants hear from the time of birth—and even before. At a very young age, infants are able to localize and discriminate sounds, and recognize the sound of their mother's voice.

LO 4.11 Describe the smell and taste capacities of infants.

The sense of smell is very well developed in infants, many of whom can distinguish their mothers on the basis of smell alone. Infants have innate taste preferences, preferring sweet tastes and showing disgust when they taste something bitter.

LO 4.12 Describe the nature of pain and touch in infants.

Infants are sensitive to pain and touch, and most medical authorities now subscribe to procedures, including anesthesia, that minimize infants' pain.

LO 4.13 Summarize the multimodal approach to perception.

Infants also have a keen ability to integrate information from more than one sense.

Journal Writing Prompt

Applying Lifespan Development: What might be the advantages and disadvantages of swaddling, a practice in which a baby is snuggly wrapped in a blanket, which usually calms an infant?

Epilogue

In this chapter, we discussed the nature and pace of infants' physical growth and the pace of less obvious growth in the brain and nervous system and in the regularity of infants' patterns and states.

We next looked at motor development, the development and uses of reflexes, the role of environmental influences on the pace and shape of motor development, and the importance of nutrition.

We closed the chapter with a look at the senses and the infant's ability to combine data from multiple sensory sources.

Turn back for a moment to the prologue of this chapter, about baby Josh's first steps, and answer these questions.

1. Which principle or principles of growth (e.g., cephalocaudal, proximodistal, hierarchical integration, independence of systems) account for the progression of physical activities that likely preceded Josh's first steps?

2. What conclusions about Josh's future physical development can be drawn based on the fact that his first steps occurred approximately 2 months early? Why?

3. What might have changed in the environment between the time Jon and Josh were born that might account for their different "first step" schedules? If you were researching this question, what environmental factors would you look for?

4. Why were Josh's parents so pleased and proud about his accomplishment, which is, after all, a routine and universal occurrence? What factors exist in U.S. culture that make the "first steps" milestone so significant?

Looking Back

LO 4.1 Describe how the human body develops in the first 2 years of life, including the four principles that govern its growth.

Human babies grow rapidly in height and weight, especially during the first 2 years of life. Major principles that govern human growth include the cephalocaudal principle, the proximodistal principle, the principle of hierarchical integration, and the principle of the independence of systems.

LO 4.2 Describe how the nervous system and brain develop in the first 2 years of life and how the environment affects such development.

The nervous system contains a huge number of neurons, more than will be needed as an adult. "Extra" connections and neurons that are not used are eliminated as an infant develops. Brain development, largely predetermined genetically, also contains a strong element of plasticity—a susceptibility to environmental influences. Many aspects of development occur during sensitive periods, when the organism is particularly susceptible to environmental influences.

LO 4.3 Explain the body rhythms and states that govern an infant's behavior the first 2 years of life.

One of the primary tasks of the infant is the development of rhythms—cyclical patterns that integrate individual behaviors. An important rhythm pertains to the infant's state—the degree of awareness of stimulation it displays.

LO 4.4 Discuss SIDS and SUID and how they can be prevented.

Sudden infant death syndrome (SIDS) is a disorder in which seemingly healthy infants die in their sleep. The American Academy of Pediatrics now suggests that babies sleep on their backs rather than on their sides or stomachs to help prevent SIDS.

LO 4.5 Explain how the reflexes that infants are born with help them adapt to their surroundings and protect themselves.

Reflexes are unlearned, automatic responses to stimuli that help newborns survive and protect themselves. Some reflexes also have value as the foundation for future, more conscious behaviors.

LO 4.6 Summarize the landmarks of motor skill development in infancy.

The development of gross and fine motor skills proceeds along a generally consistent timetable in normal children, with substantial individual and cultural variations.

LO 4.7 Summarize the role of nutrition in the physical development of infants.

Adequate nutrition is essential for physical development. Malnutrition and undernutrition affect physical aspects of growth and may also affect IQ and school performance.

LO 4.8 Summarize the benefits of breastfeeding in infancy.

Breastfeeding has distinct advantages over bottle-feeding, including the nutritional completeness of breast milk, its provision of a degree of immunity to certain childhood diseases, and its easy digestibility. In addition, breastfeeding offers significant physical and emotional benefits to both child and mother.

LO 4.9 Describe the capabilities of infants in the realm of visual perception.

Sensation, the stimulation of the sense organs, differs from perception, the interpretation and integration of sensed stimuli. Very early, infants can see depth and motion, distinguish colors and patterns, and show clear visual preferences.

LO 4.10 Describe the capabilities of infants in the realm of auditory sensation and perception.

Infants hear from the time of birth—and even before. At a very young age, infants are able to localize and discriminate sounds, and recognize the sound of their mother's voice.

LO 4.11 Describe the smell and taste capacities of infants.

The sense of smell is very well developed in infants, many of whom can distinguish their mothers on the basis of smell alone. Infants have innate taste preferences, preferring sweet tastes and showing disgust when they taste something bitter.

LO 4.12 Describe the nature of pain and touch in infants.

While at one point it was assumed that young infants do not experience pain, it is widely acknowledged today that they are born with the capacity to experience pain. One of the most highly developed sensory systems in infants, which is only now being understood, touch plays an important role in the child's future development.

LO 4.13 Summarize the multimodal approach to perception.

The multimodal approach to perception considers how information that is collected by various individual sensory systems is integrated and coordinated.

Key Terms and Concepts

cephalocaudal principle 119
proximodistal principle 119
principle of hierarchical integration 119
principle of the independence of systems 119
neuron 119
synapse 120
synaptic pruning 121
myelin 121
cerebral cortex 121
plasticity 122
sensitive period 123
rhythms 123
state 124
rapid eye movement (REM) sleep 125
sudden infant death syndrome (SIDS) 126
sudden unexpected infant death 127
reflexes 128
dynamic systems theory 132
norm 132
Brazelton Neonatal Behavioral Assessment Scale (NBAS) 133
nonorganic failure to thrive 136
sensation 139
perception 139
multimodal approach to perception 144
affordances 144

Chapter 5
Cognitive Development in Infancy

FatCamera/Getty Images

Learning Objectives

LO 5.1 Summarize the fundamental features of Piaget's theory of cognitive development.

LO 5.2 Describe Piaget's sensorimotor stage of cognitive development.

LO 5.3 Summarize the arguments both in support of and critical of Piaget's theory of cognitive development.

LO 5.4 Describe how infants process information according to information processing approaches to cognitive development.

LO 5.5 Describe the memory capabilities of infants during their first 2 years of life.

LO 5.6 Describe how infant intelligence is measured using information processing approaches.

LO 5.7 Outline the processes by which children learn to use language.

LO 5.8 Outline the major theories of language development.

LO 5.9 Describe how children influence adults' language.

Chapter Overview

Prologue: Baby Talk

Amelie Hawkins raises her eyebrows and grins broadly, leaning toward her 3-month-old daughter while shaking a baby rattle and cooing in a singsong voice, "Oooo, you like that! Yes you do! Yes you do-oo-oo! Rattle! That's a rattle!" Amelie's daughter giggles and grins, flapping her arms and kicking her legs, but that's as coherent as it gets. For now.

"I know she can't understand me, but she hears the sounds. She's learning. I can see it in her eyes. She's taking it in. She doesn't know what any of it means yet," Amelie laughs, pausing thoughtfully. "But she's aware. One day she'll say something back—that will be a very exciting day!"

Looking Ahead

How much of the world do infants understand? How do they begin to make meaning of it all? Does intellectual stimulation accelerate an infant's cognitive development? We address these and related questions in this chapter as we consider cognitive development during the first years of life. Our examination focuses on the work of developmental researchers who seek to understand how infants develop their knowledge and understanding of the world. We first discuss the work of Swiss psychologist Jean Piaget, whose theory of developmental stages served as a highly influential impetus for a considerable amount of work on cognitive development. We look at both the limitations and the contributions of this important developmental specialist.

We then cover more contemporary views of cognitive development, examining information processing approaches that seek to explain how cognitive growth occurs. After considering how learning takes place, we examine memory in infants and the ways in which infants process, store, and retrieve information. We discuss the controversial issue of the recollection of events that occurred during infancy. We also address individual differences in intelligence.

Finally, we consider language, the cognitive skill that permits infants to communicate with others. We look at the roots of language in prelinguistic speech and trace the milestones indicating the development of language skills in the progression from baby's first words to phrases and sentences. We also look at the characteristics of adults' communication addressed to infants, characteristics that are surprisingly similar across different cultures.

Tetatet/Fotolia

By interacting with their children, parents influence cognitive development during infancy.

Piaget's Approach to Cognitive Development

Olivia's dad is wiping up the mess around the base of her high chair—for the third time today! It seems to him that 14-month-old Olivia takes great delight in dropping food from the high chair. She also drops toys, spoons—anything it seems, just to watch how it hits the floor. She almost appears to be experimenting to see what kind of noise or what size of splatter is created by each item.

Swiss psychologist Jean Piaget (1896–1980) probably would have said that Olivia's dad is right in theorizing that Olivia is conducting her own series of experiments to learn more about the workings of her world. Piaget's views of the ways infants learn could be summed in a simple equation: *Action* = *Knowledge*.

Piaget argued that infants do not acquire knowledge from facts communicated by others, nor through sensation and perception. Instead, Piaget suggested that knowledge is the product of direct motor behavior. Although many of his basic explanations and propositions have been challenged by subsequent research, as we'll discuss later, the view that in significant ways infants learn by doing remains unquestioned (Piaget, 1952, 1962, 1983; Bullinger, 1997; Zuccarini et al., 2016).

Key Elements of Piaget's Theory

LO 5.1 Summarize the fundamental features of Piaget's theory of cognitive development.

As first noted in Chapter 1, Piaget's theory is based on a stage approach to development. He assumed that all children pass through a series of four universal stages in a fixed order from birth through adolescence: sensorimotor, preoperational, concrete operational, and formal operational. He also suggested that movement from one stage to the next occurs when a child reaches an appropriate level of physical maturation *and* is exposed to relevant experiences. Without such experiences, children are assumed to be incapable of reaching their cognitive potential. Some approaches to cognition focus on changes in the *content* of children's knowledge about the world, but Piaget argued that it was critical to also consider the changes in the *quality* of children's knowledge and understanding as they move from one stage to another.

schema
organized patterns of functioning that adapt and change with mental development

For instance, as they develop cognitively, infants experience changes in their understanding about what can and cannot occur in the world. Consider a baby who participates in an experiment during which she is exposed to three identical versions of her mother all at the same time, thanks to some well-placed mirrors. A 3-month-old infant will interact happily with each of these images of her mother. However, by 5 months, the child becomes quite agitated at the sight of multiple mothers. Apparently, by this time the child has figured out that she has but one mother, and viewing three at a time is thoroughly alarming (Bower, 1977). To Piaget, such reactions suggest that a baby is beginning to master principles regarding the way the world operates, indicating that she has begun to construct a mental sense of the world that she didn't have 2 months earlier.

Bill Anderson/Science Source

Swiss psychologist Jean Piaget.

Piaget believed that the basic building blocks of the way we understand the world are mental structures called **schema**—organized patterns of functioning that adapt and change with mental development. At first, schema are related to physical, or sensorimotor, activity, such as picking up or reaching for toys. As children develop, their schema move to a mental level, reflecting thought. Schema are similar to computer software: They direct and determine how data from the world, such as new events or objects, are considered and dealt with (Rakison & Oakes, 2003; Rakison & Krogh, 2012; Di Paolo, Buhrmann, & Barandiaran, 2017).

If you give a baby a new cloth book, for example, he or she will touch it, mouth it, and perhaps try to tear it or bang it on the floor. To Piaget, each of these actions may represent a scheme, and they are the infant's way of gaining knowledge and understanding of this new object. Adults, however, would use a different scheme upon encountering the book. Rather than picking it up and putting it in their mouths or banging it on the floor, they would probably be drawn to the letters on the page, seeking to understand the book through the meaning of the printed words—a very different approach.

Piaget suggested that two principles underlie the growth in children's schema: assimilation and accommodation. **Assimilation** is the process by which people understand an experience in terms of their current stage of cognitive development and way of thinking. Assimilation occurs, then, when a stimulus or an event is acted upon, perceived, and understood in accordance with existing patterns of thought. For example, an infant who tries to suck on any toy in the same way is assimilating the objects to her existing sucking scheme. Similarly, a child who encounters a flying squirrel at a zoo and calls it a "bird" is assimilating the squirrel to his existing scheme of bird.

In contrast, when we change our existing ways of thinking, understanding, or behaving in response to encounters with new stimuli or events, **accommodation** takes place. For instance, when a child sees a flying squirrel and calls it "a bird with a tail," he is beginning to *accommodate* new knowledge, modifying his scheme of bird.

Piaget believed that the earliest schema are primarily limited to the reflexes with which we are all born, such as sucking and rooting. Infants start to modify these simple early schema almost immediately, through the processes of assimilation and accommodation, in response to their exploration of the environment. Schema quickly become more sophisticated as infants become more advanced in their motor capabilities—to Piaget, a signal of the potential for more advanced cognitive development. Because Piaget's sensorimotor stage of development begins at birth and continues until the child is about 2 years old, we consider that stage here in detail. (In future chapters, we'll discuss development during the later stages.)

szefei/123RF

According to Piaget, a baby will use a sensorimotor *schema*, such as mouthing or banging, to understand a new object.

assimilation

the process by which people understand an experience in terms of their current stage of cognitive development and way of thinking

accommodation

changes in existing ways of thinking that occur in response to encounters with new stimuli or events

sensorimotor stage (of cognitive development)

Piaget's initial major stage of cognitive development, which can be broken down into six substages

The Sensorimotor Period: The Earliest Stage of Cognitive Growth

LO 5.2 Describe Piaget's sensorimotor stage of cognitive development.

Piaget suggests that the **sensorimotor stage**, the initial major stage of cognitive development, can be divided into six substages. These are summarized in Table 5-1. It is important

Table 5-1 Piaget's Six Substages of the Sensorimotor Stage

Substage	Age	Description	Example
Substage 1: Simple reflexes	First month of life	During this period, the various reflexes that determine the infant's interactions with the world are at the center of its cognitive life.	The sucking reflex causes the infant to suck at anything placed against its lips.
Substage 2: First habits and primary circular reactions	From 1 to 4 months	At this age, infants begin to coordinate what were separate actions into single integrated activities.	An infant might combine grasping an object with sucking on it, or staring at something with touching it.
Substage 3: Secondary circular reactions	From 4 to 8 months	During this period, infants take major strides in shifting their cognitive horizons beyond themselves and begin to act on the outside world.	A child who repeatedly picks up a rattle and shakes it in different ways to see how the sound changes is demonstrating her ability to modify her cognitive scheme about shaking rattles.
Substage 4: Coordination of secondary circular reactions	From 8 to 12 months	In this stage, infants begin to use more calculated approaches to producing events, coordinating several schemas to generate a single act. They achieve object performance during this stage.	An infant will push one toy out of the way to reach another toy that is lying, partially exposed, under it.
Substage 5: Tertiary circular reactions	From 12 to 18 months	At this age, infants develop what Piaget regards as the deliberate variation of actions that bring desirable consequences. Rather than just repeating enjoyable activities, infants appear to carry out miniature experiments to observe the consequences.	A child will drop a toy repeatedly, varying the position from which he drops it, carefully observing each time to see where it falls.
Substage 6: Beginnings of thought	From 18 months to 2 years	The major achievement of Substage 6 is the capacity for mental representation, or symbolic thought. Piaget argued that only at this stage can infants imagine where objects that they cannot see might be.	Children can plot in their heads unseen trajectories of objects, so that if a ball rolls under a piece of furniture, they can figure out where it is likely to emerge on the other side.

Figure 5-1 Cognitive Transitions

Infants do not suddenly shift from one stage of cognitive development to the next. Instead, Piaget argued that there is a period of transition in which some behavior reflects one stage, while other behavior reflects the more advanced stage. Does this gradualism argue against Piaget's interpretation of stages?

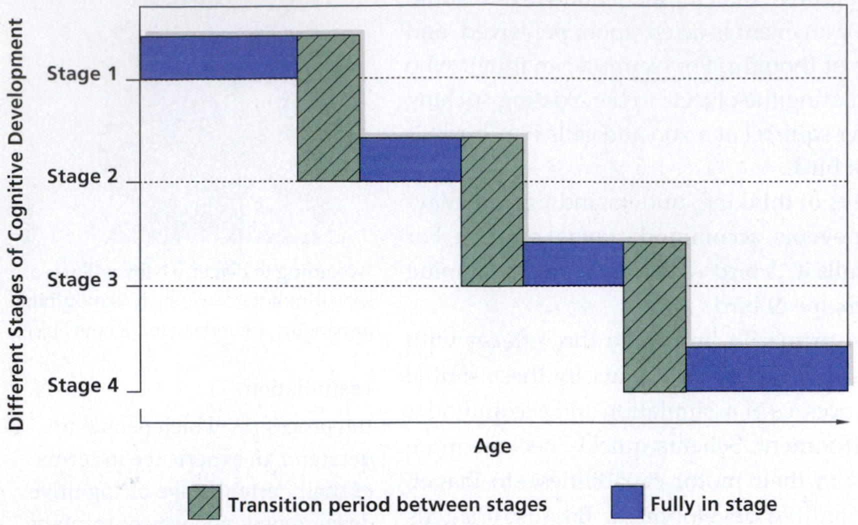

to keep in mind that although the specific substages of the sensorimotor period may at first appear to unfold with great regularity, as though infants reach a particular age and smoothly proceed into the next substage, the reality of cognitive development is somewhat different. First, the ages at which infants actually reach a particular stage vary a good deal among different children. The exact timing of a stage reflects an interaction between the infant's level of physical maturation and the nature of the social environment in which the child is being raised. Consequently, although Piaget contended that the order of the substages does not change from one child to the next, he admitted that the timing can and does vary to some degree.

Piaget viewed development as a more gradual process than the notion of different stages might seem to imply. Infants do not go to sleep one night in one substage and wake up the next morning in the next one. Instead, there is a rather gradual and steady shifting of behavior as a child moves toward the next stage of cognitive development. Infants also pass through periods of transition, in which some aspects of their behavior reflect the next higher stage, while other aspects indicate their current stage (see Figure 5-1).

SUBSTAGE 1: SIMPLE REFLEXES. The first substage of the sensorimotor period is *Substage 1: Simple reflexes*, encompassing the first month of life. During this time, the various inborn reflexes, described in Chapter 3 and Chapter 4, are at the center of a baby's physical and cognitive life, determining the nature of his or her interactions with the world. For example, the sucking reflex causes the infant to suck at anything placed against his or her lips. This sucking behavior, according to Piaget, provides the newborn with information about objects—information that paves the way to the next substage of the sensorimotor period.

At the same time, some of the reflexes begin to accommodate the infant's experience with the nature of the world. For instance, an infant who is being breastfed but who also receives supplemental bottles may start to change the way he or she sucks, depending on whether a nipple is on a breast or a bottle.

SUBSTAGE 2: FIRST HABITS AND PRIMARY CIRCULAR REACTIONS. *Substage 2: First habits and primary circular reactions*, the second substage of the sensorimotor period, occurs from 1 to 4 months of age. In this period, infants begin to coordinate what were separate actions into single integrated activities. For instance, an infant might combine grasping an object with sucking on it, or staring at something with touching it.

If an activity engages a baby's interests, he or she may repeat it over and over, simply for the sake of continuing to experience it. This repetition of a chance motor event helps the baby start building cognitive schema through a process known as a *circular reaction. Primary circular reactions* are schema reflecting an infant's repetition of interesting or enjoyable actions that focus on the infant's own body, just for the enjoyment of doing them. Thus, when an infant first puts his thumb in his mouth and begins to suck, it is a mere chance event. However, when he repeatedly sucks his thumb in the future, it represents a primary circular reaction, which he is repeating because the sensation of sucking is pleasurable.

SUBSTAGE 3: SECONDARY CIRCULAR REACTIONS. In *Substage 3: Secondary circular reactions*, the infant's actions are more purposeful. According to Piaget, this third stage of cognitive development in infancy occurs from 4 to 8 months of age. During this period, a child begins to act upon the outside world. For instance, infants now seek to repeat enjoyable events in their environments if they happen to produce them through chance activities. A child who repeatedly picks up a rattle in her crib and shakes it in different ways to see how the sound changes is demonstrating her ability to modify her cognitive scheme about shaking rattles. She is engaging in what Piaget calls secondary circular reactions.

Secondary circular reactions are schema regarding repeated actions that bring about a desirable consequence. The major difference between primary circular reactions and secondary circular reactions is whether the infant's activity is focused on the infant and his or her own body (primary circular reactions) or involves actions relating to the world outside (secondary circular reactions).

During the third substage, babies' vocalization increases substantially as infants come to notice that if they make noises, other people around them will respond with noises of their own. Similarly, infants begin to imitate the sounds made by others. Vocalization becomes a secondary circular reaction that ultimately helps lead to the development of language and the formation of social relationships.

SUBSTAGE 4: COORDINATION OF SECONDARY CIRCULAR REACTIONS. One of the major leaps forward is *Substage 4: Coordination of secondary circular reactions*, which lasts from around 8 months to 12 months. Before this stage, behavior involved direct action on objects. When something happened by chance that caught an infant's interest, she attempted to repeat the event using a single scheme. However, in Substage 4, infants begin to employ *goal-directed behavior*, in which several schema are combined and coordinated to generate a single act to solve a problem. For instance, they will push one toy out of the way to reach another toy that is lying, partially exposed, under it. They also begin to anticipate upcoming events. For instance, Piaget tells of his son Laurent, who at 8 months "recognizes by a certain noise caused by air that he is nearing the end of his feeding and, instead of insisting on drinking to the last drop, he rejects his bottle" (Piaget, 1952, pp. 248–249).

Infants' newfound purposefulness, their ability to use means to attain particular ends, and their skill in anticipating future circumstances owe their appearance in part to the developmental achievement of object permanence that emerges in Substage 4. **Object permanence** is the realization that people and objects exist even when they cannot be seen. It is a simple principle, but its mastery has profound consequences.

object permanence
the realization that people and objects exist even when they cannot be seen

Consider, for instance, 7-month-old Chu, who has yet to learn the idea of object permanence. Chu's mother shakes a rattle in front of him, then takes the rattle and places it under a blanket. To Chu, who has not mastered the concept of object permanence, the rattle no longer exists. He will make no effort to look for it.

Several months later, when he reaches Substage 4, the story is quite different (see Figure 5-2). This time, as soon as his mother places the rattle under the blanket, Chu tries to toss the cover aside, eagerly searching for the rattle. Chu clearly has learned that the object continues to exist even when it cannot be seen. For the infant who achieves an understanding of object permanence, then, out of sight is decidedly not out of mind.

The attainment of object permanence extends not only to inanimate objects, but to people, too. It gives Chu the security that his father and mother still exist even when they have left the room. This awareness is likely a key element in the development of social attachments, which we

Oksana Kuzmina/Shutterstock

Infants in Substage 4 can coordinate their secondary circular reactions, displaying an ability to plan or calculate how to produce a desired outcome.

Figure 5-2 Object Permanence

Before an infant has understood the idea of object permanence, he will not search for an object that has been hidden right before his eyes. But several months later, he will search for it, illustrating that he has attained object permanence. Why is the concept of object permanence important?

Before Object Permanence

After Object Permanence

consider in Chapter 6. The recognition of object permanence also feeds infants' growing assertiveness: As they realize that an object taken away from them doesn't just cease to exist but is merely somewhere else, their only-too-human reaction may be to want it back—and quickly.

Although the understanding of object permanence emerges in Substage 4, it is only a rudimentary understanding. It takes several months for the concept to be fully comprehended, and infants continue for several months to make certain kinds of errors relating to object permanence. For instance, they often are fooled when a toy is hidden first under one blanket and then under a second blanket. In seeking out the toy, Substage 4 infants most often turn to the first hiding place, ignoring the second blanket under which the toy is currently located—even if the hiding was done in plain view.

SUBSTAGE 5: TERTIARY CIRCULAR REACTIONS. *Substage 5: Tertiary circular reactions* is reached at around the age of 12 months and extends to 18 months. As the name of the stage indicates, during this period, infants develop tertiary circular reactions, which are schema regarding the deliberate variation of actions that bring desirable consequences. Rather than just repeating enjoyable activities, as they do with secondary circular reactions, infants appear to carry out miniature experiments to observe the consequences.

szefei/Shutterstock

With the attainment of the cognitive skill of deferred imitation, children are able to imitate people and scenes they have witnessed in the past.

For example, Piaget observed his son Laurent dropping a toy swan repeatedly, varying the position from which he dropped it, carefully observing each time to see where it fell. Instead of just repeating the action each time (as in a secondary circular reaction), Laurent made modifications in the situation to learn about their consequences. As you may recall from our discussion of research methods in Chapter 1, this behavior represents the essence of the scientific method: An experimenter varies a situation in a laboratory to learn the effects of the variation. To infants in Substage 5, the world is their laboratory, and they spend their days leisurely carrying out one miniature experiment after another. Olivia, the baby described earlier who enjoyed dropping different things from her high chair, is a little scientist in action.

What is most striking about infants' behavior during Substage 5 is their interest in the unexpected. Unanticipated events are treated not only as interesting but also as something to be explained and understood. Infants' discoveries can lead to newfound skills, some of which may cause a certain amount of chaos, as Olivia's dad realized while cleaning up around her high chair.

SUBSTAGE 6: BEGINNINGS OF THOUGHT. The final stage of the sensorimotor period is *Substage 6: Beginnings of thought*, which lasts from around 18 months to 2 years. The major achievement of Substage 6 is the capacity for mental representation, or symbolic thought. A **mental representation** is an internal image of a past event or object. Piaget argued that by this stage infants can imagine where objects might be that they cannot see. They can even plot in their heads unseen trajectories of objects, so if a ball rolls under a piece of furniture, they can figure out where it is likely to emerge on the other side.

mental representation
an internal image of a past event or object

Because of children's new abilities to create internal representations of objects, their understanding of causality also becomes more sophisticated. For instance, consider Piaget's description of his son Laurent's efforts to open a garden gate:

> *Laurent tries to open a garden gate but cannot push it forward because it is held back by a piece of furniture. He cannot account either visually or by any sound for the cause that prevents the gate from opening, but after having tried to force it he suddenly seems to understand; he goes around the wall, arrives at the other side of the gate, moves the armchair which holds it firm, and opens it with a triumphant expression. (Piaget, 1954, p. 296)*

The attainment of mental representation also permits another important development: the ability to pretend. Using the skill of what Piaget refers to as **deferred imitation**, in which a person who is no longer present is imitated later, children are able to pretend that they are driving a car, feeding a doll, or cooking dinner long after they have witnessed such scenes played out in reality. To Piaget, deferred imitation provided clear evidence that children form internal mental representations.

deferred imitation
an act in which a person who is no longer present is imitated by children who have witnessed a similar act

Appraising Piaget: Support and Challenges

LO 5.3 Summarize the arguments both in support of and critical of Piaget's theory of cognitive development.

Most developmental researchers would probably agree that in many significant ways, Piaget's descriptions of how cognitive development proceeds during infancy are generally accurate. Yet there is substantial disagreement over the validity of the theory and many of its specific predictions. (Marcovitch, Zelazo, & Schmuckler, 2003; Müller, Ten Eycke, & Baker, 2015; Barrouillet, 2015).

Let's start with what is clearly accurate about the Piagetian approach. Piaget was a masterful reporter of children's behavior, and his descriptions of growth during infancy remain a monument to his powers of observation. Furthermore, literally thousands of studies have supported Piaget's view that children learn much about the world by acting on objects in their environment. Finally, the broad outlines sketched out by Piaget of the sequence of cognitive development and the increasing cognitive accomplishments that occur during infancy are generally accurate (Bibace, 2013; Müller, Ten Eycke, & Baker, 2015; Fowler, 2017).

By contrast, specific aspects of the theory have come under increasing scrutiny—and criticism—in the decades since Piaget carried out his pioneering work. For example, some researchers question the stage conception that forms the basis of Piaget's theory. Although, as noted earlier, even Piaget acknowledged that children's transitions between stages are gradual, critics contend that development proceeds in a much more continuous fashion. Rather than showing major leaps of competence at the end of one stage and the beginning of the next, improvement comes in more gradual increments, growing step by step and skill by skill.

For instance, developmental researcher Robert Siegler suggests that cognitive development proceeds not in stages but in "waves." According to Siegler, children don't one day drop a mode of thinking and the next take up a new form. Instead, there is an ebb and flow of cognitive approaches that children use to understand the world. One day children may use one form of cognitive strategy, while another day they may choose a less advanced strategy—moving back and forth over a period of time. Although one strategy may be used most frequently at a given age, children still may have access to alternative ways of thinking. Siegler thus sees cognitive development as in constant flux (Siegler, 2012; Siegler & Lortie-Forgues, 2014; Siegler, 2016).

Other critics dispute Piaget's notion that cognitive development is grounded in motor activities. They charge that Piaget overlooked the importance of the sensory and perceptual systems that are present from a very early age in infancy—systems about which Piaget knew little, since so much of the research illustrating how sophisticated they are even in infancy was done relatively recently. Studies of children born without arms and legs (due to their mothers' unwitting use of teratogenic drugs during pregnancy, as described in Chapter 2) show that such children display normal cognitive development, despite their lack of practice with motor activities. This constitutes further evidence that the connection Piaget made between motor development and cognitive development was exaggerated (Butterworth, 1994; Houwen et al., 2016).

To bolster their perspectives, Piaget's critics also point to more recent studies that cast doubt on Piaget's view that infants are incapable of mastering the concept of object permanence until they are close to a year old. For instance, some work suggests that younger infants did not appear to understand object permanence because the techniques used to test their abilities were not sensitive enough to their true capabilities (Bremer, Slater, & Johnson, 2015; Baillargeon, 2008; Baillargeon & DeJong, 2017).

According to researcher Renée Baillargeon, infants as young as 3½ months have at least some understanding of object permanence. She argues that it may be that younger infants don't search for a rattle hidden under a blanket because they don't have the motor skills necessary to do the searching—not because they don't understand that the rattle still exists. Similarly, the apparent inability of young infants to comprehend object permanence may reflect more about infants' memory deficits than their lack of understanding of the concept: The memories of young infants may be so poor that they simply do not recall the earlier concealment of the toy (Hespos & Baillargeon, 2008).

Baillargeon has conducted ingenious experiments that demonstrate the earlier capabilities of infants in understanding object permanence. For example, in her *violation-of-expectation* studies, she repeatedly exposes infants to a physical event and then observes how they react to a variation of that event that is physically impossible. It turns out that infants as young as 3½ months show strong physiological reactions to impossible events, suggesting that they have some sense of object permanence far earlier than Piaget was able to discern (Scott & Baillargeon, 2013; Baillargeon et al., 2015; Sim & Zu, 2017).

Other types of behavior also seem to emerge earlier than Piaget suggested. For instance, recall the ability of neonates to imitate the basic facial expressions of adults just hours after birth, as discussed in Chapter 3. The presence of this skill at such an early age contradicts Piaget's view that initially infants are able to imitate only behavior that they see in others, using parts of their own body that they can plainly view—such as their hands and feet. In fact, facial imitation suggests that humans are born with a basic, innate capability for imitating others' actions, a capability that depends on certain kinds of environmental experiences, but one that Piaget believed develops later in infancy (Legerstee & Markova, 2008; Gredebäck et al., 2012; Parsons et al., 2017).

Research on babies in non-Western cultures suggests that Piaget's stages are not universal but are to some degree culturally derived.

From *a caregiver's* perspective

In general, what are some implications for childrearing practices of Piaget's observations about the ways children gain an understanding of the world? Would you use the same approaches in childrearing for a child growing up in a non-Western culture? Why or why not?

Piaget's work also seems to describe children from developed Western countries better than those in non-Western cultures. For instance, some evidence suggests that cognitive skills emerge on a different timetable for children in non-Western cultures than for children living in Europe and the United States. Infants raised in the Ivory Coast of Africa, for example, reach the various substages of the sensorimotor period at an earlier age than infants reared in France (Dasen et al., 1978; Mistry & Saraswathi, 2003; Tamis-LeMonda et al., 2012).

Despite these problems regarding Piaget's view of the sensorimotor period, even his most passionate critics concede that he has provided us with a masterful description of the broad outlines of cognitive development during infancy. His failings seem to be in underestimating the capabilities of younger infants and in his claims that sensorimotor skills develop in a consistent, fixed pattern. Still, his influence has been enormous, and although the focus of many contemporary developmental researchers has shifted to newer information processing approaches that we discuss next, Piaget remains a pioneering figure in the field of development (Kail, 2004; Maynard, 2008; Fowler, 2017).

Module 5.1 Review

LO 5.1 Summarize the fundamental features of Piaget's theory of cognitive development.

Jean Piaget's theory of human cognitive development involves a succession of stages through which children progress from birth to adolescence. As humans move from one stage to another, the way they understand the world changes.

LO 5.2 Describe Piaget's sensorimotor stage of cognitive development.

The sensorimotor stage, from birth to about 2 years, involves a gradual progression through simple reflexes, single coordinated activities, interest in the outside world, purposeful combinations of activities, manipulation of actions to produce desired outcomes, and symbolic thought. The sensorimotor stage has six substages.

LO 5.3 Summarize the arguments both in support of and critical of Piaget's theory of cognitive development.

Piaget is respected as a careful observer of children's behavior and a generally accurate interpreter of the way human cognitive development proceeds, though subsequent research on his theory does suggest several limitations.

Journal Writing Prompt

Applying Lifespan Development: Think of a common young children's toy with which you are familiar. How might its use be affected by the principles of assimilation and accommodation?

Information Processing Approaches to Cognitive Development

Amber Nordstrom, 3 months old, breaks into a smile as her brother Marcus stands over her crib, picks up a doll, and makes a whistling noise through his teeth. Amber never seems to tire of Marcus's efforts at making her smile, and soon whenever Marcus appears and simply picks up the doll, her lips begin to curl into a smile.

Clearly, Amber remembers Marcus and his humorous ways. But how does she remember him? And how much else can Amber remember?

To answer questions such as these, we need to diverge from the road that Piaget laid out for us. Rather than seeking to identify the universal, broad milestones in cognitive development through which all infants pass, as Piaget tried to do, we must consider the specific processes by which individual babies acquire and use the information to which they are exposed. We need, then, to focus less on the qualitative changes in infants' mental lives and consider more closely their quantitative capabilities, as we do in this section.

The Foundations of Information Processing

LO 5.4 Describe how infants process information according to information processing approaches to cognitive development.

information processing approaches
the model that seeks to identify the way that individuals take in, use, and store information

Information processing approaches to cognitive development seek to identify the way that individuals take in, use, and store information. According to this approach, the quantitative changes in infants' abilities to organize and manipulate information represent the hallmarks of cognitive development.

Taking this perspective, cognitive growth is characterized by increasing sophistication, speed, and capacity in processing information. Earlier, we compared Piaget's idea of schema to computer software, which directs the computer in how to deal with data from the world. We might compare the information processing perspective on cognitive growth to the improvements that come from use of more efficient programs that lead to increased speed and sophistication in the processing of information. Information processing approaches, then, focus on the types of "mental programs" that people use when they seek to solve problems (Cohen & Cashon, 2003; Fagan & Ployhart, 2015).

ENCODING, STORAGE, AND RETRIEVAL. Information processing has three basic aspects: encoding, storage, and retrieval (see Figure 5-3). *Encoding* is the process by which information is initially recorded in a form usable to memory. Infants and children—indeed, all people—are exposed to a massive amount of information; if they tried to process it all, they would be overwhelmed. Consequently, they encode selectively, picking and choosing the information to which they will pay attention.

Even if someone has been exposed to the information initially and has encoded it in an appropriate way, there is still no guarantee that he or she will be able to use it in the future. Information must also have been stored in memory adequately. *Storage* refers to the placement of material into memory. Finally, success in using the material in the future depends on retrieval processes. *Retrieval* is the process by which material in memory storage is located, brought into awareness, and used.

We can use our comparison to computers again here. Information processing approaches suggest that the processes of encoding, storage, and retrieval are analogous to different parts of a computer. Encoding can be thought of as a computer's keyboard, through which one inputs information; storage is the computer's hard drive or a zip drive, where information is stored; and retrieval is analogous to software that accesses the information for display on the screen. Only when all three processes—encoding, storage, and retrieval—are operating can information be processed.

AUTOMATIZATION. In some cases, encoding, storage, and retrieval are relatively automatic, while in other cases they are deliberate. *Automatization* is the degree to which an activity requires attention. Processes that require relatively little attention are automatic; processes that require relatively large amounts of attention are controlled. For example, some activities such as walking, eating with a fork, or reading may be automatic for you, but at first they required your full attention.

Automatic mental processes help children in their initial encounters with the world by enabling them to easily and "automatically" process information in particular ways. For instance, by age 5, children automatically encode information in terms of frequency.

Figure 5-3 Information Processing

The process by which information is encoded, stored, and retrieved.

Without a lot of attention to counting or tallying, they become aware, for example, of how often they have encountered various people, permitting them to differentiate familiar from unfamiliar people (Homae et al., 2012; Seyfarth & Cheney, 2013).

Furthermore, without intending to and without being aware of it, infants and children develop a sense of how often different stimuli are found together simultaneously. This permits them to develop an understanding of *concepts*, categorizations of objects, events, or people that share common properties. For example, by encoding the information that four legs, a wagging tail, and barking are often found together, we learn very early in life to understand the concept of "dog." Children—as well as adults—are rarely aware of how they learn such concepts, and they are often unable to articulate the features that distinguish one concept (such as a dog) from another (such as cat). Instead, learning tends to occur automatically.

szefei/Shutterstock

Many of the tasks that are now automatic for you, such as holding a cup or using a fork, at one time required your full attention.

Some of the things we learn automatically are unexpectedly complex. For example, infants have the ability to learn subtle statistical patterns and relationships; these results are consistent with a growing body of research showing that the mathematical skills of infants are surprisingly good. Infants as young as 5 months old are able to calculate the outcome of simple addition and subtraction problems.

In a study by developmental psychologist Karen Wynn, infants first were shown an object—a 4-inch-high Mickey Mouse statuette. A screen was then raised, hiding the statuette. Next, the experimenter showed the infants a second, identical Mickey Mouse and then placed it behind the same screen (Wynn, 1995, 2000). Finally, depending on the experimental condition, one of two outcomes occurred. In the "correct addition" condition, the screen dropped, revealing the two statuettes (analogous to $1 + 1 = 2$). But in the "incorrect addition" condition, the screen dropped to reveal just one statuette (analogous to the incorrect $1 + 1 = 1$).

Because infants look longer at unexpected occurrences than at expected ones, the researchers examined the pattern of infants' gazes in the different conditions. In support of the notion that infants can distinguish between correct and incorrect addition, the infants in the experiment gazed longer at the incorrect result than at the correct one, indicating they expected a different number of statuettes. In a similar procedure, infants also looked longer at incorrect subtraction problems than at correct ones. The conclusion: Infants have rudimentary mathematical skills that enable them to understand whether a quantity is accurate.

The existence of basic mathematical skills in infants has been supported by findings that nonhumans are born with some basic numeric proficiency. Even newly hatched chicks show some counting abilities. And it is not too long into infancy that children demonstrate an understanding of such basic physics as movement trajectories and gravity (van Marle & Wynn, 2011; Hespos & van Marle, 2012; Edwards et al., 2016; Christodoulou, Lac, & Moore, 2017).

The results of this growing body of research suggest that infants have an innate grasp of certain basic mathematical functions and statistical patterns. This inborn proficiency is likely to form the basis for learning more complex mathematics and statistical relationships later in life (McCrink & Wynn, 2009; van Marle & Wynn, 2009; Starr, Libertus, & Brannon, 2013; Posid & Cordes, 2015).

We turn now to several aspects of information processing, focusing on memory and individual differences in intelligence.

Memory During Infancy: They Must Remember This…

LO 5.5 Describe the memory capabilities of infants during their first 2 years of life.

Arif Terzic was born during the war in Afghanistan. He spent his first 2 years hiding in a basement with his mother. The only light he saw came from a kerosene lamp. The only sounds he heard were his mother's hushed lullabies and the explosion of shells. Someone he never saw left food for them. There was a water faucet, but sometimes the water was too filthy to drink. At one point, his mother suffered a kind of breakdown. She fed him when she remembered. But she didn't speak. Or sing.

Arif was lucky. His family emigrated to the United States when he was 2. His father found work. They rented a little house. Arif went to preschool, then kindergarten. Today, he has friends, toys, and a dog, and he loves soccer. "He doesn't remember Afghanistan," his mother says. "It's like it never happened."

How likely is it that Arif truly remembers nothing of his infancy? And if he ever does recall his first 2 years of life, how accurate will his memories be? To answer these questions, we need to consider the qualities of memory that exist during infancy.

memory
the process by which information is initially recorded, stored, and retrieved

MEMORY CAPABILITIES IN INFANCY. Certainly, infants have **memory** capabilities, defined as the process by which information is initially recorded, stored, and retrieved. As we've seen, infants can distinguish new stimuli from old, and this implies that some memory of the old must be present. Unless the infants had some memory of an original stimulus, it would be impossible for them to recognize that a new stimulus differed from the earlier one.

Infants' capability to recognize new stimuli from old tells us little, however, about how age brings about changes in the capacities of memory and in its fundamental nature. Do infants' memory capabilities increase as they get older? The answer is clearly affirmative. In one study, infants were taught that they could move a mobile hanging over the crib by kicking their legs. It took only a few days for 2-month-old infants to forget their training, but 6-month-old infants still remembered for as long as 3 weeks (Rovee-Collier, 1999; Rovee-Collier & Cuevas, 2009).

Furthermore, infants who were later prompted to recall the association between kicking and moving the mobile showed evidence that the memory continued to exist even longer. Infants who had received just two training sessions lasting 9 minutes each still recalled the association about a week later, as illustrated by the fact that they began to kick when they were placed in the crib with the mobile. Two weeks later, however, they made no effort to kick, suggesting that they had forgotten entirely.

infantile amnesia
the lack of memory for experiences that occurred prior to 3 years of age

But they hadn't forgotten: When the babies saw a reminder—a moving mobile—their memories were apparently reactivated. The infants could remember the association, following prompting, for as long as an additional month. Other evidence confirms these results, suggesting that hints can reactivate memories that at first seem lost and that the older the infant, the more effective such prompting is (DeFrancisco & Rovee-Collier, 2008; Brito & Barr, 2014; Fisher-Thompson, 2017).

StockLite/Shutterstock

Infants who have learned the association between a moving mobile and kicking showed surprising recall ability when they were exposed to a reminder.

Is infant memory qualitatively different from that in older children and adults? Researchers generally believe that information is processed similarly throughout the life span, even though the kind of information being processed changes and different parts of the brain may be used. According to memory expert Carolyn Rovee-Collier, people, regardless of their age, gradually lose memories, although, just like babies, they may regain them if reminders are provided. Moreover, the more times a memory is retrieved, the more enduring the memory becomes (Barr et al., 2007; Turati, 2008; Bell, 2012).

THE DURATION OF MEMORIES. Although the processes that underlie memory retention and recall seem similar throughout the life span, the quantity of information stored and recalled does differ markedly as infants develop. Older infants can retrieve information more rapidly, and they can remember it longer. But just how long? Can memories from infancy be recalled, for example, after babies grow up?

Researchers disagree on the age from which memories can be retrieved. Although early research supported the notion of **infantile amnesia**—the lack of memory for experiences occurring before 3 years of age—more recent research shows that infants do retain memories of these years. For example, in one study, 6-month-old infants were shown a series of unusual events, such as intermittent periods of light and dark and strange sounds. When the children were later tested at the age of 1½ years or 2½ years, they demonstrated that they recalled the experience. Other research indicates that infants show memory for behavior and situations that they have seen only once (Neisser, 2004; Callaghan, Li & Richardson, 2014; Bucci & Stanton, 2017).

Such findings are consistent with evidence that the physical trace of a memory in the brain appears to be relatively permanent; this suggests that memories, even from infancy, may be enduring. However, memories may not be easily, or accurately, retrieved. For example, memories are susceptible to interference from other, newer information, which may displace or block out the older information, thereby preventing its recall.

One reason infants appear to remember less may be because language plays a key role in determining the way in which memories from early in life can be recalled: Older children and adults may only be able to report memories using the vocabulary that they had available at the time of the initial event, when the memories were stored. Because their vocabulary at the time of initial storage may have been quite limited, they are unable to describe the event later in life, even though it is actually in their memories (Simcock & Hayne, 2002; Heimann et al., 2006).

Fuse/Getty Images

Though researchers disagree as to the age from which memories can be retrieved, people generally cannot remember events or experiences that occurred before age 3.

The question of how well memories formed during infancy are retained in adulthood remains only partially answered. Although infants' memories may be highly detailed and can be enduring if the infants experience repeated reminders, it is still not clear how accurate those memories remain over the course of the life span. Early memories are susceptible to misrecollection if people are exposed to related, and contradictory, information following the initial formation of the memory. Not only does such new information potentially impair recall of the original material, but the new material may be inadvertently incorporated into the original memory, thereby corrupting its accuracy (Cordón et al., 2004; Li, Callaghan, & Richardson, 2014).

In sum, the data suggest that although it is at least theoretically possible for memories to remain intact from a very young age—if subsequent experiences do not interfere with their recollection—in most cases memories of personal experiences in infancy do not last into adulthood. Current findings suggest that memories of personal experience seem not to become accurate before age 18 to 24 months (Howe et al., 2004; Bauer, 2007; Taylor, Liu, & Herbert, 2016.

THE COGNITIVE NEUROSCIENCE OF MEMORY. Some of the most exciting research on the development of memory is coming from studies of the neurological basis of memory. Advances in brain scan technology, as well as studies of adults with brain damage, suggest that there are two separate systems involved with long-term memory. These two systems—explicit memory and implicit memory—retain different sorts of information.

Explicit memory is memory that is conscious and can be recalled intentionally. When we try to recall a name or phone number, we're using explicit memory. In comparison, *implicit memory* consists of memories of which we are not consciously aware but that affect performance and behavior. Implicit memory consists of motor skills, habits, and activities that can be remembered without conscious cognitive effort, such as how to ride a bike or climb a stairway.

Explicit and implicit memories emerge at different rates and involve different parts of the brain. The earliest memories seem to be implicit, and they involve the cerebellum and brain stem. The forerunner of explicit memory involves the hippocampus, but true explicit memory doesn't emerge until the second half of the first year. When explicit memory does emerge, it involves an increasing number of areas of the cortex of the brain (Squire & Knowlton, 1995; Bauer, 2007; Low & Perner, 2012).

Individual Differences in Intelligence: Is One Infant Smarter Than Another?

LO 5.6 Describe how infant intelligence is measured using information processing approaches.

Maddy Rodriguez is a bundle of curiosity and energy. At 6 months old, she cries heartily if she can't reach a toy, and when she sees a reflection of herself in a mirror, she gurgles and seems, in general, to find the situation quite amusing.

Bernhard Classen/Alamy Stock Photo

Infant intelligence is difficult to define and measure. Is this infant displaying intelligent behavior?

Jared Lynch, at 6 months, is a good deal more inhibited than Maddy. He doesn't seem to care much when a ball rolls out of his reach, losing interest in it rapidly. And unlike Maddy, when he sees himself in a mirror, he pretty much ignores the reflection.

As anyone who has spent any time at all observing more than one baby can tell you, not all infants are alike. Some are full of energy and life, apparently displaying a natural-born curiosity, while others seem, by comparison, somewhat less interested in the world around them. Does this mean that such infants differ in intelligence?

Answering questions about how and to what degree infants vary in their underlying intelligence is not easy. Although it is clear that different infants show significant variations in their behavior, the issue of just what types of behavior may be related to cognitive ability is complicated. Interestingly, the examination of individual differences between infants was the initial approach taken by developmental specialists to understand cognitive development, and such issues still represent an important focus within the field.

WHAT IS INFANT INTELLIGENCE? Before we can address whether and how infants may differ in intelligence, we need to consider what is meant by the term *intelligence*. Educators, psychologists, and other experts on development have yet to agree upon a general definition of intelligent behavior, even among adults. Is it the ability to do well in scholastic endeavors? Proficiency in business negotiations? Competence in navigating across treacherous seas, such as that shown by peoples of the South Pacific who have no knowledge of Western navigational techniques?

It is even more difficult to define and measure intelligence in infants than it is in adults. Do we base it on the speed with which a new task is learned through classical or operant conditioning? How fast a baby becomes habituated to a new stimulus? The age at which an infant learns to crawl or walk? Even if we are able to identify particular behaviors that seem to differentiate one infant from another in terms of intelligence during infancy, we need to address a further, and probably more important, issue: How well do measures of infant intelligence relate to eventual adult intelligence?

Such questions are not simple, and no simple answers have been found. However, developmental specialists have devised several approaches (summarized in Table 5-2) to illuminate the nature of individual differences in intelligence during infancy.

Table 5-2 Approaches Used to Detect Differences in Intelligence During Infancy

Developmental quotient	Formulated by Arnold Gesell, the developmental quotient is an overall development score that relates to performance in four domains: motor skills (balance and sitting), language use, adaptive behavior (alertness and exploration), and personal–social behavior.
Bayley Scales of Infant Development	Developed by Nancy Bayley, the Bayley Scales of Infant Development evaluate an infant's development from 2 to 42 months. The Bayley Scales focus on two areas: mental abilities (senses, perception, memory, learning, problem solving, and language) and motor abilities (fine and gross motor skills).
Visual-recognition memory measurement	Measures of visual-recognition memory, the memory and recognition of a stimulus that has been previously seen, also relate to intelligence. The more quickly an infant can retrieve a representation of a stimulus from memory, the more efficient, presumably, is that infant's information processing.

DEVELOPMENTAL SCALES. Developmental psychologist Arnold Gesell formulated the earliest measure of infant development, which was designed to distinguish between normally developing and atypically developing babies (Gesell, 1946). Gesell based his scale on examinations of hundreds of babies. He compared their performance at different ages to learn what behaviors were most common at a particular age. If an infant varied significantly from the norms of a given age, he or she was considered to be developmentally delayed or advanced.

Following the lead of researchers who sought to quantify intelligence through a specific score (known as an intelligence quotient, or IQ, score), Gesell (1946) developed a developmental quotient, or DQ. The **developmental quotient** is an overall developmental score that relates to performance in four domains: motor skills (for example, balance and sitting), language use, adaptive behavior (such as alertness and exploration), and personal–social behavior (for example, adequately feeding and dressing oneself).

developmental quotient

an overall developmental score that relates to performance in four domains: motor skills, language use, adaptive behavior, and personal–social behavior

Later researchers have created other developmental scales. For instance, Nancy Bayley developed one of the most widely used measures for infants. The **Bayley Scales of Infant Development** evaluate an infant's development from 2 to 42 months. The Bayley Scales focus on two areas: mental abilities and motor abilities. The mental scale focuses on the senses, perception, memory, learning, problem solving, and language, while the motor scale evaluates fine and gross motor skills (see Table 5-3). Like Gesell's approach, the Bayley approach yields a developmental quotient (DQ). A child who scores at an average level—meaning average performance for other children at the same age—receives a score of 100 (Bos, 2013; Greene et al., 2013).

Bayley Scales of Infant Development

a measure that evaluates an infant's development from 2 to 42 months in two areas: mental abilities and motor abilities

The virtue of approaches such as those taken by Gesell and Bayley is that they provide a good snapshot of an infant's current developmental level. Using these scales, we can tell in an objective manner whether a particular infant falls behind or is ahead of his or her same-age peers.

The scales are particularly useful in identifying cases in which infants need immediate special attention. Tests might be administered if a parent or physician believes that an infant is suffering from developmental delays and to assess the significance of such delays. Based on the child's scores, early intervention programs can be put in place (Aylward & Verhulst, 2000; Sonne, 2012; Bode et al., 2014).

What such scales are not useful for is predicting a child's future course of development. A child whose development is identified by these measures as relatively slow at the age of 1 year will not necessarily display slow development at age 5, or 12, or 25. The association between most measures of behavior during infancy and adult intelligence, then, is minimal (Murray et al., 2007; Burakevych et al., 2017).

From *a nurse's* perspective

In what ways is the use of such developmental scales as Gesell's or Bayley's helpful? In what ways is it dangerous? How would you maximize the helpfulness and minimize the danger if you were advising a parent?

Table 5-3 Sample Items from the Bayley Scales of Infant Development

Age	2 months	6 months	12 months	17–19 months	23–25 months	38–42 months
Mental scale	Turns head to locate origin of sound; visibly responds to disappearance of face	Picks up cup by handle; notices illustrations in a book	Constructs tower of two cubes; can turn pages in a book	Mimics crayon stroke; labels objects in photo	Pairs up pictures; repeats a two-word sentence	Can identify four colors; past tense evident in speech; distinguishes gender
Motor scale	Can hold head steady and erect for 15 seconds; sits with assistance	Sits up without aid for 30 seconds; grasps foot with hands	Walks when holding onto someone's hand or furniture; holds pencil in fist	Stands on right foot without help; remains upright climbing stairs with assistance	Strings three beads; jumps length of 4 inches	Can reproduce drawing of a circle; hops two times on one foot; descends stairs, alternating feet

(**Source:** Based on Bayley, N. (2005). *Bayley Scales of Infant Development* [BSID-III], 3rd ed. San Antonio, TX: The Psychological Corporation.)

INFORMATION PROCESSING APPROACHES TO INDIVIDUAL DIFFERENCES IN INTELLIGENCE. When we speak of intelligence in everyday parlance, we often differentiate between "quick" and "slow" individuals. According to research on the speed of information processing, such terms hold some truth. Contemporary approaches to infant intelligence suggest that the speed with which infants process information may correlate most strongly with later intelligence, as measured by IQ tests administered during adulthood (Rose et al., 2012).

How can we tell whether a baby is processing information quickly? To answer this question, most researchers use habituation tests. Infants who process information efficiently ought to be able to learn about stimuli more quickly. Consequently, we would expect them to turn their attention away from a given stimulus more rapidly than those who are less efficient at information processing, leading to the phenomenon of habituation. Similarly, measures of *visual-recognition memory*, the memory and recognition of a stimulus that has been previously seen, as well as attention and representational competence, also relate to IQ. The more quickly an infant can retrieve a representation of a stimulus from memory, the more efficient, presumably, is that infant's information processing (Robinson & Pascalis, 2005; Rose et al., 2012; Trainor, 2012).

Research using an information processing framework clearly suggests a relationship between information processing efficiency and cognitive abilities: Measures of how quickly infants lose interest in stimuli that they have previously seen, as well as their responsiveness to new stimuli, correlate moderately well with later measures of intelligence. Infants who are more efficient information processors during the 6 months following birth tend to have higher intelligence scores between 2 and 12 years of age, as well as higher scores on other measures of cognitive competence (Rose, Feldman, & Jankowski, 2009; Otsuka et al., 2014).

Other research suggests that abilities related to the *multimodal approach to perception* may offer clues about later intelligence. For instance, the ability to identify a stimulus that previously has been experienced through only one sense by using another sense (called *cross-modal transference*) is associated with intelligence. A baby who is able to recognize by sight a screwdriver that she has previously only touched, but not seen, is displaying cross-modal transference. Research has found that the degree of cross-modal transference displayed by an infant at age 1—which requires a high level of abstract thinking—is associated with intelligence scores several years later (Rose, Feldman, & Jankowski, 2015).

Although information processing efficiency and cross-modal transference abilities during infancy relate moderately well to later IQ scores, we need to keep in mind two qualifications. First, even though there is an association between early information processing capabilities and later measures of IQ, the correlation is only moderately strong. Other factors, such as the degree of environmental stimulation, also play a crucial role in helping to determine adult intelligence. Consequently, we should not assume that intelligence is somehow permanently fixed in infancy.

Second, and perhaps even more important, intelligence measured by traditional IQ tests relates to a particular type of intelligence, one that emphasizes abilities that lead to academic, and certainly not artistic or professional, success. Consequently, predicting that a child may do well on IQ tests later in life is not the same as predicting that the child will be successful later in life.

Despite these qualifications, the relatively recent finding that an association exists between efficiency of information processing and later IQ scores does suggest some consistency of cognitive development across the life span. Whereas the earlier reliance on scales such as the Bayley Scales led to the misconception that little continuity existed, the more recent information processing approaches suggest that cognitive development unfolds in a more orderly, continuous manner from infancy to the later stages of life. (Also see the *Development in Your Life* feature regarding ways of promoting infants' cognitive development.)

Development in Your Life

What Can You Do to Promote Infants' Cognitive Development?

All parents want their children to reach their full cognitive potential, but sometimes efforts to reach this goal take a bizarre path. For instance, some parents spend hundreds of dollars enrolling in workshops with titles such as "How to Multiply Your Baby's Intelligence" and buying books with titles such as *How to Teach Your Baby to Read*.

Do such efforts ever succeed? Although some parents swear they do, there is no scientific support for the effectiveness of such programs. For example, despite the many cognitive skills of infants, no infant can actually read. Furthermore, "multiplying" a baby's intelligence is impossible, and such organizations as the American Academy of Pediatrics and the American Academy of Neurology have denounced programs that claim to do so.

However, certain things can be done to promote cognitive development in infants. The following suggestions, based on the findings of developmental researchers, offer a starting point:

- **Provide infants the opportunity to explore the world.** As Piaget suggests, children learn by doing, and they need the opportunity to explore and probe their environment.
- **Be responsive to infants on both a verbal and a nonverbal level.** Try to speak *with* babies, as opposed to *at* them. Ask questions, listen to their responses, and provide further communication (Merlo, Bowman, & Barnett, 2007).
- **Read to your infants.** Although they may not understand the meaning of your words, they will respond to your tone of voice and the intimacy provided by the activity. Reading together also is associated with later literacy skills and begins to create a lifelong reading habit.
- **Keep in mind that you don't have to be with an infant 24 hours a day.** Just as infants need time to explore their world on their own, parents and other caregivers need time off from child-care activities.

Even if they don't understand the meaning of the words, infants still benefit from being read to.

- **Don't push infants, and don't expect too much too soon.** Your goal should not be to create a genius; it should be to provide a warm, nurturing environment that will allow an infant to reach his or her potential.

ASSESSING INFORMATION PROCESSING APPROACHES. The information processing perspective on cognitive development during infancy is very different from Piaget's perspective. Rather than focusing on broad explanations of the *qualitative* changes that occur in infants' capabilities, as Piaget does, information processing looks at *quantitative* change. Piaget sees cognitive growth occurring in fairly sudden spurts; information processing sees more gradual, step-by-step growth. (Think of the difference between a track-and-field runner leaping hurdles and a slow-but-steady marathon racer.)

Because information processing researchers consider cognitive development in terms of a collection of individual skills, they are often able to use more precise measures of cognitive ability, such as processing speed and memory recall, than proponents of Piaget's approach. Still, the very precision of these individual measures makes it harder to get an overall sense of the nature of cognitive development, something at which Piaget was a master.

From Research to Practice

Why Formal Education Is Lost on Infants

Can you make babies smarter?

Apparently, a lot of parents think so, because collectively they're spending millions of dollars exposing infants to educational toys and media that they hope will be beneficial to their infants' cognitive growth. Parents who want to give their infant children a leg up on learning quickly find that there is no shortage of products and services that claim to do exactly that. Educational videos such as "Baby Einstein" and "Brainy Baby" promise to stimulate young minds. A wide variety of infant toys are marketed with claims that they can enhance cognitive development. And parents sometimes try implementing structured learning activities of their own design, such as flashcards, to make their babies smarter.

But do any of these strategies really work? Most evidence suggests that they don't work very well, and that in some cases their use may even backfire and impede learning. The problem stems from the faulty assumption that infants learn the way older children do—that they can benefit from structured activities that have specific learning goals. Research suggests that this approach is at odds with the way that infants actually try to make sense of their world. Whereas older children and adults take in information in a goal-directed way, looking for solutions to defined problems, infants merely explore their surroundings in an unplanned way. Structured learning experiences fail to account for this unique infant perspective (Zimmerman, Christakis & Meltzoff, 2007; Berger et al, 2015; Anderson, 2016).

Moreover, some research shows that educational media not only are ineffective in promoting cognitive development, but they actually may harm it. For example, one study showed the children who watched educational videos and DVDs between the ages of 7 and 16 months actually showed poorer language development, knowing fewer words and phrases, than those who did not watch such media. However, these results have not received consistent support (Zimmerman, Christakis, & Meltzoff, 2007; Ferguson & Donnellan, 2014).

In short, research does not consistently support the usefulness of strategies that seek to advance infants' cognitive development. For the moment, parents and other caretakers should follow the advice of the American Academy of Pediatrics, that media exposure prior to the age of 2 should be limited, particularly during meals and an hour before bedtime. Instead, it suggests using strategies that have consistently been shown to be beneficial to infant cognitive development: talking, playing, reading, and singing to infants and encouraging hands-on exploration and social interaction (AAP Council on Communications and the Media, 2016).

Shared Writing Prompt

Do you think that purchasing educational toys and media for infants is worth a try, despite the lack of scientific research supporting its use? Why? Under what conditions might its use actually have undesirable consequences?

It's as if information processing approaches focus more on the individual pieces of the puzzle of cognitive development, while Piagetian approaches focus more on the whole puzzle (Kagan, 2008; Quinn, 2008).

Ultimately, both Piagetian and information processing approaches are critical in providing an account of cognitive development in infancy. Coupled with advances in the biochemistry of the brain and theories that consider the effects of social factors on learning and cognition, the two help us paint a full picture of cognitive development. (Also see *From Research to Practice*.)

Module 5.2 Review

LO 5.4 Describe how infants process information according to information processing approaches to cognitive development.

Information processing approaches consider quantitative changes in children's abilities to organize and use information. Cognitive growth is regarded as the increasing sophistication of encoding, storage, and retrieval.

LO 5.5 Describe the memory capabilities of infants during their first 2 years of life.

Infants clearly have memory capabilities from a very early age, although the duration and accuracy of such memories are unresolved questions.

LO 5.6 Describe how infant intelligence is measured using information processing approaches.

Traditional measures of infant intelligence focus on behavioral attainments, which can help identify developmental delays or advances but are not strongly related to measures of adult intelligence. Information processing approaches to assessing intelligence rely on variations in the speed and quality with which infants process information.

Journal Writing Prompt

Applying Lifespan Development: What information from this chapter could you use to refute the claims of books or educational programs that promise to help parents increase their babies' intelligence or instill advanced intellectual skills in infants? Based on valid research, what approaches would you use for intellectual development of infants?

The Roots of Language

Vicki and Dominic were engaged in a friendly competition over whose name would be the first word their baby, Maura, said. "Say 'mama,'" Vicki would coo, before handing Maura over to Dominic for a diaper change. Grinning, he would take her and coax, "No, say 'daddy.'" Both parents ended up losing—and winning—when Maura's first word sounded more like "baba," and seemed to refer to her bottle.

Mama. No. Cookie. Dad. Jo. Most parents can remember their baby's first word, and no wonder. It's an exciting moment, this emergence of a skill that is, arguably, unique to human beings.

But those initial words are just the first and most obvious manifestations of language. Many months earlier, infants began to understand the language used by others to make sense of the world around them. How does this linguistic ability develop? What is the pattern and sequence of language development? And how does the use of language transform the cognitive world of infants and their parents? We consider these questions, and others, as we address the development of language during the first years of life.

The Fundamentals of Language: From Sounds to Symbols

LO 5.7 Outline the processes by which children learn to use language.

Language, the systematic, meaningful arrangement of symbols, provides the basis for communication. But it does more than this: It is closely tied to the way we think and how we understand the world. It enables us to reflect on people and objects and to convey our thoughts to others.

language
the systematic, meaningful arrangement of symbols, which provides the basis for communication

Language has several formal characteristics that must be mastered as linguistic competence is developed. They include:

- ***Phonology.*** Phonology refers to the basic sounds of language, called *phonemes*, that can be combined to produce words and sentences. For instance, the "a" in "mat" and the "a" in "mate" represent two different phonemes in English. Although English employs just 44 phonemes to create every word in the language, other languages have as many as 85 phonemes—and some as few as 15 (Swingley, 2017).
- ***Morphemes.*** A morpheme is the smallest language unit that has meaning. Some morphemes are complete words, while others add information necessary for interpreting a word, such as the endings "-s" for plural and "-ed" for past tense.
- ***Semantics.*** Semantics are the rules that govern the meaning of words and sentences. As their knowledge of semantics develops, children are able to understand the subtle distinction between "Ellie was hit by a ball" (an answer to the question of why Ellie doesn't want to play catch) and "A ball hit Ellie" (used to announce the current situation).

In considering the development of language, we need to distinguish between linguistic *comprehension*, the understanding of speech, and linguistic *production*, the use of language to communicate. One principle underlies the relationship between the two:

Figure 5-4 Comprehension Precedes Production

Throughout infancy, the comprehension of speech precedes the production of speech. **THINKING ABOUT THE DATA:** Choose one vocalization/speech skill and compare it to a corresponding language comprehension skill. Which skills emerges first and what is the length of time between the emergence of both skills? How might one skill rely on the other?

(**Source:** Based on Bornstein & Lamb, 1992.)

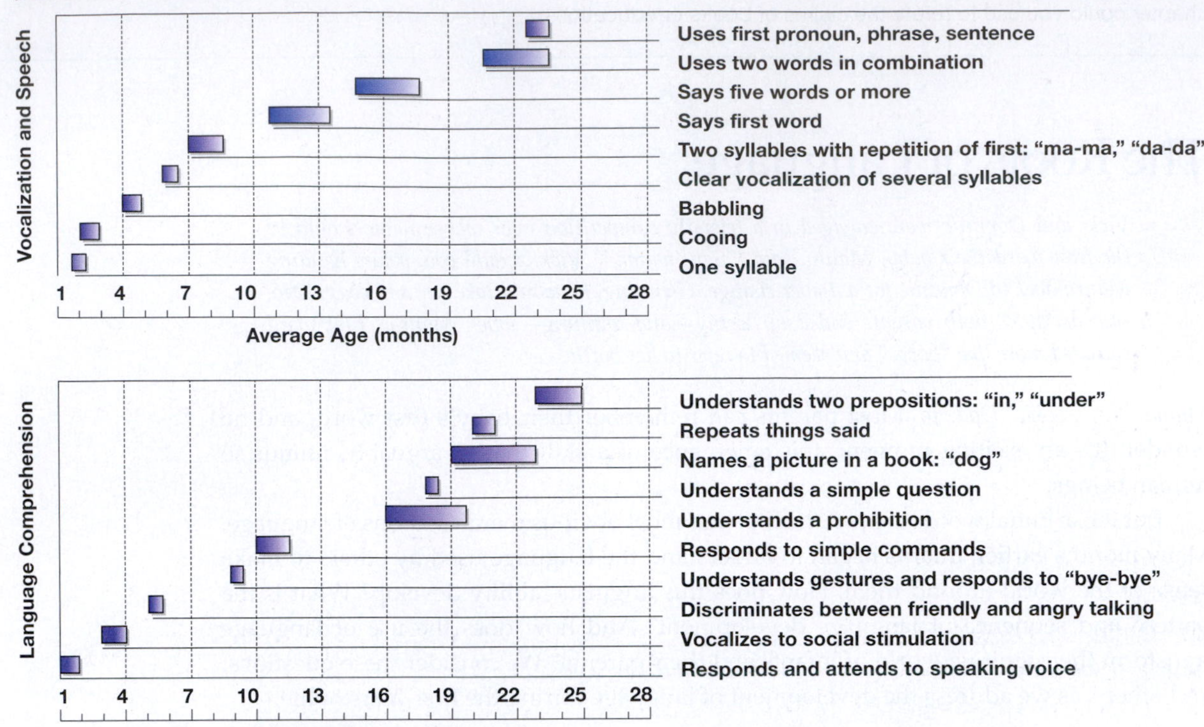

Comprehension precedes production. An 18-month-old may be able to understand a complex series of directions ("Pick up your coat from the floor and put it on the chair by the fireplace.") but may not yet have strung more than two words together when speaking for herself. Throughout infancy, comprehension also outpaces production. For instance, during infancy, comprehension of words expands at a rate of 22 new words a month, while production of words increases at a rate of about 9 new words a month, once talking begins (Shafto et al., 2012; Phung, Milojevich, & Lukowski, 2014; Swingley, 2017; see Figure 5-4).

EARLY SOUNDS AND COMMUNICATION. Spend 24 hours with even a very young infant, and you will hear a variety of sounds: cooing, crying, gurgling, murmuring, and assorted other noises. These sounds, though not meaningful in themselves, play an important role in linguistic development, paving the way for true language (O'Grady & Aitchison, 2005; Martin, Onishi & Vouloumanos, 2012).

Prelinguistic communication is communication through sounds, facial expressions, gestures, imitation, and other nonlinguistic means. When a father responds to his daughter's "ah" with an "ah" of his own, and then the daughter repeats the sound, and the father responds once again, they are engaged in prelinguistic communication. Clearly, the "ah" sound has no particular meaning. However, its repetition, which mimics the give-and-take of conversation, teaches the infant something about turn-taking and the back-and-forth of communication (Reddy, 1999).

The most obvious manifestation of prelinguistic communication is babbling. **Babbling**, making speech-like but meaningless sounds, starts at the age of 2 or 3 months and continues until around the age of 1 year. When they babble, infants repeat the same vowel sound over and over, changing the pitch from high to low (as in "ee-ee-ee," repeated at different pitches). After the age of 5 months, the sounds of babbling begin to expand, reflecting the addition of consonants (such as "bee-bee-bee-bee").

babbling
making speech-like but meaningless sounds

Babbling is a universal phenomenon, accomplished in the same way throughout all cultures. While they are babbling, infants spontaneously produce all of the sounds found in every language, not just the language they hear people around them speaking.

Even deaf children display their own form of babbling: Infants who cannot hear and who are exposed to sign language babble with their hands instead of their voices. Their gestural babbling thus is analogous to the verbal babbling of children who can hear. Furthermore, as shown in Figure 5-5, the areas of the brain activated during the production of hand gestures are similar to the areas activated during speech production, suggesting that spoken language may have evolved from gestural language (Gentilucci & Corballis, 2006; Caselli et al., 2012).

Babbling, which follows a prelinguistic stage of cooing, typically follows a progression from simple to more complex sounds. Although exposure to the sounds of a particular language does not seem to influence babbling initially, eventually experience does make a difference. By the age of 6 months, babbling reflects the sounds of the language to which infants are exposed (Blake & de Boysson-Bardies, 1992; Plummer & Beckman, 2015; McGillion et al., 2017).

The difference between cultures is so noticeable that even untrained listeners can distinguish between babbling infants who have been raised in cultures in which French, Arabic, or Cantonese languages are spoken. Furthermore, the speed at which infants begin homing in on their own language is related to the speed of later language development (Whalen, Levitt, & Goldstein, 2007; Depaolis, Vihman, & Nakai, 2013; Masapollo, Polka, & Ménard, 2015).

There are other indications of prelinguistic speech. For instance, consider 5-month-old Marta, who spies her red ball just beyond her reach. After reaching for it and finding that she is unable to get to it, she makes a cry of anger that alerts her parents that something is amiss, and her mother hands it to her. Communication has occurred.

Four months later, when Marta faces the same situation, she no longer bothers to reach for the ball and doesn't respond in anger. Instead, she holds out her arm in the direction of the ball, and with great purpose, seeks to catch her mother's eye. When her mother sees the behavior, she knows just what Marta wants. Clearly, Marta's communicative skills—though still prelinguistic—have taken a leap forward.

Even these prelinguistic skills are supplanted in just a few months, when the gesture gives way to a new communicative skill: producing an actual word. Marta's parents clearly hear her say "ball."

FIRST WORDS. When a mother and father first hear their child say "Mama" or "Dada," or even "baba," as in the case of Maura, the baby described earlier in this section, it is

Figure 5-5 Broca's Area

Areas of the brain that are activated during speech, left, are similar to areas activated during the production of hand gestures, right.

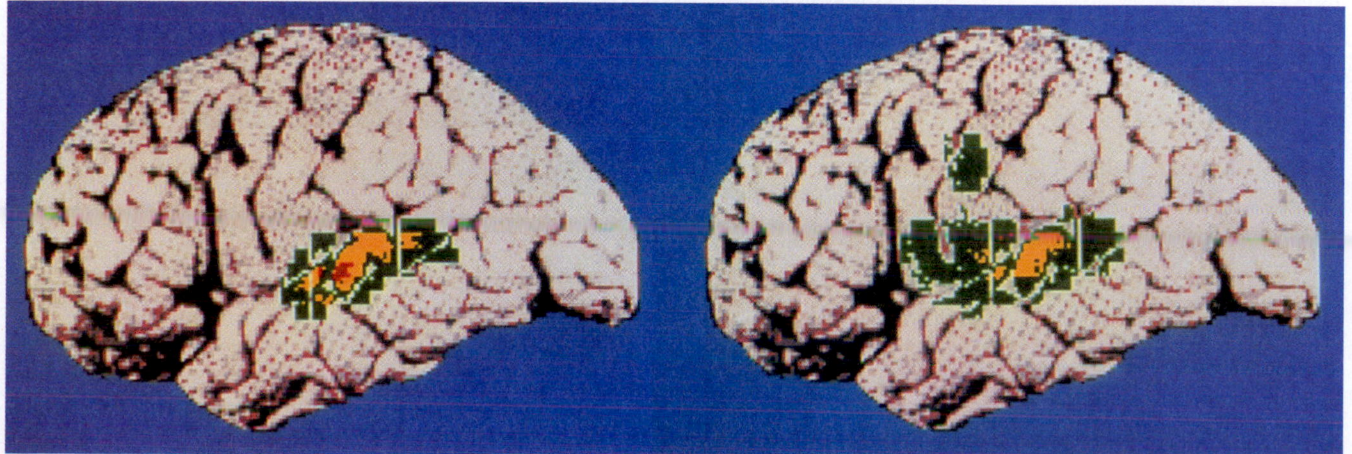

SPL/Science Source

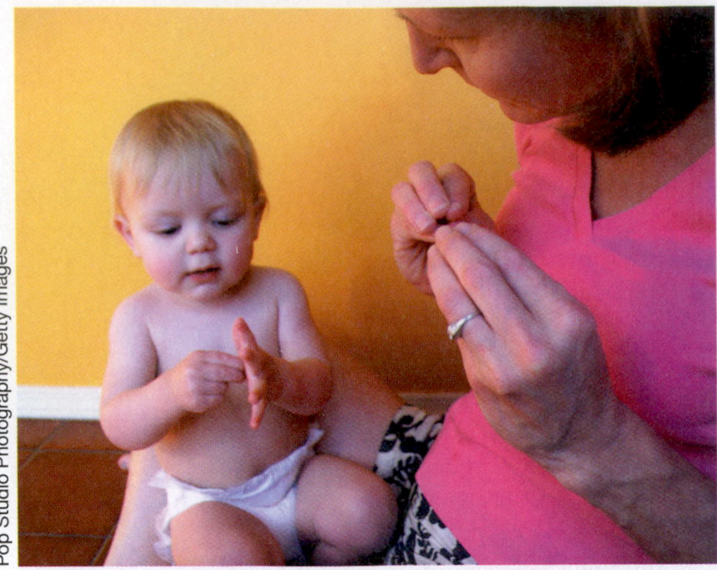

Deaf infants who are exposed to sign language do their own type of babbling, related to the use of signs.

hard to be anything but delighted. But their initial enthusiasm may be dampened a bit when they find that the same sound is used to ask for a cookie, a doll, and a ratty old blanket.

First words generally are spoken somewhere around the age of 10 to 14 months but may occur as early as 9 months. Linguists differ on just how to recognize that a first word has actually been uttered. Some say it is when an infant clearly understands words and can produce a sound that is close to a word spoken by adults, such as a child who uses "mama" for any request she may have. Other linguists use a stricter criterion for the first word; they restrict "first word" to cases in which children give a clear, consistent name to a person, event, or object. In this view, "mama" counts as a first word only if it is consistently applied to the same person, seen in a variety of situations and doing a variety of things, and is not used to label other people (Hollich et al., 2000; Masataka, 2003; Koenig & Cole, 2013).

Although there is disagreement over when we can say a first word has been uttered, no one disputes that once an infant starts to produce words, vocabulary increases at a rapid rate. By the age of 15 months, the average child has a vocabulary of 10 words and methodically expands until the one-word stage of language development ends at around 18 months. Once that happens, a sudden spurt in vocabulary occurs. In just a short period—a few weeks somewhere between 16 and 24 months of age—there is an explosion of language, in which a child's vocabulary typically increases from 50 to 400 words (Nazzi & Bertoncini, 2003; McMurray, Aslin, & Toscano, 2009; Dehaene-Lambertz, 2017).

holophrases

one-word utterances that stand for a whole phrase, whose meaning depends on the particular context in which they are used

As you can see from the list in Figure 5-6, the first words in children's early vocabularies typically regard objects and things, both animate and inanimate. Most often they refer to people or objects who constantly appear and disappear ("Mama"), to animals ("kitty"), or to temporary states ("wet"). These first words are often **holophrases**, one-word utterances that stand for a whole phrase, whose meaning depends on the particular context in which they are used. For instance, a youngster may use the phrase "ma" to mean, depending on the context, "I want to be picked up by Mom" or "I want something to eat, Mom" or "Where's Mom?" (Dromi, 1987; O'Grady & Aitchison, 2005; also see *Developmental Diversity and Your Life*).

Figure 5-6 The Top 50: The First Words Children Understand and Speak

(**Source:** Based on Benedict, 1979.)

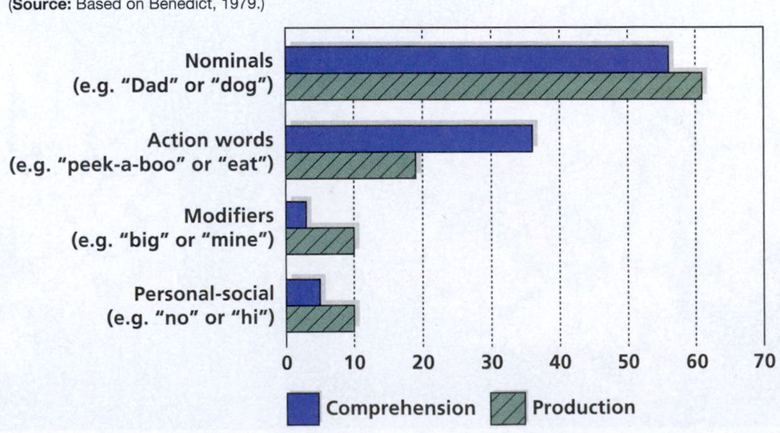

Developmental Diversity and Your Life

First Words Across the World

Does the culture and language to which infants are exposed affect their first words? The answer is clearly yes.

For example, one study looked at the first 10 words produced by infants in three cultures—North America, Hong Kong, and Beijing—who spoke English, Putonghua, and Cantonese, respectively. The researchers found that although there were commonalities ("Daddy" and "Mommy" were among the first words used in all three cultures), there were also differences. For instance, among the English-speaking infants, there were three people-related and four animal-related terms, but there were eight and nine people-related terms and no animal terms for the Cantonese and Putonghua speakers (Tardif et al., 2008; Tardif et al., 2012).

Moreover, culture has an effect on the *type* of first words spoken. For example, unlike North American English-speaking infants, who are more apt to use nouns initially, Chinese Mandarin-speaking infants use more verbs than nouns. Interestingly, by the age of 20 months, there are remarkable cross-cultural similarities in the types of words spoken. For example, a comparison of 20-month-olds in Argentina, Belgium, France, Israel, Italy, and the Republic of Korea found that children's vocabularies in every culture contained greater proportions of nouns than other classes of words (Tardif, 1996; Bornstein, Cote, & Maital, 2004; Andruski, Casielles, & Nathan, 2014).

In short, there are both similarities and differences in the earliest words spoken by infants due to the culture in which they are raised and the language spoken in their environments.

FIRST SENTENCES. When Aaron was 19 months old, he heard his mother coming up the back steps, as she did every day just before dinner. Aaron turned to his father and distinctly said, "Ma come." In stringing those two words together, Aaron took a giant step in his language development.

The explosive increase in vocabulary that comes at around 18 months is accompanied by another accomplishment: the linking together of individual words into sentences that convey a single thought. Although there is a good deal of variability in the time at which children first create two-word phrases, it is generally around 8 to 12 months after they say their first word.

The linguistic advance represented by two-word combinations is important because the linkage not only provides labels for things in the world but also indicates the relations between them. For instance, the combination may declare something about possession ("Mama key") or recurrent events ("Dog bark"). Interestingly, most early sentences don't represent demands or even necessarily require a response. Instead, they are often merely comments and observations about events occurring in the child's world (O'Grady & Aitchison, 2005; Rossi et al., 2012).

Two-year-olds using two-word combinations tend to employ particular sequences that are similar to the ways in which adult sentences are constructed. For instance, sentences in English typically follow a pattern in which the subject of the sentence comes first, followed by the verb, and then the object ("Josh threw the ball"). Children's speech most often uses a similar order, although not all the words are initially included. Consequently, a child might say "Josh threw" or "Josh ball" to indicate the same thought. What is significant is that the order is typically not "threw Josh" or "ball Josh," but rather the usual order of English, which makes the utterance much easier for an English speaker to comprehend (Hirsh-Pasek & Michnick-Golinkoff, 1995; Masataka, 2003).

Although the creation of two-word sentences represents an advance, the language used by children still is by no means adult-like. As we've just seen, 2-year-olds tend to leave out words that aren't critical to the message, similar to the way we might write a telegram for which we were paying by the word. For that reason, their talk is often called **telegraphic speech**. Rather than saying, "I put on my shoes," a child using telegraphic speech might say, "My shoes on." "I want to ride the pony" might become "I want pony" (see Table 5-4).

telegraphic speech
speech in which words not critical to the message are left out

Table 5-4 Children's Imitation of Sentences Showing Decline of Telegraphic Speech

Sample Sentences	Speaker	26 months	29 months	32 months	35 months
I put on my shoes	Kim Darden	Shoes Shoes on	My shoes My shoes on	I put on shoes Put on shoes	A Put on my shoes
I will not go to bed	Kim Darden	No bed Not go bed	Not go bed I not go bed	I not go bed I not go to bed	I not go to bed I will not go bed
I want to ride the pony	Kim Darden	Pony, pony Want pony	Want ride pony I want pony	I want ride pony I want the pony	I want to ride pony A

A = accurate imitation.

(**Source:** Based on Brown & Fraser, 1963.)

Early language has other characteristics that differentiate it from the language used by adults. For instance, consider Sarah, who refers to the blanket she sleeps with as "blankie." When her Aunt Ethel gives her a new blanket, Sarah refuses to call the new one a "blankie," restricting the word to her original blanket.

underextension
the overly restrictive use of words, common among children just mastering spoken language

Sarah's inability to generalize the label of "blankie" to blankets in general is an example of **underextension**, using words too restrictively, which is common among children just mastering spoken language. Underextension occurs when language novices think that a word refers to a specific instance of a concept, instead of to all examples of the concept (Caplan & Barr, 1989; Masataka, 2003).

overextension
the overly broad use of words, overgeneralizing their meaning

As infants like Sarah grow more adept with language, the opposite phenomenon sometimes occurs. In **overextension**, words are used too broadly, overgeneralizing their meaning. For example, when Sarah refers to buses, trucks, and tractors as "cars," she is guilty of overextension, making the assumption that any object with wheels must be a car. Although overextension reflects speech errors, it also shows that advances are occurring in the child's thought processes: The child is beginning to develop general mental categories and concepts (McDonough, 2002; Walaszewska, 2011).

referential style
a style of language use in which language is used primarily to label objects

expressive style
a style of language use in which language is used primarily to express feelings and needs about oneself and others

Infants also show individual differences in the style of language they use. For example, some use a **referential style**, in which language is used primarily to label objects. Others tend to use an **expressive style**, in which language is used mainly to express feelings and needs about oneself and others (Bates et al., 1994; Nelson, 1996; Bornstein, 2000). Language styles reflect, in part, cultural factors. For example, mothers in the United States label objects more frequently than do Japanese mothers, encouraging a more referential style of speech. In contrast, mothers in Japan are more apt to speak about social interactions, encouraging a more expressive style of speech (Fernald & Morikawa, 1993).

The Origins of Language Development

LO 5.8 Outline the major theories of language development.

The immense strides in language development during the preschool years raise a fundamental question: How does proficiency in language come about? Linguists are deeply divided on how to answer this question.

learning theory approach to language
the theory that language acquisition follows the basic laws of reinforcement and conditioning

LEARNING THEORY APPROACHES: LANGUAGE AS A LEARNED SKILL. One view of language development emphasizes the basic principles of learning. According to the **learning theory approach**, language acquisition follows the basic laws of reinforcement and conditioning discussed in Chapter 1 (Skinner, 1957). For instance, a child who articulates the word "da" may be hugged and praised by her father, who jumps to the conclusion that she is referring to him. This reaction reinforces the child, who is more likely to repeat the word. In sum, the learning theory perspective on language acquisition suggests that children learn to speak by being rewarded for making sounds that approximate speech. Through the process of *shaping*, language becomes more and more similar to adult speech.

There's a problem, though, with the learning theory approach: It doesn't seem to adequately explain how children acquire the rules of language as readily as they do. For instance, young children are reinforced when they make errors. Parents are apt to be just as responsive if their child says, "Why the dog won't eat?" as they are if the child phrases the question more correctly ("Why won't the dog eat?"). Both forms of the question are understood correctly, and both elicit the same response; reinforcement is provided for both correct and incorrect language usage. Under such circumstances, learning theory is hard-put to explain how children learn to speak properly.

Jin Yong/Shutterstock

In what ways do parents shape their children's speaking abilities?

Children are also able to move beyond specific utterances they have heard and produce novel phrases, sentences, and constructions, an ability that also cannot be explained by learning theory. Furthermore, children can apply linguistic rules to nonsense words. In one study, 4-year-old children heard the nonsense verb "to pilk" in the sentence "the bear is pilking the horse." Later, when asked what was happening to the horse, they responded by placing the nonsense verb in the correct tense and voice: "He's getting pilked by the bear."

NATIVIST APPROACHES: LANGUAGE AS AN INNATE SKILL. Such conceptual difficulties with the learning theory approach have led to the development of an alternative theory, championed by linguist Noam Chomsky and known as the nativist approach (1999, 2005). The **nativist approach** argues that there is a genetically determined, innate mechanism that directs the development of language. According to Chomsky, people are born with an innate capacity to use language, which emerges, more or less automatically, due to maturation.

nativist approach to language
the theory that a genetically determined, innate mechanism directs language development

Chomsky's analysis of different languages suggests that all the world's languages share a similar underlying structure, which he calls **universal grammar**. In this view, the human brain is wired with a neural system called the **language-acquisition device (LAD)** that both permits the understanding of language structure and provides a set of strategies and techniques for learning the particular characteristics of the language to which a child is exposed. In this view, language is uniquely human, made possible by a genetic predisposition to both comprehend and produce words and sentences (Wommacott, 2013; Bolhuis et al., 2014; Yang et al., 2017).

universal grammar
Noam Chomsky's theory that all the world's languages share a similar underlying structure

language-acquisition device (LAD)
a neural system of the brain hypothesized to permit understanding of language

Support for Chomsky's nativist approach comes from findings identifying a specific gene related to speech production. Further support comes from research showing that language processing in infants involves brain structures similar to those in adult speech processing, suggesting an evolutionary basis for language (Dehaene-Lambertz, Hertz-Pannier, & Dubois, 2006).

The view that language is an innate ability unique to humans also has its critics. For instance, some researchers argue that certain primates are able to learn at least the basics of language, an ability that calls into question the uniqueness of the human linguistic capacity. Furthermore, some critics believe that infants' use of general cognitive abilities underlies their language learning. Still others point out that although humans may be genetically primed to use language, its use still requires significant social experience in order for it to be used effectively (Savage-Rumbaugh et al., 1993; Goldberg, 2004; Ibbotson & Tomasello, 2016).

THE INTERACTIONIST APPROACHES. Neither the learning theory nor the nativist perspective fully explains language acquisition. As a result, some theorists have turned to a theory that combines both schools of thought. The **interactionist approach to language** suggests that language development is produced through a combination of genetically determined predispositions and environmental circumstances that help teach language.

interactionist approach to language
the perspective that suggests that language development is produced through a combination of genetically determined predispositions and environmental circumstances that help teach language

The interactionist perspective accepts that innate factors shape the broad outlines of language development. However, interactionists also argue that the specific course of language development is determined by the language to which children are exposed and the reinforcement they receive for using language in particular ways. Social factors are considered to be key to development, since the motivation provided by one's membership in a society and culture and one's interactions with others leads to the use of language and the growth of language skills (Dixon, 2004; Yang, 2006; Graf Estes, 2014).

Just as there is support for some aspects of learning theory and nativist positions, the interactionist perspective has also received some support. We don't know, at the moment, which of these positions will ultimately provide the best explanation. It is more likely that different factors play different roles at different times during childhood. The full explanation for language acquisition, then, remains to be found.

Speaking to Children: The Language of Infant-Directed and Gender-Related Speech

LO 5.9 Describe how children influence adults' language.

Say the following words aloud: Do you like the applesauce?

Now pretend that you are going to ask the same question of an infant, and speak it as you would for a young child's ears.

Chances are several things happened when you translated the phrase for the infant. First of all, the wording probably changed, and you may have said something like, "Does baby like the applesauce?" At the same time, the pitch of your voice probably rose, your general intonation most likely had a singsong quality, and you probably separated your words carefully.

infant-directed speech
a type of speech directed toward infants; characterized by short, simple sentences

INFANT-DIRECTED SPEECH. The shift in your language was due to your use of **infant-directed speech**, a style of speech that characterizes much of the verbal communication directed toward infants. This type of speech pattern used to be called *motherese* because it was assumed that it applied only to mothers. However, that assumption was wrong, and the gender-neutral term *infant-directed speech* is now used more frequently.

Infant-directed speech is characterized by short, simple sentences. Pitch becomes higher, the range of frequencies increases, and intonation is more varied. There is also repetition of words, and topics are restricted to items that are assumed to be comprehensible to infants, such as concrete objects in the baby's environment. (Infants are not the only ones who are the recipients of a specific form of speech: we change our style of speech when speaking to foreigners as well; Schachner & Hannon, 2011; Scott & Henderson, 2013; Hartman, Ratner, & Newman, 2017).

Sometimes infant-directed speech includes amusing sounds that are not even words, imitating the prelinguistic speech of infants. In other cases, it has little formal structure, but is similar to the kind of telegraphic speech that infants use as they develop their own language skills.

Infant-directed speech changes as children become older. Around the end of the first year, infant-directed speech takes on more adult qualities. Sentences become longer and more complex, although individual words are still spoken slowly and deliberately. Pitch is also used to focus attention on particularly important words (Soderstrom et al., 2008; Kitamura & Lam, 2009).

Infant-directed speech plays an important role in infants' acquisition of language. As discussed next, infant-directed speech occurs all over the world, though there are cultural variations. Newborns prefer such speech to regular language, a fact that suggests that they may be particularly receptive to it. Furthermore, some research suggests that babies who are exposed to a great deal of infant-directed speech early in life seem to begin to use words and exhibit other forms of linguistic competence earlier (Englund & Behne, 2006; Soderstrom, 2007; Werker et al., 2007; Bergelson & Swingley, 2012; Eaves et al., 2016).

Focus Pocus LTD/Fotolia

Zurijeta/Shutterstock

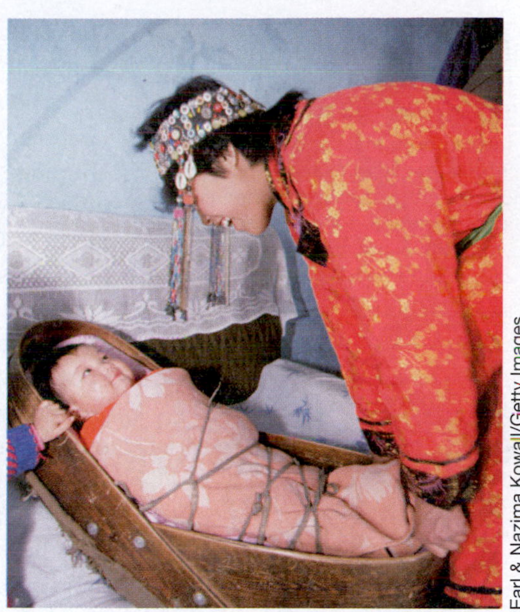
Earl & Nazima Kowall/Getty Images

Motherese, or, more precisely, infant-directed speech, includes the use of short, simple sentences and is spoken in a pitch that is higher than that used with older children and adults, and it is similar across cultures.

Developmental Diversity and Your Life

Is Infant-Directed Speech Similar in All Cultures?

Do mothers in the United States, Sweden, and Russia speak the same way to their infants?

In some respects, they clearly do. Although the words themselves differ across languages, the way the words are spoken to infants is quite similar. According to a growing body of research, there are basic similarities across cultures in the nature of infant-directed speech (Werker et al., 2007; Broesch & Bryant, 2015).

For example, 6 of the 10 most frequent major characteristics of speech directed at infants used by native speakers of English and Spanish are common to both languages: exaggerated intonation, high pitch, lengthened vowels, repetition, lower volume, and heavy stress on certain key words (such as emphasizing the word "ball" in the sentence, "No, that's a ball") (Blount, 1982). Similarly, mothers in the United States, Sweden, and Russia all exaggerate and elongate the pronunciation of the three-vowel sounds of "ee," "ah," and "oh" when speaking to infants in similar ways, despite differences in the languages in which the sounds are used (Kuhl et al., 1997).

Even deaf mothers use a form of infant-directed speech: When communicating with their infants, deaf mothers use sign language at a significantly slower tempo than when communicating with adults, and they frequently repeat the signs (Swanson, Leonard, & Gandour, 1992; Masataka, 1996, 1998, 2000).

The cross-cultural similarities in infant-directed speech are so great, in fact, that they appear in some facets of language specific to particular types of interactions. For instance, evidence comparing American English, German, and Mandarin Chinese speakers shows that in each of the languages, pitch rises when a mother is attempting to get an infant's attention or produce a response, while pitch falls when she is trying to calm an infant (Papousek & Papousek, 1991).

Why do we find such similarities across very different languages? One hypothesis is that the characteristics of infant-directed speech activate innate responses in infants. As we have noted, infants seem to prefer infant-directed speech over adult-directed speech, suggesting that their perceptual systems may be more responsive to such characteristics. Another explanation is that infant-directed speech facilitates language development, providing cues as to the meaning of speech before infants have developed the capacity to understand the meaning of words (Trainor & Desjardins, 2002; Falk, 2004; Hayashi & Mazuka, 2017).

Despite the similarities in the style of infant-directed speech across diverse cultures, there are some important cultural differences in the *quantity* of speech that infants hear from their parents. For example, although the Gusii of Kenya care for their infants in an extremely close, physical way, they speak to them less than American parents do (Levine, 1994).

There are also some stylistic differences related to cultural factors in the United States. A major factor, it seems, might be gender.

Figure 5-7 Diminishing Diminutives

Although the use of diminutives toward both male and female infants declines with age, they are consistently used more often in speech directed at females. What do you think is the cultural significance of this difference?

(**Source:** Gleason et al., 1991.)

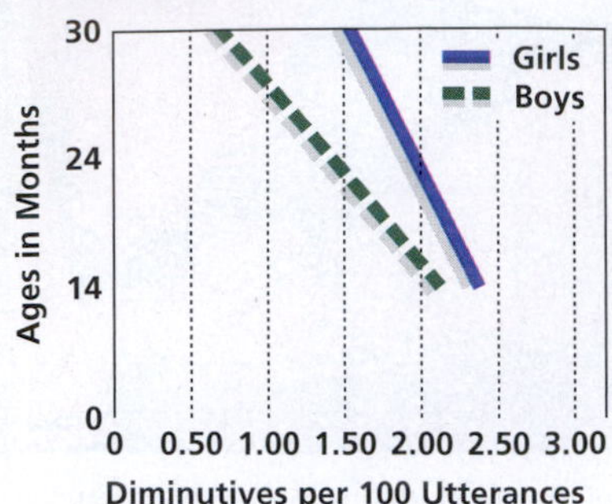

GENDER DIFFERENCES. To a girl, a bird is a birdie, a blanket a blankie, and a dog a doggy. To a boy, a bird is a bird, a blanket a blanket, and a dog a dog.

At least that's what parents of boys and girls appear to think, as illustrated by the language they use toward their sons and daughters. Virtually from the time of birth, the language parents employ with their children differs depending on the child's sex, according to research conducted by developmental psychologist Jean Berko Gleason (Gleason et al., 1994; Gleason & Ely, 2002; Arnon & Ramscar, 2012).

Gleason found that by the age of 32 months, girls hear twice as many diminutives (words such as "kitty" or "dolly" instead of "cat" or "doll") as boys hear. Although the use of diminutives declines with increasing age, their use consistently remains higher in speech directed at girls than in that directed at boys (see Figure 5-7).

Parents also are more apt to respond differently to children's requests depending on the child's gender. For instance, when turning down a child's request, mothers are likely to respond with a firm "no" to a male child but to soften the blow to a female child by providing a diversionary response ("Why don't you do this instead?") or by somehow making the refusal less direct. Consequently, boys tend to hear firmer, clearer language, while girls are exposed to warmer phrases, often referring to inner emotional states (Perlmann & Gleason, 1990).

From *an educator's* perspective

What are some implications of differences in the ways adults speak to boys and girls? How might such speech differences contribute to later differences not only in speech, but also in attitudes?

Do such differences in language directed at boys and girls during infancy affect their behavior as adults? There is no direct evidence that plainly supports such an association, but men and women do use different sorts of language as adults. For instance, as adults, women tend to use more tentative, less assertive language ("Maybe we should try to go to a movie,") than men ("I know, let's go to a movie!"). Though we don't know if these differences are a reflection of early linguistic experiences, such findings are certainly intriguing (Tenenbaum & Leaper, 2003; Hartshorne & Ullman, 2006; Plante et al., 2006).

Module 5.3 Review

LO 5.7 Outline the processes by which children learn to use language.

Before they speak, infants understand many adult utterances and engage in several forms of prelinguistic communication, including the use of facial expressions, gestures, and babbling. Children typically produce their first words between 10 and 14 months, and rapidly increase their vocabularies from that point on, especially during a spurt at about 18 months. Children's language development proceeds through a pattern of holophrases, two-word combinations, and telegraphic speech.

LO 5.8 Outline the major theories of language development.

Learning theorists believe that basic learning processes account for language development, whereas nativists like Noam Chomsky and his followers argue that humans have an innate language capacity. The interactionists suggest that language is a consequence of both environmental and innate factors.

LO 5.9 Describe how children influence adults' language.

When talking to infants, adults of all cultures tend to use infant-directed speech. An infant's gender also has an effect on his or her parents' speech.

Journal Writing Prompt

Applying Lifespan Development: What are some ways in which children's linguistic development reflects their acquisition of new ways of interpreting and dealing with their world?

Epilogue

In this chapter, we looked at infants' cognitive development using perspectives ranging from Piaget's stages to information processing theory. We examined infant learning, memory, and intelligence, and we concluded the chapter with a look at language.

Before we proceed to social and personality development in the next chapter, turn back to the prologue of this chapter, about Amelie Hawkins's conversations with her 3-month-old daughter, and answer the following questions.

1. Is Amelie correct that her daughter is learning from the baby talk that Amelie directs at her?
2. When can Amelie expect that "exciting day" when she hears her daughter's first word? What is that word likely to be?
3. If you were to advise Amelie, what would you tell her to expect in terms of her daughter's language development over time?
4. What milestones in cognitive development can Amelie expect her daughter to achieve in the coming year?

Looking Back

LO 5.1 Summarize the fundamental features of Piaget's theory of cognitive development.

According to Piaget, all children pass gradually through the four major stages of cognitive development (sensorimotor, preoperational, concrete operational, and formal operational) and their various substages when they are at an appropriate level of maturation and are exposed to relevant types of experiences. In the Piagetian view, children's understanding grows through assimilation of their experiences into their current way of thinking or through accommodation of their current way of thinking to their experiences.

LO 5.2 Describe Piaget's sensorimotor stage of cognitive development.

During the sensorimotor period (birth to about 2 years) with its six substages, infants progress from the use of simple reflexes, through the development of repeated and integrated actions that gradually increase in complexity, to the ability to generate purposeful effects from their actions. By the end of the sixth substage of the sensorimotor period, infants are beginning to engage in symbolic thought.

LO 5.3 Summarize the arguments both in support of and critical of Piaget's theory of cognitive development.

Piaget is respected as a careful observer of children's behavior and a generally accurate interpreter of the way human cognitive development proceeds, though subsequent research on his theory does suggest several limitations.

LO 5.4 Describe how infants process information according to information processing approaches to cognitive development.

Information processing approaches to the study of cognitive development seek to learn how individuals receive, organize, store, and retrieve information. Such approaches differ from Piaget's by considering quantitative changes in children's abilities to process information.

LO 5.5 Describe the memory capabilities of infants during their first 2 years of life.

Infants have memory capabilities from their earliest days, although the accuracy of infant memories is a matter of debate.

LO 5.6 Describe how infant intelligence is measured using information processing approaches.

Traditional measures of infant intelligence, such as Gesell's developmental quotient and the Bayley Scales of Infant Development, focus on average behavior observed at particular ages in large numbers of children. Information processing approaches to assessing intelligence rely on variations in the speed and quality with which infants process information.

LO 5.7 Outline the processes by which children learn to use language.

Prelinguistic communication involves the use of sounds, gestures, facial expressions, imitation, and other nonlinguistic means to express thoughts and states. Prelinguistic communication prepares the infant for speech. Infants typically produce their first words between the ages of 10 and 14 months. At around 18 months, children typically begin to link words together into primitive sentences that express single thoughts. Beginning speech is characterized by the use of holophrases, telegraphic speech, underextension, and overextension.

LO 5.8 Outline the major theories of language development.

The learning theory approach to language acquisition assumes that adults and children use basic behavioral processes—such as conditioning, reinforcement, and shaping—in language learning. A different approach proposed by Noam Chomsky holds that humans are genetically endowed with a language-acquisition device, which permits them to detect and use the principles of universal grammar that underlie all languages.

LO 5.9 Describe how children influence adults' language.

Adult language is influenced by the children to whom it is addressed. Infant-directed speech takes on characteristics, surprisingly invariant across cultures, that make it appealing to infants and that probably encourage language development. Adult language also exhibits differences based on the gender of the child to whom it is directed, which may have effects that emerge later in life.

Key Terms and Concepts

schema 150
assimilation 151
accommodation 151
sensorimotor stage (of cognitive development) 151
object permanence 153
mental representation 155
deferred imitation 155
information processing approaches 158
memory 160
infantile amnesia 160
developmental quotient 163
Bayley Scales of Infant Development 163
language 167
babbling 168
holophrases 170
telegraphic speech 171
underextension 172
overextension 172
referential style 172
expressive style 172
learning theory approach to language 172
nativist approach to language 173
universal grammar 173
language-acquisition device (LAD) 173
interactionist approach to language 173
infant-directed speech 174

Chapter 6

Social and Personality Development in Infancy

szeyuen/Fotolia

Learning Objectives

LO 6.1 Discuss how children express and experience emotions in the first 2 years of life.

LO 6.2 Differentiate stranger anxiety from separation anxiety.

LO 6.3 Discuss the development of social referencing and nonverbal decoding abilities.

LO 6.4 Describe the sense of self that children possess in the first 2 years of life.

LO 6.5 Summarize the theory of mind and evidence of infants' growing sense of mental activity by age 2.

LO 6.6 Explain attachment in infancy and how it affects a person's future social competence.

LO 6.7 Describe the roles that caregivers play in infants' social development.

LO 6.8 Discuss the development of relationships in infancy.

LO 6.9 Describe individual differences that distinguish an infant's personality.

LO 6.10 Define temperament, and describe how it affects a child in the first 2 years of life.

LO 6.11 Discuss how the gender of a child affects his or her development in the first two years of life.

LO 6.12 Describe 21st-century families and their consequences for children.

LO 6.13 Summarize how nonparental child care affects infants.

Chapter Overview

Prologue: Anarchy in the Back Seat

It was hard enough having twins without them teaching one another bad habits. But that's just what happened with Andy and Matt, twins born 2 minutes apart 10 months ago. After strapping them both into side-by-side car seats, their mother, Peggy, noticed that Andy had figured out how to unzip the Velcro strap that held his hat on his head and fling it off. She patiently put the hat back on his head, but a few minutes later Andy had managed to unzip it again and fling the hat to the floor.

But more was to come: A few days later, Andy's brother Matt, who was always attentive to his brother's often wild behavior, pulled the strap on his own hat, and then, following his brother's lead, flung the hat to the ground. Apparently his brother's achievement had not gone unnoticed.

Looking Ahead

As babies like Andy and Matt show us, children are sociable from a very early age, attentive and interacting with those around them. This anecdote also demonstrates what research is increasingly showing: Through their social interactions, babies acquire new skills and abilities from more "expert" peers. Infants, as we will see, have an amazing capacity to learn from other children, and their interactions with others can play a central role in their developing social and emotional worlds.

In this chapter, we consider social and personality development in infancy. We begin by examining the emotional lives of infants, considering which emotions they feel and how well they can read others' emotions. We also look at how others' responses shape infants' own reactions and how babies view their own and others' mental lives.

We then turn to infants' social relationships. We look at how they forge bonds of attachment and the ways they interact with family members and peers.

Finally, we cover the characteristics that differentiate one infant from another and discuss differences in the way children are treated depending on their gender. We'll consider the nature of family life and discuss how it differs from family life in earlier eras. The chapter closes with a look at the advantages and disadvantages of infant child care outside the home, a child care option that today's families increasingly employ.

Patryk Kosmider/Fotolia

Beginning at birth, boys and girls are dressed differently.

Developing the Roots of Sociability

Germaine smiles when he catches a glimpse of his mother. Tawanda looks angry when her mother takes away the spoon that she is playing with. Sydney scowls when a loud plane flies overhead.

A smile. A look of anger. A scowl. The emotions of infancy are written all over a baby's face. Yet do infants experience emotions in the same way that adults do? When do they become capable of understanding what others are experiencing emotionally? And how do they use others' emotional states to make sense of their environment? We consider some of these questions as we seek to understand how infants develop emotionally and socially.

Emotions in Infancy: Do Infants Experience Emotional Highs and Lows?

LO 6.1 Discuss how children express and experience emotions in the first 2 years of life.

Anyone who spends any time at all around infants knows they display facial expressions that seem indicative of their emotional states. In situations in which we expect them to be happy, they seem to smile; when we might assume they are frustrated, they show anger; and when we might expect them to be unhappy, they look sad.

These basic facial expressions are remarkably similar across the most diverse cultures. Whether we look at babies in India, the United States, or the jungles of New Guinea, the expression of basic emotions is the same. Furthermore, the nonverbal expression of emotion, called *nonverbal encoding*, is fairly consistent among people of all ages. These consistencies have led researchers to conclude that we are born with the capacity to display basic emotions (Ackerman & Izard, 2004; Bornstein, Suwalsky, & Breakstone, 2012; Rajhans et al., 2016).

Infants display a fairly wide range of emotional expressions. According to research on what mothers see in their children's nonverbal behavior, almost all think that by the age of 1 month, their babies have expressed interest and joy. In addition, 84 percent of mothers think their infants have expressed anger, 75 percent think their infants have expressed surprise, 58 percent think their infants have shown fear, and 34 percent think their infants have expressed sadness. Research also finds that interest, distress, and disgust are present at birth, and that other emotions emerge over the next few months (see Figure 6-1). Such findings are consistent with the work of the famous naturalist Charles Darwin, whose 1872 book, *The Expression of the Emotions in Man and Animals*, argued that humans and primates have an inborn, universal set of emotional expressions—a view consistent with today's evolutionary approach to development (Benson, 2003; MacLean et al., 2014; Smith & Weiss, 2017).

Although infants display similar *kinds* of emotions, the *degree* of emotional expressivity varies. Children in different cultures show reliable differences in emotional expressiveness, even during infancy. For example, by the age of 11 months, Chinese infants are generally less expressive than European, American, and Japanese infants (Eisenberg et al., 2000; Camras et al., 2007; Easterbrooks et al., 2013).

Blend Images/Getty Images

Across every culture, infants show similar facial expressions relating to basic emotions, such as this smile of joy. Do you think such expressions are similar in nonhuman animals?

Figure 6-1 Emergence of Emotional Expressions

Emotional expressions emerge at roughly the times shown in the figure. Keep in mind that expressions in the first few weeks after birth do not necessarily reflect particular inner feelings. **THINKING ABOUT THE DATA:** Why do you think contempt and guilt show up relatively late compared with other emotions? (Hint: Look ahead to page 186.)

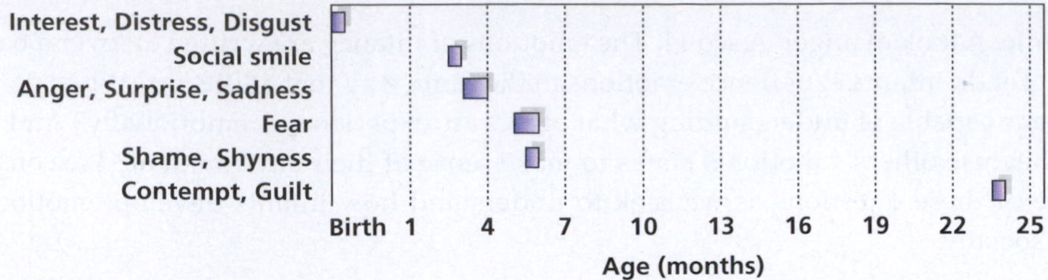

EXPERIENCING EMOTIONS. Does the capability of infants to express emotions nonverbally in a consistent, reliable manner mean that they actually *experience* emotions, and—if they do—is the experience similar to that of adults?

To answer these questions, we need to consider just what emotions are. Developmentalists believe a true *emotion* has three components: a biological arousal component (such as increased breathing rate or heartbeat), a cognitive component (awareness of feeling anger or fear), and a behavioral component (e.g., displaying that one feels unhappy by crying).

Consequently, the fact that children display nonverbal expressions in a manner similar to that of adults does not necessarily mean that their actual experience is identical. If the nature of such displays is innate, or inborn, it is possible that facial expressions can occur without any accompanying awareness of their emotional experience (the cognitive component). Nonverbal expressions, then, might be emotionless in young infants, in much the same way that your knee reflexively jerks forward when a physician taps it, without the involvement of emotions (Soussignan et al., 1997).

Most developmental researchers, however, do not think this is the case: They argue that the nonverbal expressions of infants represent actual emotional experiences. Emotional expressions may not only reflect emotional experiences but may also help regulate the emotion itself. Developmental psychologist Carroll Izard suggests that infants are born with an innate repertoire of emotional expressions, reflecting basic emotional states, such as happiness and sadness. As infants and children grow older, they expand and modify these basic expressions and become more adept at controlling their nonverbal behavioral expressions. For example, they eventually may learn that by smiling at the right time, they can increase the chances of getting their own way. Emotional expressions thus have an adaptive function, permitting infants to express their needs nonverbally to caretakers before they have developed linguistic skills.

In sum, infants do appear to experience emotions, although the range of emotions at birth is fairly restricted. However, as they get older, infants both display and experience a wider range of increasingly complex emotions. Furthermore, in addition to *expressing* a wider variety of emotions, as children develop they also *experience* a wider array of emotions (Buss & Kiel, 2004; Killeen & Teti, 2012; Soderstrom et al., 2017).

The advances in infants' emotional life are made possible by the increasing sophistication of their brains. Initially, the differentiation of emotions occurs as the cerebral cortex becomes operative in the first 3 months of life. By the age of 9 or 10 months, the structures that make up the limbic system (the site of emotional reactions) begin to grow. The limbic system starts to work in tandem with the frontal lobes, allowing for an increased range of emotions (Schore, 2003; Swain et al., 2007; Missana, Altvater-Mackensen, & Grossmann, 2017).

SMILING. As Luz lay sleeping in her crib, her mother and father caught a glimpse of the most beautiful smile crossing her face. Her parents were sure that Luz was having a pleasant dream. Were they right?

Probably not. The earliest smiles expressed during sleep probably have little meaning, although no one can be absolutely sure. By 6 to 9 weeks, babies begin to smile reliably at the sight of stimuli that please them, including toys, mobiles, and—to the delight of parents—people. The first smiles tend to be relatively indiscriminate, as infants first begin to smile at the sight of almost anything they find amusing. However, as they get older, they become more selective in their smiles.

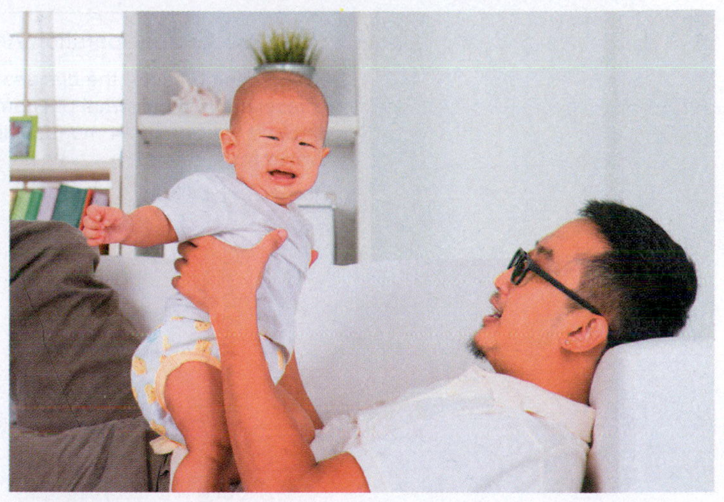

Typically, infants begin to display stranger anxiety near the end of the first year of life.

A baby's smile in response to another person, rather than to nonhuman stimuli, is considered a **social smile**. As babies get older, their social smiles become directed toward particular individuals, not just anyone. By the age of 18 months, social smiling, directed more toward caregivers, becomes more frequent than smiling directed toward nonhuman objects. Moreover, if an adult is unresponsive to a child, the amount of smiling decreases. In short, by the end of the second year, children are quite purposefully using smiling to communicate their positive emotions, and they are sensitive to the emotional expressions of others (Reissland & Cohen, 2012; Wörmann et al., 2014; Planalp et al., 2016).

social smile
smiling in response to other individuals

Stranger Anxiety and Separation Anxiety: It's Only Natural

LO 6.2 Differentiate stranger anxiety from separation anxiety.

"She used to be such a friendly baby," thought Erika's mother. "No matter whom she encountered, she had a big smile. But almost the day she turned 7 months old, she began to react to strangers as if she were seeing a ghost. Her face crinkles up with a frown, and she either turns away or stares at them with suspicion. And she doesn't want to be left with anyone she doesn't already know. It's as if she has undergone a personality transplant."

What happened to Erika is, in fact, quite typical. By the end of the first year, infants often develop both stranger anxiety and separation anxiety. **Stranger anxiety** is the caution and wariness displayed by infants when encountering an unfamiliar person. Such anxiety typically appears in the second half of the first year.

stranger anxiety
the caution and wariness displayed by infants when encountering an unfamiliar person

What brings on stranger anxiety? Here, too, brain development and the increased cognitive abilities of infants play a role. As infants' memory develops, they are able to separate the people they know from the people they don't. The same cognitive advances that allow them to respond so positively to those people with whom they are familiar also give them the ability to recognize people who are unfamiliar. Furthermore, between 6 and 9 months, infants begin trying to make sense of their world, endeavoring to anticipate and predict events. When something happens that they don't expect—such as when an unknown person appears—they experience fear. It's as if an infant has a question but is unable to answer it (Volker, 2007; Mash, Bornstein, & Arterberry, 2013).

Although stranger anxiety is common after the age of 6 months, significant differences exist between children. Some infants, particularly those who have a lot of experience with strangers, tend to show less anxiety than those whose experience with strangers is limited. Furthermore, not all strangers evoke the same reaction. For instance, infants tend to show less anxiety with female strangers than with male strangers. In addition, they react more positively to strangers who are children than to strangers who are adults, perhaps because their size is less intimidating (Swingler, Sweet, & Carver, 2007; Murray et al., 2007; Murray et al., 2008).

Separation anxiety is the distress displayed by infants when a customary care provider departs. Separation anxiety, which is also universal across cultures, usually begins

separation anxiety
the distress displayed by infants when a customary care provider departs

Figure 6-2 Separation Anxiety

Separation anxiety, the distress displayed by infants when their usual care provider leaves their presence, is a universal phenomenon beginning at around the age of 7 or 8 months. It peaks at around the age of 14 months, and then begins to decline. Does separation anxiety have survival value for humans?

(**Source:** Kagan, Kearsley, & Zelazo, 1978.)

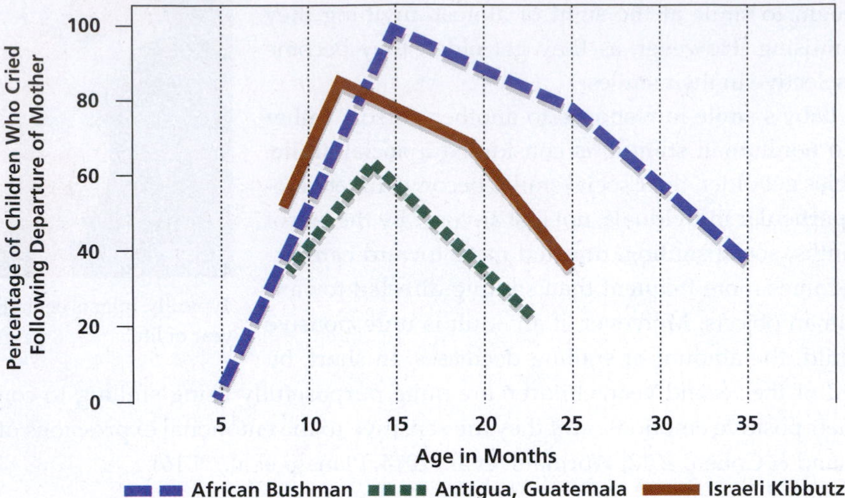

at about 7 or 8 months (see Figure 6-2). It peaks around 14 months, and then decreases. Separation anxiety is largely attributable to the same factors as stranger anxiety. Infants' growing cognitive skills allow them to ask reasonable questions, but they may be questions whose answers they are too young to understand: "Why is my mother leaving?" "Where is she going?" and "Will she come back?"

Stranger anxiety and separation anxiety represent important social progress. They reflect both cognitive advances and the growing emotional and social bonds between infants and their caregivers—bonds that we'll consider later in the chapter when we discuss infants' social relationships.

Social Referencing: Feeling What Others Feel

LO 6.3 Discuss the development of social referencing and nonverbal decoding abilities.

Twenty-three-month-old Stephania watches as her older brother Eric and his friend Chen argue loudly with each other and begin to wrestle. Uncertain of what is happening, Stephania glances at her mother. Her mother, though, wears a smile, knowing that Eric and Chen are just playing. On seeing her mother's reaction, Stephania smiles too, mimicking her mother's facial expression.

Like Stephania, most of us have been in situations in which we feel uncertain. In such cases, we sometimes turn to others to see how they are reacting. This reliance on others, known as social referencing, helps us decide what an appropriate response ought to be.

social referencing

the intentional search for information about others' feelings to help explain the meaning of uncertain circumstances and events

Social referencing is the intentional search for information about others' feelings to help explain the meaning of uncertain circumstances and events. Like Stephania, we use social referencing to clarify the meaning of a situation and thus reduce our uncertainty about what is occurring.

From *a social worker's* perspective

In what situations do adults rely on social referencing to work out appropriate responses? How might social referencing be used to influence parents' behavior toward their children?

Social referencing first occurs around the age of 8 or 9 months. It is a fairly sophisticated social ability: Infants need it to understand not only the significance of others' behavior, by using such cues as their facial expressions, but also the meaning of those behaviors within the context of a specific situation (Hepach & Westermann, 2013; Mireault et al., 2014; Walle, Reschke, & Knothe, 2017).

Infants make particular use of facial expressions in their social referencing, the way Stephania did when she noticed her mother's smile. For instance, in one study infants were given an unusual toy to play with. The amount of time they played with it depended on their mothers' facial expressions. When their mothers displayed disgust, they played with it significantly less than when their mothers appeared pleased. Furthermore, when given the opportunity to play with the same toy later, the infants remained reluctant to play with it, despite the mothers' now neutral-appearing facial reactions, suggesting that parental attitudes may have lasting consequences (Hertenstein & Campos, 2004; Pelaez, Virues-Ortega, & Gewirtz, 2012).

TWO EXPLANATIONS OF SOCIAL REFERENCING. Although it is clear that social referencing begins fairly early in life, researchers are still not certain *how* it operates. It may be that observing someone else's facial expression brings about the emotion the expression represents. That is, an infant who views someone looking sad may come to feel sad herself, and her behavior may be affected. It might also be the case that viewing another's facial expression may simply provide information. In this case, the infant does not experience the particular emotion represented by another's facial expression; she simply uses the display as data to guide her own behavior.

Both explanations for social referencing have received some support in research studies, and so we still don't know which is correct. What we do know is that social referencing is most likely to occur when a situation breeds uncertainty and ambiguity. Furthermore, infants who reach the age when they are able to use social referencing become quite upset if they receive conflicting nonverbal messages from their mothers and fathers. For example, if a mother shows with her facial expressions that she is annoyed with her son for knocking over a carton of milk, while his grandmother sees it as cute and smiles, the child receives two contradictory messages. Such mixed messages can be a real source of stress for an infant (Vaish & Striano, 2004; Schmitow & Stenberg, 2013).

DECODING OTHERS' FACIAL AND VOCAL EXPRESSIONS. The ability to employ social referencing is dependent on *nonverbal decoding* abilities to understand others' nonverbal behavior—skills that begin to emerge fairly soon after birth. Using these abilities, infants can interpret others' facial and vocal expressions that carry emotional meaning. For example, they can tell when a caregiver is happy to see them, and they pick up on worry or fear in the faces of others (Hernandez-Reif et al., 2006; Striano & Vaish, 2006; Hoehl et al., 2012).

Infants seem to be able to discriminate vocal expressions of emotion at a slightly earlier age than they discriminate facial expressions. Although relatively little attention has been given to infants' perception of vocal expressions, it does appear that they are able to discriminate happy and sad vocal expressions at the age of 5 months (Montague & Walker-Andrews, 2002; Dahl et al., 2014).

Scientists know more about the *sequence* in which nonverbal facial decoding ability progresses. In the first 6 to 8 weeks, infants' visual precision is sufficiently limited that they cannot pay much attention to others' facial expressions. But they soon begin to discriminate among different facial expressions of emotion and even seem to be able to respond to differences in emotional intensity conveyed by facial expressions. They also respond to unusual facial expressions. For instance, they show distress when their mothers pose bland, unresponsive, or neutral facial expressions (Bertin & Striano, 2006; Farroni et al., 2007; Safar & Moulson, 2017).

By the time they are midway through their first year, infants already have begun to understand the emotions that lie behind the facial and vocal expressions of others. How do we know this? One important clue comes from a study in which 7-month-old infants were shown a pair of facial expressions relating to joy and sadness, and simultaneously heard a vocalization representing either joy (a rising tone of voice) or sadness (a falling tone of voice). When the facial expression matched the tone, infants paid more attention, suggesting that they had at least a rudimentary understanding of the emotional meaning of facial expressions and voice tones (Grossmann, Striano, & Friederici, 2006; Kim & Johnson, 2013; Biro et al., 2014).

In sum, infants learn early both to produce and to decode emotions, and they begin to learn the effect of their own emotions on others. Such abilities play an important role not only in helping them experience their own emotions but also—as we see next—in using others' emotions to understand the meaning of ambiguous social situations (Buss & Kiel, 2004; Messinger et al., 2012).

The Development of Self: Do Infants Know Who They Are?

LO 6.4 Describe the sense of self that children possess in the first 2 years of life.

Elysa, 8 months old, crawls past the full-length mirror that hangs on a door in her parents' bedroom. She barely pays any attention to her reflection as she moves by. In contrast, her cousin Brianna, who is almost 2 years old, stares at herself in the mirror as she passes and laughs as she notices, and then rubs off, a smear of jelly on her forehead.

Perhaps you have had the experience of catching a glimpse of yourself in a mirror and noticing a hair out of place. You probably reacted by attempting to push the unruly hair back into place. Your reaction shows more than that you care about how you look. It implies that you have a sense of yourself, the awareness and knowledge that you are an independent social entity to which others react, and which you attempt to present to the world in ways that reflect favorably upon you.

However, we are not born with the knowledge that we exist independently from others and the larger world. Very young infants do not have a sense of themselves as individuals; they do not recognize themselves in photos or mirrors. However, the roots of **self-awareness**, knowledge of oneself, begin to grow at around the age of 12 months. We know this from a simple but ingenious experimental technique. An infant's nose is secretly colored with a dab of red powder, and the infant is seated in front of a mirror. If infants touch their noses or attempt to wipe off the rouge, we have evidence that they have at least some knowledge of their physical characteristics. For them, this awareness is one step in developing an understanding of themselves as independent objects. For instance, Brianna, in the example at the beginning of this section, showed her awareness of herself when she tried to rub the jam off her forehead (Rochat, 2004; Rochat, Broesch, & Jayne, 2012).

self-awareness
knowledge of oneself

antoniodiaz/Shutterstock

Research suggests that this 18-month-old is exhibiting a clearly developed sense of self.

Although some infants as young as 12 months seem startled on seeing the rouge spot, for most a reaction does not occur until between 17 and 24 months of age. It is also around this age that children begin to show awareness of their own capabilities. For instance, infants who participate in experiments when they are between the ages of 23 and 25 months sometimes begin to cry if the experimenter asks them to imitate a complicated sequence of behaviors involving toys, although they readily accomplish simpler sequences. Their reaction suggests that they are conscious that they lack the ability to carry out difficult tasks and are unhappy about it—a reaction that provides a clear indication of self-awareness (Legerstee et al., 1998; Asendorpf, 2002).

Children's cultural upbringing also impacts the development of self-recognition. For instance, Greek children—who experience parenting practices that emphasize autonomy and separation—show self-recognition at an earlier age than children from Cameroon. In the Cameroonian culture, parenting practices emphasize body contact and warmth, leading to more interdependence between infants and parents, and ultimately to later development of self-recognition (Keller et al., 2004; Keller, Voelker, & Yovsi, 2005; Ross et al., 2017).

In general, by the age of 18 to 24 months, infants in Western cultures have developed at least an awareness of their own physical characteristics and capabilities, and they understand that their appearance is stable over time. Although it is not clear how far this awareness extends, it is becoming increasingly evident that, as we discuss next, infants have not only a basic understanding of themselves but also the beginnings of an understanding of how the mind operates—what has come to be called a "theory of mind" (Lewis & Ramsay, 2004; Lewis & Carmody, 2008; Langfur, 2013).

Theory of Mind: Infants' Perspectives on the Mental Lives of Others—and Themselves

LO 6.5 Summarize the theory of mind and evidence of infants' growing sense of mental activity by age 2.

What are infants' thoughts about thinking? According to a growing body of research, infants begin to understand certain things about their own and others' mental processes at quite an early age. Investigators have examined children's **theory of mind**, their knowledge and beliefs about how the mind works and how it influences behavior. Theories of mind are the explanations that children use to explain how others think.

theory of mind
knowledge and beliefs about how the mind works and how it affects behavior

For instance, the cognitive advances during infancy that we discussed in Chapter 5 permit older infants to see people in a very different way from other objects. They learn to see other people as *compliant agents*, beings similar to themselves who behave under their own power and who have the capacity to respond to infants' requests. Eighteen-month-old Chris, for example, has come to realize that he can ask his father to get him more juice (Rochat, 2004; Slaughter & Peterson, 2012).

In addition, children's capacity to understand intentionality and causality grows during infancy. For example, 10- and 13-month-olds are able to mentally represent social dominance, believing that larger size is related to the ability to dominate other, smaller-sized individuals and objects. Furthermore, infants have a kind of innate morality, in which they show a preference for helpfulness (Sloane, Baillargeon, & Premack, 2012; Ruffman, 2014; Yott & Poulin-Dubois, 2016).

Furthermore, as early as 18 months, they begin to understand that others' behaviors have meaning and that the behaviors they see people enacting are designed to accomplish particular goals, in contrast to the "behaviors" of inanimate objects. For example, a child comes to understand that his father has a specific goal when he is in the kitchen making sandwiches. In contrast, his father's car is simply parked in the driveway, having no mental life or goal (Ahn, Gelman, & Amsterlaw, 2000; Wellman et al., 2008; Senju et al., 2011).

Another piece of evidence for infants' growing sense of mental activity is that by age 2, infants begin to demonstrate the rudiments of empathy. **Empathy** is an emotional response that corresponds to the feelings of another person. At 24 months of age, infants sometimes comfort others or show concern for them. In order to do this, they need to be aware of the emotional states of others. For example, 1-year-olds are able to pick up emotional cues by observing the behavior of an actress on television (Mumme & Fernald, 2003; Legerstee, Haley & Bornstein, 2013; Xu, Saether, & Sommerville, 2016).

empathy
an emotional response that corresponds to the feelings of another person

Furthermore, during their second year, infants begin to use deception, both in games of "pretend" and in outright attempts to fool others. A child who plays "pretend" and who uses falsehoods must be aware that others hold beliefs about the world—beliefs that can be manipulated. In short, by the end of infancy children have developed the rudiments of their own personal theory of mind. It helps them understand the actions of others, and it affects their own behavior (van der Mark et al., 2002; Caron, 2009).

Module 6.1 Review

LO 6.1 Discuss how children express and experience emotions in the first 2 years of life.

Infants appear to express and to experience emotions, and their emotions broaden in range to reflect increasingly complex emotional states.

LO 6.2 Differentiate stranger anxiety from separation anxiety.

As they develop cognitively and begin to distinguish familiar from unfamiliar people, infants begin to experience stranger anxiety at about 6 months and separation anxiety at around 8 months of age.

LO 6.3 Discuss the development of social referencing and nonverbal decoding abilities.

The ability to decode the nonverbal facial and vocal expressions of others develops early in infants. The use of nonverbal decoding to clarify situations of uncertainty and determine appropriate responses is called *social referencing*.

LO 6.4 Describe the sense of self that children possess in the first 2 years of life.

Infants develop self-awareness, the knowledge that they exist separately from the rest of the world, after about 12 months of age.

LO 6.5 Summarize the theory of mind and evidence of infants' growing sense of mental activity by age 2.

By age 2, children have developed the rudiments of a theory of mind.

Journal Writing Prompt

Applying Lifespan Development: Why would the sad or flat emotional expressiveness of a depressed parent be hard on an infant? How might it be counteracted?

Forming Relationships

Luis Camacho, now 38, clearly remembers the feelings that haunted him on the way to the hospital to meet his new sister Katy. Though he was only 4 at the time, that day of infamy is still vivid to him today. Luis would no longer be the only kid in the house; he would have to share his life with a baby sister. She would play with his toys, read his books, be with him in the back seat of the car.

What really bothered him, of course, was that he would have to share his parents' love and attention with a new person. And not just any new person—a girl, who would automatically have a lot of advantages. Katy would be cuter, more needy, more demanding, more interesting—more everything—than he. He would be underfoot at best, neglected at worst.

Luis also knew that he was expected to be cheerful and welcoming. So he put on a brave face at the hospital and walked without hesitation to the room where his mother and Katy were waiting.

The arrival of a newborn brings a dramatic change to a family's dynamics. No matter how welcome a baby's birth, it causes a fundamental shift in the roles that people play within the family. Mothers and fathers must start to build a relationship with their infant, and older children must adjust to the presence of a new member of the family and build their own alliance with their infant brother or sister.

Although the process of social development during infancy is neither simple nor automatic, it is crucial: The bonds that grow between infants and their parents, siblings, family, and others provide the foundation for a lifetime's worth of social relationships.

Attachment: Forming Social Bonds

LO 6.6 Explain attachment in infancy and how it affects a person's future social competence.

The most important aspect of social development that takes place during infancy is the formation of attachment. **Attachment** is the positive emotional bond that develops between a child and a particular, special individual. When children experience attachment to a given person, they feel pleasure when they are with that person and feel comforted by their presence in times of distress. As we'll see when we consider social development in early adulthood (Chapter 14), the nature of our attachment during infancy affects how we relate to others throughout the rest of our lives (Fisher, 2012; Bergman et al., 2015; Kim et al., 2017).

attachment
the positive emotional bond that develops between a child and a particular individual

To understand attachment, the earliest researchers turned to the bonds that form between parents and children in the nonhuman animal kingdom. For instance, ethologist Konrad Lorenz (1965) observed newborn goslings, which have an innate tendency to follow their mother, the first moving object to which they typically are exposed after birth. Lorenz found that goslings whose eggs were raised in an incubator and who viewed him just after hatching would follow his every movement, as if he were their mother. As discussed in Chapter 3, he labeled this process *imprinting*: behavior that takes place during a critical period and involves attachment to the first moving object that is observed.

Lorenz's findings suggested that attachment was based on biologically determined factors, and other theorists agreed. For instance, Freud suggested that attachment grew out of a mother's ability to satisfy a child's oral needs.

HARLOW'S MONKEYS. It turns out, however, that the ability to provide food and other physiological needs may not be as crucial as Freud and other theorists first thought. In a classic study, psychologist Harry Harlow gave infant monkeys the choice of cuddling a wire "monkey" that provided food or a soft terry cloth monkey that was warm but did not provide food (see Figure 6-3). Their preference was clear: Baby monkeys spent most of their time clinging to the cloth monkey, although they made occasional expeditions to the wire monkey to nurse. Harlow suggested that the preference for the warm cloth monkey provided *contact comfort* (Harlow & Zimmerman, 1959; Blum, 2002).

Figure 6-3 Monkey Mothers Matter

Harlow's research showed that monkeys preferred the warm, soft "mother" to the wire "monkey" that provided food.

Harlow Primate Laboratory

Harlow's work illustrates that food alone is not the basis for attachment. Given that the monkeys' preference for the soft cloth "mothers" developed some time after birth, these findings are consistent with the research discussed in Chapter 3, showing little support for the existence of a critical period for bonding between human mothers and infants immediately following birth.

BOWLBY'S CONTRIBUTIONS TO OUR UNDERSTANDING OF ATTACHMENT. The earliest work on human attachment, which is still highly influential, was carried out by British psychiatrist John Bowlby (1951, 2007). In Bowlby's view, attachment is based primarily on infants' needs for safety and security—their genetically determined motivation to avoid predators. As they develop, infants come to learn that their safety is best provided by a particular individual. This realization ultimately leads to the development of a special relationship with that individual, who is typically the mother. Bowlby suggested that this single relationship with the primary caregiver is qualitatively different from the bonds formed with others, including the father—a suggestion that, as we'll see later, has been a source of some disagreement.

Figure 6-4 The Ainsworth Strange Situation

In this illustration of the Ainsworth Strange Situation, the infant first explores the playroom on his own, as long as his mother is present. But when she leaves, he begins to cry. On her return, however, he is immediately comforted and stops crying. The conclusion: he is securely attached.

According to Bowlby, attachment provides a type of home base. As children become more independent, they can progressively roam further away from their secure base.

THE AINSWORTH STRANGE SITUATION AND PATTERNS OF ATTACHMENT. Developmental psychologist Mary Ainsworth built on Bowlby's theorizing to develop a widely used experimental technique to measure attachment (Ainsworth et al., 1978). The **Ainsworth Strange Situation** consists of a sequence of staged episodes that illustrate the strength of attachment between a child and (typically) his or her mother (see Figure 6-4). The "strange situation" follows this general eight-step pattern: (1) The mother and baby enter an unfamiliar room; (2) the mother sits down, leaving the baby free to explore; (3) an adult stranger enters the room and converses first with the mother and then with the baby; (4) the mother exits the room, leaving the baby alone with the stranger; (5) the mother returns, greeting and comforting the baby, and the stranger leaves; (6) the mother departs again, leaving the baby alone; (7) the stranger returns; and (8) the mother returns and the stranger leaves (Ainsworth et al., 1978; Pederson et al., 2014).

Infants' reactions to the various aspects of the Strange Situation vary considerably, depending on the nature of their attachment to their mothers. One-year-olds typically show one of four major patterns—secure, avoidant, ambivalent, and disorganized-disoriented (summarized in Table 6-1). Children who have a **secure attachment pattern** use the mother as the type of home base that Bowlby described. These children seem at ease in the Strange Situation as long as their mothers are present. They explore independently, returning to her occasionally. Although they may or may not appear upset when she leaves, securely attached children immediately go to her when she returns and seek contact. Most North American children—about two-thirds—fall into the securely attached category.

Ainsworth Strange Situation

a sequence of staged episodes that illustrates the strength of attachment between a child and (typically) his or her mother

In contrast, children with an **avoidant attachment pattern** do not seek proximity to the mother, and after she has left, they typically do not seem distressed. Furthermore, they seem to avoid her when she returns. It is as if they are indifferent to her behavior. Some 20 percent of 1-year-old children are in the avoidant category.

Table 6-1 Classifications of Infant Attachment

	Classification Criteria			
Label	**Seeking Proximity with Caregiver**	**Maintaining Contact with Caregiver**	**Avoiding Proximity with Caregiver**	**Resisting Contact with Caregiver**
Avoidant	Low	Low	High	Low
Secure	High	High (if distressed)	Low	Low
Ambivalent	High	High (often pre-separation)	Low	High
Disorganized-disoriented	Inconsistent	Inconsistent	Inconsistent	Inconsistent

Children with an **ambivalent attachment pattern** display a combination of positive and negative reactions to their mothers. Initially, ambivalent children are in such close contact with the mother that they hardly explore their environment. They appear anxious even before the mother leaves, and when she does leave, they show great distress. But upon her return, they show ambivalent reactions, seeking to be close to her but also hitting and kicking, apparently in anger. About 10 to 15 percent of 1-year-olds fall into the ambivalent classification (Cassidy & Berlin, 1994).

Although Ainsworth identified only three categories, a more recent expansion of her work finds that there is a fourth category: disorganized-disoriented. Children who have a **disorganized-disoriented attachment pattern** show inconsistent, contradictory, and confused behavior. They may run to the mother when she returns but not look at her, or seem initially calm and then suddenly break into angry weeping. Their confusion suggests that they may be the least securely attached children of all. About 5 to 10 percent of all children fall into this category (Mayseless, 1996; Cole, 2005; Bernier & Meins, 2008).

A child's attachment style would be of only minor consequence were it not for the fact that the quality of attachment between infants and their caregivers has significant consequences for relationships at later stages of life. For example, boys who are securely attached at the age of 1 year show fewer psychological difficulties at older ages than do avoidant or ambivalent children. Similarly, children who are securely attached as infants tend to be more socially and emotionally competent later, and others view them more positively. Adult romantic relationships are associated with the kind of attachment style developed during infancy (Simpson et al., 2007; MacDonald et al., 2008; Bergman, Blom, & Polyak, 2012).

At the same time, we cannot say that children who do not have a secure attachment style during infancy invariably experience difficulties later in life, nor can we say that those with a secure attachment at age 1 always have good adjustment later on. In fact, some evidence suggests that children with avoidant and ambivalent attachment—as measured by the Strange Situation—do quite well (Fraley & Spieker, 2003; Alhusen, Hayat, & Gross, 2013; Smith-Nielsen et al., 2016).

In cases in which the development of attachment has been severely disrupted, children may suffer from *reactive attachment disorder*, a psychological problem characterized by extreme problems in forming attachments to others. In young children, it can be displayed in feeding difficulties, unresponsiveness to social overtures from others, and a general failure to thrive. Reactive attachment disorder is rare and typically the result of abuse or neglect (Hornor, 2008; Schechter & Willheim, 2009; Puckering, et al., 2011).

secure attachment pattern

a style of attachment in which children use the mother as a kind of home base and are at ease when she is present; when she leaves, they become upset and go to her as soon as she returns

avoidant attachment pattern

a style of attachment in which children do not seek proximity to the mother; after the mother has left, they seem to avoid her when she returns as if they are angered by her behavior

ambivalent attachment pattern

a style of attachment in which children display a combination of positive and negative reactions to their mothers; they show great distress when the mother leaves, but upon her return they may simultaneously seek close contact but also hit and kick her

disorganized-disoriented attachment pattern

a style of attachment in which children show inconsistent, often contradictory behavior, such as approaching the mother when she returns but not looking at her; they may be the least securely attached children of all

Producing Attachment: The Roles of the Mother and Father

LO 6.7 Describe the roles that caregivers play in infants' social development.

As 5-month-old Annie cries passionately, her mother comes into the room and gently lifts her from her crib. After just a few moments, as her mother rocks Annie and speaks softly, Annie's cries cease, and she cuddles in her mother's arms. But the moment her mother places her back in the crib, Annie begins to wail again, leading her mother to pick her up once again.

The pattern is familiar to most parents. The infant cries, the parent reacts, and the child responds in turn. Such seemingly insignificant sequences as these, repeatedly occurring in the lives of infants and parents, help pave the way for the development of relationships between children, their parents, and the rest of the social world. We'll consider how each of the major caregivers and the infant play a role in the development of attachment.

MOTHERS AND ATTACHMENT. Sensitivity to their infants' needs and desires is the hallmark of mothers of securely attached infants. Such a mother tends to be aware of her child's moods, and she takes into account her child's feelings as they interact. She is also responsive during face-to-face interactions, provides feeding "on demand," and is warm and affectionate to her infant (McElwain & Booth-LaForce, 2006; Priddis & Howieson, 2009; Evans, Whittingham, & Boyd, 2012).

From *a social worker's* perspective

What might a social worker seeking to find a good home for a foster child look for when evaluating potential foster parents?

It is not only a matter of responding in *any* fashion to their infants' signals that separates mothers of securely attached and insecurely attached children. Mothers of secure infants tend to provide the appropriate level of response. Research has shown that overly responsive mothers are just as likely to have insecurely attached children as underresponsive mothers. In contrast, mothers whose communication involves *interactional synchrony*, in which caregivers respond to infants appropriately and both caregiver and child match emotional states, are more likely to produce secure attachment (Kochanska, 1998; Hane, Feldstein, & Dernetz, 2003).

The research showing the correspondence between mothers' sensitivity to their infants and the security of the infants' attachment is consistent with Ainsworth's arguments that attachment depends on how mothers react to their infants' emotional cues. Ainsworth suggests that mothers of securely attached infants respond rapidly and positively to their infants. For example, Annie's mother responds quickly to her cries by cuddling and comforting her. In contrast, mothers produce insecurely attached infants, according to Ainsworth, by ignoring their behavioral cues, behaving inconsistently with them, and ignoring and rejecting their social efforts. For example, picture a child who repeatedly and unsuccessfully tries to gain her mother's attention by calling or turning and gesturing from her stroller while her mother, engaged in conversation, ignores her. This baby is likely to be less securely attached than a child whose mother acknowledges her child more quickly and consistently (Higley & Dozier, 2009).

But how do mothers learn how to respond to their infants? One way is from their own mothers. Mothers typically respond to their infants based on their own attachment styles. As a result, there is substantial similarity in attachment patterns from one generation to the next (Peck, 2003).

It is important to realize that a mother's (and others') behavior toward infants is at least in part a reaction to the child's ability to provide effective cues. A mother may not be able to respond effectively to a child whose own behavior is unrevealing, misleading, or ambiguous. For instance, children who clearly display their anger or fear or unhappiness will be easier to read—and respond to effectively—than children whose behavior is ambiguous. Consequently, the kind of signals an infant sends may in part determine how successful the mother will be in responding.

iofoto/Shutterstock

A growing body of research highlights the importance of a father's demonstration of love for his children. In fact, certain disorders, such as depression and substance abuse, have been found to be more related to fathers' than to mothers' behavior.

FATHERS AND ATTACHMENT. Up to now, we've barely touched upon one of the key players involved in the upbringing of a child: the father. In fact, if you looked at the early theorizing and research on attachment, you'd find little mention of the father and his potential contributions to the life of the infant.

There are at least two reasons for this absence. First, John Bowlby, who provided the initial theory of attachment, suggested that there was something unique about the mother–child relationship. He believed the mother was uniquely equipped, biologically, to provide sustenance for the child, and he concluded that this capability led to the development of a special relationship between mothers and children. Second, the early work on attachment was influenced by the traditional social views of the time, which considered it "natural" for the mother to be the primary caregiver, while the father's role was to work outside the home to provide a living for his family.

Several factors led to the demise of this view. One was that societal norms changed, and fathers began to take a more active role in childrearing activities. More important, it became increasingly clear from research findings that—despite societal norms that relegated fathers to secondary childrearing roles—some infants formed their primary initial relationship with their fathers (Diener et al., 2008; McFarland-Piazza et al., 2012; Posada & Trumbell, 2017).

In addition, a growing body of research has shown that fathers' expressions of nurturance, warmth, affection, support, and concern are extremely important to their children's emotional and social well-being. Certain kinds of psychological disorders, such as substance abuse and depression, have been found to be related more to fathers' than mothers' behavior (Roelofs et al., 2006; Condon et al., 2013; Braungart-Rieker et al., 2015).

Infants' social bonds extend beyond their parents, especially as they grow older. For example, one study found that although most infants formed their first primary relationship with one person, around one-third had multiple relationships, and it was difficult to determine which attachment was primary. Furthermore, by the time the infants were 18 months old, most had formed multiple relationships. In sum, infants may develop attachments not only to their mothers but to a variety of others as well (Booth, Kelly, & Spieker, 2003; Seibert & Kerns, 2009).

Lumi Images/Alamy Stock Photo

One reason for differences in attachment involves what fathers and mothers do with their children. Mothers tend to spend more time feeding and directly nurturing their children, while fathers often spend more time playing with infants.

ARE THERE DIFFERENCES IN ATTACHMENT TO MOTHERS AND FATHERS? Although infants are fully capable of forming attachments to both mother and father—as well as to other individuals—the nature of attachment between infants and mothers, on the one hand, and infants and fathers, on the other hand, is not identical. For example, when they are in unusually stressful circumstances, most infants prefer to be soothed by their mother rather than by their father (Schoppe-Sullivan et al., 2006; Yu et al., 2012; Dumont & Paquette, 2013).

One reason for qualitative differences in attachment involves the differences in what fathers and mothers do with their children. Mothers spend a greater proportion of their time feeding and directly nurturing their children. In contrast, fathers spend more time, proportionally, playing with infants. Almost all fathers contribute to child care: Surveys show that 95 percent say they do some child care chores every day. But on average they still do less than mothers. For instance, 30 percent of fathers with wives who work do 3 or more hours of daily child care. In comparison, 74 percent of employed married mothers spend that amount of time every day in child care activities (Kazura, 2000; Whelan & Lally, 2002; Tooten et al., 2014; Luz et al., 2017).

Furthermore, fathers' play with their babies is often quite different from that of mothers. Fathers engage in more physical, rough-and-tumble activities with their children. In contrast, mothers play traditional games, such as peek-a-boo and games with more verbal elements (Paquette, Carbonneau, & Dubeau, 2003).

These differences in the ways that fathers and mothers play with their children occur even in the minority of families in the United States in which the father is the primary caregiver. Moreover, the differences occur in very diverse cultures: Fathers in Australia, Israel, India, Japan, Mexico, and even in the Aka Pygmy tribe in Central Africa all engage more in play than in caregiving, although the amount of time they spend with their infants varies widely. For instance, Aka fathers spend more time caring for their infants than members of any other known culture, holding and cuddling their babies at a rate some five times higher than anywhere else in the world (Roopnarine, 1992; Hewlett & Lamb, 2002).

These similarities and differences in childrearing practices across different societies raise an important question: How does culture affect attachment? This issue is discussed in the *Developmental Diversity and Your Life* feature.

Developmental Diversity and Your Life

Does Attachment Differ Across Cultures?

John Bowlby's observations of the biologically motivated efforts of the young of other species to seek safety and security were the basis for his views on attachment and his reason for suggesting that seeking attachment was biologically universal, a trait that we should find not only in other species but among humans of all cultures as well.

Research has shown, however, that human attachment is not as culturally universal as Bowlby predicted. Certain attachment patterns seem more likely among infants of particular cultures. For example, one study of German infants showed that most fell into the avoidant category. Other studies, conducted in Israel and Japan, have found a smaller proportion of infants who were securely attached than in the United States. Finally, comparisons of Chinese and Canadian children show that Chinese children are more inhibited than Canadians in the Ainsworth Strange Situation (Grossmann et al., 1982; Takahashi, 1986; Chen et al., 1998; Rothbaum et al., 2000; Kieffer, 2012).

AmanaimagesRF/Getty Images

Japanese parents seek to avoid separation and stress during infancy and do not foster independence. As a result, Japanese children often have the appearance of being less securely attached according to the Ainsworth Strange Situation, but using other measurement techniques, they may well score higher in attachment.

Do such findings suggest that we should abandon the notion that attachment is a universal biological tendency? Not necessarily. Though it is possible that Bowlby's claim that the desire for attachment is universal was too strongly stated, most of the data on attachment have been obtained by using the Ainsworth Strange Situation, which may not be the most appropriate measure in non-Western cultures (Dennis, Cole, & Zahn-Waxler, 2002; Mesman et al., 2016).

Attachment is now viewed as susceptible to cultural norms and expectations. Cross-cultural and intracultural differences in attachment reflect the nature of the measure employed and the expectations of various cultures. Some developmental specialists suggest that attachment should be viewed as a general tendency, but one that varies in the way it is expressed according to how actively caregivers in a society seek to instill independence in their children. Secure attachment, as defined by the Western-oriented Strange Situation, may be seen earliest in cultures that promote independence but may be delayed in societies in which independence is a less important cultural value (Rothbaum et al., 2000; Rothbaum, Rosen, & Ujiie, 2002).

Infant Interactions: Developing a Working Relationship

LO 6.8 Discuss the development of relationships in infancy.

Research on attachment is clear in showing that infants may develop multiple attachment relationships, and that over the course of time, the specific individuals with whom the infant is primarily attached may change. These variations in attachment emphasize that the development of relationships is an ongoing process, not only during infancy but throughout the life span.

PROCESSES UNDERLYING RELATIONSHIP DEVELOPMENT. Which processes underlie the development of relationships during infancy? For one thing, parents—and in fact all adults—appear to be genetically programmed to be sensitive to infants. For instance, brain-scanning techniques have found that the facial features of infants (but not adults) activate a specialized structure in the brain called the *fusiform gyrus* within a seventh of a second. Such reactions may help elicit nurturing behavior and trigger social interaction (Kringelbach et al., 2008; Zebrowitz et al., 2009; Goold & Meng, 2017).

In addition, studies have found that, across almost all cultures, mothers behave in typical ways with their infants. They tend to exaggerate their facial and vocal expressions—the nonverbal equivalent of the infant-directed speech that they use when they speak to infants (as discussed in Chapter 5). Similarly, they often imitate their infants' behavior, responding to distinctive sounds and movements by repeating them. There are even types of games, such as peek-a-boo, itsy-bitsy spider, and pat-a-cake, that are nearly universal (Harrist & Waugh, 2002; Kochanska, 2002).

Furthermore, according to the **mutual regulation model**, it is through these sorts of interactions that infants and parents learn to communicate emotional states to one another and to respond appropriately. For instance, in pat-a-cake, both infant and parent act jointly to regulate turn-taking behavior, with one individual waiting until the other completes a behavioral act before starting another. Consequently, at the age of 3 months, infants and their mothers have about the same influence on each other's behavior. Interestingly, by the age of 6 months, infants have more control over turn-taking, although by the age of 9 months, both partners once again become roughly equivalent in terms of mutual influence (Tronick, 2003).

mutual regulation model
the model in which infants and parents learn to communicate emotional states to one another and to respond appropriately

One of the ways infants and parents signal each other when they interact is through facial expressions. As we saw earlier in this chapter, even quite young infants are able to read, or decode, the facial expressions of their caregivers, and they react to those expressions.

For example, an infant whose mother, during an experiment, displays a stony, immobile facial expression reacts by making a variety of sounds, gestures, and facial expressions of her own in response to such a puzzling situation—and possibly to elicit some new response from her mother. Infants also show more happiness themselves when their mothers appear happy, and they look at their mothers longer. By contrast, infants are apt to respond with sad looks and to turn away when their mothers display unhappy expressions (Crockenberg & Leerkes, 2003; Reissland & Shepherd, 2006; Yato et al., 2008).

In short, the development of attachment in infants does not merely represent a reaction to the behavior of the people around them. Instead, there is a process of **reciprocal socialization**, in which infants' behaviors invite further responses from parents and other caregivers. In turn, the caregivers' behaviors bring about a reaction from the child, continuing the cycle. Recall, for instance, Annie, the baby who kept crying to be picked up when her mother put her in her crib. Ultimately, the actions and reactions of parents and child lead to an increase in attachment, forging and strengthening bonds between infants and caregivers as babies and caregivers communicate their needs and responses to each other. Figure 6-5 summarizes the sequence of infant–caregiver interaction (Kochanska & Aksan, 2004; Spinrad & Stifler, 2006). (Also see *From Research to Practice*.)

reciprocal socialization
a process in which infants' behaviors invite further responses from parents and other caregivers, which in turn bring about further responses from the infants

Figure 6-5 Sequence of Infant–Caregiver Interaction

The actions and reactions of caregivers and infants influence each other in complex ways. Do you think a similar pattern shows up in adult–adult interactions?

(**Source:** Adapted from Bell & Ainsworth, 1972; Tomlinson-Keasey, 1985.)

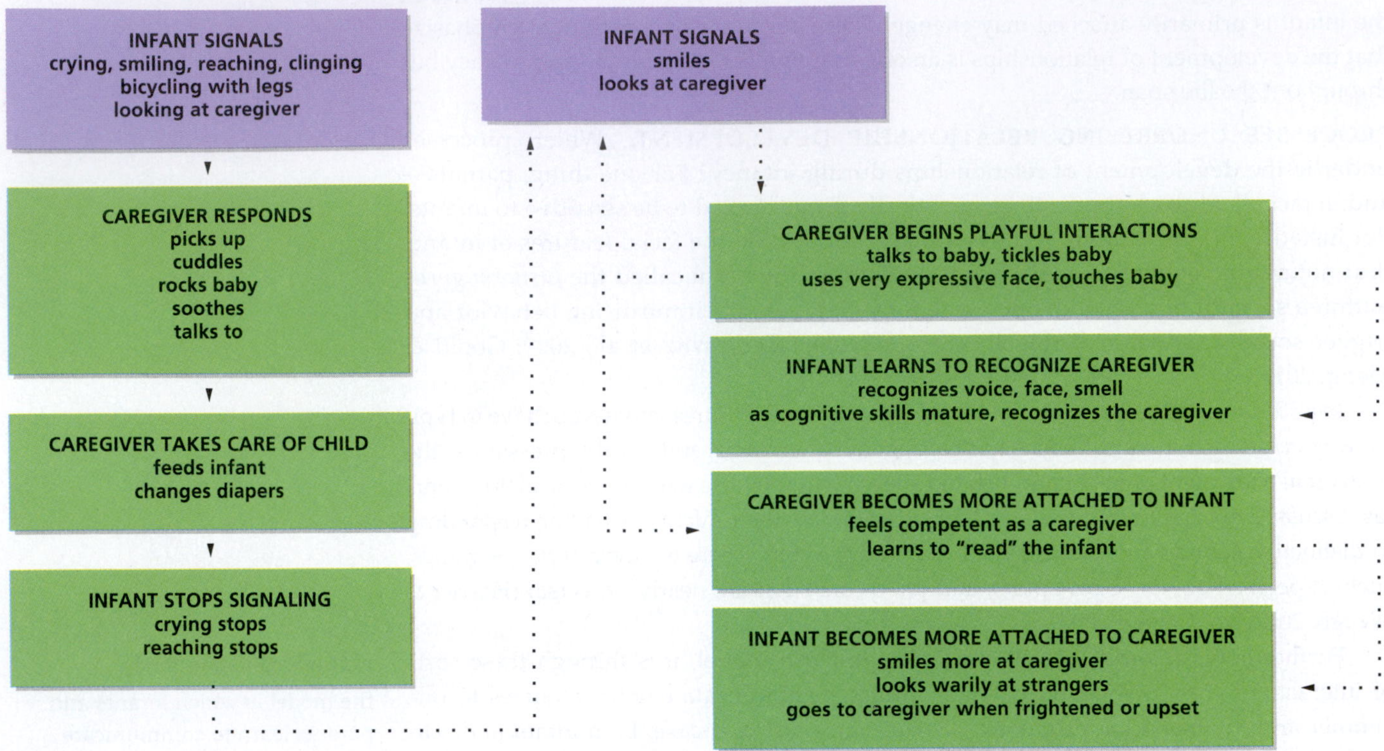

From Research to Practice

Are Infants Racist?

Many parents believe the best way to raise their children to be non-racist is by not making an issue of race at all. Promoting egalitarian values—"everyone is equal"—is assumed to be sufficient, and calling special attention to racial differences is inappropriate, the thinking goes. But does pretending that racial differences don't exist really encourage children to become colorblind?

No, it doesn't, according to a growing body of research. For example, the results of one study found that 6- to 9-month-old infants begin to associate faces of people from their own race to happy music, while they associate faces from other races with sad music. In addition, infants as young as 6 months of age are more likely to seek out information when they are uncertain from same-race adults compared with adults of a different race (Xiao et al., 2017a; Xiao et al., 2017b).

Other research shows that infants as young as 6 months notice racial differences: They stare significantly longer at photographs of people whose race is different from their parents' race. By 9 months, infants are better at distinguishing within-race faces than other-race faces (Vogel, Monesson, & Scott, 2012).

When children aren't given an explicit framework for understanding these differences they're noticing, they will try to sort them out on their own. And when they do, they start categorizing people according to race. By age 3, children who are asked to choose potential friends from a set of photographs favor their own race. By 6, children who are asked to sort out a stack of photographs of faces in any way they choose overwhelmingly choose to sort by race rather than gender. It appears that race is a central way in which to categorize the world and to differentiate individuals (Katz, 2003; Deeb et al., 2011; Johnson & Aboud, 2017).

In short, ignoring racial differences and correcting children when they make race-based observations may simply teach children that race is a taboo topic. A better approach is to treat racial differences like gender differences—to talk about them explicitly. We're comfortable teaching children that girls can grow up to be police officers just like boys, and we should be similarly comfortable teaching children that people of all races can be our friends—or even be president of the United States (Apfelbaum et al., 2010; Kurtz-Costes et al., 2011).

Shared Writing Prompt

Why do you think even young children categorize their social world in terms of similarity to themselves?

INFANTS' SOCIABILITY WITH THEIR PEERS: INFANT–INFANT INTERACTION. How sociable are infants with other children? Although they do not form "friendships" in the traditional sense, babies do react positively to the presence of peers from early in life, and they engage in rudimentary forms of social interaction.

Infants' sociability is expressed in several ways. From the earliest months of life, they smile, laugh, and vocalize while looking at their peers. They show more interest in peers than in inanimate objects, and they pay greater attention to other infants than they do to a mirror image of themselves. They also begin to show preferences for peers with whom they are familiar compared with those they do not know. For example, studies of identical twins show that twins exhibit a higher level of social behavior toward each other than toward an unfamiliar infant (Eid et al., 2003; Legerstee, 2014; Kawakami, 2014).

Infants' level of sociability generally rises with age. Nine- to 12-month-olds mutually present and accept toys, particularly if they know each other. They also play social games, such as peek-a-boo or crawl-and-chase. Such behavior is important, as it serves as a foundation for future social exchanges in which children will try to elicit responses from others and then offer reactions to those responses. These kinds of exchanges are important to learn because they continue even into adulthood. For example, someone who says, "Hi, what's up?" may be trying to elicit a response to which he or she can then reply (Endo, 1992; Eckerman & Peterman, 2001).

Finally, as infants age, they begin to imitate one another. For instance, 14-month-old infants who are familiar with one another sometimes reproduce each other's behavior. Such imitation serves a social function and can also be a powerful teaching tool (Ray & Heyes, 2011; Brownell, 2016).

According to Andrew Meltzoff, a developmental psychologist at the University of Washington, a child's ability to impart this information is only one example of how so-called "expert" babies are able to teach skills and information to other infants. According to the research of Meltzoff and his colleagues, the abilities learned from the "experts" are retained and later used to a remarkable degree. Learning by exposure starts early in life. Recent evidence shows that even 7-week-old infants can perform delayed imitation of a novel stimulus to which they have earlier been exposed, such as an adult sticking the tongue out of the side of the mouth (Meltzoff, 2002; Meltzoff, Waismeyer, & Gopnik, 2012; Waismeyer & Meltzoff, 2017).

To some developmentalists, the capacity of young children to engage in imitation suggests that imitation may be inborn. In support of this view, research has identified a class of neurons in the brain that seems to be related to an innate ability to imitate. *Mirror neurons* are neurons that fire not only when an individual enacts a particular behavior but also when the individual simply observes *another* organism carrying out the same behavior (Falck-Ytter, Gredebäck, & von Hofsten, 2006; Lepage & Théret, 2007; Paulus, 2014).

For example, research on brain functioning shows activation of the inferior frontal gyrus both when an individual carries out a particular task and when observing another individual carrying out the same task. Mirror neurons may help infants to understand others' actions, to develop a theory of mind, and to show goal-directed behavior from the time of birth. Dysfunction of mirror neurons may be related to the development of disorders involving children's theory of mind, as well as autism, a psychological disorder involving significant emotional and linguistic problems (Martineau et al., 2008; Welsh et al., 2009; von Hofsten & Rosander, 2015).

The idea that through exposure to other children infants learn new behaviors, skills, and abilities has several implications. For one thing, it suggests that interactions between infants provide more than social benefits; they may have an impact on children's future cognitive development as well. Even more important, these findings illustrate that infants may benefit from participation in child care centers (which we consider later in this chapter). Although we don't know for sure, the opportunity to learn from their peers may prove to be a lasting advantage for infants in group child care settings.

Module 6.2 Review

LO 6.6 Explain attachment in infancy and how it affects a person's future social competence.

Attachment, the positive emotional bond between an infant and a significant individual, affects a person's later social competence as an adult.

LO 6.7 Describe the roles that caregivers play in infants' social development.

Secure attachment can occur between infants and their mothers, between infants and their fathers, and between infants and other caregivers.

LO 6.8 Discuss the development of relationships in infancy.

Infants and the persons with whom they interact engage in reciprocal socialization as they mutually adjust to one another's interactions. Infants react differently to other children than to inanimate objects, and gradually they engage in increasing amounts of peer social interaction.

Journal Writing Prompt

Applying Lifespan Development: In what sort of society might an avoidant attachment style be encouraged by cultural attitudes toward childrearing? In such a society, would characterizing the infant's consistent avoidance of its mother as anger be an accurate interpretation?

Differences Among Infants

Lincoln was a difficult baby, his parents both agreed. For one thing, it seemed like they could never get him to sleep at night. He cried at the slightest noise, a problem because his crib was near the windows facing a busy street. Worse yet, once he started crying, it seemed to take forever to calm him down again. One day his mother, Aisha, was telling her mother-in-law, Mary, about the challenges of being Lincoln's mom. Mary recalled that her own son, Lincoln's father Malcom, had been much the same way. "He was my first child, and I thought this was how all babies acted. So, we just kept trying different ways until we found out how he worked. I remember, we put his crib all over the apartment until we finally found out where he could sleep, and it ended up being in the hallway for a long time. Then his sister, Maleah, came along, and she was so quiet and easy, I didn't know what to do with my extra time!"

As the story of Lincoln's family shows, babies are not all alike, and neither are their families. As we'll see, some of the differences among people seem to be present from the moment we are born. The differences among infants include overall personality and temperament, and differences in the lives they lead—differences based on their gender, the nature of their families, and the ways in which they are cared for.

Personality Development: The Characteristics that Make Infants Unique

LO 6.9 Describe individual differences that distinguish an infant's personality.

personality
the sum total of the enduring characteristics that differentiate one individual from another

The origins of **personality**, the sum total of the enduring characteristics that differentiate one individual from another, stem from infancy. From birth onward, infants begin to show unique, stable traits and behaviors that ultimately lead to their development as distinct, special individuals (Caspi, 2000; Kagan, 2000; Shiner, Masten, & Roberts, 2003).

According to psychologist Erik Erikson, whose approach to personality development we first discussed in Chapter 1, infants' early experiences are responsible for shaping one of the key aspects of their personality: whether they will be basically trusting or mistrustful.

Erikson's theory of psychosocial development
the theory that considers how individuals come to understand themselves and the meaning of others'—and their own—behavior

Erikson's theory of psychosocial development considers how individuals come to understand themselves and the meaning of others'—and their own—behavior (Erikson, 1963). The theory suggests that developmental change occurs throughout people's lives in eight distinct stages, the first of which occurs in infancy.

According to Erikson, during the first 18 months of life, we pass through the **trust-versus-mistrust stage**. During this period, infants develop a sense of trust or mistrust, largely depending on how well their needs are met by their caregivers. In the previous example, Mary's attention to Malcom's needs probably helped him develop a basic sense of trust in the world. Erikson suggests that if infants are able to develop trust, they experience a sense of hope, which permits them to feel as if they can fulfill their needs successfully. By contrast, feelings of mistrust lead infants to see the world as harsh and unfriendly, and they may have later difficulties in forming close bonds with others.

singburi/Fotolia

According to Erikson, children develop independence and autonomy if their parents encourage exploration and freedom, within safe boundaries. What does Erikson theorize happens if children are restricted and overly protected at this stage?

During the end of infancy, children enter the **autonomy-versus-shame-and-doubt stage**, which lasts from around 18 months to 3 years. During this period, children develop independence and autonomy if their parents encourage exploration and freedom within safe boundaries. However, if children are restricted and overly protected, they feel shame, self-doubt, and unhappiness.

trust-versus-mistrust stage
according to Erik Erikson, the period during which infants develop a sense of trust or mistrust, depending largely on how well their caregivers meet their needs

autonomy-versus-shame-and-doubt stage
the period during which, according to Erik Erikson, toddlers (age 18 months to 3 years) develop independence and autonomy if they are allowed the freedom to explore, or shame and self-doubt if they are restricted and overprotected

Erikson argues that personality is primarily shaped by infants' experiences. However, as we discuss next, other developmentalists concentrate on consistencies of behavior that are present at birth, even before the experiences of infancy. These consistencies are viewed largely as genetically determined and as providing the raw material of personality.

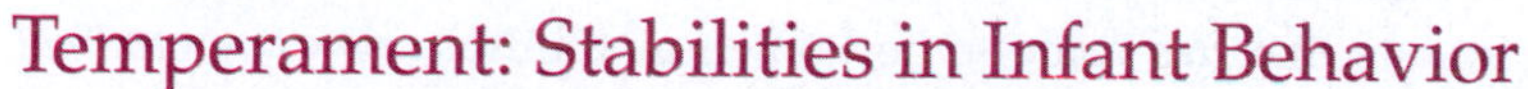

Temperament: Stabilities in Infant Behavior

LO 6.10 Define temperament, and describe how it affects a child in the first 2 years of life.

Sarah's parents thought there must be something wrong. Unlike her older brother Josh, who had been so active as an infant that he seemed never to be still, Sarah was much more placid. She took long naps and was easily soothed on those relatively rare occasions when she became agitated. What could be producing her extreme calmness?

The most likely answer: The difference between Sarah and Josh reflected differences in temperament. As we first discussed in Chapter 2, **temperament** encompasses patterns of arousal and emotionality that are consistent and enduring characteristics of an individual (Kochanska & Aksan, 2004; Rothbart, 2007; Gartstein et al., 2017).

temperament
patterns of arousal and emotionality that are consistent and enduring characteristics of an individual

Temperament refers to *how* children behave, as opposed to *what* they do or *why* they do it. Infants show temperamental differences in general disposition from the time of birth, largely due at first to genetic factors, and temperament tends to be fairly stable well into adolescence. However, temperament is not fixed and unchangeable: Childrearing practices can modify temperament significantly. In fact, some children show little consistency in temperament from one age to the next (Werner et al., 2007; de Lauzon-Guillain et al., 2012; Kusangi, Nakano, & Kondo-Ikemura, 2014).

Temperament is reflected in several dimensions of behavior. One central dimension is *activity level*, which reflects the degree of overall movement. Some babies (like Sarah) are relatively placid, and their movements are slow and almost leisurely. In contrast, the activity level of other infants (like Josh) is quite high, with strong, restless movements of the arms and legs.

Another important dimension of temperament is the nature and quality of an infant's mood, and in particular a child's *irritability*. Like Lincoln, who was described in

Table 6-2 Some Dimensions of Temperament in Infants, with Behavioral Indicators

Dimension	Behavioral Indicators
Activity level	**High:** wriggles while diaper is changed **Low:** lies still while being dressed
Approach-withdrawal	**Approach orientation:** accepts novel foods and toys easily **Withdrawal orientation:** cries when a stranger comes near
Rhythmicity	**Regular:** has consistent feeding schedule **Irregular:** has varying sleep and waking schedule
Distractibility	**Low:** continues crying even when diaper is changed **High:** stops fussing when held and rocked
Quality of mood	**Negative:** cries when carriage is rocked **Positive:** smiles or smacks lips when tasting new food
Threshold of responsiveness	**High:** not startled by sudden noises or bright lights **Low:** pauses sucking on bottle at approach of parent or slight noise

(**Source:** Based on Thomas, Chess, & Birch, 1968.)

the example at the beginning of this section, some infants are easily disturbed and cry easily, whereas others are relatively easygoing. Irritable infants fuss a great deal, and they are easily upset. They are also difficult to soothe when they do begin to cry. Such irritability is relatively stable: Infants who are irritable at birth remain irritable at age 1, and even at age 2 they are still more easily upset than infants who were not irritable just after birth (Stupica, Sherman, & Cassidy, 2011). (Other aspects of temperament are listed in Table 6-2.)

CATEGORIZING TEMPERAMENT: EASY, DIFFICULT, AND SLOW-TO-WARM BABIES. Because temperament can be viewed along so many dimensions, some researchers have asked whether broader categories can be used to describe children's overall behavior. According to Alexander Thomas and Stella Chess, who carried out a large-scale study of a group of infants that has come to be known as the *New York Longitudinal Study* (Thomas & Chess, 1980), babies can be described according to one of several profiles:

easy babies
babies who have a positive disposition; their body functions operate regularly, and they are adaptable

difficult babies
babies who have negative moods and are slow to adapt to new situations; when confronted with a new situation, they tend to withdraw

slow-to-warm babies
babies who are inactive, showing relatively calm reactions to their environment; their moods are generally negative, and they withdraw from new situations, adapting slowly

goodness-of-fit
the notion that development is dependent on the degree of match between children's temperament and the nature and demands of the environment in which they are being raised

- *Easy babies.* **Easy babies** have a positive disposition. Their body functions operate regularly, and they are adaptable. They are generally positive, showing curiosity about new situations, and their emotions are moderate or low in intensity. This category applies to about 40 percent (the largest number) of infants.
- *Difficult babies.* **Difficult babies** have more negative moods and are slow to adapt to new situations. When confronted with a new situation, they tend to withdraw. About 10 percent of infants belong in this category.
- *Slow-to-warm babies.* **Slow-to-warm babies** are inactive, showing relatively calm reactions to their environment. Their moods are generally negative, and they withdraw from new situations, adapting slowly. Approximately 15 percent of infants are slow-to-warm.

As for the remaining 35 percent, they cannot be consistently categorized. These children show a variety of combinations of characteristics. For instance, one infant may have relatively sunny moods but react negatively to new situations, while another may show little stability of any sort in terms of general temperament.

THE CONSEQUENCES OF TEMPERAMENT: DOES TEMPERAMENT MATTER? One obvious question to emerge from the findings of the relative stability of temperament is whether a particular kind of temperament is beneficial. The answer seems to be that no single type of temperament is invariably good or bad. Instead, children's long-term adjustment depends on the **goodness-of-fit** of their particular temperament and the nature and demands of the environment in which they find themselves. For instance, children with a low activity level and low irritability may do particularly well in an environment in which they are left to explore on their own and are allowed largely to direct their own behavior. In contrast, high activity level, highly irritable children may do best with greater direction, which permits them to channel their energy in particular directions (Thomas & Chess, 1980; Strelau, 1998; Schoppe-Sullivan et al., 2007). Mary, the grandmother in the earlier example, found ways to adjust the environment for her son, Malcom. Malcolm and Aisha may need to do the same for their own son, Lincoln.

Some research suggests that certain temperaments are, in general, more adaptive than others. For instance, difficult children, in general, are more likely to show behavior problems by school age than those classified in infancy as easy children. But not all difficult children experience problems. The key determinant seems to be the way parents react to their infants' difficult behavior. If they react by showing anger and inconsistency—responses that their child's difficult, demanding behavior readily evokes—then the child is ultimately more likely to experience behavior problems. In contrast, parents who display more warmth and consistency in their responses are more likely to have children who avoid later problems (Thomas, Chess, & Birch, 1968; Salley, Miller, & Bell, 2013; Sayal et al., 2014).

Furthermore, temperament seems to be at least weakly related to infants' attachment to their adult caregivers. For example, infants vary considerably in how much emotion they display nonverbally. Some are "poker-faced," showing little expressivity, while others' reactions tend to be much more easily decoded. More expressive infants may provide more easily discernible cues to others, thereby easing the way for caregivers to be more successful in responding to their needs and facilitating attachment (Feldman & Rimé, 1991; Laible, Panfile, & Makariev, 2008; Sayal et al., 2014).

Cultural differences also have a major influence on the consequences of a particular temperament. For instance, children who would be described as "difficult" in Western cultures actually seem to have an advantage in the East African Maasai culture. The reason? Mothers offer their breast to their infants only when they fuss and cry; therefore, the irritable, more difficult infants are apt to receive more nourishment than the more placid, easy infants. Particularly when environmental conditions are bad, such as during a drought, difficult babies may have an advantage (de Vries, 1984; Gaias et al., 2012; Farkas & Vallotton, 2016).

THE BIOLOGICAL BASIS OF TEMPERAMENT. Recent approaches to temperament grow out of the framework of behavioral genetics discussed in Chapter 2. From this perspective, temperamental characteristics are seen as inherited traits that are fairly stable during childhood and across the entire life span. These traits are viewed as making up the core of personality and playing a substantial role in future development (Sheese et al., 2009; Goodnight et al., 2016).

Consider, for example, the trait of physiological reactivity, characterized by a high degree of motor and muscle activity in response to novel stimuli. This high reactivity, which has been termed *inhibition to the unfamiliar,* is exhibited as shyness.

A clear biological basis underlies inhibition to the unfamiliar, in which any novel stimulus produces a rapid increase in heartbeat, blood pressure, and pupil dilation, as well as excitability of the brain's limbic system. For example, people categorized as inhibited at age 2 show high reactivity in their brain's amygdala in adulthood when viewing unfamiliar faces. The shyness associated with this physiological pattern seems to continue through childhood and even into adulthood (Propper & Moore, 2006; Kagan et al., 2007; Anzman-Frasca et al., 2013).

High reactivity to unfamiliar situations in infants has also been linked to greater susceptibility to depression and anxiety disorders in adulthood. Furthermore, infants who are highly reactive develop anterior prefrontal cortexes that are thicker than those in less reactive children when they reach adulthood. Because the prefrontal cortex is closely linked to the amygdala (which controls emotional responses) and the hippocampus (which controls fear responses), the difference in the prefrontal cortex may help explain the higher rates of depression and anxiety disorders (Schwartz & Rauch, 2004; Schwartz et al., 2008; Waters et al., 2017).

Gender: Boys in Blue, Girls in Pink

LO 6.11 Discuss how the gender of a child affects his or her development in the first 2 years of life.

"It's a boy." "It's a girl."

One of these two statements is probably the first announcement made after the birth of a child. From the moment of birth, girls and boys are treated differently. Their parents send out different kinds of birth announcements. They are dressed in different clothes and wrapped in different-colored blankets. They are given different toys (Bridges, 1993; Coltrane & Adams, 1997; Serbin, Poulin-Dubois, & Colburne, 2001).

Parents play with boy and girl babies differently: From birth on, fathers tend to interact more with sons than daughters, while mothers interact more with daughters. Because, as noted earlier in the chapter, mothers and fathers play in different ways (with fathers typically engaging in more physical, rough-and-tumble activities and mothers in traditional games, such as peek-a-boo), male and female infants are clearly exposed to different styles of activity and interaction from their parents (Clearfield & Nelson, 2006; Parke, 2007; Zosuls, Ruble, & Tamis-LeMonda, 2014).

The behavior exhibited by girls and boys is interpreted in very different ways by adults. For instance, when researchers showed adults a video of an infant whose name was given as either "John" or "Mary," adults perceived "John" as adventurous and inquisitive, while "Mary" was considered fearful and anxious, although it was the same baby performing a single set of behaviors (Condry & Condry, 1976). Clearly, adults view the behavior of children through the lens of gender. **Gender** refers to our sense of being male or female. The term *gender* is often used to mean the same thing as "sex," but they are not actually the same. *Sex* typically refers to sexual anatomy and sexual behavior, whereas *gender* refers to the social perceptions of maleness or femaleness. All cultures prescribe *gender roles* for males and females, but these roles differ greatly from one culture to another.

gender
the sense of being male or female

GENDER DIFFERENCES. There is a considerable amount of disagreement over both the extent and causes of such gender differences, even though most people agree that boys and girls do experience at least partially different worlds based on gender. Some gender differences are fairly clear from the time of birth. For example, male infants tend to be more active and fussier than female infants. Boys' sleep tends to be more disturbed than that of girls. Boys grimace more, although no gender difference exists in the overall amount of crying. There is also some evidence that male newborns are more irritable than female newborns, although the findings are inconsistent (Guinsburg et al., 2000; Losonczy-Marshall, 2008).

Differences between male and female infants, however, are generally minor. In most ways, infants seem so similar that usually adults cannot discern whether a baby is a boy or girl, as the "John" and "Mary" video research shows. Furthermore, it is important to remember that there are much greater differences among individual boys and among individual girls than there are, on average, between boys and girls (Crawford & Unger, 2004).

GENDER ROLES. Gender differences emerge more clearly as children age—and become increasingly influenced by the gender roles that society sets out for them. For instance, by age 1, infants are able to distinguish between males and females. Girls at this age prefer to play with dolls or stuffed animals, while boys seek out blocks and trucks. Often, of course, these are the only options available to them, owing to the choices their parents and other adults have made in the toys they provide (Cherney, Kelly-Vance, & Glover, 2003; Alexander, Wilcox, & Woods, 2009).

Swanlake/Fotolia

Parents of girls who play with toys related to activities associated with boys are apt to be less concerned than parents of boys who play with toys associated with girls.

Children's preferences for certain kinds of toys are reinforced by their parents. In general, however, parents of boys are more apt to be concerned about their child's choices than are parents of girls. Boys receive more reinforcement for playing with toys that society deems appropriate for boys, and this reinforcement increases with age. By contrast, a girl playing with a truck is viewed with considerably less concern than a boy playing with a doll might be. Girls who play with toys seen by society as "masculine" are less discouraged for their behavior than are boys who play with toys seen as "feminine" (Schmalz & Kerstetter, 2006; Hill & Flom, 2007; Dinella, Weisgram, & Fulcher, 2017).

By the time they reach age 2, boys behave more independently and less compliantly than girls. Much of this behavior can be traced to parental reactions to earlier behavior. For instance, when a child takes his or her first steps, parents tend to react differently, depending on the child's gender: Boys are encouraged to go off and explore the world, while girls are hugged and kept close. It is hardly surprising, then, that by age 2, girls tend to show less independence and greater compliance (Poulin-Dubois, Serbin, & Eichstedt, 2002).

Societal encouragement and reinforcement do not, however, completely explain differences in behavior between boys and girls. For example, as we'll discuss further in Chapter 8, one study examined girls who were exposed before birth to abnormally high levels of *androgen*, a male hormone, because their mothers unwittingly took a drug containing the hormone while pregnant. Later, these girls were more likely to play with toys stereotypically preferred by boys (such as cars) and less likely to play with toys stereotypically associated with girls (such as dolls). Although there are many alternative explanations for these results—you can probably think of several yourself—one possibility is that exposure to male hormones affected the brain development of the girls, leading them to favor toys that involve certain kinds of preferred skills (Mealey, 2000; Servin et al., 2003).

In sum, differences in behavior between boys and girls begin in infancy, and—as we will see in future chapters—continue throughout childhood (and beyond). Although gender differences have complex causes, representing some combination of innate, biologically related, and environmental factors, they play a profound role in the social and emotional development of infants.

Family Life in the 21st Century

LO 6.12 Describe 21st-century families and their consequences for children.

A look back at television shows from 50 years ago finds a world of families portrayed in a way that today seems oddly old-fashioned and quaint: mothers and fathers, married for years, and their good-looking children making their way in a world that seems to have few, if any, serious problems.

From *a social worker's* perspective

Imagine you are a social worker visiting a foster home. It is 11:00 A.M. You find the breakfast dishes in the sink and books and toys all over the floor. The infant you have placed in the home is happily pounding on pots and pans as his foster mother claps time. The kitchen floor is gooey under the baby's high chair. What is your assessment?

Even 50 years ago, such a view of family life was overly romantic and unrealistic. Today, however, it is broadly inaccurate, representing only a minority of families in the United States. A quick review tells the story:

- The number of single-parent families has increased significantly in the past three decades, as the number of two-parent households has declined. Currently, 65 percent of children ages 0–17 live with two married parents, down from 77 percent in 1980. Nearly a quarter of children live with only their mothers, 4 percent live with only their fathers, and 4 percent live with neither of their parents. Three-quarters of white, non-Hispanic children lived with two married parents in 2016, compared with 60 percent of Hispanic and only 34 percent of black children (Childstats.gov, 2017).
- The average size of families is shrinking. Today, on average, there are 2.5 persons per household, compared to 3.1 in 1970. The number of people living in non-family households (without any relatives) is more than 41 million (U.S. Census Bureau, 2013).
- Although the number of adolescents giving birth has declined substantially over the past 5 years, there are still nearly 10 in 1,000 births to adolescent women age 15 to 17, the vast majority of whom are unmarried (Childstats.gov, 2017).
- Fifty-seven percent of mothers of infants work outside the home (U.S. Bureau of Labor Statistics, 2013).
- Forty-three percent of children under age 18 live in low-income households, up from 40 percent in 2006. Sixty-nine percent of black children and 63 percent of Hispanic infants and toddlers live in low-income families (Jiang, Granja, & Koball, 2017).

Blend Images/Alamy Stock Photo

The number of single-parent families has increased dramatically over the past 20 years. If the current trend continues, 60 percent of all children will live at some time with a single parent.

At the very least, these statistics suggest that many infants are being raised in environments in which substantial stressors are present. Such stress makes it an unusually difficult task to raise children—which is never easy, even under the best circumstances.

At the same time, society is adapting to the new realities of family life in the 21st century. Several kinds of social support exist for the parents of infants, and society is evolving new institutions to help in their care. One example is the growing array of child care arrangements available to help working parents, as we discuss next.

How Does Infant Child Care Affect Later Development?

LO 6.13 Summarize how nonparental child care affects infants.

> *For most of the years my two kids were in child care, I worried about it. Did that weird day-care home where my daughter stayed briefly as a toddler do irreparable harm? Was my son irretrievably damaged by that child-care center he disliked? (Shellenbarger, 2003, p. D1)*

Every day, parents ask themselves questions like these. The issue of how infant child care affects later development is a pressing one for many parents, who, because of economic, family, or career demands, leave their children to the care of others for a portion of the day. Almost two-thirds of all children between 4 months and 3 years of age now spend time in nonparental child care. Overall, more than 80 percent of infants are cared for regularly by people other than their mothers at some point during their first year of life. The majority of these infants begin child care outside the home before the age of 4 months and are enrolled for almost 30 hours per week (Federal Interagency Forum on Child and Family Statistics, 2003; NICHD Early Child Care Research Network, 2006a; also see Figure 6-6). What effects do such arrangements have on later development?

Although the answer is largely reassuring, the newest research to come from the massive, long-term Study of Early Child Care and Youth Development, the longest-running examination of child care ever conducted, suggests that long-term participation in day care may have unanticipated consequences.

Figure 6-6 Where Are Children Cared For?

According to a major study by the National Institute of Child Health and Human Development (NICHD), children spend more time in some kind of child care outside the home or family as they get older.

(**Source:** NICHD Early Child Care Research Network, 2006a.)

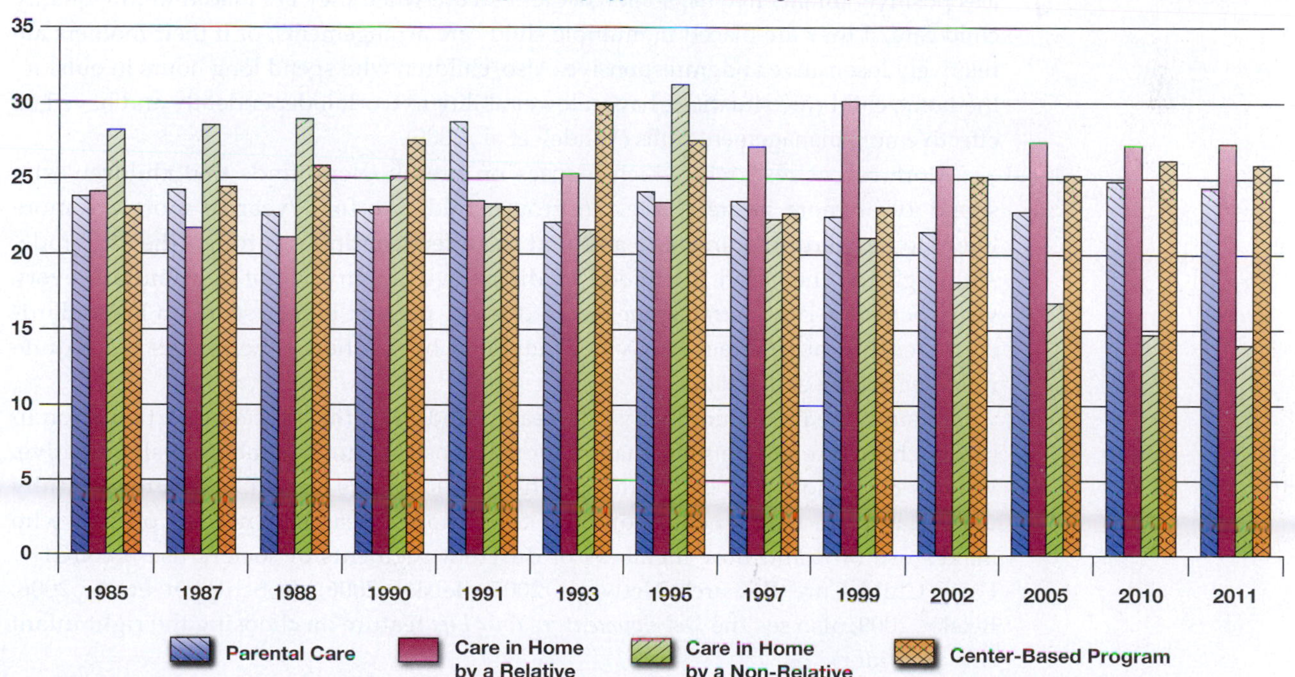

Jupiterimages/Getty Images

High-quality infant child care seems to produce only minor differences from home care in most respects, and some aspects of development may even be enhanced. What aspects of development might be enhanced by participation in infant child care outside the home?

First, the good news: According to most of the evidence, high-quality child care outside the home produces only minor differences from home care in most respects, and may even enhance certain aspects of development. For example, research finds little or no difference in the strength or nature of parental attachment bonds of infants who have been in high-quality child care compared with infants raised solely by their parents (NICHD Early Child Care Research Network, 2001; Vandell et al., 2005; Sosinsky & Kim, 2013; Ruzek et al., 2014).

In addition to the direct benefits from involvement in child care outside the home, there are indirect benefits. For example, children in lower-income households and those whose mothers are single may benefit from the educational and social experiences in child care, as well as from the higher income produced by parental employment. Furthermore, children may experience improvements in nutrition and eating habits (NICHD Early Child Care Research Network, 2003a; Dearing, McCartney, & Taylor, 2009; Dev et al., 2017).

Furthermore, children who participate in Early Head Start—a program that serves at-risk infants and toddlers in high-quality child care centers—can solve problems better, pay greater attention to others, and use language more effectively than poor children who do not participate in the program. In addition, their parents (who are also involved in the program) benefit from their participation. Participating parents talk and read more to their children, and they are less likely to spank them. Moreover, children who receive good, responsive child care are more likely to play well with other children (NICHD Early Child Care Research Network, 2001b; Maccoby & Lewis, 2003; Loeb et al., 2004; Raikes et al., 2014).

However, some of the findings on participation in child care outside the home are less positive. Infants may be somewhat less secure when they are placed in low-quality child care, if they are placed in multiple child care arrangements, or if their mothers are relatively insensitive and unresponsive. Also, children who spend long hours in outside-the-home child care situations have a lower ability to work independently and have less effective time management skills (Vandell et al., 2005).

More recent research, which focuses on preschoolers, finds that children who spend 10 or more hours a week in group child care for a year or more are more likely to be disruptive in class, and that the effect continues through the 6th grade. Although the increased likelihood of disruptive activity is not substantial—every year spent in a child care center resulted in a 1 percent higher score on a standardized measure of problem behavior completed by teachers—the results were quite reliable (Belsky et al., 2007).

In sum, the ballooning body of research finds that the effects of participation in group child care are neither unambiguously positive nor unambiguously negative. What is clear, however, is that the *quality* of child care is critical. Ultimately, to fully understand the consequences of child care, more research is needed on just who makes use of it and how members of different segments of society use it (NICHD Early Child Care Research Network, 2005; Belsky, 2006; de Schipper et al., 2006; Belsky, 2009; also see the *Development in Your Life* feature on choosing the right infant care provider).

Development in Your Life

Choosing the Right Infant Care Provider

One finding that emerges with absolute clarity from research conducted on the consequences of infant child care programs is that the benefits of child care—peer learning, greater social skills, greater independence—occur only when child care is of high quality. But what distinguishes high-quality child care from low-caliber programs? Parents should consider the following questions when they are choosing a program (American Academy of Pediatrics HealthyChildren.org, 2015):

- Are there enough providers? A desirable ratio is one adult for every three infants, although one to four can be adequate.
- Are group sizes manageable? Even with several providers, a group of infants should not be larger than eight.
- Has the center complied with all governmental regulations, and is it licensed?
- What are the hours?
- Do the people providing the care seem to like what they are doing? What are their educational qualifications? Are they experienced? Do they seem happy in the job, or is offering child care just a way to earn money?
- What do the caregivers do during the day? Do they spend their time playing with, listening and talking to, and paying attention to the children? Do they seem genuinely interested in the children, rather than merely going through the motions of caring for them? Is there a television constantly on?
- Are the children safe and clean? Does the environment allow infants to move around safely? Are the equipment and furniture in good repair? Do the providers adhere to the highest levels of cleanliness? After changing a baby's diaper, do providers wash their hands?
- What training do the providers have in caring for children? Do they demonstrate a knowledge of the basics of infant development and an understanding of how normal children develop? Do they seem alert to signs that development may depart from normal patterns?
- Finally, is the environment happy and cheerful? Is the child care more than just a babysitting service when you consider that for the time an infant is there, it is the child's whole world? You should feel fully comfortable and confident that the child care center is a place where your infant will be treated as an individual.

In addition to following these guidelines, you may contact the National Association for the Education of Young Children (NAEYC), from which you can get the name of a resource and referral agency in your area. Go to the NAEYC website at www.naeyc.org.

Module 6.3 Review

LO 6.9 Describe individual differences that distinguish an infant's personality.

According to Erik Erikson, during infancy, individuals move from the trust-versus-mistrust stage of psychosocial development to the autonomy-versus-shame-and-guilt stage.

LO 6.10 Define temperament, and describe how it affects a child in the first 2 years of life.

Temperament encompasses enduring levels of arousal and emotionality that are characteristic of an individual.

LO 6.11 Discuss how the gender of a child affects his or her development in the first 2 years of life.

Gender differences become more pronounced as infants age.

LO 6.12 Describe 21st-century families and their consequences for children.

The varieties of families, ranging from traditional two-parent to blended to same-sex couples, mirrors the complexity of modern-day society.

LO 6.13 Summarize how nonparental child care affects infants.

Child care outside of the home can have neutral, positive, or negative effects on the social development of children, depending largely on its quality. Research on the effects of child care must take into account the varying quality of different child care settings and the social characteristics of the parents who tend to use child care.

Journal Writing Prompt

Applying Lifespan Development: If you were introducing a bill in Congress regarding the minimum licensing requirements for child care centers, what would you emphasize?

Epilogue

The road infants travel as they develop as social individuals is a long and winding one. We saw in this chapter that infants begin decoding and encoding emotions early, using social referencing and eventually developing a theory of mind. We also considered how the attachment patterns that infants display can have long-term effects, influencing even what kind of parent the child eventually becomes. In addition to examining Erik Erikson's theory of psychosocial development, we also discussed temperament and explored the nature and causes of gender differences. We concluded with a discussion of infant child care options.

Return to the prologue of this chapter, which describes Andy and Matt, the 10-month-old twins who learned to undo the Velcro strap holding their hats on their heads, and answer the following questions.

1. How does this anecdote relate to the sociability of infants?
2. Is this episode evidence of self-awareness on the part of Andy or Matt? Why or why not?
3. What role do you think social referencing might have played in this scenario?
4. Can we form any opinion about Andy's or Matt's personality based on this event? Why or why not?

Looking Back

LO 6.1 Discuss how children express and experience emotions in the first 2 years of life.

Infants display a variety of facial expressions, which are similar across cultures and appear to reflect basic emotional states.

LO 6.2 Differentiate stranger anxiety from separation anxiety.

By the end of the first year, infants often develop both stranger anxiety (wariness around an unknown person) and separation anxiety (distress displayed when a customary care provider departs).

LO 6.3 Discuss the development of social referencing and nonverbal decoding abilities.

Through social referencing, infants from the age of 8 or 9 months use the expressions of others to clarify ambiguous situations and learn appropriate reactions to them. Early in life, infants develop the capability of nonverbal decoding: determining the emotional states of others based on their facial and vocal expressions.

LO 6.4 Describe the sense of self that children possess in the first 2 years of life.

Infants begin to develop self-awareness at about the age of 12 months.

LO 6.5 Summarize the theory of mind and evidence of infants' growing sense of mental activity by age 2.

Infants begin to develop a theory of mind: knowledge and beliefs about how they and others think.

LO 6.6 Explain attachment in infancy and how it affects a person's future social competence.

Attachment, a strong, positive emotional bond that forms between an infant and one or more significant persons, is a crucial factor in enabling individuals to develop social relationships.

Infants display one of four major attachment patterns: securely attached, avoidant, ambivalent, and disorganized-disoriented. Research suggests an association between an infant's attachment pattern and his or her social and emotional competence as an adult.

LO 6.7 Describe the roles that caregivers play in infants' social development.

Mothers' interactions with their babies are particularly important for social development. Mothers who respond effectively to their babies' social overtures appear to contribute to the babies' ability to become securely attached.

LO 6.8 Discuss the development of relationships in infancy.

Through a process of reciprocal socialization, infants and caregivers interact with one another and affect one another's behavior, which strengthens their mutual relationship. From an early age, infants engage in rudimentary forms of social interaction with other children, and their level of sociability rises as they age.

LO 6.9 Describe individual differences that distinguish an infant's personality.

The origins of personality, the sum total of the enduring characteristics that differentiate one individual from another, arise during infancy.

LO 6.10 Define temperament, and describe how it affects a child in the first 2 years of life.

Temperament encompasses enduring levels of arousal and emotionality that are characteristic of an individual. Temperamental differences underlie the broad classification of infants into easy, difficult, and slow-to-warm categories.

LO 6.11 Discuss how the gender of a child affects his or her development in the first 2 years of life.

As infants age, gender differences become more pronounced, mostly due to environmental influences. Differences are accentuated by parental expectations and behavior.

LO 6.12 Describe 21st-century families and their consequences for children.

The varieties of families, ranging from traditional two-parent to blended to same-sex couples, mirrors the complexity of modern-day society.

LO 6.13 Summarize how nonparental child care affects infants.

Child care, a societal response to the changing nature of the family, can be beneficial to the social development of children, fostering social interaction and cooperation, if it is of high quality.

Key Terms and Concepts

social smile 183
stranger anxiety 183
separation anxiety 183
social referencing 184
self-awareness 186
theory of mind 187
empathy 187
attachment 189
Ainsworth Strange Situation 190
secure attachment pattern 190
avoidant attachment pattern 190
ambivalent attachment pattern 191
disorganized-disoriented attachment pattern 191
mutual regulation model 195
reciprocal socialization 195
personality 198
Erikson's theory of psychosocial development 198
trust-versus-mistrust stage 199
autonomy-versus-shame-and-doubt stage 199
temperament 199
easy babies 200
difficult babies 200
slow-to-warm babies 200
goodness-of-fit 200
gender 202

Summary 2
Infancy

Ignat/Bauer-Griffin/Contributor/Getty Images

FOUR-MONTH-OLD ALEX was a model infant in almost every respect. However, there was one aspect of his behavior that posed a dilemma: how to respond when he woke up in the middle of the night and cried despondently. It usually was not a matter of being hungry, because typically he had been fed recently. And it was not caused by his diaper being soiled, because usually that had been changed recently. Instead, it seemed that Alex just wanted to be held and entertained, and when he wasn't, he cried and shrieked dramatically until someone came to him.

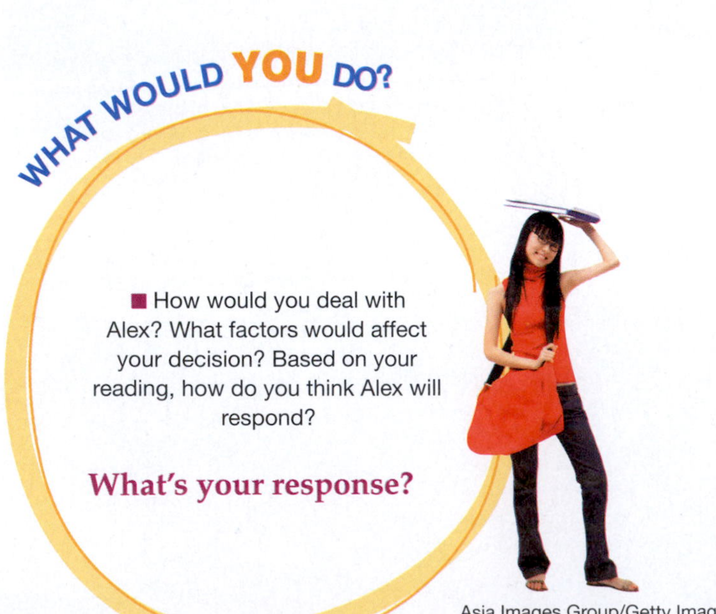

WHAT WOULD YOU DO?

■ How would you deal with Alex? What factors would affect your decision? Based on your reading, how do you think Alex will respond?

What's your response?

Asia Images Group/Getty Images

WHAT WOULD A PARENT DO?

■ What strategies would you use in dealing with Alex? Would you go to him every time he cried? Or would you try to wait him out, perhaps setting a time limit before going to him?

What's your response?

Photodisc/Getty Images

Physical Development

Ksenia Lev/Shutterstock

- Alex's body is developing various rhythms (repetitive, cyclical patterns of behavior) that are responsible for the change from sleep to wakefulness.
- Alex will sleep in spurts of around 2 hours, followed by periods of wakefulness until about 16 weeks, when he will begin to sleep as much as 6 continuous hours.
- Since Alex's sense of touch is one of his most highly developed senses (and one of the earliest developed), Alex will respond to gentle touches, such as a soothing caress, which can calm a crying, fussy infant.

Cognitive Development

FatCamera/Getty Images

- Alex has learned that his behavior (crying) can produce a desired effect (someone holding and entertaining him).
- As Alex's brain develops, he is able to separate people he knows from people he doesn't; this is why he responds so positively when someone he knows comes to comfort him during the night.

Social and Personality Development

szeyuen/Fotolia

- Alex has developed attachment (the positive emotional bond between him and particular individuals) to those who care for him.
- In order to feel secure, Alex needs to know that his caregivers will provide an appropriate response to the signals he is sending.
- Part of Alex's temperament is that he is irritable. Irritable infants can be fussy and are difficult to soothe when they do begin to cry.
- Since irritability is relatively stable, Alex will continue to display this temperament at age 1 and even age 2.

WHAT WOULD A NURSE DO?

- How would you recommend that Alex's caregivers deal with the situation? Are there any dangers that the caregivers should be aware of?

What's your response?

Mark Andersen/Rubberball/Getty Images

WHAT WOULD AN EDUCATOR DO?

- Suppose Alex spends a few hours every weekday afternoon in day care. If you were a child care provider, how would you deal with Alex if he wakes up from naps soon after falling asleep?

What's your response?

Imtmphoto/Shutterstock

Chapter 7

Physical and Cognitive Development in the Preschool Years

volkovslava/Shutterstock

Learning Objectives

LO 7.1 Describe a child's bodily growth and overall health risks during the preschool years.

LO 7.2 Summarize how preschool children's brains develop.

LO 7.3 Explain how preschool children's motor skills develop.

LO 7.4 Summarize how Piaget explains cognitive development during the preschool years.

LO 7.5 Summarize the information processing approaches to cognitive development in the preschool years.

LO 7.6 Describe Vygotsky's view of cognitive development in the preschool years.

LO 7.7 Explain how children's language develops in the preschool years.

LO 7.8 Identify the effects of digital media and television on preschoolers.

LO 7.9 Distinguish the educational programs available to children in the preschool years.

Chapter Overview

Prologue: Aaron

Aaron, a wildly energetic preschooler who just turned 3, was trying to stretch far enough to reach the bowl of cookies that he spied sitting on the kitchen counter. Because the bowl was just beyond his grasp, he pushed a chair from the kitchen table over to the counter and climbed up.

Because he still couldn't reach the cookies from the chair, Aaron climbed onto the kitchen counter and crawled over to the cookie bowl. He pried the lid off the jar, thrust his hand in, pulled out a cookie, and began to munch on it.

But not for long. His curiosity getting the better of him, he grabbed another cookie and began to work his body along the counter toward the sink. He climbed in, twisted the cold water faucet to the "on" position, and happily splashed in the cold water.

Aaron's father, who had left the room for only a moment, returned to find Aaron sitting in the sink, soaked, with a contented smile on his face.

Looking Ahead

Consider how far Aaron has come from his infancy. Just a few years earlier, he could not even lift his head. Now he's able to move with great assurance, pushing furniture, opening jars, turning knobs, and climbing on chairs. Of course, such advances in mobility also bring new challenges to parents, who must bring a new level of vigilance in order to prevent injuries, the greatest threat to preschoolers' physical well-being.

The preschool period, which extends from the end of infancy, at about age 2, to around age 6, is an exciting time in children's lives. In one sense, the preschool years mark a time of preparation: a period spent anticipating and getting ready for the start of a child's formal education, through which society will begin the process of passing on its intellectual tools to a new generation.

Gennadiy Poznyakov/Fotolia

But it is a mistake to take the label "preschool" too literally. The years between 3 and 6 are hardly a mere way station in life, an interval spent waiting for the next, more important period to start. Instead, the preschool years are a time of tremendous change and growth, where physical, intellectual, and social development proceeds at a rapid pace.

In this chapter, we focus on the physical, cognitive, and linguistic growth that occurs during the preschool years. We begin by considering the physical changes children undergo during those years. We discuss weight and height, nutrition, and health and wellness. The brain and its neural pathways change too, and we will touch on some intriguing findings relating to gender differences in the way that the brain functions. We also look at how both gross and fine motor skills change over the preschool years.

Intellectual development is the focus of much of the remainder of the chapter. We examine the major approaches to cognitive development, including the next stages of Piaget's theory, information processing approaches, and a view of cognitive development as heavily influenced by culture.

Finally, the chapter considers the important advances in language development that occur during the preschool years. We end with a discussion of several factors that influence cognitive development, including exposure to television and participation in child care and preschool programs.

Physical Growth

The advances in physical abilities that occur during the preschool period are nothing short of astounding. Just how far children develop is apparent when we look at the specific changes they have undergone in their size, shape, and physical abilities.

The Growing Body

LO 7.1 Describe a child's bodily growth and overall health risks during the preschool years.

By age 2, the average child in the United States weighs around 25 to 30 pounds and is close to 36 inches tall—around half the height of the average adult. Children grow steadily during the preschool period, and by the time they are 6 years old, they weigh, on average, about 46 pounds and stand 46 inches tall (see Figure 7-1).

INDIVIDUAL DIFFERENCES IN HEIGHT AND WEIGHT. The averages in Figure 7-1 mask great individual differences in height and weight. For instance, 10 percent of 6-year-olds weigh 55 pounds or more, and 10 percent weigh 36 pounds or less. Furthermore, average differences in height and weight between boys and girls increase during the preschool years. Although at age 2 the differences are relatively small, during the preschool years, boys start becoming taller and heavier, on average, than girls.

Global economics also affect these averages. There are profound differences in height and weight between children in economically developed countries and those in developing countries. The better nutrition and health care received by children in developed countries translates into significant differences in growth. For instance, the average Swedish 4-year-old is as tall as the average 6-year-old in Bangladesh (Leathers & Foster, 2004; Mendoza et al., 2017).

Differences in height and weight reflect economic factors within the United States as well. For instance, children in families whose incomes are below the poverty level are far more likely to be unusually short than children raised in more affluent homes (Barrett & Frank, 1987; Ogden et al., 2002).

CHANGES IN BODY SHAPE AND STRUCTURE. If we compare the bodies of a 2-year-old and a 6-year-old, we find that the bodies vary not only in height and weight, but also in shape. During the preschool years, boys and girls begin to burn off some of the fat they have carried from their infancy, and they no longer have a pot-bellied appearance. They become less round and chubby and more slender. Moreover, their arms and legs lengthen, and the size relationship between the head and the rest of the body becomes more adultlike. In fact, by the time children reach 6 years of age, their proportions are quite similar to those of adults.

Other physical changes are occurring internally. Muscle size increases, and children grow stronger. Bones become sturdier. The sense organs continue to develop.

For instance, the *eustachian tube* in the ear, which carries sounds from the external part of the ear to the internal part, moves from a position that is almost parallel to the ground at birth to a more angular position. This change sometimes leads to an increase in the frequency of earaches during the preschool years.

NUTRITION: EATING THE RIGHT FOODS. Because the rate of growth during this period is slower than during infancy, preschoolers need less food to maintain their growth. The change in food consumption may be so noticeable that parents sometimes worry that their preschooler is not eating enough. However, children tend to be quite adept at maintaining an appropriate intake of food if provided with nutritious meals. In fact, anxiously encouraging children to eat more than they seem to want naturally may lead them to increase their food intake beyond an appropriate level.

Ultimately, some children's food consumption can become so high that they become *overweight*, defined as *a body mass index* (*BMI*) between the 85th and 95th percentiles of children of the same weight and height. (BMI is calculated by dividing a child's weight in kilograms by the square of their height in meters). If the BMI is even greater, then children are considered obese. **Obesity** is defined as a BMI at or above the 95th percentile for children of the same age and sex.

The prevalence of obesity among older preschoolers increased significantly through the 1980s and 1990s. However, research released in 2014 found that the incidence of obesity declined over the prior 10 years from nearly 14 percent to just over 8 percent—a significant breakthrough in children's health (Tavernise, 2014; Miller & Brooks-Gunn, 2015).

How do parents ensure that their children have good nutrition without turning mealtimes into a tense, adversarial situation? In most cases, the best strategy is to make sure that a variety of foods low in fat and high in nutritional content is available. Foods that have a relatively high iron content are particularly important: Iron-deficiency anemia, which causes constant fatigue, is one of the prevalent nutritional problems in developed countries such as the United States. High-iron foods include dark green vegetables (such as broccoli), whole grains, and some kinds of meat, such as lean hamburger. It is also important to avoid foods with high sodium content and to include foods with low fat content (Brotanek et al., 2007; Grant et al., 2007; Jalonick, 2011).

Figure 7-1 Gaining Height and Weight

The preschool years are marked by steady increases in height and weight. The figures show the median point for boys and girls at each age, in which 50 percent of children in each category are above this height or weight level, and 50 percent are below.

(**Source:** National Center for Health Statistics in collaboration with the National Center for Chronic Disease Prevention and Health Promotion, 2000; National Center for Health Statistics, 2017)

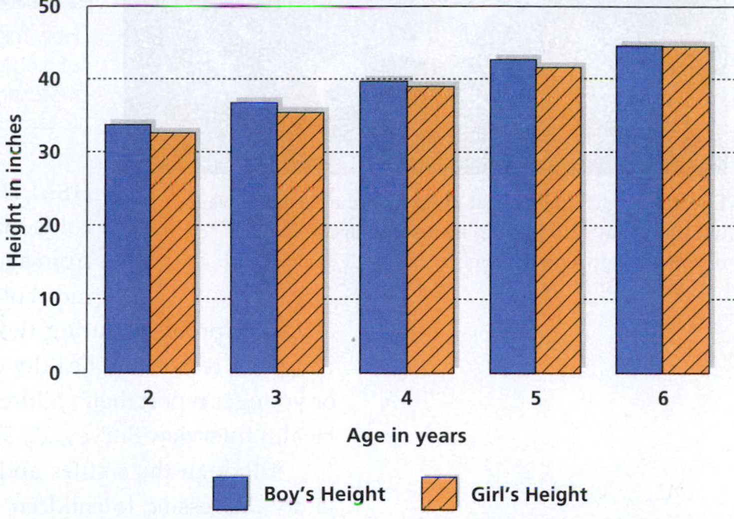

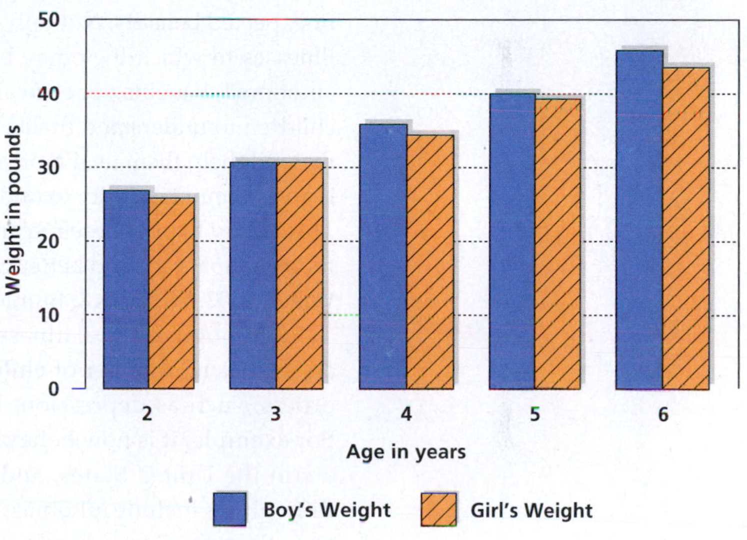

obesity

body weight more than 20 percent higher than the average weight for a person of a given age and height

Because preschool children, like adults, will not find all foods equally appealing, children should be given the opportunity to develop their own natural preferences. As long as their overall diet is adequate, no single food is indispensable. Exposing children to a wide variety of foods by encouraging them to take just one bite of new foods is a relatively low-stress way of expanding children's diets (Busick et al., 2008; Struempler et al., 2014).

In behavior called the *just-right phenomenon*, some preschool children develop strong rituals and routines about the kinds of foods they will eat. They may only eat certain

Juice Images/Alamy Stock Photo

Encouraging children to eat more than they seem to want naturally may lead them to increase their food intake beyond an appropriate level.

foods that are prepared in a particular way and presented to them in a particular manner on a plate. In adults, such rigidity would be a sign of a psychological disorder, but it is normal in young children. Almost all preschoolers eventually outgrow it (Evans et al., 1997; Evans et al., 2006).

From a *health-care worker's* perspective

How might biology and environment combine to affect the physical growth of a child adopted as an infant from a developing country and reared in a more industrialized one?

HEALTH AND ILLNESS. The average preschooler has 7 to 10 colds and other minor respiratory illnesses in each of the years from age 3 to 5. In the United States, a runny nose due to the common cold is the most frequent—and happily, the least severe—kind of health problem during the preschool years. The majority of children in the United States are reasonably healthy during this period, and 88 percent of parents of children 4 or younger report their children are in excellent or very good health (Kalb, 1997; National Health Interview Survey, 2015).

Although the sniffles and coughs that are the symptoms of such illnesses are certainly distressing to children, the unpleasantness is usually not too severe, and the illnesses usually last only a few days. What's more, such minor illnesses may offer some unexpected benefits: Not only may they help children build up immunity to more severe illnesses to which they may be exposed in the future, but they also may provide some emotional benefits. Specifically, some researchers argue that minor illness permits children to understand their bodies better. It also may permit them to learn coping skills that will help them deal more effectively with future, more severe diseases. Furthermore, it gives them the ability to understand better what others who are sick are going through. This ability to put oneself in another's shoes, known as *empathy*, may teach children to be more sympathetic and better caretakers (Notaro, Gelman, & Zimmerman, 2002; Raman & Winer, 2002; Williams & Binnie, 2002).

Although physical illness is typically a minor problem during the preschool years, an increasing number of children are being treated with drugs for psychological disorders, such as depression, formally known as *depressive disorders* (see Figure 7-2). For example, it is now believed that depression affects around 4 percent of preschoolers in the United States, and the rate of diagnosis has increased significantly. Other difficulties include phobias, anxiety disorders, and behavioral disorders. In addition, the use of drugs such as antidepressants and stimulants has grown significantly. Although it is not clear why the increase has occurred, some experts believe that parents and preschool teachers may be seeking a quick fix for behavior problems that may simply represent normal difficulties (Pozzi-Monzo, 2012; Muller, 2013; Whalen, Sylvester, & Luby, 2017).

INJURIES DURING THE PRESCHOOL YEARS: PLAYING IT SAFE. The greatest risk that preschoolers face comes from neither illness nor nutritional problems but from accidents: Before age 10, children have twice the likelihood of dying from an injury than from an illness. Children in the United States have a one in three chance every year of receiving an injury that requires medical attention (Field & Behrman, 2003; National Safety Council, 2013).

The danger of injuries during the preschool years is in part a result of the children's high levels of physical activity. A 3-year-old might think that it is perfectly reasonable to climb on an unsteady chair to get something that is out of reach, and a 4-year-old might

Figure 7-2 Numbers of Preschool Children Taking Medication for Behavioral Problems

Although there is no clear explanation as to why the use of stimulants and antidepressants has increased among children, some experts believe that medication is seen as a quick-fix solution for behavior problems that are actually normal difficulties.

(**Source:** Zito et al., 2000.)

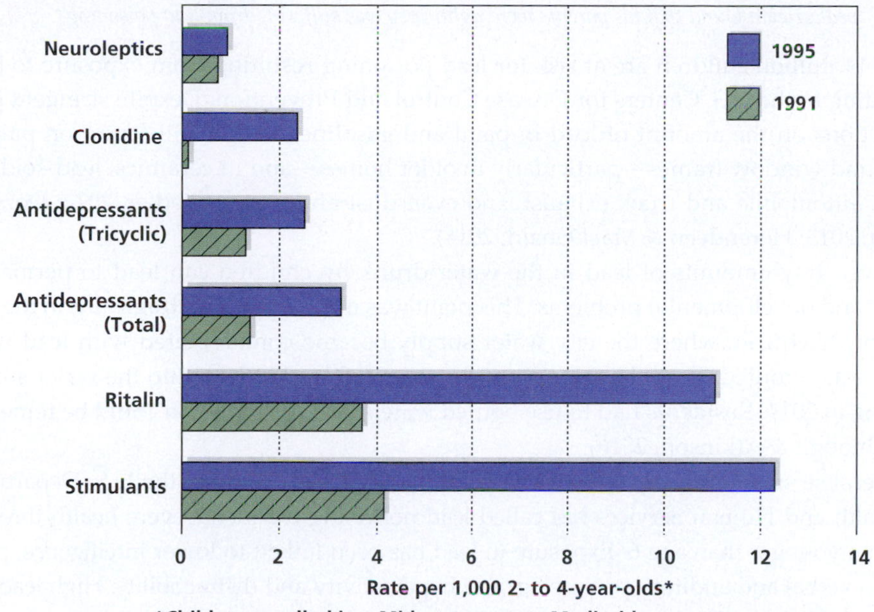

enjoy holding on to a low tree branch and swinging her legs up and down. It is this physical activity, in combination with the curiosity and lack of judgment that also characterize this age group, that makes preschoolers so accident-prone.

Furthermore, some children are more apt to take risks than others, and such preschoolers are more likely to be injured than their more cautious peers. Boys, who are often more active than girls and tend to take more risks, have a higher rate of injuries. Ethnic differences, probably due to differences in cultural norms about how closely children need to be supervised, can also be seen in accident rates. Asian American children in the United States, who tend to be supervised with particular strictness by their parents, have one of the lowest accident rates for children. Economic factors also play a role. Children raised under conditions of poverty in urban areas, whose inner-city neighborhoods may contain more hazards than more affluent areas, are two times more likely to die of injuries than children living in affluence (Morrongiello et al., 2006; Morrongiello, Klemencic, & Corbett, 2008; Sengoelge et al., 2014).

The range of dangers that preschoolers face is wide. Injuries come from falls, burns from stoves and fires, drowning in bathtubs indoors and standing water outdoors, and suffocation in places such as abandoned refrigerators. Auto accidents also account for a large number of injuries. Finally, children face injuries from poisonous substances, such as household cleaners.

Parents and caregivers of preschoolers can take several precautions to prevent injuries, although none of these measures eliminates the need for close supervision. Caregivers can start by "childproofing" preschoolers' homes and classrooms, placing covers on electrical outlets and child locks on cabinets where poisons are kept, for example. Child car seats and bike helmets can help prevent injuries in case of accidents. Parents and teachers also need to be aware of the dangers from long-term hazards, such as lead poisoning (Bull & Durbin, 2008; Morrongiello, Corbett, & Bellissimo, 2008; Morrongiello et al., 2009).

Duris Guillaume/Fotolia

The danger of injuries during the preschool years is in part a result of children's high levels of physical activity. It is important to take protective measures to reduce the hazards.

The urban environment in which poor children often live makes them especially susceptible to lead poisoning.

THE SILENT DANGER: LEAD POISONING IN YOUNG CHILDREN.

At age 3, Tory couldn't sit still. He was unable to watch a television show for more than 5 minutes, and sitting still while his mother read to him was impossible. He was often irritable, and he impulsively took risks when he was playing with other children. When his behavior reached a point where his parents thought there was something seriously wrong with him, they took him to a pediatrician for a physical examination. After testing Tory's blood, the pediatrician found that his parents were right: Tory was suffering from lead poisoning.

Some 14 million children are at risk for lead poisoning resulting from exposure to lead, according to the U.S. Centers for Disease Control and Prevention. Despite stringent legal restrictions on the amount of lead in paint and gasoline, lead is still found on painted walls and window frames—particularly in older homes—and in ceramics, lead-soldered pipes, automobile and truck exhaust, and even dust and water (Fiedler, 2012; Dozor & Amler, 2013; Herendeen & MacDonald, 2014).

Even tiny amounts of lead in the water drunk by children can lead to permanent health and developmental problems. This point was made apparent, tragically, in the case of Flint, Michigan, where the city water supply became contaminated with lead when water was rerouted through water pipes that allowed lead to leak into the water supply starting in 2014. Residents had to use bottled water until the situation could be remedied (Goodnough & Atkinson, 2016).

Because small amounts of lead can permanently harm children, the U.S. Department of Health and Human Services has called lead poisoning the most severe health threat to children younger than age 6. Exposure to lead has been linked to lower intelligence, problems in verbal and auditory processing, and hyperactivity and distractibility. High lead levels have also been linked to higher levels of antisocial behavior, including aggression and delinquency in school-age children (see Figure 7-3). At yet higher levels of exposure, lead poisoning results in illness and death (Brown, 2008; Zhang et al., 2013; Earl et al., 2016).

Poor children are particularly susceptible to lead poisoning, and the results of poisoning tend to be worse for them than for children from more affluent families. Children living in poverty are more apt to reside in housing that contains peeling and chipping lead paint, or to live near heavily trafficked urban areas with high levels of air pollution. At the same time, many families living in poverty may be less stable and unable to provide consistent opportunities for intellectual stimulation that might serve to offset some of the cognitive problems caused by the poisoning. Consequently, lead poisoning is especially harmful to poorer children (Dilworth-Bart & Moore, 2006; Polivka, 2006; Kim & Williams, 2017).

myelin

protective insulation that surrounds parts of neurons

Figure 7-3 The Consequence of Lead Poisoning

High levels of lead have been linked to higher levels of antisocial behavior, including aggression and delinquency, in school-age children.

(**Source:** Needleman et al., 1996.)

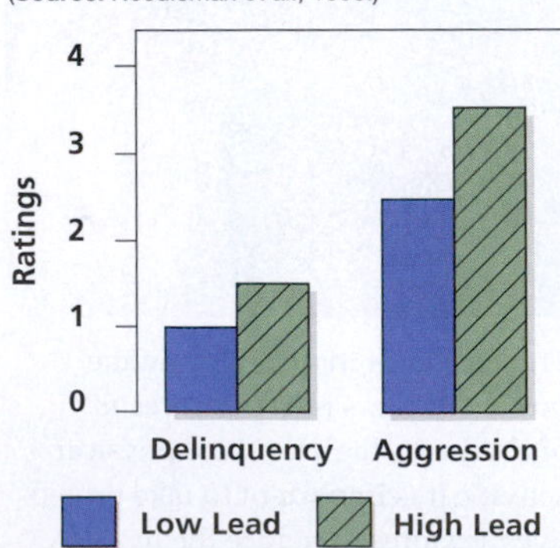

The Growing Brain

LO 7.2 Summarize how preschool children's brains develop.

The brain grows at a faster rate than any other part of the body. Two-year-olds have brains that are about three-quarters of the size and weight of an adult brain. By age 5, children's brains weigh 90 percent of average adult brain weight. In comparison, the average 5-year-old's total body weight is just 30 percent of average adult body weight (Nihart, 1993; House, 2007).

Why does the brain grow so rapidly? One reason is an increase in the number of interconnections among cells, as we saw in Chapter 4. These interconnections allow for more complex communication between neurons, and they permit the rapid growth of cognitive skills that we'll discuss later in the chapter. In addition, the amount of **myelin**—protective insulation that surrounds parts of neurons—increases, which speeds the transmission of electrical impulses along brain cells but also adds to brain weight. This rapid brain growth not only allows for increased cognitive abilities but also helps in the development of more sophisticated fine and gross motor skills (Dalton & Bergenn, 2007; Klingberg & Betteridge, 2013; Dean et al., 2014).

Development in Your Life

Keeping Preschoolers Healthy

There is no way around it: Even the healthiest preschooler occasionally gets sick. Social interaction with others ensures that illnesses will be passed from one child to another. However, some diseases are preventable, and others can be minimized if simple precautions are taken:

- Preschoolers should eat a well-balanced diet containing the proper nutrients, particularly foods containing sufficient protein. (The recommended energy intake for children at age 24 months is about 1,300 calories a day, and for those age 4 to 6, it is around 1,700 calories a day.) Although some fruit juice, such as a glass of orange juice with breakfast, is fine, generally juice has so much sugar that it should be avoided. In addition, keep offering healthy foods, even if children initially reject them; they may grow to like them.
- Preschoolers should be encouraged to exercise. Children who exercise are less likely to become obese than those who are sedentary.
- Children should get as much sleep as they wish. Being run-down from lack of either nutrition or sleep makes children more susceptible to illness.
- Children should avoid contact with others who are ill. Parents should make sure that children wash their hands after playing with other kids who are obviously sick (as well as emphasizing the importance of handwashing generally).
- Children should be placed on an appropriate schedule of immunizations. As illustrated in Figure 7-4, current recommendations state that a child should have received nine different vaccines and other preventive medicines in five to seven separate visits to the doctor. Despite the beliefs of some parents, there is no scientific basis for believing that common vaccinations should be avoided because they can increase the risk of autism. *Children should receive the recommended vaccinations outlined in the table, according to the American Academy of Pediatrics and U.S. Centers for Disease Control and Prevention,* unless otherwise told not to by a reputable medical professional (Daley & Glanz, 2011).
- Finally, if a child does get ill, remember this: Minor illnesses during childhood sometimes provide immunity to more serious illnesses later on.

Figure 7-4 Vaccination Schedule

(**Source:** http://www.cdc.gov/vaccines/parents/downloads/parent-ver-sch-0-6yrs.pdf.)

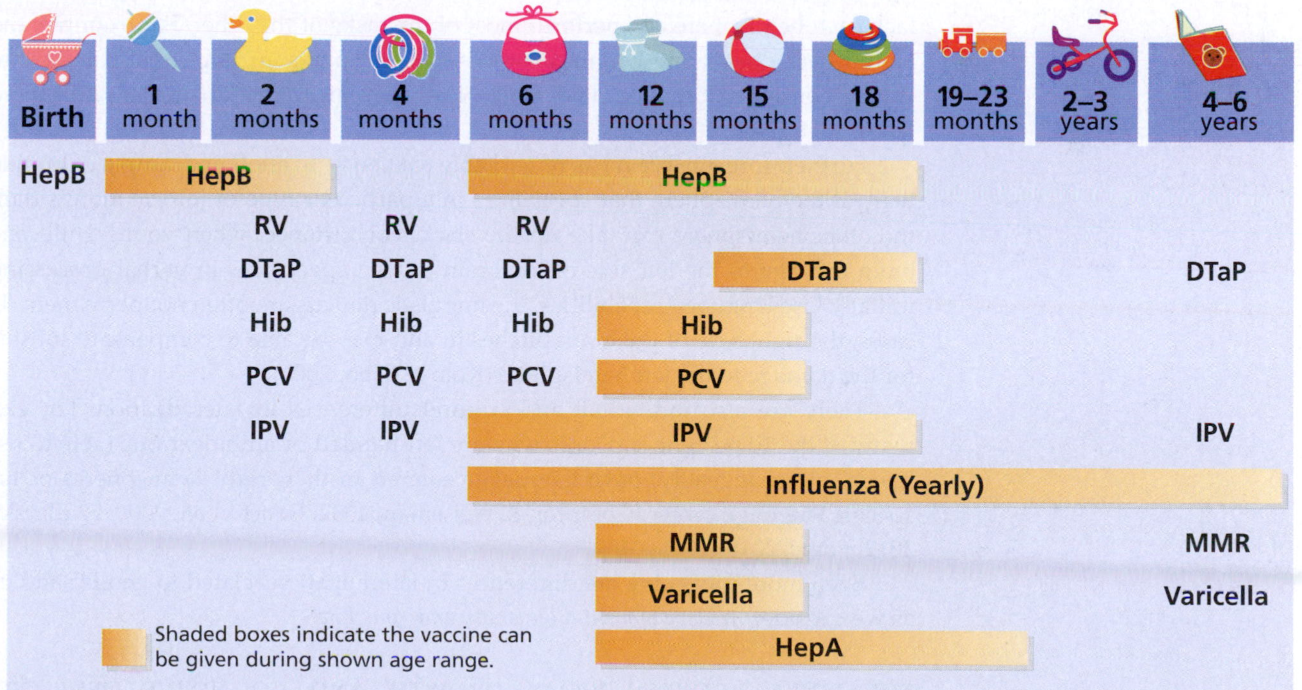

Figure 7-5 Looking into the Brain

This set of PET brain scans illustrates that activity in the right or left hemisphere of the brain differs according to the task in which a person is engaged. How might educators use this finding in their approach to teaching?

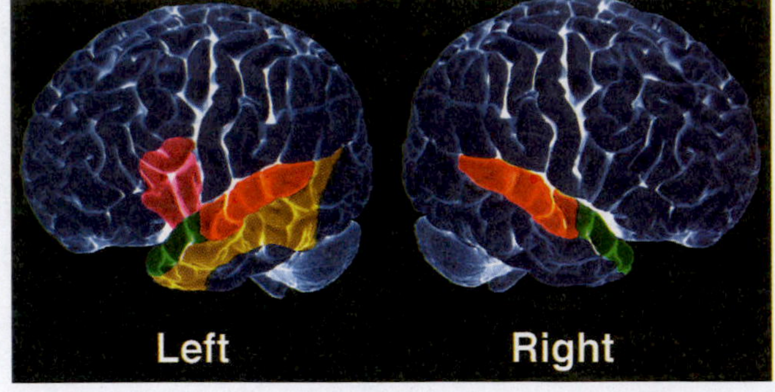

ZEPHYR/Getty Images

By the end of the preschool period, some parts of the brain have undergone particularly significant growth. For example, the *corpus callosum*, a bundle of nerve fibers that connects the two hemispheres of the brain, becomes considerably thicker, developing as many as 800 million individual fibers that help coordinate brain functioning between the two hemispheres.

In contrast, children who are malnourished show delays in brain development. For example, severely malnourished children develop less myelinization protecting their neurons (Hazin, Alves, & Rodrigues Falbo, 2007).

BRAIN LATERALIZATION. The two halves of the brain also begin to become increasingly differentiated and specialized. **Lateralization**, the process by which certain cognitive functions are located more in one hemisphere than the other, becomes more pronounced during the preschool years.

lateralization
the process by which certain cognitive functions are located more in one hemisphere of the brain than in the other

For most people, the left hemisphere is involved primarily with tasks that necessitate verbal competence, such as speaking, reading, thinking, and reasoning. The right hemisphere develops its own strengths, especially in nonverbal areas such as comprehension of spatial relationships, recognition of patterns and drawings, music, and emotional expression (Pollak, Holt, & Wismer Fries, 2004; Watling & Bourne, 2007; Dundas, Plaut, & Behrmann, 2013; see Figure 7-5).

Each of the two hemispheres also begins to process information in a slightly different manner. The left hemisphere processes information sequentially, one piece of data at a time. The right hemisphere processes information in a more global manner, reflecting on it as a whole (Ansaldo, Arguin, & Roch Locours, 2002; Holowaka & Petitto, 2002; Barber et al., 2012).

Although there is some specialization of the hemispheres, in most respects the two hemispheres act in tandem. They are interdependent, and the differences between the two are minor. Even the hemispheric specialization in certain tasks is not absolute. In fact, each hemisphere can perform most of the tasks of the other. For example, the right hemisphere does some language processing and plays an important role in language comprehension (Corballis, 2003; Hall, Neal, & Dean, 2008; Jahagirdar, 2014; Hodgson, Hirst, & Hudson, 2016).

Furthermore, the brain has remarkable resiliency. In another example of human plasticity, if the hemisphere that specializes in a particular type of information is damaged, the other hemisphere can take up the slack. For instance, when young children suffer brain damage to the left side of the brain (which specializes in verbal processing) and initially lose language capabilities, the linguistic deficits are often not permanent. In such cases, the right side of the brain pitches in and may be able to compensate substantially for the damage to the left hemisphere (Kolb & Gibb, 2006).

There are also individual and cultural differences in lateralization. For example, many of the 10 percent of people who are left-handed or ambidextrous (able to use both hands interchangeably) have language centered in their right hemispheres or have no specific language center (Compton & Weissman, 2002; Isaacs et al., 2006; Szaflarski et al., 2012; Porac, 2016).

Even more intriguing are differences in lateralization related to gender and culture, as we consider in *Developmental Diversity and Your Life*.

THE LINKS BETWEEN BRAIN GROWTH AND COGNITIVE DEVELOPMENT. Neuroscientists are just beginning to understand the ways in which brain development is related to cognitive development. For example, it appears that there are periods during

Developmental Diversity and Your Life

Are Gender and Culture Related to the Brain's Structure?

Among the most controversial findings relating to the specialization of the hemispheres of the brain is evidence that lateralization is related to gender and culture. For instance, starting during the first year of life and continuing in the preschool years, boys and girls show some hemispheric differences associated with lower body reflexes and the processing of auditory information. Boys also clearly tend to show greater specialization of language in the left hemisphere; among girls, language is more evenly divided between the two hemispheres. Such differences may help explain why—as we'll see later in the chapter—girls' language development proceeds at a more rapid pace during the preschool years than does boys' language development (Bourne & Todd, 2004; Huster, Westerhausen, & Herrmann, 2011; Allan, Joye, & Lonigan, 2017).

Before we accept a genetic explanation for the differences between female and male brains, we need to consider an equally plausible alternative: It may be that verbal abilities emerge earlier in girls because girls receive greater encouragement for verbal skills than boys do. For instance, even as infants, girls are spoken to more than boys. Such higher levels of verbal stimulation may produce growth in particular areas of the brain that does not occur in boys. Consequently, environmental factors rather than genetic ones may lead to the gender differences we find in brain lateralization (Beale, 1994; Rosenberg, 2013).

Is the culture in which one is raised related to brain lateralization? Some research suggests it is. For instance, native speakers of Japanese process information related to vowel sounds primarily in the left hemisphere of the brain. In comparison, North and South Americans and Europeans—as well as people of Japanese ancestry who learn Japanese as a second language—process vowel sounds primarily in the brain's right hemisphere.

The explanation for this cultural difference in processing of vowels seems to rest on the nature of the Japanese language. Specifically, the Japanese language allows for the expression of complex concepts using only vowel sounds. Consequently, a specific type of brain lateralization may develop while learning and using Japanese at a relatively early age (Tsunoda, 1985; Hiser & Kobayashi, 2003; Okumura, Kasai, & Murohasi, 2015).

This explanation, which is speculative, does not rule out the possibility that some type of subtle genetic difference may also be at work in determining the difference in lateralization. Once again, then, we find that teasing out the relative impact of heredity and environment is a challenging task.

childhood in which the brain shows unusual growth spurts, and these periods are linked to advances in cognitive abilities. One study that measured electrical activity in the brain across the life span found unusual spurts at between 18 months and 2 years, a time when language abilities increase rapidly. Other spurts occurred around other ages when cognitive advances are particularly intense (see Figure 7-6; Mabbott et al., 2006; Westermann et al., 2007).

Other research has suggested that increases in myelin, the protective insulation that surrounds parts of neurons, may be related to preschoolers' growing cognitive capabilities. For example, myelination of the *reticular formation*, an area of the brain associated with attention and concentration, is completed by the time children are about 5. This may be associated with children's growing attention spans as they approach school age. The improvement in memory that occurs during the preschool years may also be associated with myelination. During the preschool years, myelination is completed in the hippocampus, an area associated with memory (Rolls, 2000).

In addition, significant growth takes place in the nerves connecting the *cerebellum*, the part of the brain that controls balance and movement, to the *cerebral cortex*, the structure responsible for sophisticated information processing. The growth in these nerve

Figure 7-6 Myelin in Newborns' Brains

Myelin, the protective insulation that surrounds parts of neurons, increases with age and may be related to cognitive development. These composite scans show the distribution of myelin at birth.

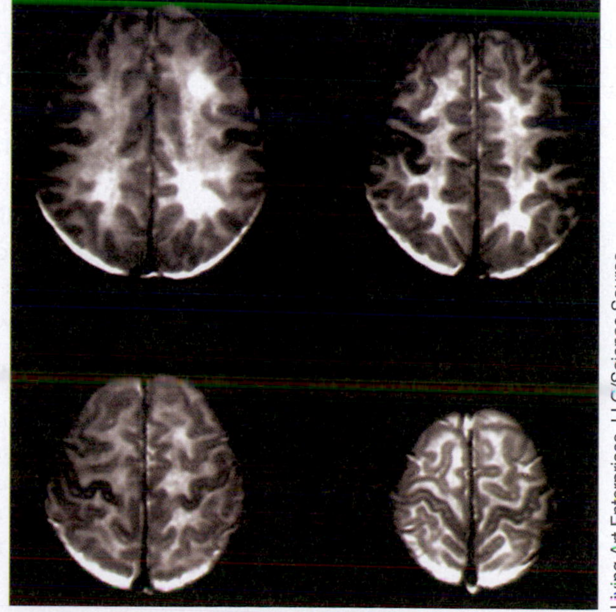

Living Art Enterprises, LLC/Science Source

fibers is related to the significant advances in motor skills that occur during the preschool years, as well as to advances in cognitive processing (Carson, 2005; Gordon, 2007).

We do not yet know the direction of causality: Does brain development produce cognitive advances, or do cognitive accomplishments fuel brain development? However, it is clear that increases in our understanding of the physiological aspects of the brain will eventually have important implications for parents and teachers.

Motor Development

LO 7.3 Explain how preschool children's motor skills develop.

Anya sat in the sandbox at the park, chatting with the other parents and playing with her two children, 5-year-old Nicholai and 13-month old Smetna. While she chatted, she kept a close eye on Smetna, who would still put sand in her mouth sometimes if she wasn't stopped. Today, however, Smetna seemed content to run the sand through her hands and try to put it into a bucket. Nicholai, meanwhile, was busy with two other boys, rapidly filling and emptying the other sand buckets to build an elaborate sand city, which they would then destroy with toy trucks.

When children of different ages gather at a playground, it's easy to see that preschool children have come a long way in their motor development since infancy. Both their gross and fine motor skills have become increasingly fine-tuned. Smetna, for example, is still mastering putting sand into a bucket, while her brother Nicholai uses that skill easily as part of his larger goal of building a sand city.

GROSS MOTOR SKILLS. By the time they are 3, children have mastered a variety of skills: jumping, hopping on one foot, skipping, and running. By 4 and 5, their skills have become more refined as they have gained increasing control over their muscles. For instance, at 4 they can throw a ball with enough accuracy that a friend can catch it, and by age 5 they can toss a ring and have it land on a peg 5 feet away. Five-year-olds can learn to ride bikes, climb ladders, and ski downhill—activities that all require considerable coordination. (Figure 7-7 summarizes major gross motor skills that emerge during the preschool years.)

These achievements may be related to brain development and myelination of neurons in areas of the brain that control balance and coordination. Another reason that motor skills develop at such a rapid clip during the preschool years is that children spend a great deal of time practicing them. During this period, the general level of activity is extraordinarily high: Preschoolers seem to be perpetually in motion. The activity level is higher at age 3 than at any other point in the entire life span.

Girls and boys differ in certain aspects of gross motor coordination, in part because of differences in muscle strength, which is somewhat greater in boys than in girls. For instance, boys can typically throw a ball farther and jump higher, and a boy's overall activity level tends to be greater than a girl's. However, girls generally surpass boys in tasks that involve the coordination of limbs. For instance, at age 5, girls are better than boys at doing jumping jacks and balancing on one foot (Largo, Fischer, & Rousson, 2003; Spessato et al., 2013).

Another aspect of muscular skills—one that parents of toddlers often find most problematic—is bowel and bladder control, as we discuss next.

POTTY WARS: WHEN—AND HOW—SHOULD CHILDREN BE TOILET TRAINED?

Sharon Bell was amazed when her daughter, Leah, just 2, announced she didn't want to wear diapers anymore. From now on, Leah said, she would only use the potty. She was even more amazed when Leah woke up with dry pajamas the next morning, and every morning after that. Three months passed without a single accident. Sharon had to admit, her 2-year-old was toilet trained.

Figure 7-7 Significant Gross Motor Skills in Early Childhood

These are important gross motor skills that develop at different ages during early childhood.

Age 3

Able to walk up stairs, alternating feet

Unable to stop or turn suddenly

Able to jump a length of 15–24 inches

Age 4

Able to walk down a long staircase, alternating feet, with assistance

Have some control in starting, stopping, and turning

Length of jump increases to 24–33 inches

Age 5

Able to walk down a long staircase, alternating feet

Capable of starting, stopping, and turning in games

Able to make a running jump of 28–36 inches

Leah's determination and success had another surprising effect. Her brother, Adam, age 4, who had never been able to give up his nighttime diaper, suddenly stopped needing one. "I'm older than she is," Adam explained when Sharon asked him about the sudden change. "If Leah doesn't wear a diaper anymore, then I'm not wearing one."

Few child care issues raise so much concern among parents as toilet training. And on few issues are there so many opposing opinions from experts and laypersons. Often, the various viewpoints are played out in the media and even take on political overtones. For instance, well-known pediatrician T. Berry Brazelton suggests a flexible approach to toilet training, advocating that it be put off until the child shows signs of readiness

Olesya Feketa/Shutterstock

Golden Pixels LLC/Shutterstock

During the preschool years, children grow in both fine and gross motor skills.

Geoff Manasse/Getty Images

Among the signs that children are ready to give up diapers is evidence that they are able to follow directions and can get to the bathroom and undress on their own.

(Brazelton, 1997; Brazelton et al., 1999). In contrast, psychologist John Rosemond, known primarily for his media advocacy of a conservative, traditional stance to childrearing, argues for a more rigid approach, saying that toilet training should be done early and quickly.

What is clear is that the age at which toilet training takes place has been rising over the past 60 years. For example, in 1957, 92 percent of children were toilet trained by age 18 months. Today, the average age of toilet training is around 30 months (Goode, 1999; Boyse & Fitzgerald, 2010).

Current guidelines of the American Academy of Pediatrics echo Brazelton's position, suggesting that there is no single time to begin toilet training and that training should begin only when children show that they are ready. The signs of readiness include staying dry at least 2 hours at a time during the day or waking up dry after naps; regular and predictable bowel movements; an indication, through facial expressions or words, that urination or a bowel movement is about to occur; the ability to follow simple directions; the ability to get to the bathroom and undress alone; discomfort with soiled diapers; asking to use the toilet or potty chair; and the desire to wear underwear.

Furthermore, children must be ready not only physically but also emotionally, and if they show strong signs of resistance to toilet training, toilet training should be put off. Children younger than 12 months have no bladder or bowel control, and they have only slight control for 6 months longer. Although some children show signs of readiness for toilet training between 18 and 24 months, some are not ready until 30 months or older (American Academy of Pediatrics, 1999; Fritz & Rockney, 2004; Connell-Carrick, 2006; Greer, Neidert, & Dozier, 2016).

Even after children are toilet trained during the day, it often takes months or years before they are able to achieve control at night. Around three-quarters of boys and most girls are able to stay dry after age 5.

Complete toilet training eventually occurs in almost all children as they mature and attain greater control over their muscles. However, delayed toilet training can be a cause for concern if a child is upset about it or if it makes the child a target of ridicule from siblings or peers. In such cases, several types of treatments have proven effective. In particular, treatments in which children are rewarded for staying dry or are awakened by a battery-powered device that senses when they have wet the bed are often effective (Houts, 2003; Vermandel et al., 2008; Millei & Gallagher, 2012).

FINE MOTOR SKILLS. At the same time that gross motor skills are developing, children are progressing in their ability to use fine motor skills, which involve more delicate, smaller body movements, such as using a fork and spoon, cutting with a scissors, tying one's shoelaces, and playing the piano.

The skills involved in fine motor movements require a good deal of practice, as anyone who has watched a 4-year-old struggling painstakingly to copy letters of the alphabet knows. The emergence of these fine motor skills shows clear developmental patterns. At age 3, children are already able to draw a circle and square with a crayon, and they can undo their clothes when they go to the bathroom. They can put a simple jigsaw puzzle together, and they can fit blocks of different shapes into matching holes. However, they do not show much precision and polish in accomplishing such tasks. For instance, they may try to force puzzle pieces into place.

By age 4, their fine motor skills are considerably better. They can draw a person that looks like a person, and they can fold paper into triangular designs. And by the time they are 5, they are able to hold and manipulate a thin pencil properly.

HANDEDNESS. How do preschoolers decide which hand to hold the pencil in as they work on their copying and other fine motor skills? For many, their choice was established soon after birth.

Beginning in early infancy, many children show signs of a preference for the use of one hand over another—the development of **handedness**. For instance, young infants may show a preference for one side of their bodies over another. By the age of 7 months, some infants seem to favor one hand by grabbing more with it than the other. Most children display a clear-cut tendency to use one hand over the other by the end of the preschool years. Some 90 percent are right-handed and 10 percent are left-handed. Furthermore, there is a gender difference: More boys than girls are left-handed. A few children remain ambidextrous even after the preschool years, using both hands with equal ease (Segalowitz, & Rapin, 2003; Marschik et al., 2008; Scharoun & Bryden, 2014).

handedness
the preference of using one hand over another

Much speculation has been devoted to the meaning of handedness, but there are few conclusions. Some research finds that left-handedness is related to higher achievements, other research shows no advantage for being left-handed, and some findings suggest that children who are ambidextrous perform less well on academic tasks. Clearly, the jury is out on the consequences of handedness (Casasanto & Henetz, 2012; Nelson, Campbell & Michel, 2013; Denny & Zhang, 2017; also see *From Research to Practice*).

From Research to Practice

How Writing by Hand Stimulates Brain Development

Are you the type of student who carries around a laptop or other mobile device and types everything, including your class notes? Or perhaps you prefer to take notes by hand because you feel that you just learn better that way? Our increasingly digital society puts pressure on schools to start children learning keyboard skills at ever younger ages, even to the point where learning to write by hand is getting pushed aside. But this would be a mistake, as research suggests that learning to write by hand plays an important role in children's cognitive development.

In a study, 5-year-old children who had not yet learned to read or write were shown a letter and asked to reproduce it. Some of the children were instructed to write the letter by hand on a blank piece of paper. Others were instructed to trace the letter over a dotted outline of it. Finally, a third group was instructed to type the letter on a keyboard. Then all of the children were again shown an image of the letter that they had just reproduced, but this time while they were undergoing a functional MRI (a scan that shows what regions of the brain are currently active).

The functional MRI revealed telling differences between the children based on how they originally reproduced the letter. The children who wrote the letter freehand showed increased activation in three regions of the brain that are associated with reading and writing in adults. The children who typed the letter on a keyboard and the children who traced an outline of the letter did not show the same activation of these brain regions. These results show that freehand writing produces changes in the brain that mere typing (or tracing) does not. The researchers theorize that the process of trying to duplicate letter shapes without assistance engages the brain in important ways—it requires careful attention to the form of the letter and planning of the steps and movements needed to recreate it (James & Engelhardt, 2012; Jao, James, & James, 2014).

Perhaps most importantly, it requires tolerance of variability in the appearance of the letters. After all, your *g* differs from your best friend's *g*, and it's likely that neither one of them bear much resemblance at all to a keyboard-generated *g*. Struggling to write your own letters, and often getting them not quite right, is likely to help you recognize letters accurately even though different sources write them differently. Merely learning to recognize letter shapes that never vary because they are printed on a keyboard isn't as likely to help with that.

Other research shows that printing, cursive writing, and typing are associated with different patterns of brain activity in young children. When the children in this study wrote their thoughts by hand, they wrote more and expressed a greater richness of ideas than did children who composed their thoughts on a keyboard. When they were thinking about writing topics during a functional MRI, children who had better hand writing skills showed greater brain activity in areas associated with memory and reading and writing. Again, learning to write by hand seems to train children's brains to think better about writing (Berninger et al., 2006; Alstad et al., 2015).

Shared Writing Prompt

If you were a parent or a teacher of young children, how might you apply these research findings to help your children learn to read and write better?

Module 7.1 Review

LO 7.1 Describe a child's bodily growth and overall health risks during the preschool years.

The preschool period is marked by steady physical growth. Preschoolers tend to eat less than they did as babies but generally regulate their food intake appropriately, given nutritious options and the freedom to develop their own choices and controls. The preschool period is generally the healthiest time of life, with only minor illnesses threatening children. Accidents and environmental hazards are the greatest threats to preschoolers' health.

LO 7.2 Summarize how preschool children's brains develop.

Brain growth is rapid during the preschool years. In addition, the brain develops lateralization, a tendency of the two hemispheres to adopt specialized tasks.

LO 7.3 Explain how preschool children's motor skills develop.

Gross and fine motor development also advances rapidly during the preschool years. Boys' and girls' gross motor skills begin to diverge, and children develop handedness.

Journal Writing Prompt

Applying Lifespan Development: What are some ways that increased understanding of issues relating to the physical development of preschoolers might help parents and caregivers in their care of children?

Intellectual Development

Three-year-old Sam was talking to himself. As his parents listened with amusement from another room, they could hear him using two very different voices. "Find your shoes," he said in a low voice. "Not today. I'm not going. I hate the shoes," he said in a higher-pitched voice. The lower voice answered, "You are a bad boy. Find the shoes, bad boy." The higher-voiced response was "No, no, no."

Sam's parents realized that he was playing a game with his imaginary friend, Gill. Gill was a bad boy who often disobeyed his mother, at least in Sam's imagination. In fact, according to Sam's musings, Gill often was guilty of the very same misdeeds for which his parents blamed Sam.

In some ways, the intellectual sophistication of 3-year-olds is astounding. Their creativity and imagination leap to new heights, their language is increasingly sophisticated, and they reason and think about the world in ways that would have been impossible even a few months earlier. But what underlies the dramatic advances in intellectual development that start in the preschool years and continue throughout that period? We have discussed the general outlines of the brain development that underlies cognitive development in preschoolers. Let's now consider several approaches to children's thinking, starting with a look at Piaget's findings on the cognitive changes that occur during the preschool years.

Piaget's Stage of Preoperational Thinking

LO 7.4 Summarize how Piaget explains cognitive development during the preschool years.

Swiss psychologist Jean Piaget, whose stage approach to cognitive development we discussed in Chapter 5, saw the preschool years as a time of both stability and great change. He suggests that the preschool years fit entirely into a single stage of cognitive development—the preoperational stage—which lasts from age 2 until around 7.

preoperational stage
according to Piaget, the stage from approximately age 2 to age 7 in which children's use of symbolic thinking grows, mental reasoning emerges, and the use of concepts increases

During the **preoperational stage**, children's use of symbolic thinking grows, mental reasoning emerges, and the use of concepts increases. Seeing Mom's car keys may prompt a question, "Go to store?" as the child comes to see the keys as a symbol of a car ride. In this way, children become better at representing events internally, and they grow less dependent on the use of direct sensorimotor activity to understand the world around them.

Yet they are still not capable of **operations**: organized, formal, logical mental processes that characterize school-age children. It is only at the end of the preoperational stage that the ability to carry out operations comes into play.

operations
organized, formal, logical mental processes

According to Piaget, a key aspect of preoperational thought is *symbolic function*, the ability to use a mental symbol, a word, or an object to stand for or represent something that is not physically present. For example, during this stage, preschoolers can use a mental symbol for a car (the word *car*), and they likewise understand that a small toy car is representative of the real thing. Because of their ability to use symbolic function, children have no need to get behind the wheel of an actual car to understand its basic purpose and use.

THE RELATIONSHIP BETWEEN LANGUAGE AND THOUGHT. Symbolic function is at the heart of one of the major advances that occurs in the preoperational period: the increasingly sophisticated use of language. As we discuss later in this chapter, children make substantial progress in language skills during the preschool period.

Piaget suggests that language and thinking are tightly interconnected and that the advances in language that occur during the preschool years reflect several improvements over the type of thinking that is possible during the earlier sensorimotor period. For instance, thinking embedded in sensorimotor activities is relatively slow because it depends on actual movements of the body that are bound by human physical limitations. In contrast, the use of symbolic thought, such as the development of an imaginary friend, allows preschoolers to represent actions symbolically, permitting much greater speed.

Even more important, the use of language allows children to think beyond the present to the future. Consequently, rather than being grounded in the immediate here and now, preschoolers can imagine future possibilities through language in the form of sometimes elaborate fantasies and daydreams.

Do the improved language abilities of preschoolers lead to improvements in thinking, or is it the other way around, with the improvements in thinking during the preoperational period leading to enhancements in language ability? This question—whether thought determines language or language determines thought—is one of the enduring and most controversial questions within the field of psychology. Piaget's answer is that language grows out of cognitive advances rather than the other way around. He argues that improvements during the earlier sensorimotor period are necessary for language development and that continuing growth in cognitive ability during the preoperational period provides the foundation for language ability.

CENTRATION: WHAT YOU SEE IS WHAT YOU THINK. Place a dog mask on a cat, and what do you get? According to 3- and 4-year-old preschoolers, a dog. To them, a cat with a dog mask ought to bark like a dog, wag its tail like a dog, and eat dog food. In every respect, the cat has been transformed into a dog (de Vries, 1969).

To Piaget, the root of this belief is centration—a key element and limitation of the thinking of children in the preoperational period. **Centration** is the process of concentrating on one limited aspect of a stimulus and ignoring other aspects.

centration
the process of concentrating on one limited aspect of a stimulus and ignoring other aspects

Preschoolers are unable to consider all available information about a stimulus. Instead, they focus on superficial, obvious elements that are within their sight. These external elements come to dominate preschoolers' thinking, leading to inaccuracy in thought.

When preschoolers are shown two rows of buttons, one with 10 buttons that are spaced closely together and the other with 8 buttons spread out to form a longer row (see Figure 7-8), and they are asked which of the rows contains more buttons, children who are 4 or 5 usually choose the row that looks longer rather than the one that actually contains more buttons. This occurs in spite of the fact that children this age know quite well that 10 is more than 8.

Figure 7-8 Which Row Contains More Buttons?

When preschoolers are shown these two rows and asked which row has more buttons, they usually respond that the lower row of buttons contains more because it looks longer. They answer in this way even though they know quite well that 10 is greater than 8. Do you think preschoolers can be *taught* to answer correctly?

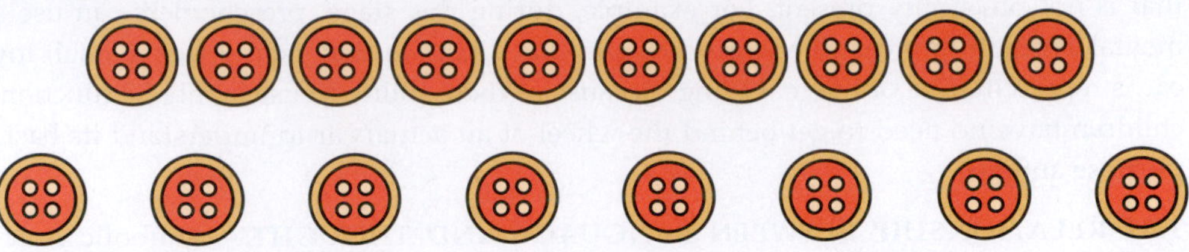

The cause of the children's mistake is that the visual image of the longer row dominates their thinking. Rather than taking into account their understanding of quantity, they focus on appearance. To a preschooler, appearance is everything. Preschoolers' focus on appearances might be related to another aspect of preoperational thought, the lack of conservation.

CONSERVATION: LEARNING THAT APPEARANCES ARE DECEIVING. Consider the following scenario:

> *Four-year-old Jaime is shown two drinking glasses of different shapes. One is short and broad; the other is tall and thin. A teacher half-fills the short, broad glass with apple juice. The teacher then pours the juice into the tall, thin glass. The juice fills the tall glass almost to the brim. The teacher asks Jaime a question: Is there more juice in the second glass than there was in the first?*

If you view this as an easy task, so do children like Jaime. They have no trouble answering the question. However, they almost always get the answer wrong.

Most 4-year-olds respond that there is more apple juice in the tall, thin glass than there was in the short, broad one. If the juice is poured back into the shorter glass, they are quick to say that there is now less juice than there was in the taller glass (see Figure 7-9).

conservation
the knowledge that quantity is unrelated to the arrangement and physical appearance of objects

The reason for the error in judgment is that children of this age have not mastered conservation. **Conservation** is the knowledge that quantity is unrelated to the arrangement and physical appearance of objects. Because they are unable to conserve, preschoolers can't understand that changes in one dimension (such as a change in appearance) do not necessarily mean that other dimensions (such as quantity) change. For example, children who do not yet understand the principle of conservation feel quite comfortable in asserting that the amount of liquid changes as it is poured between glasses of different sizes. They simply are unable to realize that the transformation in appearance does not imply a transformation in quantity.

Figure 7-9 Which Glass Contains More?

Most 4-year-old children believe that the amount of liquid in these two glasses differs because of the differences in the containers' shapes, even though they may have seen equal amounts of liquid being poured into each.

Lewis Merrim/Science Source

The lack of conservation also manifests itself in children's understanding of area, as illustrated by Piaget's cow-in-the field problem (Piaget, Inhelder, & Szeminska, 1960). In the problem, two sheets of green paper, equal in size, are shown to a child, and a toy cow is placed in each field. Next, a toy barn is placed in each field, and children are asked which cow has more to eat. The typical—and, so far, correct—response is that the cows have the same amount.

In the next step, a second toy barn is placed in each field. But in one field, the barns are placed adjacent to one another, whereas in the second field, they are separated from one another. Children who have not mastered conservation usually say that the cow in the field with the adjacent barns has more grass to eat than the cow in the field with the separated barns. In contrast,

Figure 7-10 Common Tests of Children's Understanding of the Principle of Conservation

Why is a sense of conservation important?

Type of Conservation	Modality	Change in Physical Appearance	Average Age Invariance Is Grasped
Number	Number of elements in a collection 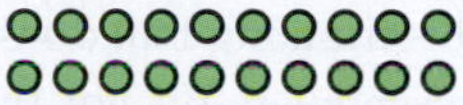	Rearranging or dislocating elements 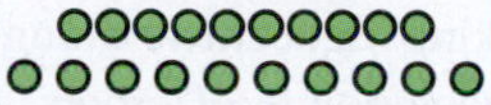	6–7 years
Substance (mass)	Amount of a malleable substance (e.g., clay or liquid) 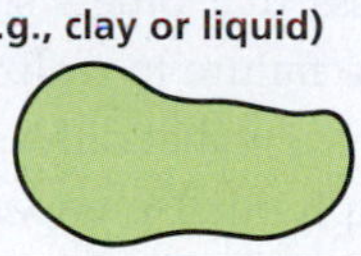	Altering shape 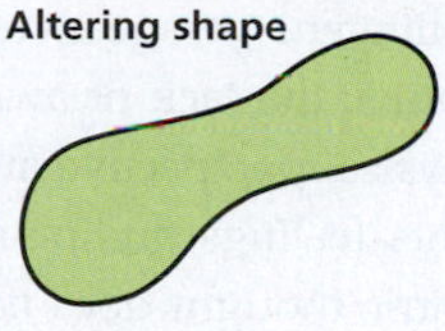	7–8 years
Length	Length of a line or object 	Altering shape or configuration 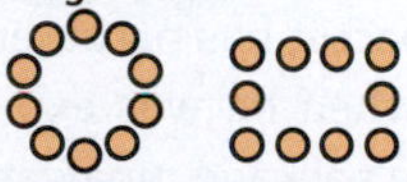	7–8 years
Area	Amount of surface covered by a set of plane figures 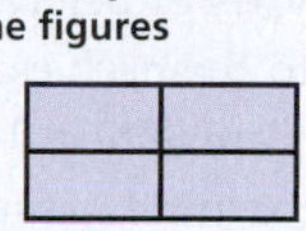	Rearranging the figures 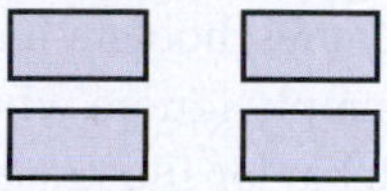	8–9 years
Weight	Weight of an object 	Altering shape 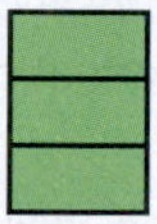	9–10 years
Volume	Volume of an object (in terms of water displacement) 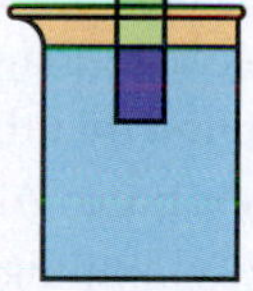	Altering shape 	14–15 years

children who can conserve answer, correctly, that the amount available is identical. (Some other conservation tasks are shown in Figure 7-10.)

Why do children in the preoperational stage make errors on tasks that require conservation? Piaget suggests that the main reason is that their tendency toward centration prevents them from focusing on the relevant features of the situation. Furthermore, they cannot follow the sequence of transformations that accompanies changes in the appearance of a situation.

INCOMPLETE UNDERSTANDING OF TRANSFORMATION. A preoperational preschool child who sees several worms during a walk in the woods may believe that they are all the same worm. The reason: She views each sighting in isolation, and she is unable to understand that a transformation would be necessary for a worm to be able to move quickly from one location to the next.

As Piaget used the term, **transformation** is the process by which one state is changed into another. For instance, adults know that if a pencil that is held upright is allowed to fall down, it passes through a series of successive stages until it reaches its final,

transformation
the process by which one state is changed into another

Figure 7-11 The Falling Pencil

Children in Piaget's preoperational stage do not understand that as a pencil falls from the upright to the horizontal position, it moves through a series of intermediary steps. Instead, they think that there are no intermediate steps in the change from the upright to horizontal position.

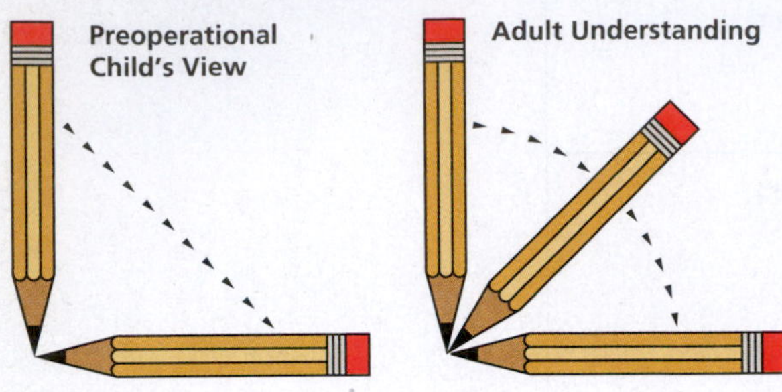

horizontal resting spot (see Figure 7-11). In contrast, children in the preoperational period are unable to envision or recall the successive transformations that the pencil followed in moving from the upright to the horizontal position. If asked to reproduce the sequence in a drawing, they draw the pencil upright and lying down, with nothing in between. Basically, they ignore the intermediate steps.

EGOCENTRISM: THE INABILITY TO TAKE OTHERS' PERSPECTIVES. Another hallmark of the preoperational period is egocentric thinking. **Egocentric thought** is thinking that does not take into account the viewpoints of others. Preschoolers do not understand that others have different perspectives from their own. Egocentric thought takes two forms: the lack of awareness that others see things from a different physical perspective and the failure to realize that others may hold thoughts, feelings, and points of view that differ from theirs. (Note what egocentric thought does *not* imply: that preoperational children intentionally think in a selfish or inconsiderate manner.)

egocentric thought
thinking that does not take into account the viewpoints of others

Egocentric thinking is what is behind children's lack of concern over their nonverbal behavior and the impact it has on others. For instance, a 4-year-old who is given an unwanted gift of socks when he was expecting something more desirable may frown and scowl as he opens the package, unaware that his face can be seen by others and may reveal his true feelings about the gift (Cohen, 2013).

Egocentrism lies at the heart of several other types of behavior during the preoperational period. For instance, preschoolers may talk to themselves, even in the presence of others, and at times they simply ignore what others are telling them. Rather than being a sign of eccentricity, such behavior illustrates the egocentric nature of preoperational children's thinking: the lack of awareness that their behavior acts as a trigger to others' reactions and responses. Consequently, a considerable amount of verbal behavior on the part of preschoolers has no social motivation behind it but is meant for the preschoolers' own consumption.

Similarly, egocentrism can be seen in hiding games with children during the preoperational stage. In a game of hide-and-seek, 3-year-olds may attempt to hide by covering their faces with a pillow—even though they remain in plain view. Their reasoning: If they cannot see others, others cannot see them. They assume that others share their view.

THE EMERGENCE OF INTUITIVE THOUGHT. Because Piaget labeled the preschool years as the "preoperational period," it is easy to assume that this is a period of marking time, waiting for the more formal emergence of operations. As if to support this view, many of the characteristics of the preoperational period highlight deficiencies, cognitive skills that the preschooler has yet to master. However, the preoperational period is far from idle. Cognitive development proceeds steadily, and in fact, several new types of ability emerge. A case in point: the development of intuitive thought.

intuitive thought
thinking that reflects preschoolers' use of primitive reasoning and their avid acquisition of knowledge about the world

Intuitive thought refers to preschoolers' use of primitive reasoning and their avid acquisition of knowledge about the world. From about age 4 through 7, children's curiosity blossoms. They constantly seek out the answers to a wide variety of questions, asking, "Why?" about nearly everything. At the same time, children may act as if they are authorities on particular topics, feeling certain that they have the correct—and final—word on an issue. If pressed, they are unable to explain how they know what they know. In other words, their intuitive thought leads them to believe that they know answers to all kinds of questions, but there is little or no logical basis for this confidence in their understanding of the way the world operates. This may lead a preschooler to state authoritatively that airplanes can fly because they move their wings up and down like a bird, even if they have never seen an airplane's wings moving in that way.

In the late stages of the preoperational period, children's intuitive thinking does have certain qualities that prepare them for more sophisticated forms of reasoning. For instance, preschoolers come to understand that pushing harder on the pedals makes a bicycle move faster, or that pressing a button on a remote control makes the television change channels. By the end of the preoperational stage, preschoolers begin to understand the notion of *functionality*, the idea that actions, events, and outcomes are related to one another in fixed patterns.

Children also begin to show an awareness of the concept of identity in the later stages of the preoperational period. *Identity* is the understanding that certain things stay the same, regardless of changes in shape, size, and appearance. For instance, knowledge of identity allows one to understand that a lump of clay contains the same amount of clay regardless of whether it is clumped into a ball or stretched out like a snake. Comprehension of identity is necessary for children to develop an understanding of conservation, the ability to understand that quantity is not related to physical appearances, as we discussed earlier. Piaget regarded children's development of conservation as a skill that marks the transition from the preoperational period to the next stage, concrete operations, which we will discuss in Chapter 9.

EVALUATING PIAGET'S APPROACH TO COGNITIVE DEVELOPMENT. Piaget, a masterful observer of children's behavior, provided a detailed portrait of preschoolers' cognitive abilities. The broad outlines of his approach have given us a useful way of thinking about the progressive advances in cognitive ability that occur during the preschool years (Siegal, 1997).

It is important, however, to consider Piaget's approach to cognitive development within the appropriate historical context and in light of more recent research findings. As we discussed in Chapter 5, his theory is based on extensive observations of relatively few children. Despite his insightful and groundbreaking observations, recent experimental investigations suggest that in certain regards, Piaget underestimated children's capabilities.

Take, for instance, Piaget's views of how children in the preoperational period understand numbers. Piaget contended that preschoolers' thinking is seriously handicapped, as evidenced by their performance on tasks involving conservation and reversibility, the understanding that a transformation can be reversed to return something to its original state. Yet more recent experimental work suggests otherwise. Developmental psychologist Rochel Gelman has found that children as young as 3 can easily tell the difference between rows of two and three toy animals, regardless of the animals' spacing. Older children are able to note differences in number, performing tasks such as identifying which of two numbers is larger and indicating that they understand some rudiments of addition and subtraction problems (Cordes & Brannon, 2009; Izard et al., 2009; Brandone et al., 2012; Dietrich et al., 2016).

Based on such evidence, Gelman concludes that children have an innate ability to count, one akin to the ability to use language that some theorists see as universal and genetically determined. Such a conclusion is clearly at odds with Piagetian notions, which suggest that children's numerical abilities do not blossom until after the preoperational period.

Some developmentalists (particularly those who favor the information processing approach, as we'll see later in the chapter) also believe that cognitive skills develop in a more continuous manner than Piaget's stage theory implies. They believe that rather than thought changing in quality, as Piaget argues, developmental changes are more quantitative in nature, improving gradually. Such critics regard the underlying processes that produce cognitive skill as undergoing only minor changes with age.

There are further difficulties with Piaget's view of cognitive development. His contention that conservation does not emerge until the end of the preoperational period, and in some cases even later, has not stood up to careful experimental scrutiny. Children can be taught to answer correctly on conservation tasks following certain training and experiences. The fact that one can improve children's performance on these tasks argues against the Piagetian view that children in the preoperational period have not reached a level of cognitive maturity that would permit them to understand conservation (Ping & Goldin-Meadow, 2008).

Clearly, children are more capable at an earlier age than Piaget's account would lead us to believe. Why did Piaget underestimate children's cognitive abilities? One answer is that his questioning of children used language that was too difficult to allow children to answer in a way that would provide a true picture of their skills. In addition, as we've seen, Piaget tended to concentrate on preschoolers' *deficiencies* in thinking, focusing his observations on children's lack of logical thought. By focusing more on children's competence, more recent theorists have found increasing evidence for a surprising degree of capability in preschoolers.

Information Processing Approaches to Cognitive Development

LO 7.5 Summarize the information processing approaches to cognitive development in the preschool years.

Even as an adult, Paco has clear recollections of his first trip to a ranch, which he took when he was 3 years old. He was visiting his godfather, who lived in New Mexico, and the two of them went to a nearby ranch. Paco recounts seeing what seemed like hundreds of cattle, and he clearly recalls his fear of the llamas, which seemed huge, smelly, and frightening. Most of all, he recalls the thrill of riding on a horse with his godfather.

The fact that Paco has a clear memory of his ranch trip is not surprising: Most people have unambiguous, and seemingly accurate, memories dating as far back as the age of 3. But are the processes used to form memories during the preschool years similar to those that operate later in life? More broadly, what general changes in the processing of information occur during the preschool years?

Information processing approaches focus on changes in the kinds of "mental programs" that children use when approaching problems. They view the changes that occur in children's cognitive abilities during the preschool years as analogous to the way a computer program becomes more sophisticated as a programmer modifies it on the basis of experience. For many child developmentalists, information processing approaches represent the dominant, most comprehensive, and ultimately the most accurate explanation of how children develop cognitively (Lacerda, von Hofsten, & Heimann, 2001).

In the next sections, we'll focus on two areas that highlight the approach taken by information processing theorists: understanding of numbers and memory development during the preschool years.

PRESCHOOLERS' UNDERSTANDING OF NUMBERS. As we saw earlier, one of the flaws critics have noticed in Piaget's theory is that preschoolers have a greater understanding of numbers than Piaget thought. Researchers using information processing approaches to cognitive development have found increasing evidence that preschoolers have a sophisticated understanding of numbers. The average preschooler is able not only to count but also to do so in a fairly systematic, consistent manner (Siegler, 1998).

For instance, developmental psychologist Rochel Gelman suggests that preschoolers follow a number of principles in their counting. Shown a group of several items, they know they should assign just one number to each item and that each item should be counted only once. Moreover, even when they get the *names* of numbers wrong, they are consistent in their usage. For instance, a 4-year-old who counts three items as "1, 3, 7" will say "1, 3, 7" when counting another group of different items. And if asked how many there are, she will probably answer that there are seven items in the group (Gallistel, 2007; Le Corre & Carey, 2007; Slusser, Ditta, & Sarnecka, 2013; Xu & LeFevre, 2016).

In short, preschoolers may demonstrate a surprisingly sophisticated understanding of numbers, although their understanding is not totally precise. Still, by the age of 4, most are able to carry out simple addition and subtraction problems by counting, and they are able to compare different quantities quite successfully (Gilmore & Spelke, 2008; Jansen et al., 2014; Harvey & Miller, 2017).

MEMORY: RECALLING THE PAST. Think back to your own earliest memory. If you are like Paco, described earlier, and most other people too, it probably is of an event that occurred after the age of 3. **Autobiographical memory**, memory of particular events from one's own life, achieves little accuracy until after 3 years of age. Accuracy then increases gradually and slowly throughout the preschool years (Nelson & Fivush, 2004; Reese & Newcombe, 2007; Wang, 2008; Valentino et al., 2014).

autobiographical memory
memory of particular events from one's own life

Preschool children's recollections of events that happened to them are sometimes, but not always, accurate. For instance, 3-year-olds can remember central features of routine occurrences, such as the sequence of events involved in getting ready for bed, fairly well. In addition, preschoolers are typically accurate in their responses to open-ended questions, such as "What rides did you like best at the amusement park?" (Wang, 2006; Pathman et al., 2013; Valentino et al., 2014; McDonnell et al., 2016).

The accuracy of preschoolers' memories is partly determined by how soon the memories are accessed. Unless an event is particularly vivid or meaningful, it is not likely to be remembered at all. Moreover, not all autobiographical memories last into later life. For instance, a child may remember the first day of kindergarten 6 months or a year later, but later in life might not remember that day at all.

Memories are also affected by cultural factors. For example, Chinese college students' memories of early childhood are more likely to be unemotional and reflect activities involving social roles, such as working in a family store, whereas U.S. college students' earliest memories are more emotionally elaborate and focus on specific events such as the birth of a sibling (Wang, 2006, 2007; Peterson, Wang, & Hou, 2009; Stevenson, Heiser, & Resing, 2016).

Not only do preschoolers' autobiographical memories fade, but what is remembered may not be wholly accurate. For example, if an event happens often, such as a trip to a grocery store, it may be hard to remember one specific time it happened. Preschoolers' memories of familiar events are often organized in terms of **scripts**, broad representations in memory of events and the order in which they occur.

scripts
broad representations in memory of events and the order in which they occur

For example, a young preschooler might represent eating in a restaurant in terms of a few steps: talking to a server, getting the food, and eating. With age, the scripts become more elaborate: getting in the car, being seated at the restaurant, choosing food, ordering, waiting for the meal to come, eating, ordering dessert, and paying for the food. Because events that are frequently repeated tend to be melded into scripts, particular instances of a scripted event are recalled with less accuracy than those that are unscripted in memory (Fivush, Kuebli, & Clubb, 1992; Sutherland, Pipe, & Schick, 2003).

There are other reasons why preschoolers may not have entirely accurate autobiographical memories. Because they have difficulty describing certain kinds of information, such as complex causal relationships, they may oversimplify recollections. For example, a child who has witnessed an argument between his grandparents may only remember that grandma took the cake away from grandpa, not the discussion of his weight and cholesterol that led up to the action.

UygarGeographic/Getty Images

This preschooler may recall this ride in 6 months, but by the time she is 12, it will probably be forgotten. Can you explain why?

INFORMATION PROCESSING THEORIES IN PERSPECTIVE. According to information processing approaches, cognitive development consists of gradual improvements in the ways people perceive, understand, and remember information. With age and practice, preschoolers process information more efficiently and with greater sophistication, and they are able to handle increasingly complex problems. In the eyes of proponents of information processing approaches, it is these quantitative advances in information processing—and not the qualitative changes suggested by Piaget—that constitute cognitive development (Zhe & Siegler, 2000; Rose, Feldman, & Jankowski, 2009).

For supporters of information processing approaches, the reliance on well-defined processes that can be tested, with relative precision, by research is one of the perspective's most important features. Rather than relying on concepts that are somewhat vague, such as Piaget's notions of assimilation and accommodation, information processing approaches provide a comprehensive, logical set of concepts.

For instance, as preschoolers grow older, they have longer attention spans, can monitor and plan what they are attending to more effectively, and become increasingly aware of their cognitive limitations. As discussed earlier in this chapter, these advances may be due to brain development. Such increasing attentional abilities place some of Piaget's findings in a different light. For instance, increased attention span allows older children to attend to both the height *and* the width of tall and short glasses into which liquid is poured. This permits them to understand that the amount of liquid in the glasses stays the same when it is poured back and forth. Preschoolers, in contrast, are unable to attend to both dimensions simultaneously and thus are less able to conserve (Hudson, Sosa, & Shapiro, 1997).

Proponents of information processing theory have also been successful in focusing on important cognitive processes to which alternative approaches traditionally have paid little attention, such as the contribution of mental skills like memory and attention to children's thinking. They suggest that information processing provides a clear, logical, and full account of cognitive development.

Yet information processing approaches have their detractors, who raise significant points. For one thing, the focus on a series of single, individual cognitive processes leaves out of consideration some important factors that appear to influence cognition. For instance, information processing theorists pay relatively little attention to social and cultural factors—a deficiency that the approach we'll consider next attempts to remedy.

An even more important criticism is that information processing approaches "lose the forest for the trees." In other words, information processing approaches pay so much attention to the detailed, individual sequence of processes that compose cognitive processing and development that they never adequately paint a whole, comprehensive picture of cognitive development—which Piaget clearly did quite well.

Developmentalists using information processing approaches respond to such criticisms by saying that their model of cognitive development has the advantage of being precisely stated and capable of leading to testable hypotheses. They also argue that there is far more research supporting their approach than there is for alternative theories of cognitive development. In short, they suggest that their approach provides a more accurate account than any other.

Information processing approaches have been highly influential over the past several decades. They have inspired a tremendous amount of research that has helped us gain some insights into how children develop cognitively.

Vygotsky's View of Cognitive Development: Taking Culture into Account

LO 7.6 Describe Vygotsky's view of cognitive development in the preschool years.

As her daughter watches, a member of the Chilcotin Indian tribe prepares a salmon for dinner. When the daughter asks a question about a small detail of the process, the mother takes out another salmon and repeats the entire process. According to the tribal view of learning, understanding and comprehension can come only from grasping the total procedure, and not from learning about the individual subcomponents of the task. (Tharp, 1989)

The Chilcotin view of how children learn about the world contrasts with the prevalent view of Western society, which assumes that only by mastering the separate parts of a problem can one fully comprehend it. Do differences in the ways particular cultures and societies approach problems influence cognitive development? According to Russian developmental psychologist Lev Vygotsky, who lived from 1896 to 1934, the answer is a clear "yes."

Vygotsky viewed cognitive development as a result of social interactions in which children learn through guided participation, working with mentors to solve problems. Instead of concentrating on individual performance, as Piagetian theory and many alternative approaches do, Vygotsky's increasingly influential view focuses on the social aspects of development and learning.

Vygotsky saw children as apprentices, learning cognitive strategies and other skills from adult and peer mentors who not only present new ways of doing things but also provide assistance, instruction, and motivation. Consequently, he focused on the child's social and cultural world as the source of cognitive development. According to Vygotsky, children gradually grow intellectually and begin to function on their own because of the assistance that adult and peer partners provide (Vygotsky, 1926/1997; Tudge & Scrimsher, 2003).

Sovfoto/Eastfoto

Russian developmental psychologist Lev Vygotsky proposed that the focus of cognitive development should be on a child's social and cultural world, as opposed to the Piagetian approach concentrating on individual performance.

Vygotsky contends that the nature of the partnership between developing children and adults and peers is determined largely by cultural and societal factors. For instance, culture and society establish the institutions, such as preschools and play groups, that promote development by providing opportunities for cognitive growth. Furthermore, by emphasizing particular tasks, culture and society shape the nature of specific cognitive advances. Unless we look at what is important and meaningful to members of a given society, we may seriously underestimate the nature and level of cognitive abilities that ultimately will be attained (Schaller & Crandall, 2004; Balakrishnan & Claiborne, 2012; Nagahashi, 2013; Veraksa et al., 2016).

For example, children's toys reflect what is important and meaningful in a particular society. In Western society, preschoolers commonly play with toy wagons, automobiles, and other vehicles, in part reflecting the mobile nature of the culture.

Societal expectations about gender also play a role in how children come to understand the world. For example, one study conducted at a science museum found that parents provided more detailed scientific explanations to boys than to girls at museum displays. Such differences in level of explanation may lead to more sophisticated understanding of science in boys and ultimately may produce later gender differences in science learning (Crowley et al., 2001).

Vygotsky's approach is therefore quite different from that of Piaget. Where Piaget looked at developing children and saw junior scientists, working by themselves to develop an independent understanding of the world, Vygotsky saw cognitive apprentices, learning from master teachers the skills that are important in the child's culture. Where Piaget saw preschoolers who were egocentric, looking at the world from their own limited vantage point, Vygotsky saw preschoolers as using others to gain an understanding of the world.

In Vygotsky's view, then, children's cognitive development is dependent on interaction with others. Vygotsky argued that it is only through partnership with other people—peers, parents, teachers, and other adults—that children can fully develop their knowledge, thinking processes, beliefs, and values (Edwards, 2004; Fleer & González Rey, 2017).

THE ZONE OF PROXIMAL DEVELOPMENT AND SCAFFOLDING: FOUNDATIONS OF COGNITIVE DEVELOPMENT. Vygotsky proposed that children's cognitive abilities increase through exposure to information that is new enough to be intriguing but not too difficult for the child to handle. He called this the **zone of proximal development (ZPD)**, the level at which a child can *almost*, but not fully, perform a task independently but can do so with the assistance of someone more competent. When appropriate instruction is offered within the zone of proximal development, children are able to increase their understanding and master new tasks. In order for cognitive development to occur, then, new information must be presented—by parents, teachers, or more skilled peers—within the zone of proximal development. For example, a preschooler might not be able to figure out by herself how to get a handle to stick on the clay pot she's building, but she could do it with some advice from her preschool teacher (Kozulin, 2004; Zuckerman & Shenfield, 2007; Norton & D'Ambrosio, 2008; Warford, 2011).

zone of proximal development (ZPD)
according to Vygotsky, the level at which a child can almost, but not fully, perform a task independently, but can do so with the assistance of someone more competent

The concept of the zone of proximal development suggests that even though two children might be able to achieve the same amount without help, if one child receives aid, he or she may improve substantially more than the other. The greater the improvement that comes with help, the larger is the zone of proximal development.

From *an educator's* perspective

If children's cognitive development is dependent on interactions with others, what obligations does society have regarding such social settings as preschools and neighborhoods?

---

scaffolding
the support for learning and problem solving that encourages independence and growth

The assistance or structuring provided by others has been termed *scaffolding*. **Scaffolding** is the support for learning and problem solving that encourages independence and growth (Puntambekar & Hübscher, 2005; Blewitt et al., 2009). To Vygotsky, the process of scaffolding not only helps children solve specific problems but also aids in the development of their overall cognitive abilities. Scaffolding takes its name from the scaffolds that are put up to aid in the construction of a building and are removed once the building is complete. In education, scaffolding involves helping children think about and frame a task in an appropriate manner. In addition, a parent or teacher is likely to provide clues to task completion that are appropriate to the child's level of development and to model behavior that can lead to completion of the task. As in construction, the scaffolding that more competent people provide to facilitate the completion of identified tasks is removed once children are able to solve a problem on their own (Taumoepeau & Ruffman, 2008; Eitel et al., 2013; Leonard & Higson, 2014; Muhonen et al., 2016).

To illustrate how scaffolding operates, consider the following conversation between mother and son:

MOTHER: Do you remember how you helped me make the cookies before?

CHILD: No.

MOTHER: We made the dough and put it in the oven. Do you remember that?

CHILD: When Grandma came?

MOTHER: Yes, that's right. Would you help me shape the dough into cookies?

CHILD: OK.

MOTHER: Can you remember how big we made the cookies when Grandma was here?

CHILD: Big.

MOTHER: Right. Can you show me how big?

CHILD: We used the big wooden spoon.

MOTHER: Good boy, that's right. We used the wooden spoon, and we made big cookies. But let's try something different today by using the ice cream scoop to form the cookies.

Although this conversation isn't particularly sophisticated, it illustrates the practice of scaffolding. The mother is supporting her son's efforts, and she gets him to respond conversationally. In the process, she not only expands her son's abilities by using a different tool (the scoop instead of the spoon) but she also models how conversations proceed.

In some societies parental support for learning differs by gender. In one study, Mexican mothers were found to provide more scaffolding than fathers. A possible explanation is that mothers may be more aware of their children's cognitive abilities than are fathers (Tenenbaum & Leaper, 1998; Tamis-LeMonda & Cabrera, 2002; de Oliveira & Jackson, 2017).

One key aspect of the aid that more accomplished individuals provide to learners comes in the form of cultural tools. *Cultural tools* are actual physical items (e.g., pencils, paper, calculators, computers, and so forth) as well as an intellectual and conceptual framework for solving problems. The intellectual and conceptual framework available to learners includes the language that is used within a culture, its alphabetical and numbering schemes, its mathematical and scientific systems, and even its religious systems. These cultural tools provide a structure that can be used to help children define and solve specific problems, as well as an intellectual point of view that encourages cognitive development.

For example, consider the cultural differences in how people talk about distance. In cities, distance is usually measured in blocks ("the store is about 15 blocks away"). To a child from a rural background, such a unit of measurement is meaningless, and more meaningful distance-related terms may be used, such as *yards, miles*, such practical rules of thumb as "a stone's throw," or references to known distances and landmarks ("about half the distance to town"). To make matters more complicated, "how far" questions are sometimes answered in terms not of distance, but of time ("it's about 15 minutes to the store"), which will be understood variously to refer to walking or riding time, depending on context—and, if riding time, to different forms of riding. For some children, the ride to the store will be conceived of as being by ox cart, and for others, by bicycle, bus, canoe, or automobile, again depending on cultural context. The nature of the tools available to children to solve problems and perform tasks is highly dependent on the culture in which they live.

EVALUATING VYGOTSKY'S CONTRIBUTIONS. Vygotsky's view—that the specific nature of cognitive development can be understood only by taking into account cultural and social context—has become increasingly influential in the past decade. In some ways, this is surprising, in light of the fact that Vygotsky died more than eight decades ago at the young age of 37 (Winsler, 2003; Gredler & Shields, 2008).

Several factors explain Vygotsky's growing influence. One is that until recently he was largely unknown to developmentalists. His writings are only now becoming widely disseminated in the United States due to the growing availability of good English translations. In fact, for most of the 20th century, Vygotsky was not widely known even within his native land. His work was banned for some time due to his reliance on Western theorists, and it was not until the breakup of the Soviet Union in 1991 that it became freely available in the formerly Soviet countries. Thus, Vygotsky, long hidden from his fellow developmentalists, didn't emerge onto the scene until long after his death (Wertsch, 2008).

Even more important, though, is the quality of Vygotsky's ideas. They represent a consistent theoretical system and help explain a growing body of research attesting to the importance of social interaction in promoting cognitive development. The idea that children's comprehension of the world is an outcome of their interactions with their parents, peers, and other members of society is both appealing and well supported by research findings. It is also consistent with a growing body of multicultural and cross-cultural research, which finds evidence that cognitive development is shaped, in part, by cultural factors (Scrimsher & Tudge, 2003; Hedegaard & Fleer, 2013; Friedrich, 2014; Yasnitsky & van der Veer, 2016).

Of course, not every aspect of Vygotsky's theorizing has been supported, and his conceptualization of cognitive growth can be criticized for its lack of precision. For instance, such broad concepts as the zone of proximal development are not terribly precise, and they do not always lend themselves to experimental tests (Daniels, 2006).

Furthermore, Vygotsky was largely silent on how basic cognitive processes, such as attention and memory, develop and how children's natural cognitive capabilities unfold. Because of his emphasis on broad cultural influences, he did not focus on how individual bits of information are processed and synthesized. These processes, which must be taken into account if we are to have a complete understanding of cognitive development, are more directly addressed by information processing theories.

Still, Vygotsky's melding of the cognitive and social worlds of children has been an important advance in our understanding of cognitive development. We can only imagine what his impact would have been if he had lived a longer life. (See Table 7-1 for a comparison of Piaget's theory, information processing theories, and Vygotskian approaches.)

Table 7-1 Comparison of Piaget's Theory, Information Processing Theories, and Vygotsky's Approach to Cognitive Development

	Piaget	Information Processing	Vygotsky
Key concepts	Stages of cognitive development; qualitative growth from one stage to another	Gradual, quantitative improvements in attention, perception, understanding, and memory	Culture and social context drive cognitive development
Role of stages	Heavy emphasis	No specific stages	No specific stages
Importance of social factors	Low	Low	High
Educational perspective	Children must have reached a given stage of development for specific types of educational interventions to be effective.	Education is reflected in gradual increments in skills.	Education is very influential in promoting cognitive growth; teachers serve as facilitators.

Module 7.2 Review

LO 7.4 Summarize how Piaget explains cognitive development during the preschool years.

According to Piaget, children in the preoperational stage develop symbolic function, a qualitative change in their thinking that is the foundation of further cognitive advances. Preoperational children use intuitive thought to explore and draw conclusions about the world, and their thinking begins to encompass the important notions of functionality and identity. Recent developmentalists, while acknowledging Piaget's gifts and contributions, take issue with his emphasis on children's limitations and his underestimation of their capabilities.

LO 7.5 Summarize the information processing approaches to cognitive development in the preschool years.

Proponents of information processing approaches argue that quantitative changes in children's processing skills largely account for their cognitive development.

LO 7.6 Describe Vygotsky's view of cognitive development in the preschool years.

Vygotsky believed that children develop cognitively within a context of culture and society. His theory includes the concepts of the zone of proximal development and scaffolding.

Journal Writing Prompt

Applying Lifespan Development: In your view, how do thought and language interact in preschoolers' development? Is it possible to think without language? How do children who have been deaf from birth think?

The Growth of Language and Learning

I tried it out and it was very great!
This is a picture of when I was running through the water with Mommy.
Where are you going when I go to the fireworks with Mommy and Daddy?
I didn't know creatures went on floats in pools.
We can always pretend we have another one.
(Shatz, 1994, p. 179)

Listen to Ricky, at age 3. In addition to recognizing most letters of the alphabet, printing the first letter of his name, and writing the word "HI," he is readily capable of producing the complex sentences quoted above.

During the preschool years, children's language skills reach new heights of sophistication. Children begin the period with reasonable linguistic capabilities, although with significant gaps in both comprehension and production. In fact, no one would mistake the language used by a 3-year-old for that of an adult. However, by the end of the preschool years, children can hold their own with adults, both comprehending and producing language that has many of the qualities of adults' language. How does this transformation occur?

Language Development

LO 7.7 Explain how children's language develops in the preschool years.

Language blooms so rapidly between the later months of age 3 and the middle months of age 3 that researchers have yet to understand the exact pattern. What is clear is that sentence length increases at a steady pace, and the ways in which children at this age combine words and phrases to form sentences—known as **syntax**—doubles each month. By the time a preschooler is 3, the various combinations reach into the thousands.

In addition to the increasing complexity of sentences, there are enormous leaps in the number of words children use. By age 6, the average child has a vocabulary of around 14,000 words. To reach this number, preschoolers acquire vocabulary at a rate of nearly one new word every 2 hours, 24 hours a day. They manage this feat through a process known as **fast mapping**, in which new words are associated with their meaning after only a brief encounter (Krcmar, Grela, & Lin, 2007; Kan & Kohnert, 2009; Marinellie & Kneile, 2012; Venker, Kover, & Weismer, 2016).

By age 3, preschoolers routinely use plurals and possessive forms of nouns (such as "boys" and "boy's"), employ the past tense (adding "ed" at the end of words), and use articles ("the" and "a"). They can ask, and answer, complex questions ("Where did you say my book is?").

Preschoolers' skills extend to the appropriate formation of words that they have never before encountered. For example, in one classic experiment, preschool children were shown cards with drawings of a cartoonish bird, such as those shown in Figure 7-12 (Berko, 1958). The experimenter told the children that the figure was a "wug," and then showed them a card with two of the cartoon figures. "Now there are two of them," the children were told, and they were then asked to supply the missing word in the sentence, "There are two________" (the answer to which, of course, is "wugs").

Not only did children show that they knew rules about the plural forms of nouns, but they understood possessive forms of nouns and the third-person singular and past-tense forms of verbs—all for words that they never had previously encountered, since they were nonsense words with no real meaning (O'Grady & Aitchison, 2005).

Preschoolers also learn what *cannot* be said as they acquire the principles of grammar. **Grammar** is the system of rules in a given language that determine how our thoughts can be expressed. (*Grammar* is a broad, general term that encompasses syntax and other linguistic rules.) For instance, preschoolers come to learn that "I am sitting" is correct, while the similarly structured "I am knowing [that]" is incorrect. Although they still make frequent mistakes of one sort or another, 3-year-olds follow the principles of grammar most of the time. Some errors are very noticeable—such as the use of *mens* and *catched*—but these errors are actually quite rare, occurring between 0.1 percent and 8 percent of the time. Put another way, young preschoolers are correct in their grammatical constructions more than 90 percent of the time (Pinker, 1994; Guasti, 2002).

PRIVATE SPEECH AND SOCIAL SPEECH. In even a short visit to a preschool, you're likely to notice some children talking to themselves during play periods. A child might be reminding a doll that the two of them are going to the grocery store later, or another child, while playing with a toy racing car, might speak of an upcoming race. In some cases, the talk is sustained, as when a child working on a puzzle says things like, "This piece goes here.... Uh-oh, this one doesn't fit.... Where can I put this piece? ... This can't be right."

Some developmentalists suggest that **private speech**, speech by children that is spoken and directed to themselves, performs an important function. For instance, Vygotsky suggested that private speech is used as a guide to behavior and thought. By communicating with themselves through private speech, children are able to try out ideas, acting

Figure 7-12 Appropriate Formation of Words

Even though no preschooler—like the rest of us—is likely to have ever before encountered a *wug*, preschoolers are able to produce the appropriate word to fill in the blank (which, for the record, is *wugs*).

(**Source:** Berko, J. (1958). The child's learning of English morphology. *Word, 14*, 150–177.)

syntax
the way in which an individual combines words and phrases to form sentences

fast mapping
a process in which new words are associated with their meaning after only a brief encounter

grammar
the system of rules that determines how our thoughts can be expressed

private speech
speech by children that is spoken and directed to themselves

as their own sounding boards. In this way, private speech facilitates children's thinking and helps them control their behavior. (Have you ever said to yourself, "Take it easy" or "Calm down" when trying to control your anger over some situation?) In Vygotsky's view, then, private speech ultimately serves an important social function, allowing children to solve problems and reflect upon difficulties they encounter. He also suggested that private speech is a forerunner to the internal dialogues that we use when we reason with ourselves during thinking (Al-Namlah, Meins, & Fernyhough, 2012; McGonigle-Chalmers, Slater, & Smith, 2014; Sawyer, 2017).

pragmatics
the aspect of language that relates to communicating effectively and appropriately with others

In addition, private speech may be a way for children to practice the practical skills required in conversation, known as *pragmatics*. **Pragmatics** is the aspect of language relating to communicating effectively and appropriately with others. The development of pragmatic abilities permits children to understand the basics of conversations—turn-taking, sticking to a topic, and what should and should not be said, according to the conventions of society. When children are taught that the appropriate response to receiving a gift is "thank you," or that they should use different language in various settings (on the playground with their friends versus in the classroom with their teacher), they are learning the pragmatics of language.

social speech
speech directed toward another person and meant to be understood by that person

The preschool years also mark the growth of social speech. **Social speech** is speech directed toward another person and meant to be understood by that person. Before the age of 3, children may seem to be speaking only for their own entertainment, apparently uncaring as to whether anyone else can understand. However, during the preschool years, children begin to direct their speech to others, wanting others to listen and becoming frustrated when they cannot make themselves understood. As a result, they begin to adapt their speech to others through pragmatics, as just discussed. Recall that Piaget contended that most speech during the preoperational period was egocentric: Preschoolers were seen as taking little account of the effect their speech was having on others. However, more recent experimental evidence suggests that children are somewhat more adept in taking others into account than Piaget initially suggested.

HOW LIVING IN POVERTY AFFECTS LANGUAGE DEVELOPMENT. The language that preschoolers hear at home has profound implications for future cognitive success, according to results of a landmark series of studies by psychologists Betty Hart and Todd Risley (Hart & Risley, 1995; Hart, 2000, 2004). The researchers studied the language used over a 2-year period by a group of parents of varying levels of affluence as they interacted with their children. Their examination of some 1,300 hours of everyday interactions between parents and children produced several major findings:

- The greater the affluence of the parents, the more they spoke to their children. As shown in Figure 7-13, the rate at which language was addressed to children varied significantly according to the economic level of the family.
- In a typical hour, parents classified as professionals spent almost twice as much time interacting with their children as parents who received welfare assistance.
- By age 4, children in families that received welfare assistance were likely to have been exposed to some 13 million fewer words than those in families classified as professionals.
- The kind of language used in the home differed among the various types of families. Children in families that received welfare assistance were apt to hear prohibitions ("no" or "stop," for example) twice as frequently as those in families classified as professionals.

Ultimately, the study found that the type of language to which children were exposed was associated with their performance on tests of intelligence. The greater the number and variety of words children heard, for instance, the better their performance at age 3 on a variety of measures of intellectual achievement.

Figure 7-13 Different Language Exposures

Parents at differing levels of affluence provide different language experiences. Professional parents and working parents address more words to their children, on average, than parents on welfare. Why do you think this is so?

(**Source:** Hart, B., and Risley, T. R. (1995). *Meaningful differences in the everyday experience of young American children.* Baltimore, MD: Paul Brookes, p. 239.)

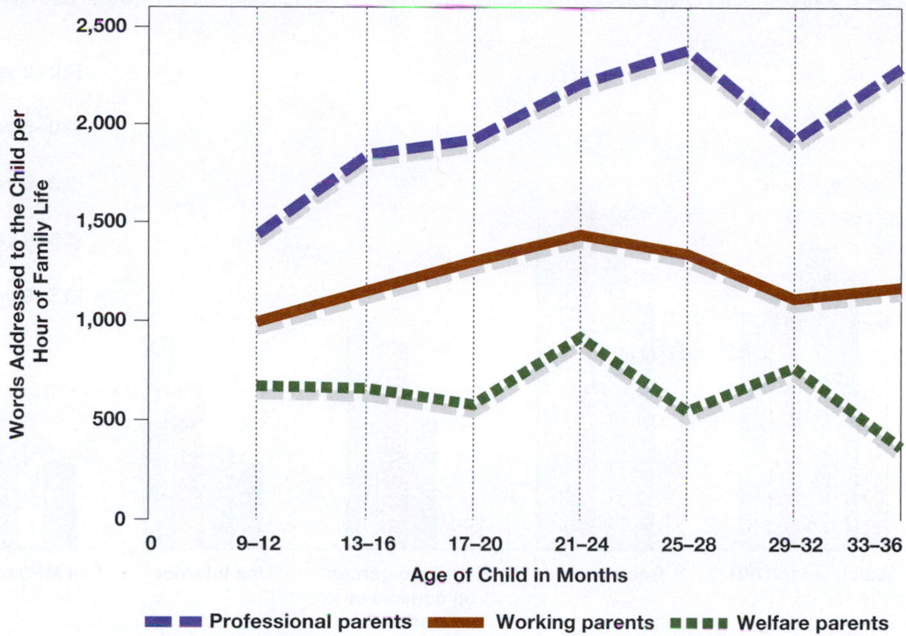

Although the findings are correlational, and thus cannot be interpreted in terms of cause and effect, they clearly suggest the importance of early exposure to language, in terms of both quantity and variety. They also suggest that intervention programs that teach parents to speak to their children more often and use more varied language may be useful in alleviating some of the potentially damaging consequences of poverty.

The research is also consistent with an increasing body of evidence that family income and poverty have powerful consequences for children's general cognitive development and behavior. By age 5, children raised in poverty tend to have lower IQ scores and do not perform as well on other measures of cognitive development as children raised in affluence. Furthermore, the longer children live in poverty, the more severe the consequences. Poverty not only reduces the educational resources available to children, but it also has such negative effects on parents that it limits the psychological support they can provide their families. In short, the consequences of poverty are severe, and they linger (Kim, Curby, & Winsler, 2014; Sharkins, Leger, & Ernest, 2016; Lipina & Evers, 2017).

Learning from the Media: Television and the Internet

LO 7.8 Identify the effects of digital media and television on preschoolers.

MEDIA CONSUMPTION. The average preschooler is exposed to over 4 hours per day of screen time, which includes watching TV and using computers. Furthermore, more than a third of households with children 2 to 7 years of age say that the television is on "most of the time" in their homes (see Figure 7-14; Bryant & Bryant, 2003; Gutnick et al., 2010; Tandon et al., 2011).

Figure 7-14 Television Time

Television is a nearly universal technology in the United States, whereas only about two-thirds of families with children age 11 or younger have computers. On a typical day, more than 80 percent of toddlers and preschoolers in the United States watch TV, and it remains the most frequently used medium by children from 0 to 11 years of age. **THINKING ABOUT THE DATA:** Compare the media use of children in their first two years of life to children ages 6-9 years old. How is their media use similar in some ways and different in others?

(**Source:** Gutnick, A. L., Robb, M., Takeuchi, L., & Kotler, J. (2010). *Always connected: The new digital media habits of young children.* New York: The Joan Ganz Cooney Center at Sesame Workshop, p. 15.)

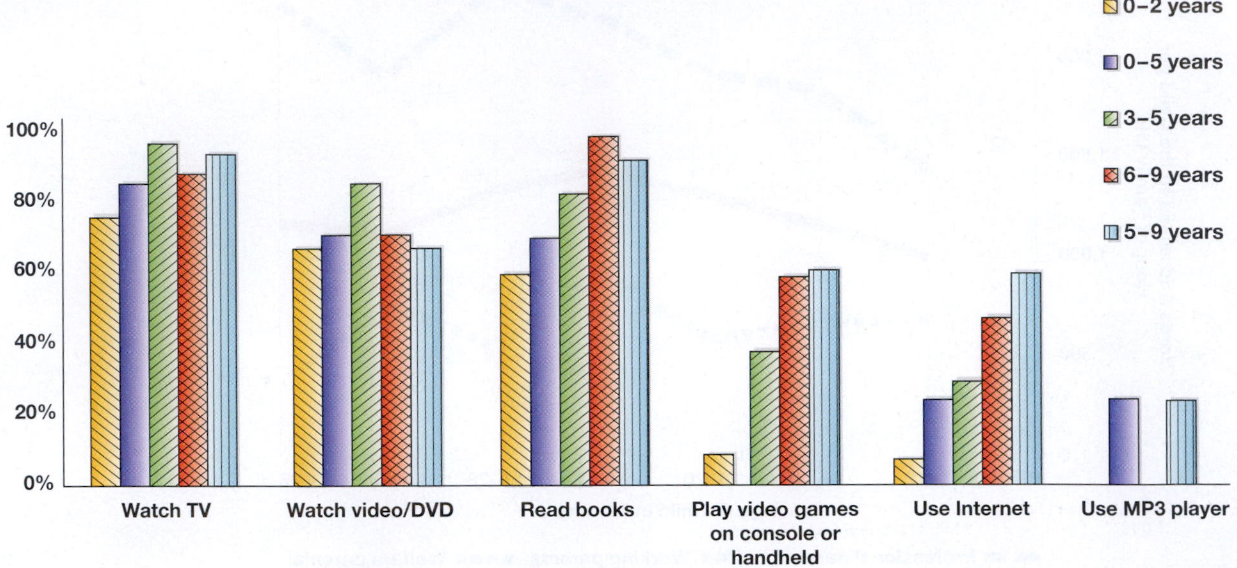

One concern about preschoolers' use of media relates to the inactivity it produces. Preschoolers who watch more than 2 hours per day of television and videos or use computers for significant amounts of time have a higher risk of obesity than those who watch less (Jordan & Robinson, 2008; Strasburger, 2009; Cox et al, 2012).

It is also unclear what, exactly, children are learning from media exposure. When they do watch television or online videos, preschool children often do not fully understand the plots of the stories they are viewing, particularly in longer programs. They are unable to recall significant story details after viewing a program, and the inferences they make about the motivations of characters are limited and often erroneous. Moreover, preschool children may have difficulty separating fantasy from reality in programming, with some believing, for example, that there is a real Big Bird living on *Sesame Street* (Wright et al., 1994).

Preschool-age children exposed to advertising are not able to critically understand and evaluate the messages to which they are exposed. Consequently, they are likely to fully accept advertisers' claims about their product. The likelihood of children believing advertising messages is so high that the American Psychological Association has recommended that television advertising targeting children under the age of 8 be restricted (Pine, Wilson, & Nash, 2007; Nash, Pine, & Messer, 2009; Nicklas et al., 2011).

In addition, the American Academy of Pediatrics recommended in 2016 that children younger than 18 months be discouraged from using screen media other than video chats. For preschoolers older than 2, they suggest limiting media to 1 hour or less of high-quality programming per day. They also recommend that no screens should be used during meals and for 1 hour before bedtime (American Academy of Pediatrics, 2016).

In short, the world to which preschoolers are exposed is imperfectly understood and unrealistic. However, as they get older and their information processing capabilities improve, preschoolers' understanding of the material they see on television and on the computer improves. They remember things more accurately, and they become better able to focus on the central message of what they're watching. This improvement suggests that the powers of media may be harnessed to bring about cognitive gains—which is exactly what the producers of *Sesame Street* set out to do (Berry, 2003; Uchikoshi, 2006; Njoroge et al., 2016).

SESAME STREET. *Sesame Street* is one of the longest-running and most popular educational programs for children in the United States, and the U.S. State Department called it the most influential children's show in the world. Almost half of all preschoolers in the United States watch the show, and it is broadcast in almost 100 different countries and in 13 languages. Characters like Big Bird and Elmo have become familiar throughout the world to both adults and preschoolers (Cole, Arafat, & Tidhar, 2003; Moran, 2006; Linebarger et al., 2017).

Sesame Street was devised with the express purpose of providing an educational experience for preschoolers. Its specific goals include teaching letters and numbers, increasing vocabulary, and teaching preliteracy skills. Has *Sesame Street* achieved its goals? Most evidence suggests that it has.

For example, preschoolers living in lower-income households who watch the show are better prepared for school, and they perform significantly higher on several measures of verbal and mathematics ability at ages 6 and 7 than those who do not watch it. Furthermore, viewers of *Sesame Street* spend more time reading than do nonviewers. And by the time they are 6 and 7, viewers of *Sesame Street* and other educational programs tend to be better readers and judged more positively by their teachers. The findings for *Sesame Street* are mirrored for other educationally oriented shows, such as *Dora the Explorer* and *Blue's Clues* (Augustyn, 2003; Linebarger, 2005).

More recent evaluations show even more positive findings. In a 2015 study, viewing *Sesame Street* was found to be as valuable as attending preschool. In fact, viewing the show was associated with increases in the likelihood of remaining at appropriate grade level by several percentage points. The effect was especially strong for boys, African Americans, and children who grow up in disadvantaged areas (Kearney & Levine, 2015).

However, *Sesame Street* has not been without its critics. For instance, some educators claim that the frenzied pace at which different scenes are shown makes viewers less receptive to the traditional forms of teaching they will experience when they begin school. Careful evaluations of the program, however, find no evidence that viewing *Sesame Street* leads to declines in enjoyment of traditional schooling. Overall, then, the most recent findings demonstrate quite positive outcomes for viewers of *Sesame Street* and other educational shows similar to it (Wright et al., 2001; Fisch, 2004; Zimmerman & Christakis, 2007; Penuel et al., 2012).

Early Childhood Education: Taking the "Pre" out of the Preschool Period

LO 7.9 Distinguish the educational programs available to children in the preschool years.

The term *preschool period* is something of a misnomer because many children engage in some form of educational experiences during this period. Almost three-quarters of children in the United States are enrolled in some form of care outside the home, much of which is designed either explicitly or implicitly to teach skills that will enhance intellectual as well as social abilities (see Figure 7-15). There are several reasons for this increase, but one major factor is the rise in the number of families in which both parents work outside the home. For instance, a high proportion of fathers work outside the home, and close to 60 percent of women with children under 6 are employed, most of them full time (Gilbert, 1994; Borden, 1998; Tamis-LeMonda & Cabrera, 2002).

Figure 7-15 Care Outside the Home

Approximately 75 percent of children in the United States are enrolled in some form of care outside the home—a trend that is the result of more parents employed full time. Evidence suggests that children can benefit from early childhood education.

(**Source:** U.S. Department of Education, National Center for Child Health, 2003.)

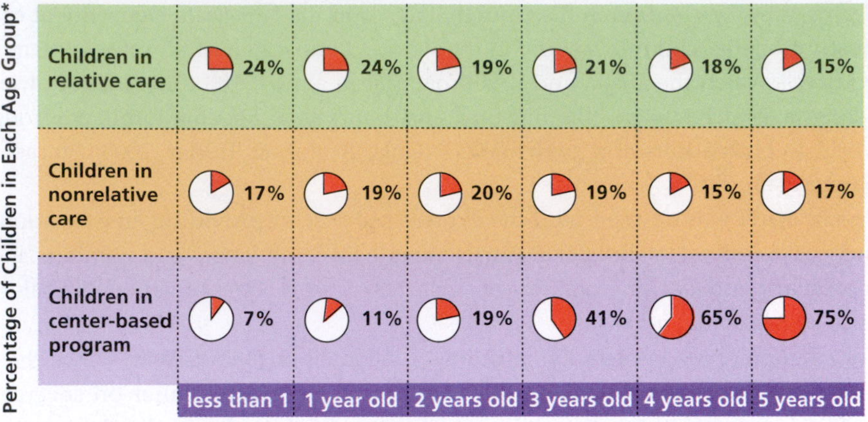

*Columns do not add up to 100 because some children participated in more than one type of child care.

However, there is another reason, one less tied to the practical considerations of child care: Developmental psychologists have found increasing evidence that children can benefit substantially from involvement in some form of educational activity before they enroll in formal schooling, which typically takes place at age 5 or 6 in the United States. When compared to children who stay at home and have no formal educational involvement, those children enrolled in good preschools experience clear cognitive and social benefits (Campbell, Ramey, & Pungello, 2002; Friedman, 2004; National Association for the Education of Young Children, 2005).

THE VARIETIES OF EARLY EDUCATION. The variety of early education alternatives is vast. Some outside-the-home care for children is little more than babysitting, while other options are designed to promote intellectual and social advances. Among the major choices of the latter type are the following:

- *Child-care centers* typically provide care for children outside the home while their parents are at work. (Child-care centers were previously referred to as day-care centers. However, because a significant number of parents work nonstandard schedules and therefore require care for their children at times other than the day, the preferred label has changed to *child-care centers*.)

  Although many child-care centers were first established as safe, warm environments where children could be cared for and could interact with other children, today their purpose tends to be broader, aimed at providing some form of intellectual stimulation. Still, their primary purpose tends to be more social and emotional than cognitive.

- Some child care is provided in *family child-care centers*, small operations run in private homes. Because centers in some areas are unlicensed, the quality of care can be uneven, and parents should consider whether a family child-care center is licensed before enrolling their children. In contrast, providers of center-based care, which is offered in institutions such as school classrooms, community centers, and churches and synagogues, are typically licensed and regulated by governmental authorities. Because teachers in such programs are more often trained professionals than those who provide family child care, the quality of care is often higher.

- *Preschools* are explicitly designed to provide intellectual and social experiences for children. They tend to be more limited in their schedules than family child-care centers, typically providing care for only 3 to 5 hours per day. Because of this limitation, preschools mainly serve children from middle and higher socioeconomic levels, in cases where parents don't need to work full time.

  Like child-care centers, preschools vary enormously in the activities they provide. Some emphasize social skills, whereas others focus on intellectual development. Some do both. For instance, Montessori preschools, which use a method developed by Italian educator Maria Montessori, employ a carefully designed set of materials to create an environment that fosters sensory, motor, and language development. Children are provided with a variety of activities to choose from, with the option of moving from one to another (Gutek, 2003).

  Similarly, in the Reggio Emilia preschool approach—another Italian import—children participate in what is called a *negotiated curriculum* that emphasizes the joint participation of children and teachers. The curriculum builds on the interests of children, promoting their cognitive development through the integration of the arts and participation in weeklong projects (Hong & Trepanier-Street, 2004; Rankin, 2004; Paolella, 2013; Mages, 2016).

- *School child care* is provided by some local school systems in the United States. Almost half the states in the United States fund prekindergarten programs for 4-year-olds, often aimed at disadvantaged children. Because they typically are staffed by better-trained teachers than less-regulated child-care centers, school child-care programs are often of higher quality than other early education alternatives.

THE EFFECTIVENESS OF CHILD CARE. How effective are such programs? Most research suggests that preschoolers enrolled in child-care centers show intellectual development that at least matches that of children at home and often is better. For instance, some studies find that preschoolers in child care are more verbally fluent, show memory and comprehension advantages, and even achieve higher IQ scores than at-home children. Other studies find that early and long-term participation in child care is particularly helpful for children from impoverished home environments or who are otherwise at risk. Some research even shows that child-care programs can have positive consequences 25 years later (Vandell, 2004; Mervis, 2011; Reynolds et al., 2011; Vivanti et al., 2014).

Similar advantages are found for social development. Children in high-quality programs tend to be more self-confident, independent, and knowledgeable about the social world in which they live than those who do not participate. However, not all the outcomes of outside-the-home care are positive: Children in child care have been found to be less polite, less compliant, less respectful of adults, and sometimes more competitive and aggressive than their peers (Clarke-Stewart & Allhusen, 2002; NICHD Early Child Care Research Network, 2003b; Belsky et al., 2007; Douglass & Klerman, 2012).

Another way to consider the effectiveness of child care is to take an economic approach. For instance, one study of prekindergarten education in Texas found that every $1 invested in high-quality preschool programs produced $3.50 in benefits. Benefits included increased graduation rates, higher earnings, savings in juvenile crime, and reductions in child welfare costs (Aguirre et al., 2006).

It is important to keep in mind that not all early childhood care programs are equally effective. As we observed of infant child care in Chapter 6, one key factor is program *quality:* High-quality care provides intellectual and social benefits, while low-quality care not only is unlikely to furnish benefits but actually may harm children (Votruba-Drzal, Coley, & Chase-Lansdale, 2004; NICHD Early Child Care Research Network, 2006; Dearing, McCartney, & Taylor, 2009).

THE QUALITY OF CHILD CARE. How can we define "high quality"? Several characteristics are important; they are analogous to those that pertain to infant child care (see Chapter 6). The major characteristics of high-quality care include the following (Vandell, Shumow, & Posner, 2005; Lavzer & Goodson, 2006; Leach et al., 2008; Rudd, Cain, & Saxon, 2008; Lloyd, 2012):

- The care providers are well trained, preferably with bachelor's degrees.
- The child-care center has an appropriate overall size and ratio of care providers to children. Single groups should not have many more than 14 to 20 children, and there should be no more than 5 to 10 three-year-olds per caregiver, or 7 to 10 four- or five-year-olds per caregiver.
- The child–teacher ratio should be 10:1 or better.
- The curriculum of a child-care facility is carefully planned out and coordinated among the teachers.
- The language environment is rich, with a great deal of conversation.
- The caregivers are sensitive to children's emotional and social needs, and they know when and when not to intervene.
- Materials and activities are age appropriate.
- Basic health and safety standards are followed.
- Children should be screened for vision, hearing, and health problems.
- At least one meal a day should be served.
- The facility should provide at least one family support service.

No one knows how many programs in the United States can be considered "high quality," but there are many fewer than desirable. In fact, the United States lags behind almost every other industrialized country in the quality of its child care, as well as in its quantity and affordability, as we discuss further in the *Developmental Diversity and Your Life* feature (Muenchow & Marsland, 2007; Pianata et al., 2009).

Developmental Diversity and Your Life

Preschools Around the World: Why Does the United States Lag Behind?

In France and Belgium, access to preschool is a legal right. Sweden and Finland provide child care for preschoolers whose parents want it. Russia has an extensive system of state-run *yasli-sads*, nursery schools and kindergartens, attended by 75 percent of children age 3 to 7 in urban areas.

In contrast, the United States has no coordinated national policy on preschool education—or on the care of children in general. There are several reasons for this. For one, decisions about education have traditionally been left to the states and to local school districts. For another, the United States has no tradition of teaching preschoolers, unlike other countries in which preschool-age children have been enrolled in formal programs for decades. Finally, the status of preschools in the United States has been traditionally low. Consider, for instance, that preschool and nursery school teachers are the lowest-paid of all teachers. (Teacher salaries increase as the age of students rises. Thus, college and high school teachers are paid the highest salaries, while preschool and elementary school teachers are paid the lowest salaries.)

Preschools also differ significantly from one country to another, reflecting their differing societal views of the purpose of early childhood education. For instance, in a cross-country comparison of preschools in China, Japan, and the United States, researchers found that parents in the three countries view the purpose of preschools very differently. Whereas parents in China tend to see preschools primarily as a way of giving children a good start academically, Japanese parents view them primarily as a way of giving children the opportunity to be members of a group. In the United States, in comparison, parents regard the primary purpose of preschools as making children more independent and self-reliant, although obtaining a good academic start and having group experience are also seen as important (Huntsinger et al., 1997; Johnson et al., 2003).

PREPARING PRESCHOOLERS FOR ACADEMIC PURSUITS: DOES HEAD START TRULY PROVIDE A HEAD START? Although many programs designed for preschoolers focus primarily on social and emotional factors, some are geared primarily toward promoting cognitive gains and preparing preschoolers for the more formal instruction they will experience when they start kindergarten. In the United States, the best-known program designed to promote future academic success is Head Start. Born in the 1960s during the height of the War on Poverty, the program has served over 30 million children and their families; each year, nearly 1 million children age 3 and 4 are in Head Start. The program, which stresses parental involvement, was designed to serve the "whole child," including children's physical health, self-confidence, social responsibility, and social and emotional development (Gupta et al., 2009; Zhai, Raver, & Jones, 2012; Office of Head Start, 2015).

Whether Head Start is seen as successful or not depends on the lens through which one is looking. If, for instance, the program is expected to provide long-term increases in IQ scores, it is a disappointment. Although graduates of Head Start programs tend to show immediate IQ gains, these increases do not last.

On the positive side, it is clear that Head Start is meeting its goal of getting preschoolers ready for school. Preschoolers who participate in Head Start are better prepared for future schooling—in terms of health, social, emotional, and cognitive factors—than those who do not. Furthermore, graduates of Head Start programs have better future school adjustment than their peers, and they are less likely to be in special education classes or to be retained in their grade. Finally, some research suggests that Head Start graduates even show higher academic performance at the end of high school, although the gains are modest (Bierman et al., 2009; Mervis, 2011b; Goble et al., 2017).

In addition to Head Start programs, other types of preschool readiness programs also provide advantages throughout the school years. Studies show that those who participate and graduate from such preschool programs are less likely to repeat grades, and they complete school more frequently than those who are not in the programs. Preschool readiness programs also appear to be cost-effective. According to a cost-benefit analysis of one readiness program, for every $1 spent on the program, taxpayers saved $7 by the time the graduates reached the age of 27 (Friedman, 2004; Gormley et al., 2005; Lee et al., 2014).

A comprehensive evaluation of early intervention programs suggests that, taken as a group, they can provide significant benefits and that government funds invested early in life may ultimately lead to a reduction in future costs. For instance, compared with children who did not participate in early intervention programs, participants in various programs showed gains in emotional or cognitive development, better educational outcomes, increased economic self-sufficiency, reduced levels of criminal activity, and improved health-related behaviors. Although not every program produced all these benefits, and not every child benefited to the same extent, the results of the evaluation suggested that the potential benefits of early intervention can be substantial (NICHD Early Child Care Research Network & Duncan, 2003; Love et al., 2006; Izard et al., 2008; Mervis, 2011a).

ARE WE PUSHING CHILDREN TOO HARD AND TOO FAST? Not everyone agrees that programs that seek to enhance academic skills during the preschool years are a good thing. According to developmental psychologist David Elkind, U.S. society tends to push children so rapidly that they begin to feel stress and pressure at a young age (Elkind, 2007).

Elkind argues that academic success is largely dependent on factors out of parents' control, such as inherited abilities and a child's rate of maturation. Consequently, children of a particular age cannot be expected to master educational material without taking into account their current level of cognitive development. In short, children require **developmentally appropriate educational practice**, which is education that is based on both typical development and the unique characteristics of a given child (Robinson & Stark, 2005).

developmentally appropriate educational practice
education that is based on both typical development and the unique characteristics of a given child

From *an educator's* perspective

Do you accept the view that children in U.S. society are "pushed" academically to the extent that they feel too much stress and pressure at a young age? Why?

Rather than arbitrarily expecting children to master material at a particular age, Elkind suggests that a better strategy is to provide an environment in which learning is encouraged but not pushed. By creating an atmosphere in which learning is facilitated—for instance, by reading to preschoolers—parents will allow children to proceed at their own pace rather than at one that pushes them beyond their limits (Reese & Cox, 1999; van Kleeck & Stahl, 2003).

Although Elkind's suggestions are appealing—it is certainly hard to disagree that increases in children's anxiety levels and stress should be avoided—they are not without their detractors. For instance, some educators have argued that pushing children is largely a phenomenon of the middle and higher socioeconomic levels, possible only if parents are relatively affluent. For poorer children, whose parents may not have substantial resources available to push their children nor the easy ability to create an environment that promotes learning, the benefits of formal programs that promote learning are likely to outweigh their drawbacks. Furthermore, developmental researchers have found that there are ways for parents to prepare their children for future educational success.

Module 7.3 Review

LO 7.7 Explain how children's language develops in the preschool years.

In the preschool years, children rapidly increase in linguistic ability, developing an improved sense of grammar and shifting gradually from private to social speech. Poverty can affect children's language development by limiting the opportunities for parents and other caregivers to interact linguistically with children.

LO 7.8 Identify the effects of digital media and television on preschoolers.

Preschoolers watch television at high levels. The effects of television on preschoolers are mixed, with benefits from some programs and clear disadvantages due to other aspects of viewing.

LO 7.9 Distinguish the educational programs available to children in the preschool years.

Preschool educational programs are beneficial if they are of high quality, with trained staff, good curriculum, proper group sizes, and small staff-to-student ratios. Preschool children are likely to benefit from a developmentally appropriate, individualized, and supportive environment for learning.

Journal Writing Prompt

Applying Lifespan Development: Imagine that you are the parent of a preschooler. What have you learned in this module that might improve your parenting?

Epilogue

In this chapter, we looked at children in the preschool years, focusing on their physical development, growth, nutritional needs, overall health, brain growth, and advances in gross and fine motor skills. We discussed cognitive development from the Piagetian perspective, with its description of the characteristics of thought in the preoperational stage, and from the perspective of information processing theorists and Lev Vygotsky, who emphasized the social and cultural influences on cognitive development. We then discussed the burst in linguistic ability that occurs during the preschool years and the influence of television on preschoolers' development. We concluded with a discussion of preschool education and its effects.

Before moving on to a discussion of children's cognitive development in the next chapter, turn back for a moment to this chapter's prologue, which describes Aaron's excursion across the kitchen counter and into the sink (with a stop along the way at the cookie jar). Consider these questions:

1. Why, specifically, do you think Aaron climbed up on the counter? Was it merely to get a cookie?
2. What gross and fine motor skills were involved in Aaron's journey across the counter and into the sink?
3. What dangers did Aaron face in this incident?
4. What could Aaron's father, who had left the room for only a moment, have done to prevent Aaron from climbing into the sink?

Looking Back

LO 7.1 Describe a child's bodily growth and overall health risks during the preschool years.

In addition to gaining height and weight, the bodies of preschool children undergo changes in shape and structure. Children grow more slender, and their bones and muscles strengthen. Children in the preschool years are generally quite healthy. Obesity in these years is caused by genetic and environmental factors. The greatest health threats are accidents and environmental factors.

LO 7.2 Summarize how preschool children's brains develop.

Brain growth is particularly rapid during the preschool years, with the number of interconnections among cells and the amount of myelin around neurons increasing greatly. The halves of the brain begin to specialize in somewhat different tasks—a process called lateralization.

LO 7.3 Explain how preschool children's motor skills develop.

Both gross and fine motor skills advance rapidly during the preschool years. Gender differences begin to emerge, fine motor skills are honed, and handedness begins to assert itself.

LO 7.4 Summarize how Piaget explains cognitive development during the preschool years.

During the stage that Jean Piaget has described as *preoperational*, children are not yet able to engage in organized, formal, logical thinking. However, their development of symbolic function permits quicker and more effective thinking as they are freed from the limitations of sensorimotor learning. According to Piaget, children in the preoperational stage engage in intuitive thought for the first time, actively applying rudimentary reasoning skills to the acquisition of world knowledge.

LO 7.5 Summarize the information processing approaches to cognitive development in the preschool years.

A different approach to cognitive development is taken by proponents of information processing theories, who focus on preschoolers' storage and recall of information and on quantitative changes in information processing abilities (such as attention).

LO 7.6 Describe Vygotsky's view of cognitive development in the preschool years.

Lev Vygotsky proposed that the nature and progress of children's cognitive development are dependent on the children's social and cultural context.

LO 7.7 Explain how children's language develops in the preschool years.

Children rapidly progress from two-word utterances to longer, more sophisticated expressions that reflect their growing vocabularies and emerging grasp of grammar. The development of linguistic abilities is affected by socioeconomic status. The result can be lowered linguistic—and, ultimately, academic—performance by poorer children.

LO 7.8 Identify the effects of digital media and television on preschoolers.

The effects of television are mixed. Preschoolers' sustained exposure to emotions and situations that are not representative of the real world have raised concerns. By contrast, preschoolers can derive meaning from such targeted programs as *Sesame Street*, which are designed to bring about cognitive gains.

LO 7.9 Distinguish the educational programs available to children in the preschool years.

Early childhood educational programs, offered as center-based or school-based child care or as preschool, can lead to cognitive and social advances. The United States lacks a coordinated national policy on preschool education. The major federal initiative in U.S. preschool education has been the Head Start program, which has yielded mixed results.

Key Terms and Concepts

obesity 215
myelin 218
lateralization 220
handedness 225
preoperational stage 226
operations 227
centration 227
conservation 228
transformation 229
egocentric thought 230
intuitive thought 230
autobiographical memory 233
scripts 233
zone of proximal development (ZPD) 235
scaffolding 236
syntax 239
fast mapping 239
grammar 239
private speech 239
pragmatics 240
social speech 240
developmentally appropriate educational practice 247

Chapter 8

Social and Personality Development in the Preschool Years

OJO Images Ltd/Alamy Stock Photo

Learning Objectives

LO 8.1 Describe the major developmental challenges that preschool-age children face.

LO 8.2 Explain how preschool-age children develop a concept of themselves.

LO 8.3 Explain how preschool-age children develop a sense of racial identity and gender.

LO 8.4 Describe the sorts of social relationships that preschool-age children engage in.

LO 8.5 Explain how and why preschool-age children play.

LO 8.6 Summarize how thinking changes in the preschool years.

LO 8.7 Describe the types of disciplinary styles parents employ and the effects they have on their children.

LO 8.8 List the factors that contribute to child abuse and neglect.

LO 8.9 Define resilience, and describe how it can help abused children.

LO 8.10 Explain how preschool-age children develop a moral sense.

LO 8.11 Describe how aggression develops in preschool-age children.

Chapter Overview

Prologue: A Marvelous Julian

Lincoln and Beth Avery had expected their son Julian to be just like his older brother, Carl. Carl was bold and adventurous, a climber of trees and a leader on the playground. By age 4, however, it was clear Julian had his own personality. He liked to sit on the front steps of their brownstone looking at picture books. He liked to draw and make things with clay. He was a calm, thoughtful child who chose to watch others more often than interact with them.

The Averys were surprised by the preferences of their younger son and voiced their concerns to his preschool teacher. The teacher confirmed that Julian was indeed a quiet child. No, he was not a leader on the playground, but he did have several friends in the class, and he seemed content most of the time, especially when he was creating something out of cardboard or construction paper, or making a story with pictures. The teacher urged the Averys not to worry. "Julian is developing a sense of who he is and what he can do, what he likes to do. He won't be Carl. He can't be. But I think he'll be a marvelous Julian."

Looking Ahead

Like most preschool-age children, Julian is only just beginning to show the personality that will develop over the rest of his life. Although he is his parents' son, he is not his brother. He may not even share many of his parents' personality traits, but with their love and support, he will, as his teacher put it, become a marvelous Julian.

In this chapter, we address social and personality development during the preschool period, a time of enormous growth and change. We begin by examining how preschool-age children continue to form a sense of self, focusing on how they develop their self-concepts. We especially examine issues of self relating to gender, a central aspect of children's views of themselves and others.

Preschoolers' social lives are the focus of the next part of the chapter. We look at how children play with one another, examining the various types of play. We consider how parents and other authority figures use discipline to shape children's behavior.

Finally, we examine two key aspects of preschool-age children's social behavior: moral development and aggression. We consider how children develop a notion of right and wrong and how that development can lead them to be helpful to others. We also look at the other side of the coin—aggression—and examine the factors that lead preschool-age children to behave in a way that hurts others. We end on an optimistic note: considering how we may help preschool-age children to be more moral and less aggressive individuals.

Phase4Studios/Shutterstock

During the preschool years, a child's ability to understand others' emotions begins to grow.

Forming a Sense of Self

Although the question "Who am I?" is not explicitly posed by most preschool-age children, it underlies a considerable amount of development during the preschool years. During this period, children wonder about the nature of the self, and the way they answer the "Who am I?" question may affect them for the rest of their lives.

Psychosocial Development: Resolving the Conflicts

LO 8.1 Describe the major developmental challenges that preschool-age children face.

Mary-Alice's preschool teacher raised her eyebrows slightly when the 4-year-old took off her coat. Mary-Alice, usually dressed in well-matched playsuits, was a medley of prints. She had on a pair of flowered pants along with a completely clashing plaid top. The outfit was accessorized with a striped headband, socks in an animal print, and Mary-Alice's polka-dotted rain boots. Mary-Alice's mom gave a slightly embarrassed shrug. "Mary-Alice got dressed all by herself this morning," she explained as she handed over a bag containing spare shoes, just in case the rain boots became uncomfortable during the day.

Psychoanalyst Erik Erikson may well have praised Mary-Alice's mother for helping Mary-Alice develop a sense of initiative (if not of fashion). The reason: Erikson (1963) suggested that, during the preschool years, children face a key conflict relating to psychosocial development that involves the development of initiative.

psychosocial development
according to Erikson, development that encompasses changes both in the understanding individuals have of themselves as members of society and in their comprehension of the meaning of others' behavior

As we discussed in Chapter 6, **psychosocial development** encompasses changes in individuals' understanding of themselves as well as their understanding of others' behavior. According to Erikson, society and culture present the developing person with particular challenges, which shift as people age. Erikson believed that people pass through eight distinct stages, each characterized by a crisis or conflict that the person must resolve. Our experiences as we try to resolve these conflicts lead us to develop ideas about ourselves that can last for the rest of our lives.

In the early part of the preschool period, children are ending the autonomy-versus-shame-and-doubt stage, which lasts from around 18 months to 3 years. In this period, children either become more independent and autonomous if their parents encourage exploration and freedom or they experience shame and self-doubt if they are restricted and overprotected.

initiative-versus-guilt stage
according to Erikson, the period during which children between age 3 and age 6 experience conflict between independence of action and the sometimes negative results of that action

The preschool years largely encompass what Erikson called the **initiative-versus-guilt stage**, which lasts from around age 3 to age 6. During this period, children's views of themselves change as preschool-age children face conflicts between, on the one hand, the desire to act independently of their parents and do things on their own, and, on the other hand, the guilt that comes from failure when they don't succeed. They are eager to do things on their own ("Let *me* do it" is a popular refrain among preschoolers), but they feel guilt if their efforts fail. They come to see themselves as persons in their own right, and they begin to make decisions on their own.

Indeed/Getty Images

Deciding what clothes to wear can be part of the initiative-versus-guilt stage for preschool-age children.

From a *child-care provider's* perspective

How would you relate Erikson's stages of trust versus mistrust, autonomy versus shame and doubt, and initiative versus guilt to the issue of secure attachment discussed in an earlier chapter?

Parents, such as Mary-Alice's mother, who react positively to this transformation toward independence can help their children resolve the opposing feelings that are characteristic of this period. By providing their children with opportunities to act self-reliantly, while still giving them direction and guidance, parents can support and encourage their children's initiative. In contrast, parents who discourage their children's efforts to seek independence may contribute to a sense of guilt that persists throughout their lives as well as affects their self-concept, which begins to develop during this period.

Self-Concept in the Preschool Years: Thinking About the Self

LO 8.2 Explain how preschool-age children develop a concept of themselves.

If you ask preschool-age children to specify what makes them different from other kids, they readily respond with answers like "I'm a good runner" or "I like to color" or "I'm a big girl." Such answers relate to **self-concept**—their identity, or their set of beliefs about what they are like as individuals (Brown, 1998; Marsh, Ellis, & Craven, 2002; Bhargava, 2014; Crampton & Hall, 2017).

self-concept
a person's identity, or set of beliefs about what one is like as an individual

The statements that describe children's self-concepts are not necessarily accurate. In fact, preschool children typically overestimate their skills and knowledge across all domains of expertise. Consequently, their view of the future is quite rosy: They expect to win the next game they play, to beat all opponents in an upcoming race, to write great stories when they grow up. Even when they have just experienced failure at a task, they are likely to expect to do well in the future. This optimistic view is held, in part, because they have not yet started to compare themselves and their performance against others. Their inaccuracy is also helpful, freeing them to take chances and try new activities (Verschueren, Doumen, & Buyse, 2012; Ehm, Lindberg, & Hasselhorn, 2013; Jia, Lang, & Schoppe-Sullivan, 2016).

Preschool-age children's view of themselves also reflects the way their particular culture considers the self. For example, many Asian societies tend to have a **collectivistic orientation**, promoting the notion of interdependence. People in such cultures tend to regard themselves as parts of a larger social network in which they are interconnected with and responsible to others. In contrast, children in Western cultures are more likely to develop a view of the self reflecting an **individualistic orientation** that emphasizes personal identity and the uniqueness of the individual. They are more apt to see themselves as self-contained and autonomous, in competition with others for scarce resources. Consequently, children in Western cultures are more likely to focus on what sets them apart from others—what makes them special.

collectivistic orientation
a philosophy that promotes the notion of interdependence

individualistic orientation
a philosophy that emphasizes personal identity and the uniqueness of the individual

Such views pervade a culture, sometimes in subtle ways. For instance, one well-known saying in Western cultures states that "the squeaky wheel gets the grease." Preschoolers who are exposed to this perspective are encouraged to gain the attention of others by standing out and making their needs known. In contrast, children in Asian cultures are exposed to a different perspective; they are told that "the nail that stands out gets pounded down." This perspective suggests to preschoolers that they should attempt to blend in and refrain from making themselves distinctive (Lehman, Chiu, & Schaller, 2004; Wang, 2006; Akyil et al., 2016).

Racial, Ethnic, and Gender Awareness

LO 8.3 Explain how preschool-age children develop a sense of racial identity and gender.

During the preschool period, children's sense of who they are becomes more refined. Two particularly important aspects of self are race and gender.

RACIAL IDENTITY: DEVELOPING SLOWLY. Preschoolers' developing self-concepts can be affected by their culture's attitudes toward various racial and ethnic groups. As we'll see in the *Developmental Diversity and Your Life* feature, preschoolers' awareness of their ethnic or racial identity develops slowly and is subtly influenced by the attitudes of the people, schools, and other cultural institutions with which they come into contact in their community.

Developmental Diversity and Your Life

Developing Racial, Ethnic, and Socioeconomic Awareness

The preschool years mark an important turning point for children. Their answer to the question "Who am I?" begins to take into account their racial and ethnic identity.

For most preschool-age children, racial awareness is already present, as we discussed in prior chapters. Certainly, even infants are able to distinguish different skin colors; their perceptual abilities allow for such color distinctions quite early in life. However, it is only later that children begin to attribute meaning to different racial characteristics.

By the time they are 3 or 4 years old, preschool-age children notice differences among people based on skin color, and they begin to identify themselves as a member of a particular group, such as "Hispanic" or "black." Although early in the preschool years they do not realize that ethnicity and race are enduring features of who they are, later they begin to develop an understanding of the significance that society gives to ethnic and racial membership (Quintana et al., 2008; Guerrero, Enseco, & Lam, 2011; Setoh et al., 2017).

Some preschoolers have mixed feelings about their racial and ethnic identity. Some experience **race dissonance**, the phenomenon in which minority children indicate preferences for majority values or people. For instance, some studies find that as many as 90 percent of African American children, when asked about their reactions to drawings of black and white children, react more negatively to the drawings of black children than to those of white children. However, these negative reactions did not translate into lower self-esteem for the African American subjects. Instead, their preferences appear to be a result of the powerful influence of the dominant white culture, rather than a disparagement of their own racial characteristics (Holland, 1994; Quintana, 2007).

Ethnic identity emerges somewhat later than racial identity because ethnicity is usually less conspicuous than race. For instance, in one study of Mexican American ethnic awareness, preschoolers displayed only a limited knowledge of their ethnic identity. However, as they became older, they grew more aware of the significance of their ethnicity. Preschoolers who were bilingual, speaking both Spanish and English, were most apt to be aware of their ethnic identity. (Bernal, 1994; Quintana et al., 2006; Grey & Yates, 2014; Mesinas & Perez, 2016).

Furthermore, racial socialization is a particular issue for children who are adopted into families in which the parents and/or other siblings are of different races and ethnicities. Some researchers suggest that children in transracial families may hold more egalitarian attitudes regarding race (Langrehr, Thomas, & Morgan, 2016).

Preschool children are also sensitive to differences in socioeconomic status. Although they don't understand the abstract concepts of socioeconomic status, they can articulate a difference between those who are "rich" and those who are "poor" (Bienvenu & Ramsey, 2006; Goodman et al., 2007).

race dissonance
the phenomenon in which minority children indicate preferences for majority values or people

GENDER IDENTITY: DEVELOPING FEMALENESS AND MALENESS

Boys' awards: Very Best Thinker, Most Eager Learner, Most Imaginative, Most Enthusiastic, Most Scientific, Best Friend, Mr. Personality, Hardest Worker, Best Sense of Humor.

Girls' awards: All-Around Sweetheart, Sweetest Personality, Cutest Personality, Best Sharer, Best Artist, Biggest Heart, Best Manners, Best Helper, Most Creative.

What's wrong with this picture? To one parent, whose daughter received one of the girls' awards during a kindergarten graduation ceremony, quite a bit. While the girls were getting pats on the back for their pleasing personalities, the boys were receiving awards for their intellectual and analytic skills (Deveny, 1994).

Such a situation is not rare: Girls and boys often live in very different worlds. Differences in the ways males and females are treated begin at birth, continue during the preschool years, and—as we'll see later—extend into adolescence and beyond (Bornstein et al., 2008; Brinkman et al., 2014).

Gender, the sense of being male or female, is well established by the time children reach the preschool years. (As we first noted in Chapter 6, "gender" and "sex" do not mean the same thing. *Sex* typically refers to sexual anatomy and sexual behavior, whereas *gender* refers to the perception of maleness or femaleness related to membership in a given society.) By age 2, children consistently label themselves and those around them as male or female (Raag, 2003; Campbell, Shirley, & Candy, 2004; Dinella, Weisgram, & Fulcher, 2017).

Sergiyn/Fotolia

Cantor Pannatto/Fotolia

During the preschool period, differences in play according to gender become more pronounced. In addition, boys tend to play with boys, and girls with girls.

One way gender shows up is in play. Preschool boys spend more time than girls in rough-and-tumble play, while preschool girls spend more time than boys in organized games and role-playing. Rough-and-tumble play is important because it promotes the development of the prefrontal cortex and helps teach preschoolers to regulate their emotions (Kestly, 2014).

During this time boys begin to play more with boys, and girls play more with girls, a trend that increases during middle childhood. Girls begin to prefer same-sex playmates a little earlier than boys. They first have a clear preference for interacting with other girls at age 2, while boys don't show much preference for same-sex playmates until age 3 (Martin & Fabes, 2001; Raag, 2003).

Such same-sex preferences appear in many cultures. For instance, studies of kindergartners in mainland China show no examples of mixed-gender play. Similarly, gender "outweighs" ethnic variables when it comes to play: A Hispanic boy would rather play with a white boy than with a Hispanic girl (Whiting & Edwards, 1988; Aydt & Corsaro, 2003).

Preschool-age children often have very strict ideas about how boys and girls are supposed to act. Their expectations about gender-appropriate behavior are even more gender-stereotyped than those of adults and may be less flexible during the preschool years than at any other point in the life span. Beliefs in gender stereotypes become increasingly pronounced up to age 5, and although they become somewhat less rigid by age 7, they do not disappear. In fact, the gender stereotypes held by preschoolers resemble those held by traditional adults in society (Halim, Ruble, & Tamis-LeMonda, 2013; Halim et al., 2014; Emilson, Folkesson, & Lindberg, 2016).

From *a child-care provider's* perspective

If a girl in a preschool child care setting loudly tells a boy that he can't play with the dolls in the play area because he's a boy, what is the best way to handle the situation?

And what is the nature of preschoolers' gender expectations? Like adults, preschoolers expect that males are more apt to have traits involving competence, independence, forcefulness, and competitiveness. In contrast, females are viewed as more likely to have traits such as warmth, expressiveness, nurturance, and submissiveness. Although these are *expectations*, and they say nothing about the way that men and women actually behave, such expectations provide the lens through which preschool-age children view the world and thus affect their behavior as well as the way they interact with peers and adults (Blakemore, 2003; Gelman, Taylor, & Nguyen, 2004; Martin & Dinella, 2012).

The prevalence and strength of preschoolers' gender expectations, and differences in behavior between boys and girls, have proven puzzling. Why should gender play such a powerful role during the preschool years (as well as during the rest of the life span)? Developmentalists have proposed several explanations, including the biological and psychoanalytic perspectives.

BIOLOGICAL PERSPECTIVES ON GENDER. Since gender relates to the sense of being male or female, and sex refers to the physical characteristics that differentiate males and females, it would hardly be surprising to find that the biological characteristics associated with sex might themselves lead to gender differences. This has been shown to be true.

Hormones are one sex-related biological characteristic that have been found to affect gender-based behaviors. Girls exposed to unusually high levels of *androgens* (male hormones) prenatally are more likely to display behaviors associated with male stereotypes than are their sisters who were not exposed to androgens (Knickmeyer & Baron-Cohen, 2006; Burton et al., 2009; Mathews et al., 2009).

Androgen-exposed girls preferred boys as playmates and spent more time than other girls playing with toys associated with the male role, such as cars and trucks. Similarly, boys exposed prenatally to atypically high levels of female hormones are apt to display more behaviors that are stereotypically female than is usual (Servin et al., 2003; Knickmeyer & Baron-Cohen, 2006).

Moreover, some research suggests that biological differences exist in the structure of female and male brains. For instance, part of the *corpus callosum*, the bundle of nerves that connects the hemispheres of the brain, is proportionally larger in women than in men. To some theoreticians, evidence such as this suggests that gender differences may be produced by biological factors like hormones (Westerhausen et al., 2004).

Before accepting such contentions, however, it is important to note that alternative explanations abound. For example, it may be that the corpus callosum is proportionally larger in women as a result of certain kinds of experiences that influence brain growth in particular ways. We know that girls are spoken to more than boys as infants, which might produce certain kinds of brain development. If this is true, environmental experience produces biological change—and not the other way around.

Other developmentalists see gender differences as serving the biological goal of survival of the species through reproduction. Basing their work on an evolutionary approach, these theorists suggest that our male ancestors who showed more stereotypically masculine qualities, such as forcefulness and competitiveness, may have been able to attract females who were able to provide them with hardy offspring. Females who excelled at stereotypically feminine tasks, such as nurturing, may have been valuable partners because they could increase the likelihood that children would survive the dangers of childhood (Browne, 2006; Ellis, 2006).

As in other domains that involve the interaction of inherited biological characteristics and environmental influences, it is difficult to attribute behavioral characteristics unambiguously to biological factors. Because of this problem, we must consider other explanations for gender differences.

PSYCHOANALYTIC PERSPECTIVES. You may recall from Chapter 1 that Sigmund Freud's psychoanalytic theory suggests that we move through a series of stages related to biological urges. To Freud, the preschool years encompass the *phallic stage*, in which the focus of a child's pleasure relates to genital sexuality.

Freud argued that the end of the phallic stage is marked by an important turning point in development: the Oedipal conflict. According to Freud, the *Oedipal conflict* occurs at around age 5, when the anatomical differences between males and females become particularly evident. Boys begin to develop sexual interests in their mothers, viewing their fathers as rivals.

As a consequence, boys conceive a desire to kill their fathers—just as Oedipus did in the ancient Greek tragedy. However, because they view their fathers as all-powerful, boys develop a fear of retaliation, which takes the form of *castration anxiety*. In order to overcome this fear, boys repress their desires for their mothers and instead begin to identify with their fathers, attempting to be as similar to them as possible. **Identification** is the process through which children attempt to be similar to their same-sex parent, incorporating the parent's attitudes and values.

identification
the process through which children attempt to be similar to their same-sex parent, incorporating the parent's attitudes and values

Girls, according to Freud, go through a different process. They begin to feel sexual attraction toward their fathers and experience *penis envy*—a view that not unexpectedly has led to accusations that Freud viewed women as inferior to men. In order to resolve their penis envy, girls ultimately identify with their mothers, attempting to be as similar to them as possible.

In the cases of both boys and girls, the ultimate result of identifying with the same-sex parent is that children adopt their parents' gender attitudes and values. In this way, says Freud, society's expectations about the ways females and males "ought" to behave are perpetuated into new generations.

You may find it difficult to accept Freud's elaborate explanation of gender differences. So do most developmentalists, who believe that gender development is best explained by other mechanisms. In part, they base their criticisms of Freud on the lack of scientific support for his theories. For example, children learn gender stereotypes much earlier than age 5. Furthermore, this learning occurs even in single-parent households. However, some aspects of psychoanalytic theory have been supported, such as findings indicating that preschool-age children whose same-sex parents support sex-stereotyped behavior tend to demonstrate that behavior also. Still, far simpler processes can account for this phenomenon, and many developmentalists have searched for explanations of gender differences other than Freud's (Martin & Ruble, 2004).

SOCIAL LEARNING APPROACHES. As their name implies, social learning approaches see children as learning gender-related behavior and expectations by observing others. Children watch the behavior of their parents, teachers, siblings, and even peers. A little boy sees the glory of a major league baseball player and becomes interested in sports. A little girl watches her high school neighbor practicing cheerleading moves and begins to try them herself. The observation of the rewards that these others attain for acting in a gender-appropriate manner leads the children to conform to such behavior themselves (Rust et al., 2000).

Books and the media, and in particular television and video games, also play a role in perpetuating traditional views of gender-related behavior from which preschoolers may learn. Analyses of the most popular television shows, for example, find that male characters outnumber female characters by two to one. Furthermore, females are more apt to appear with males, whereas female–female relationships are relatively uncommon (Calvert et al., 2003; Chapman, 2016).

Television also presents men and women in traditional gender roles. Television shows typically define female characters in terms of their relationships with males. Females are more likely to appear as victims than are males. They are less likely to be presented as productive or as decision makers and more likely to be portrayed as characters interested in romance, their homes, and their families. Such models, according to social learning theory, are apt to have a powerful influence on preschoolers' definitions of appropriate behavior (Nassif & Gunter, 2008; Prieler et al., 2011; Matthes, Prieler, & Adam, 2016).

In some cases, learning of social roles does not involve models but occurs more directly. For example, many of us may have heard preschool-age children being told by their parents to act like a "little lady" or "man." What this generally means is that girls should behave politely and courteously or that boys should be tough and stoic—traits associated with society's traditional stereotypes of women and men. Such direct training sends a clear message about the behavior expected of a preschool-age child (Leaper, 2002; Williams, Sheridan, & Sandberg, 2014).

According to social learning approaches, children learn gender-related behavior and expectations from their observations of others.

gender identity
the perception of oneself as male or female

gender schema
a cognitive framework that organizes information relevant to gender

COGNITIVE APPROACHES. In the view of some theorists, one aspect of preschoolers' desire to form a clear sense of identity is the wish to establish a **gender identity**, a perception of themselves as male or female. To do this, they develop a **gender schema**, a cognitive framework that organizes information relevant to gender (Martin & Ruble, 2004; Signorella & Frieze, 2008; Halim et al., 2013).

Gender schemas are developed early in life and serve as a lens through which preschoolers view the world. For instance, preschoolers use their increasing cognitive abilities to develop "rules" about what is appropriate and what is inappropriate for males and females. Thus, some girls decide that wearing pants is inappropriate for a female and apply the rule so rigidly that they refuse to wear anything but dresses. Or a preschool boy may reason that because makeup is typically worn by females, it is inappropriate for him to wear makeup even when he is in a preschool play and all the other boys and girls are wearing it (Frawley, 2008).

According to *cognitive-developmental theory*, proposed by Lawrence Kohlberg, this rigidity is in part a reflection of preschoolers' understanding of gender (Kohlberg, 1966). Rigid gender schemas are influenced by the preschooler's erroneous beliefs about sex differences. Specifically, young preschoolers believe that sex differences are based not on biological factors but on differences in appearance or behavior. Employing this view of the world, a girl may reason that she can be a father when she grows up, or a boy may think he could turn into a girl if he put on a dress and tied his hair in a ponytail. However, by the time they reach age 4 or 5, children develop an understanding of **gender constancy**, the awareness that people are permanently males or females, depending on fixed, unchangeable biological factors.

gender constancy
the belief that people are permanently males or females, depending on fixed, unchangeable biological factors

For some children, gender identification is particularly challenging. *Transgender children* believe that they are trapped in the body of the other gender. There are some reports of transgender children expressing to their parents that they believe their gender identity is different from that assigned at birth as early as they learn to talk, starting at 18 to 24 months. But there is relatively little research on the issue, and little guidance exists for parents about how to deal with preschoolers who express the conviction that they identify with the other gender (Prince-Embury & Saklofske, 2014; Fast & Olson, 2017).

Interestingly, research on typical children's growing understanding of gender constancy during the preschool period indicates that it has no particular effect on

Table 8-1 Four Approaches to Gender Development

Perspective	Key Concepts	Applying the Concepts to Preschool Children
Biological	Our ancestors who behaved in ways that are now stereotypically feminine or masculine may have been more successful in reproducing. Brain differences may lead to gender differences.	Girls may be genetically "programmed" by evolution to be more expressive and nurturing, while boys are "programmed" to be more competitive and forceful. Abnormal hormone exposure before birth has been linked to both boys and girls behaving in ways typically expected of the other gender.
Psychoanalytic	Gender development is the result of identification with the same-sex parent, achieved by moving through a series of stages related to biological urges.	Girls and boys whose parents of the same sex behave in stereotypically masculine or feminine ways are likely to do so, too, perhaps because they identify with those parents.
Social Learning	Children learn gender-related behavior and expectations from their observation of others' behavior.	Children notice that other children and adults are rewarded for behaving in ways that conform to standard gender stereotypes—and sometimes punished for violating those stereotypes.
Cognitive	Through the use of gender schemas, developed early in life, preschoolers form a lens through which they view the world. They use their increasing cognitive abilities to develop "rules" about what is appropriate for males and females.	Preschoolers are more rigid in their rules about proper gender behavior than people at other ages, perhaps because they have just developed gender schemas that don't yet permit much variation from stereotypical expectations.

gender-related behavior. In fact, the appearance of gender schemas occurs well before children understand gender constancy. Even young preschool-age children assume that certain behaviors are appropriate—and that others are not—on the basis of stereotypic views of gender (Ruble et al., 2007; Karniol, 2009; Halim et al., 2014).

Is it possible to avoid viewing the world in terms of gender schemas? According to Sandra Bem (1987), one way is to encourage children to be **androgynous**, a state in which gender roles encompass characteristics thought typical of both sexes. For instance, parents and caregivers can encourage preschool children to see males as assertive (typically viewed as a male-appropriate trait) but at the same time warm and tender (usually viewed as female-appropriate traits). Similarly, girls might be encouraged to see the female role as both empathetic and tender (typically seen as female-appropriate traits) and competitive, assertive, and independent (typical male-appropriate traits).

androgynous
a state in which gender roles encompass characteristics thought typical of both sexes

Like the other approaches to gender development (summarized in Table 8-1), the cognitive perspective does not imply that differences between the two sexes are in any way improper or inappropriate. Instead, it suggests that preschoolers should be taught to treat others as individuals. Furthermore, preschoolers need to learn the importance of fulfilling their own talents, acting as individuals and not as representatives of a particular gender.

Module 8.1 Review

LO 8.1 Describe the major developmental challenges that preschool-age children face.

According to Erik Erikson's psychosocial development theory, preschool-age children move from the autonomy-versus-shame-and-doubt stage to the initiative-versus-guilt stage.

LO 8.2 Explain how preschool-age children develop a concept of themselves.

During the preschool years, children develop their self-concepts, beliefs about themselves that they derive from their own perceptions, their parents' behaviors, and society.

LO 8.3 Explain how preschool-age children develop a sense of racial identity and gender.

Racial and ethnic awareness begins to form in the preschool years. Gender awareness also develops in the preschool years. Explanations of this phenomenon include biological, psychoanalytical, learning, and cognitive approaches.

Journal Writing Prompt

Applying Lifespan Development: What sorts of activities might you suggest a preschool boy or girl undertake to encourage him or her to adopt a less stereotypical gender schema?

Friends and Family: Preschoolers' Social Lives

When Juan was 3, he had his first best friend, Emilio. Juan and Emilio, who lived in the same apartment building in San Jose, were inseparable. They played incessantly with toy cars, racing them up and down the apartment hallways until some of the neighbors began to complain about the noise. They pretended to read to one another, and sometimes they slept over at each other's home—a big step for a 3-year-old. Neither boy seemed more joyful than when he was with his "best friend"—the term each used of the other.

An infant's family can provide nearly all the social contact he or she needs. As preschoolers, however, many children, like Juan and Emilio, begin to discover the joys of friendship with their peers. Although they may expand their social circles considerably, parents and family nevertheless remain very influential in the lives of preschoolers. Let's take a look at both of these sides of preschoolers' social development: friends and family.

The Development of Friendships

LO 8.4 Describe the sorts of social relationships that preschool-age children engage in.

Before age 3, most social activity involves simply being in the same place at the same time, without real social interaction. However, at around age 3, children begin to develop real friendships like Juan and Emilio's as peers come to be seen as individuals who hold some special qualities and rewards. While preschoolers' relations with adults reflect children's needs for care, protection, and direction, their relations with peers are based more on the desire for companionship, play, and fun.

As preschoolers age, their ideas about friendship gradually evolve. They come to view friendship as a continuing state, a stable relationship that not only takes place in the immediate moment but also offers the promise of future activity (Proulx & Poulin, 2013; Paulus & Moore, 2014; Paulus, 2016).

The quality and kinds of interactions children have with friends change during the preschool period. For 3-year-olds, the focus of friendship is the enjoyment of carrying out shared activities—doing things together and playing jointly, as when Juan and Emilio played with their toy cars in the hallway. Older preschoolers, however, pay more attention to abstract concepts, such as trust, support, and shared interests (Park, Lay, & Ramsay, 1993). Throughout the preschool years, playing together remains an important part of all friendships. Like friendships, these play patterns change during the preschool years.

functional play
play that involves simple, repetitive activities typical of 3-year-olds

constructive play
play in which children manipulate objects to produce or build something

Playing by the Rules: The Work of Play

LO 8.5 Explain how and why preschool-age children play.

In Rosie Graiff's class of 3-year-olds, Minnie bounces her doll's feet on the table as she sings softly to herself. Ben pushes his toy car across the floor, making motor noises. Sarah chases Abdul around and around the perimeter of the room.

Play is more than what children of preschool age do to pass the time. Instead, play helps preschoolers develop socially, cognitively, and physically. It even performs an important role in brain growth and development (McGinnis, 2012; Holmes & Romeo, 2013; Fleer, 2017).

Jamie Grill/Blend Images/Age Fotostock

As preschoolers get older, their conception of friendship evolves and the quality of their interactions changes.

CATEGORIZING PLAY. At the beginning of the preschool years, children engage in **functional play**—simple, repetitive activities typical of 3-year-olds. Functional play may involve objects, such as dolls or cars, or repetitive muscular movements, such as skipping, jumping, or rolling and unrolling a piece of clay. Functional play, then, involves doing something for the sake of being active rather than with the aim of creating some end product (Bober, Humphry, & Carswell, 2001; Kantrowitz & Evans, 2004).

As children get older, functional play declines. By the time they are 4, children become involved in a more sophisticated form of play. In **constructive play** children manipulate objects to produce or build something. A child who builds a house out of Legos or puts a puzzle together is involved in constructive play: He or she has an ultimate goal—to produce something. Such play is not necessarily aimed at creating something novel, since children may repeatedly build a house of blocks, let it fall into disarray, and then rebuild it.

Constructive play gives children a chance to test their developing physical and cognitive skills and to practice their fine muscle movements. They gain experience in solving problems about the ways and the sequences in which things fit together. They also learn to cooperate with others—a development we observe as the social nature of play shifts during the preschool period. Consequently, it's important for adults who care for preschoolers to provide a variety of toys that allow for both functional and constructive play (Shi, 2003; Love & Burns, 2006; Oostermeijer, Boonen, & Jolles, 2014).

FatCamera/Getty Images

In parallel play, children play with similar toys, in a similar manner, but don't necessarily interact with one another.

THE SOCIAL ASPECTS OF PLAY. If two preschoolers are sitting at a table side by side, each putting a different puzzle together, are they engaged jointly in play?

According to pioneering work done by Mildred Parten (1932), the answer is "yes." She suggests that these preschoolers are engaged in **parallel play**, in which children play with similar toys, in a similar manner, but do not interact with each other. Parallel play is typical for children during the early preschool years. Preschoolers also engage in another form of play, a highly passive one: onlooker play. In **onlooker play**, children simply watch others at play but do not actually participate themselves. They may look on silently, or they may make comments of encouragement or advice.

As they get older, however, preschool-age children engage in more sophisticated forms of social play that involve a greater degree of interaction. In **associative play**, two or more children actually interact with one another by sharing or borrowing toys or materials, although they do not do the same thing. In **cooperative play**, children genuinely play with one another, taking turns, playing games, or devising contests.

Usually associative and cooperative play do not typically become common until children reach the end of the preschool years. But children who have had substantial preschool experience are more apt to engage in more social forms of behavior, such as associative and cooperative play, earlier in the preschool years than those with less experience (Brownell, Ramani, & Zerwas, 2006; Dyer & Moneta, 2006). (The various types of play are summarized in Table 8-2.)

Solitary and onlooker play continue in the later stages of the preschool period. There are simply times when children prefer to play by themselves. And when newcomers join a group, one strategy—often a successful strategy—for becoming part of the group is to engage in onlooker play, waiting for an opportunity to join the play more actively (Lindsey & Colwell, 2003).

The nature of pretend, or make-believe, play also changes during the preschool period. In some ways, pretend play becomes increasingly *un*realistic—and even more imaginative—as preschoolers change from using only realistic objects to using less concrete ones. Thus, at the start of the preschool period, children may pretend to listen to a radio only if they actually have a plastic radio that looks realistic. Later, however, they are more likely to use an entirely different object, such as a cardboard box, as a pretend radio (Parsons & Howe, 2013; Russ, 2014; Thibodeau et al., 2016).

Russian developmentalist Lev Vygotsky, whom we discussed in Chapter 7, argued that pretend play, particularly if it involves social play, is an important means for expanding preschool-age children's cognitive skills. Through make-believe play, children are able to "practice" activities (such as pretending to use a computer) that are a part of their particular culture and broaden their understanding of the way the world functions.

Furthermore, play helps the brain develop, as we discuss in *From Research to Practice*.

parallel play
action in which children play with similar toys, in a similar manner, but do not interact with each other

onlooker play
action in which children simply watch others at play, but do not actually participate themselves

associative play
play in which two or more children actually interact with one another by sharing or borrowing toys or materials, although they do not do the same thing

cooperative play
play in which children genuinely interact with one another, taking turns, playing games, or devising contests

Table 8-2 Preschoolers' Play

Type of Play	Description	Examples
General Categories		
Functional play	Simple, repetitive activities typical of 3-year-olds. May involve objects or repetitive muscular movements.	Moving dolls or cars repetitively. Skipping, jumping, rolling or unrolling a piece of clay.
Constructive play	More sophisticated play in which children manipulate objects to produce or build something. Developed by age 4, constructive play lets children test physical and cognitive skills and practice fine muscle movements.	Building a dollhouse or car garage out of Legos, putting together a puzzle, making an animal out of clay.
Social Aspects of Play (Parten's Categories)		
Parallel play	Children use similar toys in a similar manner at the same time, but do not interact with each other. Typical of children during the early preschool years.	Children sitting side by side, each playing with their own toy car, putting together their own puzzle, or making an individual clay animal.
Onlooker play	Children simply watch others at play, but do not actually participate. They may look on silently or they may make comments of encouragement or advice. Common among preschoolers and can be helpful when a child wishes to join a group already at play.	One child watches as a group of others plays with dolls, cars, or clay; builds with Legos; or works on a puzzle together.
Associative play	Two or more children interact, sharing or borrowing toys or materials, although they do not do the same thing.	Two children, each building their own Lego garage, may trade bricks back and forth.
Cooperative play	Children genuinely play with one another, taking turns, playing games, or devising contests.	A group of children working on a puzzle may take turns fitting in the pieces. Children playing with dolls or cars may take turns making the dolls talk or may agree on rules to race the cars.

From Research to Practice

Does Play Promote Brain Development?

As Janet took a lump of soft clay and pounded it into the shape of a long, curly snake, Franklin moved a toy truck across a tabletop so quickly that it flew off the side. He laughed, quickly picked it up off the floor, and repeatedly made it fly off the table while his friend Jason watched and giggled. At another table, Helena pretended to read a book, quietly talking to herself as she flipped from one page to another

A growing amount of research suggests that play like this, found in preschool classrooms around the world, goes well beyond simple fun and games. In fact, play not only leads to increases in self-control and the ability to plan ahead, but it may even promote the development of the brain.

For example, play helps children learn self-regulation skills by teaching them the importance of controlling their impulses. By playing games in which they must plan out strategies, they learn the importance of planning ahead and regulating their emotions. Furthermore, play helps children develop verbal self-regulation (Diamond & Amso, 2008; Savina, 2014; Kroll, 2017).

Even more intriguing, some researchers believe that play helps the brain to develop and become more sophisticated. Based on experiments with non-humans, neuroscientist Sergio Pellis has found not only that certain sorts of damage to the brain leads to abnormal sorts of play, but that depriving animals of the ability to play affects the course of brain development (Bergen, Davis, & Abbitt, 2016; Himmler et al., 2016).

For instance, in one experiment, Pellis and his colleagues observed rats under two different conditions. In the control condition, a juvenile target rat was housed with three other young females, allowing them the opportunity to engage in the equivalent of rat play. In the experimental condition, the young target rats were housed with three adult females. Although young rats caged with adults don't have the opportunity to play, they do encounter social experiences with the adults, who will groom and touch them. When Pellis examined the brains of the rats, he found that the play-deprived rats showed deficiencies in the development of their prefrontal cortex (Pellis & Pellis, 2007; Bell, Pellis, & Kolb, 2009; Pellis & Burghardt, 2017).

Although it's a big leap from rat play to toddler play, the results of the study do suggest the significance of play in promoting brain and cognitive development. Ultimately, play may be one of the engines that fuels the intellectual development of preschoolers.

Shared Writing Prompt

Based on these research findings, what would you say to educators who reduce the amount of recess for budgetary reasons or to include more time for academic subjects?

Culture also affects children's styles of play. For example, Korean American children engage in a higher proportion of parallel play than their Anglo-American counterparts, while Anglo-American preschoolers are involved in more pretend play (see Figure 8-1; Farver, Kim, & Lee-Shin, 1995; Farver & Lee-Shin, 2000; Bai, 2005).

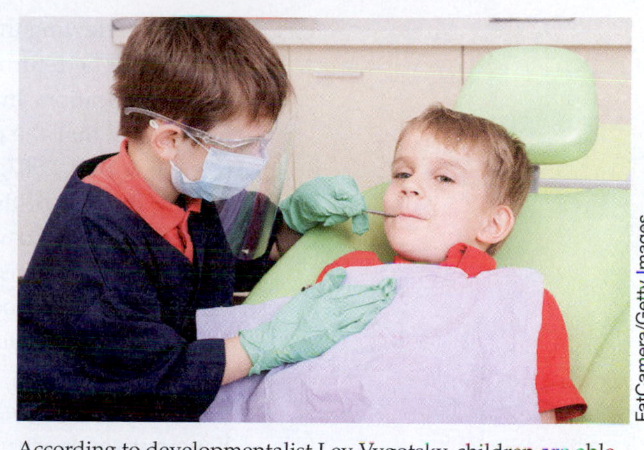

According to developmentalist Lev Vygotsky, children are able, through make-believe play, to practice activities that are part of their particular culture and broaden their understanding of the way the world functions.

Preschoolers' Theory of Mind: Understanding What Others Are Thinking

LO 8.6 Summarize how thinking changes in the preschool years.

One reason behind the changes in children's play is the continuing development of preschoolers' theory of mind. As we first discussed in Chapter 6, *theory of mind* refers to knowledge and beliefs about how the mind operates. Using their theory of mind, preschool children are able to come up with explanations for how *others* think and reasons for why they behave the way they do.

One of the main reasons for children's emerging play and social skills is that during the preschool years, children increasingly can see the world from others' perspectives. Even children as young as 2 are able to understand that others have emotions. By age 3 or 4, preschoolers can distinguish between something in their minds and physical actuality. For instance, 3-year-olds know that they can imagine something that is not physically present, such as a zebra, and that others can do the same. They can also pretend that something has happened and react as if it really had occurred, a skill that becomes part of their imaginative play. And they know that others have the same capability (Andrews, Halford, & Bunch, 2003; Wellman, 2012; Wu & Su, 2014).

Preschool-age children also become more insightful regarding the motives and reasons behind people's behavior. They begin to understand that their mother is angry because she was late for an appointment, even if they themselves haven't seen her be late. Furthermore, by age 4, preschool-age children's understanding that people can be fooled and mistaken by physical reality (such as magic tricks involving sleight of hand) becomes surprisingly sophisticated. This increase in understanding helps children become more socially skilled as they gain insight into what others are thinking (Fitzgerald & White, 2002; Eisbach, 2004; Fernández, 2013).

There are limits, however, to 3-year-olds' theory of mind. Although they understand the concept of "pretend" by age 3, children's understanding of "belief" is still not complete. The difficulty experienced by 3-year-olds in comprehending "belief" is illustrated by their performance on the *false belief* task. In the false belief task, preschoolers are shown a doll named Maxi who places chocolate in a cabinet and then leaves. After Maxi is gone, though, his mother moves the chocolate somewhere else.

Figure 8-1 Comparing Play Complexity

An examination of Korean American and Anglo-American preschoolers' play complexity finds clear differences in patterns of play. Can you think of any explanation for this finding?

(**Source:** Based on Farver, Kim, & Lee-Shin, 1995.)

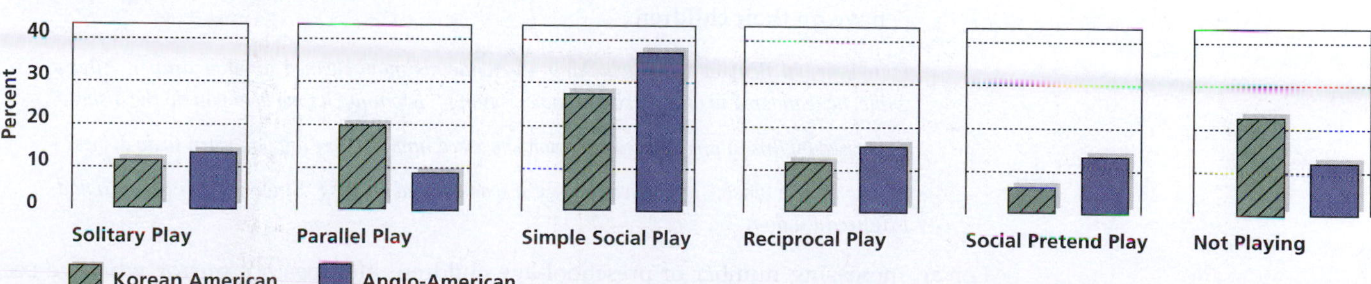

After viewing these events, a preschooler is asked where Maxi will look for the chocolate when he returns. Three-year-olds answer (erroneously) that Maxi will look for it in the new location. In contrast, 4-year-olds correctly realize that Maxi has the erroneous false belief that the chocolate is still in the cabinet, and that's where he will look for it (Brown & Bull, 2007; Lecce et al., 2014; Ornaghi, Pepe, & Grazzini, 2016).

By the end of the preschool years, most children easily solve false belief problems. However, children with autism spectrum disorder have considerable difficulties with false belief problems throughout their lifetimes. *Autism spectrum disorder* is a psychological disorder that produces significant language and emotional difficulties.

Children with autism spectrum disorder find it particularly difficult to relate to others, in part because they find it difficult to understand what others are thinking. According to the Centers for Disease Control and Prevention, about 1 in 68 children (primarily males) have autism spectrum disorder, which is characterized by a lack of connection to other people, even parents, and an avoidance of interpersonal situations. Individuals with autism spectrum disorder are bewildered by false belief problems no matter how old they are (Begeer et al., 2012; Carey, 2012; Miller, 2012; Peterson, 2014).

THE EMERGENCE OF THEORY OF MIND. What factors are involved in the emergence of theory of mind? Certainly, brain maturation is an important factor. As myelination within the frontal lobes becomes more pronounced, preschoolers develop more emotional capacity involving self-awareness. In addition, hormonal changes seem to be related to emotions that are more evaluative in nature (Davidson, 2003; Schore, 2003; Sabbagh et al., 2009).

Developing language skills are also related to the increasing sophistication of children's theory of mind. In particular, the ability to understand the meaning of words such as *think* and *know* is important in helping preschool-age children understand the mental lives of others (Farrant, Fletcher, & Maybery, 2006; Farrar et al., 2009; LaBounty et al., 2017).

As much as the child's developing theory of mind promotes more engaged social interactions and play, the process is reciprocal: Opportunities for social interaction and make-believe play are also critical in promoting the development of theory of mind. For example, preschool-age children with older siblings (who provide high levels of social interaction) have more sophisticated theories of mind than those without older siblings. In addition, abused children show delays in their ability to correctly answer the false belief task, in part due to reduced experience with normal social interaction (Nelson, Adamson, & Bakeman, 2008; Müller et al., 2012; O'Reilly & Peterson, 2015).

Cultural factors also play an important role in the development of theory of mind and the interpretations that children bring to bear on others' actions. For example, children in more industrialized Western cultures may be more likely to see others' behavior as due to the kind of people they are, a function of the people's personal traits and characteristics ("She won the race because she is really fast"). In contrast, children in non-Western cultures may see others' behavior as produced by forces that are less under their personal control ("She won the race because she was lucky") (Tardif, Wellman, & Cheung, 2004; Wellman et al., 2006; Liu et al., 2008).

Preschoolers' Family Lives

LO 8.7 Describe the types of disciplinary styles parents employ and the effects they have on their children.

Four-year-old Benjamin was watching TV while his mom cleaned up after dinner. After a while, he wandered in and grabbed a towel, saying, "Mommy, let me help you do the dishes."

Surprised by this unprecedented behavior, she asked him, "Where did you learn to do dishes?"

"I saw it on a video," he replied, "Only it was the dad helping. Since we don't have a dad, I figured I'd do it."

For an increasing number of preschool-age children, life does not mirror what we see in reruns of old sitcoms. Many face the realities of an increasingly complicated world.

For instance, children are increasingly likely to live with only one parent. In 1960, less than 10 percent of all children under age 18 lived with one parent. Three decades later, a single parent heads a quarter of all families. There are also large racial disparities: Nearly half of all African American children and a quarter of Hispanic children live with a single parent, compared with 22 percent of white children (Grall, 2009).

Still, for most children the preschool years are not a time of upheaval and turmoil. Instead, the period encompasses a growing interaction with the world at large. As we've seen, for instance, preschoolers begin to develop genuine friendships with other children, in which close ties emerge. One central factor leading preschoolers to develop friendships comes when parents provide a warm, supportive home environment. Strong, positive relationships between parents and children encourage children's relationships with others. How do parents nurture that relationship? Consider the following:

While she thinks no one is looking, Maria goes into her brother Alejandro's bedroom, where he has been saving the last of his Halloween candy. Just as she takes his last Reese's Peanut Butter Cup, the children's mother walks into the room and immediately takes in the situation.

If you were Maria's mother, which of the following reactions seems most reasonable?

1. Tell Maria that she must go to her room and stay there for the rest of the day and that she is going to lose access to her favorite blanket, the one she sleeps with every night and during naps.
2. Mildly tell Maria that what she did was not such a good idea and she shouldn't do it in the future.
3. Explain why her brother Alejandro would be upset by her actions and tell her that she must go to her room for an hour as punishment.
4. Forget about it and let the children sort it out themselves.

Each of these four alternative responses represents one of the major parenting styles identified by Diana Baumrind and updated by Eleanor Maccoby and colleagues (Maccoby & Martin, 1983; Baumrind, 1980, 2005).

Authoritarian parents respond as in the first alternative. They are controlling, punitive, rigid, and cold. Their word is law, and they value strict, unquestioning obedience from their children. They also do not tolerate expressions of disagreement.

authoritarian parents
parents who are controlling, punitive, rigid, and cold, and whose word is law

Permissive parents, in contrast, provide lax and inconsistent feedback, as in the second alternative. They require little of their children, and they don't see themselves as holding much responsibility for how their children turn out. They place little or no limits or control on their children's behavior.

permissive parents
parents who provide lax and inconsistent feedback and require little of their children

Authoritative parents are firm, setting clear and consistent limits. Although they tend to be relatively strict, like authoritarian parents, they are loving and emotionally supportive. They also try to reason with their children, giving explanations for why they should behave in a particular way ("Alejandro is going to be upset"), and communicating the rationale for any punishment they may impose. Authoritative parents encourage their children to be independent.

authoritative parents
parents who are firm, setting clear and consistent limits, but who try to reason with their children, giving explanations for why they should behave in a particular way

Finally, **uninvolved parents** show virtually no interest in their children, displaying indifferent, rejecting behavior. They are detached emotionally and see their role as no more than feeding, clothing, and providing shelter for their child. In its most extreme form, uninvolved parenting results in *neglect*, a form of child abuse. (The four patterns are summarized in Table 8-3.)

uninvolved parents
parents who show almost no interest in their children and display indifferent, rejecting behavior

Does the particular style of discipline that parents use result in differences in children's behavior? The answer is very much yes (Cheah et al., 2009; Lin, Chiu, & Yeh, 2012; Flouri & Midouhas, 2017):

- Children of authoritarian parents tend to be withdrawn, showing relatively little sociability. They are not very friendly, often behaving uneasily around their peers. Girls who are raised by authoritarian parents are especially dependent on their parents, whereas boys are unusually hostile.

Table 8-3 Parenting Styles

How Demanding Parents Are of Children ▶	Demanding	Undemanding
How Responsive Parents Are to a Child ▼	**Authoritative**	**Permissive**
Highly Responsive	**Characteristics:** firm, setting clear and consistent limits **Relationship with Children:** Although they tend to be relatively strict, they are loving and supportive and encourage independence. They try to reason with their children, giving explanations for why they should behave in a particular way, and they communicate the rationale for punishments they impose.	**Characteristics:** lax and inconsistent feedback **Relationship with Children:** They require little of their children, and they don't see themselves as holding much responsibility for how their children turn out. They place little or no limits or control on their children's behavior.
	Authoritarian	**Uninvolved**
Low Responsive	**Characteristics:** controlling, punitive, rigid, cold **Relationship with Children:** Their word is law, and they value strict, unquestioning obedience from their children. They also do not tolerate expressions of disagreement.	**Characteristics:** displaying indifferent, rejecting behavior **Relationship with Children:** They are detached emotionally and see their role as only providing food, clothing, and shelter. In its extreme form, this parenting style results in neglect, a form of child abuse.

- Permissive parents have children who, in many ways, share the undesirable characteristics of children of authoritarian parents. Children with permissive parents tend to be dependent and moody, and they are low in social skills and self-control.
- Children of authoritative parents fare best. They generally are independent, friendly with their peers, self-assertive, and cooperative. They have strong motivation to achieve, and they are typically successful and likable. They regulate their own behavior effectively, both in terms of their relationships with others and emotional self-regulation. Some authoritative parents also display several characteristics that have come to be called *supportive parenting*, including parental warmth, proactive teaching, calm discussion during disciplinary episodes, and interest and involvement in children's activities. Children whose parents engage in such supportive parenting show better adjustment and are better protected from the consequences of later adversity they may encounter (Belluck, 2000; Kaufmann et al., 2000).
- Children whose parents show uninvolved parenting styles are the worst off. Their parents' lack of involvement disrupts their emotional development considerably, leading them to feel unloved and emotionally detached, and their physical and cognitive development is adversely affected as well.

Although such classification systems are useful ways of categorizing and describing parents' behavior, they are not a recipe for success. Parenting and growing up are more complicated than that! For instance, in a significant number of cases the children of authoritarian and permissive parents develop quite successfully. Furthermore, most parents are not entirely consistent: Although the authoritarian, permissive, authoritative, and uninvolved patterns describe general styles, sometimes parents switch from their dominant mode to one of the others. For instance, when a child darts into the street, even the most laid-back and permissive parent is likely to react in a harsh, authoritarian manner, laying down strict demands about safety. In such cases, authoritarian styles may be most effective (Eisenberg & Valiente, 2002; Gershoff, 2002).

Paul Catalin Pop/Alamy Stock Photo

Children with authoritarian parents tend to be withdrawn and unsociable. What are the consequences of parents who are too permissive? Too uninvolved?

CULTURAL DIFFERENCES IN CHILDREARING PRACTICES. It's important to keep in mind that the findings regarding childrearing styles we have been discussing are chiefly applicable to Western societies. The style of parenting that is most successful may depend quite heavily on the norms of a particular culture—and what parents in a particular culture are taught regarding appropriate childrearing practices (Yagmurlu & Sanson, 2009; Calzada et al., 2012; Dotti Sani & Treas, 2016).

For example, the Chinese concept of *chiao shun* suggests that parents should be strict, firm, and in tight control of their children's behavior. Parents are seen to have a duty to train their children to adhere to socially and culturally desirable standards of behavior, particularly those manifested in good school performance. Children's acceptance of such an approach to discipline is seen as a sign of parental respect (Chao, 1994; Lui & Rollock, 2013; Frewen et al., 2015).

Typically, parents in China are highly directive with their children, pushing them to excel and controlling their behavior to a considerably higher degree than parents do in Western countries. And it works: Children of Asian parents tend to be quite successful, particularly academically (Steinberg, Dornbusch, & Brown, 1992; Nelson et al., 2006; Kim et al., 2017).

In contrast, U.S. parents are generally advised to use authoritative methods and explicitly to avoid authoritarian measures. It is interesting to note that it wasn't always this way. Until World War II, the point of view that dominated the advice literature was authoritarian, apparently founded on Puritan religious influences that suggested that children had "original sin" or that they needed to have their wills broken (Smuts & Hagen, 1985).

Tom Wang/Fotolia

The style of parenting that is most effective depends on what parents in a particular culture are taught regarding appropriate childrearing practices.

For Hispanic parents, one central value relates to the concept of respect. Hispanic parents believe that children should listen to rules and should be obedient to authority figures (O'Connor et al., 2013).

In short, the childrearing practices that parents follow reflect cultural perspectives about the nature of children as well as about the appropriate role of parents and their support system. No single parenting pattern or style, then, is likely to be universally appropriate or invariably to produce successful children. For example, parents who are immigrants often hold different views of appropriate childrearing practices than natives in a country, and yet raise children who are quite successful (Wang, Pomerantz, & Chen, 2007; Pomerantz et al., 2011; Chen, Sun, & Yu, 2017).

Similarly, it is important to keep in mind that childrearing practices are not the sole influence on children's development. For example, sibling and peer influences play a significant role in children's development. Furthermore, children's behavior is in part produced by their unique genetic endowments, and their behavior can in turn shape parental behavior. In sum, parents' childrearing practices are just one of a rich array of environmental and genetic influences that affect children (Boivin et al., 2005; Loehlin, Neiderhiser, & Reiss, 2005; Rossi, 2014).

Child Abuse and Psychological Maltreatment: The Grim Side of Family Life

LO 8.8 List the factors that contribute to child abuse and neglect.

The figures are gloomy and disheartening: In the United States, at least five children are killed by their parents or caretakers every day, and 140,000 others are physically injured every year. Around 3 million children are abused or neglected in the United States each year. The abuse takes several forms, ranging from physical abuse to psychological mistreatment (see Figure 8-2; National Clearinghouse on Child Abuse and Neglect Information, 2004; U.S. Department of Health and Human Services, 2007).

Figure 8-2 Child Fatalities by Maltreatment Type

The graph below indicates the type of maltreatment involved in child maltreatment fatalities. Some fatalities involve multiple types of maltreatment. **THINKING ABOUT THE DATA:** What are some surprising facts represented in this graph?

(**Source:** Child Welfare Information Gateway. https://www.childwelfare.gov/pubs/factsheets/fatality/, 2015.)

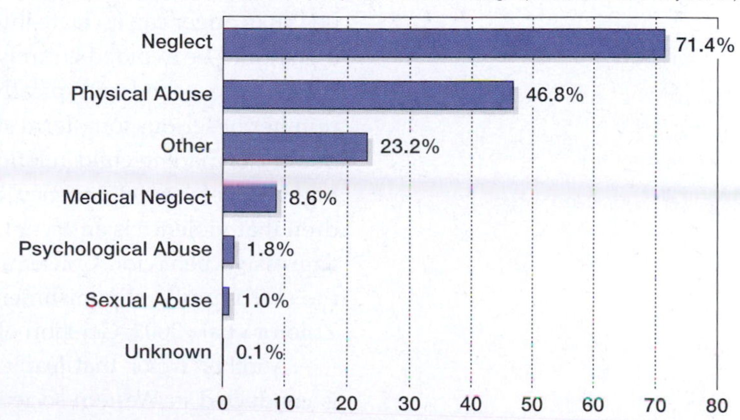

PHYSICAL ABUSE. Child abuse can occur in any household, regardless of economic well-being or the social status of the parents. It is most frequent in families living in stressful environments. Poverty, single parenthood, and higher-than-average levels of marital conflict help create

Table 8-4 What Are the Warning Signs of Child Abuse?

Because child abuse is typically a secret crime, identifying the victims of abuse is particularly difficult. Still, there are several signs in a child that indicate that he or she is the victim of violence (Robbins, 1990):

- Visible, serious injuries that have no reasonable explanation
- Bite or choke marks
- Burns from cigarettes or immersion in hot water
- Feelings of pain for no apparent reason
- Fear of adults or care providers
- Inappropriate attire in warm weather (long sleeves, long pants, high-necked garments)—possibly to conceal injuries to the neck, arms, and legs
- Extreme behavior—highly aggressive, extremely passive, extremely withdrawn
- Fear of physical contact
- In cases of sexual abuse: the use of new words for private body parts, mimicking sexual acts with toys or stuffed animals, or showing resistance at removing clothes

If you suspect a child is a victim of aggression, it is your responsibility to act. Call your local police or the department of social services in your city or state, or call Child Help U.S.A. at 1-800-422-4453. Talk to a teacher or a member of the clergy. Remember, by acting decisively, you can literally save someone's life.

such environments. Stepfathers are more likely to commit abuse against stepchildren than genetic fathers are against their own offspring. Child abuse is also more likely when there is a history of violence between spouses (Osofsky, 2003; Evans, 2004; Ezzo & Young, 2012). Table 8-4 lists some of the warning signs of abuse.

Abused children are more likely to be fussy, resistant to control, and not readily adaptable to new situations. They have more headaches and stomachaches, experience more bed-wetting and are generally more anxious than other children, and they may show developmental delays. Children in certain age groups are also more likely to be the targets of abuse: Three- and 4-year-olds and 15- to 17-year-olds are somewhat more likely to be abused by their parents than children of other ages (Ammerman & Patz, 1996; Haugaard, 2000; Carmody et al., 2014).

As you consider this information about the characteristics of abused children, keep in mind that labeling children as being at higher risk for receiving abuse does not make them responsible for their abuse; the family members who carry out the abuse are at fault. Statistical findings simply suggest that children with such characteristics are more at risk of being the recipients of family violence.

Reasons for Physical Abuse Why does physical abuse occur? Most parents certainly do not intend to hurt their children. Indeed, most parents who abuse their children later express bewilderment and regret about their own behavior.

One reason for child abuse is the vague demarcation between permissible and impermissible forms of physical violence. Societal folklore in the United States says that spanking is not merely acceptable but is often necessary and desirable. Almost half of mothers with children younger than 4 have spanked their child in the previous week, and close to 20 percent of mothers believe it is appropriate to spank a child less than 1 year old. In some other cultures, physical discipline is even more common (Lansford et al., 2005; Deb & Adak, 2006; Shor, 2006).

Unfortunately, the line between "spanking" and "beating" is not clear, and spankings begun in anger can escalate into abuse. Increasing scientific evidence suggests that spanking should be avoided entirely. Although physical punishment may produce immediate compliance—children typically stop the behavior spanking is meant to end—there are a number of serious long-term side effects. For example, spanking is associated with lower quality of parent–child relationships, poorer mental health for both child and parent, higher levels of delinquency, and more antisocial behavior. Spanking also teaches children that violence is an acceptable solution to problems by serving as a model of violent, aggressive behavior. Consequently, according to the American Academy of Pediatrics, the use of physical punishment of any sort is *not* recommended (Benjet & Kazdin, 2003; Zolotor et al., 2008; Gershoff et al., 2012).

Another factor that leads to high rates of abuse is the privacy in which child care is conducted in Western societies. In many other cultures, childrearing is seen as the joint responsibility of several people and even society as a whole. In most Western cultures—and particularly in the United States—children are raised in private, isolated households. Because child care is seen as the sole responsibility of the parent, other people are typically not available to help out when a parent's patience is tested (Chaffin, 2006; Elliott & Urquiza, 2006).

Sometimes abuse is the result of an adult's unrealistically high expectations regarding children's abilities to be quiet and compliant at a particular age. Children's failure to meet these unrealistic expectations may provoke abuse (Peterson, 1994).

Increasingly, spanking and other forms of physical violence are being seen as a human rights violation. The United Nations Committee on the Rights of the Child has called physical punishment "legalized violence against children," and the organization has called for its elimination. A treaty supporting this view has been ratified by 192 countries, with the exception of the United States and Somalia (Smith, 2012).

The Cycle of Violence Hypothesis Many times, those who abuse children were themselves abused as children. According to the **cycle of violence hypothesis**, the abuse and neglect that children suffer predispose them as adults to abuse and neglect their own children (Widom, 2000; Heyman & Slep, 2002).

cycle of violence hypothesis
the theory that the abuse and neglect that children suffer predispose them as adults to abuse and neglect their own children

According to this hypothesis, victims of abuse have learned from their childhood experiences that violence is an appropriate and acceptable form of discipline. Violence may be perpetuated from one generation to another, as each generation learns to behave abusively (and fails to learn the skills needed to solve problems and instill discipline without resorting to physical violence) through its participation in an abusive, violent family (Blumenthal, 2000; Ethier, Couture, & Lacharite, 2004; Ehrensaft et al., 2015).

Being abused as a child does not inevitably lead to abuse of one's own children. Statistics show that only about one-third of people who were abused or neglected as children abuse their own children; the remaining two-thirds of people abused as children do not turn out to be child abusers. Clearly, suffering abuse as a child is not the full explanation for child abuse in adults (Straus & McCord, 1998).

PSYCHOLOGICAL MALTREATMENT. Children may also be the victims of more subtle forms of mistreatment. **Psychological maltreatment** occurs when parents or other caregivers harm children's behavioral, cognitive, emotional, or physical functioning. It may be the result of either overt behavior or neglect (Higgins & McCabe, 2003; Garbarino, 2013).

psychological maltreatment
abuse that occurs when parents or other caregivers harm children's behavioral, cognitive, emotional, or physical functioning

For example, abusive parents may frighten, belittle, or humiliate their children, thereby intimidating and harassing them. Children may be made to feel like disappointments or failures, or they may be constantly reminded that they are a burden to their parents. Parents may tell their children that they wish they had never had children and specifically that they wish that their children had never been born. Children may be threatened with abandonment or even death. In other instances, older children may be exploited. They may be forced to seek employment and then to give their earnings to their parents.

In other cases of psychological maltreatment, the abuse takes the form of neglect. Parents may ignore their children or be emotionally unresponsive to them. In such cases, children may be given unrealistic responsibilities or may be left to fend for themselves.

No one is certain how much psychological maltreatment occurs each year because figures separating psychological maltreatment from other types of abuse are not routinely gathered. Most maltreatment occurs in the privacy of people's homes. Furthermore, psychological maltreatment typically causes no physical damage, such as bruises or broken bones, to alert physicians, teachers, and other authorities. Consequently, many cases of psychological maltreatment probably are not identified. However, it is clear that profound neglect that involves children who are unsupervised or uncared for is the most frequent form of psychological maltreatment (Scott et al., 2012).

Guntmar Fritz/Getty Images

Sometimes abuse is the result of an adult's unrealistic expectations regarding children's abilities to be quiet and compliant at a particular age.

Figure 8-3 Abuse Alters the Brain

The limbic system, composed of the hippocampus and amygdala, can be permanently altered as a result of childhood abuse.

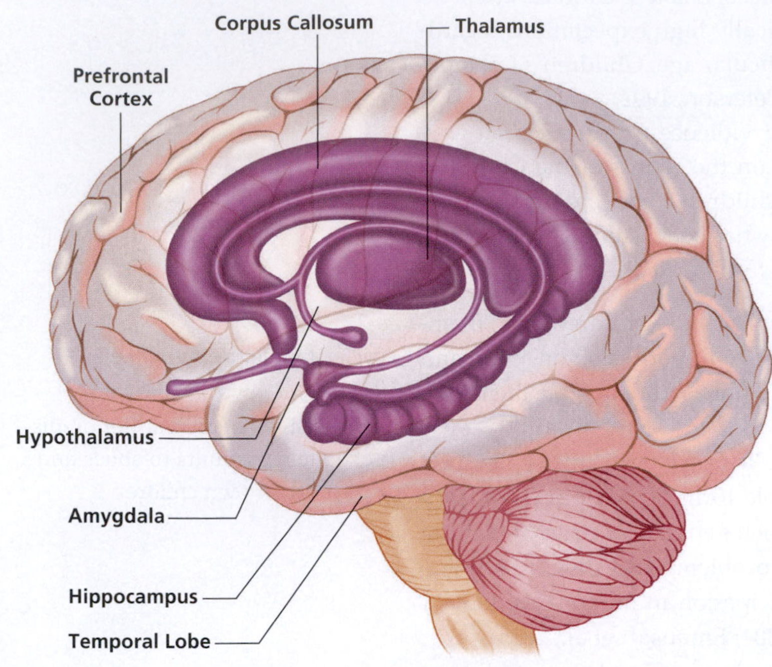

What are the consequences of psychological maltreatment? Some children are sufficiently resilient to survive the abuse and grow into psychologically healthy adults. In many cases, however, lasting damage results. For example, psychological maltreatment has been associated with low self-esteem, lying, misbehavior, and underachievement in school. In extreme cases, it can produce criminal behavior, aggression, and murder. In other instances, children who have been psychologically maltreated become depressed and even commit suicide (Allen, 2008; Palusci & Ondersma, 2012; Spinazzola et al., 2014).

One reason that psychological maltreatment—as well as physical abuse—produces so many negative consequences is that the brains of victims undergo permanent changes due to the abuse (see Figure 8-3). For example, childhood maltreatment can lead to reductions in the size of the amygdala and hippocampus in adulthood. The stress, fear, and terror produced by abuse may also produce permanent changes in the brain due to overstimulation of the limbic system. Because the limbic system is involved in the regulation of memory and emotion, the result can be antisocial behavior during adulthood (Rick & Douglas, 2007; Twardosz & Lutzker, 2009; Presseau et al., 2017).

Resilience: Overcoming the Odds

LO 8.9 Define resilience, and describe how it can help abused children.

Given the seriousness of child abuse in all its forms, and the physical, psychological, and neurological damage it can cause, it's remarkable that not all children who have been abused are permanently scarred by it. Actually, some do surprisingly well, considering the type of problems they have encountered. What enables some children to overcome the stress and trauma that in most cases haunts others for life?

The answer appears to be a quality that psychologists have termed resilience. **Resilience** is the ability to overcome circumstances that place a child at high risk for psychological or physical damage, such as extremes of poverty, prenatal stress, or homes that are racked with violence or other forms of social disorder. Several factors seem to reduce and, in certain cases, eliminate some children's reactions to difficult circumstances that produce profoundly negative consequences in others (Collishaw et al., 2007; Monahan, Beeber, & Harden, 2012; Sciaraffa, Zeanah, & Zeanah, 2017).

resilience
the ability to overcome circumstances that place a child at high risk for psychological or physical damage

According to developmental psychologist Emmy Werner, resilient children tend to have temperaments that evoke positive responses from a wide variety of caregivers. They tend to be affectionate, easygoing, and good-natured. They are easily soothed as infants, and they are able to elicit care from the most nurturant people in any environment in which they find themselves. In a sense, then, resilient children are successful in making their own environments by drawing out behavior in others that is necessary for their own development (Werner & Smith, 2002; Martinez-Torteya et al., 2009; Newland, 2014).

Similar traits are associated with resilience in older children. The most resilient school-age children are those who are socially pleasant, outgoing, and have good communication skills. They tend to be relatively intelligent, and they are independent, feeling that they can shape their own fate and are not dependent on others or on luck (Curtis & Cicchetti, 2003; Kim & Cicchetti, 2003; Haskett et al., 2006).

The characteristics of resilient children suggest ways to improve the prospects of children who are at risk from a variety of developmental threats. For instance, in addition

Development in Your Life

Disciplining Children

The question of how best to discipline children has been raised for generations. Answers from developmentalists today include the following advice (Brazelton & Sparrow, 2003; Flouri, 2005):

- For most children in Western cultures, authoritative parenting works best. Parents should be firm and consistent, providing clear direction for desirable behavior. Authoritative disciplinarians provide rules, but they explain why those rules make sense, using language that children can understand.
- Spanking is *never* an appropriate discipline technique, according to the American Academy of Pediatrics. Not only is spanking less effective than other techniques in curbing undesirable behavior, but it leads to additional, unwanted outcomes, such as the potential for more aggressive behavior. Even though most Americans were spanked as children, the research is abundantly clear in demonstrating that spanking is inappropriate (Bell & Roman, 2012; American Academy of Pediatrics, 1998, 2012).
- Use *time-out* for punishment, in which children are removed from a situation in which they have misbehaved and are not permitted to engage in enjoyable activities for a set period of time.
- Tailor parental discipline to the characteristics of the child and the situation. Try to keep the child's particular personality in mind, and adapt discipline to it.
- Use routines (such as a bath routine or a bedtime routine) to avoid conflict. For instance, bedtime can be the source of a nightly struggle between a resistant child and an insistent parent. Parental strategies for gaining compliance that involve making the situation predictably enjoyable—such as routinely reading a bedtime story or engaging in a nightly "wrestling" match with the child—can defuse potential battles.

to decreasing their exposure to factors that put them at risk in the first place, we need to increase their competence by teaching them ways to deal with their situation. Programs that have been successful in helping especially vulnerable children have a common thread: They provide competent and caring adult models who can teach the children problem-solving skills and help them to communicate their needs to those who are in a position to help them (Maton et al., 2004; Condly, 2006; Goldstein & Brooks, 2013).

Module 8.2 Review

LO 8.4 Describe the sorts of social relationships that preschool-age children engage in.

In the preschool years, children develop their first true friendships on the basis of personal characteristics, trust, and shared interests.

LO 8.5 Explain how and why preschool-age children play.

The character of preschoolers' play changes over time, growing more sophisticated, interactive, and cooperative, and relying increasingly on social skills.

LO 8.6 Summarize how thinking changes in the preschool years.

During the preschool years, children's theory of mind begins to encompass the thoughts and feelings of others.

LO 8.7 Describe the types of disciplinary styles parents employ and the effects they have on their children.

Whatever the changes in the structure of families in recent years, the importance of a warm family environment to children's social development cannot be overstated.

There are several distinct childrearing styles, including authoritarian, permissive, authoritative, and uninvolved. Childrearing styles show strong cultural influences.

LO 8.8 List the factors that contribute to child abuse and neglect.

Some children suffer abuse from their own family members, especially in families living in stressful circumstances. In the United States, a folklore of discipline that views spanking as beneficial, together with an insistence on family privacy, can lead some parents to go over the line and abuse their children.

LO 8.9 Define resilience, and describe how it can help abused children.

Resilience, the ability to overcome highly unfavorable circumstances, is an important temperamental characteristic that can help children overcome abuse and neglect.

Journal Writing Prompt

Applying Lifespan Development: What cultural and environmental factors in the United States may have contributed to the shift from an authoritarian parenting style to an authoritative one since World War II? Is another shift underway?

Moral Development and Aggression

Lena and Carrie were part of a group of preschoolers who wanted to act out Goldilocks and the Three Bears. *The teacher began assigning parts. "Carrie, you can be Baby Bear. And Lena, you be Goldilocks."*

Tears welled up in Carrie's eyes. "I don't want to be Baby Bear," she sobbed.

Lena put her arms around Carrie. "You can be Goldilocks, too. We'll be the Goldilocks twins." Carrie cheered up at once, grateful that Lena had understood her feelings and responded with kindness.

In this short scenario we see many of the key elements of morality, as it is played out among preschool-age children. Changes in children's views of what is ethically right and what is the right way to behave are an important element of growth during the preschool years.

At the same time, the kind of aggression displayed by preschoolers is also changing. We can consider the development of morality and aggression as two sides of the coin of human conduct, and both involve a growing awareness of others.

Developing Morality: Following Society's Rights and Wrongs

LO 8.10 Explain how preschool-age children develop a moral sense.

moral development
the changes in people's sense of justice and of what is right and wrong, and in their behavior related to moral issues

Moral development refers to changes in people's sense of justice and of what is right and wrong, and in their behavior related to moral issues. Developmentalists have considered moral development in terms of children's reasoning about morality, their attitudes toward moral lapses, and their behavior when faced with moral issues. In the process of studying moral development, psychologists have evolved several approaches.

PIAGET'S VIEW OF MORAL DEVELOPMENT. Child psychologist Jean Piaget was one of the first to study questions of moral development. He suggested that moral development, like cognitive development, proceeds in stages (Piaget, 1932). The earliest stage is a broad form of moral thinking he called *heteronomous morality*, in which rules are seen as invariant and unchangeable. During this stage, which lasts from about age 4 through age 7, children play games rigidly, assuming that there is one, and only one, way to play and that every other way is wrong. At the same time, though, preschool-age children may not even fully grasp game rules. Consequently, a group of children may be playing together, with each child playing according to a slightly different set of rules. Nevertheless, they enjoy playing with others. Piaget suggests that every child may "win" such a game because winning is equated with having a good time, as opposed to truly competing with others.

This rigid heteronomous morality is ultimately replaced by two later stages of morality: incipient cooperation and autonomous cooperation. As its name implies, in the *incipient cooperation stage*, which lasts from around age 7 to age 10, children's games become more clearly social. Children learn the actual formal rules of games, and they play according to this shared knowledge. Consequently, rules are still seen as largely unchangeable. There is a "right" way to play the game, and children in the incipient cooperation stage play according to these formal rules.

It is not until the *autonomous cooperation stage*, which begins at about age 10, that children become fully aware that formal game rules can be modified if the people who play the game agree. The later transition into more sophisticated forms of moral development—which we will consider in Chapter 12—also is reflected in school-age children's understanding that rules of law are created by people and are subject to change according to the will of people.

Until these later stages are reached, however, children's reasoning about rules and issues of justice is bounded in the concrete. For instance, consider the following two stories:

> *Pedro comes home from preschool. On the table where he usually has his afternoon snack, there is a plate of cookies. Thinking they are for him, he eats four cookies. His mother comes in and says she made the cookies for a bake sale to raise money for his school.*
>
> *Steven's preschool class is having a party. Each child has been given two cookies and a cup of punch. Steven eats his two cookies. When he sees another child, Lizzie, leave her seat, he takes one of her cookies and eats it.*

Piaget found that a preschool child in the heteronomous morality stage would judge the child who took four cookies as being worse than the one who took just one cookie. In contrast, children who have moved beyond the heteronomous morality stage would consider the child who took one cookie as being naughtier. The reason: Children in the heteronomous morality stage do not take *intention* into account.

Preschoolers believe in immanent justice. This child may worry that she will be punished instantly even if no one sees her carrying out the misdeed.

Children in the heteronomous stage of moral development also believe in immanent justice. *Immanent justice* is the notion that rules that are broken earn immediate punishment. Preschool children believe that if they do something wrong, they will be punished instantly—even if no one sees them carrying out their misdeeds. In contrast, older children understand that punishments for misdeeds are determined and meted out by people. Children who have moved beyond the heteronomous morality stage have come to understand that one must make judgments about the severity of a transgression based on whether the person intended to do something wrong.

EVALUATING PIAGET'S APPROACH TO MORAL DEVELOPMENT. Recent research suggests that although Piaget was on the right track in his description of how moral development proceeds, his approach suffers from the same problem we encountered in his theory of cognitive development. Specifically, Piaget underestimated the age at which children's moral skills are honed.

It is now clear that preschool-age children understand the notion of intentionality by about age 3, and this allows them to make judgments based on intent at an earlier age than Piaget supposed. Specifically, when provided with moral questions that emphasize intent, preschool children judge someone who is intentionally bad as more "naughty" than someone who is unintentionally bad but who creates more objective damage. Moreover, by age 4, they judge intentional lying as being wrong (Bussey, 1992).

SOCIAL LEARNING APPROACHES TO MORALITY. Social learning approaches to moral development stand in stark contrast to Piaget's approach. While Piaget emphasizes how limitations in preschoolers' cognitive development lead to particular forms of moral *reasoning*, social learning approaches focus more on how the environment in which preschoolers operate produces **prosocial behavior**, helping behavior that benefits others (Caputi et al., 2012; Schulz et al., 2013; Buon, Habib, & Frey, 2017).

prosocial behavior
helping behavior that benefits others

Social learning approaches build upon the behavioral approaches that we first discussed in Chapter 1. They acknowledge that some instances of children's prosocial behavior stem from situations in which they have received positive reinforcement for acting in a morally appropriate way. For instance, when Claire's mother tells her she has been a "good girl" for sharing a box of candy with her brother Dan, Claire's behavior has been reinforced. As a consequence, she is more likely to engage in sharing behavior in the future (Ramaswamy & Bergin, 2009).

Social learning approaches go a step further, however, arguing that not all prosocial behavior has to be directly performed and subsequently reinforced for learning to occur. According to social learning approaches, children also learn moral behavior more indirectly by observing the behavior of others, called *models* (Bandura, 1977). Children imitate models who receive reinforcement for their behavior, and ultimately they learn to perform the behavior themselves. For example, when Claire's friend Jake watches Claire share her candy with her brother, and Claire is praised for her behavior, Jake is more likely to engage in sharing behavior himself at some later point.

Quite a few studies illustrate the power of models and of social learning more generally in producing prosocial behavior in preschool-age children. For example, experiments have shown that children who view someone behaving generously or unselfishly are apt to follow the model's example, subsequently behaving in a generous or unselfish manner themselves when put in a similar situation. The opposite also holds true: If a model behaves selfishly, children who observe such behavior tend to behave more selfishly themselves (Hastings et al., 2007).

Not all models are equally effective in producing prosocial responses. For instance, preschoolers are more apt to model the behavior of warm, responsive adults than of adults who appear colder. Furthermore, models viewed as highly competent or high in prestige are more effective than others.

Children do more than simply mimic unthinkingly behavior that they see rewarded in others. By observing moral conduct, they are reminded of society's norms about the importance of moral behavior as conveyed by parents, teachers, and other powerful authority figures. They notice the connections between particular situations and certain kinds of behavior. This increases the likelihood that similar situations will elicit similar behavior in the observer.

abstract modeling
the process in which modeling paves the way for the development of more general rules and principles

Consequently, modeling paves the way for the development of more general rules and principles in a process called **abstract modeling**. Rather than always modeling the particular behavior of others, older preschoolers begin to develop generalized principles that underlie the behavior they observe. After observing repeated instances in which a model is rewarded for acting in a morally desirable way, children begin the process of inferring and learning the general principles of moral conduct (Bandura, 1991).

From *an educator's* perspective

How might a preschool school teacher encourage a shy child to join a group of preschoolers who are playing together?

GENETIC APPROACHES TO MORALITY. A highly controversial recent approach to morality suggests that particular genes may underlie some aspects of moral behavior. According to this view, preschoolers have a genetic predisposition to behave generously or selfishly.

In one study designed to illustrate this approach, researchers gave preschoolers the opportunity to behave generously by sharing stickers. Those who were more selfish and less generous were more likely to have a variation in a gene called AVPR1A, which regulates a hormone in the brain that is related to social behavior (Avinun et al., 2011).

empathy
the understanding of what another individual feels

It is unlikely that the gene mutation fully accounts for the preschoolers' lack of generosity. The environment in which the children were raised is also likely to play a significant, and perhaps predominant, role in determining moral behavior. Still, the findings are provocative in showing that generosity may have genetic roots.

lofoto/Shutterstock

The roots of empathy grow early, and by the time children reach age 2 or 3, they are able to offer gifts and spontaneously share with other children and adults.

EMPATHY AND MORAL BEHAVIOR. **Empathy** is the understanding of what another individual feels. According to some developmentalists, empathy lies at the heart of moral behavior.

The roots of empathy grow early. One-year-old infants cry when they hear other infants crying. By ages 2 and 3, toddlers will offer gifts and spontaneously share toys with other children and adults, even if they are strangers (Ruffman, Lorimer, & Scarf, 2017).

During the preschool years, empathy continues to grow as children's ability to monitor and regulate their emotional and cognitive responses increases. Some theorists believe that increasing empathy—as well as other positive emotions, such as sympathy and admiration—leads children to behave in a more moral fashion.

In addition, some negative emotions—such as anger at an unfair situation or shame over previous transgressions—also may promote moral behavior (Decety & Jackson, 2006; Bischof-Köhler, 2012; Eisenberg, Spinrad, & Morris, 2014).

The notion that negative emotions may promote moral development is one that Freud first suggested in his theory of psychoanalytic personality development. Recall from Chapter 1 that Freud argued that a child's *superego*, the part of the personality that represents societal do's and don'ts, is developed through resolution of the *Oedipal conflict*. Children come to identify with their same-sex parent, incorporating that parent's standards of morality in order to avoid unconscious guilt raised by the Oedipal conflict.

Whether or not we accept Freud's account of the Oedipal conflict and the guilt it produces, his theory is consistent with more recent findings. These suggest that preschoolers' attempts to avoid experiencing negative emotions sometimes lead them to act in more moral, helpful ways. For instance, one reason children help others is to avoid the feelings of personal distress that they experience when they are confronted with another person's unhappiness or misfortune (Eisenberg, Valiente, & Champion, 2004; Cushman et al., 2013).

Aggression and Violence in Preschoolers: Sources and Consequences

LO 8.11 Describe how aggression develops in preschool-age children.

Four-year-old Duane could not contain his anger and frustration anymore. Although he usually was mild mannered, when Eshu began to tease him about the split in his pants and kept it up for several minutes, Duane finally snapped. Rushing over to Eshu, Duane pushed him to the ground and began to hit him with his small, closed fists. Because he was so distraught, Duane's punches were not terribly effective, but they were severe enough to hurt Eshu and bring him to tears before the preschool teachers could intervene.

Aggression among preschoolers is quite common, though attacks such as this are not. The potential for verbal hostility, shoving matches, kicking, and other forms of aggression is present throughout the preschool period, although the degree to which aggression is acted out changes as children become older.

Eshu's taunting is also a form of aggression. **Aggression** is intentional injury or harm to another person. Infants don't act aggressively; it is hard to contend that their behavior is *intended* to hurt others, even if they inadvertently manage to do so. In contrast, by the time they reach preschool age, children demonstrate true aggression.

aggression
intentional injury or harm to another person

emotional self-regulation
the capability to adjust emotions to a desired state and level of intensity

During the early preschool years, some of the aggression is addressed at attaining a desired goal, such as getting a toy away from another person or using a particular space occupied by another person. Consequently, in some ways the aggression is inadvertent, and minor scuffles may in fact be a typical part of early preschool life. It is the rare child who does not demonstrate at least an occasional act of aggression.

However, extreme and sustained aggression is a cause of concern. In most children, the amount of aggression declines as they move through the preschool years, as do the frequency and average length of episodes of aggressive behavior (Persson, 2005).

The child's personality and social development contribute to this decline in aggression. Throughout the preschool years, children become better at controlling the emotions that they are experiencing. **Emotional self-regulation** is the capability to adjust emotions to a desired state and level of intensity. Starting at age 2, children are able to talk about their feelings, and they engage in strategies to regulate them. As they get older, they develop more effective strategies, learning to better cope with negative emotions. In addition to

Oleg Mikhaylov/Shutterstock

Aggression, both physical and verbal, is present throughout the preschool period.

their increasing self-control, children are also, as we've seen, developing sophisticated social skills. Most learn to use language to express their wishes, and they become increasingly able to negotiate with others (Philippot & Feldman, 2005; Cole et al., 2009; Helmsen, Koglin, & Petermann, 2012; Rose et al., 2016).

Despite these typical declines in aggression, some children remain aggressive throughout the preschool period. Furthermore, aggression is a relatively stable characteristic: The most aggressive preschoolers tend to be the most aggressive children during the school-age years, and the least aggressive preschoolers tend to be the least aggressive school-age children (Tremblay, 2001; Schaeffer, Petras, & Ialongo, 2003; Davenport & Bourgeois, 2008).

Boys typically show higher levels of physical, instrumental aggression than girls. **Instrumental aggression** is aggression motivated by the desire to obtain a concrete goal, such as playing with a desirable toy that another child is playing with.

instrumental aggression
aggression motivated by the desire to obtain a concrete goal

relational aggression
nonphysical aggression that is intended to hurt another person's feelings

Although girls show lower levels of instrumental aggression, they may be just as aggressive but in different ways from boys. Girls are more likely to practice **relational aggression**, which is nonphysical aggression that is intended to hurt another person's feelings. Such aggression may be demonstrated through name-calling, withholding friendship, or simply saying mean, hurtful things that make the recipient feel bad (Werner & Crick, 2004; Murray-Close, Ostrov, & Crick, 2007; Valles & Knutson, 2008).

THE ROOTS OF AGGRESSION. How can we explain the aggression of preschoolers? Some theoreticians suggest that to behave aggressively is an instinct, part and parcel of the human condition. For instance, Freud's psychoanalytic theory suggests that we all are motivated by sexual and aggressive instincts (Freud, 1920). According to ethologist Konrad Lorenz, an expert in animal behavior, animals—including humans—share a fighting instinct that stems from primitive urges to preserve territory, maintain a steady supply of food, and weed out weaker animals (Lorenz, 1974).

Similar arguments are made by evolutionary theorists and *sociobiologists*, scientists who consider the biological roots of social behavior. They argue that aggression leads to increased opportunities to mate, improving the likelihood that one's genes will be passed on to future generations. In addition, aggression may help to strengthen the species and its gene pool as a whole, because the strongest survive. Ultimately, then, aggressive instincts promote the survival of one's genes to pass on to future generations (Archer, 2009).

Although instinctual explanations of aggression are logical, most developmentalists believe they are not the whole story. Not only do instinctual explanations fail to take into account the increasingly sophisticated cognitive abilities that humans develop as they get older, but they also have relatively little experimental support. Moreover, they provide little guidance in determining when and how children, as well as adults, will behave aggressively, other than noting that aggression is an inevitable part of the human condition. Consequently, developmentalists have turned to other approaches to explain aggression and violence.

SOCIAL LEARNING APPROACHES TO AGGRESSION. The day after Duane lashed out at Eshu, Lynn, who had watched the entire scene, got into an argument with Ilya. They verbally bickered for a while, and suddenly Lynn balled her hand into a fist and tried to punch Ilya. The preschool teachers were stunned: It was rare for Lynn to get upset, and she had never displayed aggression before.

Is there a connection between the two events? Most of us would answer yes, particularly if we subscribed to the view, suggested by social learning approaches, that aggression is largely a learned behavior. Social learning approaches to aggression contend that aggression is based on observation and prior learning. To understand the causes of aggressive behavior, then, we should look at the system of rewards and punishments that exists in a child's environment.

Social learning approaches to aggression emphasize how social and environmental conditions teach individuals to be aggressive. These ideas grow out of behavioral perspectives, which suggest that aggressive behavior is learned through direct reinforcement. For instance, preschool-age children may learn that they can continue to play with the most desirable toys by aggressively refusing their classmates' requests for sharing. In the parlance of traditional learning theory, they have been reinforced for acting aggressively (by continued use of the toy), and they are more likely to behave aggressively in the future.

But social learning approaches suggest that reinforcement also comes in less direct ways. A good deal of research suggests that exposure to aggressive models leads to increased aggression, particularly if the observers are themselves angered, insulted, or frustrated. For example, Albert Bandura and his colleagues illustrated the power of models in a classic study of preschool-age children (Bandura, Ross, & Ross, 1963). One group of children watched a film of an adult playing aggressively and violently with a Bobo doll (a large, inflated plastic clown designed as a punching bag for children that always returns to an upright position after being pushed down). In comparison, children in another group watched a film of an adult playing sedately with a set of Tinkertoys (see Figure 8-4). Later, the preschool-age children were allowed to play with a number of toys, which included both the Bobo doll and the Tinkertoys. But first, the children were led to feel frustration by being refused the opportunity to play with a favorite toy.

As predicted by social learning approaches, the preschool-age children modeled the behavior of the adult. Those who had seen the aggressive model playing with the Bobo doll were considerably more aggressive than those who had watched the calm, unaggressive model playing with the Tinkertoys.

Later research has supported this early study, and it is clear that exposure to aggressive models increases the likelihood that aggression on the part of observers will follow. These findings have profound consequences, particularly for children who live in communities in which violence is prevalent. For instance, one survey conducted in a city public hospital found that 1 in 10 children under age 6 said they had witnessed a shooting or stabbing. Other research indicates that one-third of the children in some urban neighborhoods have seen a homicide and that two-thirds have seen a serious assault. Such frequent exposure to violence increases the probability that observers will behave aggressively themselves (Farver et al., 1997; Evans, 2004; Dubow et al., 2016).

Figure 8-4 Modeling Aggression

This series of photos is from Albert Bandura's classic Bobo doll experiment, designed to illustrate social learning of aggression. The photos clearly show how the adult model's aggressive behavior (in the first row) is imitated by children who had viewed the aggressive behavior (second and third rows).

Albert Bandura

VIEWING VIOLENCE ON TV: DOES IT MATTER? Even the majority of preschool-age children who are not witnesses to real-life violence are typically exposed to aggression via the medium of television. Children's television programs actually contain higher levels of violence (69 percent) than other types of programs (57 percent). In an average hour, children's programs contain more than twice as many violent incidents as other types of programs (Wilson, 2002).

This high level of televised violence and Bandura and others' research findings on modeling violence raise a significant question: Does viewing aggression increase the likelihood that children (and later adults) will enact actual—and ultimately deadly—aggression? It is hard to answer the question definitively, primarily because scientists are unable to conduct true experiments outside laboratory settings.

Although it is clear that laboratory observation of aggression on television leads to higher levels of aggression, evidence showing that real-world viewing of aggression is associated with subsequent aggressive behavior is correlational. (Think, for a moment, of what would be required to conduct a true experiment involving children's viewing habits. It would require that we control children's viewing of television in their homes for extended periods, exposing some to a steady diet of violent shows and others to nonviolent ones—something that most parents would not agree to.)

Despite the fact, then, that the results are primarily correlational, the overwhelming weight of research evidence is clear in suggesting that observation of televised aggression does lead to subsequent aggression. Longitudinal studies have found that children's preferences for violent television shows at age 8 are related to the seriousness of criminal convictions by age 30. Other evidence supports the notion that observation of media violence can lead to a greater readiness to act aggressively, bullying, and an insensitivity to the suffering of victims of violence (Ostrov, Gentile, & Crick, 2006; Christakis & Zimmerman, 2007; Kirsh, 2012; Merritt et al., 2016).

Television is not the only source of media violence. Many video games contain a significant amount of aggressive behavior, and children are playing such games at high rates. For example, 14 percent of children age 3 and younger and around 50 percent of those age 4 to 6 play video games. Because research conducted with adults shows that playing violent video games is associated with behaving aggressively, children who play video games containing violence may be at higher risk for behaving aggressively (Bushman, Gollwitzer, & Cruz, 2014; Linebarger, 2015).

Fortunately, social learning principles that lead preschoolers to learn aggression from television and video games suggest ways to reduce the negative influence of the medium. For instance, children can be explicitly taught to view violence with a more skeptical, critical eye. Being taught that violence is not representative of the real world, that the viewing of violence can affect them negatively, and that they should refrain from imitating the behavior they have seen on television can help children interpret the violent programs differently and be less influenced by them (Persson & Musher-Eizenman, 2003; Donnerstein, 2005).

Furthermore, just as exposure to aggressive models leads to aggression, observation of *non*aggressive models can *reduce* aggression. Preschoolers don't just learn from others how to be aggressive; they can also learn how to avoid confrontation and to control their aggression, as we'll discuss later.

COGNITIVE APPROACHES TO AGGRESSION: THE THOUGHTS BEHIND VIOLENCE. Two children, waiting for their turn in a game of kickball, inadvertently knock into one another. One child's reaction is to apologize; the other's is to shove, saying angrily, "Cut it out." Despite the fact that each child bears the same responsibility for the minor event, very different reactions result. The first child interprets the event as an accident, while the second sees it as a provocation and reacts with aggression.

The cognitive approach to aggression suggests that the key to understanding moral development is to examine preschoolers' interpretations of others' behavior and of the environmental context in which a behavior occurs. According to developmental psychologist Kenneth Dodge and his colleagues, some children are more prone than others to assume that actions are aggressively motivated. They are unable to pay attention to the appropriate cues in a situation and are unable to interpret the behaviors in a given situation accurately. Instead, they assume—often erroneously—that what is happening is related to others' hostility. Subsequently, in deciding how to respond, they base their behavior on their inaccurate interpretation of others' behavior. In sum, they may behave aggressively in response to a situation that never, in fact, existed (Petit & Dodge, 2003).

For example, consider Jake, who is drawing at a table with Gary. Jake reaches over and takes a red crayon that Gary had just decided he was going to use next. Gary is instantly certain that Jake "knew" that he was going to use the red crayon and that Jake is taking it just to be mean. With this interpretation in mind, Gary hits Jake for "stealing" his crayon.

Although the cognitive approach to aggression provides a description of the process that leads some children to behave aggressively, it is less successful in explaining how certain children come to be inaccurate perceivers of situations in the first place. Furthermore, it fails to explain why such inaccurate perceivers so readily respond with aggression and why they assume that aggression is an appropriate and even desirable response.

However, cognitive approaches to aggression are useful in pointing out a means to reduce aggression: By teaching preschool-age children to be more accurate interpreters of a situation, we can induce them to be less prone to view others' behavior as motivated by hostility, and consequently less likely to respond with aggression themselves. The guidelines in the *Development in Your Life* box are based on the various theoretical perspectives on aggression and morality that we've discussed in this chapter.

Development in Your Life

Increasing Moral Behavior and Reducing Aggression in Preschool-Age Children

The numerous points of view on the causes of aggression in preschool children are useful for the various methods for encouraging preschoolers' moral conduct and reducing the incidence of aggression they suggest. Here are some of the most practical and readily accomplished strategies (Bor & Bor, 2004; Eisenberg, 2012):

- Provide opportunities for preschool-age children to observe others acting in a cooperative, helpful, prosocial manner. Encourage them to interact with peers in joint activities in which they share a common goal. Such cooperative activities can teach the importance and desirability of working with—and helping—others.
- Encourage children to engage in activities that benefit others, such as sharing. But don't directly reward them for doing it with concrete reinforcements, such as candy or money. Verbal praise is fine.
- Talk to preschoolers about how others must feel in difficult situations, thereby fostering empathy.
- Do not ignore aggressive behavior. Parents and teachers should intervene when they see aggression in preschoolers, and send a clear message that aggression is an unacceptable means to resolve conflicts.
- Help preschoolers devise alternative explanations for others' behavior. This strategy is particularly important for children who are prone to aggression and who may be apt to view others' conduct as more hostile than it actually is. Parents and teachers should help such children see that the behavior of their peers has several possible interpretations.
- Monitor preschoolers' television viewing, particularly the violence that they view. There is good evidence that observation of televised aggression results in subsequent increases in children's levels of aggression. Encourage preschoolers to watch particular shows that are designed, in part, to increase the level of moral conduct, such as *Sesame Street, Dora the Explorer*, or *Daniel Tiger*.
- Help preschoolers understand their feelings. When children become angry—and all children do—they need to learn how to deal with their feelings in a constructive manner. Tell them *specific* things they can do to improve the situation ("I see you're really angry with Jake for not giving you a turn. Don't hit him, but tell him you want a chance to play with the game.")
- Explicitly teach reasoning and self-control. Preschoolers can understand the rudiments of moral reasoning, and they should be reminded why certain behaviors are desirable. For instance, explicitly saying, "If you take all the cookies, others will have no dessert" is preferable to saying, "Good children don't eat all the cookies."

Module 8.3 Review

LO 8.10 Explain how preschool-age children develop a moral sense.

Piaget believed that preschoolers are in the heteronomous morality stage of moral development, in which rules are seen as invariant and unchangeable. Social learning approaches to moral development emphasize the importance of reinforcement for moral actions and the observation of models of moral conduct. Psychoanalytical and other theories focus on children's empathy with others and their wish to help others so they can avoid unpleasant feelings of guilt themselves.

LO 8.11 Describe how aggression develops in preschool-age children.

Aggression typically declines in frequency and duration as children become more able to regulate their emotions and to use language to negotiate disputes. Ethologists and sociobiologists regard aggression as an innate human characteristic, while proponents of social learning and cognitive approaches focus on learned aspects of aggression.

Journal Writing Prompt

Applying Lifespan Development: If high-prestige models of behavior are particularly effective in influencing moral attitudes and actions, are there implications for individuals in such industries as sports, advertising, and entertainment?

Epilogue

This chapter examined the social and personality development of preschool-age children, including their development of self-concept. The changing social relationships of preschool-age children can be seen in the changing nature of play. We considered typical styles of parental discipline and their effects later in life, and we examined the factors that lead to child abuse. We discussed the development of a moral sense from several developmental perspectives, and we concluded with a discussion of aggression.

Before moving on to the next chapter, take a moment to reread the prologue about Julian Avery, whose personality was so different from his older brother's. Then answer the following questions:

1. In what critical ways does Julian differ from his older brother, and what do you think are the implications for Julian's future development?
2. What kind of disciplinary style would be best suited to Julian? Do you think that style would differ from what would be optimal for his older brother?
3. What clues to Julian's self-concept do you see in the story? How do you think Julian would answer the question, "Who am I?" How might that answer differ from that his parents might give in describing Julian?
4. What do the differences between Julian's and his older brother's behavior suggest about the relative importance of nature and nurture in determining personality?

Looking Back

LO 8.1 Describe the major developmental challenges that preschool-age children face.

According to Erik Erikson, preschool-age children initially are in the autonomy-versus-shame-and-doubt stage (18 months to 3 years) in which they develop independence and mastery over their physical and social worlds or feel shame, self-doubt, and unhappiness. Later, in the initiative-versus-guilt stage (ages 3 to 6), preschool-age children face conflicts between the desire to act independently and the guilt that comes from the unintended consequences of their actions.

LO 8.2 Explain how preschool-age children develop a concept of themselves.

Preschoolers' self-concepts are formed partly from their own perceptions and estimations of their characteristics, partly from their parents' behavior toward them, and partly from cultural influences.

LO 8.3 Explain how preschool-age children develop a sense of racial identity and gender.

Preschool-age children form racial attitudes largely in response to their environment, including parents and other influences. Gender differences emerge early and conform to social stereotypes about what is appropriate and inappropriate for each sex. The strong gender expectations held by preschoolers are explained in different ways by different theorists. Some point to genetic factors as evidence for a biological explanation of gender expectations. Freud's psychoanalytic theories use a framework based on the subconscious. Social learning theorists focus on environmental influences, including parents, teachers, peers, and the media, while cognitive theorists propose that children form gender schemas, cognitive frameworks that organize information that the children gather about gender.

LO 8.4 Describe the sorts of social relationships that preschool-age children engage in.

Preschool social relationships begin to encompass genuine friendships, which involve trust and endure over time.

LO 8.5 Explain how and why preschool-age children play.

Older preschoolers engage in more constructive play than functional play. They also engage in more associative and cooperative play than younger preschoolers, who do more parallel and onlooker playing.

LO 8.6 Summarize how thinking changes in the preschool years.

Preschoolers begin to understand how others think and why they do the things they do. Children begin to grasp the difference between reality and imagination and begin to take part consciously in imaginative play.

LO 8.7 Describe the types of disciplinary styles parents employ and the effects they have on their children.

Disciplinary styles differ both individually and culturally. In the United States and other Western societies, parents' styles tend to be mostly authoritarian, permissive, uninvolved, and authoritative. The authoritative style is regarded as the most effective. Children of authoritarian and permissive parents may develop dependency, hostility, and low self-control, while children of uninvolved parents may feel unloved and emotionally detached. Children of authoritative parents tend to be more independent, friendly, self-assertive, and cooperative.

LO 8.8 List the factors that contribute to child abuse and neglect.

Child abuse, which may be either physical or psychological, occurs especially in stressful home environments. Firmly held notions regarding family privacy and the use of physical punishment in childrearing contribute to the high rate of abuse in the United States. Moreover, the cycle of violence hypothesis points to the likelihood that persons who were abused as children may turn into abusers as adults.

LO 8.9 Define resilience, and describe how it can help abused children.

Children who have been abused often survive their backgrounds by relying on the temperamental quality of resilience.

LO 8.10 Explain how preschool-age children develop a moral sense.

Piaget believed that preschool-age children are in the heteronomous morality stage of moral development, characterized by a belief in external, unchangeable rules of conduct and sure, immediate punishment for all misdeeds. In contrast, social learning approaches to morality emphasize interactions between environment and behavior in moral development, in which models of behavior play an important role. Some developmentalists believe that moral behavior is rooted in a child's development of empathy. Other emotions, including the negative emotions of anger and shame, may also promote moral behavior.

LO 8.11 Describe how aggression develops in preschool-age children.

Aggression, which involves intentional harm to another person, begins to emerge in the preschool years. As children age and improve their language skills, acts of aggression typically decline in frequency and duration. Some ethologists, such as Konrad Lorenz, believe that aggression is simply a biological fact of human life—a belief held also by many sociobiologists, who focus on competition within species to pass genes on to the next generation. Social learning theorists focus on the role of the environment, including the influence of models and social reinforcement, as factors influencing aggressive behavior. The cognitive approach to aggression emphasizes the role of interpretations of the behaviors of others in determining aggressive or nonaggressive responses.

Key Terms and Concepts

Summary 3
The Preschool Years

Cute_photos/Shutterstock

JULIE, a 3-year-old in her first days of preschool, was initially shy and passive. She appeared to accept that older and larger children, particularly boys, had a right to tell her what to do and to take things from her that they wanted. She saw little choice but to let these things happen, since she was powerless to stop them. However, in the span of one short year, Julie decided that she had enough. Instead of accepting the "rule" that bigger kids could do whatever they wanted, she would protest against its unfairness. Instead of silently allowing other kids to dominate her, she would use her newfound moral sense, together with her evolving language skills, to warn them off. Julie had put together all the developmental tools that she had to make her world a fairer and better place.

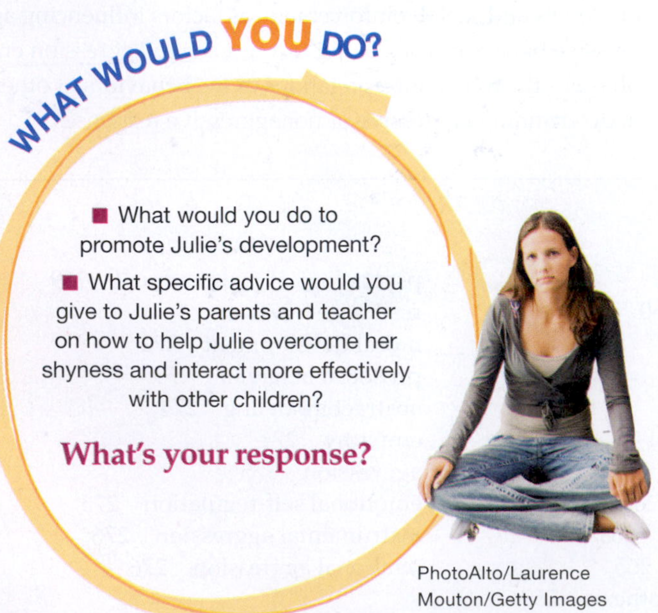

PhotoAlto/Laurence Mouton/Getty Images

Photodisc/Getty Images

Physical Development

volkovslava/Shutterstock

- Julie grew bigger, heavier, and stronger during the preschool years.
- Her brain grew, and with it her cognitive abilities, including the ability to plan and to use language as a tool.
- She learned to use and control her gross and fine motor skills.

Cognitive Development

Lew Merrim/Science Source

- During the preschool years, Julie's memory capabilities increased.
- She watched others and learned from her peers and from adults how to handle different situations.
- She also used her growing language skills to function more effectively.

Social and Personality Development

OJO Images Ltd/Alamy Stock Photo

- As with other preschool-age children, Julie's play was a way to grow socially, cognitively, and physically.
- Julie learned the rules of play, such as taking turns and playing fairly.
- She also developed theories of mind that help her to understand what others are thinking.
- She developed the beginnings of a sense of justice and moral behavior.
- Julie was able to adjust her emotions to a desired intensity level and can use language to express her wishes and deal with others.

WHAT WOULD A NURSE DO?

- How would you help Julie's parents to provide appropriate kinds of discipline for Julie?
- How would you help her parents to optimize their home environment to promote physical, cognitive, and social development for their children?

What's your response?

Sheer Photo, Inc/Getty Images

WHAT WOULD AN EDUCATOR DO?

- What strategies would you use to promote cognitive and social development?
- How would you deal with instances of bullying in your preschool classroom, both in terms of children who were victimized as well as dealing with the bully?

What's your response?

Tom Baker/123RF

Chapter 9

Physical and Cognitive Development in Middle Childhood

Blend Images/Age Fotostock

Learning Objectives

LO 9.1 Describe ways in which children grow during middle childhood and factors that influence their growth.

LO 9.2 Outline the course of motor development in middle childhood.

LO 9.3 Summarize the main physical and mental health concerns of school-age children.

LO 9.4 Describe the sorts of special needs that may become apparent in school-age children and how can they be met.

LO 9.5 Summarize the Piagetian view of cognitive development in middle childhood.

LO 9.6 Explain how children develop cognitively in middle childhood according to information processing approaches.

LO 9.7 Summarize Vygotsky's interpretation of cognitive development during middle childhood.

LO 9.8 Describe how language develops during middle childhood.

LO 9.9 Explain how children learn to read.

LO 9.10 Summarize what schools teach beyond the basics in middle childhood.

LO 9.11 Describe how intelligence is measured and what controversies arise from measuring it.

LO 9.12 Describe how children with intellectual disabilities and children who are intellectually gifted are educated in middle childhood.

Chapter Overview

Prologue: Seeding a Garden

In his third-grade math class, Danny Nunes is introducing his students to word problems. After they work through some problems together, Danny asks, "How would *you* write a word problem?"

Silence. Finally one student ventures, "Well, they're about normal things, like the size of a rug or something." Then the class takes off.

"Yeah, or painting a wall or dividing up a pizza."

"But you have to tell people what to do, and it has to have math."

"Let's make it about pizza."

"How about a garden?"

"Yeah, like how many bags of seeds you need to cover it."

Eventually a plausible word problem emerges.

"Word problems are scary," Danny says later, "so I make students think about how they're made—a form of metacognition. Writing a problem cooperatively reveals the main features of such problems, and those are the keys to solving them. After writing some problems, students approach solving them in a much more mindful way."

Looking Ahead

Middle childhood is characterized by milestones like this one as children's physical, cognitive, and social skills ascend to new heights. Beginning at age 6 and continuing to the start of adolescence at around age 12, the period of middle childhood is often referred to as the "school years" because it marks the beginning of formal education for most children. Sometimes the physical and cognitive growth that occurs during middle childhood is gradual, and other times it is sudden—but it is always remarkable.

We begin our consideration of middle childhood by examining physical and motor development. We discuss how children's bodies change and the problems of malnutrition and—the other side of the coin—childhood obesity. We also consider the development of children with special needs.

Next, we turn to the development of children's cognitive abilities in middle childhood. We examine several approaches put forward to describe and explain cognitive development, including Piagetian and information processing theories and the important ideas of Vygotsky. We look at language development and the questions surrounding bilingualism—an increasingly pressing social policy issue in the United States.

Finally, we consider several issues involving schooling. After discussing the scope of education throughout the world, we examine the critical skill of reading and the nature of multicultural education. The chapter ends with a discussion of intelligence, a characteristic closely tied to school success. We look at the nature of IQ tests and at the education of children who are either significantly below or above the intellectual norm.

Blend Images/Age Fotostock

During middle childhood, children's physical, cognitive, and social skills ascend to new heights.

Physical Development

Cinderella, dressed in yella,
went upstairs to kiss her fellah.
But she made a mistake and she kissed a snake.
How many doctors did it take? One, two, . . .

While the other girls chanted the classic jump-rope rhyme, Kat proudly displayed her newly developed ability to jump backward. In second grade, Kat was starting to get quite good at jumping rope. In first grade, she simply had not been able to master it. But over the summer, she had spent many hours practicing, and now that practice seemed to be paying off.

As Kat is gleefully experiencing, middle childhood is a time when children make great physical strides, mastering all kinds of new skills as they grow bigger and stronger. How does this progress occur? We'll first consider typical physical growth during middle childhood and then turn our attention to a look at children with special needs.

The Growing Body

LO 9.1 Describe ways in which children grow during middle childhood and factors that influence their growth.

Slow but steady. If three words could characterize the nature of growth during middle childhood, it would be these. Especially when compared to the swift growth during the first five years of life and the remarkable growth spurt characteristic of adolescence, middle childhood is relatively tranquil. On the other hand, the body has not shifted into neutral. Physical growth continues, although at a more stately pace than it did during the preschool years.

HEIGHT AND WEIGHT CHANGES. While they are in elementary school, children in the United States grow, on average, 2 to 3 inches a year. By age 11, the average height for girls is 4 feet, 10 inches and the average height for boys is slightly shorter at 4 feet, 9 1/2 inches. This is the only time during the life span when girls are, on average, taller than boys. This height difference reflects the slightly more rapid physical development of girls, who start their adolescent growth spurt around age 10.

Weight gain follows a similar pattern. During middle childhood, both boys and girls gain around 5 to 7 pounds a year. Weight is also redistributed. As the rounded look of "baby fat" disappears, children's bodies become more muscular, and their strength increases.

These average height and weight increases disguise significant individual differences, as anyone who has seen a line of fourth graders walking down a school corridor has doubtless noticed. It is not unusual to see children of the same age who are 6 or 7 inches apart in height. (Also see the *Developmental Diversity and Your Life* feature.)

Laurence Mouton/Getty Images

Variations of 6 inches in height between children of the same age are not unusual and are well within normal ranges.

PROMOTING GROWTH WITH HORMONES: SHOULD SHORT CHILDREN BE MADE TO GROW TALLER? Being tall is considered an advantage in most of U.S. society. Because of this cultural preference, parents sometimes worry about their children's growth if their children are short. To the manufacturers of Protropin, an artificial human growth hormone that can make short children taller, there's a simple solution: Administer the drug to make the children grow taller than they naturally would (Lagrou et al., 2008; Pinquart, 2013; Brod et al., 2017).

Should children be given such drugs? The question is a relatively new one: Artificial hormones to promote growth have become available only in the past two decades. Although tens of thousands of children who have insufficient natural growth hormone are taking such drugs, some observers question whether shortness is a serious

Developmental Diversity and Your Life

The Impact of Culture on Growth

Most children in North America receive sufficient nutrients to grow to their full potential. In other parts of the world, however, inadequate nutrition and disease take their toll, producing children who are shorter and who weigh less than they would if they had sufficient nutrients. The discrepancies can be dramatic: Children in poorer areas of cities, such as Calcutta, Hong Kong, and Rio de Janeiro, are smaller than their counterparts in affluent areas of the same cities.

America/Alamy Stock Photo

Inadequate nutrition and disease affect growth significantly. Children in poorer areas of cities such as Calcutta, Hong Kong, and Rio de Janeiro are smaller than their counterparts in affluent areas of the same cities.

In the United States, most variations in height and weight are the result of different people's unique genetic inheritance, including genetic factors relating to racial and ethnic background. For instance, children from Asian and Oceanic Pacific backgrounds tend to be shorter, on average, than those with northern and central European heritages. In addition, the rate of growth during childhood is generally more rapid for blacks than for whites (Deurenberg, Deurenberg-Yap, & Guricci, 2002; Deurenberg et al., 2003).

In addition, culture determines what mothers feel is an appropriate diet to feed their children. For example, Hmong immigrants in California believe that rice should play an important part in their children's diets, not only for its nutrient value but because it is representative of the Hmong culture and serves to support identification as a member of the culture (Vue, Wolff, & Goto, 2011).

Of course, even within particular racial and ethnic groups, there is significant variation between individuals. Moreover, we cannot attribute racial and ethnic differences solely to genetic factors because dietary customs as well as possible variations in levels of affluence also may contribute to the differences. In addition, severe stress—brought on by factors such as parental conflict or alcoholism—can affect the functioning of the pituitary gland, thereby affecting growth (Koska et al., 2002).

enough problem to warrant the use of the drug. Certainly, one can function well in society without being tall. Furthermore, the drug is costly and has potentially dangerous side effects. In some cases, the drug may lead to the premature onset of puberty, which may—ironically—restrict later growth.

From a *health-care provider's* perspective

Under what circumstances would you recommend the use of a growth hormone such as Protropin? Is shortness primarily a physical or a cultural problem?

However, there is no denying that artificial growth hormones are effective in increasing children's height, in some cases adding well over a foot in height to extremely short children, placing them within normal height ranges. Ultimately, until long-term studies of the safety of such treatments are completed, parents and medical personnel must carefully weigh the pros and cons before administering the drug to their children (Webb et al., 2012; Poidvin et al., 2014; Dykens, Roof, & Hunt-Hawkins, 2016).

NUTRITION. As we discussed earlier, there is a rather obvious relationship between size and nutrition. But size isn't the only area affected by children's levels of nutrition. For instance, longitudinal studies over many years in Guatemalan villages show that children's nutritional backgrounds are related to several dimensions of social and emotional functioning at school age. Children who had received more nutrients were more involved with their peers, showed more positive emotion, and had less anxiety than their peers who had received less adequate nutrition. Better nutrition also made children more eager to explore

Figure 9-1 Nutritional Benefits

Children who received higher levels of nutrients had more energy and felt more self-confident than those whose nutritional intake was lower. What policy implications does this finding suggest?

(**Source:** Based on Barrett, D. E., & Radke-Yarrow, M. R. (1985). Effects of nutritional supplementation on children's responses to novel, frustrating, and competitive situations. American Journal of Clinical Nutrition, 42, 102–120.

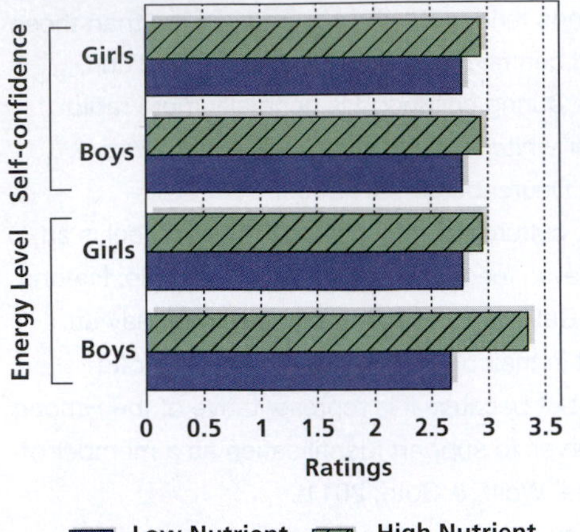

new environments, more persistent in frustrating situations, and more alert at some types of activities, and these children displayed generally higher energy levels and more self-confidence (Barrett & Frank, 1987; Nyaradi et al., 2013; see Figure 9-1).

Nutrition is also linked to cognitive performance. For instance, in one study, children in Kenya who were well nourished performed better on a test of verbal abilities and on other cognitive measures than those who had mild to moderate undernutrition. Other research suggests that malnutrition may influence cognitive development by dampening children's curiosity, responsiveness, and motivation to learn (Grigorenko, 2003; Jackson, 2015; Tooley, Makhoul, & Fisher, 2016).

CHILDHOOD OBESITY. In spite of a widely held view that thinness is a virtue, at least in the United States, increasing numbers of children are becoming obese. *Obesity* is defined as a BMI at or above the 95th percentile for children of the same age and sex. (BMI is calculated by dividing a child's weight in kilograms by the square of their height in meters). By this definition, 17 percent of U.S. children are obese—a proportion that has more than tripled since the 1970s. And it's not only a problem in the United States; the number of children ages 5–19 who are obese has increased 1,000% from 1975 to 2016 (see Figure 9-2; Ogden et al., 2015; NCD Risk Factor Collaboration, 2017).

Obesity is found more often in children in low-income families. In addition, the prevalence of obesity is related to ethnicity in the United States: Hispanic and American Indian/Alaska Native younger children show greater levels of obesity than whites and blacks (Ogden et al., 2015).

The costs of childhood obesity last a lifetime. Children who are obese are more likely to be overweight as adults and have a greater risk of developing heart disease, type 2 diabetes, cancer, and other diseases. Some scientists believe that an epidemic of obesity may be leading to a decline in life span in the United States (Park, 2008; Mehlenbeck, Farmer, & Ward, 2014).

Obesity is caused by a combination of genetic and social characteristics as well as diet. Particular inherited genes are related to obesity and predispose certain children to be overweight. For example, adopted children tend to have weights that are more similar to those of their birth parents than to those of their adoptive parents (Bray, 2008; Skledar et al., 2012; Maggi et al., 2015).

Social factors also enter into children's weight problems. Children need to learn to control their own eating. Parents who are particularly controlling and directive regarding their children's eating may produce children who lack internal controls to regulate their own food intake (Wardle, Guthrie, & Sanderson, 2001; Gomes, Barros, & Pereira, 2017).

Figure 9-2 Obesity in Children

Percentage of children ages 2 to 19 who are obese, by age.

(Child Trends Data Bank, 2014).

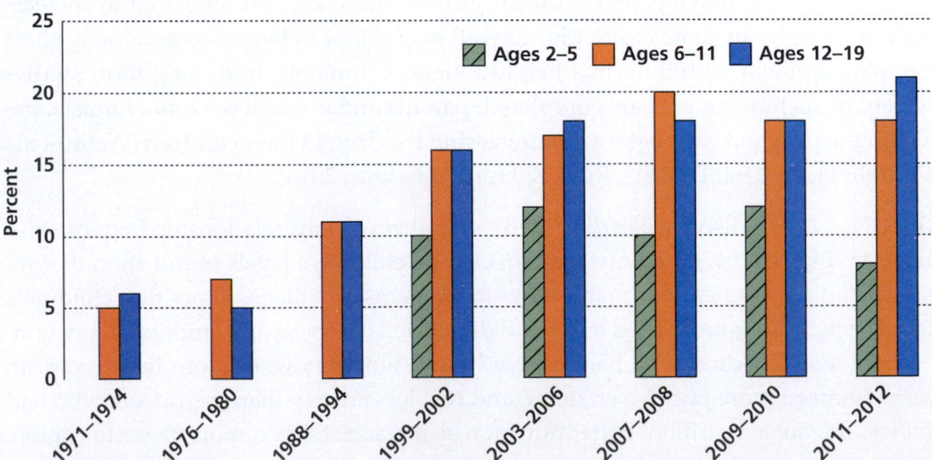

Poor diets also contribute to obesity. Despite their knowledge that certain foods are necessary for a balanced, nutritious diet, many parents provide their children with too few fruits and vegetables and more fats and sweets than recommended (see Figure 9-3). School lunch programs have sometimes contributed to the problem by failing to provide nutritious options (Johnston, Delva, & O'Malley, 2007; Story, Nanney, & Schwartz, 2009).

Given how energetic children in middle childhood can be, it is surprising that a major factor in childhood obesity is a lack of exercise. School-age children, by and large, tend to engage in relatively little exercise and are not particularly fit. For instance, around 40 percent of boys age 6 to 12 are unable to do more than one pull-up, and a quarter can't do any. Furthermore, children have shown little or no improvement in the amount of exercise they get, despite national efforts to increase the level of fitness of school-age children, in part because many schools have reduced the time available for recess and gym classes. From age 6 to 18, boys decrease their physical activity by 24 percent and girls by 36 percent (Sallis & Glanz, 2006; Weiss & Raz, 2006; Ige, DeLeon, & Nabors, 2017).

Why, when our visions of childhood include children running happily on school playgrounds, playing sports, and chasing one another in games of tag, is the actual level of exercise relatively low? One answer is that many kids are inside their homes, watching television and computer screens. Such sedentary activities not only keep children from exercising but often also encourage them to snack while viewing TV or surfing the Web (Goldfield, 2012; Cale & Harris, 2013; Lambrick et al., 2016; also see the *Development in Your Life* feature).

Figure 9-3 Balanced Diet?

Recent studies have found that the diet of children is almost the opposite of that recommended by the U.S. Department of Agriculture, a situation that can lead to an increase in obesity. The typical 10-year-old is 10 pounds heavier than a decade ago.

(**Source:** USDA, 2017.)

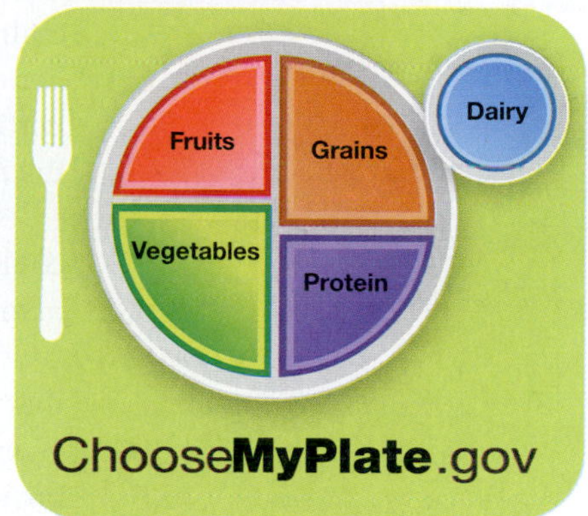

Development in Your Life

Keeping Children Fit

> *Here is a brief portrait of a contemporary American: Sam works all week at a desk and gets no regular physical exercise. On weekends he spends many hours sitting in front of the TV, often snacking on sodas and sweets. Both at home and at restaurants, his meals feature high-calorie, fat-saturated foods. (Segal & Segal, 1992, p. 235)*

Although this sketch could apply to many adult men and women, Sam is actually a 6-year-old. He is one of many school-age children in the United States who get little or no regular exercise and who consequently are physically unfit and at risk for obesity and other health problems.

Several things can be done to encourage children to become more physically active (Tyre & Scelfo, 2003; Okie, 2005):

- **Make exercise fun.** In order for children to build the habit of exercising, they need to find it enjoyable. Activities that keep children on the sidelines or that are overly competitive may give children with inferior skills a lifelong distaste for exercise.
- **Be an exercise role model.** Children who see that exercise is a regular part of the lives of their parents, teachers, or adult friends may come to think of fitness as a regular part of their lives, too.
- **Gear activities to the child's physical level and motor skills.** For instance, use child-size equipment that can make participants feel successful.
- **Encourage the child to find a partner.** It could be a friend, a sibling, or a parent. Exercising can involve a variety of activities, such as snowboarding or hiking, but almost all activities are carried out more readily if someone else is doing them too.
- **Start slowly.** Sedentary children—those who aren't used to regular physical activity—should start off gradually. For instance, they could start with 5 minutes of exercise a day, seven days a week. Over 10 weeks, they could move toward a goal of 30 minutes of exercise three to five days a week.
- **Urge participation in organized sports activities, but do not push too hard.** Not every child is athletically inclined, and pushing too hard for involvement in organized sports may backfire. Make participation and enjoyment the goals of such activities, not winning.
- **Don't make physical activity, such as jumping jacks or push-ups, a punishment for unwanted behavior.** Instead, schools and parents should encourage children to participate in organized programs that seek to involve children in ways that are enjoyable.
- **Provide a healthy diet.** Children who eat a healthy diet will have more energy to engage in physical activity than those who have a diet heavy in soda and snack foods.

Motor Development

LO 9.2 Outline the course of motor development in middle childhood.

The fact that the fitness level of school-age children is not as high as we would desire does not mean that such children are physically incapable. In fact, even without regular exercise, children's gross and fine motor skills develop substantially over the course of the school years.

GROSS MOTOR SKILLS. One important improvement in gross motor skills is in the realm of muscle coordination. When watching a softball player pitch a ball past a batter to her catcher, a runner reach the finish line in a race, or Kat, the jump-roper described earlier in the chapter, we are struck by the huge strides that these children have made since the more awkward days of preschool.

During middle childhood, children master many types of skills that earlier they could not perform well. For instance, most school-age children can readily learn to ride a bike, ice skate, swim, and skip rope (Cratty, 1986; see Figure 9-4).

Do boys and girls differ in their motor skills? Years ago developmentalists concluded that gender differences in gross motor skills became increasingly pronounced during these years, with boys outperforming girls. However, when comparisons are made between boys and girls who regularly take part in similar activities—such as softball—gender variations in gross motor skills are minimal (Hall & Lee, 1984; Jurimae & Saar, 2003).

Why the change? Expectations probably played a role. Society did not expect girls to be highly physically active and told girls that they would do worse than boys in sports, and the girls' performance reflected that message.

Today, however, society's message has changed, at least officially. For instance, the American Academy of Pediatrics suggests that boys and girls should engage in the same

Figure 9-4 Gross Motor Skills

Gross motor skills developed by children between the ages of 6 and 12.

(**Source:** Adapted from Cratty, 1979, p. 222.)

6 Years	7 Years	8 Years	9 Years	10 Years	11 Years	12 Years
Girls superior in accuracy of movement; boys superior in more forceful, less complex acts. Can throw with the proper weight shift and step. Acquire the ability to skip.	Can balance on one foot with eyes closed. Can walk on a 2-inch-wide balance beam without falling off. Can hop and jump accurately into small squares (hopscotch). Can correctly execute a jumping-jack exercise.	Can grip objects with 12 pounds of pressure. Can engage in alternate rhythmical hopping in a 2-2, 2-3, or 3-3 pattern. Girls can throw a small ball 33 feet; boys can throw a small ball 59 feet. The number of games participated in by both sexes is the greatest at this age.	Girls can jump vertically 8.5 inches over their standing height plus reach; boys can jump vertically 10 inches. Boys can run 16.6 feet per second; girls can run 16 feet per second.	Can judge and intercept directions of small balls thrown from a distance. Both girls and boys can run 17 feet per second.	Boys can achieve standing broad jump of 5 feet; girls can achieve standing broad jump of 4.5 feet.	Can achieve high jump of 3 feet.

sports and games, and that they can do so together in mixed-gender groups. There is no reason to separate the sexes in physical exercise and sports until puberty, when the smaller size of females begins to make them more susceptible to injury in contact sports (American Academy of Pediatrics, 2004; Kanters et al., 2013; Deaner, Balish, & Lombardo, 2016).

During middle childhood, children master many types of skills that earlier they could not perform well, such as those that depend on fine motor coordination.

FINE MOTOR SKILLS. Typing at a computer keyboard. Writing in cursive with pen and pencil. Drawing detailed pictures. These are just some of the accomplishments that depend on improvements in fine motor coordination that occur during early and middle childhood. Six- and 7-year-olds are able to tie their shoes and fasten buttons; by age 8, children can use each hand independently; and by 11 and 12, they can manipulate objects with almost as much capability as they will show in adulthood.

One reason for advances in fine motor skills is that the amount of myelin in the brain increases significantly between ages 6 and 8 (Lecours, 1982). *Myelin* provides protective insulation that surrounds parts of nerve cells. Because increased levels of myelin raise the speed at which electrical impulses travel between neurons, messages can reach muscles more rapidly and control them better.

Physical and Mental Health During Middle Childhood

LO 9.3 Summarize the main physical and mental health concerns of school-age children.

Imani was miserable. Her nose was running, her lips were chapped, and her throat was sore. Although she had been able to stay home from school and spend the day watching TV, she still felt that she was suffering mightily.

Despite her misery, Imani's situation is not so bad. She'll get over the cold in a few days and be no worse for having experienced it. In fact, she may be a little *better* off, for she is now immune to the specific cold germs that made her ill in the first place.

Imani's cold may end up being the most serious illness that she gets during middle childhood. For most children, this is a period of robust health, and most of the ailments they do contract tend to be mild and brief. Routine immunizations during childhood have produced a considerably lower incidence of the life-threatening illnesses that 50 years ago claimed the lives of a significant number of children.

Illness is not uncommon, however. For instance, more than 90 percent of children are likely to have at least one serious medical condition over the six-year period of middle childhood, according to the results of one large survey. And although most children have short-term illnesses, about one in nine has a chronic, persistent condition, such as repeated migraine headaches. And some illnesses are actually becoming more prevalent (Dey & Bloom, 2005).

ASTHMA. Asthma is among the diseases that have shown a significant increase in prevalence over the past several decades. **Asthma** is a chronic condition characterized by periodic attacks of wheezing, coughing, and shortness of breath. More than 7 million U.S. children suffer from the disorder, and worldwide the number is more than 150 million (Bowen, 2013; Koinis-Mitchell et al., 2014; Gandhi et al., 2016).

asthma
a chronic condition characterized by periodic attacks of wheezing, coughing, and shortness of breath

Racial and ethnic minorities are particularly at risk for the disease, because they are more at risk for exposure to environmental factors due to higher rates of poverty. Because they may live in poorer areas, they are more at risk for exposure to poor air quality and chemicals, factors that increase the risk of asthma. But genetic factors also seem to be at work (Forno & Celedon, 2009; Fedele et al., 2016).

Asthma occurs when the airways leading to the lungs constrict, partially blocking the passage of oxygen. Because the airways are obstructed, more effort is needed to push air through them, making breathing more difficult. The air being forced through the obstructed airways results in the whistling sound called wheezing.

Asthma attacks are triggered by a variety of factors. Among the most common are respiratory infections (such as colds or flu), allergic reactions to airborne irritants (such as pollution, cigarette smoke, dust mites, and animal dander and excretions), stress, and exercise. Sometimes even a sudden change in air temperature or humidity is enough to bring on an attack (Noonan & Ward, 2007; Marin et al., 2009; Ross et al., 2012).

One of the most puzzling questions about asthma is why more and more children are suffering from it. Some researchers suggest that increasing air pollution has led to the rise; others believe that cases of asthma that might have been missed in the past are being identified more accurately. Still others have suggested that exposure to "asthma triggers," such as dust, may be increasing because new buildings are more weatherproof—and therefore less drafty—than old ones, and consequently the flow of air within them is more restricted.

Although asthma and other illnesses are threats to children's well-being during middle childhood, the greater potential risk comes from the possibility of injury. During this period, children are more likely to suffer a life-threatening injury from an accident than a severe illness, as we discuss next (Woolf & Lesperance, 2003).

ACCIDENTS. The increasing independence and mobility of school-age children lead to new safety issues. Between ages 5 and 14, the rate of injury for children increases. Boys are more apt to be injured than girls, probably because their overall level of physical activity is greater. Some ethnic and racial groups are at greater risk than others: Injury death rates are highest for American Indian and Alaska Natives, and lowest for Asians and Pacific Islanders. Whites and African Americans have approximately the same death rates from injuries (see Figure 9-5; Noonan, 2003; Borse et al., 2008).

Figure 9-5 Injury Death Rates by Age

During middle childhood, the most frequent causes of accidental death are transportation-related. **THINKING ABOUT THE DATA:** Why do you think transportation-related deaths soar just after middle childhood?

(**Source:** Borse et al., 2008.)

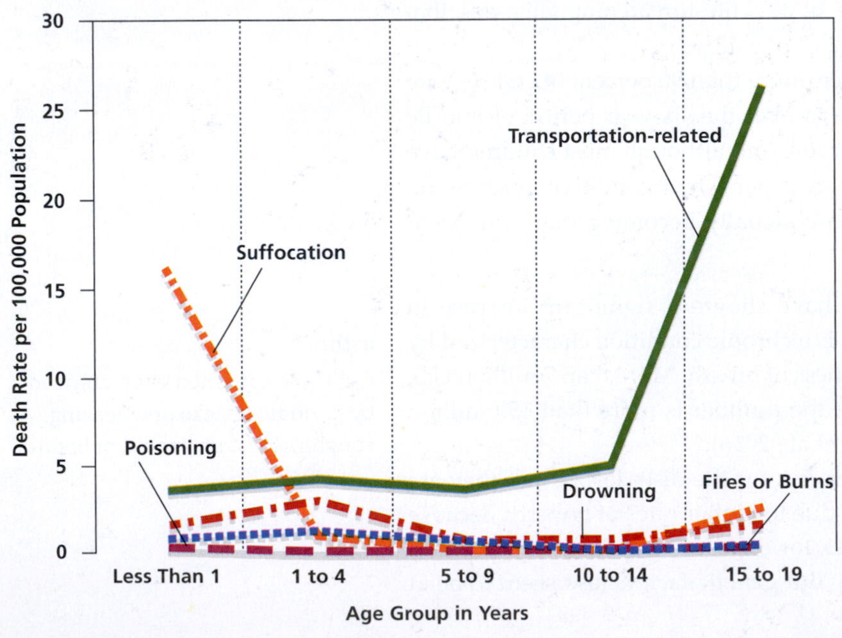

The increased mobility of school-age children is a source of several kinds of accidents. For instance, children who regularly walk to school on their own, many traveling such a distance alone for the first time in their lives, face the risk of being hit by cars and trucks. Because of their lack of experience, they may misjudge distances when calculating just how far they are from an oncoming vehicle. Furthermore, bicycle accidents pose an increasing risk, particularly as children more frequently venture out onto busy roads (Schnitzer, 2006).

The most frequent sources of injury to children are automobile accidents and other transportation injuries. Auto crashes annually kill 4 out of every 100,000 children between ages 5 and 9. Fires and burns, drowning, and gun-related deaths follow in frequency (Field & Behrman, 2002; Schiller & Bernadel, 2004).

Two ways to reduce auto and bicycle injuries are to use seat belts consistently inside the car and to wear appropriate protective gear outside. Bicycle helmets have significantly reduced head injuries, and in many localities their use is mandatory. Similar protection is available for other activities; for example, knee and elbow pads have proven to be important sources of injury reduction for roller-blading and skateboarding (Blake et al., 2008; Lachapelle, Noland, & Von Hagen, 2013).

SAFETY IN CYBERSPACE. One contemporary threat to the safety of school-age children comes from the Internet. Cyberspace makes available material that many parents find objectionable.

Although certain programs can be used to automatically block known sites that are dangerous to children or that contain objectionable material, most experts feel that the most reliable safeguard is close supervision by parents. According to the National Center for Missing and Exploited Children, a nonprofit organization that works with the U.S. Department of Justice, parents should warn their children never to provide personal information, such as home addresses or telephone numbers, to people on public computer "bulletin boards" or in chat rooms. In addition, children should not be allowed to hold face-to-face meetings with people they meet via computer, at least not without a parent present.

There are no reliable statistics that provide a true sense of the risk presented by exposure to cyberspace. But certainly a potential hazard exists, and parents must offer their children guidance. It is wrong to assume that just because children are in the supposed safety of their own bedrooms, logged on to home computers, they are truly safe (Mitchell et al., 2011; Reio & Ortega, 2016).

PSYCHOLOGICAL DISORDERS

Ben Cramer, 8, loves baseball and mystery stories. He has a dog, Frankie, and a blue racing bike. Ben also has bipolar disorder, a serious psychological disorder. Engaged in his schoolwork one minute, he'll refuse to even look at his teacher the next. Often a good friend, he'll suddenly lash out at the other children in the class. Sometimes, he believes he can do anything: touch fire and not get burned or jump off the roof and fly. Other times, he feels so sad and small, he writes poems about dying.

Bipolar disorder such as Ben's is diagnosed when a person cycles back and forth between two emotional states: unrealistically high spirits and energy at one extreme, and depression at the other. For years most people neglected the symptoms of such psychological disorders in children, and even today parents and teachers may overlook their presence. Yet it is a common problem: One in five children and adolescents has a psychological disorder that produces at least some impairment. For example, about 5 percent of preteens suffer from childhood depressive disorder, and 13 percent of children between 9 and 17 experience an anxiety disorder. The estimated cost of treatment of children's psychological disorders is $250 billion (Cicchetti & Cohen, 2006; Kluger, 2010; Holly et al., 2015).

In part, the neglect of children's psychological disorders occurs because children's symptoms are not entirely consistent with the ways adults express similar disorders. Even when childhood psychological disorders are diagnosed, the correct treatment is not always apparent. For example, the use of antidepressant drugs has become a popular treatment for a variety of childhood psychological disorders, including depression and anxiety. More than 10 million prescriptions are written annually for children under 18. Surprisingly, though, antidepressant drugs have never been approved by governmental regulators for use with children. Still, because the drugs have received approval for adult use, it is perfectly legal for physicians to write prescriptions for children (Goode, 2004).

Advocates for the increased use of antidepressants, such as Prozac, Zoloft, Paxil, and Wellbutrin, for children suggest that depression and other psychological disorders can be treated quite successfully using drug therapies. In many cases, more traditional nondrug therapies that largely employ traditional psychotherapy simply are ineffective. In such cases, drugs can provide the only form of relief. Furthermore, at least one clinical test

Psychological disorders, such as bipolar disorder and depression, can impair children's thinking and behavior.

has shown that the drugs are effective with children (Lovrin, 2009; Hirschtritt et al., 2012; Lawrence et al., 2017).

Critics, however, contend that there is little evidence for the long-term effectiveness of antidepressants in children. Even worse, no one knows the consequences of the use of antidepressants on children's developing brains nor the long-term consequences more generally. Little is known about the correct dosages for children of given ages or sizes. Furthermore, some observers suggest that the use of special children's versions of the drugs, in orange- or mint-flavored syrups, might lead to overdoses or perhaps eventually encourage the use of illegal drugs (Cheung, Emslie, & Mayes, 2006; Rothenberger & Rothenberger, 2013; Seedat, 2014).

Finally, there is some evidence linking the use of antidepressant medication with an increased risk of suicide. Although the link has not been firmly established, the U.S. Food and Drug Administration issued a warning about the use of a class of antidepressants known as selective serotonin reuptake inhibitors (SSRIs) in 2004. Some experts have urged that the use of these antidepressants in children and adolescents be banned completely (Bostwick, 2006; Sammons, 2009).

Although the use of antidepressant drugs to treat children is controversial, it is clear that childhood depression and other psychological disorders remain a significant problem for many children. Childhood psychological disorders must not be ignored. Not only are the disorders disruptive during childhood, but those who suffer from psychological problems as children are at risk for future disorders during adulthood (Gören, 2008; Sapyla & March, 2012; Palanca-Maresca et al., 2017).

Children with Special Needs

LO 9.4 Describe the sorts of special needs that may become apparent in school-age children and how can they be met.

Karen Avery was a happy-go-lucky child—until she got to first grade. A reading assessment put Karen in the lowest reading group. Despite lots of one-on-one time with her teacher, Karen's reading did not improve. She couldn't recognize words she'd seen the day before or the day before that. Her retention problems soon became apparent across the curriculum. Karen's parents agreed to let the school give her some diagnostic tests. The results suggested Karen's brain had problems transferring information from her short-term (working) memory to her long-term memory. She was labeled with a learning-disability. By law, she could now get the help she really needed.

Karen Avery joined millions of other children who are classified as having a *specific learning disorder*, one of several types of special needs that children can have. Although every child has different specific capabilities, children with *special needs* differ significantly from typical children in terms of physical attributes or learning abilities. Furthermore, their needs present major challenges for both care providers and teachers.

SENSORY DIFFICULTIES: VISUAL, AUDITORY, AND SPEECH PROBLEMS. Anyone who has temporarily lost his or her eyeglasses or a contact lens has had a glimpse of how difficult even rudimentary, everyday tasks must be for those with sensory impairments. To function with less than typical vision, hearing, or speech can be a tremendous challenge.

visual impairment
a difficulty in seeing that may include blindness or partial sightedness

Visual impairment can be considered in both a legal and an educational sense. The definition of legal impairment is quite straightforward: *Blindness* is visual acuity of less than 20/200 after correction (meaning the inability to see even at 20 feet what a typical person can see at 200 feet), whereas *partial sightedness* is visual acuity of less than 20/70 after correction.

Even if individuals are not so severely impaired as to be legally blind, their visual problems may still seriously affect schoolwork. For one thing, the legal criterion pertains solely to distance vision, while most educational tasks require close-up vision. In addition, the legal definition does not consider abilities in the perception of color, depth, and light—all of which might influence a student's educational success. About one student in a thousand requires special education services relating to a visual impairment.

Most severe visual problems are identified fairly early, but it sometimes happens that an impairment goes undetected. Visual problems can also emerge gradually as children develop physiologically and changes occur in the visual apparatus of the eyes.

AMELIE-BENOIST/BSIP/Getty Images

Auditory impairments can produce both academic and social difficulties, and they may lead to speech difficulties.

Auditory impairments can also cause academic problems, and they can produce social difficulties as well, since considerable peer interaction takes place through informal conversation. Hearing loss, which affects some 1 to 2 percent of the school-age population, is not simply a matter of not hearing enough. Rather, auditory problems can vary along a number of dimensions (Yoshinaga-Itano, 2003; Smith, Bale, & White, 2005; Martin-Prudent et al., 2016).

auditory impairment
a special need that involves the loss of hearing or some aspect of hearing

In some cases of hearing loss, the child's hearing is impaired at only a limited range of frequencies, or pitches. For example, the loss may be great at pitches in the normal speech range yet quite minor in other frequencies, such as those of very high or low sounds. A child with this kind of loss may require different levels of amplification at different frequencies; a hearing aid that indiscriminately amplifies all frequencies equally may be ineffective because it will amplify the sounds the person can hear to an uncomfortable degree.

How a child adapts to this impairment depends on the age at which the hearing loss begins. If the loss of hearing occurs in infancy, the effects will probably be much more severe than if it occurs after age 3. Children who have had little or no exposure to the sound of language are unable to understand or produce oral language themselves. By contrast, loss of hearing after a child has learned language will not have serious consequences on subsequent linguistic development.

Severe and early loss of hearing is also associated with difficulties in abstract thinking. Because children with hearing impairment may have limited exposure to language, they may have more trouble mastering abstract concepts that can be understood fully only through the use of language than concrete concepts that can be illustrated visually. For example, it is difficult to explain the concept of "freedom" or "soul" without use of language (Marschark, Spencer, & Newsom, 2003; Meinzen-Derr et al., 2014; Fitzpatrick et al., 2017).

Auditory difficulties are sometimes accompanied by speech impairments, one of the most public types of exceptionality: Every time the child speaks aloud, the impairment is obvious to listeners. The definition of **speech impairment** suggests that speech is impaired when it deviates so much from the speech of others that it calls attention to itself, interferes with communication, or produces maladjustment in the speaker. In other words, if a child's speech sounds impaired, it probably is. Speech impairments are present in around 3 to 5 percent of the school-age population (Bishop & Leonard, 2001).

speech impairment
speech that deviates so much from the speech of others that it calls attention to itself, interferes with communication, or produces maladjustment in the speaker

Childhood-onset fluency disorder, or *stuttering*, involves a substantial disruption in the rhythm and fluency of speech and is the most common speech impairment. Despite a great deal of research, no specific cause has been identified. Occasional stuttering is not unusual in young children—and occasionally occurs in normal adults—but chronic stuttering can be a severe problem. Not only does stuttering hinder communication, but it can produce embarrassment and stress in children, who may become inhibited from conversing with others and speaking aloud in class (Altholz & Golensky, 2004; Sasisekaran, 2014).

childhood-onset fluency disorder (stuttering)
substantial disruption in the rhythm and fluency of speech; the most common speech impairment

Parents and teachers can adopt several strategies for dealing with stuttering. For starters, attention should not be drawn to the stuttering, and children should be given sufficient time to finish what they begin to say, no matter how protracted the statement becomes. It does not help stutterers to finish their sentences for them or otherwise correct their speech (Ryan, 2001; Beilby, Byrnes, & Young, 2012).

LEARNING DISABILITIES: DISCREPANCIES BETWEEN ACHIEVEMENT AND CAPACITY TO LEARN. Like Karen Avery, who was described at the beginning of this section, some 1 in 10 school-age children are labeled as having specific learning disorders. **Specific learning disorders** are characterized by difficulties in the acquisition and use of listening, speaking, reading, writing, reasoning, or mathematical abilities. A somewhat ill-defined, grab-bag category, learning disorders are diagnosed when there is a discrepancy between children's actual academic performance and their apparent potential to learn (Lerner, 2002; Bos & Vaughn, 2005; Bonifacci et al., 2016).

specific learning disorders
difficulties in the acquisition and use of listening, speaking, reading, writing, reasoning, or mathematical abilities

Such a broad definition encompasses a wide and extremely varied range of difficulties. For instance, some children suffer from *dyslexia*, a reading disability that can result in the misperception of letters during reading and writing, unusual difficulty in sounding out letters, confusion between left and right, and difficulties in spelling. Dyslexia is sometimes thought of as a language-based learning disability because it affects so many language-related skills, including reading comprehension, recall, writing, and spelling.

Although dyslexia is not fully understood, one likely explanation for the disorder is a problem in the part of the brain responsible for breaking words into the sound elements that make up language (Lachmann et al., 2005; Sumner, Connelly, & Barnett, 2014).

Some children have *auditory processing disorder* (APD), which impedes the way that sound is processed or interpreted by the brain. Children with APD have trouble making discriminations between different sounds, despite the sounds being loud enough to be heard. This can make it difficult to determine where sounds are coming from (Bartlett et al., 2017).

There are a number of other types of specific learning disorders including those relating to math (*dyscalculia*), handwriting (*dysgraphia*), and abilities to recognize facial expressions and other nonverbal cues (*non-verbal learning disabilities*). One feature they share is that the causes of specific learning disorders are not well understood. Although they are generally attributed to some form of brain dysfunction, probably due to genetic factors, some experts suggest that they are produced by such environmental causes as poor early nutrition or allergies (Shaywitz et al., 2004; Lafay, St-Pierre, & Macoir, 2017).

ATTENTION-DEFICIT/HYPERACTIVITY DISORDER

Troy Dalton, 7, exhausted his teacher. Unable to sit still, he roamed the classroom all day, distracting the other children. In reading group, he jumped up and down in his seat, dropping his book and knocking over the whiteboard. During read aloud, he ran around the room, humming noisily and shouting, "I'm a jet plane!" Once, he flung himself through the air, landing on another boy and breaking his arm. "He's the definition of perpetual motion," the teacher told Troy's mother (who looked pretty exhausted herself). The school finally decided to split Troy's day between the three second-grade classrooms. It was not a perfect solution, but it did allow his primary teacher to do some actual teaching.

Seven-year-old Troy Dalton's high energy and low attention span are caused by attention-deficit/hyperactivity disorder, which occurs in 3 to 5 percent of the school-age population. **Attention-deficit/hyperactivity disorder (ADHD)**, is marked by inattention, impulsiveness, a low tolerance for frustration, and generally a great deal of inappropriate activity. All children show such traits some of the time, but for those diagnosed with ADHD, such behavior is common and interferes with their home and school functioning (American Academy of Pediatrics, 2000; Whalen et al., 2002; Van Neste et al., 2015).

attention-deficit/hyperactivity disorder (ADHD)
a learning disability marked by inattention, impulsiveness, a low tolerance for frustration, and generally a great deal of inappropriate activity

What are the most common signs of ADHD? It is often difficult to distinguish between children who simply have a high level of activity and those with ADHD. Some of the most common symptoms include:

- Persistent difficulty in finishing tasks, following instructions, and organizing work
- Inability to watch an entire television program
- Frequent interruption of others or excessive talking
- A tendency to jump into a task before hearing all the instructions
- Difficulty in waiting or remaining seated
- Fidgeting, squirming

Figure 9-6 Rising Diagnoses of ADHD

Over the past 20 years, diagnoses of ADHD have increased for boys and girls.

(**Source:** CDC/NCHS, Health Data Interactive and National Health Interview Survey. http://www.cdc.gov/nchs/data/databriefs/db70.htm)

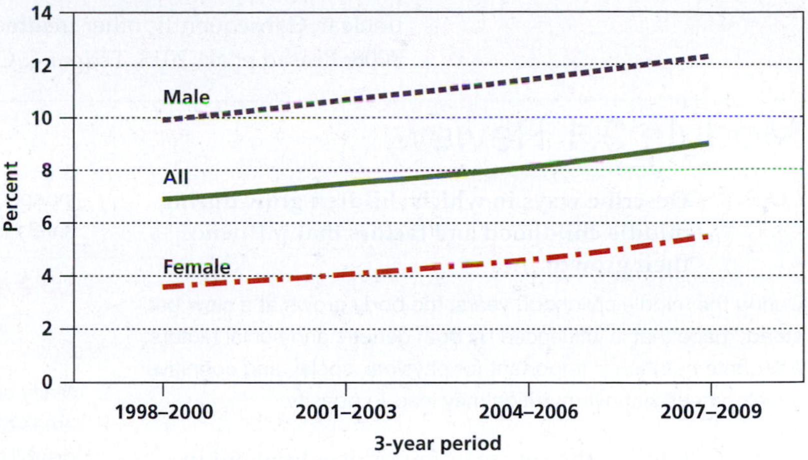

Percent: 0, 2, 4, 6, 8, 10, 12, 14

Male

All

Female

1998–2000, 2001–2003, 2004–2006, 2007–2009

3-year period

Because there is no simple test to identify whether a child has ADHD, it is hard to know for sure how many children have the disorder. The Centers for Disease Control and Prevention put the proportion of children ages 3 to 17 with ADHD at 9 percent, with boys being twice as likely to be diagnosed with the disorder as girls. Other estimates are lower. What is clear is that the incidence of diagnoses of ADHD has increased significantly in recent decades (see Figure 9-6). It is unclear whether the increase is due to an actual increase in the disorder or instead to an increase in its labeling. In any case, only a trained clinician can make an accurate diagnosis following an extensive evaluation of the child and interviews with parents and teachers (Sax & Kautz, 2003; CDC, 2010).

The causes of ADHD are not clear, although some research finds that it is related to a delay in neural development. Specifically, it may be that the thickening of the brain's cortex in children with ADHD lags three years behind that of children without the disorder (see Figure 9-7).

The treatment of children with ADHD has been a source of considerable controversy. Because it has been found that doses of Ritalin or Dexedrine (which, paradoxically, are stimulants) reduce activity levels in hyperactive children, many physicians routinely

Figure 9-7 The Brains of Children with ADHD

The brains of children with ADHD (in the top row) show less thickening of the cortex compared to the brains of typical children at the same age.

(**Source:** Shaw et al., 2007.)

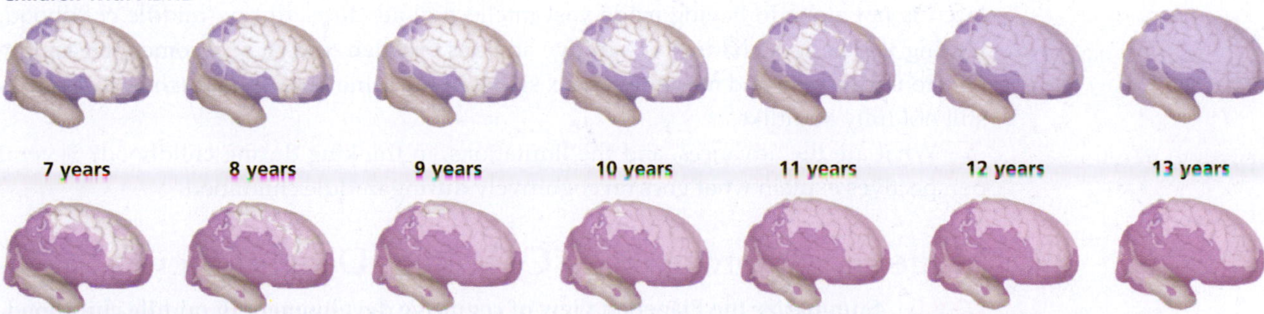

prescribe drug treatment (Arnsten, Berridge, & McCracken, 2009; Weissman et al., 2012; Pelham et al., 2016).

Although in many cases such drugs are effective in increasing attention span and compliance, in some cases the side effects (such as irritability, reduced appetite, and depression) are considerable, and the long-term health consequences of this treatment are unclear. Consequently, other treatments, such as behavioral therapy, are also used (Rose, 2008; Prasad et al., 2013; Thapar & Cooper, 2016).

Module 9.1 Review

LO 9.1 Describe ways in which children grow during middle childhood and factors that influence their growth.

During the middle childhood years, the body grows at a slow but steady pace that is influenced by both genetic and social factors. Adequate nutrition is important for physical, social, and cognitive development, but overnutrition may lead to obesity.

LO 9.2 Outline the course of motor development in middle childhood.

Children substantially improve their gross and fine motor skills during the school years, with muscular coordination and manipulative skills advancing to near-adult levels.

LO 9.3 Summarize the main physical and mental health concerns of school-age children.

The incidence of asthma and childhood depression has increased significantly over the past several decades. The increasing independence and mobility of school-age children lead to new safety issues.

LO 9.4 Describe the sorts of special needs that may become apparent in school-age children and how can they be met.

Many school-age children have special needs, particularly in the areas of vision, hearing, and speech. Some also have learning disabilities. Attention-deficit/hyperactivity disorder, marked by attention, organization, and activity problems, affects between 3 and 5 percent of the school-age population. Treatment through the use of drugs is highly controversial.

Journal Writing Prompt

Applying Lifespan Development: What are some aspects of U.S. culture that may contribute to obesity among school-age children?

Intellectual Development

Jared's parents were delighted when he came home from kindergarten one day and explained that he had learned why the sky was blue. He talked about the earth's atmosphere—although he didn't pronounce the word correctly—and how tiny bits of moisture in the air reflected the sunlight. Although his explanation had rough edges (he couldn't quite grasp what the "atmosphere" was), he still had the general idea, and that, his parents felt, was quite an achievement for their 5-year-old.

Fast-forward six years. Jared, now 11, had already spent an hour laboring over his evening's homework. After completing a two-page worksheet on multiplying and dividing fractions, he had begun work on his U.S. Constitution project. He was taking notes for his report, which would explain what political factions had been involved in the writing of the document and how the Constitution had been amended since its creation.

Jared is not alone in having made vast intellectual advances during middle childhood. During this period, children's cognitive abilities broaden, and they become increasingly able to understand and master complex skills. At the same time, though, their thinking is still not fully adultlike.

What are the advances, and the limitations, in thinking during childhood? Several perspectives explain what goes on cognitively during middle childhood.

Piagetian Approaches to Cognitive Development

LO 9.5 Summarize the Piagetian view of cognitive development in middle childhood.

Let's return for a moment to Jean Piaget's view of the preschooler, which we considered in Chapter 7. From Piaget's perspective, the preschooler thinks *preoperationally*.

This type of thinking is largely egocentric, and preoperational children lack the ability to use *operations*—organized, formal, logical mental processes.

THE RISE OF CONCRETE OPERATIONAL THOUGHT. All this changes, according to Piaget, during the concrete operational period, which coincides with the school years. The **concrete operational stage**, which occurs between ages 7 and 12, is characterized by the active, and appropriate, use of logic.

concrete operational stage
the period of cognitive development between ages 7 and 12, which is characterized by the active, and appropriate, use of logic

Concrete operational thought involves applying *logical operations* to concrete problems. For instance, when children in the concrete operational stage are confronted with a conservation problem (such as determining whether a constant amount of liquid poured from one container to another container of a different shape stays the same), they use cognitive and logical processes to answer, no longer being influenced solely by appearance. They are able to reason correctly that since none of the liquid has been lost, the amount stays the same. Because they are less egocentric, they can take multiple aspects of a situation into account, an ability known as **decentering**. Jared, the sixth grader described at the beginning of this section, was using his decentering skills to consider the views of the different factions involved in creating the U.S. Constitution.

decentering
the ability to take multiple aspects of a situation into account

The shift from preoperational thought to concrete operational thought does not happen overnight, of course. During the two years before children move firmly into the concrete operational period, they shift back and forth between preoperational and concrete operational thinking. For instance, they typically pass through a period when they can answer conservation problems correctly but can't articulate why they did so. When asked to explain the reasoning behind their answers, they may respond with an unenlightening, "Because."

Once concrete operational thinking is fully engaged, however, children show several cognitive advances. For instance, they attain the concept of *reversibility*, which is the notion that processes transforming a stimulus can be reversed, returning the stimulus to its original form. Grasping reversibility permits children to understand that a ball of clay that has been squeezed into a long, snake-like rope can be returned to its original state. More abstractly, it allows school-age children to understand that if $3 + 5 = 8$, then $5 + 3$ also $= 8$—and, later during the period, that $8 - 3 = 5$.

Concrete operational thinking also permits children to understand such concepts as the relationship between time and speed. For instance, consider the problem shown in Figure 9-8 in which two cars start and finish at the same points in the same amount of

Figure 9-8 Routes to Conservation

After being told that the two cars traveling on routes 1 and 2 start and end their journeys in the same amount of time, children who are just entering the concrete operational period still reason that the cars are traveling at the same speed. Later, however, they reach the correct conclusion: that the car traveling the longer route must be moving at a higher speed if it starts and ends its journey at the same time as the car traveling the shorter route.

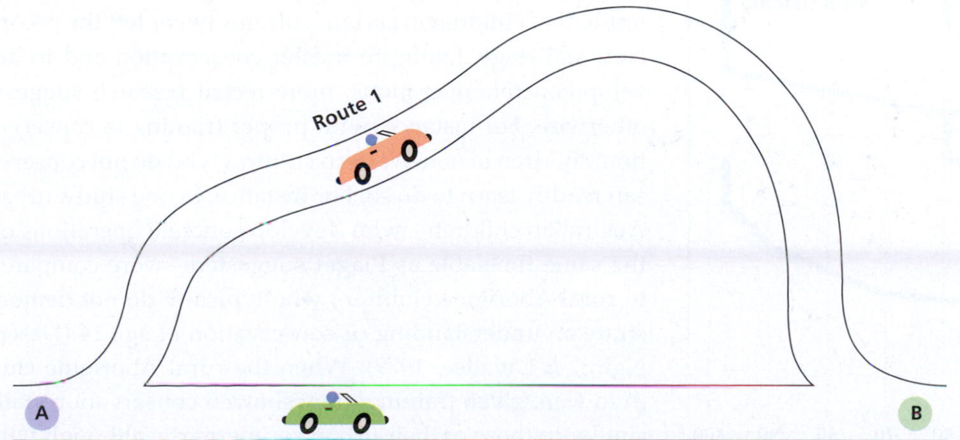

Cognitive development makes substantial advances in middle childhood.

time, but travel different routes. Children who are just entering the concrete operational period reason that the cars are traveling at the same speed. However, between the ages of 8 and 10, children begin to draw the right conclusion: that the car traveling the longer route must be moving faster if it arrives at the finish point at the same time as the car traveling the shorter route.

Despite the advances that occur during the concrete operational stage, children still experience one critical limitation in their thinking: They remain tied to concrete, physical reality. Furthermore, they are unable to understand truly abstract or hypothetical questions, or ones that involve formal logic.

PIAGET IN PERSPECTIVE: PIAGET WAS RIGHT, PIAGET WAS WRONG. As we learned in our prior consideration of Piaget's views in Chapter 5 and Chapter 7, researchers following in Piaget's footsteps have found much to cheer about—as well as much to criticize.

Piaget was a virtuoso observer of children, and his many books contain pages of brilliant, careful observations of children at work and play. Furthermore, his theories have powerful educational implications, and many schools employ principles derived from his views to guide the nature and presentation of instructional materials (Flavell, 1996; Siegler & Ellis, 1996; Brainerd, 2003).

In some ways, then, Piaget's approach was quite successful in describing cognitive development. At the same time, though, critics have voiced compelling and seemingly legitimate grievances about his approach. As we have noted before, many researchers argue that Piaget underestimated children's capabilities, in part because of the limited nature of the mini-experiments he conducted. When a broader array of experimental tasks is used, children show less consistency within stages than Piaget would predict (Bjorklund, 1997b; Bibace, 2013; Siegler, 2016).

Furthermore, Piaget seems to have misjudged the age at which children's cognitive abilities emerge. As might be expected from our earlier discussions of Piaget's stages, increasing evidence suggests that children's capabilities emerge earlier than Piaget envisioned. Some children show evidence of a form of concrete operational thinking before age 7, the time at which Piaget suggested these abilities first appear.

Still, we cannot dismiss the Piagetian approach. Although some early cross-cultural research seemed to imply that children in certain cultures never left the preoperational stage, failing to master conservation and to develop concrete operations, more recent research suggests otherwise. For instance, with proper training in conservation, children in non-Western cultures who do not conserve can readily learn to do so. For instance, in one study, urban Australian children—who develop concrete operations on the same timetable as Piaget suggested—were compared to rural Aborigine children, who typically do not demonstrate an understanding of conservation at age 14 (Dasen, Ngini, & Lavallee, 1979). When the rural Aborigine children were given training, they showed conservation skills similar to those of their urban counterparts, although with a time lag of around three years (see Figure 9-9).

Figure 9-9 Conservation Training

Rural Australian Aborigine children trail their urban counterparts in the development of their understanding of conservation; with training, they later catch up. Without training, around half of 14-year-old Aborigines do not have an understanding of conservation. What can be concluded from the fact that training influences the understanding of conservation?

(**Source:** Based on Dasen, Ngini, & Lavallee, 1979.)

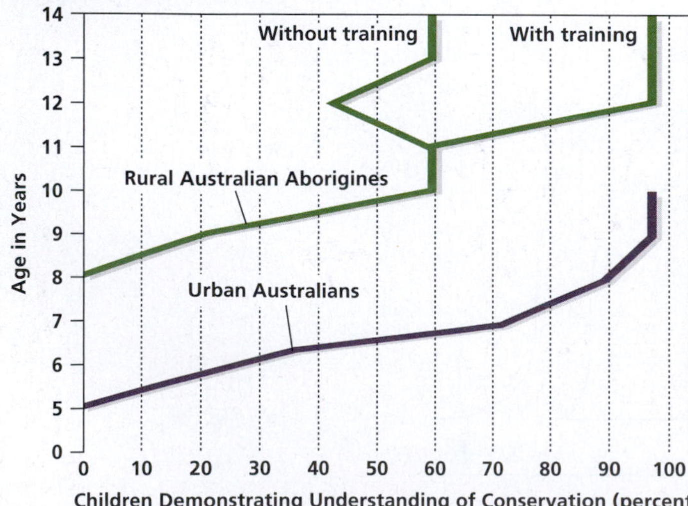

Furthermore, when children are interviewed by researchers from their own culture, who know the language and customs of the culture well and who use reasoning tasks that are related to domains important to the culture, the children are considerably more likely to display concrete operational thinking (Jahoda, 1983). Ultimately, such research suggests that Piaget was right when he argued that concrete operations were universally achieved during middle childhood. Although school-age children in some cultures may differ from Westerners in the demonstration of certain cognitive skills, the most probable explanation of the difference is that the non-Western children have had different sorts of experiences from those that permit children in Western societies to perform well on Piagetian measures of conservation and concrete operations. The progress of cognitive development, then, cannot be understood without looking at the nature of a child's culture (Lau, Lee, & Chiu, 2004; Maynard, 2008; Wang et al., 2016).

Information Processing in Middle Childhood

LO 9.6 Explain how children develop cognitively in middle childhood according to information processing approaches.

It is a significant achievement for first graders to learn basic math tasks, such as addition and subtraction of single-digit numbers, as well as the spelling of simple words such as *dog* and *run*. But by the time they reach sixth grade, children are able to work with fractions and decimals, like the fractions worksheet that Jared, the boy in the example at the start of this section, completed for his sixth-grade homework. They can also spell such words as *exhibit* and *residence*.

According to *information processing approaches*, children become increasingly sophisticated in their handling of information. Like computers, they can process more data as the size of their memories increases and the "programs" they use to process information become increasingly sophisticated (Kuhn et al., 1995; Kail, 2003; Zelazo et al., 2003).

MEMORY. As we saw in Chapter 5, **memory** in the information processing model is the ability to encode, store, and retrieve information. For a child to remember a piece of information, the three processes must all function properly. Through *encoding*, the child initially records the information in a form usable to memory. Children who were never taught that 5 + 6 = 11, or who didn't pay attention when they were exposed to this fact, will never be able to recall it. They never encoded the information in the first place.

memory
the process by which information is initially encoded, stored, and retrieved

But mere exposure to a fact is not enough; the information also has to be *stored*. In our example, the information that 5 + 6 = 11 must be placed and maintained in the memory system. Finally, proper functioning of memory requires that material that is stored in memory must be *retrieved*. Through retrieval, material in memory storage is located, brought into awareness, and used.

During middle childhood, the capacity of short-term memory (also referred to as *working memory*) improves significantly. For instance, children are increasingly able to hear a string of digits ("1-5-6-3-4") and then repeat the string in reverse order ("4-3-6-5-1"). At the start of the preschool period, they can remember and reverse only about two digits; by the beginning of adolescence, they can perform the task with as many as six digits. In addition, they use more sophisticated strategies for recalling information, which can be improved with training (Jack, Simcock, & Hayne, 2012; Jarrold & Hall, 2013; Resing et al., 2017).

Memory capacity may shed light on another issue in cognitive development. Some developmental psychologists suggest that the difficulty children experience in solving conservation problems during the preschool period may stem from memory limitations (Siegler & Richards,

Penny Tweedie/Getty Images

Although some early cross-cultural research seemed to imply that children in certain cultures never left the preoperational stage, more recent research suggests otherwise.

1982). They argue that young children simply may not be able to recall all the necessary pieces of information that enter into the correct solution of conservation problems.

metamemory

an understanding about the processes that underlie memory, which emerges and improves during middle childhood

Metamemory, an understanding about the processes that underlie memory, also emerges and improves during middle childhood. By the time they enter first grade and their theory of mind becomes more sophisticated, children have a general notion of what memory is, and they are able to understand that some people have better memories than others (Cherney, 2003; Ghetti & Angelini, 2008; Jaswal & Dodson, 2009).

School-age children's understanding of memory becomes more sophisticated as children grow older and increasingly engage in *control strategies*—conscious, intentionally used tactics to improve cognitive processing. For instance, school-age children are aware that rehearsal, the repetition of information, is a useful strategy for improving memory, and they increasingly employ it over the course of middle childhood. Similarly, they progressively make more effort to organize material into coherent patterns, a strategy that permits them to recall it better. For instance, when faced with remembering a list including cups, knives, forks, and plates, older school-age children are more likely than children just entering the school-age years to group the items into coherent patterns—cups and plates, forks and knives (Sang, Miao, & Deng, 2002; Dionne & Cadoret, 2013).

Similarly, children in middle childhood increasingly use *mnemonics* (pronounced "neh MON ix"), which are formal techniques for organizing information in a way that makes it more likely to be remembered. For instance, they may learn that the spaces on the music staff spell the word *FACE* or learn the rhyme "Thirty days hath September, April, June, and November ..." to try to recall the number of days in each month (Bellezza, 2000; Carney & Levin, 2003; Sprenger, 2007; also see the *From Research to Practice* box.)

From Research to Practice

The Key to Better Math Skills Is at Children's Fingertips

When you learned to do simple arithmetic, did you start by learning to count on your fingers? And did your parents or teachers at some point actively discourage you from doing that? Perhaps even today you still mentally count up or down to do addition and subtraction (and maybe even feel an occasional twinge of guilt about it)? If so, fear not—what you're doing is common and natural, and research suggests that it's just part of how we learn to think about numbers as young children.

Counting objects—whether they are beads, coins, fingers, or something else—is an important tactic for giving children a concrete understanding of simple mathematical operations. Educators emphasize that it's perfectly appropriate for children to use this strategy and to continue using it until they develop the ability to mentally manipulate numbers and no longer need the crutch (Berteletti & Booth, 2016).

Recent research confirms the importance of finger counting to the development of math skill. Children ages 8 to 13 were subjected to functional magnetic resonance imaging (fMRI) scans while they mentally solved simple arithmetic problems involving subtraction and multiplication. Regions of the brain associated with the fingers lit up when the children were doing subtraction—one in the somatosensory cortex and one in the motor cortex—as if the children were counting on their fingers, although none of them were. Solving multiplication problems did not activate these finger-associated regions of the brain, suggesting that multiplication and subtraction involve different neural networks in the brain. This makes sense given that multiplication is usually learned by rote memorization rather than by counting (Berteletti & Booth, 2015; Sella et al., 2017).

Moreover, children who are more skilled at finger perception—that is, who are better able to accurately detect which finger is being touched without looking—tend to be more skilled at math. Indeed, finger perception is a good predictor of future math success, and training in finger perception improves math performance. While researchers can't say for sure whether this association means that the development of math skills definitely depends on finger perception, it is consistent with the observation that visualization facilitates understanding of mathematical concepts. It seems that while most of us outgrow counting on our fingers, our brains never really do (Berteletti & Booth, 2016).

Shared Writing Prompt

How might a parent or a. teacher apply this research to help children develop stronger math skills?

IMPROVING MEMORY. Can children be trained to be more effective in the use of control strategies? Definitely. School-age children can be taught to use particular strategies, although such teaching is not a simple matter. For instance, children need to know not only how to use a memory strategy but also when and where to use it most effectively.

Take, for example, an innovative technique called the *key word strategy*, which can help students learn the vocabulary of a foreign language, the capitals of the states, or other information in which two sets of words or labels are paired. In the key word strategy, one word is paired with another that sounds like it (Wyra, Lawson, & Hungi, 2007). For instance, in learning foreign language vocabulary, a foreign word is paired with a common English word that has a similar sound. The English word is the key word. Thus, to learn the Spanish word for duck (*pato*, pronounced *pot-o*), the key word might be "pot"; for the Spanish word for horse (*caballo*, pronounced *cob-eye-yo*), the key word might be "eye." Once the key word is chosen, children then form a mental image of the two words interacting with one another. For instance, a student might use an image of a duck taking a bath in a pot to remember the word *pato*, or a horse with bulging eyes to remember the word *caballo*.

Vygotsky's Approach to Cognitive Development and Classroom Instruction

LO 9.7 Summarize Vygotsky's interpretation of cognitive development during middle childhood.

Learning environments can encourage children to learn these strategies as well. Recall from Chapter 7 that Russian developmentalist Lev Vygotsky proposed that cognitive advances occur through exposure to information within a child's *zone of proximal development* (ZPD). The ZPD is the level at which a child can almost, but not quite, understand or perform a task.

Vygotsky's approach has been particularly influential in the development of several classroom practices based on the proposition that children should actively participate in their educational experiences. Consequently, classrooms are seen as places where children should have the opportunity to experiment and try out new activities (Vygotsky, 1926/1997; Gredler, 2012; Danish et al., 2017).

From *an educator's* perspective

Suggest how a teacher might use Vygotsky's approach to teach 10-year-olds about colonial America.

According to Vygotsky, education should focus on activities that involve interaction with others. Both child–adult and child–child interactions can provide the potential for cognitive growth. The nature of the interactions must be carefully structured to fall within each individual child's zone of proximal development.

Several current and noteworthy educational innovations have borrowed heavily from Vygotsky's work. For example, *cooperative learning*, in which children work together in groups to achieve a common goal, incorporates several aspects of Vygotsky's theory. Students working in cooperative groups benefit from the insights of others, and if they get onto the wrong track, they may be brought back to the correct course by others in their group. However, not every peer is equally helpful to members of a cooperative learning group: As Vygotsky's approach would imply, individual children benefit most when at least some of the other members of the group are more competent at the task and can act as experts (DeLisi, 2006; Slavin, 2013; Gillies, 2014).

Reciprocal teaching is another educational practice that reflects Vygotsky's approach to cognitive development. *Reciprocal teaching* is a technique to teach reading comprehension

Students working in cooperative groups benefit from the insights of others.

strategies. Students are taught to skim the content of a passage, raise questions about its central point, summarize the passage, and finally predict what will happen next. A key to this technique is its reciprocal nature, its emphasis on giving students a chance to take on the role of teacher. In the beginning, teachers lead students through the comprehension strategies. Gradually, students progress through their zones of proximal development, taking more and more control over use of the strategies, until the students are able to take on a teaching role. The method has shown impressive success in raising reading comprehension levels, particularly for students experiencing reading difficulties (Greenway, 2002; Takala, 2006; Spörer, Brunstein, & Kieschke, 2009; Lundberg & Reichenberg, 2013; Davis & Voirin, 2016).

Language Development: What Words Mean

LO 9.8 Describe how language develops during middle childhood.

If you listen to what school-age children say to one another, their speech, at least at first hearing, sounds not too different from that of adults. However, the apparent similarity is deceiving. The linguistic sophistication of children—particularly at the start of the school-age period—still requires refinement to reach adult levels of expertise.

MASTERING THE MECHANICS OF LANGUAGE. Vocabulary continues to increase during the school years at a fairly rapid clip. For instance, the average 6-year-old has a vocabulary of 8,000 to 14,000 words, whereas the vocabulary grows by another 5,000 words between ages 9 and 11.

School-age children's mastery of grammar also improves. For instance, the use of the passive voice is rare during the early school-age years (as in "The dog was walked by Jon," compared with the active-voice "Jon walked the dog"). Six- and 7-year-olds only infrequently use conditional sentences, such as "If Sarah will set the table, I will wash the dishes." However, over the course of middle childhood, the use of both passive voice and conditional sentences increases. In addition, children's understanding of *syntax*, the rules that indicate how words and phrases can be combined to form sentences, grows during middle childhood.

By the time they reach first grade, most children pronounce words quite accurately. However, certain *phonemes*, units of sound, remain troublesome. For instance, the ability to pronounce *j, v, th,* and *zh* sounds develops later than the ability to pronounce other phonemes.

School-age children also may have difficulty decoding sentences when the meaning depends on *intonation*, or tone of voice. For example, consider the sentence, "George gave a book to David and he gave one to Bill." If the word *he* is emphasized, the meaning is "George gave a book to David and David gave a different book to Bill." But if the intonation emphasizes the word *and*, then the meaning changes to "George gave a book to David and George also gave a book to Bill." School-age children cannot easily sort out subtleties such as these (Wells, Peppé, & Goulandris, 2004; Bosco et al., 2013).

In addition to language skills, conversational skills also develop during middle childhood. Children become more competent in their use of *pragmatics*, the rules governing the use of language to communicate in a given social setting.

For example, although children are aware of the rules of conversational turn-taking at the start of the early childhood period, their use of these rules is sometimes primitive. Consider the following conversation between 6-year-olds Yonnie and Max:

YONNIE: My dad drives a FedEx truck.
MAX: My sister's name is Molly.
YONNIE: He gets up really early in the morning.
MAX: She wet her bed last night.

Later, however, conversations show more give and take, with the second child actually responding to the comments of the first. For instance, this conversation between 11-year-olds Mia and Josh reflects a more sophisticated mastery of pragmatics:

MIA: I don't know what to get Claire for her birthday.
JOSH: I'm getting her earrings.
MIA: She already has a lot of jewelry.
JOSH: I don't think she has that much.

METALINGUISTIC AWARENESS. One of the most significant developments in middle childhood is children's increasing understanding of their own use of language, or **metalinguistic awareness**. By the time children are 5 or 6, they understand that language is governed by a set of rules. Whereas in the early years they learn and comprehend these rules implicitly, during middle childhood children come to understand them more explicitly (Benelli et al., 2006; Saiegh-Haddad, 2007).

metalinguistic awareness
an understanding of one's own use of language

Metalinguistic awareness helps children achieve comprehension when information is fuzzy or incomplete. For instance, when preschoolers are given ambiguous or unclear information, such as directions for how to play a complicated game, they rarely ask for clarification, and they tend to blame themselves if they do not understand. By the time they reach age 7 or 8, children realize that miscommunication may be due to factors attributable not only to themselves but to the person communicating with them as well. Consequently, school-age children are more likely to ask for clarifications of information that is unclear to them (Apperly & Robinson, 2002; van den Herik, 2017).

HOW LANGUAGE PROMOTES SELF-CONTROL. The growing sophistication of their language helps school-age children control and regulate their behavior. For instance, in one experiment, children were told that they could have one marshmallow treat if they chose to eat one immediately, but two treats if they waited. Most of the children, who ranged in age from 4 to 8, chose to wait, but the strategies they used while waiting differed significantly.

The 4-year-olds often chose to look at the marshmallows while waiting, a strategy that was not terribly effective. In contrast, 6- and 8-year-olds used language to help them overcome temptation, although in different ways. The 6-year-olds spoke and sang to themselves, reminding themselves that if they waited, they would get more treats in the end. The 8-year-olds focused on aspects of the marshmallows that were not related to taste, such as their appearance, which helped them to wait.

In short, children used "self-talk" to help regulate their own behavior. Furthermore, the effectiveness of their self-control grew as their linguistic capabilities increased.

BILINGUALISM: SPEAKING IN MANY TONGUES

John Dewey Elementary is a school known for its progressive and democratic attitudes. On the campus of a large university, it boasts a staff of classroom aides who in sum speak 15 different languages, including Hindi and Hausa. The challenge is that there are more than 30 languages spoken by the students.

From the smallest towns to the biggest cities, the voices with which children speak are changing. Nearly one in five people in the United States—some 62 million—speak a language other than English at home, and that percentage is growing. **Bilingualism**—the use of more than one language—is growing increasingly common (Graddol, 2004; Hoff & Core, 2013; see Figure 9-10).

bilingualism
the use of more than one language

Children who enter school with little or no English proficiency must learn both the standard curriculum and the language in which that curriculum is taught. One approach to educating non-English speakers is *bilingual education*, in which children are initially taught in their native language, while at the same time learning English. With bilingual

Figure 9-10 Percentage of People 5 Years and Over Who Spoke a Language Other Than English at Home

(Source: U.S. Census Bureau, 2011 American Community Survey.)

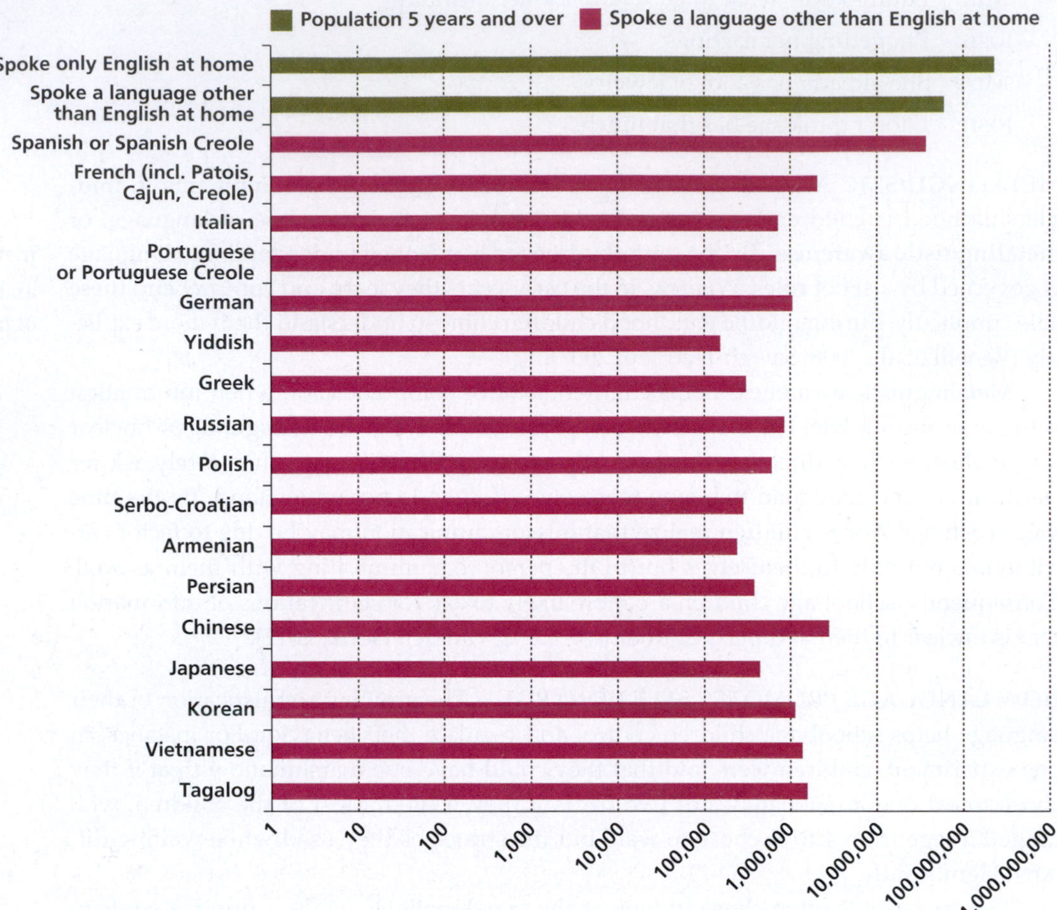

instruction, students are able to develop a strong foundation in basic subject areas using their native language. The ultimate goal of most bilingual education programs is to gradually shift instruction into English.

An alternative approach is to immerse students in English, teaching solely in that language. To proponents of this approach, initially teaching students in a language other than English hinders students' efforts to learn English and slows their integration into society.

The two quite different approaches have been highly politicized, with some politicians arguing in favor of "English-only" laws, while others urge school systems to respect the challenges faced by nonnative speakers by offering some instruction in their native language. Still, the psychological research is clear in suggesting that knowing more than one language offers several cognitive advantages. Because they have a wider range of linguistic possibilities to choose from as they assess a situation, speakers of two languages show greater cognitive flexibility. They can solve problems with greater creativity and versatility. Furthermore, learning in one's native tongue is associated with higher self-esteem in minority students (Hermanto, Moreno, & Bialystok, 2012; Hsin & Snow, 2017).

Module 9.2 Review

LO 9.5 Summarize the Piagetian view of cognitive development in middle childhood.

According to Piaget, school-age children are in the concrete operational stage, characterized by the application of logical processes to concrete problems.

LO 9.6 Explain how children develop cognitively in middle childhood according to information processing approaches.

Information processing approaches focus on quantitative improvements in memory and in the sophistication of the mental programs that school-age children use. The memory processes—encoding, storage, and retrieval—come under increasing control during the school years, and the development of metamemory improves cognitive processing and memorization.

LO 9.7 Summarize Vygotsky's interpretation of cognitive development during middle childhood.

According to Vygotsky's approach, children in the school years should have the opportunity to experiment and participate actively with their colleagues in their educational experiences.

LO 9.8 Describe how language develops during middle childhood.

Language development is characterized by improvements in vocabulary, syntax, and pragmatics; by the growth of metalinguistic awareness; and by the use of language as a self-control device. Bilingualism can produce improvements in cognitive flexibility and metalinguistic awareness.

Journal Writing Prompt

Applying Lifespan Development: Do children use language (and talking to themselves) as a self-control device? How?

Schooling: The Three Rs (and More) of Middle Childhood

As the eyes of the six other children in his reading group turned to him, Glenn shifted uneasily in his chair. Reading had never come easily to him, and he always felt anxious when it was his turn to read aloud. But as his teacher nodded in encouragement, he plunged in, hesitantly at first, then gaining momentum as he read the story about a mother's first day on a new job. He found that he could read the passage quite nicely, and he felt a surge of happiness and pride at his accomplishment. When he was done, he broke into a broad smile as his teacher said simply, "Well done, Glenn."

Small moments such as these, repeated over and over, make—or break—a child's educational experience. Schooling marks a time when society formally attempts to transfer to new generations its accumulated body of knowledge, beliefs, values, and wisdom. The success with which this transfer is managed determines, in a very real sense, the future fortunes of the world.

In the United States, as in most developed countries, a primary school education is both a universal right and a legal requirement. Virtually all children are provided with a free education through the 12th grade.

Children in other parts of the world are not so fortunate. More than 160 million of the world's children do not have access to even a primary school education. An additional 100 million children do not progress beyond a level comparable to our elementary school education, and close to a billion individuals (two-thirds of them women) are illiterate throughout their lives (see Figure 9-11; International Literacy Institute, 2001).

In almost all developing countries, fewer females than males receive formal education, a discrepancy found at every level of schooling. Even in developed countries, women lag behind men in their exposure to science and technological topics. These differences reflect widespread and deeply held cultural and parental biases that favor males over females. Educational levels in the United States are more nearly equal between men and women. Especially in the early years of school, boys and girls share equal access to educational opportunities.

Figure 9-11 The Plague of Illiteracy

Illiteracy remains a significant worldwide problem, particularly for women. Across the world, close to a billion people are illiterate throughout their lives.

(**Source:** UNESCO, 2016.)

Adult literacy rate by country, 2014

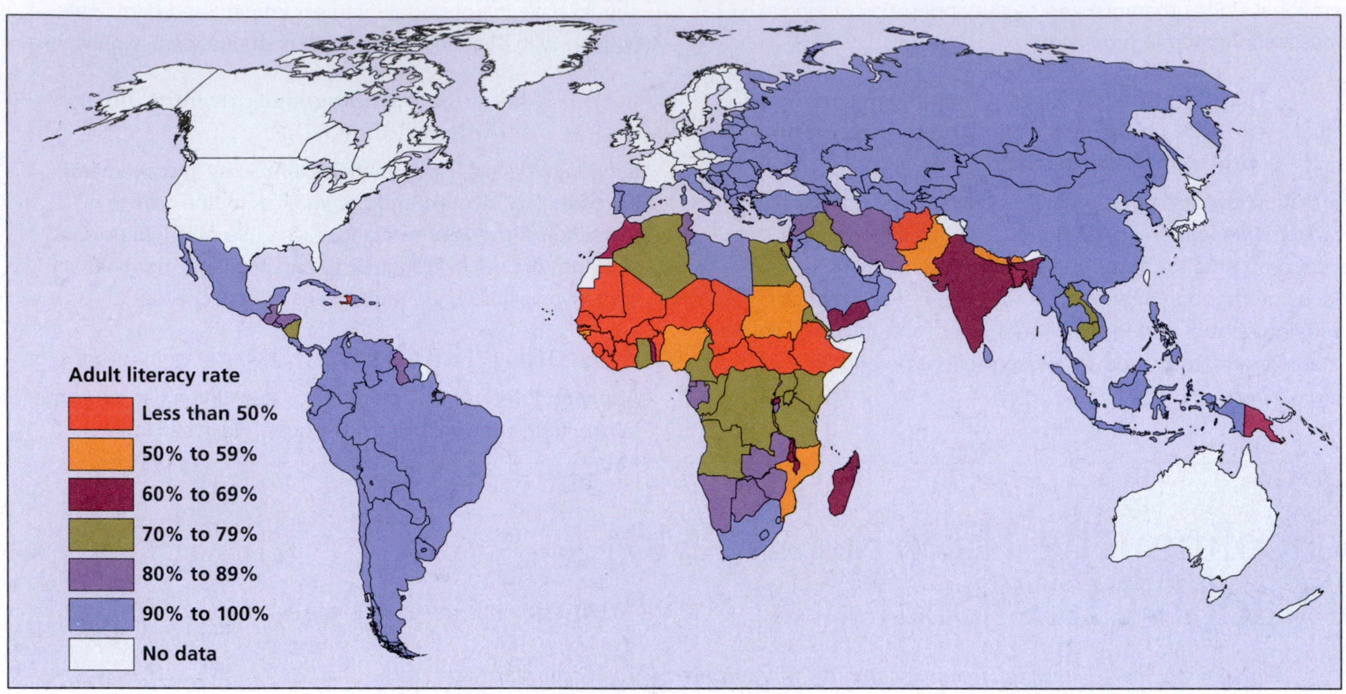

Youth literacy rate by country, 2014

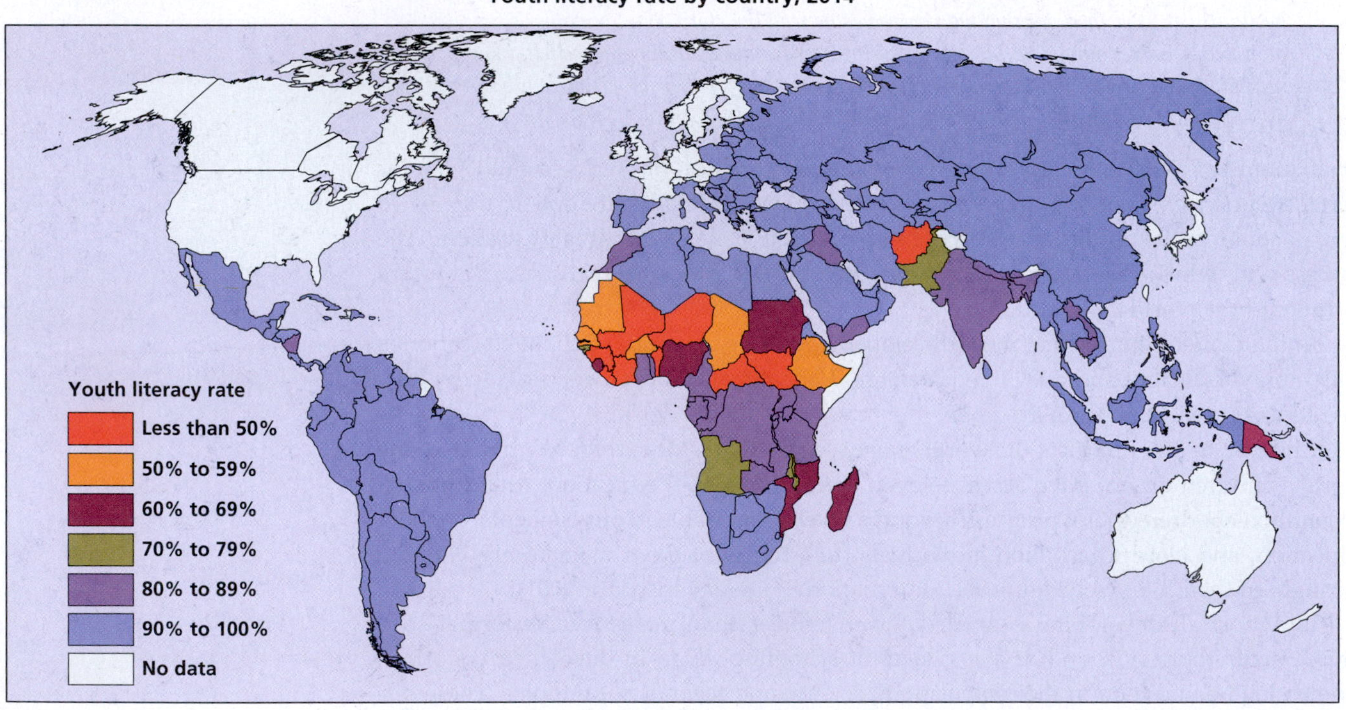

Reading: Learning to Decode the Meaning Behind Words

LO 9.9 Explain how children learn to read.

There is no other task that is more fundamental to schooling than learning to read. Reading involves a significant number of skills, from low-level cognitive skills (the identification of single letters and associating letters with sounds) to higher-level skills (matching written words with meanings located in long-term memory and using context and background knowledge to determine the meaning of a sentence).

READING STAGES. The development of reading skills generally occurs in several broad and frequently overlapping stages (Chall, 1979, 1992; see Table 9-1). In *Stage 0*, which lasts from birth to the start of first grade, children learn the essential prerequisites for reading, including identification of the letters in the alphabet, sometimes writing their names, and reading a few very familiar words (such as their own names or *stop* on a stop sign).

Stage 1 brings the first real type of reading, but it largely involves *phonological recoding* skill. At this stage, which usually encompasses the first and second grade, children can sound out words by blending the letters together. Children also complete the job of learning the names of letters and the sounds that go with them.

In *Stage 2*, typically around second and third grades, children learn to read aloud with fluency. However, they do not attach much meaning to the words because the effort involved in simply sounding out words is usually so great that relatively few cognitive resources are left over to process the meaning of the words.

The next period, *Stage 3*, extends from fourth to eighth grade. Reading becomes a means to an end—in particular, a way to learn. Whereas earlier reading was an accomplishment in and of itself, by this point children use reading to learn about the world. However, even at this age, understanding gained from reading is not complete. For instance, one limitation children have at this stage is that they are able to comprehend information only when it is presented from a single perspective.

In the final period, *Stage 4*, children are able to read and process information that reflects multiple points of view. This ability, which begins during the transition into high school, permits children to develop a far more sophisticated understanding of material. This explains why great works of literature are not read at an earlier stage of education. It is not so much that younger children do not have the vocabulary to understand such works (although this is partially true); it is that they lack the ability to understand the multiple points of view that sophisticated literature invariably presents.

HOW SHOULD WE TEACH READING? Educators have long been engaged in a debate regarding the most effective means of teaching reading. At the heart of this debate is a disagreement about the nature of the mechanisms by which information is processed during reading. According to proponents of *code-based approaches to reading*, reading should be taught by presenting the basic skills that underlie reading. Code-based approaches emphasize the components of reading, such as the sounds of letters and their

Table 9-1 Development of Reading Skills

Stage	Age	Key Characteristics
Stage 0	Birth to start of first grade	Learns prerequisites for reading, such as identification of the letters
Stage 1	First and second grades	Learns phonological recoding skills, starts reading
Stage 2	Second and third grades	Reads aloud fluently, but without much meaning
Stage 3	Fourth to eighth grades	Uses reading as a means for learning
Stage 4	Eighth grade and beyond	Understands reading in terms of reflecting multiple points of view

(**Source:** Based on Chall, J.S. (1979). The great debate: Ten years later with a modest proposal for reading stages. In L.G. Resnick & P.A. Wreaver (Eds),Theory and practice of early reading (Vol. 1, pp.29-56). Hillsdale, NJ: Lawrence Erlbaum Associates.)

combinations—phonics—and how letters and sounds are combined to make words. They suggest that reading consists of processing the individual components of words, combining them into words, and then using the words to derive the meaning of written sentences and passages (Jimenez & Guzman, 2003; Gray et al., 2007; Hagan-Burke, 2013; Cohen et al., 2016).

In contrast, some educators argue that reading is taught most successfully by using a whole-language approach. In *whole-language approaches to reading*, reading is viewed as a natural process, similar to the acquisition of oral language. According to this view, children should learn to read through exposure to complete writing—sentences, stories, poems, lists, charts, and other examples of actual uses of writing. Instead of being taught to sound out words, children are encouraged to make guesses about the meaning of words based on the context in which they appear. Through such a trial-and-error approach, children come to learn whole words and phrases at a time, gradually becoming proficient readers (Shaw, 2003; Sousa, 2005; Donat, 2006).

Figure 9-12 Reading and the Brain

The act of reading involves activation of significant areas of the brain, as these scans illustrate. In the top scan, an individual is reading aloud; in the bottom scan, the person is reading silently.

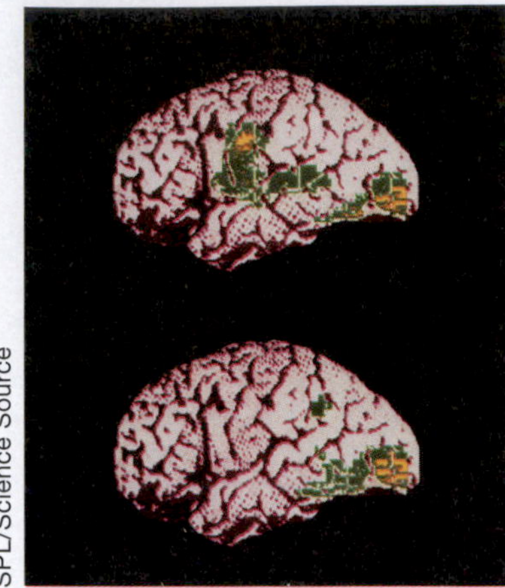

SPL/Science Source

A growing body of research suggests that the code-based approach to reading instruction is superior to whole-language approaches. For example, one study found not only that a group of children tutored in phonics for a year improved substantially in their reading, compared to a group of good readers, but also that the neural pathways involved in reading became closer to those of good readers (Shaywitz et al., 2004; Shapiro & Solity, 2008, 2016; Vaish, 2014).

Based on research such as this, the National Reading Panel and National Research Council now support reading instruction using code-based approaches. Their position signals that an end may be near to the debate over which approach to teaching reading is most effective (Rayner et al., 2002; Brady, 2011).

Whatever approach is used to teach reading, reading produces significant changes in the wiring of the brain. It boosts the organization of the visual cortex of the brain, and it improves the processing of spoken language (see Figure 9-12; Dejaeme et al., 2010).

Educational Trends: Beyond the Three Rs

LO 9.10 Summarize what schools teach beyond the basics in middle childhood.

Schooling in the 21st century is very different from what it was as little as a few decades ago. U.S. schools are experiencing a return to the educational fundamentals embodied in the traditional three Rs (reading, writing, and arithmetic). The focus on the fundamentals marks a departure from educational trends of prior decades when the emphasis was on social well-being and on allowing students to choose study topics on the basis of their interests instead of following a set curriculum (Schemo, 2003; Yinger, 2004; Merrow, 2012).

Elementary school classrooms today also stress individual accountability, both for teachers and for students. Teachers are more likely to be held responsible for their students' learning, and both students and teachers are more likely to be required to take tests, developed at the state or national level, to assess their competence. Consequently, pressures on students to succeed have grown (McDonnell, 2004).

As the U.S. population has become more diverse, elementary schools have also paid increased attention to issues involving student diversity and multiculturalism. And with good reason: Cultural, as well as language, differences affect students socially and educationally. The demographic makeup of students in the United States is undergoing an extraordinary shift. For instance, the proportion of Hispanics will in all likelihood more than double in the next 50 years. Moreover, by the year 2050, non-Hispanic Caucasians will likely become a minority of the total population of the United States (Colby & Ortman, 2015; see Figure 9-13). Consequently, educators have been increasingly serious about multicultural concerns. The following *Developmental Diversity and Your Life* feature, on multicultural education, discusses how the goals for educating students from different cultures have changed significantly over the years and are still being debated today (Brock et al., 2007).

Figure 9-13 The Changing Face of America

Current projections of the population makeup of the United States show that by the year 2050, the proportion of non-Hispanic whites will decline as the proportion of minority group members increases. What will be some of the impacts of changing demographics on social workers?

(**Source:** U.S. Census Bureau, 2000.)

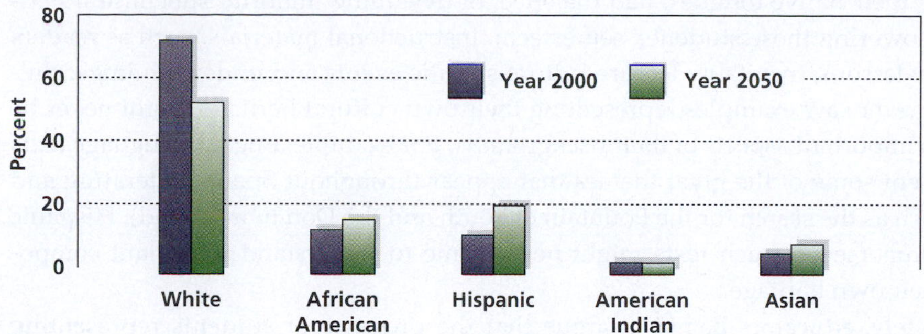

multicultural education

a form of education in which the goal is to help minority students develop competence in the culture of the majority group while maintaining positive group identities that build on their original cultures

Developmental Diversity and Your Life

Multicultural Education

It has always been the case that classrooms in the United States have been populated by individuals from a broad range of backgrounds and experiences. Yet it is only recently that variations in student backgrounds have been viewed as one of the major challenges—and opportunities—that educators face.

The diversity of background and experience in the classroom relates to a fundamental objective of education, which is to provide a formal mechanism to transmit the information a society deems important. As the famous anthropologist Margaret Mead (1942, p. 633) once said, "In its broadest sense, education is the cultural process, the way in which each newborn human infant, born with a potentiality for learning greater than that of any other mammal, is transformed into a full member of a specific human society, sharing with the other members of a specific human culture."

Culture, then, can be thought of as a set of behaviors, beliefs, values, and expectations shared by members of a particular society. But although culture is often thought of in a relatively broad context (as in "Western culture" or "Asian culture"), it is also possible to focus on particular *subcultural* groups within a larger, more encompassing culture. For example, we can consider particular racial, ethnic, religious, socioeconomic, or even gender groups in the United States as manifesting characteristics of a subculture.

E. D. Torial/Alamy

Pupils and teachers exposed to a diverse group could better understand the world and gain a greater sensitivity to the values and needs of others. What are some ways of developing greater sensitivity in the classroom?

Membership in a cultural or subcultural group might be of only passing interest to educators were it not for the fact that students' cultural backgrounds have a substantial impact on the way that they—and their peers—are educated. In recent years, a considerable amount of thought has gone into establishing **multicultural education**, a form of education in which the goal is to help minority students develop competence in the culture of the majority group while maintaining positive group identities that build on their original cultures (Nieto, 2005).

CULTURAL ASSIMILATION OR PLURALISTIC SOCIETY? Multicultural education developed in part as a reaction to a **cultural assimilation model** in which the goal of education was to assimilate individual cultural identities into a unique, unified American culture. In practical terms this meant, for example, that non-English-speaking students were discouraged from speaking their native tongues and were totally immersed in English.

cultural assimilation model

a model in which the goal of education is to assimilate individual cultural identities into a unique, unified American culture

In the early 1970s, however, educators and members of minority groups began to suggest that the cultural assimilation model ought to be replaced by a **pluralistic society model**. According to this conception, American society is made up of diverse, coequal cultural groups that should preserve their individual cultural features.

pluralistic society model
the concept that American society is made up of diverse, coequal cultural groups that should preserve their individual cultural features

The pluralistic society model grew in part from the belief that teachers, by emphasizing the dominant culture and discouraging students who were nonnative speakers from using their native tongues, had the effect of devaluing minority subcultural heritages and lowering those students' self-esteem. Instructional materials, such as readers and history lessons, inevitably feature culture-specific events and understandings; children who never saw examples representing their own cultural heritage might never be exposed to important aspects of their backgrounds. For example, English-language texts rarely present some of the great themes that appear throughout Spanish literature and history (such as the search for the Fountain of Youth and the Don Juan legend). Hispanic students immersed in such texts might never come to understand important components of their own heritage.

Ultimately, educators began to argue that the presence of students representing diverse cultures enriched and broadened the educational experience of all students. Pupils and teachers exposed to people from different backgrounds could better understand the world and gain greater sensitivity to the values and needs of others (Zirkel & Cantor, 2004; Levin et al., 2012; Thijs & Verkuyten, 2013; Theodosiou-Zipiti & Lamprianou, 2016).

FOSTERING A BICULTURAL IDENTITY. Today, most educators agree that minority children should be encouraged to develop a **bicultural identity**. They recommend that school systems encourage children to maintain their original cultural identities while they integrate themselves into the dominant culture. This view suggests that an individual can live as a member of two cultures, with two cultural identities, without having to choose one over the other (Lu, 2001; Oyserman et al., 2003; Vyas, 2004; Collins, 2012).

bicultural identity
maintaining one's original cultural identity while integrating oneself into the dominant culture

From *an educator's* perspective

Should one goal of society be to foster cultural assimilation in children from other cultures? Why or why not?

The best way to achieve this goal of biculturalism is not clear. Consider, for example, children who enter a school speaking only Spanish. The traditional "melting-pot" technique would be to immerse the children in classes taught in English while providing a crash course in English-language instruction (and little else) until the children demonstrate a suitable level of proficiency. Unfortunately, the traditional approach has a considerable drawback: Until the children master English, they fall further and further behind their peers who entered school already knowing English.

More contemporary approaches emphasize a bicultural strategy in which children are encouraged to maintain simultaneous membership in more than one culture. In the case of Spanish-speaking children, for example, instruction begins in the child's native language and shifts as rapidly as possible to include English. At the same time, the school conducts a program of multicultural education for all students, in which teachers present material on the cultural backgrounds and traditions of all the students in the school. Such instruction is designed to enhance the self-image of speakers from both majority and minority cultures (Bracey, Bamaca, & Umana-Taylor, 2004; Fowers & Davidov, 2006; Mok & Morris, 2012).

Although most educational experts favor bicultural approaches, the general public does not always agree. For instance, the national "English-only" movement mentioned earlier has as one of its goals the prohibition of school instruction in any language other than English. Whether such a perspective will prevail remains to be seen.

Intelligence: Determining Individual Strengths

LO 9.11 Describe how intelligence is measured and what controversies arise from measuring it.

"Why should you tell the truth?"

"How far is Los Angeles from New York?"

"A table is made of wood; a window of ____."

As 10-year-old Hyacinth sat hunched over her desk, trying to answer a long series of questions like these, she tried to guess the point of the test she was taking in her fifth-grade classroom. Clearly, the test didn't cover material that her teacher, Ms. White-Johnston, had talked about in class.

"What number comes next in this series: 1, 3, 7, 15, 31, ____ ?"

As she continued to work her way through the questions, she gave up trying to guess the rationale for the test. She'd leave that to her teacher, she sighed to herself. Rather than attempting to figure out what it all meant, she simply tried to do her best on the individual test items.

Hyacinth was taking an intelligence test. She might be surprised to learn that she was not alone in questioning the meaning and import of the items on the test. Intelligence test items are painstakingly prepared, and intelligence tests show a strong relationship to success in school (for reasons we'll soon discuss). Many developmentalists, however, would admit to harboring their own doubts as to whether questions such as those on Hyacinth's test are entirely appropriate to the task of assessing intelligence.

Understanding just what is meant by the concept of intelligence has proven to be a major challenge for researchers interested in delineating what separates intelligent from unintelligent behavior. Although nonexperts have their own conceptions of intelligence (one survey found, for instance, that laypersons believe that intelligence consists of three components: problem-solving ability, verbal ability, and social competence), it has been more difficult for experts to concur (Sternberg et al., 1981; Howe, 1997). Still, a general definition of intelligence is possible: **Intelligence** is the capacity to understand the world, think with rationality, and use resources effectively when faced with challenges (Wechsler, 1975).

intelligence
the capacity to understand the world, think with rationality, and use resources effectively when faced with challenges

Part of the difficulty in defining intelligence stems from the many—and sometimes unsatisfactory—paths that have been followed over the years in the quest to distinguish more intelligent people from less intelligent ones. To understand how researchers have approached the task of assessing intelligence by devising *intelligence tests*, we need to consider some of the historical milestones in the area of intelligence.

INTELLIGENCE BENCHMARKS: DIFFERENTIATING THE INTELLIGENT FROM THE UNINTELLIGENT. The Paris school system was faced with a problem at the turn of the 20th century: A significant number of children were not benefiting from regular instruction. Unfortunately, these children—many of whom we would now call intellectually disabled—were generally not identified early enough to shift them to special classes. The French minister of instruction approached psychologist Alfred Binet with this problem and asked him to devise a technique for the early identification of students who might benefit from instruction outside the regular classroom.

Binet's Test. Binet tackled his task in a thoroughly practical manner. His years of observing school-age children suggested to him that previous efforts to distinguish intelligent from unintelligent students—some of which were based on reaction time or keenness of sight—were off the mark. Instead, he launched a trial-and-error process in which items and tasks were administered to students who had been previously identified by teachers as being either "bright" or "dull." Tasks that the bright students completed correctly and the dull students failed to complete correctly were retained for the test. Tasks that did not discriminate between the two groups were discarded. The end result of this process was a test that reliably distinguished students who had previously been identified as fast or slow learners.

Binet's pioneering efforts in intelligence testing left three important legacies. The first was his pragmatic approach to the construction of intelligence tests. Binet did not have theoretical preconceptions about what intelligence was. Instead, he used a trial-and-error approach to psychological measurement that continues to serve as the predominant approach to test construction today. His definition of intelligence as *that which his test measured* has been adopted by many modern researchers, and it is particularly popular among test developers who respect the widespread utility of intelligence tests but wish to avoid arguments about the underlying nature of intelligence.

Binet's legacy extends to his linking of intelligence and school success. Binet's procedure for constructing an intelligence test ensured that intelligence—defined as performance on the test—and school success would be virtually one and the same. Thus, Binet's intelligence test, and today's tests that follow in the footsteps of that test, have become reasonable indicators of the degree to which students possess attributes that contribute to successful school performance. Notably, however, these tests do not provide useful information regarding a vast number of other attributes that are largely unrelated to academic proficiency, such as social skills or personality characteristics.

mental age
the typical intelligence level found for people at a given chronological age

Finally, Binet developed a procedure of linking each intelligence test score with a **mental age**, the age of the children taking the test who, on average, achieved that score. For example, if a 6-year-old girl received a score of 30 on the test, and this was the average score received by 10-year-olds, her mental age would be considered 10 years. Similarly, a 15-year-old boy who scored a 90 on the test—thereby matching the mean score for 15-year-olds—would be assigned a mental age of 15 years (Wasserman & Tulsky, 2005).

chronological (or physical) age
the actual age of the child taking the intelligence test

Although assigning a mental age to students provides an indication of whether or not they are performing at the same level as their peers, it does not permit adequate comparisons between students who each have different **chronological (or physical) age**. By using mental age alone, for instance, it would be assumed that a 15-year-old responding with a mental age of 17 years would be as bright as a 6-year-old responding with a mental age of 8 years, when actually the 6-year-old would be showing a much greater *relative* degree of brightness.

intelligence quotient (IQ score)
a measure of intelligence that takes into account a student's mental and chronological age

A solution to this problem comes in the form of the **intelligence quotient (IQ score)**, a measure that takes into account a student's mental *and* chronological age. The traditional method of calculating an IQ score uses the following formula, in which MA stands for mental age and CA for chronological age:

$$\text{IQ score} = \frac{\text{MA}}{\text{CA}} \times 100$$

As a bit of trial and error with this formula demonstrates, people whose mental age (MA) is equal to their chronological age (CA) will always have an IQ of 100. Furthermore, if the chronological age exceeds the mental age—implying below-average intelligence—the score will be below 100; and if the chronological age is lower than the mental age—suggesting above-average intelligence—the score will be above 100.

Using this formula, we can return to our earlier example of a 15-year-old who scores at a 17-year-old mental age. This student's IQ is $17/15 \times 100$, or 113. In comparison, the IQ of a 6-year-old scoring at a mental age of 8 is $8/6 \times 100$, or 133—a higher IQ score than the 15-year-old's.

IQ scores today are calculated in a more mathematically sophisticated manner and are known as *deviation IQ scores*. The average deviation IQ score remains set at 100, but tests are now devised so that the degree of deviation from this score permits the calculation of the proportion of people who have similar scores. For instance, approximately two-thirds of all people fall within 15 points of the average score of 100, achieving scores between 85 and 115. As scores rise or fall beyond this range, the percentage of people in the same score category drops significantly.

Measuring IQ: Present-Day Approaches to Intelligence. Since the time of Binet, tests of intelligence have become increasingly accurate measures of IQ. Most of them can still trace their roots to his original work in one way or another. For example, one of the most widely used tests—the **Stanford-Binet Intelligence Scales, Fifth Edition (SB5)**—began as an American revision of Binet's original test. The test consists of a series of items that vary according to the age of the person being tested. For instance, young children are asked to answer questions about everyday activities or to copy complex figures. Older people are asked to explain proverbs, solve analogies, and describe similarities between groups of words. The test is administered orally, and test-takers are given progressively more difficult problems until they are unable to proceed.

The **Wechsler Intelligence Scale for Children, Fourth Edition (WISC-IV)** is another widely used intelligence test. The test (which stems from its adult counterpart, the *Wechsler Adult Intelligence Scale*) provides measures of verbal and nonverbal skills, as well as a total score. As you can see from the sample items in Figure 9-14, the test includes a variety of types of items, allowing for easier identification of any specific problems a test-taker may have (Zhu & Weiss, 2005).

The **Kaufman Assessment Battery for Children, Second Edition (KABC-II)** takes a different approach than the SB5 and WISC-IV. In the KABC-II, children are tested on their ability to integrate different kinds of stimuli simultaneously and to use step-by-step thinking. A special virtue of the KABC-II is its flexibility. It allows the person giving the test to use alternative wording or gestures, or even to pose questions in a different

Stanford-Binet Intelligence Scales, Fifth Edition (SB5)
a test that consists of a series of items that vary according to the age of the person being tested

Wechsler Intelligence Scale for Children, Fourth Edition (WISC-IV)
a test for children that provides separate measures of verbal and performance (or nonverbal) skills, as well as a total score

Kaufman Assessment Battery for Children, Second Edition (KABC-II)
an intelligence test that measures children's ability to integrate different stimuli simultaneously and to use step-by-step thinking

Figure 9-14 Measuring Intelligence

The Wechsler Intelligence Scales for Children (WISC-IV) includes items such as these. What do such items cover? What do they miss?

Name	Goal of Item	Example
Information	Assess general information	How many nickels make a dime?
Comprehension	Assess understanding and evaluation of social norms and past experience	What is the advantage of keeping money in the bank?
Arithmetic	Assess math reasoning through verbal problems	If two buttons cost 15 cents, what will be the cost of a dozen buttons?
Similarities	Test understanding of how objects or concepts are alike, tapping abstract reasoning	In what way are an hour and a week alike?
Digit symbol	Assess speed of learning	Match symbols to numbers using key. 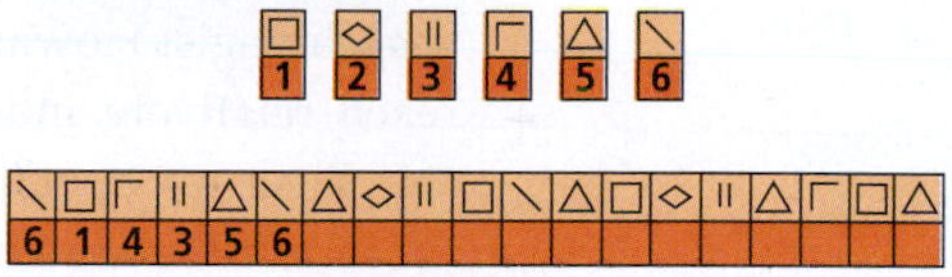
Picture completion	Visual memory and attention	Identify what is missing. 
Object assembly	Test understanding of relationship of parts to wholes	Put pieces together to form a whole. 

language, in order to maximize a test-taker's performance. This capability of the KABC-II makes testing more valid and equitable for children to whom English is a second language (Kaufman et al., 2005; McGill & Spurgin, 2016).

What do the IQ scores derived from IQ tests mean? For most children, IQ scores are reasonably good predictors of their school performance. That's not surprising, given that the initial impetus for the development of intelligence tests was to identify children who were having difficulties in school (Sternberg & Grigorenko, 2002).

But when it comes to performance outside of academic spheres, the story is different. For instance, although people with higher IQ scores are apt to finish more years of schooling, once this is statistically controlled for, IQ scores are not closely related to income and later success in life. Furthermore, IQ scores are frequently inaccurate when it comes to predicting a particular individual's future success. For example, two people with different IQ scores may both finish their bachelor's degrees at the same college, and the person with a lower IQ might end up with a higher income and a more successful career. Because of these difficulties with traditional IQ scores, researchers have turned to alternative approaches to intelligence (McClelland, 1993).

WHAT IQ TESTS DON'T TELL: ALTERNATIVE CONCEPTIONS OF INTELLIGENCE. The intelligence tests used most frequently in school settings today are based on the idea that intelligence is a single factor, a unitary mental ability. This one main attribute has commonly been called *g* (Spearman, 1927; Lubinski, 2004). The *g* factor is assumed to underlie performance on every aspect of intelligence, and it is the *g* factor that intelligence tests presumably measure.

Many theorists, however, dispute the notion that intelligence is unidimensional. Some developmentalists suggest that two kinds of intelligence exist: fluid intelligence and crystallized intelligence. **Fluid intelligence** reflects information processing capabilities, reasoning, and memory. For example, a student asked to group a series of letters according to some criterion or to remember a set of numbers would be using fluid intelligence (Cattell, 1987; Salthouse, Pink, & Tucker-Drob, 2008; Shangguan & Shi, 2009; Ziegler et al., 2012; Kenett et al., 2016).

fluid intelligence
intelligence that reflects information processing capabilities, reasoning, and memory

In contrast, **crystallized intelligence** is the accumulation of information, skills, and strategies that people have learned through experience and that they can apply in problem-solving situations. A student would likely be relying on crystallized intelligence to solve a puzzle or deduce the solution to a mystery, in which it was necessary to draw on past experience (Hill et al., 2013; Thorsen, Gustafsson, & Cliffordson, 2014; Hülür et al., 2017).

crystallized intelligence
the accumulation of information, skills, and strategies that people have learned through experience and that they can apply in problem-solving situations

Other theorists divide intelligence into an even greater number of parts. For example, psychologist Howard Gardner suggests that we have at least eight distinct intelligences, each relatively independent (see Figure 9-15). Gardner suggests that these separate intelligences operate not in isolation, but together, depending on the type of activity in which we are engaged (Chen & Gardner, 2005; Gardner & Moran, 2006; Roberts & Lipnevich, 2012).

From *an educator's* perspective

Does Howard Gardner's theory of multiple intelligences suggest that classroom instruction should be modified from an emphasis on the traditional three Rs of reading, writing, and arithmetic?

Russian psychologist Lev Vygotsky, whose approach to cognitive development we discussed in Chapter 7, took a very different approach to intelligence. He suggested that to assess intelligence, we should look not only at those cognitive processes that are fully developed but at those that are currently being developed as well. To do this, Vygotsky contended that assessment tasks should involve cooperative interaction between the individual who is being assessed and the person who is doing the assessment—a process called *dynamic assessment*. In short, intelligence is seen as being reflected not only in how

Figure 9-15 Gardner's Eight Intelligences

Howard Gardner has theorized that there are eight distinct intelligences, each relatively independent.

(**Source:** Based on Walters & Gardner, 1986.)

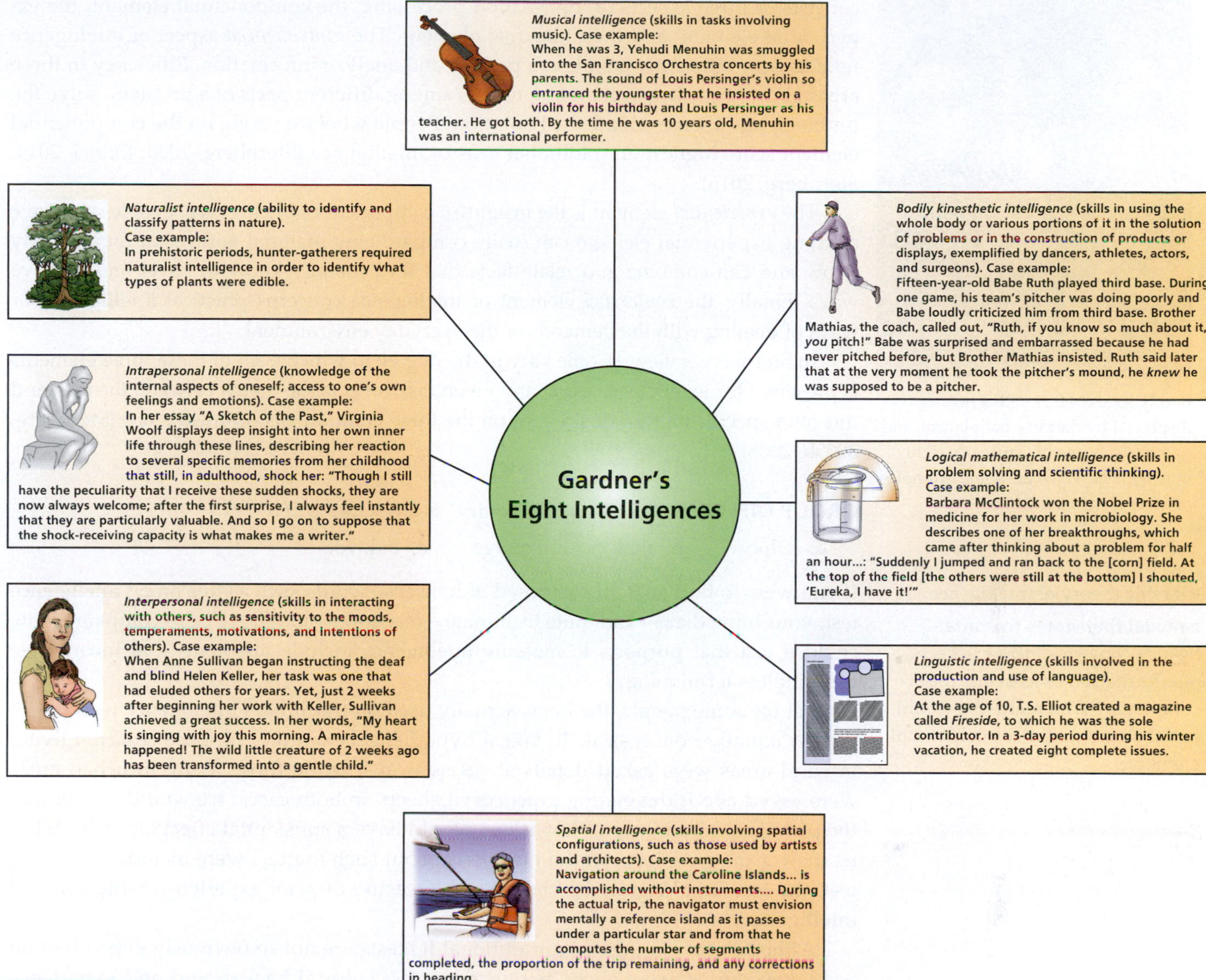

children can perform on their own but also in terms of how well they perform when helped by adults (Vygotsky, 1927/1976; Lohman, 2005).

Taking yet another approach, psychologist Robert Sternberg (1990, 2003a) suggests that intelligence is best thought of in terms of information processing. In this view, the way in which people store material in memory and later use it to solve intellectual tasks provides the most precise conception of intelligence. Rather than focusing on the various subcomponents that make up the *structure* of intelligence, then, information processing approaches examine the *processes* that underlie intelligent behavior (Floyd, 2005).

Studies of the nature and speed of problem-solving processes show that people with higher intelligence levels differ from others not only in the number of problems they ultimately are able to solve but in their method of solving the problems as well. People with high IQ scores spend more time on the initial stages of problem solving, retrieving relevant information from memory. In contrast, those who score lower on traditional IQ tests tend to spend less time on the initial stages, instead skipping ahead and making less informed guesses. The processes used in solving problems, then, may reflect important differences in intelligence (Sternberg, 2005).

Sternberg's work on information processing approaches to intelligence led him to develop the **triarchic theory of intelligence**. According to this model, intelligence consists of three aspects of information processing: the componential element, the experiential element, and the contextual element. The *componential* aspect of intelligence reflects how efficiently people can process and analyze information. Efficiency in these areas allows people to infer relationships among different parts of a problem, solve the problem, and then evaluate their solution. People who are strong on the componential element score highest on traditional tests of intelligence (Sternberg, 2005; Ekinci, 2014; Sternberg, 2016).

Pearson Education, Inc.

Bodily kinesthetic intelligence, as displayed by dancers, ballplayers, and gymnasts, is one of Gardner's eight intelligences. What are some examples of other Gardner intelligences?

The *experiential* element is the insightful component of intelligence. People who have a strong experiential element can easily compare new material with what they already know and can combine and relate facts that they already know in novel and creative ways. Finally, the *contextual* element of intelligence concerns practical intelligence, or ways of dealing with the demands of the everyday environment.

In Sternberg's view, people vary in the degree to which each of these three elements is present. Our level of success at any given task reflects the match between the task and our own specific pattern of strength on the three components of intelligence (Sternberg, 2003b, 2008).

triarchic theory of intelligence

a model that states that intelligence consists of three aspects of information processing: the componential element, the experiential element, and the contextual element

GROUP DIFFERENCES IN IQ. A "jontry" is an example of a

a. rulpow **b.** flink **c.** spudge **d.** bakwoe

If you were to find an item composed of nonsense words such as this on an intelligence test, your immediate—and quite legitimate—reaction would likely be to complain. How could a test that purports to measure intelligence include test items that incorporate meaningless terminology?

Yet for some people, the items actually used on traditional intelligence tests might appear equally nonsensical. To take a hypothetical example, suppose children living in rural areas were asked details about subways, while those living in urban areas were asked about the mating practices of sheep. In both cases, we would expect that the previous experiences of test-takers would have a substantial effect on their ability to answer the questions. And if questions about such matters were included on an IQ test, the test could rightly be viewed as a measure of prior experience rather than of intelligence.

Although the questions on traditional IQ tests are not so obviously dependent on test-takers' prior experiences as our examples, cultural background and experience do have the potential to affect intelligence test scores. Many educators suggest that traditional measures of intelligence are subtly biased in favor of white upper- and middle-class students and against groups with different cultural experiences (Ortiz & Dynda, 2005).

EXPLAINING RACIAL DIFFERENCES IN IQ. The issue of how cultural background and experience influence IQ test performance has led to considerable debate among researchers. The debate has been fueled by the finding that IQ scores of certain racial groups are consistently lower, on average, than the IQ scores of other groups. For example, the mean score of African Americans tends to be about 15 IQ points lower than the mean score of whites—although the measured difference varies a great deal depending on the particular IQ test employed (Fish, 2001; Maller, 2003).

The question that emerges from such differences, of course, is whether they reflect actual differences in intelligence or, instead, are caused by bias in the intelligence tests themselves in favor of majority groups and against minorities. For example, if whites perform better on an IQ test than African Americans because of their greater familiarity with the language used in the test items, the test hardly can be said to provide a fair measure of the intelligence of African Americans. Similarly, an intelligence test that solely used African American Vernacular English could not be considered an impartial measure of intelligence for whites.

The question of how to interpret differences between intelligence scores of different cultural groups lies at the heart of one of the major controversies in child development: To what degree is an individual's intelligence determined by heredity and to what degree by environment? The issue is important because of its social implications. For instance, if intelligence is primarily determined by heredity and is therefore largely fixed at birth, attempts to alter cognitive abilities later in life, such as schooling, will meet with limited success. By contrast, if intelligence is largely environmentally determined, modifying social and educational conditions is a more promising strategy for bringing about increases in cognitive functioning (Weiss, 2003; Nisbett et al., 2012).

Howard Grey/Getty Images

The issue of whether racial differences in IQ exist is highly controversial and ultimately relates to questions of the genetic and environmental determinants of intelligence.

***THE BELL CURVE* CONTROVERSY.** Although investigations into the relative contributions of heredity and environment to intelligence have been conducted for decades, the smoldering debate became a raging fire with the publication of *The Bell Curve*, a book by Richard J. Herrnstein and Charles Murray (1994). In the book, Herrnstein and Murray argue that the average 15-point IQ difference between whites and African Americans is due primarily to heredity rather than environment. Furthermore, they argue that this IQ difference accounts for the higher rates of poverty, lower employment, and higher use of welfare among minority groups as compared with majority groups.

The conclusions reached by Herrnstein and Murray raised a storm of protest, and many researchers who examined the data reported in the book came to conclusions that were quite different. Most developmentalists and psychologists responded by arguing that the racial differences in measured IQ can be explained by environmental differences between the races. In fact, when a variety of indicators of economic and social factors are statistically taken into account simultaneously, mean IQ scores of black and white children turn out to be actually quite similar. For instance, children from similar middle-class backgrounds, whether African American or white, tend to have similar IQ scores (Brooks-Gunn, Klebanov, & Duncan, 1996; Alderfer, 2003).

Furthermore, critics maintained that there is little evidence to suggest that IQ is a cause of poverty and other social ills. Some critics suggested, as mentioned earlier in this discussion, that IQ scores were unrelated in meaningful ways to later success in life (e.g., Nisbett, 1994; Reifman, 2000; Sternberg, 2005).

Finally, members of cultural and social minority groups may score lower than members of the majority group due to the nature of the intelligence tests themselves. It is clear that traditional intelligence tests may discriminate against minority groups who have not had exposure to the same environment that majority group members have experienced (Fagan & Holland, 2007; Razani et al., 2007).

Most traditional intelligence tests are constructed using white, English-speaking, middle-class populations as their test subjects. As a result, children from different cultural backgrounds may perform poorly on the tests—not because they are less intelligent but because the tests use questions that are culturally biased in favor of majority group members. A classic study found that in one California school district, Mexican American students were 10 times more likely than whites to be placed in special education classes (Mercer, 1973; Hatton, 2002).

More recent findings show that nationally, twice as many African American students as white students are classified as mildly intellectually disabled, a difference that experts attribute primarily to cultural bias and poverty. Although certain IQ tests (such as the *System of Multicultural Pluralistic Assessment*, or *SOMPA*) have been designed to be equally valid regardless of the cultural background of test-takers, no test can be completely without bias (Reschly, 1996; Sandoval et al., 1998; Hatton, 2002).

In short, most experts in the area of IQ were not convinced by the contention in *The Bell Curve* that differences in group IQ scores are largely determined by genetic factors. Still, we cannot put the issue to rest, largely because it is impossible to design a definitive experiment that can determine the cause of differences in IQ scores between members of different groups. (Thinking about how such an experiment might be designed shows the futility of the enterprise: One cannot ethically assign children to different living conditions to find the effects of environment, nor would one wish to genetically control or alter intelligence levels in unborn children.)

Today, IQ is seen as the product of *both* nature and nurture interacting with one another in a complex manner. Rather than seeing intelligence as produced by either genes or experience, genes are considered to affect experiences, and experiences are viewed as influencing the expression of genes. For instance, psychologist Eric Turkheimer has found evidence that while environmental factors play a larger role in influencing the IQ of poor children, genes are more influential in the IQ of affluent children (Harden, Turkheimer, & Loehlin, 2007; Turkheimer et al., 2017).

Ultimately, it may be less important to know the absolute degree to which intelligence is determined by genetic and environmental factors than it is to learn how to improve children's living conditions and educational experiences. By enriching the quality of children's environments, we will be in a better position to permit all children to reach their full potential and to maximize their contributions to society, whatever their individual levels of intelligence (Wickelgren, 1999; Posthuma & de Geus, 2006; Nisbett, 2008).

Below and Above Intelligence Norms: Intellectual Disabilities and the Intellectually Gifted

LO 9.12 Describe how children with intellectual disabilities and children who are intellectually gifted are educated in middle childhood.

Although Connie kept pace with her classmates in kindergarten, by the time she reached first grade, she was academically the slowest in almost every subject. It was not that she didn't try, but rather that it took her longer than other students to catch on to new material, and she regularly required special attention to keep up with the rest of the class.

In some areas she excelled: When asked to draw or produce something with her hands, she not only matched her classmates' performance but exceeded it, producing beautiful work that was much admired by her classmates. Although the other students in the class felt that there was something different about Connie, they were hard-pressed to identify the source of the difference, and in fact they didn't spend much time pondering the issue.

Connie's parents and teacher, though, knew what made her special. Extensive testing in kindergarten had shown that Connie's intelligence was well below normal, and she was officially classified as a special needs student.

If Connie had been attending school before 1975, she would most likely have been removed from her regular class as soon as her low IQ was identified, and placed in a class taught by a special needs teacher. Such classes, often consisting of students with a hodgepodge of afflictions, including emotional difficulties, severe reading problems, and physical disabilities such as multiple sclerosis, as well those with lower IQs, were traditionally kept separate and apart from the regular educational process.

All that changed in 1975 when Congress passed Public Law 94–142, the Education for All Handicapped Children Act. The intent of the law—an intent that has been largely realized—was to ensure that children with special needs received a full education in the **least restrictive environment**, the setting most similar to that of children without special needs (Yell & Drasgow, 2010; Yell, 2015).

In practice, the law has meant that children with special needs must be integrated into regular classrooms and regular activities to the greatest extent possible, as long as doing so is educationally beneficial. Children are to be isolated from the regular classroom only for those subjects that are specifically affected by their exceptionality; for all other subjects, they are to be taught with nonexceptional children in regular classrooms. Of course, some children with severe handicaps still need a mostly or entirely separate education, depending on the extent of their condition. But the goal of the law is to integrate exceptional children and typical children to the fullest extent possible (Yell, 2015).

Robin Nelson/PhotoEdit

This girl with Down syndrome is mainstreamed into this class.

This educational approach to special education, designed to end the segregation of exceptional students as much as possible, has come to be called mainstreaming. In **mainstreaming**, exceptional children are integrated as much as possible into the traditional educational system and are provided with a broad range of educational alternatives (Belkin, 2004; Crosland & Dunlap, 2012).

least restrictive environment
the setting that is most similar to that of children without special needs

mainstreaming
an educational approach in which exceptional children are integrated to the extent possible into the traditional educational system and are provided with a broad range of educational alternatives

ENDING SEGREGATION BY INTELLIGENCE LEVELS: THE BENEFITS OF MAINSTREAMING. In many respects, the introduction of mainstreaming—while clearly increasing the complexity of classroom teaching—was a reaction to failures of traditional special education. For one thing, there was little research support for the advisability of special education for exceptional students. Research that examined such factors as academic achievement, self-concept, social adjustment, and personality development generally failed to discern any advantages for special needs children placed in special, as opposed to regular, education classes. Furthermore, systems that compel minorities to be educated separately from majorities historically tend to be less effective—as an examination of schools that were once segregated on the basis of race clearly demonstrates (Wehmeyer & Lee, 2017).

Ultimately, however, the most compelling argument in favor of mainstreaming is philosophical: Because special needs students must ultimately function in a normal environment, greater experience with their peers ought to enhance their integration into society, as well as positively affect their learning. Mainstreaming, then, provides a mechanism to equalize the opportunities available to all children. The ultimate objective of mainstreaming is to ensure that all persons, regardless of ability or disability, have access to a full range of educational opportunities and, ultimately, a fair share of life's rewards (Scherer, 2004).

Does the reality of mainstreaming live up to its promise? To some extent, the benefits extolled by proponents have been realized. However, classroom teachers must receive substantial support in order for mainstreaming to be effective. It is not easy to teach a class in which students' abilities are significantly different from one another (Wehmeyer & Shogren, 2017).

The benefits of mainstreaming have led some professionals to promote an alternative educational model known as full inclusion. *Full inclusion* is the integration of all students, even those with the most severe disabilities, into regular classes. In such a system, separate special education programs would cease to operate. Full inclusion is controversial, and it remains to be seen how widespread such a practice will become (Mangiatordi, 2012; Justice et al., 2014; Bešić et al., 2017).

BELOW THE NORM: INTELLECTUAL DISABILITY. Approximately 1 to 3 percent of the school-age population is considered to be intellectually disabled. Estimates vary so widely because the most commonly accepted definition of intellectual disability, which was previously referred to professionally as *mental retardation*, is one that leaves a great deal of room for interpretation. According to the American Association on Intellectual and Developmental Disabilities, **intellectual disability** is a disability characterized by significant limitations both in intellectual functioning and in adaptive behavior, which covers many everyday social and practical skills. (American Association on Intellectual and Developmental Disabilities, 2012).

intellectual disability
a disability characterized by significant limitations both in intellectual functioning and in adaptive behavior, which covers many everyday social and practical skills

Most cases of intellectual disability are classified as *familial intellectual disability*, in which no cause is apparent, but there is a history of intellectual disability in the family. In other cases, there is a clear biological cause. The most common biological causes are *fetal alcohol syndrome*, which is produced by a mother's use of alcohol while pregnant, and *Down syndrome*, which results from the presence of an extra chromosome. Birth complications, such as a temporary lack of oxygen, may also produce intellectual disabilities (Plomin, 2005; West & Blake, 2005; Manning & Hoyme, 2007).

Although limitations in intellectual functioning can be measured in a relatively straightforward manner—using standard IQ tests—it is more difficult to determine how to gauge limitations in other areas. Ultimately, this imprecision leads to a lack of uniformity in the ways experts apply the label of "intellectual disability." Furthermore, it has resulted in significant variation in the abilities of people who are categorized as experiencing intellectual disability. Accordingly, intellectually disabled people range from those who can be taught to work and function with little special attention to those who are virtually untrainable and who never develop speech or such basic motor skills as crawling or walking.

The vast majority of the intellectually disabled—some 90 percent—have relatively low levels of deficits. Classified with **mild intellectual disability**, they score in the range of 50 or 55 to 70 on IQ tests. Typically, their intellectual disability is not even identified before they reach school, although their early development often is slower than average. Once they enter elementary school, their need for special attention usually becomes apparent, as it did with Connie, the first grader profiled at the beginning of this discussion. With appropriate training, these students can reach a third- to sixth-grade educational level, and although they cannot carry out complex intellectual tasks, they are able to hold jobs and function quite independently and successfully.

mild intellectual disability
intellectual disability in which IQ scores fall in the range of 50 or 55 to 70

Intellectual and adaptive limitations become more apparent, however, at higher levels of intellectual disabilities. People whose IQ scores range from around 35 or 40 to 50 or 55 are classified with **moderate intellectual disability**. Accounting for 5 to 10 percent of those classified as intellectually disabled, the moderately intellectually disabled display distinctive behavior early in their lives. They are slow to develop language skills, and their motor development is also affected. Regular schooling is usually not effective in training people with moderate intellectual disabilities to acquire academic skills, because generally they are unable to progress beyond the second-grade level. Still, they are capable of learning occupational and social skills, and they can learn to travel independently to familiar places. Typically, they require moderate levels of supervision.

moderate intellectual disability
intellectual disability in which IQ scores range from around 35 or 40 to 50 or 55

At the most significant levels of intellectual disability—those who are classified with **severe intellectual disability** (IQs ranging from around 20 or 25 to 35 or 40) and **profound intellectual disability** (IQs below 20 or 25)—the ability to function is severely limited. Usually, such people have little or no speech, have poor motor control, and may need 24-hour nursing care. At the same time, however, some people with severe intellectual disability are capable of learning basic self-care skills, such as dressing and eating, and they may even develop the potential to become partially independent as adults. Still, the need for relatively high levels of care continues throughout the life span, and most severely and profoundly intellectually disabled people are institutionalized for the majority of their lives.

severe intellectual disability
intellectual disability in which IQ scores range from around 20 or 25 to 35 or 40

profound intellectual disability
intellectual disability in which IQ scores fall below 20 or 25

ABOVE THE NORM: THE GIFTED AND TALENTED

Amy Leibowitz picked up reading at age 3. By 5, she was writing her own books. First grade bored her within a week. As her school had no program for gifted children, it was suggested she skip to second grade. From there, she went to fifth grade. Her parents were proud but concerned. When they asked the fifth-grade teacher where she felt Amy really belonged, the teacher said she was ready, academically, for high school.

It sometimes strikes people as curious that the gifted and talented are considered to have a form of exceptionality. Yet the 3 to 5 percent of school-age children who are gifted and talented present special challenges of their own.

Which students are considered to be **gifted and talented**? Little agreement exists among researchers on a single definition of this rather broad category of students. However, the federal government considers the term *gifted* to include "children who give evidence of high performance capability in areas such as intellectual, creative, artistic, leadership capacity, or specific academic fields, and who require services or activities not ordinarily provided by the school in order to fully develop such capabilities" (Sec 582, P. L. 97–35-Education and Consolidation Act). Intellectual capabilities, then, represent only one type of exceptionality; unusual potential in areas outside the academic realm are also included in the concept. Gifted and talented children have so much potential that they, no less than students with low IQs, warrant special concern—although special school programs for them are often the first to be dropped when school systems face budgetary problems (Schemo, 2004; Mendoza, 2006; Olszewski-Kubilius & Thomson, 2013).

gifted and talented
children who show evidence of high-performance capability in areas such as intellectual, creative, artistic, leadership capacity, or specific academic fields

People who are described as *gifted*—especially when the term is applied to those with exceptionally high intelligence—are often stereotyped as "unsociable," "poorly adjusted," and "neurotic." However, most research suggests that highly intelligent people tend to be outgoing, well adjusted, and popular (Bracken & Brown, 2006; Shaughnessy et al., 2006; Cross et al., 2008).

For instance, one landmark, long-term study of 1,500 gifted students, which began in the 1920s, found that not only were the gifted smarter than average, but they were also healthier, better coordinated, and psychologically better adjusted than their less intelligent classmates. Furthermore, their lives played out in ways that most people would envy. The subjects received more awards and distinctions, earned more money, and made many more contributions in art and literature than the average person. For instance, by the time they had reached age 40, they had collectively produced more than 90 books, 375 plays and short stories, and 2,000 articles, and they had registered more than 200 patents. Perhaps not surprisingly, they reported greater satisfaction with their lives than the nongifted (Reis & Renzulli, 2004; Duggan & Friedman, 2014).

Yet being gifted and talented is no guarantee of success in school, as we can see if we consider the particular components of the category. For example, the verbal abilities that allow the eloquent expression of ideas and feelings can equally permit the expression of glib and persuasive statements that happen to be inaccurate. Furthermore, teachers may sometimes misinterpret the humor, novelty, and creativity of unusually gifted children and see their intellectual fervor as disruptive or inappropriate. And peers are not always sympathetic: Some very bright children try to hide their intelligence in an effort to fit in better with other students (Swiatek, 2002).

EDUCATING THE GIFTED AND TALENTED. Educators have devised two approaches to teaching the gifted and talented: acceleration and enrichment. **Acceleration** allows gifted students to move ahead at their own pace, even if this means skipping to higher grade levels. The materials that students receive under acceleration programs are not necessarily different from what other students receive; they simply are provided at a faster pace than for the average student (Smutny, Walker, & Meckstroth, 2007; Wells, Lohman, & Marron, 2009; Lee, Olszewski-Kubilius, & Thomson, 2012).

acceleration
special programs that allow gifted students to move ahead at their own pace, even if this means skipping to higher grade levels

enrichment
an approach through which students are kept at grade level but are enrolled in special programs and given individual activities to allow greater depth of study on a given topic

An alternative approach is **enrichment**, through which students are kept at grade level but are enrolled in special programs and given individual activities to allow greater depth of study on a given topic. In enrichment, the material provided to gifted students differs not only in the timing of its presentation but in its sophistication as well. Thus, enrichment materials are designed to provide an intellectual challenge to the gifted student, encouraging higher-order thinking (Worrell, Szarko, & Gabelko, 2001; Rotigel, 2003).

Acceleration programs can be remarkably effective. Most studies have shown that gifted students who begin school considerably earlier than their age-mates do as well as or better than those who begin at the traditional age. One of the best illustrations of the benefits of acceleration is the Study of Mathematically Precocious Youth, an ongoing program at Vanderbilt University. In this program, seventh and eighth graders who have unusual abilities in mathematics participate in a variety of special classes and workshops. The results have been nothing short of sensational, with students successfully completing college courses and sometimes even enrolling in college early. Some students have even graduated from college before age 18. And the accomplishments of those students is not unique to graduates of the program; additional research shows that, in general, profoundly gifted children later become profoundly accomplished in their chosen career paths (Lubinski & Benbow, 2006; Peters et al., 2014; Makel et al., 2016).

Module 9.3 Review

LO 9.9 Explain how children learn to read.

The development of reading skills generally occurs in several stages. A combination of elements from code-based (i.e., phonics) approaches and whole-language approaches appears to offer the most promise.

LO 9.10 Summarize what schools teach beyond the basics in middle childhood.

Multicultural education is in transition from a melting-pot model of cultural assimilation to a pluralistic society model.

LO 9.11 Describe how intelligence is measured and what controversies arise from measuring it.

The measurement of intelligence has traditionally been a matter of testing skills that promote academic success. Recent theories of intelligence suggest that there may be several distinct intelligences or several components of intelligence that reflect different ways of processing information.

LO 9.12 Describe how children with intellectual disabilities and children who are intellectually gifted are educated in middle childhood.

U.S. educators are attempting to deal with substantial numbers of exceptional persons whose intellectual and other skills are significantly lower or higher than normal.

Journal Writing Prompt

Applying Lifespan Development: Should one goal of society be to foster the cultural assimilation of children from other cultures? Why or why not?

Epilogue

In this chapter, we discussed children's physical and cognitive development during the middle childhood years. We considered physical growth and its related nutrition and health concerns. We also looked at the intellectual growth that occurs at this time as interpreted by Piaget, information processing approaches, and Vygotsky. Children at this age show increased capabilities in memory and language, which facilitate and support gains in many other areas. We looked at some aspects of schooling worldwide and, especially, in the United States, concluding with an examination of intelligence: how it is defined, how it is tested, and how children who fall significantly below or above the intellectual norm are educated and treated.

Look back to the prologue about Danny Nunes teaching his third-grade class to solve math word problems by having them write one, and answer the following questions:

1. Danny calls his approach to word problems an example of "metacognition." What does he mean by this? How would metacognition help his third graders learn to solve such problems?
2. Relate Danny's method of teaching word problems to the developmental theories of Piaget, information processing, and Vygotsky. Which approach do you think most clearly describes what Danny is doing in this lesson?

3. Some teachers might consider Danny's approach to teaching word problems ambitious, and yet his students seem to "get it." Can you think of other teaching approaches that might take into account the cognitive abilities of his middle-school-age students?

4. In solving word problems in this way, do you think Danny's students are relying more on fluid or crystallized intelligence? Why?

Looking Back

LO 9.1 Describe ways in which children grow during middle childhood and factors that influence their growth.

The middle childhood years are characterized by slow and steady growth. Weight is redistributed as baby fat disappears. In part, growth is genetically determined, but societal factors such as affluence, dietary habits, nutrition, and disease also contribute significantly.

LO 9.2 Outline the course of motor development in middle childhood.

During the middle childhood years, great improvements occur in gross motor skills. Cultural expectations appear to underlie most gross motor skill differences between boys and girls. Fine motor skills also develop rapidly.

LO 9.3 Summarize the main physical and mental health concerns of school-age children.

Adequate nutrition is important because of its contributions to growth, health, social and emotional functioning, and cognitive performance. Obesity is partially influenced by genetic factors but is also associated with children's failure to develop internal controls, overeating, overindulgence in sedentary activities such as television viewing, and lack of physical exercise. Asthma and childhood depression are fairly prevalent among children of school age.

LO 9.4 Describe the sorts of special needs that may become apparent in school-age children and how can they be met.

Visual, auditory, and speech impairments, as well as other learning disabilities, can lead to academic and social problems and must be handled with sensitivity and appropriate assistance. Children with attention-deficit/hyperactivity disorder exhibit another form of special need. ADHD is characterized by inattention, impulsiveness, failure to complete tasks, lack of organization, and excessive amounts of uncontrollable activity. Treatment of ADHD by drugs is highly controversial because of unwanted side effects and doubts about long-term consequences.

LO 9.5 Summarize the Piagetian view of cognitive development in middle childhood.

According to Piaget, school-age children enter the concrete operational period and for the first time become capable of applying logical thought processes to concrete problems.

LO 9.6 Explain how children develop cognitively in middle childhood according to information processing approaches.

According to information processing approaches, children's intellectual development in the school years can be attributed to substantial increases in memory capacity and the sophistication of the "programs" children can handle.

LO 9.7 Summarize Vygotsky's interpretation of cognitive development during middle childhood.

Vygotsky recommends that students focus on active learning through child–adult and child–child interactions that fall within each child's zone of proximal development.

LO 9.8 Describe how language develops during middle childhood.

The language development of children in the school years is substantial, with improvements in vocabulary, syntax, and pragmatics. Children learn to control their behavior through linguistic strategies, and they learn more effectively by seeking clarification when they need it. Bilingualism can be beneficial in the school years. Children who are taught all subjects in the first language, with simultaneous instruction in English, appear to experience few deficits and attain several linguistic and cognitive advantages.

LO 9.9 Explain how children learn to read.

The development of reading skills, which is fundamental to schooling, generally occurs in several stages: identifying letters, reading highly familiar words, sounding out letters and blending sounds into words, reading words with fluency but with little comprehension, reading with comprehension and for practical purposes, and reading material that reflects multiple points of view.

LO 9.10 Summarize what schools teach beyond the basics in middle childhood.

Multiculturalism and diversity are significant issues in U.S. schools, where the melting-pot society, in which minority cultures are assimilated to the majority culture, is being replaced by the pluralistic society, in which individual cultures maintain their own identities while participating in the definition of a larger culture.

LO 9.11 Describe how intelligence is measured and what controversies arise from measuring it.

Intelligence testing has traditionally focused on factors that differentiate successful academic performers from unsuccessful ones. The intelligence quotient, or IQ score, reflects the ratio of a person's mental age to his or her chronological age. Other conceptualizations of intelligence focus on different types of intelligence or on different aspects of the information processing task.

LO 9.12 Describe how children with intellectual disabilities and children who are intellectually gifted are educated in middle childhood.

In today's schools, exceptional children—including children with intellectual deficits—are to be educated in the least restrictive environment, typically the regular classroom. If done properly, this strategy can benefit all students and permit exceptional students to focus on strengths rather than weaknesses. Gifted and talented children can benefit from special educational programs, including acceleration programs and enrichment programs.

Key Terms and Concepts

asthma 291
visual impairment 294
auditory impairment 295
speech impairment 295
childhood-onset fluency disorder (stuttering) 295
specific learning disorders 296
attention-deficit/hyperactivity disorder (ADHD) 296
concrete operational stage 299
decentering 299
memory 301
metamemory 302
metalinguistic awareness 305
bilingualism 305
multicultural education 311
cultural assimilation model 311
pluralistic society model 312
bicultural identity 312
intelligence 313
mental age 314
chronological (or physical) age 314
intelligence quotient (IQ score) 314
Stanford-Binet Intelligence Scales, Fifth Edition (SB5) 315
Wechsler Intelligence Scale for Children, Fourth Edition (WISC-IV) 315
Kaufman Assessment Battery for Children, Second Edition (KABC-II) 315
fluid intelligence 316
crystallized intelligence 316
triarchic theory of intelligence 318
least restrictive environment 321
mainstreaming 321
intellectual disability 322
mild intellectual disability 322
moderate intellectual disability 322
severe intellectual disability 322
profound intellectual disability 322
gifted and talented 323
acceleration 323
enrichment 324

Chapter 10

Social and Personality Development in Middle Childhood

imageBROKER/Age Fotostock

Learning Objectives

LO 10.1 Describe the major developmental challenges of middle childhood.

LO 10.2 Summarize ways in which children's views of themselves change during middle childhood.

LO 10.3 Explain why self-esteem is important during middle childhood.

LO 10.4 Describe how children's sense of right and wrong changes in middle childhood.

LO 10.5 Describe the sorts of relationships and friendships that are typical of middle childhood.

LO 10.6 Describe what makes a child popular and why popularity is important in middle childhood.

LO 10.7 Describe how gender affects friendships in middle childhood.

LO 10.8 Describe how friendships between the races change during the school years.

LO 10.9 Summarize how today's diverse family and care arrangements affect children in middle childhood.

LO 10.10 Describe how children's social and emotional lives affect their school performance in middle childhood.

Chapter Overview

Prologue: New Kid in Town

When 9-year-old Matt Donner's family relocated from Topeka, Kansas, to Providence, Rhode Island, after his father was promoted, Matt was both excited and fearful. Moving to a new part of the country was exciting. But Matt had been a quiet and unassuming fourth grader in his old hometown with a small circle of friends. How well would he make the adjustment to fifth grade in his new home?

Not well, it turns out. His shy manner got in the way of making new friends. Instead of sitting with other kids at lunchtime, Matt sat alone with a book. "They all knew each other already. That made it really hard," Matt lamented. "I just didn't fit in."

Matt's regional accent and small stature didn't help matters. It wasn't long before classmates were mocking his speech and tripping him in the halls. His locker was broken into so many times that Matt gave up using it and just carried his books with him. Teachers either didn't care, or more likely didn't notice—the bullying rarely happened in front of them. Matt's greatest fear was that his parents would find out and be disappointed in him. He didn't want them to know that he had let himself become a victim.

Looking Ahead

Matt's experience is, sadly, not uncommon. As children grow into middle childhood, the way they relate to others and the way they think of themselves undergo significant transformations. Sometimes, these transformations are fairly smooth. However, as Matt's story shows, they can also present children and parents with new and unexpected challenges.

Sergey Novikov/123RF GB Ltd

Children's understanding of themselves continues to change during middle childhood.

In this chapter, we focus on social and personality development during middle childhood. It is a time when children's views of themselves change, they form new bonds with friends and family, and they become increasingly attached to social institutions outside the home.

We start our consideration of personality and social development during middle childhood by examining the changes that occur in the ways children see themselves. We discuss how they view their personal characteristics, and we examine the complex issue of self-esteem.

Next, the chapter turns to relationships during middle childhood. We discuss the stages of friendship and the ways gender and ethnicity affect how and with whom children interact. We also examine how to improve children's social competence.

The last part of the chapter explores the central societal institution in children's lives: the family. We consider the consequences of divorce, self-care children, and the phenomenon of group care.

The Developing Self

Karla Holler sits comfortably in the treehouse she built in a tall apple tree growing in her suburban home's backyard. At age 9, she's just finished the latest addition, nailing pieces of wood together, expertly wielding a hammer. She and her father started building the treehouse when she was 5 years old, and she has been making small additions to it ever since. By this point, she has developed a clear sense of pride regarding the treehouse, and she spends hours in it, savoring the privacy it provides.

Karla's growing sense of competence is reflected in this passage. Conveying what psychologist Erik Erikson calls "industriousness," Karla's quiet pride in her accomplishment illustrates one of the ways in which children's views of themselves evolve.

Rob Marmion/Shutterstock

According to Erik Erikson, middle childhood encompasses the industry-versus-inferiority stage, characterized by a focus on meeting the challenges presented by the world.

Psychosocial Development in Middle Childhood

LO 10.1 Describe the major developmental challenges of middle childhood.

According to Erik Erikson, whose approach to psychosocial development we last discussed in Chapter 8, middle childhood is very much about competence. Lasting from roughly age 6 to age 12, the **industry-versus-inferiority stage** is characterized by a focus on efforts to meet the challenges presented by parents, peers, school, and the other complexities of the modern world.

industry-versus-inferiority stage
according to Erikson, the period from age 6 to 12 characterized by a focus on efforts to attain competence in meeting the challenges presented by parents, peers, school, and the other complexities of the modern world

As children move through middle childhood, school presents enormous challenges. They must direct their energies not only to mastering what they are presented in school, which encompasses an enormous body of information, but also to making a place for themselves in their social worlds. They increasingly work with others in group activities and must navigate among different social groups and roles, including relationships involving teachers, friends, and families.

Success in the industry-versus-inferiority stage brings with it feelings of mastery and proficiency and a growing sense of competence, like that expressed by Karla when she talks about her building experience. By contrast, difficulties in this stage lead to feelings of failure and inadequacy. As a result, children may withdraw both from academic pursuits, showing less interest and motivation to excel, and from interactions with peers.

Children may find that attaining a sense of industry during the middle childhood years has lasting consequences. For example, one study examined how childhood industriousness and hard work were related to adult behavior by following a group of 450 men over a 35-year period, starting in early childhood (Vaillant & Vaillant, 1981). The men who were most industrious and hardworking during childhood were most successful as adults, both in occupational attainment and in their personal lives. In fact, childhood industriousness was more closely associated with adult success than was intelligence or family background.

Understanding Oneself: A New Response to "Who Am I?"

LO 10.2 Summarize ways in which children's views of themselves change during middle childhood.

During middle childhood, children continue their efforts to answer the question "Who am I?" as they seek to understand the nature of the self. Although the question does not yet have the urgency it will assume in adolescence, children in middle childhood still seek to pin down their place in the world.

THE SHIFT IN SELF-UNDERSTANDING FROM THE PHYSICAL TO THE PSYCHOLOGICAL. Children are on a quest for self-understanding during middle childhood. Helped by the cognitive advances that we discussed Chapter 9, they begin to view themselves less in terms of external physical attributes and more in terms of psychological traits (Bosacki, 2014; Aronson & Bialostok, 2016; Thomaes, Brummelman, & Sedikides, 2017).

For instance, 6-year-old Carey describes herself as "a fast runner and good at drawing"—both characteristics dependent on skill in external activities relying on motor skills. In contrast, 11-year-old Meiping characterizes herself as "pretty smart, friendly, and helpful to my friends." Meiping's view of herself is based on psychological characteristics, inner traits that are more abstract than the younger child's descriptions. The use of inner traits to determine self-concept results from the child's increasing cognitive skills, a development that we discussed in Chapter 9.

In addition to shifting focus from external characteristics to internal psychological traits, children's views of who they are become less simplistic and have greater complexity. In Erikson's view, children are seeking endeavors where they can be successfully industrious. As they get older, children discover that they may be good at some things and not so good at others. Ten-year-old Ginny, for instance, comes to understand that she is good at arithmetic but not very good at spelling; 11-year-old Alberto determines that he is good at softball but doesn't have the stamina to play soccer very well.

Children's self-concepts become divided into personal and academic spheres. As can be seen in Figure 10-1, children evaluate themselves in four major areas, and each of these areas can be broken down even further. For instance, the nonacademic self-concept includes the components of physical appearance, peer relations, and physical ability. Academic self-concept is similarly divided. Research on students' self-concepts in English, mathematics, and nonacademic realms has found that the separate self-concepts are not always correlated, although there is overlap among them. For example, a child who sees herself as a star math student is not necessarily going to feel she is great at English (Marsh & Hau, 2004; Ehm, Lindberg, & Hasselhorn, 2013; Lohbeck, Tietjens, & Bund, 2016).

SOCIAL COMPARISON. If someone asks you how good you are at math, how would you respond? Most of us would compare our performance to that of others who are roughly the same age and educational level. It is unlikely that we'd answer the question by comparing ourselves either to Albert Einstein or to a kindergartner just learning about numbers.

Children in middle childhood begin to follow the same sort of reasoning when they seek to understand how able they are. When they were younger, they tended to consider their abilities in terms of some hypothetical standard, making a judgment that they are good or bad in an absolute sense. Now they begin to use social comparison processes, comparing themselves to others, to determine their levels of accomplishment (Weiss, Ebbeck, & Horn, 1997).

social comparison
the desire to evaluate one's own behavior, abilities, expertise, and opinions by comparing them to those of others

Social comparison is the desire to evaluate one's own behavior, abilities, expertise, and opinions by comparing them to those of others. According to a theory first suggested by psychologist Leon Festinger (1954), when concrete, objective measures of ability are lacking, people turn to *social reality* to evaluate themselves. Social reality refers to understanding that is derived from how others act, think, feel, and view the world.

But who provides the most adequate comparison? When they cannot objectively evaluate their ability, children during middle childhood increasingly look to others who are similar to themselves. In addition, children may use *upward social comparison,* in which they evaluate their abilities against those who appear to be more proficient and successful than they are. While using upward social comparison may provide aspirational models, it can sometimes make individuals feel worse about themselves as they fear they can never be as good as their more successful peers (Summers, Schallert, & Ritter, 2003; Boissicat et al., 2012).

Downward Social Comparison. Although children typically compare themselves to others who are similar, in some cases—particularly when their self-esteem is at stake—they choose to make *downward social comparisons* with others who are obviously less competent or successful. Such downward social comparison protects children's self-esteem.

Figure 10-1 Looking Inward: The Development of Self

As children get older, their views of self become more differentiated, comprising several personal and academic spheres. What cognitive changes make this possible?

(**Source:** Based on Shavelson, Hubner, & Stanton, 1976.)

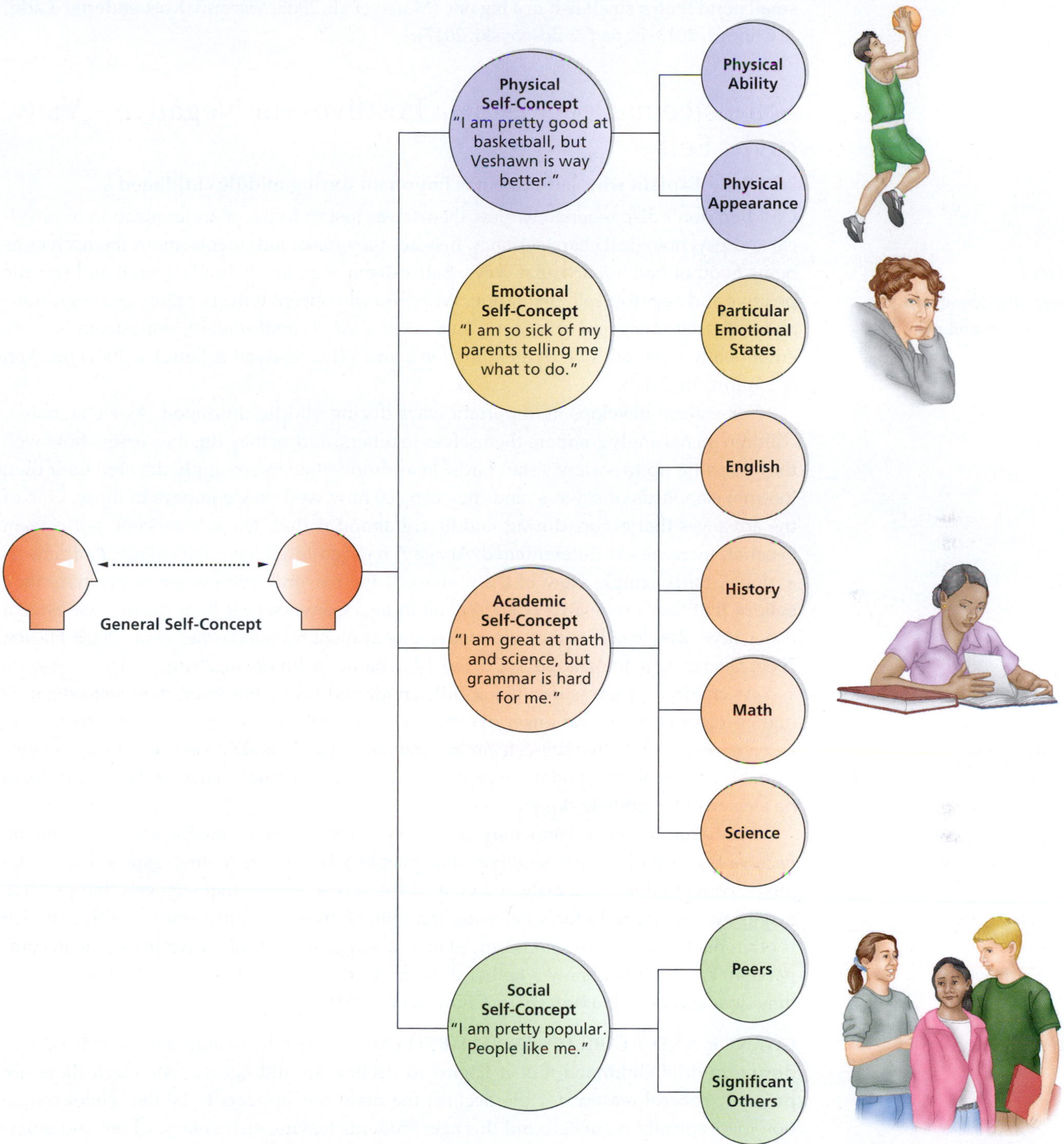

By comparing themselves to those who are less able, children ensure that they will come out on top and thereby preserve an image of themselves as successful (Hui et al., 2006; Hosogi et al., 2012; Sheskin, Bloom, & Wynn, 2014).

Downward social comparison helps explain why some students in elementary schools with generally low achievement levels are found to have stronger academic self-esteem than very capable students in schools with high achievement levels. The reason seems to be that students in the low-achievement schools observe others who are not doing terribly well academically, and they feel relatively good by comparison. In contrast, students in the high-achievement schools may find themselves competing with a more academically proficient group of students, and their perception of their performance may suffer in comparison. At least in terms of self-esteem, then, it is better to be a big fish in a small pond than a small fish in a big one (Marsh et al., 2008; Visconti, Kochenderfer-Ladd, & Clifford, 2013; Lapan & Boseovski, 2017).

Self-Esteem: Developing a Positive—or Negative—View of the Self

LO 10.3 Explain why self-esteem is important during middle childhood.

self-esteem
an individual's overall and specific positive and negative self-evaluation

Children don't dispassionately view themselves just in terms of an itemization of physical and psychological characteristics. Instead, they make judgments about themselves as being good or bad in particular ways. **Self-esteem** is an individual's overall and specific positive and negative self-evaluation. Whereas self-concept reflects beliefs and cognitions about the self (*I am good at trumpet; I am not so good at social studies*), self-esteem is more emotionally oriented (*Everybody thinks I'm a nerd.*) (Davis-Kean & Sandler, 2001; Bracken & Lamprecht, 2003).

Self-esteem develops in important ways during middle childhood. As we've noted, children increasingly compare themselves to others, and as they do, they assess how well they measure up to society's standards. In addition, they increasingly develop their own internal standards of success, and they can see how well they compare to those. One of the advances that occurs during middle childhood is that, like self-concept, self-esteem becomes increasingly differentiated. At age 7, most children have self-esteem that reflects a global, fairly simple view of themselves. If their overall self-esteem is positive, they believe that they are relatively good at all things. Conversely, if their overall self-esteem is negative, they feel that they are inadequate at most things (Lerner et al., 2005; Harter, 2006; Hoersting & Jenkins, 2011; Coelho, Marchante, & Jimerson, 2016).

As children progress into the middle childhood years, however, their self-esteem is higher for some areas and lower in others. For example, a boy's overall self-esteem may be composed of positive self-esteem in some areas (such as the positive feelings he gets from his artistic ability) and more negative self-esteem in others (such as the unhappiness he feels over his athletic skills).

Furthermore, self-esteem may be associated with social media use. Research on Facebook use with adults suggests that people who are frequently exposed to social media come to develop a distorted view of the world, a view that suggests that positive events are the norm. In turn, believing that others' lives are consistently positive (which is often the view they present on social media) suggests that their own lives pale in comparison. We don't yet know whether these findings hold for children, but it seems likely they do (Ozimek & Bierhoff, 2016; Chow & Wan, 2017).

CHANGE AND STABILITY IN SELF-ESTEEM. Generally, overall self-esteem is high during middle childhood, but it begins to decline around age 12. Although there are probably several reasons for the decline, the main one appears to be the school transition that typically occurs around this age: Students leaving elementary school and entering either middle school or junior high school show a decline in self-esteem, which then gradually rises again (Twenge & Campbell, 2001; Robins & Trzesniewski, 2005; Poorthuis et al., 2014).

From *an educator's* perspective

What can teachers do to help children whose low self-esteem is causing them to fail? How can this cycle of failure be broken?

However, some children have chronically low self-esteem. Children with low self-esteem face a tough road, in part because their self-esteem becomes enmeshed in a cycle of failure that grows increasingly difficult to break. Assume, for instance, that Harry, a student with chronically low self-esteem, is facing an important test. Because of his low self-esteem, he expects to do poorly. As a consequence, he is quite anxious—so anxious that he is unable to concentrate well and study effectively. Furthermore, he may decide not to study much because he figures that if he's going to do badly anyway, why bother studying?

Ultimately, of course, Harry's high anxiety and lack of effort bring about the result he expected: He does poorly on the test. This failure, which confirms Harry's expectation, reinforces his low self-esteem, and the cycle of failure continues (see Figure 10-2).

In contrast, students with high self-esteem travel a more positive path, falling into a cycle of success. Having higher expectations leads to increased effort and lower anxiety, increasing the probability of success. In turn, this helps affirm their higher self-esteem, which began the cycle.

Parents can help break the cycle of failure by promoting their children's self-esteem. The best way to do this is through the use of the *authoritative* childrearing style that we discussed in Chapter 8. Authoritative parents are warm and emotionally supportive, while still setting clear limits for their children's behavior. In contrast, other parenting styles have less positive effects on self-esteem. Parents who are highly punitive and controlling send a message to their children that they are untrustworthy and unable to make good decisions—a message that can undermine children's sense of adequacy. Highly indulgent parents, who indiscriminately praise and reinforce their children regardless of their actual performance, can create a false sense of self-esteem in their children, which ultimately may be just as damaging to children (Raboteg-Saric & Sakic, 2013; Harris et al., 2015; Orth, 2017).

Figure 10-2 A Cycle of Low Self-Esteem

Because children with low self-esteem may expect to do poorly on a test, they may experience high anxiety and not work as hard as those with higher self-esteem. As a result, they actually do perform badly on the test, which in turn confirms their negative view of themselves. In contrast, those with high self-esteem have more positive expectations, which leads to lower anxiety and higher motivation. As a consequence, they perform better, reinforcing their positive self-image. How would a teacher help students with low self-esteem break out of their negative cycle?

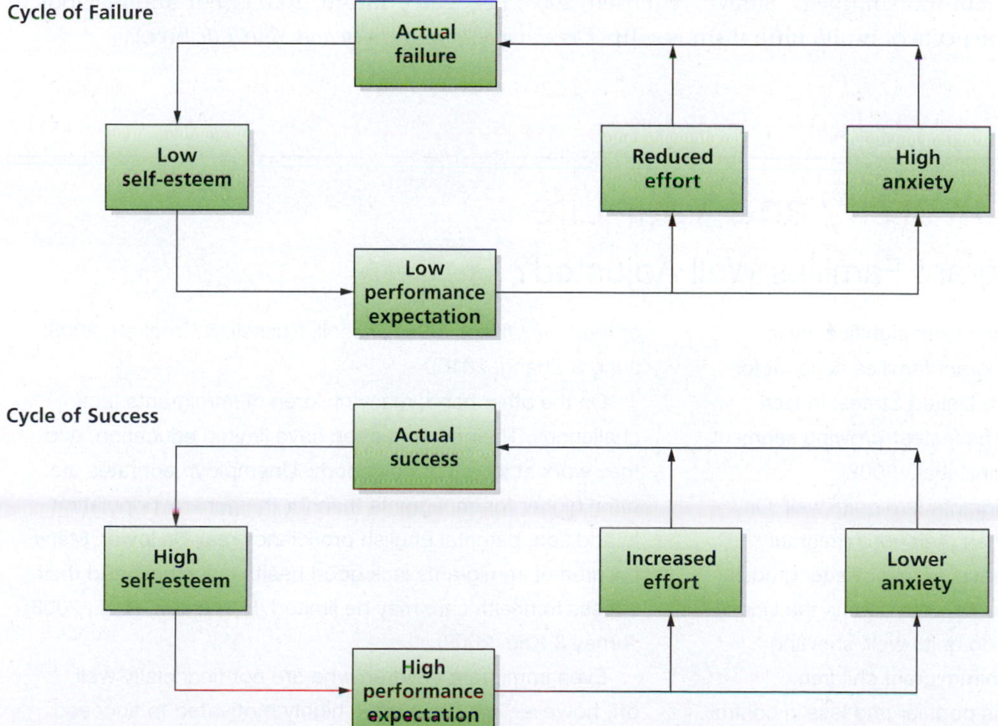

Knape/Getty Images

In pioneering research conducted several decades ago, African American girls' preference for white dolls was viewed as an indication of low self-esteem. More recent evidence, however, suggests that white and African American children show little difference in self-esteem.

RACE AND SELF-ESTEEM. If you were part of a racial group whose members routinely experienced prejudice and discrimination, it seems reasonable to predict that your self-esteem would be affected. Early research confirmed that hypothesis and found that African Americans had lower self-esteem than whites. For example, a set of pioneering studies a generation ago found that African American children shown black and white dolls preferred the white dolls over the black ones (Clark & Clark, 1947). The interpretation that was drawn from the study: The self-esteem of the African American children was low.

However, more recent research has shown these early assumptions to be overstated. The picture is more complex regarding relative levels of self-esteem between members of different racial and ethnic groups. For example, although white children initially show higher self-esteem than black children, black children begin to show slightly higher self-esteem than white children around age 11. This shift occurs as African American children become more closely identified with their racial group, develop more complex views of racial identity, and increasingly view the positive aspects of their group membership (Tatum, 2007; Sprecher, Brooks, & Avogo, 2013; Davis et al., 2017).

Hispanic children also show an increase in self-esteem toward the end of middle childhood, although even in adolescence their self-esteem still trails that of whites. In contrast, Asian American children show the opposite pattern: Their self-esteem in elementary school is higher than that of whites and blacks, but by the end of childhood, their self-esteem is lower than that of whites (Tropp & Wright, 2003; Verkuyten, 2008; Kapke, Gerdis, & Lawton, 2017).

One explanation for the complex relationship between self-esteem and minority group status comes from *social identity theory*. According to the theory, members of a minority group are likely to accept the negative views held by a majority group only if they perceive that there is little realistic possibility of changing the power and status differences between the groups. If minority group members feel that prejudice and discrimination can be reduced, and they blame society for the prejudice and not themselves, self-esteem should not differ between majority and minority groups (Tajfel & Turner, 2004; Thompson, Briggs-King, & LaTouche-Howard, 2012).

As group pride and ethnic awareness among minority group members has grown, differences in self-esteem between members of different ethnic groups have narrowed. This trend has been supported by an increased sensitivity to the importance of multiculturalism (Negy, Shreve, & Jensen, 2003; Lee, 2005; Tatum, 2007). (For another look at aspects of multiculturalism, see the *Developmental Diversity and Your Life* box.)

Developmental Diversity and Your Life

Are Children of Immigrant Families Well Adjusted?

Immigration to the United States has risen significantly in the past 50 years. Children in immigrant families account for almost 25 percent of children in the United States. In fact, children of immigrant families are the fastest-growing segment of children in the country (Hernandez et al., 2008).

In many ways, children of immigrants fare quite well. On the one hand, they are better off than their nonimmigrant peers. For example, they tend to have equal or better grades in school than children whose parents were born in the United States. Psychologically, they also do quite well, showing similar levels of self-esteem as nonimmigrant children, although they do report feeling less popular and less in control of their lives (Kao, 2000; Driscoll, Russell, & Crockett, 2008; Jung & Zhang, 2016).

On the other hand, many children of immigrants face challenges. Their parents often have limited education, and they work at jobs that pay poorly. Unemployment rates are often higher for immigrants than for the general population. In addition, parental English proficiency may be lower. Many children of immigrants lack good health insurance, and their access to health care may be limited (Hernandez et al., 2008; Turney & Kao, 2009).

Even immigrant children who are not financially well off, however, are often more highly motivated to succeed and place greater value on education than do children in nonimmigrant families. Moreover, many immigrant children come from societies that emphasize collectivism, and consequently they may feel they have a greater obligation and duty to their family to succeed. Finally, their country of origin may give some immigrant children a strong enough cultural identity to prevent them from adopting undesirable "American" behaviors—such as materialism or selfishness (Fuligni & Yoshikawa, 2003; Suárez-Orozco, Suárez-Orozco, & Todorova, 2008).

During the middle childhood years, it thus appears that children in immigrant families often do quite well in the United States. The story is less clear, however, when immigrant children reach adolescence and adulthood. For instance, some research shows higher rates of obesity (a key indicator of physical health) in immigrant adolescents. Research is just beginning to clarify how effectively immigrants cope over the course of the life span (Fuligni & Fuligni, 2008; Perreira & Ornelas, 2011; Fuligni, 2012).

Ira Berger/Alamy Stock Photo

Immigrant children tend to fare quite well in the United States, partly because many come from societies that emphasize collectivism, and consequently they may feel more obligation and duty to their family to succeed. What are some other cultural differences that can lead to the success of immigrant children?

Moral Development

LO 10.4 Describe how children's sense of right and wrong changes in middle childhood.

Your wife is near death from an unusual kind of cancer. One drug exists that the physicians think might save her—a form of radium that a scientist in a nearby city has recently developed. The drug, though, is expensive to manufacture, and the scientist is charging 10 times what the drug costs him to make. He pays $1,000 for the radium and charges $10,000 for a small dose. You have gone to everyone you know to borrow money, but you can get together only $2,500—one-quarter of what you need. You've told the scientist that your wife is dying and asked him to sell it more cheaply or let you pay later. But the scientist has said, "No, I discovered the drug, and I'm going to make money from it." In desperation, you consider breaking into the scientist's laboratory to steal the drug for your wife. Should you do it?

According to developmental psychologist Lawrence Kohlberg and his colleagues, the answer that children give to this question reveals central aspects of their sense of morality and justice. He suggests that people's responses to moral dilemmas such as this one reveal the stage of moral development they have attained—as well as yield information about their general level of cognitive development (Kohlberg, 1984; Colby & Kohlberg, 1987; Buon, Habib, & Frey, 2017).

Kohlberg contends that people pass through a series of stages as their sense of justice evolves and in the kind of reasoning they use to make moral judgments. Primarily because of the cognitive characteristics we discussed earlier, younger school-age children tend to think either in terms of concrete, unvarying rules ("It is always wrong to steal" or "I'll be punished if I steal") or in terms of the rules of society ("Good people don't steal" or "What if everyone stole?").

By the time they reach adolescence, however, individuals are able to reason on a higher plane, typically having reached Piaget's stage of formal operations. They are capable of comprehending abstract, formal principles of morality, and they consider cases such as the one just presented in terms of broader issues of morality and of right and wrong ("Stealing may be acceptable if you are following your own conscience and doing the right thing").

Kohlberg suggests that moral development emerges in a three-level sequence, which is further subdivided into six stages (see Table 10-1). At the lowest level, *preconventional morality* (Stages 1 and 2), people follow rigid rules based on punishments or rewards. For example, a student at the preconventional level might evaluate the moral dilemma posed in the story by saying that it was not worth stealing the drug because if you were caught, you would go to jail.

In the next level, that of *conventional morality* (Stages 3 and 4), people approach moral problems in terms of their own position as good, responsible members of society. Some at this level would decide *against* stealing the drug because they think they would feel guilty or dishonest for violating social norms. Others would decide *in favor* of stealing the drug because if they did nothing in this situation, they would be unable to face others. All of these people would be reasoning at the conventional level of morality.

Finally, individuals using *postconventional morality* (Level 3; Stages 5 and 6) invoke universal moral principles that are considered broader than the rules of the particular society in which they live. People who feel that they would condemn themselves if they did not steal the drug because they would not be living up to their own moral principles would be reasoning at the postconventional level.

Kohlberg's theory proposes that people move through the periods of moral development in a fixed order and that they are unable to reach the highest stage until adolescence, due to deficits in cognitive development that are not overcome until then

Table 10-1 Kohlberg's Sequence of Moral Reasoning

		SAMPLE MORAL REASONING	
Level	**Stage**	**In Favor of Stealing**	**Against Stealing**
LEVEL 1 **Preconventional morality** The main considerations are the avoidance of punishment and the desire for rewards.	**STAGE 1** Obedience and punishment orientation: People obey rules to avoid being punished. Obedience is its own reward.	"You shouldn't just let your wife die. People will blame you for not doing enough, and they'll blame the scientist for not selling you the drug for less money."	"You can't steal the drug because you'll be arrested and go to jail. Even if you aren't caught, you'll feel guilty, and you'll always worry that the police may figure out what you did."
	STAGE 2 Reward orientation: People obey rules in order to earn rewards for their own benefit.	"Even if you get caught, the jury will understand and give you a short sentence. Meanwhile, your wife is alive. And if you're stopped before you get the drug to your wife, you could probably just return the drug without penalty."	"You shouldn't steal the drug because you're not responsible for your wife's cancer. If you get caught, your wife will still die, and you'll be in jail."
LEVEL 2 **Conventional morality** Membership in society becomes important. People behave in ways that will win the approval of others.	**STAGE 3** "Good boy" morality: People want to be respected by others and try to do what they're supposed to do.	"Who will blame you if you steal a life-saving drug? But if you just let your wife die, you won't be able to hold your head up in front of your family or your neighbors."	"If you steal the drug, everyone will treat you like a criminal. They will wonder why you couldn't have found some other way to save your wife."
	STAGE 4 Authority and social-order-maintaining morality: People believe that only society, not individuals, can determine what is right. Obeying society's rules is right in itself.	"A husband has certain responsibilities toward his wife. If you want to live an honorable life, you can't let fear of the consequences get in the way of saving her. If you ever want to sleep again, you have to save her."	"You shouldn't let your concern for your wife cloud your judgment. Stealing the drug may feel right at the moment, but you'll live to regret breaking the law."
LEVEL 3 **Postconventional morality** People accept that there are certain ideals and principles of morality that must govern our actions. These ideals are more important than any particular society's rules.	**STAGE 5** Morality of contract, individual rights, and democratically accepted law: People rightly feel obligated to follow the agreed rules of society. But as societies develop over time, rules have to be updated to make societal changes reflect underlying social principles.	"If you simply follow the law, you will violate the underlying principle of saving your wife's life. If you do take the drug, society will understand your actions and respect them. You can't let an outdated law prevent you from doing the right thing."	"Rules represent society's thinking on the morality of actions. You can't let your short-term emotions interfere with the more permanent rules of society. If you do, society will judge you negatively, and in the end you will lose self-respect."
	STAGE 6 Morality of individual principles and conscience: People accept that laws are attempts to write down specific applications of universal moral principles. Individuals must test these laws against their consciences, which tend to express an inborn sense of those principles.	"If you allow your wife to die, you will have obeyed the letter of the law, but you will have violated the universal principle of life preservation that resides within your conscience. You will blame yourself forever if your wife dies because you obeyed an imperfect law."	"If you become a thief, your conscience will blame you for putting your own interpretation of moral issues above the legitimate rule of law. You will have betrayed your own standards of morality."

(**Source:** Based on Kohlberg, 1969.)

(Kurtines & Gewirtz, 1987). However, not everyone is presumed to reach the highest stages: Kohlberg found that postconventional reasoning is relatively rare.

Although Kohlberg's theory provides a good account of the development of moral *judgments*, the links with moral *behavior* are less strong. Still, students at higher levels of moral reasoning are less likely to engage in antisocial behavior at school (such as breaking school rules) and in the community (such as engaging in juvenile delinquency) (Langford, 1995; Carpendale, 2000; Wu & Liu, 2014).

Furthermore, one experiment found that 15 percent of students who reasoned at the postconventional level of morality—the highest category—cheated when given the opportunity, although they were not as likely to cheat as those at lower levels, where more than half of the students cheated. Clearly, however, knowing what is morally right does not always mean acting in accordance (Snarey, 1995; Hart, Burock, & London, 2003; Semerci, 2006; Prohaska, 2012).

Kohlberg's theory has also been criticized because it is based solely on observations of members of Western cultures. Cross-cultural research finds that members of more industrialized, technologically advanced cultures move through the stages more rapidly than members of nonindustrialized countries. Why? One explanation is that Kohlberg's higher stages are based on moral reasoning involving governmental and societal institutions, such as the police and the court system. In less industrialized areas, morality may be based more on relationships between people in a particular village. In short, the nature of morality may differ in diverse cultures, and Kohlberg's theory is more suited for Western cultures (Fu et al., 2007).

An aspect of Kohlberg's theory that has proved even more problematic is the difficulty it has explaining *girls'* moral judgments. Because the theory initially was based largely on data from males, some researchers have argued that it does a better job describing boys' moral development than girls' moral development. This would explain the surprising finding that women typically score at a lower level than men on tests of moral judgments using Kohlberg's stage sequence. This result has led to an alternative account of moral development for girls.

MORAL DEVELOPMENT IN GIRLS. Psychologist Carol Gilligan (1982, 1987) has suggested that differences in the ways boys and girls are raised in our society lead to basic distinctions in how men and women view moral behavior. According to Gilligan, boys view morality primarily in terms of broad principles, such as justice or fairness, whereas girls see it in terms of responsibility toward individuals and willingness to sacrifice themselves to help specific individuals within the context of particular relationships. Compassion for individuals, then, is a more prominent factor in moral behavior for women than it is for men (Gilligan, Lyons, & Hammer, 1990; Gump, Baker, & Roll, 2000).

Gilligan views morality as developing among females in a three-stage process (summarized in Table 10-2). In the first stage, called "orientation toward individual survival," females first concentrate on what is practical and best for them, gradually making a transition from selfishness to responsibility, in which they think about what would be best for

Table 10-2 Gilligan's Three Stages of Moral Development for Women

Stage	Characteristics	Example
Stage 1 Orientation toward individual survival	Initial concentration is on what is practical and best for self. Gradual transition from selfishness to responsibility, which includes thinking about what would be best for others.	A first grader may insist on playing only games of her own choosing when playing with a friend.
Stage 2 Goodness as self-sacrifice	Initial view is that a woman must sacrifice her own wishes for what other people want. Gradual transition from "goodness" to "truth," which takes into account needs of both self and others.	Now older, the same girl may believe that to be a good friend, she must play the games her friend chooses, even if she herself doesn't like them.
Stage 3 Morality of nonviolence	A moral equivalence is established between self and others. Hurting anyone—including oneself—is seen as immoral. Most sophisticated form of reasoning, according to Gilligan.	The same girl may realize that both friends must enjoy their time together and look for activities that both she and her friend can enjoy.

(**Source:** Gilligan, 1982.)

others. In the second stage, termed "goodness as self-sacrifice," females begin to think that they must sacrifice their own wishes for what other people want. Ideally, women make a transition from "goodness" to "truth," in which they take into account their own needs plus those of others. This transition leads to the third stage, "morality of nonviolence," in which women come to see that hurting anyone is immoral—including hurting themselves. This realization establishes a moral equivalence between themselves and others and represents, according to Gilligan, the most sophisticated level of moral reasoning.

It is obvious that Gilligan's sequence of stages is quite different from Kohlberg's, and some developmentalists have suggested that her rejection of Kohlberg's work is too sweeping and that gender differences are not as pronounced as first thought (Colby & Damon, 1987). For instance, some researchers argue that both males and females use similar "justice" and "care" orientations in making moral judgments. Clearly, the question of how boys and girls differ in their moral orientations, as well as the nature of moral development in general, is far from settled (Weisz & Black, 2002; Jorgensen, 2006; Tappan, 2006; Donleavy, 2008).

Module 10.1 Review

LO 10.1 Describe the major developmental challenges of middle childhood.

According to Erikson, children in the middle childhood years are in the industry-versus-inferiority stage.

LO 10.2 Summarize ways in which children's views of themselves change during middle childhood.

In the middle childhood years, children begin to use social comparison and self-concepts based on psychological rather than physical characteristics.

LO 10.3 Explain why self-esteem is important during middle childhood.

During the middle childhood years, self-esteem is based on comparisons with others and internal standards of success; if self-esteem is low, the result can be a cycle of failure.

LO 10.4 Describe how children's sense of right and wrong changes in middle childhood.

According to Kohlberg, moral development proceeds from a concern with rewards and punishments, through a focus on social conventions and rules, toward a sense of universal moral principles. Gilligan has suggested, however, that girls may follow a somewhat different progression of moral development.

Journal Writing Prompt

Applying Lifespan Development: Kohlberg and Gilligan each suggest there are three major levels of moral development. Are any of their levels comparable? In which level of either theory do you think that the largest discrepancy between males and females would be observed?

Relationships: Building Friendship in Middle Childhood

In Lunch Room Number Two, Jamillah and her new classmates chew slowly on sandwiches and sip quietly on straws from cartons of milk.... Boys and girls look timidly at the strange faces across the table from them, looking for someone who might play with them in the schoolyard, someone who might become a friend.

For these children, what happens in the schoolyard will be just as important as what happens in the school. And when they're out on the playground, there will be no one to protect them. No child will hold back to keep from beating them at a game, humiliating them in a test of skill, or harming them in a fight. No one will run interference or guarantee membership in a group. Out on the playground, it's sink or swim. No one automatically becomes your friend. (Kotre & Hall, 1990, pp. 112–113)

As Jamillah and her classmates demonstrate, friendship comes to play an increasingly important role during middle childhood. Children grow progressively more sensitive to the importance of friends, and building and maintaining friendships becomes a large part of children's social lives.

Friends influence children's development in several ways. For instance, friendships provide children with information about the world and other people as well as about themselves. Friends provide emotional support that allows children to respond more effectively to stress. Having friends makes a child less likely to be the target of aggression, and it can teach children how to manage and control their emotions and help them interpret their own emotional experiences (Berndt, 2002; Lundby, 2013).

Friendships in middle childhood also provide a training ground for communicating and interacting with others. They can also foster intellectual growth by increasing children's range of experiences (Nangle & Erdley, 2001; Gifford-Smith & Brownell, 2003; Majors, 2012).

Although friends and other peers become increasingly influential throughout middle childhood, they are not more important than parents and other family members. Most developmentalists believe that children's psychological functioning and their development in general is the product of a combination of factors, including peers and parents (Vandell, 2000; Parke, Simpkins, & McDowell, 2002; Laghi et al., 2014). For that reason, we'll talk more about the influence of family later in this chapter.

Stages of Friendship: Changing Views of Friends

LO 10.5 Describe the sorts of relationships and friendships that are typical of middle childhood.

During middle childhood, a child's conception of the nature of friendship undergoes some profound changes. According to developmental psychologist William Damon, a child's view of friendship passes through three distinct stages (Damon & Hart, 1988).

STAGE 1: BASING FRIENDSHIP ON OTHERS' BEHAVIOR. In the first stage, which ranges from around 4 to 7 years of age, children see friends as others who like them and with whom they share toys and other activities. They view the children with whom they spend the most time as their friends. For instance, a kindergartner who is asked, "How do you know that someone is your best friend?" may say that his best friend is someone who plays games with him and who likes him back (Damon, 1983; Erdley & Day, 2017).

What children in this first stage don't do much of, however, is to take others' personal qualities into consideration. For instance, they don't see their friendships as being based on their peers' unique positive personal traits. Instead, they use a very concrete approach to deciding who is a friend, primarily dependent on others' behavior. They like those who share and with whom they can share, while they don't like those who don't share, who hit, or who don't play with them. In sum, in the first stage, friends are viewed largely in terms of presenting opportunities for pleasant interactions.

STAGE 2: BASING FRIENDSHIP ON TRUST. In the next stage, however, children's view of friendship becomes more complicated. Lasting from around age 8 to age 10, this stage covers a period in which children take others' personal qualities and traits, as well as the rewards they provide, into consideration. But the centerpiece of friendship in this second stage is mutual trust. Friends are seen as those who can be counted on to help out when they are needed. This means that violations of trust are taken very seriously, and friends cannot make amends for such violations just by engaging in positive play, as they might at earlier ages. Instead, the expectation is that formal explanations and formal apologies must be provided before a friendship can be reestablished.

Alistair Berg/Getty Images

Mutual trust is considered to be the centerpiece of friendship during middle childhood.

STAGE 3: BASING FRIENDSHIP ON PSYCHOLOGICAL CLOSENESS. The third stage of friendship begins toward the end of middle childhood, from 11 to 15 years of age.

Table 10-3 The Most-Liked and Least-Liked Behaviors That Fifth and Sixth Graders Note in Their Friends, in Order of Importance

Most-Liked Behaviors	Least-Liked Behaviors
Having a sense of humor	Verbal aggression
Being nice or friendly	Expressions of anger
Being helpful	Dishonesty
Being complimentary	Being critical or criticizing
Inviting one to participate in games, etc.	Being greedy or bossy
Sharing	Physical aggression
Avoiding unpleasant behavior	Being annoying or bothersome
Giving one permission or control	Teasing
Providing instructions	Interfering with achievements
Loyalty	Unfaithfulness
Performing admirably	Violating of rules
Facilitating achievements	Ignoring others

(**Source:** Adapted from Zarbatany, Hartmann, & Rankin, 1990.)

During this period, children begin to develop the view of friendship that they hold during adolescence. Although we'll discuss this perspective in detail in Chapter 12, the main criteria for friendship shift toward intimacy and loyalty. Friendship at this stage is characterized by feelings of closeness, usually brought on by sharing personal thoughts and feelings through mutual disclosure. They are also somewhat exclusive. By the time they reach the end of middle childhood, children seek out friends who will be loyal, and they come to view friendship not so much in terms of shared activities as in terms of the psychological benefits that friendship brings.

Children also develop clear ideas about which behaviors they seek in their friends—and which they dislike. As can be seen in Table 10-3, fifth and sixth graders most enjoy others who invite them to participate in activities and who are helpful, both physically and psychologically. In contrast, displays of physical or verbal aggression, among other behaviors, are disliked.

status
the evaluation of a role or person by other relevant members of a group

Individual Differences in Friendship: What Makes a Child Popular?

LO 10.6 Describe what makes a child popular and why popularity is important in middle childhood.

Monkey Business/Fotolia

A variety of factors lead some children to be unpopular and socially isolated from their peers.

Why is it that some children are the schoolyard equivalent of the life of the party, while others are social isolates whose overtures toward their peers are dismissed or disdained?

Developmentalists have attempted to answer this question by examining individual differences in popularity, seeking to identify the reasons why some children climb the ladder of popularity while others remain firmly on the ground.

STATUS AMONG SCHOOL-AGE CHILDREN: ESTABLISHING ONE'S POSITION. Who's on top? Although school-age children are not likely to articulate such a question, the reality of children's friendships is that they exhibit clear hierarchies in terms of status. **Status** is the evaluation of a role or person by other relevant members of a group. Children who have higher status have greater access to available resources, such as games, toys, books, and information. In contrast, lower-status children are more likely to follow the lead of children of higher status.

Status can be measured in several ways. Most frequently, children are asked directly how much they like or dislike particular classmates. They may also be asked whom they would most (and least) like to play with or to carry out some task with.

Status is an important determinant of children's friendships. High-status children tend to form friendships with higher-status individuals, while lower-status children are more likely to have friends of lower status. Status is also related to the number of friends a child has: Higher-status children are more apt to have a greater number of friends than lower-status children.

But it is not only the quantity of social interactions that separates high-status children from lower-status children; the nature of their interactions is also different. Higher-status children are more likely to be viewed as friends by other children. They are more likely to form cliques, groups that are viewed as exclusive and desirable, and they tend to interact with a greater number of other children. In contrast, children of lower status are more likely to play with younger or less popular children (McQuade et al., 2014; van den Berg et al., 2017).

In short, popularity is a reflection of children's status. School-age children who are average to high in status are more likely to initiate and coordinate joint social behavior, making their general level of social activity higher than that of children low in social status (Erwin, 1993; Shutts, 2015).

WHAT PERSONAL CHARACTERISTICS LEAD TO POPULARITY? Popular children share several personality characteristics. They are usually helpful, cooperating with others on joint projects. Popular children are also funny, tending to have good senses of humor and to appreciate others' attempts at humor. Compared with children who are less popular, they are better able to read others' nonverbal behavior and understand others' emotional experiences. They can also control their nonverbal behavior more effectively, thereby presenting themselves well. In short, popular children are high in **social competence**, the collection of individual social skills that permits individuals to perform successfully in social settings (Feldman, Tomasian, & Coats, 1999; McQuade et al., 2016; Erdley & Day, 2017).

social competence
the collection of social skills that permits individuals to perform successfully in social settings

Although, generally, popular children are friendly, open, and cooperative, one subset of popular boys (but not popular girls) displays an array of negative behaviors, including being aggressive, disruptive, and causing trouble. Despite these behaviors, these boys may be viewed as cool and tough by their peers, and they are often remarkably popular. This popularity may occur in part because they are seen as boldly breaking rules that others feel constrained to follow (Woods, 2009; Schonert-Reichl et al., 2012; Scharf, 2014).

SOCIAL PROBLEM-SOLVING ABILITIES. Another factor that relates to children's popularity is their skill at social problem solving. **Social problem solving** refers to the use of strategies for solving social conflicts in ways that are satisfactory both to oneself and to others. Because social conflicts among school-age children are a frequent occurrence—even among the best of friends—successful strategies for dealing with them are an important element of social success (Murphy & Eisenberg, 2002; Dereli-Iman, 2013).

social problem solving
the use of strategies for solving social conflicts in ways that are satisfactory both to oneself and to others

According to developmental psychologist Kenneth Dodge, successful social problem solving proceeds through a series of steps that correspond to children's information processing strategies (see Figure 10-3). Dodge argues that the manner in which children solve social problems is a consequence of the decisions they make at each point in the sequence (Dodge, Lansford, & Burks, 2003; Lansford et al., 2006; Lansford et al., 2014).

By carefully delineating each of the stages, Dodge provides a means by which interventions can be targeted toward a specific child's deficits. For instance, some children routinely misinterpret the meaning of other children's behavior (Step 2) and then respond according to their misinterpretation.

Suppose Max, a fourth grader, is playing a game with Will. While playing the game, Will begins to get angry because he is losing and complains about the rules. If Max is not able to understand that much of Will's anger is frustration at not winning, he is likely to react in an angry way himself, defending the rules, criticizing Will, and making the situation worse. If Max interprets the source of Will's anger more accurately, Max may be able to behave in a more effective manner, perhaps by reminding Will, "Hey, you beat me at Connect Four," thereby defusing the situation.

Figure 10-3 Problem-Solving Steps

Children's problem solving proceeds through several steps involving different information processing strategies.

(**Source:** Based on Dodge, 1985.)

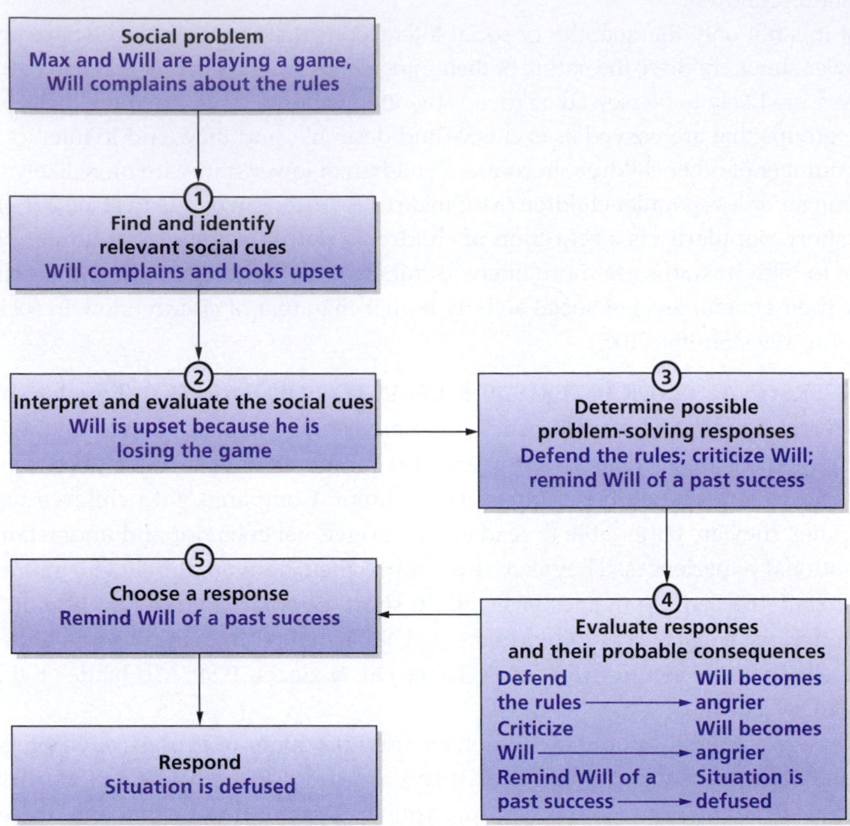

Generally, children who are popular are better at interpreting the meaning of others' behavior accurately. Furthermore, they possess a wider inventory of techniques for dealing with social problems. In contrast, less popular children tend to be less effective at understanding the causes of others' behavior, and as a result their reactions to others may be inappropriate. In addition, their strategies for dealing with social problems are more limited; they sometimes simply don't know how to apologize or help someone who is unhappy feel better (Rose & Asher, 1999; Rinaldi, 2002; Lahat et al., 2014).

Unpopular children may become victims of a phenomenon known as *learned helplessness*. Because they don't understand the root causes of their unpopularity, children may feel that they have little or no ability to improve their situation. As a result, they may simply give up and not even try to become more involved with their peers. In turn, their learned helplessness becomes a self-fulfilling prophecy, reducing the chances that they will become more popular in the future (Seligman, 2007; Aujoulat, Luminet, & Deccache, 2007; Altermatt & Broady, 2009).

TEACHING SOCIAL COMPETENCE. Can anything be done to help unpopular children learn social competence? Happily, the answer appears to be yes. Several programs have been developed to teach children a set of social skills that seem to underlie general social competence. For example, in one experimental program, a group of unpopular fifth and sixth graders was taught how to hold a conversation with friends. They were taught ways to disclose material about themselves, to learn about others by asking questions, and to offer help and suggestions to others in a nonthreatening way.

Compared with a group of children who did not receive such training, the children who were in the experiment interacted more with their peers, held more

Development in Your Life

Increasing Children's Social Competence

Building and maintaining friendships is critical in children's lives. Is there anything that parents and teachers can do to increase children's social competence?

The answer is a clear yes. Among the strategies that can work are the following:

- Encourage social interaction. Teachers can devise ways in which children are led to take part in group activities, and parents can encourage membership in such groups as Brownies and Cub Scouts or participation in team sports.
- Teach listening skills to children. Show them how to listen carefully and respond to the underlying meaning of a communication as well as its overt content.
- Make children aware that people display emotions and moods nonverbally and that consequently they should pay attention to others' nonverbal behavior, not just to what they are saying on a verbal level.
- Teach conversational skills, including the importance of asking questions and self-disclosure. Encourage students to use "I" statements in which they clarify their own feelings or opinions and to avoid making generalizations about others.
- Don't ask children to choose teams or groups publicly. Instead, assign children randomly: It works just as well in ensuring a distribution of abilities across groups and avoids the public embarrassment of a situation in which some children are chosen last.

conversations, developed higher self-esteem, and—most critically—were more accepted by their peers than before training (Asher & Rose, 1997; Bierman, 2004; Fransson et al., 2016). (For more on increasing children's social competence, see the *Development in Your Life* feature.)

SCHOOLYARD—AND CYBER-YARD—BULLIES

> *Austin Rodriguez, an Ohio teen, attempted suicide after classmates bullied him for being gay. They reportedly hid his gym clothes and tried to prevent him from entering the locker room or the lunchroom. They made nasty remarks on the Internet.*
>
> *Rachel Ehmke, a Minnesota seventh grader, hung herself when the bullying got too awful to live with. The 13-year-old had been hounded for months by a group of girls who called her "prostitute," scrawled "slut" all over her notebook, and harassed her online.*

Austin and Rachel are not alone in facing the torment of bullying, whether it comes at school or online. Almost 85 percent of girls and 80 percent of boys report experiencing some form of harassment in school at least once, and 160,000 U.S. schoolchildren stay home from school each day because they are afraid of being bullied. Others encounter bullying online, which may be even more painful because often the bullying is done anonymously or may involve public postings (Mishna, Saini, & Solomon, 2009; Law et al., 2012; Barlett & Chamberlin, 2017).

There are four general types of bullying. In *verbal bullying*, victims are called names, threatened, or made fun of because of physical or other attributes. *Physical bullying* represents actual aggression, in which children may be hit, pushed, or touched inappropriately. *Relational bullying* may be more subtle; it occurs when children are socially attacked, by deliberately excluding them from social activities. Finally, *cyberbullying* occurs when victims are attacked online or by the spreading of malicious lies meant to damage their reputation (Espelage & Colbert, 2016; Osanloo, Reed, & Schwartz, 2017).

Children who experience frequent bullying are most often loners who are fairly passive. They often cry easily, and they tend to lack the social skill that might otherwise defuse a bullying situation. For example, they are unable to think of humorous comebacks to bullies' taunts. But though children such as these are more likely to be bullied, even children without these characteristics occasionally are bullied during their school careers: Some 90 percent of middle school students report being bullied at some point in their time at school, beginning as early as the preschool years (Katzer, Fetchenhauer, & Belschak, 2009; Lapidot-Lefler & Dolev-Cohen, 2014; Jansen et al., 2016).

About 10 to 15 percent of students bully others at one time or another. About half of all bullies come from abusive homes—meaning, of course, that half don't. They tend to watch more television containing violence, and they misbehave more at home and at school than do nonbullies. When their bullying gets them into trouble, they may try to lie their way out of the situation, and they show little remorse for their victimization of others. Furthermore, bullies, compared with their peers, are more likely to break the law as adults. Although bullies are sometimes popular among their peers, some ironically themselves become victims of bullying (Ireland & Archer, 2004; Barboza et al., 2009; Reijntjes et al., 2015).

One of the most effective ways to reduce the incidence of bullying is through school programs that enlist and involve students. For example, schools can train students to intervene when they see an instance of bullying, rather than watching passively. Empowering students to stand up for victims has been shown to reduce bullying significantly (Storey et al., 2008; Munsey, 2012; Juvonen et al., 2016).

How can children in middle childhood deal with bullying? Among the strategies experts suggest are refusing to engage when provocations occur, speaking up against bullying (saying something such as "stop it"), and talking with parents, teachers, and other trusted adults to get their help. Ultimately, children need to recognize that one has the right *not* to be bullied. (The U.S. government website StopBullying.gov provides extensive information about bullying; NCB Now, 2011; Saarento, Boulton, & Salmivalli, 2014.)

Gender and Friendships: The Sex Segregation of Middle Childhood

LO 10.7 Describe how gender affects friendships in middle childhood.

Girls rule; boys drool.
Boys are idiots. Girls have cooties.
Boys go to college to get more knowledge; girls go to Jupiter to get more stupider.

At least, those are some of the views of boys and girls regarding members of the other sex during the elementary school years. Avoidance of the other sex becomes quite pronounced during those years, to the degree that the social networks of most boys and girls consist almost entirely of same-sex groupings (Mehta & Strough, 2009; Rancourt et al., 2012; Zosuls et al., 2014; Braun & Davidson, 2016).

Interestingly, the segregation of friendships according to gender occurs in almost all societies. In nonindustrialized societies, same-gender segregation may be the result of the types of activities that children engage in. For instance, in many cultures, boys are assigned one type of chore and girls another. Participation in different activities may not provide the whole explanation for sex segregation, however: Even children in more developed countries, who attend the same schools and participate in many of the same activities, still tend to avoid members of the other gender (Whiting & Edwards, 1988; Steinmetz et al., 2014).

When boys and girls make occasional forays into the other gender's territory, the action often has romantic overtones. For instance, girls may threaten to kiss a boy, or boys might try to lure girls into chasing them. Such behavior, termed "border work," helps to emphasize the clear boundaries that exist between the two sexes. In addition, it may pave the way for future interactions that do involve romantic or sexual interests, when school-age children reach adolescence and cross-sex interactions become more socially endorsed (Beal, 1994; Lindsey, 2012).

The lack of cross-gender interaction in the middle childhood years means that boys' and girls' friendships are restricted to members of their own sex. Furthermore, the nature of friendships within these two groups is quite different. Boys typically have larger networks of friends than girls, and they tend to play in groups rather than pairing off. Differences in status within the group are usually quite pronounced, with an acknowledged leader and members falling into particular levels of status. Because of the fairly rigid rankings that represent the relative social power of those in the group, known as the **dominance hierarchy**, members of higher status can safely question and oppose children lower in the hierarchy (Pedersen et al., 2007; Pun, Birch & Baron, 2017).

Cathy Yeulet/123RF GB Ltd

Though same-sex groupings dominate in middle childhood, when boys and girls do make occasional forays into each other's territory, there are often romantic overtones. Such behavior has been termed *border work*.

Boys tend to be concerned with their place in the dominance hierarchy, and they attempt to maintain their status and improve upon it. This makes for a style of play known as *restrictive*. In restrictive play, interactions are interrupted when a child feels that his status is challenged. Thus, a boy who feels that he is unjustly challenged by a peer of lower status may attempt to end the interaction by scuffling over a toy or otherwise behaving assertively. Consequently, boys' play tends to come in bursts, rather than in more extended, tranquil episodes (Benenson & Apostoleris, 1993; Estell et al., 2008; Cheng et al., 2016).

The language of friendship used among boys reflects their concern over status and challenge. For instance, consider this conversation between two boys who were good friends:

dominance hierarchy
rankings that represent the relative social power of those in a group

Child 1: Why don't you get out of my yard?

Child 2: Why don't you *make* me get out of the yard?

Child 1: I *know* you don't want that.

Child 2: You're not gonna make me get out the yard cuz you can't.

Child 1: Don't force me.

Child 2: You can't. Don't force me to hurt you (*snickers*). (Goodwin, 1990, p. 37)

Friendship patterns among girls are quite different. Rather than having a wide network of friends, school-age girls focus on one or two "best friends" who are of relatively equal status. In contrast to boys, who seek out status differences, girls profess to avoid differences in status, preferring to maintain friendships at equal status levels.

Conflicts among school-age girls are usually solved through compromise, by ignoring the situation, or by giving in, rather than by seeking to make one's own point of view prevail. In sum, the goal is to smooth over disagreements, making social interaction easy and nonconfrontational (Noakes & Rinaldi, 2006).

The motivation of girls to solve social conflict indirectly does not stem from a lack of self-confidence or from apprehension over the use of more direct approaches. Actually, when school-age girls interact with other girls who are not considered friends or with boys, they can be quite confrontational. However, among friends their goal is to maintain equal-status relationships—relationships lacking a dominance hierarchy (Beale, 1994; Zahn-Waxler et al., 2008).

The language used by girls tends to reflect their view of relationships. Rather than blatant demands ("Give me the pencil"), girls are more apt to use language that is less confrontational and directive. Girls tend to use indirect forms of verbs, such as "Let's go to the movies" or "Would you want to trade books with me?" rather than "I want to go to the movies" or "Let me have these books" (Goodwin, 1990; Besag, 2006).

Cross-Race Friendships: Integration in and out of the Classroom

LO 10.8 Describe how friendships between the races change during the school years.

Are friendships colorblind? For the most part, the answer is no. Children's closest friendships tend largely to be with others of the same race. As children age, there is a decline in

As children age, there is a decline in the number and depth of friendships outside their own racial group. What are some ways in which schools can foster mutual acceptance?

the number and depth of friendships outside their own racial group. By the time they are 11 or 12, it appears that African American children become particularly aware of and sensitive to the prejudice and discrimination directed toward members of their race. At that point, they are more likely to make distinctions between members of ingroups (groups to which people feel they belong) and members of outgroups (groups to which people do not perceive membership) (Rowley et al., 2008; McDonald et al., 2013; Bagci et al., 2014).

For instance, when third graders from one long-integrated school were asked to name a best friend, around one-quarter of white children and two-thirds of African American children chose a child of the other race. In contrast, by the time they reached 10th grade, less than 10 percent of whites and 5 percent of African Americans named a different-race best friend (McGlothlin & Killen, 2005; Rodkin & Ryan, 2012; Munniksma et al., 2017).

From *a social worker's* perspective

How might it be possible to decrease the segregation of friendships along racial lines? What factors would have to change in individuals or in society?

Although they may not choose each other as best friends, whites and African Americans—as well as members of other minority groups—can show a high degree of mutual acceptance. This pattern is particularly true in schools with ongoing integration efforts. This makes sense: A good deal of research supports the notion that contact between majority and minority group members can reduce prejudice and discrimination (Hewstone, 2003; Quintana et al., 2008).

Module 10.2 Review

LO 10.5 Describe the sorts of relationships and friendships that are typical of middle childhood.

Children's understanding of friendship changes from the sharing of enjoyable activities, through the consideration of personal traits that can meet their needs, to a focus on intimacy and loyalty.

LO 10.6 Describe what makes a child popular and why popularity is important in middle childhood.

Friendships in childhood display status hierarchies. Social competence and social problem-solving skills contribute toward a child's popularity. Many children, especially loners, are the victims of bullies during their school years. Programs that involve students in intervening in bullying acts are most effective in reducing its incidence.

LO 10.7 Describe how gender affects friendships in middle childhood.

Boys and girls engage increasingly in same-sex friendships, with boys' friendships involving group relationships and girls' friendships characterized by pairings of girls with equal status.

LO 10.8 Describe how friendships between the races change during the school years.

Interracial friendships decrease in frequency as children age, but contact as peers among members of different races can promote mutual acceptance and appreciation.

Journal Writing Prompt

Applying Lifespan Development: Do you think the stages of friendship are a childhood phenomenon, or do adults' friendships display similar stages?

Family and School: Shaping Children's Behavior in Middle Childhood

Tamara's mother, Brenda, waited outside the door of her daughter's second-grade classroom for the end of the school day. Tamara came over to greet her mother as soon as she spotted her. "Mom, can Anna come over to play today?" Tamara demanded. Brenda had been looking forward to spending some time alone with Tamara, who had spent the last three days at her dad's house. But, Brenda reflected, Tamara hardly ever got to ask kids over after school, so she agreed to the request. Unfortunately, it turned out today wouldn't work for Anna's family, so they tried to find an alternate date. "How about Thursday?" Anna's mother suggested. Before Tamara could reply, her mother reminded her, "You'll have to ask your dad. You're at his house that night." Tamara's expectant face fell. "OK," she mumbled.

How will Tamara's adjustment be affected by dividing her time between the two homes where she lives with her divorced parents? What about the adjustment of her friend, Anna, who lives with both her parents, both of whom work outside the home? These are just a few of the questions we need to consider as we look at the ways that children's schooling and home life affect their lives during middle childhood.

Families: The Changing Home Environment

LO 10.9 Summarize how today's diverse family and care arrangements affect children in middle childhood.

Ms. Herald's first graders are making family trees to honor the diversity of the children's families. And what diversity there is! Paul has two dads. Jorge's mom remarried after her divorce, and his new dad came with two daughters. Mary's dad died. Now she has a mom and twin brothers. Demetri lives with his grandparents and his aunt and her son. Beth lives with her dad and his girlfriend. The girlfriend is pregnant, so Beth writes "Baby???" on her tree. And Jonas lives in a foster home: two moms, three kids.

We've noted in earlier chapters that changes have occurred in the structure of the family over the past few decades. With an increase in the number of parents who both work outside of the home, a soaring divorce rate, and a rise in single-parent families, the environment faced by children passing through middle childhood in the 21st century is very different from that faced by prior generations.

One of the biggest challenges facing children and their parents is the increasing independence that characterizes children's behavior during middle childhood. During the period, children move from being almost completely controlled by their parents to increasingly controlling their own destinies—or at least their everyday conduct. Middle childhood, then, is a period of **coregulation** in which children and parents jointly control behavior. Increasingly, parents provide broad, general guidelines for conduct, while children have control over their everyday behavior. For instance, parents may urge their daughter to buy a balanced, nutritious school lunch each day, but their daughter's decision to regularly buy pizza and two desserts is very much her own.

coregulation
a period in which parents and children jointly control children's behavior

FAMILY LIFE: STILL CENTRAL TO CHILDREN'S LIVES. During the middle years of childhood, children spend significantly less time with their parents. Still, parents remain the major influence in their children's lives, and they are seen as providing essential assistance, advice, and direction (Parke, 2004).

Siblings also have an important influence on children during middle childhood, for good and for bad. Although brothers and sisters can provide support, companionship, and a sense of security, they can also be a source of strife.

Sibling rivalry can occur, with siblings competing or quarreling with one another. Such rivalry can be most intense when siblings are similar in age and of the same sex. Parents may intensify sibling rivalry by being perceived as favoring one child over another. Such perceptions may or may not be accurate. For example, older siblings may be permitted more freedom, which the younger sibling may interpret as favoritism. In some cases, perceived favoritism not only leads to sibling rivalry but may also damage the self-esteem of the younger sibling. However, sibling rivalry is not inevitable, and many siblings get along with each other quite well (McHale, Updegraff, & Whiteman, 2012; Edward, 2013; Skrzypek, Maciejewska-Sobczak, & Stadnicka-Dmitriew, 2014).

Cultural differences are linked to sibling experiences. For example, in Mexican American families, which have particularly strong values regarding the importance of family, siblings are less likely to respond negatively when younger siblings receive preferential treatment (McHale et al., 2005; McGuire & Shanahan, 2010).

What about children who have no siblings? The only child has no opportunity to develop sibling rivalry but also misses out on the benefits that siblings can bring. Generally, despite the stereotype that only children are spoiled and self-centered, the reality is that they are as well adjusted as children with brothers and sisters. In some ways, only children are better adjusted, often having higher self-esteem and stronger motivation to achieve. This had been particularly good news for parents in the People's Republic of China, where until fairly recently a strict one-child policy was in effect. Studies there show that Chinese only children often academically outperform children with siblings (Miao & Wang, 2003; Liu et al., 2017).

WHEN BOTH PARENTS WORK OUTSIDE THE HOME: HOW DO CHILDREN FARE? In most cases, children whose parents both work full time outside of the home fare quite well. Children whose parents are loving, are sensitive to their children's needs, and provide appropriate substitute care typically develop no differently from children in families in which one of the parents does not work (Hadzic, Magee, & Robinson, 2013).

The good adjustment of children whose mothers and fathers both work relates to the psychological adjustment of the parents, especially mothers. In general, women who are satisfied with their lives tend to be more nurturing with their children. When work provides a high level of satisfaction, then, mothers who work outside of the home may be more psychologically supportive of their children. Thus, it is not so much a question of whether a mother chooses to work full time, to stay at home, or to arrange some combination of the two. What matters is how satisfied she is with the choices she has made (Haddock & Rattenborg, 2003; Heinrich, 2014).

Although we might expect that children whose parents both work would spend comparatively less time with their parents than children with one parent at home full time, research suggests otherwise. Children with mothers and fathers who work full time spend essentially the same amount of time with family, with friends in class, and alone as children in families where one parent stays at home (Gottfried, Gottfried, & Bathurst, 2002).

self-care children

children who let themselves into their homes after school and wait alone until their caretakers return from work; previously known as *latchkey children*

HOME AND ALONE: WHAT DO CHILDREN DO?

When 10-year-old Johnetta Colvin comes home after finishing a day at Martin Luther King Elementary School, the first thing she does is grab a few cookies and turn on the computer. She spends some time texting with her friends and then goes over to the television and typically spends the next hour watching. During commercials, she takes a look at her homework. What she doesn't do is chat with her parents, neither of whom is there. She's home alone.

Johnetta is a **self-care child**, the term for children who let themselves into their homes after school and wait alone until their parents return from work. Some 12 to 14 percent of children in the United States between the ages of 5 and 12 spend some time alone after school, without adult supervision. Moreover, three states have a minimum age for leaving a child home alone. Illinois law requires children to be 14 years old; in Maryland, the minimum age is 8, while in Oregon, children must be 10 before being left home alone (Berger, 2000; Child Welfare Information Gateway, 2013).

Melanie Jensen/Getty Images

The consequences of being a self-care child are not necessarily harmful, and they may even lead to a greater sense of independence and competence.

In the past, concern about self-care children centered on their lack of supervision and the emotional costs of being alone. Such children were previously called *latchkey children*, evoking images of sad, pathetic, and neglected children. However, an alternative view of self-care children is that a few hours alone may provide a helpful period of decompression. Furthermore, it may give children the opportunity to develop a greater sense of autonomy (Hofferth & Sandberg, 2001).

Research has identified few differences between self-care children and children who return to homes with parents. Although some children report negative experiences while at home by themselves (such as loneliness), they do not seem emotionally damaged by the experience. In addition, if they stay at home by themselves rather than "hanging out" unsupervised with friends, they may avoid involvement in activities that can lead to difficulties (Goyette-Ewing, 2000; Klein, 2017).

In sum, being a self-care child is not necessarily harmful. In fact, children may develop an enhanced sense of independence and competence. Furthermore, the time spent alone provides an opportunity to work uninterrupted on homework and school or personal projects. Children with employed parents may have higher self-esteem because they feel they are contributing to the household in significant ways (Goyette-Ewing, 2000; Child Welfare Information Gateway, 2013).

DIVORCE. Having divorced parents, like Tamara, the second grader who was described earlier, is no longer very distinctive. Only around half the children in the United States spend their entire childhoods living in the same household with both their parents. The rest will live in single-parent homes or with stepparents, grandparents, or other nonparental relatives; and some will end up in foster care (Harvey & Fine, 2004; Nicholson et al., 2014).

How do children react to divorce? The answer depends on how soon you ask the question following a divorce, as well as how old the children are at the time of the divorce. Immediately after a divorce, both children and parents may show several types of psychological maladjustment for a period that may last from 6 months to 2 years. For instance, children may be anxious, experience depression, or show sleep disturbances and phobias. Even though children most often live with their mothers following a divorce, the quality of the mother–child relationship declines in the majority of cases, often because children see themselves as caught in the middle between their mothers and fathers (Lansford, 2009; Maes, De Mol, & Buysse, 2012; Weaver & Schofield, 2015).

From a *health-care worker's* perspective

How might the development of self-esteem in middle childhood be affected by a divorce? Can constant hostility and tension between parents lead to a child's health problems?

During the early stage of middle childhood, children whose parents are divorcing often blame themselves for the breakup. By age 10, children feel pressure to choose sides, taking the position of either the mother or the father. As a result, they experience some degree of divided loyalty (Hipke, Wolchik, & Sandler, 2010).

Although researchers agree that the short-term consequences of divorce can be quite difficult, the longer-term effects are less clear. Some studies have found that 18 months to 2 years later, most children begin to return to their predivorce state of psychological adjustment. For many children, there are minimal long-term consequences (Hetherington & Kelly, 2002; Guttmann & Rosenberg, 2003; Harvey & Fine, 2004; Schaan & Vögele, 2016).

Other evidence, however, suggests that the fallout from divorce lingers. For example, twice as many children of divorced parents enter psychological counseling as children from intact families (although sometimes a judge will mandate counseling as part of the divorce). In addition, people who have experienced parental divorce are more at risk for experiencing divorce themselves later in life (Huurre, Junkkari, & Aro, 2006; Uphold-Carrier & Utz, 2012; South, 2013; Mahrer & Wolchik, 2017).

How children react to divorce depends on several factors. One is the economic standing of the family the child is living with. In many cases, divorce brings a decline in both parents' standards of living. When this occurs, children may be thrown into poverty (Ozawa & Yoon, 2003; Fischer, 2007).

In other cases, the negative consequences of divorce are less severe because the divorce reduces the hostility and anger in the home. If the household before the divorce was overwhelmed by parental strife—as is the case in around 30 percent of divorces—the greater calm of a postdivorce household may be beneficial to children. This is particularly true for children who maintain a close, positive relationship with the parent with whom they do not live (Davies et al., 2002).

For some children, then, divorce is an improvement over living with parents who have an intact but unhappy marriage, high in conflict. But in about 70 percent of divorces, the predivorce level of conflict is not high, and children in these households may have a more difficult time adjusting to divorce (Amato & Booth, 1997; Amato & Afifi, 2006).

SINGLE-PARENT FAMILIES. Although the majority of children in the United States (69 percent) live with two parents, the remaining 31 percent live in some other arrangement, such as living with a single parent or grandparents (see Figure 10-4). There are also some significant racial disparities: Seventy-four percent of white children live with two married parents, compared with 60 percent of Hispanic and 34 percent of black children (ChildStats.gov, 2017).

In rare cases, death is the reason for single parenthood. More frequently, either no spouse was ever present (i.e., the mother never married), the parents have divorced, or the spouse is absent. In the vast majority of cases, the single parent who is present is the mother.

What consequences are there for children living in homes with just one parent? This is a difficult question to answer. Much depends on whether a second parent was present earlier and the nature of the parents' relationship at that time. Furthermore, the economic status of the single-parent family plays a role in determining the consequences for children. Single-parent families are often less well-off financially than two-parent families, and living in relative poverty has a negative impact on children (Davis, 2003; Harvey & Fine, 2004; Nicholson et al., 2014).

In sum, the impact of living in a single-parent family is not, by itself, invariably negative or positive. Given the large number of single-parent households, the stigma that was once attached to such families has largely declined. The ultimate consequences for children depend on a variety of factors that accompany single parenthood, such as the

Figure 10-4 Living Arrangements of Children: 1960 to Present

Although the number of children living with single parents increased dramatically for several decades, it has leveled off in recent years. **THINKING ABOUT THE DATA:** In comparing 1968 to 2014, how much does the rate of children living with two parents decline? What living arrangement is the two-parent home being replaced by?

(**Sources:** U.S. Census Bureau Decennial Census, 1960, and Current Population Survey, Annual Social and Economic Supplements, 1968–2014.)

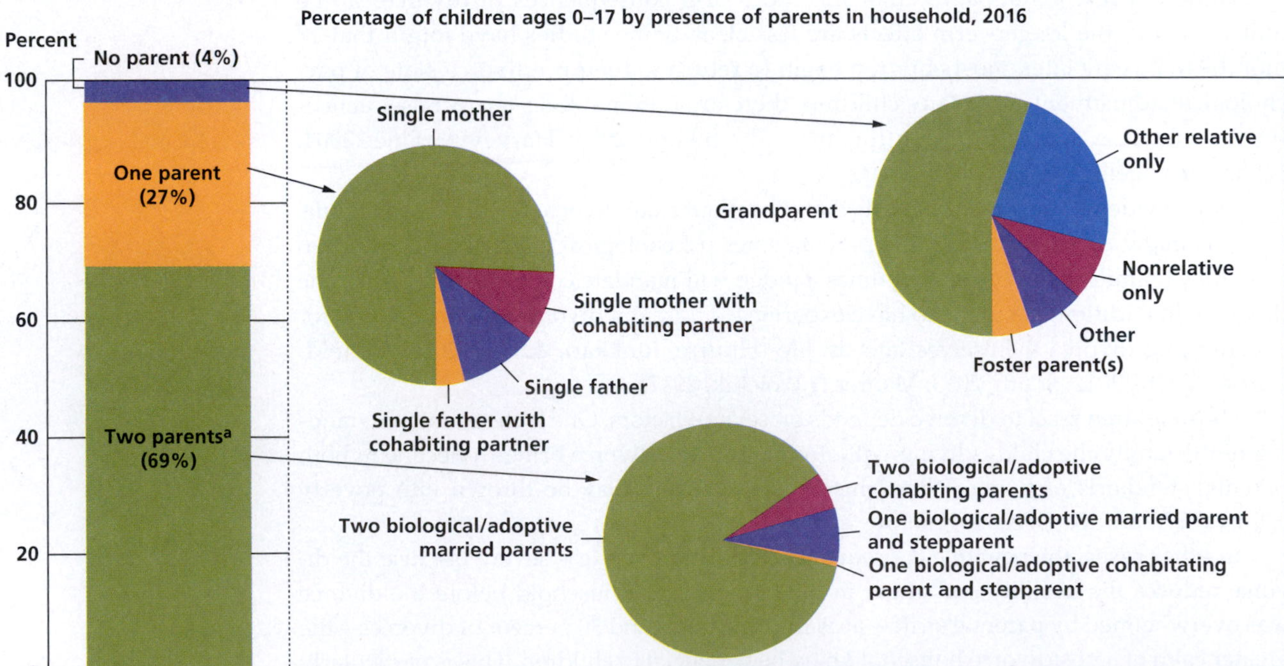

[a]Children living with two stepparents are included here, in either of the categories where one parent is biological/adoptive and one is a stepparent.

economic status of the family, the amount of time that the parent is able to spend with the child, and the degree of stress in the household.

MULTIGENERATIONAL FAMILIES. Some households consist of several generations, in which children, parents, and grandparents live together. The number of multigenerational families is growing; some 19 percent of the U.S. population lived in households with multiple generations in 2014, up from 17 percent just 5 years earlier. The number of multigenerational families grew in part because of the economic downturn in 2008, as well as increases in the cost of housing (Carrns, 2016).

The presence of multiple generations in the same house can make for a rich living experience for children, who experience the influence both of their parents and grandparents. At the same time, multigenerational families also have the potential for conflict, with several adults acting as disciplinarians without coordinating what they do.

The prevalence of three-generation families who live together is greater among African Americans than among Caucasians. In addition, African American families, which are more likely than white families to be headed by single parents, often rely substantially on the help of grandparents in everyday child care, and cultural norms tend to be highly supportive of grandparents taking an active role (Oberlander, Black, & Starr, 2007; Pittman & Boswell, 2007; Kelch-Oliver, 2008).

LIVING IN BLENDED FAMILIES. For many children, the aftermath of divorce includes the subsequent remarriage of one or both parents. More than 10 million households in the United States contain at least one spouse who has remarried. More than 5 million remarried couples have at least one stepchild living with them in what has come to be called a **blended family**. Overall, 17 percent of all children in the United States live in blended families (U.S. Bureau of the Census, 2001; Bengtson et al., 2004).

blended family

a remarried couple that has at least one stepchild living with them

Living in a blended family is challenging for the children involved. There often is a fair amount of *role ambiguity*, in which roles and expectations are unclear. Children may be uncertain about their responsibilities, how to behave toward stepparents and stepsiblings, and how to make a host of decisions that have wide-ranging implications for their role in the family. For instance, a child in a blended family may have to choose which parent to spend each vacation and holiday with, or to decide between the conflicting advice coming from biological parent and stepparent (Cath & Shopper, 2001; Belcher, 2003; Guadalupe & Welkley, 2012; Mundy & Wofsy, 2017).

In many cases, however, elementary-school-age children in blended families often do surprisingly well. In comparison to adolescents, who have more difficulties, elementary-school-age children often adjust with relative ease to blended arrangements, for several reasons. For one thing, the family's financial situation often improves after a parent remarries. In addition, in a blended family there are more people to share the burden of household chores. Finally, the simple fact that the family contains more individuals increases the opportunities for social interaction (Greene, Anderson, & Hetherington, 2003; Hetherington & Elmore, 2003; Purswell & Dillman Taylor, 2013).

Of course, not all children adjust well to life in a blended family. Some find the disruption of routine and of established networks of family relationships difficult. For instance, a child who is used to having her mother's complete attention may find it difficult to observe her mother showing interest and affection to a stepchild. The most successful blending of families occurs when the parents create an environment that supports children's self-esteem and that permits all family members to feel a sense of togetherness. Generally, the younger the children, the easier the transition is within a blended family (Jeynes, 2007; Kirby, 2006.)

(For a look at how children of gay, lesbian, and transgender parents fare, see the *From Research to Practice* Box).

From Research to Practice

Two Moms, Two Dads: How Do Children Fare with Gay, Lesbian, and Transgender Parents?

An increasing number of children have two mothers or two fathers. Estimates suggest that between 1 million and 5 million families are headed by two lesbian or two gay parents in the United States, and some 6 million children have lesbian or gay parents (Patterson, 2007, 2009; Gates, 2013).

How do children in lesbian, gay, and transgender households fare? Although there is little data on the effects of a transgender parent on children, a growing body of research on the effects of same-sex parenting on children shows that children develop similarly to the children of heterosexual families. Their sexual orientation is unrelated to that of their parents, their behavior is no more or less gender-typed, and they seem equally well adjusted (Fulcher, Sutfin, & Patterson, 2008; Patterson, 2009; Goldberg, 2010).

One large-scale analysis examined 33 studies of the effects of parental gender and sexual identity on their children's outcomes. No overall effects were found for children's sexual orientation cognitive abilities or gender identity. There were some differences in terms of parent–child relationships, in which the relationship between parent and child was perceived to *better* among same-gender parents, compared with different-gender parents. The research also found that children of same-gender parents showed more typical gender play and behavior than children of different-gender parents. Finally, children with lesbian or gay parents had higher levels of psychological adjustment than children with heterosexual parents (Fedewa, Black, & Ahn, 2015).

Other research shows that children of lesbian and gay parents have similar relationships with their peers as children of heterosexual parents. They also relate to adults—both those who are gay and those who are straight—no differently from children whose parents are heterosexual. And when they reach adolescence, their romantic relationships and sexual behavior are no different from those of adolescents living with opposite-sex parents (Patterson, 2009; Golombok et al., 2003; Wainright, Russell, & Patterson, 2004; Wainright & Patterson, 2008).

In short, research shows that there is little developmental difference between children whose parents are gay and lesbian and those who have heterosexual parents. There is insufficient research to make the same statement about transgender parenting; more studies need to be conducted before conclusions can be drawn. What is clearly different for children with same-sex parents is the possibility of discrimination and prejudice due to their parents' sexual orientation, although U.S. society has become considerably more tolerant of such unions. In fact, the 2015 U.S. Supreme Court ruling legalizing same-sex marriages should accelerate the trend of acceptance of such unions (Davis, Saltzburg, & Locke, 2009; Biblarz & Stacey, 2010; Kantor, 2015; Miller, Kors, & Macfie, 2017).

Shared Writing Prompt

How might gay and lesbian parents prepare their children to deal with the prejudice and discrimination that they potentially may face?

RACE AND FAMILY LIFE. Although there are as many types of families as there are individuals, research does find some consistencies related to race (Parke, 2004). For example, African American families often have a particularly strong sense of family. Members of African American families are frequently willing to offer welcome and support to extended family members in their homes. Because there is a relatively high level of female-headed households among African Americans, the social and economic support of extended family often is critical. In addition, there is a relatively high proportion of families headed by older adults, such as grandparents, and some studies find that children in grandmother-headed households are particularly well adjusted (McLoyd et al., 2000; Smith & Drew, 2002; Taylor, 2002).

Eric Audras/Getty Images

Children with gay or lesbian parents develop similarly to children with heterosexual parents.

Hispanic families also often stress the importance of family life, as well as community and religious organizations. Children are taught to value their ties to their families, and they come to see themselves as a central part of an extended family. Ultimately, their sense of who they are becomes tied to the family. Hispanic families also tend to be relatively larger, with an average size of 3.71, compared to 2.97 for Caucasian families and 3.31 for African American families (Cauce & Domenech-Rodriguez, 2002; U.S. Bureau of the Census, 2003; Halgunseth, Ispa, & Rudy, 2006).

Although relatively little research has been conducted on Asian American families, emerging findings suggest that fathers are more apt to be powerful figures, maintaining discipline. In keeping with the more collectivist orientation of Asian cultures, children tend to believe that family needs have a higher priority than personal needs, and males, in particular, are expected to care for their parents throughout their lifetimes (Ishii-Kuntz, 2000).

POVERTY AND FAMILY LIFE. Regardless of race, children living in families that are economically disadvantaged face significant hardships. Poor families have fewer basic everyday resources, and there are more disruptions in children's lives. For example, parents may be forced to look for less expensive housing or may move the entire household in order to find work. The result frequently is family environments in which parents are less responsive to their children's needs and provide less social support (Evans, 2004; Duncan, Magnuson & Votruba-Drzal, 2014).

The stress of difficult family environments, along with other stresses in the lives of poor children—such as living in unsafe neighborhoods with high rates of violence and attending inferior schools—ultimately takes its toll. Economically disadvantaged children are at risk for poorer academic performance, higher rates of aggression, and conduct problems. In addition, declines in economic well-being are linked to physical and mental health problems. Specifically, the chronic stress associated with poverty makes children more susceptible to cardiovascular disease, depression, and Type 2 diabetes (Sapolsky, 2005; Morales & Guerra, 2006; Tracy et al., 2008; Duncan, Magnuson & Votruba-Drzal, 2017).

GROUP CARE: ORPHANAGES IN THE 21ST CENTURY. The term *orphanage* evokes images of pitiful youngsters clothed in rags, eating porridge out of tin cups, and housed in huge, prison-like institutions. The reality today is different. Even the word *orphanage* is rarely used, having been replaced by *group home* or *residential treatment center*. Typically housing a relatively small number of children, group homes are used for children whose parents are no longer able to care for them adequately. They are usually funded by a combination of federal, state, and local aid.

Group care has grown significantly in the past decade. In the period from 1995 to 2000, the number of children in foster care increased by more than 50 percent. Today, more than 400,000 children in the United States live in foster care (see Figure 10-5; Child Welfare Information Gateway, 2017).

Keystone-France/Getty Images

Alexander Alland, Jr./Getty Images

Although the orphanages of the early 1900s were crowded and institutional (left), today the equivalent, called group homes or residential treatment centers (right), are much more pleasant.

Figure 10-5 Children in Foster Care

Although the number of children in foster care has declined over the past decade, the numbers are still significant.

(**Source:** Child Welfare Information Gateway. (2017). *Foster Care Statistics 2015*. Washington, DC: U.S. Department of Health and Human Services, Children's Bureau.)

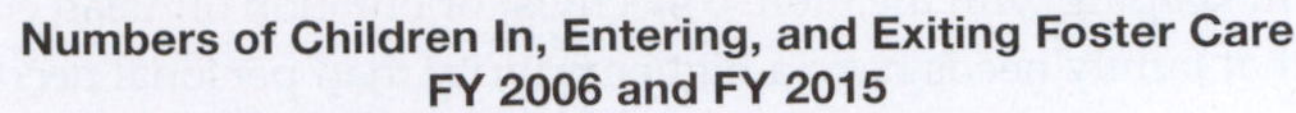

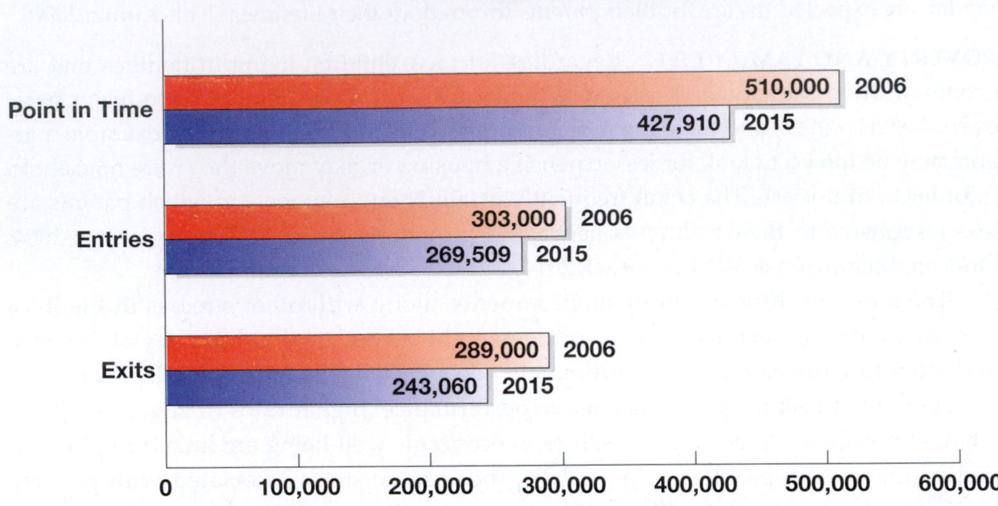

About three-quarters of children in group care are victims of neglect and abuse. Each year, 300,000 children are removed from their homes. Most of them can be returned to their homes following intervention with their families by social service agencies. But the remaining one-quarter are so psychologically damaged due to abuse or other causes that once they are placed in group care, they are likely to remain there throughout childhood. Children who have developed severe problems, such as high levels of aggression or anger, have difficulty finding adoptive families, and it is often difficult to find even temporary foster families who are able to cope with their emotional and behavior problems (Bass, Shields, & Behrman, 2004; Chamberlain et al., 2006; Leloux-Opmeer, 2016).

Although some politicians have suggested that an increase in group care is a solution to complex social problems associated with unwed mothers who become dependent on welfare, experts in providing social services and psychological treatment are not so sure. For one thing, group homes cannot always consistently provide the support and love potentially available in a family setting. Moreover, group care is hardly cheap: It can cost some $40,000 per year to support a child in group care—about 10 times the cost of maintaining a child in foster care or on welfare (Roche, 2000; Allen & Bissell, 2004).

Other experts argue that group care is neither inherently good nor inherently bad. Instead, the consequences of living away from one's family may be quite positive, depending on the particular characteristics of the staff of the group home and whether child and youth care workers are able to develop an effective, stable, and strong emotional bond with a specific child. Of course, if a child is unable to form a meaningful relationship with a worker in a group home, the results may well be harmful (Hawkins-Rodgers, 2007; Knorth et al., 2008).

School: The Academic Environment

LO 10.10 Describe how children's social and emotional lives affect their school performance in middle childhood.

Children spend more of their day in the classroom than anywhere else. It is not surprising, then, that schools have a profound impact on children's lives, shaping and molding not only their ways of thinking but the ways they view the world. We turn now to a number of aspects of schooling in middle childhood that can have a profound effect on children.

HOW CHILDREN EXPLAIN ACADEMIC SUCCESS AND FAILURE. Most of us, at one time or another, have done poorly on a test. Think back to how you felt when you received a bad grade. Did you feel shame? Anger at the teacher? Fear of the consequences?

How you react is a reflection of your **attributions**, the explanations for the reasons behind your behavior. People generally react to failure (as well as success) by considering whether the cause is due to *dispositional factors* ("I'm not such a smart person") or due to *situational* factors ("I didn't get enough sleep last night"). For example, when a success is attributed to internal factors ("I'm smart"), students tend to feel pride; but failure attributed to internal factors ("I'm so stupid") causes shame (Weiner, 2007; Hareli & Hess, 2008; Healy et al., 2015; Lohbeck, Grube, & Moschner, 2017).

attributions

people's explanations for the reasons behind their behavior

CULTURAL COMPARISONS: INDIVIDUAL DIFFERENCES IN ATTRIBUTION. Not everyone comes to the same conclusions about the sources of success and failure. In addition to individual differences, among the strongest influences on people's attributions are their race, ethnicity, and socioeconomic status. Attribution is a two-way street. While our attributions can affect our future performance, it is also true that different experiences give us different perceptions about the ways things in the world fit together. For this reason, it is not surprising that there are subcultural differences in how achievement-related behaviors are understood and explained.

One important difference is related to racial factors: African Americans are less likely than whites to attribute success to internal rather than external causes. African American children tend to feel that aspects such as how difficult a task is and luck (external causes) are the major determinants of their performance outcomes. They are likely to believe that even if they put in maximum effort, prejudice and discrimination (external causes) will prevent them from succeeding (Graham, 1994; Rodgers & Summers, 2008).

Such an attributional pattern, one that overemphasizes the importance of external causes, reduces a student's sense of personal responsibility for success or failure. When attributions are based on internal factors, they suggest that a change in behavior—such as increased effort—can bring about a change in success (Glasgow et al., 1997).

African Americans are not the only group susceptible to maladaptive attributional patterns. Women, for example, often attribute their unsuccessful performance to low ability, an uncontrollable factor. Ironically, though, they do not attribute successful performance to high ability, but rather to factors outside their control. A belief in this pattern suggests the conclusion that even with future effort, success will be unattainable. Females who hold these views may be less inclined to expend the effort necessary to improve their rate of success (Dweck, 2002). By contrast, the success rate of Asian students in school, as described in the following *Developmental Diversity and Your Life* section, illustrates the power of internal attributions.

Developmental Diversity and Your Life

Explaining Asian Academic Success

Consider two students, Ben and Hannah, each performing poorly in school. Suppose you thought that Ben's poor performance was due to unalterable, stable causes, such as a lack of intelligence, while Hannah's was produced by temporary causes, such as a lack of hard work. Who would you think would ultimately do better in school?

If you are like most people, you'd probably predict that the outlook was better for Hannah. After all, Hannah could always work harder, but it is hard for someone like Ben to develop higher intelligence.

According to psychologist Harold Stevenson, this reasoning lies at the heart of the superior school performance of Asian students compared with students in the United States. Stevenson's research suggests that teachers, parents, and students in the United States are likely to attribute school performance to stable, internal causes, while people in Japan, China, and other East Asian countries are more likely to see temporary, situational factors as the cause of their performance. The Asian view, which stems in part from ancient

Confucian writings, tends to accentuate the necessity of hard work and perseverance (Stevenson, Lee, & Mu, 2000; Yang & Rettig, 2004; Phillipson, 2006).

This cultural difference in attributional styles is displayed in several ways. For instance, surveys show that mothers, teachers, and students in Japan and Taiwan all believe strongly that students in a typical class tend to have the same amount of ability. In contrast, mothers, teachers, and students in the United States are apt to disagree, arguing that there are significant differences in ability among the various students (see Figure 10-6).

It is easy to imagine how such different attributional styles can influence teaching approaches. If, as in the United States, students and teachers seem to believe that ability is fixed and locked in, poor academic performance will be greeted with a sense of failure and reduced motivation to work harder to overcome it. In contrast, Japanese teachers and students are apt to see failure as a temporary setback due to their lack of hard work. After making such an attribution, they are more apt to expend increased effort on future academic activities.

These different attributional orientations may explain the fact that Asian students frequently outperform American students in international comparisons of student achievement, according to some developmentalists. Because Asian students tend to assume that academic success results from hard work, they may put greater effort into their schoolwork than American students, who believe that their inherent ability determines their performance. These arguments suggest that the attributional style of students and teachers in the United States might well be maladaptive. They also argue that the attributional styles taught to children by their parents may have a significant effect on their future success (Little, Miyashita, & Karasawa, 2003; Muramoto, Yamaguchi, & Kim, 2009).

Figure 10-6 Mothers' Beliefs in Children's Ability

Compared to mothers in Taiwan and Japan, U.S. mothers were less apt to believe that all children have the same degree of underlying, innate ability. Subjects responded using a 7-point scale, where 1 = strongly disagree and 7 = strongly agree. What are the implications of this finding for schooling in the United States?

(**Sources:** Stevenson & Lee, 1990.)

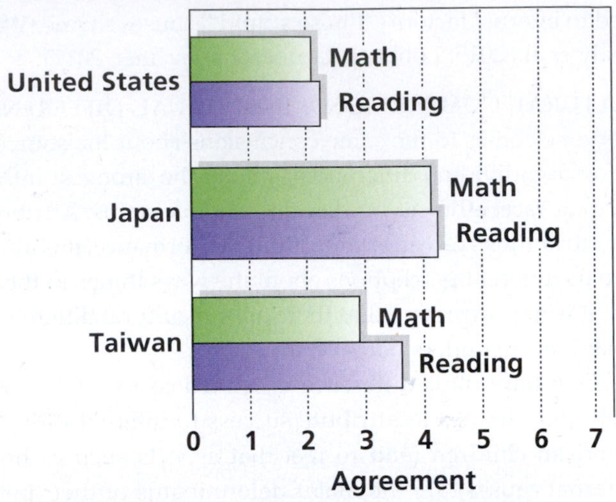

However, the relative success of Asian students has brought about some undesirable consequences. Specifically, Asians have been stereotyped as a "model minority," suggesting that Asians are hardworking overachievers. The "model minority" stereotype produces anti-Asian sentiments that students must navigate (Kiang, Witkow, & Thompson, 2016; Parks & Yoo, 2016).

emotional intelligence
the set of skills that underlies the accurate assessment, evaluation, expression, and regulation of emotions

BEYOND THE THREE RS: SHOULD SCHOOLS TEACH EMOTIONAL INTELLIGENCE? In many elementary schools, the hottest topic in the curriculum has little to do with the traditional three Rs. Instead, a significant educational trend for educators in many elementary schools throughout the United States is the use of techniques to increase students' **emotional intelligence**, the skills that underlie the accurate assessment, evaluation, expression, and regulation of emotions (Salovey & Pizarro, 2003; Mayer, Salovey, & Caruso, 2000, 2008; Mpofu et al., 2017).

Some educators argue that emotional literacy should be a standard part of the school curriculum, and several programs have been effective in teaching students to manage their emotions more effectively. For instance, in one program, children are provided with lessons in empathy, self-awareness, and social skills. In another, children are taught about caring and friendship as early as first grade through exposure to stories in which characters exhibit these positive qualities (Zautra et al., 2015).

Programs meant to increase emotional intelligence have not met with universal acceptance. Critics suggest that the nurturance of emotional intelligence is best left to students' families and that schools ought to concentrate on more traditional curriculum matters. Others suggest that adding emotional intelligence to an already crowded curriculum may reduce time spent on academics. Finally, some critics argue that there is no well-specified set of criteria for what constitutes emotional intelligence, and consequently, it is difficult to develop appropriate, effective curriculum materials (Humphrey et al., 2007).

Still, most people consider emotional intelligence to be worthy of nurturance. Certainly, it is clear that emotional intelligence is quite different from traditional conceptions of intelligence. For example, most of us can think of individuals who, while quite intelligent in a traditional sense, are also insensitive and socially unskilled. The goal of emotional intelligence training is to produce people who are not only cognitively sophisticated but are also able to manage their emotions effectively (Nelis et al., 2009).

Module 10.3 Review

LO 10.9 Summarize how today's diverse family and care arrangements affect children in middle childhood.

Self-care children may develop independence and enhanced self-esteem from their experience. How divorce affects children depends on such factors as financial circumstances and the comparative levels of tension in the family before and after the divorce. The effects of being raised in a single-parent household depend on financial circumstances, the amount of parent–child interaction, and the level of tension in the family.

LO 10.10 Describe how children's social and emotional lives affect their school performance in middle childhood.

Attributional patterns differ along individual, cultural, and gender dimensions. Emotional intelligence—the skills that underlie the accurate assessment, evaluation, expression, and regulation of emotions—is becoming accepted as an important aspect of social intelligence.

Journal Writing Prompt

Applying Lifespan Development: Politicians often speak of "family values." How does this term relate to the diverse family situations covered in this chapter, including divorced parents, single parents, blended families, working parents, self-care children, abusive families, and group care?

Epilogue

Self-esteem and moral development are two key areas in social and personality development in the middle childhood years. Children at this age tend to develop and rely on deeper relationships and friendships, and we looked at the ways gender and race can affect friendships. The changing nature of family arrangements can also affect social and personality development. So can the ways children and teachers explain school successes and failures. Finally, we concluded with a discussion of emotional intelligence, a set of qualities that enhances children's ability to feel empathy for others and to control and express their emotions.

Return to the prologue—about Matt Donner's social struggles—and answer the following questions.

1. Why do you think Matt seems to blame himself for being the victim of bullies?
2. What might be the motivation for other kids to bully Matt? How might it make them feel about themselves?
3. If a school guidance counselor wanted to help Matt adjust to his new school and make friends, what advice could she give him?
4. Why might Matt's parents be so in the dark about what was going on with their son at his new school? Why do you think Matt wanted to keep it that way?

Looking Back

LO 10.1 Describe the major developmental challenges of middle childhood.

According to Erikson, children in the middle childhood years are in the industry-versus-inferiority stage, focusing on achieving competence and responding to a wide range of personal challenges.

LO 10.2 Summarize ways in which children's views of themselves change during middle childhood.

Children in the middle childhood years begin to view themselves in terms of psychological characteristics and to differentiate their self-concepts into separate areas. They use social comparison to evaluate their behavior, abilities, expertise, and opinions.

LO 10.3 Explain why self-esteem is important during middle childhood.

Children in these years are developing self-esteem; those with chronically low self-esteem can become trapped in a cycle of failure in which low self-esteem feeds on itself by producing low expectations and poor performance.

LO 10.4 Describe how children's sense of right and wrong changes in middle childhood.

According to Kohlberg, people pass from preconventional morality (motivated by rewards and punishments), through conventional morality (motivated by social reference), to postconventional morality (motivated by a sense of universal moral principles). Gilligan has sketched out an alternative progression for girls, from an orientation toward individual survival, through goodness as self-sacrifice, to the morality of nonviolence.

LO 10.5 Describe the sorts of relationships and friendships that are typical of middle childhood.

Children's friendships display status hierarchies, and their understanding of friendship passes through stages, from a focus on mutual liking and time spent together, through the consideration of personal traits and the rewards that friendship provides, to an appreciation of intimacy and loyalty.

LO 10.6 Describe what makes a child popular and why popularity is important in middle childhood.

Popularity in children is related to traits that underlie social competence. Because of the importance of social interactions and friendships, developmental researchers have engaged in efforts to improve social problem-solving skills and the processing of social information.

LO 10.7 Describe how gender affects friendships in middle childhood.

Boys and girls in middle childhood increasingly prefer same-gender friendships. Male friendships are characterized by groups, status hierarchies, and restrictive play. Female friendships tend to involve one or two close relationships, equal status, and a reliance on cooperation.

LO 10.8 Describe how friendships between the races change during the school years.

Cross-race friendships diminish in frequency as children age. Equal-status interactions among members of different racial groups can lead to improved understanding, mutual respect and acceptance, and a decreased tendency to stereotype.

LO 10.9 Summarize how today's diverse family and care arrangements affect children in middle childhood.

Children in families in which both parents work outside the home generally fare well. Self-care children who fend for themselves after school may develop independence and a sense of competence and contribution. Immediately after a divorce, the effects on children in the middle childhood years can be serious, depending on the financial condition of the family and the hostility level between spouses before the divorce. The consequences of living in a single-parent family depend on the financial condition of the family and, if there had been two parents, the level of hostility that existed between them. Blended families present challenges to the child but can also offer opportunities for increased social interaction. Children in group care tend to have been victims of neglect and abuse. Many can be helped and placed with their own or other families, but about 25 percent of them will spend their childhood years in group care.

LO 10.10 Describe how children's social and emotional lives affect their school performance in middle childhood.

People attach attributions to their academic successes and failures. Differences in attributional patterns are not only individual but also appear to be influenced by culture and gender as well. Emotional intelligence is the set of skills that permits people to manage their emotions effectively.

Key Terms and Concepts

industry-versus-inferiority stage 329
social comparison 330
self-esteem 332
status 340
social competence 341
social problem solving 341
dominance hierarchy 345
coregulation 347
self-care children 348
blended family 351
attributions 355
emotional intelligence 356

Summary 4
Middle Childhood

RYAN entered first grade with boundless hope and a keen desire to read. Unfortunately, an undiagnosed vision problem interfered with his reading, and fine motor deficits made writing difficult. In most other ways, Ryan was at least the equal of his peers: physically active, imaginative, and highly intelligent. Socially, however, he was hampered by spending time in special education classes. Because he had been singled out and because he could not do some of the things his classmates could do, he was ignored, even bullied, by some of them. When he finally got the right treatment, though, most of his problems vanished. His physical and social skills advanced to match his cognitive abilities. He became more engaged in his schoolwork and more open to friendships. Ryan's story had a happy ending.

Mike Kemp/Getty Images

■ How would you deal with a situation in which your child had physical disabilities that would prevent him or her from progressing in school? How would you encourage your child? How would you deal with your child's frustration at falling behind in school?

What's your response?

Asia Images Group/Getty Images

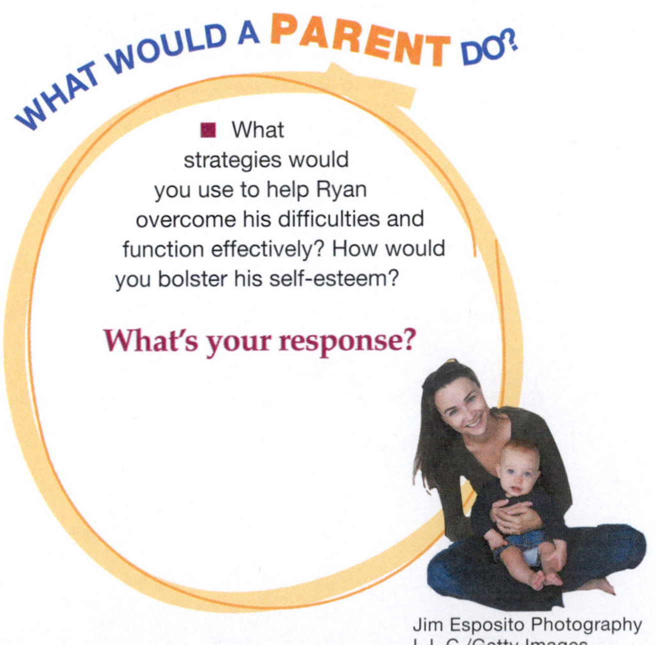

■ What strategies would you use to help Ryan overcome his difficulties and function effectively? How would you bolster his self-esteem?

What's your response?

Jim Esposito Photography L.L.C./Getty Images

Physical Development

Blend Images/Age Fotostock

- Steady growth and increased abilities characterized Ryan's physical development in these years.
- Ryan's gross and fine motor skills developed as muscle coordination improved and he practiced new skills.
- Ryan's sensory problems interfered with his schoolwork.

Cognitive Development

Rob Marmion/Shutterstock

- Ryan's intellectual abilities, such as language and memory, increased in middle childhood.
- One of the key academic tasks for Ryan was to read fluently and with appropriate comprehension.
- Ryan displayed many components and types of intelligence, and the development of his intellectual skills was aided by his social interactions.

Social and Personality Development

imageBROKER/Age Fotostock

- In this period, Ryan mastered many of the challenges presented by school and peers, which took on central importance in his life.
- The development of Ryan's self-esteem was particularly crucial; when Ryan felt himself inadequate, his self-esteem suffered.
- Ryan's friendships helped provide emotional support and fostered intellectual growth.

WHAT WOULD A HEALTH CARE PROVIDER DO?

- How might you respond to Ryan's vision and motor problems? What if Ryan's parents had refused to believe that there was anything physically wrong with Ryan? How would you convince them to get treatment for Ryan?

What's your response?

Photodisc/Getty Images

WHAT WOULD AN EDUCATOR DO?

- How would you deal with Ryan's difficulties in reading and writing? What would you do to help integrate him into his class and help him make friends with his classmates? What would you recommend in terms of educational specialists to deal with his problems?

What's your response?

Mel Yates/Getty Images

Chapter 11

Physical and Cognitive Development in Adolescence

PhotoAlto/Getty Images

Learning Objectives

LO 11.1 Describe the physical changes adolescents experience as the body reaches puberty.

LO 11.2 Explain the nutritional needs and concerns of adolescents.

LO 11.3 Summarize the ways in which the brain develops in adolescence.

LO 11.4 Describe how cognitive development proceeds during adolescence according to Piaget.

LO 11.5 Summarize how information processing approaches explain adolescent cognitive development.

LO 11.6 Describe how adolescent egocentrism affects thinking and behavior.

LO 11.7 Analyze the factors that affect adolescent school performance.

LO 11.8 Describe how adolescents use the Internet and social media.

LO 11.9 Analyze what illegal drugs adolescents use and why.

LO 11.10 Discuss how adolescents use and abuse alcohol.

LO 11.11 Summarize how and why adolescents use tobacco.

LO 11.12 Describe the dangers adolescent sexual practices present and how these dangers can be avoided.

Chapter Overview

Prologue: A Jury of Their Peers

Best friends Jade and Maya, 14, take several selfies after getting their hair cut and styled. In a trendy clothing store, they snap another dozen pics of themselves modeling the lacy tees they just bought. From the shop, the girls go to Maya's house, where they dress up and put on lots of makeup. After taking loads of selfies, they each choose their best shot and post it in a beauty contest on Instagram. They also post the pics on Facebook and Tumblr.

The feedback starts pouring in. Jade gets some "likes," but Maya gets three times as many. While Maya is garnering comments like "hot" and "eye candy," Jade's photo elicits only "cute" or a smiley face.

Jade stares at herself in the mirror. The makeup covers most of her acne but not all. Her blue eyes are bright but too small for her round face. And she's not exactly a size 0. *I'm hopeless,* Jade thinks.

Looking Ahead

Many adolescents struggle to meet society's—and their own—demands as they traverse the challenges of the teenage years. These challenges extend far beyond managing an overstuffed schedule. With bodies that are conspicuously changing; the temptations of sex, alcohol, and other drugs; cognitive advances that make the world seem increasingly complex; social networks that are in constant flux; and careening emotions, adolescents find themselves in a period of life that evokes excitement, anxiety, glee, and despair, sometimes in equal measure.

In this chapter and the next, we consider the basic issues and questions that underlie adolescence. This chapter focuses on physical and cognitive growth during adolescence. As we will see, it is a time of extraordinary physical maturation, triggered by the onset of puberty. We discuss the consequences of early and late maturation, as well as nutrition and eating disorders.

Next, we turn to a consideration of cognitive development during adolescence. After reviewing several approaches to understanding changes in cognitive capabilities, we examine school performance, focusing on the ways that socioeconomic status, ethnicity, and race affect scholastic achievement.

Tetra Images/Alamy Stock Photo

During adolescence, teenagers' lives become increasingly complex.

The chapter concludes with a discussion of several of the major threats to adolescents' well-being. We will focus on drug, alcohol, and tobacco use, as well as sexually transmitted infections.

Physical Maturation

For the male members of the Awa tribe, the beginning of adolescence is signaled by an elaborate and—to Western eyes—gruesome ceremony marking the transition from childhood to adulthood. The boys are whipped for two or three days with sticks and prickly branches. Through the whipping, the boys atone for their previous infractions and honor tribesmen who were killed in warfare. But that's just for starters; the ritual continues for days more.

Most of us probably feel gratitude that we did not have to endure such physical trials when we entered adolescence. But members of Western cultures do have their own rites of passage into adolescence, admittedly less fearsome, such as bar mitzvahs and bat mitzvahs at age 13 for Jewish boys and girls, and confirmation ceremonies in many Christian denominations (Dunham, Kidwell, & Wilson, 1986; Delaney, 1995; Herdt, 1998; Eccles, Templeton, & Barber, 2003; Hoffman, 2003).

From *an educator's* perspective

Why do you think the passage to adolescence is regarded in many cultures as such a significant transition that it calls for unique ceremonies?

Regardless of the nature of the ceremonies celebrated by various cultures, their underlying purpose tends to be similar from one culture to the next: symbolically celebrating the onset of the physical changes that turn a child's body into an adult body capable of reproduction. With these changes the child exits childhood and arrives at the doorstep of adulthood.

Growth During Adolescence: The Rapid Pace of Physical and Sexual Maturation

LO 11.1 Describe the physical changes adolescents experience as the body reaches puberty.

adolescence
the developmental stage that lies between childhood and adulthood

Adolescence is the developmental stage that lies between childhood and adulthood. It is generally viewed as starting just before the teenage years and ending just after them. It is a transitional stage. Adolescents are considered no longer children, but not yet adults. It is a time of considerable physical and psychological growth and change. In fact, in only a few months, adolescents can grow several inches and require a virtually new wardrobe as they are transformed, at least in physical appearance, from children to young adults. One aspect of this transformation is the adolescent growth spurt, a period of very rapid growth in height and weight. On average, boys grow 4.1 inches a year and girls 3.5 inches a year. Some adolescents grow as much as 5 inches in a single year (Tanner, 1972; Caino et al., 2004).

Boys' and girls' adolescent growth spurts begin at different times. As you can see in Figure 11-1, girls begin their spurts around age 10, while boys start at about age 12. During the two-year period starting at age 11, girls tend to be taller than boys. But by age 13, boys, on average, are taller than girls—a state of affairs that persists for the remainder of the life span.

puberty
the period during which the sexual organs mature

Puberty, the period during which the sexual organs mature, begins when the pituitary gland in the brain signals other glands in children's bodies to begin producing the sex hormones, *androgens* (male hormones) or *estrogens* (female hormones), at adult levels. (Males and females produce both types of sex hormones, but males have a higher

Figure 11-1 Growth Patterns

Patterns of growth are depicted in two ways. The first figure shows height at a given age, while the second shows the height *increase* that occurs from birth through the end of adolescence. Notice that girls begin their growth spurt around age 10, while boys begin the growth spurt at about age 12. However, by age 13, boys tend to be taller than girls. **THINKING ABOUT THE DATA:** What are the social consequences for boys and girls of being taller or shorter than average?

(**Source:** Adapted from Cratty, 1986.)

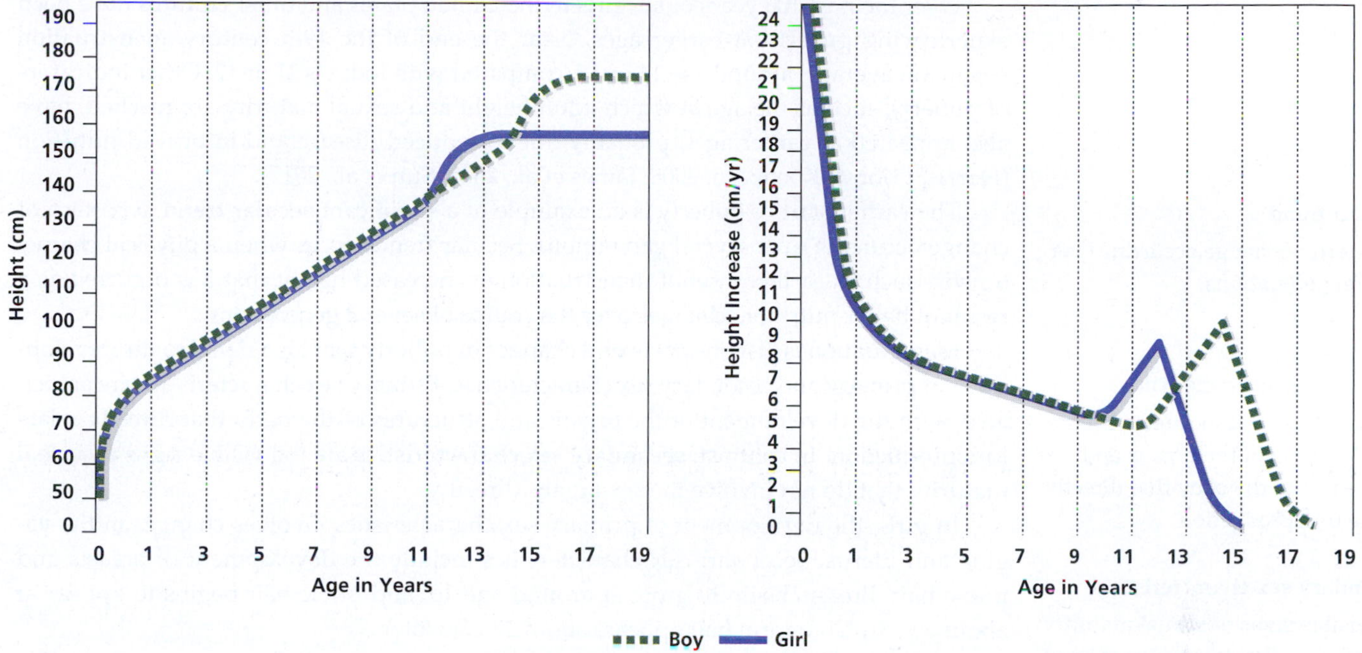

concentration of androgens and females a higher concentration of estrogens.) The pituitary gland also signals the body to increase production of growth hormones that interact with the sex hormones to cause the growth spurt and puberty. In addition, the hormone *leptin* appears to play a role in the start of puberty.

menarche
the onset of menstruation

Like the growth spurt, puberty begins earlier for girls than for boys. Girls start puberty at around age 11 or 12, and boys begin at around age 13 or 14. However, there are wide variations among individuals. For example, some girls begin puberty as early as 7 or 8 or as late as 16.

PUBERTY IN GIRLS. It is not clear why puberty begins at a particular time. What is clear is that environmental and cultural factors play a role. For example, **menarche**, the onset of menstruation and probably the most obvious signal of puberty in girls, varies greatly in different parts of the world. In poorer, developing countries, menstruation begins later than in more economically advantaged countries. Even within wealthier countries, girls in more affluent groups begin to menstruate earlier than less affluent girls (see Figure 11-2).

Consequently, it appears that girls who are better nourished and healthier are more apt to start menstruation at an earlier age than those who suffer from malnutrition or chronic disease. In fact, some studies have suggested that weight or the proportion of fat to muscle in the body might play a critical role in the timing of menarche. For example, in the United States, athletes with a low percentage of body fat may start menstruating later than less active girls. Conversely, obesity—which results in an increase

Figure 11-2 Onset of Menstruation

The onset of menstruation occurs earlier in more economically advantaged countries than in those that are poorer. But even in wealthier countries, girls living in more affluent circumstances begin to menstruate earlier than those living in less affluent situations. Why is this the case?

(**Source:** Adapted from Eveleth & Tanner, 1976.)

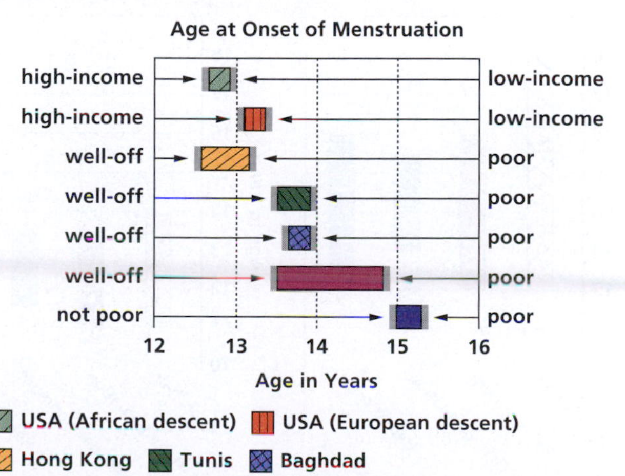

in the secretion of leptin, a hormone associated with the onset of menstruation—leads to earlier puberty (Woelfle, Harz, & Roth, 2007; Sanchez-Garrido & Tena-Sempere, 2013; Shen et al., 2016).

Other factors can affect the timing of menarche. For instance, environmental stress caused by such factors as parental divorce or high levels of family conflict can bring about an early onset (Kaltiala-Heino, Kosunen, & Rimpela, 2003; Ellis, 2004; Belsky et al., 2007).

Over the past 100 years or so, girls in the United States and other cultures have been experiencing puberty at earlier ages. Near the end of the 19th century, menstruation began, on average, around age 14 or 15, compared with today's 11 or 12. Other indicators of puberty, such as the age at which adult height and sexual maturity are reached, have also appeared at earlier ages, probably due to reduced disease and improved nutrition (Harris, Prior, & Koehoorn, 2008; James et al., 2012; Sun et al., 2017).

secular trend
a pattern of change occurring over several generations

The earlier start of puberty is an example of a significant **secular trend**, a pattern of change occurring over several generations. Secular trends occur when a physical characteristic, such as earlier onset of menstruation or increased height that has occurred as a result of better nutrition, changes over the course of several generations.

primary sex characteristics
characteristics associated with the development of the organs and structures of the body that directly relate to reproduction

secondary sex characteristics
the visible signs of sexual maturity that do not directly involve the sex organs

Menstruation is just one of several changes in puberty that are related to the development of primary and secondary sex characteristics. **Primary sex characteristics** are associated with the development of the organs and structures of the body that directly relate to reproduction. In contrast, **secondary sex characteristics** are the visible signs of sexual maturity that do not involve the sex organs directly.

In girls, the development of primary sex characteristics involves changes in the vagina and uterus. Secondary sex characteristics include the development of breasts and pubic hair. Breasts begin to grow at around age 10, and pubic hair begins to appear at about age 11. Underarm hair appears about 2 years later.

For some girls, indications of puberty start unusually early. One out of seven Caucasian girls develops breasts or pubic hair by age 8. Even more surprisingly, the figure is one out of two for African American girls. The reasons for this earlier onset of puberty are unclear, and the demarcation between normal and abnormal onset of puberty is a point of controversy among specialists (Ritzen, 2003; Mensah et al., 2013; Mrug et al., 2014).

PUBERTY IN BOYS. Boys' sexual maturation follows a somewhat different course. The penis and scrotum begin to grow at an accelerated rate around age 12, and they reach adult size about 3 or 4 years later. As boys' penises enlarge, other primary sex characteristics are developing with enlargement of the prostate gland and seminal vesicles, which produce semen (the fluid that carries sperm). A boy's first ejaculation, known as *spermarche*, usually occurs around age 13, more than a year after the body has begun producing sperm. At first, the semen contains relatively few sperm, but the amount of sperm increases significantly with age. Secondary sex characteristics are also developing. Pubic hair begins to grow around age 12, followed by the growth of underarm and facial hair. Finally, boys' voices deepen as the vocal cords become longer and the larynx larger. (Figure 11-3 summarizes the changes that occur in sexual maturation during early adolescence.)

Figure 11-3 Sexual Maturation

The changes in sexual maturation that occur for males and females during early adolescence.

(**Source:** Based on Tanner, 1978.)

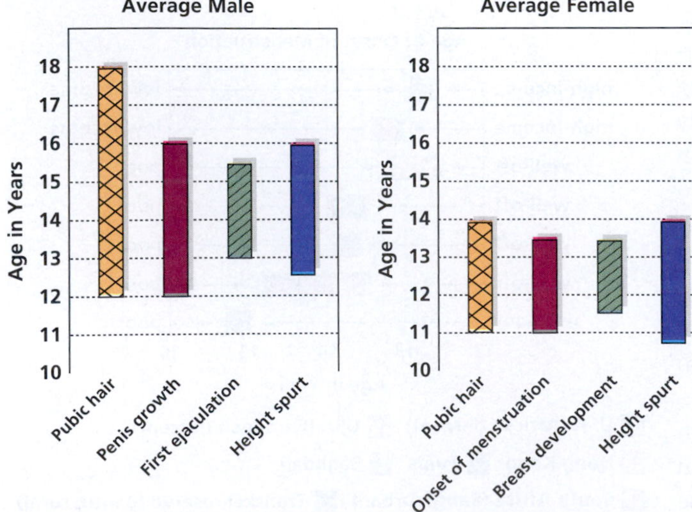

The surge in production of hormones that triggers the start of adolescence may also lead to rapid swings in mood. For example, boys may have feelings of anger and annoyance that are associated with higher hormone levels. In girls, the emotions produced by hormone production are somewhat different: Higher levels of hormones are associated with anger and depression (Buchanan, Eccles, & Becker, 1992; Fujisawa & Shinohara, 2011; Sun et al., 2016).

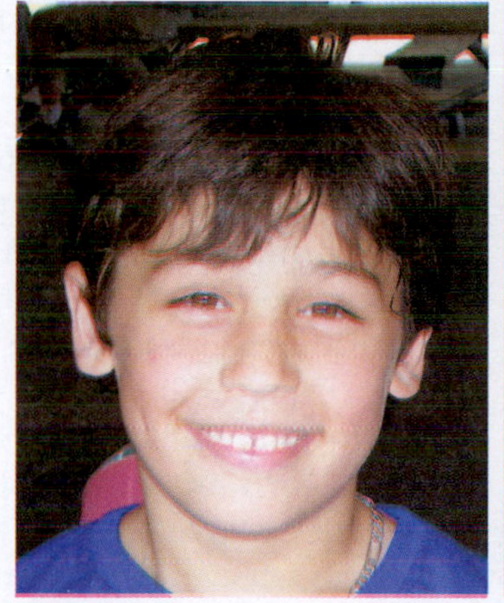

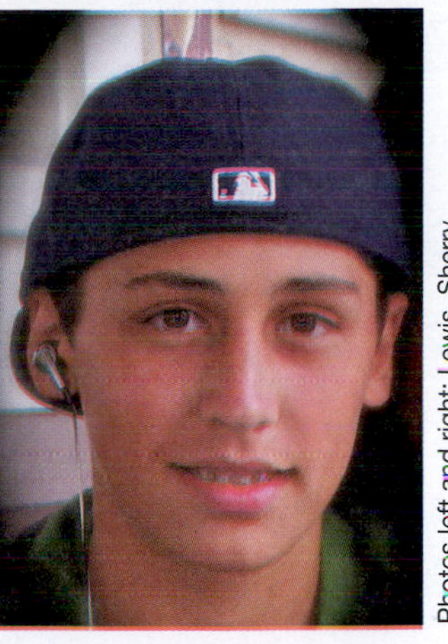

Photos left and right: Lewis, Sherry

Note the changes that have occurred in just a few years in these pre- and post-puberty photos of the same boy.

BODY IMAGE: REACTIONS TO PHYSICAL CHANGES IN ADOLESCENCE. Unlike infants, who also undergo extraordinarily rapid growth, adolescents are well aware of what is happening to their bodies, and they may react with horror or joy, spending long periods in front of mirrors. Few, though, are neutral about the changes they are witnessing.

Some of the changes of adolescence do not show up in physical changes but carry psychological weight. In the past, girls tended to react to menarche with anxiety because Western society tended to emphasize the more negative aspects of menstruation, such as the potential of cramps and messiness. Today, however, society's view of menstruation is more positive, in part because menstruation has been demystified and discussed more openly. (For instance, television commercials for tampons are commonplace.) As a consequence, menarche is typically accompanied by an increase in self-esteem, a rise in status, and greater self-awareness, as adolescent girls see themselves as becoming adults (Matlin, 2003; Yuan, 2012; Chakraborty & De, 2014).

A boy's first ejaculation is roughly equivalent to menarche in a girl. However, while girls generally tell their mothers about the onset of menstruation, boys rarely mention their first ejaculation to their parents or even their friends (Stein & Reiser, 1994). Why? One reason is that girls require tampons or sanitary napkins, and mothers provide them. It also may be that boys see the first ejaculation as an indication of their budding sexuality, an area about which they are quite uncertain and therefore reluctant to discuss with others.

Menstruation and ejaculations occur privately, but changes in body shape and size are quite public. Consequently, teenagers entering puberty frequently are embarrassed by the changes that are occurring. Girls, in particular, are often unhappy with their new bodies. Ideals of beauty in many Western countries call for an unrealistic thinness that is quite different from the actual shape of most women. Puberty brings a considerable increase in the amount of fatty tissue, as well as enlargement of the hips and buttocks—a far cry from the slenderness that society seems to demand (Cotrufo et al., 2007; Kretsch et al., 2016; Senín-Calderón et al., 2017).

How children react to the onset of puberty depends in part on when it happens. Girls and boys who mature either much earlier or later than most of their peers are especially affected by the timing of puberty.

THE TIMING OF PUBERTY: THE CONSEQUENCES OF EARLY AND LATE MATURATION. Why does it matter when a boy or girl reaches puberty? It matters because early or late maturation has social consequences. And as we shall see, social consequences are very important to adolescents.

Kuvien/Fotolia

Boys who mature early tend to be more successful in athletics and have a more positive self-concept. But what might be the downside to early maturation?

Early Maturation. For boys, early maturation is largely a plus. Early maturing boys tend to be more successful at athletics, presumably because of their larger size. They also tend to be more popular and to have a more positive self-concept.

Early maturation in boys does have a downside, however. Boys who mature early are more apt to have difficulties in school, and they are more likely to become involved in delinquency and substance abuse. The reason: Their larger size makes it more likely that they will seek out the company of older boys who may involve them in activities that are inappropriate for their age. Overall, though, the pluses seem to outweigh the minuses for early maturing boys (Costello et al., 2007; Lynne et al., 2007; Beltz et al., 2014).

The story is a bit different for early maturing girls. For them, the obvious changes in their bodies—such as the development of breasts—may lead them to feel uncomfortable and different from their peers. Moreover, because girls, in general, mature earlier than boys, early maturation tends to come at a very young age in the girl's life. Early maturing girls may have to endure ridicule from their less mature classmates (Olivardia & Pope, 2002; Mendle, Turkheimer, & Emery, 2007; Hubley & Arim, 2012; Skoog & Özdemir, 2016).

Early maturation is not a completely negative experience for girls. Girls who mature earlier tend to be sought after more as potential dates, and their popularity may enhance their self-concept. This attention has a price, however. They may not be socially ready to participate in the kind of one-on-one dating situations that most girls deal with at a later age, and such situations may be psychologically challenging for early maturing girls. Moreover, the conspicuousness of their deviance from their later-maturing classmates may have a negative effect, producing anxiety, unhappiness, and depression (Kaltiala-Heino et al., 2003; Galvao et al., 2013).

Cultural norms and standards regarding how women should look play a big role in how girls experience early maturation. For instance, in the United States, the notion of female sexuality is looked upon with a degree of ambivalence, being promoted in the media yet frowned upon socially. Girls who appear "sexy" attract both positive and negative attention.

Consequently, unless a young girl who has developed secondary sex characteristics early can handle the disapproval she may encounter when she conspicuously displays her growing sexuality, the outcome of early maturation may be negative. In countries in which attitudes about sexuality are more liberal, the results of early maturation may be more positive. For example, in Germany, which has a more open view of sex, early maturing girls have higher self-esteem than such girls in the United States. Furthermore, the consequences of early maturation vary even within the United States, depending on the views of girls' peer groups and on prevailing community standards regarding sex (Petersen, 2000; Güre, Uçanok, & Sayil, 2006).

Late Maturation. As with early maturation, the situation with late maturation is mixed, although in this case boys fare worse than girls. For instance, boys who are smaller and lighter than their more physically mature peers tend to be viewed as less attractive. Because of their smaller size, they are at a disadvantage when it comes to sports activities. Furthermore, boys are expected to be bigger than their dates, so the social lives of late-maturing boys may suffer. Ultimately, if the difficulties in adolescence lead to a decline in self-concept, the disadvantages of late maturation for boys could extend well into adulthood. However, coping with the challenges of late maturation may actually help males in some ways. For example, late-maturing boys grow up to have several positive qualities, such as assertiveness and insightfulness (Kaltiala-Heino et al., 2003; Benoit, Lacourse, & Claes, 2014).

The picture for late-maturing girls is generally more positive. In the short term, girls who mature later may be overlooked in dating and other mixed-sex activities during junior high school and middle school, and they may have relatively low social status. However, by the time they are in the tenth grade and have begun to mature visibly, late-maturing-girls' satisfaction with themselves and their bodies may be greater than that of early maturers. In fact, late-maturing girls may end up with fewer emotional problems. The reason? Late-maturing girls are more apt to fit the societal ideal of a slender, "leggy" body type than early maturers, who tend to look heavier in comparison (Peterson, 1988; Kaminaga, 2007; Leen-Feldner, Reardon, & Hayward, 2008).

In sum, the reactions to early and late maturation present a complex picture. As we have seen repeatedly, we need to take into consideration the complete constellation of factors affecting individuals in order to understand their development. Some developmentalists suggest that other factors, such as changes in peer groups, family dynamics, and particularly schools and other societal institutions, may be more pertinent in determining an adolescent's behavior than early and later maturation, and the effects of puberty in general (Stice, 2003; Mendle, Turkheimer, & Emery, 2007; Hubley & Arim, 2012).

Nutrition, Food, and Eating Disorders: Fueling the Growth of Adolescence

LO 11.2 Explain the nutritional needs and concerns of adolescents.

At 16, Ariel Porter was pretty, outgoing, and popular, but when a boy she liked kidded her about being "too fat" to take out, she took it seriously. She began to obsess about food, using her mom's food scale to plan her meals compulsively. She kept charts of portion sizes, weights, and calories, cutting her food into tiny morsels and placing minuscule amounts of meat, vegetables, and fruit into an array of zip-up bags labeled with the days of the week and acceptable times of consumption.

In a few months, Ariel went from 101 pounds to 83. Her hips and ribs became clearly visible, and her fingers and knees ached constantly. Her menstrual periods stopped flat, her hair developed split ends, and her fingernails broke easily. Still, Ariel insisted she was overweight, pinching imaginary pockets of fat on her body to prove her point. What finally got her to accept that she had a problem was the return of her older sister from college. At first sight of Ariel, her sister gasped audibly, dropped to her knees, and broke down crying.

Ariel's problem: anorexia nervosa, a severe eating disorder. As we have seen, the cultural ideal of slim and fit favors late-developing girls. But when those developments do occur, how do girls—and, increasingly, boys—cope when the image in the mirror deviates from the ideal presented in the popular media?

The rapid physical growth of adolescence is fueled by an increase in food consumption. Particularly during the growth spurt, adolescents eat substantial quantities of food, increasing their intake of calories rather dramatically. During the teenage years, the average girl requires some 2,200 calories a day, and the average boy requires 2,800.

Of course, not just any calories help nourish adolescents' growth. Several key nutrients are essential, including, in particular, calcium and iron. The calcium provided by milk helps bone growth, which may prevent the later development of osteoporosis—the thinning of bones—that affects 25 percent of women later in their lives. Similarly, iron is necessary to prevent iron-deficiency anemia, an ailment that is not uncommon among teenagers.

For most adolescents, the major nutritional issue is ensuring the consumption of a sufficient balance of appropriate foods. Two extremes of nutrition can be a major concern for a substantial minority and can create a real threat to health. Among the most prevalent problems: obesity and eating disorders like the one afflicting Ariel Porter.

OBESITY. The most common nutritional concern during adolescence is obesity. One in five adolescents is overweight, and 1 in 20 can be formally classified as obese (body weight that is more than 20 percent above average). Moreover, the proportion of female adolescents who are classified as obese increases over the course of adolescence (Kimm, 2003; Mikulovic et al., 2011; U.S. Preventive Services Task Force, 2017).

Although adolescents are obese for the same reasons as younger children, the psychological consequences may be particularly severe during a time of life when body image is of special concern. Furthermore, the potential health consequences of obesity during adolescence are also problematic. For instance, obesity taxes the circulatory system, increasing the likelihood of high blood pressure and type 2 diabetes. Finally, obese adolescents stand an 80 percent chance of becoming obese adults (Goble, 2008; Wang et al., 2008; Morrison et al., 2015; Gowey et al., 2016).

Figure 11-4 No Sweat

Physical activity among both white and black adolescent females declines substantially over the course of adolescence. What might be the reasons for this decline?

(**Source:** Based on Kimm et al., 2002.)

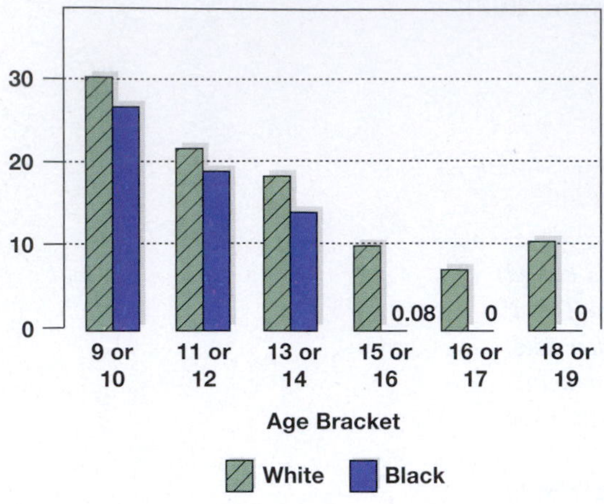

Lack of exercise is one of the main culprits. One survey found that by the end of the teenage years, most females get virtually no exercise outside of physical education classes in school. The older they are, the less exercise female adolescents engage in. The problem is particularly pronounced for older black female adolescents, more than half of whom report *no* physical exercise outside of school, compared with about a third of white adolescents who report no exercise (see Figure 11-4; Delva, O'Malley, & Johnston, 2006; Reichert et al., 2009; Nicholson & Browning, 2012; Puterman et al., 2016).

Why do adolescent girls get so little exercise? It may reflect a lack of organized sports or good athletic facilities for girls. It may even be the result of lingering cultural norms suggesting that athletic participation is more the realm of boys than girls.

There are additional reasons for the high rate of obesity during adolescence. One is the availability of fast foods, which deliver large portions of high-calorie, high-fat cuisine at prices adolescents can afford. In addition, many adolescents spend a significant proportion of their leisure time inside their homes using social media, watching television, and playing video games. Such sedentary activities not only keep adolescents from exercising, but they often are also accompanied by snacks of junk foods (Thivel et al., 2011; Laska et al., 2012; Bailey-Davis et al., 2017).

ANOREXIA NERVOSA AND BULIMIA. The fear of fat and the desire to avoid obesity sometimes become so strong that they turn into a problem. For instance, Ariel Porter suffered from **anorexia nervosa**, a severe eating disorder in which individuals refuse to eat. Their troubled body image leads them to deny that their behavior and appearance, which may become skeletal, are out of the ordinary.

anorexia nervosa

a severe eating disorder in which individuals refuse to eat, while denying that their behavior and appearance, which may become skeletal, are out of the ordinary

Anorexia is a dangerous psychological disorder; some 15 to 20 percent of its victims literally starve themselves to death. It primarily afflicts women between ages 12 and 40; those most susceptible are intelligent, successful, and attractive white adolescent girls from affluent homes. Anorexia is also becoming a problem for more boys. About 10 percent of victims are male, a percentage that is increasing and is associated with the use of steroids (Crisp et al., 2006; Scheckmann et al., 2012; Herpertz-Dahlmann, 2015).

Even though they eat little, individuals with anorexia are often focused on food. They may go shopping often, collect cookbooks, talk about food, or cook huge meals for others. Although they may be incredibly thin, their body image is so distorted that they see themselves as disgustingly fat and try to lose more and more weight. Even when they look like skeletons, they are unable to see how thin they have become.

Bulimia, another eating disorder, is characterized by *binging*, eating large quantities of food, followed by *purging* of the food through vomiting or the use of laxatives. People with bulimia may eat an entire gallon of ice cream or a whole package of tortilla chips. But after such a binge, sufferers experience powerful feelings of guilt and depression, and they intentionally rid themselves of the food.

bulimia

an eating disorder characterized by binges on large quantities of food, followed by purges of the food through vomiting or the use of laxatives

Although the weight of a person with bulimia remains fairly normal, the disorder is quite hazardous. The constant vomiting and diarrhea of the binge-and-purge cycles may produce a chemical imbalance that can lead to heart failure.

The exact reasons for the occurrence of eating disorders are not clear, although several factors play a role. Dieting often precedes the development of eating disorders, as even normal-weight individuals are spurred on by societal standards of slenderness to seek to lower their weight. The feelings of control and success may encourage them to lose more and more weight. Furthermore, girls who mature earlier than their peers and who have a higher level of body fat are more susceptible to eating disorders during later adolescence as they try to bring their maturing bodies back into line with the cultural standard of a thin, boyish physique. Adolescents who are clinically depressed are also more likely to develop eating disorders later (Santos, Richards, & Bleckley, 2007; Courtney, Gamboz, & Johnson, 2008; Wade & Watson, 2012; Schvey, Eddy, & Tanofsky-Kraff, 2016).

Some experts suggest that a biological cause lies at the root of both anorexia nervosa and bulimia. Twin studies indicate that there are genetic components to the disorders. In addition, hormonal imbalances sometimes occur in sufferers (Wade et al., 2008; Baker et al., 2009; Xu et al., 2017).

Other attempts to explain the eating disorders emphasize psychological and social factors. For instance, some experts suggest that the disorders are a result of perfectionistic, overdemanding parents or byproducts of other family difficulties. Culture also plays a role. Anorexia nervosa, for instance, is found only in cultures that idealize slender female bodies. Because in most places such a standard does not hold, anorexia is not prevalent outside the United States (Harrison & Hefner, 2006; Bennett, 2008; Bodell, Joiner, & Ialongo, 2012).

This young woman suffers from anorexia nervosa, a severe eating disorder in which people refuse to eat, while denying that their behavior and appearance are out of the ordinary.

For example, anorexia is quite rare in Asia, with two interesting exceptions: the upper classes of Japan and of Hong Kong, where Western influence is greatest. Furthermore, anorexia nervosa is a fairly recent disorder. It was not seen in the 17th and 18th centuries, when the ideal of the female body was a plump corpulence. The increasing number of boys with anorexia in the United States may be related to a growing emphasis on a muscular male physique that features little body fat (Mangweth, Hausmann, & Walch, 2004; Makino et al., 2006; Greenberg, Cwikel, & Mirsky, 2007).

Because anorexia nervosa and bulimia are products of both biological and environmental causes, treatment typically involves a mix of approaches. For instance, both psychological therapy and dietary modifications are likely to be needed for successful treatment. In more extreme cases, hospitalization may be necessary (Stein, Latzer, & Merrick, 2009; Doyle et al., 2014; Graves et al., 2017).

Brain Development and Thought: Paving the Way for Cognitive Growth

LO 11.3 Summarize the ways in which the brain develops in adolescence.

Adolescence brings greater independence. Teenagers tend to assert themselves more and more. This independence is, in part, the result of changes in the brain that pave the way for the significant advances that occur in cognitive abilities during adolescence, as we'll consider in the next part of the chapter. As the number of neurons (the cells of the nervous system) continue to grow, and their interconnections become richer and more complex, adolescent thinking also becomes more sophisticated (Toga & Thompson, 2003; Petanjek et al., 2008; Blakemore, 2012; Konrad, Firk, & Uhlhaas, 2013).

The brain produces an oversupply of gray matter during adolescence, which is later pruned back at the rate of 1 to 2 percent per year (see Figure 11-5). *Myelination*—the process in which nerve cells are insulated by a covering of fat cells—increases and continues to make the transmission of neural messages more efficient. Both the pruning process and increased myelination contribute to the growing cognitive abilities of adolescents (Sowell et al., 2001; Sowell et al., 2003; Mychasiuk & Metz, 2016).

Figure 11-5 Pruning Gray Matter

As children grow into adulthood, gray matter is pruned from the brain. These composite scans show changes in gray matter and other physical changes in the cortex from age 4 through 21.

(**Source:** Gogtay et al., 2004.)

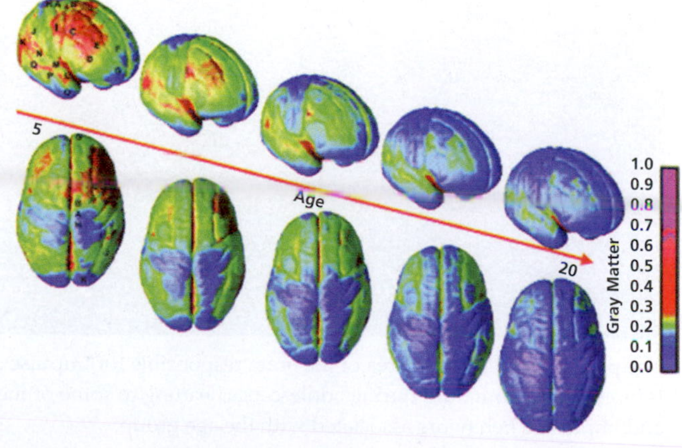

One specific area of the brain that undergoes considerable development throughout adolescence is the prefrontal cortex, which is not fully developed until around the early 20s. The *prefrontal cortex* is the part of the brain that allows people to think, evaluate, and make complex judgments in a uniquely human way. It underlies the increasingly complex intellectual achievements that are possible during adolescence.

During adolescence, the prefrontal cortex becomes increasingly efficient in communicating with other parts of the brain.

This helps build a communication system within the brain that is more distributed and sophisticated, permitting the different areas of the brain to process information more effectively (Scherf, Sweeney, & Luna, 2006; Hare et al., 2008; Wiggins et al., 2014).

The prefrontal cortex also provides for impulse control. Rather than simply reacting to emotions such as anger or rage, an individual with a fully developed prefrontal cortex is able to inhibit the desire for action that stems from such emotions.

Because during adolescence the prefrontal cortex is biologically immature, the ability to inhibit impulses is not fully developed. This brain immaturity may lead to some of the risky and impulsive behaviors that are characteristic of adolescence. Furthermore, some researchers theorize that not only do adolescents underestimate the risks of risky behavior, but they also overestimate the rewards that will come from the behavior. Regardless of the causes of risk-taking in adolescents, this understanding of brain development has led to a heated discussion of whether the death penalty should be applied to adolescents, as we discuss next (Steinberg & Scott, 2003; Casey, Jones, & Somerville, 2011; Gopnik, 2012).

THE IMMATURE BRAIN ARGUMENT: TOO YOUNG FOR THE DEATH PENALTY? Consider the following case:

> *It was a horrible crime. Seventeen-year-old Christopher Simmons, along with Charles Benjamin, 15 years old, broke into the home of a 46-year-old woman, stealing $6. They tied up the woman, put duct tape over her eyes and mouth, and dumped her into the back of her car. Then they drove to a bridge and dropped her into the river below. Her dead body was found in the river the next day. After being tracked down by the police, both confessed. (Raeburn, 2004)*

In this horrific case, Benjamin was sentenced to life in prison, and Simmons was given the death penalty. But Simmons's lawyers appealed, and ultimately the U.S. Supreme Court ruled that he—and anyone else under age 18—could not be executed because of their youth.

Among the facts that the Supreme Court weighed in its decision was evidence from neuroscientists and child developmentalists that the brains of adolescents are still developing in important ways and that therefore they lack judgment because of this brain immaturity. According to this reasoning, adolescents are not fully capable of making reasonable decisions because their brains are not yet wired like those of adults.

The argument that adolescents may not be as responsible for their crimes as adults stems from research showing that the brain continues to grow and mature during the teenage years, and sometimes beyond. For example, neurons that make up unnecessary gray matter of the brain begin to disappear during adolescence. In their place, the volume of white matter of the brain begins to increase. The decline in gray matter and the increase in white matter permit more sophisticated, thoughtful cognitive processing (Beckman, 2004; Ferguson, 2013; Maier-Hein et al., 2014; Luna & Wright, 2016).

Are the brains of adolescents so immature that teenage offenders should receive less harsh punishment for their crimes than those with older, and therefore more mature, brains? It is not a simple question, and the answer probably will come more from those studying morality than from scientists (Aronson, 2007).

Ayush Garg

The prefrontal cortex, the area of the brain responsible for impulse control, is biologically immature during adolescence, leading to some of the risky and impulsive behaviors associated with the age group.

SLEEP DEPRIVATION. With increasing academic and social demands placed on them, adolescents go to bed later and get up earlier. As a result, they often lead their lives in something of a sleep-deprived daze.

The sleep deprivation comes at a time when adolescents' internal clocks shift. Older adolescents in particular experience the need to go to bed later and to sleep later in the morning, and they require 9 hours of sleep each night to feel rested. Yet half of adolescents sleep 7 hours or less each night, and almost one in five gets less than 6 hours. Because they typically have early morning classes but don't feel sleepy until late at night, they end up getting far less sleep than their bodies crave (Loessl et al., 2008; Wolfson & Richards, 2011; Dagys et al., 2012; Cohen-Zion et al., 2016).

Sleep deprivation takes its toll. Sleepy teens have lower grades, are more depressed, and have greater difficulty controlling their moods. In addition, they are at great risk for car accidents (Roberts, Roberts, & Duong, 2009; Roberts, Roberts, & Xing, 2011; Louca & Short, 2014).

Module 11.1 Review

LO 11.1 Describe the physical changes adolescents experience as the body reaches puberty.

Adolescence is a period of rapid physical growth, including the changes associated with puberty. Puberty can cause reactions in adolescents ranging from confusion to increased self-esteem. Early or late maturation can bring advantages and disadvantages, depending on gender as well as emotional and psychological maturity.

LO 11.2 Explain the nutritional needs and concerns of adolescents.

Adequate nutrition is essential in adolescence because of the need to fuel physical growth. Changing physical needs and environmental pressures can induce obesity or eating disorders.

The two most common eating disorders are anorexia nervosa and bulimia. Both must be treated with a combination of physical and psychological therapies.

LO 11.3 Summarize the ways in which the brain develops in adolescence.

Brain development paves the way for significant cognitive growth, although the brain is not fully developed until the early 20s.

Journal Writing Prompt

Applying Lifespan Development: How can societal and environmental influences contribute to the emergence of an eating disorder?

Cognitive Development and Schooling

Ms. Mejia smiled as she read a particularly creative paper. As part of her eighth-grade American Government class every year, she asked students to write about what their lives would be like if America had not won its war for independence from Britain. She had tried something similar with her sixth graders, but many of them seemed unable to imagine anything different from what they already knew. By eighth grade, however, they were able to come up with some very interesting scenarios. One boy imagined that he would be known as Lord Lucas; a girl imagined that she would be a servant to a rich landowner; another, that she would be helping to plot an overthrow of the government.

What is it that sets adolescents' thinking apart from that of younger children? One of the major changes is the ability to think beyond the concrete, current situation to what *might* or *could* be. Adolescents are able to keep a variety of abstract possibilities in their heads, and they can see issues in relative, as opposed to absolute, terms. Instead of viewing problems as having black-and-white solutions, they are capable of perceiving shades of gray.

Once again we can use several approaches to explain adolescents' cognitive development. We'll begin by returning to Piaget's theory, which has had a significant influence on how developmentalists think about thinking during adolescence.

Piagetian Approaches to Cognitive Development: Using Formal Operations

LO 11.4 Describe how cognitive development proceeds during adolescence according to Piaget.

Fourteen-year-old Leigh is asked to solve a problem that anyone who has seen a grandfather clock may have pondered: What determines the speed at which a pendulum moves back and forth? In the version of the problem that she is asked to solve, Leigh is given a weight hanging from a string. She is told that she can vary several things: the length of the string, the weight of the object at the end of the string, the amount of force used to push the string, and the height to which the weight is raised in an arc before it is released.

Leigh doesn't remember, but she was asked to solve the same problem when she was 8 years old, as part of a longitudinal research study. At that time, she was in the concrete operational period, and her efforts to solve the problem were not very successful. She approached the problem haphazardly, with no systematic plan of action. For instance, she simultaneously tried to push the pendulum harder *and* shorten the length of the string *and* increase the weight on the string. Because she was varying so many factors at once, when the speed of the pendulum changed, she had no way of knowing which factor or factors made a difference.

Now, however, Leigh is much more systematic. Rather than immediately beginning to push and pull at the pendulum, she stops a moment and thinks about what factors to take into account. She considers how she might test which of those factors is important, forming a hypothesis about which is most important. Then, just like a scientist conducting an experiment, she varies only one factor at a time. By examining each variable separately and systematically, she is able to come to the correct solution: The length of the string determines the speed of the pendulum.

USING FORMAL OPERATIONS TO SOLVE PROBLEMS. Leigh's approach to the pendulum question, a problem devised by Jean Piaget, illustrates that she has moved into the formal operational period of cognitive development (Piaget & Inhelder, 1958). The **formal operational stage** is the stage at which people develop the ability to think abstractly. Piaget suggested that people reach this stage at the start of adolescence, around age 12. Leigh was able to think about the various aspects of the pendulum problem in an abstract manner and to understand how to test out the hypotheses that she had formed.

formal operational stage
the stage at which people develop the ability to think abstractly

By bringing formal principles of logic to bear on problems they encounter, adolescents are able to consider problems in the abstract rather than only in concrete terms. They are able to test their understanding by systematically carrying out rudimentary experiments on problems and situations, and observing what their experimental "interventions" bring about.

Adolescents are able to use formal reasoning, in which they start with a general theory about what produces a particular outcome and then deduce explanations for specific situations in which they see that particular outcome. Like the scientists who form hypotheses that we discussed in Chapter 1, they can then test their theories. What distinguishes this kind of thinking from earlier cognitive stages is the ability to start with abstract possibilities and move to the concrete; in previous stages, children are tied to the concrete here and now. For example, at age 8, Leigh just started moving things around to see what would happen in the pendulum problem, a concrete approach. At age 12, however, she started with the abstract idea that each variable—the string, the size of the weight, and so forth—should be tested separately.

Hero Images/Getty Images

Like scientists who form hypotheses, adolescents in the formal operational stage use systematic reasoning. They start with a general theory about what produces a particular outcome, and then deduce explanations for specific situations in which they see that particular outcome.

Adolescents also are able to employ propositional thought during the formal operational stage. *Propositional thought* is reasoning that uses abstract logic in the absence of concrete examples. For example, propositional thinking allows adolescents to understand that if certain premises are true, then a conclusion must also be true. For example, consider the following:

All teachers are mortal.	*[premise]*
Ms. Gonzales is a teacher.	*[premise]*
Therefore, Ms. Gonzales is mortal.	*[conclusion]*

Not only can adolescents understand that if both premises are true, then so is the conclusion, but they are also capable of using similar reasoning when premises and conclusions are stated more abstractly, as follows:

All As are B.	*[premise]*
C is an A.	*[premise]*
Therefore, C is a B.	*[conclusion]*

Although Piaget proposed that children enter the formal operational stage at the beginning of adolescence, you may recall that he also hypothesized that—as with all the stages of cognitive development—full capabilities do not emerge suddenly, at one stroke. Instead, they gradually unfold through a combination of physical maturation and environmental experiences. According to Piaget, it is not until adolescents are around 15 years old that they are fully settled in the formal operational stage.

Some evidence suggests that a sizable proportion of people hone their formal operational skills at a later age, and in some cases, never fully employ formal operational thinking at all. For instance, most studies show that only 40 to 60 percent of college students and adults achieve formal operational thinking completely, and some estimates run as low as 25 percent. But many of those adults who do not show formal operational thought in every domain are fully competent in *some* aspects of formal operations (Sugarman, 1988; Keating, 1990, 2004).

One of the reasons adolescents differ in their use of formal operations relates to the culture in which they were raised. For instance, people who live in isolated, scientifically unsophisticated societies and who have little formal education are less likely to perform at the formal operational level than are formally educated persons living in more technologically sophisticated societies (Segall et al., 1990; Commons, Galaz-Fontes, & Morse, 2006; Asadi, Amiri, & Molavi, 2014).

Does this mean that adolescents (and adults) from cultures in which formal operations tend not to emerge are incapable of attaining them? Not at all. A more probable conclusion is that the scientific reasoning that characterizes formal operations is not equally valued in all societies. If everyday life does not require or promote a certain type of reasoning, it is unreasonable to expect people to employ that type of reasoning when confronted with a problem (Gauvain, 1998).

THE CONSEQUENCES OF ADOLESCENTS' USE OF FORMAL OPERATIONS. Adolescents' ability to reason abstractly, embodied in their use of formal operations, leads to a change in their everyday behavior. Whereas earlier they may have unquestioningly accepted rules and explanations set out for them, their increased abstract reasoning abilities may lead them to question their parents and other authority figures far more strenuously. Advances in abstract thinking also lead to greater idealism, which may make adolescents impatient with imperfections in institutions, such as schools and the government.

In general, adolescents become more argumentative. They enjoy using abstract reasoning to poke holes in others' explanations, and their increased abilities to think critically make them acutely sensitive to parents' and teachers' perceived shortcomings. For instance, they may note the inconsistency in their parents' arguments against using drugs, such as when they know that their parents used drugs when they were adolescents and nothing much came of it. At the same time, adolescents can be indecisive, as they are able to see the merits of multiple sides to issues (Elkind, 1996; Alberts, Elkind, & Ginsberg, 2007; Knoll et al., 2016).

Coping with the increased critical abilities of adolescents can be challenging for parents, teachers, and other adults who deal with adolescents. But it also makes adolescents more interesting, as they actively seek to understand the values and justifications that they encounter in their lives.

EVALUATING PIAGET'S APPROACH. Each time we've considered Piaget's theory in previous chapters, several concerns have cropped up. Let's summarize some of the issues here:

- Piaget suggests that cognitive development proceeds in universal, step-like advances that occur at particular stages. Yet we find significant differences in cognitive abilities from one person to the next, especially when we compare individuals from different cultures. Furthermore, we find inconsistencies even within the same individual. People may be able to accomplish some tasks that indicate they have reached a certain level of thinking, but not other tasks. If Piaget were correct, a person ought to perform uniformly well once she or he reaches a given stage (Siegler, 1994).
- The notion of stages proposed by Piaget suggests that cognitive abilities do not grow gradually or smoothly. Instead, the stage point of view implies that cognitive growth is typified by relatively rapid shifts from one stage to the next. In contrast, many developmentalists argue that cognitive development proceeds in a more continuous fashion, increasing not so much in qualitative leaps forward as in quantitative accumulations. They also contend that Piaget's theory is better at *describing* behavior at a given stage than *explaining* why the shift from one stage to the next occurs (Case, 1999).
- Because of the nature of the tasks Piaget employed to measure cognitive abilities, critics suggest that he underestimated the age at which certain capabilities emerge. It is now widely accepted that infants and children are more sophisticated at an earlier age than Piaget asserted (Bornstein & Lamb, 2005; Kenny, 2013).
- Piaget had a relatively narrow view of what is meant by *thinking* and *knowing*. In Piagetian theory, knowledge consists primarily of the kind of understanding displayed in the pendulum problem. However, as we discussed in Chapter 9, developmentalists such as Howard Gardner suggest that we have many kinds of intelligence, separate from and independent of one another (Gardner, 2000, 2006).
- Finally, some developmentalists argue that formal operations do not represent the epitome of thinking and that more sophisticated forms of thinking do not actually emerge until early adulthood. For instance, developmental psychologist Giesela Labouvie-Vief (1980, 1986) argues that the complexity of society requires thought that is not necessarily based on pure logic. Instead, a kind of thinking is required that is flexible, allows for interpretive processes, and reflects the fact that reasons behind events in the real world are subtle—something that Labouvie-Vief calls *postformal thinking* (Labouvie-Vief & Diehl, 2000; Hamer & Van Rossum, 2016).

On one hand, these criticisms and concerns regarding Piaget's approach to cognitive development have considerable merit. On the other hand, Piaget's theory has been the impetus for an enormous number of studies on the development of thinking capacities and processes, and it also spurred a good deal of classroom reform. Finally, his bold statements about the nature of cognitive development provided a fertile soil from which many opposing positions on cognitive development bloomed, such as the information processing perspective, to which we turn next (Taylor & Rosenbach, 2005; Kuhn, 2008; Bibace, 2013).

Information Processing Perspectives: Gradual Transformations in Abilities

LO 11.5 Summarize how information processing approaches explain adolescent cognitive development.

From the perspective of proponents of information processing approaches to cognitive development, adolescents' mental abilities grow gradually and continuously. Unlike Piaget's view that the increasing cognitive sophistication of the adolescent is a reflection of stage-like spurts, the **information processing perspective** sees changes in adolescents' cognitive abilities as evidence of gradual transformations in the capacity to take in, use, and store information. A number of progressive changes occur in the ways people organize their thinking about the world, develop strategies for dealing with new situations, sort facts, and achieve advances in memory capacity and perceptual abilities (Pressley & Schneider, 1997; Wyer, 2004).

information processing perspective
the model that seeks to identify the way that individuals take in, use, and store information

Adolescents' general intelligence—as measured by traditional IQ tests—remains stable, but there are dramatic improvements in the specific mental abilities that underlie intelligence. Verbal, mathematical, and spatial abilities increase, making many adolescents quicker with a comeback, impressive sources of information, and accomplished athletes. Memory capacity grows, and adolescents become more adept at effectively dividing their attention across more than one stimulus at a time—such as simultaneously studying for a biology test and listening to music.

Furthermore, as Piaget noted, adolescents grow increasingly sophisticated in their understanding of problems, their ability to grasp abstract concepts and to think hypothetically, and their comprehension of the possibilities inherent in situations. This permits them, for instance, to endlessly dissect the course that their relationships might hypothetically take.

Adolescents know more about the world, too. Their store of knowledge increases as the amount of material to which they are exposed grows and their memory capacity enlarges. Taken as a whole, the mental abilities that underlie intelligence show a marked improvement during adolescence (Kail, 2004; Kail & Miller, 2006; Atkins et al., 2012).

metacognition
the knowledge that people have about their own thinking processes and their ability to monitor their cognition

According to information processing explanations of cognitive development during adolescence, one of the most important reasons for advances in mental abilities is the growth of metacognition. **Metacognition** is the knowledge that people have about their own thinking processes and their ability to monitor their cognition. Although school-age children can use some metacognitive strategies, adolescents are much more adept at understanding their own mental processes.

For example, as adolescents improve their understanding of their memory capacity, they get better at gauging how long they need to study a particular kind of material to memorize it for a test. Furthermore, they can judge when they have fully memorized the material considerably more accurately than they could when they were younger. These improvements in metacognitive abilities permit adolescents to comprehend and master school material more effectively (Thielsch, Andor, & Ehring, 2015; Rahko et al., 2016; Zakrzewski, Johnson, & Smith, 2017).

These new abilities also can make adolescents particularly introspective and self-conscious—two hallmarks of the period, which, as we see next, may produce a high degree of egocentrism.

Max Whittaker/Getty Images

Adolescents' ability to reason abstractly leads them to question accepted rules and explanations.

Egocentrism in Thinking: Adolescents' Self-Absorption

LO 11.6 Describe how adolescent egocentrism affects thinking and behavior.

Carlos thinks of his parents as "control freaks"; he cannot figure out why his parents insist that when he borrows their car, he call home and let them know where he is. Jeri is thrilled that Molly bought earrings just like hers, thinking it is the ultimate compliment, even though it's not clear that Molly even knew that Jeri had a similar pair when she bought them. Lu is upset with his biology teacher, Ms. Sebastian, for giving a long, difficult midterm exam on which he didn't do well.

Adolescents' newly sophisticated metacognitive abilities enable them to readily imagine that others are thinking about them, and they may construct elaborate scenarios about others' thoughts. It is also the source of the egocentrism that sometimes dominates adolescents' thinking. **Adolescent egocentrism** is a state of self-absorption in which the world is viewed as focused on oneself. This egocentrism makes adolescents highly critical of authority figures such as parents and teachers, unwilling to accept criticism, and quick to find fault with others' behavior (Schwartz, Maynard, & Uzelac, 2008; Inagaki, 2013; Rai et al., 2014; Lin, 2016).

adolescent egocentrism
a state of self-absorption in which the world is viewed as focused on oneself

From *a social worker's* perspective

In what ways does adolescent egocentrism complicate adolescents' social and family relationships? Do adults entirely outgrow egocentrism and personal fables?

The kind of egocentrism we see in adolescence helps explain why adolescents sometimes perceive that they are the focus of everyone else's attention. Adolescents may develop what has been called an **imaginary audience**, fictitious observers who pay as much attention to the adolescents' behavior as adolescents do themselves.

imaginary audience
an adolescent's belief that his or her own behavior is a primary focus of others' attentions and concerns

The imaginary audience is usually perceived as focusing on the one thing that adolescents think most about: themselves. Unfortunately, these scenarios may suffer from the same kind of egocentrism as the rest of their thinking. For instance, a student sitting in a class may be sure a teacher is focusing on her, and a teenager at a basketball game is likely to be convinced that everyone around is focusing on the pimple on his chin.

Egocentrism leads to a second distortion in thinking: the notion that one's experiences are unique. Adolescents develop **personal fables**, the view that what happens to them is unique, exceptional, and shared by no one else. For instance, teenagers whose romantic relationships have ended may feel that no one has ever experienced the hurt they feel, that no one has ever been treated so badly, that no one can understand what they are going through (Alberts, Elkind, & Ginsberg, 2007; Rai et al., 2016).

personal fables
the view held by some adolescents that what happens to them is unique, exceptional, and shared by no one else

Personal fables may also make adolescents feel invulnerable to the risks that threaten others. Much of adolescents' risk-taking may well be traced to the personal fables they construct for themselves. They may think that there is no need to use condoms during sex because, in the personal fables they construct, pregnancy and sexually transmitted infections such as AIDS only happen to other kinds of people, not to them. They may drive after drinking because their personal fables paint them as careful drivers, always in control (Greene et al., 2000; Vartanian, 2000; Reyna & Farley, 2006).

School Performance

LO 11.7 Analyze the factors that affect adolescent school performance.

Do the advances that occur in metacognition, reasoning, and other cognitive abilities during adolescence translate into improvements in school performance? If grades are used as the measure, the clear answer is yes. Grades awarded to high school students have shifted upward in the past decade. The mean high school grade point average went up from 3.27 to 3.38 from 1998 to 2016. And the greatest amount of grade inflation occurred in high schools with students who are wealthier, and where most students are white (College Board, 2005; Buckley, Letukas, & Wildavsky, 2018).

At the same time, however, independent measures of achievement, such as SAT scores, have not risen. Consequently, a more likely explanation for the higher grades is the phenomenon of grade inflation. According to this view, it is not that students have changed. Instead, instructors have become more lenient, awarding higher grades for the same performance (Cardman, 2004).

Further evidence for grade inflation comes from the relatively poor achievement of students in the United States when compared to students in other countries. For instance, students in the United States score lower on standardized math and science tests when compared to students in many other industrialized countries (see Figure 11-6; OECD, 2014).

Jackf/Fotolia

Adolescents' egocentrism affects their thinking and behavior.

There is no single reason for this gap in the educational achievement of U.S. students, but several factors, such as less time spent in classes and less intensive instruction, are at work. Furthermore, the broad diversity of the U.S. school population may affect performance relative to other countries, in which the population attending school is more homogeneous and affluent (Stedman, 1997; Schemo, 2001).

The poorer accomplishments of U.S. students is also reflected in high school graduation rates. Although the United States once stood first in the percentage of the population graduating from high school, it has dropped to 24th among industrialized countries. Only 79 percent of U.S. high school students graduate—a rate considerably lower than those of other developed countries. Certainly, as we discuss next, differences in socioeconomic status are reflected in school performance within the United States (Stedman, 1997; Schemo, 2001; OECD, 2001, 2014).

SOCIOECONOMIC STATUS AND SCHOOL PERFORMANCE: INDIVIDUAL DIFFERENCES IN ACHIEVEMENT. All students are entitled to the same opportunity in the classroom, but it is very clear that certain groups have more educational advantages than others. One of the most telling indicators of this reality is the relationship between educational achievement and socioeconomic status (SES).

Middle- and high-SES students, on average, earn higher grades, score higher on standardized tests of achievement, and complete more years of schooling than students

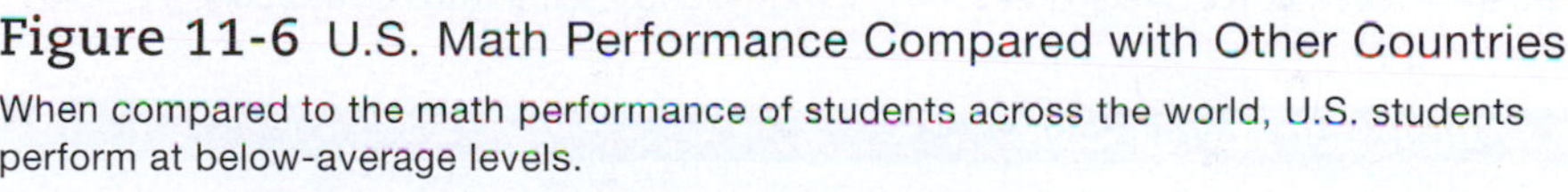

Figure 11-6 U.S. Math Performance Compared with Other Countries

When compared to the math performance of students across the world, U.S. students perform at below-average levels.

(**Source:** Based on OECD, 2014.)

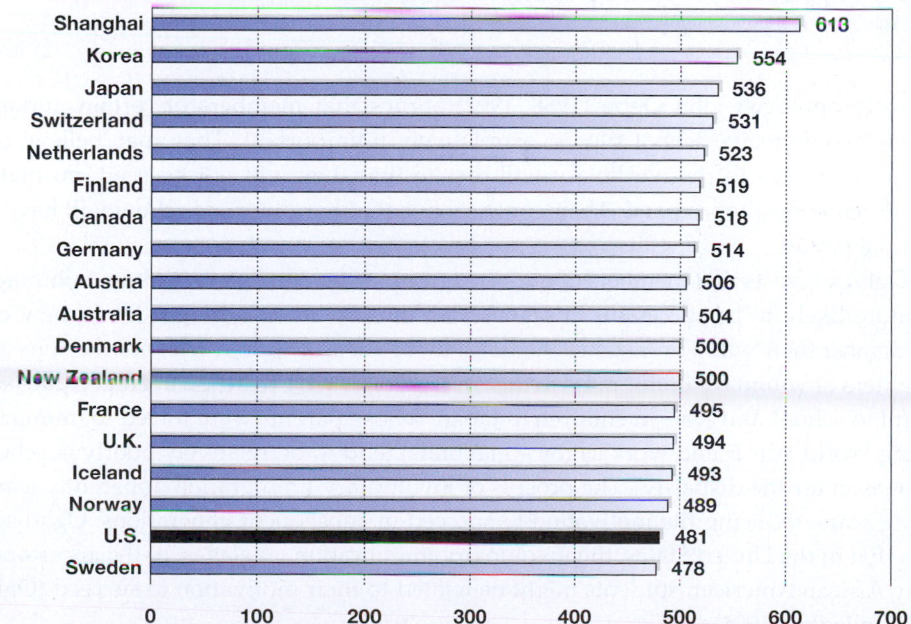

from lower-SES homes. Of course, this disparity does not start in adolescence; the same findings hold for children in lower grades. However, by the time students are in high school, the effects of socioeconomic status become even more pronounced (Tucker-Drob & Harden, 2012; Roy & Raver, 2014; Li, Allen, & Casillas, 2017).

Why do students from middle- and high-SES homes show greater academic success? There are several reasons. For one thing, children living in poverty lack many of the advantages enjoyed by other children. Moreover, their nutrition and health may be less adequate. Often living in crowded conditions and attending inadequate schools, they may have few places to do homework. Their homes may lack the books and computers commonplace in more economically advantaged households (Prater, 2002; Chiu & McBride-Chang, 2006).

For these reasons, students from impoverished backgrounds may be at a disadvantage from the day they begin their schooling. As they grow older, their school performance may continue to lag, and their disadvantage may snowball. Because later school success builds heavily on basic skills presumably learned early in school, children who experience early problems may find themselves falling increasingly behind the academic eight ball as adolescents (Biddle, 2001; Hoff, 2012; Duncan, Magnuson, & Votruba-Drzal, 2017).

ETHNIC AND RACIAL DIFFERENCES IN SCHOOL ACHIEVEMENT. Achievement differences between ethnic and racial groups are significant, and they paint a troubling picture of American education. For instance, data on school achievement indicate that, on average, African American and Hispanic students tend to perform at lower levels, receive lower grades, and score lower on standardized tests of achievement than Caucasian students. In contrast, Asian American students tend to receive higher grades than Caucasian students (Shernoff & Schmidt, 2008; Byun & Park, 2012; Kurtz-Costes, Swinton, & Skinner, 2014).

What is the source of such ethnic and racial differences in academic achievement? Clearly, much of the difference is due to socioeconomic factors: Because a higher proportion of African American and Hispanic families live in poverty than the proportion of whites, their economic disadvantage may be reflected in their school performance. When we take socioeconomic levels into account by comparing different ethnic and racial groups at the same socioeconomic level, achievement differences diminish, but they do not vanish (Meece & Kurtz-Costes, 2001; Cokley, 2003; Guerrero et al., 2006).

From *an educator's* perspective

Why might descendants of people who were forced to immigrate to a country be less successful academically than those who came voluntarily? What approaches might be used to overcome this obstacle?

isacg/Getty Images

John Ogbu notes that Korean children whose parents emigrated voluntarily to the United States do better in school than their counterparts in Japan, whose parents were forced to emigrate from Korea to Japan during World War II.

Anthropologist John Ogbu (1988, 1992) argues that members of certain minority groups may perceive school success as relatively unimportant. They may believe that societal prejudice in the workplace will dictate that they will not succeed, no matter how much effort they expend. Their conclusion is that hard work in school will have no eventual payoff.

Ogbu suggests that members of minority groups who enter a new culture voluntarily are more likely to be successful in school than those who are brought into a new culture against their will. For instance, he notes that Korean children who are the sons and daughters of voluntary immigrants to the United States tend to be, on average, quite successful in school. But Korean children in Japan, whose parents were forced to immigrate during World War II and work as forced laborers, tend to do relatively poorly in school. The reason for the disparity? The process of involuntary immigration apparently leaves lasting scars, reducing the motivation to succeed in subsequent generations. Ogbu suggests that in the United States, the involuntary immigration, as slaves, of the ancestors of many African American students might be related to their motivation to succeed (Ogbu, 1992; Gallagher, 1994).

Another factor in the differential success of various ethnic and racial group members has to do with attributions for academic success. As we discussed in Chapter 10, students from many Asian cultures tend to view achievement as the consequence of temporary situational factors, such as how hard they work. In contrast, African American students are more apt to view success as the result of external causes over which they have no control, such as luck or societal biases. Students who subscribe to the belief that effort will lead to success, and then expend that effort, are more likely to do better in school than students who believe that effort makes less of a difference (Stevenson, Chen, & Lee, 1992; Fuligni, 1997; Saunders, Davis, & Williams, 2004).

DROPPING OUT OF SCHOOL. Most students complete high school, but each year some half million students drop out prior to graduating. The consequences of dropping out are severe. High school dropouts earn 42 percent less than high school graduates, and the unemployment rate for dropouts is 50 percent.

Adolescents who leave school do so for a variety of reasons. Some leave because of pregnancy or problems with the English language. Others must leave for economic reasons, including needing to support themselves or their families.

Dropout rates differ according to gender and ethnicity. Males are more likely to drop out of school than females. In addition, although the dropout rate for all ethnicities has been declining somewhat over the past two decades, particularly for Hispanics, there are

Developmental Diversity and Your Life

Academic Performance and Stereotype Threat

Consider this fact: when women take college classes in math, science, and engineering, they are more likely to do poorly than are men who enter college with the same level of preparation and identical SAT scores. Strangely, however, this phenomenon does not hold true for other areas of the curriculum, where men and women perform at similar levels.

According to psychologist Claude Steele, the reason behind women's declining levels of performance is *academic disidentification*, a lack of personal identification with an academic domain. For women, disidentification is specific to math and science. Negative societal stereotypes produce a state of *stereotype threat* in which members of the group fear that their behavior will indeed confirm the stereotype (Carr & Steele, 2009).

For instance, women seeking to achieve in nontraditional fields that rely on math and science may be hindered as they become distracted by worries about the failure that society predicts for them. In some cases, a woman may decide that failure in a male-dominated field, because it would confirm societal stereotypes, presents such great risks that, paradoxically, the struggle to succeed is not worth the effort. In that instance, the woman may not even try very hard (Inzlicht & Ben-Zeev, 2000).

But there is a bright side to Steele's analysis: If women can be convinced that societal stereotypes regarding achievement are invalid, their performance improves. In short, women are vulnerable to expectations regarding their future success, whether the expectations come from societal stereotypes or from information about the prior performance of women on similar tasks. More encouraging, the evidence suggests that if women can be convinced that others have been successful in given domains, they may overcome even longstanding societal stereotypes (Croizet et al., 2004; Davies, Spencer, & Steele, 2005; Good, Aronson, & Harder, 2008).

We should also keep in mind that women are not the only group susceptible to society's stereotyping. Members of minority groups, such as African Americans and Hispanic Americans, are also vulnerable to stereotypes about academic success. In fact, Steele suggests that African Americans may work under the pressure of feeling that they must disconfirm the negative stereotype regarding their academic performance. The pressure can be anxiety-provoking and threatening and can reduce their performance below their true ability level. Ironically, stereotype threat may be most severe for better, more confident students, who have not previously internalized the negative stereotype to the extent of questioning their own abilities (Carr & Steele, 2009; McClain & Cokley, 2017).

In addition, African Americans may "disidentify" with academic success by putting forth less effort on academic tasks and generally downgrading the importance of academic achievement. Ultimately, such disidentification may act as a self-fulfilling prophecy, increasing the chances of academic failure (Davis, Aronson, & Salinas, 2006; Kellow & Jones, 2008; Kronberger & Horwath, 2013).

Figure 11-7 Dropout Rates of 16- Through 24-Year-Olds by Race/Ethnicity: 1990–2013

Dropout Rates of 16- Through 24-Year-Olds by Race/Ethnicity: 1990–2013. Dropout rates have generally declined in the past 25 years, particularly for Hispanics.

(**Source:** U.S. Department of Education, 2015.)

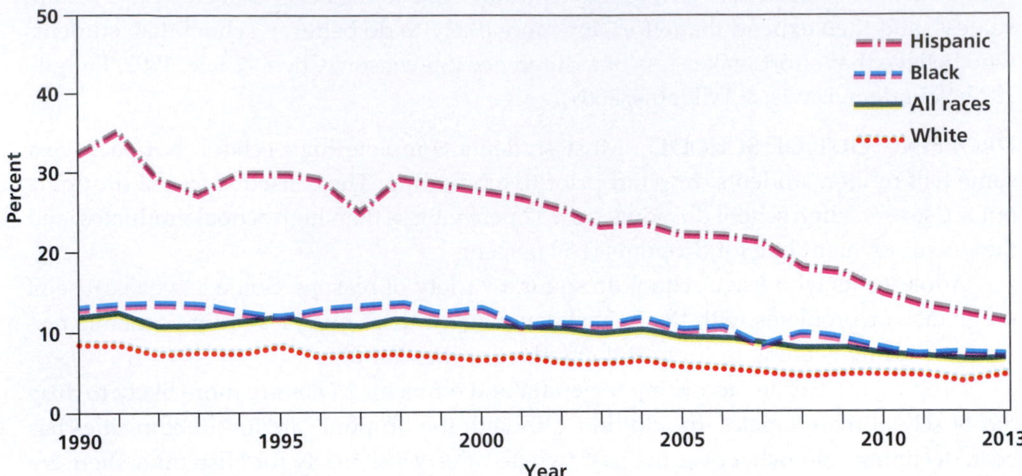

still discrepancies according to race (see Figure 11-7). Not all minority groups, however, show higher dropout rates than Caucasians: Asians, for instance, drop out at a lower rate (National Center for Education Statistics, 2003; Stearns & Glennie, 2006; U.S. Department of Education, 2015).

Poverty plays a large role in determining whether a student completes high school. Students from lower-income households are three times more likely to drop out than those from middle- and upper-income households. Because economic success is so dependent on education, dropping out often perpetuates a cycle of poverty (National Center for Education Statistics, 2002).

Cyberspace: Adolescents Online

LO 11.8 Describe how adolescents use the Internet and social media.

Prakash Subhani faces a choice: study for his chemistry final or check out Facebook. Prakash needs to do well on the test to raise his grade. But he also needs to keep up with his friends in India. Finally, he decides to compromise. He'll spend a half hour on Facebook and devote the rest of the night to study. But the next time he looks at his watch, nearly four hours have passed and he is too tired to study. Prakash has to face his chemistry test unprepared.

Like Prakash Subhani, most adolescents make use of social media and other technologies to a staggering degree. In fact, according to a comprehensive survey using a sample of boys and girls 8 to 18 years old conducted by the Kaiser Family Foundation (a well-respected think tank), young people spend an average of 6.5 hours a day with media. Furthermore, because for around a quarter of the time they are using more than one form of medium simultaneously, they are actually being exposed to the equivalent of 8.5 hours per day (Boneva et al., 2006; Jordan et al., 2007).

The amount of media use can be extraordinary. For example, some teenagers send nearly 30,000 texts a month, often carrying on multiple conversations simultaneously. The use of texting often supplants other forms of social interaction, such as telephone calls or even face-to-face interactions (Lenhart, 2010; Richtel, 2010; see Figure 11-8).

Adolescents are also likely to use multiple social platforms, with Facebook, Instagram, and Snapchat being most popular. There are also gender differences; boys are more likely to use Facebook, while girls are more likely to use visually oriented platforms such as

Tumblr, Pinterest, and Instagram. Both boys and girls have few privacy concerns: Surveys show that nearly all share their names, birthdates, and photos of themselves. Finally, adolescents use social media to advance their romantic interests (Lenhart, Smith, & Anderson, 2015; Office of Adolescent Health, 2016).

For many adolescents, another form of social media involves engagement in online video games. In addition to their gaming aspects, video games provide a means to communicate with peers. Furthermore, some research suggests that video games provide cognitive stimulation. For example, even violent action or "shooter" video games produce improvements in attention, visual processing, spatial skills, and mental rotation abilities (Wait et al., 2010; Green & Bavelier, 2012; Uttal et al., 2013).

There are clear downsides to the social media use of adolescents. For example, some developmentalists suggest that the high frequency of social media use is related to a decline in face-to-face social competence. In this view, online involvement reduces the opportunities to learn social skills. However, some aspects of social media use may actually help adolescents learn certain types of social skills and thereby enhance their overall social competence (Yang & Brown, 2015; Reich, 2017).

Figure 11-8 Teenagers and Social Media Use

Adolescents' use of social media is frequent even at the start of the teenage years and becomes more frequent as they become older.

(**Source:** Madden et al., 2013.)

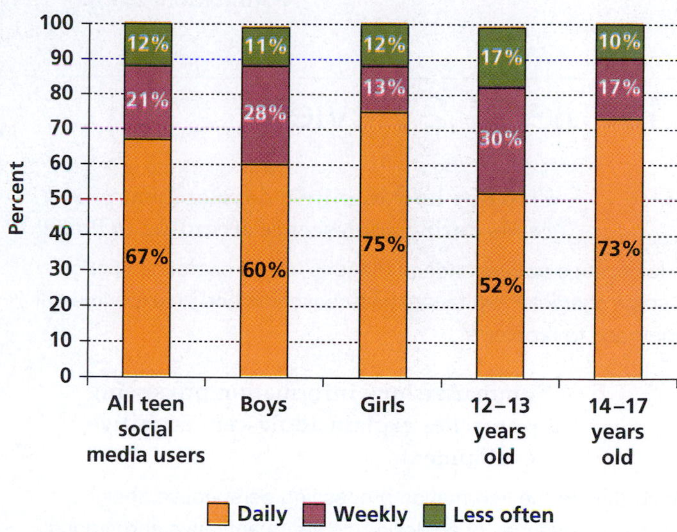

Furthermore, some forms of online activities can be mean-spirited. For example, some teenagers make use of the Web to bully others—a process in which victims are repeatedly texted or emailed with hurtful messages. The source of such *cyberbullying* can remain anonymous, and the messages may be particularly abusive. Although they do not inflict physical harm, they can be psychologically damaging (Zacchilli & Valerio, 2011; Best, Manktelow, & Taylor, 2014; Bartlett et al., 2017).

MEDIA AND EDUCATION. The widespread availability of the Web also has produced considerable changes in education, allowing adolescents to tap into a vast array of information. However, it is not yet obvious how web access will change education or whether the impact will be uniformly positive. For instance, schools must change their curricula to include specific instruction in a key skill for deriving value from the Web: learning to sort through huge bodies of information to identify what is most useful and discard what is not. To obtain the full benefits of the Web, then, students must obtain the ability to search, choose, and integrate information in order to create new knowledge (Trotter, 2004; Guilamo-Ramos et al., 2015).

Despite the substantial benefits of the Web, its use also has a downside. Claims that cyberspace is overrun with child molesters may be exaggerated, but it is true that cyberspace makes available material that many parents and other adults find highly objectionable. In addition, there is the growing problem of online gambling. High school and college students can easily bet on sports events and participate in games such as poker on the Web using credit cards (Winters, Stinchfield, & Botzet, 2005; Fleming et al., 2006; Mitchell, Wolak, & Finkelhor, 2007).

The growing use of computers also presents a challenge involving socioeconomic status, race, and ethnicity. Poorer adolescents and members of minority groups have less access to computers than more affluent adolescents and members of socially advantaged groups—a phenomenon known as the *digital divide.*

For example, 17 percent of households with school-age children lack regular access to the Web. And there are stark racial and ethnic differences: 77 percent of black students reported using a personal computer frequently, compared with 87 percent of white students and 81 percent of Hispanic/Latino students. Asian American students had the highest rate of use, at 91.2 percent. Furthermore, only 18 percent of teachers believe that their students have the digital resources available to complete assignments at home, and students agree: 42 percent of students say they received a lower grade on an assignment because they did not have Internet access. How society reduces these discrepancies is a matter of considerable importance (Olsen, 2009; Purcell et al., 2013; Hispanic Heritage Foundation, 2015).

Module 11.2 Review

LO 11.4 Describe how cognitive development proceeds during adolescence according to Piaget.

Adolescence corresponds to Piaget's formal operations period, a stage characterized by abstract reasoning and an experimental approach to problems.

LO 11.5 Summarize how information processing approaches explain adolescent cognitive development.

According to the information processing perspective, the cognitive advances of adolescence are quantitative and gradual, involving improvements in many aspects of thinking and memory. Improved metacognition enables the monitoring of thought processes and of mental capacities.

LO 11.6 Describe how adolescent egocentrism affects thinking and behavior.

Adolescents are susceptible to adolescent egocentrism and the perception that an imaginary audience is constantly observing their behavior. They also construct personal fables that stress their uniqueness and immunity to harm.

LO 11.7 Analyze the factors that affect adolescent school performance.

Academic performance is linked in complex ways to socioeconomic status and to race and ethnicity.

LO 11.8 Describe how adolescents use the Internet and social media.

Adolescents spend a great deal of time online interacting with friends, finding information, and entertaining themselves. Internet-related concerns focus on unequal access to computers, called the digital divide, and the misuse of social media for cyberbullying.

Journal Writing Prompt

Applying Lifespan Development: When faced with complex problems, such as what kind of computer or car to buy, do you think most adults spontaneously apply formal operations like those used to solve the pendulum problem? Why or why not?

Threats to Adolescents' Well-Being

It took a car crash to wake Tom Jansen up—literally and figuratively. The police called at 12:30 a.m. and told him to pick up his 13-year-old daughter Roni at the hospital. The accident wasn't serious, but what Tom learned that night might have saved Roni's life. The police found alcohol on her breath and on that of every other occupant of the car, including the driver.

Tom always knew that someday he'd have to have the "alcohol and drug talk" with Roni, but he had hoped it would be in high school, not middle school. Thinking back, he saw that he had been wrong to chalk up the classic signs of a drug or alcohol problem—school absences, declining grades, general listlessness—to "adolescent angst." It was time to face facts.

He and Roni met with a counselor weekly for several months. At first Roni was hostile, but one evening she started sobbing while they were doing the dishes. Tom simply held her, never saying a word. But from that moment, he knew his Roni was back.

Tom Jansen learned that alcohol was not the only drug Roni was using. As her friends later admitted, Roni had all the signs of becoming what they called a "garbage head"—someone who would try anything. Had the accident never happened, Roni might have gotten into very serious trouble or even lost her life.

Few cases of adolescent alcohol use produce such extreme results, but the use of alcohol, as well as other kinds of substance use and abuse, is one of several kinds of threats to health during adolescence, usually one of the healthiest periods of life. While the extent of risky behavior is difficult to gauge, preventable problems, such as drug, alcohol, and tobacco use, as well as sexually transmitted infections, represent serious threats to adolescents' health and well-being.

Illegal Drugs

LO 11.9 Analyze what illegal drugs adolescents use and why.

How common is illegal drug use during adolescence? Very. For example, 1 in 15 high school seniors smokes marijuana on a daily or near-daily basis. Furthermore, marijuana usage has remained at fairly high levels over the past decade, and attitudes about its use have become more positive as marijuana has been legalized in a number of states for adult use (Nanda & Konnur, 2006; Tang & Orwin, 2009; Johnston et al., 2016; see Figure 11-9).

Figure 11-9 Marijuana Use Remains Steady

According to an annual survey, the proportion of students reporting marijuana use over the past 12 months has remained steady at fairly high levels.

(**Source:** Johnston et al., 2016.)

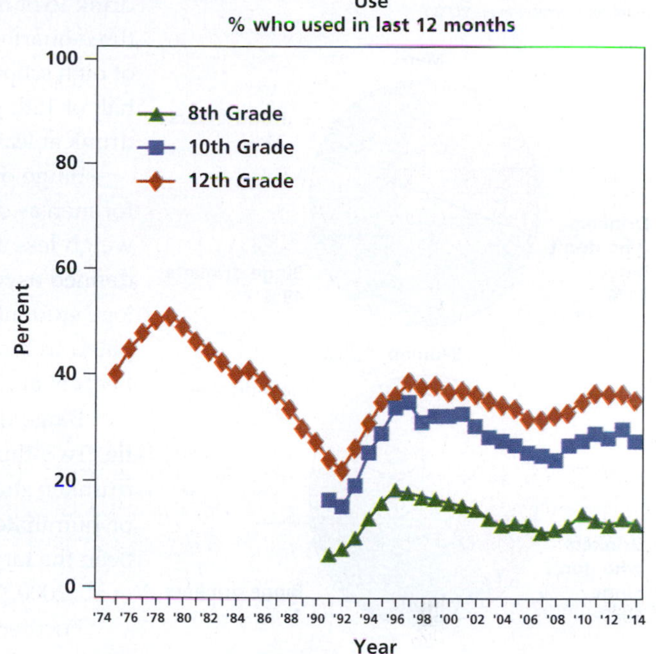

Adolescents have a variety of reasons for using drugs. Some use them for the pleasurable experience they supposedly provide. Others use them to try to escape from the pressures of everyday life, however temporarily. Some adolescents try drugs simply for the thrill of doing something illegal.

One of the newest reasons for using drugs is to enhance academic performance. A growing number of high school students are using drugs, such as Adderall, an amphetamine prescribed for attention deficit hyperactivity disorder. When used illegally, Adderall is assumed to increase focus and is thought to increase the ability to study and allow users to study for long hours (Schwarz, 2012; Munro et al., 2017).

The alleged drug use of well-known celebrities also contributes to adolescent drug use. Finally, peer pressure plays a role: Adolescents, as we'll discuss in greater detail in Chapter 12, are particularly susceptible to the perceived standards of their peer groups (Urberg, Luo, & Pilgrim, 2003; Nation & Heflinger, 2006; Young et al., 2006).

The use of illegal drugs is dangerous in several respects. For instance, some drugs are addictive. **Addictive drugs** are drugs that produce a biological or psychological dependence in users, leading to increasingly powerful cravings for them.

addictive drugs

drugs that produce a biological or psychological dependence in users, leading to increasingly powerful cravings for them

When drugs produce a biological addiction, their presence in the body becomes so common that the body is unable to function in their absence. Furthermore, addiction causes actual physical—and potentially lingering—changes in the nervous system. In such cases, drug intake no longer may provide a "high" but may be necessary simply to maintain the perception of everyday normalcy (Cami & Farré, 2003; Munzar, Cami, & Farré, 2003).

In addition to physical addiction, drugs also can produce psychological addiction. In such cases, people grow to depend on drugs to cope with the everyday stress of life. If drugs are used as an escape, they may prevent adolescents from confronting—and potentially solving—the problems that led them to drug use in the first place. Finally, drugs may be dangerous because even casual users of less hazardous drugs can escalate to more dangerous forms of substance abuse.

Adolescent drug use makes up a large part of the current opioid epidemic that is affecting the United States. As we will discuss later in the book, the rate of overdoses due to opioid use has increased dramatically in the past decade. (Opioids include both legal drugs such as codeine and OxyContin, and illegal drugs such as heroin and fentanyl.) Almost 100 Americans die every day from an opioid overdose, and the number of drug overdose deaths among 15- to 19-year-olds has increased 15 percent for males from 2014 to 2015, and 35 percent for females from 2013 to 2015 (Katz, 2017).

Figure 11-10 Binge Drinking Among College Students

For men, binge drinking is defined as consuming five or more drinks in one sitting; for women, the total is four or more. Why is binge drinking popular?

(**Source:** Wechsler et al., 2003.)

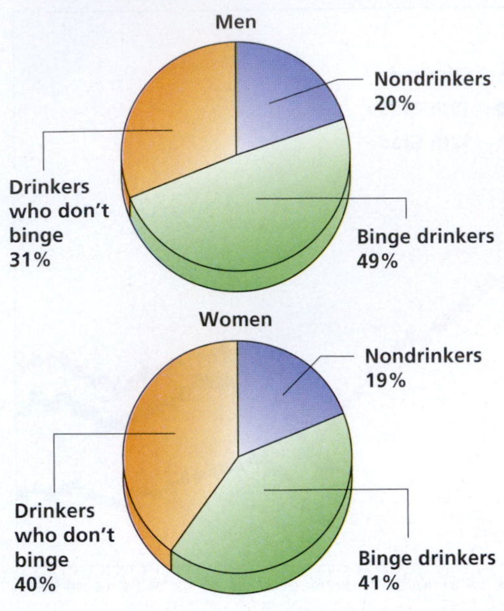

Alcohol: Use and Abuse

LO 11.10 **Discuss how adolescents use and abuse alcohol.**

Three-fourths of college students have something in common: They've consumed at least one alcoholic drink during the past 30 days. More than 40 percent say they've had five or more drinks within the past 2 weeks, and some 16 percent drink 16 or more drinks per week. High school students, too, are drinkers: Nearly three-quarters of high school seniors report having consumed alcohol by the end of high school, and about two-fifths have done so by the eighth grade. More than half of 12th graders and nearly a fifth of eighth graders say that they have been drunk at least once in their lives (Ford, 2007; Johnston et al., 2015).

Binge drinking is a particular problem on college campuses. It is defined for men as drinking five or more drinks in one sitting; for women, who tend to weigh less and whose bodies absorb alcohol less efficiently, binge drinking is defined as four drinks in one sitting. Surveys find that almost half of male college students and over 40 percent of female college students say they participated in binge drinking during the previous 2 weeks (Harrell & Karim, 2008; Beets et al., 2009; see Figure 11-10).

Binge drinking affects even those who don't drink or who drink very little. Two-thirds of lighter drinkers reported that they had been disturbed by drunken students while sleeping or studying. Around a third had been insulted or humiliated by a drunken student, and 25 percent of women said they had been the target of an unwanted sexual advance by a drunk classmate (Wechsler et al., 2000, 2002, 2003; McQueeny, 2009; Squeglia et al., 2012; Spear et al., 2013).

Furthermore, brain scans show damaged tissue in teenage binge drinkers compared to non-binge drinkers. They have thinner and lower-volume regions in the prefrontal cortex and cerebellar regions, and their white matter is reduced. Such findings suggest that alcohol has toxic effects on the brain during a period in which the brain is particularly susceptible to damage, and it may lead to permanent damage to the structure of neurons in the brain (Cservenka & Brumback, 2017).

Why do adolescents start to drink in the first place? For some—especially male athletes, whose rate of drinking tends to be higher than that of the general adolescent population—drinking is seen as a way of proving they can drink as much as anybody. Others drink for the same reason that some use drugs: It releases inhibitions and tension, and it reduces stress. Many begin because the conspicuous examples of drunkenness strewn around campus cause them to assume that everyone is drinking heavily, something known as the *false consensus effect* (Dunn et al., 2012; Archimi & Kuntsche, 2014; Drane, Modecki, & Barber, 2017).

alcoholics

persons with alcohol problems who have learned to depend on alcohol and are unable to control their drinking

For some adolescents, alcohol use becomes a habit that cannot be controlled. **Alcoholics**, those with alcohol problems, learn to depend on alcohol and are unable to control their drinking. They also become increasingly able to tolerate alcohol and therefore need to drink ever-larger amounts of liquor in order to bring about the positive effects they crave. Some drink throughout the day, while others go on binges in which they consume huge quantities of alcohol.

The reasons that some adolescents—or anyone—become alcoholics are not fully known. Genetics plays a role: Alcoholism runs in families. At the same time, not all alcoholics have family members with alcohol problems. For those adolescents with a family history of alcohol problems, alcoholism may be triggered by efforts to deal with the stress that having an alcoholic parent or family member can cause (Berenson, 2005; Clarke et al., 2008).

The origins of an adolescent's problems with alcohol or drugs are less important than getting help. Parents, teachers, and friends can provide the help a teen needs to address the problem—if they realize there is a problem. How can concerned friends and family members tell if an adolescent they know is having difficulties with alcohol or drugs? Some of the telltale signs are described in the following *Development and Your Life* box.

Development in Your Life

Hooked on Drugs or Alcohol?

It is not always easy to determine whether an adolescent has a drug or alcohol abuse problem, but there are some warning signs. Red flags include:

Feeling Connected to or Identifying with the Drug Culture

- Frequent references to drugs in conversation or jokes
- Interest in or familiarity with drug paraphernalia
- Antagonism to discussing drugs
- Drug-related posters or magazines, or clothing with drug references

Marked Changes in School Performance

- Notable drop in grades—not just from C's to F's, but from A's to B's and C's
- Assignments repeatedly turned in late or not completed
- Lack of motivation or self-discipline; appears indifferent or "spaced out"
- Increased absenteeism or tardiness

Physical Deterioration

- Easily distracted, unable to concentrate, prone to memory lapses
- Impaired coordination; tremors, slurred or incoherent speech
- Unhealthy appearance; indifference to hygiene or grooming
- Bloodshot eyes, dilated pupils
- Changes in appetite or sleep patterns; sudden weight loss or gain

Behavioral Changes

- Frequent dishonesty (lying, stealing, cheating); trouble with the police
- Sudden change in friends; reluctance to talk about new ones
- Possession of or unexplained need for large amounts of money
- Sudden mood swings, inappropriate anger, unusual hyperactivity or agitation
- Reduced self-esteem; appears fearful or anxious with no reason
- Diminished interest in extracurricular activities and hobbies (based on Franck & Brownstone, 1991, pp. 593–594)

If an adolescent—or anyone else, for that matter—fits any of these descriptors, help is probably needed. A good place to start is a hotline run by the National Institute on Drug Abuse at (800) 662-4357 or its website at www.nida.nih.gov. In addition, those who need advice can find a local listing for Alcoholics Anonymous online.

Tobacco: The Dangers of Smoking

LO 11.11 Summarize how and why adolescents use tobacco.

Most adolescents are well aware of the dangers of smoking, but many still indulge in it. Recent figures show that, overall, a smaller proportion of adolescents smoke than in prior decades, but the numbers remain substantial, and within certain groups the numbers are increasing. Smoking is on the rise among girls, and in several countries, including Austria, Norway, and Sweden, the proportion of girls who smoke is higher than the proportion of boys. There are racial differences as well: White children and children in lower-socioeconomic-status households are more likely to experiment with cigarettes and to start smoking earlier than African American children and children living in higher-socioeconomic-status households. Also, significantly more white males of high school age smoke than do African American males in high school, although the differences have narrowed in recent years (Harrell et al., 1998; Stolberg, 1998; Baker, Brandon, & Chassin, 2004; Fergusson et al., 2007; Proctor, Barnett, & Muilenburg, 2012).

Smoking is becoming a habit that is hard to maintain. There are growing social sanctions against it. It's becoming more difficult to find a comfortable place to smoke: More places, including schools and places of business, have become "smoke-free." Even so, a good number of adolescents still smoke, despite knowing the dangers of smoking and of secondhand smoke. Why, then, do adolescents begin to smoke and maintain the habit?

Developmental Diversity and Your Life

Selling Death: Pushing Smoking to the Less Advantaged

According to a U.S. Cancer Institute report, each major U.S. tobacco company has a leading "youth brand" (Marlboro, Camel, Newport), which it promotes heavily.

Caribbean Chill, Midnight Berry, Mocha Taboo, and Mintrigue, and Skoal chewing tobacco come in fruity flavors, just like candy.

If you are a cigarette manufacturer and you find that the number of people using your product is declining, what do you do? U.S. companies have sought to carve out new markets by turning to a young and impressionable market, especially among the least advantaged groups of people. In addition to seeking new converts in the United States, tobacco companies aggressively recruit adolescent smokers abroad. In many developing countries, the number of smokers is still low. Tobacco companies are seeking to increase this number through marketing strategies designed to hook adolescents on the habit by means of free samples. In addition, in countries where American culture and products are held in high esteem, advertising suggests that the use of cigarettes is an American—and consequently prestigious—habit (Boseley, 2008; Hakim, 2015).

The strategy is effective. For instance, in some Latin American cities, as many as 50 percent of teenagers smoke. According to the World Health Organization, smoking will prematurely kill some 1 billion people in the 21st century (Picard, 2008).

One reason is that for some adolescents, smoking is seen as an adolescent rite of passage, a sign of growing up. In addition, seeing influential models, such as celebrities, parents, and peers, smoking increases the chances that an adolescent will take up the habit. Cigarettes are also very addictive. Nicotine, the active chemical ingredient of cigarettes, can produce biological and psychological dependency very quickly. Although one or two cigarettes generally do not produce a lifetime smoker, it takes only a little more to start the habit. People who smoke as few as 10 cigarettes early in their lives stand an 80 percent chance of becoming habitual smokers (West, Romero, & Trinidad, 2007; Tucker et al., 2008; Wills et al., 2008; Holliday & Gould, 2016).

A popular trend in smoking is the use of e-cigarettes. *E-cigarettes* are battery-powered cigarette-shaped devices that deliver nicotine that is vaporized to form a mist. Not unlike the experience of smoking actual tobacco, they appear to be less harmful than traditional cigarettes. However, as we consider in the *From Research to Practice* box, their health effects are unclear, and the U.S. government has sought to regulate their sale (Tavernise, 2013; Lanza, Russell, & Braymiller, 2017).

From Research to Practice

Vaping and Dripping

Vaping, the inhalation of nicotine vapor generated by electronic cigarettes, is rapidly growing in popularity among U.S. teenagers. In just 4 years the percentage of high school students who reported using one of these devices in the past month increased by more than tenfold, from 1.5 percent in 2011 to 16 percent in 2015. This translates to millions of adolescents who are vaping, raising important questions about the effects of this practice on their health (Centers for Disease Control and Prevention, 2018).

The good news is that e-cigarettes have been shown to be a lot safer than conventional cigarettes, which are associated with various cancers and serious lung diseases. The harmful effects of conventional cigarettes are caused by tar and other toxic chemicals that are present in cigarette smoke. While e-cigarettes aren't entirely toxin-free—the nicotine fluid contains flavorings and other additives that may not be safe to inhale—the vapor they produce is much less toxic than cigarette smoke is (Pisinger & Dossing, 2014).

Of course, that's when the e-cigarettes are used as designed. But many adolescents have discovered a new way to vape. It's called *dripping*, and it entails hacking an e-cigarette to expose the heat coil and then dripping the nicotine fluid directly onto it. This produces a concentrated vapor cloud that gives the user a stronger and more flavorful hit. One study showed that of the high school student participants who had ever tried vaping, about one in four had also tried dripping. Little is known about the effects of dripping, but some experts believe that the higher temperature at which it vaporizes the nicotine fluid may release more toxins (Krishnan-Sarin et al., 2017).

Whether they are vaped or dripped, it's clear that e-cigarettes aren't harmless, as a growing body of research suggests that use of e-cigarettes may encourage adolescents to take up smoking conventional cigarettes. Furthermore, nicotine can have harmful effects on the still-developing brains of adolescents. And of course, becoming addicted to nicotine at any age makes ongoing use of tobacco more likely. While some argue that in an imperfect world an adolescent taking up vaping is far preferable to an adolescent taking up smoking, public health experts' best advice is still not to use nicotine products at all (England et al., 2015; Centers for Disease Control, 2018).

Shared Writing Prompt

Do you think vaping is a realistically acceptable alternative to smoking for adolescents, or do you think that teens should be prohibited from all nicotine use? Why or why not?

Sexually Transmitted Infections

LO 11.12 Describe the dangers adolescent sexual practices present and how these dangers can be avoided.

When her doctor informed her that she had AIDS, Cheryl Mundt, age 17, thought immediately of her first boyfriend. He had broken up with her a year ago without any explanation, and Cheryl could never contact him afterward. Now she was faced with having to tell her new boyfriend about her condition, and she wasn't sure what his reaction would be. She only knew that she had to tell him right away, whatever the consequences.

AIDS. Cheryl Mundt was not alone: *Acquired immunodeficiency syndrome (AIDS)* is one of the leading causes of death among young people worldwide. AIDS has no cure and ultimately brings death to those who are infected with the HIV virus that produces the disease.

Because AIDS is spread primarily through sexual contact, it is classified as a **sexually transmitted infection (STI)**. Although it began as a problem that primarily affected gays, it has spread to other populations, including heterosexuals and intravenous drug users. Minorities have been particularly hard hit: African Americans and Hispanics account for 70 percent of new AIDS cases in the United States, while African American males have almost eight times the prevalence of AIDS as white males. Over 25 million people have died from AIDS worldwide, and people living with the disease number 34 million worldwide (see Figure 11-11; UNAIDS, 2011).

sexually transmitted infection (STI)
an infection that is spread through sexual contact

Figure 11-11 AIDS Around the World

The number of people carrying the AIDS virus varies substantially by geographic region. By far the most cases are found in Africa and the Middle East, although the disease is a growing problem in Asia.

(**Source:** UNAIDS & World Health Organization, 2009.)

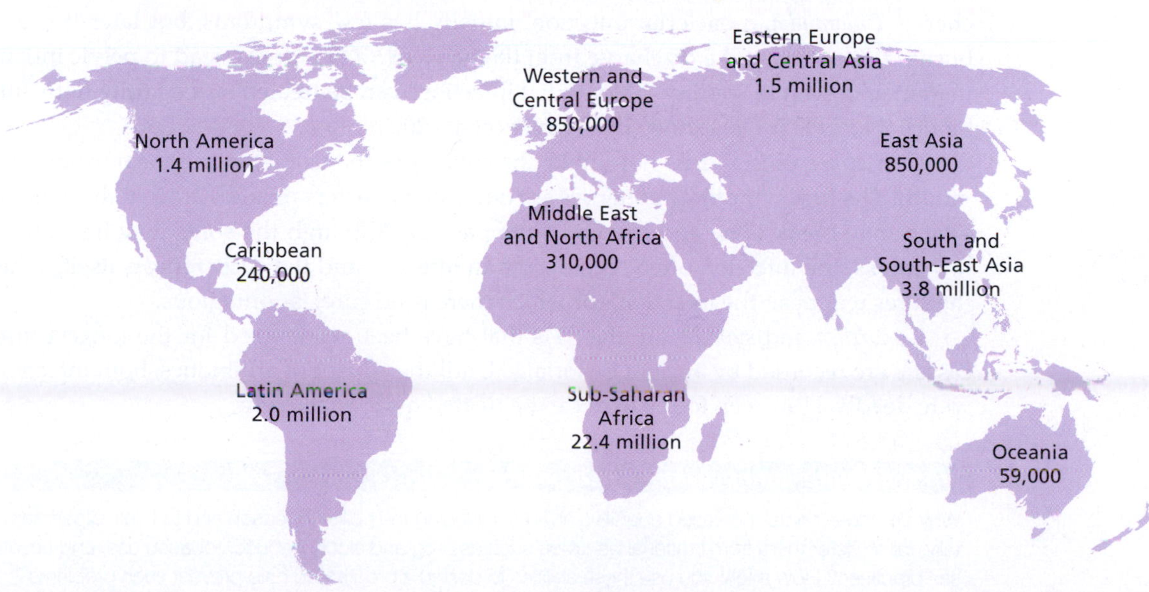

Figure 11-12 Sexually Transmitted Infections (STIs) Among Adolescents

Why are adolescents in particular in danger of contracting an STI?

(**Sources:** Guttmacher Institute, 2004; Weinstock, Berman, & Cates, 2006.)

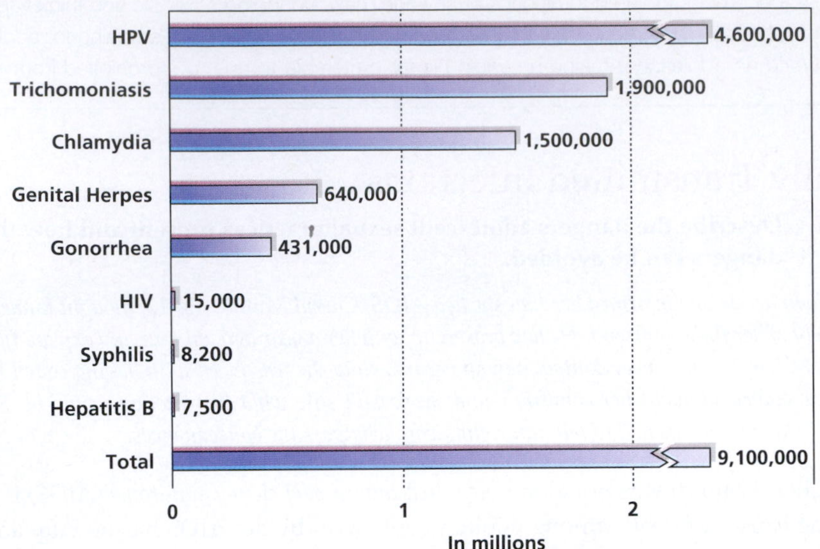

OTHER SEXUALLY TRANSMITTED INFECTIONS. AIDS is the deadliest of sexually transmitted infections, but a number of other STIs are far more common (see Figure 11-12). One out of four adolescents contracts an STI before graduating from high school. Overall, around 2.5 million teenagers contract an STI, such as the ones listed in Figure 11-12, each year (Weinstock, Berman, & Cates, 2004).

The most common STI is *human papillomavirus (HPV)*. HPV can be transmitted through genital contact without intercourse. Most infections do not have symptoms, but HPV can produce genital warts and in some cases lead to cervical cancer. A vaccine that protects against some kinds of HPV is available. The U.S. Centers for Disease Control and Prevention recommends it be routinely administered to girls and boys 11 to 12 years old—a recommendation that has provoked considerable political reaction (Schwarz et al., 2012; Thomas et al., 2013; Wilson et al., 2017).

Another common STI is *trichomoniasis*, an infection in the vagina or penis that is caused by a parasite. Initially without symptoms, it can eventually cause a painful discharge. *Chlamydia*, a bacterial infection, initially has few symptoms, but later it causes burning urination and a discharge from the penis or vagina. It can lead to pelvic inflammation and even to sterility. Chlamydial infections can be treated successfully with antibiotics (Nockels & Oakeshott, 1999; Fayers et al., 2003).

Genital herpes is a virus not unlike the cold sores that sometimes appear around the mouth. The first symptoms of herpes are often small blisters or sores around the genitals, which may break open and become quite painful. Although the sores may heal after a few weeks, the infection often recurs after an interval, and the cycle repeats itself. When the sores reappear, the infection, for which there is no cure, is contagious.

Gonorrhea and *syphilis* are the STIs that have been recognized for the longest time; cases were recorded by ancient historians. Until the advent of antibiotics, both infections were deadly. However, today both can be treated quite effectively.

From a *health-care provider's* perspective

Why do adolescents' increased cognitive abilities, including the ability to reason and to think experimentally, fail to deter them from irrational behavior, such as drug and alcohol abuse, tobacco use, and unsafe sex practices? How might you use these abilities to design a program to help prevent such problems?

Table 11-1 Safer Sex Practices

The only foolproof method of avoiding a sexually transmitted infection (STI) is abstinence. However, by following the "safer sex" practices listed here, one can significantly reduce the risk of contracting an STI:

- *Know your sexual partner well.* Before having sex with someone, learn about his or her sexual history.
- *Use condoms.* For those in sexual relationships, condoms are the most reliable means of preventing transmission of STIs.
- *Avoid the exchange of bodily fluids, particularly semen.* In particular, avoid anal intercourse. The AIDS virus in particular can spread through small tears in the rectum, making anal intercourse without condoms particularly dangerous. Oral sex, once thought relatively safe, is now viewed as potentially dangerous for contracting the AIDS virus.
- *Stay sober.* Using alcohol and drugs impairs judgment and can lead to poor decisions—and it makes using a condom correctly more difficult.
- *Consider the benefits of monogamy.* People in long-term, monogamous relationships with partners who have been faithful are at a lower risk of contracting STIs.

AVOIDING STIs. Short of abstinence, there is no certain way to avoid STIs. However, there are things that can be done to make sex safer; these are listed in Table 11-1.

Still, even when adolescents have been exposed to substantial sex education, the use of safer sex practices is far from universal. As we discussed earlier in the chapter, teens are prone to feel invulnerable and are therefore more likely to engage in risky behavior, believing their chances of contracting STIs are minimal. This is particularly true when adolescents perceive that their partner is "safe"—someone they know well and with whom they are involved in a relatively long-term relationship (Tinsley, Lees, & Sumartojo, 2004; Widman et al., 2014).

Unfortunately, unless an individual knows the complete sexual history and STI status of a partner, unprotected sex remains a risky business. And learning a partner's complete sexual history is difficult. Not only is it embarrassing to ask, but partners may not be accurate reporters, whether from ignorance of their own exposure, embarrassment, a sense of privacy, or simply forgetfulness. As a result, STIs remain a significant problem among adolescents.

Module 11.3 Review

LO 11.9 Analyze what illegal drugs adolescents use and why.

Illegal drug use is prevalent among adolescents as a way to find pleasure, avoid pressure, or gain the approval of peers.

LO 11.10 Discuss how adolescents use and abuse alcohol.

The use of alcohol is also popular among adolescents, often to appear adult or to lessen inhibitions.

LO 11.11 Summarize how and why adolescents use tobacco.

Despite the well-known dangers of smoking, adolescents often smoke to enhance their image or to emulate adults.

LO 11.12 Describe the dangers adolescent sexual practices present and how these dangers can be avoided.

AIDS is the most serious of the sexually transmitted infections, ultimately causing death. Safe-sex practices or sexual abstinence can prevent AIDS, although adolescents often ignore these strategies. Other sexually transmitted infections affect adolescents, such as chlamydia, genital herpes, trichomoniasis, gonorrhea, and syphilis.

Journal Writing Prompt

Applying Lifespan Development: How do adolescents' concerns about self-image and their perception that they are the center of attention contribute to smoking and alcohol use?

Epilogue

To call adolescence a period of great change in people's lives is an understatement. This chapter looked at the significant physical, psychological, and cognitive changes that adolescents undergo and at some of the consequences of entering and living through adolescence.

Before turning to the next chapter, return for the moment to the opening prologue of this chapter, about Jade and Maya, two girls seeking approval for their appearance from their peers online. In light of what you now know about adolescence, consider the following questions about Jade and Maya.

1. Jade worries that she's not a size 0. What health problems does Jade risk if she becomes fixated on dropping a lot of weight? What suggestions would you make to help her focus on maintaining a healthy body instead of worrying about her dress size?

2. Cyber beauty pageants place a lot of stress on teen girls to look and dress to maximize sex appeal. What messages does this give to young girls about their self-worth? How would you counter these messages?

3. Social media is a fact of life for all teens. What suggestions could you make to Jade to bolster her self-esteem while still being able to interact with friends online?

4. Fourteen-year-old Maya is a very attractive girl. She receives positive feedback from friends and strangers whenever she posts her picture on social media sites. Do you think there may be a negative side to Maya's online popularity? Explain your answer.

Looking Back

LO 11.1 Describe the physical changes adolescents experience as the body reaches puberty.

The adolescent years are marked by a physical growth spurt, which for girls begins around age 10, and for boys around age 12. Puberty begins in girls at around age 11 and in boys at around age 13. The physical changes of puberty often have psychological effects, such as an increase in self-esteem and self-awareness, as well as confusion and uncertainty about sexuality. Early maturation has different effects on boys and girls. For boys, being bigger and more developed can lead to increased athleticism, greater popularity, and a more positive self-concept. For girls, early maturation can lead to increased popularity and an enhanced social life but also embarrassment over their bodies, which suddenly look different from everyone else's. For the short term, late maturation can be a physical and social disadvantage that affects boys' self-concept. Girls who mature late may suffer neglect by their peers, but ultimately they appear to suffer no lasting ill effects and may even benefit.

LO 11.2 Explain the nutritional needs and concerns of adolescents.

While most adolescents have no greater nutritional worries other than fueling their growth with appropriate foods, some are obese or overweight. Excessive concern about obesity can cause some adolescents, especially girls, to develop an eating disorder, such as anorexia nervosa or bulimia.

LO 11.3 Summarize the ways in which the brain develops in adolescence.

Changes in the brain pave the way for the rapid cognitive growth of adolescence, especially changes in the prefrontal cortex. These changes permit sophisticated thought, evaluation, and judgment, enabling the complex intellectual achievements of adolescence.

LO 11.4 Describe how cognitive development proceeds during adolescence according to Piaget.

Adolescence coincides with Piaget's formal operations period of development, when people begin to engage in abstract thought and scientific reasoning.

LO 11.5 Summarize how information processing approaches explain adolescent cognitive development.

According to information processing approaches, cognitive growth during adolescence is gradual and quantitative, involving improvements in memory capacity, mental strategies, metacognition, and other aspects of cognitive functioning. Adolescents also grow in the area of metacognition, which permits them to monitor their thought processes and accurately assess their cognitive capabilities.

LO 11.6 Describe how adolescent egocentrism affects thinking and behavior.

Adolescents' developing cognitive abilities may also promote a form of adolescent egocentrism, a self-absorption related to their developing sense of themselves as independent identities. This can make it hard for adolescents to accept criticism and tolerate authority figures. Adolescents may play to an imaginary audience of critical observers, and they may develop personal fables.

LO 11.7 Analyze the factors that affect adolescent school performance.

School performance tends to decline during the adolescent years. School achievement is linked with socioeconomic status, race, and ethnicity. While many academic achievement differences are due to socioeconomic factors, attributional patterns regarding success factors and belief systems regarding the link between school success and success in life also play a part.

LO 11.8 Describe how adolescents use the Internet and social media.

Adolescents are avid Internet users, spending significant portions of each day using social media, information resources, and entertainment outlets. The Internet also supports abuse, such as cyberbullying.

LO 11.9 Analyze what illegal drugs adolescents use and why.

The use of illicit drugs is widespread among adolescents, who are motivated by pleasure seeking, pressure avoidance, the desire to flout authority, or the imitation of role models.

LO 11.10 Discuss how adolescents use and abuse alcohol.

Many adolescents use alcohol for social reasons and to experience a readily available high. Binge drinking is a particular hazard among college students.

LO 11.11 Summarize how and why adolescents use tobacco.

Despite social sanctions against it, many adolescents continue to use tobacco products—or e-cigarettes—as a rite of passage into adulthood.

LO 11.12 Describe the dangers adolescent sexual practices present and how these dangers can be avoided.

AIDS is one of the leading causes of death among young people, affecting minority populations with particular severity. Adolescent behavior patterns and attitudes, such as shyness, self-absorption, and a belief in personal invulnerability, work against the use of safe-sex practices that can prevent the disease. Other sexually transmitted infections, including chlamydia, genital herpes, trichomoniasis, gonorrhea, and syphilis, occur frequently among the adolescent population and can also be prevented by safe-sex practices or abstinence.

Key Terms and Concepts

Chapter 12

Social and Personality Development in Adolescence

DGLimages/Shutterstock

Learning Objectives

LO 12.1 Describe how self-concept and self-esteem develop during adolescence.

LO 12.2 Summarize how Erikson explains identity formation during adolescence.

LO 12.3 Explain Marcia's categories of adolescent identity.

LO 12.4 Describe the role religion and spirituality play in identity formation in adolescence.

LO 12.5 Discuss the challenges ethnic and minority groups face in identity formation in adolescence.

LO 12.6 Identify the dangers adolescents face as they deal with the stresses of their age.

LO 12.7 Describe what family relationships are like during adolescence.

LO 12.8 Explain how relationships with peers change during adolescence.

LO 12.9 Discuss what it means to be popular and unpopular in adolescence and how adolescents respond to peer pressure.

LO 12.10 Describe the functions and characteristics of dating during adolescence and how sexuality develops.

LO 12.11 Explain how sexual orientation develops in adolescence.

LO 12.12 Summarize the challenges of teen pregnancy and the types of programs that are most effective in preventing it.

Chapter Overview

Prologue: Satellite Vision

Could satellites in space help the visually impaired navigate through daily life?

That's what Ameen Abdulrasool, when he was an 18-year-old high school student, figured when he invented a system that promises independence for the visually impaired. Ameen, who attended high school in Chicago, was inspired by automobile navigation systems that use Global Positioning System satellites to help car drivers avoid getting lost.

Ameen, whose father and several other relatives are blind, wanted to devise a system that would let the visually impaired know where they were and how to reach particular destinations. To do this, he put together an iPod-size instrument that would receive the satellite signals, bracelets to be worn on each arm, and earphones. After users program in a destination, they receive voice commands telling them what direction to turn. At the same time, the bracelets vibrate to indicate the right direction.

It took 3 years of trial and error, but the system has proven highly effective. It promises to expand the world of the visually impaired, who now may be able to plot a course through the world as never before (Kemker, 2017).

Looking Ahead

What drove Ameen to invent his device? What was it about his personality and identity that led him to try to help his blind relatives? What inspired him to act in a selfless and even heroic way?

In this chapter, we discuss personality and social development during adolescence. We begin by considering how adolescents form their views of themselves. We look at self-concept, self-esteem, and identity development. We also examine two major psychological difficulties: depression and suicide.

Next, we discuss relationships during adolescence. We consider how adolescents reposition themselves within the family and how the influence of family members declines in some spheres as peers take on new importance. We also examine the ways in which adolescents interact with their friends and the ways in which popularity is determined.

Finally, the chapter considers dating and sexual behavior. We look at the role of dating and close relationships in adolescents'

KidStock/Getty Images

The social lives of adolescents take varied forms.

lives, and we consider sexual behavior and the standards that govern adolescents' sex lives. We conclude by looking at teenage pregnancy and at programs that seek to prevent unwanted pregnancy.

Identity: Asking "Who Am I?"

You have no idea how much pressure a 13-year-old has to deal with. You've got to look cool, act cool, wear the right clothes, wear your hair a certain way—and your friends have different ideas about all these things than your parents, know what I mean? And you've got to have friends or you're nobody. And then some of your friends say you're not cool if you don't drink or do drugs, but what if you don't want that?—Anton Merced

The thoughts of 13-year-old Anton Merced demonstrate a clear awareness—and self-consciousness—regarding his newly forming place in society and life. During adolescence, questions like "Who am I?" and "Where do I belong in the world?" begin to take a front seat.

Why should issues of identity become so important during adolescence? One reason is that adolescents' intellectual capacities become more adult-like. They are able to see how they stack up against others and become aware that they are individuals, apart not just from their parents but from all others. The dramatic physical changes during puberty make adolescents acutely aware of their own bodies and aware that others are reacting to them in ways to which they are unaccustomed. Whatever the cause, adolescence often brings substantial changes in teenagers' self-concepts and self-esteem—in sum, their notions of their own identity.

Self-Concept and Self-Esteem

LO 12.1 Describe how self-concept and self-esteem develop during adolescence.

Who are you, and how do you feel about yourself? Questions like these present important challenges during adolescence.

SELF-CONCEPT: ASKING "WHAT AM I LIKE?" Ask Valerie to describe herself, and she says, "Others look at me as laid-back, relaxed, and not worrying too much. But really, I'm often nervous and emotional."

The fact that Valerie distinguishes others' views of her from her own perceptions represents a developmental advance of adolescence. In childhood, Valerie would have characterized herself according to a list of traits that would not differentiate her view of herself and others' perspectives. However, adolescents are able to make the distinction, and when they try to describe who they are, they take both their own and others' views into account (Preckel et al., 2013; McLean & Syed, 2015; Griffin, Adams, & Little, 2017).

This broader view of themselves is one aspect of adolescents' increasing understanding of who they are. They can see various aspects of the self simultaneously, and this view of the self becomes more organized and coherent. They look at the self from a psychological perspective, viewing traits not as concrete entities but as abstractions (Adams, Montemayor, & Gullotta, 1996). For example, teenagers are more likely than younger children to describe themselves in terms of their ideology (saying something like "I'm an environmentalist") than in terms of physical characteristics (such as "I'm the fastest runner in my class").

In some ways, this broader, more multifaceted self-concept is a mixed blessing, especially during the earlier years of adolescence. At that time, adolescents may be troubled by the multiple aspects of their personalities. During the beginning of adolescence, for instance, teenagers may want to view themselves in a certain way ("I'm a sociable person and love to be with people"), and they may become concerned when their behavior is inconsistent with that view ("Even though I want to be sociable, sometimes I can't stand being around my friends and just want to be alone"). By the end of adolescence, however, teenagers find it easier to accept that different situations elicit different behaviors and feelings (Trzesniewski, Donnellan, & Robins, 2003; Hitlin, Brown, & Elder, 2006).

PhotoAlto/Getty Images

Adolescents' sense of who they are takes their own and others' views into account.

SELF-ESTEEM: ASKING "HOW DO I LIKE MYSELF?" *Knowing* yourself and *liking* yourself are two different things. Although adolescents become increasingly accurate in understanding who they are (their self–concept), this knowledge does not guarantee that they like themselves (their self-esteem) any better. In fact, their increasing accuracy in understanding themselves permits them to see themselves fully—warts and all. It's what they do with these perceptions that leads them to develop a sense of their self-esteem.

The same cognitive sophistication that allows adolescents to differentiate various aspects of the self also leads them to evaluate those aspects in different ways (Chan, 1997; J. Cohen, 1999). For instance, an adolescent may have high self-esteem in terms of academic performance but lower self-esteem in terms of relationships with others. Or it may be just the opposite, as articulated by this adolescent:

> Do I *like* myself? What a question! Well, let's see. I like some of what I am, like I'm a good listener and a good friend, but I don't like other things, like my jealous side. I'm no genius at schoolwork—my parents would like me to do better—but if you're too smart you don't have a lot of friends. I'm pretty good at sports, especially swimming. But the best thing about me is that I'm a good friend, you know, loyal. I'm pretty well known for that, and pretty popular.

GENDER DIFFERENCES IN SELF-ESTEEM. What determines an adolescent's self-esteem? Several factors make a difference. One is gender: Particularly during early adolescence, girls' self-esteem tends to be lower and more vulnerable than boys' self-esteem. One reason for this difference is that, compared to boys, girls tend to be more concerned about physical appearance and social success—in addition to academic achievement. Although boys are also concerned about these things, their attitudes are often more casual. In addition, societal messages suggesting that female academic achievement is a roadblock to social success can put girls in a difficult bind: If they do well academically, they jeopardize their social success. No wonder that the self-esteem of adolescent girls is more fragile than that of boys (Ayres & Leaper, 2013; Jenkins & Demaray, 2015; Ra & Cho, 2017).

Although generally self-esteem is higher in adolescent boys than in girls, boys do have vulnerabilities of their own. For example, society's stereotypical gender expectations may lead boys to feel that they should be confident, tough, and fearless all the time. Boys facing difficulties, such as not making a sports team or being rejected by a girl they wanted to date, are likely to feel not only miserable about the defeat they face but also incompetent because they don't measure up to the stereotype (Pollack, Shuster, & Trelease, 2001; Witt, Donnellan, & Trzesniewski, 2011; Levant et al., 2016).

SOCIOECONOMIC STATUS AND RACE DIFFERENCES IN SELF-ESTEEM. Socioeconomic status (SES) and race also influence self-esteem. Adolescents of higher SES generally have higher self-esteem than those of lower SES, particularly during middle and later adolescence. It may be that the social status factors that especially enhance one's standing and self-esteem—such as having more expensive clothes or a car—become more conspicuous in the later periods of adolescence (Dai et al., 2012; Cuperman, Robinson, & Ickes, 2014).

Race and ethnicity also play a role in self-esteem, but their impact has declined as prejudicial treatment of minorities has eased. Early studies found that minority status led to lower self-esteem. African Americans and Hispanics, researchers explained, had lower self-esteem than Caucasians because prejudicial attitudes in society made them feel disliked and rejected, and this feeling was incorporated into their self-concepts. More recent research paints a different picture. Most findings suggest that African American adolescents differ little from whites in their levels of self-esteem (Harter, 1990). Why should this be? One explanation is that social movements within the African American community bolster racial pride help support African American adolescents. Research finds

Daniel M Ernst/Shutterstock

A strong sense of racial identity during adolescence is tied to higher levels of self-esteem.

that a stronger sense of racial identity is related to a higher level of self-esteem in African Americans and Hispanics (Verkuyten, 2003; Phinney, 2008; Kogan et al., 2014).

Another reason for overall similarity in self-esteem levels between adolescents of different racial groups is that teenagers in general focus their preferences and priorities on those aspects of their lives at which they excel. Consequently, African American youths may concentrate on the things that they find most satisfying and gain self-esteem from being successful at them (Yang & Blodgett, 2000; Phinney, 2005; Aoyagi, Santos, & Updegraff, 2017).

Finally, self-esteem may be influenced not by race alone but by a complex combination of factors. For instance, some developmentalists have considered race and gender simultaneously, coining the term *ethgender* to refer to the joint influence of race and gender. One study that simultaneously took both race and gender into account found that African American and Hispanic males had the highest levels of self-esteem, while Asian and Native American females had the lowest levels (Saunders, Davis, & Williams, 2004; Biro et al., 2006; Park et al., 2012).

Identity Formation: Change or Crisis?

LO 12.2 Summarize how Erikson explains identity formation during adolescence.

According to Erik Erikson, whose theory we last discussed in Chapter 10, the search for identity inevitably leads some adolescents into substantial psychological turmoil as they encounter the adolescent identity crisis (Erikson, 1963). Erikson's theory regarding this stage, which is summarized with his other stages in Table 12-1, suggests that teenagers try to figure out what is unique and distinctive about themselves—something they are able to do with increasing sophistication because of the cognitive gains that occur during adolescence.

Erikson argues that adolescents strive to discover their particular strengths and weaknesses and the roles they can best play in their future lives. This discovery process often involves "trying on" different roles or choices to see if they fit an adolescents' capabilities and views about themselves. Through this process, adolescents seek to understand who they are by narrowing and making choices about their personal, occupational, sexual, and political commitments. Erikson calls this the **identity-versus-identity-confusion stage**.

identity-versus-identity-confusion stage
the period during which teenagers seek to determine what is unique and distinctive about themselves

In Erikson's view, adolescents who stumble in their efforts to find a suitable identity may go off course in several ways. They may adopt socially unacceptable

Table 12-1 A Summary of Erikson's Stages

Stage	Approximate Age	Positive Outcomes	Negative Outcomes
1. Trust versus mistrust	Birth–1.5 years	Feelings of trust from others' support	Fear and concern regarding others
2. Autonomy versus shame and doubt	1.5–3 years	Self-sufficiency if exploration is encouraged	Doubts about self; lack of independence
3. Initiative versus guilt	3–6 years	Discovery of ways to initiate actions	Guilt from actions and thoughts
4. Industry versus inferiority	6–12 years	Development of sense of competence	Feelings of inferiority; little sense of mastery
5. Identity versus identity confusion	Adolescence	Awareness of uniqueness of self; knowledge of roles	Inability to identify appropriate roles in life
6. Intimacy versus isolation	Early adulthood	Development of loving, sexual relationships and close friendships	Fear of relationships with others
7. Generativity versus stagnation	Middle adulthood	Sense of contribution to continuity of life	Trivialization of one's activities
8. Ego-integrity versus despair	Late adulthood	Sense of unity in life's accomplishments	Regret over lost opportunities of life

(**Source:** Erikson, 1963.)

roles as a way of expressing what they do *not* want to be, or they may have difficulty forming and maintaining long-lasting close personal relationships. In general, their sense of self becomes "diffuse," failing to organize around a central, unified core identity.

In contrast, those who are successful in forging an appropriate identity set a course that provides a foundation for future psychosocial development. They learn their unique capabilities and believe in them, and they develop an accurate sense of who they are. They are prepared to set out on a path that takes full advantage of what their unique strengths permit them to do (Allison & Schultz, 2001).

Lawrence Manning/Getty Images

During the identity-versus-identity-confusion stage, U.S. teenagers seek to understand who they are by narrowing and making choices about their personal, occupational, sexual, and political commitments. Can this stage be applied to teenagers in other cultures? Why or why not?

SOCIETAL PRESSURES AND RELIANCE ON FRIENDS AND PEERS. As if teenagers' self-generated identity issues were not difficult enough, societal pressures are also high during the identity-versus-identity-confusion stage, as any student knows who has been repeatedly asked by parents and friends "What's your major?" and "What are you going to do when you graduate?" Adolescents feel pressure to decide whether their post–high school plans include work or college and, if they choose work, which occupational track to follow. Up to this point in their development, their educational lives have been pretty much programmed by U.S. society, which lays out a universal educational track. However, the track ends at high school, and consequently, adolescents face difficult choices about which of several possible future paths they will follow.

During this period, adolescents increasingly rely on their friends and peers as sources of information. At the same time, their dependence on adults declines. As we discuss later in the chapter, this increasing dependence on the peer group enables adolescents to forge close relationships. Comparing themselves to others helps them clarify their own identities.

This reliance on peers to help adolescents define their identities and learn to form relationships is the link between this stage of psychosocial development and the next stage Erikson proposed, known as *intimacy versus isolation*. It also relates to the subject of gender differences in identity formation. When Erikson developed his theory, he suggested that males and females move through the identity-versus-identity-confusion period differently. He argued that males are more likely to proceed through the social development stages in the order they are shown in Table 12-1, developing a stable identity before committing to an intimate relationship with another person. In contrast, he suggested that females reverse the order, seeking intimate relationships and then defining their identities through these relationships. These ideas largely reflect the social conditions at the time Erikson was writing, when women were less likely to go to college or establish their own careers and instead often married early. Today, however, the experiences of boys and girls seem relatively similar during the identity-versus-identity-confusion period.

PSYCHOLOGICAL MORATORIUM. Because of the pressures of the identity-versus-identity-confusion period, Erikson suggested that many adolescents pursue a "psychological moratorium." The *psychological moratorium* is a period during which adolescents take time off from the upcoming responsibilities of adulthood and explore various roles and possibilities. For example, many college students take a semester or year off to travel, work, or find some other way to examine their priorities.

However, many adolescents cannot, for practical reasons, pursue a psychological moratorium involving a relatively leisurely exploration of various identities. Some adolescents, for economic reasons, must work part time after school and then take jobs immediately after graduation from high school. As a result, they have little time to experiment with identities and engage in a psychological moratorium. Does this mean such adolescents will be psychologically damaged in some way? Probably not. The satisfaction that can come from successfully holding a part-time job while attending school may be a sufficient psychological reward to outweigh the inability to try out various roles.

LIMITATIONS OF ERIKSON'S THEORY. One criticism that has been raised regarding Erikson's theory is that he uses male identity development as the standard against which to compare female identity. To critics, Erikson's view is based on male-oriented concepts of individuality and competitiveness. In an alternative conception, psychologist Carol Gilligan has suggested that women develop identity through the establishment of relationships. In this view, a key component of a woman's identity is the building of caring networks between herself and others (Gilligan, 2004; Kroger, 2006).

Marcia's Approach to Identity Development: Updating Erikson

LO 12.3 Explain Marcia's categories of adolescent identity.

Using Erikson's theory as a springboard, psychologist James Marcia suggests that identity can be seen in terms of which of two characteristics—crisis or commitment—is present or absent. *Crisis* is a period of identity development in which an adolescent consciously chooses between various alternatives and makes decisions. *Commitment* is psychological investment in a course of action or an ideology. We can see the difference between an adolescent who careens from one activity to another, with nothing lasting more than a few weeks, compared with one who becomes totally absorbed in volunteer work at a homeless shelter, for example (Peterson, Marcia, & Carpendale, 2004; Marcia, 2007; Crocetti, 2017).

After conducting lengthy interviews with adolescents, Marcia proposed four categories of adolescent identity (see Table 12-2).

identity achievement
the status of adolescents who commit to a particular identity following a period of crisis during which they consider various alternatives

identity foreclosure
the status of adolescents who prematurely commit to an identity without adequately exploring alternatives

moratorium
the status of adolescents who may have explored various identity alternatives to some degree, but have not yet committed themselves

1. **Identity achievement**. Teenagers within this identity status have successfully explored and thought through who they are and what they want to do. Following a period of crisis during which they considered various alternatives, these adolescents have committed to a particular identity. Teens who have reached this identity status tend to be the most psychologically healthy, higher in achievement motivation and moral reasoning than adolescents of any other status.
2. **Identity foreclosure**. These are adolescents who have committed to an identity but who did not do it by passing through a period of crisis in which they explored alternatives. Instead, they accepted others' decisions about what was best for them. Typical adolescents in this category are a son who enters the family business because it is expected of him and a daughter who decides to become a physician simply because her mother is one. Although foreclosers are not necessarily unhappy, they tend to have what can be called "rigid strength": Happy and self-satisfied, they also have a high need for social approval and tend to be authoritarian.
3. **Moratorium**. Although adolescents in the moratorium category have explored various alternatives to some degree, they have not yet committed themselves. As a

Table 12-2 Marcia's Four Categories of Adolescent Development

CRISIS/EXPLORATION	COMMITMENT: Present	COMMITMENT: Absent
PRESENT	**Identity achievement** "I enjoyed working at an advertising company the last two summers, so I plan to go into advertising."	**Moratorium** "I'm taking a job at my mom's bookstore until I figure out what I really want to do."
ABSENT	**Identity foreclosure** "My dad says I'm good with kids and would be a good teacher, so I guess that's what I'll do."	**Identity diffusion** "Frankly, I have no idea what I'm going to do."

(**Source:** Based on Marcia, 1980.)

consequence, Marcia suggests, they show relatively high anxiety and experience psychological conflict. However, they are often lively and appealing, seeking intimacy with others. Adolescents of this status typically settle on an identity but only after something of a struggle.

4. **Identity diffusion.** Adolescents in this category neither explore nor commit to considering various alternatives. They tend to be flighty, shifting from one thing to the next. While they may seem carefree, according to Marcia, their lack of commitment impairs their ability to form close relationships. In fact, they are often socially withdrawn.

identity diffusion
the status of adolescents who consider various identity alternatives, but never commit to one or never even consider identity options in any conscious way

It is important to note that adolescents are not necessarily stuck in one of the four categories. Some move back and forth between moratorium and identity achievement in what has been called a "MAMA" cycle (moratorium—identity achievement—moratorium—identity achievement). For instance, even though a forecloser may have settled on a career path during early adolescence with little active decision making, he or she may reassess the choice later and move into another category. For some individuals, then, identity formation may take place beyond the period of adolescence. However, identity gels in the late teens and early 20s for most people (Al-Owidha, Green, & Kroger, 2009; Duriez et al., 2012; Mrazek, Harada, & Chiao, 2014).

From *a social worker's* perspective

Do you believe that all four of Marcia's identity statuses can lead to reassessment and different choices later in life? Are there stages in Marcia's theory of development that may be more difficult to achieve for adolescents who live in poverty? Why?

In some ways, Marcia's identity status perspective foreshadows what other researchers have called emerging adulthood. **Emerging adulthood** is the period beginning in the late teenage years and extending into the mid-20s. It is a transitional stage between adolescence and adulthood that spans the third decade of life (Arnett, 2011, 2016).

Emerging adulthood
the period beginning in the late teenage years and extending into the mid-20s

As we will discuss in greater detail when we consider early adulthood social and personality development, emerging adulthood is a period in which teenagers have left adolescence, although brain growth continues and neural circuits become more complex. But it is typically a period of uncertainty, in which post-adolescents are working to determine who they are and their path forward (Verschueren et al., 2017).

Religion and Spirituality

LO 12.4 Describe the role religion and spirituality play in identity formation in adolescence.

Ever wonder why God made mosquitos? How about why God gave Adam and Eve the ability to rebel if He knew how much of a mess it would cause? Can someone be saved and later lose their salvation? Do pets go to Heaven?

As exemplified in this blog post, questions of religion and spirituality begin to be asked during adolescence. Religion is important to many people because it offers a formal means of satisfying spirituality needs. *Spirituality* is a sense of attachment to some higher power, such as God, nature, or something sacred. Although spirituality needs are typically tied to religious beliefs, they may be independent. Many people who consider themselves to be spiritual individuals do not participate in formal religious practices or are not affiliated with any particular religion.

Because their cognitive abilities increase during adolescence, teenagers are able to think more abstractly about religious matters. Furthermore, as they grapple with general questions of identity, they may question their religious identity. After having accepted their religious identity in an unquestioning manner during childhood, adolescents may view religion more critically and seek to distance themselves from formal religion. In other cases, they may be drawn more closely to their religious affiliation because it offers answers to such abstract questions as "Why am I here on this earth?" and "What is the meaning of life?" Religion provides a way of viewing the world and universe as having intentional design—a place that was created by something or someone (Yonker, Schnabelrauch, & DeHaan, 2012; Levenson, Aldwin, & Igarashi, 2013; Longo, Bray, & Kim-Spoon, 2017).

According to theologian James Fowler, our understanding and practice of faith and spirituality proceeds through a series of stages that extend throughout the lifetime. During childhood, individuals hold a fairly literal view of God and biblical figures. For example, children may think of God as living at the top of the earth and being able to see what everyone is doing (Fowler & Dell, 2006; Boyatzis, 2013).

In adolescence, the view of spirituality becomes more abstract. As they build their identity, adolescents typically develop a core set of beliefs and values. However, in many cases, adolescents do not consider their views either deeply or systematically, and it is not until later that they become more reflective.

As they leave adolescence, people typically move into the *individuative-reflective stage* of faith, in which they reflect on their beliefs and values. They understand that their views are one of many, and that multiple views of God are possible. Ultimately, the final stage of faith development is the *conjunctive stage*, in which individuals develop a broad, inclusive view of religion and all humanity. They see humanity as a whole, and they may work to promote a common good. In this stage, they may move beyond formal religion and hold a unified view of people across the globe.

Identity, Race, and Ethnicity

LO 12.5 Discuss the challenges ethnic and minority groups face in identity formation in adolescence.

Although the path to forming an identity is often difficult for adolescents, it presents a particular challenge for members of racial and ethnic groups that have traditionally been discriminated against. Society's contradictory values are one part of the problem. On the one hand, adolescents are told that society should be color-blind, that race and ethnic background should not matter in terms of opportunities and achievement, and that if they do achieve, society will accept them. Based on a traditional *cultural assimilation model*, this view holds that individual cultural identities should be assimilated into a unified culture in the United States—the proverbial melting-pot model.

The *pluralistic society model* suggests that U.S. society is made up of diverse, coequal cultural groups that should preserve their individual cultural features. The pluralistic society model grew in part from the belief that the cultural assimilation model denigrates the cultural heritage of minorities and lowers their self-esteem.

According to this view, then, racial and ethnic factors become a central part of adolescents' identity and are not submerged in an attempt to assimilate into the majority culture. From this perspective, identity development includes development of *racial and ethnic identity*—the sense of membership in a racial or ethnic group and the feelings that are associated with that membership. It includes a sense of commitment and ties with a particular racial or ethnic group (Phinney, 2008; Gfellner & Armstrong, 2013; Umaña-Taylor et al., 2014; Wang, Douglass & Yip, 2017).

There is a middle ground. Minority group members can form a *bicultural identity* in which they draw from their own cultural identity while integrating themselves into the dominant culture. This view suggests that an individual can live as a member of two cultures, with two cultural identities, without having to choose one over the other (LaFromboise, Coleman, & Gerton, 1993; Shi & Lu, 2007).

Figure 12-1 Bicultural Identity in the United States

The number of Americans who identified themselves as belonging to more than one race grew substantially between 2000 and 2010. Almost 10 percent report belonging to three or more races.

(**Source:** U.S. Bureau of the Census, 2011.)

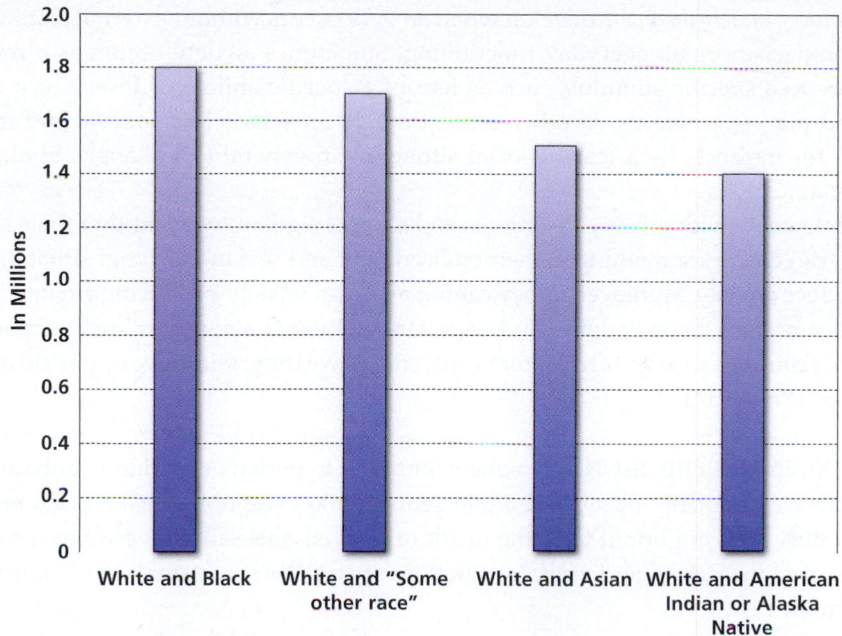

The choice of a bicultural identity is increasingly common. In fact, the number of people who identify themselves as belonging to more than one race is considerable, increasing 134 percent from 2000 to 2010 (see Figure 12-1; U.S. Census Bureau, 2011).

The process of identity formation is not simple for anyone and may be doubly difficult for minority group members. Racial and ethnic identity takes time to form, and for some individuals it may occur over a prolonged period. Still, the ultimate result can be the formation of a rich, multifaceted identity (Quintana, 2007; Jensen, 2008; Klimstra et al., 2012; Yoon et al., 2017).

Depression and Suicide: Psychological Difficulties in Adolescence

LO 12.6 Identify the dangers adolescents face as they deal with the stresses of their age.

As she entered ninth grade, it struck Leanne Taunton that she was stuck without hope inside a dreadful world. "It was like the air was a big weight pressing in on me from all sides." A friend listened to her sympathetically and invited her to her basement. "We started doing drugs, using whatever was in the medicine cabinet. At first it seemed to offer some relief, but in the end we both had to go home again, if you know what I mean."

One day Leanne grabbed her father's razor, filled up the tub, and slashed her wrists. At age 14, she had had enough.

Although by far the majority of teenagers weather the search for identity—as well as the other challenges presented by the period—without major psychological difficulties, some find adolescence particularly stressful. Some, in fact, develop severe psychological problems. Three of the most serious are adolescent anxiety, depression, and suicide.

ADOLESCENT ANXIETY. All adolescents occasionally experience anxiety, a feeling of apprehension or tension in reaction to stressful situations; it is a totally normal reaction to stress.

In some cases, though, adolescents develop anxiety disorders, which are the most prevalent psychological disorders in the age group, striking around 8 percent of the population. *Anxiety disorders* develop when anxiety occurs without external justification, and it impacts normal, everyday functioning. Sometimes anxiety occurs as a result of exposure to a specific stimulus, such as fear of a specific animal or insect, or a fear of crowded places or heights. In other cases, though, anxiety is less specific and may be caused, for instance, by a fear of social situations in general (Merikangas et al., 2009; Stopa et al., 2013).

Adolescents with anxiety disorders can be hypervigilant, worried that their anxiety will be triggered by something in their environment and seeking to avoid situations that can produce anxiety. Moreover, if they cannot avoid an anxiety-producing circumstances, they may become overwhelmed and experience physical symptoms such as panic attacks that produce a range of symptoms, including sweating, faintness, or gastric distress (Carleton et al., 2014).

ADOLESCENT DEPRESSION. No one is immune to periods of sadness, unhappiness, and feeling emotionally upset, and adolescents are no exception. The end of a relationship, failure at an important task, the death of a loved one—all may produce profound feelings of sadness, loss, and grief. In situations such as these, depression is a fairly typical reaction.

How common are feelings of depression in adolescence? More than a quarter of adolescents report feeling so sad or hopeless for 2 or more weeks in a row that they stop doing their normal activities. Almost two-thirds of teenagers say they have experienced such feelings at one time or another. However, only a small minority of adolescents—some 3 percent—experience *major depressive disorder*, a full-blown psychological disorder in which depression is severe and lingers for long periods (Grunbaum et al., 2001; Galambos, Leadbeater, & Barker, 2004).

Gender, ethnic, and racial differences are also found in depression rates. As is the case among adults, adolescent girls, on average, experience depression more often than boys. Some studies have found that African American adolescents have higher rates of depression than white adolescents, although not all research supports this conclusion. Native Americans, too, have higher rates of depression (Zahn-Waxler, Shirtcliff, & Marceau, 2008; Sanchez, Lambert, & Ialongo, 2012; English, Lambert & Ialongo, 2014; Blom et al., 2016).

zea_lenanet/Fotolia

Between 25 and 40 percent of girls, and 20 to 35 percent of boys, experience occasional episodes of depression during adolescence, although the incidence of major depression is far lower.

In cases of severe, long-term depression, biological factors are often involved. Although some adolescents seem to be genetically predisposed to experience depression, environmental and social factors relating to the extraordinary changes in the social lives of adolescents are also important influences. An adolescent who experiences the death of a loved one, for example, or one who grows up with an alcoholic or a depressed parent is at a higher risk of depression. In addition, being unpopular, having few close friends, and experiencing rejection are associated with adolescent depression (Eley, Liang, & Plomin, 2004; Zalsman et al., 2006; Herberman Mash et al., 2014).

One of the most puzzling questions about depression is why its incidence is higher among girls than boys. There is little evidence that it is linked to hormone differences or a particular gene. Instead, some psychologists speculate that stress is more pronounced for girls than for boys in adolescence due to the many, sometimes conflicting, demands of the traditional female gender role. Recall, for instance, the situation of the adolescent girl who was quoted in our discussion of self-esteem. She worries not only about doing well in school but also about being popular. If she feels that academic success undermines her popularity, she is placed in a bind that can leave her feeling helpless. Added to this is that traditional gender roles still give higher status to men than to women (Hyde, Mezulis, & Abramson, 2008; Chaplin, Gillham, & Seligman, 2009; Castelao & Kröner-Herwig, 2013).

Girls' generally higher levels of depression during adolescence may also reflect gender differences in ways of coping with stress rather than gender differences in mood. Girls may be more apt than boys to react to stress by turning inward, thereby experiencing a sense of helplessness and hopelessness. In contrast, boys more often react by externalizing the stress and acting more impulsively or aggressively, or by turning to drugs and alcohol (Wisdom & Agnor, 2007; Wu et al., 2007; Brown et al., 2012; Anyan & Hjemdal, 2016).

Lee Young Ho/Sipa USA/Newscom

The rate of adolescent suicide has tripled in the last 30 years. These students mourn following the suicide of a classmate.

ADOLESCENT SUICIDE. The rate of adolescent suicide in the United States has tripled in the past 30 years. Overall, one teenage suicide occurs every 90 minutes, for an annual rate of 12.2 suicides per 100,000 adolescents. Moreover, the reported rate may actually understate the true number of suicides; parents and medical personnel are often reluctant to report a death as suicide, preferring to label it an accident (Joe & Marcus, 2003; Conner & Goldston, 2007; Healthychildren.org, 2016).

Even with underreporting, suicide is the third most common cause of death in the 15- to 24-year-old age group, after accidents and homicide. It is important to keep in mind, however, that although the suicide rate has risen more for adolescents than for other age groups, the highest rate of suicide is found in the period of late adulthood.

In adolescence, the rate of suicide is higher for boys than girls, although girls *attempt* suicide more frequently. Suicide attempts among males are more likely to result in death because of the methods they use: Boys tend to use more violent means, such as guns, while girls are more apt to choose a drug overdose. Some estimates suggest that there are as many as 200 attempted suicides by both sexes for every successful one (Dervic et al., 2006; Pompili et al., 2009; Payá-González et al., 2015).

The reasons behind the increase in adolescent suicide over past decades are unclear. The most obvious explanation is that the stress experienced by teenagers has increased, leading those who are most vulnerable to be more likely to commit suicide. But why should stress have increased only for adolescents given that the suicide rate for other segments of the population has remained fairly stable over the same time period?

Although we are not yet sure why adolescent suicide has increased, it is clear that certain factors heighten the risk of suicide. One factor is depression. Depressed teenagers who are experiencing a profound sense of hopelessness are at greater risk of committing suicide (although most depressed individuals do not commit suicide). In addition, social inhibition, perfectionism, and a high level of stress and anxiety are related to a greater risk of suicide. The easy availability of guns—which are more prevalent in the United States than in other industrialized nations—also contributes to the suicide rate (Wright, Wintemute, & Claire, 2008; Hetrick et al., 2012).

In addition to depression, some cases of suicide are associated with family conflicts and relationship or school difficulties. Others stem from a history of abuse and neglect. The rate of suicide among drug and alcohol abusers is also relatively high. As can be seen in Figure 12-2, teens who called in to a hotline because they were thinking of killing

Figure 12-2 Adolescent Difficulties

Family, peer relationships, and self-esteem problems were most often mentioned by adolescents contemplating suicide, according to a review of phone calls to a telephone help line.

(**Source:** Based on Boehm & Campbell, 1995.)

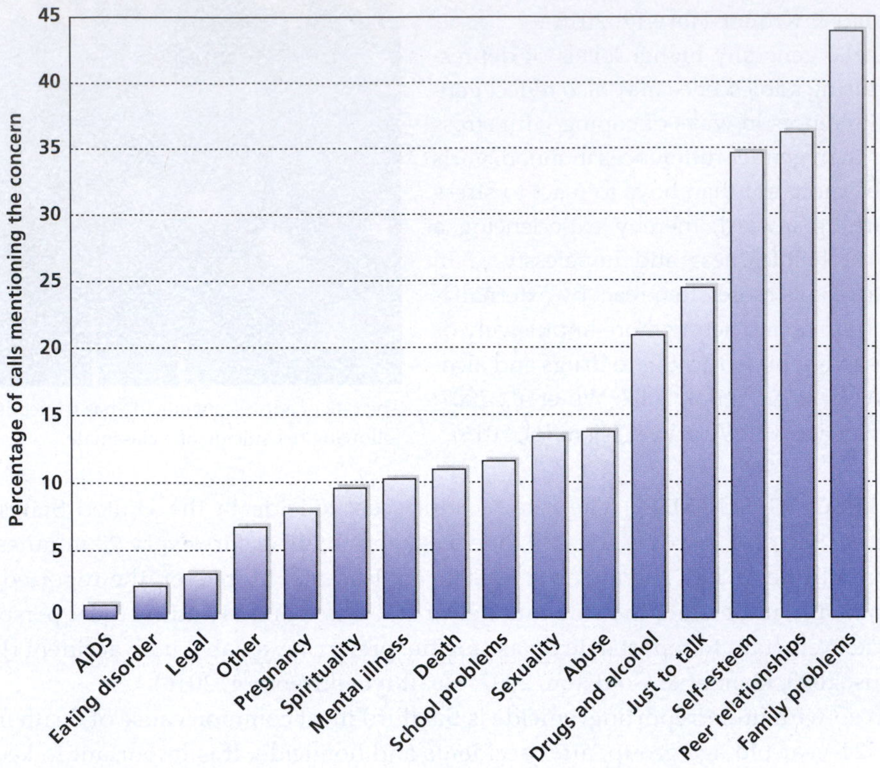

themselves mentioned several other factors as well (Bergen, Martin, & Richardson, 2003; Wilcox, Conner, & Caine, 2004; Jacobson et al., 2013).

Some suicides appear to be caused by exposure to the suicide of others. In *cluster suicide*, one suicide leads to attempts by others to kill themselves. For instance, some high schools have experienced a series of suicides following a well-publicized case. As a result, many schools have established crisis intervention teams to counsel students when a student commits suicide (Insel & Gould, 2008; Daniel & Goldston, 2009; Abrutyn & Mueller, 2014).

Several warning signs should sound an alarm regarding the possibility of suicide, including the following:

- Direct or indirect talk about suicide, such as "I wish I were dead" or "You won't have me to worry about any longer"
- School difficulties, such as missed classes or a decline in grades
- Making arrangements as if preparing for a long trip, such as giving away prized possessions or arranging for the care of a pet
- Writing a will
- Loss of appetite or excessive eating
- General depression, including a change in sleeping patterns, slowness and lethargy, and uncommunicativeness
- Dramatic changes in behavior, such as a shy person suddenly acting outgoing
- Preoccupation with death in music, art, or literature

Development in Your Life

Adolescent Suicide: How to Help

If you suspect that an adolescent, or anyone else for that matter, is contemplating suicide, don't stand idly by. Act! Here are several suggestions:

- Talk to the person, listen without judging, and give the person an understanding forum in which to try to talk things through.
- Talk specifically about suicidal thoughts, asking such questions as: Does the person have a plan? Has he or she bought a gun? Where is it? Has he or she stockpiled pills? Where are they? The Public Health Service notes that "contrary to popular belief, such candor will not give a person dangerous ideas or encourage a suicidal act."
- Evaluate the situation, trying to distinguish between general upset and more serious danger, as when suicide plans *have* been made. If the crisis is acute, *do not leave the person alone.*
- Be supportive, let the person know you care, and try to break down his or her feelings of isolation.
- Take charge of finding help, without concern about invading the person's privacy. Do not try to handle the problem alone; get professional help immediately.
- Make the environment safe, removing from the premises (not just hiding) weapons such as guns, razors, scissors, medication, and other potentially dangerous household items.
- Do not keep suicide talk or threats secret; these are calls for help and call for immediate action.
- Do not challenge, dare, or use verbal shock treatment on suicidal persons in an effort to make them realize the errors in their thinking. These can have tragic effects.
- Make a contract with the person, getting a promise or commitment, preferably in writing, not to make a suicide attempt until you have talked further.
- Don't be overly reassured by a sudden improvement of mood. Such seemingly quick recoveries sometimes reflect the relief of finally deciding to commit suicide or the temporary release of talking to someone, but most likely the underlying problems have not been resolved.

For immediate help with a suicide-related problem, call (800) 273-8255 (the National Suicide Prevention Lifeline) or (800) 621-4000 (the National Runaway Switchboard). Both hotlines are staffed with trained counselors. You can also contact the Lifeline Crisis chat line at http://chat.suicidepreventionlifeline.org/GetHelp/LifelineChat.aspx.

Module 12.1 Review

LO 12.1 Describe how self-concept and self-esteem develop during adolescence.

Self-concept during adolescence grows more differentiated as the view of the self becomes more organized, broader, and more abstract, and takes account of the views of others. Self-esteem, too, grows increasingly differentiated as the adolescent develops the ability to place different values on different aspects of the self.

LO 12.2 Summarize how Erikson explains identity formation during adolescence.

Erikson's identity-versus-identity-confusion stage focuses on the adolescent's struggle to determine an identity and a role in society. Those who are successful in forming an identity prepare themselves for future development.

LO 12.3 Explain Marcia's categories of adolescent identity.

Marcia's four categories of adolescent identity—identity achievement, identity foreclosure, moratorium, and identity diffusion—are based on the presence or absence of crisis and commitment. The most psychologically healthy adolescents are in the identity achievement category.

LO 12.4 Describe the role religion and spirituality play in identity formation in adolescence.

Increased cognitive abilities allow adolescents to think more abstractly about religious and spiritual matters. As they question their religious identity, they may draw a distinction between organized religion and a personal sense of spirituality.

LO 12.5 Discuss the challenges ethnic and minority groups face in identity formation in adolescence.

Ethnic and minority adolescents must navigate a course through two models of societal acceptance: the cultural assimilation model and the pluralistic society model. For these teenagers, identity development includes the development of a racial and ethnic identity. A third model—forming a bicultural identity—is available to them.

LO 12.6 Identify the dangers adolescents face as they deal with the stresses of their age.

One of the dangers that adolescents face is depression, which affects girls more than boys. Suicide is the third most common cause of death among 15- to 24-year-olds.

Journal Writing Prompt

Applying Lifespan Development: What are some consequences of the shift from reliance on adults to reliance on peers? Are there advantages? Dangers?

Relationships: Family and Friends

When 13-year-old Emma tells her father about her friend Nia's upcoming dance party, he says he'll pick her up at 1 a.m. Emma goes ballistic. "One a.m.!" she scoffs, "Dad, it's a SLEEPover! Everybody's getting picked up at noon the next day." Her father asks, "And when will the boys be going home?"

Emma looks at him with disbelief. "Noon the next day, same as everyone."

Her father sighs. "There is no way you are going to sleep over anywhere where there are boys."

Emma's disbelief is palpable. "But Dad," she explains impatiently, "Nia's mother will be there. Nothing's going to happen. Nobody's going to sleep anyway."

Speechless, Emma's father signals time out, resolving to talk to other parents about this strange new world he has somehow landed in.

The social world of adolescents is considerably wider than that of younger children. As adolescents' relationships with people outside the home grow increasingly important, their interactions with their families evolve and take on a new, and sometimes difficult, character (Collins, Gleason, & Sesma, 1997; Collins & Andrew, 2004).

Family Ties: Changing Relations with Relations

LO 12.7 Describe what family relationships are like during adolescence.

When Paco Lizzagara entered junior high school, his relationship with his parents changed drastically. What had been a good relationship had become tense by the middle of seventh grade. Paco felt his parents always seemed to be "on his case." Instead of giving him more freedom, which he felt he deserved at age 13, they actually seemed to be becoming more restrictive.

Paco's parents would probably see things differently. They would likely suggest that they were not the source of the tension in the household—Paco was. From their point of view, Paco, with whom they'd established what seemed to be a close, stable, loving relationship throughout much of his childhood, suddenly seemed transformed. They felt he was shutting them out of his life, and when he did speak with them, it was merely to criticize their politics, their dress, their preferences in TV shows. To his parents, Paco's behavior was upsetting and bewildering.

THE QUEST FOR AUTONOMY. Parents are sometimes angered, and even more frequently puzzled, by adolescents' conduct. Children who have previously accepted their parents' judgments, declarations, and guidelines begin to question—and sometimes rebel against—their parents' views of the world.

autonomy
independence and a sense of control over one's life

These clashes are caused in part by the shifting roles that both children and parents must deal with during adolescence. Adolescents increasingly seek **autonomy**, independence and a sense of control over their lives. Most parents intellectually realize that this shift is a normal part of adolescence, representing one of the primary developmental tasks of the period, and in many ways they welcome it as a sign of their children's growth. However, in many cases the day-to-day realities of adolescents' increasing autonomy may prove difficult for them to handle (Smetana, 1995). But understanding this growing independence intellectually and agreeing to allow a teen to attend a party when no parents will be present are two different things. To the adolescent, her parents' refusal indicates a lack of trust or confidence. To the parent, it's simple good sense: "I trust you," they may say. "It's everyone else who will be there that I worry about."

In most families, teenagers' autonomy grows gradually over the course of adolescence. For instance, one study of changes in adolescents' views of their parents found that increasing autonomy led them to perceive parents less in idealized terms and more as persons in their own right. For example, rather than seeing their parents as authoritarian disciplinarians mindlessly reminding them to do their homework, they may come to see their parents' emphasis on excelling in school as evidence of parental regrets about their own lack of education and a wish to see their children have more options in life. At the same time, adolescents come to depend more on themselves and to feel more like separate individuals (see Figure 12-3).

Figure 12-3 Changing Views of Parents

As adolescents become older, they come to perceive their parents in less idealized terms and more as individuals. **THINKING ABOUT THE DATA:** What effect is this likely to have on family relations?

(**Source:** Based on Steinberg & Silverberg, 1986.)

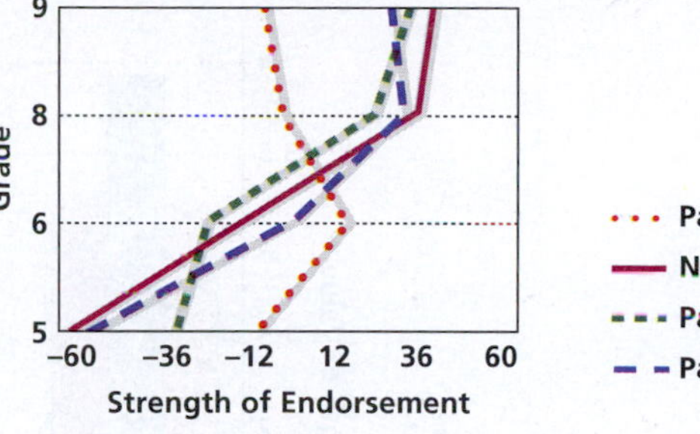

The increase in adolescent autonomy changes the relationship between parents and teenagers. At the start of adolescence, the relationship tends to be asymmetrical: Parents hold most of the power and influence over the relationship. By the end of adolescence, however, power and influence have become more balanced, and parents and children end up in a more symmetrical, or egalitarian, relationship. Power and influence are shared, although parents typically retain the upper hand (Goede, Branje, & Meeus, 2009; Inguglia et al., 2014).

CULTURE AND AUTONOMY. The degree of autonomy that is eventually achieved varies from one family and one child to the next. Cultural factors play an important role. In Western societies, which tend to value individualism, adolescents seek autonomy at a relatively early stage of adolescence. In contrast, Asian societies are collectivistic; they promote the idea that the well-being of the group is more important than that of the individual. In such societies, adolescents' aspirations to achieve autonomy are less pronounced (Supple et al., 2009; Perez-Brena, Updegraff, & Umaña-Taylor, 2012; Czerwińska-Jasiewicz, 2017).

Adolescents from different cultural backgrounds also vary in their feelings of obligation to their family. More than those from more individualistic societies, adolescent in more collectivistic cultures tend to feel greater obligation to their families, in terms of fulfilling their expectations about their duty to provide assistance, show respect, and support their families in the future. In collectivistic societies, the push for autonomy is less strong, and the timetable during which autonomy is expected to develop is slower (see Figure 12-4; Fuligni & Zhang, 2004; Leung, Pe-Pua, & Karnilowicz, 2006; Chan & Chan, 2013; Hou, Kim, & Wang, 2016).

For example, when asked at what age an adolescent would be expected to carry out certain behaviors (such as going to a concert with friends), adolescents and parents provide different answers depending on their cultural background. In comparison to Asian adolescents and parents, Caucasian adolescents and parents indicate an earlier timetable, anticipating greater autonomy at an earlier age (Feldman & Wood, 1994).

Does the more extended timetable for the development of autonomy in more collectivistic cultures have negative consequences for adolescents in those cultures? Apparently not. The more important factor is the degree of match between cultural expectations and developmental patterns. What probably matters most is how well the development of autonomy matches societal expectations, not the specific timetable of autonomy (Rothbaum et al., 2000; Zimmer-Gembeck & Collins, 2003; Updegraff et al., 2006).

In addition to cultural factors affecting autonomy, gender also plays a role. In general, male adolescents are permitted more autonomy at an earlier age than female adolescents. The encouragement of male autonomy is consistent with more general traditional male stereotypes, in which males are perceived as more independent and females, conversely, as more dependent on others. The more parents hold traditional stereotypical views of gender, the less likely they are to encourage their daughters' autonomy (Bumpus, Crouter, & McHale, 2001).

Figure 12-4 Family Obligations

Adolescents from Asian and Latin American groups feel a greater sense of respect and obligation toward their families than adolescents with European backgrounds.

(**Source:** Fuligni, Tseng, & Lam, 1999.)

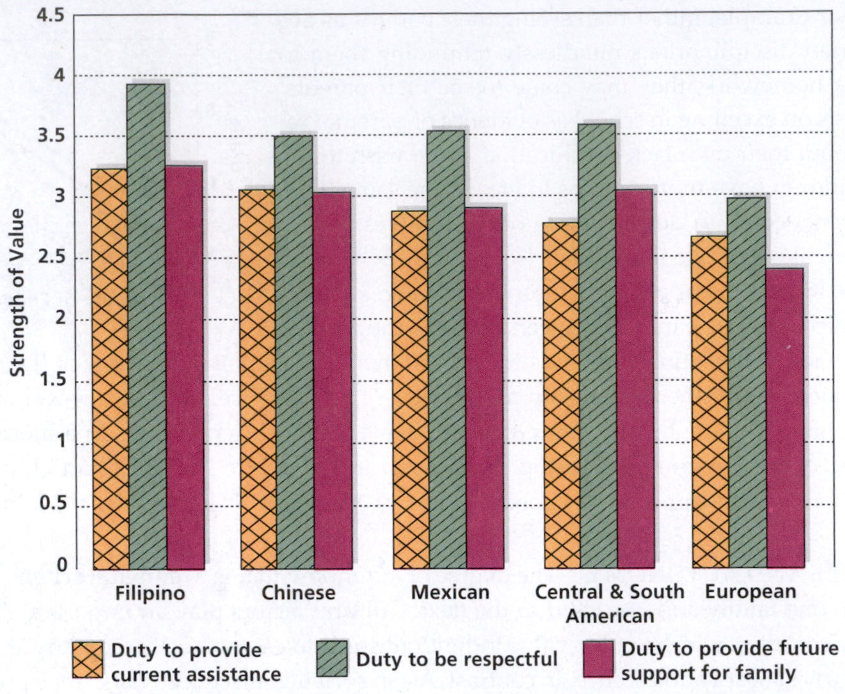

THE MYTH OF THE GENERATION GAP. Teen movies often depict adolescents and their parents with totally opposing points of view about the world. For example, the parent of an environmentalist teen might turn out to own a polluting factory. These exaggerations are often funny because we assume there is a kernel of truth in them, in that parents and teenagers often don't see things the same way. According to this argument, there is a **generation gap**, a deep divide between parents and children in attitudes, values, aspirations, and worldviews.

generation gap
a divide between parents and adolescents in attitudes, values, aspirations, and worldviews

The reality, however, is quite different. The generation gap, when it exists, is really quite narrow. Adolescents and their parents tend to see eye to eye in a variety of domains. Republican parents generally have Republican children; members of the Christian right have children who espouse similar views; parents who advocate for abortion rights have children who are pro-choice. On social, political, and religious issues, parents and adolescents tend to be in synch, and children's worries mirror those of their parents. Adolescents' concerns about society's problems (see Figure 12-5) are those with which most adults would probably agree (Knafo & Schwartz, 2003; Smetana, 2005; Grønhøj & Thøgersen, 2012).

As we have stated, most adolescents and their parents get along quite well. Despite their quest for autonomy and independence, most adolescents have deep love, affection, and respect for their parents—and parents feel the same way about their children. Although some parent–adolescent relationships are seriously troubled, the majority of relationships are more positive than negative and help adolescents avoid the kind of peer pressure we'll discuss later in the chapter (Resnick et al., 1997; Black, 2002; Coleman, 2014).

Even though adolescents spend decreasing amounts of time with their families in general, the amount of time they spend alone with each parent remains remarkably stable across adolescence (see Figure 12-6). In short, there is no evidence suggesting that family problems are worse during adolescence than at any other stage of development (Larson et al., 1996; Granic, Hollenstein, & Dishion, 2003).

Figure 12-5 What's the Problem?

Parents are most likely to agree with their adolescents' views of society's ills.

(**Source:** Based on PRIMEDIA/Roper National Youth Survey, 1999.)

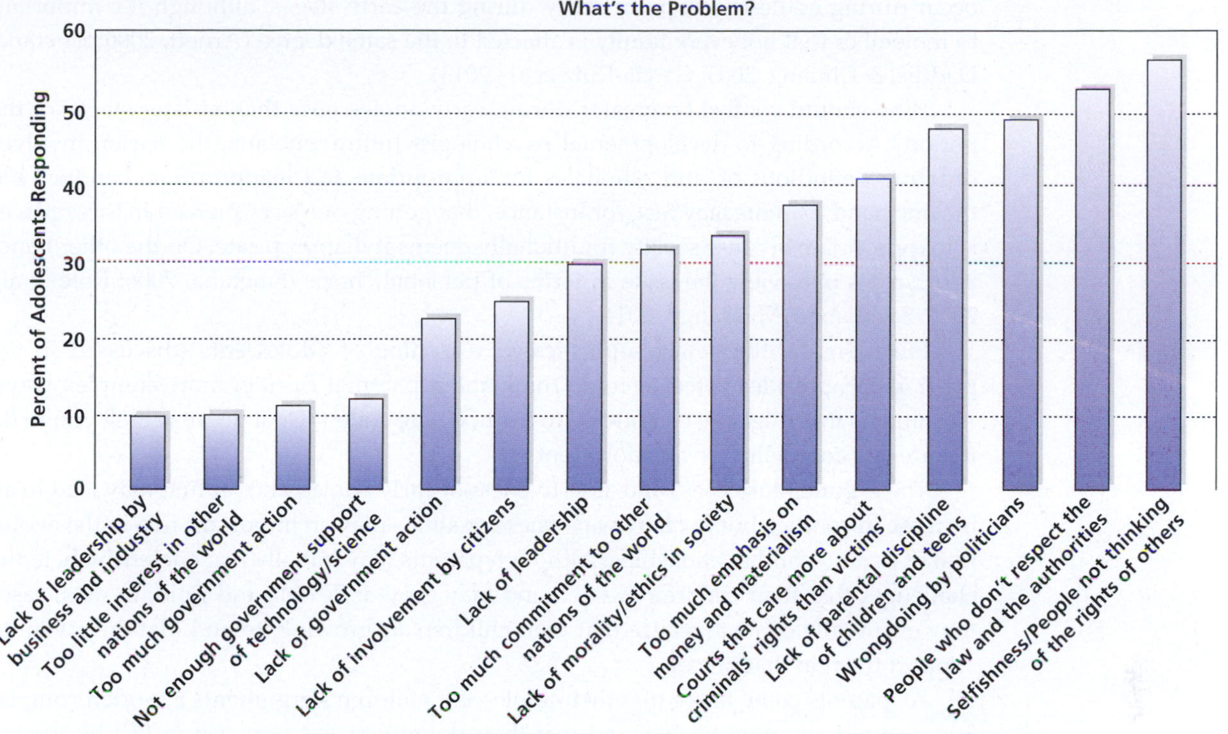

CONFLICTS WITH PARENTS. Of course, if most adolescents get along with their parents most of the time, that means some of the time they don't. No relationships are always sweetness and light. Parents and teens may hold similar attitudes about social and

Figure 12-6 Time Spent by Adolescents with Parents

Despite their quest for autonomy and independence, most adolescents have deep love, affection, and respect for their parents, and the amount of time they spend alone with each parent (the lower two segments) remains remarkably stable across adolescence.

(**Source:** Larson et al., 1996.)

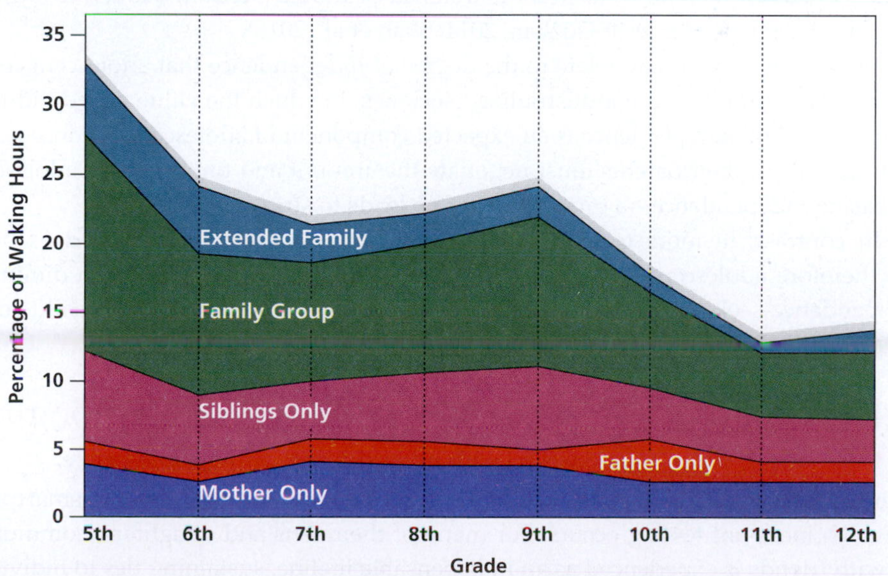

political issues, but they often hold different views on matters of personal taste, such as music preferences and styles of dress. Also, as we've seen, parents and children may run into disagreements when children seek to achieve autonomy and independence sooner than parents feel is right. Consequently, parent–child conflicts are more likely to occur during adolescence, particularly during the early stages, although it's important to remember that not every family is affected to the same degree (Arnett, 2000; Smetana, Daddis, & Chuang, 2003; García-Ruiz et al., 2013).

Why should conflict be greater during early adolescence than at later stages of the period? According to developmental psychologist Judith Smetana, the reason involves differing definitions of, and rationales for, appropriate and inappropriate conduct. On the one hand, parents may feel, for instance, that getting one's ear pierced in three places is inappropriate because society traditionally deems it inappropriate. On the other hand, adolescents may view the issue in terms of personal choice (Smetana, 2006; Rote et al., 2012; Sorkhabi & Middaugh, 2014).

Furthermore, the newly sophisticated reasoning of adolescents (discussed in the previous chapter) leads teenagers to think about parental rules in more complex ways. Arguments that might be convincing to a school-age child ("Do it because I tell you to do it") are less compelling to an adolescent.

The argumentativeness and assertiveness of early adolescence at first may lead to an increase in conflict, but in many ways these qualities play an important role in the evolution of parent–child relationships. Although parents may initially react defensively to the challenges that their children present, and may grow inflexible and rigid, in most cases they eventually come to realize that their children *are* growing up and that they want to support them in that process.

As parents come to see that their adolescent children's arguments are often compelling and not so unreasonable, and that their daughters and sons can in fact be trusted with more freedom, they become more yielding, allowing, and eventually perhaps even encouraging independence. As this process occurs during the middle stages of adolescence, the combativeness of early adolescence declines.

This pattern does not apply for all adolescents. Although the majority of teenagers maintain stable relations with their parents throughout adolescence, as many as 20 percent pass through a fairly rough time (Dmitrieva, Chen, & Greenberg, 2004).

CULTURAL DIFFERENCES IN PARENT–CHILD CONFLICTS DURING ADOLESCENCE. Although parent–child conflicts are found in every culture, there does seem to be less conflict between parents and their teenage children in "traditional," preindustrial cultures. Teens in such traditional cultures also experience fewer mood swings and instances of risky behavior than do teens in industrialized countries (Nelson, Badger, & Wu, 2004; Kapadia, 2008; Jensen & Dost-Gözkan, 2014; Shah et al., 2016).

Why? The answer may relate to the degree of independence that adolescents expect and adults permit. In more industrialized societies, in which the value of individualism is typically high, independence is an expected component of adolescence. Consequently, adolescents and their parents must negotiate the amount and timing of the adolescent's increasing independence—a process that often leads to strife.

In contrast, in more traditional societies, individualism is not valued as highly, and therefore adolescents are less inclined to seek out independence. With diminished independence-seeking on the part of adolescents, the result is less parent–child conflict (Dasen & Mishra, 2000).

Relationships with Peers: The Importance of Belonging

LO 12.8 Explain how relationships with peers change during adolescence.

In the eyes of many parents, the most fitting symbol of adolescence is the smartphone, on which incessant texting occurs. For many of their sons and daughters, communicating with friends is experienced as an indispensable lifeline, sustaining ties to individuals with whom they may have already spent many hours earlier in the day.

The seemingly compulsive need to communicate with friends demonstrates the role that peers play in adolescence. Continuing the trend that began in middle childhood, adolescents spend increasing amounts of time with their peers, and the importance of peer relationships grows as well. There is probably no period of life in which peer relationships are as important as they are in adolescence.

SOCIAL COMPARISON. Peers become more important in adolescence for a number of reasons. For one thing, they provide each other with the opportunity to compare and evaluate opinions, abilities, and even physical changes—a process called *social comparison.* Because the physical and cognitive changes of adolescence are so unique to this age group and so pronounced, especially during the early stages of puberty, adolescents turn increasingly to others who share, and consequently can shed light on, their own experiences (Li & Wright, 2013; Schaefer & Salafia, 2014; Tian, Yu & Huebner, 2017).

Parents are unable to provide social comparison. Not only are they well beyond the changes that adolescents undergo, but also adolescents' questioning of adult authority and their motivation to become more autonomous make parents, other family members, and adults in general inadequate and invalid sources of knowledge. Who is left to provide such information? Peers.

REFERENCE GROUPS. As we have said, adolescence is a time of experimentation, of trying out new identities, roles, and conduct. Peers provide information about what roles and behavior are most acceptable by serving as a reference group. **Reference groups** are groups of people with whom one compares oneself. Just as a professional ballplayer is likely to compare his performance against that of other professional players, so do teenagers compare themselves to those who are similar to them.

reference groups
groups of people with whom one compares oneself

Reference groups present a set of *norms*, or standards, against which adolescents can judge their abilities and social success. An adolescent need not even belong to a group for it to serve as a reference group. For instance, unpopular adolescents may find themselves belittled and rejected by members of a popular group, yet use that more popular group as a reference group (Berndt, 1999).

CLIQUES AND CROWDS: BELONGING TO A GROUP. One of the consequences of the increasing cognitive sophistication of adolescents is the ability to group others in more discriminating ways. Consequently, even if they do not belong to the group they use for reference purposes, adolescents typically are part of some identifiable group. Rather than defining people in concrete terms relating to what they do ("football players" or "musicians") as a younger school-age child might, adolescents use more abstract terms packed with greater subtleties ("jocks" or "skaters" or "stoners") (Brown, 2004).

Adolescents tend to belong to two types of groups: cliques and crowds. **Cliques** are groups of 2 to 12 people whose members have frequent social interactions with one another. In contrast, **crowds** are larger, comprising individuals who share particular characteristics but who may not interact with one another. For instance, "jocks" and "nerds" are representative of crowds found in many high schools.

cliques
groups of 2 to 12 people whose members have frequent social interactions with one another

crowds
larger groups than cliques, composed of individuals who share particular characteristics but who may not interact with one another

Membership in particular cliques and crowds is often determined by the degree of similarity with members of the group. One of the most important dimensions of similarity relates to substance use; adolescents tend to choose friends who use alcohol and other drugs to the same extent that they do. Their friends are also often similar in terms of their academic success, although this is not always true. For instance, during early adolescence, attraction to peers who are particularly well behaved seems to decrease, while, at the same time, those who behave more aggressively become more attractive (Kupersmidt & Dodge, 2004; Hutchinson & Rapee, 2007; Kiuru et al., 2009).

The emergence of distinct cliques and crowds during adolescence reflects in part the increased cognitive capabilities of adolescents. Group labels are abstractions, requiring teens to make judgments of people with whom they may interact only rarely and of whom they have little direct knowledge. It is not until mid-adolescence that teenagers are sufficiently

Yellow Dog Productions/Getty Images

The sex segregation of childhood continues during the early stages of adolescence. However, by the time of middle adolescence, this segregation decreases, and boys' and girls' cliques begin to converge.

sophisticated cognitively to make the subtle judgments that underlie distinctions between different cliques and crowds (Burgess & Rubin, 2000; Brown & Klute, 2003).

GENDER RELATIONS. As children enter adolescence from middle childhood, their groups of friends are composed almost universally of same-sex individuals. Boys hang out with boys; girls hang out with girls. Technically, this sex segregation is called the **sex cleavage**.

This situation changes as members of both sexes enter puberty. Boys and girls experience the hormonal surge that marks puberty and causes the maturation of the sex organs (see Chapter 11). At the same time, societal pressures suggest that the time is appropriate for romantic involvement. These developments lead to a change in the ways adolescents view the opposite sex. Whereas a 10-year-old is likely to see every member of the other sex as "annoying" and "a pain," heterosexual teenage boys and girls begin to regard each other with greater interest in terms of both personality and sexuality. (For gays and lesbians, pairing off holds other complexities, as we will discuss later when we consider adolescent dating.)

sex cleavage
sex segregation in which boys interact primarily with boys and girls primarily with girls

As they move into puberty, boys' and girls' cliques, which previously had moved along parallel but separate tracks, begin to converge. Adolescents begin to attend boy–girl dances or parties, although mostly the boys still spend their time with boys, and the girls with girls (Richards et al., 1998).

A little later, however, adolescents increasingly spend time with members of the other sex. New cliques emerge, composed of both males and females. Not everyone participates initially: Early on, the teenagers who are leaders of the same-sex cliques and who have the highest status lead the way. Eventually, however, most adolescents find themselves in cliques that include boys and girls.

Cliques and crowds undergo yet another transformation at the end of adolescence: They become less influential and may dissolve as a result of the increased pairing off that occurs. Furthermore, they are affected by diversity issues, as we discuss in the *Developmental Diversity and Your Life* feature.

Developmental Diversity and Your Life

Race Segregation: The Great Divide of Adolescence

When Robert Corker, a student at Tufts University, first stepped into the gym, he was immediately pulled into a pickup basketball game. "The guys thought I'd be good at basketball just because I'm tall and black. Actually, I stink at sports and quickly changed their minds. Fortunately, we all laughed about it later," Robert says.

* * *

When Sandra Cantú, a Puerto Rican nursing student at the University of Alabama, entered the cafeteria wearing her hospital whites, two female students assumed she was a cafeteria worker and asked her to clear off their table.

* * *

Race relations are no easier for white students to manage. Ted Connors, a white senior at Southern Methodist, recalls the day he asked a student in his dorm for help with his Spanish homework. "He laughed in my face," Ted recalls, "I assumed he spoke Spanish just because his name was Hector Gonzalez. Actually, he had grown up in Michigan and spoke only English. It took quite a while to live that one down."

* * *

The pattern of racial misunderstanding experienced by these students is repeated over and over in schools and colleges throughout the United States: Even when they attend desegregated schools with significant ethnic and racial diversity, people of different ethnicities and races interact relatively little. Moreover, even if they have a friend of a different ethnicity within the confines of a school, most adolescents don't interact with cross-race friends outside of school (Hamm, Brown, & Heck, 2005; Benner & Wang, 2017).

It doesn't start out this way. During elementary school and even during early adolescence, there is a fair amount of integration among students of differing ethnicities. However, by middle and late adolescence, the amount of segregation is striking (Ennett & Bauman, 1996; Knifsend & Juvonen, 2014).

Why should racial and ethnic segregation be the rule, even in schools that have been desegregated for some time? One reason is that minority students may actively seek support from others who share their minority status (where "minority" is used in its sociological sense to indicate a subordinate group whose members lack power, compared to members of a dominant group). By associating primarily with other members of their own group, members of minority groups are able to affirm their own identity.

Members of different racial and ethnic groups may be segregated in the classroom as well. As we discussed in Chapter 10, because certain groups have been historically discriminated against, members of these minority groups tend to experience less school success than members of the majority group. It may be that ethnic and racial segregation in high school is based not on ethnicity itself but on academic achievement.

If minority group members experience less academic success, they may find themselves in classes with proportionally fewer majority group members. Similarly, majority students may be in classes with few minority students. Such class assignment practices, then, may inadvertently maintain and promote racial and ethnic segregation. This pattern would be particularly prevalent in schools where rigid academic tracking is practiced, with students assigned to "low," "medium," and "high" tracks depending on their prior achievement (Lucas & Berends, 2002).

The lack of contact among students of different racial and ethnic backgrounds in school may also reflect prejudice, both perceived and real, toward members of other groups. Students of color may feel that the white majority is prejudiced, discriminatory, and hostile, and they may prefer to stick to same-race groups. Conversely, white students may assume that minority group members are antagonistic and unfriendly. Such mutually destructive attitudes reduce the likelihood that meaningful interaction can take place (Phinney, Ferguson, & Tate, 1997; Tropp, 2003).

Is this sort of voluntary segregation along racial and ethnic lines found during adolescence inevitable? No. Adolescents who have interacted regularly and extensively with those of different races earlier in their lives are more likely to have friends of different races. Schools that actively promote contact among members of different ethnicities in classes help create an environment in which cross-race friendships can flourish. Furthermore, having friends of another race helps minority group members deal with discrimination they may encounter (Hewstone, 2003; Davies et al., 2011; Benner & Wang, 2017).

Still, the task is daunting. Many societal pressures act to keep members of different races from interacting with one another. Peer pressure, too, may encourage this as some cliques may actively promote norms that discourage group members from crossing racial and ethnic lines to form new friendships.

Popularity and Conformity

LO 12.9 Discuss what it means to be popular and unpopular in adolescence and how adolescents respond to peer pressure.

If you think back to your own adolescence, you'll probably have a good sense of your own popularity. You're not alone: Popularity is an important dimension of adolescent life.

POPULARITY AND REJECTION. Most adolescents have well-tuned antennae when it comes to determining who is popular and who is not. For some teenagers, concerns over popularity—or lack of it—may be a central focus of their lives.

Actually, the social world of adolescents is not divided solely into popular and unpopular individuals; the differentiations are more complex (see Figure 12-7). For instance, some adolescents are controversial; in contrast to *popular* adolescents, who are mostly liked, **controversial adolescents** are liked by some and disliked by others. For example, a controversial adolescent may be highly popular within a particular group, such as the string orchestra, but not popular among other classmates. Furthermore, there are **rejected adolescents**, who are uniformly disliked, and **neglected adolescents**, who are neither liked nor disliked. Neglected adolescents are the forgotten students—the ones whose status is so low that they are overlooked by almost everyone.

In most cases, popular and controversial adolescents tend to be similar in that their overall status is higher, while rejected and neglected adolescents share a generally

controversial adolescents
children who are liked by some peers and disliked by others

rejected adolescents
children who are actively disliked and whose peers may react to them in an obviously negative manner

neglected adolescents
children who receive relatively little attention from their peers in the form of either positive or negative interactions

Figure 12-7 The Social World of Adolescence

An adolescent's popularity can fall into one of four categories, depending on the opinions of his or her peers. Popularity is related to differences in status, behavior, and adjustment.

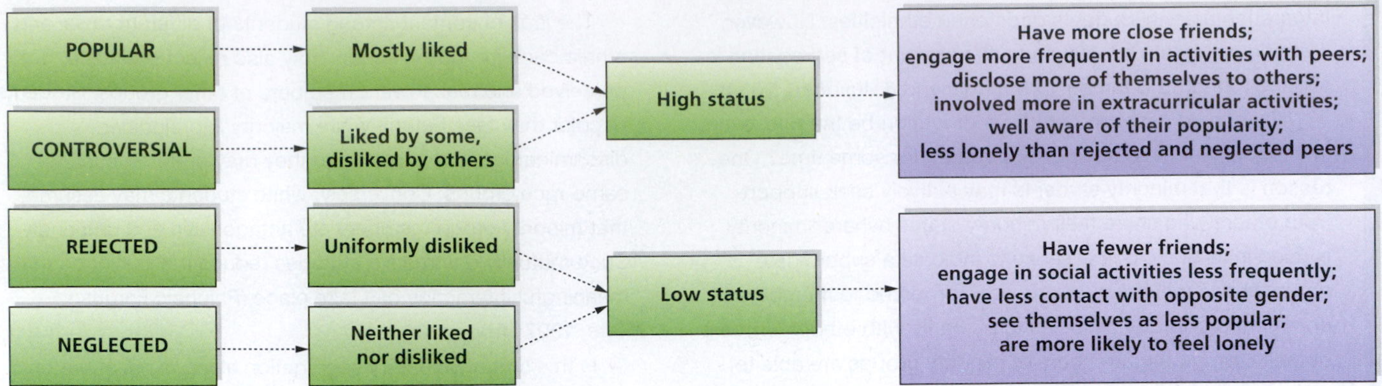

lower status. Popular and controversial adolescents have more close friends, engage more frequently in activities with their peers, and disclose more about themselves to others than less popular students. They are also more involved in extracurricular school activities. In addition, they are well aware of their popularity, and they are less lonely than their less popular classmates (Becker & Luthar, 2007; Closson, 2009; Estévez, et al., 2014).

In contrast, the social world of rejected and neglected adolescents is considerably less pleasant. They have fewer friends, engage in social activities less frequently, and have less contact with the opposite sex. They see themselves—accurately, it turns out—as less popular, and they are more likely to feel lonely. They may find themselves in conflicts with others, some of which escalate into full-blown fights that require mediation (McElhaney, Antonishak, & Allen, 2008; Woodhouse, Dykas, & Cassidy, 2012).

What is it that determines status in high school? As illustrated in Table 12-3, men and women have different perceptions. For example, college men suggest that physical attractiveness is the most important factor in determining high school girls' status, while college women believe it is a high school girl's grades and intelligence (Suitor et al., 2001; Gommans et al., 2017).

CONFORMITY: PEER PRESSURE IN ADOLESCENCE. Whenever Aldos Henry said he wanted to buy a particular brand of sneakers or a certain style of shirt, his parents complained that he was just giving in to peer pressure and told him to make up his own mind about things.

Table 12-3 High School Status

According to college men		According to college women	
High-status high school girls:	**High-status high school boys:**	**High-status high school girls:**	**High-status high school boys:**
1. Are good-looking	1. Take part in sports	1. Have high grades and are intelligent	1. Take part in sports
2. Have high grades and are intelligent	2. Have high grades and are intelligent	2. Participate in sports	2. Have high grades and are intelligent
3. Take part in sports	3. Are popular with girls	3. Are sociable	3. Are sociable
4. Are sociable	4. Are sociable	4. Are good-looking	4. Are good-looking
5. Are popular with boys	5. Have nice cars	5. Have nice clothes	5. Participate in school clubs or government

Note: Results are based on responses from students at Louisiana State University, Southeastern Louisiana University, State University of New York at Albany, State University of New York at Stony Brook, University of Georgia, and the University of New Hampshire.

(**Source:** Based on Suitor et al., 2001.)

In arguing with Aldos, his parents were subscribing to a view of adolescence that is quite prevalent in U.S. society: that teenagers are highly susceptible to **peer pressure**, the influence of one's peers to conform to their behavior and attitudes. Were his parents correct?

peer pressure
the influence of one's peers to conform to their behavior and attitudes

The research suggests that in some cases, adolescents *are* highly susceptible to the influence of their peers. For instance, when considering what to wear, whom to date, and what movies to see, adolescents are apt to follow the lead of their peers. Wearing the right clothes, down to a particular brand, sometimes can be a ticket to membership in a popular group. It shows you know what's what. When it comes to many nonsocial matters, however, such as choosing a career path or trying to solve a problem, adolescents are more likely to turn to an experienced adult (Phelan, Yu, & Davidson, 1994).

In short, particularly in middle and late adolescence, teenagers turn to those they see as experts on a given dimension. If they have social concerns, they turn to the people most likely to be experts—their peers. If the problem is one about which parents or other adults are most likely to have expertise, teenagers tend to turn to them for advice and are most susceptible to their opinions (Perrine & Aloise-Young, 2004).

Overall, then, it does not appear that susceptibility to peer pressure suddenly soars during adolescence. Instead, adolescence brings about a change in the people to whom an individual conforms. Whereas children conform fairly consistently to their parents during childhood, in adolescence conformity shifts to the peer group, in part because pressures to conform to peers increase as adolescents seek to establish their identity apart from their parents.

Ultimately, however, adolescents conform less to both peers *and* adults as they develop increasing autonomy in their lives. As they grow in confidence and in the ability to make their own decisions, adolescents are more apt to remain independent and to reject pressures from others, no matter who those others are. Before they learn to resist the urge to conform to their peers, however, teenagers may get into trouble, often along with their friends (Cook, Buehler, & Henson, 2009; Monahan, Steinberg, & Cauffman, 2009; Meldrum, Miller, & Flexon, 2013).

undersocialized delinquents
adolescent delinquents who are raised with little discipline or with harsh, uncaring parental supervision

JUVENILE DELINQUENCY: THE CRIMES OF ADOLESCENCE. Adolescents, along with young adults, are more likely to commit crimes than any other age group. This is a misleading statistic in some respects: Because certain behaviors (such as drinking) are illegal for adolescents but not for older individuals, it is rather easy for adolescents to break the law by doing something that, were they a few years older, would be legal. But even when such crimes are disregarded, adolescents are disproportionately involved in violent crimes, such as murder, assault, and rape, and in property crimes involving theft, robbery, and arson.

Although the number of violent crimes committed by U.S. adolescents over the past decade has declined, delinquency among some teenagers remains a significant problem. Violence is a major cause of nonfatal injuries among adolescents, and it is the third leading cause of death among youth age 10 to 24 years in the United States (National Center for Injury Prevention and Control, 2016).

Why do adolescents become involved in criminal activity? Some offenders, known as **undersocialized delinquents**, are adolescents who are raised with little discipline or with harsh, uncaring parental supervision. Although they are influenced by their peers, these children have not been socialized appropriately by their parents and were not taught standards of conduct to regulate their own behavior. Undersocialized delinquents typically begin criminal activities at an early age, well before the onset of adolescence (Hoeve et al., 2008; Barrett & Katsiyannis, 2017).

David Young-Wolff/Getty Images

Undersocialized delinquents are raised with little discipline or by harsh, uncaring parents, and they begin antisocial activities at a relatively early age. In contrast, socialized delinquents know and usually follow the norms of society, and they are highly influenced by their peers.

Undersocialized delinquents share several characteristics. They tend to be relatively aggressive and violent fairly early in life, characteristics that lead to rejection by peers and academic failure. They are also more likely to have been diagnosed with attention deficit disorder as children, and they tend to be less intelligent than average (Silverthorn & Frick, 1999; Rutter, 2003; Peach & Gaultney, 2013).

Undersocialized delinquents often suffer from psychological difficulties, and as adults they fit a psychological pattern called antisocial personality disorder. They are relatively unlikely to be successfully rehabilitated, and many undersocialized delinquents live on the margins of society throughout their lives (Lynam, 1996; Frick et al., 2003).

socialized delinquents
adolescent delinquents who know and subscribe to the norms of society and who are fairly normal psychologically

A larger group of adolescent offenders are socialized delinquents. **Socialized delinquents** know and subscribe to the norms of society; they are fairly normal psychologically. For them, transgressions committed during adolescence do not lead to a life of crime. Instead, most socialized delinquents pass through a period during adolescence when they engage in some petty crimes (such as shoplifting), but they do not continue lawbreaking into adulthood.

Typically, socialized delinquents are highly influenced by their peers, and their delinquency often occurs in groups. In addition, some research suggests that parents of socialized delinquents supervise their children's behavior less closely than other parents. But like other aspects of adolescent behavior, these minor delinquencies are often a result of giving in to group pressure or seeking to establish one's identity as an adult (Fletcher et al., 1995; Thornberry & Krohn, 1997).

Module 12.2 Review

LO 12.7 Describe what family relationships are like during adolescence.

The search for autonomy may cause a readjustment in relations between teenagers and their parents, but the generation gap is less wide than is generally thought.

LO 12.8 Explain how relationships with peers change during adolescence.

Cliques and crowds serve as reference groups in adolescence and offer a ready means of social comparison. Sex cleavage gradually diminishes, until boys and girls begin to pair off. Racial separation increases during adolescence, bolstered by socioeconomic status differences, different academic experiences, and mutually distrustful attitudes.

LO 12.9 Discuss what it means to be popular and unpopular in adolescence and how adolescents respond to peer pressure.

Degrees of popularity in adolescence include popular, controversial, neglected, and rejected adolescents. Adolescents tend to conform to their peers in areas in which they regard their peers as experts, and to adults in areas of perceived adult expertise. Adolescents are disproportionately involved in criminal activities, although most do not commit crimes. Juvenile delinquents can be categorized as undersocialized or socialized delinquents.

Journal Writing Prompt

Applying Lifespan Development: Thinking back to your own high school days, what were the dominant cliques in your school? How were they related to gender and race?

Dating, Sexual Behavior, and Teenage Pregnancy

It took him almost a month, but Sylvester Chiu finally got up the courage to ask Jackie Durbin to go to the movies. It was hardly a surprise to Jackie, though. Sylvester had first told his friend Erik about his resolve to ask Jackie out, and Erik had told Jackie's friend Cynthia about Sylvester's plans. Cynthia, in turn, had told Jackie, who was primed to say "yes" when Sylvester finally did call.

Welcome to the complex world of dating, an important and changing ritual of adolescence. We'll consider dating, as well as several other aspects of adolescents' relationships with one another, in the remainder of the chapter.

Dating and Sexual Relationships in the 21st Century

LO 12.10 Describe the functions and characteristics of dating during adolescence and how sexuality develops.

When and how adolescents begin to date is determined by cultural factors that change from one generation to another. Until fairly recently, exclusively dating a single individual was seen as something of a cultural ideal, viewed in the context of romance. Society often encouraged dating in adolescence, in part as a way for adolescents to explore relationships that might eventually lead to marriage.

Today, some adolescents believe that the concept of dating is outmoded and limiting, and in some places the practice of "hooking up"—a vague term that covers everything from kissing to sexual intercourse—is viewed as more appropriate. Still, despite changing cultural norms, dating remains the dominant form of social interaction that leads to intimacy among adolescents (Denizet-Lewis, 2004; Bogle, 2008; Rice, McGill, & Adler-Baeder, 2017).

Dating is also being changed through the use of social media. For example, although only 8 percent of teenagers have met a romantic partner online, expressing interest in a partner and flirting are common. Half of all teens ages 13 to 17 have let someone know they are interested in them by friending them on Facebook or another social media site, and 47 percent have expressed their attraction by liking or otherwise interacting with them on social media. Around a third have sent them flirtatious messages online. And in some cases, as we discuss in the *From Research to Practice* box, these messages become quite explicit (Lenhart, Smith, & Anderson, 2015).

THE FUNCTIONS OF DATING. Although on the surface dating is part of a pattern of courtship that can potentially lead to marriage, it serves other functions as well, especially early on. Dating is a way to learn how to establish intimacy with another individual. It can provide entertainment and, depending on the status of the person one is dating, prestige. It even can be used to develop a sense of one's own identity (Zimmer-Gembeck & Gallaty, 2006; Friedlander et al., 2007; Paludi, 2012; Kreager et al., 2016).

From Research to Practice

When Texting Turns Explicit: Sexting

> *One day last winter Margarite posed naked before her bathroom mirror, held up her cell phone, and took a picture. Then she sent the full-length frontal photo to Isaiah, her new boyfriend. Both were in eighth grade. (Hoffman, 2011, p. A1)*

For an increasing number of adolescents, *sexting* (the sending of texts that contain explicit, sexually provocative photos or text) is commonplace. It is easy to do and can be used in an effort to demonstrate one's affection or loyalty to a partner in an established relationship. Sexting also may be used instead of having actual sex, or as a prelude to sex. In some cases, sexting is used to indicate interest in starting a relationship (Strassberg, Cann, & Velarde, 2017; van Oosten & Vandenbosch, 2017).

Sexting has become commonplace: According to the results of one poll, 24 percent of 14- to 17-year-olds were involved in some form of naked sexting, either using cell phones or the Web. Another survey found that 4 percent of adolescents in the same age range admitted to sending naked photos or video by cell phone, and 15 percent had received them (Quaid, 2011; Lippman & Campbell, 2014; Vanden Abeele, Campbell, & Eggermont, 2014).

Sexting is also related to risky sexual behavior: Males who sext are four times more likely, and females are twice as likely, to have had multiple sexual relationships at the same time compared to those who don't engage in sexting. In addition, males who sext are 40 percent less likely to regularly use condoms compared to those who don't sext. Moreover, compared with those who don't report sexting, teenagers who sext are considerably more likely to have low self-esteem (Mitchell, Ybarra, & Korchmaros, 2014).

The consequences of sexting can be devastating. It is not uncommon for texts to be forwarded, and there are numerous incidents in which recipients of explicit photos have sent the images to friends. Ultimately, a photo may be forwarded to hundreds of others. There is also a double standard: When boys are caught sending photos of themselves, they are typically viewed more positively than girls, who may be labeled as slutty (Hoffman, 2011; Lippman & Campbell, 2014; Van Oosten & Vandenbosch, 2017).

Sexting not only may produce considerable psychological harm to the person who is depicted in sexually explicit photos, but there can be legal consequences. If the image involves anyone under the age of 18 (including the subject depicted, the photographer, someone who forwards the text, or even the recipient), child pornography laws come into play. An increasing number of prosecutions have occurred as a result of sexting (Lorang, McNiel, & Binder, 2016).

Shared Writing Prompt

Is it reasonable for prosecutors to use child pornography laws to deal with the problem of sexting?

Just how well dating serves such functions, particularly the development of psychological intimacy, is an open question. What specialists in adolescence do know, however, is surprising: Dating in early and middle adolescence is not terribly successful at facilitating intimacy. On the contrary, dating is often a superficial activity in which the participants so rarely let down their guards that they never become truly close and never expose themselves emotionally to each other. Psychological intimacy may be lacking even when sexual activity is part of the relationship (Collins, 2003; Furman & Shaffer, 2003; Tuggle, Kerpelman, & Pittman, 2014).

True intimacy becomes more common during later adolescence. At that point, the dating relationship may be taken more seriously by both participants, and it may be seen as a way to select a mate and as a potential prelude to marriage (an institution we consider in Chapter 14).

For homosexual adolescents, dating presents special challenges. In some cases, blatant homophobic prejudice expressed by classmates may lead gays and lesbians to date members of the other sex in an effort to fit in. If they do seek relationships with other gays and lesbians, they may find it difficult to find partners, who may not openly express their sexual orientation. Homosexual couples who do openly date face possible harassment, making the development of a relationship all the more difficult (Savin-Williams, 2003a).

DATING, RACE, AND ETHNICITY. Culture influences dating patterns among adolescents of different racial and ethnic groups, particularly those whose parents have immigrated to the United States from other countries. Parents may try to control their children's dating behavior in an effort to preserve their culture's traditional values or to ensure that their child dates within his or her racial or ethnic group.

For example, some immigrant parents may be especially conservative in their attitudes and values, in part because they themselves may have had no experience of dating and also because of religious considerations, such as in observant Muslim and Orthodox Jewish households. (In many cases, the parents' marriage was arranged by others, and the entire concept of dating is unfamiliar.) They may insist that dating be conducted with chaperones, or not at all. As a consequence, they may find themselves involved in substantial conflict with their children (Hoelter, Axinn, & Ghimire, 2004; Lau et al., 2009; Shenhav, Campos & Goldberg, 2017).

SEXUAL BEHAVIOR. The hormonal changes of puberty not only trigger the maturation of the sexual organs but also produce a new range of feelings in the form of sexuality. Sexual behavior and thoughts are among the central concerns of adolescents. Almost all adolescents think about sex, and many think about it a good deal of the time (Kelly, 2001; Ponton, 2001).

masturbation
sexual self-stimulation

The first type of sex in which adolescents engage is often solitary sexual self-stimulation, or **masturbation**. By age 15, some 80 percent of teenage boys and 20 percent of teenage girls report that they have masturbated. Masturbation in males occurs more frequently in the early teens and then begins to decline, while in females, the frequency is lower initially and increases throughout adolescence. In addition, patterns of masturbation frequency show differences according to race. For example, African American men and women masturbate less than whites (Schwartz, 1999; Hyde & DeLamater, 2004).

Although masturbation is widespread, it still may produce feelings of shame and guilt. There are several reasons for this. One is that adolescents may believe that masturbation signifies the inability to find a sexual partner—an erroneous assumption, since statistics show that three-quarters of married men and two-thirds of married women report masturbating between 10 and 24 times a year (Das, 2007; Gerressu et al., 2008).

For some, the sense of shame about masturbation is the result of a lingering legacy of misguided views of masturbation, in part based on religious prohibitions, cultural and social norms, and bad science. For instance, physician J. W. Kellogg believed in the 1800s that masturbation was detrimental to physical and emotional health. One of his solutions: he invented corn flakes, thinking that certain grains would be less likely to provoke sexual excitation (Michael et al., 1994).

The reality of masturbation is different. Today, experts on sexual behavior view it as a normal, healthy, and harmless activity. Some even suggest that it provides a useful way to learn about one's own sexuality (Hyde & DeLamater, 2004; Levin, 2007).

Figure 12-8 Adolescents and Sexual Activity

The age at which adolescents have sexual intercourse for the first time is declining, and around three-quarters have had sex before age 20.

(**Source:** Finer & Philbin, 2013.)

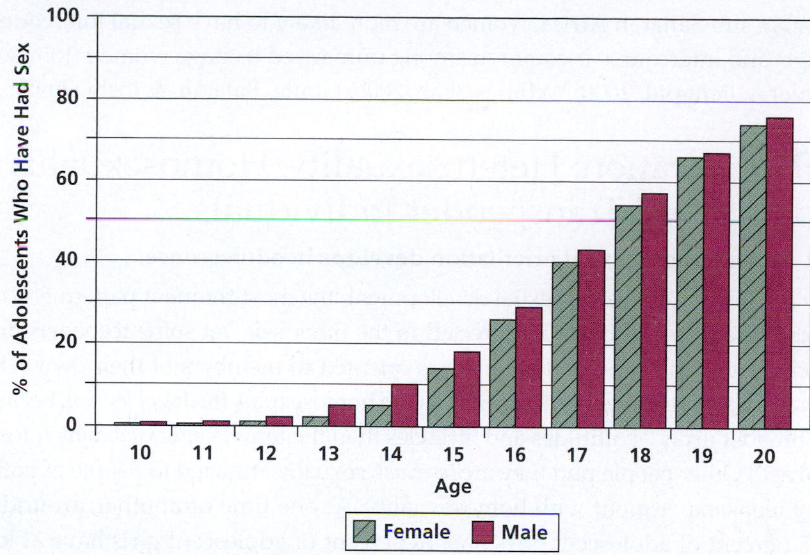

SEXUAL INTERCOURSE. Although it may be preceded by many different types of sexual intimacy, including deep kissing, massaging, petting, and oral sex, sexual intercourse remains a major milestone in the perceptions of most adolescents. Consequently, the main focus of researchers investigating sexual behavior has been on the act of heterosexual intercourse.

The average age at which adolescents first have sexual intercourse has been steadily declining over the past 50 years, and about 13 percent of adolescents have had sex before age 15. Overall, the average age of first sexual intercourse is 17, and around 70 percent of adolescents have had sex before age 20 (see Figure 12-8). At the same time, though, many teenagers are postponing sex, and the number of adolescents who say they have never had sexual intercourse increased by 13 percent from 1991 to 2007 (MMWR, 2008; Guttmacher Institute, 2012).

There are also racial and ethnic differences in the timing of initial sexual intercourse: African Americans generally have sex for the first time earlier than do Puerto Ricans, who have sex earlier than do whites. These racial and ethnic differences likely reflect differences in socioeconomic conditions, cultural values, and family structure (Singh & Darroch, 2000; Hyde, 2008).

From a *medical-care* provider's perspective

A parent asks you how to prevent her 14-year-old son from engaging in sexual activity until he is older. What would you tell her?

It is impossible to consider sexual activities without also looking at the societal norms governing sexual conduct. The prevailing norm several decades ago was the *double standard* in which premarital sex was considered permissible for males but not for females. Women were told by society that "nice girls don't," while men heard that premarital sex was permissible—although they should be sure to marry virgins.

Today the double standard has begun to give way to a new norm, called *permissiveness with affection.* According to this standard, premarital intercourse is viewed as permissible for both men and women if it occurs in the context of a long-term, committed, or loving relationship (Hyde & DeLamater, 2004; Earle et al., 2007).

The demise of the double standard is far from complete, however. Attitudes toward sexual conduct are still typically more lenient for males than for females, even in relatively socially liberal cultures. And in some cultures, the standards for men and women are quite distinct. For example, in North Africa, the Middle East, and the majority of Asian countries, most women conform to societal norms suggesting that they abstain from sexual intercourse until they are married. In Mexico, where there are strict standards against premarital sex, males are also considerably more likely than females to have premarital sex. In contrast, in sub-Saharan Africa, women are more likely to have sexual intercourse prior to marriage, and intercourse is common among unmarried teenage women (Johnson et al., 1992; Peltzer & Pengpid, 2006; Wellings et al., 2006; Ghule, Balaiah, & Joshi, 2007).

Sexual Orientation: Heterosexuality, Homosexuality, Bisexuality, and Transgender Individuals

LO 12.11 Explain how sexual orientation develops in adolescence.

When we consider adolescents' sexual development, the most frequent pattern is *heterosexuality*, sexual attraction and behavior directed to the other sex. Yet some teenagers are *homosexual*; their sexual attraction and behavior is oriented to members of their own sex. (Most male homosexuals prefer the term *gay* and female homosexuals the label *lesbian*, because they refer to a broader array of attitudes and lifestyles than the term *homosexual*, which focuses on the sexual act.) Other people find they are *bisexual*, sexually attracted to people of both sexes.

Many teens experiment with homosexuality. At one time or another, around 20 percent to 25 percent of adolescent boys and 10 percent of adolescent girls have at least one same-sex sexual encounter. In fact, homosexuality and heterosexuality are not completely distinct sexual orientations. Alfred Kinsey, a pioneer sex researcher, argued that sexual orientation should be viewed as a continuum in which "exclusively homosexual" is at one end and "exclusively heterosexual" is at the other (Kinsey, Pomeroy, & Martin, 1948). In between are people who show both homosexual and heterosexual behavior. Although accurate figures are difficult to obtain, most experts believe that between 4 and 10 percent of both men and women are exclusively homosexual during extended periods of their lives (Diamond, 2003a, 2003b; Russell & Consolacion, 2003; Pearson & Wilkinson, 2013).

The determination of sexual orientation is further complicated by distinctions between sexual orientation and gender identity. While sexual orientation relates to the object of one's sexual interests, *gender identity* is the gender a person believes he or she is psychologically. Sexual orientation and gender identity are not necessarily related to one another: A man who has a strong masculine gender identity may be attracted to other men. Consequently, the extent to which men and women enact traditional "masculine" or "feminine" behavior is not necessarily related to their sexual orientation or gender identity (Hunter & Mallon, 2000; Greydanus & Pratt, 2016).

Some individuals identify as transgender. *Transgender* individuals feel that they are trapped in the body of the other gender. Transgender individuals have a gender issue involving their sexual identity. Transgender individuals may seek sex-change operations in which their genitals are surgically removed and the genitals of the desired sex are created. It is a difficult path, one involving counseling, hormone injections, and living as a member of the desired sex for several years prior to surgery. Ultimately, though, the outcome can be very positive.

Transgender individuals are different from those who are called *intersex* or the older term *hermaphrodite*. An intersex person is born with an atypical combination of sexual organs or chromosomal or gene patterns. For instance, they may be born with both male and female sex organs, or ambiguous organs. Only 1 in 4,500 births results in an intersex infant (Diamond, 2013).

WHAT DETERMINES SEXUAL ORIENTATION? The factors that induce people to develop as heterosexual, homosexual, or bisexual are not well understood. Evidence suggests that genetic and biological factors may play an important role. Studies of twins show that identical twins are more likely to both be homosexual than pairs of siblings who don't share their genetic makeup. Other research finds that various structures of the brain are different in homosexuals and heterosexuals, and hormone production also seems to be linked to sexual orientation (Ellis et al., 2008; Fitzgerald, 2008; Santtila et al., 2008).

Other researchers have suggested that family or peer environmental factors play a role. For example, Sigmund Freud argued that homosexuality was the result of inappropriate identification with the opposite-sex parent (Freud, 1922/1959). The difficulty with Freud's theoretical perspective and other, similar perspectives that followed is that there simply is no evidence to suggest that any particular family dynamic or childrearing practice is consistently related to sexual orientation. Similarly, explanations based on learning theory, which suggest that homosexuality arises because of rewarding, pleasant homosexual experiences and unsatisfying heterosexual ones, do not appear to be the complete answer (Isay, 1990; Golombok & Tasker, 1996).

In short, there is no accepted explanation of why some adolescents develop a heterosexual orientation and others a homosexual orientation. Most experts believe that sexual orientation develops out of a complex interplay of genetic, physiological, and environmental factors (LeVay & Valente, 2003; Mustanski, Kuper, & Greene, 2014).

What is clear is that adolescents who find themselves attracted to members of the same sex may face a more difficult time than other teens. U.S. society still harbors great ignorance and prejudice regarding homosexuality, persisting in the belief that people have a choice in the matter—which they do not. Gay and lesbian teens may be rejected by their family or peers, or even harassed and assaulted if they are open about their orientation. The result is that homosexual adolescents are at greater risk for depression, and suicide rates are significantly higher for homosexual adolescents than for heterosexual adolescents. Gays and lesbians who do not conform to gender stereotypes are particularly susceptible to victimization, and they have lower rates of adjustment (Toomey et al., 2010; Madsen & Green, 2012; Mitchell, Ybarra, & Korchmaros, 2014).

The good news is that most people ultimately come to grips with their sexual orientation and become comfortable with it. Although lesbian, gay, and bisexual individuals may experience mental health difficulties as a result of the stress, prejudice, and discrimination they face, homosexuality is not considered a psychological disorder by any major psychological or medical association. All of them endorse efforts to reduce discrimination against homosexuals. Furthermore, society's attitudes toward homosexuality are changing, particularly among younger individuals. For example, a majority of U.S. citizens favor the practice of gay marriage, which became legal in 2015 (Baker & Sussman, 2012; Patterson, 2013; Hu, Xu & Tornello, 2016).

Teenage Pregnancies

LO 12.12 Summarize the challenges of teen pregnancy and the types of programs that are most effective in preventing it.

Feedings at 3:00 a.m., diaper changes, and visits to the pediatrician are not part of most people's vision of adolescence. Yet every year, tens of thousands of adolescents in the United States give birth.

The good news, though, is that the number of teenage pregnancies has decreased significantly in the past two decades. In fact, in 2014, the birth rate for U.S. teenagers was the lowest level ever reported in the seven decades that the government has been tracking pregnancies (see Figure 12-9). Birth rates declined to historic lows in all racial and ethnic groups, but disparities remain, with non-Hispanic black and Hispanic teen birth rates more than two times greater than the rate for whites. In addition, American Indian/Alaska Native teen birth rates are more than 1.5 times higher than the white teen birth rate. Overall, the pregnancy rate of teenagers is 24.2 births per 1,000 (Hamilton & Ventura, 2012; CDC, 2016).

Several factors explain the drop in teenage pregnancies:

- New initiatives have raised awareness among teenagers of the risks of unprotected sex. For example, about two-thirds of high schools in the United States have established comprehensive sex education programs (Villarosa, 2003; Corcoran & Pillai, 2007).

Figure 12-9 Teenage Pregnancy Rates

The rate of teenage pregnancies has dropped dramatically among all ethnic groups since the early 1990s.

(**Source:** Hamilton et al., 2015.)

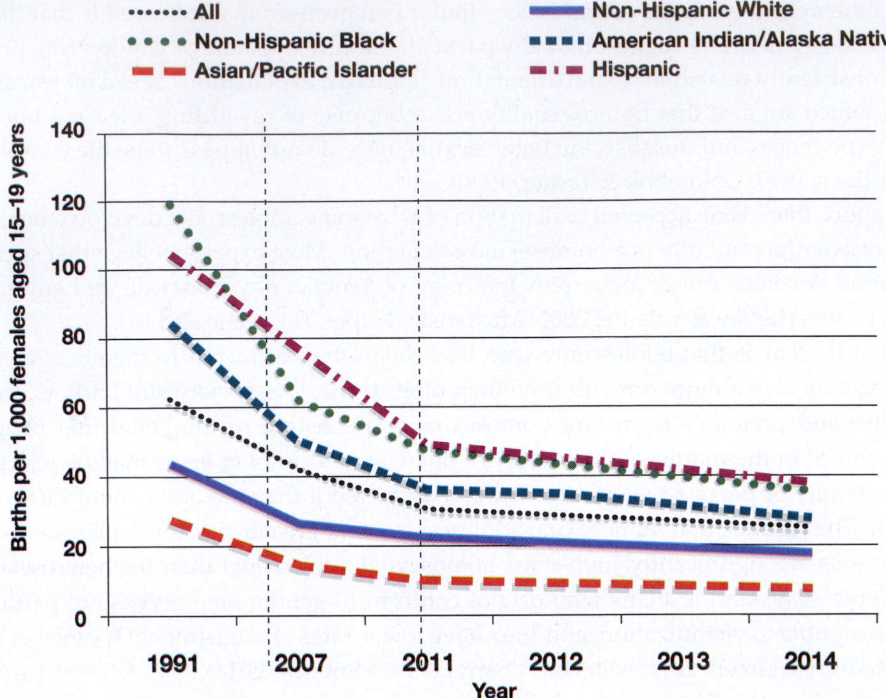

- The rates of sexual intercourse among teenagers have declined. The percentage of teenage girls who have ever had sexual intercourse dropped from 51 percent in 1988 to 43 percent in 2006–2010 (Martinez, Copen, & Abma, 2011).
- The use of condoms and other forms of contraception has increased. For example, virtually all sexually experienced girls age 15–19 have used some method of contraception (Martinez, Copen, & Abma, 2011).
- Substitutes for sexual intercourse may be more prevalent. For example, oral sex, which many teenagers do not even consider "sex," may increasingly be viewed as an alternative to sexual intercourse (Bernstein, 2004; Chandra et al., 2011).

One thing that apparently *hasn't* led to a reduction in teenage pregnancies is asking adolescents to take a virginity pledge. Public pledges to refrain from premarital sex—a centerpiece of some forms of sex education—have been shown to be ineffective. For example, in one study of 12,000 teenagers, 88 percent reported eventually having sexual intercourse. However, pledges did delay the start of sex an average of 18 months (Bearman & Bruckner, 2004).

Even with the decline in the birth rate for U.S. teenagers, the rate of teenage pregnancy in the United States is 2 to 10 times higher than that of other industrialized countries. The results of an unintended pregnancy can be devastating to both mother and child. In comparison to earlier times, teenage mothers today are much less likely to be married. In a high percentage of cases, mothers care for their children without the help of the father. Without financial or emotional support, a mother may have to abandon her own education, and consequently she may be relegated to unskilled, poorly paying jobs for the rest of her life. In other cases, she may develop long-term dependency on welfare. An adolescent mother's physical and mental health may suffer as she faces unrelenting stress due to continual demands on her time (Manlove et al., 2004; Gillmore et al., 2006; Oxford et al., 2006).

Module 12.3 Review

LO 12.10 Describe the functions and characteristics of dating during adolescence and how sexuality develops.

Dating in adolescence serves a number of functions, including intimacy, entertainment, and prestige. Masturbation, once viewed very negatively, is now generally regarded as a normal and harmless practice that continues into adulthood. Sexual intercourse is a major milestone that most people reach during adolescence. The age of first intercourse reflects cultural differences and has been declining over the past 50 years.

LO 12.11 Explain how sexual orientation develops in adolescence.

Sexual orientation, which is most accurately viewed as a continuum rather than categorically, develops as the result of a complex combination of factors.

LO 12.12 Summarize the challenges of teen pregnancy and the types of programs that are most effective in preventing it.

Teenage pregnancy has negative consequences for adolescent mothers and their children. The incidence of teenage pregnancies has declined because awareness among adolescents has increased, as have the use of condoms and reliance on substitutes for intercourse.

Journal Writing Prompt

Applying Lifespan Development: What aspects of the social world of adolescents work against the achievement of true intimacy in dating?

Epilogue

We continued our consideration of adolescence in this chapter, looking at social and personality issues. Self-concept, self-esteem, and identity develop during adolescence, which can be a period of self-discovery. We looked at adolescents' relationships with family and peers, and at gender, race, and ethnic relations during adolescence. Our discussion concluded with a look at dating, sexuality, and sexual orientation.

Before turning to the next chapter, think back to the Prologue. There we met Ameen Abdulrasool, who while an adolescent developed a promising new way to help the visually impaired navigate through the world. Consider the following questions relating to his social and personality development:

1. What aspects of Abdulrasool's personality might have caused him to seek out a way to help the visually impaired?
2. How do you think Abdulrasool's self-esteem affected his efforts to develop the navigation system?
3. Based on his motivation to support his blind relatives by developing the navigation system, what do you think his relationship with his family was like?
4. Do you think advances in Abdulrasool's social and personality development, as well as advances in his cognitive development, allowed him to successfully develop the navigation system?

Looking Back

LO 12.1 Describe how self-concept and self-esteem develop during adolescence.

During adolescence, self-concept differentiates to encompass others' views as well as one's own and to include multiple aspects simultaneously. Differentiation of self-concept can cause confusion as behaviors reflect a complex definition of the self. Adolescents also differentiate their self-esteem, evaluating particular aspects of themselves differently.

LO 12.2 Summarize how Erikson explains identity formation during adolescence.

According to Erik Erikson, adolescents are in the identity-versus-identity-confusion stage, seeking to discover their individuality and identity. They may become confused and exhibit dysfunctional reactions, and they may rely for help and information more on friends and peers than on adults.

LO 12.3 Explain Marcia's categories of adolescent identity.

James Marcia identifies four identity statuses that individuals may experience in adolescence and in later life: identity achievement, identity foreclosure, identity diffusion, and moratorium.

LO 12.4 Describe the role religion and spirituality play in identity formation in adolescence.

Many adolescents begin to think abstractly and critically about religion and spirituality and come to form their own religious identity.

LO 12.5 Discuss the challenges ethnic and minority groups face in identity formation in adolescence.

The formation of an identity is challenging for members of racial and ethnic minority groups, many of whom appear to be embracing a bicultural identity approach.

LO 12.6 Identify the dangers adolescents face as they deal with the stresses of their age.

Many adolescents have feelings of sadness and hopelessness, and some experience major depression. Biological, environmental, and social factors contribute to depression, and there are gender, ethnic, and racial differences in its occurrence. The rate of adolescent suicide is rising, with suicide now the third most common cause of death in the 15- to 24-year-old bracket.

LO 12.7 Describe what family relationships are like during adolescence.

Adolescents' quest for autonomy often brings confusion and tension to their relationships with their parents, but the actual "generation gap" between parents' and teenagers' attitudes is usually small.

LO 12.8 Explain how relationships with peers change during adolescence.

Peers are important during adolescence because they provide social comparison and reference groups against which to judge social success. Relationships among adolescents are characterized by the need to belong. During adolescence, boys and girls begin to spend time together in groups and, toward the end of adolescence, to pair off. In general, segregation between people of different races and ethnicities increases in middle and late adolescence, even in schools with a diverse student body.

LO 12.9 Discuss what it means to be popular and unpopular in adolescence and how adolescents respond to peer pressure.

Degrees of popularity during adolescence include popular and controversial adolescents (on the high end of popularity) and neglected and rejected adolescents (on the low end). Peer pressure is not a simple phenomenon. Adolescents conform to their peers in areas in which they feel their peers are expert, and to adults in areas of adult expertise. As adolescents grow in confidence, their conformity to both peers and adults declines. Although most adolescents do not commit crimes, adolescents are disproportionately involved in criminal activities. Juvenile delinquents can be categorized as undersocialized or socialized delinquents.

LO 12.10 Describe the functions and characteristics of dating during adolescence and how sexuality develops.

During adolescence, dating provides intimacy, entertainment, and prestige. Achieving psychological intimacy, which is difficult at first, becomes easier as adolescents mature, gain confidence, and take relationships more seriously. For most adolescents, masturbation is often the first step into sexuality. The age of first intercourse, which is now in the teens, has declined as the double standard has faded and the norm of permissiveness with affection has gained ground. However, the rate of sexual intercourse has also declined.

LO 12.11 Explain how sexual orientation develops in adolescence.

Sexual orientation develops out of a complex interplay of genetic, physiological, and environmental factors.

LO 12.12 Summarize the challenges of teen pregnancy and the types of programs that are most effective in preventing it.

Teenage pregnancy has been declining in the United States for two decades, but it remains a problem because of its serious and long-term consequences for both mother and child. The most effective means for preventing teen pregnancy is the provision of accurate information, the availability of condoms and other forms of pregnancy avoidance, and the practice of alternative forms of sexuality.

Key Terms and Concepts

identity-versus-identity-confusion stage 398
identity achievement 400
identity foreclosure 400
moratorium 400
identity diffusion 401
emerging adulthood 401
autonomy 408
generation gap 410
reference groups 413
cliques 413
crowds 413
sex cleavage 414
controversial adolescents 415
rejected adolescents 415
neglected adolescents 415
peer pressure 417
undersocialized delinquents 417
socialized delinquents 418
masturbation 420

Summary 5
Adolescence

David De Lossy/Getty Images

FROM AGE 13 TO AGE 18, Mariah changed from a seemingly "together" teenager to a troubled young adolescent to an increasingly confident and independent late adolescent. Early in her adolescence, she struggled to define herself and responded to the "Who am I?" question with some decidedly unwise answers. She dabbled with—and then nearly drowned in—drugs, and she attempted suicide. At last, seeking help for her difficulties, she kicked her bad habits, began to work on her self-concept, returned to school and became interested in photography, repaired her family life, and entered a positive relationship with a boyfriend.

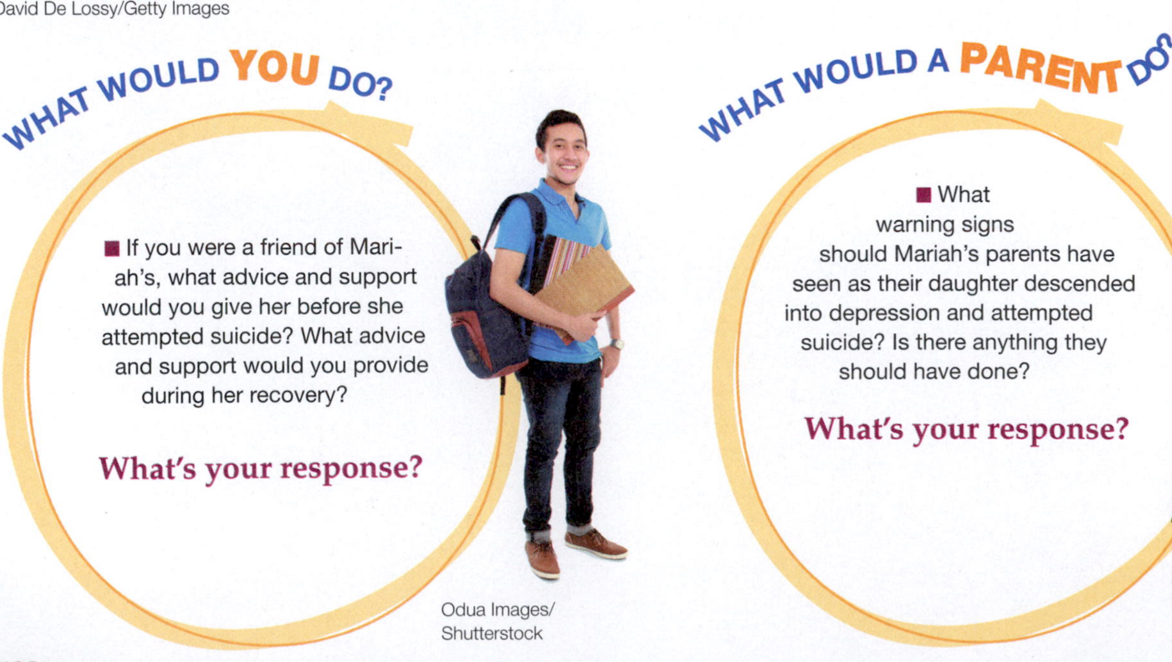

WHAT WOULD YOU DO?

■ If you were a friend of Mariah's, what advice and support would you give her before she attempted suicide? What advice and support would you provide during her recovery?

What's your response?

Odua Images/Shutterstock

WHAT WOULD A PARENT DO?

■ What warning signs should Mariah's parents have seen as their daughter descended into depression and attempted suicide? Is there anything they should have done?

What's your response?

Photodisc/Getty Images

Physical Development

PhotoAlto/Getty Images

- Adolescents have many physical issues to deal with.
- Mariah's resort to drugs is a strategy used by some adolescents for coping with the stresses of the period.
- Adolescent brain development permits Mariah to engage in complex thinking, which can sometimes lead to confusion.
- Mariah displays a lack of impulse control, which is typical of a not yet fully developed prefrontal cortex.

Cognitive Development

Photodisc/Getty Images

- Adolescents' personal fables include a sense of invulnerability, which probably contributed to Mariah's impulsive decisions.
- Mariah's depression may stem from the adolescent tendency toward introspection and self-consciousness.
- Mariah may have used drugs to escape the pressures of everyday life.
- It is not unusual for an adolescent like Mariah to have school difficulties.

Social and Personality Development

DGLimages/Shutterstock

- Mariah's struggles with identity represent the characteristic internal conflict of adolescence.
- In balancing friendships with the desire to be alone, Mariah is struggling to accommodate her increasingly complex personality.
- Her more accurate self-concept may in fact lower Mariah's self-esteem.
- In relying on her "cool" crowd, Mariah is defining her identity in terms of a questionable reference group.
- Mariah's struggle with depression reflects the higher incidence of this ailment among adolescent girls.
- Mariah benefited from a moratorium that enabled her to reestablish connection with her "clueless" parents and begin to assume true independence.
- Her relationship with her boyfriend indicates a return to a normal social pattern.

WHAT WOULD A SOCIAL WORKER DO?

■ When an adolescent such as Mariah shows a definite decline in academic performance, are the symptoms likely to be interpreted differently depending on whether the adolescent comes from an affluent or impoverished background? How can a professional care provider prevent different interpretation and treatment?

What's your response?

Sheer Photo, Inc/ stockbyte/Getty Images

WHAT WOULD AN EDUCATOR DO?

■ What signals might a teacher have observed in Mariah's classroom performance to suggest that she was having a drug problem? What steps might the teacher have taken?

What's your response?

Tom Baker/123RF

Chapter 13

Physical and Cognitive Development in Early Adulthood

Ascent Xmedia/Getty Images

Learning Objectives

LO 13.1 Describe how the body develops and stays healthy during early adulthood.

LO 13.2 Explain why a healthy diet is particularly important in early adulthood.

LO 13.3 Describe the challenges people with physical disabilities face in early adulthood.

LO 13.4 Summarize the effects of stress and what can be done about it.

LO 13.5 Describe how cognitive development continues in young adulthood.

LO 13.6 Compare and contrast Perry's and Schaie's approaches to cognitive development in young adulthood.

LO 13.7 Explain how intelligence is defined today and how life events cause cognitive growth in young adults.

LO 13.8 Describe who attends college today and how the college population is changing.

LO 13.9 Summarize the difficulties students face as they enter college.

LO 13.10 Describe how gender affects the treatment of college students.

Chapter Overview

Prologue: A Tale of Two Students

For Enrico Vasquez, there was never any doubt: He was headed for college. Enrico, the son of a wealthy Cuban immigrant who had made a fortune in the medical supply business after fleeing Cuba 5 years before Enrico's birth, had always had the importance of education drummed into him by his family. In fact, the question was never *whether* he would go to college, but what college he would be able to get into. As a consequence, Enrico found high school to be a pressure cooker: Every grade and extracurricular activity was seen as helping—or hindering—his chances of admission to a "good" college.

***

Armando Williams's letter of acceptance to Dallas County Community College is framed on the wall of his mother's apartment. To her, the letter represents nothing short of a miracle, an answer to her prayers. Growing up in a neighborhood saturated with drugs and drive-by shootings, Armando had always been a hard worker and a "good boy," in his mother's view. But when he was growing up, she never even entertained the possibility of his making it to college. To see him reach this stage in his education fills her with joy.

Looking Ahead

Although Enrico Vasquez's and Armando Williams's lives followed two very different paths, they share the single goal of obtaining a college education. They represent the increasing diversity in family background, socioeconomic status, race, and ethnicity that is coming to characterize college populations today.

As we see in this and the following chapter, considerable development goes on during early adulthood, which starts at the end of adolescence (around age 20) and continues until roughly the start of middle age (around age 40). Significant changes—and challenges—occur as new opportunities arise and people choose to take on (or to forgo) a new set of roles as spouse, parent, and worker.

This chapter focuses on physical and cognitive development during this period. It begins with a look at the physical changes that extend into early adulthood. Though more subtle than the physical changes of adolescence, growth continues, and various motor skills change as well. We look at diet and weight, examining the prevalence of obesity in this age group. We also consider stress and coping during the early years of adulthood.

The chapter then turns to cognitive development. Although traditional approaches to cognitive development regarded adulthood as an inconsequential plateau, we will examine some new theories suggesting that significant cognitive growth occurs during adulthood. We also consider the nature of adult intelligence and the impact of life events on cognitive development.

Graduating from college is a significant milestone for some young adults.

The last part of the chapter focuses on college, the institution that shapes intellectual growth for those who attend. We examine who goes to college, and we explore how gender and race can influence achievement. We end by looking at some reasons why students drop out of college and discussing some of the adjustment problems that college students face.

Physical Development

Grady McKinnon grinned as his mountain bike left the ground briefly. The 27-year-old financial auditor was delighted to be out for a camping and biking weekend with four of his college buddies. Grady had been worried that an upcoming deadline at work would make him miss this trip. When they were still in school, Grady and his friends used to go biking nearly every weekend. But jobs, marriage—and even a child for one of the guys—started taking up a lot of their attention. This was their only trip this summer. He was glad he hadn't missed it.

Grady and his friends were probably in the best physical condition of their lives when they first started to go mountain biking regularly in college. Even now, as Grady's life becomes more complicated and sports start to take a backseat to work and other personal demands, he is still enjoying one of the healthiest periods of his life. As we will see, although most people, like Grady, reach the height of their physical capacities in young adulthood, at the same time, they must try to cope with the stress produced by the challenges of their adult lives.

Physical Development, Fitness, and Health

LO 13.1 Describe how the body develops and stays healthy during early adulthood.

In most respects, physical development and maturation are complete at early adulthood. Most people are at the peak of their physical capabilities. They have attained their full height, and their limbs are proportional to their size, rendering the gangliness of adolescence a memory. People in their early 20s tend to be healthy, vigorous, and energetic. Although **senescence**, the natural physical decline brought about by increasing age, has already begun, age-related changes are not usually very obvious to people until later in their lives.

senescence
the natural physical decline brought about by aging

At the same time, some growth continues during early adulthood. For example, some people, particularly late maturers, continue to gain height in their early 20s.

Certain parts of the body also reach full maturity now. For example, the brain grows in both size and weight, reaching its maximum during early adulthood (and then subsequently contracting in size later in life). The gray matter of the brain continues to be pruned back, and myelination (the process by which nerve cells are insulated by a covering of fat cells) continues to increase. These changes in the brain help support the cognitive advances that occur during early adulthood. Furthermore, the changes in the brain mean that young adults' minds are still malleable and adaptive to new experiences. For example, learning a new language, musical instrument, or job skill is easier for young adults than it is for older adults (Li, 2012; Schwarz & Bilbo, 2014; Knežević & Marinković, 2017).

One part of the brain in particular, the prefrontal cortex, doesn't mature until well into young adulthood. This region is responsible for such higher-order mental functions as planning, decision making, and impulse control. It's not surprising, then, that the greatest risks to health and well-being in this stage of life mainly involve poor judgment—motor vehicle accidents, violence, drug abuse, and excessive drinking chief among them (Giedd, 2012; Steinberg, 2014; Tamnes et al., 2017).

THE SENSES. In early adulthood, the senses are as sharp as they will ever be. Although there are changes in the elasticity of the eye—a continuation of an aging process that may begin as early as age 10—they are so minor that they produce no deterioration in vision. It is not until the 40s that eyesight changes sufficiently to be noticeable—as we will see in Chapter 15.

Hearing, too, is at its peak. However, a gender difference emerges: Women can detect higher tones more readily than men (McGuinness, 1972). In general, though, the hearing of both men and women is quite good. Under quiet conditions, the average young adult can hear the ticking of a watch 20 feet away.

The other senses, including taste, smell, and sensitivity to touch and pain, are quite good, and they remain that way throughout early adulthood. These senses maintain their acuity until the 40s or 50s, when they begin to decline.

PHYSICAL FITNESS. If you are a professional athlete, most people probably consider you to be over the hill by the time you leave your 20s. Although there are notable exceptions (think of baseball star Derek Jeter, who continued playing professionally until he was 40), even athletes who train constantly tend to lose their physical edge once they reach their 30s. In some sports, the peak passes even sooner. Swimmers are at their best in their late teens, and gymnasts peak even earlier.

The rest of us are also at the height of our psychomotor abilities during early adulthood. Reaction time is quicker, muscle strength is greater, and eye–hand coordination is better than at any other period (Sliwinski et al., 1994).

The physical prowess that typically characterizes early adulthood doesn't come naturally, however, nor does it come to everyone. In order to reach their physical potential, people must exercise and maintain a proper diet.

The benefits of exercise are hardly secret: In the United States, yoga and Pilates classes and jogging and swimming are common activities. Yet the conspicuousness of exercise activities is misleading. Less than 10 percent of Americans are involved in sufficient regular exercise to keep them in good physical shape, and less than a quarter engage in even moderate regular exercise. Furthermore, the opportunity to exercise is largely an upper- and middle-class phenomenon; people of lower socioeconomic status (SES) often have neither the time nor the money to engage in regular exercise (Delva, O'Malley, & Johnston, 2006; Proper, Cerin, & Owen, 2006; Farrell et al., 2014).

The amount of exercise required to yield significant health benefits is not enormous. According to recommendations from the American College of Sports Medicine and the Centers for Disease Control and Prevention, people should accumulate at least 150 minutes of moderate-intensity physical activity per week. The time spent exercising can be continuous or occur in bouts of at least 10 minutes. Moderate-intensity activity includes walking briskly at 3 to 4 mph, biking at speeds up to 10 mph, golfing while carrying or pulling clubs, fishing by casting from shore, playing ping pong, or canoeing at 2 to 4 mph. Even common household chores, such as weeding, vacuuming, and mowing with a power mower, provide moderate exercise (American College of Sports Medicine, 2011; DeBlois & Lefferts, 2017).

Jim McIsaac/Getty Images

It's not just professional athletes, such as baseball star Derek Jeter shown here, who are at the height of athleticism in early adulthood. Almost everyone reaches their peak of physical fitness during this period.

Figure 13-1 The Result of Fitness: Longevity

The greater the fitness level, as measured by adherence to the Health and Human Services (HHS) guidelines, the higher the gains in life expectancy due to physical activity.

(**Source:** National Cancer Institute, 2012.)

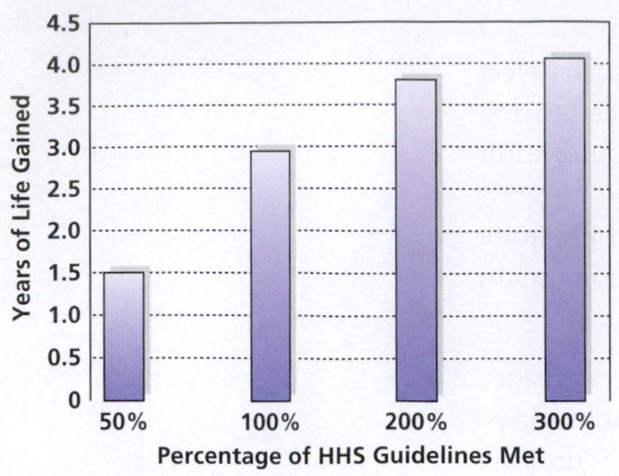

From *an educator's* perspective

Can people be taught the lifelong advantages of regular exercise? Should school-based physical education programs be changed to foster a lifelong commitment to exercise?

The advantages to those who do become involved in regular exercise programs are many. Exercise increases cardiovascular fitness, meaning that the heart and circulatory system operate more efficiently. Furthermore, lung capacity increases, raising endurance. Muscles become stronger, and the body is more flexible and maneuverable. The range of movement is greater, and the muscles, tendons, and ligaments are more elastic. Moreover, exercise during this period helps reduce *osteoporosis*, the thinning of the bones, in later life.

Exercise also may optimize the immune response of the body, helping it fight off disease. Exercise may even decrease stress and anxiety and reduce depression. It can provide people with a sense of control over their bodies, as well as impart a feeling of accomplishment (Wise et al., 2006; Rethorst, Wipfli, & Landers, 2009; Treat-Jacobson, Bronäs, & Salisbury, 2014).

Regular exercise offers the possibility of another, ultimately more important, reward: It is associated with increased longevity (see Figure 13-1; Stevens et al., 2002; Fisher et al., 2017).

HEALTH. Although a lack of exercise may produce poor health (and worse), health risks in general are relatively slight during early adulthood. During this period, people are less susceptible to colds and other minor illnesses than they were as children, and when they do come down with illnesses, they usually get over them quickly.

Adults in their 20s and 30s stand a higher risk of dying from accidents, primarily those involving automobiles, than from most other causes. But there are other killers: Among the leading causes of death for people ages 25 to 34 are suicide, homicide, cancer, and heart disease. (National Vital Statistics System, 2015).

Not all people fare equally well during early adulthood. Lifestyle decisions, including the use—or abuse—of alcohol, tobacco, or drugs or engaging in unprotected sex, can hasten *secondary aging*, physical declines brought about by environmental factors or an individual's behavioral choices. Such lifestyle decisions can also increase a young adult's risk of dying from illness and disease.

As the definition of secondary aging implies, cultural factors, including gender and race, are also related to the risk of dying in young adulthood. For instance, men are more apt to die than women, primarily due to their higher involvement in automobile accidents. Furthermore, African Americans have twice the death rate of Caucasians, and minorities in general have a higher likelihood of dying than the Caucasian majority.

Another major cause of death for men in this age group is violence, particularly in the United States. The homicide rate is higher in the United States than in many other developed countries (see Figure 13-2). Racial factors are also related to the homicide rate in the United States.

Although homicide is the third most frequent cause of death for white males between ages 25 and 34, it is *the* most frequent cause of death for black males and the second most frequent cause of death for Hispanic males in that same age range.

Race and culture are related not only to the causes of death, but, as we see in the *Developmental Diversity and Your Life* feature, also to young adults' lifestyles and health-related behavior.

Figure 13-2 Tracking Murder

The murder rate is far higher in the United States than in many other developed countries. What features of U.S. society contribute to this state of affairs?

(**Source:** Based on UNODC, 2013.)

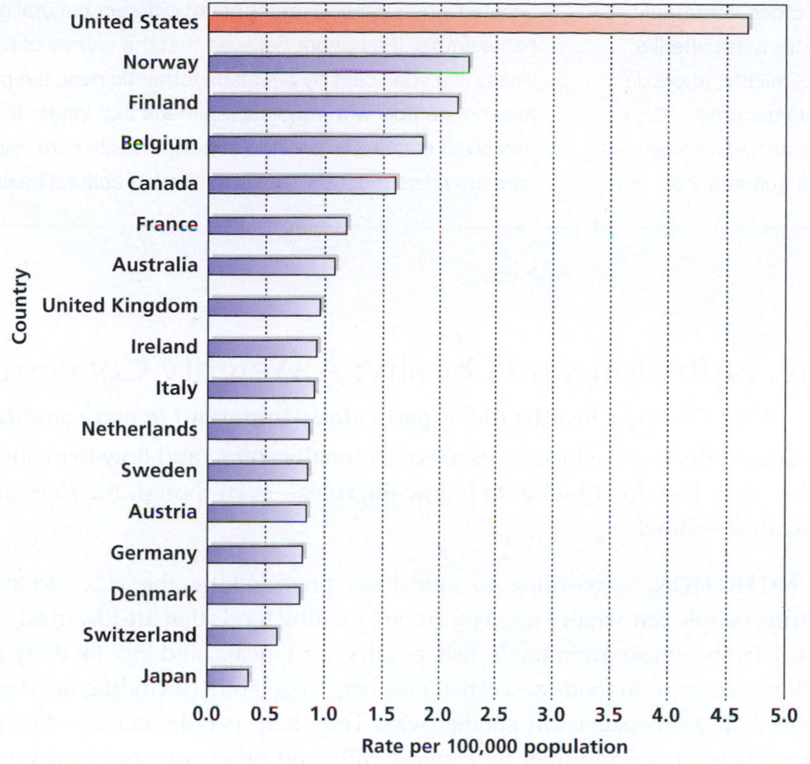

Developmental Diversity and Your Life

How Cultural Beliefs Influence Health and Health Care

Manolita recently suffered a heart attack. She was advised by her doctor to change her eating and activity habits or face the risk of another life-threatening heart attack. During the period that followed, Manolita dramatically changed her eating and activity habits. She also began going to church and praying extensively. After a recent checkup, Manolita is in the best shape of her life. What are some of the reasons for Manolita's amazing recovery? (Murguia, Peterson, & Zea, 1997, 16)

***

After reading this passage, would you conclude that Manolita recovered her health because (a) she changed her eating and activity habits, (b) she became a better person, (c) God was testing her faith, or (d) her doctor prescribed the correct changes?

In response to a survey asking this question, more than two-thirds of Latino immigrants from Central America, South America, or the Caribbean believed that "God was testing her faith" had a moderate or great effect on her recovery, although most also agreed that a change in eating and activity habits was important (Murguia et al., 1997; Yang et al., 2016).

The findings of this study help explain why Latinos are the least likely of any Western ethnic group to seek the help of a physician when they are ill. According to psychologists Alejandro Murguia, Rolf Peterson, and Maria Zea (1997), cultural health beliefs, along with demographic and psychological barriers, reduce people's use of physicians and medical care.

Specifically, they suggest that Latinos, as well as members of some non-Western groups, are more likely than non-Hispanic whites to believe in supernatural causes of illness. For instance, members of these groups may attribute illness to a punishment from God, a lack of faith, or a hex. Such beliefs may reduce the motivation to seek medical care from a physician (Landrine & Klonoff, 1994; Yang et al., 2016).

Money also plays a role. Lower socioeconomic status reduces the ability to pay for traditional medical care, which is expensive and may indirectly encourage the continued reliance on less traditional and less expensive methods. In addition, the lower level of involvement in the mainstream culture that is characteristic of recent immigrants to the United States is

(*continued*)

associated with a lower likelihood of visiting a physician and obtaining mainstream medical care (Pachter & Weller, 1993; Landrine & Klonoff, 1994; Antshel & Antshel, 2002).

Furthermore, cultural differences play a role in how psychological disorders are viewed and experienced. For example, members of some Plains Indians tribes commonly hear the voices of the dead calling to them from the afterlife, and that is seen as normal in their culture. Similarly, anorexia nervosa—an eating disorder in which people become obsessed with their weight and body image and sometimes may starve themselves—is seen primarily in cultures that hold strict societal standards relating to weight and slimness. In cultures in which body standards are different, anorexia nervosa is not seen (Lopez & Guarnaccia, 2000; Jacob, 2014: Munro, Randell, & Lawrie, 2017).

Health care providers need to take cultural beliefs into account when treating members of different cultural groups. For example, if a patient believes that the source of his or her illness is a spell cast by a jealous romantic rival, the patient may not comply with medical regimens that ignore that perceived source. To provide effective health care, then, health care providers must be sensitive to such cultural health beliefs.

Eating, Nutrition, and Obesity: A Weighty Concern

LO 13.2 Explain why a healthy diet is particularly important in early adulthood.

Most young adults know which foods are nutritionally sound and how to maintain a balanced diet; they just don't bother to follow the rules—even though the rules are not all that difficult to follow.

GOOD NUTRITION. According to guidelines provided by the U.S. Department of Agriculture, people can achieve good nutrition by eating foods that are low in fat, including vegetables, fruits, whole-grain foods, fish, poultry, lean meats, and low-fat dairy products. In addition, whole-grain foods and cereal products, vegetables (including dried beans and peas), and fruit are beneficial in another way: They help people increase the amount of complex carbohydrates and fiber they ingest. Milk and other sources of calcium are also needed to prevent osteoporosis. Finally, people should reduce salt intake (Jones et al., 2012; Tyler et al., 2014).

Figure 13-3 Obesity on the Rise

In spite of greater awareness of the importance of good nutrition, the percentage of adults with weight problems in the United States has risen dramatically over the past few decades. Why do you think this rise has occurred?

(**Source:** National Health and Nutrition Examination Survey, 2014.)

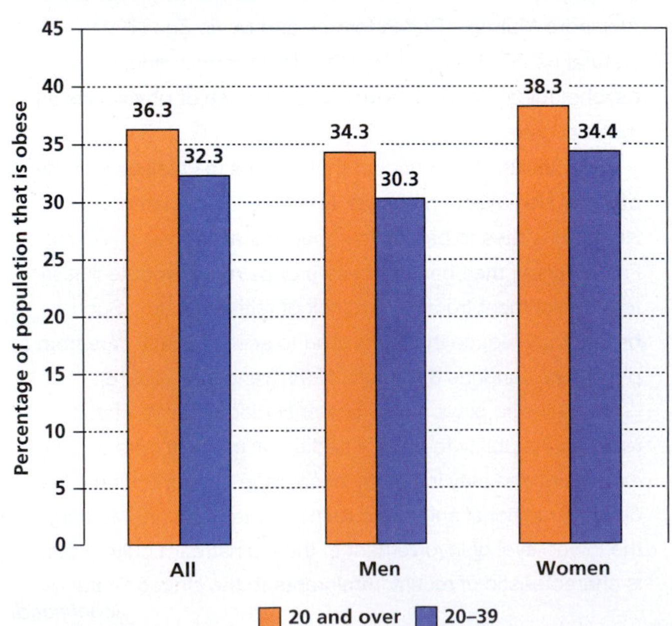

During adolescence, a poor diet does not always present a significant problem. For instance, teenagers don't suffer too much from a diet high in junk foods and fat because they are undergoing such tremendous growth. The story changes when they reach young adulthood, however. With growth tapering off, young adults must reduce the caloric intake they were used to during adolescence.

Many do not. Although most people enter young adulthood with bodies of average height and weight, they gradually put on weight if their poor dietary habits remain unchanged.

OBESITY. The adult population of the United States is growing—in more ways than one. Obesity, defined as a body mass index (BMI) at or above the 95th percentile for adults of the same age and sex, is on the rise in the United States. Just over 36 percent of adults are obese, a percentage that has nearly tripled since the 1960s. Furthermore, as age increases, more and more people are classified as obese. And 70 percent of adults age 20 and over are overweight (see Figure 13-3; Centers for Disease Control and Prevention, 2010; Ogden et al., 2015).

Weight control is a difficult—and often losing—battle for many young adults. Most people who diet ultimately regain the weight they have lost, and they become involved in a seesaw cycle of weight gain and loss. Some obesity experts now argue that the rate of dieting failure is so great that people may want to avoid dieting altogether. Instead, if people eat the foods they really want in moderation, they may be able to avoid the binge eating that often occurs when diets fail. Even though obese people may never reach their desired weight, they may, according to this reasoning, ultimately control their weight more effectively (Roehrig et al., 2009; Tremblay & Chaput, 2012; Chapuis-de-Andrade, de Araujo, & Lara, 2017).

Obesity is particularly prevalent in the United States. The world average weight for adults is 137 pounds; in the United States, the average is 180 (Walpole, 2012; see Figure 13-4).

Figure 13-4 First in Obesity

Obesity is particularly prevalent in the United States. The world average weight for adults is 137 pounds; in the United States, the average is 180.

(**Source:** Walpole, 2012; OECD, 2017.)

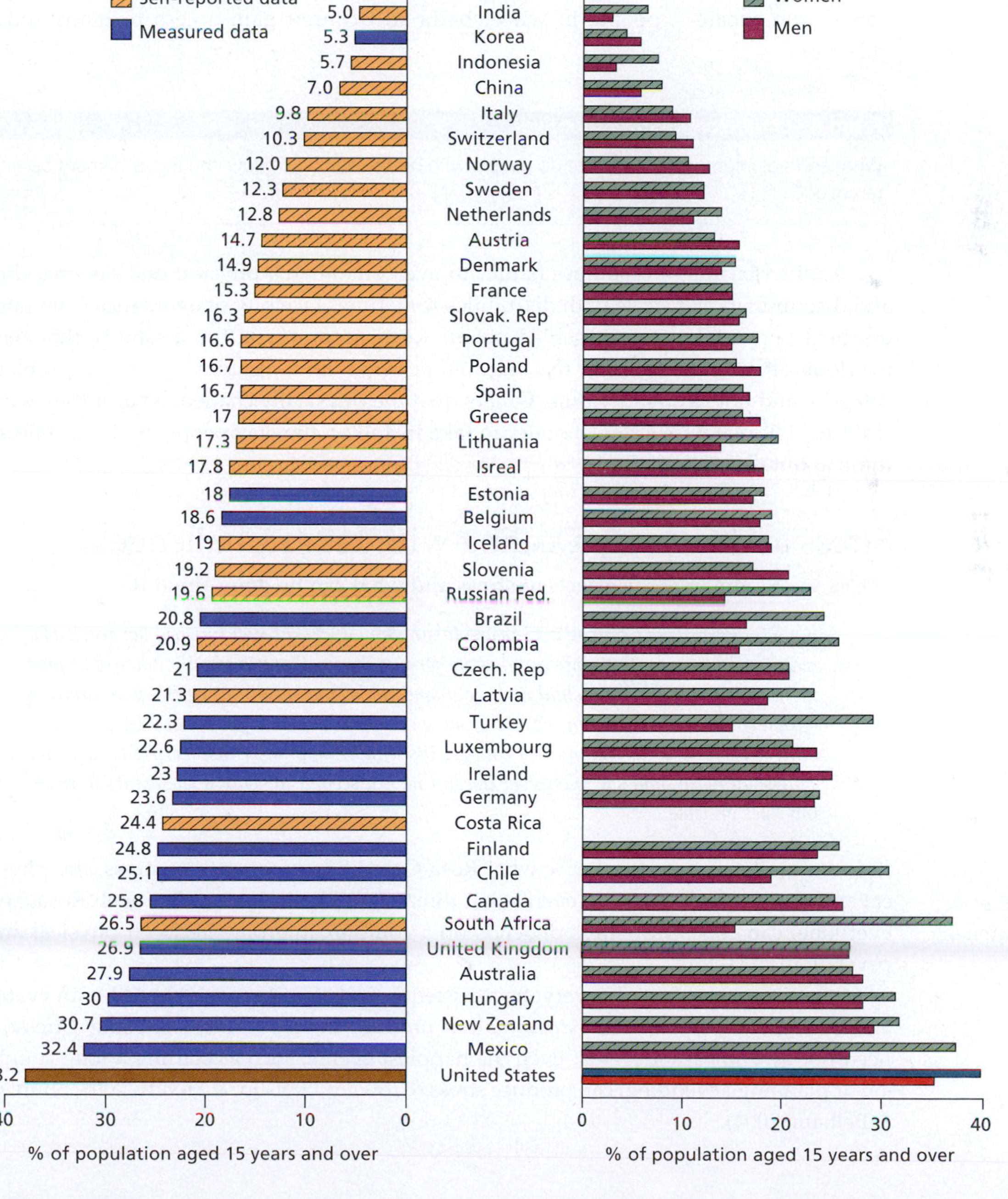

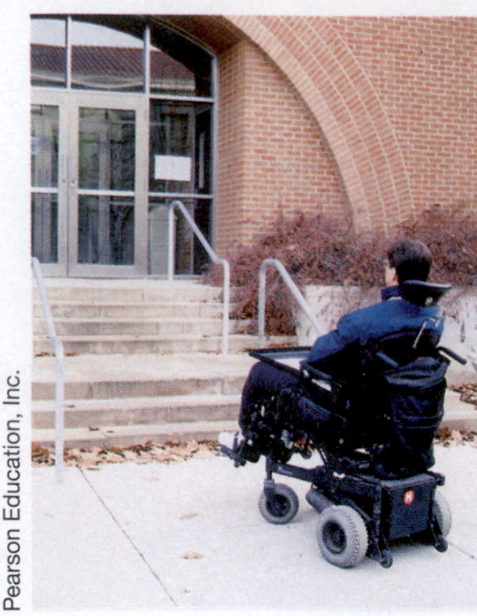

Despite the passage of the Americans with Disabilities Act (ADA), people with physical disabilities still cannot gain access to many older buildings.

Physical Disabilities: Coping with Physical Challenges

LO 13.3 Describe the challenges people with physical disabilities face in early adulthood.

Over 50 million people in the United States are physically or mentally challenged, according to the official definition of *disability*—a condition that substantially limits a major life activity, such as walking or vision. People with disabilities face a difficult, challenging path.

Statistics on people with disabilities paint a picture of a minority group that is undereducated and underemployed. Fewer than 10 percent of those with major handicaps have finished high school, fewer than 25 percent of disabled men and 15 percent of disabled women work full time, and unemployment rates are high. Furthermore, even if people with disabilities do find work, the positions they find are often routine and low-paying (Albrecht, 2005).

Individuals with disabilities face several kinds of barriers to leading full lives that are completely integrated into the broader society. Some barriers are physical. Despite passage in 1990 of the landmark Americans with Disabilities Act (ADA), which mandates full access to public establishments such as stores, office buildings, hotels, and theaters, people in wheelchairs still cannot gain access to many older buildings.

From *a social worker's* perspective

What sorts of interpersonal barriers do people with disabilities face? How can those barriers be removed?

Another barrier—sometimes harder to overcome than a physical one—is prejudice and discrimination. People with disabilities sometimes face pity or avoidance from nondisabled people. Some nondisabled people focus so much on the disability that they overlook other characteristics, reacting to a person with a disability only as a problem category and not as an individual. Others treat the physically challenged as if they were children. Ultimately, such treatment can take its toll on the way people with disabilities think about themselves.

Stress and Coping: Dealing with Life's Challenges

LO 13.4 Summarize the effects of stress and what can be done about it.

It's 5:00 P.M. Rosa Convoy, a 25-year-old single mother, has just finished her work as a receptionist at a dentist's office and is on her way home. She has exactly 2 hours to pick up her daughter Zoe from child care, get home, make and eat dinner, pick up and return with a babysitter from down the street, say goodbye to Zoe, and get to her 7:00 programming class at a local community college. It's a marathon she runs every Tuesday and Thursday night, and she knows she doesn't have a second to spare if she wants to reach the class on time.

stress
the physical and emotional response to events that threaten or challenge us

It doesn't take an expert to know what Rosa Convoy is experiencing: **stress**, the physical and emotional response to events that threaten or challenge us. How well Rosa, and everyone, can cope with stress depends on a complex interplay between physical and psychological factors.

Stress is a part of nearly everyone's existence, and our lives are crowded with events and circumstances, known as *stressors*, that produce threats to our wellbeing. Stressors need not be unpleasant events: Even the happiest events, such as starting a long-sought job or planning a wedding, can produce stress (Crowley, Hayslip, & Hobdy, 2003; Shimizu & Pelham, 2004).

Researchers in the field of **psychoneuroimmunology (PNI)**—the study of the relationship among the brain, the immune system, and psychological factors—have found that stress produces several outcomes. The most immediate is typically a biological reaction, as certain hormones, secreted by the adrenal glands, cause a rise in heart rate, blood pressure, respiration rate, and sweating. In some situations, these immediate effects may be beneficial because they produce an "emergency reaction" in the sympathetic nervous system by which people are better able to defend themselves from a sudden, threatening situation (Kiecolt-Glaser, 2009; Janusek, Cooper, & Mathews, 2012; Irwin, 2015).

psychoneuroimmunology (PNI)
the study of the relationship among the brain, the immune system, and psychological factors

At the same time, long-term, continuous exposure to stressors may result in a reduction of the body's ability to deal with stress. As stress-related hormones are constantly secreted, the heart, blood vessels, and other body tissues may deteriorate. As a consequence, people become more susceptible to diseases as their ability to fight off germs declines. In short, both *acute stressors* (sudden, one-time events) and *chronic stressors* (long-term, continuing events) have the potential to produce significant physiological consequences (Graham, Christian, & Kiecolt-Glaser, 2006; Rohleder, 2012; Maimari, 2017).

THE ORIGINS OF STRESS. Experienced job interviewers, college counselors, and owners of bridal shops all know that not everyone reacts the same way to a potentially stressful event. What makes the difference in people's reactions? According to psychologists Arnold Lazarus and Susan Folkman, people move through a series of stages, depicted in Figure 13-5, that determine whether they will experience stress (Lazarus, 1968; Lazarus & Folkman, 1984, 1991).

Figure 13-5 Steps in the Perception of Stress

The way we appraise a potential stressor determines whether we will experience stress.

(**Source:** Based on Kaplan, Sallis, & Patterson, 1993.)

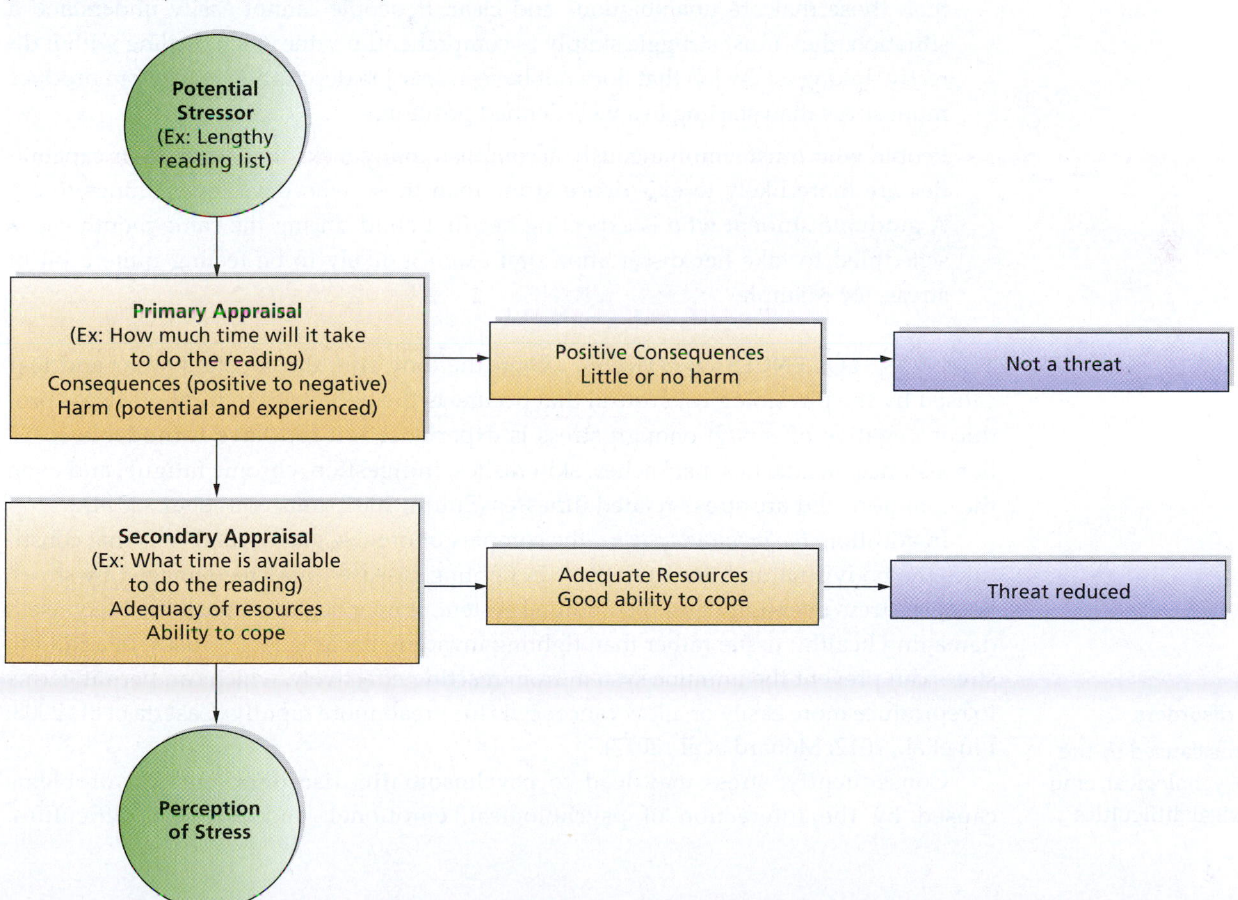

primary appraisal
the assessment of an event to determine whether its implications are positive, negative, or neutral

Primary appraisal is the first step—the individual's assessment of an event to determine whether its implications are positive, negative, or neutral. If a person sees the event as primarily negative, he or she appraises it in terms of the harm that it has caused in the past, how threatening it is likely to be, and how likely it is that the challenge can be resisted successfully. For example, you are likely to feel differently about an upcoming French test if you passed the last one with flying colors than you would if you did poorly.

secondary appraisal
the assessment of whether one's coping abilities and resources are adequate to overcome the harm, threat, or challenge posed by the potential stressor

Secondary appraisal follows. **Secondary appraisal** is the person's answer to the question "Can I handle it?"—an assessment of whether his or her coping abilities and resources are adequate to overcome the challenge posed by the potential stressor. At this point in the process, people try to determine if they will be able to meet the dangers in the situation. If resources are lacking, and the potential threat is great, they will experience stress. A traffic ticket is upsetting to anyone, but to those for whom the fine is an economic hardship, the stress is considerably greater.

Stress varies with the person's appraisal, and that appraisal varies with the person's temperament and circumstances. There are some general principles that help predict when an event will be appraised as stressful. Psychologist Shelley Taylor (2009) suggests the following:

- Events and circumstances that produce negative emotions are more likely to lead to stress than events that are positive. For example, planning for the adoption of a new baby produces less stress than dealing with the illness of a loved one.
- Situations that are uncontrollable or unpredictable are more likely to produce stress than those that can be controlled and predicted. Professors who give surprise quizzes in their classes, then, produce more stress than those whose quizzes are scheduled in advance.
- Events and circumstances that are ambiguous and confusing produce more stress than those that are unambiguous and clear. If people cannot easily understand a situation, they must struggle simply to comprehend it rather than dealing with it directly. Taking a new job that does not have a clear job description is likely to produce more stress than starting in a well-defined position.
- People who must simultaneously accomplish many tasks that strain their capabilities are more likely to experience stress than those who have fewer things to do. A graduate student who is expecting her first child during the same month she is scheduled to take her dissertation oral exam is likely to be feeling quite a bit of stress, for example.

THE CONSEQUENCES OF STRESS. Over the long run, the constant wear and tear caused by the physiological arousal that occurs as the body tries to fight off stress produces negative effects. If enough stress is experienced, it can have formidable costs. For instance, headaches, backaches, skin rashes, indigestion, chronic fatigue, and even the common cold are stress-related illnesses (Suinn, 2001; Andreotti et al., 2014).

In addition, *the immune system*—the complex of organs, glands, and cells that constitutes the body's natural line of defense in fighting disease—may be damaged by stress. Because stress overstimulates the immune system, it may begin to attack the body itself, damaging healthy tissue rather than fighting invading bacteria and viruses. In addition, stress can prevent the immune system from reacting effectively, which can permit germs to reproduce more easily or allow cancer cells to spread more rapidly (Caserta et al., 2008; Liu et al., 2012; Ménard et al., 2017).

psychosomatic disorders
medical problems caused by the interaction of psychological, emotional, and physical difficulties

Consequently, stress may lead to **psychosomatic disorders**, medical problems caused by the interaction of psychological, emotional, and physical difficulties.

For instance, ulcers, asthma, arthritis, and high blood pressure may—though not invariably—be produced by stress (Davis et al., 2008; Marin et al., 2009; Wippert & Niemeyer, 2014).

In sum, stress affects people in a number of ways. It can increase the risk of becoming ill, it may actually produce illness, it makes it more difficult to recover from illness, and it may reduce one's ability to cope with future stress. (To get a sense of how much stress you have in your own life, complete the questionnaire in Table 13-1.) Keep in mind that although stress occurs at all stages of life, as we age, we may learn to cope with stress better. As we see next, coping takes a variety of forms.

COPING WITH STRESS. Stress is a normal part of life, something that everyone encounters. Yet some young adults are better than others at **coping**, the effort to control, reduce, or learn to tolerate the threats that lead to stress (Taylor & Stanton, 2007). What is the key to successful coping?

coping
the effort to control, reduce, or learn to tolerate the threats that lead to stress

Some people use *problem-focused coping*, by which they attempt to manage a stressful problem or situation by directly changing the situation to make it less stressful. For example, a man who is having on-the-job difficulties may speak to his boss and ask that his responsibilities be modified, or he may look for another job.

Other people employ *emotion-focused coping*, which involves the conscious regulation of emotion. For instance, a mother who is having trouble finding appropriate care for her child while she is at work may tell herself that she should look at the bright side: At least she has a job in a difficult economy (Master et al., 2009; Folkman, 2011; Pow & Cashwell, 2017).

Table 13-1 How Stressed Are You?

The statements below will help you determine your level of stress. Mark the appropriate number in each box, then add up those numbers to find your score. Your answers should reflect your experiences in the past month only. To help you rate the extent of your stress, use the key at the bottom.

1. I become upset when something happens unexpectedly.
☐ 0 = never, 1 = almost never, 2 = sometimes, 3 = fairly often, 4 = very often

2. I feel I'm unable to control the things that are most important in my life.
☐ 0 = never, 1 = almost never, 2 = sometimes, 3 = fairly often, 4 = very often

3. I feel nervous and "stressed."
☐ 0 = never, 1 = almost never, 2 = sometimes, 3 = fairly often, 4 = very often

4. I feel confident about my ability to handle my personal problems.
☐ 4 = never, 3 = almost never, 2 = sometimes, 1 = fairly often, 0 = very often

5. In general, I feel things are going my way.
☐ 4 = never, 3 = almost never, 2 = sometimes, 1 = fairly often, 0 = very often

6. I'm able to control irritations in my life.
☐ 4 = never, 3 = almost never, 2 = sometimes, 1 = fairly often, 0 = very often

7. I feel I cannot cope with all the things I need to do.
☐ 0 = never, 1 = almost never, 2 = sometimes, 3 = fairly often, 4 = very often

8. Generally, I feel on top of things.
☐ 4 = never, 3 = almost never, 2 = sometimes, 1 = fairly often, 0 = very often

9. I get angry at things that are beyond my control.
☐ 0 = never, 1 = almost never, 2 = sometimes, 3 = fairly often, 4 = very often

10. I feel problems pile up to such an extent that I cannot overcome them.
☐ 0 = never, 1 = almost never, 2 = sometimes, 3 = fairly often, 4 = very often

How Do You Measure Up?

Stress levels vary from person to person, but you can compare your total score to the averages below:

Age		Gender	
18–29	14.2	Men	12.1
30–44	13.0	Women	13.7
45–54	12.6		
55–64	11.9		
65 and older	12.0		

Marital Status	
Widowed	12.6
Married or living with partner	12.4
Single or never wed	14.1
Divorced	14.7
Separated	16.6

(**Source:** Based on Sheldon Cohen, Dept. of Psychology, Carnegie Mellon University.)

Sometimes people acknowledge that they are in a stressful situation that cannot be changed, but they cope by managing their reactions. For example, they may take up meditation or exercise to reduce their physical reactions.

Coping is also aided by the presence of *social support*, assistance and comfort supplied by others. Turning to others in the face of stress can provide both emotional support (in the form of a shoulder to cry on) and practical, tangible support (such as a temporary financial loan). In addition, others can provide information, offering specific advice on how to deal with stressful situations. The ability to learn from others' experiences is one of the reasons that people use the Web to connect with people who have similar experiences (Kim, Sherman, & Taylor, 2008; Green, DeCourville, & Sadava, 2012; Vallejo-Sánchez & Pérez-García, 2015).

Finally, even if people do not consciously cope with stress, some psychologists suggest that they may use unconscious defensive coping mechanisms of which they are unaware and that aid in stress reduction. **Defensive coping** involves unconscious strategies that distort or deny the true nature of a situation. For instance, people may deny the seriousness of a threat, trivialize a life-threatening illness, or tell themselves that academic failure on a series of tests is unimportant.

defensive coping
coping that involves unconscious strategies that distort or deny the true nature of a situation

Another type of defensive coping is emotional insulation. In *emotional insulation*, people unconsciously try to prevent themselves from experiencing emotions. By attempting to remain unaffected by negative (or positive) experiences, they try to avoid the pain brought about by the experience. If defensive coping becomes a habitual response to stress, it can prevent the person from dealing with the reality of the situation by offering a way to avoid or ignore the problem (Ormont, 2001).

In some cases, people use drugs or alcohol to escape from stressful situations. Like defensive coping, drinking and drug use do not help address the situation causing the stress, and they can increase a person's difficulties. For example, people may become addicted to the substances that initially provided them with a pleasurable sense of escape.

HARDINESS, RESILIENCE, AND COPING. The success with which young adults deal with stress depends in part on their *coping style*, their general tendency to deal with stress in a particular way. For example, people with a "hardy" coping style are especially successful in dealing with stress. **Hardiness** is a personality characteristic associated with a lower rate of stress-related illness.

hardiness
a personality characteristic associated with a lower rate of stress-related illness

Hardy individuals are take-charge people who revel in life's challenges. It is not surprising, then, that people who are high in hardiness are more resistant to stress-related illness than those who show less hardiness. Hardy people react to potentially threatening stressors with optimism, feeling that they can respond effectively. By turning threatening situations into challenging ones, they are less apt to experience high levels of stress (Maddi et al., 2006; Andrew et al., 2008; Maddi, 2014).

For people who face the most profound of life's difficulties—such as the unexpected death of a loved one or a permanent injury, such as spinal cord damage—a key factor in their reactions is their level of resilience. As we first discussed in Chapter 8, *resilience* is the ability to withstand, overcome, and actually thrive following profound adversity (Werner, 2005; Kim-Cohen, 2007; Lipsitt & Demick, 2012).

Resilient young adults tend to be easygoing, good-natured, and have good social and communication skills. They are independent, feeling that they can shape their own fate, and they are not dependent on others or on luck. In short, they work with what they have, and they make the best of whatever situation in which they find themselves (Deshields et al., 2005; Friborg et al., 2005; Clauss-Ehlers, 2008). (Also see the *Development in Your Life* feature.)

Development in Your Life

Coping with Stress

Although no single formula can cover all cases of stress, some general guidelines can help all of us cope with the stress that is part of our lives. Among them are the following (Sacks, 1993; Kaplan, Sallis, & Patterson, 1993; Bionna, 2006).

- Seek control over the situation producing the stress. Putting yourself in charge of a situation that is producing stress can take you a long way toward coping with it. For example, if you are feeling stress about an upcoming test, do something about it—such as starting to study.
- Redefine "threat" as "challenge." Changing the definition of a situation can make it seem less threatening. "Look for the silver lining" is not bad advice. For example, if you get fired, look at it as an opportunity to get a new, and potentially better, job.
- Use mindfulness. Mindfulness stress reduction techniques involve learning to become aware of one's surroundings, making every moment count, and observing one's thoughts and feelings without judging them. Research has demonstrated that getting into a mindful state helps manage and reduce stress responses (Meland et al., 2015; Ramasubramanian, 2017).
- Find social support. Almost any difficulty can be faced more easily with the help of others. Friends, family members, and even telephone hotlines staffed by trained counselors can provide significant support. (For help in identifying appropriate hotlines, the U.S. Public Health Service maintains a "master" toll-free number that can provide the phone numbers and addresses of many national groups. Call 800-336-4794.)
- Use relaxation techniques. Reducing the physiological arousal brought about by stress can be a particularly effective way of coping with stress. A variety of techniques that produce relaxation, such as transcendental meditation, yoga, progressive muscle relaxation, and even hypnosis, have been shown to be effective in reducing stress. One technique that works particularly well was devised by physician Herbert Benson and is illustrated in Table 13-2 (Benson, 1993).
- Try to maintain a healthy lifestyle that will reinforce your body's natural coping mechanisms. Exercise, eat nutritiously, get enough sleep, and avoid or moderate your use of alcohol, tobacco, or other drugs.
- If all else fails, keep in mind that a life without any stress at all would be a dull one. Stress is a natural part of life, and successfully coping with it can be a gratifying experience.

Table 13-2 How to Elicit the Relaxation Response

Some general advice on regular practice of the relaxation response:

- Try to find 10 to 20 minutes in your daily routine; before breakfast is a good time.
- Sit comfortably.
- For the period you will practice, try to arrange your life so you won't have distractions. Turn off your cell phone, and ask someone else to watch the kids.
- Time yourself by glancing periodically at a clock or watch (but don't set an alarm). Commit yourself to a specific length of practice, and try to stick to it.

There are several approaches to eliciting the relaxation response. Here is one standard set of instructions:

Step 1. Pick a focus word or short phrase that's firmly rooted in your personal belief system. For example, a nonreligious individual might choose a neutral word like *one* or *peace* or *love*. A Christian person desiring to use a prayer could pick the opening words of Psalm 23, *The Lord is my shepherd*; a Jewish person could choose *Shalom*.
Step 2. Sit quietly in a comfortable position.
Step 3. Close your eyes.
Step 4. Relax your muscles.
Step 5. Breathe slowly and naturally, repeating your focus word or phrase silently as you exhale.
Step 6. Throughout, assume a passive attitude. Don't worry about how well you're doing. When other thoughts come to mind, simply say to yourself, "Oh, well," and gently return to the repetition.
Step 7. Continue for 10 to 20 minutes. You may open your eyes to check the time, but do not use an alarm. When you finish, sit quietly for a minute or so, at first with your eyes closed and later with your eyes open. Then do not stand for 1 or 2 minutes.
Step 8. Practice the technique once or twice a day.

(**Source:** Benson, 1993.)

Module 13.1 Review

LO 13.1 Describe how the body develops and stays healthy during early adulthood.

By young adulthood, the body and the senses are at their peak, but growth is proceeding, particularly in the brain. Even though young adults are generally as fit and healthy as they will ever be, accidents present the greatest risk of death. In the United States, violence is also a significant risk, particularly for nonwhite males.

LO 13.2 Explain why a healthy diet is particularly important in early adulthood.

Even in young adulthood, health must be maintained by proper diet and exercise. Obesity is increasingly a problem for young adults.

LO 13.3 Describe the challenges people with physical disabilities face in early adulthood.

People with physical disabilities face not only physical barriers but also psychological barriers caused by prejudice and discrimination.

LO 13.4 Summarize the effects of stress and what can be done about it.

Stress, which is a healthy reaction in small doses, can be harmful to body and mind if it is frequent or of long duration. The effort to control, reduce, or learn to tolerate stress is called *coping*. Coping strategies include problem-focused coping, emotion-focused coping, and relying on social support.

Journal Writing Prompt

Applying Lifespan Development: Describe and discuss your own coping style(s). What do you do when faced with stress? What works and what doesn't?

Cognitive Development

Ben is known to be a heavy drinker, especially when he goes to parties. Tyra, Ben's wife, warns him that if he comes home drunk one more time, she will leave him and take the children. Tonight Ben is out late at an office party. He comes home drunk. Does Tyra leave Ben?

An adolescent who hears this situation (drawn from research by Adams and Labouvie-Vief, 1986) may find the case to be open and shut: Tyra leaves Ben. But in early adulthood, the answer becomes a bit less clear. As people enter adulthood, they become less concerned with the sheer logic of situations and instead take into account real-life concerns that may influence and temper behavior in particular instances.

Intellectual Growth in Early Adulthood

LO 13.5 Describe how cognitive development continues in young adulthood.

If cognitive development were to follow the same pattern as physical development, we would expect to find little new intellectual growth in early adulthood. In fact, Jean Piaget, whose theory of cognitive development played such a prominent role in our earlier discussions of intellectual change, argued that by the time people left adolescence, their thinking, at least qualitatively, had largely become what it would be for the rest of their lives. People might gather more information, but the ways in which they think about it would not change.

Was Piaget's view correct? Increasing evidence suggests that he was mistaken.

Design Pics Inc/Alamy Stock Photo

The nature of thought changes qualitatively during early adulthood.

POSTFORMAL THOUGHT. Developmental psychologist Gisela Labouvie-Vief suggests that the nature of thinking changes qualitatively during early adulthood. She asserts that thinking based solely on formal operations (Piaget's final stage, reached during adolescence) is insufficient to meet the demands placed on young adults. The complexity of society, which requires specialization, and the increasing challenge of finding one's way through all that complexity require thought that is not necessarily based on logic alone but also on practical experience, moral judgments, and values (Labouvie-Vief, 2006, 2009).

For example, imagine a young, single woman in her first job. Her boss, a married man whom she respects greatly and who is in a position to help her career, invites her to go with him to make an important presentation to a client. When the presentation, which has gone very well, is over, he suggests they go out to dinner and celebrate. Later that evening, after sharing a bottle of wine, he asks if he can walk her back to her hotel room to make sure she gets back safely. How should she handle the situation?

Logic alone doesn't answer such questions. Labouvie-Vief suggests that as young adults are increasingly exposed to difficult and ambiguous situations like these, their thinking must develop to handle them. She suggests that young adults learn to use analogies and metaphors to make comparisons, confront society's paradoxes, and become comfortable with a more subjective understanding. Such thinking requires weighing all the aspects of a situation according to one's values and beliefs. It allows for interpretive processes and reflects the fact that reasons behind events in the real world are subtle, painted in shades of gray rather than in black and white (Thornton, 2004; Labouvie-Vief, 2015; Sinnott et al., 2017).

To demonstrate how this sort of thinking develops, in an experiment, Labouvie-Vief presented participants, ranging in age from 10 to 40, with scenarios similar to the Ben and Tyra scenario at the beginning of this section. Each story had a clear, logical conclusion. However, the story could be interpreted differently if real-world demands and pressures were taken into account.

In responding to the scenarios, adolescents relied heavily on the logic inherent in formal operations. For instance, they would predict that Tyra would immediately pack up her bags and leave with the children when Ben came home drunk. After all, that's what she said she would do.

In contrast, young adults were less prone to use strict logic in determining a character's likely course of action. Instead, they would consider various possibilities that might come into the picture in a real-life situation: Would Ben be apologetic and beg Tyra not to leave? Did Tyra really mean it when she said she would leave? Does Tyra have some alternative place to go?

Young adults exhibited what Labouvie-Vief calls postformal thought. **Postformal thought** is thinking that goes beyond Piaget's formal operations. Rather than being based on purely logical processes, with absolutely right and wrong answers to problems, postformal thought acknowledges that adult predicaments must sometimes be solved in relativistic terms.

postformal thought
thinking that acknowledges that adult predicaments must sometimes be solved in relativistic terms

According to psychologist Jan Sinnott (1998a, 2009), postformal thought also takes into account real-world considerations when solving problems. Postformal thinkers can shift back and forth between an abstract, ideal solution and real-world constraints that might prevent the solution from being successfully implemented. In addition, postformal thinkers understand that just as there can be multiple causes of a situation, there can be multiple solutions.

In short, postformal thought and dialectical thinking acknowledge a world that sometimes lacks clearly right and wrong solutions to problems, a world in which logic may fail to resolve complex human questions. Instead, finding the best resolution to difficulties may involve drawing upon and integrating prior experiences.

Approaches to Postformal Thinking

LO 13.6 Compare and contrast Perry's and Schaie's approaches to cognitive development in young adulthood.

In addition to Labouvie-Vief's approach to postformal thoughts, psychologists William Perry and K. Warner Schaie have proposed alternative approaches to postformal thought.

PERRY'S RELATIVISTIC THINKING. To psychologist William Perry (1981), early adulthood represents a period of developmental growth that encompasses mastery not just of particular bodies of knowledge but of ways of understanding the world. Perry examined the ways in which students grew intellectually and morally during college. In comprehensive interviews with a group of students at Harvard University, he found that students entering college tended to use *dualistic thinking* in their views of the world. For instance, they reasoned that something was right or it was wrong; people were good or they were bad; and others were either for them or against them.

As these students encountered new ideas and points of view from other students and their professors, however, their dualistic thinking declined. Consistent with the notion of changes in postformal thinking, students increasingly realized that issues can have more than one plausible side. Furthermore, they understood more clearly that it is possible to hold multiple perspectives on an issue. This multiple thinking was characterized by a shift in the way the students viewed authorities: Instead of presupposing that experts had all the answers, they began to assume that their own thinking on an issue had validity if their position was well thought out and rational.

From *an educator's* perspective

Can you think of situations that you would deal with differently as an adult than as an adolescent? Do the differences reflect postformal thinking?

According to Perry, they had entered a stage in which knowledge and values were regarded as relativistic. Rather than seeing the world as having absolute standards and values, they argued that different societies, cultures, and individuals could have different standards and values, and all of them could be equally valid.

It's important to keep in mind that Perry's theory is based on a sample of interviews conducted with well-educated students attending an elite college. His findings may not apply as well to people who are not taught to examine multiple points of view, as is common in a college setting. Still, his notion that thinking continues to develop during early adulthood is widely accepted. As we consider next, other theories suggest that thinking changes in significant ways throughout adulthood.

SCHAIE'S STAGES OF DEVELOPMENT. Developmental psychologist K. Warner Schaie offers another perspective on postformal thought. Taking up where Piaget left off, Schaie suggests that adults' thinking follows a set pattern of stages (illustrated in Figure 13-6). But Schaie focuses on the ways in which information is *used* during adulthood rather than on changes in the acquisition and understanding of new information, as in Piaget's approach (Schaie & Willis, 1993; Schaie & Zanjani, 2006; Schaie, 2016).

Schaie suggests that before adulthood, the main cognitive developmental task is acquisition of information. Consequently, he labels the first stage of cognitive development, which encompasses all of childhood and adolescence, the **acquisitive stage**. Information gathered before we grow up is largely squirreled away for future use. In fact, much of the rationale for education during childhood and adolescence is to prepare people for future activities.

acquisitive stage
according to Schaie, the first stage of cognitive development, encompassing all of childhood and adolescence, in which the main developmental task is to acquire information

The situation changes considerably in early adulthood, however. Instead of targeting the future use of knowledge, the focus shifts to the "here and now." According to Schaie, young adults are in the achieving stage, applying their intelligence to attaining long-term

Figure 13-6 Schaie's Stages of Adult Development

(**Source:** Based on Schaie, 1977–1978.)

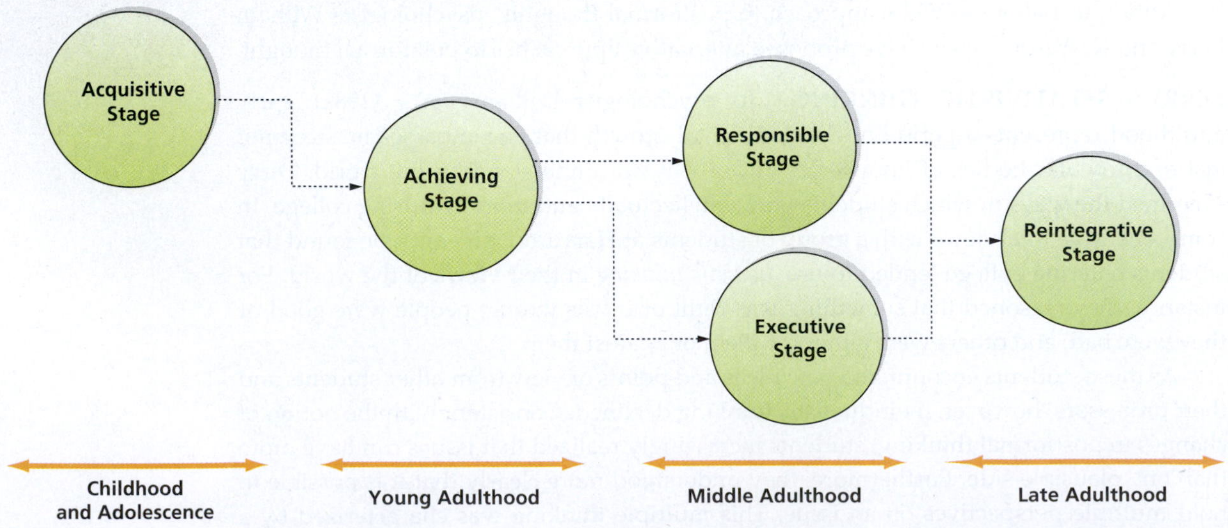

goals regarding their careers, family, and contributions to society. During the **achieving stage**, young adults must confront and resolve several major issues, and the decisions they make—such as what job to take and whom to marry—have implications for the rest of their lives.

achieving stage
the point reached by young adults in which intelligence is applied to specific situations involving the attainment of long-term goals regarding careers, family, and societal contributions

During the late stages of early adulthood and in middle adulthood, people move into what Schaie calls the responsible and executive stages. In the **responsible stage**, middle-aged adults are mainly concerned with protecting and nourishing their spouses, families, and careers.

responsible stage
the stage in which the major concerns of middle-aged adults relate to their personal situations, including protecting and nourishing their spouses, families, and careers

Sometime later, further into middle adulthood, many people (but not all) enter the **executive stage** in which they take a broader perspective, becoming more concerned about the larger world. Rather than focusing only on their own lives, people in the executive stage also put energy into nourishing and sustaining societal institutions. They may become involved in town government, religious congregations, service clubs, charitable groups, factory unions—organizations that have a larger purpose in society. People in the executive stage, then, look beyond their individual situations.

executive stage
the period in middle adulthood when people take a broader perspective than earlier, including concerns about the world

Late adulthood, according to Schaie's model, marks entry into the final period, the **reintegrative stage**, the period of late adulthood during which people focus on tasks that have personal meaning. In this stage, they no longer focus on acquiring knowledge as a means of solving potential problems that they may encounter. Instead, their information acquisition is directed toward particular issues that specifically interest them.

reintegrative stage
the period of late adulthood during which the focus is on tasks that have personal meaning

Furthermore, they have less interest in—and patience for—things that they do not see as having some immediate application to their lives. Thus, the abstract issue of whether the federal budget should be balanced may be of less concern to an elderly individual than whether the government should provide universal health care.

Schaie's perspective on cognitive development reminds us that cognitive change doesn't stop at adolescence, as Piaget would contend. Instead, there are significant changes that continue throughout early adulthood and onward.

From *an educator's* perspective

Do you think educators can teach people to be more intelligent? Are there components or varieties of intelligence that might be more "teachable" than others?

Intelligence: What Matters in Early Adulthood?

LO 13.7 Explain how intelligence is defined today and how life events cause cognitive growth in young adults.

You've had a pretty good year at your job. You've got two assistants who help you; one is quite good, but the other doesn't work very hard. Although you're well-liked in the company, there's not much to distinguish you from your peers. Although you want to move up quickly in the company and become an executive, you're just not sure how you can you meet your goals.

The way adults respond to this situation has a great deal to do with their future success, according to psychologist Robert Sternberg. The scenario is one of a series designed to assess a particular type of intelligence that may have more of an impact on future success than the type of intelligence measured by traditional IQ tests of the sort we discussed in Chapter 9 (Wagner & Sternberg, 1985; Sternberg, 2015).

In his **triarchic theory of intelligence**, Sternberg suggests that intelligence is made up of three major components: componential, experiential, and contextual (see Figure 13-7). The *componential* aspect includes the mental components involved in analyzing data used in solving problems, especially problems involving rational behavior. It relates to people's ability to select and use formulas, to choose appropriate problem-solving strategies, and in general to make use of what they have been taught. The *experiential* component refers to the relationship between intelligence, people's prior experience, and their

triarchic theory of intelligence
Sternberg's theory that intelligence is made up of three major components: componential, experiential, and contextual

Figure 13-7 Sternberg's Triarchic Theory of Intelligence

(**Source:** Based on Sternberg, 1985, 1991.)

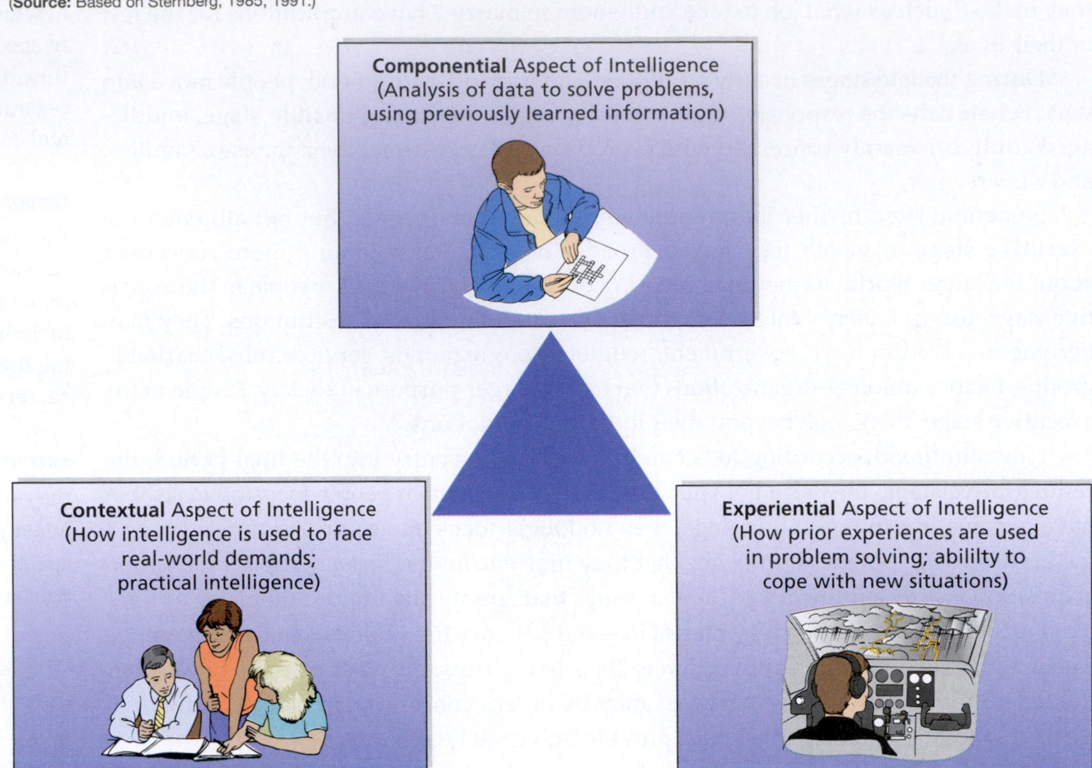

ability to cope with new situations. This is the insightful aspect of intelligence, which allows people to relate what they already know to a new situation and an array of facts never before encountered. Finally, the *contextual* component of intelligence involves the degree of success people demonstrate in facing the demands of their everyday, real-world environments. For instance, the contextual component is involved in adapting to on-the-job professional demands (Sternberg, 2005, 2015).

Traditional intelligence tests, which yield an IQ score, tend to focus on the componential aspect of intelligence. Yet increasing evidence suggests that a more useful measure, particularly when one is looking for ways to compare and predict adult success, is the contextual component—the aspect of intelligence that has come to be called practical intelligence.

PRACTICAL AND EMOTIONAL INTELLIGENCE. According to Sternberg, the IQ score that most traditional tests produce relates quite well to academic success. However, IQ seems to be unrelated to other types of achievement, such as career success. For example, although it is clear that success in business settings requires some minimal level of the sort of intelligence measured by IQ tests, the rate of career advancement and the ultimate success of business executives are only marginally related to IQ scores (Sternberg, 2006; Grigorenko et al., 2009; Ekinci, 2014).

Sternberg contends that success in a career necessitates a type of intelligence called practical intelligence, which is substantially different from that involved in traditional academic pursuits (Sternberg et al., 1997). While academic success is based on knowledge of particular types of information, obtained largely from reading and listening, **practical intelligence** is learned primarily by observing others and modeling their behavior. People who are high in practical intelligence have a good "social radar." They are able to understand and handle even new situations effectively, reading people and circumstances insightfully, based on their previous experiences.

practical intelligence
according to Sternberg, intelligence that is learned primarily by observing others and modeling their behavior

Related to this sort of mental ability is another type of intelligence involving emotional domains. **Emotional intelligence** is the set of skills that underlies the accurate assessment, evaluation, expression, and regulation of emotions. Emotional intelligence is what gives some people the ability to get along well with others, to understand what others are feeling and experiencing, and to respond appropriately to the needs of others. It permits a person to tune into others' feelings, allowing an individual to respond appropriately. Emotional intelligence is also of obvious value to career and personal success as a young adult (Nelis et al., 2009; Kross & Grossmann, 2012; Szczygieł & Mikolajczak, 2017).

emotional intelligence
the set of skills that underlie the accurate assessment, evaluation, expression, and regulation of emotions

CREATIVITY: NOVEL THOUGHT. The hundreds of musical compositions of Wolfgang Amadeus Mozart, who died at age 35, were largely written during early adulthood. The same is true of many other creative individuals: Many mathematicians and physicists produce their major works during early adulthood. Overall, creative productivity seems to peak in the late 30s and early 40s, and then slowly decline. But there are many exceptions, and the most creative people maintain their creativity throughout their life span (Simonton, 2017; see Figure 13-8).

One reason for the higher creativity of early adulthood may be that *after* early adulthood, creativity can be stifled by the fact that the more people know about a subject, the less likely they are to be creative in that area. According to such reasoning, people in early adulthood may be at the peak of their creativity because many of the problems they encounter on a professional level are novel—or at least new to them. As they get older, however, and become more familiar with the problems, their creativity may be stymied. In addition, as we age, we become less flexible in our thinking, and we are less likely to adopt unfamiliar hypotheses and assumptions (Gopnik et al, 2017).

Figure 13-8 Creativity and Age

The period of maximum creativity differs depending on the particular field. The percentages refer to the percent of total lifetime major works produced during the particular age period. Why do poets peak earlier than novelists?

(**Source:** Based on Dennis, 1966.)

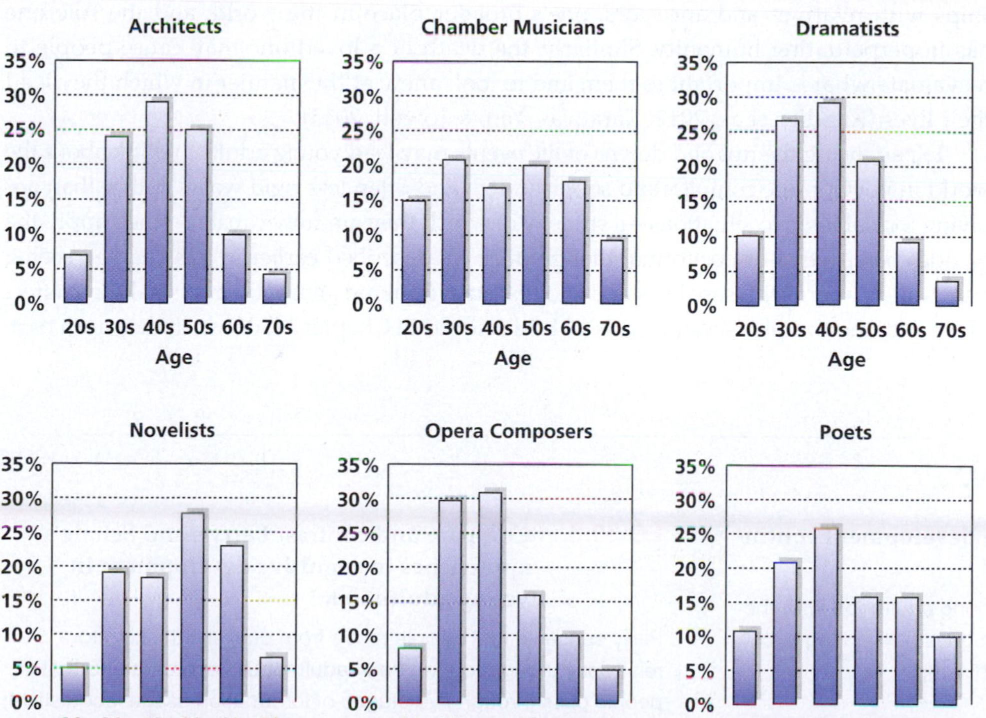

However, many people do not reach their pinnacle of creativity until later in life. For instance, Buckminster Fuller did not devise his major contribution, the geodesic dome, until he was in his 50s. Frank Lloyd Wright designed the Guggenheim Museum in New York at age 70. Charles Darwin and Jean Piaget were still writing influential works well into their 70s, and Pablo Picasso was painting in his 90s. Furthermore, when we look at overall productivity, as opposed to the period of a person's most important output, we find that productivity remains fairly steady throughout adulthood, particularly in the humanities (Simonton, 2009; 2017).

creativity
the combination of responses or ideas in novel ways

One reason for the difficulty in determining the relationship between age and creativity is just what constitutes an instance of **creativity**, which is defined as the combination of responses or ideas in novel ways. Because definitions of what is "novel" may vary from one person to the next, it is hard to identify a particular behavior unambiguously as creative.

That ambiguity hasn't stopped psychologists from trying. For instance, one important component of creativity is a person's willingness to take risks that may result in potentially high payoffs. Creative people are analogous to successful stock market investors, who try to follow the "buy low, sell high" rule. Creative people develop and endorse ideas that are unfashionable or regarded as wrong ("buying low"). They assume that eventually others will see the value of the ideas and embrace them ("selling high"). According to this theory, creative adults take a fresh look at ideas or problem solutions that might initially be discarded, particularly if the problem is a familiar one. They are flexible enough to move away from the way they have typically done things and to consider new approaches and opportunities (Sternberg, Kaufman, & Pretz, 2002; Sawyer, 2012; Sternberg, 2017).

IMAGEMORE Co, Ltd./Getty Images

Profound events such as the birth of a child or the death of a loved one can stimulate cognitive development by offering an opportunity to reevaluate our place in the world. What are some other profound events that might stimulate cognitive development?

LIFE EVENTS AND COGNITIVE DEVELOPMENT. Marriage. The death of a parent. Starting a first job. The birth of a child. Buying a house. The course of life comprises many events such as these—important milestones on the path through the life span. Such occurrences, whether they are welcome or unwanted, clearly may bring about stress, as we saw earlier in this chapter. But do they also cause cognitive growth?

Although the research is still spotty and largely based on case studies, some evidence suggests that major life events may lead to cognitive growth. For instance, the birth of a child—a profound event—may trigger fresh insights into the nature of one's relationships with relatives and ancestors, one's broader place in the world, and the role one has in perpetuating humanity. Similarly, the death of a loved one may cause people to reevaluate what is important to them and to look anew at the manner in which they lead their lives (Kandler et al., 2012; Karatzias, Yan, & Jowett, 2015).

Experiencing the ups and downs of life events may lead young adults to think about the world in novel, more complex and sophisticated, and often less rigid ways. Rather than applying formal logic to situations—a strategy of which they are fully capable—they apply the broader perspective of postformal thought that we described earlier in this chapter, seeing trends and patterns, personalities and choices. Such thinking allows them to deal more effectively with the complex social worlds (to be discussed in Chapter 14) of which they are a part.

Module 13.2 Review

LO 13.5 Describe how cognitive development continues in young adulthood.

Cognitive development continues into young adulthood with the emergence of postformal thought, which goes beyond logic to encompass interpretive and subjective thinking.

LO 13.6 Compare and contrast Perry's and Schaie's approaches to cognitive development in young adulthood.

Perry suggests that people move from dualistic thinking to relativistic thought during early adulthood. According to Schaie, people pass through five stages of information usage: acquisitive, achieving, responsible, executive, and reintegrative.

LO 13.7 Explain how intelligence is defined today and how life events cause cognitive growth in young adults.

New views of intelligence encompass the triarchic theory, practical intelligence, and emotional intelligence. Creativity seems to peak during early adulthood, with young adults viewing even long-standing problems as novel situations. Major life events contribute to cognitive growth by providing opportunities and incentives to rethink oneself and one's world.

Journal Writing Prompt

Applying Lifespan Development: What does "familiarity breeds rigidity" mean? Can you think of examples of this phenomenon from your own experience?

College: Pursuing Higher Education

Attending—and completing—college is a significant accomplishment. Although you may believe that college attendance is commonplace, this is not the case at all: Nationwide, high school graduates who enter college are actually in the minority.

The Demographics of Higher Education

LO 13.8 Describe who attends college today and how the college population is changing.

What types of students enter college? As in the U.S. population as a whole, U.S. college students are primarily white and middle class. About 58 percent of the college population age 18 to 24 years old is white, compared with 19 percent Hispanic, 14 percent black, 7 percent Asian, and 2 percent other races or ethnicities (U.S. Department of Education, 2012; see Figure 13-9 and the *From Research to Practice* box).

Figure 13-9 College Enrollment Rates by Racial Group

The proportion of nonwhites who attend college is lower than the proportion of whites, except for Asians. The percentages refer to total college enrollment rates of 18- to 24-year-olds in degree-granting institutions.

(**Source:** Musu-Gillette et al., 2016.)

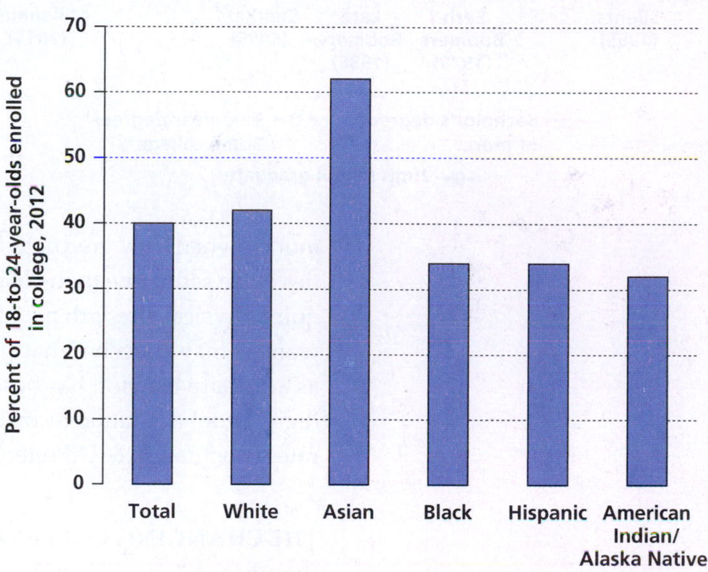

From Research to Practice

Does a Racially Diverse College Campus Make for a Richer Learning Environment?

One factor students sometimes consider in choosing a college to attend is the diversity of the student body. Some applicants—perhaps those seeking to learn about people from different backgrounds—are attracted to campuses with a diverse ethnic mixture. But the benefits of studying in a racially diverse environment may actually extend beyond learning about others, and may actually help students to think more effectively and critically.

It seems reasonable that diversity should stimulate critical thinking, and research has been supportive of this hypothesis. For example, in homogenous settings, in which students have similar backgrounds and perspectives, students bring similarities in thinking to situations in which they engage in problem solving. By contrast, diverse groups, whose members represent a variety of backgrounds and perspectives, bring greater variety in ideas and perspectives that the group must integrate in their discussions. This engagement with different outlooks on a problem tends to increase the complexity of the group members' thinking (Gurin et al., 2003; Roksa et al., 2017).

These findings are consistent with a growing body of research that finds that exposure to other students who represent the range of cultures, ethnicities, and races has important consequences. Not only do students benefit socially in terms of increased multicultural understanding, but their cognitive development is also enhanced. In short, diversity has significant cognitive benefits, leading to more critical thinking and other sorts of cognitive advances (Gurin, Nagda, & Lpez, 2004; Nagda, Gurin, & Johnson, 2005; Pascarella et al., 2014).

Shared Writing Prompt

How might you counter concerns that greater classroom diversity could make students feel less comfortable and therefore less willing to engage and able to learn effectively?

Figure 13-10 Education and Economic Security

The disparity in earnings between those who have a college degree and those who don't has grown over the past 50 years.

(**Source:** Taylor, Fry, & Oates, 2014.)

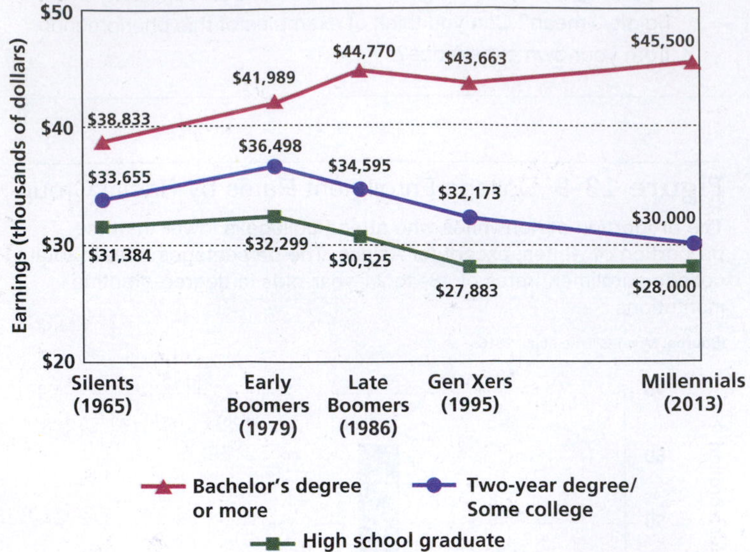

For students who do not attend or complete college, the consequences can be significant. Higher education is an important way for people to improve their economic well-being. Just 3 percent of adults who have a college education live below the poverty line. Compare that with high school dropouts: They are 10 times more likely to be living in poverty (see Figure 13-10; U.S. Bureau of Labor Statistics, 2012).

THE GENDER GAP IN COLLEGE ATTENDANCE. More women than men attend college, with 71 percent of female high school graduates enrolled in college the fall following graduation, compared with only 61 percent of males. The gender gap is even greater for minority students, with 69 percent of black women enrolled compared to 57 percent of black men, and 76 percent of Hispanic women enrolled compared to 62 percent of Hispanic men. Furthermore, projections show that the gap between women and men is expected to grow over the next decade (Adebayo, 2008; Lopez & Gonzalez-Barrera, 2014).

Why is there a gender gap in college attendance? It may be that men have more opportunities to earn money when they graduate from high school, and they find these immediate opportunities more seductive than college. For instance, the military, trade unions, and jobs that require physical strength may be more attractive to men, and consequently more men than women may perceive that good options other than college are available. Furthermore, as affirmative action has become less of a factor in admissions, women often have better high school academic records than men, and they may be admitted to college at greater rates (Buchmann & DiPrete, 2006; England & Li, 2006; Rocheleau, 2016).

THE CHANGING COLLEGE STUDENT: NEVER TOO LATE TO GO TO COLLEGE? If the phrase "average college student" brings to mind an image of an 18- or 19-year-old, you should begin to rethink your view. Increasingly, students are older. In fact, a quarter of students taking college courses for credit in the United States are between the ages of 25 and 35—like Laura Twombly, the 30-year-old student profiled earlier. Two-thirds of community college students are age 22 or older, and 14 percent are 40+ years old (U.S. Department of Education, 2005; American Association of Community Colleges, 2015).

Why are so many older, nontraditional students taking college courses? One reason is economic. As a college degree becomes increasingly important in obtaining a job, some workers feel compelled to get the credential. Many employers encourage or require workers to undergo training to learn new skills or update their old ones.

In addition, as people age, they may begin to feel the need to settle down with a family. This change in attitude can reduce their risk-taking behavior and make them focus more on acquiring the ability to support their family—a phenomenon that has been labeled *maturation reform*.

From *an educator's* perspective

How is the growing number of older, nontraditional students likely to affect the college classroom, given what you know about human development? Why?

According to developmental psychologist Sherry Willis (1985), several broad goals underlie adults' participation in learning experiences. First, adults may be seeking to understand their own aging. As they get older, they try to figure out what is happening to them and what to expect in the future. Second, adults seek education in order to understand more fully the rapid technological and cultural changes that characterize modern life.

Furthermore, adult learners may be seeking a practical edge in combating obsolescence on the job. Some individuals also may be attempting to acquire new vocational skills. Finally, adult educational experiences may be seen as helpful in preparing for future retirement. As adults get older, they become increasingly concerned with shifting from a work orientation to a leisure orientation, and they may see education as a means of broadening their possibilities.

College Adjustment: Reacting to the Demands of College Life

first-year adjustment reaction
a cluster of psychological symptoms, including loneliness, anxiety, withdrawal, and depression, relating to the college experience suffered by first-year college students

LO 13.9 Summarize the difficulties students face as they enter college.

When you began college, did you feel depressed, lonely, anxious, and withdrawn from others? If you did, you weren't alone. Many students, particularly those who are recent high school graduates and who are living away from home for the first time, experience difficulties in adjustment during their first year in college. The **first-year adjustment reaction** is a cluster of psychological symptoms, including loneliness, anxiety, and depression, relating to the college experience. Although any first-year student may suffer from one or more of the symptoms of first-year adjustment reaction, it is particularly likely to occur among students who have been unusually successful, either academically or socially, in high school. When they begin college, their sudden change in status may cause them distress.

Mark Bowden/Getty Images

Students who have been successful and popular in high school are particularly vulnerable to the first-year adjustment reaction in college. Counseling, as well as increasing familiarity with campus life, can help a student adjust.

First-generation college students, who are the first in their families to attend college, are particularly susceptible to difficulties during their first year of college. They may arrive at college without a clear understanding of how the demands of college differ from those of high school, and the social support they have from their families may be inadequate. In addition, they may be less well prepared for college work (Barry et al., 2009; Credé & Niehorster, 2012).

Most often, the first-year adjustment reaction passes as students make friends, experience academic success, and integrate themselves into campus life. In other cases, though, the problems remain and may fester, leading to more serious psychological difficulties. (Also see the *Development in Your Life* box.)

Development in Your Life

When Do College Students Need Professional Help with Their Problems?

A college friend comes to you and says that she has been feeling depressed and unhappy and can't seem to shake the feeling. She doesn't know what to do and thinks that she may need professional help. How do you answer her?

Although there are no hard-and-fast rules, several signals can be interpreted to determine whether professional help is warranted (Engler & Goleman, 1992). Among them are the following:

- Psychological distress that lingers and interferes with a person's sense of well-being and ability to function (such as depression so great that someone has trouble completing his or her work)

(Continued)

- Feeling that one is unable to cope effectively with the stress
- Hopeless or depressed feelings, with no apparent reason
- Inability to build close relationships with others
- Physical symptoms such as headaches, stomach cramps, and skin rashes that have no apparent underlying cause

If some of these signals are present, it would be helpful to discuss them with some kind of help provider—such as a counseling psychologist, clinical psychologist, or other mental health worker. The best place to start is the campus medical center. A personal physician, neighborhood clinic, or local board of health can also provide a referral.

How prevalent are concerns about psychological problems? Surveys find that almost half of college students report having at least one significant psychological issue. Other research found that almost a third of students reported being depressed (see Figure 13-11; Benton et al., 2003; Gruttadaro & Crudo, 2012).

Figure 13-11 College Problems

The primary mental health issue experienced by college students is depression.

(**Source:** Gruttadaro & Crudo, 2012.)

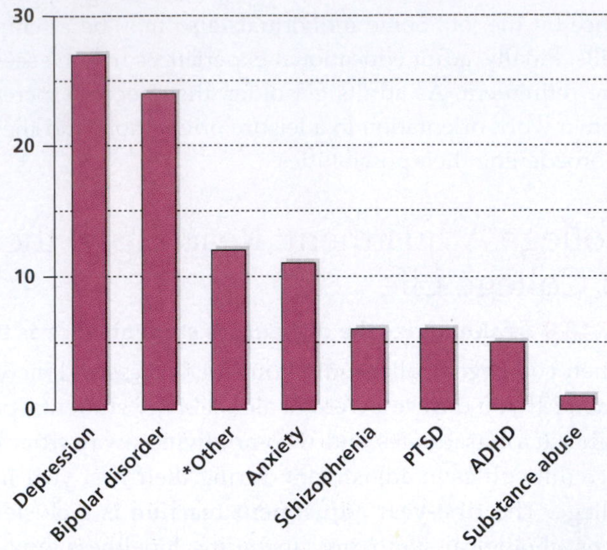

***Other diagnoses include borderline personality disorder, dysthymia, eating disorders, obsessive-compulsive disorder, schizoaffective disorder and autism spectrum disorder.**

DROPPING OUT OF COLLEGE. The proportion of students who enter college but ultimately never graduate is substantial. Only around 40 percent of those who start college finish 4 years later with a degree. Although about half of those who don't receive a degree in 4 years eventually do finish, the other half never obtain a college degree. For minorities, the picture is even worse: The national dropout rate for African American college students stands at 60 percent, as measured by the number of African American students who graduate within 6 years of starting college (Casselman, 2014).

Why is the college dropout rate so high? There are several reasons. One has to do with finances: Given the high cost of college, many students are unable to afford the continued expense or the strain of juggling the demands of a job and the demands of college. Other people leave college because of changes in their life situations, such as marriage, the birth of a child, or the death of a parent.

Academic difficulties also may play a role. Some students simply find that they are not successful in their studies, and they are either forced by academic authorities to drop out or they leave on their own. However, in most cases, students who drop out are not in academic jeopardy (Feldman, 2018).

College students who drop out in early adulthood—intending to return one day but never making it back because they become enmeshed in the nitty-gritty of everyday life—can experience real difficulties. They may become stuck as young adults in undesirable, low-paying jobs for which they are intellectually overqualified. A college education becomes a lost opportunity.

Yet dropping out is not always a step backward in a young adult's life path. In some cases, it gives people breathing room to reassess their goals. For instance, students who view the college experience as simply marking time until they can get on with their "real" lives by earning a living can sometimes benefit from a period of full-time work. During the hiatus from college, they often get a different perspective on the realities of both work and school. Other individuals simply benefit by having some time off from school in which to mature socially or psychologically, as we'll discuss further in the next chapter.

Gender and College Performance

LO 13.10 Describe how gender affects the treatment of college students.

> *I registered for a calculus course my first year at DePauw. Even 20 years ago I was not timid, so on the very first day I raised my hand and asked a question. I still have a vivid memory of the professor rolling his eyes, hitting his head with his hand in frustration, and announcing to everyone, "Why do they expect me to teach calculus to girls?" I never asked another question.* (Sadker & Sadker, 1994, p. 162)

Although such incidents of blatant sexism are less likely to occur today, prejudice and discrimination directed at women are still a fact of college life. For instance, the next time you are in class, consider the gender of your classmates—and the subject matter of the class. Although men and women attend college in roughly equal proportions, there is significant variation in the classes they take. Classes in education and the social sciences, for instance, typically have a larger proportion of women than men; and classes in engineering, the physical sciences, and mathematics tend to have more men than women.

Even women who start out in mathematics, engineering, and the physical sciences are more likely than men to drop out or change majors. For instance, the attrition rate for women in such fields during the college years is 2.5 times greater than the rate for men. And although the number of women seeking graduate degrees in science and engineering has been increasing, women still lag behind men in the numbers seeking to enter those fields (National Science Foundation, 2002; York, 2008; Halpern, 2014).

The differences in gender distribution and attrition rates across subject areas are no accident. They reflect the powerful influence of gender stereotypes that operate throughout the world of education—and beyond. For instance, when women in their first year of college are asked to name a likely career choice, they are much less apt to choose careers that have traditionally been dominated by men, such as engineering or computer programming, and more likely to choose professions that have traditionally been populated by women, such as nursing and social work. Furthermore, even when they do choose to enter math- and science-related fields, they may face sex discrimination (CIRE, 1990; Ceci & Williams, 2010; Lane, Goh, & Driver-Linn, 2012).

Women also expect to earn less than men, both when they start their careers and when they are at their peaks. These expectations jibe with reality: On average, women earn 82 cents for every dollar that men earn (Bureau of Labor Statistics, 2012; DeNavas-Walt, Proctor, & Smith, 2013; Catalyst, 2015).

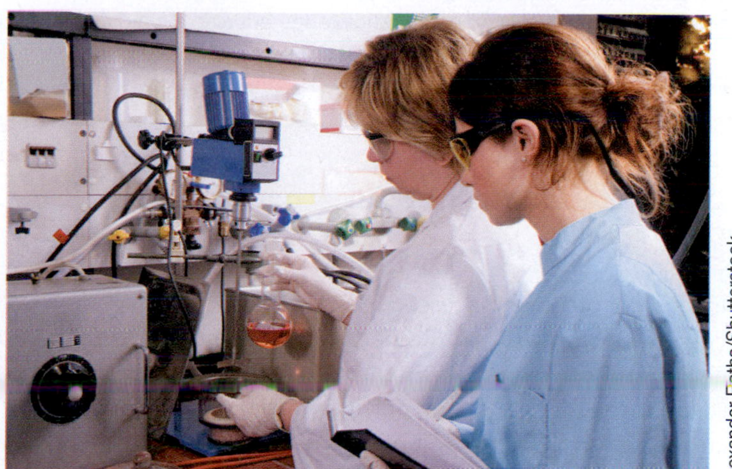

As a result of the powerful influence of gender stereotypes in the world of education, women are underrepresented in the areas of physical science, math, and engineering. What can be done to reverse this trend?

Alexander Faths/Shutterstock

Male and female college students also have different expectations regarding their areas of competence. For instance, one survey asked first-year college students whether they were above or below average on a variety of traits and abilities. As shown in Figure 13-12, men were more likely than women to think of themselves as above average in overall academic and mathematical ability, competitiveness, and emotional health.

Both male and female college professors treat men and women differently in their classes, even though the different treatment is largely unintentional and the professors are unaware of their actions. For instance, professors may call on men in class more frequently

Figure 13-12 The Great Gender Divide

During their first year of college, men, compared to women, are more apt to view themselves as above average on several spheres relevant to academic success. **THINKING ABOUT THE DATA:** What is the root of this difference?

(**Source:** Astin, Korn, & Berz, 1989.)

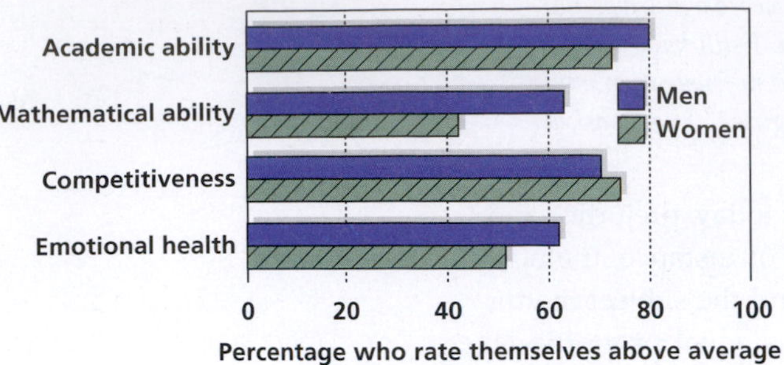

than women, and they make more eye contact with men than with women. Furthermore, male students are more likely than female students to receive extra help from their professors. Finally, the quality of the responses received by male and female students differs, with male students receiving more positive reinforcement for their comments than female students, particularly in science and math fields (Sadker et al., 2007; D'Lima, Winsler, & Kitsantas, 2014).

BENEVOLENT SEXISM: WHEN BEING NICE IS NOT SO NICE. Although some cases of unequal treatment of women represent *hostile sexism*, in which people treat women in a way that is overtly harmful, in other cases women are the victims of benevolent sexism. *Benevolent sexism* is a form of sexism in which women are placed in stereotyped and restrictive roles that appear, on the surface, to be positive.

Benevolent sexism even seems, at first, to be beneficial to women. For instance, a male college professor may compliment a female student on her good looks or offer to give her an easier research project so she won't have to work so hard. Although the professor may feel that he is merely being thoughtful, in fact he may be making the woman feel that she is not being taken seriously, and he may be undermining her view of her competence. In short, benevolent sexism can be just as harmful as hostile sexism (Glick & Fiske, 2012; Rudman & Fetterolf, 2014; Glick & Raberg, 2017).

Module 13.3 Review

LO 13.8 Describe who attends college today and how the college population is changing.

Rates of college enrollment differ across racial and ethnic lines. The average age of college students is steadily increasing as more adults return to college.

LO 13.9 Summarize the difficulties students face as they enter college.

New students often find the transition to college difficult and experience the first-year adjustment reaction. In college, students learn not only a body of knowledge but also a way of understanding the world that generally accepts more viewpoints and sees values in relativistic terms.

LO 13.10 Describe how gender affects the treatment of college students.

Gender differences in treatment and expectations cause men and women to make different choices and engage in different behaviors in college.

Journal Writing Prompt

Applying Lifespan Development: How would you educate college professors who behave differently toward male and female students? What factors contribute to this phenomenon? Can this situation be changed?

Epilogue

In this chapter we discussed physical and cognitive development in early adulthood. We looked at overall health and fitness and at intellectual growth, which proceeds through stages that profit from young adults' increasing experience and subtlety. We also examined the college scene, noting demographic trends and differences in treatment and academic performance that affect some groups of college students. We discussed the advantages of college and the adjustment reaction that some first-year college students experience as they encounter the new realities of college life.

Return to the prologue of this chapter, in which we met college students Enrico Vasquez and Armando Williams. In light of what you now know about physical and cognitive development in early adulthood, answer the following questions.

1. How do you think family expectations about education affected the two students' decisions to enroll in college?
2. As a Hispanic American student from a wealthy background, what challenges is Enrico likely to encounter if he enters a college in which Hispanic students are a small minority?
3. Is academic disidentification likely to be a problem for Armando, with his "mean streets" background? Why or why not?
4. How might the phenomenon of stereotype threat affect both Enrico and Armando?
5. Which student do you think may have the more difficult adjustment to college? Which is more likely to drop out of college? Why?

Looking Back

LO 13.1 Describe how the body develops and stays healthy during early adulthood.

The body and the senses generally reach their peak in early adulthood. Health risks are minimal, with accidents presenting the greatest risk of death. In the United States, violence is a significant cause of death, particularly among nonwhite segments of the population.

LO 13.2 Explain why a healthy diet is particularly important in early adulthood.

Many young adults begin to put on weight because they fail to change poor eating habits developed earlier, and the percentage of obese adults increases with every year of aging.

LO 13.3 Describe the challenges people with physical disabilities face in early adulthood.

People with physical disabilities face physical and material difficulties as well as psychological difficulties, including prejudice and discrimination.

LO 13.4 Summarize the effects of stress and what can be done about it.

Moderate, occasional stress is biologically healthy, but long exposure to stressors produces damaging physical and psychosomatic effects. In reacting to potentially stressful situations, people pass through primary appraisal of the situation itself and secondary appraisal of their own coping abilities. People cope with stress in a number of healthy and unhealthy ways, including problem-focused coping, emotion-focused coping, social support, and defensive coping.

LO 13.5 Describe how cognitive development continues in young adulthood.

Some theorists find increasing evidence of postformal thought, which goes beyond formal logic to produce more flexible and subjective thinking that takes account of real-world complexity and yields subtler answers than those found during adolescence.

LO 13.6 Compare and contrast Perry's and Schaie's approaches to cognitive development in young adulthood.

To Perry's thinking, cognitive growth in early adulthood involves developing deeper ways of understanding the world, including a progression from dualistic thinking to the realization that it is possible to hold multiple perspectives on issues. According to Schaie, the development of thinking follows a set pattern of stages: the acquisitive stage, the achieving stage, the responsible stage, the executive stage, and the reintegrative stage.

LO 13.7 Explain how intelligence is defined today and how life events cause cognitive growth in young adults.

Traditional views that equated IQ with intelligence are being questioned. According to Sternberg's triarchic theory, intelligence is made up of componential, experiential, and contextual aspects. Practical intelligence seems to be related most closely with career success, and emotional intelligence underlies social interactions and responsiveness to others' needs. Creativity often peaks in young adulthood, possibly because young people view problems in novel ways rather than in the familiar ways of their older peers. Important life events, such as births and deaths, seem to contribute to cognitive growth by generating new insights into the self and revised views of the world.

LO 13.8 Describe who attends college today and how the college population is changing.

The profile of the U.S. college student has been changing, with many students beyond the traditional 18- to 22-year-old age range. Compared to white high school graduates, a smaller percentage of African American and Hispanic American high school graduates enter college.

LO 13.9 Summarize the difficulties students face in college.

Many college students, particularly those who experience a decline in status from their high school days, fall victim to the first-year adjustment reaction—feelings of depression, anxiety, and withdrawal that typically pass quickly as the students integrate themselves into their new surroundings. Students who end up dropping out of college usually have the intention of returning at a later time. Reasons for dropping out include academic unreadiness, financial constraints, and changes in life circumstances.

LO 13.10 Describe how gender affects the treatment of college students.

Gender differences exist in the fields of study chosen by students, in students' expectations regarding their future careers and earnings, and in professors' treatment of students.

Key Terms and Concepts

senescence 432
stress 438
psychoneuroimmunology (PNI) 439
primary appraisal 440
secondary appraisal 440
psychosomatic disorders 440
coping 441
defensive coping 442
hardiness 442
postformal thought 445
acquisitive stage 446
achieving stage 447
responsible stage 447
executive stage 447
reintegrative stage 447
triarchic theory of intelligence 447
practical intelligence 448
emotional intelligence 449
creativity 450
first-year adjustment reaction 453

Chapter 14

Social and Personality Development in Early Adulthood

Zachary Miller/Getty Images

Learning Objectives

LO 14.1 Describe what makes young adults happy, what is meant by the social clock, and the concept of emerging adulthood.

LO 14.2 Explain how young adults respond to the need for intimacy and friendship and how liking turns to loving.

LO 14.3 Differentiate the different kinds of love.

LO 14.4 Describe how young adults choose spouses.

LO 14.5 Explain how infant attachment styles are related to romantic relationships as adults.

LO 14.6 Describe the sorts of relationships people enter into in early adulthood and what makes these relationships work or cease to work.

LO 14.7 Describe how the arrival of children affects a relationship in early adulthood.

LO 14.8 Compare gay and lesbian parents to heterosexual parents.

LO 14.9 Explain why some people choose to remain single in early adulthood.

LO 14.10 Explain the role of careers in the lives of young adults.

LO 14.11 List factors that influence the choice of a career in early adulthood.

LO 14.12 Describe how gender affects work choices and the work environment.

LO 14.13 Explain why people work and what elements of a job bring satisfaction.

Chapter Overview

Prologue: Paul and Mario

Paul Gerard and Mario Deluca are recalling how they first met 5 years ago in freshman biology lab in college. "Our usual lab partners were out that day, so we kind of got stuck together," remembers Mario. "We were just making small talk at first, but then it kept going."

"It was so amazing," Paul continues. "That day started just like any other, but by the time I went to bed that night I knew I had met my soul mate. We just had so much in common! But it was more than that—it was the way I felt while we were together. It was like a drug. I can't even explain it." He pauses thoughtfully, then answers with conviction, "In that moment, nothing else mattered. Not the exam I had the next day, not the people who were staring at us—it was me and Mario. We felt connected. It felt ... it felt right."

Diane Diederich/Getty Images

Forming relationships is an important part of early adulthood for many people.

Looking Ahead

Early adulthood is a period that poses a variety of developmental tasks (see Table 14-1). During this period, we come to grips with the notion that we are no longer other people's children. We begin to perceive ourselves as adults, as full members of society with significant responsibilities (Arnett, 2000). Many, but not all, of us form romantic relationships that will last, we hope, until the end of our lives.

This chapter examines the challenges of early adulthood, concentrating on the development and course of relationships with others. We will first consider how we establish and maintain love for others, looking at the differences between liking and loving as well as the different types of love. In doing so, we will examine how people choose partners and how their choices are influenced by societal and cultural factors.

Table 14-1 The Developmental Tasks of Adulthood

Adulthood (Ages 20–40)	Middle Adulthood (Ages 40–60)	Late Adulthood (Age 60+)
• Taking responsibility for yourself • Understanding that you have a unique history and that it is not permanent • Managing the separation from your parents • Redefining the relationship with your parents • Gaining and interpreting your sexual experiences • Becoming capable of intimacy with another (nonfamily) person • Managing money • Developing skills that can lead to a career • Considering career possibilities • Considering parenthood and possibly becoming a parent • Defining your values • Finding a place in society	• Understanding that time is passing and accepting it • Accepting that you are aging • Accepting changes in your body, including appearance and health • Developing an acceptable work identity • Becoming a member of society • Understanding that society is constantly changing • Keeping old friends and making new ones • Coping with changes in your sexuality • Continuously reworking your spousal or partner relationship • Altering your relationship with your children as they age • Passing on knowledge, skills, and values to the next generation • Managing money effectively for short- and long-term goals • Experiencing the illness and death of persons close to you, especially parents • Finding a place in society	• Spending time well • Remaining social rather than isolated • Making friends and new connections • Adjusting to changing sexuality • Staying healthy • Managing physical pain, ailments, and limitations • Making life without work a comfortable lifestyle • Using time wisely for engaging work and recreation • Managing finances effectively for yourself and your dependents • Focusing on the present and future, not dwelling on the past • Adjusting to ongoing losses of close connections • Accepting care from children and grandchildren

(**Source:** Based on Colarusso & Nemiroff, 1981.)

Close relationships are a major preoccupation for most young adults. We will examine the choice of whether to marry and the factors that influence the course and success of marriage. We will also consider how having a child influences a couple's happiness and the kinds of roles children play within a marriage. Families today come in all shapes and sizes, representing the complexity of relationships that are central to life for most people during early adulthood.

Careers are another preoccupation of young adulthood. We will see how identity during early adulthood is often tied to one's job and how people decide on the kind of work they wish to do. The chapter ends with a discussion of the reasons people work—not only to earn money—and how people go about choosing a career.

Forging Relationships: Intimacy, Liking, and Loving During Early Adulthood

Dianne Maher swept Thad Ramon off his feet—literally. "I was setting up the cafeteria for a dance, and she was sweeping the floor. Next thing I knew a push broom was under my heels and down I went. I didn't hurt myself or anything, and my pride wasn't injured, but you could say my heart took a beating. There she was, sly grin on her face, and all I could do was stare and laugh. We started talking and laughing some more, and soon we discovered we had a lot more than silliness in common. We've been together ever since."

Thad followed his heart and in senior year of college publicly proposed to Dianne in that same cafeteria. They plan to get married beside the college duck pond and at the end of the ceremony march beneath crossed push brooms held by their ushers and bridesmaids.

Not everyone falls in love quite as easily as Dianne and Thad. For some, the road to love is tortuous, meandering through soured relationships and fallen dreams; for others, it is a road never taken. For some, love leads to marriage and a life befitting society's storybook view of home, children, and long years together as a couple. For many, it leads to a less happy ending, prematurely concluding in divorce and custody battles.

Intimacy and forming relationships are major considerations during early adulthood. Young adults' happiness stems, in part, from their relationships, and many worry about whether they are developing serious relationships "on time." Even those who are not interested in forming a long-term relationship typically are focused, to some extent, on connecting with others.

The Components of Happiness: Fulfilling Psychological Needs

LO 14.1 Describe what makes young adults happy, what is meant by the social clock, and the concept of emerging adulthood.

Think back over the past 7 days of your life. What made you happiest? According to research on young adults, it probably wasn't money or material objects that brought you happiness. Instead, happiness usually is derived from feelings of independence, competence, self-esteem, or relating well to other people (Bergsma & Ardelt, 2012; Bojanowska & Zalewska, 2015; Norona, Roberson, & Welsh, 2017).

If you ask young adults to recall a time when they were happy, they are most likely to mention an experience or moment when they felt their psychological needs rather than material needs had been satisfied. Being chosen for a new job, developing a deep relationship, or moving into their own apartment or home are examples of the kinds of experiences that might be recalled. Conversely, when they remember times when they were least satisfied, they mention incidents in which basic psychological needs were left unfulfilled.

It's interesting to compare these findings, based on research in the United States, with studies conducted in Asian countries. For example, young adults in Korea more often associate satisfaction with experiences involving other people, whereas young adults in the United States experienced satisfaction from experiences relating to the self and self-esteem. Apparently, culture influences which psychological needs are most important in determining happiness (Sedikides, Gaertner, & Toguchi, 2003; Jongudomkarn & Camfield, 2006; Demir et al., 2012).

THE SOCIAL CLOCKS OF ADULTHOOD. Having children. Receiving a promotion. Getting divorced. Changing jobs. Becoming a grandparent. Each of these events marks a moment on what has been called the social clock of life.

social clock
the culturally determined psychological timepiece providing a sense of whether we have reached the major benchmarks of life at the appropriate time in comparison to our peers

The **social clock** is a term used to describe the psychological timepiece that records the major milestones in people's lives. Each of us has such a social clock that provides us with a sense of whether we have reached the major benchmarks of life early, late, or right on time in comparison to our peers. Our social clocks are culturally determined: They reflect the expectations of the society in which we live.

Until the middle of the 20th century, the social clocks of adulthood were fairly uniform—at least for upper-class and middle-class people in Western society. Most people moved through a series of developmental stages closely aligned with particular ages. For example, the typical man completed his education by his early 20s, started a career, married in his mid-20s, and was working to provide for a growing family by the time he was in his 30s. Women also followed a set pattern, which focused on getting married and raising children—but not, in most cases, entering a profession and developing a career.

Today, there is considerably more heterogeneity in the social clocks of both men and women. The timing at which major life events occur has changed considerably. Furthermore, as we consider next, women's social clocks have changed dramatically as a result of social and cultural changes (Goldberg, 2014).

WOMEN'S SOCIAL CLOCKS. Developmental psychologist Ravenna Helson and colleagues suggest that people have several social clocks from which to choose, and the selection they make has substantial implications for personality development during early and middle adulthood. Focusing on a sample of women who graduated from college during the early 1960s, Helson's longitudinal research has examined women whose social clocks were focused either on their families, on careers, or on a more individualistic target (Helson & McCabe, 1994; Society for Personality and Social Psychology, 2017).

Helson found several broad patterns. Over the course of the study, which assessed participants at ages 21, 27, and 43, the women generally became more self-disciplined and committed to their duties. They also felt greater independence and confidence, and they were able to cope with stress and adversity more effectively. Finding a spouse and embarking on a journey toward motherhood meant that many women exhibited what Helson called traditional feminine behavior from about age 21 to 27. But as children grew up and maternal duties diminished, women took on less traditional roles. The study also found some intriguing similarities in personality development in women who chose to focus on family compared with those who focused on career. Both groups tended to show generally positive changes. In contrast, women who had no strong focus on either family or career tended to show either little change or more negative shifts in personality development, such as becoming less satisfied over time.

Helson's conclusion is that the particular social clock that a woman chooses may not be the critical factor in determining the course of personality development. Instead, the process of choosing a particular social clock may be important in producing growth, whether that social clock involves motherhood or a career path. It is less important whether a woman chooses to first develop a career and then embark toward motherhood, or chooses the opposite pattern, or follows some other path entirely. What is more critical is investing in and focusing on a particular trajectory.

It is important to keep in mind that social clocks are culturally determined. The timing of motherhood and the type and course of a woman's career are both influenced by the social, economic, and cultural worlds in which the woman lives.

EMERGING ADULTHOOD: NOT QUITE THERE YET? Do you feel as though you're not really an "adult," despite having reached an age where you are legally an adult? Are you still unsure of who you are and what you want to do with your life, and feeling unready to go out in the world on your own? If so, what you're experiencing is a developmental period known as **emerging adulthood**—a transitional stage between adolescence and adulthood that spans the third decade of life. Researchers are increasingly considering emerging adulthood to be a distinct developmental period during which the brain is still growing and modifying its neural pathways. It's typically a time of uncertainty and self-discovery during which the emerging adult is still figuring out the world and his or her place in it (Arnett, 2014a).

emerging adulthood
the period from the late teenage years extending to the mid-20s in which people are still sorting out their options for the future

Emerging adulthood is marked by five features. *Identity exploration* entails learning to make important decisions about love, work, and one's core beliefs and values. In one comprehensive survey of over 1,000 diverse emerging adults age 18 to 29 throughout the United States, 77 percent agreed with the statement "This is a time of life for finding out who I really am." Another feature of emerging adulthood is *instability*, which can be represented as changes in life plans or goals, fluctuating career and educational paths, rocky relationships, and even shifts in ideologies. In the survey, 83 percent of respondents agreed that "This time of my life is full of changes" (Arnett, 2014b).

A third feature of emerging adulthood is *self-focus*: It's a time of life that comes between parental control and the obligations of childrearing and career. With fewer people to answer to, emerging adults enjoy the luxury of focusing on themselves for a while before making any serious commitments. "This is a time of my life for focusing on myself" was a statement with which 71 percent of respondents agreed. Given all this, it's probably not surprising that a fourth feature of emerging adulthood is *feeling in-between*, a sense of being no longer an adolescent but not yet really an adult either. For some emerging adults the feeling is enhanced by remaining dependent in some ways on their parents, and for others it's more a sense of uncertainty and hesitation in accepting full adulthood just yet. Half of the respondents to the survey were unwilling to agree completely that they had reached adulthood (Arnett, 2014b).

Finally, despite the stress and anxiety that are associated with the uncertainties of emerging adulthood, it is also a time of *optimism*. Nearly 90 percent of survey respondents agreed that "I am confident that someday I will get what I want out of life" and 83 percent agreed "At this time of my life, anything is possible." Part of the reason for this optimism is the tendency for young adults today to be better educated than their parents were, such that their optimism has a basis in reality. And happily, by the time they are 30, most emerging adults have found their way and have settled more comfortably into their adult roles (Arnett, 2014b, 2015; Ozmen, Brelsford, & Danieu, 2017).

The existence of the period of emerging adulthood is driven by the nature of economic changes in industrialized countries in the past several decades. As these economies continue to shift toward technology and information, an increasing time has to be spent becoming educated. Furthermore, the age of marriage has risen, as has the timing of the birth of children (Arnett, 2016).

Furthermore, both men and women have increasing ambivalence about becoming adults. Surveys show that people in their late teens and early 20s respond with "yes and no" most frequently when asked if they have reached adulthood (Arnett, 2006; Verschueren et al., 2017).

Intimacy, Friendship, and Love

LO 14.2 Explain how young adults respond to the need for intimacy and friendship and how liking turns to loving.

Despite ongoing changes in the nature of women's (and men's) social clocks, one aspect of adulthood remains a central feature: the development and maintenance of relationships with others. As we consider next, those relationships are a key part of development during early adulthood.

intimacy-versus-isolation stage according to Erikson, the period from postadolescence into the early 30s that focuses on developing close relationships with others

SEEKING INTIMACY: ERIKSON'S VIEW OF YOUNG ADULTHOOD. Erik Erikson regarded young adulthood as the **intimacy-versus-isolation stage**, which spans the period of postadolescence into the early 30s. During this period, the focus is on developing close, intimate relationships with others.

Erikson's idea of intimacy comprises several aspects. One is a degree of selflessness, involving the sacrifice of one's own needs to those of another. A further component involves sexuality, the experience of joint pleasure from focusing not just on one's own gratification but also on that of one's partner. Finally, there is deep devotion, marked by efforts to fuse one's identity with the identity of a partner.

According to Erikson, those who experience difficulties during this stage are often lonely, isolated, and fearful of relationships with others. Their difficulties may stem from an earlier failure to develop a strong identity. In contrast, young adults who are able to form intimate relationships with others on a physical, intellectual, and emotional level successfully resolve the crisis posed by this stage of development.

Although Erikson's approach has been influential, some aspects of his theory trouble today's developmentalists. For instance, Erikson's view of healthy intimacy was limited to adult heterosexuality, the goal of which was to produce children. Consequently, homosexual partnerships, couples who were childless by choice, and other relationships that deviated from what Erikson saw as the ideal were thought of as less than satisfactory. Furthermore, Erikson focused more on men's development than on women's and did not consider racial and ethnic identity, thereby greatly limiting the applicability of his theory (Yip, Sellers, & Seaton, 2006).

Still, Erikson's work has been influential historically because of its emphasis on examining the continued growth and development of personality throughout the life span. Furthermore, it inspired other developmentalists to consider psychosocial growth during young adulthood and the range of intimate relationships we develop, from friendship to mates for life (Whitbourne, Sneed, & Sayer, 2009).

FRIENDSHIP. Most of our relationships with others involve friends, and for most people maintaining such relationships is an important part of adult life. Why? One reason is that there is a basic *need for belonging* that leads people in early adulthood to establish and maintain at least a minimum number of relationships with others. Most people are driven toward forming and preserving relationships that allow them to experience a sense of belonging with others (Manstead, 1997; Rice, 1999).

But how do particular people end up becoming our friends? One of the most important reasons is simple proximity—people form friendships with others who live nearby and with whom they come in contact most frequently. Because of their accessibility, people who are in close proximity can obtain rewards of friendship, such as companionship, social approval, and the occasional helping hand, at relatively little cost.

People are most attracted to those who can keep confidences and are loyal, warm, and affectionate.

Similarity also plays an important role in friendship formation. Birds of a feather *do* flock together: People are more attracted to others who hold attitudes and values similar to their own (Selfhout et al., 2009; Preciado et al., 2012; Mikulincer et al., 2015; Wrzus et al., 2017).

The importance of similarity becomes particularly evident when we consider cross-race friendships. By the time of adolescence, the number of cross-race close friendships dwindles, a pattern that continues throughout the remainder of the life span. In fact, although most adults claim on surveys to have a close friend of a different race, when they are queried regarding the names of close friends, few include a person of a different race.

We also choose friends on the basis of their personal qualities. What's most important? People are most attracted to others who keep confidences and are loyal, warm, and affectionate. In addition, we like those who are supportive, helpful, and provide a sense of security (Hartup & Stevens, 1999; You & Bellmore, 2012).

Defining the Indefinable: What Is Love?

LO 14.3 Differentiate the different kinds of love.

> *After a few chance encounters at the laundromat where they wash their clothes each week, Rebecca and Jerry begin to talk with one another. They find they have a lot in common, and they begin to look forward to what are now semi-planned meetings. After several weeks, they go out on their first official date and discover that they are well suited to each other.*

If such a pattern seems predictable, it is: Most relationships develop in a fairly similar way, following a surprisingly regular progression (Burgess & Huston, 1979; Berscheid, 1985):

- Two people interact with each other more often and for longer periods of time. Furthermore, the range of settings increases.
- The two people increasingly seek out each other's company.
- They open up to each other more and more, disclosing more intimate information about themselves. They begin to share physical intimacies.
- The couple is more willing to share both positive and negative feelings, and they may offer criticism in addition to praise.
- They begin to agree on the goals they hold for the relationship.
- Their reactions to situations become more similar.
- They begin to feel that their own psychological well-being is tied to the success of the relationship, viewing it as unique, irreplaceable, and cherished.
- Finally, their definition of themselves and their behavior changes: They begin to see themselves and act as a couple rather than as two separate individuals.

Is the "love" that Rebecca and Jerry are feeling just a lot of "liking"? Most developmental psychologists would answer negatively; love not only differs quantitatively from liking, it represents a qualitatively different state. For example, love, at least in its early stages, involves relatively intense physiological arousal, an all-encompassing interest in another individual, recurrent fantasies about the other individual, and rapid swings of emotion. As distinct from liking, love includes elements of closeness, passion, and exclusivity (Hendrick & Hendrick, 2003; Silton & Ferris, 2017).

Not all love is the same, of course. We don't love our mothers the same way we love girlfriends or boyfriends, brothers or sisters, or lifelong friends. What distinguishes these different types of love? Some psychologists suggest that our love relationships can fall into two different categories: passionate or companionate.

passionate (or romantic) love
a state of powerful absorption in someone

companionate love
the strong affection for those with whom our lives are deeply involved

labeling theory of passionate love
the theory that individuals experience romantic love when two events occur together: intense physiological arousal and situational cues suggesting that the arousal is due to love

PASSIONATE AND COMPANIONATE LOVE: THE TWO FACES OF LOVE. **Passionate (or romantic) love** is a state of powerful absorption in someone. It includes intense physiological interest and arousal, and caring for another's needs. In comparison, **companionate love** is the strong affection that we have for those with whom our lives are deeply involved (Hendrick & Hendrick, 2003; Barsade & O'Neill, 2014).

What is it that fuels the fires of passionate love? According to one theory, anything that produces strong emotions—even negative ones, such as jealousy, anger, or fear of rejection—may be the source of deepening passionate love.

In psychologists Elaine Hatfield and Ellen Berscheid's **labeling theory of passionate love**, individuals experience romantic love when two events occur together: intense physiological arousal and situational cues that indicate that "love" is the appropriate label for the feelings they are experiencing (Berscheid & Walster, 1974). The physiological arousal can be produced by sexual arousal, excitement, or even negative emotions such as jealousy. Whatever the cause, if that arousal is subsequently labeled as "I must be falling in love" or "she makes my heart flutter" or "he really turns me on," then the experience is attributed to passionate love.

The theory is particularly useful in explaining why people may feel deepened love even when they experience continual rejection or hurt from their assumed lover. It suggests that such negative emotions can produce strong physiological arousal. If this arousal is interpreted as being caused by "love," then people may decide that they are even more in love than they were before they experienced the negative emotions.

But why should people label an emotional experience as "love" when there are so many possible alternatives? One answer is that in Western cultures, romantic love is seen as possible, acceptable, desirable—an experience to be sought. The virtues of passion are extolled in love ballads, commercials, television shows, and films. Consequently, young adults are primed and ready to experience love in their lives (Dion & Dion, 1988; Hatfield & Rapson, 1993; Florsheim, 2003).

It is interesting to note that this is not the way it is in every culture. For instance, in many cultures, passionate, romantic love is a foreign concept. Marriages may be arranged on the basis of economic and status considerations. Even in Western cultures, the concept of love is of relatively recent origin. For instance, the notion that couples need to be in love was not "invented" until the Middle Ages, when social philosophers first suggested that love ought to be a requirement for marriage. Their goal in making such a proposal: to provide an alternative to the raw sexual desire that had served as the primary basis for marriage before (Xiaohe & Whyte, 1990; Haslett, 2004; Moore & Wei, 2012).

intimacy component
the component of love that encompasses feelings of closeness, affection, and connectedness

passion component
the component of love that comprises the motivational drives relating to sex, physical closeness, and romance

STERNBERG'S TRIANGULAR THEORY: THE THREE FACES OF LOVE. To psychologist Robert Sternberg, love is more complex than a simple division into passionate and companionate types. He suggests instead that love is made up of three components: intimacy, passion, and decision/commitment. The **intimacy component** encompasses feelings of closeness, affection, and connectedness. The **passion component** comprises the motivational drives relating to sex, physical closeness, and romance. This component is exemplified by intense, physiologically arousing feelings of attraction. Finally, the third

Table 14-2 The Combinations of Love

	Component			
Type of Love	**Intimacy**	**Passion**	**Decision/Commitment**	**Example**
Nonlove	Absent	Absent	Absent	The way you might feel about the person who takes your ticket at the movies
Liking	Present	Absent	Absent	Good friends who have lunch together at least once or twice a week
Infatuated love	Absent	Present	Absent	A "fling" or short-term relationship based only on sexual attraction
Empty love	Absent	Absent	Present	An arranged marriage or a couple who have decided to stay married "for the sake of the children"
Romantic love	Present	Present	Absent	A couple who have been happily dating a few months, but have not made any plans for a future together
Companionate love	Present	Absent	Present	A couple who enjoy each other's company and their relationship, although they no longer feel much sexual interest in each other
Fatuous love	Absent	Present	Present	A couple who decides to move in together after knowing each other for only 2 weeks
Consummate love	Present	Present	Present	A loving, sexually vibrant, long-term relationship

aspect of love, the **decision/commitment component**, embodies both the initial cognition that one loves another person and the longer-term determination to maintain that love (Sternberg, 1986, 1988; Sternberg & Hojjat, 1997b).

decision/commitment component
the third aspect of love that embodies both the initial cognition that one loves another person and the longer-term determination to maintain that love

These components can be combined to form eight different types of love depending on which of the three components is either present or missing from a relationship (see Table 14-2). For instance, *nonlove* refers to people who have only the most casual of relationships; it consists of the absence of the three components of intimacy, passion, and decision/commitment. *Liking* develops when only intimacy is present; *infatuated love* exists when only passion is felt; and *empty love* exists when only decision/commitment is present.

Other types of love involve a mix of two or more components. For instance, romantic love occurs when intimacy and passion are present, and *companionate love* when intimacy and decision/commitment occur jointly. When two people experience *romantic love*, they are drawn together physically and emotionally, but they do not necessarily view the relationship as lasting. Companionate love, by contrast, may occur in long-lasting relationships in which physical passion has taken a back seat.

Fatuous love exists when passion and decision/commitment, without intimacy, are present. Fatuous love is a kind of mindless loving in which there is no emotional bond between the partners.

Finally, the eighth kind of love is *consummate love.* In consummate love, all three components of love are present. Although we might assume that consummate love represents the "ideal" love, such a view may well be mistaken. Many long-lasting and entirely satisfactory relationships are based on types of love other than consummate love. Furthermore, the type of love that predominates in a relationship varies over time. As shown in Figure 14-1, in strong, loving relationships, the level of decision/commitment peaks and remains fairly stable. By contrast, passion tends to peak early in a relationship and then decline and level off. Intimacy also increases fairly rapidly but can continue to grow over time.

Choosing a Partner: Recognizing Mr. or Ms. Right

LO 14.4 Describe how young adults choose spouses.

For many young adults, the search for a partner is a major pursuit during early adulthood. Certainly, society offers a great deal of advice on how to succeed in this endeavor, as a glance at the array of magazines at any supermarket checkout counter confirms. Despite all the counsel, the road to identifying an individual to share one's life is not always easy.

Figure 14-1 The Shape of Love

Over the course of a relationship, the three aspects of love—intimacy, passion, and decision/commitment—vary in strength. How do these change as a relationship develops?

(**Source:** Sternberg, 1986.)

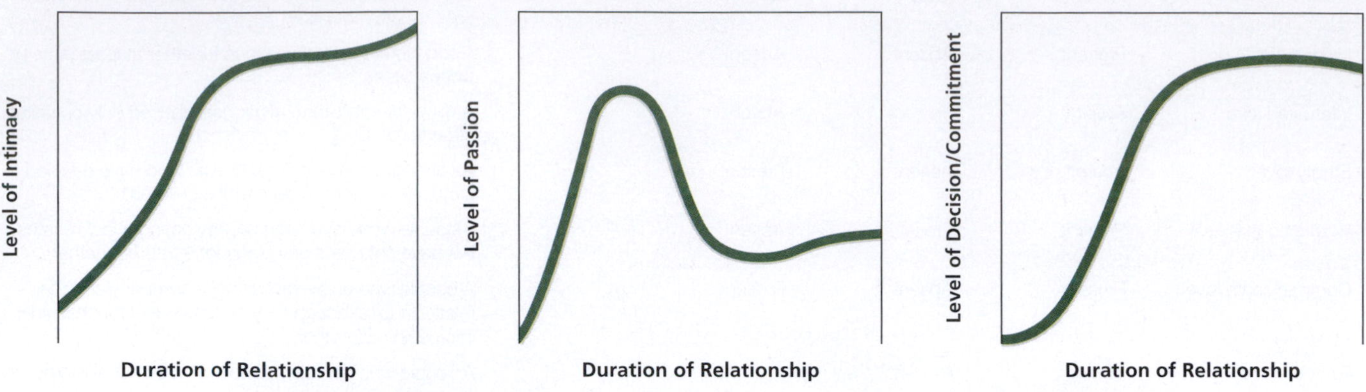

SEEKING A SPOUSE: IS LOVE THE ONLY THING THAT MATTERS? Most people have no hesitation in articulating that the major factor in choosing a husband or wife is love. Most people in the United States, that is: If we ask people in other societies, love becomes a secondary consideration. For instance, consider the results of a survey in which college students were asked if they would marry someone they did not love. On the one hand, hardly anyone in the United States, Japan, or Brazil would consider it. On the other hand, a goodly proportion of college students in Pakistan and India would find it acceptable to marry without love (Levine, 1993).

If love is not the only important factor, what else matters? The characteristics differ considerably from one culture to another. For instance, a survey of nearly 10,000 people from around the world found that although people in the United States believed that love and mutual attraction were the primary characteristics, in China men ranked good health most important, and women rated emotional stability and maturity most critical. In contrast, in South Africa men from a Zulu background rated emotional stability first, and Zulu women rated dependable character as being of greatest concern (Buss et al., 1990; Buss, 2003).

Yet there are commonalities across cultures. For instance, love and mutual attraction, even if not at the top of a specific culture's list, were highly desired across all cultures. Furthermore, traits such as dependability, emotional stability, pleasing disposition, and intelligence were highly valued almost universally.

Certain gender differences in the preferred characteristics of a mate were similar across cultures—findings that have been confirmed by other surveys (e.g., Sprecher, Sullivan, & Hatfield, 1994). Men, more than women, prefer a potential marriage partner who is physically attractive. In contrast, women, more than men, prefer a potential spouse who is ambitious and industrious.

One explanation for cross-cultural similarities in gender differences rests on evolutionary factors. According to psychologist David Buss and colleagues (Buss, 2004; Buss & Shackelford, 2008), human beings, as a species, seek out certain characteristics in their mates that are likely to maximize the availability of beneficial genes. He argues that males in particular are genetically programmed to seek out mates with traits that indicate they have high reproductive capacity. Consequently, physically attractive younger women might be more desirable since they are more capable of having children over a longer time period.

In contrast, women are genetically programmed to seek out men who have the potential to provide scarce resources in order to increase the likelihood that their offspring will survive. Consequently, they are attracted to mates who offer the highest potential of providing economic well-being (Walter, 1997; Kasser & Sharma, 1999; Li et al., 2002).

The evolutionary explanation for gender differences has come under heavy fire from critics. First, there is the problem that the explanation is untestable. Furthermore, the similarities across cultures relating to different gender preferences may simply reflect similar patterns of gender stereotyping that have nothing to do with evolution. In addition, although some of the gender differences in what men and women prefer are consistent across cultures, there are numerous inconsistencies as well.

Finally, some critics of the evolutionary approach suggest that the finding that women prefer a partner who has good earning potential may have nothing to do with evolution and everything to do with the fact that men generally hold more power, status, and other resources fairly consistently across different cultures. Consequently, it is a rational choice for women to prefer a high-earning-potential spouse. Conversely, because men don't need to take economic considerations into account, they can use more inconsequential criteria—like physical attractiveness—in choosing a spouse. In short, the consistencies that are found across cultures may be the result of the realities of economic life that are similar throughout different cultures (Eagly & Wood, 2003).

Figure 14-2 Filtering Potential Marriage Partners

According to one approach, we screen potential mates through successively finer-grained filters in order to settle on an appropriate spouse.

(**Source:** Based on Janda & Klenke-Hamel, 1980.)

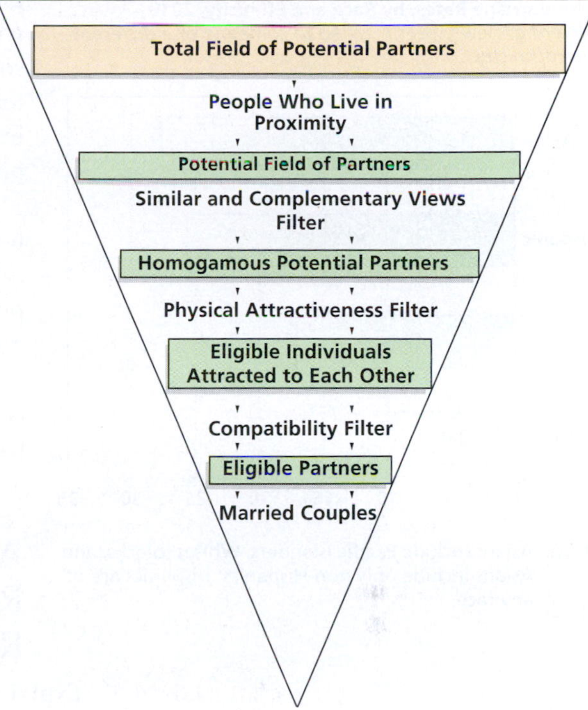

FILTERING MODELS: SIFTING OUT A SPOUSE. Although surveys assist in identifying the characteristics that are highly valued in a potential spouse, they are less helpful in determining how a specific individual is chosen as a partner. One approach that helps explain this is the filtering model developed by psychologists Louis Janda and Karen Klenke-Hamel (1980). They suggest that people seeking a mate screen potential candidates through successively finer-grained filters, just as we sift flour in order to remove undesirable material (see Figure 14-2).

The model assumes that people first filter for factors relating to broad determinants of attractiveness. Once these early screens have done their work, more sophisticated types of screening are used. The end result is a choice based on compatibility between the two individuals.

What determines compatibility? It is not only a matter of pleasing personality characteristics; several cultural factors also play an important role. For instance, people often marry according to the principle of homogamy. **Homogamy** is the tendency to marry someone who is similar in age, race, education, religion, and other basic demographic characteristics. Homogamy has traditionally been the dominant standard for most marriages in the United States.

homogamy
the tendency to marry someone who is similar in age, race, education, religion, and other basic demographic characteristics

From *a social worker's* perspective

How do the principles of homogamy and the marriage gradient work to limit options for high-status women? How do they affect men's options?

The importance of homogamy is declining, however, particularly among certain ethnic groups. For example, the rate of intermarriage among African American men tripled from 1980 to 2010. Still, for other groups—such as Hispanic and Asian immigrants—the principle of homogamy still has considerable influence (see Figure 14-3; Fu & Heaton, 2008; Wang/Pew Research Center, 2012; Mu & Xie, 2014).

The marriage gradient represents another societal standard that determines who marries whom. The **marriage gradient** is the tendency for men to marry women who are slightly younger, smaller, and lower in status, and women to marry men who are slightly older, larger, and higher in status (Bernard, 1982).

marriage gradient
the tendency for men to marry women who are slightly younger, smaller, and lower in status, and women to marry men who are slightly older, larger, and higher in status

Figure 14-3 Marriage Outside of Racial/ Ethnic Group

Although homogamy has been the standard for most marriages in the United States, the rate of marriages crossing ethnic and racial lines is substantial.

(**Source:** Wang/Pew Research Center, 2012.)

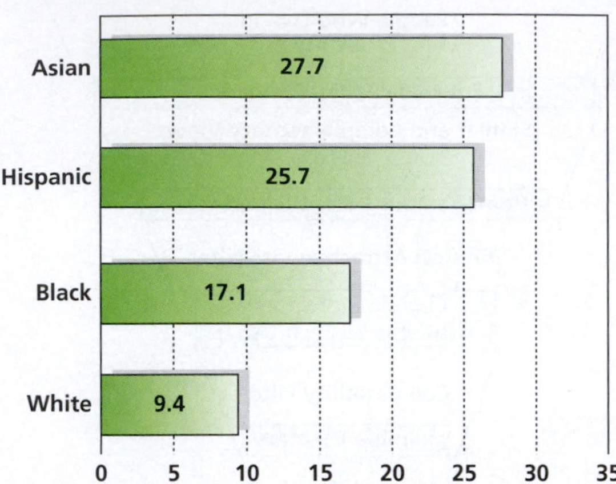

Note: Asians include Pacific Islanders. Whites, blacks, and Asians include only non-Hispanics. Hispanics are of any race.

The marriage gradient, which has a powerful influence on marriage in the United States, has important, and unfortunate, effects on partner choice. For one thing, it limits the number of potential mates for women, especially as they age, while allowing men a wider choice of partners as their age increases. Furthermore, some men do not marry because they cannot find women of low enough status to meet the demands of the gradient or cannot find women of the same or higher status who are willing to accept them as mates. Consequently, they are, in the words of sociologist Jessie Bernard (1982), "bottom of the barrel" men. By the same token, some women will be unable to marry because they are higher in status or seek someone of higher status than anyone in the available pool of men—"cream of the crop" women, in Bernard's words.

The marriage gradient makes finding a spouse particularly difficult for well-educated African American women. Fewer African American men attend college than African American women, making the potential pool of men who are suitable—as defined by society and the marriage gradient—relatively small. Consequently, relative to women of other races, African American women are more apt to marry men who are less educated than they are—or not marry at all (Willie & Reddick, 2003). (Also see the *Developmental Diversity and Your Life box*.)

Attachment Styles and Romantic Relationships: Do Adult Loving Styles Reflect Attachment in Infancy?

LO 14.5 Explain how infant attachment styles are related to romantic relationships as adults.

"I want a girl just like the girl that married dear old Dad." So go the lyrics of an old song, suggesting that the songwriter would like to find someone who loves him as much as his mother did. Is this just a corny tune, or is there a kernel of truth in this sentiment? Put more broadly, is the kind of attachment that people experience during infancy reflected in their adult romantic relationships?

Increasing evidence suggests that it very well may be. As you may recall, *attachment* refers to the positive emotional bond that develops between a child and a particular individual. Most infants fall into one of three attachment categories: securely attached children, who have healthy, positive, trusting relationships with their caregivers; avoidant infants, who are relatively indifferent to caregivers and who avoid interactions with them; and ambivalent infants, who show great distress when separated from a caregiver but who appear angry upon the caregiver's return.

According to psychologist Phillip Shaver and his colleagues, attachment styles continue into adulthood and affect the nature of romantic relationships (Dinero et al., 2008; Frías, Shaver, & Mikulincer, 2015; Shaver et al., 2017). For instance, consider the following statements:

1. I find it relatively easy to get close to others and am comfortable depending on them and having them depend on me. I don't often worry about being abandoned or about someone getting too close to me.
2. I am somewhat uncomfortable being close to others; I find it difficult to trust them completely, difficult to allow myself to depend on them. I am nervous when anyone gets too close, and often love partners want me to be more intimate than I feel comfortable being.
3. I find that others are reluctant to get as close as I would like. I often worry that my partner doesn't really love me or won't want to stay with me. I want to merge completely with another person, and this desire sometimes scares people away (Shaver, Hazan, & Bradshaw, 1988).

Developmental Diversity and Your Life

Gay and Lesbian Relationships: Men with Men and Women with Women

Most research conducted by developmental psychologists has examined heterosexual relationships, but an increasing number of studies have looked at relationships involving gay men and those involving lesbian women. The findings suggest that gay and lesbian relationships are quite similar to relationships between heterosexuals.

For example, gay men describe successful relationships in ways that are similar to heterosexual couples' descriptions. They believe that successful relationships involve greater appreciation for the partner and the couple as a whole, less conflict, and more positive feelings toward the partner. Similarly, lesbian women in a relationship show high levels of attachment, caring, intimacy, affection, and respect (Beals, Impett, & Peplau, 2002; Kurdek, 2006).

Furthermore, the age preferences expressed in the marriage gradient for heterosexuals also extend to partner preferences for homosexual men. Like heterosexual men, homosexual men prefer partners who are the same age or younger. In contrast, lesbians' age preferences fall somewhere between those of heterosexual women and heterosexual men (Kenrick et al., 1995).

Finally, despite the stereotype that gay males, in particular, find it difficult to form relationships and are more interested in sexual alliances, the reality is different. Most gays and lesbians seek loving, long-term, and meaningful relationships that differ little qualitatively from those desired by heterosexuals. Although some research suggests that homosexual relationships are less long-lasting than heterosexual relationships, the factors that lead to relationship stability—partners' personality traits, support for the relationship from others, and dependence on the relationship—are similar for homosexual and heterosexual couples (Diamond & Savin-Williams, 2003; Kurdek, 2005, 2008; Barelds et al., 2017).

Opinions on very few social issues have changed as much as attitudes toward same-sex marriage, which the Supreme Court in 2015 ruled legal in the United States. A majority of Americans support same-sex marriage, a significant shift in sentiment over the past 20 years. Furthermore, there are significant generational differences: whereas two-thirds of people under 30 support same-sex marriage, only 38 percent of those older than 65 support the legalization of gay marriage (Pew Research Center, 2014).

Stockbyte/Getty Images

Research finds that the quality of lesbian and gay relationships differs little from that of heterosexual relationships.

According to Shaver's research, agreement with the first statement reflects a secure attachment style. Adults who agree with this statement readily enter into relationships and feel happy, energized, and confident about the future success of their relationships. Most young adults—just over half—display the secure style of attachment (Hazan & Shaver, 1987; Luke, Sedikides, & Carnelley, 2012).

In contrast, adults who agree with the second statement typically display the avoidant attachment style. These individuals, who make up about a quarter of the population, tend to be less invested in relationships, have higher breakup rates, and often feel lonely.

Finally, agreement with the third category is reflective of an ambivalent style. Adults with an ambivalent style have a tendency to become overly invested in relationships, have repeated breakups with the same partner, and have relatively low self-esteem. Around 20 percent of adults fall into this category (Simpson, 1990; Li & Chan, 2012).

Iofoto/Fotolia

Some psychologists believe that our attachment style as infants is repeated in the quality of our intimate relationships as adults.

Attachment style is also related to the nature of care that adults give to their romantic partners when they need assistance. For instance, secure adults tend to provide more sensitive and supportive care, being responsive to their partner's psychological needs. In comparison, anxious adults are more likely to provide compulsive, intrusive (and ultimately less helpful) aid to partners (Feeney & Collins, 2003; Gleason, Iida, & Bolger, 2003; Mikulincer & Shaver, 2009).

It seems clear that there are continuities between infants' attachment styles and their behavior as adults. People who are having difficulty in relationships might look back to their infancy to identify the root of their problem (Simpson et al., 2007; Berlin, Cassidy, & Appleyard, 2008; Draper et al., 2008).

Module 14.1 Review

LO 14.1 Describe what makes young adults happy, what is meant by the social clock, and the concept of emerging adulthood.

Happiness in young adulthood is derived from the fulfillment of psychological rather than material needs. The social clock refers to the timing of major life events. Young adults can also be viewed as entering emerging adulthood, the period from the late teenage years extending to the mid-20s in which people are still sorting out their options for the future.

LO 14.2 Explain how young adults respond to the need for intimacy and friendship and how liking turns to loving.

According to Erikson, young adults are in the intimacy-versus-isolation stage. The course of relationships typically follows a pattern of increasing interaction, intimacy, and redefinition.

LO 14.3 Differentiate the different kinds of love.

According to the labeling theory of passionate love, people experience love when intense physiological arousal is accompanied by situational cues that the experience should be labeled "love." Types of love include passionate and companionate love. Sternberg's triangular theory identifies three basic components (intimacy, passion, and decision/commitment).

LO 14.4 Describe how young adults choose spouses.

In many Western cultures, love is the most important factor in selecting a partner. According to filtering models, people apply increasingly fine filters to potential partners, eventually choosing a mate according to the principles of homogamy and the marriage gradient. In general, the nature of relationships in heterosexual, gay, and lesbian couples is more similar than different.

LO 14.5 Explain how infant attachment styles are related to romantic relationships as adults.

Attachment styles in infants appear to be linked to the ability to form romantic relationships in adulthood.

Journal Writing Prompt

Applying Lifespan Development: Consider a long-term marriage with which you are familiar. Do you think the relationship involves passionate love or companionate love (or both)? What changes when a relationship moves from passionate to companionate love? From companionate to passionate love? In which direction is it more difficult for a relationship to move? Why?

The Course of Relationships

He wasn't being a chauvinist or anything, expecting me to do everything and him nothing. He just didn't volunteer to do things that obviously needed doing, so I had to put down some ground rules. Like if I'm in a bad mood, I may just yell: "I work 8 hours just like you. This is half your house and half your child, too. You've got to do your share!" Jackson never changed the kitty litter box once in 4 years, but he changes it now, so we've made great progress. I just didn't expect it to take so much work. We planned this child together and we went through Lamaze together, and Jackson stayed home for the first 2 weeks. But then—wham—the partnership was over. (Cowan & Cowan, 1992, p. 63)

Relationships, like the individuals who make them up, face a variety of challenges. As men and women move through early adulthood, they encounter significant changes in their lives as they work at starting and building their careers, having children, and establishing, maintaining, and sometimes ending relationships with others. One of the primary questions young adults face is whether and when to marry.

Cohabitation, Marriage, and Other Relationship Choices: Sorting Out the Options of Early Adulthood

LO 14.6 Describe the sorts of relationships people enter into in early adulthood and what makes these relationships work or cease to work.

For some people, the primary issue is not identifying a potential spouse but whether to marry at all. Although surveys show that most heterosexuals (and a growing number of gays and lesbians) say they want to get married, a significant number choose some other route. For instance, the past half-century has seen both a decline in the number of married couples and a huge, 1,500 percent rise in couples living together without being married, a status known as **cohabitation**. In fact, today, some 7.5 million people are cohabiting in the United States (see Figure 14-4). Married couples now make up a minority of households (Doyle, 2004b; Roberts, 2006; Jay, 2012).

Figure 14-4 Cohabitation

The number of couples living together prior to marriage increased by 41 percent from 2000 to 2010.

(**Source:** U.S. Bureau of the Census, 2010.)

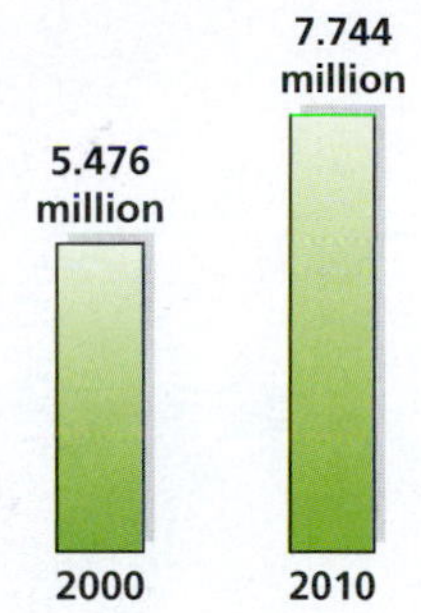

cohabitation
couples living together without being married

Most young adults will live with a romantic partner for at least one period of time during their 20s. Furthermore, most marriages today occur after a period in which the couple has cohabited. Why do so many couples choose to cohabit rather than to marry? Some feel they are not ready to make a lifelong commitment. Others feel that cohabitation provides "practice" for marriage. This is more likely for women than men. Women tend to see cohabitation as a step toward marriage; men are more likely to view it as a way to test a relationship (Jay, 2012; Perelli-Harris & Styrc, 2017).

Some couples cohabitate because they reject the institution of marriage altogether, maintaining that marriage is outmoded and that it is unrealistic to expect a couple to spend a lifetime together (Martin, Martin, & Martin, 2001; Guzzo, 2009; Miller, Sassler, & Kus-Appough, 2011).

Statistics suggest that those who feel that cohabiting increases their subsequent chances of a happy marriage are incorrect. On the contrary, the chances of divorce are somewhat higher for those who have previously cohabited, according to data collected in both the United States and Western Europe (Hohmann-Marriott, 2006; Rhoades, Stanley, & Markman, 2006, 2009; Tang, Curran, & Arroyo, 2014).

MARRIAGE. Despite the prevalence of cohabitation, marriage ultimately remains the preferred alternative for most people during early adulthood. Many see marriage as the appropriate culmination of a loving relationship, while others feel it is the "right" thing to do after reaching a particular age in early adulthood. Others seek marriage because of the various roles that a spouse can fill. For instance, a spouse can play an economic role, providing security and financial well-being. Spouses also fill a sexual role, offering a means of sexual gratification and fulfillment that is fully accepted by society. Another role is therapeutic and recreational: Spouses provide a sounding board to discuss one another's problems and act as partners for activities. Marriage also offers the only means of having children that is fully accepted by all segments of society. Finally, marriage offers legal benefits and protections, such as being eligible for medical insurance under a spouse's policy and eligibility for survivor benefits, such as Social Security benefits (Furstenberg, 1996).

Although marriage remains important, it is not a static institution. For example, fewer U.S. citizens are now married than at any time since the late 1890s. Part of this decline in marriage is attributable to higher divorce rates, but the decision of people to marry later in life is also a contributing factor. The median age of first marriage in the United States is now 28.7 for men and 26.5 for women—the oldest age for women since national statistics were first collected in the 1880s (see Figure 14-5; U.S. Bureau of the Census, 2010).

Figure 14-5 Postponing Marriage

THINKING ABOUT THE DATA: The age at which women and men first marry is the highest since national statistics were first collected in the late 1800s. What factors account for this?

(**Source:** U.S. Bureau of the Census, 2011.)

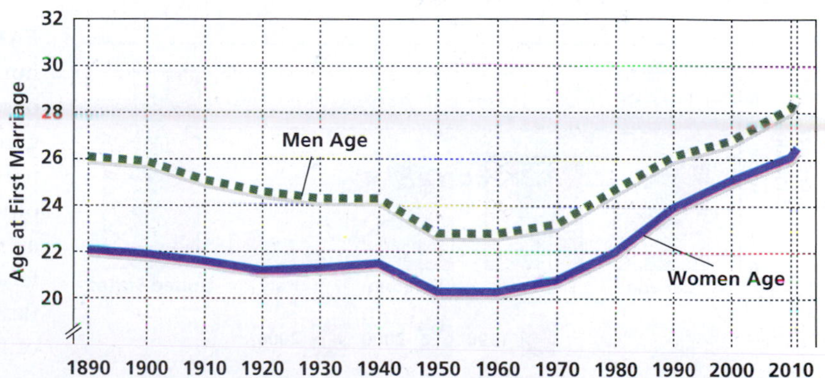

In many European countries, legal alternatives to marriage are growing. For instance, France offers "civil solidarity pacts," in which couples receive many of the same legal rights as married couples. What differs is that there is no legal lifetime commitment that they would be asked to make if they married; civil solidarity pacts can be dissolved more easily than marriages (Lyall, 2004).

Does this mean that marriage is losing its viability as a social institution? Probably not. Most people eventually do marry, and national polls find that almost everyone endorses the notion that a good family life is important (Newport & Wilke, 2013).

Why are people getting married later in life? The delay in part reflects economic concerns and the commitment to establishing a career. Choosing and starting a career presents an increasingly difficult series of decisions for young adults, and some feel that until they get a foothold on a career path and begin to earn an adequate salary, marriage plans should be put on hold (Dreman, 1997).

From *a social worker's* perspective

Why do you think society has established such a powerful norm in favor of marriage? What effects might such a norm have on a person who prefers to remain single?

WHAT MAKES MARRIAGES WORK? Partners in successful marriages display several characteristics. They visibly show affection to one another, and they communicate relatively little negativity. Happily married couples tend to perceive themselves as part of an interdependent couple rather than as one of two independent individuals. They also experience social homogamy, a similarity in leisure activity and role preferences. They hold similar interests, and they agree on a distribution of roles—such as who takes out the garbage and who takes care of the children (Carrere et al., 2000; Huston et al., 2001; Stutzer & Frey, 2006; Cordova, 2014).

Our awareness of the characteristics displayed by husbands and wives in successful marriages has not, however, helped prevent what can only be called an epidemic of divorce. The statistics on divorce are grim: Only about half of all marriages in the United States remain intact. Over 800,000 marriages end in divorce each year, and there are 3.2 divorces for every 1,000 individuals. This figure actually represents a decline from the peak in the mid-1970s of 5.3 divorces per 1,000 people, and most experts think that the rate is leveling off (National Center for Health Statistics, 2017).

Divorce is not just a problem in the United States. Countries around the world, both rich and poor, have substantial divorce rates, although in some places the rate is declining (see Figure 14-6).

Figure 14-6 Divorce Around the World

Countries around the world have substantial divorce rates, although in some places the rate is declining.

(**Source:** Adapted from Population Council Report, 2009.)

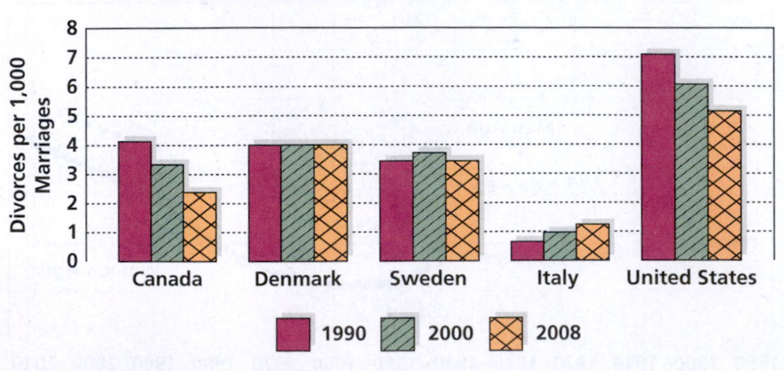

Although we discuss the consequences of divorce in greater detail in Chapter 16 when we consider middle age, divorce is a problem that has its roots in early adulthood and the early years of marriage. In fact, most divorces occur during the first 10 years of marriage.

EARLY MARITAL CONFLICT. Conflict in marriage is not unusual. According to some statistics, nearly half of newly married couples experience a significant degree of conflict. One of the major reasons is that partners may initially idealize one another, perceiving each other through the proverbial "starry eyes." However, as the realities of day-to-day living together and interacting begin to sink in, they become more aware of flaws, like the wife whose quotation began this section of the chapter. Perceptions of marital quality over the first 10 years of marriage on the part of both wives and husbands show a decline in the early years, followed by a period of stabilization, and then additional decline (see Figure 14-7; Huston et al., 2001; Karney & Bradbury, 2005; Kulik, Walfisch, & Liberman, 2016).

Figure 14-7 Perceptions of Marital Quality

At the beginning of marriage, partners see each other in a more idealized manner. But as time passes, the perception of the quality of the marriage declines.

(**Source:** Kurdek, 1999.)

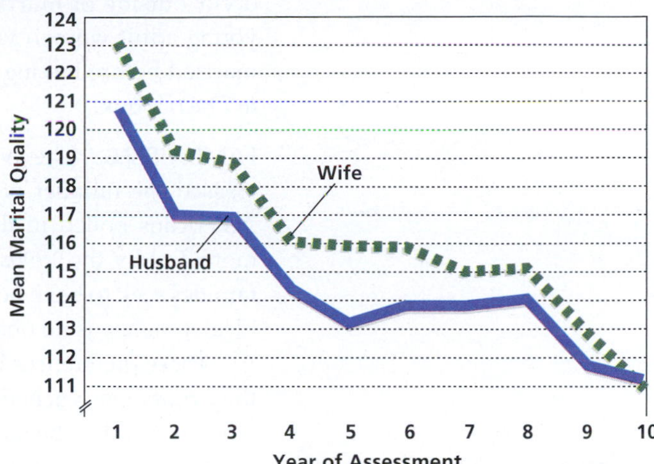

There are many sources of marital conflict. Husbands and wives may have difficulty making the transition from being children of their parents to being autonomous adults. Others have difficulty developing an identity apart from their spouses, while some struggle to find a satisfactory allocation of time to share with the spouse, compared with time spent with friends and other family members (Crawford, Houts, & Huston, 2002; Murray, Bellavia, & Rose, 2003; Madigan, Plamondon, & Jenkins, 2017).

Most married couples, however, view the early years of marriage as deeply satisfying. For them, marriage can be a kind of extension of courtship. As they negotiate changes in their relationship and learn more about each other, many couples find themselves more deeply in love than they were before marriage. For many couples, the newlywed period is one of the happiest of their entire married lives (Orbuch et al., 1996; McNulty & Karney, 2004).

Kayte Deioma/Alamy Stock Photo

Successful marriage involves companionship and mutual enjoyment of various activities.

Parenthood: Choosing to Have Children

LO 14.7 Describe how the arrival of children affects a relationship in early adulthood.

Having—or not having—children is one of the most important decisions couples make. What makes a couple decide to have children? Childrearing decidedly isn't economically advantageous: According to the U.S. government, a middle-class family with two children spends around $235,000 for each child by the time the child reaches age 18. Add in the costs of college and the figure comes to over $300,000 per child. And if you take into account the cost of care provided by families for their children, the total costs of caring for children are at least twice as high as the government estimates (Lino & Carlson, 2009; Folbre, 2012).

Instead, young adults typically cite psychological reasons for having children. They expect to derive pleasure from watching their children grow, fulfillment from their children's accomplishments, satisfaction from seeing them become successful, and enjoyment from forging a close bond with their children. But there also may be a self-serving element in the decision to have children. For example, parents-to-be may hope that their children will provide for them in their old age, maintain a family business or farm, or simply offer companionship. Others have children because to do so is such a strong societal norm: More than 90 percent of all married couples have at least one child, although most Americans prefer smaller families over larger ones (Saad, 2011).

For some couples, there is no decision to have children. Some children are unplanned, the result of the failure or absence of birth control methods. In some cases, the couple may have planned to have children at some point in the future, and so the pregnancy is not regarded as particularly undesirable and may even be welcomed. But in families that had actively not wanted to have children or already had what they considered "enough" children, a pregnancy can be viewed as problematic (Leathers & Kelley, 2000; Pajulo, Helenius, & Mayes, 2006).

The couples who are most likely to have unwanted pregnancies are often the most vulnerable in society. Unplanned pregnancies occur most frequently in younger, poorer, and less-educated couples. Happily, there has been a dramatic rise in the use and effectiveness of contraceptives, and the incidence of undesired pregnancies has declined in the past several decades (Centers for Disease Control, 2003; Villarosa, 2003).

For many young adults, the decision to have children is independent of the decision to marry. Although overall most women (59 percent) are married when they have children, more than half of births to women in the United States under age 30 now occur outside of marriage. The only demographic group for which this is not true is young adult women with a college education; they overwhelmingly still choose to be married before having children (DeParle & Tavernise, 2012; also see the *From Research to Practice* box).

FAMILY SIZE. The availability and use of effective contraceptives has dramatically decreased the number of children in the average American family. Almost 70 percent of Americans polled in the 1930s agreed that the ideal number of children was three or more, but by the 1990s the percentage had shrunk to less than 40 percent. Today, most families seek to have no more than two children—although most say that three or more is ideal if money is no object (see Figure 14-8; Gallup Poll, 2004; Saad, 2011).

These preferences have been translated into changes in the actual birth rate. In 1957, the *fertility rate* reached a post–World War II peak in the United States of 3.7 children per woman and then began to decline. Today, the rate is at 1.9 children per woman, which is less than the *replacement level*, the number of children that one generation must produce to

From Research to Practice

Children May Be Hazardous to Your Happiness

It's the American dream—getting married, buying a home, and settling down to have children. Everyone knows that parenthood is one of the great joys of life and that it contributes greatly to one's happiness and sense of well-being. But in that regard, everyone may be wrong: Research shows that not only does having children not necessarily produce increased happiness, in some cases it may actually reduce it (Brooks, 2008; Knopp et al., 2017).

Sociologist Robin Simon, who studied thousands of American families, summarized her findings this way: "Parents experience lower levels of emotional well-being, less frequent positive emotions and more frequent negative emotions than their childless peers. In fact, no group of parents—married, single, step or even empty nest—reported significantly greater emotional well-being than people who never had children" (Ali, 2008, p. 62; Simon, 2008, 2014).

Of course, parenthood is not without its rewards. Despite lower happiness, parents also report more purpose, more meaning, and ultimately more satisfaction with life than non-parents. But research data do not show that children bring greater happiness to their parents (Simon, 2008, 2014).

Why, then, does the belief that children bring great happiness persist? One possible reason is that we learn them from our parents. People who believe that parenting is a satisfying, life-enhancing experience are more likely to have children than are people who don't. The former group has more children to whom to pass on their beliefs, while the latter group's less rosy perspective is less likely to get transmitted to the subsequent generation (Gilbert, 2006; Knopp et al., 2017).

Another reason for people's continued faith in the joys of parenting has to do with selective recall. When people conjure up memories of their parenting experiences, they are likely to focus on the relatively rare best of times: a baby's first words or first smile, a fun day at the park, or graduation day. The stresses of parenthood—nighttime feedings, dirty diapers, fighting siblings, piles of dirty laundry, and so forth—may be much more common but tend to recede into the background when parents reflect on the experience. So when parents are asked whether having children enriched their lives, they tend to respond in the affirmative (Powdthavee, 2009).

But when parents' current sense of well-being is actually measured at various points in time, the truth emerges: Parents are not actually happier than people who do not have children, and on some measures the parents actually seem to do worse. Again, the culprit seems to be the day-to-day stresses that parenthood brings. On any given day, parents have fewer freedoms, more worries, and more domestic drudgery to deal with than do their childless peers (Evenson & Simon, 2005; Powdthavee, 2008, 2009; Chen, Lin, & Hsiao, 2016).

Ultimately, of course, many worthwhile pursuits in life, such as marriage or a career (not to mention pursuing a college education), bring their fair share of daily hassles and headaches. The hope is that in the balance, the occasional moments of joy and accomplishment make it all worthwhile.

Shared Writing Prompt

What are some benefits of parenthood that researchers might be overlooking?

be able to replenish its numbers. In contrast, in some underdeveloped countries, the fertility rate is as high as 6.5 (in Niger; *World Factbook*, 2017).

What has produced this decline in the fertility rate? In addition to the availability of more reliable birth control methods, one reason is that increasing numbers of women have joined the workforce. The pressures of simultaneously holding a job and raising a child have convinced many women to have fewer children.

Furthermore, many women who work outside the home are choosing to have children later in their childbearing years in order to develop their careers. Women between the ages of 30 and 34 are the only ones whose rate of births has actually increased over earlier decades. Still, because women who have their first children in their 30s have fewer years in which to have children, they ultimately cannot have as many children as women who begin childbearing in their 20s. Research suggesting that there are health benefits for mothers in terms of spacing children further apart may lead families to ultimately have fewer children (Marcus, 2004).

Figure 14-8 Smaller Is Better

Continuing trends over the past 75 years, U.S. parents prefer families with fewer children. What do you think is the ideal number of children for a family to have?

(**Source:** Saad, 2011.)

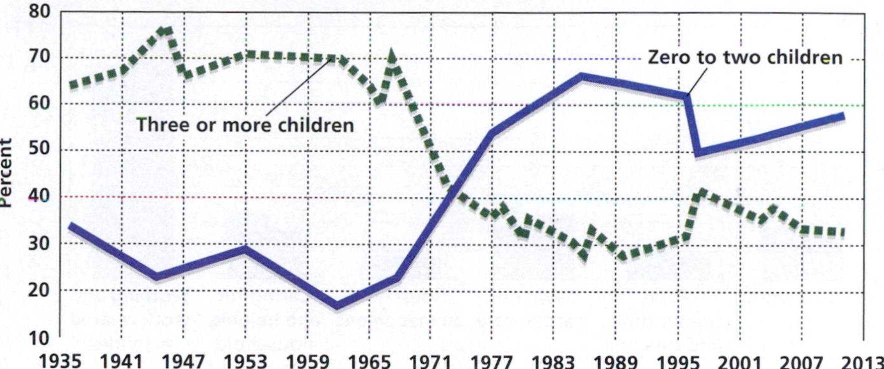

Some of the traditional incentives for having children—such as their potential for providing economic support in old age—may also no longer be as attractive. Potential parents may view Social Security and other pensions as a more predictable means of support when they are elderly than relying on their children. There is also, as mentioned earlier, the sheer cost of raising a child, particularly the well-publicized increase in the cost of college. This enormous cost, too, may act as a disincentive for bearing larger numbers of children.

Finally, some couples avoid having children because they fear they will not be good parents or simply because they don't want the work and responsibility involved in childrearing. Women may also fear that they will share a disproportionate amount of the effort involved in childrearing—a perception that may be an accurate reading of reality, as we consider next.

DUAL-EARNER COUPLES. One of the major historical shifts affecting young adults that began in the last half of the 20th century is the increase in the number of families in which both parents work. Close to three-quarters of married women with school-age children are employed outside the home, and more than half of mothers with children under age 6 are working. In the mid-1960s, only 17 percent of mothers of 1-year-olds worked full time; now, more than 50 percent do. In the majority of families, both husband and wife work (Carnegie Task Force, 1994; Barnett & Hyde, 2001; Matias et al., 2017).

For married couples who both work and have no children, the combined total of paid (in the office) and unpaid work (the chores at home) is nearly identical, at 8 hours 11 minutes for men, and 8 hours 3 minutes for women. And even for those families who have children under age 18, women who are employed full time do only 20 minutes more of combined paid and unpaid work (Konigsberg, 2010).

However, the nature of husbands' contributions to the household often differs from that of wives. For instance, husbands tend to carry out chores such as mowing the lawn or house repairs that are more easily scheduled in advance (or sometimes postponed) and often can be carried out on the weekend. In contrast, women's household chores tend to be devoted to things that need immediate attention, such as child care and meal

Figure 14-9 Division of Labor

Although husbands and wives generally work at their paying jobs a similar number of hours each week, wives are apt to spend more time than their husbands doing home chores and child-care activities. Why do you think this pattern exists?

(**Source:** Bureau of Labor Statistics, 2012.)

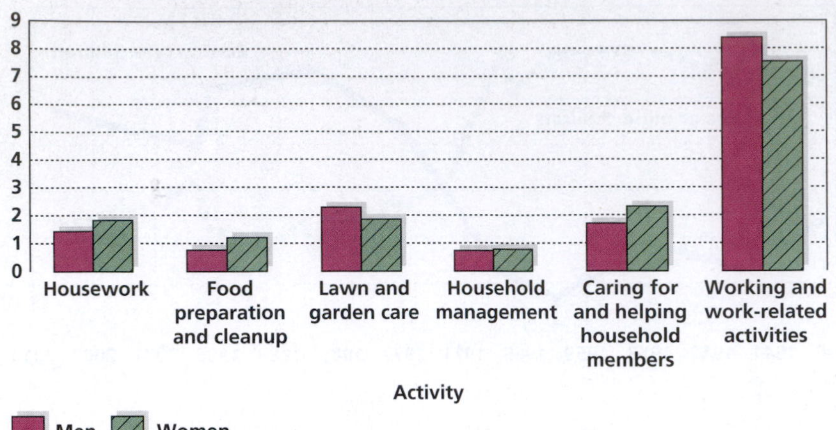

Note: Figures refer to average hours per day for persons who engaged in the activity.

preparation, and often can't be scheduled on the weekend or put off. As a result, wives experience greater levels of anxiety and stress (Lee, Vernon-Feagans, & Vazquez, 2003; Bureau of Labor Statistics, 2012; Ogolsky, Dennison, & Monk, 2014; see Figure 14-9).

THE TRANSITION TO PARENTHOOD: TWO'S A COUPLE, THREE'S A CROWD?

We had no idea what we were getting into when our first child was born. We certainly prepared for the event, reading magazine articles and books and even attending a class on child care. But when Sheanna was actually born, the sheer enormity of the task of taking care of her, her presence at every moment of the day, and the awesome responsibility of raising another human being weighed on us like nothing else we'd ever faced. Not that it was a burden. But it did make us look at the world with an entirely different perspective.

The arrival of a child alters virtually every aspect of family life, in positive and, sometimes, negative ways. The addition of a child to a household brings about a dramatic shift in the roles spouses must play. They are suddenly placed in new roles—"mother" and "father"—and these new positions may overwhelm their ability to respond in their older, though continuing, roles of "wife" and "husband." In addition, the birth of a child produces significant physical and psychological demands, including near-constant fatigue, new financial responsibilities, and an increase in household chores (Meijer & van den Wittenboer, 2007).

Dragon Images/Shutterstock

As increasing numbers of women have joined the workforce, more are choosing to have fewer children and to have them later.

Furthermore, in contrast to many non-Western cultures, in which childrearing is seen as a task that involves the entire community, Western culture's emphasis on individualism views childrearing as a primarily private enterprise. Thus, mothers and fathers in Western society are largely left to forge their own paths after the birth of a child, often without significant community support (Rubin & Chung, 2006; Lamm & Keller, 2007).

Consequently, for many couples, the strains accompanying the birth of a child produce the lowest level of marital satisfaction of any point in their marriage. This is particularly true for women, who tend to be more dissatisfied than men with their marriages after the arrival of children. The most likely reason for this gender difference is that wives often experience a greater increase in their responsibilities than husbands do, even in families in which parents seek to share childrearing chores (Laflamme, Pomerleau, & Malcuit, 2002; Lu, 2006).

This is not to say that all couples experience a decrease in marital satisfaction upon the birth of a child. According to work by John Gottman and colleagues (Shapiro, Gottman, & Carrère, 2000), marital satisfaction can remain steady, and actually rise, with the birth of a child. They identified three factors that permitted couples to successfully weather the increased stress that follows the birth of a child:

- Working to build fondness and affection toward one's partner
- Remaining aware of events in one's spouse's life and responding to those events
- Considering problems as controllable and solvable

In particular, those couples who were well satisfied with their marriages as newlyweds were more likely to continue to be satisfied as they raised their children. Couples who harbor realistic expectations regarding the extent of childrearing effort and other household responsibilities they face when children are born also tend to be more satisfied after they become parents. Furthermore, parents who work together as a *coparenting team*, in which they thoughtfully adopt common childrearing goals and strategies, are more apt to be satisfied with their parenting roles (Schoppe-Sullivan et al., 2006; McHale & Rotman, 2007).

In short, having children can well lead to greater marital satisfaction—at least for couples who are already satisfied with their marriage. For marriages in which satisfaction is low, having children may make a bad situation worse (Shapiro et al., 2000; Driver, Tabares, & Shapiro, 2003; Lawrence et al., 2008).

Gay and Lesbian Parents

LO 14.8 Compare gay and lesbian parents to heterosexual parents.

In increasing numbers, children are being raised in families in which there are two moms or two dads. Rough estimates suggest that around 16 to 20 percent of same-sex couples are parents (Gates, 2012).

How do lesbian and gay households compare to heterosexual households? To answer the question, we first need to consider some characteristics of gay and lesbian couples without children. According to studies comparing gay, lesbian, and heterosexual couples, labor tends to be divided more evenly in homosexual households than in heterosexual households. Each partner in a homosexual relationship is more likely to carry out approximately the same number of different chores, compared with heterosexual partners. Furthermore, gay and lesbian couples cling more strongly to the ideal of an egalitarian allocation of household work than heterosexual couples do (Kurdek, 2003, 2007).

Parenthood expands the roles of both husbands and wives into that of fathers and mothers, a process that can have profound effects on couples' relationships.

As with heterosexual couples, however, the arrival of a child (usually through adoption or artificial insemination) changes the dynamics of household life considerably in homosexual couples. As it does in heterosexual unions, a specialization of roles develops. According to recent research on lesbian mothers, for instance, childrearing tends to fall more to one member of the couple, while the other spends more time in paid employment. Although both partners usually say they share household tasks and decision making equally, biological mothers are more involved in child care. Conversely, the nonbiological mother in the couple is more likely to report spending greater time in paid employment (Patterson, 2013).

The evolution of the relationship between homosexual couples when children arrive appears to be more similar to that of heterosexual couples than dissimilar, particularly in the increased role specialization occasioned by the requirements of child care. The experience for children of being in a household with two parents of the same sex is also similar. Most research suggests that children raised in households in which the parents are homosexual show no differences in terms of eventual adjustment from those raised in heterosexual households. Although they may face greater challenges from a society in which the roots of prejudice against homosexuality are deep, children who have two moms or two dads ultimately seem to fare well (Patterson, 2009; Weiner & Zinner, 2015; Farr, 2017).

Staying Single: I Want to Be Alone

LO 14.9 Explain why some people choose to remain single in early adulthood.

For some people, neither marriage nor cohabitation is the preferred option. To them, living alone represents a good path, consciously chosen, through life. *Singlehood*, living alone without an intimate partner, has increased significantly in the past several decades, encompassing around 20 percent of women and 30 percent of men. Almost 20 percent will probably spend their entire lives in singlehood (U.S. Bureau of the Census, 2012).

People who choose not to marry or live with a partner give several reasons for their decision. One is that they view marriage negatively. Rather than seeing marriage in the idealized terms presented in the media of the 1950s, they focus more on high divorce rates and marital strife. Ultimately, they conclude that the risks of forming a lifetime union may be too high.

Others view marriage as too restrictive. These individuals place great value on personal change and growth, which would be impeded by the stable, long-term commitment implied by marriage. Finally, some people simply do not encounter anyone with whom they wish to spend the remainder of their lives. Instead, they value their independence, autonomy, and freedom (DePaulo, 2004, 2006).

Despite the advantages of singlehood, there are also drawbacks. Society often stigmatizes single individuals, particularly women, holding up marriage as the idealized norm. Furthermore, there can be a lack of companionship and sexual outlets, and singles may feel that their futures are less secure financially (Byrne, 2000; Schachner, Shaver, & Gillath, 2008).

Module 14.2 Review

LO 14.6 Describe the sorts of relationships people enter into in early adulthood and what makes these relationships work or cease to work.

Cohabitation is an increasingly popular option for young adults, but most still choose to marry. Divorce is prevalent in the United States, particularly within the first 10 years of marriage. Partners in successful relationships share interests, affection, communication, and household responsibilities.

LO 14.7 Describe how the arrival of children affects a relationship in early adulthood.

Couples overwhelmingly desire to produce children, although the availability of contraception and changes in women's roles in the workplace have combined to decrease average family size.

LO 14.8 Compare gay and lesbian parents to heterosexual parents.

Children bring pressures to both heterosexual and homosexual relationships, causing changes in focus, roles, and responsibilities.

LO 14.9 Explain why some people choose to remain single in early adulthood.

An increasing number of people in recent decades have chosen singlehood. Reasons include a negative view of marriage and a preference for independence. Single people often face societal suspicion and may experience a lack of companionship and financial insecurity.

Journal Writing Prompt

Applying Lifespan Development: In what ways do you think cognitive changes in early adulthood (e.g., the emergence of postformal thought and practical intelligence) affect how young adults deal with questions of marriage, divorce, and childrearing?

Work: Choosing and Embarking on a Career

Why did I decide that I wanted to be a lawyer? The answer is a bit embarrassing. When I got to my senior year of college, I began to worry about what I was going to do when I graduated. My parents were asking, with increasing frequency, what kind of work I was thinking about, and I felt the pressure rising with each phone call from home. So I began to think seriously about the problem. At the time, there was some big trial in the news all the time, and it got me to thinking about what it might be like to be an attorney. And I had always been fascinated by Law and Order *when it had been on television. For these reasons, and just about none other, I decided to take the law boards and apply to law school.*

For almost all of us, early adulthood is a period of decisions with lifelong implications. One of the most critical is choosing a career path. The choice we make goes well beyond determining how much money we will earn; it also relates to our status, our sense of self-worth, and the contribution that we will make in life. In sum, decisions about work go to the very core of a young adult's identity.

Identity During Young Adulthood: The Role of Work

LO 14.10 Explain the role of careers in the lives of young adults.

According to psychiatrist George Vaillant, young adulthood is marked by a stage of development called career consolidation. During **career consolidation**, a stage that begins between ages 20 and 40, young adults become centered on their careers. Based on a comprehensive longitudinal study of a large group of male graduates of Harvard, begun when they were freshmen in the 1930s, Vaillant found a general pattern of psychological development (Vaillant, 1977; Vaillant & Vaillant, 1990).

career consolidation
a stage that is entered between ages 20 and 40, when young adults become centered on their careers

In their early 20s, the men tended to be influenced by their parents' authority. But in their late 20s and early 30s, they started to act with greater autonomy. They married and began to have and raise children. At the same time, they began to focus on their careers—the period of career consolidation.

Based on his data, Vaillant drew a relatively uninspiring portrait of people in the career consolidation stage. The participants in his study worked very hard because they were working their way up the corporate ladder. They tended to be rule-followers who sought to conform to the norms of their professions. Rather than showing the independence and questioning that they had displayed earlier, while still in college, they threw themselves unquestioningly into their work.

Vaillant argues that work played such an important role in the lives of the men he studied that the career consolidation stage should be seen as an addition to Erikson's intimacy-versus-isolation stage of psychosocial identity. In Vaillant's view, career concerns come to supplant the focus on intimacy, and the career consolidation stage marks a bridge between Erikson's intimacy-versus-isolation stage and Erikson's next period, that of generativity-versus-stagnation stage. (*Generativity* refers to an individual's contribution to society.)

Reactions to Vaillant's viewpoint are mixed. Critics point out, for instance, that Vaillant's sample, though relatively large, comprised a highly restricted, unusually bright group of people, all of them men. It is hard to know how generalizable the results are. Furthermore, societal norms have changed considerably since the time the study was begun in the late 1930s, and people's views of the importance of work may have shifted. In addition, the lack of women in the sample and the fact that there have been major changes in the role of work in *women's* lives make Vaillant's conclusions even less generalizable.

Furthermore, research on what has been called the *millennial generation*—those born after 1980 and who entered young adulthood around the millennium in 2000—seem to have different views of work than earlier generations. They are much more likely to expect to change jobs multiple times; the idea of working for life for a single company is less attractive than it was to previous generations. They also have high (and sometimes unrealistic) expectations about how successful they will be, but don't necessarily feel that they will need to work hard to achieve that success. In fact, work-life balance is of considerable importance to millennials, who see employment as just one facet of a well-rounded life (Kuron et al., 2015; Deal & Levenson, 2016).

Still, whatever their attitudes about work, it is clear that employment plays an important role in young adults' lives and that it makes up a significant part of both men's and women's identity—if for no other reason than that many people spend more time working than they do on any other activity. We turn now to how people decide what careers to follow—and the implications of that decision.

Picking an Occupation: Choosing Life's Work

LO 14.11 List factors that influence the choice of a career in early adulthood.

Some people know from childhood that they want to be physicians or firefighters or to go into business, and they follow invariant paths toward their goals. For others, the choice of a career is very much a matter of chance, of turning to the want ads and seeing what's available. Many of us fall somewhere between these two extremes.

fantasy period
according to Ginzberg, the period, lasting until about age 11, when career choices are made, and discarded, without regard to skills, abilities, or available job opportunities

tentative period
the second stage of Ginzberg's theory, which spans adolescence, when people begin to think in pragmatic terms about the requirements of various jobs and how their own abilities might fit with them

realistic period
the third stage of Ginzberg's theory, which occurs in early adulthood, when people begin to explore specific career options, either through actual experience on the job or through training for a profession, and then narrow their choices and make a commitment

GINZBERG'S CAREER CHOICE THEORY. According to Eli Ginzberg (1972), people typically move through a series of stages in choosing a career. The first stage is the **fantasy period**, which lasts until a person is around 11. During the fantasy period, career choices are made, and discarded, without regard to skills, abilities, or available job opportunities. Instead, choices are made solely on the basis of what sounds appealing. Thus, a child may decide he wants to be a rock star—despite the fact that he cannot carry a tune.

People begin to take practical considerations into account during the **tentative period**, which spans adolescence. They begin to think more practically about the requirements of various jobs and how their own abilities and interests might fit with them. They also consider their personal values and goals, exploring how well a particular occupation might satisfy them.

Finally, in early adulthood, people enter the realistic period. In the **realistic period**, young adults explore specific career options either through actual experience on the job or through training for a profession. After initially exploring what they might do, people begin to narrow their choices to a few alternative careers and eventually make a commitment to a particular one.

Although Ginzberg's theory makes sense, critics have charged that it oversimplifies the process of choosing a career. Because Ginzberg's research was based on subjects from middle socioeconomic levels, it may overstate the choices and options available to people in lower socioeconomic levels. Furthermore, the ages associated with the various stages may be too rigid. For instance, a person who does not attend college but begins to work immediately after high-school graduation is likely to be making serious career decisions at a much earlier point than a person who attends college. In addition, economic shifts have caused many people to change careers at different points in their adult lives.

HOLLAND'S PERSONALITY TYPE THEORY. Other theories of career choice emphasize how an individual's personality affects decisions about a career. According to John Holland, for instance, certain personality types match particularly well with certain careers. If the correspondence between personality and career is good, people will enjoy their careers more and be more likely to stay in them; but if the match is poor, they will be unhappy and more likely to shift into other careers (Holland, 1997).

Blue jean images/Getty Images

According to one theory, people move through a series of life stages in choosing a career. The first stage is the fantasy period, which lasts until a person is around 11 years old.

According to Holland, six personality types are important in career choice:

- ***Realistic.*** Realistic people are down-to-earth, practical problem-solvers, and physically strong, but their social skills are mediocre. They make good farmers, laborers, and truck drivers.
- ***Intellectual.*** Intellectual types are oriented toward the theoretical and abstract. Although they are not particularly good with people, they are well suited to careers in math and science.
- ***Social.*** The traits associated with the social personality type are related to verbal skills and interpersonal relations. Social types are good at working with people, and consequently make good salespeople, teachers, and counselors.
- ***Conventional.*** Conventional individuals prefer highly structured tasks. They make good clerks, secretaries, and bank tellers.
- ***Enterprising.*** These individuals are risk-takers and take-charge types. They are good leaders and may be particularly effective as managers or politicians.
- ***Artistic.*** Artistic types use art to express themselves, and they often prefer the world of art to interactions with people. They are best suited to occupations involving art.

Development in Your Life

Choosing a Career

One of the greatest challenges people face in early adulthood is making a decision that will have lifelong implications: their career. Although there is no single correct choice—most people can be happy in any of several different jobs—the options can be daunting. Following are some guidelines for at least starting to come to grips with the question of what occupational path to follow:

- Systematically evaluate a variety of choices. Online sites such as LinkedIn.com and Monster.com contain a wealth of information about potential career paths, and most colleges and universities have career centers that can provide occupational data and guidance.
- Know yourself. Evaluate your strengths and weaknesses, perhaps by completing a questionnaire at a college career center that can provide insight into your interests, skills, and values.
- Create a "balance sheet" listing the potential gains and losses that you will incur from a particular profession. First, list the gains and losses that you will experience directly, and then list gains and losses for others, such as family members. Next, write down your projected self-approval or self-disapproval from the potential career. Finally, write down the projected social approval or disapproval you are likely to receive from others. By systematically evaluating a set of potential careers according to each of these criteria, you will be in a better position to compare different possibilities.
- "Try out" different careers through paid or unpaid internships. By seeing a job firsthand, interns are able to get a better sense of what an occupation is truly like.
- Remember that if you make a mistake, you can change careers. People today increasingly change careers in early adulthood and even beyond. No one should feel locked into a decision made earlier in life. As we have seen throughout this book, people develop substantially over the course of their lives.
- It is reasonable to expect that shifting values, interests, abilities, and life circumstances might make a different career more appropriate later in life than the one chosen during early adulthood.

Holland's personality categories form the basis of a number of measures often used in college career centers to help students identify appropriate careers. Rather than providing a single personality type, most measures based on Holland's categories provide a score for each of the categories, assuming that individuals vary in the degree to which a particular type applies.

Although Holland's enumeration of personality types is sensible, it suffers from a central flaw: Not everyone fits neatly into particular personality types. Furthermore, there are certainly exceptions to the typology, with jobs being held by people who don't have the particular personality that Holland would predict. Still, the basic notions of the theory have been validated, and they form the foundation of several of the "job quizzes" that people can take to see what occupations they might especially enjoy (Armstrong, Rounds, & Hubert, 2008; Martincin & Stead, 2015). (Also see the *Development in Your Life* box.)

Gender and Career Choices: Women's Work

LO 14.12 Describe how gender affects work choices and the work environment.

> *WANTED: Full-time employee for small family firm. DUTIES: Including but not limited to general cleaning, cooking, gardening, laundry, ironing and mending, purchasing, bookkeeping and money management. Child care may also be required. HOURS: Avg. 55/wk but standby duty required 24 hours/day, 7 days/wk. Extra workload on holidays. SALARY AND BENEFITS: No salary, but food, clothing, and shelter provided at employer's discretion; job security and benefits depend on continued goodwill of employer. No vacation. No retirement plan. No opportunities for advancement. REQUIREMENTS: No previous experience necessary, can learn on the job. Only women need apply.* (Unger & Crawford, 1992, p. 446)

Two generations ago, many women entering early adulthood assumed that this admittedly exaggerated job description matched the work for which they were best suited and to which they aspired: housewife. Even those women who sought work outside the home were relegated to certain professions. For instance, until the 1960s, employment ads in newspapers throughout the United States were almost always divided into two sections: "Help Wanted: Male" and "Help Wanted: Female." The men's job listings encompassed such professions as police officer, construction worker, and legal counsel; the women's listings were for secretaries, teachers, cashiers, and librarians.

communal professions
occupations that are associated with relationships

agentic professions
occupations that are associated with getting things accomplished

The breakdown of jobs deemed appropriate for men and women reflected society's traditional view of what the two genders were best suited for. Traditionally, women were considered most appropriate for **communal professions**, occupations associated with relationships, such as nursing. In contrast, men were perceived as best suited for agentic professions. **Agentic professions** are associated with getting things accomplished, such as carpentry. It is probably no coincidence that communal professions typically have lower status and pay than agentic professions (Eagly & Steffen, 1986; Trapnell & Paulhus, 2012; Locke & Heller, 2017).

From a *social worker's* perspective

How does the division of work into communal jobs (associated with relationships) and agentic jobs (associated with getting things done) relate to traditional views of male–female differences?

Although discrimination based on gender is far less blatant today than it was several decades ago—it is now illegal, for instance, to advertise a position specifically for a man or a woman—remnants of traditional gender-role prejudice persist. As we discussed in Chapter 13, women are less likely to be found in traditionally male-dominated professions such as engineering and computer programming.

Although significant progress in closing the gender wage gap was made in the past 40 years, women's earnings still lag behind those of men. Women earn an average of 82 cents for every dollar that men earn. Women who are members of certain minority groups are even worse off: Black women earn 63 cents for every dollar that white men earn. And women in many professions earn significantly less than men in identical jobs, as shown in Figure 14-10 (Frome et al., 2006; U.S. Bureau of Labor Statistics, 2014, 2017).

Figure 14-10 The Gender Wage Gap

These occupations are those in which women's earnings as a percentage of men's earnings were the lowest.

(**Source:** Bureau of Labor Statistics, 2017.)

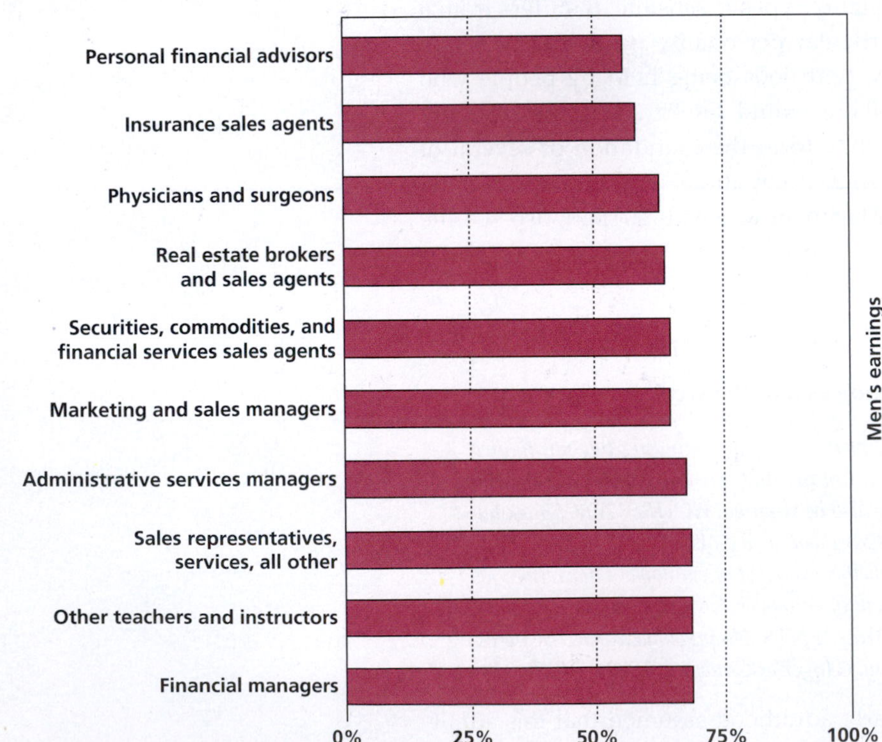

More women are working outside the home than ever before, despite status and pay that are often lower than men's. Between 1950 and 2010, the percentage of the female population (age 16 and over) in the U.S. labor force increased from 35 percent to close to 60 percent, and women today make up around 47 percent of the labor force. Almost all women expect to earn a living, and almost all do at some point in their lives. Furthermore, in 24 percent of U.S. households, women earn more than their husbands (U.S. Bureau of Labor Statistics, 2010, 2013; DeWolf, 2017).

Opportunities for women are considerably greater than they were in earlier years. Women are more likely to be physicians, lawyers, insurance agents, and bus

Figure 14-11 Shares of Employment by Gender for Selected Occupations

For many occupations, there are marked gender discrepancies in terms of employment.

(**Source:** Department of Labor Women's Bureau, 2017.)

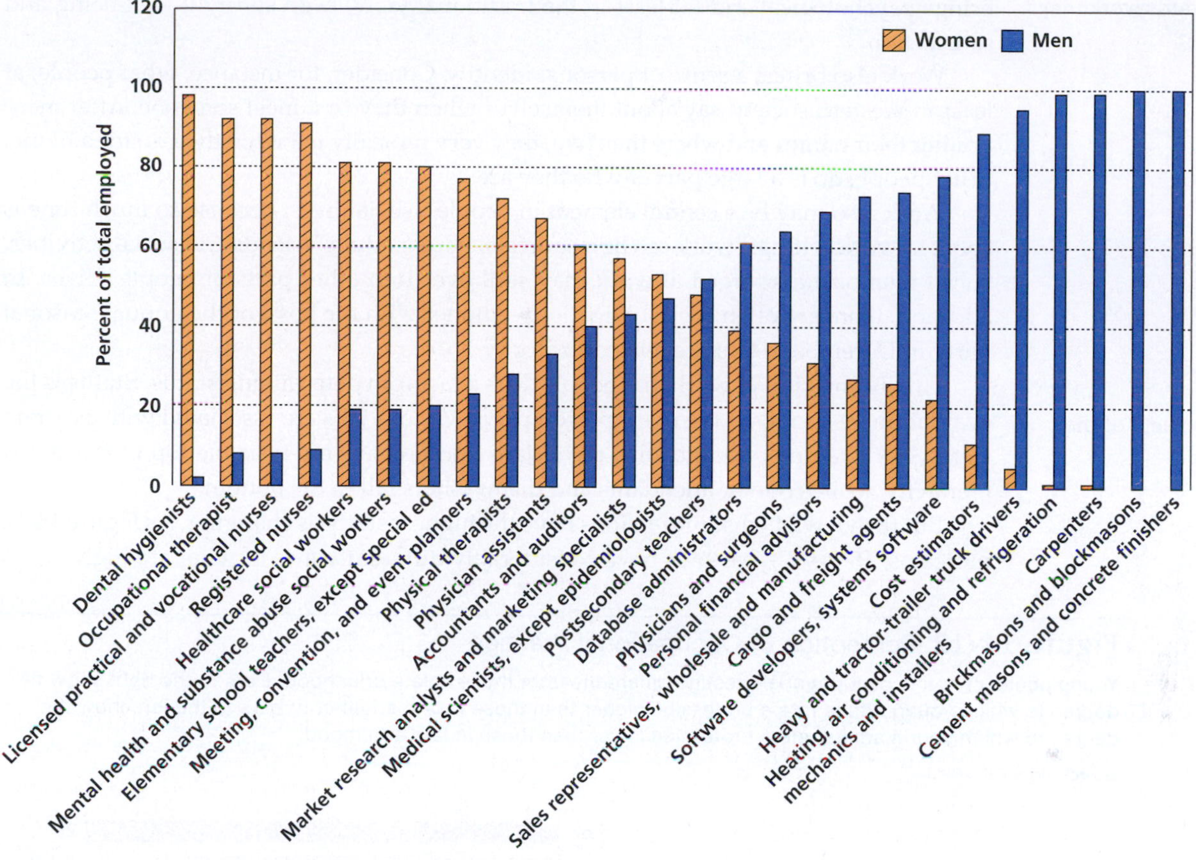

drivers than they were in the past. However, as noted earlier, within specific job categories, there are still notable gender differences. For example, female bus drivers are more apt to have part-time school bus routes, whereas men hold better-paying full-time routes in cities. Similarly, female pharmacists are more likely to work in hospitals, whereas men work in higher-paying jobs in retail stores (Unger & Crawford, 2003; also see Figure 14-11).

In the same way, women (and minorities, too) in high-status, visible professional roles may hit what has come to be called the *glass ceiling*. The glass ceiling is an invisible barrier within an organization that, because of discrimination, prevents individuals from being promoted beyond a certain level. It operates subtly, and often the people responsible for keeping the glass ceiling in place are unaware of how their actions perpetuate discrimination against women and minorities (Goodman, Fields, & Blum, 2003; Stockdale & Crosby, 2004; Dobele, Rundle-Thiele, & Kopanidis, 2014).

Why Do People Work? More Than Earning a Living

LO 14.13 Explain why people work and what elements of a job bring satisfaction.

This may seem an easy question to answer: People work to earn a living. Yet the reality is different; young adults express many reasons for seeking a job.

INTRINSIC AND EXTRINSIC MOTIVATION. Certainly, people work in order to obtain various concrete rewards, or out of extrinsic motivation. **Extrinsic motivation** drives people to obtain tangible rewards, such as money and prestige (D'Lima, Winsler, & Kitsantas, 2014).

extrinsic motivation
motivation that drives people to obtain tangible rewards, such as money and prestige

intrinsic motivation
motivation that causes people to work for their own enjoyment, not just for the rewards work may bring

People also work for their own enjoyment, for personal rewards—not just for the financial rewards a job may bring. This is known as **intrinsic motivation**. People in many Western societies tend to subscribe to the Puritan work ethic, the notion that work is important in and of itself. According to this view, working is a meaningful act that brings psychological and (at least in the traditional view) even spiritual well-being and satisfaction.

Work also brings a sense of personal identity. Consider, for instance, what people, at least in Western society, say about themselves when they first meet someone. After mentioning their names and where they live, they very typically tell what they do for a living. What people do is a large part of who they are.

Work also may be a central element in people's social lives. Because so much time is spent in work settings, work can be a source of young adults' friends and social activities. Social relationships forged at work may spill over into other parts of people's lives. In addition, there are often social obligations—dinner with the boss, or the annual seasonal party in December—that are related to work.

status
the evaluation by society of the role a person plays

Finally, the kind of work that people do is a factor in determining status. **Status** is the evaluation by society of the role a person plays. Various jobs are associated with a certain status. For example, traditionally, physicians and lawyers are near the top of the status hierarchy, while counter attendants and dishwashers fall to the bottom.

But the view of what professions have the highest status is changing. As Figure 14-12 indicates, 18- to 37-year-olds have considerably different views of what are high-status

Figure 14-12 Perception of Occupational Prestige

Young adults perceive occupational prestige differently from those in late adulthood. Bars to the right show the degree to which young adults rate a profession higher than those in late adulthood; bars to the left show the degree to which young adults rate a profession lower than those in late adulthood.

(**Source:** Harris Poll, 2014.)

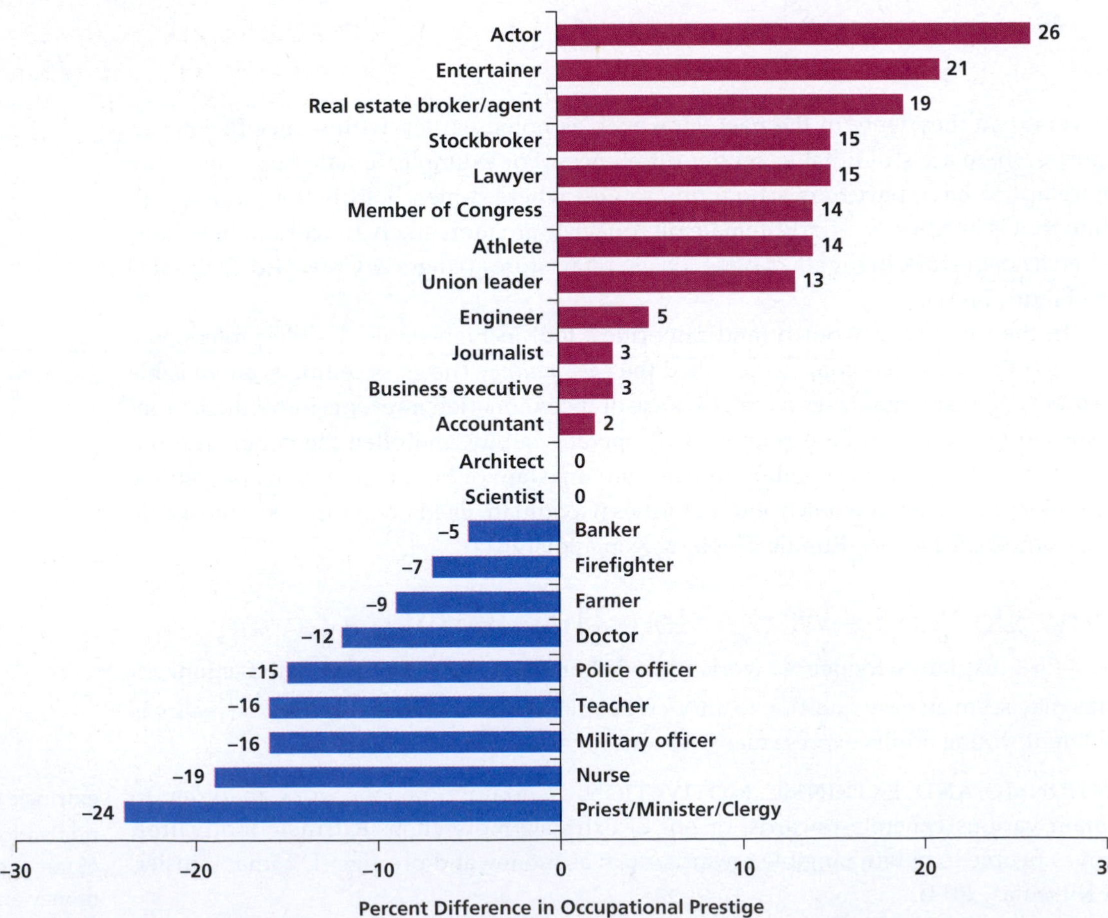

jobs from those in late adulthood. For example, 18- to 37-year-olds are more likely to view professions that provide fame, such as acting, as having high prestige (Harris Poll, 2014).

SATISFACTION ON THE JOB. The status associated with particular jobs affects people's satisfaction with their work. As might be expected, the higher the status of the job, the more satisfied people tend to be. Furthermore, the status of the job of the major wage-earner can affect the status of the other members of the family (Green, 1995; Schieman, McBrier, & van Gundy, 2003).

Of course, status isn't everything: Worker satisfaction depends on a number of factors, not the least of which is the nature of the job itself. For example, some people who work at computers are monitored on a minute-by-minute basis; supervisors can consistently see how many keystrokes they are entering. In some firms in which workers use the phone for sales or to take customer orders, conversations are monitored by supervisors. Workers' Web use and e-mail are also monitored or restricted by a large number of employers. Not surprisingly, such forms of job stress produce worker dissatisfaction (MacDonald, 2003).

Job satisfaction is higher when workers have input into the nature of their jobs and feel their ideas and opinions are valued. They also prefer jobs that offer variety, requiring many different types of skills, over those that require only a few. Finally, the more influence employees have over others, either directly as supervisors or more informally, the greater their job satisfaction (Peterson & Wilson, 2004; Thompson & Prottas, 2006; Carton & Aiello, 2009).

Module 14.3 Review

LO 14.10 Explain the role of careers in the lives of young adults.

Choosing a career is an important step in early adulthood, so important that George Vaillant considers career consolidation a developmental stage on a par with Erikson's intimacy-versus-isolation stage.

LO 14.11 List factors that influence the choice of a career in early adulthood.

According to Eli Ginzberg, people pass through three stages in considering careers: the fantasy period, the tentative period, and the realistic period. Other theories of career choice, such as John Holland's, attempt to match personality types to suitable careers.

LO 14.12 Describe how gender affects work choices and the work environment.

Gender stereotypes are changing, but women still experience subtle prejudice in career choices, roles, and wages.

LO 14.13 Explain why people work and what elements of a job bring satisfaction.

People work because of both extrinsic and intrinsic motivation factors.

Journal Writing Prompt

Applying Lifespan Development: If Vaillant's study were performed today on women, in what ways do you think the results would be similar to or different from those of the original study?

Epilogue

Our examination of early adulthood revealed a period less dramatic than others in terms of evident growth, but no less important or less characterized by change and development. We witnessed individuals at the peak of health and the height of their intellectual powers entering a period of their lives in which true independence is the challenge and the goal.

In this chapter, we looked at some of the most significant issues of early adulthood: forming relationships, falling in love and potentially getting married, and finding a career. We explored the factors that lead to loving relationships, the considerations that affect the choice of whether and whom to marry, and the characteristics of good—and not so good—marriages. We also discussed factors that people consider in choosing careers and the features of careers that make them satisfying.

Before we move on to middle adulthood in the next chapter, recall the prologue that began this chapter, about the relationship between Paul Gerard and Mario DeLuca. In light of your knowledge of relationships and careers in early adulthood, answer the following questions.

1. Is Paul and Mario's story of falling in love on the day they met typical of how most couples fall in love?
2. How might Robert Sternberg label the kind of love that Paul and Mario seem to be describing? How might the love that they felt for each other have changed between then and now?
3. Do you think that the labeling theory of passionate love describes Paul and Mario's experience, and why?
4. Paul and Mario are considering adopting a child together. How might that decision affect their relationship?

Looking Back

LO 14.1 Describe what makes young adults happy, what is meant by the social clock, and the concept of emerging adulthood.

For young adults, happiness is related to psychological factors, such as independence, competence, self-esteem, and relationships with others. The social clock is a term used to describe the psychological timepiece that records the major milestones in people's lives. Young adults can also be viewed as entering emerging adulthood, the period from the late teenage years extending to the mid-20s in which people are still sorting out their options for the future.

LO 14.2 Explain how young adults respond to the need for intimacy and friendship and how liking turns to loving.

Young adults face Erik Erikson's intimacy-versus-isolation stage, with those who resolve this conflict being able to develop intimate relationships with others.

LO 14.3 Differentiate the different kinds of love.

Passionate love is characterized by intense physiological arousal, intimacy, and caring, while companionate love is characterized by respect, admiration, and affection. Psychologist Robert Sternberg suggests that three components of love (intimacy, passion, and decision/commitment) combine to form eight types of love through which a relationship can dynamically evolve.

LO 14.4 Describe how young adults choose spouses.

Although in Western cultures love tends to be the most important factor in selecting a partner, other cultures emphasize other factors. According to filtering models, people filter potential partners initially for attractiveness and then for compatibility, generally conforming to the principle of homogamy and the marriage gradient. Gays and lesbians generally seek the same qualities in relationships as heterosexual men and women: attachment, caring, intimacy, affection, and respect.

LO 14.5 Explain how infant attachment styles are related to romantic relationships as adults.

Evidence suggests that people's attachment styles in infancy can affect the nature of their future romantic relationships as adults.

LO 14.6 Describe the sorts of relationships people enter into in early adulthood and what makes these relationships work or cease to work.

In young adulthood, while cohabitation is popular, marriage remains the most attractive option. The median age of first marriage is rising for both men and women. Partners in successful marriages visibly show affection to one another, communicate relatively little negativity, and see themselves as part of an interdependent couple rather than as one of two independent individuals. Divorce is prevalent in the United States, affecting nearly half of all marriages.

LO 14.7 Describe how the arrival of children affects a relationship in early adulthood.

More than 90 percent of married couples have at least one child, but the size of the average family has decreased, due partly to birth control and partly to the changing roles of women in the workforce. Children bring pressures to any marriage, shifting the focus of the marriage partners, changing their roles, and increasing their responsibilities.

LO 14.8 Compare gay and lesbian parents to heterosexual parents.

Gay and lesbian parents have more similarities with heterosexual parents than differences. When gay and lesbian parents have children, they experience changes in their relationships that mirror those in heterosexual couples.

LO 14.9 Explain why some people choose to remain single in early adulthood.

Singlehood is the choice of increasing numbers of people. Those who choose to remain single generally seek independence and wish to avoid the hazards of marriage.

LO 14.10 Explain the role of careers in the lives of young adults.

According to George Vaillant, career consolidation is a developmental stage in which young adults are involved in defining their careers and themselves.

LO 14.11 List factors that influence the choice of a career in early adulthood.

A model developed by Eli Ginzberg suggests that people typically move through three stages in choosing a career: the fantasy period of youth, the tentative period of adolescence, and the realistic period of young adulthood. Other approaches, such as that of John Holland, attempt to match people's personality types with suitable careers. This sort of research underlies most career-related inventories and measures used in career counseling.

LO 14.12 Describe how gender affects work choices and the work environment.

Gender-role prejudice and stereotyping remain a problem in the workplace and in preparing for and selecting careers. Women tend to be pressured into certain occupations and out of others, and they earn less money for the same work.

LO 14.13 Explain why people work and what elements of a job bring satisfaction.

People are motivated to work by both extrinsic factors, such as the need for money and prestige, and intrinsic factors, such as the enjoyment of work and its personal importance. Work helps determine a person's identity, social life, and status. Job satisfaction is the result of many factors, including the nature and status of one's job, the amount of input one has into its nature, the variety of one's responsibilities, and the influence one has over others.

Key Terms and Concepts

social clock 462
emerging adulthood 463
intimacy-versus-isolation stage 464
passionate (or romantic) love 466
companionate love 466
labeling theory of passionate love 466
intimacy component 466
passion component 466
decision/commitment component 467
homogamy 469
marriage gradient 469
cohabitation 473
career consolidation 481
fantasy period 482
tentative period 482
realistic period 482
communal professions 484
agentic professions 484
extrinsic motivation 485
intrinsic motivation 486
status 486

Summary 6
Early Adulthood

Laurence Mouton/PhotoAlto/Getty Images

BELLA ARNOFF AND THEODORE CHOI face many developmental issues typical of young adults. They have to consider the questions of health and aging, and the unspoken admission that they do not have all the time in the world. They have to look at their relationship and decide whether to take what society and nearly all their friends consider the next logical step: marriage. They have to face the question of children and career, and the possibility of giving up the luxury of being a two-earner family. They even have to reconsider Theodore's intention to continue his education. Fortunately, they have each other to help deal with the stress of this weighty combination of questions and decisions—and a considerable developmental arsenal of useful skills and abilities.

WHAT WOULD YOU DO?

■ If you were a friend of Bella and Theodore, what factors would you advise them to consider as they contemplate moving from cohabitation to marriage? Would your advice be the same if only Bella or Theodore asked you?

What's your response?

Ascent Xmedia/Getty Images

WHAT WOULD A HEALTH-CARE PROVIDE DO?

■ Given that Bella and Theodore are young, in good health, and physically fit, what strategies would you advise them to pursue to stay that way?

What's your response?

Zoonar GmbH/Age Fotostock

Physical Development

Ascent Xmedia/Getty Images

- Bella and Theodore's bodies and senses are at their peak, with their physical development nearly complete.
- During this period the couple will increasingly need to pay attention to diet and exercise.
- Because they face so many important decisions, Bella and Theodore are prime candidates for stress.

Cognitive Development

Zoonar/Jannis Werner/Age Fotostock

- Bella and Theodore are in K. Warner Schaie's achieving stage, confronting major life issues, including career and marriage.
- They are able to apply postformal thought to the complex issues they face.
- Dealing with major life events, while causing stress, may also foster cognitive growth in both of them.
- Theodore's desire to return to college is not unusual today, when colleges are serving a diversity of students, including many older students.

Social and Personality Development

Zachary Miller/Getty Images

- Bella and Theodore are at a time when love and friendship relationships are of major importance.
- The couple are likely to be experiencing a combination of intimacy, passion, and decision/commitment.
- Bella and Theodore have been cohabiting and are now exploring marriage as a relationship option.
- Bella and Theodore are not unusual in taking on decisions about marriage and children—decisions with major implications for the relationship.
- The couple must also decide how to handle the shift from two careers to one, at least temporarily—a decision that is far more than financial.

WHAT WOULD A CAREER COUNSELOR DO?

- Assuming Bella and Theodore decide to have children, what advice would you give them about handling the major expenses they face and the impact of children on their careers? Would you advise one of them to put his or her career on hold and pursue childrearing full time? If so, how would you counsel them to decide which career should be put on hold?

What's your response?

Sheer Photo, Inc/stockbyte/Getty Images

WHAT WOULD AN EDUCATOR DO?

- A friend of Theodore's has told him that he would be a "fish out of water" if he went back to graduate school a long time after getting his undergraduate degree. Do you agree? Would you advise Theodore to pursue his graduate school studies right away, before he gets too old, or to wait until his life settles down?

What's your response?

Tom Baker/123RF

Chapter 15

Physical and Cognitive Development in Middle Adulthood

Mats Silvan/Getty Images

Learning Objectives

LO 15.1 Describe the physical changes that affect people in middle adulthood.

LO 15.2 Explain how the senses change in middle adulthood.

LO 15.3 Explain how reaction time changes during middle adulthood.

LO 15.4 Compare how middle-aged men and middle-aged women experience changes in sexuality.

LO 15.5 Describe changes in health that occur in middle adulthood.

LO 15.6 Describe the risk factors related to coronary heart disease.

LO 15.7 Summarize what causes cancer and what tools are available to diagnose and treat it.

LO 15.8 Describe what happens to a person's intelligence in middle adulthood.

LO 15.9 Explain the role of expertise in middle adulthood.

LO 15.10 Describe how aging affects memory and how memory can be improved.

Chapter Overview

Prologue: Faster, Higher, Older

Since she began racing 4 years ago, Deborah Thelonius has won around a dozen long-distance competitions, including a 26.2-mile marathon. Her specialty is high-altitude running, and she holds the record at the Pikes Peak Marathon, where she had to climb 20 miles to a height of more than 14,000 feet above sea level.

Thelonius is 48.

But her running hasn't come without a price. She trains 6 days a week, and the arthritis in her knees creates a lot of pain. But she's not about to give up running. As she says, "It brings me a kind of satisfaction that I can't get from anything else. I'm going to keep at it as long as my body holds out."

Looking Ahead

Thelonius's success at high-altitude running is indicative of a revolution that is occurring in terms of the physical activity of people in middle adulthood. People reaching the mid-century mark are joining health clubs in record numbers, seeking to maintain their health and agility as they age.

They are doing this because it is during middle adulthood, roughly defined as the period from 40 to 65 years of age, that many people first face visible reminders that time is passing. Their bodies and, to some extent, their cognitive abilities begin to change in unwelcome ways. Many people make adjustments to meet the changing demands of middle age, but others, like Deborah Thelonius, view age as a challenge they can rise to meet through exercise, diet, and continued professional success. As we look at the physical, cognitive, and social changes of middle adulthood in this chapter and the next, we see that the period brings good news as well as bad. Many individuals are at the height of their capabilities, engaged in the process of shaping their lives as never before.

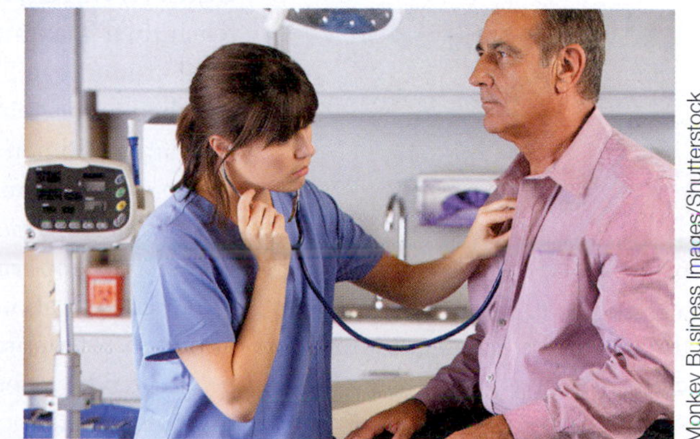
Monkey Business Images/Shutterstock

For some people, middle adulthood is a period in which unwelcome health problems begin to affect daily life.

We begin the chapter by considering physical development. We consider changes in height, weight, and strength, and discuss the subtle declines in various senses. We also look at the role of sexuality in middle adulthood.

We examine both health and illness during middle age and pay particular attention to two of the major health problems of the period, heart disease and cancer.

The second part of the chapter focuses on cognitive development in middle age. We look at the tricky question of whether or what kind of intelligence declines during the period, and we consider the difficulty of answering the question fully. We also look at memory, examining the ways in which memory capabilities change during middle adulthood.

Physical Development

It crept up gradually on Sharon Boker-Tov. Soon after reaching age 40, she noticed that it took her a bit longer to bounce back from minor illnesses, such as colds and the flu. Then she became conscious of changes in her eyesight: She needed more light to read fine print, and she had to adjust how far she held newspapers from her face in order to read them easily. Finally, she couldn't help but notice that the strands of gray hair on her head, which had begun to appear gradually when she was in her late 20s, were becoming a virtual forest.

Physical Transitions: The Gradual Change in the Body's Capabilities

LO 15.1 Describe the physical changes that affect people in middle adulthood.

Middle adulthood is the time when most people become increasingly aware of the gradual changes in their bodies that mark the aging process. As we saw in Chapter 13, some of the aging that people experience is the result of *senescence*, or naturally occurring declines related to age. Other changes, however, are the result of lifestyle choices, such as diet, exercise, smoking, and alcohol or drug use. As we'll see throughout this chapter, people's lifestyle choices can have a major impact on their physical, and even cognitive, fitness during middle age.

Of course, physical changes occur throughout the entire life span. Yet these changes take on new significance during middle adulthood, particularly in Western cultures that place a high value on youthful appearance. For many people, the psychological significance of such changes far exceeds the relatively minor and gradual changes that they are experiencing. Sharon Boker-Tov had found gray hairs even in her 20s, but in her 40s they multiplied in a way that she could not ignore. She was no longer young.

People's emotional reactions to the physical changes of middle adulthood depend in part on their self-concepts. For those whose self-image is tied closely to their physical attributes—such as highly athletic men and women or those who are physically quite attractive—middle adulthood can be particularly difficult. The signs of aging they see in the mirror signal aging and mortality but also may lead to the perception of a reduction in physical attractiveness. Those middle-aged adults, however, whose views of themselves are not so closely tied to physical attributes generally report no less satisfaction with their body images than younger adults (Eitel, 2003; Hillman, 2012; Murray & Lewis, 2014).

Physical appearance often plays an especially important role in determining how women see themselves. This is particularly true in Western cultures, where women face strong societal pressure to retain a youthful appearance. Society applies a double standard to men and women in terms of appearance: Whereas older women tend to be viewed in unflattering terms, aging men are more frequently perceived as displaying a maturity that enhances their stature (Hofmeier et al., 2017).

HEIGHT, WEIGHT, AND STRENGTH: THE BENCHMARKS OF CHANGE. Most people reach their maximum height during their 20s and remain relatively close to that height until around age 55. At that point, people begin a "settling" process in which the bones attached to the spinal column become less dense. Although the loss of height is very slow, ultimately women average a 2-inch decline and men a 1-inch decline over the rest of the life span (Rossman, 1977; Bennani et al., 2009).

osteoporosis
a condition in which the bones become brittle, fragile, and thin, often brought about by a lack of calcium in the diet

Women are more prone to a decline in height because they are at greater risk of osteoporosis. **Osteoporosis**, a condition in which the bones become brittle, fragile, and thin, is often brought about by a lack of calcium in the diet. As we discuss further in Chapter 17, although osteoporosis has a genetic component, it is one of the aspects of aging that can be affected by a person's lifestyle choices. Women—and men, for that matter—can reduce the risk of osteoporosis by maintaining a diet high in calcium (which is found in milk, yogurt, cheese, and some leafy greens) and by exercising regularly (Prentice et al., 2006; Swaim, Barner, & Brown, 2008; Rizzoli, Abraham, & Brandi, 2014).

During middle adulthood the amount of body fat also tends to grow in the average person. "Middle-age spread" is a visible symptom of this problem. Even those who have been relatively slim all their lives may begin to put on weight. Because height is not increasing, and actually may be declining, these weight and body fat gains lead to an increase in the number of people who become obese.

This weight gain usually doesn't have to happen. Lifestyle choices play a major role. People who maintain an exercise program during middle age tend to avoid obesity, as do individuals living in cultures where the typical life is more active and less sedentary than that of many Western cultures.

Changes in height and weight are also accompanied by declines in strength. Throughout middle adulthood, strength gradually decreases, particularly in the back and leg muscles. By the time they are 60, people have lost, on average, about 10 percent of their maximum strength. Still, such a loss in strength is relatively minor, and most people are easily able to compensate for it (Spence, 1989). Again, lifestyle choices can make a difference. People who exercise regularly are likely to feel stronger and to have an easier time compensating for any losses than those who are sedentary.

The Senses: The Sights and Sounds of Middle Age

LO 15.2 Explain how the senses change in middle adulthood.

Sharon Boker-Tov's experiences with needing extra light to read and holding the newspaper a little farther away are so common that reading glasses and bifocals have become almost a stereotypical emblem of middle age. Like Sharon, most people notice unmistakable changes in the sensitivity not only of their eyes but also of other sense organs. Although all the organs seem to shift at roughly the same rate, the changes are particularly noticeable in vision and hearing.

presbyopia
a nearly universal change in eyesight during middle adulthood that results in some loss of near vision

glaucoma
a condition in which pressure in the fluid of the eye increases, either because the fluid cannot drain properly or because too much fluid is produced

VISION. Starting at around age 40, *visual acuity*—the ability to discern fine spatial detail in both close and distant objects—begins to decline (see Figure 15-1). The shape of the eye's lens changes, and its elasticity deteriorates, which makes it harder to focus images sharply onto the retina. The lens becomes less transparent, so less light passes through the eye (DiGiovanna, 1994).

A nearly universal change in eyesight during middle adulthood is the loss of near vision, called **presbyopia**. Even people who have never needed glasses or contact lenses find themselves holding reading matter at an increasing distance from their eyes in order to bring it into focus. Eventually, they need reading glasses. For those who were previously nearsighted, presbyopia may require bifocals or two sets of glasses (Kalsi, Heron, & Charman, 2001; Koopmans & Kooijman, 2006; Kemper, 2012).

Figure 15-1 The Decline of Visual Acuity

Beginning around age 40, the ability to discern fine detail begins to drop.

(**Source:** Based on Pitts, 1982.)

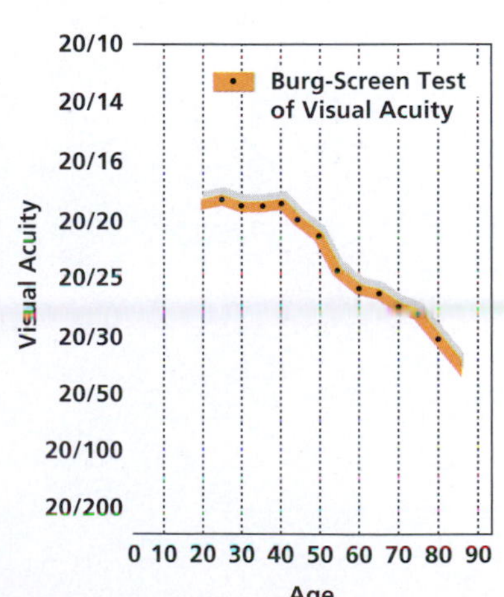

Other changes in vision also begin in middle adulthood. There are declines in depth perception, distance perception, and the ability to view the world in three dimensions. The loss of elasticity in the lens also means that people's ability to adapt to darkness is impaired, and they are less able to see in dimly lit environments. Such visual reductions may make it more difficult to climb stairs or to navigate around a dark room (Spear, 1993; Andrews, d'Avossa & Sapir, 2017).

Although changes in vision are most often brought about by the gradual processes of normal aging, in some cases disease is involved. One of the most frequent causes of eye problems is glaucoma, which may, if left untreated, ultimately produce blindness. **Glaucoma** occurs when pressure in the fluid of the eye increases, either because the fluid cannot drain properly or because too much is produced. Around 1 to 2 percent of people over age 40 are afflicted by the disorder, and African Americans are particularly susceptible.

Initially, the increased pressure in the eye may constrict the neurons involved in peripheral vision and lead to tunnel vision. Ultimately, the pressure can become so great that all nerve cells are constricted, which causes complete blindness. Fortunately, glaucoma can be treated if it is detected early enough. Medication can reduce the pressure in the eye, as can surgery to restore normal drainage of eye fluid (Plosker & Keam, 2006; Lambiase et al., 2009; Sleath et al., 2017).

HEARING. Like vision, hearing undergoes a gradual decline in acuity starting in middle adulthood. For the most part, however, the changes are less evident than those involving eyesight.

Some of the hearing losses of middle adulthood result from environmental factors. For instance, people whose professions keep them near loud noises—such as airplane mechanics and construction workers—are more apt to suffer debilitating and permanent hearing loss.

Many changes, however, are simply related to aging. For instance, age brings a loss of *cilia* or *hair cells* in the inner ear, which transmit neural messages to the brain when vibrations bend them. Like the lens of the eye, the eardrum also becomes less elastic with age, reducing sensitivity to sound (Wiley et al., 2005).

presbycusis
loss of the ability to hear sounds of high frequency

The ability to hear high-pitched, high-frequency sounds usually degrades first, a problem called **presbycusis**. About 12 percent of people between ages 45 and 65 suffer from presbycusis. There is also a gender difference: Men are more prone to hearing loss than women, starting at around age 55. People who have hearing difficulties may also have problems identifying the direction and origin of a sound, a process called *sound localization*. Sound localization can deteriorate because it depends on comparing the discrepancy in sound perceived by the two ears. For example, a sound on the right will stimulate the right ear first and then, a tiny time later, register in the left ear. Because hearing loss may not affect both ears equally, sound localization can suffer (Veras & Mattos, 2007; Gopinath et al., 2012; Koike, 2014).

Declines in sensitivity to sounds do not markedly affect most people in middle adulthood. Most people are able to compensate for the losses that do occur relatively easily—by asking people to speak up, turning up the volume of a television set, or paying greater attention to what others are saying.

Reaction Time: Not-So-Slowing Down

LO 15.3 Explain how reaction time changes during middle adulthood.

One common concern about aging is the notion that people begin to slow down once they reach middle adulthood. How valid is such a worry?

In most cases, not very. There is an increase in reaction time (meaning that it takes longer to react to a stimulus), but usually the increase is fairly mild and hardly noticeable. For instance, reaction time on simple tasks, such as reacting to a loud noise, increases by around 20 percent from age 20 to 60. More complex tasks, which require the coordination of various skills—such as driving a car—show less of an increase. Still, it takes a bit more time for drivers to move the foot from the gas pedal to the brake when they are faced with an emergency situation. Increases in reaction time are largely produced by changes in the speed with which the nervous system processes nerve impulses (Roggeveen, Prime, & Ward, 2007; Wolkorte, Kamphuis, & Zijdewind, 2014).

Despite the increase in reaction time, middle-aged drivers have fewer accidents than younger ones. Why would this be? Part of the reason is that older drivers tend to be more careful and to take fewer risks than younger ones. Much of the cause for their better performance, however, is older drivers' greater amount of practice in the skill. The minor slowing of reaction time is made up for by their expertise. In the case of reaction time, then, practice may indeed make perfect (Cantin et al., 2009; Endrass, Schreiber, & Kathmann, 2012; Meador, Boyd, & Loring, 2017).

Can slowing down be slowed down? In many cases, the answer is yes. Lifestyle choices once more come into play. Specifically, involvement in an active exercise program retards the effects of aging, producing several important outcomes, such as better health and improved muscle strength and endurance (see Figure 15-2). "Use it or lose it" is an aphorism with which developmentalists would agree (Conn, 2003).

Figure 15-2 The Benefits of Exercise

Many benefits accrue from maintaining a high level of physical activity throughout life.

(**Source:** DiGiovanna, 1994.)

The Advantages of Exercise

Muscle System

Slower decline in energy molecules, muscle cell thickness, number of muscle cells, muscle thickness, muscle mass, muscle strength, blood supply, speed of movement, stamina

Slower increase in fat and fibers, reaction time, recovery time, development of muscle soreness

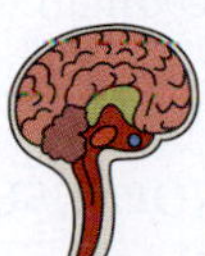

Nervous System

Slower decline in processing impulses by the central nervous system

Slower increase in variations in speed of motor neuron impulses

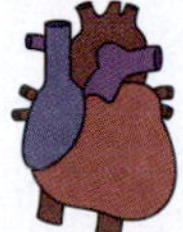

Circulatory System

Maintenance of lower levels of LDLs and higher HDL/cholesterol and HDL/LDL ratios

Decreased risk of high blood pressure, atherosclerosis, heart attack, stroke

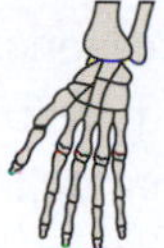

Skeletal System

Slower decline in bone minerals

Decreased risk of fractures and osteoporosis

Psychological Benefits

Enhanced mood

Feelings of well-being

Reduces stress

Sex in Middle Adulthood: The Ongoing Sexuality of Middle Age

LO 15.4 Compare how middle-aged men and middle-aged women experience changes in sexuality.

Sexuality remains an important part of life for most middle-aged people. Although the frequency of sexual intercourse declines with age (see Figure 15-3), sexual pleasure remains a vital part of most middle-aged adults' lives. About half of men and women age 45 to 59 report having sexual intercourse about once a week or more. Close to three-quarters of men and more than half of women age 50 to 59 report masturbating. Half of men age 50 to 59 and a third of women in that age group have received oral sex from a sex partner in the past year. Similarly, sex remains an important activity for gay and lesbian couples during middle adulthood (Duplassie & Daniluk, 2007; Herbenick et al., 2010; Koh & Sewell, 2015).

For many, middle adulthood brings a kind of sexual enjoyment and freedom that was missing during their earlier lives. With their children grown and away from home, middle-aged married couples have more time to engage in uninterrupted sexual activities. Women who have passed through menopause are liberated from the fear of pregnancy and no longer need to employ birth control techniques (Lamont, 1997; DeLamater, 2012).

Figure 15-3 Reported Frequency of Sexual Intercourse

As people age, the frequency of sexual intercourse declines.

(**Source:** Karraker, DeLamater, & Schwartz, 2011.)

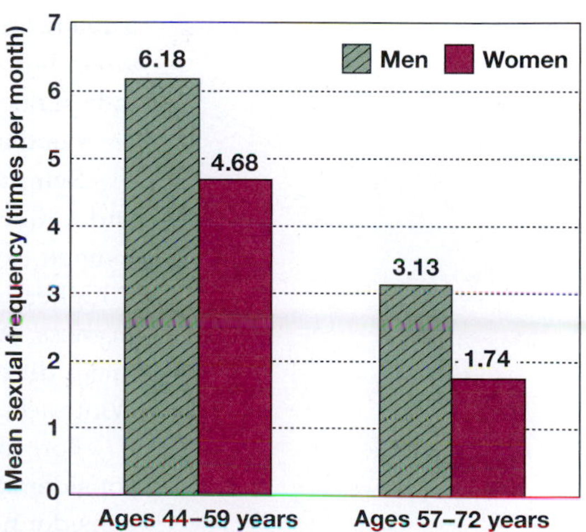

Both men and women can face some challenges to their sexuality during middle adulthood. For instance, a man typically needs more time to achieve an erection, and it takes longer after an orgasm to have another. The volume of fluid that is ejaculated declines. Finally, the production of *testosterone*, the male sex hormone, declines with age (Hyde & DeLamater, 2003).

For women, the walls of the vagina become thinner and less elastic. The vagina begins to shrink, and its entrance becomes compressed, which can make intercourse painful. For most women, though, the changes are not so great as to reduce sexual pleasure. Those women who do experience declines in enjoyment from sexual intercourse can find help from an increasing array of drugs, such as topical creams and testosterone patches, being developed to increase sexual pleasure (Freedman & Ellison, 2004; Nappi & Polatti, 2009; Spring, 2015).

female climacteric

the period that marks the transition from being able to bear children to being unable to do so

menopause

the cessation of menstruation

THE FEMALE CLIMACTERIC AND MENOPAUSE. Starting at around age 45, women enter a period known as the climacteric that lasts for some 15 to 20 years. The **female climacteric** marks the transition from being able to bear children to being unable to do so.

The most notable sign of the female climacteric is menopause. **Menopause** is the cessation of menstruation. For most women, menstrual periods begin to occur irregularly and less frequently during a 2-year period starting at around age 47 or 48, although this process may begin as early as age 40 or as late as age 60. After a year goes by without a menstrual period, menopause is said to have occurred.

Menopause is important for several reasons. For one thing, it marks the point at which a traditional pregnancy is no longer possible (although eggs implanted in a postmenopausal woman can produce a pregnancy). In addition, the production of estrogen and progesterone, the female sex hormones, begins to drop, producing a variety of hormone-related age changes (Schwenkhagen, 2007).

The changes in hormone production may produce a variety of symptoms, although the degree to which a woman experiences them varies significantly. One of the best-known and most prevalent symptoms is "hot flashes," in which a woman senses an unexpected feeling of heat from the waist up. A woman may get red and begin to sweat when a hot flash occurs. Afterward, she may feel chilled. Some women experience hot flashes several times a day; others never experience hot flashes. In one survey, for instance, only half of the women reported experiencing hot flashes.

During menopause, headaches, feelings of dizziness, heart palpitations, and aching joints are other relatively common symptoms, though far from universal. In general, only about one-tenth of all women experience severe distress during menopause. And many—perhaps as many as half—have no significant symptoms at all (Ishizuka, Kudo, & Tango, 2008; Levin, 2015; Guérin, Goldfield & Prud'homme, 2017).

For many women, symptoms of menopause may begin a decade before menopause actually occurs. *Perimenopause* is the period beginning around 10 years prior to menopause when hormone production begins to change. Perimenopause is marked by sometimes radical fluctuations in hormone production, resulting in some of the same symptoms that are found in menopause.

Symptoms of menopause also differ by race. Compared with Caucasians, Japanese and Chinese women generally report fewer overall symptoms. African American women experience more hot flashes and night sweats, and Hispanic women report a higher level of several other symptoms, including heart pounding and vaginal dryness. Although the reason for these differences is unclear, it may be related to racial differences in hormonal levels or perhaps diet (Cain, Johannes, & Avis, 2003; Winterich, 2003; Shea, 2006).

For some women, the symptoms of perimenopause and menopause can be considerable. Treating those problems, though, has proven to be no easy task, as we consider next.

THE DILEMMA OF HORMONE THERAPY: NO EASY ANSWER

Forty-six-year-old Sara Kendrick was certain she was having a heart attack. She had been weeding her garden when suddenly she couldn't get enough air into her lungs. She felt as if she were on fire, becoming lightheaded and dizzy. A feeling of nausea came over her. She made it to the kitchen to call 911 and then fell to the floor. When the emergency team examined her, she was both relieved and embarrassed to learn that her symptoms indicated not a heart attack but her first hot flash.

A decade ago, physicians would have had a straightforward remedy for hot flashes and other uncomfortable symptoms caused by the onset of menopause: They would have prescribed regular doses of a hormone replacement drug.

For millions of women who experienced similar difficulties, it was a solution that worked. In *hormone therapy (HT)*, estrogen and progesterone are administered to alleviate the worst of the symptoms experienced by menopausal women. HT clearly reduces a variety of problems, such as hot flashes and loss of skin elasticity. In addition, HT may reduce coronary heart disease by changing the ratio of "good" cholesterol to "bad" cholesterol. HT also decreases the thinning of the bones related to osteoporosis, which, as we discussed, becomes a problem for many people in late adulthood (Alexandersen, Karsdal, & Christiansen, 2009; Lisabeth & Bushnell, 2012; Braden et al., 2017).

Furthermore, some studies show that HT is associated with reduced risks of stroke and colon cancer. Estrogen may improve memory and cognitive performance in healthy women, as well as reduce depression. Finally, increased estrogen may lead to a greater sex drive (Schwenkhagen, 2007; Cumming et al., 2009; Garcia-Portilla, 2009).

Although hormone therapy may sound like a cure-all, in fact, since it became popular in the early 1990s, it has been well understood that there were risks involved. For instance, it seemed to increase the risk of breast cancer and blood clots. The thinking was, though, that the benefits of HT outweighed the risks. All that changed after 2002, when a large study conducted by the Women's Health Initiative determined that the long-term risks of HT outweighed the benefits. Women taking a combination of estrogen and progestin were found to be at higher risk for breast cancer, stroke, pulmonary embolism, and heart disease. Increased risk of stroke and pulmonary embolism were later found to be associated with estrogen-alone therapy (Lobo, 2009).

The results of the Women's Health Initiative study led to a profound rethinking of the benefits of HT, calling into question the wisdom that HT could protect postmenopausal women against chronic disease. Many women stopped taking hormone replacement drugs. Statistics tell the story: 40 percent of postmenopausal women in the United States were using hormone therapy in 2002; it was down to 20 percent a decade later (Newton et al., 2006; Michael et al., 2009; Beck, 2012).

The sharp decline among menopausal women using HT is probably an overreaction, however. The most recent thinking among medical experts is that it's not a simple all-or-nothing proposition; some women are simply better candidates for HT than others. While HT seems to be less appropriate for older, postmenopausal women (such as those who participated in the Women's Health Initiative study) because of the increased risk of coronary heart disease and other health complications, younger women at the onset of menopause and who are experiencing severe symptoms might still benefit from the therapy, at least on a short-term basis (Rossouw et al., 2007; Lewis, 2009; Beck, 2012).

Ultimately, HT presents a risk, although one that many physicians believe is worth taking. Women nearing menopause need to read literature on the topic, consult their physicians, and ultimately come to an informed decision about how to proceed.

THE PSYCHOLOGICAL CONSEQUENCES OF MENOPAUSE. Traditionally, experts, as well as the general population, believed that menopause was linked directly to depression, anxiety, crying spells, lack of concentration, and irritability. Some researchers estimated that as many as 10 percent of menopausal women suffered severe

Developmental Diversity and Your Life

The Experience of Menopause Across Cultures

If you're an American woman, one symptom of menopause that you might look forward to least are the hot flashes that are often viewed as a primary symptom. Yet if you are Japanese, the symptom you might fear most is shoulder stiffness. And if you live in India, you might not worry about menopause at all, because many women report no symptoms at all other than a change in menstrual patterns (Lock, 1993; Pote, 2017).

The nature and extent of menopausal symptoms clearly differ according to a woman's ethnic and cultural background. Women in non-Western cultures often have vastly different menopausal experiences from those in Western cultures. For instance, women of high castes in India report few symptoms of menopause. In fact, they look forward to menopause because being postmenopausal produces several social advantages, such as an end to taboos associated with menstruation and a perception of increased wisdom due to age. Similarly, Mayan women have no notion of hot flashes, and they generally look forward to the end of their childbearing years (Robinson, 2002; Dillaway et al., 2008; Marvan, Rosa, & Arroyo, 2013).

Not only does culture impact the symptoms women expect and experience, it is reflected in the meaning that women give to the period of menopause. In some cultures, menopause produces respect and freedom. For instance, the inability to become pregnant following menopause allows women to socialize more freely with men—something they couldn't do when they could still become pregnant (Stefanopoulou & Grunfeld, 2017).

DavidDennisPhotos/Getty Images

While women in some cultures anticipate menopause with dread, Mayan women have no notion of hot flashes, and they generally look forward to the end of their childbearing years.

depression. It was assumed that physiological changes in menopausal women's bodies brought about such disagreeable outcomes (DeAngelis, 2010; Mauas, Kopala-Sibley, & Zuroff, 2014).

Today, however, most researchers view menopause from a different perspective. It now seems more reasonable to regard menopause as a normal part of aging that does not, by itself, produce psychological symptoms. Certainly, some women experience psychological difficulties, but they do at other points in life as well (Matthews et al., 2000; Freeman, Sammel, & Liu, 2004; Somerset et al., 2006).

A woman's expectations about menopause can make a significant difference in her experience of it, according to research. On the one hand, women who expect to have difficulties during menopause are more likely to attribute every physical symptom and emotional swing to it. On the other hand, those with more positive attitudes toward menopause may be less apt to attribute physical sensations to menopausal physiological changes. A woman's attribution of physical symptoms, then, may affect her perception of the rigors of menopause—and ultimately her actual experience of the period. In fact, as we consider in *Developmental Diversity and Your Life*, menopause is viewed, and experienced, in very different ways across different cultures (Breheny & Stephens, 2003; Bauld & Brown, 2009; Strauss, 2011).

From *a health-care professional's* perspective

What cultural factors in the United States might contribute to a woman's negative experience of menopause? How?

THE MALE CLIMACTERIC. Do men experience the equivalent of menopause? Not really. Because they have never weathered anything akin to menstruation, they would have difficulty experiencing its discontinuation. At the same time, men do experience some changes during middle age that are collectively referred to as the male climacteric. The **male climacteric** is the period of physical and psychological change in the reproductive system that occurs during late middle age, typically in the 50s.

male climacteric
the period of physical and psychological change relating to the male reproductive system that occurs during late middle age

Because the changes happen gradually, it is hard to pinpoint the exact period of the male climacteric. For instance, despite progressive declines in the production of testosterone and sperm, men continue to be able to father children throughout middle age. However, about 10 percent of men have atypically low levels of testosterone by age 50. For these men, testosterone replacement therapy is sometimes used (Fennell et al., 2009).

One physical change that does occur quite frequently is enlargement of the *prostate gland*. By age 40, around 10 percent of men have enlarged prostates, and the percentage increases to half of all men by age 80. Enlargement of the prostate produces problems with urination, including difficulty starting urination or a need to urinate frequently at night.

Furthermore, sexual problems increase as men age. In particular, *erectile dysfunction*, in which men are unable to achieve or maintain an erection, becomes more common. Drugs such as Viagra, Levitra, and Cialis, as well as patches that deliver doses of the hormone testosterone, often are effective in treating the problem (Abdo et al., 2008; Glina, Cohen, & Vieira, 2014; Wentzell, 2017).

Although the physical changes associated with middle age are unequivocal, it's not clear whether they are the direct cause of any particular psychological symptoms or changes. Men, like women, clearly undergo psychological development during middle adulthood, but the extent to which psychological changes—which we discuss more in the next chapter—are associated with changes in reproductive or other physical capabilities remains an open question.

Module 15.1 Review

LO 15.1 Describe the physical changes that affect people in middle adulthood.

People in middle adulthood experience gradual changes in physical characteristics and appearance.

LO 15.2 Explain how the senses change in middle adulthood.

The acuity of the senses, particularly vision and hearing, declines slightly during middle age.

LO 15.3 Explain how reaction time changes during middle adulthood.

Reaction time slows slightly during middle adulthood, but this decline is compensated for by increased care and expertise and a decrease in risk-taking.

LO 15.4 Compare how middle-aged men and middle-aged women experience changes in sexuality.

Sexuality in middle adulthood changes slightly, but middle-aged couples, freed from concerns about children, can often progress to a new level of intimacy and enjoyment. Physiological changes relating to sexuality occur in both men and women. Both the female climacteric, which includes menopause, and the male climacteric seem to have physical and perhaps psychological symptoms.

Journal Writing Prompt

Applying Lifespan Development: Would you rather fly on an airplane with a middle-aged pilot or a young one? Why?

Health

It was an average exercise session for Jerome Yanger. After the alarm went off at 5:30 A.M., he climbed onto his exercise bike and began vigorously peddling, trying to maintain, and exceed, his average speed of 14 miles per hour. Stationed in front of the television set, he used the remote control to tune to the morning business news. Occasionally glancing up at the television, he began reading a report he had not finished the night before, swearing under his breath at some of the poor sales figures he was seeing. By the time he had completed exercising a half-hour later, he had gotten through the report, had managed to sign a few letters his administrative assistant had typed for him, and had even left two voicemail messages for some colleagues.

Most of us would be ready to head back to bed after such a packed half-hour. For Jerome Yanger, however, it was routine: He consistently tried to accomplish several activities at the same time. Jerome thought of such behavior as efficient. Developmentalists might view it in another light, however: as symptomatic of a style of behavior that makes Jerome a likely candidate for coronary heart disease.

Although most people are relatively healthy in middle adulthood, they also become increasingly susceptible to a variety of health-related concerns. We will consider some of the typical health problems of middle age, focusing in particular on coronary heart disease and cancer.

Wellness and Illness: The Ups and Downs of Middle Adulthood

LO 15.5 Describe changes in health that occur in middle adulthood.

Health concerns become increasingly important to people during middle adulthood. Surveys asking adults what they worry about show that health—along with safety and money—is an issue of concern. For instance, more than half of adults surveyed say they are either "afraid" or "very afraid" of having cancer (see Figure 15-4).

For most people, however, middle age is a period of health. According to census figures, the vast majority of middle-aged adults report no chronic health difficulties and face no limitations on their activities.

Actually, in some ways people are better off, healthwise, in middle adulthood than in earlier periods of life. People between the ages of 45 and 65 are less likely than younger adults to experience infections, allergies, respiratory diseases, and digestive problems. They may contract fewer of these diseases now because they may have already experienced them and built up immunities during younger adulthood.

Certain chronic diseases do begin to appear during middle adulthood. Arthritis typically begins after age 40, and type 2 diabetes is most likely to occur in people between ages 50 and 60, particularly if they are overweight. Hypertension (high blood pressure) is one of the most frequent chronic disorders found in middle age. Sometimes called the "silent killer" because it is symptomless, hypertension, if left untreated, greatly increases the risk of strokes and heart disease. For such reasons, a variety of preventive and diagnostic medical tests are routinely recommended for adults during middle adulthood (Walters & Rye, 2009; see Table 15-1).

Figure 15-4 Worries of Adulthood

As people enter middle adulthood, health and safety concerns become increasingly important, followed by financial worries.

(**Source:** *USA Weekend*, 1997.)

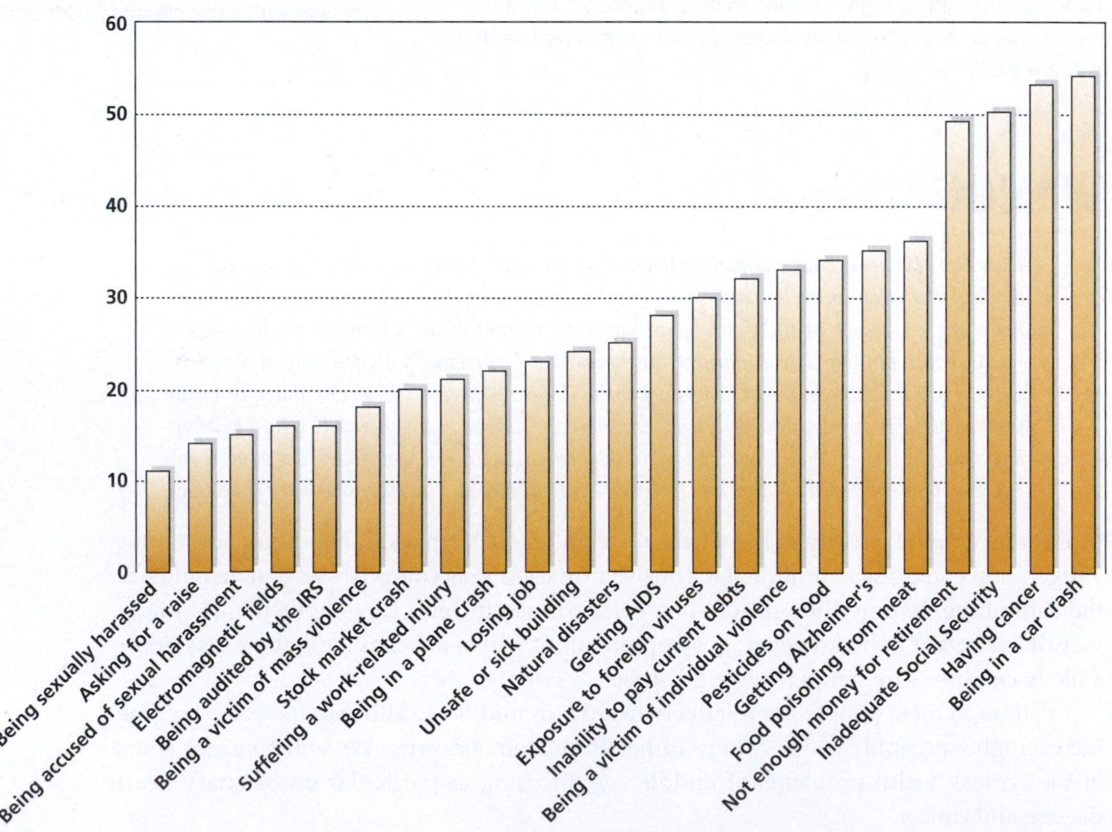

Table 15-1 Adult Preventive Care Schedules

(**Source:** Swenson & Ebell, 2016.)

Age	*18*	*20*	*21*	*24*	*25*	*35*	*40*	*45*	*50*	*55*	*59*	*65*	*70*	*74*	*75*	*80*
USPSTF screening recommendations																
Alcohol misuse	(B)															
Depression	(B)															
Hypertension	(A)															
Obesity	(B)															
Tobacco use and cessation	(A)															
HIV infection	(A)												(A) ***if at increased risk***			
Hepatitis B virus infection	(B) ***if at increased risk***															
Syphilis	(A) ***if at increased risk***															
Tuberculosis	(B) ***if at increased risk***															
BRCA gene screening	(B) ***if appropriate family history***															
Chlamydia and gonorrhea	(B) if sexually active				(B) ***if at increased risk***											
Intimate partner violence	(B) childbearing-aged women															
Cervical cancer			(A) Pap smer every 3 years, or every 5 years with human papillomavirus cotesting starting at age 30													
Lipid disorder		(B) ***if increased CHD risk***				(A)										
		(B) ***if increased CHD risk***						(A) ***if increased CHD risk***								
Abnormal glucose/diabetes							(B) if overweight or obese									
Hepatitis C virus infection	(B) ***if at high risk***								(B) birth years 1945–1965					(B) ***if at high risk***		
Colorectal cancer									(A)							
Breast cancer									(B) biennial screening							
Lung cancer										(B) if 30 pack-years and current or former smoker (quit in past 15 years)						
Osteoporosis								(B) if ≥ 9.3% 10-year fracture risk				(B)				
Abdominal aortic aneurysm												(B) if an "ever smoker"				
USPSTF preventive medications recommendations																
Primary prevention breast cancer	(B) ***if at increased risk*** and only after shared decision making															
Folic acid supplementation	(A) if capable of conceiving															
Statins for primary prevention of CVD							(B)									
Aspirin for primary prevention of CVD and colorectal cancer									(B) if ≥ 10% 10-year CVD risk							
Fall prevention (vitamin D)												(B) if community dwelling and increased fall risk				
USPSTF counseling recommendations																
Sexually transmitted infection prevention	(B) ***if at increased risk***															
Diet/activity for CVD prevention	(B) if overweight or obese and with ***additional CVD risk***															
Skin cancer prevention	(B) if fair skinned															

Legend	*Normal risk*	*With specific risk factor*
Recommendation for men and women		
Recommendation for men only		
Recommendation for women only		

Recommendation grades	
A	Recommended (likely significant benefit)
B	Recommended (likely moderate benefit)
C	Do not use routinely (benefit is likely small)
D	Recommended against (likely harm or no benefit)
I	Insufficient evidence to recommend for or against

CHD = coronary heart disease; CVD = cardiovascular disease; HIV = human immunodeficiency virus; USPSTF = U.S. Preventive Services Task Force.

Visual adaptation from recommendation statements by Swenson PF, Lindberg C, Carrilo C, and Clutter J.

As a result of the onset of chronic diseases, the death rate among middle-aged individuals is higher than it is in earlier periods of life. Still, death remains a rare occurrence: Statistically, only three out of every hundred 40-year-olds would be expected to die before age 50, and eight out of every hundred 50-year-olds would be expected to die before age 60. Furthermore, the death rate for people between 40 and 60 has declined dramatically over the past 75 years. For instance, the death rate now stands at just half of what it was in the 1940s. There also are socioeconomic status and gender variations in health, as we consider in the *Developmental Diversity and Your Life* box (Smedley & Syme, 2000).

STRESS IN MIDDLE ADULTHOOD. Stress continues to have a significant impact on health during middle adulthood, as it did in young adulthood, although the nature of what is stressful may have changed. For example, parents may experience stress over their adolescent children's potential drug use rather than worry about whether their toddler is ready to give up his pacifier.

Developmental Diversity and Your Life

Individual Variations in Health: Socioeconomic Status and Gender Differences

Masked by the overall figures describing the health of middle-aged adults are vast individual differences. While most people are relatively healthy, some are beset by a variety of ailments. Part of the cause is genetic. For instance, hypertension often runs in families.

Some of the causes of poor health are related to social and environmental factors. For instance, the death rate for middle-aged African Americans in the United States is twice the rate for Caucasians. Why should this be true?

Socioeconomic status (SES) seems to play a large role. For instance, when whites and African Americans of the same SES level are compared, the death rate for African Americans actually falls below that of whites. But the lower a family's income, the more likely it is that a member will experience a disabling illness and at an earlier age. In fact, one study found that the gap in life expectancy between the richest 1 percent and poorest 1 percent was 14.6 years. As can be seen in Figure 15-5, the higher the income level, the longer the life expectancy for both men and women (Chetty et al., 2016; Link et al., 2017).

There are a number of reasons for this. People living in lower SES households are more apt to work in occupations that are dangerous, such as mining or construction work. Lower income also often translates into inferior health-care coverage. In addition, the crime rates and environmental pollutants are generally higher in lower-income neighborhoods.

Figure 15-5 Life Expectancy and Income

For both men and women, the higher the income level, the longer the life span.

(**Source:** Chetty et al., 2016.)

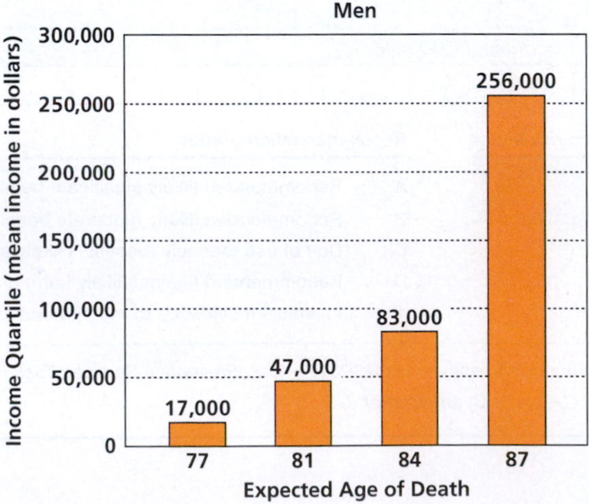

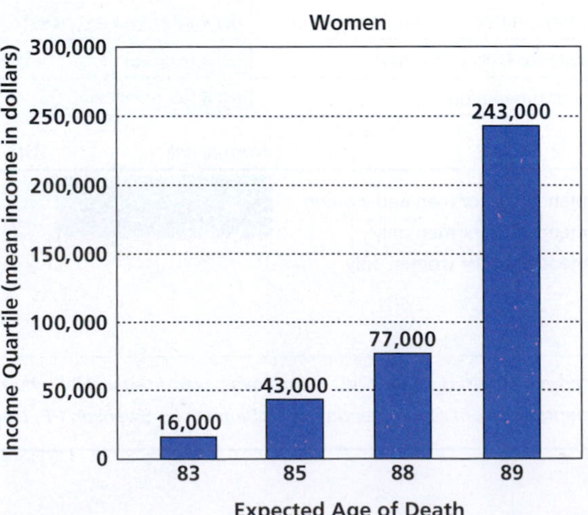

(continued)

Ultimately, then, a higher incidence of accidents and health hazards, and thus a higher death rate, are linked to lower levels of income (Dahl & Birkelund, 1997; Hendren, Humiston, & Fiscella, 2012).

Gender, like socioeconomic status, also makes a difference in health. Even though women's overall mortality rate is lower than men's—a trend that holds true from the time of infancy—the incidence of illness among middle-aged women is higher than it is among men.

Women are more likely to experience minor, short-term illness and chronic but non-life-threatening diseases, such as migraine headaches, and men are more apt to experience more serious illnesses, such as heart disease. Furthermore, the rate of cigarette smoking is lower among women than men, which reduces their susceptibility to cancer and heart disease; women drink less alcohol than men, which reduces the risk of cirrhosis of the liver and auto accidents; and women tend to work at less dangerous jobs than men.

Another possible reason for the higher incidence of illness in women may be the greater medical research targeted toward men and the types of disorders from which they suffer. The vast majority of medical research money is aimed at preventing life-threatening diseases faced mostly by men rather than at chronic conditions, such as heart disease, that may cause disability and suffering but not necessarily death. Typically, when research is carried out on diseases that strike both men and women, much of it has focused on men as subjects rather than on women. Although this bias is now being addressed in initiatives announced by the U.S. National Institutes of Health, the historical pattern has been one of gender discrimination by the traditionally male-dominated research community (Vidaver et al., 2000; Westervelt, 2015).

No matter what events trigger stress, the results are similar. As we first discussed in Chapter 13, *psychoneuroimmunologists*, who study the relationship among the brain, the immune system, and psychological factors, note that stress produces three main consequences, summarized in Figure 15-6. First, stress has direct physiological outcomes, ranging from increased blood pressure and hormonal activity to decreased immune system response. Second, stress also leads people to engage in unhealthy behaviors, such as cutting back on sleep, smoking, drinking, or taking other drugs. Finally, stress has indirect effects on health-related behavior. People under a lot of stress may be less likely to seek out good medical care, exercise, or comply with medical advice (Dagher et al., 2009; Ihle et al., 2012; de Frias & Whyne, 2015). All of these can lead to or affect serious health conditions, including such major problems as heart disease.

Figure 15-6 The Consequences of Stress

Stress produces three major consequences: direct physiological effects, harmful behaviors, and indirect health-related behaviors.

(**Source:** Adapted from Baum, 1994.)

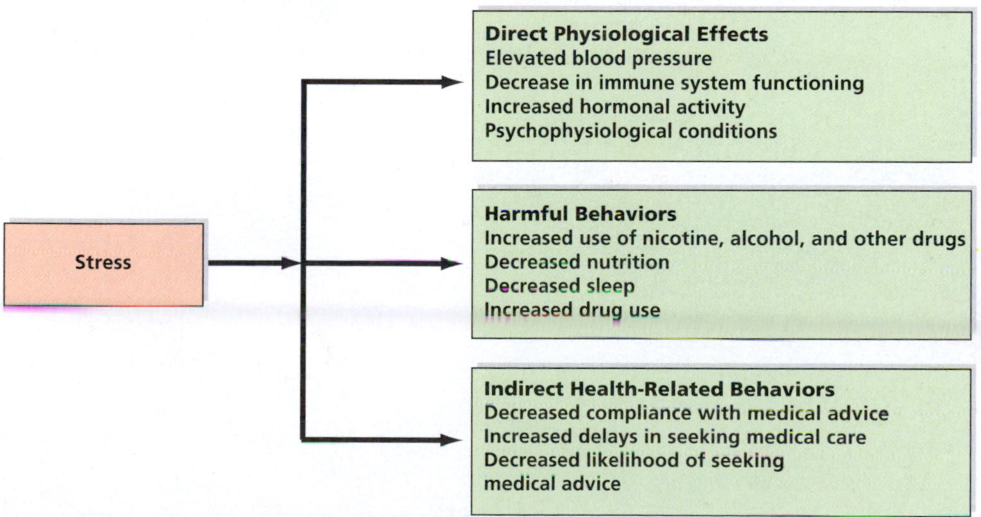

The A's and B's of Coronary Heart Disease: Linking Health and Personality

LO 15.6 Describe the risk factors related to coronary heart disease.

More men die in middle age from diseases relating to the heart and circulatory system than from any other cause. Women are less vulnerable, as we'll see, but they are not immune. Each year such diseases kill around 151,000 people under age 65, and they are responsible for more loss of work and disability days due to hospitalization than any other cause (American Heart Association, 2010).

RISK FACTORS FOR HEART DISEASE. Although heart and circulatory diseases are a major problem, they are not an equal threat for all people—some people have a much lower risk than others. For instance, the death rate in some countries, such as Japan, is only a quarter of the rate in the United States (also see Figure 15-7). Why should this be true?

The answer is that both genetic and experiential characteristics are involved. Some people seem genetically predisposed to develop heart disease. If a person's parents suffered from it, the likelihood is greater that she or he will too. Similarly, sex and age are risk factors: Men are more likely to suffer from heart disease than women, and the risk rises as people age.

Figure 15-7 Death from Heart Disease Worldwide

The risk of dying from cardiovascular disease differs significantly depending on the country in which one lives. What cultural or environmental factors might help to explain this fact?

(**Source:** Meyers, 2015.)

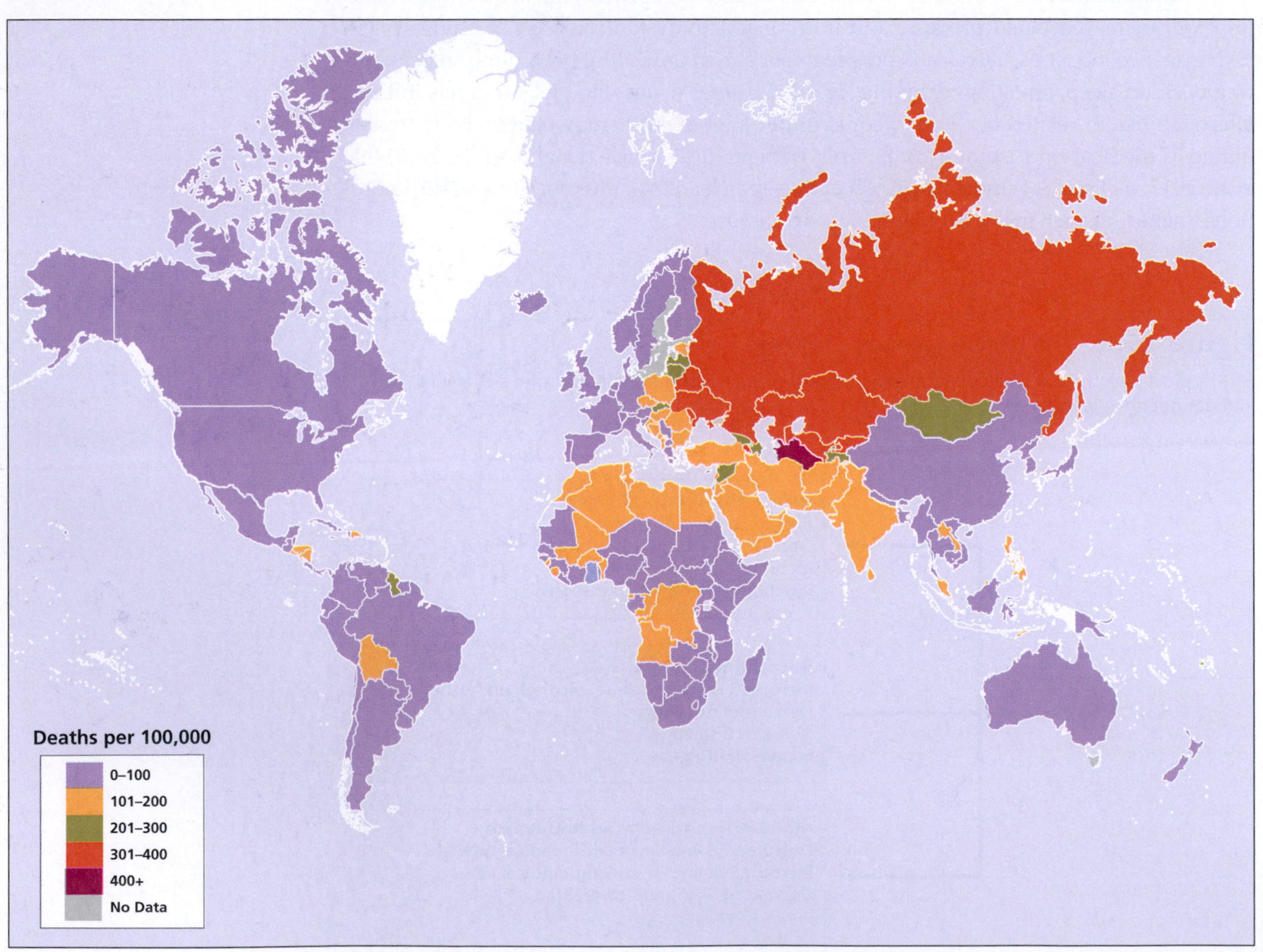

However, environment and lifestyle choices are also important. Cigarette smoking, a diet high in fats and cholesterol, and a relative lack of physical exercise all increase the likelihood of heart disease. Such factors may explain country-to-country variations in the incidence of heart disease. For example, the death rate attributable to heart disease in Japan is relatively low and may be attributable to differences in diet: The typical diet in Japan is much lower in fat than the typical diet in the United States (Scarborough et al., 2012; Platt et al., 2014; Hirsch & Morlière, 2017).

But diet is not the only factor. Psychological factors, particularly those related to the perception and experience of stress, appear to be associated with heart disease. In particular, a set of personality characteristics appears to be related to the development of middle-aged adults' coronary heart disease—the Type A behavior pattern.

TYPE A AND TYPE B. For a certain proportion of adults, waiting patiently in a long line at the grocery store is a near impossibility. Sitting in their cars at a long red light makes them seethe. And an encounter with a slow, inept clerk at a retail store makes them furious.

People like this—and those similar to Jerome Yanger, who uses his exercise program as an opportunity to accomplish more work—have a set of characteristics known as the Type A behavior pattern. The **Type A behavior pattern** is characterized by competitiveness, impatience, and a tendency toward frustration and hostility. Type A people are driven to accomplish more than others, and they engage in *polyphasic activities*—multiple activities carried out simultaneously. They are the true multitaskers whom you might see talking on their phones while working on their laptop computers while riding the commuter train—and eating breakfast. They are easily angered and become both verbally and nonverbally hostile if they are prevented from reaching a goal they seek to accomplish.

Type A behavior pattern
behavior characterized by competitiveness, impatience, and a tendency toward frustration and hostility

In contrast to the Type A behavior pattern, many people have virtually the opposite characteristics in a pattern known as the Type B behavior pattern. The **Type B behavior pattern** is characterized by noncompetitiveness, patience, and a lack of aggression. In contrast to Type A individuals, Type B individuals experience little sense of time urgency, and they are rarely hostile.

Type B behavior pattern
behavior characterized by noncompetitiveness, patience, and a lack of aggression

Most people are not purely Type A or Type B. In fact, Type A and Type B represent the ends of a continuum, with most people falling somewhere in between the two endpoints. Still, most people come closer to one or the other of the two categories. Which category a person falls into is of some importance, particularly by middle adulthood, because a great deal of research suggests that the distinction is related to the incidence of coronary heart disease. For example, Type A men have twice the rate of coronary heart disease, a greater number of fatal heart attacks, and five times as many heart problems overall as Type B men (Rosenman, 1990; Wielgosz & Nolan, 2000).

Although it is not certain why Type A behavior increases the risk of heart problems, the most likely explanation is that when Type A individuals are in stressful situations, they become excessively aroused physiologically. Heart rate and blood pressure rise, and production of the hormones epinephrine and norepinephrine increases. The wear and tear on the body's circulatory system is what seems to ultimately produce coronary heart disease (Williams, Barefoot, & Schneiderman, 2003).

It's important to note that not every component of the Type A behavior pattern is harmful. The key component that links Type A behavior and heart disease is *hostility*. Furthermore, the links between Type A behavior and coronary heart disease are correlational. No definitive evidence has been found that Type A behavior *causes* coronary heart disease. In fact, some evidence suggests that only certain components of Type A behavior are most involved in producing disease, and not the entire constellation of behaviors associated with the pattern (Demaree & Everhart, 2004; Eaker et al., 2004; Kahn, 2004; Myrtek, 2007).

killerb10/Getty Images

In addition to being characterized as competitive, people with Type A personalities also tend to engage in polyphasic activities, or doing a number of things at once. Does a Type A personality deal with stress differently than a Type B personality?

Although the relationship between at least some Type A behaviors and heart disease is clear, this does not mean that all middle-aged adults who can be characterized as Type A are destined to suffer from coronary heart disease. For one thing, almost all the research conducted to date has focused on men, primarily because the incidence of coronary heart disease is much higher for males than for females. In addition, other types of negative emotions besides the hostility found in Type A behavior have been linked to heart disease. For example, psychologist Johan Denollet has identified behavior he calls *Type D*—for "distressed"—that is linked to coronary heart disease. He believes that insecurity, anxiety, and having a negative outlook put people at risk for heart attacks (Schiffer et al., 2008; Pedersen et al., 2009; Lin et al., 2017).

The Threat of Cancer

LO 15.7 Summarize what causes cancer and what tools are available to diagnose and treat it.

Brenda surveyed the crowd as she stood in line to start the annual Race for the Cure, a running and walking event that raised funds to fight breast cancer. It was a sobering sight. She spotted a group of five women, all wearing the bright pink shirts that marked them as cancer survivors. Several other racers had photos of loved ones who had lost their battles with the disease pinned to their jerseys.

Few diseases are as frightening as cancer, and many middle-aged individuals view a cancer diagnosis as a death sentence. Although the reality is different—many forms of cancer respond quite well to medical treatment, and two-thirds of people diagnosed with the disease are still alive 5 years later—the disease raises many fears. And there is no denying that cancer is the second-leading cause of death in the United States (CDC, 2015).

The precise trigger for cancer is still not known, but the process by which cancer spreads is straightforward. For some reason, particular cells in the body begin to multiply uncontrollably and rapidly. As they increase in number, these cells form tumors. If left unimpeded, they draw nutrients from healthy cells and body tissue. Eventually, they destroy the body's ability to function properly.

Like heart disease, cancer is associated with a variety of risk factors, some genetic and others environmental. Some kinds of cancer have clear genetic components. For example, a family history of breast cancer—which is the most common cause of cancer death among women—raises the risk for a woman.

Several environmental and behavioral factors are also related to the risk of cancer. For instance, poor nutrition, smoking, alcohol use, exposure to sunlight, exposure to radiation, and particular occupational hazards (such as exposure to certain chemicals or asbestos) are all known to increase the chances of developing cancer.

From *a health-care professional's* perspective

Does the effect of psychological attitudes on cancer survival suggest that nontraditional healing techniques—such as the use of meditation—might have a place in cancer treatment? Why or why not?

After a diagnosis of cancer, several forms of treatment are possible, depending on the type of cancer. One treatment is *radiation therapy*, in which the tumor is the target of radiation designed to destroy it. Patients undergoing *chemotherapy* ingest controlled doses of toxic substances meant, in essence, to poison the tumor. Finally, surgery may be used to remove the tumor (and often the surrounding tissue). The exact form of treatment is a result of how far the cancer has spread throughout a patient's body when it is first identified.

Because early cancer detection improves a patient's chances, diagnostic techniques that help identify the first signs of cancer are of great importance. This is particularly true during middle adulthood, when the risk of contracting certain kinds of cancer increases.

Consequently, physicians urge that women routinely examine their breasts and men regularly check their testicles for signs of cancer. In addition, cancer of the prostate gland, which is the most frequent type of cancer in men, can be detected by routine rectal exams and by a blood test to identify the presence of prostate-specific antigens (PSA).

Mammograms, which provide internal scans of women's breasts, also help identify early stage cancer. However, the question of when women should begin to routinely have the procedure has been controversial. As shown in Figure 15-8, the risk of breast cancer begins to grow at around age 30, and then becomes increasingly more likely; but as we discuss in *From Research to Practice*, when to begin—and end—routine mammogram screening is controversial.

Figure 15-8 Age and the Risk of Breast Cancer

Starting around age 30, the risk of breast cancer becomes increasingly likely, as these annual incidence figures show.

(**Source:** SEER, 2014.)

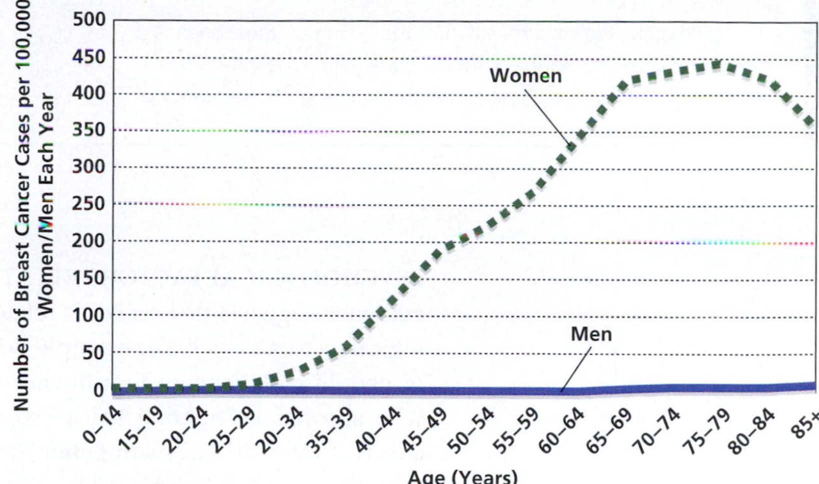

From Research to Practice

Routine Mammograms: At What Age Should Women Start?

I eat right, exercise, breast-fed my children, and buy organic when I can. I have never lived on a Superfund site, and I do not have cancer in my family line. The chance of me finding a lump in my breasts were—I thought—slim to none.

But 5 years ago, on a quiet Sunday morning at the start of spring in New England, everything I believed about my life changed forever. My husband and our two children, ages 4 and 1, were downstairs in the kitchen making breakfast. I was upstairs enjoying a much-needed hot shower. ... As I let the water flow down my aching back, I started my usual self-breast exam. ... I felt a lump.

In some ways, this 38-year-old woman was lucky: She found her cancer early. Statistically, the earlier breast cancer is diagnosed, the better a woman's chances of survival. But just how to accomplish early identification has produced some degree of contention in the medical field. In particular, controversy surrounds the age at which *mammograms*, a kind of weak X-ray used to examine breast tissue, should be routinely administered to women.

Mammograms are among the best means of detecting breast cancer in its earliest stages. The technique allows physicians to identify tumors while they are still very small. Patients have time for treatment before the tumor grows and spreads to other parts of the body. Mammograms have the potential for saving many lives, and nearly all medical professionals suggest that at some point during middle adulthood women should routinely obtain them.

But at what age should women start having annual mammograms? The risk of breast cancer begins to grow at around age 30, and then cancer becomes increasingly more likely. Ninety-five percent of new cases occur in women age 40 and above (Howlader et al., 2017).

Determining the age to begin routine screening mammograms is complicated by two considerations. First, there is the problem of *false positives*, instances in which the test suggests something is wrong when in fact there is no problem. Because the breast tissue of younger women is denser than that of older women, younger women are more likely to have false positives. In fact, some estimates suggest that as many as a third of all younger women who have repeated mammograms are likely to have a false positive that necessitates further testing or a biopsy. Furthermore, the opposite problem also may occur: *false negatives*, in which a mammogram does not detect indications of cancer (Destounis et al, 2009; Elmore et al., 2009; Posso et al., 2017).

The American Cancer Society guidelines suggest that women ages 40 to 44 should have the choice to start annual breast cancer mammogram screenings if they wish to do so. Between the ages 45 and 54, it is recommended that they have an annual mammogram. Women age 55 and older should switch to mammograms every 2 years, or they can have annual screenings if they wish. Finally, women should continue to have mammograms as long as they are in good health and expected to live 10 more years or longer (American Cancer Society, 2017).

The American Cancer Society recommendation is controversial. For example, the American College of Radiology argues that women age 40 and above should receive annual screenings. They note that the 10-year risk a 40-year-old woman is 1 in 69, and that one in six breast cancers occur in women 40 to 49 years of age (Kopans, 2017).

Ultimately, the determination of the timing of screenings is a highly personal one. Women should consult their health-care providers and discuss the latest research regarding the frequency of mammograms. For women who have a history of breast cancer in their families or a mutation in a gene called BRCA, the evidence is clear that mammograms starting at age 40 are beneficial (Grady, 2009; Winters et al., 2017).

Shared Writing Prompt

Would your advice regarding the frequency of screening for breast cancer to a 40-year-old who was a family member differ from advice to a stranger? Why and how?

PSYCHOLOGICAL FACTORS RELATING TO CANCER: MIND OVER TUMOR? Some evidence suggests that cancer is related not only to physiological causes but to psychological factors as well. For example, some research indicates that the emotional responses of people with cancer can influence their recovery. In one study, for instance, women who showed a "fighting spirit" coped better with their cancer. However, long-term survival rates do not seem better for patients who have a positive attitude compared with those with a less positive attitude. For the moment, then, the jury is out in terms of the degree to which psychological factors affect cancer (Rom, Miller, & Peluso, 2009; Azlan et al., 2017).

Personality factors may also play a role in cancer. For example, cancer patients who are habitually optimistic report less physical and psychological distress than those who are less optimistic (Gerend, Aiken, & West, 2004; Shelby et al., 2008; Cassileth, 2014).

Related to the idea that psychological factors can help prevent or improve cancer treatment success is evidence that participation in psychological therapy may give cancer patients an edge in treatment. For example, one study found that women in the advanced stages of breast cancer who participated in group therapy lived at least 18 months longer than those who did not participate in therapy. Furthermore, the women who participated also experienced less anxiety and pain (Spiegel & Giese-Davis, 2003; Spiegel, 2011).

How, exactly, might a person's psychological state be linked to his or her prognosis with cancer? Cancer treatment is intricate, complex, and often unpleasant. It may be that patients who have the most positive attitudes and are involved in therapy might be more likely to adhere to medical treatments. Consequently, such patients are more likely to experience treatment success (Sheridan & Radmacher, 2003; Sephton et al., 2009).

There's another possibility: It may be that a positive psychological outlook bolsters the body's immune system, the natural line of defense against disease. A positive outlook may energize the immune system to produce "killer" cells that fight the cancerous cells. In contrast, negative emotions and attitudes may impair the ability of the body's natural killer cells to fight off the cancer (Ironson & Schneiderman, 2002; Gidron et al., 2006).

It is important to keep in mind that the link between attitudes, emotions, and cancer is far from proven. Furthermore, it is unjustified and unfair to assume that a cancer patient would be doing better if only he or she had a more positive attitude. What the data do suggest is that psychological therapy might be warranted as a routine component of cancer treatment, even if it does nothing more than improve the patient's psychological state and raise his or her morale (Hart et al., 2012; Bower et al., 2014; Garland et al., 2017).

Norman Pogson/Shutterstock

Although some studies suggest that the degree of social support in a person's life may be related to a decreased risk of cancer, the link between attitudes, emotions, and cancer is far from proven.

Module 15.2 Review

LO 15.5 Describe changes in health that occur in middle adulthood.

In general, middle adulthood is a period of good health, although susceptibility to chronic diseases, such as arthritis, type 2 diabetes, and hypertension, increases.

LO 15.6 Describe the risk factors related to coronary heart disease.

Heart disease is a risk for middle-aged adults. Both genetic and environmental factors contribute to heart disease, including the Type A behavior pattern.

LO 15.7 Summarize what causes cancer and what tools are available to diagnose and treat it.

The incidence of cancer begins to be significant in middle adulthood. Therapies such as radiation therapy, chemotherapy, and surgery can successfully treat cancer, and psychological factors, such as a fighting attitude and a refusal to accept the finality of cancer, can influence survival rates.

Journal Writing Prompt

Applying Lifespan Development: What social policies might be developed to lower the incidence of disabling illness among members of lower socioeconomic groups?

Cognitive Development

It began innocently enough. Forty-five-year-old Bina Clingman couldn't remember whether she had mailed the letter that her husband had given her, and she wondered, in passing, whether this was a sign of aging. The very next day, her feelings were reinforced when she had to spend 20 minutes looking for a phone number that she knew she had written down on a piece of paper—somewhere. By the time she had found it, she was surprised and even a little anxious. "Am I losing my memory?" she asked herself, with both annoyance and some degree of concern.

Many people in their 40s will tell you that they feel more absentminded than they did 20 years earlier and that they harbor at least some concern about becoming less mentally able than when they were younger. Common wisdom suggests that people lose some mental sharpness as they age. But how accurate is this notion?

Does Intelligence Decline in Adulthood?

LO 15.8 Describe what happens to a person's intelligence in middle adulthood.

For years, experts provided a clear, unwavering response when asked whether intelligence declined during adulthood. It was a response that most adults were not happy to hear: Intelligence peaks at age 18, stays fairly steady until the mid-20s, and then begins a gradual decline that continues until the end of life.

Today, however, developmentalists have come to see that the answers to questions about changes in intelligence across the life span are more complicated—and they have come to different, and more complex, conclusions.

THE DIFFICULTIES IN ANSWERING THE QUESTION. The conclusion that intelligence starts to diminish in the mid-20s was based on extensive research. In particular, *cross-sectional studies*—which test people of different ages at the same point in time—clearly showed that older subjects were more likely to score less well than younger subjects on traditional intelligence tests.

But consider the drawbacks of cross-sectional research—in particular the possibility that it may suffer from cohort effects. Recall that *cohort effects* are influences associated with growing up at a particular historical time that affect persons of a particular age. For instance, suppose that compared to the younger people, the older people in a cross-sectional study had had less adequate educations, were exposed to less stimulation in their jobs, or were relatively less healthy. In that case, the lower IQ scores of the

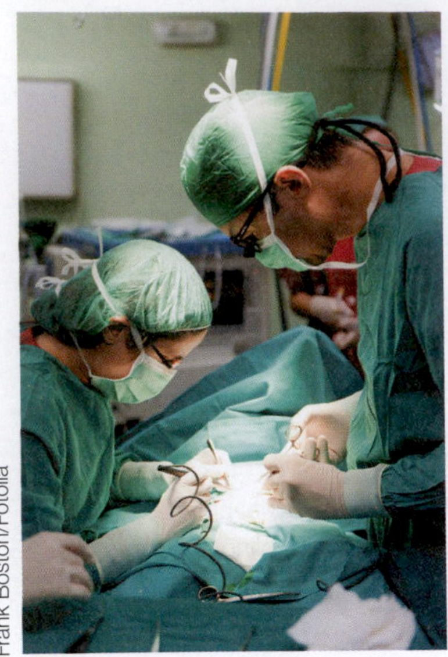

Frank Boston/Fotolia

It is difficult to evaluate cognitive abilities in middle adulthood. While some types of mental abilities may begin to decline, other types hold steady and actually may increase.

older group could hardly be attributed solely, or perhaps even partially, to differences in intelligence between younger and older individuals. In sum, because they do not control for cohort effects, cross-sectional studies may well *underestimate* intelligence in older subjects.

In an effort to overcome the cohort problems of cross-sectional studies, developmentalists began to turn to *longitudinal studies,* in which the same people are studied periodically over a span of time. These studies began to reveal a different developmental pattern for intelligence: Adults tended to show fairly stable and even increasing intelligence test scores until they reached their mid-30s, and in some cases up to their 50s. At that point, though, scores began to decline (Bayley & Oden, 1955).

But let's step back a moment and consider the drawbacks of longitudinal studies. For instance, people who take the same intelligence test repeatedly may perform better simply because they become more familiar—and comfortable—with the testing situation. Similarly, because they have been exposed to the same test regularly over the years, they may even begin to remember some of the test items. Consequently, practice effects may account for the relatively superior performance of people on longitudinal measures of intelligence as opposed to cross-sectional measures (Salthouse, 2009).

Furthermore, it is difficult for researchers using longitudinal studies to keep their samples intact. Participants in a study may move away, decide they no longer want to participate, or become ill and die. As time goes on, the participants who remain in the study may represent a healthier, more stable, and more psychologically positive group of people than those who are no longer part of the sample. If this is the case, then longitudinal studies may mistakenly *overestimate* intelligence in older subjects.

CRYSTALLIZED AND FLUID INTELLIGENCE. The ability of developmentalists to draw conclusions about age-related changes in intelligence faces still more hurdles. For instance, many IQ tests include sections based on physical performance, such as arranging a group of blocks. These sections are timed and scored on the basis of how quickly a question is completed. If older people take longer on physical tasks—and remember that reaction time slows with age, as we discussed earlier in the chapter—then their poorer performance on IQ tests may be a result of physical rather than cognitive changes.

To complicate the picture even further, many researchers believe that there are two kinds of intelligence: fluid intelligence and crystallized intelligence. As we first noted in Chapter 9, **fluid intelligence** reflects information processing capabilities, reasoning, and memory. For instance, a person who is asked to arrange a series of letters according to some rule or to memorize a set of numbers uses fluid intelligence. In contrast, **crystallized intelligence** is the information, skills, and strategies that people have learned and accumulated through experience and that they can apply in problem-solving situations. Someone who is solving a crossword puzzle or attempting to identify the murderer in a mystery story is using crystallized intelligence, relying on his or her past experience as a resource.

fluid intelligence
reflects information processing capabilities, reasoning, and memory

crystallized intelligence
the accumulation of information, skills, and strategies that people have learned through experience and that they can apply in problem-solving situations

Initially, researchers believed that fluid intelligence was largely determined by genetic factors, and crystallized intelligence primarily by experiential, environmental factors. However, they later abandoned this distinction, largely because they found that crystallized intelligence is determined in part by fluid intelligence. For instance, a person's ability to solve a crossword puzzle (which involves crystallized intelligence) is a result of that person's proficiency with letters and patterns (a manifestation of fluid intelligence).

When developmentalists looked at the two kinds of intelligence separately, they arrived at a new answer to the question of whether intelligence declines with age. Actually, they arrived at two answers: yes and no. Yes, because in general, fluid intelligence does decline with age; and no, because crystallized intelligence holds steady and in some cases

Figure 15-9 Changes in Crystallized and Fluid Intelligence

Although crystallized intelligence increases with age, fluid intelligence begins to decline in middle age. What are the implications for general competence in middle adulthood?

(**Source:** Schaie, 1985.)

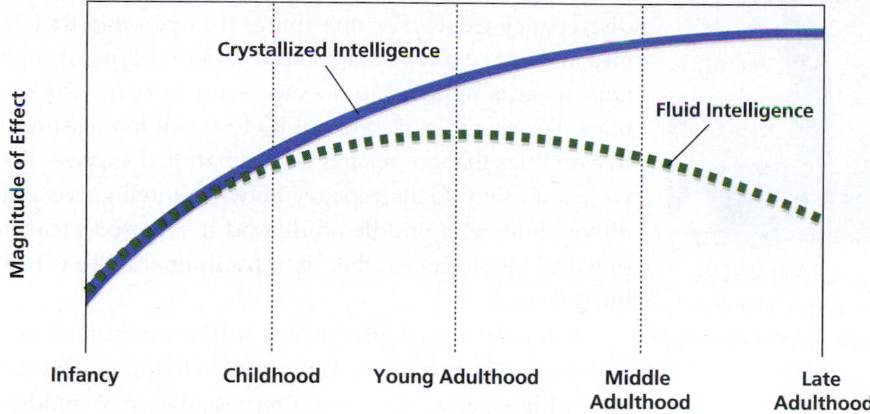

actually improves (Salthouse, Pink, & Tucker-Drob, 2008; Manard et al., 2015; Wettstein et al., 2017; see Figure 15-9).

If we look at more specific types of intelligence, true age-related differences and developments in intelligence begin to show up. According to developmental psychologist K. Warner Schaie (1994), who has conducted extensive longitudinal research on the course of adult intellectual development, we should consider many particular types of ability, such as spatial orientation, numeric ability, verbal ability, and so on, rather than the broad divisions of crystallized and fluid intelligence.

When looked at in this way, the question of how intelligence changes in adulthood yields yet another answer, a more specific one. Schaie has found that certain abilities, such as inductive reasoning, spatial orientation, perceptual speed, and verbal memory, begin to decline very gradually at around age 25 and continue to decline through old age. Numeric and verbal abilities show a quite different pattern. Numeric ability tends to increase until the mid-40s, is lower at age 60, and then stays steady throughout the rest of life. Verbal ability rises until about the start of middle adulthood, around age 40, and stays fairly steady throughout the rest of the life span (Schaie, 1994).

Why do these changes occur? One reason is that brain functioning begins to change in middle adulthood. For example, researchers have found that 20 genes that are vital to learning, memory, and mental flexibility begin to function less efficiently as early as age 40. Furthermore, as people age, the specific areas of their brains used to accomplish particular tasks change. For instance, older adults use both brain hemispheres for tasks that in younger people involve just one hemisphere (Lu et al., 2004; Fling et al., 2011; Phillips, 2011).

From *an educator's* perspective

How do you think the apparent discrepancy between declining IQ scores and continuing cognitive competence in middle adulthood would affect the learning ability of middle adults who return to school?

REFRAMING THE ISSUE: WHAT IS THE SOURCE OF COMPETENCE DURING MIDDLE ADULTHOOD? Despite the gradual declines in particular cognitive abilities during middle adulthood, it is during this part of the life span that people come to hold

Hill Street Studios/Age Fotostock

Cognitive development during middle and later adulthood is a mixture of growth and decline. As people begin to lose certain abilities as a result of biological deterioration, they also advance in other areas by strengthening their skills.

some of the most important and powerful positions in society. How can we explain such continuing, and even growing, competence in the face of apparently ongoing declines in certain cognitive skills?

One answer comes from psychologist Timothy Salthouse (1994), who suggests that there are four reasons why this discrepancy exists. For one thing, it is possible that typical measures of cognitive skills tap a different type of cognition than what is required to be successful in particular occupations. For example, traditional IQ tests fail to measure cognitive abilities that are related to occupational success. Perhaps we would find no discrepancy between intelligence and cognitive abilities in middle adulthood if we used measures of practical intelligence rather than traditional IQ tests to assess intelligence.

A second factor also relates to the measurement of IQ and occupational success. It is possible that the most successful middle-aged adults are not representative of middle-aged adults in general. It may be that only a small proportion of people are highly successful, and the rest, who experience only moderate or little success, may have changed occupations, retired, or become sick and died. If we look at highly successful people, then, we are examining an unrepresentative sample of individuals.

It is also conceivable that the degree of cognitive ability required for professional success is simply not that high. According to this argument, people can be quite successful professionally and still be on the decline in certain kinds of cognitive abilities. In other words, their cognitive declines are not all that important; they have brains to spare.

Finally, it may be that older people are successful because they have developed specific kinds of expertise and particular competencies. Whereas IQ tests measure reactions to novel situations, occupational success may be influenced by very specific sorts of well-practiced abilities. Consequently, although their overall intellectual skills may show a decline, middle-aged individuals may maintain and even expand the distinctive talents they need for professional accomplishment. This explanation has generated a whole area of research on expertise, as we'll see later in the chapter.

selective optimization

the process by which people concentrate on particular skill areas to compensate for losses in other areas

For example, developmental researchers Paul Baltes and Margaret Baltes (1990) have studied a strategy called selective optimization. **Selective optimization** is the process by which people concentrate on particular skill areas to compensate for losses in other areas. The researchers suggest that cognitive development during middle and later adulthood is a mixture of growth and decline. As people begin to lose certain abilities as a result of biological deterioration, they advance in other areas by strengthening their skills. Because they are able to compensate for their losses, they avoid showing any practical deterioration. Overall cognitive competence, then, ultimately remains stable and may even improve (Deary, 2012; Hahn & Lachman, 2015; Palmore, 2017).

For instance, recall that reaction time lengthens as people get older. Because reaction time is a component of typing skill, we would expect that older typists would be slower than younger ones. However, this is not the case. Why? The answer is that while their reaction time is increasing, older typists look further ahead in the material they are to type. This allows them to compensate for their lengthier reaction time. Similarly, although a business executive may be less quick in recalling names, he may have a mental file of deals he has completed in the past and be able to forge new agreements easily because of it.

Selective optimization is only one of the strategies adults with expertise in various fields use to maintain high performance. What are some other characteristics of experts?

The Development of Expertise: Separating Experts from Novices

LO 15.9 Explain the role of expertise in middle adulthood.

If you were ill and needed a diagnosis, would you prefer to visit a newly minted young physician who had just graduated from medical school or a more experienced, middle-aged physician?

If you chose the older physician, it's probably because you assumed that he or she would have a higher level of expertise. **Expertise** is the acquisition of skill or knowledge in a particular area. More focused than broader intelligence, expertise develops as people devote attention and practice to particular domains and, in so doing, gain experience, either because of their profession or because they simply enjoy a given area. For example, physicians become better at diagnosing the symptoms of a medical problem in their patients as they gain experience. Similarly, a person who enjoys cooking and does a lot of it begins to know beforehand how a recipe will taste if certain modifications are made (Morita et al., 2008; Reuter et al., 2012, 2014).

expertise
the acquisition of skill or knowledge in a particular area

What separates experts from those who are less skilled in a given area? While beginners use formal procedures and rules, often following them very strictly, experts rely on experience and intuition, and they often bend the rules. Because experts have so much experience, their processing of information is often automatic, performed without the need for much thought. Experts often are not very articulate at explaining how they draw conclusions; their solutions often just seem right to them—and *are* more likely to be right. Brain imaging studies show that experts, compared to novices, use different neural pathways to solve problems (Grabner, Neubauer, & Stern, 2006).

Finally, when difficulties arise, experts develop better strategies for solving them than nonexperts, and they're more flexible in approaching problems. Their experience has provided them with alternative routes to the same solution, and this increases the probability of success (Willis, 1996; Clark, 1998; Arts, Gijselaers, & Boshuizen, 2006).

Of course, not everyone develops expertise in some particular area during middle adulthood. Professional responsibilities, amount of leisure time, educational level, income, and marital status all affect the development of expertise.

Memory: You Must Remember This

LO 15.10 Describe how aging affects memory and how memory can be improved.

Whenever Mary Donovan can't find her car keys, she mutters to herself that she is "losing her memory." Like Bina Clingman, who was worried about forgetting things like letters and phone numbers, Mary probably believes that memory loss is pretty common in middle age.

However, if she fits the pattern of most people in middle adulthood, her assessment is not necessarily accurate. According to research on memory changes in adulthood, most people show only minimal memory losses, and many people exhibit none at all, during middle adulthood. Furthermore, because of societal stereotypes about aging, people in middle adulthood may be prone to attribute their absentmindedness to aging, even though they have been absentminded throughout their lives. Consequently, it is the *meaning* they give to their forgetfulness that changes rather than their actual ability to remember (Chasteen et al., 2005; Hoessler & Chasteen, 2008; Hess, Hinson, & Hodges, 2009).

TYPES OF MEMORY. To understand the nature of memory changes, it is necessary to consider the different types of memory. Memory is traditionally viewed in terms of three sequential components: sensory memory, short-term memory (also called working memory), and long-term memory. *Sensory memory* is an initial, momentary storage of information that lasts only an instant. Information is recorded by an individual's sensory system as a raw, meaningless stimulus. Next, information moves into *short-term memory*, which holds it for 15 to 25 seconds. Finally, if the information is rehearsed, it is moved into *long-term memory*, where it is stored on a relatively permanent basis.

Both sensory memory and short-term memory show virtually no weakening during middle adulthood. The story is a bit different for long-term memory, which declines with age for some people. It appears, however, that the reason for the decline is not a fading or a complete loss of memory, but rather that with age, people register and store information less efficiently. In addition, age makes people less efficient in retrieving information that is stored in memory. In other words, even if the information was adequately stored in long-term memory, it may become more difficult to locate or isolate it (Salthouse, 1994).

It is important to keep in mind that memory declines in middle age are relatively minor, and most can be compensated for by various cognitive strategies. As mentioned earlier, paying greater attention to material when it is first encountered can aid in its later recall. Your lost car keys may have relatively little to do with memory declines, instead reflecting your inattentiveness when you put them down.

Many middle-aged adults find it hard to pay attention to particular things for some of the same reasons that expertise develops. They are used to using memory shortcuts, *schemas*, to ease the burden of remembering all the many things that each of us experiences every day.

schemas
organized bodies of information stored in memory

MEMORY SCHEMAS. One of the ways that people recall information is through the use of **schemas**, organized bodies of information stored in memory. Schemas help people represent the way the world is organized and allow them to categorize and interpret new information (Fiske & Taylor, 1991). For example, we may have a schema for eating out in a restaurant. We don't need to treat a meal in a new restaurant as a completely new experience. We know that when we go there, we will be seated at a table or counter and offered a menu from which to select food. Our schema for eating out tells us how to relate to the server, what sorts of food to eat first, and that we should leave a tip at the end of the meal.

People hold schemas for particular individuals (such as the particular behavior patterns of one's mother, wife, or child) as well as for categories of people (mail carriers, lawyers, or professors) and behaviors or events (dining in a restaurant or visiting the dentist). People's schemas serve to organize their behavior into coherent wholes and help them to interpret social events. For example, a person who knows the schema for a visit to the doctor is not likely to be surprised when he is asked to remove his clothes.

Schemas also convey cultural information. Psychologists Susan Fiske and Shelley Taylor (1991) give an example of an old Native American folktale in which the hero participates with several companions in a battle and is shot by an arrow. However, he feels no pain from the arrow. When he returns to his home and tells the story, something black emerges from his mouth, and he dies the next morning.

This tale is puzzling to most Westerners because they are unschooled in the particular Native American culture to which the story belongs. However, to someone familiar with the Native American culture, the story makes perfect sense: The hero feels no pain because his companions are ghosts, and the "black thing" coming from his mouth is his departing soul.

For a Native American, it may be relatively easy to later recall the story, because it makes sense in a way that it doesn't to members of other cultures. Furthermore, material that is consistent with existing schemas is more likely to be recalled than material that is inconsistent (Van Manen & Pietromonaco, 1993). For example, a person who usually puts her keys in a certain spot may lose them because she doesn't recall putting them down somewhere other than in the usual place. (Also see the *Development in Your Life* Box.)

mnemonics
formal strategies for organizing material in ways that make it more likely to be remembered

Development in Your Life

Effective Strategies for Remembering

All of us are forgetful at one time or another. However, there are techniques that can help us remember more effectively and make it less likely that we will forget things that we wish to remember. **Mnemonics** (pronounced "nee-MON-iks") are formal strategies for organizing material in ways that make it more likely to be remembered. Among the mnemonics that work not only in middle adulthood but also at other points of the life span are the following (Bellezza, Six, & Phillips, 1992; Guttman, 1997; Bloom & Lamkin, 2006; Morris & Fritz, 2006):

- *Get organized.* For people who have trouble keeping track of where they left their keys or remembering appointments, the simplest approach is for them to become more organized. Using an appointment book, hanging one's keys on a hook, or using Post-It notes can help jog one's memory.
- *Pay attention.* You can improve your recall by initially paying attention when you are exposed to new information and by purposefully thinking that you wish to recall it in the future. If you are particularly concerned about remembering something, such as where you parked your car, pay particular attention at the moment you park the car, and remind yourself that you really want to remember.
- *Use the encoding specificity phenomenon.* According to the encoding specificity phenomenon, people are most likely to recall information in environments that are similar to those in which they initially learned ("encoded") it (Tulving & Thompson, 1973). For instance, people are best able to recall information on a test if the test is held in the room in which they studied the material on the test.
- *Visualize.* Making mental images of ideas can help you recall them later. For example, if you want to remember that global warming may lead to rising oceans, think of yourself on a beach on a hot day, with the waves coming closer and closer to where you've set out your beach blanket.
- *Rehearse.* In the realm of memory, practice makes perfect, or if not perfect, at least better. Adults of all ages can improve their memories if they expend more effort in rehearsing what they want to remember. By practicing what they wish to recall, people can substantially improve their recall of the material.

Module 15.3 Review

LO 15.8 Describe what happens to a person's intelligence in middle adulthood.

The question of whether intelligence declines in middle adulthood is complicated by limitations in cross-sectional studies and longitudinal studies. Intelligence appears to be divided into components, some of which decline while others hold steady or even improve. In general, cognitive competence in middle adulthood holds fairly steady despite declines in some areas of intellectual functioning.

LO 15.9 Explain the role of expertise in middle adulthood.

Expertise, the application of skill or knowledge in practical areas of life, increases in middle adulthood because of gains in experience. Experts rely less on formal procedures and more on intuition, and they are better at problem solving than non-experts.

LO 15.10 Describe how aging affects memory and how memory can be improved.

Memory may appear to decline in middle age, but in fact long-term memory deficits are probably the result of ineffective strategies of storage and retrieval. Memory strategies have been shown to be effective in improving memorization and recall of information.

Journal Writing Prompt

Applying Lifespan Development: How might crystallized and fluid intelligence work together to help middle-aged people deal with novel situations and problems?

Epilogue

People's physical abilities and health in middle adulthood are generally still good. Subtle changes are occurring, but individuals often find it easy to compensate for them because of the strengths of other cognitive skills. The incidence of chronic and life-threatening diseases increases, especially heart disease and cancer. In the cognitive realm, intelligence and memory decline very gradually in some areas, but this decline is hidden by compensatory strategies and gains in other areas.

Return to the prologue of this chapter, about Deborah Thelonius's high-altitude racing, and answer these questions:

1. What changes in physical functioning during middle adulthood are likely to affect Thelonius's performance?

2. What adjustments could Thelonius make to compensate for changes in her capabilities?
3. What physical and psychological benefits might Thelonius be gaining from her running?
4. If Thelonius were to return to school in middle adulthood, what cognitive challenges would she face compared with her younger classmates?

Looking Back

LO 15.1 Describe the physical changes that affect people in middle adulthood.

During middle adulthood, roughly the period from 40 to 65, people typically decline slowly in height and strength, and gain in weight. Height loss, especially in women, may be associated with osteoporosis, a thinning of the bones brought about by a lack of calcium in the diet. The best antidote for physical and psychological deterioration appears to be a healthful lifestyle, including regular exercise.

LO 15.2 Explain how the senses change in middle adulthood.

Visual acuity declines during this period as the eyes' lens changes. People in middle adulthood tend to experience declines in near vision, depth and distance perception, adaptation to darkness, and the ability to perceive in three dimensions. In addition, the incidence of glaucoma, a disease that can cause blindness, increases in middle adulthood. Hearing acuity also declines slightly in this period, typically involving some loss of the ability to hear high-frequency sounds and a deterioration of sound localization.

LO 15.3 Explain how reaction time changes during middle adulthood.

Reaction time of middle-aged people begins to increase gradually, but slower reactions are largely offset in complex tasks by increased skill due to years of task rehearsal.

LO 15.4 Compare how middle-aged men and middle-aged women experience changes in sexuality.

Adults in middle age experience changes in sexuality, but these are less dramatic than commonly supposed, and many middle-aged couples experience new sexual freedom and enjoyment. Women in middle age experience the female climacteric, the change from being able to bear children to no longer being able to do so. The most notable sign is menopause, which is often accompanied by physical and emotional discomfort. Therapies and changing attitudes toward menopause appear to be lessening women's fears and experience of difficulty regarding menopause. Men also undergo changes in their reproductive systems, sometimes referred to as the male climacteric. Generally, the production of sperm and testosterone declines and the prostate gland enlarges, causing difficulties with urination.

LO 15.5 Describe changes in health that occur in middle adulthood.

Middle adulthood is generally a healthy period, but people become more susceptible to chronic diseases, including arthritis, type 2 diabetes, and hypertension, and they have a higher death rate than before. However, the death rate among people in middle adulthood in the United States has been steadily declining. Overall health in middle adulthood varies according to socioeconomic status and gender. People of higher SES are healthier and have lower death rates than people of lower SES. Women have a lower mortality rate than men but a higher incidence of illness. Researchers have generally paid more attention to the life-threatening diseases experienced by men than to the less fatal but chronic diseases typically experienced by women.

LO 15.6 Describe the risk factors related to coronary heart disease.

Heart disease begins to be a significant factor in middle adulthood. Genetic characteristics, such as age, gender, and a family history of heart disease, are associated with the risk of heart disease, as are environmental and behavioral factors, including smoking, a diet high in fats and cholesterol, and a lack of exercise. Psychological factors also play a role in heart disease. A pattern of behaviors associated with competitiveness, impatience, frustration, and particularly hostility—called the Type A behavior pattern—is associated with a high risk of heart problems.

LO 15.7 Summarize what causes cancer and what tools are available to diagnose and treat it.

Like heart disease, cancer becomes a threat in middle adulthood and is related to genetic and environmental factors. Treatments include radiation therapy, chemotherapy, and surgery. Psychological factors may play a role in cancer, although the research is mixed. Furthermore, persons with strong family and social ties appear to be less likely to develop cancer than persons who lack such ties. Breast cancer is a significant risk for women in middle adulthood. Mammography can help identify cancerous tumors early enough for successful treatment, but the age at which women should begin to have routine mammograms—40 or 50—is a matter of controversy.

LO 15.8 Describe what happens to a person's intelligence in middle adulthood.

The question of whether intelligence declines in middle adulthood is challenging to answer because the two basic methods of addressing it have significant limitations. Cross-sectional methods, which study many subjects of different ages at one point in time, suffer from cohort effects. Longitudinal studies, which focus on the same subjects at several different points in time, are plagued by the difficulty of keeping a sample of subjects intact over many years. Those who divide intelligence into two main types—fluid and crystallized—generally find that fluid intelligence slowly declines through middle adulthood while crystallized intelligence holds steady or improves. Those who divide intelligence into greater numbers of components find an even more complicated pattern. People in middle adulthood generally display a high degree of overall cognitive competence despite demonstrated declines in particular areas of intellectual functioning. People tend to focus on and exercise specific areas of competence that generally compensate for areas of loss, a strategy known as selective optimization.

LO 15.9 Explain the role of expertise in middle adulthood.

Experts maintain, and even increase, cognitive competence in a particular subject through attention and practice. Experts process information about their field significantly differently from novices.

LO 15.10 Describe how aging affects memory and how memory can be improved.

Memory in middle adulthood may seem to be on the decline, but the problem is not with either sensory memory or short-term memory. Even apparent problems with long-term memory may have more to do with people's storage and retrieval strategies rather than with overall memory deterioration, and the problems are minor and relatively easy to overcome. People interpret, store, and recall information in the form of memory schemas, which organize related bits of information, set up expectations, and add meaning to phenomena. Mnemonic devices can help people improve their ability to recall information by forcing them to pay attention to information as they store it (the keyword technique), to use cues to enable retrieval (the encoding specificity phenomenon), or to practice information retrieval (rehearsal).

Key Terms and Concepts

osteoporosis 494
presbyopia 495
glaucoma 495
presbycusis 496
female climacteric 498
menopause 498
male climacteric 500
Type A behavior pattern 507
Type B behavior pattern 507
fluid intelligence 512
crystallized intelligence 512
selective optimization 514
expertise 515
schemas 516
mnemonics 517

Chapter 16

Social and Personality Development in Middle Adulthood

kali9/Getty Images

Learning Objectives

LO 16.1 Describe ways in which personality develops during middle adulthood.

LO 16.2 Summarize Erikson's view of development during middle adulthood and how others have expanded on his ideas.

LO 16.3 Discuss the nature of continuity in personality development during middle adulthood.

LO 16.4 Describe typical patterns of marriage and divorce in middle adulthood.

LO 16.5 Differentiate the changing family situations middle-aged adults face.

LO 16.6 Describe how people in middle adulthood react to becoming grandparents.

LO 16.7 List the causes and characteristics of family violence in the United States.

LO 16.8 Summarize characteristics of work and career in middle adulthood.

LO 16.9 Describe the effect losing one's job has on a person in middle adulthood.

LO 16.10 Explain how and why people change careers in middle adulthood.

LO 16.11 Describe how people experience leisure time in middle adulthood.

Chapter Overview

Prologue: From Clothes to Rock to Talk

To say that Mirandi Babitz's career path has taken a lot of twists would be an understatement. Her work has spanned from a fashionable Hollywood clothing boutique to a therapist's office, with a lot of rock 'n' roll in between.

After getting married for the first time in the 1960s, Mirandi opened a clothing store in Los Angeles with her husband. The couple met with a lot of success. Mirandi helped design clothes for Jim Morrison of The Doors, Eric Clapton, and other prominent musicians of the era.

When Mirandi's marriage ended, though, she left the fashion industry. Through her connections in the music world, she became a road manager. Again, Mirandi found success, and worked with major acts such as Bonnie Raitt and Crosby, Stills, and Nash. But increasingly Mirandi found that the rock 'n' roll lifestyle was something she was not just managing, but living. After struggling with substance abuse, she entered rehab.

After getting sober, Mirandi left the music business, but found that as she approached 40 she didn't know the direction she wanted her career to take next. A psychologist friend suggested she consider therapy. Mirandi took to the idea, and earned her master's degree in clinical psychology. Today, Mirandi has been a therapist for more than two decades (Nishi, 2008; Babitz, 2016).

Looking Ahead

The twists and turns in Mirandi Babitz's life may be a bit extreme, but they are not unique: Few lives follow a set, predictable pattern through middle adulthood. In fact, one of the remarkable characteristics of middle age is its variety, as the paths that different people travel continue to diverge.

In this chapter, we focus on the personality and social development that occurs in midlife. We begin by examining the personality changes that typify this period. We also explore some of the controversies that underlie developmental psychologists' understandings of midlife, including whether the midlife crisis, a phenomenon popularized in modern media, is fact or fiction.

Next we consider the relationships that evolve during middle adulthood, the various familial ties that bind people together (or come unglued) during this period, including marriage, divorce, the empty nest, and grandparenting. We also look at a bleaker side of family relations: family violence, which is surprisingly prevalent.

Finally, the chapter examines the role of work and leisure during middle adulthood. We will examine the changing role of work in people's lives and some of the difficulties associated with work, such as burnout and unemployment. The chapter concludes with a discussion of leisure time, which becomes more important during middle age.

Pressmaster/Fotolia

During middle age, adults' relationships with others continue to evolve.

Personality Development

My 40th birthday was not an easy one. It's not that I woke up one morning and felt different—that's never been the case. But what did happen during my 40th year was that I came to the realization of the finiteness of life, and that the die was cast. I began to understand that I probably wasn't going to be president of the United States—a secret ambition—or a CEO of a major corporation. Time was no longer on my side, but something of an adversary. But it was curious: Rather than following my traditional pattern of focusing on the future, planning to do this or do that, I began to appreciate what I had. I looked around at my life, was pretty well satisfied with some of my accomplishments, and began to focus on the things that were going right, not the things that I was lacking. But this state of mind didn't happen in a day; it took several years after turning 40 before I felt this way. Even now, it is hard to fully accept that I am middle-aged.

As this 47-year-old man suggests, the realization that one has entered middle adulthood does not always come easily, nor is it generally welcome. In many Western societies, age 40 has special meaning, bringing with it the inescapable fact that one is now middle-aged—at least in the view of others—and the suggestion, embodied in everyday common wisdom, that one is about to experience the throes of a "midlife crisis." Is this view correct? As we'll see, it depends on your perspective.

Two Perspectives on Adult Personality Development: Normative Crisis Versus Life Events

LO 16.1 Describe ways in which personality develops during middle adulthood.

normative–crisis models
the approach to personality development that is based on fairly universal stages tied to a sequence of age-related crises

life events models
the approach to personality development that is based on the timing of particular events in an adult's life rather than on age per se

Traditional views of personality development during adulthood have suggested that people move through a fixed series of stages, each tied fairly closely to age. These stages are related to specific crises in which an individual goes through an intense period of questioning and even psychological turmoil. This traditional perspective is a feature of what are called normative-crisis models of personality development. **Normative-crisis models** see personality development in terms of fairly universal stages, tied to a sequence of age-related crises. For example, Erik Erikson's psychosocial theory predicts that people move through a series of stages and crises throughout the life span.

In contrast, some critics suggest that normative-crisis approaches may be outmoded. They arose at a time when society had fairly rigid and uniform roles for people. Traditionally, men were expected to work and support a family; women were expected to stay at home, be housewives, and take care of the children. And the roles of men and women played out at relatively uniform ages.

Today, however, there is considerable variety in both the roles and the timing. Some people marry and have children at 40. Others have children and marry later. Still others never marry, but live with a partner of the same or opposite sex and perhaps adopt a child or forego children altogether. In sum, changes in society have called into question normative-crisis models that are tied closely to age (Fugate & Mitchell, 1997; Barnett & Hyde, 2001; Fraenkel, 2003).

Dave Parker/Alamy Stock Photo

In Western society, turning 40 represents an important milestone.

From a *social worker's* perspective

In what ways might normative-crisis models of personality development be specific to Western culture?

Because of all this variation, some theorists, such as Ravenna Helson, focus on what may be called **life events models**, which suggest that it is the particular events in an adult's life, rather than age per se, that determines the course of personality development. For instance, a woman who has her first child at age 21 may experience psychological forces similar to those experienced by a woman who has her first child at age 39.

The result is that the two women, despite their very different ages, share certain commonalities of personality development (Helson & Srivastava, 2001; Roberts, Helson, & Klohnen, 2002; Hentschel, Eid, & Kutscher, 2017).

It is not clear whether the normative-crisis view or the life events perspective will ultimately paint the more accurate picture of personality development and change during the course of adulthood. What is clear is that developmental theorists from a range of perspectives all agree that middle adulthood is a time of continuing—and significant—psychological growth.

Erikson's Stage of Generativity Versus Stagnation

LO 16.2 Summarize Erikson's view of development during middle adulthood and how others have expanded on his ideas.

As we first discussed in Chapter 12, psychoanalyst Erik Erikson suggested that middle adulthood encompasses a period he characterized as the **generativity-versus-stagnation stage**. One's middle adulthood, according to Erikson, is spent either in what he called generativity, making a personal contribution to family, community, work, and society as a whole, or in stagnation. Generative people strive to play a role in guiding and encouraging future generations. Often, people find generativity through parenting, but other roles can fill this need too. People may work directly with younger individuals, acting as mentors, or they may satisfy their need for generativity through creative and artistic output, seeking to leave a lasting contribution. The focus of those who experience generativity, then, is beyond themselves, as they look toward the continuation of their own lives through others (Penningroth & Scott, 2012; Schoklitsch & Baumann, 2012; Serrat et al., 2017).

generativity-versus-stagnation stage
according to Erikson, the stage during middle adulthood in which people consider their contributions to family and society

In contrast, a lack of psychological growth in this period means that people become stagnant. Focusing on the triviality of their own activity, people may come to feel that they have made only limited contributions to the world, that their presence has counted for little. Some individuals find themselves floundering, still seeking new and potentially more fulfilling careers. Others become frustrated and bored.

Although Erikson provides a broad overview of personality development, some psychologists have suggested that we need a more precise look at changes in personality during middle adulthood. We'll consider three alternative approaches.

BUILDING ON ERIKSON'S VIEWS: VAILLANT AND GOULD. Developmentalist George Vaillant (1977) argues that an important period between about ages 45 and 55 is "keeping the meaning" versus rigidity. During that period, adults seek to extract the meaning from their lives, and to "keep the meaning" by developing an acceptance of the strengths and weaknesses of others. Although they recognize that the world is not perfect and has many shortcomings, they strive to safeguard their world, and they are relatively content. The man quoted at the beginning of this section, for example, seems to be content with the meaning he has found in his life. People who are not able to keep the meaning in their lives risk becoming rigid and increasingly isolated from others.

Psychiatrist Roger Gould (1978, 1980) offered an alternative to both Erikson's and Vaillant's views. While he agrees that people move through a series of stages and potential crises, he suggests that adults pass through a series of seven stages associated with specific age periods (see Table 16-1). According to Gould, people in their late 30s and early 40s begin to feel a sense of urgency in terms of attaining life's goals as they realize that their time is limited. Coming to grips with the reality that life is finite can propel people toward adult maturity.

Gould based his model of adult development on a relatively small sample and relied heavily on his own clinical judgments. Little research has supported his description of the various stages, which was heavily influenced by the psychoanalytic perspective.

Table 16-1 Summary of Gould's Transformations in Adult Development

Stage	Approximate Age Range	*At this stage, people typically:*
1	16 to 18	plan to leave home and terminate parental control
2	18 to 22	leave the family and begin to reorient toward peers
3	22 to 28	become independent and commit to career and (often) spouse and children
4	29 to 34	question themselves and experience confusion; they may become dissatisfied with marriage and career
5	35 to 43	feel an urgent need to achieve life goals, becoming increasingly aware of the passage and limits of time; they often realign life goals
6	43 to 53	settle down at last, with acceptance of their lives
7	53 to 60	grow more tolerant, accepting their past; they become less negative and generally more mellow

(**Source:** Based on Gould, 1978.)

BUILDING ON ERIKSON'S VIEWS: LEVINSON'S SEASON OF LIFE THEORY. Another alternative to Erikson's work is psychologist Daniel Levinson's *seasons of life* theory. According to Levinson (1986, 1992), who intensively interviewed a group of men, the early 40s are a period of transition and crisis. Levinson suggests that adult men pass through a series of stages beginning with their entry into early adulthood at around age 20 and continuing into middle adulthood. The beginning stages have to do with leaving one's family and entering the adult world.

At around age 40 or 45, however, people move into a period that Levinson calls the midlife transition. The *midlife transition* is a time of questioning. People begin to focus on the finite nature of life, and they begin to question some of their everyday, fundamental assumptions. They experience the first signs of aging, and they confront the knowledge that they will be unable to accomplish all their aims before they die.

midlife crisis
a stage of uncertainty and indecision brought about by the realization that life is finite

In Levinson's view, this period of assessment may lead to a **midlife crisis**, a stage of uncertainty and indecision brought about by the realization that life is finite. Facing signs of physical aging, men may also discover that even the accomplishments of which they are proudest have brought them less satisfaction than they expected. Looking toward the past, they may seek to define what went wrong and look for ways to correct their past mistakes. The midlife crisis, then, is a painful and tumultuous period of questioning.

Levinson's view is that most people are susceptible to a fairly profound midlife crisis. But before accepting his perspective, we need to consider some critical drawbacks in his research. First, his initial theorizing was based on a group of only 40 men, and his work with women was carried out years later and once again on only a small sample. Furthermore, Levinson overstated the consistency and generality of the patterns he found in the samples he used to derive his theory. In fact, as we consider next, the notion of a universal midlife crisis has come under considerable criticism (McFadden & Rawson Swan, 2012; Thorpe et al., 2014; Etaugh, 2017).

THE MIDLIFE CRISIS: REALITY OR MYTH? Central to Levinson's model of the seasons of life is the concept of *midlife crisis*, a period in the early 40s presumed to be marked by intense psychological turmoil. The notion has taken on a life of its own: There is a general expectation in U.S. society that age 40 represents an important psychological juncture.

There's a problem, though, with such a view: The evidence for a widespread midlife crisis is simply lacking. Rather, most research suggests that, for most people, the passage into middle age is relatively tranquil. The majority of people regard midlife as a particularly rewarding time. If they are parents, for example, their children often have passed the period when childrearing is physically demanding, and in some cases children have left the home altogether, allowing parents the opportunity to rekindle an intimacy that they may have lost. Many middle-aged people find that their careers have blossomed—as we discuss later in this chapter—and far from being in crisis, they may feel quite content with their lot in life. Rather than looking toward the future, they focus on the present, seeking to maximize their ongoing involvement with family, friends, and other social groups. Those who feel regret over the course of their lives may be motivated to change the direction of their lives, and those who do change their lives end up better off psychologically (Stewart & Vandewater, 1999; Robinson, Demetre, & Litman, 2017).

Figure 16-1 Feeling Younger and Age of Death

People who said they felt younger than their chronological age were more likely to live longer than those who felt older than their chronological death. The average actual age of participants in the study was 66.

(**Source:** Based on Rippon & Steptoe, 2015.)

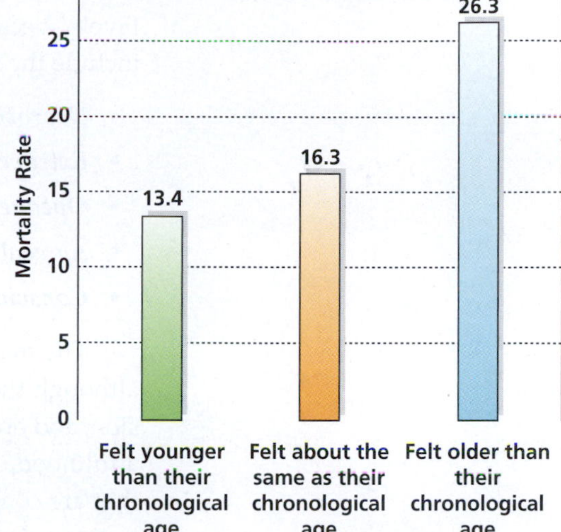

Furthermore, how one feels about one's age is actually associated with health outcomes. People who feel younger than their chronological age are more likely to avoid death than those who feel older than their chronological age. In other words, the younger people felt, the less likely they were to die within an 8-year period following being asked the question of how old they felt (see Figure 16-1; Miche et al., 2014; Rippon & Steptoe, 2015).

In short, the evidence for a midlife crisis experienced by most people is no more compelling than the evidence for a stormy adolescence. Yet, like that notion, the idea that the midlife crisis is nearly universal seems unusually well entrenched in "common wisdom." Why is this the case?

One reason may be that people who do experience turmoil during middle age tend to be relatively obvious and easily remembered by observers. For instance, a 40-year-old man who divorces his wife, replaces his sedate Volvo station wagon with a red Audi convertible, and marries a much younger woman is likely to be more conspicuous than a happily married man who remains with his spouse (and Chevrolet) throughout middle adulthood. As a consequence, we are more likely to notice and recall marital difficulties than the lack of them. In this way, the myth of a blustery and universal midlife crisis is perpetuated. The reality, though, is quite different: For most people, a midlife crisis is more the stuff of fiction than of reality. For some people midlife may not bring many changes at all. And as we consider in the *Developmental Diversity and Your Life* box in some cultures, middle age is not even considered a separate period of life.

Stability Versus Change in Personality

LO 16.3 Discuss the nature of continuity in personality development during middle adulthood.

Jane Hennesey, age 53 and a vice president of an investment banking firm, says that inside, she still feels like a kid.

Many middle-aged adults would agree with such a sentiment. Although most people tend to say that they have changed a good deal since they reached adolescence—and mostly for the better—many also contend that in terms of basic personality traits, they perceive important similarities between their present selves and their younger selves.

The degree to which personality is stable across the life span or changes as we age is one of the major issues of personality development during middle adulthood. Theorists such as Erikson and Levinson clearly suggest that there is substantial change over time. Erikson's stages and Levinson's seasons describe set patterns of change. The change may be predictable and related to age, but it is substantial.

Conversely, an impressive body of research suggests that at least in terms of individual traits, personality is quite stable and continuous over the life span. Developmental psychologists Paul Costa and Robert McCrae find remarkable stability in particular traits. Even-tempered 20-year-olds are even-tempered at age 75; affectionate 25-year-olds become affectionate 50-year-olds; and disorganized 26-year-olds are still disorganized at age 60. Similarly, self-concept at age 30 is a good indication of self-concept at age 80 (Terracciano, McCrae, & Costa, 2009; Debast et al., 2014; Mõttus et al., 2017; also see Figure 16-2).

There is also evidence that people's traits actually become more ingrained as they age. For instance, some research suggests that confident adolescents become more confident in their mid-50s, while shy people become more diffident over the same time frame.

STABILITY AND CHANGE IN THE "BIG FIVE" PERSONALITY TRAITS. Quite a bit of research has centered on the personality traits that have come to be known as the "Big Five"—because they represent the five major clusters of personality characteristics. These include the following:

- ***Neuroticism,*** the degree to which a person is moody, anxious, and self-critical
- ***Extroversion,*** how outgoing or shy a person is
- ***Openness,*** a person's level of curiosity and interest in new experiences
- ***Agreeableness,*** how easygoing and helpful a person tends to be
- ***Conscientiousness,*** a person's tendencies to be organized and responsible

The majority of studies find that the Big Five traits are relatively stable past age 30, although there are some variations in specific traits. In particular, neuroticism, extraversion, and openness to experience decline somewhat from early adulthood through middle adulthood, while agreeableness and conscientiousness increase to a degree—findings that are consistent across cultures. The basic pattern, however, is one of stability in these basic traits through adulthood (Hahn, Gottschling, & Spinath, 2012; Curtis, Windsor, & Soubelet, 2015; Wettstein et al., 2017).

Does evidence for the stability of personality traits contradict the perspective of personality change championed by theorists such as Erikson, Gould, and Levinson? Not necessarily, for on closer inspection, the contradictions of the two approaches may be more apparent than real.

On the one hand, people's basic traits do appear to show continuity, particularly over the course of their adult lives. On the other hand, people are also susceptible to changes in their lives, and adulthood is jam-packed with major events, such as changes in family status, career, and even the economy. Furthermore, physical changes due to aging, illness, the death of a loved one, and an increased understanding of a finite life span can provide the impetus for changes in the ways people view themselves and the world at large (Roberts, Walton, & Viechtbauer, 2006; Iveniuk et al., 2014).

In support of this view, new research on a group of baby boomers that stretches back to their college years traces changes in their personality that extend over the course of their adult lives, as we discuss in the *From Research to Practice* box.

Figure 16-2 The Stability of Personality

According to Paul Costa and Robert McCrae, basic personality traits such as neuroticism, extroversion, and openness are stable and consistent throughout adulthood.

(**Source:** Based on Costa et al., 1986, p. 148.)

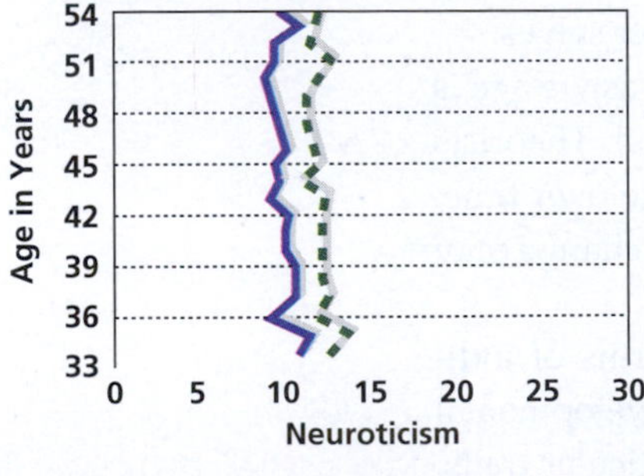

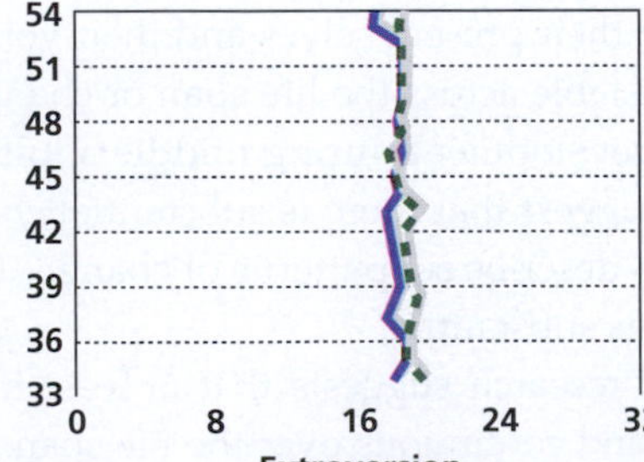

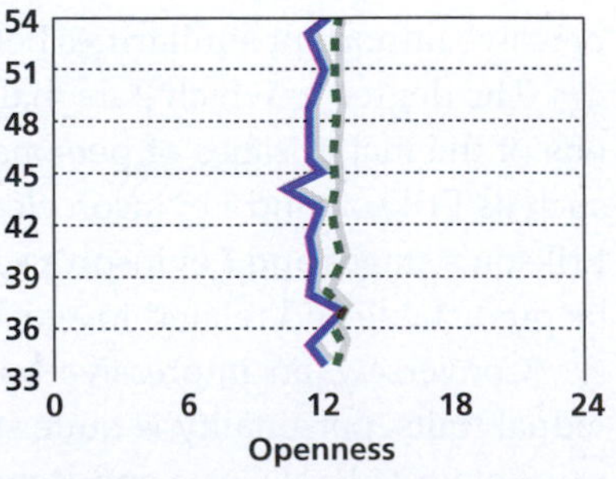

Developmental Diversity and Your Life

Middle Age: In Some Cultures, It Doesn't Exist

There's no such thing as middle age.

At least one can draw that conclusion by looking at the lives of women living in the Oriya culture in Orissa, India. According to research carried out by developmental anthropologist Richard Shweder, who studied how high-caste Hindu women viewed the process of aging, a distinct period of middle age does not exist. These women view their life course not on the basis of chronological age, but on the nature of one's social responsibility, family management issues, and moral sense at a given time (Shweder, 1998, 2003).

ephotocorp/Alamy Stock Photo

Some women living in the Oriya culture in Orissa, India, view their life course not on the basis of chronological age but on the nature of one's social responsibility, family management issues, and moral sense at a given period.

The model of aging of the Oriyan woman is based on two phases of life: life in her father's house (*bapa gharo*), followed by life in her husband's mother's house (*sasu gharo*). These two segments make sense in the context of Oriyan family life, which consists of multigenerational households in which marriages are arranged. After they are married, husbands remain with their parents, and wives are expected to move into the husband's parents' household. At the time of marriage, a wife's social status is seen as having changed from a child (someone's daughter) to a sexually active female (a daughter-in-law).

The shift from child to daughter-in-law typically occurs around age 18 to 20. However, chronological age per se does not mark significant boundaries in life for Oriyan women, nor do physical changes, such as the onset of menstruation and its cessation at menopause. Instead, it is the change from daughter to daughter-in-law that brings about a significant alteration in social responsibility. For instance, women must shift their focus from their own parents to the parents of their husband, and they must become sexually active in order to reproduce the husband's family line.

To a Western eye, the description of the life course of these Indian women suggests that they might perceive their lives as restricted because in most cases they have no careers outside the home, but they do not see themselves in this light. In fact, in the Oriya culture, domestic work is highly respected and valued. Furthermore, Oriyan women perceive themselves as more cultured and civilized than men, who must work outside the home.

In short, the notion of a separate middle age is clearly a cultural construction. The significance of a particular age range differs significantly depending on the culture in which one lives.

From Research to Practice

Evolving Circumstances, Evolving Personality: How Personality Changes Through Adulthood and Beyond

I feel like I've grown and changed a lot over the past 20 years. After facing a bout of cancer in my mid-40s, and then being involved as one of my children struggled with a drug problem, and experiencing a merger at work in which my job changed radically, how could I not have become a different person in some important ways?

As this 58-year-old's comment illustrates, personality change is often precipitated by life events over which we have no control. Our personalities change as a combination of our basic personality traits and the events that we encounter as part of everyday life. Even more intriguing, personality seems to show generational shifts.

The fluidity of personality is illustrated in a study by researcher Susan Whitbourne and colleagues that followed two groups of baby boomers from their college years until their mid-40s and mid-50s, respectively, on a measure of Erikson's stages. Changes over time in participants' responses on the measure showed personality development throughout adulthood. The childhood stages of trust, autonomy, and initiative continued to grow slowly through the mid-50s, suggesting that these qualities are not set in stone early in life but that they continue to be revisited throughout life as new challenges and life events emerge (Whitbourne & Sliwinski, 2012; Sneed et al., 2012; Dezutter et al., 2014; Whitbourne & Whitbourne, 2016).

Moreover, the study found that personality development does not progress the same way for everyone. For one thing, psychosocial growth occurs at different rates for different people, a finding that is consistent with Erikson's assertion that personality development is a personal process that depends in part on people's life experiences.

Furthermore, research shows that personality changes from one generation to another. For example, a group of researchers, taking advantage of Finland's long history of compulsory military service, used personality tests administered to 80 percent of all Finnish men as part of their entry into the military. Using data from 400,000 men born between 1962 and 1976, they were able to examine personality trends over that period. What they found was that each new group of soldiers showed increasing levels of self-confidence, sociability, leadership motivation, achievement striving, and several other traits—a change in personality across generations (Jokela et al., 2017).

Taken together, these findings suggest that personality change occurs throughout adulthood, as well as across generations. The possibility of change is with us not only through our own life spans, but across generations.

Shared Writing Prompt

What kinds of life events might you expect to affect personality the most during adulthood? Why?

Module 16.1 Review

LO 16.1 Describe ways in which personality develops during middle adulthood.

Normative-crisis models portray people as passing through age-related stages of development; life events models focus on specific changes in response to varying life events.

LO 16.2 Summarize Erikson's view of development during middle adulthood and how others have expanded on his ideas.

According to Erik Erikson, middle adulthood encompasses the generativity-versus-stagnation stage, while George Vaillant sees it as the "keeping the meaning versus rigidity" period. Roger Gould suggests that people move through seven stages during adulthood. Daniel Levinson argues that the midlife transition can lead to a midlife crisis, but there is little evidence for this in the majority of middle-aged people.

LO 16.3 Discuss the nature of continuity in personality development during middle adulthood.

Broad, basic personality characteristics are relatively stable. Specific aspects of personality do seem to change in response to life events.

Journal Writing Prompt

Applying Lifespan Development: How do you think the midlife transition is different for a middle-aged person whose child has just entered adolescence versus a middle-aged person who has just become a parent for the first time?

Relationships: Family in Middle Age

For Kathy and Bob, accompanying their son Jon to his college orientation was like nothing they had ever experienced before. When Jon had been accepted at a college on the other side of the country, the reality that he would be leaving home didn't really register. It wasn't until the time came to leave him on his new campus that the sense that their family would be changing in ways they could barely fathom hit them. It was a wrenching experience. Not only did Kathy and Bob worry about their son as parents tend to do, but they felt a sense of profound loss—that, to a large extent, their job of raising their son was over. Now he was on his own. It was a thought that filled them with pride but with great sadness as well.

For members of many non-Western cultures who live in traditional extended families in which multiple generations spend their lives in the same household or village, middle adulthood is not particularly special. But in Western cultures, family dynamics undergo significant change during middle adulthood. It is in middle age that most parents experience major changes in their relationships not only with their children but with other family members as well. It is a period of shifting role relationships that, in 21st-century Western cultures, encompasses an increasing number of combinations and permutations. We'll start by looking at the ways in which marriage develops and changes over this period, and then consider some of the many alternative forms that family life takes today (Kaslow, 2001).

Marriage and Divorce

LO 16.4 Describe typical patterns of marriage and divorce in middle adulthood.

Two of the largest transitions that can occur during middle adulthood are marriage and divorce. Let's consider how they unfold.

MARRIAGE. Fifty years ago, midlife was similar for most people. Men and women who had married during early adulthood were still married to one another. One hundred years ago, when life expectancy was much shorter than it is today, people in their 40s were most likely married—but not necessarily to the same person they had first married. Spouses often died; people might be well into their second marriage by the time of middle age.

Today the story is different and, as we said earlier, more varied. More people are single during middle adulthood, having never married. Single people may live alone or with a partner. Some have divorced, lived alone, and then remarried. During middle adulthood, many people's marriages end in divorce, and many families "blend" together into new households, containing children and stepchildren from previous marriages. Other couples still spend between 40 and 50 years together, the bulk of those years during middle adulthood. Many people experience the peak of marital satisfaction during middle age.

THE UPS AND DOWNS OF MARRIAGE. Even for happily married couples, marriage has its ups and downs, with satisfaction rising and falling over the course of the marriage. In the past, most research has suggested that marital satisfaction follows the U-shaped configuration shown in Figure 16-3 (Figley, 1973). Specifically, marital satisfaction begins to decline just after the marriage, and it continues to fall until it reaches its lowest point following the births of the couple's children. However, at that

Figure 16-3 The Phases of Marital Satisfaction

For many couples, marital satisfaction falls and rises in a U-shaped configuration. Satisfaction begins to decline after marriage, and continues to fall until the births of children. But then it begins to rise and eventually returns to a level of satisfaction similar to that at the start of marriage. Why do you think this pattern of satisfaction occurs?

(**Source:** Based on Rollins & Cannon, 1974.)

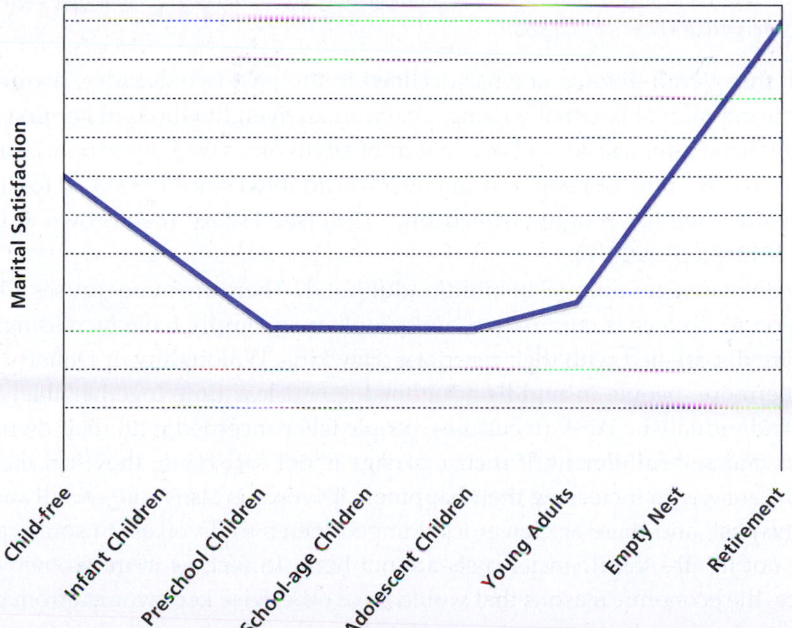

point, satisfaction begins to grow, eventually returning to the same level that it held at the start of marriage (Gorchoff, John, & Helson, 2008; Medina, Lederhos, & Lillis, 2009; Stroope, McFarland, & Uecker, 2015).

Middle-aged couples cite several sources of marital satisfaction. For instance, both men and women typically state that their spouse is their "best friend" and that they like their spouses as people. They also view marriage as a long-term commitment and agree on their aims and goals. Finally, most also feel that their spouses have grown more interesting over the course of the marriage (Levenson, Carstensen, & Gottman, 1993; Baker, McNulty & VanderDrift, 2017).

Sexual satisfaction is related to general marital satisfaction. What matters is not how often married people have sex. Instead, satisfaction is related to *agreeing* about the quality of their sex lives (Litzinger & Gordon, 2005; Butzer & Campbell, 2008; Schoenfeld et al., 2017).

Are there "secrets" to successful marriages? Not really. However, there are proven coping mechanisms that allow couples to remain together happily. Among them are (Orbuch, 2009; Bernstein, 2010):

- ***Holding realistic expectations.*** Successful couples understand that there are some things about their partner that they may not like all that much. They accept that their partner will do things that they don't like some of the time.
- ***Focusing on the positive.*** Thinking about the things that they like about their partner helps them to accept the things that bother them.
- ***Compromising.*** Partners in successful marriages understand that they are not going to win every argument, and they don't keep score.
- ***Avoiding suffering in silence.*** If something does bother them, they let their partner know about it. But they don't bring it up in an accusatory way. Instead, they talk about it at a time when they are both calm.

DIVORCE

Louise knew after 2 months that the marriage was doomed. Tom never listened to a word she said, never asked her how her day had been, never lifted a hand to help around the house. He was completely self-centered and seemingly unaware of her existence. Still, it took 23 years before she got up the nerve to tell him she wanted a divorce. His response was casual: "What took you so long? I always wondered why you stayed with me." After her initial relief that there would be no resistance, she felt betrayed and foolish. All the anguish, all the trying to make a go of it, all the pain of a bad marriage—and they both knew all along that there was no point.

Although the overall divorce rate has declined in the past two decades, divorce among couples during midlife is actually rising. One woman in eight who is in her first marriage will get divorced after age 40, and one in four of all divorces were by people 50 and older. In fact, the divorce rate for people 50 and over has doubled since 1990. And for those over 65, the divorce rate has roughly tripled since 1990 (see Figure 16-4; Brown & Lin, 2012; Thomas, 2012; Stepler, 2017).

Why do marriages unravel in middle adulthood? There are many causes. One is that the decision to divorce is cumulative, and people may simply have increasingly grown apart or are dissatisfied with their marriage (Hawkins, Willoughby, & Doherty, 2012).

Furthermore, people in middle adulthood spend less time together than in earlier years. In individualistic Western cultures, people feel concerned with their own personal happiness and self-fulfillment. If their marriage is not satisfying, they feel that divorce may be the answer to increasing their happiness. Divorce is also more socially acceptable than in the past, and there are fewer legal impediments to divorces. In some cases—but certainly not in all—the financial costs are not high. In fact, as more women enter the workforce, the economic reasons that would have otherwise kept women from divorcing their husbands are no longer strong enough to keep the marriage together. Consequently, as opportunities for women grow, wives may feel less dependent on their husbands, both from an emotional and an economic standpoint (Brown & Lin, 2012; Canham et al., 2014; Crowley, 2018).

Another reason for divorce is that, as we discussed in Chapter 14, feelings of romantic, passionate love may subside over time. Because Western culture emphasizes the importance of romance and passion, members of marriages in which passion has declined may feel that that is a sufficient reason to divorce. In some marriages, it is a lack of excitement and an increase in boredom that leads to marital dissatisfaction. Finally, there is a great deal of stress in households in which both parents work, and this stress puts a strain on marriages. Much of the energy directed toward families and maintaining relationships in the past is now directed toward work and other institutions outside the home (Macionis, 2001; Tsapelas, Aron, & Orbuch, 2009).

Finally, some marriages end because of *infidelity*, in which a spouse engages in sexual activity with a person outside of the marriage. Although statistics are highly suspect—if you lie to your spouse, why would you be truthful to a pollster?—one survey found that in a given year, about 12 percent of men and 7 percent of women say they have had sex outside their marriage (Atkins & Furrow, 2008; Steiner et al., 2015).

Figure 16-4 Rising Divorces in Middle Adulthood

The divorce rate for adults 50 and older has doubled in the past 25 years. The graph shows the number of persons who divorced per 1,000 married persons in each age group.

(**Source:** Pew Research Center, 2017.)

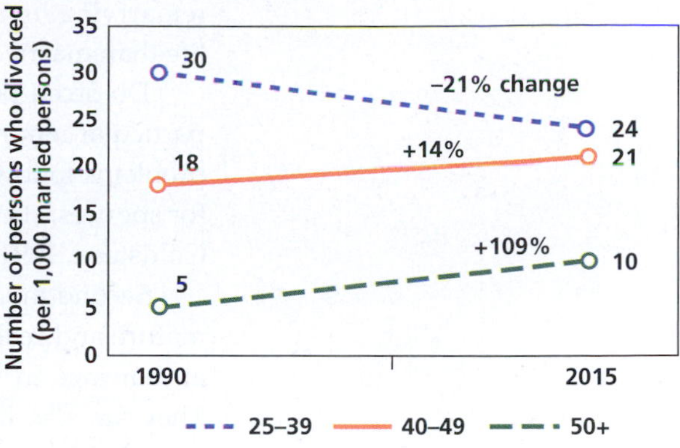

Whatever the causes, divorce can be especially difficult for men and women in midlife. It can be particularly hard for women who have followed the traditional female role of staying with the children and never performing substantial work outside the home. These women may face prejudice against older workers, finding that they are less likely to be hired than younger people, even in jobs with minimal requirements. Without a good deal of training and support, these divorced women, lacking recognized job skills, may remain virtually unemployable (Williams & Dunne-Bryant, 2006; Hilton & Anderson, 2009; Bowen & Jensen, 2017).

At the same time, many people who divorce in midlife end up happy with the decision. Women, in particular, are apt to find that developing a new, independent self-identity is a positive outcome. Furthermore, both men and women who divorce during midlife are likely to enter new relationships, and—as we will see—they typically remarry (Enright, 2004; Koren, 2014).

REMARRIAGE. Many of the people who divorce—some 75 to 80 percent—end up marrying again, usually within 2 to 5 years. In fact, 4 in 10 new marriages involve remarriage (also see Figure 16-5). Divorced people are most likely to marry people who have also been divorced, partly because divorced people tend to be the ones in the available pool, but also because those who have gone through divorce share similar experiences (Pew Research Center, 2014; Lamidi & Cruz, 2014).

Although the overall rate of remarriage is high, it is far higher in some groups than in others. For instance, it is harder for women to remarry than men, particularly older women. Whereas 90 percent of women under age 25 remarry after divorce, less than one-third of women over age 40 remarry (Bumpass, Sweet, & Martin, 1990; Besharov & West, 2002).

The reason for this age difference stems from the *marriage gradient*: Societal norms push men to marry women who are younger, smaller, and lower in status than themselves. As a consequence, the older a woman is, the fewer the socially acceptable men she has available to her because those men her age are likely to be looking for younger women. In addition,

Figure 16-5 Remarriage Rates per 1,000 Men and Women by Age, 2012

The proportion of people who remarry declines with age, with men consistently more likely to remarry at a higher rate than women remarry.

(**Source:** Lamidi & Cruz, 2014.)

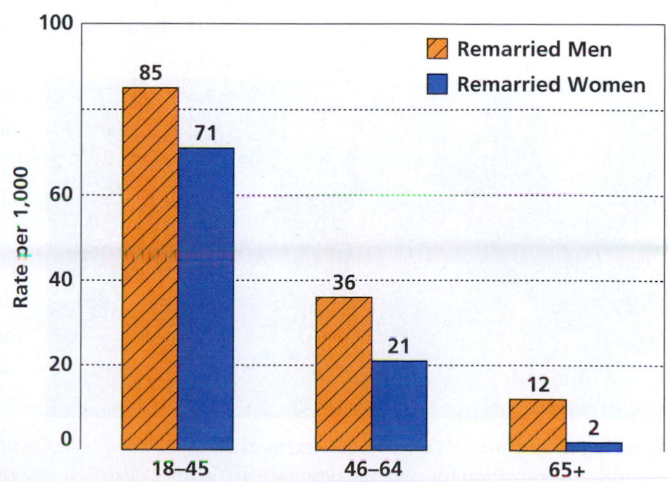

women have the disadvantage of societal double standards regarding physical attractiveness. Older women tend to be perceived as unattractive, while older men tend to be seen as "distinguished" and "mature" (Buss, 2003; Doyle, 2004a; Khodarahimi & Fathi, 2017).

There are several reasons divorced people may find getting married again more appealing than remaining single. One motivation to remarry is to avoid the social consequences of divorce. Even in the 21st century, when the breakup of marriages is common, divorce carries with it a certain stigma that people may attempt to overcome by remarrying. In addition, divorced people overall report lower levels of satisfaction with life than married people (Lucas, 2005).

Divorced people miss the companionship that marriage provides. Divorced men in particular report feeling lonely and experience an increase in physical and mental health problems following divorce. Finally, marriage provides clear economic benefits reserved for spouses, such as sharing the cost of a house and medical benefits (Ross, Microwsky, & Goldsteen, 1991; Stewart et al., 1997).

Second marriages are not the same as first marriages. Older couples tend to be more mature and realistic in their expectations of a partner and a marriage. They tend to look at marriage in less romantic terms than younger couples, and they are more cautious. They are also likely to show greater flexibility in terms of roles and duties; they share household chores more equitably and make decisions in a more participatory manner (Hetherington, 1999).

Unfortunately, however, this doesn't make second marriages more durable than first ones. In fact, the divorce rate for second marriages is slightly higher than for first marriages. Several factors explain this phenomenon. One is that second marriages may be subject to stresses that are not present in first marriages, such as the strain of blending different families. For another, having experienced and survived divorce before, partners in second marriages may be less committed to relationships and more ready to walk away from unsatisfactory ones. Finally, they may have personality and emotional characteristics that don't make them easy to live with (Warshak, 2000; Coleman, Ganong, & Weaver, 2001).

Despite the high divorce rate for second marriages, many people settle into remarriage quite successfully. In such cases, remarried couples report as great a degree of satisfaction as couples in successful first marriages (Michaels, 2006; Ayalon & Koren, 2015).

Family Evolutions: From Full House to Empty Nest

LO 16.5 Differentiate the changing family situations middle-aged adults face.

empty nest syndrome
the experience that relates to parents' feelings of unhappiness, worry, loneliness, and depression resulting from their children's departure from home

For many parents, a major transition that typically occurs during middle adulthood is the departure of children, who may be going to college, getting married, joining the military, or taking a job far from home. Even people who become parents at relatively late ages are likely to experience this transition at some point during middle adulthood, since the period spans nearly a quarter-century. As we saw in the description of Kathy and Bob, a child's departure can be a wrenching experience—so wrenching, in fact, that it has been labeled the "empty nest syndrome." The **empty nest syndrome** refers to instances in which parents experience unhappiness, worry, loneliness, and depression from their children's departure from home (Lauer & Lauer, 1999).

Ariel Skelley/Getty Images

Leaving their youngest child at college marks the start of a significant transition for parents, who face an "empty nest."

Many parents report that major adjustments are required. Particularly for women who have stayed home to rear their children, the loss can be difficult. Certainly, if traditional homemakers have little or nothing else in their lives except their children, they do face a challenging period.

While coping with the feelings of loss can be difficult, parents can also find that some aspects of this era of middle adulthood are quite positive. Even mothers who have not worked outside the home find that after the children leave, they have time for other outlets for their physical and psychological energies, such as community or recreational activities. Moreover, they may feel that they now have the opportunity to get a job or to go back to school. Finally, many mothers find that the period of motherhood is not easy; surveys show that most people feel that being a mother is harder than it used to be. Such mothers may now feel liberated from a comparatively difficult set of responsibilities (Heubusch, 1997; Morfei et al., 2004; Chen, Yang, & Aagard, 2012).

Consequently, although some feelings of loss over the departure of children are common for most people, there is little, if any, evidence to suggest that the departure of children produces anything more than temporary feelings of sadness and distress. This is especially true for women who have been working outside the home (Antonucci, 2001; Crowley, Hayslip, & Hobdy, 2003; Kadam, 2014).

In fact, there are some discernible benefits when children leave home. Married spouses have more time for one another. Married or unmarried people can throw themselves into their own work without having to worry about helping the kids with homework, carpools, and the like (Gorchoff, John, & Helson, 2008).

Keep in mind that most research examining the so-called empty nest syndrome has focused on women. Because men traditionally are not as involved as women in childrearing, it was assumed that the transition when children left home would be relatively smooth for men. However, men also may experience feelings of loss when their children depart, although the nature of that loss may be different from that experienced by women.

One survey of fathers whose children had left home found that although most fathers expressed either happy or neutral feelings about the departure of their children, almost a quarter felt unhappy (Lewis, Freneau, & Roberts, 1979). Those fathers tended to mention lost opportunities, regretting things that they had not done with their children. For instance, some felt that they had been too busy for their children or hadn't been sufficiently nurturing or caring.

Some parents react to the departure of their children by becoming *helicopter parents*, parents who intrusively intervene in their children's lives. Helicopter parenting is seen when parents micromanage their children's college careers, complaining to instructors and administrators about poor grades that their children received or seeking to get them into certain classes. In some cases, the phenomenon has started earlier: Parents of elementary school children sometimes exhibit the same tendencies.

In extreme cases, helicopter parenting extends to the workplace; some employers complain that parents call human relations departments to extol the virtues of their children as potential employees. Although statistics about the prevalence of helicopter parenting are hard to come by, it is clear that the phenomenon is real. One survey of 799 employers found that nearly a third said that parents had submitted resumes for their child, sometimes not even informing their son or daughter. One-quarter said that parents had contacted them, urging them to hire their son or daughter. And 4 percent said that a parent had accompanied the child on a job interview. Some parents even help their children complete work assignments once they get a job (Gardner, 2007; Ludden, 2012).

In most cases, though, parents permit their children to develop independently once they leave home. However, children may not always leave home for good, and the empty nest sometimes becomes replenished with what have been called "boomerang children," as we discuss next.

BOOMERANG CHILDREN: REFILLING THE EMPTY NEST

Carole Olis doesn't know what to make of her 23-year-old son, Rob. He has been living at home since his graduation from college more than 2 years ago. "I ask him, 'Why don't you move out with your friends?'" says Carole, shaking her head. Rob has a ready answer: "They all live at home, too."

Carole Olis is not alone in being surprised and somewhat perplexed by the return of her son. There has been a significant increase in the United States in the number of young adults who come back to live in the homes of their middle-aged parents.

boomerang children
young adults who return, after leaving home for some period, to live in the homes of their middle-aged parents

Known as **boomerang children**, these returning offspring typically cite economic issues as the main reason for coming back home. Because of a difficult economy, many young adults cannot find jobs after college, or the positions they do find pay so little that they have difficulty making ends meet. Others return home after the breakup of a marriage. Overall, close to one-third of young adults ages 25 to 34 are living with their parents. In some European countries, the proportion is even higher (Roberts, 2009; Parker, 2012).

Because about half of boomerang children pay rent to their parents, parental finances may benefit. The arrangement doesn't seem to affect social relationships within the family: Half say it makes no difference or is a plus. Only a quarter of boomerang children find the arrangement has been bad for their relationship with their parents (Parker, 2012; see Figure 16-6).

sandwich generation
couples who in middle adulthood must fulfill the needs of both their children and their aging parents

THE SANDWICH GENERATION: BETWEEN CHILDREN AND PARENTS. At the same time children are leaving the nest, or perhaps even returning as boomerang children, many middle-aged adults face another challenge: growing responsibility for the care of their own aging parents. The term **sandwich generation** has come to be applied to these middle-aged adults who feel squeezed between the needs of their children and their aging parents (Grundy & Henretta, 2006; Chassin et al., 2009; Steiner & Fletcher, 2017).

Being part of the sandwich generation is a relatively new phenomenon, produced by several converging trends. First, both men and women are marrying later and having children at an older age. At the same time, people are living longer. Consequently, the likelihood is growing that those in middle adulthood will simultaneously have children who still require a significant amount of nurturing and parents who are still alive and in need of care.

The care of aging parents can be psychologically tricky. For one thing, there is a significant degree of role reversal, with children taking on the parental role and parents in a more dependent position. Furthermore, older people, who were previously independent, may resent and resist their children's efforts to help. They certainly do not want to be burdens on their children. For instance, almost all elderly people who live alone report that they do not wish to live with their children (Merrill, 1997).

People in middle adulthood provide a range of care for their parents. In some cases, the care is merely financial, such as helping them make ends meet on meager pensions. In other situations, it takes the form of help in managing a household, such as taking down storm windows in the spring or shoveling snow in the winter.

In more extreme cases, elderly parents may be invited to live in the home of a son or daughter. Census data reveal that the multigenerational household, which includes three or more generations, is the fastest-growing household arrangement of any sort. As of 2016, almost 20 percent of the U.S. population lived with multiple generations under the same roof—almost 61 million people. The number of multigenerational households has increased by more than 50 percent since 1980 (Carrns, 2016).

Figure 16-6 Boomerang Children's Views of Their Situation

The percentage of those saying that living with their parents at this stage of life has been bad, good, or no different in terms of their relationship.

(**Source:** Parker, 2012.)

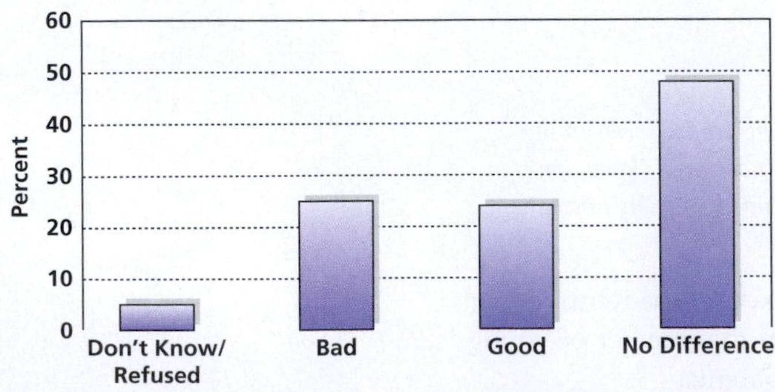

Multigenerational families present a tricky situation, as parents' and children's roles are renegotiated. Typically, the adult children in the middle generation—who, after all, are no longer children—are in charge of the household. Both they and their parents must adjust to the changing relationships and find some common ground in making decisions. Elderly parents may find the loss of independence particularly difficult, and this can be wrenching for their adult child as well. The youngest generation may resist the inclusion of the oldest generation.

In many cases, the burden of caring for aging parents is not shared equally, with the larger share most often taken on by women. Even in married couples where both husband and wife are in the labor force, middle-aged women tend to be more involved in the day-to-day care of aging parents, even when the parent or parents are their in-laws (Putney & Bengtson, 2001; Corry et al., 2015).

Culture also influences how caregivers view their roles. For example, members of Asian cultures, which are more collectivistic, are more likely to view caregiving as a traditional and not-out-of-the-ordinary duty. In contrast, members of more individualistic cultures may perceive familial ties as less central, and caring for a member of an older generation may be experienced as more burdensome (Ho et al., 2003; Kim & Lee, 2003; Ron, 2014).

Lisa Peardon/Getty Images

Living in a multigenerational setting with children and their children and their families can be rewarding for all three generations. Are there any disadvantages to this type of situation for the sandwich generation?

Despite the burden of being sandwiched in the middle of two generations, which can stretch the caregiving child's resources, there are also significant rewards. The psychological attachment between middle-aged children and their elderly parents can continue to grow. Both partners in the relationship can see each other more realistically. They can become closer, more accepting of each other's weaknesses, and more appreciative of each other's strengths (Mancini & Blieszner, 1991; Vincent, Phillipson, & Downs, 2006).

Becoming a Grandparent: Who, Me?

LO 16.6 Describe how people in middle adulthood react to becoming grandparents.

When her eldest son and daughter-in-law had their first child, Leah couldn't believe it. At age 54, she had become a grandmother! She kept telling herself that she felt far too young to be considered anybody's grandparent.

Middle adulthood often brings one of the unmistakable symbols of aging: becoming a grandparent. For some people, becoming a grandparent has been eagerly awaited. They may miss the energy and excitement and even demands of young children, and they may see grandparenthood as the next stage in the natural progression of life. Others are less pleased with the prospect of grandparenthood, seeing it as a clear signpost of aging.

Grandparenting tends to fall into different styles. *Involved* grandparents are actively engaged in grandparenting and have influence over their grandchildren's lives. They hold clear expectations about the ways their grandchildren should behave. A retired grandmother or grandfather who takes care of a grandchild several days a week while her parents are at work is an example of an involved grandparent (Mueller, Wilhelm, & Elder, 2002; Fergusson, Maughan, & Golding, 2008).

In contrast, *companionate* grandparents are more relaxed. Rather than taking responsibility for their grandchildren, companionate grandparents act as supporters and buddies to them. Grandparents who visit and call frequently, and perhaps occasionally take their grandchildren on vacations or invite them to visit without their parents, are practicing the companionate style of grandparenting.

Finally, the most aloof type of grandparents are *remote*. Remote grandparents are detached and distant, and they show little interest in their grandchildren. Remote grandparents, for example, would rarely make visits to see their grandchildren and might complain about their childish behavior when they did see them.

There are marked gender differences in the extent to which people enjoy grandparenthood. Generally, grandmothers are more interested and experience greater satisfaction than grandfathers, particularly when they have a high level of interaction with younger grandchildren (Smith & Drew, 2002).

Furthermore, African American grandparents are more apt to be involved with their grandchildren than white grandparents. The most reasonable explanation for this phenomenon is that the prevalence of three-generation families who live together is greater among African Americans than among Caucasians. In addition, African American families, which are more likely than white families to be headed by single parents, often rely substantially on the help of grandparents in everyday child care, and cultural norms tend to be highly supportive of grandparents taking an active role (Stevenson, Henderson, & Baugh, 2007; Keene, Prokos, & Held, 2012; Cox & Miner, 2014).

Family Violence: The Hidden Epidemic

LO 16.7 List the causes and characteristics of family violence in the United States.

After finding an unidentified earring, the wife accused her husband of being unfaithful. His reaction was to throw her against the wall of their apartment, and then to toss her clothes out the window. In another incident, the husband became angry. Screaming at his wife, he threw her against a wall, and then picked her up and literally threw her out of the house. Another time, the wife called 911, begging for the police to protect her. When the police came, the woman, with a black eye, a cut lip, and swollen cheeks, hysterically screamed, "He's going to kill me."

Unfortunately, the scene described above is far from rare. Violence, both physical and psychological, is part of many relationships.

THE PREVALENCE OF SPOUSAL ABUSE. Domestic violence is one of the ugly truths about marriage in the United States, occurring at epidemic levels. Some form of violence happens in one-fourth of all marriages, and more than half the women who were murdered in one recent 10-year period were murdered by a partner. Between 21 and 34 percent of women will be slapped, kicked, beaten, choked, or threatened or attacked with a weapon at least once by an intimate partner. In fact, close to 15 percent of all marriages in the United States are characterized by continuing, severe violence. Furthermore, domestic violence is a worldwide problem. Estimates suggest that one in three women throughout the globe experience some form of violent victimization during their lives (Garcia-Moreno et al., 2005; also see Figure 16-7).

In the United States, no segment of society is immune from spousal abuse. Violence occurs across social strata, races, ethnic groups, and religions. Both gay and straight partnerships can be abusive. Violence also occurs across genders: Although in the vast majority of cases of abuse a husband batters a wife, in about 8 percent of the cases wives physically abuse their husbands (Cameron, 2003; Dixon & Browne, 2003; Yon et al., 2014).

Figure 16-7 Violent Victimization by Victim–Offender Relationship, 2003–2012

(**Source:** Truman & Morgan, 2014.)

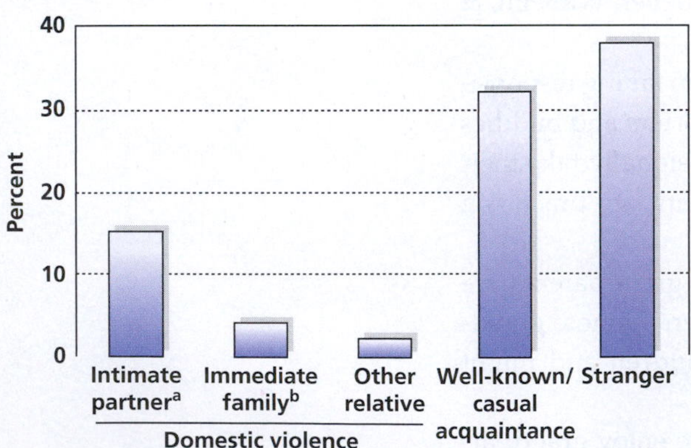

[a]Includes current or former spouses, boyfriends, and girlfriends.

[b]Includes parents, children, and siblings.

Certain factors increase the likelihood of abuse. For instance, spousal abuse is more likely to occur in large families in which there is continuing economic concern and a high level of verbal aggression than families in which such factors are not present. Those husbands and wives who grew up in families where violence was present are more likely to be violent themselves (Ehrensaft, Cohen, & Brown, 2003; Lackey, 2003).

The factors that put a family at risk are similar to those associated with child abuse, another form of family violence. Child abuse occurs most frequently in stressful environments, in lower socioeconomic levels, in single-parent families, and in situations with high levels of marital conflict. Families with four or more children have higher rates of abuse, and those with incomes lower than $15,000 a year have abuse rates that are seven times higher than families with higher incomes. But not all types of abuse are higher in poorer families: Incest is more likely to occur in affluent families (Cox, Kotch, & Everson, 2003; Ybarra & Thompson, 2017).

THE STAGES OF SPOUSAL ABUSE. Marital aggression by a husband typically occurs in three stages (Walker, 1989; see Figure 16-8). The first is the *tension-building* stage in which a batterer becomes upset and shows dissatisfaction initially through verbal abuse. He may also show some preliminary physical aggression in the form of shoving or grabbing. The wife may desperately try to avoid the impending violence, attempting to calm her spouse or withdraw from the situation. Such behavior may serve only to enrage the husband, who senses his wife's vulnerability, and her efforts to escape may lead to an escalation of his anger.

Figure 16-8 The Stages of Violence

(**Source:** Adapted from Walker, 1984, 1989; Gondolf, 1985.)

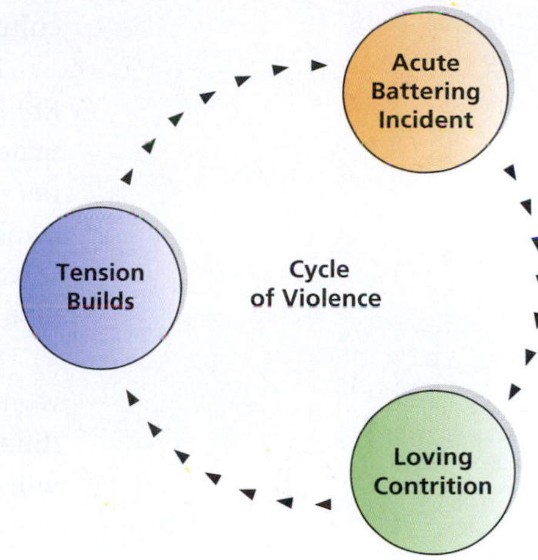

The next stage consists of an *acute battering incident*, when the physical abuse actually occurs. It may last from several minutes to hours. Wives may be shoved against walls, choked, slapped, punched, kicked, and stepped on. Their arms may be twisted or broken, they may be shaken severely, thrown down a flight of stairs, or burned with cigarettes or scalding liquids. About a quarter of wives are forced to engage in sexual activities during this period, which takes the form of aggressive sexual acts and rape.

Finally, in some—but not all—cases, the episode moves into the *loving contrition* stage. At this point, the husband feels remorse and apologizes for his actions. He may minister to his wife, providing first aid and sympathy, and assuring her that he will never act violently again. Because wives may feel that in some way they were partly at fault in triggering the aggression, they may be motivated to accept the apology and forgive their husbands. They want to believe that the aggression will never occur again.

The loving contrition stage helps explain why many wives remain with abusive husbands and are the continuing victims of abuse. Wishing desperately to keep their marriages intact, and believing that they have no good alternatives, some wives remain out of a vague sense that they are responsible for the abuse. Others remain out of fear: They are afraid their husbands may come after them if they leave.

THE CYCLE OF VIOLENCE. Still other wives stay with batterers because they, like their husbands, have learned a seemingly unforgettable lesson from childhood: Violence is an acceptable means of settling disputes.

Individuals who abuse their spouses and children were often as children the victims of abuse themselves. According to the **cycle of violence hypothesis**, abuse and neglect of children leads them to be predisposed to abusiveness as adults. In line with social learning theory, the cycle of violence hypothesis suggests that family aggression is perpetuated from one generation to another as family members follow the lead of the previous generation. It is a fact that individuals who abuse their wives often were raised in households in which they witnessed spousal abuse, just as parents who abuse their children frequently were the victims of abuse themselves as children (Renner & Slack, 2006; Whiting et al., 2009; Eriksson & Mazerolle, 2015).

cycle of violence hypothesis
the theory that abuse and neglect of children leads them to be predisposed to abusiveness as adults

From *a health-care provider's* perspective

What can be done to end the cycle of violence, in which people who were abused as children grow up to be abusers of others?

Growing up in a home where abuse occurs does not invariably lead to abusiveness as an adult. Only about one-third of people who were abused or neglected as children abuse their own children as adults, and two-thirds of abusers were not themselves abused as children. The cycle of violence, then, does not tell the full story of abuse (Maxwell et al., 2016).

Whatever the causes of abuse, there are ways to deal with it, as we consider next.

SPOUSAL ABUSE AND SOCIETY: THE CULTURAL ROOTS OF VIOLENCE. Although the tendency often is to see marital violence and aggression as a particularly North American phenomenon, in fact other cultures have traditions in which violence is regarded as acceptable (Rao, 1997). For instance, wife battering is particularly prevalent in cultures in which women are viewed as inferior to men and are treated as property.

In Western societies too, wife beating was acceptable at one time. According to English common law, which formed the foundation of the legal system in the United States, husbands were allowed to beat their wives. In the 1800s, this law was modified to permit only certain kinds of beating. Specifically, a husband could not beat his wife with a stick or rod that was thicker than his thumb—the origin of the phrase "rule of thumb." It was not until the late 19th century that spousal abuse was made illegal in the United States (Davidson, 1977).

Some experts on abuse suggest that the traditional power structure under which women and men function is a root cause of abuse. They argue that the more a society differentiates between men and women in terms of status, the more likely it is that abuse will occur.

As evidence, they point to research examining the legal, political, educational, and economic roles of women and men. For example, some research has compared battering statistics across the various states in the United States. Abuse is more likely to occur in states where women are of particularly low or high status compared with women's status in other states. Apparently, relatively low status makes women easy targets of violence. Conversely, unusually high status may make husbands feel threatened and consequently more likely to behave abusively (Vandello & Cohen, 2003). (Also see the *Development in Your Life* box.)

Development in Your Life

Dealing with Spousal Abuse

Despite the fact that spousal abuse occurs in some 25 percent of all marriages, efforts to deal with victims of abuse are underfunded and inadequate to meet current needs. Some psychologists argue that the same factors that led society to underestimate the magnitude of the problem for many years now hinder the development of effective interventions. Still, there are several measures to help the victims of spousal abuse (Lambert, 2016; Mugai, 2016; Klika & Conte, 2017)

- Teach both wives and husbands a basic premise: Physical violence is *never*, under *any* circumstances, an acceptable means of resolving disagreements.
- Call the police. It is against the law to assault another person, including a spouse. Although it may be difficult to involve law enforcement officers, this is a realistic way of dealing with domestic abuse. Judges can also issue restraining orders requiring abusive husbands to stay away from their wives.
- Understand that the remorse shown by a spouse, no matter how heartfelt, may have no bearing on the possibility of future violence. Even if a husband shows loving regret after a battering session and vows that he will never be violent again, such a promise is no guarantee against future abuse.
- If you are a victim of abuse, seek a safe haven. Many communities have shelters for the victims of domestic violence that can house women and their children. Because addresses of shelters are kept confidential, an abusive spouse will not be able to find you. Telephone numbers are on the Web (start with www.thehotline.org for the National Domestic Violence Hotline), and local police should also have the numbers.
- If you feel in danger from an abusive partner, seek a restraining order from a judge in court. Under a restraining order a spouse is forbidden to come near you, under penalty of law.
- Call the National Domestic Violence Hotline at 1-800-799-7233 for immediate advice.

Module 16.2 Review

LO 16.4 Describe typical patterns of marriage and divorce in middle adulthood.

For most couples, marital satisfaction rises during middle adulthood.

LO 16.5 Differentiate the changing family situations middle-aged adults face.

Family changes in middle adulthood include the departure of children. In recent years, the phenomenon of "boomerang children" has emerged. Middle-aged adults often have increasing responsibilities for their aging parents.

LO 16.6 Describe how people in middle adulthood react to becoming grandparents.

Many middle-aged adults experience grandparenthood for the first time. Typically, grandparents may be involved, companionate, or remote.

LO 16.7 List the causes and characteristics of family violence in the United States.

Marital violence tends to pass through three stages: tension building, an acute battering incident, and loving contrition. The incidence of family violence is highest in families of lower socioeconomic status. A "cycle of violence" affords a partial explanation. Cultural norms may also play a role.

Journal Writing Prompt

Applying Lifespan Development: Are the phenomena of the empty nest, boomerang children, the sandwich generation, and grandparenting culturally dependent? Why might such phenomena be different in societies where multigenerational families are the norm?

Work and Leisure

Enjoying a weekly game of golf…starting a neighborhood watch program…coaching a Little League baseball team…joining an investment club…traveling…taking a cooking class…attending a theater series…running for the local town council…going to the movies with friends…hearing lectures on Buddhism…fixing up a porch in the back of the house…chaperoning a high school class on an out-of-state trip…lying on a beach in Duck, North Carolina, reading a book during an annual vacation…

When we look at what people in the middle years of adulthood actually do, we find activities as varied as the individuals themselves. Although for most people middle adulthood represents the peak of on-the-job success and earning power, it is also a time when people throw themselves into leisure and recreational activities. In fact, middle age may be the period when work and leisure activities are balanced most easily. No longer feeling that they must prove themselves on the job, and increasingly valuing the contributions they are able to make to family, community, and—more broadly—society, middle-aged adults may find that work and leisure complement one another in ways that enhance overall happiness.

Work and Careers: Jobs at Midlife

LO 16.8 Summarize characteristics of work and career in middle adulthood.

For many, middle age is the time of greatest productivity, success, and earning power. It is also a time when occupational success may become considerably less alluring than it once was. This is particularly the case for those who may not have achieved the occupational success they had hoped for when they began their careers. In such cases, work becomes less valued, while family and other off-the-job interests become more important (Howard, 1992; Simonton, 1997).

The factors that make a job satisfying change during middle age. Younger adults are interested in abstract and future-oriented concerns, such as the opportunity for advancement or the possibility of recognition and approval. Middle-aged employees care more about the here-and-now qualities of work. For instance, they are more concerned with pay, working conditions, and specific policies, such as the way vacation time is calculated. Furthermore, as at earlier stages of life, changes in overall job quality are associated with changes in stress levels for both men and women (Cohrs, Abele, & Dette, 2006; Rantanen et al., 2012; Hamlet & Herrick, 2014).

In general, though, the relationship between age and work seems to be positive: The older workers are, the more overall job satisfaction they experience. This pattern is not altogether surprising, since younger adults who are dissatisfied with their positions will quit them and find new positions that they like better. Furthermore, older workers have fewer opportunities to change positions. Consequently, they may learn to live with what they have, and accept that the position they have is the best they are likely to get. Such acceptance may ultimately be translated into satisfaction (Tangri, Thomas, & Mednick, 2003).

CHALLENGES OF WORK: ON-THE-JOB DISSATISFACTION

For 44-year-old Peggy Augarten, early morning shifts in the intensive care unit of the suburban hospital where she worked were becoming increasingly difficult. Although it had always been hard to lose a patient, recently she found herself breaking into tears over her patients at the strangest moments: while she was doing the laundry, washing the dishes, or watching TV. When she began to dread going to work in the morning, she knew that her feelings about her job were undergoing a fundamental change.

Job satisfaction is not universal in middle adulthood. For some people, work becomes increasingly stressful as dissatisfaction with working conditions or with the nature of the job mounts. In some cases, conditions become so bad that the result is burnout or a decision to change jobs. Peggy Augarten's response can probably be traced to the phenomenon of burnout. **Burnout** occurs when workers experience dissatisfaction, disillusionment, frustration, and weariness from their jobs. It occurs most often in jobs that involve helping others, and it often strikes professionals who initially were the most idealistic and driven (see Table 16-2). In some ways, such workers may be overcommitted to their jobs, and the realization that they can make only minor dents in huge societal problems, such as poverty and medical care, can be disappointing and demoralizing. Furthermore, many such professions require long hours, and the difficulty of achieving success can lead to burnout (Dunford et al., 2012; Rössler et al., 2015; Miyasaki et al., 2017).

burnout
a situation that occurs when workers experience dissatisfaction, disillusionment, frustration, and weariness from the job

One of the consequences of burnout is a growing cynicism about one's work. For instance, an employee might say to himself, "What am I working so hard on this for? No one is even going to notice that I've come in on budget for the past 2 years." In addition, workers may feel indifference and lack of concern about how well they do their job. The idealism with which a worker may have entered a profession is replaced by pessimism and the attitude that it is impossible to provide any kind of meaningful solution to a problem.

People can combat burnout, even those in professions with high demands and seemingly insurmountable burdens. For example, the nurse who despairs of not having enough time for every patient can be helped to realize that a more feasible goal—such as giving patients a quick backrub—can be equally important.

Table 16-2 High-Burnout Careers

1. Physician
2. Nurse
3. Social Worker
4. Teacher
5. School Principal
6. Attorney
7. Police Officer
8. Public Accountant
9. Fast-Food Worker
10. Retail Worker

Source: White, 2017.

Jobs can also be structured so that workers (and their supervisors) pay attention to small victories in their daily work, such as the pleasure of a client's gratitude, even though the "big picture" of disease, poverty, racism, and an inadequate educational system may look gloomy. Furthermore, engaging in "best practices" on the job, and knowing that one is doing one's best, can decrease burnout. Finally, mentally disengaging from work during leisure time is helpful in reducing the consequences of burnout (Peisah et al., 2009; Sonnentag, 2012; Wilkinson, Infantolino, & Wacha-Montes, 2017).

Unemployment: The Dashing of the Dream

LO 16.9 Describe the effect losing one's job has on a person in middle adulthood.

> *The dream is gone—probably forever. And it seems like it tears you apart. It's just disintegrating away. You look alongside the river banks... there's all flat ground. There used to be a big scrap pile there where steel and iron used to be melted and used over again, processed. That's all leveled off. Many a time I pass through and just happen to see it. It's hard to visualize it's not there anymore. (Kotre & Hall, 1990, p. 290)*

It is hard not to view 52-year-old Matt Nort's description of an obsolete Pittsburgh steel mill as symbolic of his own life. Because he has been unemployed for several years, Matt's dreams for occupational success in his own life have died along with the mill in which he once worked.

For many workers, unemployment is a hard reality of life, and the implications of not being able to find work are as much psychological as they are economic. For those who have been fired, laid off by corporate downsizing, or forced out of jobs by technological advances, being out of work can be psychologically and even physically devastating (Sharf, 1992).

Unemployment can leave people feeling anxious, depressed, and irritable. Their self-confidence may plummet, and they may be unable to concentrate. According to one analysis, every time the unemployment rate goes up 1 percent, there is a 4 percent rise in suicide, and admissions to psychiatric facilities go up by some 4 percent for men and 2 percent for women (Inoue et al., 2006; Paul & Moser, 2009).

Even aspects of unemployment that might at first seem positive, such as having more time, can produce disagreeable consequences. Perhaps because of feelings of depression and having too much time on one's hands, unemployed people are less apt to participate in community activities, use libraries, and read than employed people. They are more likely to be late for appointments and even for meals (Ball & Orford, 2002; Tyre & McGinn, 2003).

And these problems may linger. Middle-aged adults who lose their jobs tend to stay unemployed longer than younger workers and have fewer opportunities for gratifying work as they age. Furthermore, employers may discriminate against older job applicants and make it more difficult to obtain new employment. Ironically, such discrimination is not only illegal but is based on misguided assumptions: Research finds that older workers show less absenteeism than younger ones, hold their jobs longer, are more reliable, and are more willing to learn new skills (Bernard, 2012).

In sum, midlife unemployment is a shattering experience. And for some people, especially those who never find meaningful work again, it taints their entire view of the world. For people forced into such involuntary—and premature—retirement, the loss of a job can lead to pessimism, cynicism, and despondency. Overcoming such feelings often takes time and a good deal of psychological adjustment to come to terms with the situation. Yet there are also challenges for those who *do* find a new career, too (Waters & Moore, 2002; Pelzer, Schaffrath, & Vernaleken, 2014).

Switching—and Starting—Careers at Midlife

LO 16.10 Explain how and why people change careers in middle adulthood.

For some people, middle adulthood brings with it a hunger for change. For such individuals, who may be experiencing dissatisfaction with their jobs, switching careers after a period of unemployment, or simply returning to a job market they left years before, their developmental paths lead to new careers.

People who change careers in middle adulthood do so for several reasons. It may be that their jobs offer little challenge; they have achieved mastery, and what was once difficult is now routine. Other people change because their jobs have changed in ways they do not like, or they may have lost their job. They may be asked to accomplish more with fewer resources, or technological advances may have made such drastic changes in their day-to-day activities that they no longer enjoy what they do.

Still others are unhappy with the status they have achieved and wish to make a fresh start. Some are burned out or feel that they are on a treadmill. In addition, some people simply do not like to think of themselves doing the same thing for the rest of their lives. For them, middle age is seen as the last point at which they can make a meaningful occupational change (Steers & Porter, 1991).

Finally, a significant number of people, almost all of them women, return to the job market after having taken time off to raise children. Some may need to find paying work after a divorce. Since the mid-1980s, the number of women in the workforce who are in their 50s has grown significantly. Around half of women between the ages of 55 and 64—and an even larger percentage of those who graduated from college—are now in the workforce (see Figure 16-9).

People may enter new professions with unrealistically high expectations and be disappointed by the realities of the situation. Furthermore, middle-aged people who start new careers may find themselves in entry-level positions. As a consequence, their peers on the job may be considerably younger than they are (Sharf, 1992; Barnett & Hyde, 2001). But in the long run, taking on a new career in middle adulthood can be invigorating. Those who switch or start new careers may be especially valued employees (Adelmann, Antonucci, & Crohan, 1990; Connor, 1992; Bromberger & Matthews, 1994).

Some forecasters suggest that career changes may become the rule rather than the exception. According to this point of view, technological advances will occur so rapidly that people will be forced periodically to change what they do to earn a living, often dramatically. In such a scenario, people will have not one, but several, careers during their lifetimes. As the following *Developmental Diversity and Your Life* box makes clear, this is especially true for those who make a major life and career change: immigrating to another country as adults.

Figure 16-9 Women at Work

The percentage of women who are in the labor force has steadily increased since the middle of the past century.

(**Source:** Hipple, 2016).

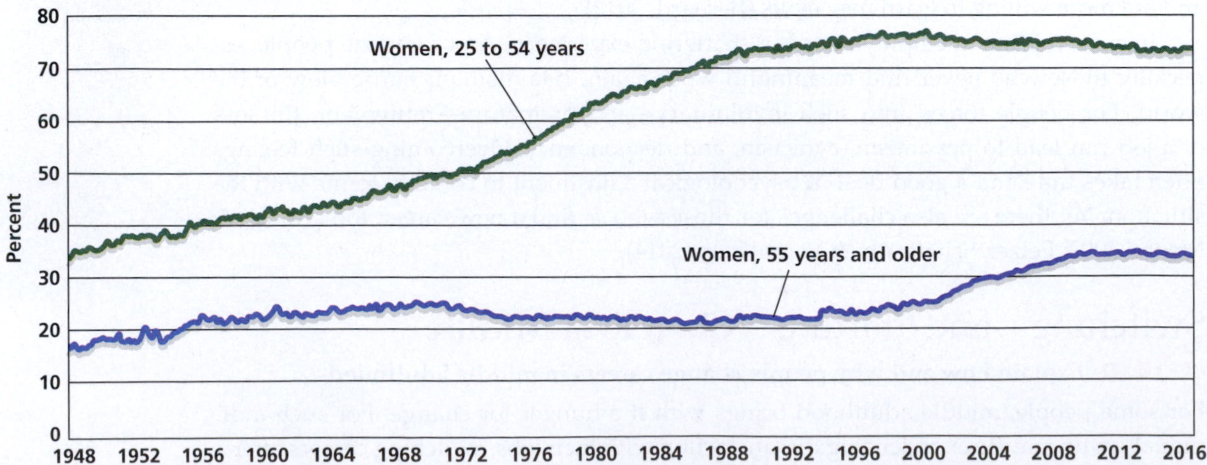

Developmental Diversity and Your Life

Immigrants on the Job: Making It in America

If we rely solely on much of what we hear from certain anti-immigrant politicians in the United States, we would probably view immigrants to the United States as straining the educational, prison, welfare, and health-care systems while contributing little to U.S. society. But the assumptions that underlie anti-immigrant sentiment are in fact quite wrong.

Some 43 million people in the United States were born outside the country, representing close to 14 percent of the population, nearly three times the percentage in 1970. First- and second-generation immigrants comprise almost a quarter of the population of the United States (see Figure 16-10; Congressional Budget Office, 2013).

Today's immigrants are somewhat different from those of the earlier waves at the beginning of the 20th century. Only a third are white, compared with almost 90 percent of immigrants who arrived before 1960. Critics argue that many new immigrants lack the skills that will allow them to make a contribution to the high-tech economy of the 21st century.

The critics are wrong in many fundamental respects. For instance, consider the following data (Flanigan, 2005; Gorman, 2010; Camarota & Zeigler, 2015):

- Most legal and illegal immigrants ultimately succeed financially. For example, although they initially experience higher rates of poverty than native-born Americans, immigrants who arrived in the United States prior to 1980 and have had a chance to establish themselves actually have a higher average family income than native-born Americans. Immigrants are twice as likely to start businesses as citizens born in the United States. Furthermore, companies owned by immigrants are more likely to hire employees than companies owned by native-born citizens (ADL, 2017).
- Most of the projected increase in immigration comes from increases in legal immigrants, not illegal immigrants.
- Few immigrants come to the United States to get on welfare. Instead, most say they come because of opportunities to work and prosper in the United States. Nonrefugee

Figure 16-10 Immigrants in the United States

Since 1970 the number of immigrants in the United States has steadily climbed and, barring changes in immigration policy, immigrants who arrive in the future plus their descendants will account for roughly three-fourths of future U.S. population increases.

(**Source:** Camarota & Zeigler, 2015).

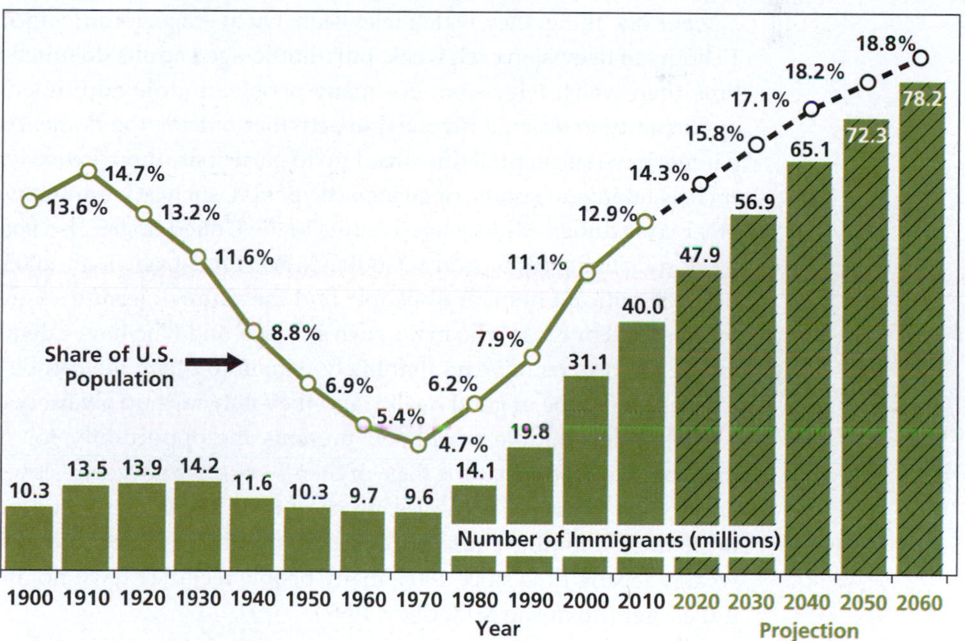

immigrants who are old enough to work are less likely to be on welfare than native-born U.S. citizens.

- Given time, immigrants contribute more to the economy than they take away. Although initially costly to the government, often because they hold low-paying jobs and therefore pay no income taxes, immigrants become more productive as they get older.

Why are immigrants often ultimately financially successful? One explanation is that immigrants who voluntarily choose to leave their native countries are particularly motivated and driven to be successful, whereas those who choose *not* to immigrate may be relatively less motivated.

In short, the reality is that the majority of immigrants ultimately become contributing members of U.S. society. For instance, they may alleviate labor shortages, and the money they send to relatives who remain at home may invigorate the world economy.

From *a social worker's* perspective

Why do you think immigrants' ambition and achievements are widely underestimated? Does the occurrence of conspicuous negative examples play a role (as it does in perceptions of the midlife crisis and stormy adolescence)?

Leisure Time: Life Beyond Work

LO 16.11 Describe how people experience leisure time in middle adulthood.

With the typical workweek hovering between 35 and 40 hours—and becoming shorter for most people—most middle-aged adults have some 70 waking hours per week at their disposal (Kacapyr, 1997). What do they do with their leisure time?

For one thing, they watch television. On average, middle-aged people watch around 15 hours of television each week. But middle-aged adults do much more with their leisure time than watch television. For many people, middle adulthood represents a renewed opportunity to become involved in activities outside the home. As children leave home, parents have substantial time freed up to participate more extensively in leisure activities, such as taking up sports, or civic participation, such as joining town committees or doing other civic duties. Middle-aged adults in the United States also spend about 6 hours each week socializing (Robinson & Godbey, 1997; Lindstrom et al., 2005).

A significant number of people find the allure of leisure so great that they take early retirement. For those who make such a choice, and who have adequate financial resources to last the dozens of years that likely remain to them, life can be quite gratifying. Early retirees tend to be in good health, and they may take up a variety of new activities.

Although middle adulthood presents the opportunity for more leisure activities, most people report that the pace of their lives does not seem slower. Because they are involved in a variety of activities, much of their free time is scattered throughout the week in 15- and 30-minute chunks. Consequently, despite a documented increase of 5 hours of weekly leisure time since 1965, many people feel they have no more free time than they did earlier (Robinson & Godbey, 1997).

One reason why extra leisure time may not be noticeable is that the pace of life in the United States is still considerably faster than in many countries. By measuring the length of time average pedestrians cover 60 feet, the time it takes for a customer to purchase a stamp, and the accuracy of public clocks, research has compared the tempo of living in a variety of countries. According to a composite of these measures, the United States has a quicker tempo than many other countries, particularly Latin American, Asian, Middle Eastern, and African countries. However, many countries outpace the United States. For example, Western European countries and Japan operate more quickly than the United States, with Switzerland ranking first (see Table 16-3; Levine, 1997a, 1997b).

Table 16-3 Comparative Pace of Life (Rank #1 = Highest Pace)

Rank of 31 countries for overall pace of life and for three measures: minutes downtown pedestrians take to walk 60 feet; minutes it takes a postal clerk to complete a stamp purchase transaction; and accuracy in minutes of public clocks.

Rank	Overall Pace of Life	Time to Walk 60 Feet	Time to Buy a Postage Stamp	Accuracy of Public Clocks
1	Switzerland	Ireland	Germany	Switzerland
2	Ireland	Netherlands	Switzerland	Italy
3	Germany	Switzerland	Ireland	Austria
4	Japan	England	Japan	Singapore
5	Italy	Germany	Sweden	Romania
6	England	United States	Hong Kong	Japan
7	Sweden	Japan	Taiwan	Sweden
8	Austria	France	Austria	Germany
9	Netherlands	Kenya	England	Poland
10	Hong Kong	Italy	Costa Rica	France
11	France	Canada	Singapore	Ireland
12	Poland	Poland	Italy	China
13	Costa Rica	Sweden	Greece	England
14	Taiwan	Hong Kong	Netherlands	Hong Kong
15	Singapore	Greece	Poland	Costa Rica
16	United States	Costa Rica	El Salvador	South Korea
17	Canada	Mexico	Czech Republic	Bulgaria
18	South Korea	Taiwan	France	Hungary
19	Hungary	Hungary	Hungary	Jordan
20	Czech Republic	South Korea	South Korea	United States
21	Greece	Czech Republic	Canada	Taiwan
22	Kenya	El Salvador	Bulgaria	Canada
23	China	Austria	United States	Czech Republic
24	Bulgaria	China	Brazil	Kenya
25	Romania	Singapore	China	Netherlands
26	Jordan	Indonesia	Indonesia	Mexico
27	Syria	Bulgaria	Jordan	Syria
28	El Salvador	Jordan	Syria	Brazil
29	Brazil	Syria	Romania	Greece
30	Indonesia	Romania	Kenya	Indonesia
31	Mexico	Brazil	Mexico	El Salvador

(**Source:** Based on Levine, 1997a.)

Module 16.3 Review

LO 16.8 Summarize characteristics of work and career in middle adulthood.

People in middle age look at their jobs differently than before, placing more emphasis on short-term factors and less on career striving and ambition. Job satisfaction tends to be high for most middle-aged people, but some are dissatisfied because of disappointment with their accomplishments and for other reasons. Burnout is a factor, especially for people in the helping professions.

LO 16.9 Describe the effect losing one's job has on a person in middle adulthood.

Unemployment in midlife can have negative economic, psychological, and physical effects.

LO 16.10 Explain how and why people change careers in middle adulthood.

Midlife career changes are becoming more prevalent, motivated usually by dissatisfaction, the need for more challenge or greater status, or the desire to return to the workforce after childrearing.

LO 16.11 Describe how people experience leisure time in middle adulthood.

People in middle adulthood usually have more leisure time than they had at earlier ages. Often they use it to become more involved outside the home in recreational and community activities.

Journal Writing Prompt

Applying Lifespan Development: Why might striving for occupational success be less appealing in middle age than before? What cognitive and personality changes might contribute to this phenomenon?

Epilogue

Despite the lingering belief that middle adulthood is a time of stagnation, crisis, and dissatisfaction, we have seen that people continue to grow and change during this period. Physically, they experience gradual declines and become more susceptible to some diseases. Cognitively, middle-aged adults experience gains in some areas and losses in others, and generally they learn to compensate rather well for any declining capacities.

As for the realm of social and personality development, we witnessed people facing and dealing successfully with a large number of changes in family relationships and work life. We also saw that to characterize this as a time of crisis is to overstate the negative and to ignore the positive aspects of the period, which is usually characterized by satisfaction and successful adjustment. Most typically, people in middle age fill many roles successfully, engaging with others from many periods of the life span, including their children, parents, spouses, friends, and coworkers.

In this chapter, we examined theories of the stages of midlife development and viewed some of the major controversies that emerge from this period of life. We have also considered the status of relationships during middle adulthood, particularly relationships with children, parents, and spouses. We have seen that changes in these areas are especially likely to affect adults at this time of their lives. Finally, we discussed work and leisure time during midlife—a time when career and retirement issues are likely to be uniquely salient.

Before turning to the next chapter, recall the prologue to this one, about Mirandi Babitz's career journey. Using your knowledge of the midlife period, consider these questions:

1. Do Mirandi Babitz's reasons for changing careers in midlife seem typical or unusual? Does it seem that dissatisfaction played an important role in his particular career trajectory?
2. Does Babitz's experience seem to fit best with Erikson's, Vaillant's, or Levinson's view on midlife? Why do you think so?
3. Does Babitz display any of the signs of a midlife crisis? Why or why not?
4. Can you interpret Babitz's life more accurately in terms of a normative-crisis model of personality development or a life events model? Why?

Looking Back

LO 16.1 Describe ways in which personality develops during middle adulthood.

There are differing opinions as to whether people pass through age-related developmental stages in a more or less uniform progression, as normative-crisis models indicate, or respond to a varying series of major life events at different times and in different orders, as life events models suggest.

LO 16.2 Summarize Erikson's view of development during middle adulthood and how others have expanded on his ideas.

Erik Erikson suggests that the developmental conflict of the age is generativity versus stagnation, involving a shift in focus from oneself to the world beyond. George Vaillant views the main developmental issue as keeping the meaning versus rigidity, in which people seek to extract meaning from their lives and accept the strengths and weaknesses of others. According to Roger Gould, people move through seven stages during adulthood. Daniel Levinson's theory of the seasons of life focuses on the creation of a global vision of one's future in early adulthood, followed by the midlife transition of the early 40s, during which people confront their mortality and question their accomplishments, often inducing a midlife crisis. Levinson has been criticized for the methodological limitations of his study, which focused on a small sample of men. The notion of the midlife crisis has been discredited for lack of evidence. Even the concept of a distinct "middle age" appears to be cultural in nature, achieving significance in some cultures and not in others.

LO 16.3 Discuss the nature of continuity in personality development during middle adulthood.

It appears that, in general, the broad personality may be relatively stable over time, with particular aspects changing in response to life changes.

LO 16.4 Describe typical patterns of marriage and divorce in middle adulthood.

Middle adulthood is, for most married couples, a time of satisfaction, but for many couples marital satisfaction declines steadily and divorce results. Most people who divorce remarry, usually to another divorced person. Because of the marriage gradient, women over 40 find it harder to remarry than men. People who marry for a second time tend to be more realistic and mature than people in first marriages, and they tend to share roles and responsibilities more equitably. However, second marriages end in divorce even more often than first marriages.

LO 16.5 Differentiate the changing family situations middle-aged adults face.

The empty nest syndrome, a supposed psychological upheaval following the departure of children from the home, is probably exaggerated. The permanent departure of children is often delayed as "boomerang" children return home for a number of years after having faced the harsh economic realities of life. Adults in the middle years often face responsibilities for their children and for their aging parents. Such adults, who have been called the sandwich generation, face significant challenges.

LO 16.6 Describe how people in middle adulthood react to becoming grandparents.

Many middle-aged adults become grandparents for the first time. Researchers have identified three grandparenting styles: involved, companionate, and remote. Styles tend to differ by gender and race.

LO 16.7 List the causes and characteristics of family violence in the United States.

Family violence in the United States has reached epidemic proportions, with some form of violence occurring in a quarter of all marriages. The likelihood of violence is highest in families that are subject to economic or emotional stresses. In addition, people who were abused as children have a higher likelihood of becoming abusers as adults—a phenomenon termed the "cycle of violence." Marital aggression typically proceeds through three stages: a tension-building stage, an acute battering incident, and a loving contrition stage. Despite contrition, abusers tend to remain abusers unless they get effective help.

LO 16.8 Summarize characteristics of work and career in middle adulthood.

For most persons, midlife is a time of job satisfaction. Career ambition becomes less of a force in the lives of middle-aged workers, and outside interests begin to be more valued. Job dissatisfaction can result from disappointment with one's achievements and position in life or from the feeling that one has failed to make a difference in the insurmountable problems of the job. This latter phenomenon, termed *burnout*, often affects those in the helping professions.

LO 16.9 Describe the effect losing one's job has on a person in middle adulthood.

Some people in middle adulthood must face unexpected unemployment, which brings economic, psychological, and physical consequences.

LO 16.10 Explain how and why people change careers in middle adulthood.

A growing number of people voluntarily change careers in midlife, some to increase job challenge, satisfaction, and status, and others to return to a workforce they left years earlier to rear children.

LO 16.11 Describe how people experience leisure time in middle adulthood.

Middle-aged people have substantial leisure time at their disposal, which many spend in social, recreational, and community activities. Leisure activities in midlife serve as a good preparation for retirement.

Key Terms and Concepts

normative-crisis models 522
life events models 522
generativity-versus-stagnation stage 523
midlife crisis 524
empty nest syndrome 532
boomerang children 534
sandwich generation 534
cycle of violence hypothesis 537
burnout 540

Summary 7
Middle Adulthood

Mike Harrington/Getty Images

LEIGH RYAN, active physically and mentally and unsure about her marriage, is at 50 chronologically and developmentally right in the middle of middle adulthood. She has continued to grow through the first half of middle adulthood, and she has firm plans to keep developing through the second half. She is active and engaged in her hobbies of dance and gardening, and she is pursuing further education in sociology while working full time and teaching part time. Socially, she enjoys entertaining her friends and giving back to her community, but she finds that her long marriage is unsatisfying, and she is quietly working to resolve that matter. In midlife she is feeling the pull of family connections in Montreal and may in fact make a move in that direction. Undoubtedly, her development will continue wherever she chooses to live, with or without her husband.

- Would you advise Leigh to consider lightening her schedule, perhaps by giving up her teaching job or reducing her course load? Why or why not?

What's your response?

Laurence Mouton/PhotoAlto/Getty Images

WHAT WOULD A MARRIAGE COUNSELOR DO?

- What factors in her marriage would you advise Leigh to consider as she contemplates divorce, given her age and situation? How can she tell if her marital discontent is a genuine issue to resolve or just a "midlife crisis"?

What's your response?

Imagemore Co., Ltd/Getty Images

Physical Development

Mats Silvan/Getty Images

- Leigh shows few signs of the physical declines of midlife, and she has maintained a high activity level.
- The fact that she is keeping physically fit may help her stave off osteoporosis and other ailments.
- It is possible that Leigh's marital discontent may reflect changes in her or her husband's sexuality.
- Leigh appears to be generally healthy, and her many activities seem to be life-enhancing rather than stress-inducing.

Cognitive Development

iofoto/Shutterstock

- Leigh is pursuing a doctoral degree, which demands intellectual alertness and activity.
- Leigh's love of teaching indicates an active mind and a commitment to using her intelligence.
- It is likely that Leigh has a great deal of practical intelligence in addition to the more traditional kind.
- Her memory shows little sign of decline and allows for new skills to be learned.

Social and Personality Development

kali3/Getty Images

- Leigh shares with many people in middle adulthood the experience of raising children and seeing them off to college.
- Her contributions to her community and her family indicate that she is successfully managing Erikson's generativity-versus-stagnation stage.
- Leigh is working on her marital situation, which shows clear signs of a gradual decline rather than a reawakening.
- Leigh faces the prospect of an empty nest, which may have an effect on whether she decides to stay married.

WHAT WOULD A HEALTH-CARE PROVIDER DO?

- How would you check that Leigh's many activities are healthful for her and not potentially stress-inducing and harmful?

What's your response?

Rubberball/Mark Andersen/Getty Images

WHAT WOULD AN EDUCATIONAL COUNSELOR DO?

- Would you advise Leigh to consider studying something other than sociology—perhaps something more practical—given her age? Is she too old for a doctorate? Will she be able to keep up with younger students?

What's your response?

Connection Blue/Alamy Stock Photo

Chapter 17

Physical and Cognitive Development in Late Adulthood

Echo/Getty Images

Learning Objectives

LO 17.1 Describe what it is like to grow old in the United States today.

LO 17.2 Summarize the physical changes that occur in old age.

LO 17.3 Explain the extent to which people slow down as they age and the consequences of this slowing.

LO 17.4 Describe how the senses are affected by aging.

LO 17.5 Describe the general state of health of older people and the disorders to which they are susceptible.

LO 17.6 Summarize how wellness can be maintained in old age.

LO 17.7 Describe how sexuality is affected by aging.

LO 17.8 Identify the factors involved with the life span and the causes of death.

LO 17.9 Discuss the possible extension of the life span through scientific advances and the implications of this extension.

LO 17.10 Describe how well older adults function cognitively.

LO 17.11 Discuss the ways memory does and does not decline in late adulthood.

LO 17.12 Describe how learning and education continue in late adulthood.

Chapter Overview

Prologue: A Better Way to Shell a Nut

Jock Brandis had spent 30 years working in the film industry, solving tricky engineering problems as a lighting director. After a 2001 visit to Africa, though, Brandis turned his career in a new direction. While visiting a friend in the Peace Corps in Malawi, Brandis saw native women shelling peanuts, an important cash crop, with fingers bloodied from carrying out the repetitive task for hours each day. Jock realized that the local economy would be helped immeasurably if they had a machine that did the shelling for them.

When Brandis, now age 71, returned to the United States, though, he found out that such a machine simply didn't exist. Undaunted, he set out to invent a machine that could shell nuts, and he created the Universal Nut Sheller, a simple apparatus that costs $28 to build. He also founded a nonprofit organization, the Full Belly Project, to help distribute the device. Today, the Universal Nut Sheller is used in 43 countries, and the Full Belly Project continues its work to help those in developing nations get the tools they need to run successful and profitable farms (Brandis, 2010; Kenney, 2015).

Looking Ahead

Jock Brandis is not alone when it comes to showing extraordinary vitality in late adulthood. Increasingly, older people are pioneering new fields, achieving new athletic endeavors, and generally reshaping how we perceive the later stages of life. For a growing number of people in late adulthood, vigorous mental and physical activity remains an important part of daily life.

In this chapter, we will consider both physical and cognitive development during late adulthood. We begin with a discussion of the myths and realities of aging, examining some of the stereotypes that color our understanding of late adulthood. We look at the outward and inward signs of aging and the ways the nervous system and senses change with age.

Next, we consider health and well-being in late adulthood. After examining some of the major disorders that affect older people, we look at what determines wellness and what it is about aging that makes old people susceptible to disease. We also focus on various theories that seek to explain the aging process, as well as on gender, race, and ethnic differences in life expectancy.

Finally, the chapter discusses intellectual development during late adulthood. We look at the nature of intelligence in older people and the various ways cognitive abilities change. We also assess how different types of memory fare during late adulthood, and we consider ways to reverse intellectual declines in older people.

Juice Images Ltd/Getty Images

Gerontologists have found that people in late adulthood can be as vigorous and active as those many years younger.

Physical Development in Late Adulthood

Let's start our journey through late adulthood by considering the physical changes that occur.

Aging: Myth and Reality

LO 17.1 Describe what it is like to grow old in the United States today.

gerontologists
specialists who study aging

Old age used to be equated with loss: loss of brain cells, loss of intellectual capabilities, loss of energy, loss of sex drive. However, as people like Jock Brandis show, that view is being steadily displaced as **gerontologists**, specialists who study aging, paint a new picture of late adulthood. Rather than being viewed as a period of decline, late adulthood is now seen as a stage in which people continue to change—to grow in some areas and, yes, to decline in others.

Late adulthood holds a unique distinction among the periods of human life: Because people are living longer, late adulthood is actually increasing in length. Whether we peg the start of the period at age 65 or 70, there is today a greater proportion of people alive in late adulthood than at any time in world history.

Because many older adults are as vigorous and involved with life as people several decades younger, we cannot define old age by chronological years alone; we also must take into account people's physical and psychological well-being, their *functional ages.* Some researchers of aging divide people into three groups according to their functional ages: the *young old* are healthy and active; the *old old* have some health problems and difficulties with daily activities; and the *oldest old* are frail and in need of care. Although a person's chronological age can predict which functional group he or she is most likely to fall into, it is not a sure thing. An active, healthy 100-year-old would be considered young old by researchers on aging. In comparison, a 60-year-old in the late stages of emphysema would be considered among the oldest old, according to functional age.

Like researchers of aging, demographers have taken to dividing their measurements of the elderly population by age. They use the same terms as researchers who refer to functional aging but with different meanings (so be sure to clarify if someone is using one of these terms). For demographers, the *young old* are those 65 to 74 years old. The *old old* are between 75 and 84, and the *oldest old* are people 85 and older.

THE DEMOGRAPHICS OF LATE ADULTHOOD. One out of every eight people in the United States is 65 or older. However, projections suggest that by the year 2060, nearly one-quarter of the population will be age 65 and above. The number of people over age 85 is projected to increase from the current 6 million to 20 million by 2060 (see Figure 17-1; Mather, Jacobsen, & Pollard, 2015).

The fastest-growing segment of the population is the oldest old—people who are 85 or older. In the past two decades, the size of this group has nearly doubled. The population explosion among older people is not limited to the United States. In fact, the rate of increase is much higher in developing countries. As can be seen in Figure 17-2, the sheer numbers of elderly are increasing substantially in countries around the globe. By 2050, the number of adults worldwide over age 60 will exceed the number of people under age 15 for the first time in history (Sandis, 2000; United Nations, Department of Economic and Social Affairs, Population Division, 2013).

Figure 17-1 The Flourishing Elderly

The number of people in the United States over age 65 is projected to double by the year 2060 from the number in 2014. What are the factors that contribute to this increase?

(**Source:** Adapted from Mather, Jacobsen, & Pollard, 2015.)

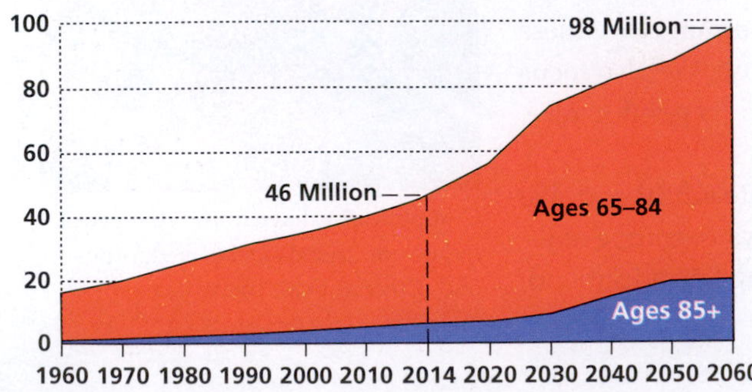

AGEISM: CONFRONTING THE STEREOTYPES OF LATE ADULTHOOD. Crotchety. Old codger. Old coot. Senile. Geezer. Old hag. Such are the labels of late adulthood. If you find that

Figure 17-2 The Elderly Population Worldwide

Longer life is transforming population profiles worldwide, with the proportion of those over age 60 predicted to increase substantially by the year 2050.

(**Source:** Based on United Nations, Department of Economic and Social Affairs, Population Division, 2013.)

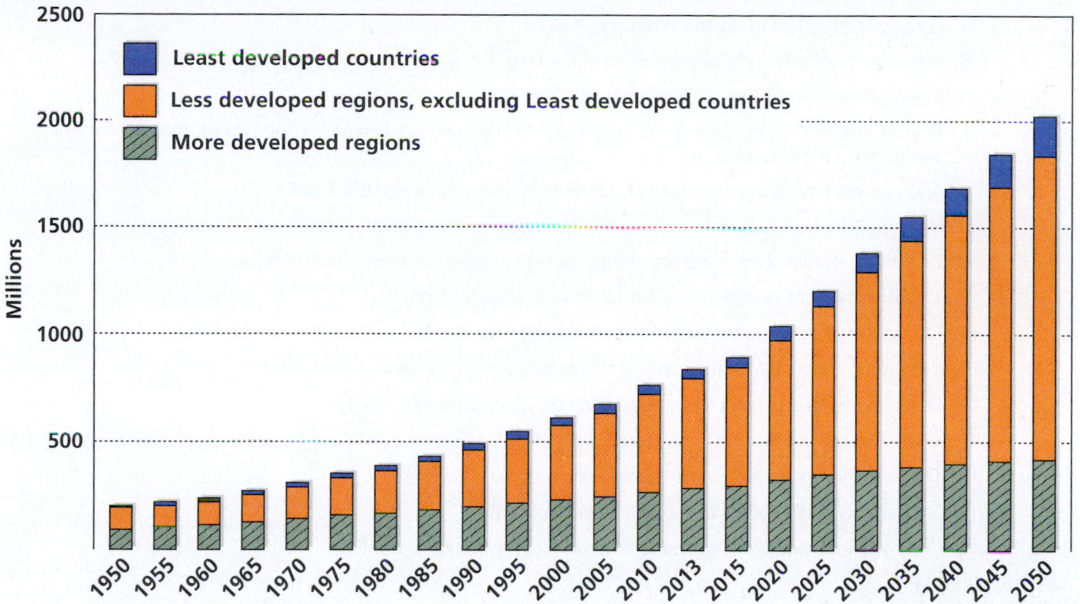

they don't draw a pretty picture, you're right: Such words are demeaning and biased, representing both overt and subtle ageism. **Ageism** is prejudice and discrimination directed at older people.

ageism
prejudice and discrimination directed at older people

Ageism is manifested in several ways. It is found in widespread negative attitudes toward older people, suggesting that they are in less than full command of their mental faculties. For example, the results of many attitude studies have found that older adults are viewed more negatively than younger ones on a variety of traits, particularly those having to do with general competence and attractiveness (Woodspring, 2012; Jesmin, 2014; Ayalon & Tesch-Römer, 2017).

Furthermore, identical behavior carried out by an older and a younger person often is interpreted quite differently. Imagine you hear someone describing his search for his house keys. How would your perception of the person change if you knew he was 20 or 80? Older adults who show memory lapses are viewed as chronically forgetful and likely to be suffering from some mental disorder. Similar behavior on the part of young adults is judged more charitably, merely as evidence of temporary forgetfulness produced by having too much on their minds (Nelson, 2004; Lassonde et al., 2012).

Monkey Business Images/Shutterstock

What do you see when you look at this woman? Ageism is found in widespread negative attitudes toward older people, suggesting that they are in less than full command of their faculties.

This negative view of older people is connected to the reverence of youth and youthful appearance that characterizes many Western societies. It is the rare advertisement that includes an elderly person, unless it is for a product specifically designed for older adults. And when older persons are portrayed in television programming, they are often presented as someone's mother, father, grandmother, or grandfather rather than as individuals in their own right (McVittie, McKinlay, & Widdicombe, 2003; Swift et al., 2017).

The ageism that produces such negative views of older people is reflected in the way they are treated. For instance, elderly individuals seeking jobs may face open prejudice, being told in job interviews that they lack the stamina for particular jobs. Or they

Table 17-1 The Myths of Aging

1. The majority of old people (age 65 and older) have defective memory, are disoriented, or are demented. T or F?
2. The five senses (sight, hearing, taste, touch, and smell) all tend to weaken in old age. T or F?
3. The majority of old people have no interest in, nor capacity for, sexual relations. T or F?
4. Lung capacity tends to decline in old age. T or F?
5. The majority of old people are sick most of the time. T or F?
6. Physical strength tends to decline in old age. T or F?
7. At least one-tenth of the aged are living in long-stay institutions (such as nursing homes, mental hospitals, and homes for the aged). T or F?
8. Aged drivers have fewer accidents per driver than those under age 65. T or F?
9. Older workers usually cannot work as effectively as younger workers. T or F?
10. Over three-fourths of the aged are healthy enough to carry out their normal activities. T or F?
11. The majority of old people are unable to adapt to change. T or F?
12. Old people usually take longer to learn something new. T or F?
13. It is almost impossible for the average old person to learn something new. T or F?
14. Older people tend to react more slowly than do younger people. T or F?
15. In general, old people tend to be pretty much alike. T or F?
16. The majority of old people say they are seldom bored. T or F?
17. The majority of old people are socially isolated. T or F?
18. Older workers have fewer accidents than do younger workers. T or F?
Scoring
All odd-numbered statements are false; all even-numbered statements are true. Most college students miss about six, and high school students miss about nine. Even college instructors miss an average of about three.

(**Source:** Adapted from Palmore, 1988; Rowe & Kahn, 1999.)

sometimes are relegated to jobs for which they are overqualified. In addition, such stereotypes are accepted by people in late adulthood, becoming self-fulfilling prophecies that hinder performance (Rupp, Vodanovich, & Credé, 2006; Levy, 2009; Wiener et al., 2014).

The ageism directed toward people in late adulthood is, in some ways, a peculiarly modern and Western cultural phenomenon. In the colonial period of U.S. history, a long life was an indication that a person had been particularly virtuous, and older people were held in high esteem. Similarly, people in most Asian societies venerate those who have reached old age because elders have attained special wisdom as a consequence of living so long. Likewise, many Native American societies traditionally have viewed older people as storehouses of information about the past (Bodner, Bergman, & Cohen-Fridel, 2012; Maxmen, 2012).

Today, however, negative views of older people prevail in U.S. society, and they are based on widespread misinformation. For instance, to test your knowledge about aging, try answering the questions posed in Table 17-1. Most people score no higher than chance on the items, averaging about 50 percent correct (Palmore, 1992). Given the prevalence of ageist stereotypes in Western societies today, it is reasonable to ask how accurate these views are. Is there a kernel of truth in them?

The answer is largely no. Aging produces consequences that vary greatly from one person to the next. Although some elderly people are in fact physically frail, have cognitive difficulties, and require constant care, others are vigorous and independent—and sharp, brilliant, and shrewd thinkers. Furthermore, some problems that at first glance seem attributable to old age are actually a result of illness, improper diet, or insufficient nutrition. As we will see, the autumn and winter of life can bring change and growth on a par with—and sometimes even greater than—earlier periods of the life span (Whitbourne, 2007).

From *a social worker's* perspective

When older people win praise and attention for being "vigorous," "active," and "youthful," is this a message that combats or supports ageism?

Physical Transitions in Older People

LO 17.2 Summarize the physical changes that occur in old age.

"Feel the burn." That's what the teacher says, and many of the 14 women in the class are doing just that. As the teacher continues through a variety of exercises, the women participate to varying degrees. Some stretch and reach vigorously, while others just move in time to the beat of the music. It's not much different from thousands of exercise classes all over the United States, yet to the youthful observer there is one surprise: The youngest woman in this class is 66 years old, and the oldest, dressed in a sleek black leotard, is 81.

The surprise registered by this observer reflects a popular stereotype of elderly persons. Many people view those over 65 as sedentary and sedate, an image that certainly does not incorporate involvement in vigorous exercise.

The reality, however, is different. Although the physical capabilities of elderly people are not the same as they were in earlier stages of life, many older persons remain remarkably agile and physically fit in later life (Riebe, Burbank, & Garber, 2002; Sargent-Cox, Anstey, & Luszcz, 2012).

Still, the changes in the body that began subtly during middle adulthood become unmistakable during old age. Both the outward indications of aging and those related to internal functioning become incontestable.

As we discuss aging, it is important to remember the distinction, introduced in Chapter 13 and Chapter 15, between primary and secondary aging. **Primary aging**, or *senescence*, involves the universal and irreversible changes that occur as people get older due to genetic programming. It reflects the inevitable changes that all of us experience from the time we are born. In contrast, **secondary aging** encompasses changes that result from illness, health habits, and other individual differences but that are not caused by increased age itself and are not inevitable. Although the physical and cognitive changes that involve secondary aging are more common as people become older, they are potentially avoidable and can sometimes be reversed.

primary aging

aging that involves universal and irreversible changes that, due to genetic programming, occur as people get older

secondary aging

changes in physical and cognitive functioning that result from illness, health habits, and other individual differences, but that are not caused by increased age itself and are not inevitable

OUTWARD SIGNS OF AGING. One of the most obvious signs of aging is the changes in a person's hair. Most people's hair becomes distinctly gray and eventually white, and it may thin out. The face and other parts of the body become wrinkled as the skin loses elasticity and *collagen*, the protein that forms the basic fibers of body tissue.

People may become noticeably shorter, with some shrinking as much as 4 inches. Although this shortening is partially to the result of changes in posture, the primary cause is that the cartilage in the discs of the backbone has become thinner. This is particularly true for women, who are more susceptible than men to **osteoporosis**, or thinning of the bones, largely because of reduced production of estrogen.

osteoporosis

a condition in which the bones become brittle, fragile, and thin, often brought about by a lack of estrogen in the diet

Osteoporosis affects 25 percent of women over age 60 and is a primary cause of broken bones among elderly women and men. It is largely preventable if people's calcium and protein intake are sufficient in earlier parts of life and if they have engaged in adequate exercise. In addition, osteoporosis can be treated and even prevented through use of drugs such as Fosamax (alendronate) (Tadic et al., 2012; Hansen et al., 2014; Braun et al., 2017).

Although negative stereotypes against appearing old operate for both men and women, they are particularly potent for women. In Western cultures there is a *double standard* for appearance, by which women who show signs of aging are judged more harshly than men. For instance, gray hair in men is often viewed as "distinguished," a sign of character; the same characteristic in women is a signal that they are "over the hill."

As a consequence of the double standard, women are considerably more likely than men to feel compelled to hide the signs of aging. For instance, older women are much more likely than men

Tetra Images/Alamy Stock Photo

Even in late adulthood, exercise is possible—and beneficial.

Figure 17-3 Changing Physical Capacities

As people age, significant changes occur in the functioning of various systems of the body.

(**Source:** Based on Whitbourne, 2001.)

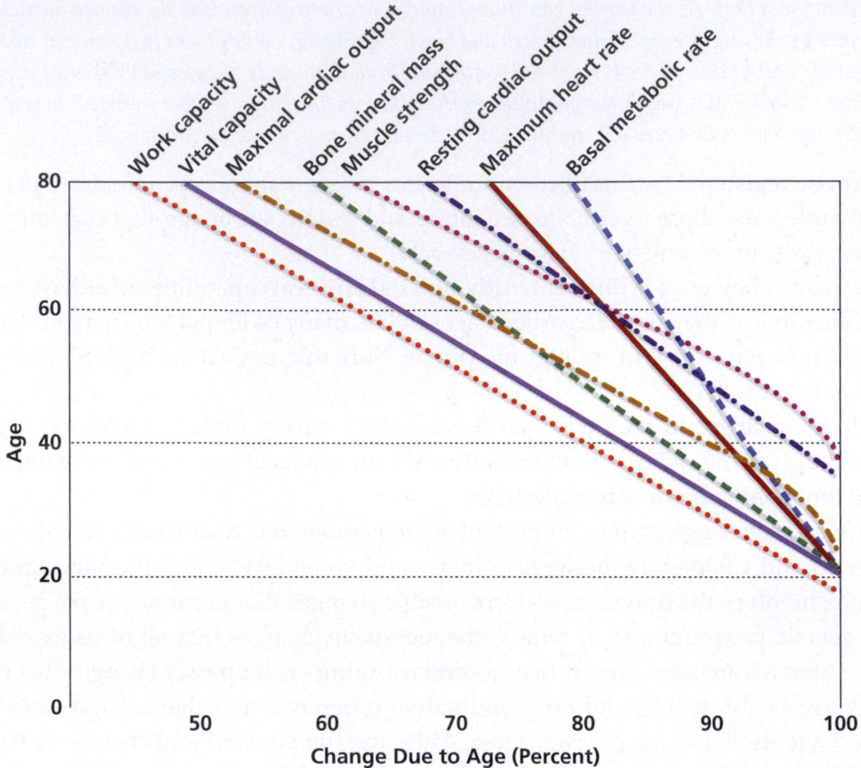

to dye their hair and to have cosmetic surgery, and women's use of cosmetics is designed to make them look younger (Crawford & Unger, 2004).

This is changing, however. Men are also becoming more interested in maintaining a youthful appearance, another sign of the dominance of a youth orientation in Western culture. For example, more cosmetic products, such as wrinkle creams, are available for men. This may be interpreted as a sign both that the double standard is easing and that ageism is becoming more of a concern for both sexes.

INTERNAL AGING. As the outward physical signs of aging become increasingly apparent, significant changes occur in the internal functioning of the organ systems. The capacities of many functions decline with age (see Figure 17-3; Whitbourne, 2001; Aldwin & Gilmer, 2004).

The brain becomes smaller and lighter with age, although, in the absence of disease, it retains its structure and function. As the brain shrinks, it pulls away from the skull, and the amount of space between brain and skull doubles from age 20 to age 70. Blood flow is reduced within the brain, which also uses less oxygen and glucose. The number of neurons, or brain cells, declines in some parts of the brain, although not as many as was once thought. For instance, recent research suggests that the number of cells in the brain's cortex may drop only minimally or not at all. In fact, some evidence suggests that certain types of neuronal growth may continue throughout the life span (Jäncke et al., 2015; Goyal et al., 2017; see Figure 17-4).

The reduced flow of blood in the brain is due in part to the heart's reduced capacity to pump blood throughout the circulatory system. Because of hardening and shrinking of blood vessels throughout the body, the heart is forced to work harder, and it is typically

Figure 17-4 Brain Decline

These PET scan composite images show the differences in metabolism, indicated by the dramatic reduction in aerobic glycolysis (shown in yellow), between young and old adults.

(**Source:** Goyal et al., 2017.)

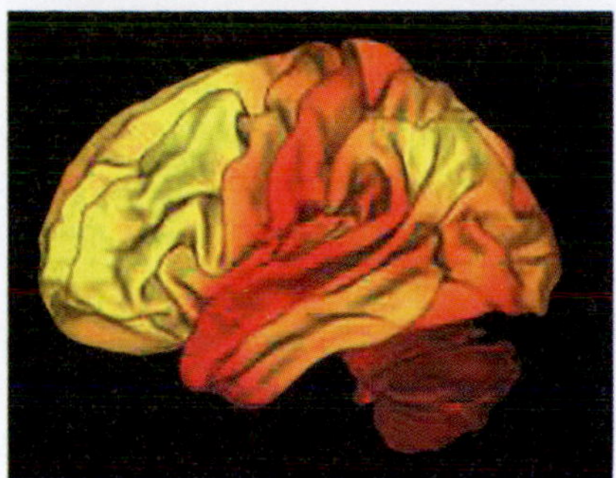

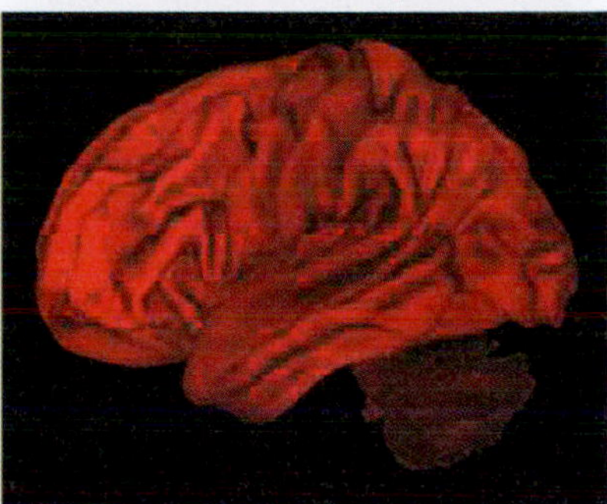

unable to compensate fully. A 75-year-old man pumps less than three-quarters of the blood that he was able to pump during early adulthood (Yildiz, 2007).

Other bodily systems work at lower capacity than they did earlier in life. For instance, the respiratory system is less efficient with age. The digestive system produces less digestive juice and is less efficient in pushing food through the system—which produces a higher incidence of constipation. Some hormones are produced at lower levels with increasing age. Furthermore, muscle fibers decrease both in size and in amount, and they become less efficient at using oxygen from the bloodstream and storing nutrients (Deruelle et al., 2008; Morley, 2012).

Although all of these changes are part of the normal process of aging, they often occur earlier in people who have less healthy lifestyles. For example, smoking accelerates declines in cardiovascular capacity at any age.

Lifestyle factors can also slow the changes associated with aging. For instance, people whose exercise program includes weightlifting may lose muscle fiber at a slower rate than those who are sedentary. Similarly, physical fitness is related to better performance on mental tests, may prevent a loss of brain tissue, and may even aid in the development of new neurons. An increasing number of studies suggest that sedentary older adults who begin aerobic fitness training ultimately show cognitive benefits (Pereira et al., 2007; Lin et al., 2014; Bonavita & Tedeschi, 2017).

Slowing Reaction Time

LO 17.3 Explain the extent to which people slow down as they age and the consequences of this slowing.

Karl winced as the "game over" message came up on his grandson's video game system. He enjoyed trying out their games, but he just couldn't shoot down those bad guys as quickly as his grandkids could.

As people get older, they take longer: longer to put on a tie, longer to reach a ringing phone, longer to press the buttons in a video game. One reason for this slowness is a lengthening of reaction time. Reaction time begins to increase in middle age, and by late adulthood the rise can be significant (Benjuya, Melzer, & Kaplanski, 2004; Der & Deary, 2006).

peripheral slowing hypothesis
the theory suggesting that overall processing speed declines in the peripheral nervous system with increasing age

It is not clear why people slow down. One explanation, known as the **peripheral slowing hypothesis**, suggests that overall processing speed declines in the peripheral nervous system. According to this notion, the peripheral nervous system, which encompasses the nerves that branch out from the spinal cord and brain and reach the extremities of the body, becomes less efficient with age. Because of this decrease in efficiency, it takes longer for information from the environment to reach the brain and longer for commands from the brain to be transmitted to the body's muscles (Salthouse, 2006, 2017).

generalized slowing hypothesis
the theory that processing in all parts of the nervous system, including the brain, is less efficient

Other researchers have proposed an alternative explanation. According to the **generalized slowing hypothesis**, processing in all parts of the nervous system, including the brain, is less efficient. As a consequence, slowing occurs throughout the body, including the processing of both simple and complex stimuli and the transmission of commands to the muscles of the body (Harada, Natelson Love, & Triebel, 2013).

Although we don't know which explanation provides the more accurate account, it is clear that the slowing of reaction time and general processing results in a higher incidence of accidents for elderly persons. Because their reaction and processing time is slowed, they are unable to efficiently receive information from the environment that may indicate a dangerous situation, their decision-making processes may be slower, and ultimately their ability to remove themselves from harm's way is impaired. Still, drivers over age 70 have fewer auto accidents than teenagers when accidents are figured in terms of miles of driving (Tefft, 2012; see Figure 17-5).

Although it takes older individuals longer to respond, the *perception* of time seems to increase with age. The days and weeks seem to go by more quickly; generally, time seems to rush by faster for older adults than younger ones. The reason may be due to changes in the way the brain coordinates its internal time clock (Facchini & Rampazi, 2009; Jones Ross, Cordazzo, & Scialfa, 2014).

The Senses: Sight, Sound, Taste, and Smell

LO 17.4 Describe how the senses are affected by aging.

Old age brings with it distinct declines in the sense organs of the body, although in this area there is a great deal of variation. Sensory declines are of major psychological consequence because the senses serve as people's link with the world outside the mind.

Figure 17-5 Vehicle Crashes Across the Life Span, 2008–2009

Drivers over age 70 have a superior crash record to drivers 19 and younger when crashes are calculated per mile of driving. Why is this the case? **THINKING ABOUT THE DATA:** At what age do fatalities begin to approach those of 16 year olds? What factors lead to this increase?

(**Source:** Tefft, 2012.)

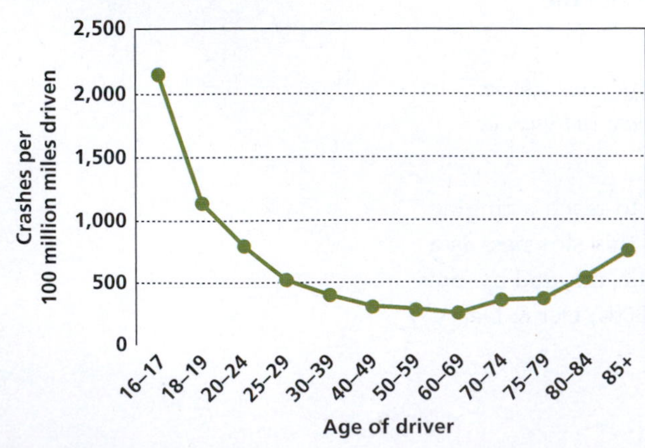

VISION. Age-related changes in the physical apparatus of the eye—the cornea, lens, retina, and optic nerve—lead to a decrease in visual abilities. For instance, the lens becomes considerably less transparent: The amount of light arriving at the retina of a healthy 60-year-old is only a third as much as that of a 20-year-old. The optic nerve becomes less efficient in transmitting nerve impulses (Gawande, 2007).

As a result, vision declines along several dimensions. We see distant objects less clearly and need more light to see clearly, and it takes longer to adjust from dark to light places and vice versa.

These changes in vision produce everyday difficulties. Driving, particularly at night, becomes more challenging. Similarly, reading requires more lighting, and eye strain occurs more easily. Eyeglasses and contact lenses can correct many of these problems, however, and the majority of older people can see reasonably well (Owsley, Stalvey, & Phillips, 2003).

Several eye diseases become more common during late adulthood. For instance, *cataracts*—cloudy or opaque areas on the lens of the eye that interfere with passing light—frequently develop. People with cataracts have blurred vision and tend to experience glare in bright light. If cataracts are left untreated, the lens becomes milky white, and blindness is the eventual result. However, cataracts can

Figure 17-6 The World Through Macular Degeneration

(a) Age-related macular degeneration affects the macula, a yellowish area of the eye located near the retina. Eyesight gradually deteriorates once a portion of the macula thins and degenerates. (b) Macular degeneration leads to a gradual deterioration of the center of the retina, leaving only peripheral vision. This is an example of what a person with macular degeneration might see.

(**Source:** AARP, 2005, p. 34.)

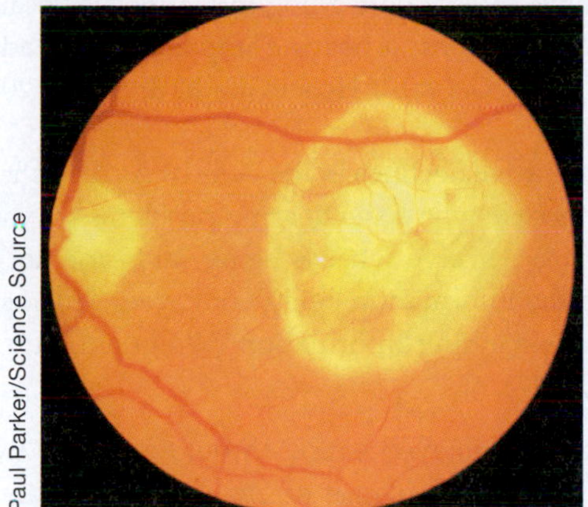

Paul Parker/Science Source

Pearson Education

be surgically removed, and eyesight can be restored through the use of eyeglasses, contact lenses, or *intraocular lens implants*, in which a plastic lens is permanently placed in the eye (Walker, Anstey, & Lord, 2006).

Another serious problem that afflicts many elderly individuals is glaucoma. As we noted first in Chapter 15, *glaucoma* occurs when pressure in the fluid of the eye increases, either because the fluid cannot drain properly or because too much fluid is produced. Glaucoma, too, can be treated with drugs or surgery if it is detected early enough.

The most common cause of blindness in people over the age of 60 is *age-related macular degeneration (AMD)*. This disorder affects the *macula*, a yellowish area of the eye located near the retina at which visual perception is most acute. When a portion of the macula thins and degenerates, eyesight gradually deteriorates (see Figure 17-6). If diagnosed early, macular degeneration can sometimes be treated with medication or lasers. In addition, there is some evidence that a diet rich in antioxidant vitamins (C, E, and A) can reduce the risk of the disease (Wiggins & Uwaydat, 2006; Coleman et al., 2008; Jager, Mieler, & Miller, 2008).

HEARING. Around 30 percent of adults between ages 65 and 74 have some degree of hearing loss, and the figure rises to 50 percent among people over age 75. Overall, more than 10 million elderly people in the United States have hearing impairments of one kind or another (Chisolm, Willott, & Lister, 2003; Pacala & Yueh, 2012; Bainbridge & Wallhagen, 2014).

Aging particularly affects a person's ability to hear higher frequencies. Loss of these frequencies makes it hard to hear conversations when there is considerable background noise or when several people are speaking simultaneously. Furthermore, some elderly persons actually find loud noises painful.

Although hearing aids can help compensate for these losses and would probably be helpful in around 75 percent of the cases of permanent hearing loss, only 20 percent of elderly people wear them. One reason is that hearing aids are far from perfect. They amplify background noises as much as they amplify conversations, making it difficult for wearers to separate what they want to hear from other sounds. An elderly person trying to follow a conversation in a restaurant may be jolted by the sound of a fork clattering onto a plate. Many elderly people feel that the use of hearing aids makes them appear even older than they really are and encourages others to treat them as if their minds were disabled (Lesner, 2003; Meister & von Wedel, 2003).

Hearing loss can be especially damaging to the social lives of older people. Unable to hear conversations fully, some elderly people with hearing problems withdraw from others, avoiding situations in which many people are present. They may also be unwilling to respond to others, since they are unsure of what was said to them. Hearing loss can lead to feelings of paranoia as the person fills in the blanks according to his or her mental fears rather than reality. For example, someone may say "I *hate* going to the mall," and the impaired listener may decide that they have said, "I hate going to Maude's." Because they are able to catch only fragments of conversations, a hearing-impaired older adult can easily feel left out and lonely (Myers, 2000; Goorabi, Hoseinabadi, & Share, 2008; Mikkola et al., 2014).

Furthermore, hearing loss may hasten cognitive declines in the elderly. As they struggle to understand what is being said, older people who have hearing problems may use considerable mental resources simply to try to perceive what is being said—mental resources that might otherwise be processing the information being conveyed. The result can be difficulties in remembering and understanding information (Wingfield, Tun, & McCoy, 2005; Moser, Luxenberger, & Freidl, 2017).

TASTE AND SMELL. Elderly people who have enjoyed eating throughout their lives may experience a real decline in the quality of life because of changes in sensitivity to taste and smell. Both senses become less discriminating in old age, causing food to taste and smell less appetizing than it did earlier (Kaneda et al., 2000; Nordin, Razani, & Markison, 2003; Murphy, 2008).

The reason for the decrease in taste and smell sensitivity can be traced to physical changes. Most older people have fewer taste buds in the tongue than they did when they were younger. Furthermore, the olfactory bulbs in the brain begin to shrivel, which reduces the ability to smell. Because smell is responsible in part for taste, the shrinkage of the olfactory bulbs makes food taste even blander.

The loss of taste and smell sensitivity has an unfortunate side effect: Because food does not taste as good, people eat less and open the door to malnutrition. They may also over-salt their food to compensate for the loss of taste buds, thereby increasing their chances of developing *hypertension*, or high blood pressure, one of the most common health problems of old age (Smith et al., 2006).

Module 17.1 Review

LO 17.1 Describe what it is like to grow old in the United States today.

Because many older adults are as vigorous and involved with life as people several decades younger, we cannot define old age by chronological years alone; we also must take into account people's physical and psychological well-being, their *functional ages*. Yet despite many older people being vigorous, older people are often the victims of ageism—prejudice and discrimination against old people.

LO 17.2 Summarize the physical changes that occur in old age.

Old age brings both external changes (thinning and graying hair, wrinkles, and shorter stature) and internal changes (decreased brain size, reduced blood flow within the brain, and diminished efficiency in circulation, respiration, and digestion).

LO 17.3 Explain the extent to which people slow down as they age and the consequences of this slowing.

The two main hypotheses to explain the increase in reaction time in old age are the peripheral slowing hypothesis and the generalized slowing hypothesis.

LO 17.4 Describe how the senses are affected by aging.

Vision may become more difficult at distances, in dim light, and when moving from darkness to light and vice versa. Hearing, especially of high frequencies, may diminish, causing social and psychological difficulties, and taste and smell may become less discriminating, leading to nutritional problems.

Journal Writing Prompt

Applying Lifespan Development: Should strict examinations for renewal of driver's licenses be imposed on older people? What issues should be taken into consideration?

Health and Wellness in Late Adulthood

Sandra Frye passes around a photo of her father. "He was 75 when this was taken. He looks great, and he could still sail back then, but he was already forgetting things like what he'd done yesterday or what he'd eaten for breakfast."

Frye takes part in a support group for family members of Alzheimer's patients. The second picture she shares shows her father 10 years later. "It was sad. He'd start talking to me and his words would jumble. Then he'd forget who I was. He forgot he had a younger brother or that he'd been a pilot in World War II. A year after this photo, he was bedridden. Six months later, he died."

When Sandra Frye's father was diagnosed with Alzheimer's, he joined the 5.3 million Americans who suffer from this debilitating condition, a disease that saps both the physical and mental powers of its victims. In some ways, Alzheimer's disease symbolizes our view of elderly people, who, according to popular stereotypes, are more apt to be ill than healthy.

However, the reality is different: Most elderly people are in relatively good health for most of old age. According to surveys conducted in the United States, almost three-quarters of people 65 and older rate their health as good, very good, or excellent. However, to be old is to be susceptible to a host of diseases, and maintaining their physical and mental health is a major concern of older adults. We now consider some of the major physical and psychological problems that beset older people (Kahn & Rowe, 1999; National Council on Aging, 2015).

Health Problems in Older People: Physical and Psychological Disorders

LO 17.5 Describe the general state of health of older people and the disorders to which they are susceptible.

Most of the illnesses and diseases found in late adulthood are not peculiar to old age; people of all ages suffer from cancer and heart disease, for instance. However, the incidence of these and many other diseases rises with age, increasing the odds that an elderly person will be ill during the period. Moreover, while younger people can readily rebound from a variety of health problems, older persons bounce back more slowly from illnesses. And ultimately, the illness may get the best of an older person, preventing a full recovery.

COMMON PHYSICAL DISORDERS. The leading causes of death in elderly people are heart disease, cancer, and stroke. Close to three-quarters of people in late adulthood die from these problems. Because aging is associated with a weakening of the body's immune system, older adults are also more susceptible to infectious diseases (Feinberg, 2000).

In addition to their risk of fatal diseases and conditions, most older people have at least one chronic, long-term condition. For instance, *arthritis*, an inflammation of one or more joints, afflicts roughly half of older people. Arthritis can cause painful swelling in various parts of the body, and it can be disabling. Sufferers can find themselves unable to carry out the simplest of everyday activities, such as unscrewing the cap of a jar of food or turning a key in a lock. Although aspirin and other drugs can relieve some of the swelling and reduce the pain, the condition cannot be cured (Sun, Wu, & Kalunian, 2007).

Around one-third of older people have *hypertension*, or high blood pressure. Many people who have high blood pressure are unaware of their condition because it does not have any symptoms, which makes it more dangerous. Over time, higher tension within the circulatory system can result in deterioration of the blood vessels and heart, and can raise the risk of cerebrovascular disease, or stroke, if it is not treated (Wiggins & Uwaydat, 2006; Oliveira, de Menezes, & de Olinda, 2017).

PSYCHOLOGICAL AND MENTAL DISORDERS. Some 15 to 25 percent of those over age 65 are thought to show some symptoms of a psychological disorder, although this

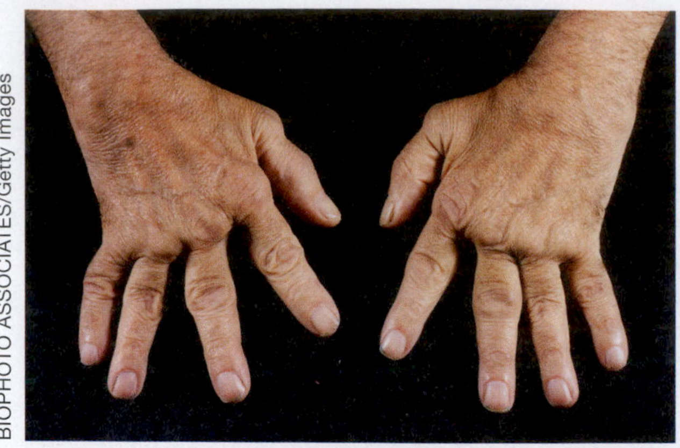
BIOPHOTO ASSOCIATES/Getty Images

Arthritis can produce swelling and inflammation in the joints of the hands.

represents a lower prevalence rate than in younger adults. The behavioral symptoms related to these disorders are sometimes different in those over 65 from those displayed by younger adults (Haight, 1991; Whitbourne, 2001).

One of the more prevalent problems is major depression, which is characterized by feelings of intense sadness, pessimism, and hopelessness. One obvious reason older people may become depressed is because they suffer cumulative losses with the death of spouses and friends. Their own declining health and physical capabilities, which may make them feel less independent and in control, may contribute to the prevalence of depression (Menzel, 2008; Vink et al., 2009; Taylor, 2014).

These explanations make sense, but it is not yet entirely clear that depression is a significantly worse problem in late adulthood than it is earlier in life. Some studies suggest that the rate of depression actually may be lower during late adulthood. One reason for this contradictory finding is that there may be two kinds of depression in older adulthood: depression that continues from earlier stages of life and depression that occurs as a result of aging (Gatz, 1997).

It is not unusual for some elderly people to suffer from drug-induced psychological disorders brought about by combinations of drugs they may be taking for various medical conditions. Because of changes in metabolism, a dose of a particular drug that would be appropriate for a 25-year-old might be much too high for a 75-year-old. The effects of drug interactions can be subtle, and they can manifest themselves in a variety of psychological symptoms, such as drug intoxication or anxiety. Because of these possibilities, older people who take medications must be careful to inform their physicians and pharmacists of every drug they take. They should also avoid medicating themselves with over-the-counter drugs because a combination of nonprescription and prescription drugs may be dangerous or even deadly.

dementia
the most common mental disorder of the elderly, it covers several diseases, each of which includes serious memory loss accompanied by declines in other mental functioning

The most common mental disorder of elderly people is **dementia**, a broad category of serious memory loss accompanied by declines in other mental functioning, which encompasses a number of diseases. Although dementia has many causes, the symptoms are similar: declining memory, lessened intellectual abilities, and impaired judgment. The chances of experiencing dementia increase with age. Less than 2 percent of people between 60 and 65 years are diagnosed with dementia, but the percentages double for every 5-year period past 65. There are some ethnic differences, too, with African Americans and Hispanics showing higher levels of dementia than Caucasians (Alzheimer's Association, 2017).

The most common form of dementia is Alzheimer's disease. Alzheimer's represents one of the most serious mental health problems faced by the aging population.

Alzheimer's disease
a progressive brain disorder that produces loss of memory and confusion

ALZHEIMER'S DISEASE. **Alzheimer's disease**, a progressive brain disorder that produces loss of memory and confusion, leads to the deaths of 100,000 people in the United States each year. One in 10 people age 65 and older has Alzheimer's; 19 percent of those age 75 to 84 have disease, and nearly half of people over age 85 are affected by the disease. Unless a cure is found, some 14 million people will be victims of Alzheimer's by 2050—more than three times the current number (Park et al., 2014; Alzheimer's Association, 2017).

The symptoms of Alzheimer's disease develop gradually. Generally, the first sign is unusual forgetfulness. A person may stop at a grocery store several times during the week, forgetting that he or she has already done the shopping. People may also have trouble recalling particular words during conversations. At first, recent memories are affected, and then older memories fade. Eventually, people with the disease are totally confused, unable to speak intelligibly or to recognize even their closest family and friends. In the final stages of the disease, they lose voluntary control of their muscles and are bedridden. Because victims of the disorder are initially aware that their memories are failing and often understand quite well the future course of the disease, they may suffer from anxiety, fear, and depression—emotions not difficult to understand, given the grim prognosis.

Biologically, Alzheimer's occurs when production of *beta amyloid precursor protein*—a protein that normally helps the production and growth of neurons—goes awry, producing large clumps of cells called plaque that trigger inflammation and deterioration of nerve cells. The brain shrinks, and several areas of the hippocampus and frontal and temporal lobes show deterioration. Furthermore, certain neurons die, which leads to a shortage of various neurotransmitters, such as acetylcholine (Wolfe, 2006; Medeiros et al., 2007; Bredesen, 2009).

Figure 17-7 A Different Brain?

Brain scans show differences between the brains of those with Alzheimer's disease and those who do not suffer from it.

(**Source:** Booheimer et al., 2000.)

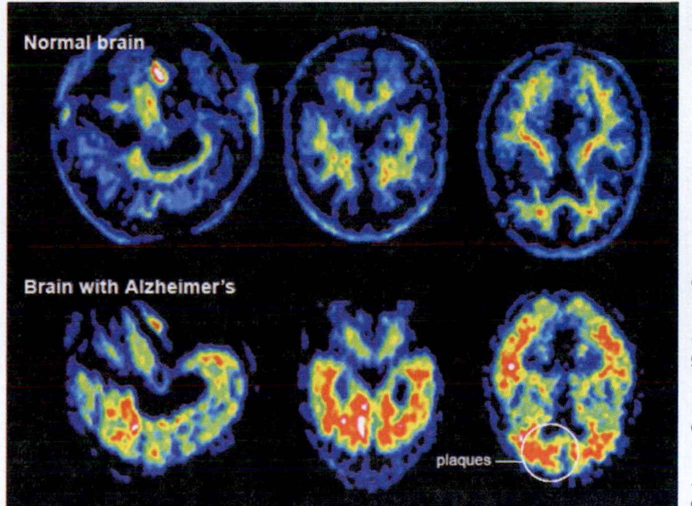

Science Source/Science Source

Although the physical changes in the brain that produce the symptoms of Alzheimer's are clear (see Figure 17-7), what is not known is what triggers the problem in the first place. Several explanations have been advanced. For instance, as we saw in Chapter 2, genetics clearly plays a role, with some families showing a much higher incidence of Alzheimer's than others. In certain families, half the children appear to inherit the disease from their parents. Furthermore, years before the actual symptoms of Alzheimer's emerge, people who are genetically at high risk for the disease show differences in brain functioning (Coon et al., 2007; Thomas & Fenech, 2007; Baulac et al., 2009).

Most evidence suggests that Alzheimer's is an inherited disorder, but nongenetic factors, such as high blood pressure or diet, may increase susceptibility to the disease. In one cross-cultural study, poor black residents in a Nigerian town were less likely to develop Alzheimer's than a comparable sample of African Americans living in the United States. The researchers speculate that variations in diet between the two groups—the residents of Nigeria ate mainly vegetables—might account for the differences in the Alzheimer's rates (Lahiri et al., 2007; Fuso et al., 2012; Roussotte et al., 2014).

Other explanations for the disease have also been investigated. For example, scientists are studying certain kinds of viruses, dysfunctions of the immune system, and hormone imbalances that may produce the disease. Other studies have found that lower levels of linguistic ability in the early 20s are associated with declines in cognitive capabilities due to Alzheimer's much later in life (Alisky, 2007; Carbone et al., 2014).

At the present time, there is no cure for Alzheimer's disease; treatment deals only with the symptoms. While understanding of the causes of Alzheimer's is incomplete, several drug treatments for Alzheimer's appear promising, although none is effective in the long term. The most promising drugs are related to the loss of the neurotransmitter acetylcholine (Ach) that occurs in some forms of Alzheimer's disease. Donepezil (Aricept) and Rivastigmine (Exelon) are among the most common drugs prescribed, and they alleviate some of the symptoms of the disease. Still, they are effective in only half of Alzheimer's patients, and only temporarily (Gauthier & Scheltens, 2009).

Other drugs being studied include anti-inflammatory drugs, which may reduce the brain inflammation that occurs in Alzheimer's. In addition, the chemicals in vitamins C and E are being tested, since some evidence suggests that people who take such vitamins are at lower risk for developing the disorder. Still, at this point, it is clear that no drug treatment is truly effective (Alzheimer's Association, 2004; Mohajeri & Leuba, 2009; Sabbagh, 2009)

As victims lose the ability to feed and clothe themselves, or even to control bladder and bowel functions, they must be cared for 24 hours a day. Because such care is typically impossible for even the most dedicated families, most Alzheimer's victims end their lives

Development in Your Life

Caring for People with Alzheimer's Disease

Alzheimer's disease is one of the most difficult illnesses to deal with, as a friend or loved one progressively deteriorates both mentally and physically. However, several steps can be taken to help both patient and caregiver deal with Alzheimer's:

- Make patients feel secure in their home environments by keeping them occupied in everyday tasks of living as long as possible.
- Provide labels for everyday objects, furnish calendars and detailed but simple lists, and give oral reminders of time and place.
- Keep clothing simple: Provide clothes with few zippers and buttons, and lay them out in the order in which they should be put on.
- Put bathing on a schedule. People with Alzheimer's may be afraid of falling and of hot water, and may therefore avoid needed bathing.
- Prevent people with the disease from driving. Although patients often want to continue driving, their accident rate is high—some 20 times higher than average.
- Monitor the use of the telephone. Alzheimer patients who answer the phone have been victimized by agreeing to requests of telephone salespeople and investment counselors.
- Provide opportunities for exercise, such as a daily walk. This prevents muscle deterioration and stiffness.
- Caregivers should remember to take time off. Although caring for an Alzheimer's patient can be a full-time chore, caregivers need to lead their own lives. Seek out support from community service organizations.
- Call or write the Alzheimer's Association, which can provide support and information. The Association can be reached at 225 N. Michigan Ave. FL. 17, Chicago, IL 60601-7633; Tel. 1-800-272-3900; http://www.alz.org.

in nursing homes. Patients with Alzheimer's make up some two-thirds of those in nursing homes (Prigerson, 2003).

People who care for the victims of Alzheimer's often become secondary victims of the disease. It is easy to become frustrated, angry, and exhausted by the demands of Alzheimer's patients, whose needs may be overpowering. In addition to the physical chore of providing total care, caregivers face the loss of a loved one, who not only is visibly deteriorating but can also act emotionally unstable and even fly into rages. The burdens of caring for a person with Alzheimer's can be overwhelming (Ott, Sanders, & Kelber, 2007; Sanders et al., 2008; Iavarone et al., 2014). (Also see the *Development in Your Life* box.)

Wellness in Late Adulthood: The Relationship Between Aging and Illness

LO 17.6 Summarize how wellness can be maintained in old age.

Is getting sick an inevitable part of old age? Not necessarily. Whether an older person is ill or well depends less on age than on a variety of factors, including genetic predisposition, past and present environmental factors, and psychological factors.

Certain diseases, such as cancer and heart disease, have a clear genetic component. Some families have a higher incidence of breast cancer, for instance, than others. At the same time, though, a genetic predisposition does not automatically mean that a person will get a particular illness. People's lifestyles—whether or not they smoke, the nature of their diets, their exposure to cancer-causing agents, such as sunlight or asbestos—may raise or lower their chances of coming down with such a disease.

Furthermore, economic well-being also plays a role. For instance, as at all stages of life, living in poverty restricts access to medical care. Even relatively well-off people may have difficulties finding affordable health care. For example, the average 65-year-old couple retiring in 2013 is estimated to need $220,000 to pay for medical costs through their retirement. Furthermore, older people spend almost 13 percent of their total expenditures on health care, more than two times what younger individuals spend (Administration on Aging, 2003; Wild et al., 2014).

Finally, psychological factors play an important role in determining people's susceptibility to illness—and ultimately their likelihood of death. For example, having a sense of control over one's environment, even in terms of making choices involving everyday matters, leads to a better psychological state and superior health outcomes (Taylor, 1991; Levy et al., 2002).

PROMOTING GOOD HEALTH. People can do specific things to enhance their physical well-being—as well as their longevity—during old age. It is probably no surprise that the right things to do are no different from what people should do during the rest of the life span: Eat a proper diet, exercise, and avoid obvious threats to health, such as smoking (see Figure 17-8). Medical and social services providers who work with elderly people have begun to emphasize the importance of these lifestyle choices for older adults. The goal of many such professionals has become not just to keep older adults from illness and death, but to extend people's *active life spans*, the amount of time they remain healthy and able to enjoy their lives (Sawatzky & Naimark, 2002; Gavin & Myers, 2003; Katz & Marshall, 2003).

Sometimes, however, older people experience difficulties that prevent them from following even these simple guidelines. For instance, varying estimates suggest that between 15 and 50 percent of elderly people do not have adequate nutrition, and several million experience hunger every day (deCastro, 2002; Donini, Savina, & Cannella, 2003; Strohl, Bednar, & Longley, 2012).

The reasons for such malnutrition and hunger are varied. Some elderly people are too poor to purchase adequate food, and some are too frail to shop or cook for themselves. Others feel little motivation to prepare and eat proper meals, particularly if they live alone or are depressed. For those who have experienced significant declines in taste and smell sensitivity, eating well-prepared food may no longer be enjoyable. And some older people may never have eaten well-balanced meals in earlier periods of their lives (Vandenberghe-Descamps et al., 2017).

Obtaining sufficient exercise may also prove problematic for older persons. Physical activity increases muscle strength and flexibility, reduces blood pressure and the risk of heart attack, and produces several other benefits, but many older people do not get

Figure 17-8 Benefits of Exercise and a Healthy Diet

A study of more than 7,000 men, age 40 to 59, found that not smoking, keeping weight down, and exercising regularly can greatly reduce the risk of coronary heart disease, stroke, and diabetes. Although the study included only men, a healthy lifestyle can benefit women too. (To find your body mass index [BMI], multiply your weight in pounds by 705. Divide the result by your height in inches, then divide by your height again.)

(**Source:** Based on Wannamethee et al., 1998.)

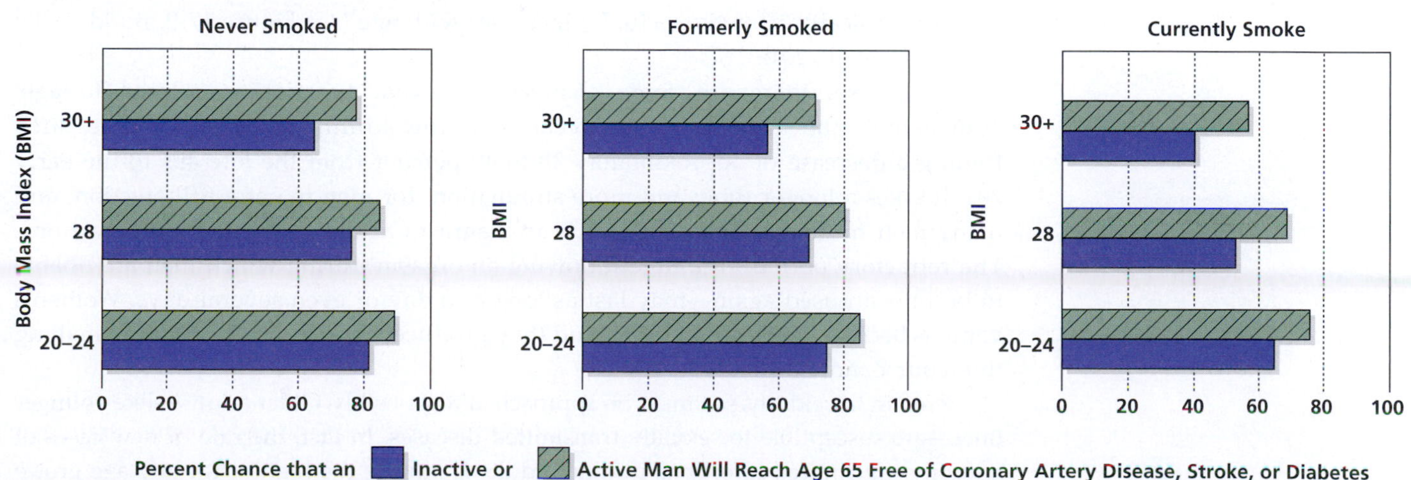

Artfamily/Fotolia

Economic well-being and diet are important factors in the relationship between aging and illness.

sufficient exercise to experience any of these benefits (Hardy & Grogan, 2009; Kamijo et al., 2009; Kelley et al., 2009).

For instance, illness may prevent older adults from exercising, and even inclement weather during the winter may restrict a person's ability to get out of the house. Furthermore, problems can combine: A poor person with insufficient money to eat properly may as a consequence have little energy to put into physical activity (Traywick & Schoenberg, 2008; Logsdon et al., 2009).

Sexuality in Old Age: Use It or Lose It

LO 17.7 Describe how sexuality is affected by aging.

Do your grandparents have sex? Quite possibly, yes. Although the answer may surprise you, increasing evidence suggests that people are sexually active well into their 80s and 90s. This happens in spite of societal stereotypes suggesting that it is somehow improper for two 75-year-olds to have sexual intercourse, and even worse for a 75-year-old to masturbate. Such negative attitudes are a function of societal expectations in the United States. In many other cultures, elderly people are expected to remain sexually active, and in some societies, people are expected to become less inhibited as they age (Hillman, 2000; Lindau et al., 2007; De Conto, 2017).

Two major factors determine whether an elderly person will engage in sexual activity. One is good physical and mental health. People need to be physically healthy and to hold generally positive attitudes about sexual activity in order for sex to take place. The other determinant of sexual activity during old age is previous regular sexual activity. The longer elderly men and women have gone without sexual activity, the less likely is future sexual activity. "Use it or lose it" seems an accurate description of sexual functioning in older people. Sexual activity can and often does continue throughout the life span. Furthermore, there's some intriguing evidence that having sex may have some unexpected side benefits: One study found that having sex regularly is associated with a lower risk of death (Henry & McNab, 2003; Huang et al., 2009; Hillman, 2012; McCarthy & Pierpaoli, 2015)!

Masturbation is the most common sexual practice in late adulthood. One survey found that 43 percent of men and 33 percent of women over age 70 masturbated. The average frequency for those who masturbated was once per week. Around two-thirds of married men and women had sex with their spouses, again averaging around once per week. In addition, the percentage of people who view their sexual partners as physically attractive actually increases with age (see Figure 17-9; Budd, 1999; Herbenick et al., 2010).

Of course, there are some changes in sexual functioning related to age. Testosterone, the male hormone, declines during adulthood, with some research finding a decrease of approximately 30 to 40 percent from the late 40s to the early 70s. It takes a longer time, and more stimulation, for men to get a full erection, and many men routinely take drugs such as Viagra to achieve and maintain erections. The refractory period—the time following an orgasm during which men are unable to become aroused again—may last as long as a day or even several days. Women's vaginas become thin and inelastic, and they produce less natural lubrication, making intercourse more difficult.

Even in the elderly, sex must be approached responsibly. Older adults—like younger ones—are susceptible to sexually transmitted diseases. In fact, the rate of new cases of sexually transmitted infections in older adults is among the highest for any age group (Seidman, 2003; National Institute of Aging, 2004).

Figure 17-9 Attractiveness over Time

More than 50 percent of Americans over age 45 find their partners attractive, and as time goes on, they find their partners more attractive.

(**Source:** AARP/Modern Maturity Sexuality Study, 1999.)

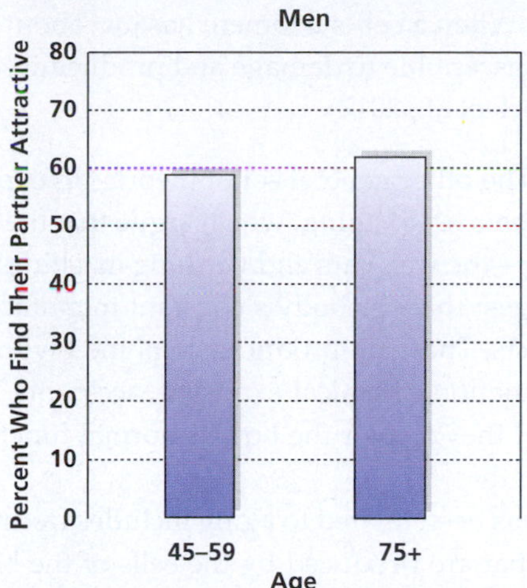

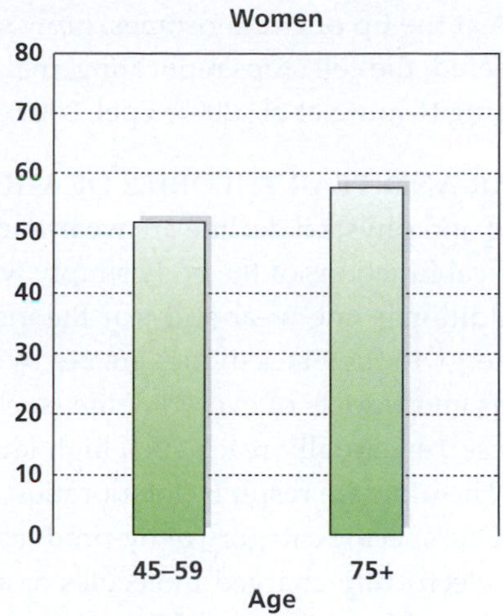

Approaches to Aging: Why Is Death Inevitable?

LO 17.8 Identify the factors involved with the life span and the causes of death.

Hovering over our discussion of health in late adulthood is the specter of death. At some point, no matter how healthy we have been throughout life, we know that we will experience physical declines and that life will end. But why?

There are two major approaches to explaining why we undergo physical deterioration and death: genetic programming theories and wear-and-tear theories.

GENETIC PROGRAMMING THEORIES OF AGING. **Genetic programming theories of aging** suggest that human DNA genetic code contains a built-in time limit for the reproduction of human cells. After a certain amount of time has gone by—determined genetically—the cells are no longer able to divide, and the individual begins to deteriorate (Rattan, Kristensen, & Clark, 2006).

genetic programming theories of aging
theories that suggest that human DNA genetic code contains a built-in time limit for the reproduction of human cells

There are actually several variations of the genetic programming approach. One is that the genetic material contains a "death gene" that is programmed to direct the body to deteriorate and die. Researchers who take an evolutionary viewpoint, described first in Chapter 1, suggest that survival of the species would require that people live long enough to reproduce. A long life span after the reproductive years, however, would be unnecessary. According to this view, genetically related diseases that tend to strike later in life would continue to exist because they allow people time to have children, thus passing along genes that are "programmed" to cause diseases and death.

A variation of the genetic programming view is that the cells of the body can only duplicate a certain number of times. Throughout our lives, new cells are being made, through cell duplication, to repair and replenish all of our various tissues and organs. According to this view, however, the genetic instructions for running the body can be read only a certain number of times before they become illegible. (Think of a computer disk containing a program that is used over and over and eventually just gives out.) As these instructions become incomprehensible, cells stop reproducing. Because the body is

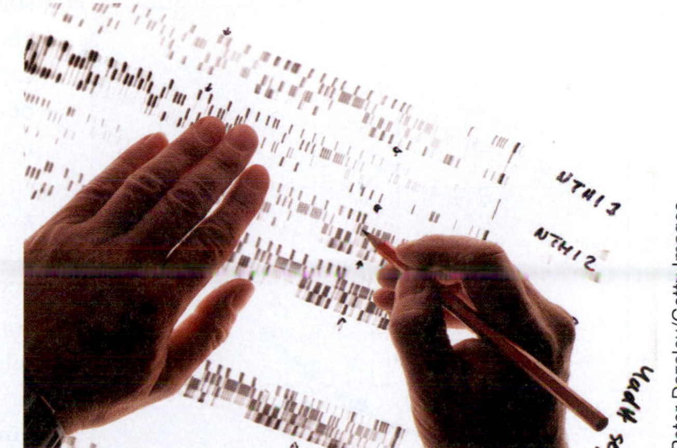
Peter Dazeley/Getty Images

According to genetic preprogramming theories of aging, our DNA contains a built-in limit on the length of life.

not being renewed at the same rate, people begin to experience bodily deterioration and ultimately death (Hayflick, 2007; Thoms, Kuschel, & Emmert, 2007).

Evidence for the genetic programming theory comes from research showing that when human cells are permitted to divide in the laboratory, they can do so successfully only around 50 times. Each time they divide, *telomeres*, which are tiny, protective areas of DNA at the tip of chromosomes, grow shorter. When a cell's telomere has just about disappeared, the cell stops replicating, making it susceptible to damage and producing signs of aging (Chung et al., 2007; Epel, 2009; Murdock et al., 2017).

wear-and-tear theories of aging
theories that the mechanical functions of the body simply wear out with age

WEAR-AND-TEAR THEORIES OF AGING. The other general set of theories to explain aging and physical decline are **wear-and-tear theories of aging**, which argue that the mechanical functions of the body simply wear out—the way cars and washing machines do. In addition, some wear-and-tear theorists suggest that the body's constant manufacture of energy to fuel its activities creates by-products. These by-products, combined with the toxins and threats of everyday life (such as radiation, chemical exposure, accidents, and disease), eventually reach such high levels that they impair the body's normal functioning. The ultimate result is deterioration and death.

One specific category of by-products that has been related to aging includes free radicals, electrically charged molecules or atoms that are produced by the cells of the body. Because of their electrical charge, free radicals may cause negative effects on other cells of the body. A great deal of research suggests that oxygen free radicals may be implicated in a number of age-related problems, including cancer, heart disease, and diabetes (Sierra, 2006; Hayflick, 2007; Sonnen et al., 2009).

RECONCILING THE THEORIES OF AGING. Genetic programming theories and wear-and-tear theories make different suggestions about the inevitability of death. Genetic programming theories suggest that there is a built-in time limit to life—it's programmed in the genes, after all. Wear-and-tear theories, particularly those that focus on the toxins that are built up during the course of life, paint a somewhat more optimistic view. They suggest that if a means can be found to eliminate the toxins produced by the body and by exposure to the environment, aging might well be slowed. For example, certain genes seem to slow aging and increase people's ability to withstand age-related diseases (Ghazi, Henis-Korenblit, & Kenyon, 2009; Aldwin & Igarashi, 2015).

life expectancy
the average age of death for members of a population

We don't know which class of theories provides the more accurate account of the reasons for aging. Each is supported by some research, and each seems to explain certain aspects of aging. Ultimately, then, just why the body begins to deteriorate and die remains something of a mystery (Horiuchi, Finch, & Mesle, 2003).

Figure 17-10 Living to Age 100

If increases in life expectancy continue, it may be a common occurrence for people to live to be 100. What implications does this have for society?

(**Source:** United Nations, Department of Economic and Social Affairs, "World Population Prospects: 2015 Revision," cited in Stepler, 2016).

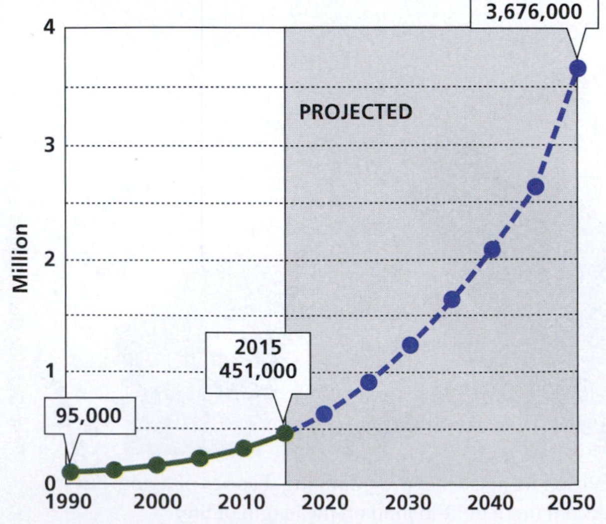

LIFE EXPECTANCY: HOW LONG HAVE I GOT? Although the reasons for deterioration and death are not fully apparent, conclusions about average life expectancy can be stated quite clearly: Most of us can expect to live into old age. The **life expectancy**—the average age of death for members of a population—of a person born in 2010, for instance, is 78 years.

Average life expectancy has been steadily increasing. In 1776, average life expectancy in the United States was just 35. By the early 1900s, it had risen to 47. And in only four decades, from 1950 to 1990, it increased from 68 to over 75 years. Predictions are that it will continue to rise steadily, possibly reaching age 80 by the year 2050 (also see Figure 17-10).

There are several reasons for the steady increase in life expectancy over the past 200 years. Health and sanitation conditions are generally better, with many diseases, such as smallpox, wiped out entirely. Other diseases that used to kill people at early ages, such as measles and mumps, are now better controlled through vaccines and preventive measures. People's working conditions are generally better, and many products are safer than they once were. As we've seen, many people are becoming aware of lifestyle choices, such as keeping their weight down, eating lots of fresh fruit and vegetables, and exercising, which can extend their lives. As environmental factors continue to improve, we can predict that life expectancy will continue to increase. Also, as we've seen, many people are becoming aware of the importance of lifestyle choices for extending not just the length of their lives, but their active life spans, the years they spend in health and enjoyment of life.

One major question for gerontologists is just how far the life span can be increased. The most common answer is that the upper limit of life hovers around 120 years, the age reached by Jeanne Calment, who was the oldest person in the world until she died in 1997 at age 122. Living beyond this age would probably require some major genetic alterations in humans, because every species seems to have biological constraints that keep them from growing old beyond a particular life span (see Figure 17-11). Furthermore, there

Figure 17-11 Animal Life Spans

Maximum recorded life spans for animals found in the wild.

(**Source:** Based on Kirkwood, 2010).

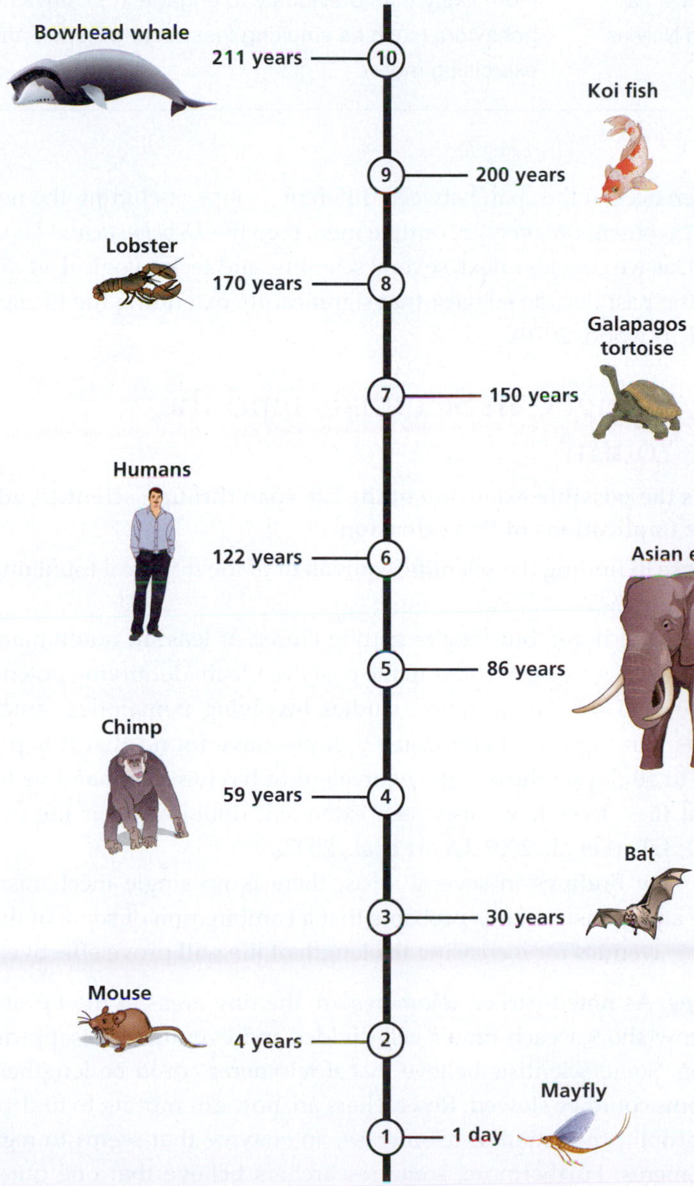

Bowhead whale
211 years — 10
Koi fish
9 — 200 years
Lobster
170 years — 8
Galapagos tortoise
7 — 150 years
Humans
122 years — 6
Asian elephant
5 — 86 years
Chimp
59 years — 4
Bat
3 — 30 years
Mouse
4 years — 2
Mayfly
1 — 1 day

Developmental Diversity and Your Life

Gender Differences in Average Life Expectancy: Why Do Women Live Longer Than Men?

The average life expectancy of a male in the United States is 76.9 years. In comparison, a female has a life expectancy of 81.6, a difference of almost 5 years. Similar discrepancies, favoring females, are found throughout the world. Why?

It turns out that there are several reasons for these discrepancies. Consider, for example, the gender gap in life expectancy, which is particularly pronounced. Across the industrialized world, women live longer than men by some 4 to 10 years. This female advantage begins just after conception: Although slightly more males are conceived, males are more likely to die during the prenatal period, infancy, and childhood. Consequently, by age 30 there are roughly equal numbers of men and women. But by age 65, 84 percent of females and only 70 percent of males are still alive. For those over 85, the gender gap widens: For every male, 2.57 women are still alive (United Nations World Population Prospects, 2006; *World Factbook*, 2012).

There are several explanations for the gender gap. One is that the naturally higher levels of the hormones estrogen and progesterone in women provide some protection from diseases, such as heart attacks. It is also possible that women engage in healthier behavior during their lives, such as eating well. However, no conclusive evidence supports any of these explanations fully (DiGiovanna, 1994; Emslie & Hunt, 2008).

Whatever its cause, the gender gap has continued to increase. During the early part of the 20th century, there was only a 2-year difference in favor of women, but in the 1980s, this gap grew to 7 years. The size of the gap now seems to have leveled off, largely because men are more likely than previously to engage in positive health behaviors (such as smoking less, eating better, and exercising more).

are persistent differences in life span between different groups, including the nearly universal finding that women, on average, outlive men. (See the *Developmental Diversity and Your Life* box.) Still, as we consider next, several scientific and technological advances that have occurred in the past decade suggest that significantly extending the life span is not an impossibility (Kirkwood, 2010).

Postponing Aging: Can Scientists Find the Fountain of Youth?

LO 17.9 Discuss the possible extension of the life span through scientific advances and the implications of this extension.

Are researchers close to finding the scientific equivalent of the mythical fountain of youth that can postpone aging?

They haven't found it yet, but they're getting closer, at least in nonhuman species. Researchers have made significant strides in the past decade in identifying potential ways that aging may be held off. For instance, studies involving nematodes—microscopic, transparent worms that typically live for just 9 days—have found that it is possible to extend their lives to 50 days, which is the equivalent of having a human live to the age of 420 years. Fruit flies' lives have also been extended, doubling their life expectancy (Whitbourne, 2001; Libert et al., 2007; Ocorr et al., 2007).

According to new findings in several areas, there is no single mechanism that is likely to postpone aging. Instead, it is probable that a combination of some of the following most promising avenues for increasing the length of life will prove effective:

- *Telomere therapy.* As noted earlier, telomeres are the tiny areas at the tip of chromosomes that grow shorter each time a cell divides and eventually disappear, ending cell replication. Some scientists believe that if telomeres could be lengthened, age-related problems could be slowed. Researchers are now attempting to find genes that control the natural production of telomerase, an enzyme that seems to regulate the length of telomeres. Furthermore, some researchers believe that one can lengthen telomeres, and hence lengthen life, by following good health practices (Chung et al., 2007; Reynolds, 2016; Blackburn & Epel, 2017).

- *Drug therapy.* Scientists have discovered that the drug rapamycin could extend life in mice by 14 percent by interfering with the activity of the protein mTOR. This finding suggests the drug may have an effect on expanding the life span and improving memory. Another substance, GDF11, appears to restore muscle strength and slow deterioration of neurons, at least in mice (Santos et al., 2011; Stipp, 2012; Katsimpardi et al., 2014; Zhang et al., 2014).
- *Unlocking longevity genes.* Certain genes control the body's ability to overcome environmental challenges, making it better able to overcome physical adversity. If those genes can be harnessed, they may provide a way of increasing the life span. One particularly promising family of genes is sirtuins, which may regulate and promote longer life (Sinclair & Guarente, 2006; Glatt et al., 2007; Fujitsuka et al., 2016).
- *Reducing free radicals through antioxidant drugs.* As mentioned earlier, free radicals are unstable molecules that are a by-product of normal cell functioning; free radicals may drift through the body, damaging other cells and leading to aging. Although antioxidant drugs designed to reduce the number of free radicals have not yet been proven effective, some scientists think that they may eventually be perfected. Furthermore, some speculate it may be possible to insert in human cells genes that produce enzymes that act as antioxidants. In the meantime, nutritionists urge a diet rich in antioxidant vitamins, which are found in fruits and vegetables (Kedziora-Kornatowska et al., 2007; Haleem et al., 2008; Kolling & Knopf, 2014).
- *Restricting calories.* For at least the past decade, researchers have known that laboratory rats who are fed an extremely low-calorie diet, one that provides 30 to 50 percent of their normal intake, often live 30 percent longer than better-fed rats, provided that they obtain all the vitamins and minerals that they require. The reason appears to be that fewer free radicals are produced in the hungry rats. Researchers hope to develop drugs that mimic the effects of calorie restriction without forcing people to feel hungry all the time (Mattson, 2003; Ingram, Young, & Mattison, 2007; Cuervo, 2008).
- *The bionic solution: replacing worn-out organs.* Heart transplants, liver transplants, lung transplants: We live in an age where the removal of damaged or diseased organs and their replacement with better-functioning ones seems nearly routine.

However, despite significant advances in organ transplantation, transplants frequently fail because the body rejects the foreign tissue. To overcome this problem, some researchers suggest that replacement organs can be grown from a recipient's cloned cells, thereby solving the rejection problem. In an even more radical advance, genetically engineered cells from nonhumans that do not evoke rejection could be cloned, harvested, and transplanted into people who require transplants. Finally, it is possible that technical advances permitting the development of artificial organs that can completely replace diseased or damaged ones will become common (Cascalho, Ogle, & Platt, 2006; Kwant et al., 2007; Li & Zhu, 2007).

From *a health-care professional's* perspective

Given what you've learned about explanations of life expectancy, what might you do to try to extend your own life?

Unfortunately, all these possibilities for the extension of the human life span remain unproven. Furthermore, a more immediate problem to solve is the reduction in the significant disparities in life expectancies between members of different racial and ethnic groups, which we discuss in the following *Developmental Diversity and Your Life* segment.

Developmental Diversity and Your Life

Racial and Ethnic Differences in Life Expectancy

- The average white child born in the United States is likely to live 78 years. The average African American child is likely to live 3.4 years less.
- A child born in Japan has a life expectancy of more than 85 years; for a child born in Chad, life expectancy is just over 50 years (*World Factbook*, 2017).

Such racial and ethnic differences are troubling. They point out the disparities in socioeconomic well-being of various groups in the United States, illustrated in Figure 17-12.

Why does this gap exist? In many cases, economic and health factors explain the gap. For example, in the case of the black population in the United States, certain diseases that lead to death are more prevalent than in the white population. The rate of heart disease, cancer, and diabetes is higher in blacks than whites. And economic disparities often lead blacks to receive medical care that is inferior to that of whites, also pushing down life expectancy.

The good news is that the gap in life expectancy is decreasing. The suicide rate for black men has declined, unlike that of whites and other racial groups. Furthermore, mortality among black infants has declined, and births to teenage mothers (who often have higher infant mortality rates) have declined faster for blacks than whites. There also has been a decline in homicides, which have fallen faster for blacks than for whites (Tavernise, 2016).

Although racial disparities in life span may be declining for blacks in the United States, the same is not true for other racial and ethnic minority groups—especially Native Americans. For example, the county in which the Pine Ridge Native American reservation is located has the lowest life expectancy in the country—66.8 years, and some 20 years lower than people living in the counties with the highest life expectancy in the country (Dwyer-Lindgren et al., 2017).

There are also significant differences in life expectancy globally. Specifically, there are wide life expectancy discrepancies related to health-care access, child-care services, prevalence of smoking and other unhealthy practices, hospital capacity, and a host of additional socioeconomic factors. Until such factors are addressed, disparities in life span are likely to persist.

Figure 17-12 Life Expectancy of African Americans and Whites

Both male and female African Americans have a shorter life expectancy than male and female Caucasians. Are the reasons for this genetic, cultural, or both?

(**Source:** Kochanek, Arias, & Anderson, 2013.)

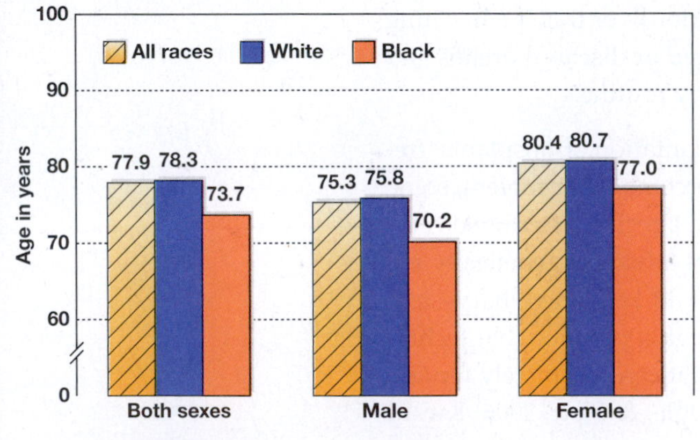

Liba Taylor/Robert Harding

A child born in Japan has a life expectancy of 83 years. In countries like Gambia, people have an average life expectancy of 45.

Module 17.2 Review

LO 17.5 Describe the general state of health of older people and the disorders to which they are susceptible.

Although most older people are healthy, the incidence of some serious diseases rises in old age, and most people have at least one chronic ailment before they die. Older people are susceptible to psychological disorders, such as depression. The most prevalent and damaging brain disorder among older people is Alzheimer's disease.

LO 17.6 Summarize how wellness can be maintained in old age.

Proper diet, exercise, and avoidance of health risks can lead to prolonged wellness during old age.

LO 17.7 Describe how sexuality is affected by aging.

Sexuality can continue throughout the life span in healthy adults. People who enjoy sex before old age are most likely to continue doing so as they age further.

LO 17.8 Identify the factors involved with the life span and the causes of death.

Whether death is caused by genetic programming or by general physical wear and tear is an unresolved question. Life expectancy, which has risen for centuries, varies with gender, race, and ethnicity.

LO 17.9 Discuss the possible extension of the life span through scientific advances and the implications of this extension.

New approaches to increasing life expectancy include telomere therapy, reducing free radicals through antioxidant drugs, restricting caloric intake, and replacing worn-out organs.

Journal Writing Prompt

Applying Lifespan Development: In what ways is socioeconomic status related to wellness in old age and to life expectancy?

Cognitive Development in Late Adulthood

Three women were talking about the inconveniences of growing old.

"Sometimes," one of them confessed, "when I go to my refrigerator, I can't remember if I'm putting something in or taking something out."

"Oh, that's nothing," said the second woman. "There are times when I find myself at the foot of the stairs wondering if I'm going up or if I've just come down."

"Well, my goodness!" exclaimed the third woman. "I'm certainly glad I don't have any problems like that"—and she knocked on wood. "Oh," she said, starting up out of her chair, "there's someone at the door." (Dent, 1984, p. 38)

This old joke sums up the stereotypic view of aging. In fact, not too long ago many gerontologists would have subscribed to the view that older people are befuddled and forgetful.

Today, however, the view has changed dramatically. Researchers no longer see the cognitive abilities of older people as inevitably declining. Overall intellectual ability and specific cognitive skills, such as memory and problem solving, are more likely to remain strong. With the appropriate practice and exposure to certain kinds of environmental stimuli, cognitive skills can actually improve.

Intelligence in Older People

LO 17.10 Describe how well older adults function cognitively.

The notion that older people become less cognitively adept initially arose from misinterpretations of research evidence. As we first noted in Chapter 15, early research on how intelligence changed as a result of aging typically drew a simple comparison between younger and older people's performance on the same IQ test, using traditional cross-sectional experimental methods. For example, a group of 30-year-olds and a group of 70-year-olds might have been given the same test and had their performance compared.

Such a procedure, however, presents several drawbacks, as we noted in Chapter 1. One is that cross-sectional methods do not take into account *cohort effects*—influences attributable to growing up in a particular era. For example, if the younger group—because of when they grew up—has more education, on average, than the older group, we might expect the younger group to do better on the test for that reason alone. Furthermore, because some traditional intelligence tests include timed portions or reaction-time components, the slower reaction time of older people might account for their inferior performance.

To try to overcome such problems, developmental psychologists turned to longitudinal studies, which followed the same individuals for many years. However, because of repeated exposure to the same test, subjects may, over time, become familiar with the test items. Furthermore, participants in longitudinal studies may move away, stop participating, become ill, or die, leaving a smaller and possibly more cognitively skilled group of people. In short, longitudinal studies have their drawbacks, and their use initially led to some erroneous conclusions about older people.

RECENT FINDINGS ABOUT INTELLIGENCE IN OLDER PEOPLE. More recent research has attempted to overcome the drawbacks of both cross-sectional and longitudinal methods. In what is probably the most ambitious—and still ongoing—study of intelligence in older people, developmental psychologist K. Warner Schaie has employed sequential methods. As we discussed in Chapter 1, *sequential studies* combine cross-sectional and longitudinal methods by examining several different age groups at a number of points in time.

In Schaie's massive study, a battery of tests of cognitive ability was given to a group of 500 randomly chosen individuals. The people belonged to different age groups, starting at age 20 and extending at 5-year intervals to age 70. The participants were tested, and continue to be tested, every 7 years, and more people are recruited to participate every year. At this point, more than 5,000 participants have been tested (Schaie, 1994; Schaie & Willis, 2011).

The study, along with other research, supports several generalizations about the nature of intellectual change during old age. Among the major changes are the following (Schaie, 1994; Craik & Salthouse, 1999; Salthouse, 2006):

- Some abilities gradually decline throughout adulthood, starting at around age 25, while others stay relatively steady (see Figure 17-13). There is no uniform pattern in adulthood of age-related changes across all intellectual abilities. In addition, as we discussed in Chapter 15, fluid intelligence (the ability to deal with new problems and situations) declines with age, while crystallized intelligence (the store of information, skills, and strategies that people have acquired) remains steady and in some cases actually improves (Baltes & Schaie, 1974; Schaie, 1993; Deary, 2014).
- For the average person, some cognitive declines are found in all abilities by age 67. However, these declines are minimal until the 80s. Even at age 81, less than half of the people tested showed consistent declines over the previous 7 years.

Figure 17-13 Changes in Intellectual Functioning

Although some intellectual abilities decline across adulthood, others stay relatively steady.

(**Source:** Schaie, 1994, p. 307.)

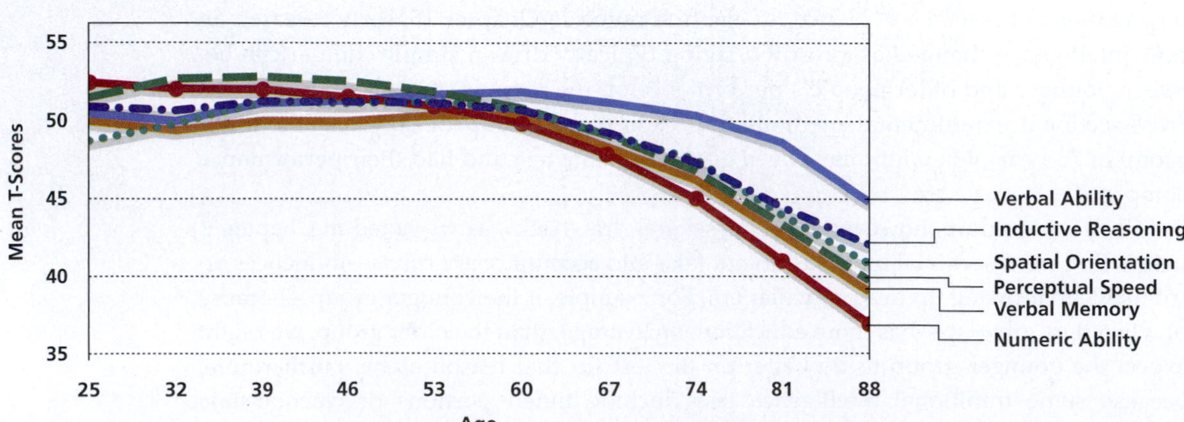

- Significant individual differences are found in the patterns of change in intelligence. Some people begin to show intellectual declines in their 30s, whereas others do not experience any decreases until they are in their 70s. In fact, around a third of those in their 70s score higher than the average young adult.
- Environmental and cultural factors play a role in intellectual decline. People with an absence of chronic disease, higher socioeconomic status (SES), involvement in an intellectually stimulating environment, a flexible personality style, marriage to a bright spouse, maintenance of good perceptual processing speed, and feelings of self-satisfaction with one's accomplishments in midlife or early old age showed less decline.

The relationship between environmental factors and intellectual skills suggests that with the proper stimulation, practice, and motivation, older people can maintain their mental abilities. Such **plasticity** in cognitive skills illustrates that there is nothing fixed about the changes that occur in intellectual abilities during late adulthood. In mental life, as in so many other areas of human development, the motto "use it or lose it" is quite fitting. Based on this principle, some developmentalists have sought to develop interventions to help older adults maintain their information processing skills, as we discuss in the *From Research to Practice* box.

plasticity
the degree to which a developing structure or behavior is susceptible to experience

From Research to Practice

Can We Train the Brain? Interventions to Improve Cognitive Functioning

Can we improve cognitive functioning through training? Well-designed research suggests that the answer is "yes," although many questions remain to be answered.

In a 10-year groundbreaking federally sponsored study of nearly 3,000 adults, the Advance Cognitive Training for Independent and Vital Elderly (ACTIVE), researchers looked at nearly 3,000 participants with a mean age of 74 at the start of the study. Participants received 10 cognitive training sessions lasting about an hour each, with each successive session becoming increasingly challenging. Three groups of participants received memory training (such as mnemonic strategies for memorizing word lists), reasoning training (such as finding the pattern in a series of numbers), or processing speed training (such as identifying objects that flashed briefly on a computer screen). Some participants also received "booster" training 1 year later and again 3 years later, each time consisting of four more sessions (Willis et al., 2006).

Remarkably, cognitive benefits were evident 5 years after the original training sessions. Compared to a control group that received no training, participants who received reasoning training performed 40 percent better on reasoning tasks at the 5-year mark, those who received memory training performed 75 percent better on memory tasks, and those who received speed training performed a staggering 300 percent better on speed tasks (Vedantam, 2006; Willis et al., 2006).

Even more surprising, some of the improvements were evident 10 years after the initial treatment. The improvements persisted both for those who received the reasoning and processing speed training. Furthermore, participants who received training reported that it was easier for them to manage their daily activities, such as handling their finances and medications, although standardized tests did not show a difference among groups (Rebok et al., 2013; Rebok et al., 2014; Parisi et al., 2017).

Overall, the findings are quite promising. Yet some caveats are in order. First, the results are from a single study, and much more research needs to be conducted. Second, the findings do not suggest that the use of commercially available apps that purport to improve memory and cognitive functioning, such as those sold by Lumosity or Clockwork Brain, are effective. In fact, the U.S. Federal Trade Commission rebuked Lumosity and ordered that rebates be sent to customers who were duped by exaggerated advertising claims. There is yet to be definitive evidence that apps actually produce greater cognitive ability in older adults—or younger ones, for that matter (Robbins, 2016).

It is also important to note that not all developmentalists believe the "use it or lose it" hypothesis. For example, developmental psychologist Timothy Salthouse suggests that the rate of true, underlying cognitive decline in late adulthood is unaffected by mental exercise. Instead, he argues that some people—the kind who have consistently engaged throughout their lives in high levels of mental activity, such as completing crossword puzzles—enter late adulthood with a "cognitive reserve." This cognitive reserve allows them to continue to perform at relatively high mental levels, even though underlying declines are actually happening. His hypothesis is controversial, though, and most developmentalists accept the hypothesis that mental exercise is beneficial (Salthouse, 2012, 2016).

Shared Writing Prompt

What advice would you give people in late adulthood about the steps they should take to avoid loss of cognitive skills?

Memory: Remembrance of Things Past—and Present

LO 17.11 Discuss the ways memory does and does not decline in late adulthood.

Composer Aaron Copland summed up what had happened to his memory in old age by remarking, "I have no trouble remembering everything that had happened 40 or 50 years ago—dates, places, faces, music. But I'm going to be 90 my next birthday, November 14th, and I find I can't remember what happened yesterday" (Time, 1980, p. 57). *Our confidence in the accuracy of Copland's analysis is strengthened by an error in his statement: On his next birthday, he would be only 80 years old!*

Is memory loss an inevitable part of aging? Not necessarily. For instance, cross-cultural research reveals that in societies where older people are held in relatively high esteem, such as in China, people are less likely to show memory losses than in societies where they are held in less regard. In such cultures, the more positive expectations regarding aging may lead people to think more positively about their own capabilities (Levy & Langer, 1994; Hess, Auman, & Colcombe, 2003).

From *a health-care professional's* perspective

How might cultural factors, such as the esteem in which a society holds its older members, work to affect an older person's memory performance?

Even when the declines in memory that can be directly traced to aging do occur, they are limited primarily to *episodic memories*, which relate to specific life experiences, such as recalling the year you first visited New York City. In contrast, other types of memory, such as *semantic memories* (general knowledge and facts, such as the fact that 2 + 2 = 4 or the name of the capital of North Dakota) and *implicit memories* (memories about which people are not consciously aware, such as how to ride a bike), are largely unaffected by age (Dixon & Cohen, 2003; Nilsson, 2003).

Memory capacities do change during old age. For instance, *short-term memory* slips gradually during adulthood until age 70, when the decline becomes more pronounced. The largest drop is for information that is presented quickly and verbally, such as when someone staffing a computer helpline rattles off a series of complicated steps for fixing a problem with a computer. In addition, information about things that are completely unfamiliar is more difficult to recall. For example, declines occur in memory for prose passages, names and faces of people, and even such critical information as the directions on a medicine label, possibly because new information is not registered and processed as effectively when it is initially encountered. Although these age-related changes are generally minor, and their impact on everyday life is negligible (because most elderly people automatically learn to compensate for them), memory losses are real (Carroll, 2000; Light, 2000; Carmichael et al., 2012; Klaming et al., 2017).

autobiographical memory
memories of information about one's own life

Monkey Business/Fotolia

Memory loss is not as common among Chinese elderly as it is in elderly people in the West. What are some factors that contribute to cultural differences in memory loss of the elderly?

AUTOBIOGRAPHICAL MEMORY: RECALLING THE DAYS OF OUR LIVES. When it comes to **autobiographical memory**, memories of information about one's own life, older people are subject to some of the same principles of recall as younger individuals. For instance, memory recall frequently follows the *Pollyanna principle*, in which pleasant memories are more likely to be recalled than unpleasant memories. Similarly, people tend to forget information about their past that is not congruent with the way they currently see themselves. They are more likely to make the material that they do recall "fit" their current conception of themselves, like a strict parent who forgets that she got drunk at her high school prom (Rubin & Greenberg, 2003; Skowronski, Walker, & Betz, 2003; Loftus, 2003).

Everyone tends to recall particular periods of life better than others. As can be seen in Figure 17-14, 70-year-olds tend to recall autobiographical details from their 20s and 30s best. In contrast, 50-year-olds are likely to have more memories of their teenage years and their 20s. In both cases, recall of earlier years is better than recall of somewhat more recent decades but not as complete as recall of very recent events (Rubin, 2000).

People in late adulthood also use information that they recall in different ways from younger individuals when they make decisions. For example, they process information more slowly and may make poorer judgments when complex rules are involved, and they focus more on emotional content than younger people. However, the accumulated knowledge and experience of people in late adulthood can compensate for their deficits, particularly if they are highly motivated to make good decisions (Peters et al., 2007).

Figure 17-14 Remembrances of Things Past

Recall of autobiographical memories varies with age, with 70-year-olds recalling details from their 20s and 30s best, and 50-year-olds recalling memories from their teenage years and 20s. People of both ages also recall more recent memories best of all.

(**Source:** Rubin, 1986.)

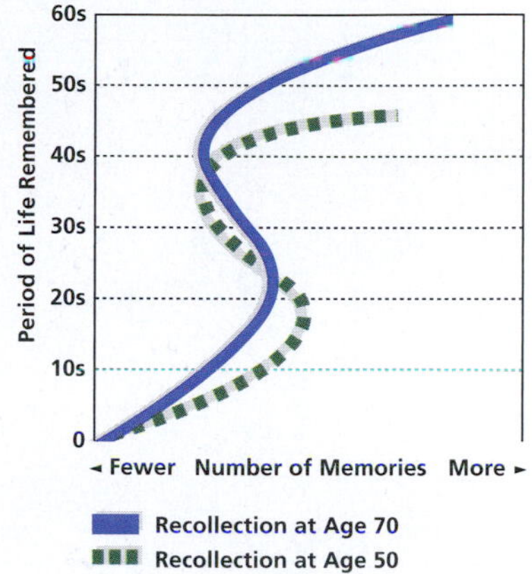

EXPLAINING MEMORY CHANGES IN OLD AGE. Explanations for apparent changes in memory among older people tend to focus on three main categories: environmental factors, information processing deficits, and biological factors.

- *Environmental factors*. Certain short-term factors that cause declines in memory may be found more frequently in older people. For example, older people are more apt than younger ones to take the kinds of prescription drugs that hinder memory. The lower performance of older people on memory tasks may be related to drug taking and not to age per se.

  Similarly, declines in memory can sometimes be traced to life changes in late adulthood. For instance, retirees, no longer facing intellectual challenges from their jobs, may become less practiced in using memory. Also, their motivation to recall information may be lower than previously, accounting for lower performance on tasks involving memory. They may also be less motivated than younger people to do their best in testing situations in experiments.

- *Information processing deficits*. Memory declines may also be linked to changes in information processing capabilities. For example, as we reach later adulthood, our ability to inhibit irrelevant information and thoughts may decrease, and these irrelevant thoughts interfere with successful problem solving. Similarly, the speed of information processing may decline, perhaps in a similar way to the slowing of reaction times that we discussed earlier, leading to the memory impairments observed in old age (Palfai, Halperin, & Hoyer, 2003; Salthouse, Atkinson, & Berish, 2003; Ising et al., 2014).

  Another information processing view suggests that older adults concentrate on new material less effectively than younger individuals and have greater difficulty paying att1ention to appropriate stimuli and organizing material in memory. This information processing deficit approach, which has received the most research support, suggests that memory declines are the result of changes in the ability to pay attention to and organize tasks involving memory skills. According to this view, older people also use less efficient processes to retrieve information from memory. These information processing deficits subsequently lead to declines in recall abilities (Castel & Craik, 2003; Luo & Craik, 2008, 2009).

- *Biological factors*. The last of the major approaches to explaining changes in memory during late adulthood concentrates on biological factors. According to this view, memory changes are a result of brain and body deterioration.

  For instance, declines in episodic memory may be related to the deterioration of the frontal lobes of the brain or a reduction in estrogen. Some studies also show a loss of cells in the hippocampus, which is critical to memory. However, specific sorts of memory deficits occur in many older people without any evidence of underlying biological deterioration (Eberling et al., 2004; Lye et al., 2004; Stevens et al., 2008).

Never Too Late

LO 17.12 Describe how learning and education continue in late adulthood.

Martha Tilden and Jim Hertz, both 71, loved the Metropolitan Opera House tour, the talk by the famous tenor, the ballet, and the lectures they attended during the "Lincoln Center Festival" trip they are just finishing.

Martha and Jim are veterans of Road Scholar (formerly Elderhostel), which has scrapped any suggestion of "elderness" or cheap student housing. All the educational programs they have taken have featured comfortable hotel or dorm rooms and mixed-age events. Now Martha and Jim are discussing their next program, trying to decide between a wildlife trip to Ontario and a "Building Bridges to Islam" program in Virginia.

More than 100,000 people enroll annually in thousands of classes organized by the Road Scholar program, the largest educational program for people in late adulthood. Represented on college campuses across the world, the Road Scholar movement is among the increasing evidence that intellectual growth and change continue to be important throughout people's lives, including in late adulthood. As we saw in our examination of research on cognitive training, exercising specific cognitive skills may be especially important to older adults who want to maintain their intellectual functioning (Simson, Wilson, & Harlow-Rosentraub, 2006; Li et al., 2017).

The popularity of programs such as Road Scholar is part of a growing trend among older people. Because the majority of older people have retired, they have time to pursue further education and delve into subjects in which they have always been interested.

Although not everyone is able to afford tuitions charged by Road Scholar, many public colleges provide free tuition to those 65 and older. In addition, some retirement communities are located at or near college campuses, such as those constructed by the University of Michigan and Penn State University (Powell, 2004; Forbes, 2014).

Although some elderly people are doubtful about their intellectual capabilities and consequently avoid regular college classes in which they compete with younger students, their concern is largely misplaced. Older adults often have no trouble maintaining their standing in rigorous college classes. Furthermore, professors and other students generally find the presence of older people, with their varied and substantial life experiences, a real educational benefit (Simpson, Simon, & Wilson, 2001; Simson, Wilson, & Harlow-Rosentraub, 2006).

TECHNOLOGY AND LEARNING IN LATE ADULTHOOD. One of the biggest generational divides involves the use of technology. People 65 and older are less likely to use technology than younger individuals, although the gap is not as large as it once was. Around 40 percent of older adults use smartphones, up from 18 percent in 2013. (see Figure 17-15).

Still, many older adults are not participating in the digital revolution. A third of adults above age 65 never use the Internet, and about half don't have home broadband. Moreover, the proportion of those who own smartphones is 42 percentage points lower than younger Americans (Anderson & Perrin, 2017).

Why are older people less likely to use technology? One reason is that they are less interested and motivated, in part because they are less likely to be working and therefore less in need of learning new technology skills. But another barrier is cognitive. For example, because fluid intelligence (the ability to deal with new problems and situations) shows some declines with age, this may impact the ability to learn new technology (Charness & Boot, 2009; Erickson & Johnson, 2011).

Figure 17-15 Technology Use and Age

Older individuals in the United States are less likely to use the Internet and have a broadband connection at home than those who are younger, although the gap is decreasing.

(**Source:** Anderson & Perrin, 2017.)

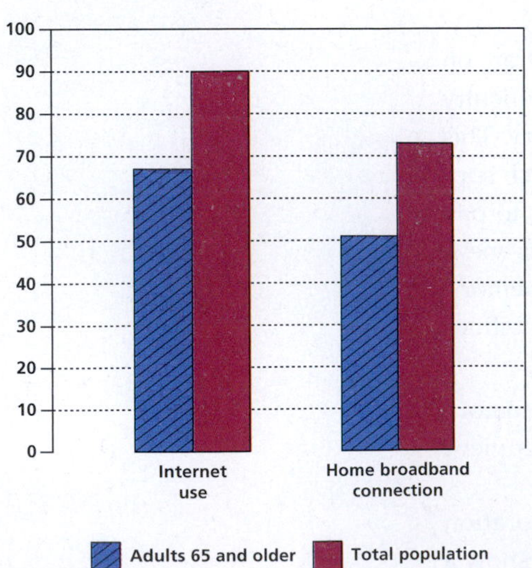

This hardly means that people in late adulthood are unable to learn to use technology. An increasing number of individuals are using e-mail and social networking sites, such as Facebook. It is likely that the lag in the adoption of technology between younger and older adults will continue to decline as technology use becomes even more widespread in the general society (Costa & Veloso, 2016).

Module 17.3 Review

LO 17.10 Describe how well older adults function cognitively.

Although some intellectual abilities gradually decline throughout adulthood, starting at around age 25, others stay relatively steady. The intellect retains considerable plasticity and can be maintained with stimulation, practice, and motivation.

LO 17.11 Discuss the ways memory does and does not decline in late adulthood.

Declines in memory affect mainly episodic memories and short-term memory. Explanations of memory changes in old age have focused on environmental factors, information processing declines, and biological factors.

LO 17.12 Describe how learning and education continue in late adulthood.

Older people can enjoy and participate actively in college-level and other classes, and their presence in classes with younger people adds a different and welcome perspective.

Journal Writing Prompt

Applying Lifespan Development: Do you think steady or increasing crystallized intelligence can partially or fully compensate for declines in fluid intelligence? Why or why not?

Epilogue

Who are the old, and how old are they? In this chapter, we began by reviewing the demographics of old age and looking at the phenomenon of ageism. We discussed health and wellness during late adulthood and found that older people can extend their well-being through good diet, good habits, and regular exercise. We also discussed the length of the life span and explored some of the reasons why life expectancy has been increasing. We ended with an examination of cognitive abilities among the elderly and evidence showing that there are considerable discrepancies between stereotypical views of older people's intellectual abilities and memory and reality.

Return to the prologue of this chapter, about Jock Brandis's invention of the Universal Nut Sheller, and answer the following questions:

1. In what ways does Brandis contradict the stereotypes of older people and life in late adulthood?
2. In what ways does he confirm these stereotypes?
3. What elements of Brandis's life may have contributed to his high level of activity? What do you think he was like as a younger person?
4. What steps could Brandis take to maintain his high level of cognitive functioning?

Looking Back

LO 17.1 Describe what it is like to grow old in the United States today.

The number and proportion of older people in the United States and many other countries are larger than ever, and elderly people are the fastest-growing segment of the U.S. population. Older people as a group are subjected to stereotyping and discrimination, a phenomenon referred to as *ageism*.

LO 17.2 Summarize the physical changes that occur in old age.

Old age is a period in which outward physical changes unmistakably indicate aging, but many older people remain fit, active, and agile well into the period. Older people experience a decrease in brain size and a reduction of blood flow (and oxygen) to all parts of the body, including the brain. The circulatory, respiratory, and digestive systems all work with less efficiency.

LO 17.3 Explain the extent to which people slow down as they age and the consequences of this slowing.

Reaction time among the elderly is slower, a fact that is explained by the peripheral slowing hypothesis (processing speed in the peripheral nervous system slows down) and the generalized slowing hypothesis (processing in all parts of the nervous system slows down).

LO 17.4 Describe how the senses are affected by aging.

Physical changes in the eye bring declines in vision, and several eye diseases become more prevalent in old age, including cataracts, glaucoma, and age-related macular degeneration (AMD). Hearing also declines, particularly the ability to hear higher frequencies. Hearing loss has psychological and social consequences, since it discourages older people from engaging in social interactions. Declines in the senses of taste and smell also occur in late adulthood.

LO 17.5 Describe the general state of health of older people and the disorders to which they are susceptible.

Although some people are healthy, the incidence of certain serious diseases rises in old age, and the ability to recuperate declines. Most older people suffer from at least one long-term ailment. The leading causes of death in old age are heart disease, cancer, and stroke. Older people are also susceptible to psychological disorders, such as depression, and brain disorders, especially Alzheimer's disease.

LO 17.6 Summarize how wellness can be maintained in old age.

Psychological and lifestyle factors can influence wellness in old age. A sense of control over one's life and environment can have positive effects, as can a proper diet, exercise, and the avoidance of risk factors, such as smoking.

LO 17.7 Describe how sexuality is affected by aging.

Despite some changes in sexual functioning, sexuality continues throughout old age, provided both physical and mental health are good.

LO 17.8 Identify the factors involved with the life span and the causes of death.

The inevitability of death is unquestioned but unexplained. Genetic programming theories claim that the body has a built-in time limit on life, while wear-and-tear theories maintain that the body simply wears out. Life expectancy has been rising steadily for centuries and continues to do so, with differences according to gender, race, and ethnicity.

LO 17.9 Discuss the possible extension of the life span through scientific advances and the implications of this extension.

The life span may be further increased by technological advances such as telomere therapy, the use of antioxidant drugs to reduce free radicals, development of low-calorie diets, and organ replacement.

LO 17.10 Describe how well older adults function cognitively.

According to sequential studies, such as those conducted by developmental psychologist K. Warner Schaie, intellectual abilities tend to decline slowly throughout old age, but different abilities change in different ways. Training, stimulation, practice, and motivation can help older people maintain their mental abilities.

LO 17.11 Discuss the ways memory does and does not decline in late adulthood.

Loss of memory in late adulthood is not general but specific to certain kinds of memory. Episodic memories are most affected, while semantic and implicit memories are largely unaffected. Short-term memory declines gradually until age 70, then deteriorates quickly. Explanations of memory changes may focus on environmental factors, information processing declines, and biological factors. Which approach is most accurate is not entirely settled.

LO 17.12 Describe how learning and education continue in late adulthood.

The popularity of programs like Road Scholar attests to the desire of many older people to continue learning. Older students can significantly enhance college courses by bringing their experiences and prior learning to the classroom.

Key Terms and Concepts

Chapter 18

Social and Personality Development in Late Adulthood

santypan/Shutterstock

Learning Objectives

LO 18.1 Describe ways in which personality develops during late adulthood.

LO 18.2 Explain how age relates to the distribution of resources, power, and privilege.

LO 18.3 Define wisdom and describe how it is correlated with age.

LO 18.4 Differentiate the theories of aging.

LO 18.5 Describe the circumstances in which older people live and the difficulties they face.

LO 18.6 Discuss how financially secure older people are in the United States today.

LO 18.7 Summarize the positives and negatives of retiring as well as typical stages retired people pass through.

LO 18.8 Describe how marriages fare in late adulthood.

LO 18.9 Describe the typical reactions to the death of a spouse during late adulthood.

LO 18.10 Discuss the nature of relationships in late adulthood.

LO 18.11 Explain how aging affects family relationships.

LO 18.12 Discuss what causes elder abuse and how it can be prevented.

Chapter Overview

Prologue: Late Love

They met at a singles picnic when Geraldine Mooers was 76 and Richard Thomas was 73. They were an unlikely couple from the start: She was a liberal Democrat who, as a retired dietician, loved to exercise. He was a staunch Republican who was an overweight retired cook. They both were widowed and had children and grandchildren.

But something clicked, and they soon became a couple. Richard moved into Geraldine's condo, and eventually they married in a church, but without a marriage license, because their accountant and lawyer said marriage would complicate their financial lives. They said the formalities didn't matter; in their hearts, they were married.

Health was an issue: Richard had a pacemaker, and he had surgery to lose weight. And then there was the penile implant he received, because he wanted to have sex with Gerry.

Having both lost spouses, they both knew the end to their story, and they knew that one would go through a wrenching loss. And that happened 10 years after they met, when Richard died peacefully at age 83. In his obituary, Richard was quoted as saying that he was the luckiest man in the world to have had two women to love him (Wolfe, 2007; *Star Tribune*, 2016).

Looking Ahead

The warmth and affection between Geraldine and Richard were unmistakable. Their relationship was central to their lives, and their mutual love and admiration reached the heights of human interconnectedness.

We turn in this chapter to the social and emotional aspects of late adulthood, which remain as central an aspect of life as in earlier stages of the life span. We begin by considering how personality continues to develop in elderly individuals, and then turn to an examination of various ways people can age successfully.

Monkey Business/Fotolia

Many grandparents include their grandchildren as an integral part of their social networks.

Next, we consider how various societal factors affect the day-to-day living conditions of older adults. We discuss options in living arrangements, as well as ways economic and financial issues influence people's lives. We also look at how culture governs the way we treat older people, and we examine the influence of work and retirement on elderly individuals, considering the ways retirement can be optimized.

Finally, we consider relationships in late adulthood, not only among married couples but also among other relatives and friends. We will see how the social networks of late adulthood continue to play an important—and sustaining—role in people's lives. We examine how events such as the divorce of a parent, decades earlier, can still have a critical impact on the course of people's lives. We end with a discussion of the growing phenomenon of elder abuse.

Personality Development and Successful Aging

Greta Roach has a puckish manner, a habit of nudging you when she is about to say something funny. This happens often, because that is how she views the world. Even last year's knee injury, which forced her to drop out of her bowling league and halted the march of blue-and-chrome trophies across her living-room table, is not—in her mind—a frailty of age.

Roach, 93, takes the same spirited approach to life in her 90s as she did in her 20s, something not all elders can do .... "I enjoy life. I belong to all the clubs. I love to talk on the telephone. I write to my old friends." She pauses. "Those that are still alive." (Pappano, 1994, pp. 19, 30)

In many ways, Greta Roach, with her wit, high spirits, and enormous activity level, is much the same person she was in earlier years. Yet for other older adults, time and circumstances seem to bring changes in their outlook on life, in their views of themselves, and perhaps even in their basic personalities. One of the fundamental questions asked by lifespan developmentalists concerns the degree to which personality either remains stable or changes in later adulthood.

Continuity and Change in Personality During Late Adulthood

LO 18.1 Describe ways in which personality develops during late adulthood.

Is personality relatively stable throughout adulthood, or does it vary in significant ways? The answer, it turns out, depends on which facets of personality we wish to consider. According to developmental psychologists Paul Costa and Robert McCrae, the "big five" basic personality traits (neuroticism, extroversion, openness, agreeableness, and conscientiousness) are remarkably stable across adulthood. For instance, even-tempered people at age 20 are still even-tempered at age 75, and people who hold positive self-concepts early in adulthood still view themselves positively in late adulthood (Costa & McCrae, 1997; McCrae & Costa, 2003; Curtis, Windsor, & Soubelet, 2015; Kahlbaugh & Huffman, 2017).

For example, at age 93, Greta Roach is still active and humorous, as she was in her 20s. Similarly, other longitudinal investigations have found that personality traits remain quite stable. Consequently, there seems to be a fundamental continuity to personality (Field & Millsap, 1991).

Despite this general stability of basic personality traits, there is still the possibility of change over time. As we noted in Chapter 16, the profound changes that occur throughout adulthood in people's social environments may produce fluctuations and changes in personality. What is important to a person at age 80 is not necessarily the same as what was important at age 40.

In order to account for these sorts of changes, some theorists have focused their attention on the discontinuities of development. As we'll see next, the work of Erik Erikson, Robert Peck, Daniel Levinson, and Bernice Neugarten has examined the changes in personality that occur as a result of new challenges that appear in later adulthood.

EGO INTEGRITY VERSUS DESPAIR: ERIKSON'S FINAL STAGE. Psychoanalyst Erik Erikson's final word on personality concerns late adulthood—the time, he suggested, when elderly people move into the last of life's eight stages of psychosocial development. Labeled the **ego-integrity-versus-despair stage**, this last period is characterized by a process of looking back over one's life, evaluating it, and coming to terms with it.

ego-integrity-versus-despair stage
Erikson's final stage of life, characterized by a process of looking back over one's life, evaluating it, and coming to terms with it

People who are successful in this stage of development experience a sense of satisfaction and accomplishment, which Erikson terms "integrity." When people achieve integrity, they feel that they have realized and fulfilled the possibilities that have come their way in life, and they have few regrets. However, some people look back on their lives with dissatisfaction. They may feel that they have missed important opportunities and have not accomplished what they wished. Such individuals may be unhappy, depressed, angry, or despondent over what they have done or failed to do with their lives—in short, they despair.

PECK'S DEVELOPMENTAL TASKS. Although Erikson's approach provides a picture of the broad possibilities of later adulthood, other theorists offer a more differentiated view of what occurs in the final stage of life. For instance, psychologist Robert Peck (1968) suggests that personality development in elderly people is occupied by three major developmental tasks or challenges.

In Peck's view—which is part of a comprehensive description of change across adulthood—the first task in old age is that people must redefine themselves in ways that do not relate to their work roles or occupations. He labels this stage **redefinition of self versus preoccupation with work role**. As we will see when we discuss retirement, the changes that occur when people stop working can trigger a difficult adjustment that has a major impact on the way people view themselves. Peck suggests that people must adjust their values to place less emphasis on themselves as workers or professionals and more on attributes that don't involve work, such as being a grandparent or a gardener.

redefinition of self versus preoccupation with work role
the theory that those in old age must redefine themselves in ways that do not relate to their work roles or occupations

The second major developmental task in late adulthood, according to Peck, is **body transcendence versus body preoccupation**. As we saw in Chapter 17, elderly individuals can undergo significant changes in their physical capabilities as a result of aging. In the body-transcendence-versus-body-preoccupation stage, people must learn to cope with and move beyond (transcend) those physical changes. If they don't, they become preoccupied with their physical deterioration, to the detriment of their personality development. Greta Roach, who just gave up bowling in her 90s, is an example of someone who is coping well with the physical changes of aging.

body transcendence versus body preoccupation
a period in which people must learn to cope with and move beyond changes in physical capabilities as a result of aging

Finally, the third developmental task faced by those in old age is **ego transcendence versus ego preoccupation**, in which elderly people must come to grips with their coming death. They need to understand that although death is inevitable, and probably not too far off, they have made contributions to society. If people in late adulthood see these contributions, which can take the form of children or work- and civic-related activities, as lasting beyond their own lives, they will experience ego transcendence. If not, they may become preoccupied with the question of whether their lives had value and worth to society.

ego transcendence versus ego preoccupation
the period in which elderly people must come to grips with their coming death

LEVINSON'S FINAL SEASON: THE WINTER OF LIFE. Daniel Levinson's theory of adult development does not focus as much as Erikson's and Peck's theories on the challenges that aging adults must overcome. Instead, he looks at the processes that can lead to personality change as we grow old. According to Levinson, people enter late adulthood by passing through a transition stage that typically occurs around age 60 to 65 (Levinson, 1986, 1992). During this transition period, people come to view themselves as entering late adulthood—or, ultimately, as being "old." Knowing full well what society's stereotypes about elderly individuals are, and how negative they can be, people struggle with the notion that they are now in this category.

According to Levinson, with age people come to realize that they are no longer on the center stage of life but are increasingly playing bit parts. This loss of power, respect, and authority may be difficult for individuals accustomed to having control in their lives.

Semmick Photo/Shutterstock

In late adulthood, many people find fulfillment and satisfaction through volunteer, and sometimes paid, activities.

On the positive side, people in late adulthood can serve as resources to younger individuals, and they may find themselves regarded as "venerated elders" whose advice is sought and relied upon. Furthermore, old age can bring with it a new freedom to do things for the simple sake of the enjoyment and pleasure they bring rather than because they are obligations.

COPING WITH AGING: NEUGARTEN'S STUDY. Rather than focusing on the commonalities of aging, or the processes and tasks involved in aging, Bernice Neugarten (1972, 1977)—in what became a classic study—examined the different ways that people cope with aging. Neugarten found four different personality types in her research on people in their 70s:

- *Disintegrated and disorganized personalities.* Some people are unable to accept aging, and they experience despair as they get older. They are often found in nursing homes or are hospitalized.
- *Passive-dependent personalities.* Others become fearful with age—they have a fear of falling ill, fear of the future, fear of their own inability to cope. They are so fearful that they may seek out help from family and care providers, even when they don't need it.
- *Defended personalities.* Others respond to the fear of aging in a quite different manner: They try to stop it in its tracks. They may attempt to act young, exercising vigorously and engaging in youthful activities. Unfortunately, they may set up unrealistic expectations for themselves and run the risk of feeling disappointed as a result.
- *Integrated personalities.* The most successful individuals cope comfortably with aging. They accept becoming older and maintain a sense of self-dignity.

Neugarten found that the majority of the people she studied fell into the final category. They acknowledged aging and were able to look back at their lives and gaze into the future with acceptance.

LIFE REVIEW AND REMINISCENCE: THE COMMON THEME OF PERSONALITY DEVELOPMENT. Looking back over one's life is a major thread running through the work of Erikson, Peck, Levinson, and Neugarten's views of personality development in old age. Indeed, **life review**, in which people examine and evaluate their lives, is a common theme for most personality theorists who focus on late adulthood.

life review
the point in life at which people examine and evaluate their lives

According to gerontologist Robert Butler (2002), life review is triggered by the increasingly obvious prospect of one's death. As people age, they look back on their lives, remembering and reconsidering what has happened to them. We might at first suspect that such reminiscence may be harmful, as people relive the past, wallow in past problems, and revive old wounds, but this is not the case at all. By reviewing the events of their lives, elderly people often come to a better understanding of their past. They may be able to resolve lingering problems and conflicts that they had with particular people, such as an estrangement from a child, and they may feel they can face their current lives with greater serenity (Korte, Westerhof, & Bohlmeijer, 2012; Latorre et al., 2015; Bergström, 2017).

Life review offers other benefits. For example, reminiscence may lead to a sense of sharing and mutuality, a feeling of interconnectedness with others. Moreover, it can be a source of social interaction as older adults seek to share their prior experiences with others (Parks, Sanna, & Posey, 2003).

Hill Street Studios/Blend Images/Getty Images

The process of life review can improve memory and foster feelings of interconnectedness.

Reminiscence may even have cognitive benefits, improving memory in older people. By reflecting on the past, people activate a variety of memories about people and events in their lives. In turn, these memories may trigger other, related memories and may bring back sights, sounds, and even smells of the past.

The outcomes of life review and reminiscence are not always positive. People who become obsessive about the past, reliving old insults and mistakes that cannot be rectified, may end up feeling guilt, depression, and anger against people from the past who may not even still be alive. In such cases, reminiscence produces declines in psychological functioning (DeGenova, 1993; Cappeliez, Guindon, & Robitaille, 2008).

Overall, however, the process of life review and reminiscence can play an important role in the ongoing lives of elderly individuals. It provides continuity between past and present, and may increase awareness of the contemporary world. It also can provide new insights into the past and into others, allowing people to continue personality growth and to function more effectively in the present (Coleman, 2005; Haber, 2006; Alwin, 2012).

Age Stratification Approaches to Late Adulthood

LO 18.2 Explain how age relates to the distribution of resources, power, and privilege.

age stratification theories
the view that an unequal distribution of economic resources, power, and privilege exists among people at different stages of the life course

Age, like race and gender, provides a way of ranking people within a given society. **Age stratification theories** suggest that economic resources, power, and privilege are distributed unequally among people at different stages of the life course. Such inequality is particularly pronounced during late adulthood.

Even as advances in medical technologies have led to a longer life span, power and prestige for the elderly have eroded, at least in industrialized societies. For example, the peak earning years are the 50s; later, earnings tend to decline. Furthermore, younger people have more independence and are often physically removed from their elders, making them less dependent on older adults. In addition, rapidly changing technology causes older adults to be seen as lacking important skills. Ultimately, older adults are regarded as not particularly productive members of society and in some cases are seen as simply irrelevant (Macionis, 2001). As Levinson's theory emphasizes, people are certainly aware of the declines in status that accompany growing old in Western societies. Levinson considers adjusting to them to be the major transition of late adulthood.

Age stratification theories help explain why aging is viewed more positively in less industrialized societies. For example, in cultures in which agricultural activities predominate, older people can accumulate control over important resources, such as animals and land. In such societies, in which the concept of retirement is unknown, older individuals (especially older males) are exceptionally respected, in part because they continue to be involved in daily activities central to the society. Furthermore, because agricultural practices change at a less rapid pace than the technological advances that characterize more industrialized societies, people in late adulthood are seen as possessing considerable wisdom. Cultural values that stress respect for elders are not limited to less industrialized countries. They shape how elderly adults are treated in a variety of societies, as discussed in the *Developmental Diversity and Your Life* feature.

Does Age Bring Wisdom?

LO 18.3 Define wisdom and describe how it is correlated with age.

One of the benefits of age is supposed to be wisdom. But does the average elderly person have wisdom, and do people gain wisdom as they become older?

wisdom
expert knowledge in the practical aspects of life

Although it seems reasonable to believe that we get wiser as we get older, we don't know for sure because the concept of **wisdom**—expert knowledge in the practical aspects of life—has, until recent years, received little attention from gerontologists and other researchers. In part, this lack of attention stems from the difficulty in defining and measuring the concept, which is unusually vague (Baltes & Smith, 2008; Meeks & Jeste, 2009; Montepare, Kempler, & McLaughlin-Volpe, 2014).

Developmental Diversity and Your Life

How Culture Shapes the Way We Treat People in Late Adulthood

The view we hold of late adulthood is colored by the culture in which we live. For example, Asian societies, in general, hold elderly people, particularly members of their own families, in higher esteem than Western cultures tend to. Although the strength of this standard has been declining in areas of Asia in which industrialization has been increasing rapidly, such as Japan, the view of aging and the treatment of people in late adulthood still tend to be more positive than in Western cultures (Cobbe, 2003; Degnen, 2007; Smith & Hung, 2012).

What is it about Asian cultures that leads to higher levels of esteem for old age? In general, cultures that hold the elderly in high regard are relatively homogeneous in socioeconomic terms. In addition, the roles that people play in those societies entail greater responsibility with increasing age, and elderly people control resources to a relatively large extent.

Moreover, the roles played by people in Asian society display more continuity throughout the life span than in Western cultures, and older adults continue to engage in activities that are valued by society. Finally, Asian cultures are more organized around extended families in which the older generations are well integrated into the family structure (Fry, 1985; Sangree, 1989). In such an arrangement, younger family members may come to see older members as having accumulated a great deal of wisdom, which they can share.

However, even those societies that articulate strong ideals regarding the treatment of older adults do not always live up to those standards. For instance, research on the Chinese people, whose admiration, respect, and even worship for individuals in late adulthood are strong, shows that people's actual behavior, in almost every segment of the society except for the most elite, fails to be as positive as their attitudes are. Furthermore, it is typically sons and their wives who are expected to care for elderly parents; parents with just daughters may find themselves with no one to care for them in late adulthood. In short, conduct toward elderly people in particular cultures is not uniform, and it is important not to make broad, global statements about how older adults are treated in a given society (Comunian & Gielen, 2000; Li, Ji & Chen, 2014; Vauclair et al., 2017).

It is not just Asian cultures that hold the elderly in particular esteem. For example, in Latino cultures, the elderly are thought to have a special inner strength, and they are assumed to be a valuable resource for younger individuals in a family. In many African cultures, reaching an old age is seen as a sign of divine intervention, and the elderly are called "big person" in a number of African languages (Diop, 1989; Holmes & Holmes, 1995; Lehr, Seiler, & Thomae, 2000).

Monkey Business/Fotolia

What aspects of Asian cultures lead them to hold higher levels of esteem for people in old age?

Wisdom can be seen as reflecting an accumulation of knowledge, experience, and contemplation, and by this definition, older age may be necessary, or at least helpful, to acquiring true wisdom (Staudinger, 2008; Randall, 2012; Rakoczy et al., 2017).

Wisdom is not the same as intelligence, but distinguishing these two qualities can be tricky. Some researchers suggest that a primary distinction is related to timing: Whereas knowledge that is derived from intelligence is related to the here and now, wisdom is a more timeless quality. Intelligence may permit a person to think logically and systematically, but wisdom provides an understanding of human behavior. According to psychologist Robert Sternberg, who has conducted considerable research related to practical intelligence, intelligence permits humans to invent the atom bomb, whereas wisdom prevents them from using it (Karelitz, Jarvin, & Sternberg, 2010; Wink & Staudinger, 2015).

Measuring wisdom is difficult. Ursula Staudinger and Paul Baltes (2000) designed a study showing that it is possible to assess people reliably on the concept. Pairs of people ranging in age from 20 to 70 years discussed difficulties relating to life events. One problem involved someone who gets a phone call from a good friend who says that he or she is planning to commit suicide. Another involved a 14-year-old girl who wants to move out of her family home immediately. Participants were asked what they should do and consider.

Although there were no absolute right or wrong answers to these problems, the responses were evaluated against several criteria, including the amount of factual knowledge the participants brought to bear on the problem; their knowledge about decision-making strategies, such as considering the consequences of a decision; how well the participants considered the problem within the context of the central character's life span and the values that the central character may hold; and whether the participants recognized that there may not be a single, absolute solution.

Using these criteria, participants' responses were rated as relatively wise or unwise. For instance, an example of a response to the suicide problem rated as particularly wise is the following:

> *On the one hand, this problem has a pragmatic side; one has to react one way or another. On the other hand, it also has a philosophical side—whether human beings are allowed to kill themselves etc .... First one would need to find out whether this decision is the result of a longer process or whether it is a reaction to a momentary life situation. In the latter case, it is uncertain how long this condition will last. There can be conditions that make suicide conceivable. But I think no one should be easily released from life. They should be forced to "fight" for their death if they really want it .... It seems that one has a responsibility to try to show the person alternative pathways. Currently, for example, there seems to be a trend in our society that it becomes more and more accepted that old people commit suicide. This can also be viewed as dangerous. Not because of the suicide itself but because of its functionality for society.* (Staudinger & Baltes, 1996, p. 762)

The Staudinger and Baltes study also found that the older participants benefited more from an experimental condition designed to promote wise thinking, and other research suggests that the very wisest individuals may be older adults.

Other research has looked at wisdom in terms of the development of theory of mind—the ability to make inferences about others' thoughts, feelings, and intentions, their mental states. Although the research findings are mixed, some research finds that older adults, with their added years of experience to draw upon, utilize a more sophisticated theory of mind (Karelitz, Jarvin, & Sternberg, 2010; Rakoczy, Harder-Kasten, & Sturm, 2012).

Successful Aging: What Is the Secret?

LO 18.4 Differentiate the theories of aging.

> *At age 77, Elinor Reynolds spends most of her time at home, leading a quiet, routine existence. Never married, Elinor receives visits from her two sisters every few weeks, and some of her nieces and nephews stop by on occasion. But for the most part, she keeps to herself. When asked, she says she is quite happy.*
>
> *In contrast, Carrie Masterson, also 77, is involved in something different almost every day. If she is not visiting the senior center, participating in some kind of activity, she is out shopping. Her daughter complains that Carrie is "never home" when she tries to reach her by phone, and Carrie replies that she has never been busier—or happier.*

Clearly, there is no single way to age successfully. How people age depends on personality factors and the circumstances in which people find themselves. Some people become progressively less involved with day-to-day events, whereas others maintain active ties to people and their areas of personal interest. Three major approaches provide explanations: disengagement theory, activity theory, and continuity theory. While disengagement theory suggests that successful aging is characterized by gradual withdrawal, activity theory argues that successful aging occurs when people maintain their engagement with the world. Continuity theory takes a compromise position, suggesting that what is important is maintaining a desired level of involvement. We'll consider each approach in turn.

DISENGAGEMENT THEORY: GRADUAL RETREAT. According to **disengagement theory**, late adulthood often involves a gradual withdrawal from the world on physical, psychological, and social levels (Cummings & Henry, 1961). On a physical level, elderly people have lower energy levels and tend to slow down progressively. Psychologically, they begin to withdraw from others, showing less interest in the world around them and spending more time looking inward. Finally, on a social level, they engage in less interaction with others, in terms of both day-to-day, face-to-face encounters and participation in society as a whole. Some older adults also become less involved and invested in the lives of others.

disengagement theory
theory suggesting that late adulthood is marked by a gradual withdrawal from the world on physical, psychological, and social levels

Disengagement theory suggests that withdrawal is a mutual process. Because of norms and expectations about aging, society in general begins to disengage from those in late adulthood. For example, mandatory retirement ages compel elderly people to withdraw from work-related roles, thereby accelerating the process of disengagement.

Although there is some logic to disengagement theory, research has not been supportive. Furthermore, the theory has been criticized because it takes the failure of society to provide sufficient opportunities for meaningful engagement during late adulthood and then, in a sense, blames people in this age group for not being engaged.

Of course, some degree of disengagement is not necessarily negative. For example, a gradual withdrawal in late adulthood may permit people to become more reflective about their own lives and less constrained by social roles. Furthermore, people can become more discerning in their social relationships, focusing on those who best meet their needs (Settersten, 2002; Wrosch, Bauer, & Scheier, 2005; Liang & Luo, 2012).

Still, most gerontologists reject disengagement theory, pointing out that disengagement is relatively uncommon. In most cases, people remain engaged, active, and busy throughout old age, and (especially in non-Western cultures) the expectation is that people will remain actively involved in everyday life. Clearly, disengagement is not an automatic, universal process (Bergstrom & Holmes, 2000; Crosnoe & Elder, 2002).

ACTIVITY THEORY: CONTINUED INVOLVEMENT. The lack of support for disengagement theory led to an alternative, known as activity theory. **Activity theory** suggests that successful aging occurs when people maintain the interests and activities they pursued during middle age and resist any decrease in the amount and type of social interaction they have with others. According to this perspective, happiness and satisfaction with life are assumed to spring from a high level of involvement with the world. Moreover, successful aging occurs when older adults adapt to inevitable changes in their environments not by withdrawing but by resisting reductions in their social involvement (Consedine, Magai, & King, 2004; Hutchinson & Wexler, 2007; Rebok et al., 2014).

activity theory
the theory suggesting that successful aging occurs when people maintain the interests, activities, and social interactions with which they were involved during middle age

Activity theory suggests that successful aging in late adulthood reflects a continuation of activities in which elderly people participated earlier. Even in cases in which it is no longer possible to participate in certain activities—such as work, following retirement—activity theory argues that successful aging occurs when replacement activities are found.

But activity theory is not the full story. For one thing, activity theory makes little distinction between various types of activities. Surely not every activity will have an equal impact on a person's happiness and satisfaction with life, and being involved in various activities just for the sake of remaining engaged is unlikely to be satisfying. In sum, the specific nature and quality of the activities in which people engage are likely to be more critical than the mere quantity or frequency of their activities (Adams, 2004).

Tina7si/Fotolia

Pressmaster/Fotolia

While disengagement theory suggests that people in late adulthood begin to gradually withdraw from the world, activity theory argues that successful aging occurs when people maintain their involvement with others.

From *a social worker's* perspective

How might cultural factors affect an older person's likelihood of pursuing either the disengagement strategy or the activity strategy?

A more significant concern is that for some people in late adulthood, the principle of "less is more" clearly holds. For such individuals, less activity brings greater enjoyment of life. They are able to slow down and do only the things that bring them the greatest satisfaction. In fact, some people view the ability to moderate their pace as one of the bounties of late adulthood. For them, a relatively inactive, and perhaps even solitary, existence is welcomed.

In short, neither disengagement theory nor activity theory provides a complete picture of successful aging. For some people, a gradual disengagement occurs, and this leads to relatively high levels of happiness and satisfaction. For others, preserving a significant level of activity and involvement leads to greater satisfaction (Ouwehand, de Ridder, & Bensing, 2007).

CONTINUITY THEORY: A COMPROMISE POSITION. The current view of successful aging is a compromise between a certain degree of disengagement and activity. **Continuity theory** suggests that people simply need to maintain their desired level of involvement in society in order to maximize their sense of well-being and self-esteem (Whitbourne, 2001; Atchley, 2003; Carmel, 2017).

continuity theory
the theory suggesting that people need to maintain their desired level of involvement in society in order to maximize their sense of well-being and self-esteem

According to continuity theory, those who were highly active and social will be happiest if they largely remain so. Those more retiring individuals, who enjoy solitude and solitary interests, such as reading or walks in the woods, will be happiest if they are free to pursue that level of sociability (Holahan & Chapman, 2002; Wang et al., 2014).

It is also clear that, regardless of the level of activity in which older adults engage, most experience positive emotions as frequently as younger individuals. Furthermore, they become more skilled in regulating their emotions.

Other factors enhance feelings of happiness during late adulthood. For instance, good physical and mental health is clearly important in determining an elderly person's overall sense of well-being. Similarly, having enough financial security to provide for basic needs, including food, shelter, and medical care, is critical. In addition, a sense of autonomy, independence, and personal control over one's life is a significant advantage (Charles & Carstensen, 2010; Vacha-Haase, Hill, & Bermingham, 2012; Sutipan, Intarakamhang & Macaskill, 2017).

More specifically, developmental psychologist Laura Carstensen has suggested in her *socioemotional selectivity theory* that as the time horizon of older adults decreases, they become increasingly selective in the goals and activities in which they invest. Furthermore, as they become older and their time horizons are constrained, people in late adulthood become invested in present-oriented goals that provide emotional satisfaction and meaning, compared with longer-term goals (Charles & Carstensen, 2010, 2014).

Furthermore, socioemotional selectivity theory suggests that as they age, people develop a preference for seeking out positive information, compared with negative information. They are more likely to involve themselves with familiar individuals who provide positive experiences and who are more likely to fulfil their emotional needs. In short, they become more selective in their emotional engagements with others (Reed & Carstensen, 2012; English & Carstensen, 2016).

Other research finds that the way elderly people perceive old age can influence their happiness and satisfaction. Those who view late adulthood in terms of positive attributes—such as the possibility of gaining knowledge and wisdom—are apt to perceive themselves in a more positive light than those who view old age in a more pessimistic and unfavorable way (Levy, Slade, & Kasl, 2002; Levy, 2003).

selective optimization
the process by which people concentrate on selected skill areas to compensate for losses in other areas

Ultimately, as a group, people in late adulthood report being happier than younger people, according to the results of surveys. And it's not that those over 65 have always been happier. Instead, being older seems to bring a degree of contentment in the majority of people (Yang, 2008).

SELECTIVE OPTIMIZATION WITH COMPENSATION: A GENERAL MODEL OF SUCCESSFUL AGING. In considering the factors that lead to successful aging, developmental psychologists Paul Baltes and Margret Baltes focus on the *selective optimization with compensation model* (summarized in Figure 18-1). As we first noted in Chapter 15, the assumption underlying the model is that late adulthood brings with it changes and losses in underlying capabilities, which vary from one person to another. However, it is possible to overcome such shifts in capabilities through selective optimization.

Selective optimization is the process by which people concentrate on particular skill areas to compensate for losses in other areas. They do this by seeking to fortify their general motivational, cognitive, and physical resources while also, through a process of selection, focusing on particular areas of special interest. A person who has run marathons all her life may have to cut back or give up entirely other activities in order to increase her training. By giving up other activities, she may be able to maintain her running skills through concentration on them (Burnett-Wolle & Godbey, 2007; Scheibner & Leathem, 2012; Hahn & Lachman, 2015).

At the same time, the model suggests that elderly individuals engage in compensation for the losses that they have sustained due to aging. Compensation may take the form, for instance, of employing a hearing aid to offset losses in hearing. Piano virtuoso Arthur Rubinstein provides another example of selective optimization with compensation. In his later years, he maintained his concert career and was acclaimed for his playing. To manage this, he used several strategies that illustrate the model of selective optimization with compensation.

First, Rubinstein reduced the number of pieces he played at concerts—an example of being selective in what he sought to accomplish. Second, he practiced those pieces more often, thus using optimization. Finally, in an example of compensation, he slowed down the tempo of musical passages immediately preceding faster passages, thereby fostering the illusion that he was playing just as fast as he had ever played (Baltes & Baltes, 1990).

Figure 18-1 Selective Optimization with Compensation

According to the model proposed by Paul Baltes and Margret Baltes, successful aging occurs when an older adult focuses on his or her most important areas of functioning and compensates for losses in other areas. Is this unique to old age?

(**Source:** Based on Baltes & Baltes, 1990.)

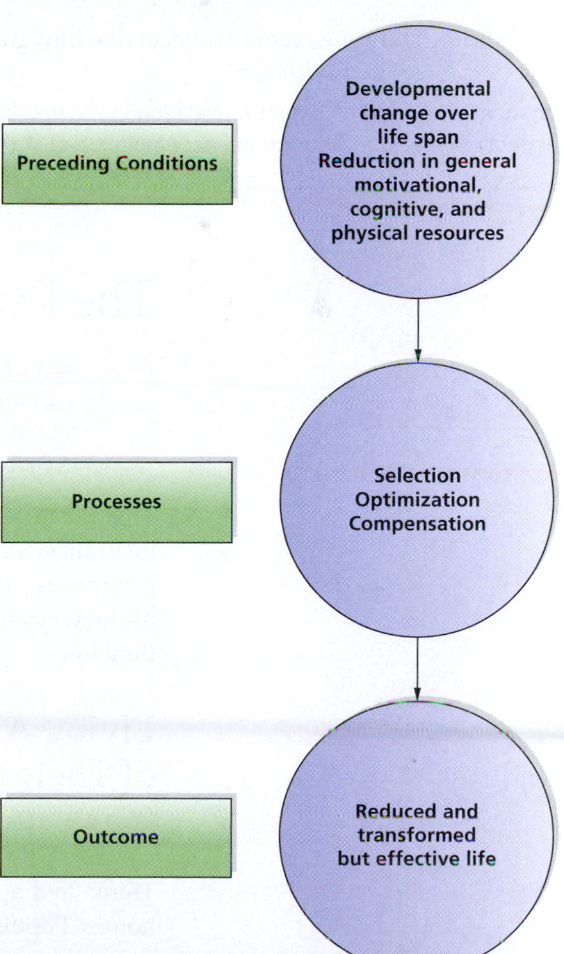

In short, the model of selective optimization with compensation illustrates the fundamentals of successful aging. Although late adulthood may bring about various changes in underlying capabilities, people who focus on making the most of their achievements in particular areas may well be able to compensate for any limitations and losses that do occur. The outcome is a life that is reduced in some areas but is also transformed and modified and, ultimately, is effective and successful.

Module 18.1 Review

LO 18.1 Describe ways in which personality develops during late adulthood.

While some aspects of personality remain stable, others change to reflect the social environments through which people pass as they age. Erik Erikson calls older adulthood the ego-integrity-versus-despair stage, focusing on individuals' feelings about their lives, while Robert Peck focuses on three tasks that define the period. According to Daniel Levinson, after struggling with the notion of being old, people can experience liberation and self-regard. Bernice Neugarten focuses on the ways people cope with aging.

LO 18.2 Explain how age relates to the distribution of resources, power, and privilege.

Age stratification theories suggest that the unequal distribution of economic resources, power, and privilege becomes particularly pronounced during late adulthood.

LO 18.3 Define wisdom and describe how it is correlated with age.

Wisdom is defined as expert knowledge in the practical aspects of life, won through the accumulation of knowledge, experience, and contemplation. Because it is experience-based, wisdom may be dependent on aging. Societies in which elderly people are respected for their wisdom are generally characterized by social homogeneity, extended families, responsible roles for older people, and control of significant resources by older people.

LO 18.4 Differentiate the theories of aging.

Disengagement theory suggests that older people gradually withdraw from the world, which can lead to reflection and satisfaction. In contrast, activity theory suggests that the happiest people continue to be engaged with the world. A compromise position—continuity theory—may be the most useful approach. The most successful model for aging may be selective optimization with compensation.

Journal Writing Prompt

Applying Lifespan Development: How might personality traits account for success or failure in achieving satisfaction through the life review process?

The Daily Life of Late Adulthood

Before I retired 10 years ago, everyone told me I'd miss work, get lonely, and feel flat without the challenges of business. Baloney! This is the best time of my life! Miss work? No way. What's to miss? Meetings? Training sessions? Evaluations? Sure, there's less money and people, but I have all I need with my savings, my hobbies, and my traveling.

This positive view of life in late adulthood was expressed by a 75-year-old retired insurance worker. Although the story is certainly not the same for all retirees, many, if not most, find their post-work lives happy and involving. We will consider some of the ways in which people lead their lives in late adulthood, beginning with where they live.

Living Arrangements: The Places and Spaces of Their Lives

LO 18.5 Describe the circumstances in which older people live and the difficulties they face.

Think "old age," and if you are like most people, your thoughts soon turn to nursing homes. Popular stereotypes place most elderly people in lonely, unpleasant, institutional surroundings under the care of strangers.

The reality, however, is quite different. Although it is true that some people finish their lives in nursing homes, they are a tiny minority—only 5 percent. Most people live out their entire lives in home environments, typically in the company of at least one other family member.

LIVING AT HOME. A large number of older adults live alone. People over 65 represent a quarter of America's 9.6 million single-person households. Roughly two-thirds of people over age 65 live with other members of the family. In most cases they live with spouses. Some older adults live with their siblings, and others live in multigenerational settings with their children, grandchildren, and even occasionally great-grandchildren.

The consequences of living with a family member are quite varied, depending on the nature of the setting. For married couples, living with a spouse represents continuity with earlier life. For people who move in with their children, the adjustment to life in a multigenerational setting can be jarring. Not only is there a potential loss of independence and privacy, but older adults may feel uncomfortable with the way their children are raising their grandchildren. Unless there are some ground rules about the specific roles that people are to play in the household, conflicts can arise (Navarro, 2006).

Living in extended families is more typical for some groups than for other groups. For instance, African Americans are more likely than whites to live in multigenerational families. Furthermore, the amount of influence that family members have over one another and the interdependence of extended families are generally greater in African American, Asian American, and Hispanic families than in Caucasian families (Becker, Beyene, & Newsom, 2003).

SPECIALIZED LIVING ENVIRONMENTS. For some 10 percent of those in late adulthood, home is an institution. As we'll see, elderly people live in a broad range of different types of specialized environments.

One of the more recent innovations in living arrangements is the **continuing-care community**. Such communities typically offer an environment in which all the residents are of retirement age or older. Residents may need various levels of care, which is provided by the community. Residents sign contracts under which the community makes a commitment to provide care at whatever level is needed. In many such communities, people start out living in separate houses or apartments, either independently or with occasional home care. As they age and their needs increase, residents may eventually move into *assisted living*, in which people live in independent housing but are supported by medical providers to the extent required. Continuing care ultimately extends all the way to fulltime nursing care, which is often provided at an on-site nursing home.

Continuing-care communities tend to be fairly homogeneous in terms of religious, racial, and ethnic backgrounds, and they are often organized by private or religious organizations. Because joining may involve a substantial initial payment, members of such communities tend to be relatively well-off financially. Increasingly, though, continuing-care communities are making efforts to raise the level of diversity. Furthermore, they are attempting to increase opportunities for intergenerational interaction by establishing day-care centers on the premises and developing programs that involve younger populations (Chaker, 2003; Berkman, 2006).

Several types of nursing institutions exist, ranging from those that provide part-time day care to homes that offer 24-hour-a-day, live-in care. In **adult day-care facilities**, elderly individuals receive care only during the day but spend nights and weekends in their own homes. During the time that they are at the facility, people receive nursing care, take their meals, and participate in scheduled activities. Sometimes adult facilities are combined with infant and child day-care programs, an arrangement that allows for interaction between the old and the young (Gitlin et al., 2006; Dabelko & Zimmerman, 2008; Teitelman et al., 2017).

Other institutional settings offer more extensive care. The most intensive institutions are **skilled-nursing facilities**, which provide full-time nursing care for

continuing-care community
a community that offers an environment in which all the residents are of retirement age or older and need various levels of care

adult day-care facilities
settings in which elderly individuals receive care only during the day, but spend nights and weekends in their own homes

skilled-nursing facilities
settings that provide full-time nursing care for people who have chronic illnesses or are recovering from a temporary medical condition

Maskot/Getty Images

So-called "granny units" are one way that older people can get the support and assistance of family while still maintaining privacy and independence.

people who have chronic illnesses or are recovering from a temporary medical condition. Although only 4.5 percent of those age 65 and older live in nursing homes, the number increases dramatically with age. Around 3 percent of the over-65 population lives in nursing homes, while around 10 percent of the over-85 population lives in nursing homes (Administration on Aging, 2006; *Nursing Home Data Compendium*, 2013).

The greater the extent of nursing home care, the greater the adjustment required of residents. Although some newcomers adjust relatively rapidly, the loss of independence brought about by institutional life may lead to difficulties. In addition, elderly people are as susceptible as other people to society's stereotypes about nursing homes, and their expectations may be particularly negative. They may see themselves as just marking time until they eventually die, forgotten and discarded by a society that venerates youth (Biedenharn & Normoyle, 1991; Baltes, 1996).

institutionalism
a psychological state in which people in nursing homes develop apathy, indifference, and a lack of caring about themselves

INSTITUTIONALISM AND LEARNED HELPLESSNESS. Although the fears of those in nursing homes may be exaggerated, they can lead to **institutionalism**, a psychological state in which people develop apathy, indifference, and a lack of caring about themselves. Institutionalism is brought about, in part, by a sense of *learned helplessness*, a belief that one has no control over one's environment (Peterson & Park, 2007).

The sense of helplessness brought about by institutionalism can literally have deadly consequences. Consider, for instance, what happens when people enter nursing homes in late adulthood. One of the most conspicuous changes from their independent past is that they no longer have control over their most basic activities. They may be told when and what to eat, their sleeping schedules may be arranged by others, and even their visits to the bathroom may be regulated (Wolinsky, Wyrwich, & Babu, 2003; Iecovich & Biderman, 2012; de Oliveira Brito et al., 2014).

A classic experiment showed the consequences of such a loss of control. Psychologists Ellen Langer and Irving Janis (1979) divided elderly residents of a nursing home into two groups. One group of residents was encouraged to make a variety of choices about their day-to-day activities. The other group was given no choices and was encouraged to let the nursing home staff care for them. The results were clear. The participants who had choices were not only happier, they were also healthier: 18 months after the experiment began, only 15 percent of the choice group had died—compared to 30 percent of the comparison group.

In short, the loss of control over certain aspects of their daily life experienced by residents of nursing homes and other institutions can have a profound effect on their well-being. Keep in mind that not all nursing homes are the same, however. The best go out of their way to permit residents to make basic life decisions, and they attempt to give people in late adulthood a sense of control over their lives.

ASTIER/BSIP/Getty Images

Elderly people in adult day-care facilities socialize with others during meals and activities.

From *a health-care professional's* perspective

What policies might a nursing home institute to minimize the chances that its residents will develop institutionalism? Why are such policies relatively uncommon?

Financial Issues: The Economics of Late Adulthood

LO 18.6 Discuss how financially secure older people are in the United States today.

People in late adulthood, like people in all other stages of life, range from one end of the socioeconomic spectrum to the other. Like the man quoted earlier in this section of the chapter, those who were relatively affluent during their working years tend to remain relatively affluent, while those who were poor at earlier stages of life tend to remain poor when they reach late adulthood.

However, the social inequities that various groups experience during their earlier lives become magnified with increasing age. At the same time, people who reach late adulthood today may experience growing economic pressure as a result of the ever-increasing human life span, which means it is more likely they will run through their savings.

Overall, just under 10 percent of people age 65 and older live in poverty, a proportion that is quite close to that for people younger than 65. However, there are significant differences in gender and racial groups. For instance, women are almost twice as likely as men to be living in poverty. Of those elderly women living alone, around one-fourth live on incomes below the poverty line. A married woman may also slip into poverty if she becomes widowed, for she may have used up savings to pay for her husband's final illness, and the husband's pension may cease with his death (Spraggins, 2003; DeNavas-Walt & Proctor, 2014; see Figure 18-2).

Furthermore, 8 percent of whites in late adulthood live below the poverty level, compared with 19 percent of Hispanics and 24 percent of African Americans. Minority women fare the worst of any category. For example, divorced black women age 65 to 74 have a poverty rate of 47 percent (Federal Interagency Forum on Age-Related Statistics, 2000; U.S. Bureau of the Census, 2013).

One source of financial vulnerability for people in late adulthood is the reliance on a fixed income for support. Unlike that of a younger person, the income of an elderly person, which typically comes from a combination of Social Security benefits, pensions, and savings, rarely keeps up with inflation. Consequently, as inflation drives up the price of goods such as food and clothing, income does not rise as quickly. What may have been a reasonable income at age 65 is worth much less 20 years later, as the elderly person gradually slips into poverty.

The rising cost of health care is another source of financial vulnerability in older adults. The average older person spends close to 20 percent of his or her income for health-care costs. For those who require care in nursing home facilities, the financial costs can be staggering, running an average of close to $80,000 a year (MetLife Mature Market Institute, 2009).

Figure 18-2 Poverty in Late Adulthood

Although women are more likely than men to be living in poverty at every age after 18, women over age 75 are particularly at risk. Why do you think this discrepancy is so pronounced at this age?

(**Source:** DeNavas-Walt & Proctor, 2015.)

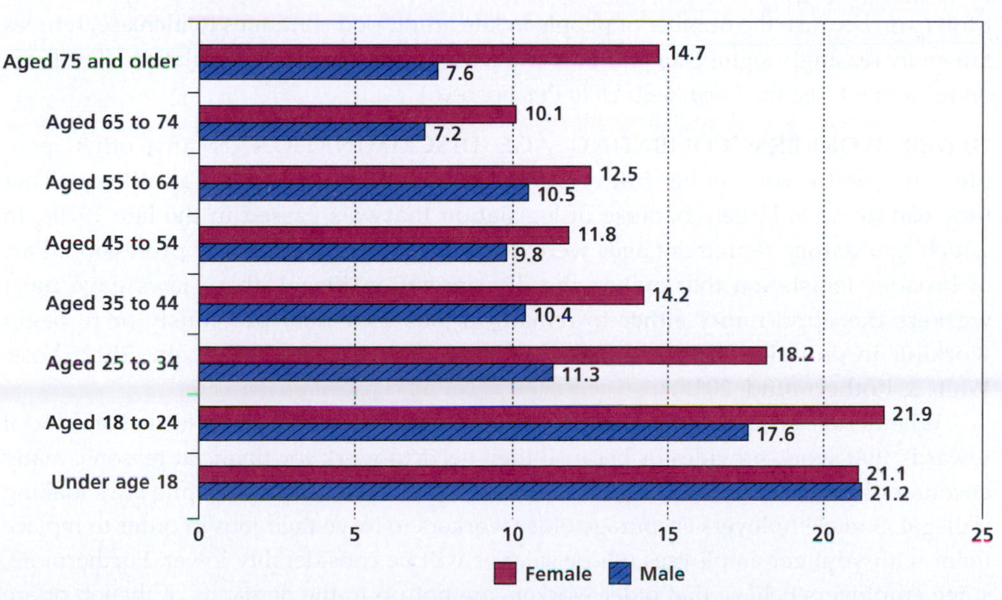

Unless major changes are made in the way that Social Security and Medicare are financed, the costs borne by younger U.S. citizens in the workforce must rise significantly. Increasing expenditures mean that a larger proportion of younger people's pay must be taxed to fund benefits for the elderly. Such a situation is apt to lead to increasing friction and segregation between younger and older generations. Indeed, as we'll see, Social Security payments are one key factor in many people's decisions about how long to work.

Work and Retirement in Late Adulthood

LO 18.7 Summarize the positives and negatives of retiring as well as typical stages retired people pass through.

"Don't forget your change, Mrs. Brody," Jim Hardy reminds his customer. "And enjoy your grandkids' visit." Hardy waves goodbye, and the woman smiles as she waves back.

Jim Hardy turned 84 last month, and he works 24 hours a week at the local supermarket. "I wasn't always a cashier," Hardy says. "I've done lots of work in my time. Started out on a logging operation, first in Vancouver, then up in Maine. But I got married and the missus wanted me to do something steady, so I got a job doing repairs for the telephone company. Worked that job for more than 40 years."

When Hardy's wife died 5 years ago, he thought about retiring and moving to Hawaii. "Beautiful country out there and the people are friendly." But Hardy didn't retire. He took the supermarket job instead.

"I like it here" he says. "I see folks. Talk to 'em. I'm not sure I'd know what to do if I wasn't working."

Retirement is a major decision faced by the majority of individuals in late adulthood. Some, like Jim Hardy, wish to work as long as they can. Others retire the moment their financial circumstances permit it.

When they do retire, many people experience a fair amount of difficulty in making the identity shift from "worker" to "retiree." They lack a professional title, they may no longer have people asking them for advice, and they can't say "I work for the Diamond Company."

For others, though, retirement represents a major opportunity, offering the chance to lead, perhaps for the first time in adulthood, a life of leisure. Because a significant number of people retire as early as age 55 or 60, and because people's life spans are expanding, many people spend far more time in retirement than in previous generations. Moreover, because the number of people in late adulthood continues to increase, retirees are an increasingly significant and influential segment of the U.S. population. (For more on retirement, see the *From Research to Practice* box.)

OLDER WORKERS: COMBATING AGE DISCRIMINATION. Many other people continue to work, either full or part time, for some part of late adulthood. That they can do so is largely because of legislation that was passed in the late 1970s, in which mandatory retirement ages were made illegal in almost every profession. Part of broader legislation that makes age discrimination illegal, these laws gave most workers the opportunity either to remain in jobs they held previously or to begin working in entirely different fields (Lindemann & Kadue, 2003; Lain, 2012; Voss, Wolff & Rothermund, 2017).

Whether older adults continue to work because they enjoy the intellectual and social rewards that work provides or because they need to work for financial reasons, many encounter age discrimination. Age discrimination remains a reality despite laws making it illegal. Some employers encourage older workers to leave their jobs in order to replace them with younger employees whose salaries will be considerably lower. Furthermore, some employers believe that older workers are not up to the demands of the job or are

From Research to Practice

Retirement: Looking Back and Looking Forward

Many people think of retirement as a time of slowing down, perhaps withdrawing from an active lifestyle to sit out the rest of one's days in a rocking chair. But the reality is that there are many different possible approaches to retirement, including options for staying just as active while retired as in the pre-retirement years. Rather than the closing of a book, retirement represents the turning of a new chapter—and the story that unfolds in that new chapter has a lot to do with the retiree's expectations, goals, and pre-retirement plans.

Based on an extensive series of interviews, psychologist Nancy Schlossberg (2004, 2017) has identified six basic paths of retirement:

- *Continuers* use part-time or volunteer work to remain at least partially active in their pre-retirement work.
- *Involved spectators* take more of a back-seat role in staying connected with their previous fields.
- *Adventurers* use retirement as a time to explore entirely new pursuits, perhaps including a new field of work.
- *Searchers* try different activities in search of a suitable way to spend their retirement.
- *Easy gliders* don't fret about retirement much and take each day as it comes.
- *Retreaters* become depressed and withdrawn and stop searching for a meaningful pathway through retirement.

The path that a person takes can change over the course of retirement, too, underscoring another fundamental point: Retirement is less of a destination than it is a journey. People who negotiate retirement most successfully are those who see it not as a time of withdrawal and stagnation but as an opportunity for development and exploration (Brucker & Leppel, 2013; Sherry et al., 2017).

For many people, retirement occurs in stages as they withdraw slowly from work—perhaps by dropping to part-time work for a period before retiring altogether. Others put off retirement as long as they can; some simply enjoy their work, while others are increasingly finding that they simply do not have the financial means to retire as employers scale back pension plans and health benefits for retirees (Harrison & Newman, 2013; Muratore & Earl, 2015).

Research suggests that it's just as important to prepare psychologically for retirement as it is to prepare financially. It's important for older adults to keep in mind that they don't just retire from work, but they also retire to a new lifestyle. Planning for what that lifestyle will be like—whether it will include part-time work, volunteer work, travel, or other activities, for example—can make a difference in adjustment to retirement (Froidevaux, Hirschi, & Wang, 2016; Leandro-Franca et al., 2016).

Shared Writing Prompt

What factors might contribute to the specific retirement path a given person takes?

less willing to adapt to a changing workplace—stereotypes about the elderly that are enduring, despite legislative changes.

There is little evidence to support the idea that older workers' ability to perform their jobs declines. In many fields, such as art, literature, science, politics, and even entertainment, it is easy to find examples of people who have made some of their greatest contributions during late adulthood. Even in those few professions that were specifically exempted from laws prohibiting mandatory retirement ages—those involving public safety—the evidence does not support the notion that workers should be retired at an arbitrary age.

For instance, one large-scale, careful study of older police officers, firefighters, and prison guards came to the conclusion that age was not a good predictor of the general level of a worker's performance or whether he or she was likely to be incapacitated on the job. Instead, a case-by-case analysis of individual workers' performance was a more accurate predictor (Landy & Conte, 2004).

Although age discrimination remains a problem, market forces may help reduce its severity. As baby boomers retire and the workforce drastically shrinks, companies may begin to offer incentives to older adults to either remain in the workforce or to return to it after they have retired. Still, for most older adults, retirement is the norm.

RETIREMENT: FILLING A LIFE OF LEISURE. Why do people decide to retire? Although the basic reason seems apparent—to stop working—the retirement decision is actually based on a variety of factors. For instance, sometimes workers are burned out after a lifetime of work; they seek a respite from the tension and frustration of their jobs and from the sense that they are not accomplishing as much as they once wished they could. Others retire because their health has declined, and still others because they are offered incentives by their employers in the form of bonuses or increased pensions if they retire by a certain age. Finally, some people have planned for years to retire and intend to use their increased leisure to travel, study, or spend more time with their children and grandchildren (Nordenmark & Stattin, 2009; Petkoska & Earl, 2009; Müller et al., 2014).

Whatever the reason they retire, people often pass through a series of retirement stages, summarized in Figure 18-3. Retirement may begin with a *honeymoon* period, in which former workers engage in a variety of activities, such as travel, that were previously hindered by full-time work. The next phase may be *disenchantment*, in which retirees conclude that retirement is not all they thought it would be. They may miss the stimulation and companionship of their previous jobs, or they may find it hard to keep busy (Osborne, 2012; Schlosser, Zinni, & Armstrong-Stassen, 2012; Rafalski et al., 2017).

The next phase is *reorientation*, in which retirees reconsider their options and become engaged in new, more fulfilling activities. If successful, this leads to the *retirement routine* stage, in which they come to grips with the realities of retirement and feel fulfilled in this new phase of life. Not all people reach this stage; some may feel disenchanted with retirement for years.

Figure 18-3 Stages of Retirement

(**Source:** Based on Atchley, 1982.)

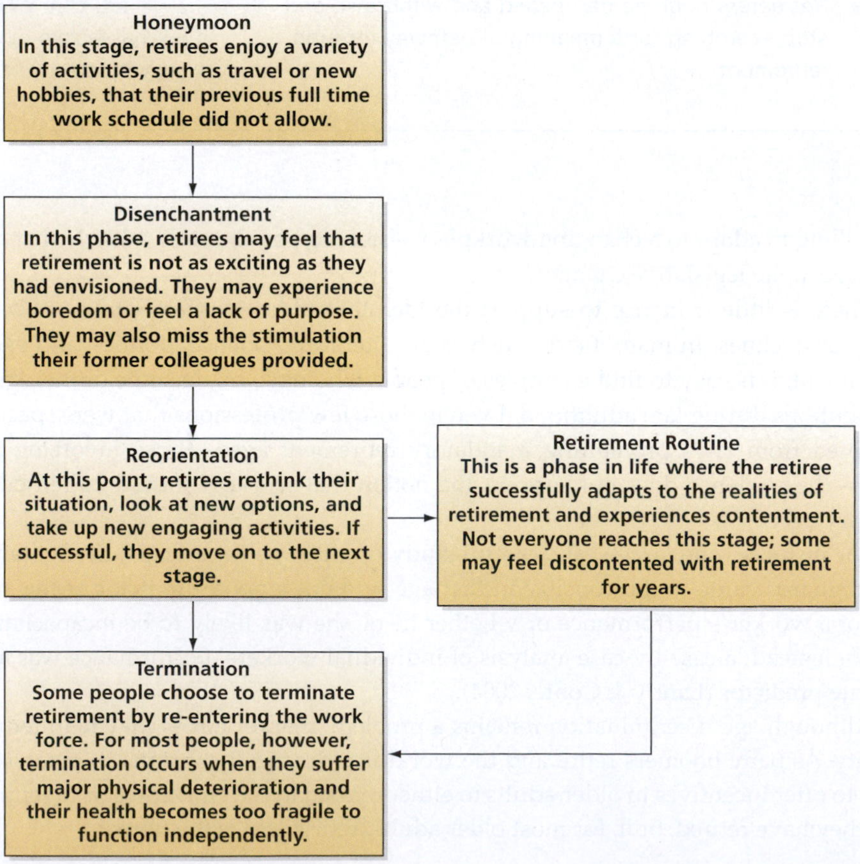

Honeymoon
In this stage, retirees enjoy a variety of activities, such as travel or new hobbies, that their previous full time work schedule did not allow.

Disenchantment
In this phase, retirees may feel that retirement is not as exciting as they had envisioned. They may experience boredom or feel a lack of purpose. They may also miss the stimulation their former colleagues provided.

Reorientation
At this point, retirees rethink their situation, look at new options, and take up new engaging activities. If successful, they move on to the next stage.

Retirement Routine
This is a phase in life where the retiree successfully adapts to the realities of retirement and experiences contentment. Not everyone reaches this stage; some may feel discontented with retirement for years.

Termination
Some people choose to terminate retirement by re-entering the work force. For most people, however, termination occurs when they suffer major physical deterioration and their health becomes too fragile to function independently.

Development in Your Life

Planning for—and Living—a Good Retirement

What makes for a good retirement? Gerontologists suggest that several factors are related to success (Rowe & Kahn, 1998; Noone, Stephens, & Alpass, 2009):

- Plan ahead financially. Because most financial experts suggest that Social Security pensions will be inadequate in the future, personal savings are critical. Similarly, having adequate health-care insurance is essential.
- Consider tapering off from work gradually. Sometimes it is possible to enter into retirement by shifting from full-time to part-time work. Such a transition may be helpful in preparing for eventual fulltime retirement.
- Explore your interests before you retire. Assess what you like about your current job and think about how that might be translated into leisure activities.
- If you are married or in a long-term partnership, spend some time discussing your views of the ideal retirement with your partner. You may find that you need to negotiate a vision that will suit you both.
- Consider where you want to live. Try out, temporarily, a community to which you are thinking of moving.
- Determine the advantages and disadvantages of downsizing your current home. You may need less space than you did earlier in life, and you might welcome fewer maintenance chores.
- Plan to volunteer your time. People who retire have an enormous wealth of skills, and these are often needed by nonprofit organizations and small businesses. Organizations such as the Retired Senior Volunteer Program and the Foster Grandparent Program can help match your skills with people who need them.

Finally, the last phase of the retirement process is *termination*. Although some people terminate retirement by going back to work, termination for most people results from major physical deterioration. In this case, health becomes so bad that the person can no longer function independently. Obviously, not everyone passes through all these stages, and the sequence is not universal. In large measure, a person's reactions to retirement stem from the reasons he or she retired in the first place. For example, a person forced into retirement for health reasons will have a very different experience from a person who eagerly chose to retire at a particular age. Similarly, the retirement of people who loved their jobs may be a quite different experience from that of people who despised their work.

In short, the psychological consequences of retirement vary a great deal from one individual to the next. For many people, though, retirement is a continuation of a life well lived, and they use it to the fullest. Moreover, as we see in the *Development in Your Life* feature, one can do several things to plan a good retirement.

Module 18.2 Review

LO 18.5 Describe the circumstances in which older people live and the difficulties they face.

Elderly people live in a variety of settings, although most live at home with a family member.

LO 18.6 Discuss how financially secure older people are in the United States today.

Financial issues can trouble older people, largely because their incomes are fixed, health-care costs are increasing, and the life span is lengthening.

LO 18.7 Summarize the positives and negatives of retiring as well as typical stages retired people pass through.

People may pass through stages, including a honeymoon period, disenchantment, reorientation, retirement routine, and termination, as they adjust to retirement.

Journal Writing Prompt

Applying Lifespan Development: Based on the research on successful aging, what advice would you give someone who is nearing retirement?

Relationships: Old and New

Leonard Timbola, 94, describes how he met his wife, Ellen, 90.

"I was 23 when Pearl Harbor happened and I enlisted right away. I was sent to Fort Bragg and I was lonely. I'd often go into Fayetteville and just poke around. One day I was in a bookstore reaching for a book. You remember what it was?"

"Out of the Silent Planet," *Ellen says. "I happened to be reaching for it at the same time. Our hands met, and then our eyes."*

"And that was the end of my bachelorhood," says Leonard. "Fate sent me to that bookstore."

Ellen continues. "We shared that book and everything else from then on. We were married 4 months later."

"Just before I shipped out," says Leonard.

This is the way they are: He starts a thought, she finishes it. Unless it's the other way around.

"She wrote every day. I got her letters in bunches, and that was the best reading I ever did." He places his hand on Ellen's knee. Her hand joins his there.

"You weren't nearly as frequent a writer," she reminds him gently. "But when I did get one from you, I read it every day."

"Well that's the same thing," he laughs.

The warmth and affection between Leonard and Ellen are unmistakable. Their relationship, spanning eight decades, continues to bring them quiet joy, and their life is the sort to which many couples aspire. Yet it is also something of a rarity for those in the last stage of life. For every older person who is part of a couple, many more are alone.

What is the nature of the social world of people in late adulthood? To answer the question, we will first consider the nature of marriage in the period.

Marriage in the Later Years: In Sickness and in Health

LO 18.8 Describe how marriages fare in late adulthood.

It's a man's world—at least when it comes to marriage after age 65. The proportion of men who are married at this age is far greater than that of women. One reason for this disparity is that 70 percent of women outlive their husbands by at least a few years. Because there are fewer men available (many have died), these women are unlikely to remarry (also see Figure 18-4).

Figure 18-4 Living Patterns of Older Americans

(Source: Stepler, 2016.)

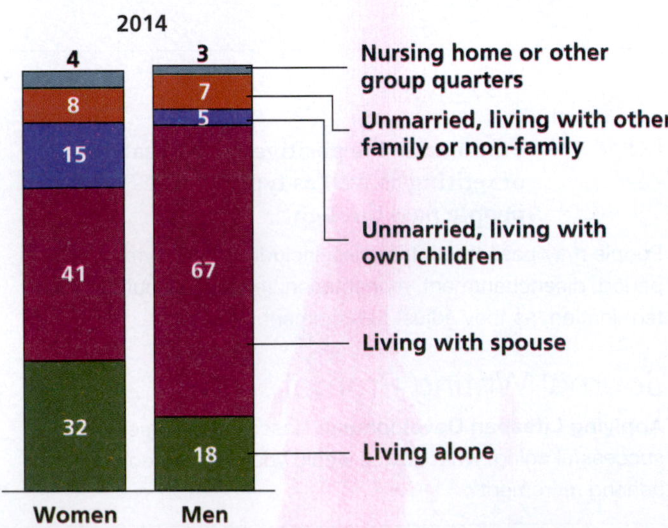

Furthermore, the marriage gradient that we first discussed in Chapter 14 is still a powerful influence. Reflecting societal norms that suggest that women should marry men older than themselves, the marriage gradient works to keep women single even in the later years of life. At the same time, it makes remarriage for men much easier, since the available pool of eligible partners is much larger (Treas & Bengtson, 1987; AARP, 1990).

The vast majority of people who are still married in later life report that they are satisfied with their marriages. Their partners provide substantial companionship and emotional support. Because at this period in life they have typically been together for a long time, they have great insight into their partners (Jose & Alfons, 2007; Petrican, Moscovitch, & Grady, 2014).

At the same time, not every aspect of marriage is equally satisfying, and marriages may undergo severe stress as spouses experience changes in their lives. For instance, the retirement of one or both spouses can bring about a shift in the nature of a couple's relationship (Henry, Miller, & Giarrusso, 2005).

DIVORCE. For some couples, the stress is so great that one spouse or the other seeks a divorce. Some 15 percent of Americans over age 50 are divorced. The divorce rate has doubled since 1990 (Roberts, 2013).

The reasons for divorce at such a late stage of life are varied. Often, women who divorce do so because their husbands are abusive or alcoholic. But in the more frequent case of a husband seeking a divorce from his wife, the reason is often that he has found a younger woman. Often the divorce occurs soon after retirement, when men who have been highly involved in their careers are in psychological turmoil (Solomon et al., 1998).

Divorce so late in life is particularly difficult for women. Between the marriage gradient and the limited size of the potential pool of eligible men, it is unlikely that an older divorced woman will remarry. Divorce in late adulthood can be devastating. For many women, marriage has been their primary role and the center of their identities, and they may view divorce as a major failure. As a consequence, happiness and the quality of life for divorced women often plummet (Goldscheider, 1994; Davies & Denton, 2002).

Seeking a new relationship becomes a priority for many men and women who are divorced or whose spouses have died. As in earlier stages of life, people seeking to develop relationships use a variety of strategies to meet potential partners, such as joining singles organizations or using the Internet to seek out companionship (Durbin, 2003; Dupuis, 2009).

It is important to keep in mind that some people enter late adulthood having never married. For those who have remained single throughout their lives—about 5 percent of the population—late adulthood may bring fewer transitions, since the status of living alone does not change. In fact, never-married individuals report feeling less lonely than do most people their age, and they have a greater sense of independence (Newston & Keith, 1997).

DEALING WITH RETIREMENT: TOO MUCH TOGETHERNESS?

> *When Morris Abercrombie finally stopped working full time, his wife, Roxanne, found some aspects of his increased presence at home troubling. Although their marriage was strong, his intrusion into her daily routine and his constant questioning about whom she was on the phone with and where she was going when she went out were irksome. Finally, she began to wish he would spend less time around the house. It was an ironic thought: She had passed much of Morris's pre-retirement years wishing that he would spend more time at home.*

The situation in which Morris and Roxanne found themselves is not unique. For many couples, retirement means that relationships need to be renegotiated. In some cases, retirement results in a couple spending more time together than at any other point in their marriage. In others, retirement alters the long-standing distribution of household chores, with men taking on more responsibility than before for the everyday functioning of the household.

Research suggests that an interesting role reversal often takes place. In contrast to the early years of marriage, when wives, more than husbands, typically desire greater companionship with their spouses, in late adulthood husbands' companionship needs tend to be greater than their wives'. The power structure of marriage also changes: Men become more affiliative and less competitive following retirement. At the same time, women become more assertive and autonomous (Kulik, 2002).

CARING FOR AN AGING SPOUSE OR PARTNER. The shifts in health that accompany late adulthood sometimes require women and men to care for their spouses or partners in ways that they never envisioned. Health issues may force them into nearly full-time caretaking, a role they may have never envisioned for themselves.

At the same time, some people view caring for an ailing and dying spouse or partner in a more positive light, regarding it in part as a final opportunity to demonstrate love and devotion. Some caregivers report feeling quite satisfied as a result of fulfilling what they see as their responsibility to their spouse. And some of those who experience emotional distress initially find that the distress declines as they successfully adapt to the stress of caregiving.

Yet even if giving care is viewed in such a light, without doubt it is an arduous chore, made more difficult by the fact that the spouses providing the care are probably not in

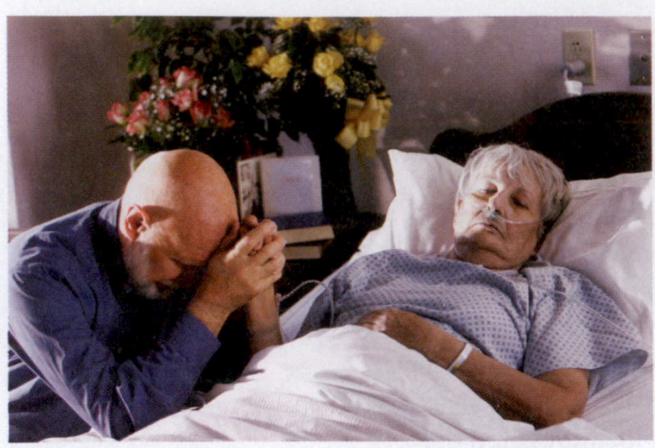
Photodisc/Getty Images

One of the most difficult responsibilities of later adulthood can be caring for one's ill spouse.

the peak of physical health themselves. Caregiving may indeed be detrimental to the provider's own physical and psychological health. For instance, caregivers report lower levels of satisfaction with life than do non-caregivers (Mausbach et al., 2012; Davis et al., 2014; Glauber, 2017).

In most cases, it should be noted, the care provider is the wife. Just under three-quarters of people who provide care to a spouse are women. Part of the reason is demographic: Men tend to die earlier than women, and consequently they contract the diseases leading to death earlier than women. A second reason relates to society's traditional gender roles, which view women as "natural" caregivers. As a consequence, health-care providers may be more likely to suggest that a wife cares for her husband than that a husband cares for his wife.

The Death of a Spouse: Becoming Widowed

LO 18.9 Describe the typical reactions to the death of a spouse during late adulthood.

Hardly any event is more painful and stressful than the death of one's spouse. Especially for those who married young, the death of a spouse leads to profound feelings of loss and often brings about drastic changes in economic and social circumstances. If the marriage has been a good one, the death of the partner means the loss of a companion, a lover, a confidante, a helper.

Upon a partner's death, spouses suddenly assume a new and unfamiliar societal role: widowhood. At the same time, they lose the role with which they were most familiar: spouse. Abruptly, widowed people are no longer part of a couple; instead they are viewed by society, and themselves, solely as individuals. All this occurs as they are dealing with profound and sometimes overwhelming grief.

Widowhood brings a variety of new demands and concerns. There is no longer a companion with whom to share the day's events. If the deceased spouse primarily carried out household chores, the surviving spouse must learn how to do these tasks and must perform them every day. Although initially family and friends provide a great deal of support, this assistance quickly fades into the background, and newly widowed people are left to make the adjustment to being single on their own (Hanson & Hayslip, 2000; Smith, J. M., 2012; Isherwood, King & Luszcz, 2017).

People's social lives often change drastically following the death of a spouse. Married couples tend to socialize with other married couples; widowed individuals may feel like "fifth wheels" as they seek to maintain the friendships they enjoyed as a member of a couple. Eventually, such friendships may cease, although they may be replaced by friendships with other single people (Fry & Debats, 2010).

Economic issues are of major concern to many widowed people. Although many have insurance, savings, and pensions to provide economic security, some individuals, most often women, experience a decline in their economic well-being as the result of a spouse's death, as noted earlier in this chapter. In such cases, the change in financial status can force distressing decisions, such as selling the house in which the couple spent their entire married lives (Meyer, Wolf, & Himes, 2006).

The process of adjusting to widowhood encompasses three stages (see Figure 18-5). In the first stage, *preparation*, spouses prepare, in some cases years and even decades ahead of time, for the eventual death of the partner. Consider, for instance, the purchase of life insurance, the preparation of a will, and the decision to have children, who may eventually provide care in one's old age. Each of these actions helps prepare for the eventuality that one will be widowed and will require some degree of assistance (Roecke & Cherry, 2002).

Figure 18-5 Process of Adjustment to Widowhood

Do you think the process of adjustment is identical for men and women?

(**Source:** Based on Heinemann & Evans, 1990.)

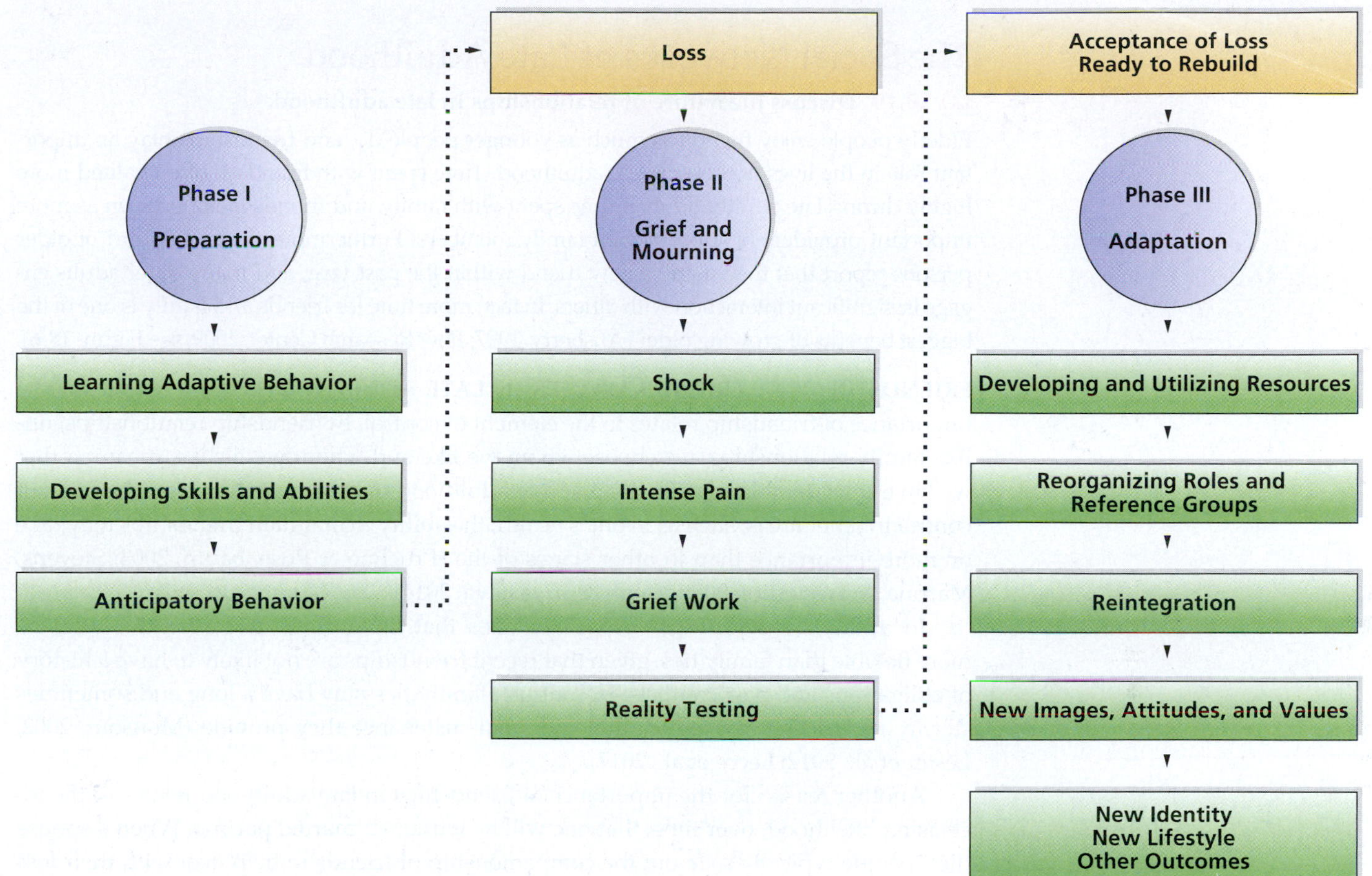

The second stage of adjustment to widowhood, *grief and mourning*, is an immediate reaction to the death of a spouse. It starts with the shock and pain of loss and continues as the survivor works through the period of emotions the loss brings up. The length of time a person spends in grief and mourning depends on the degree of support received from others, as well as on personality factors. In some cases, the grief and mourning period may last for years, while in others, it lasts a few months.

The last stage of adjustment to the death of a spouse is *adaptation*. In adaptation, the widowed individual starts a new life. The period begins with the acceptance of one's loss and continues with the reorganization of roles and the formation of new friendships. The adaptation stage also encompasses a period of reintegration in which a new identity—as an unmarried person—is developed.

It is important to keep in mind that this three-stage model of loss and change does not apply to everyone, and the timing of the stages varies considerably. Moreover, some people experience *complicated grief*, a form of unrelenting mourning that continues sometimes for months and even years. In complicated grief, people find it difficult to let go of a loved one, and they have intrusive memories of the deceased that impede normal functioning (Holland et al., 2009; Piper et al., 2009; Zisook & Shear, 2009).

From *a social worker's* perspective

What are some factors that can combine to make older adulthood a more difficult time for women than for men?

For most people, though, life returns to normal and becomes enjoyable once again after the death of a spouse. Still, the death of a spouse is a profound event in any period of life. During late adulthood, its implications are particularly powerful, since it can be seen as a forewarning of one's own mortality.

The Social Networks of Late Adulthood

LO 18.10 Discuss the nature of relationships in late adulthood.

Elderly people enjoy friends as much as younger people do, and friendships play an important role in the lives of those in late adulthood. Time spent with friends is often valued more highly during late adulthood than time spent with family, and friends are often seen as more important providers of support than family members. Furthermore, around a third of older persons report that they made a new friend within the past year, and many older adults engage in significant interaction with others. In fact, more time for friends and family is one of the biggest benefits of growing older (Ansberry, 1997; Pew Research Center, 2009; see Figure 18-6).

FRIENDSHIP: WHY FRIENDS MATTER IN LATE ADULTHOOD. One reason for the importance of friendship relates to the element of control. In friendship relationships, unlike family relationships, we choose whom we like and whom we dislike, meaning that we have considerable control. Because late adulthood may bring with it a gradual loss of control in other areas, such as in one's health, the ability to maintain friendships may take on more importance than in other stages of life (Pruchno & Rosenbaum, 2003; Stevens, Martina, & Westerhof, 2006; Singh & Srivastava, 2014).

In addition, friendships—especially ones that have developed recently—may be more flexible than family ties, given that recent friendships are not likely to have a history of obligations and past conflicts. In contrast, family ties may have a long and sometimes stormy record that can reduce the emotional sustenance they provide (Monsour, 2002; Lester et al., 2012; Lecce et al., 2017).

Another reason for the importance of friendships in late adulthood relates to the increasing likelihood, over time, that one will be without a marital partner. When a spouse dies, people typically seek out the companionship of friends to help deal with their loss and also for some of the companionship that was provided by the deceased spouse.

Of course, it isn't only spouses who die during old age; friends die too. The way adults view friendship in late adulthood determines how vulnerable they are to the death of a friend. If the friendship has been defined as irreplaceable, then the loss of the friend may be quite difficult. In contrast, if the friendship is defined as one of many friendships,

Figure 18-6 Benefits of Growing Older

People 65 and older cite a number of aspects of growing old that are positive. Chief among them are more time with family. **THINKING ABOUT THE DATA:** Individuals in late adulthood participate in a variety of social activities and this participation changes over time. What are some of the most prevalent social activities that older adults engage in? Describe how this social activity participation changes over time.

(**Source:** Pew Research Center, 2009.)

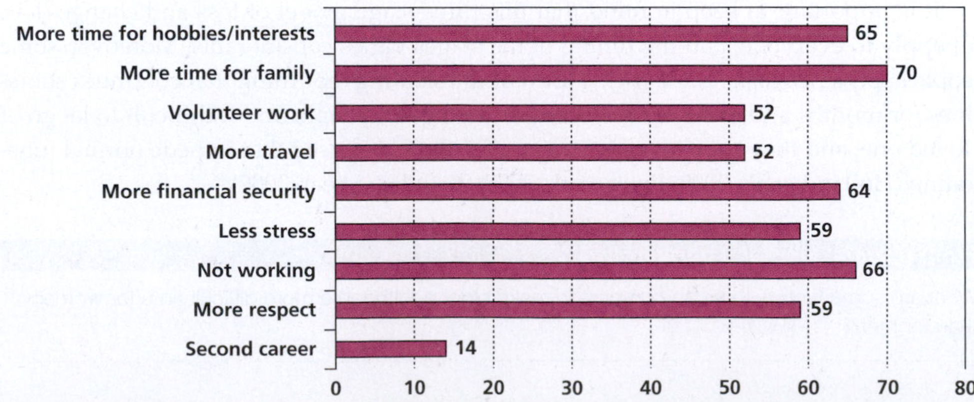

then the death of a friend may be less traumatic. In such cases, older adults are more likely to become involved subsequently with new friends.

SOCIAL SUPPORT: THE SIGNIFICANCE OF OTHERS. Friendships also provide one of the basic social needs: social support. **Social support** is assistance and comfort supplied by a network of caring, interested people. Such support plays a critical role in successful aging (Avlund, Lund, & Holstein, 2004; Gow et al., 2007; Evans, 2009; Li, Xu, & Li, 2014).

social support
assistance and comfort supplied by a network of caring, interested people

The benefits of social support are considerable. For instance, people can provide emotional support by lending a sympathetic ear and providing a sounding board for one's concerns. Furthermore, social support from people who are experiencing similar problems—such as the loss of a spouse—can provide an unmatched degree of understanding and a pool of helpful suggestions for coping strategies that would be less credible coming from others.

Finally, people can furnish material support, such as helping with rides or picking up groceries. They can provide help in solving problems, such as dealing with a difficult landlord or fixing a broken appliance.

The benefits of social support extend not only to the recipient of the support but also to the provider. People who offer support experience feelings of usefulness and heightened self-esteem, knowing that they are making a contribution to others' welfare.

What kinds of social support are most effective and appropriate? It can vary from preparing food, accompanying someone to a movie, or inviting someone to dinner. But the opportunity for reciprocity is important, too. Reciprocity is the expectation that if someone provides something positive to another person, eventually, the favor will be returned. In Western societies, older adults—like younger people—value relationships in which reciprocity is possible (Becker, Beyene, & Newsom, 2003).

With increasing age, it may be progressively more difficult to reciprocate the social support that one receives. As a consequence, relationships may become more asymmetrical, placing the recipient in a difficult psychological position.

Family Relationships: The Ties That Bind

LO 18.11 Explain how aging affects family relationships.

Even after the death of a spouse, most older adults are part of a larger family unit. Connections with siblings, children, grandchildren, and even great-grandchildren continue, and they may provide an important source of comfort to adults in the last years of their lives.

Siblings may provide unusually strong emotional support during late adulthood. Because they often share old, pleasant memories of childhood, and because they usually represent the oldest existing relationships a person has, siblings can provide important support. While not every memory of childhood may be happy, continuing interaction with brothers and sisters still provides substantial emotional support during late adulthood.

CHILDREN. Even more important than siblings are children and grandchildren. Even in an age in which geographic mobility is high, most parents and children remain fairly close, both geographically and psychologically. Some 75 percent of children live within a 30-minute drive of their parents, and parents and children visit and talk with one another frequently. Daughters tend to be in more frequent contact with their parents than sons, and mothers tend to receive communication more frequently than fathers (Ji-liang, Li-qing, & Yan, 2003; Diamond, Fagundes, & Butterworth, 2010; Byrd-Craven et al., 2012).

Because the great majority of older adults have at least one child who lives fairly close by, family members still provide significant aid to one another. Moreover, parents and children tend to share similar views of how adult children should behave toward their parents (see Table 18-1). In particular, they expect that children should help their parents understand their resources, provide emotional support, and talk over matters of importance, such as medical issues. Furthermore, it is most often children who end up caring for their aging parents when they require assistance (Dellmann-Jenkins & Brittain, 2003; Ron, 2006; Funk, 2010).

Table 18-1 Views of Parents and Children Regarding Behavior of Adult Children Toward Parents

Rank	Children's Ranking	Parent's Ranking
1	Help understand resources	Discuss matters of importance
2	Give emotional support	Help understand resources
3	Discuss matters of importance	Give emotional support
4	Make room in home in emergency	Give parents advice
5	Sacrifice personal freedom	Be together on special occasions
6	Give care when sick	Sacrifice personal freedom
7	Be together on special occasions	Make room in home in emergency
8	Provide financial help	Feel responsible for parent
9	Give parents advice	Give care when sick
10	Adjust family schedule to help	Adjust family schedule to help
11	Feel responsible for parent	Visit once a week
12	Adjust work schedule to help	Adjust work schedule to help
13	Believe that parent should live with child	Provide financial help
14	Visit once a week	Write once a week
15	Live close to parent	Believe that parent should live with child
16	Write once a week	Live close to parent

(**Source:** Based on Hamon & Blieszner, 1990.)

The bonds between parents and children are sometimes asymmetrical, with parents seeking a closer relationship and children a more distant one. Parents have a greater *developmental stake* in close ties, since they see their children as perpetuating their beliefs, values, and standards. Meanwhile, children are motivated to maintain their autonomy and live independently from their parents. These divergent perspectives make parents more likely to minimize conflicts they experience with their children, and children more likely to maximize them.

For parents, their children remain a source of great interest and concern. Some surveys show, for instance, that even in late adulthood parents talk about their children nearly every day, particularly if the children are having some sort of problem. At the same time, children may turn to their elderly parents for advice, information, and sometimes tangible help, such as money (Diamond, Fagundes, & Butterworth, 2010).

GRANDCHILDREN AND GREAT-GRANDCHILDREN. As we discussed first in Chapter 16, not all grandparents are equally involved with their grandchildren. Even those grandparents who take great pride in their grandchildren may be relatively detached from them, avoiding any direct care role. However, many grandparents include their grandchildren as an integral part of their social networks (Coall & Hertwig, 2011; Geurts, van Tilburg, & Poortman, 2012; Moore & Rosenthal, 2017).

As we saw, grandmothers tend to be more involved with their grandchildren than grandfathers; similarly, there are gender differences in the feelings grandchildren have toward their grandparents. Specifically, most young adult grandchildren feel closer to their grandmothers than to their grandfathers. In addition, most express a preference for their maternal grandmothers over their paternal grandmothers (Hayslip, Shore, & Henderson, 2000; Lavers-Preston & Sonuga-Barke, 2003; Bishop et al., 2009).

African American grandparents tend to be more involved with their grandchildren than white grandparents, and African American grandchildren often feel closer to their grandparents. Moreover, grandfathers seem to play a more central role in the lives of African American children than in the lives of white children. The reason for these racial differences probably stems in large measure from the higher proportion of multigenerational families among African Americans than among whites. In such families, grandparents usually play a central role in childrearing (Crowther & Rodriguez, 2003; Stevenson, Henderson, & Baugh, 2007; Gelman et al., 2014).

Great-grandchildren play less of a role in the lives of both white and African American great-grandparents. Most great-grandparents do not have close relationships with their great-grandchildren. Close relationships tend to occur only when the great-grandparents and great-grandchildren live relatively near one another (McConnell, 2012).

There are several explanations for the relative lack of involvement of great-grandparents with great-grandchildren. One is that by the time they reach great-grandparenthood, older adults are so old that they do not have much physical or psychological energy to expend on forming relationships with their great-grandchildren. Another is that there may be so many great-grandchildren that great-grandparents do not feel strong emotional ties to them. It is not uncommon for a great-grandparent who has had a large number of children to have so many great-grandchildren that they are difficult to keep track of.

Still, even though most great-grandparents may not have close relationships with their great-grandchildren, they profit emotionally from the mere fact that they have great-grandchildren. For instance, great-grandparents may see their great-grandchildren as representing both their own and their family's continuation, as well as providing a concrete sign of their longevity. Furthermore, as health advances in late adulthood continue to increase, great-grandparents are physically able to contribute more to the lives of their great-grandchildren (McConnell, 2012).

Elder Abuse: Relationships Gone Wrong

LO 18.12 Discuss what causes elder abuse and how it can be prevented.

When Lorene Templeton was 74, her son Aaron moved in with her. "I was lonely and welcomed the company. When Aaron offered to take care of my finances, I gave him my power of attorney."

For the next 3 years, Aaron cashed Lorene's checks, withdrew her money, and used her credit card. "When I found out, Aaron apologized. He said he needed the money to get out of trouble. He promised to stop."

But he didn't. Aaron emptied Lorene's accounts and then demanded the key to her safe deposit box. When she refused, he beat her until she lost consciousness.

"His problem was drugs," Lorene says. "Finally, I called the police and they arrested him. Now I feel free for the first time in years."

It would be easy to assume that such cases are rare. The truth of the matter, however, is that they are considerably more common than we would like to believe. According to some estimates, **elder abuse**, the physical or psychological mistreatment or neglect of elderly individuals, had been experienced by as many as 11 percent of the elderly consulted during the previous year. Even these estimates may be too low, since people who are abused are often too embarrassed or humiliated to report their plight. And as the number of elderly people increases, experts believe that the number of cases of elder abuse will also rise (Acierno et al., 2010; Dow & Joosten, 2012; Jackson, 2018).

elder abuse
the physical or psychological mistreatment or neglect of elderly individuals

Elder abuse is most frequently directed at family members and particularly at elderly parents. Those most at risk are likely to be less healthy and more isolated than the average person in late adulthood, and they are more likely to be living in a caregiver's home. Although there is no single cause for elder abuse, it often is the result of a combination of economic, psychological, and social pressures on caregivers who must provide high levels of care 24 hours a day. Thus, people with Alzheimer's disease or other sorts of dementia are particularly likely to be targets of abuse (Tauriac & Scruggs, 2006; Baker, 2007; Lee, 2008).

The best approach to dealing with elder abuse is to prevent it from occurring in the first place. Family members caring for an older adult should take occasional breaks. Social support agencies can be contacted; they can provide advice and concrete support. For instance, the National Family Caregivers Association (800-896-3650) maintains a caregivers' network and publishes a newsletter. Anyone suspecting that an elderly person is being abused should contact local authorities, such as their state's Adult Protective Services or Elder Protective Services.

Module 18.3 Review

LO 18.8 Describe how marriages fare in late adulthood.

While marriages in older adulthood are generally happy, stresses due to aging can bring divorce. Retirement often requires a reworking of power relationships within the marriage.

LO 18.9 Describe the typical reactions to the death of a spouse during late adulthood.

The death of a spouse brings highly significant psychological, social, and material changes to the survivor.

LO 18.10 Discuss the nature of relationships in late adulthood.

Friendships are very important in later life, providing social support and companionship from peers who are likely to understand the older adult's feelings and problems.

LO 18.11 Explain how aging affects family relationships.

Family relationships are a continuing part of most older people's lives, especially relationships with siblings and children.

LO 18.12 Discuss what causes elder abuse and how it can be prevented.

Elder abuse typically involves a socially isolated elderly parent in poor health and a caregiver who feels burdened by the parent. The best way to prevent abuse is to provide relief for the caregiver in the form of breaks and social support.

Journal Writing Prompt

Applying Lifespan Development: What are some ways the retirement of a spouse can bring stress to a marriage? Is retirement likely to be less stressful in households where both spouses work, or twice as stressful?

Epilogue

Social and personality development continues in the last years of life. In this chapter, we focused on the question of change versus stability in personality and the sorts of life events that can affect personality development. We debunked a few stereotypes as we looked at the ways older people live and at the effects of retirement. Relationships, especially marital and family relationships but also friendships and social networks, are important to the well-being of older adults. We closed the chapter with a look at the troubling phenomenon of elder abuse.

Turn back to the prologue to this chapter, about the late-in-life marriage of Geraldine Mooers and Richard Thomas, and answer the following questions.

1. What aspects of Geraldine's and Richard's personalities can be deduced from the prologue?
2. Based on evidence in the prologue, how do you think they are managing what Erikson calls the ego-integrity-versus-despair stage? How about Peck's developmental tasks?
3. In what ways are they accomplishing life review? Does this process appear to be harmful or helpful to them?
4. If Geraldine and Richard chose disengagement as a strategy in late adulthood, what would you expect their lives to be like? What if they chose the activity strategy? Is there evidence to suggest which approach they took?

Looking Back

LO 18.1 Describe ways in which personality develops during late adulthood.

In Erik Erikson's ego-integrity-versus-despair stage of psychosocial development, as people reflect on their lives, they may feel either satisfaction, which leads to integration, or dissatisfaction, which can lead to despair and a lack of integration. Robert Peck identifies the three main tasks of this period as redefinition of self versus preoccupation with work role, body transcendence versus body preoccupation, and ego transcendence versus ego preoccupation. Daniel Levinson identifies a transitional stage that people pass through on the way to late adulthood, during which they struggle with being "old" and with societal stereotypes. A successful transition can lead to liberation and self-respect. Bernice Neugarten identified four personality types according to the way they cope with aging: disintegrated and disorganized, passive-dependent, defended, and integrated. Life review, a common theme of developmental theories of late adulthood, can help people resolve past conflicts and achieve wisdom and serenity, but some people become obsessive about past errors and slights.

LO 18.2 Explain how age relates to the distribution of resources, power, and privilege.

Age stratification theories suggest that the unequal distribution of economic resources, power, and privilege is particularly pronounced during late adulthood. In general, Western societies do not hold elderly people in as high esteem as many Asian societies.

LO 18.3 Define wisdom and describe how it is correlated with age.

Wisdom reflects the accumulation of knowledge related to human behavior. Because it is gathered through experience, it appears to be correlated with age.

LO 18.4 Differentiate the theories of aging.

Disengagement theory and activity theory present opposite views of ways to deal successfully with aging. People's choices depend partly on their prior habits and personalities. The model of selective optimization with compensation involves focusing on personally important areas of functioning and compensating for ability losses in those areas.

LO 18.5 Describe the circumstances in which older people live and the difficulties they face.

Living arrangement options include staying at home, living with family members, participating in adult day care, residing in continuing-care communities, and living in skilled-nursing facilities.

LO 18.6 Discuss how financially secure older people are in the United States today.

Elderly people may become financially vulnerable because they must cope with rising health-care expenses and other costs on a fixed income.

LO 18.7 Summarize the positives and negatives of retiring as well as typical stages retired people pass through.

People who retire must fill an increasingly longer span of leisure time. Those who are most successful plan ahead and have varied interests. People who retire often pass through stages, including a honeymoon period, disenchantment, reorientation, a retirement routine stage, and termination.

LO 18.8 Describe how marriages fare in late adulthood.

Marriages in later life generally remain happy, although stresses brought about by major life changes that accompany aging can cause rifts. Divorce is usually harder on the woman than the man, partly because of the continuing influence of the marriage gradient. Deterioration in the health of a spouse can cause the other spouse—typically the wife—to become a caregiver, which can bring both challenges and rewards.

LO 18.9 Describe the typical reactions to the death of a spouse during late adulthood.

The death of a spouse forces the survivor to assume a new societal role, accommodate to the absence of a companion and chore-sharer, create a new social life, and resolve financial problems. Sociologists Gloria Heinemann and Patricia Evans have identified three stages in adjusting to widowhood: preparation, grief and mourning, and adaptation. Some people never reach the adaptation stage.

LO 18.10 Discuss the nature of relationships in late adulthood.

Friendships are important in later life because they offer personal control, companionship, and social support.

LO 18.11 Explain how aging affects family relationships.

Family relationships, especially with siblings and children, provide a great deal of emotional support for people in later life.

LO 18.12 Discuss what causes elder abuse and how it can be prevented.

In the increasingly prevalent phenomenon of elder abuse, parents who are socially isolated and in poor health may be abused by children who are forced to act as caregivers. The best defense against elder abuse is prevention by ensuring that caregivers receive time off and have access to social support.

Key Terms and Concepts

ego-integrity-versus-despair stage 583
redefinition of self versus preoccupation with work role 584
body transcendence versus body preoccupation 584
ego transcendence versus ego preoccupation 584
life review 585
age stratification theories 586
wisdom 586
disengagement theory 589
activity theory 589
continuity theory 590
selective optimization 591
continuing-care community 593
adult day-care facilities 593
skilled-nursing facilities 593
institutionalism 594
social support 605
elder abuse 607

Chapter 19

Death and Dying

Danny E. Martindale/Getty Images

Learning Objectives

LO 19.1 Review the difficulties in defining death.

LO 19.2 Describe what death means at different stages of the life span.

LO 19.3 Describe how dying is affected by culture.

LO 19.4 Summarize how we can prepare for death.

LO 19.5 Describe ways in which people face the prospect of their own death.

LO 19.6 Describe ways in which people exercise control over the death decision.

LO 19.7 Compare and contrast the advantages of hospice and home care for the end of life.

LO 19.8 Describe how survivors react to and cope with death.

LO 19.9 Describe ways in which people experience grief and the functions it serves.

Chapter Overview

Prologue: A Good Death

Jackson LeRoi knew that he'd be dying soon—very soon. At the age of 71, he'd been diagnosed with a particularly aggressive form of brain cancer, and his doctors were clear that his time was limited.

LeRoi made a choice: Rather than endure grueling rounds of chemotherapy, which would only extend his life for a few months at best, he chose to refuse treatment, except for drugs that would keep his final days pain-free.

"I've led a good life. I'm happy with what I've accomplished," he said. And he had a lot of friends, many of whom attended a party he threw when his doctor told him he had less than two weeks to live. People laughed, people cried, but, for LeRoi, it's what he wanted: a celebration of a life well lived.

Looking Ahead

Death is an experience that will happen to all of us at some time, as universal to the human condition as birth. As such, it is a milestone of life that is central to an understanding of the life span.

Lisa F. Young/Fotolia

Quality of life becomes an increasingly important issue as people reach the end of the life span.

Only in the past several decades have lifespan developmentalists given serious study to the developmental implications of dying. In this chapter, we discuss death and dying from several perspectives. We begin by considering how we define death—a determination that is more complex than it seems. We then examine how people view and react to death at different points in the life span. We also consider the very different views of death held by various societies.

Next, we look at how people confront their own deaths. We discuss one theory that people move through several stages as they come to grips with their approaching death. We also look at how people use living wills and assisted suicide.

Finally, we consider bereavement and grief. We examine the difficulties in distinguishing normal from unhealthy grief, and we discuss the consequences of a loss. The chapter also looks at mourning and funerals, discussing how people can prepare themselves for the inevitability of death.

Dying and Death Across the Life Span

It took a major legal and political battle, but eventually Terri Schiavo's husband won the right to remove a feeding tube that had been keeping her alive for 15 years. Lying in a hospital bed all those years in what physicians called a "persistent vegetative state," Schiavo was never expected to regain consciousness after suffering brain damage due to respiratory and cardiac arrest. After a series of court battles, her husband—despite the wishes of her parents—was allowed to direct caretakers to remove the feeding tube; Schiavo died soon afterward.

Was Schiavo's husband right in seeking to remove her feeding tube? Was she already dead when it was removed? Were her constitutional rights unfairly ignored by her husband's action?

The difficulty of answering such questions illustrates the complexity of what are, literally, matters of life and death. Death is not only a biological event; it involves psychological aspects as well. We need to consider not only issues relating to the definition of death but also the ways in which our conception of death changes across various points in the life span.

Defining Death: Determining the Point at Which Life Ends

LO 19.1 Review the difficulties in defining death.

What is death? Although the question seems straightforward, defining the point at which life ceases and death occurs is surprisingly complex. Over the past few decades, medicine has advanced to the point where some people who would have been considered dead a few years ago would now be considered alive.

functional death
the absence of a heartbeat and breathing

Functional death is defined by an absence of heartbeat and breathing. Although this definition seems unambiguous, it is not completely straightforward. For example, a person whose heart has stopped beating and whose breathing has ceased for as long as 5 minutes may be resuscitated and suffer little damage as a consequence of the experience. Does this mean that the person who is now alive was dead, as the functional definition would have it?

brain death
a diagnosis of death based on the cessation of all signs of brain activity, as measured by electrical brain waves

Because of this imprecision, heartbeat and respiration are no longer used to determine the moment of death. Medical experts now measure brain functioning. In **brain death**, all signs of brain activity, as measured by electrical brain waves, have ceased. When brain death occurs, there is no possibility of restoring brain functioning.

Some medical experts suggest that a definition of death that relies only on a lack of brain waves is too restrictive. They argue that losing the ability to think, reason, feel, and experience the world may be sufficient to declare a person dead. In this view, which takes psychological considerations into account, a person who suffers irreversible brain damage, who is in a coma, and who will never experience anything approaching a human life can be considered dead. In such a case, the argument goes, death can be judged to have arrived, even if some sort of primitive brain activity is still occurring (Burkle, Sharp, & Wijdicks, 2014; Wang et al., 2017).

Not surprisingly, such an argument, which moves us from strictly medical criteria to moral and philosophical considerations, is controversial. As a result, the legal definition of death in most localities in the United States relies on the absence of brain functioning, although some laws still include a definition relating to the absence of respiration and heartbeat. The reality is that no matter where a death occurs, in most cases people do not bother to measure brain waves. Usually, the brain waves are closely monitored only in certain circumstances—when the time of death is significant, when organs may potentially be transplanted, or when criminal or legal issues might be involved.

The difficulty in establishing legal and medical definitions of death may reflect some of the changes in understanding and attitudes about death that occur over the course of people's lives.

Death Across the Life Span: Causes and Reactions

LO 19.2 Describe what death means at different stages of the life span.

Death is something we associate with old age. However, for many individuals, death comes earlier. In such cases, in part because it seems unnatural for a younger person to die, the reactions to death are particularly extreme. In the United States today, in fact, some people believe that children should be sheltered—that it is wrong for them to know much about death. Yet people of every age can experience the death of friends and family members, as well as their own death. How do our reactions to death evolve as we age? We will consider several age groups.

DEATH IN INFANCY AND CHILDHOOD. Despite its economic wealth, the United States has a relatively high infant mortality rate. Some 55 countries have a smaller percentage of infants who die in the first year of birth than the United States (*World Factbook*, 2017).

As these statistics indicate, the number of parents who experience the death of an infant is substantial, and their reactions may be profound. The loss of a child typically brings up all the same reactions one would experience upon the death of an older person, and sometimes even more severe effects as family members struggle to deal with a death at such an early age. One of the most common reactions is extreme depression (Murphy, Johnson, & Wu, 2003; Christiansen, 2017).

One kind of death that is exceptionally difficult to deal with is prenatal death, or *miscarriage*, a topic touched on in Chapter 2. Parents typically form psychological bonds with their unborn child, and consequently they often feel profound grief if the child dies before birth. Moreover, friends and relatives often fail to understand the emotional impact of miscarriage on parents, making parents feel their loss all the more keenly (Wheeler & Austin, 2001; Nikčević & Nicolaides, 2014).

Another form of death that produces extreme stress, in part because it is so unanticipated, is sudden infant death syndrome. In **sudden infant death syndrome (SIDS)**, a seemingly healthy baby stops breathing and dies of unexplained causes. Usually occurring between the ages of 2 and 4 months, SIDS strikes unexpectedly; a robust, hardy baby is placed into a crib at naptime or nighttime and never wakes up.

sudden infant death syndrome (SIDS)
the unexplained death of a seemingly healthy baby

In cases of SIDS, parents often feel intense guilt, and acquaintances may be suspicious of the "true" cause of death. As we discussed in Chapter 4, however, there is no known cause for SIDS, which seems to strike randomly, and parents' guilt is unwarranted (Kinney & Thach, 2009; Mitchell, 2009; Horne, 2017).

During childhood, the most frequent cause of death is accidents, most of them due to motor vehicle crashes, fires, and drowning. However, a substantial number of children in the United States are victims of homicides, which have nearly tripled in number since 1960. Homicide is among the top four causes of death for children between the ages of 1 and 24, and the leading cause of death for 15- to 24-year-old African Americans (Centers for Disease Control and Prevention, 2016).

For parents, the death of a child produces the most profound sense of loss and grief. In the eyes of most parents, there is no worse death, including the loss of a spouse or of one's own parents. Parents' extreme reaction is partly based on the sense that the natural order of the world, in which children *should* outlive their parents, has somehow collapsed. Their reaction is often coupled with the feeling that it is their primary responsibility to protect their children from any harm, and they may feel that they have failed in this task when a child dies (Granek et al., 2015).

Parents are almost never well equipped to deal with the death of a child, and they may obsessively ask themselves afterward, over and over, why the death occurred. Because the bond between children and parents is so strong, parents sometimes feel that a part of themselves has died as well. The stress is so profound that the loss of a child significantly increases the chances of admission to a hospital for a mental disorder (Feigelman, Jordan, & Gorman, 2009; Fox, Cacciatore, & Lacasse, 2014).

CHILDHOOD CONCEPTIONS OF DEATH. Children themselves do not really begin to develop a concept of death until around age 5. Although they are well aware of death before that time, they are apt to think of it as a temporary state that involves a reduction in living rather than a cessation. For instance, a preschool-age child might say, "Dead people don't get hungry—well, maybe a little" (Kastenbaum, 1985, p. 629).

Some preschool-age children think of death in terms of sleep—with the consequent possibility of waking up, just as Sleeping Beauty was awakened in the fairy tale. For children who believe this, death is not particularly fearsome; rather, it is something of a curiosity. If people merely tried hard enough—by administering medicine, providing food, or using magic—dead people might "return" (Russell, 2017).

From *an educator's* perspective

Given their developmental level and understanding of death, how do you think preschool children react to the death of a parent?

In some cases, children's misunderstanding of death can produce devastating emotional consequences. Children sometimes leap to the erroneous conclusion that they are somehow responsible for a person's death. For instance, they may assume they could have prevented the death by being better behaved. In the same way, they may think that if the person who died really wanted to, she or he could return.

Around age 5, children better understand the finality and irreversibility of death. In some cases, children personify death as some kind of ghostlike or devilish figure. At first, though, they do not think of death as universal but rather as something that happens only to certain people. By about age 9, however, they come to accept the universality of death and its finality (Nagy, 1948). By middle childhood, children also learn about some of the customs involved with death, such as funerals, cremation, and cemeteries (Hunter & Smith, 2008).

For children who are themselves dying, death can be a very real concept. In a groundbreaking study, anthropologist Myra Bluebond-Langner (2000) found that some children were able to articulate that they were dying very directly, saying "I am going to die." Other children were more indirect, noting that they were never going back to school, expecting not to be around for someone's birthday party, or considering burying their dolls. Children may also be well aware that adults don't like to talk about their illness or of their possibility of dying.

DEATH IN ADOLESCENCE. We might expect the significant advances in cognitive development that occur during adolescence to bring about a sophisticated, thoughtful, and reasoned view of death. However, in many ways, adolescents' views of death are as unrealistic as those of younger children, although along different lines.

Although adolescents clearly understand the finality and irreversibility of death, they tend not to think it can happen to them, a fact that can lead to risky behavior. Adolescents develop a *personal fable*, a set of beliefs that causes them to feel unique and special—so special, in fact, that they may believe they are invulnerable and that the bad things that happen to other people won't happen to them.

Many times, the risky behavior that results from these beliefs causes death in adolescence. For instance, the most frequent cause of death among adolescents is accidents, most often involving motor vehicles. Other frequent causes include homicide, suicide, cancer, and AIDS (National Center for Health Statistics, 2015).

When adolescent feelings of invulnerability confront the likelihood of death due to an illness, the results can be shattering. Adolescents who learn that they have a terminal illness often feel angry and cheated—that life has been unjust to them. Because they feel—and act—so negatively, it may be difficult for medical personnel to treat them effectively.

In contrast, some adolescents diagnosed with a terminal illness react with total denial. Feeling indestructible, they may find it impossible to accept the seriousness of their illness. If it does not interfere with their acceptance of medical treatment, some degree of denial may actually be useful, as it allows adolescents to continue with their normal lives as long as possible (Beale, Baile, & Aaron, 2005; Cullen, 2017).

DEATH IN YOUNG ADULTHOOD. Young adulthood is the time when most people feel primed to begin their lives. Past the preparatory time of childhood and adolescence, they are on the threshold of making their mark on the world. Because death at such a point in life seems close to unthinkable, its occurrence is particularly difficult. Actively pursuing their goals for life, they are angry and impatient with any illness that threatens their future.

In early adulthood, death is most likely to occur due to accidents, followed by suicide, homicide, AIDS, and cancer. By the end of early adulthood, however, disease becomes a more prevalent cause of death.

For those people facing death in early adulthood, several concerns are of particular importance. One is the desire to develop intimate relationships and express sexuality, both of which are inhibited, if not completely prevented, by a terminal illness. For instance, people who test positive for the AIDS virus may find it quite difficult to start new relationships. The role of sexual activities within evolving relationships presents even more challenging issues.

Another particular concern during young adulthood involves future planning. At a time when most people are mapping out their careers and deciding at what point to start a family, young adults who have a terminal illness face additional burdens. Should they marry, even though it is likely that the partner will soon end up widowed? Should a couple seek to conceive a child if the child is likely to be raised by only one parent? How soon should one's employer be told about a terminal illness, when it is clear that employers sometimes discriminate against unhealthy workers? None of these questions is easily answered.

Like adolescents, young adults sometimes make poor patients. They are outraged at their plight and feel the world is unfair, and they may direct their anger at care providers and loved ones. In addition, they may make the medical staff who provide direct care—nurses and orderlies—feel particularly vulnerable, since the staff themselves are often young.

DEATH IN MIDDLE ADULTHOOD. For people in middle adulthood, the shock of a life-threatening disease—which is the most common cause of death in this period—is not so great. By this point, people are well aware that they are going to die sometime, and they may be able to consider the possibility of death in a fairly realistic manner.

Their sense of realism doesn't make the possibility of dying any easier, however. In fact, fears about death are often greater in middle adulthood than at any time previously—or even in later life. These fears may lead people to look at life in terms of the number of years they have remaining as opposed to their earlier orientation toward the number of years they have already lived.

The most frequent cause of death in middle adulthood is heart attack or stroke. Although the unexpectedness of such a death does not allow for preparation, in some ways it is easier than a slow and painful death from a disease such as cancer. It is certainly the kind of death that most people prefer: When asked, they say they would like an instant and painless death that does not involve loss of any body part (Taylor, 2015).

DEATH IN LATE ADULTHOOD. By the time they reach late adulthood, people know with some certainty that their time is coming to an end. Furthermore, they face an increasing number of deaths in their environment. Spouses, siblings, and friends may have already died—a constant reminder of their own mortality.

The most likely causes of death are cancer, stroke, and heart disease during late adulthood. What would happen if these causes of death were eliminated? According to demographers' estimates, the average 70-year-old's life expectancy would increase around 7 years (Hayward, Crimmins, & Saito, 1997).

The prevalence of death in the lives of elderly people makes them less anxious about dying than they were at earlier stages of life. This does not mean that people in late adulthood welcome death. Rather, it implies that they are more realistic and reflective about it. They think about death, and they may begin to make preparations for it. Some begin to pull away from the world due to diminishing physical and psychological energy.

Impending death is sometimes accompanied by acceleration of declines in cognitive functioning. In what is known as the *terminal decline*, a significant drop in performance in cognitive areas such as memory and reading may foreshadow death within the next few years (Thorvaldsson et al., 2008; Wilson et al., 2015; Brandmaier et al., 2017).

Some elderly individuals actively seek out death, turning to suicide. In fact, the suicide rate for men climbs steadily during the course of late adulthood, and no age group has a higher rate of suicide than white men over the age of 85. (Adolescents and young adults commit suicide in greater numbers, but their *rate* of suicide—the number of suicides as a proportion of the general adolescent population—is actually lower.) Suicide is often a consequence of severe depression or some form of dementia, or it can be due to the loss of a spouse. And, as we will discuss later in the chapter, some individuals, struck down with a terminal illness, seek the assistance of others in committing suicide (Mezuk et al., 2008; Dombrovski et al., 2012; McCue & Balasubramaniam, 2017).

One particularly important issue for older adults suffering from a terminal illness is whether their lives still have value. More than younger individuals, elderly people who are dying harbor concerns that they are burdens to their family or to society. Furthermore, they may be given the message, sometimes inadvertently, that their value to society has ended and that they have attained the status of "dying" as opposed to being "very sick" (Kastenbaum, 2000).

Do older people wish to know if death is impending? The answer, in most cases, is yes. Like younger patients, who usually state that they wish to know the true nature of an ailment, older people want the details of their illnesses. Ironically, candor is not something caregivers wish to provide: Physicians usually prefer to avoid telling dying patients that their illnesses are terminal (Goold, Williams, & Arnold, 2000; Hagerty et al., 2004). However, not all people wish to learn the truth about their condition or to know that they are dying.

Cultural Responses to Death

LO 19.3 Describe how dying is affected by culture.

It is important to keep in mind that individuals react to death in substantially different ways. In part, their reaction is produced by personality factors. For example, people who are generally anxious are more concerned about death. In addition to personal differences, there are significant cultural differences in how people view and react to death (see the *Developmental Diversity and Your Life* feature).

People's responses to death take many forms across different cultures, but even within Western societies, reactions to death and dying are quite diverse. For instance, consider which is better: for a man to die after a full life in which he has raised a family and been successful in his job, or for a courageous and valiant young soldier to die defending his country in wartime. Has one person died a better death than the other?

The answer depends on one's values, which are largely shaped by cultural and subcultural teachings, often shared through religious beliefs. For instance, some societies view death as a punishment or as a judgment about one's contributions to the world. Others see death as redemption from an earthly life of travail. Some view death as the start of an eternal life, while others believe that there is no heaven or hell and that an earthly life is all there is (Bryant, 2003).

Developmental Diversity and Your Life

Differing Conceptions of Death

In the midst of a tribal celebration, an older man waits for his oldest son to place a cord around his neck. The older man has been sick, and he is ready to relinquish his ties to this earthly world. He asks that his son lift him to his death, and the son complies.

To Hindus in India, death is not an ending but rather part of a continual cycle. Because they believe in reincarnation, death is thought to be followed by rebirth into a new life. Death, then, is seen as a companion to life.

***

Given that religious teachings regarding the meaning of life and death are quite diverse, it is not surprising that views of death and dying vary substantially. For instance, one study found that Christian and Jewish 10-year-olds viewed death from a more "scientific" vantage point (in terms of the cessation of physical activity in the body) than Sunni Muslim and Druze children of the same age, who are more likely to see death in spiritual terms. We cannot be sure whether such differences are the result of the different religious and cultural backgrounds of the children or whether differences in exposure to dying people influence the rate at which the understanding of death develops. However, it is clear that members of the various groups have very different conceptions of death (Thorson et al., 1997; Aiken, 2000; Xiao et al., 2012).

For members of Native American tribes, death is seen as a continuation of life. For example, Lakota parents will tell their children, "Be kind to your brother, for someday he will die." When people die, they are assumed to move to a spirit land called "Wanagi Makoce," inhabited by all people and animals. Death, then, is not viewed with anger or seen as unfair (Huang, 2004).

Members of some cultures learn about death at an earlier age than others. For instance, cultures with exposure to high levels of violence and death may lead to an awareness of death earlier than in cultures in which violence is less a part of everyday life. For example, children in Israel understand the finality, irreversibility, and inevitability of death at an earlier age than children in the United States and Britain (McWhirter, Young, & Majury, 1983; Atchley, 2000; Braun, Pietsch, & Blanchette, 2000).

Anne-Marie Palmer/Alamy

Differing conceptions of death lead to different rituals. For example, in India, bodies may be floated in the Ganges River following death.

Cultural differences are also reflected in the nature of care provided to the dying. For example, in traditional Thai cultures, members of the community participate in care by praying for the patient, and they attach strings to the patient, symbolically seeking to reattach the soul to the body. In some Native American cultures, spirit dancers may burn gifts for ancestors to help in treatment (Putsch & Joyce, 2017).

Furthermore, in traditional multigenerational Asian families, who live together under one roof, younger generations were expected to provide care for dying older generations. But as modernization has occurred, more elderly people live by themselves, and there are fewer societal networks in place to care for the dying (Hatton, 2015).

Can Death Education Prepare Us for the Inevitable?

LO 19.4 Summarize how we can prepare for death.

"When will Mom come back from being dead?"

"Why did Barry have to die?"

"Did Grandpa die because I was bad?"

Children's questions such as these illustrate why many developmentalists, as well as **thanatologists**, people who study death and dying, have suggested that death education should be an important component of everyone's schooling. Consequently, a relatively new area of instruction, termed death education, has emerged. *Death education* encompasses programs that teach about death, dying, and grief. Death education is designed to help people of all ages deal better with death and dying—both others' deaths and their own personal mortality.

thanatologists
people who study death and dying

Death education has evolved in part as a response to the way we hide death, at least in most Western societies. We typically give hospitals the task of dealing with dying people, and we do not talk to children about death or allow them to go to funerals for fear of upsetting them. Even those most familiar with death, such as emergency workers and medical specialists, are uncomfortable talking about the subject. Because it is discussed so little and is so removed from everyday life, people of all ages may have little opportunity to confront their feelings about death or to gain a more realistic sense of it (Kim & Lee, 2009; Waldrop & Kirkendall, 2009; Kellehear, 2015; Chapple et al., 2017).

Several types of death education programs exist. Among them are the following:

- **Crisis intervention education.** After the 2012 mass shooting at Sandy Hook Elementary School in Newtown, Connecticut, surviving children received crisis intervention designed to deal with their anxieties. Younger children, whose conceptions of death were shaky at best, needed explanations of the loss of life that day geared to their levels of cognitive development. Crisis intervention education is used in less extreme times as well. For example, it is common for schools to make emergency counseling available if a student is killed or commits suicide (Sandoval, Scott, & Padilla, 2009; Reeves & Fernandez, 2017).
- **Routine death education.** Although relatively little curricular material on death is available at the elementary school level, coursework in high schools is becoming increasingly common. For instance, some high schools have specific courses on death and dying. Furthermore, colleges and universities increasingly include courses relating to death in such departments as psychology, human development, sociology, and education (Eckerd, 2009; Corr, 2015).
- **Death education for members of the helping professions.** Professionals who will deal with death, dying, and grief as part of their careers have a special need for death education. Almost all medical and nursing schools now offer some form of death education to help their students. The most successful programs not only supply ways for providers to help patients deal with their own impending deaths and those of family members but also allow students to explore their feelings about the topic (Haas-Thompson, Alston, & Holbert, 2008; Kehl & McCarty, 2012).

Although no single form of death education will be sufficient to demystify death, the kinds of programs just described may help people come to grips more effectively with what is, along with birth, the most universal—and certain—of all human experiences.

Module 19.1 Review

LO 19.1 Review the difficulties in defining death.

Death has been defined as the cessation of heartbeat and respiration (functional death), the absence of electrical brain waves (brain death), and the loss of human qualities.

LO 19.2 Describe what death means at different stages of the life span.

The death of an infant or a young child can be particularly difficult for parents, and for an adolescent, death appears to be unthinkable. Death in young adulthood can appear unfair, while people in middle adulthood have begun to understand the reality of death. By the time they reach late adulthood, people know they will die and begin to make preparations.

LO 19.3 Describe how dying is affected by culture.

Cultural differences in attitudes and beliefs about death strongly influence people's reactions to it.

LO 19.4 Summarize how we can prepare for death.

Thanatologists recommend that death education become a normal part of learning.

Journal Writing Prompt

Applying Lifespan Development: Do you think people who are going to die should be told? Does your response depend on the person's age?

Confronting Death

Carol Reyes had been active all her life. When she broke her pelvis at 89, she was determined to walk again. With 6 months of intensive physical therapy, she did. At 93, she came down with pneumonia. After a month in the hospital, she returned home to the things she loved—her cat, her books, and taking an active part in local politics—a little weaker but basically sound.

Three years later, Carol's doctor told her she had ALS, a disease in which the motor neurons in the brain and spinal cord slowly die. She could take a drug called Rilutek to slow its progress, but eventually her muscles would atrophy, making it hard to use her hands or walk. She'd have trouble speaking and swallowing. In the end, her lungs would be paralyzed.

Carol agreed to try the drug but told her doctor she wanted a DNR—a Do Not Resuscitate order—for when her lungs began seizing up and breathing became difficult. "That's not a life I'd like to be living," she said.

Four months later, Carol Reyes found herself gasping for breath. She refused oxygen. She refused to go to the hospital. She died quickly, in her own bed.

Like other deaths, Reyes's raises a myriad of difficult questions. Was her refusal to take oxygen equivalent to suicide? Should the ambulance medic have complied with the request? Was she coping with her impending death effectively? How do people come to terms with death, and how do they react and adapt to it? Lifespan developmentalists and other specialists in death and dying have struggled to find answers to such questions.

Understanding the Process of Dying: Are There Steps Toward Death?

LO 19.5 Describe ways in which people face the prospect of their own death.

No individual has had a greater influence on our understanding of the way people confront death than Elisabeth Kübler-Ross. A psychiatrist, Kübler-Ross developed a theory of death and dying, built on extensive interviews with people who were dying and with those who cared for them (Kübler-Ross, 1969, 1982).

Based on her observations, Kübler-Ross initially suggested that people pass through five basic steps as they move toward death (summarized in Figure 19-1).

DENIAL. "No, I can't be dying. There must be some mistake." It is typical for people to protest in such a manner on learning that they have a terminal disease. Such objections represent the first stage of dying, *denial*. In denial, people resist the idea that they are going to die. They may argue that their test results have been mixed up, that an X-ray has been read incorrectly, or that their physician does not know what he or she is talking about (Teutsch, 2003).

ANGER. After they move beyond denial, people may be likely to express *anger*. A dying person may be angry at everyone: people who are in good health, their spouses and other family members, those who are caring for them, their children. They may lash out at others, and wonder—sometimes aloud—why *they* are dying and not someone else. They may be furious at God, reasoning that they have led good lives and that there are far worse people in the world who should be dying.

Figure 19-1 Moving Toward the End of Life

There are five steps toward death, according to Kübler-Ross (1975).

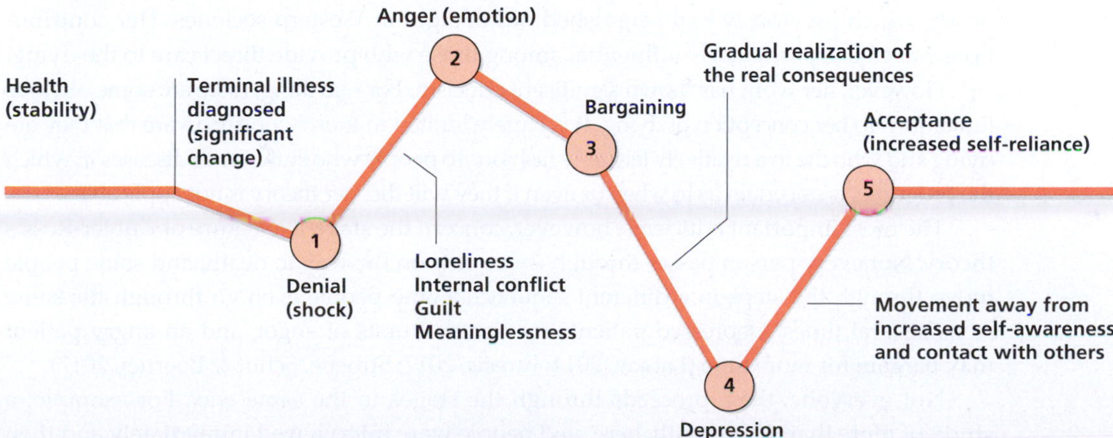

BARGAINING. "If you're good, you'll be rewarded." Most people learn this equation in childhood, and many try to apply it to their impending death. In this case, "good" means promising to be a better person, and the "reward" is staying alive.

In *bargaining*, dying people try to negotiate their way out of death. They may declare that they will dedicate their lives to the poor if God saves them. They may promise that if they can just live long enough to see a son married, they will willingly accept death later.

However, the promises that are part of the bargaining process are rarely kept. If one request appears to be granted, people typically seek another, and yet another. Furthermore, they may be unable to fulfill their promises because their illnesses keep progressing and prevent them from achieving what they said they would do.

In the end, of course, all the bargaining in the world is unable to overcome the inevitability of death. When people eventually realize that death is unavoidable, they often move into a stage of depression.

From *an educator's* perspective

Do you think Kübler-Ross's five steps of dying might be subject to cultural influences? Age differences? Why or why not?

DEPRESSION. Many dying people experience phases of *depression*. Realizing that the issue is settled and they cannot bargain their way out of death, people are overwhelmed with a deep sense of loss. They know that they are losing their loved ones and that their lives really are coming to an end.

The depression they experience may be of two types. In *reactive depression*, the feelings of sadness are based on events that have already occurred: the loss of dignity that may accompany medical procedures, the end of a job, or the knowledge that one will never return from the hospital to one's home.

Dying people also experience preparatory depression. In *preparatory depression*, people feel sadness over future losses. They know that death will bring an end to their relationships with others and that they will never see future generations. The reality of death is inescapable in this stage, and it brings about profound sadness over the unalterable conclusion of one's life.

ACCEPTANCE. Kübler-Ross suggested that the final step of dying is *acceptance*. People who have developed a state of acceptance are fully aware that death is impending. Unemotional and uncommunicative, they have virtually no feelings—positive or negative—about the present or future. They have made peace with themselves, and they may wish to be left alone. For them, death holds no sting.

EVALUATING KÜBLER-ROSS'S THEORY. Kübler-Ross has had an enormous impact on the way we look at death. As one of the first people to observe systematically how people approach their own deaths, she is recognized as a pioneer. Kübler-Ross was almost single-handedly responsible for bringing into public awareness the phenomenon of death, which previously had languished out of sight in Western societies. Her contributions have been particularly influential among those who provide direct care to the dying.

However, her work has drawn significant criticism. For one thing, there are some obvious limitations to her conception of dying. It is largely limited to those who are aware that they are dying and who die in a relatively leisurely fashion. To people who suffer from diseases in which the prognosis is uncertain as to when or even if they will die, her theory is not applicable.

The most important criticisms, however, concern the stage-like nature of Kübler-Ross's theory. Not every person passes through every step on the way to death, and some people move through the steps in a different sequence. Some people even go through the same steps several times. Depressed patients may show bursts of anger, and an angry patient may bargain for more time (Larson, 2014; Jurecic, 2017; Stroebe, Schut & Boerner, 2017).

Not everyone, then, proceeds through the stages in the same way. For example, a study of more than 200 recently bereaved people were interviewed immediately and then several months later. If Kübler-Ross's theory was correct, the final stage of acceptance comes at the end of a lengthy grieving process. But most of the participants expressed acceptance of the passing of their loved one right from the beginning. Moreover, rather than feeling anger or depression, two of the other putative stages of grief, participants reported mostly feeling a yearning for the deceased person. Rather than a series of fixed stages, grief looks more like an assortment of symptoms that rise and fall and eventually dissipate (Maciejewski et al., 2007; Genevro & Miller, 2010; Gamino & Ritter, 2012).

The finding that people often follow their own unique personal trajectories of grief has been especially important for medical and other caregivers who work with dying people. Because Kübler-Ross's stages have become so well known, well-meaning caregivers have sometimes tried to encourage patients to work through the steps in a prescribed order, without enough consideration for their individual needs.

Finally, there are substantial differences in people's reactions to impending death. The specific cause of dying; how long the process of dying lasts; a person's age, sex, and personality; and the social support available from family and friends all influence the course of dying and people's responses to it (Carver & Scheier, 2002).

Ultimately, there are significant concerns about the accuracy of Kübler-Ross's account of how people react to impending death. In response to some of these concerns, other theorists have developed alternative ideas. Psychologist Edwin Shneidman, for example suggests that there are "themes" in people's reactions to dying that can occur—and recur—in any order throughout the dying process. These include such feelings and thoughts as incredulity, a sense of unfairness, fear of pain or even general terror, and fantasies of being rescued (Shneidman, 2007).

Another theorist, Charles Corr, suggests that, as in other periods of life, people who are dying face a set of psychological tasks. These include minimizing physical stress, maintaining the richness of life, continuing or deepening their relationships with other people, and fostering hope, often through spiritual searching (Corr, Nabe, & Corr, 2006; Corr, 2015).

Choosing the Nature of Death: Is DNR the Way to Go?

LO 19.6 Describe ways in which people exercise control over the death decision.

The letters "DNR" written on a patient's medical chart have a simple and clear meaning. Standing for "Do Not Resuscitate," DNR signifies that rather than administering any and every procedure that might possibly keep a patient alive, no extraordinary means are to be taken. For terminally ill patients, DNR may mean the difference between dying immediately or living additional days, months, or even years, kept alive only by the most extreme, invasive, and even painful medical procedures.

The decision to use or not to use extreme medical interventions entails several issues. One is the differentiation of "extreme" and "extraordinary" measures from those that are simply routine. There are no hard-and-fast rules; people making the decision must consider the needs of the specific patient, his or her prior medical history, and factors such as age and even religion. For instance, different standards might apply to a 12-year-old patient and an 85-year-old patient with the same medical condition.

Other questions concern quality of life. How can we determine an individual's current quality of life and whether it will be improved or diminished by a particular medical intervention? Who makes such decisions—the patient, a family member, or medical personnel?

One thing is clear: Medical personnel are reluctant to carry out the wishes of the terminally ill and their families to suspend aggressive treatment. Even when it is certain that a patient is going to die, and patients determine that they do not wish to receive further treatment, physicians often claim to be unaware of their patients' wishes. For instance, although one-third of the patients ask not to be resuscitated, less than half of these people's physicians state that they know of their patients' preference (see Figure 19-2). In addition, only 49 percent of patients have their wishes

Figure 19-2 Dying Hard: Experiences of 4,301 Patients with End-of-Life Care

THINKING ABOUT THE DATA: What percent of the total patient sample have a preference to not be resuscitated? What factors would affect your personal decision to have or not have a do not resuscitate order?

(**Source:** Based on Knaus et al., 1995.)

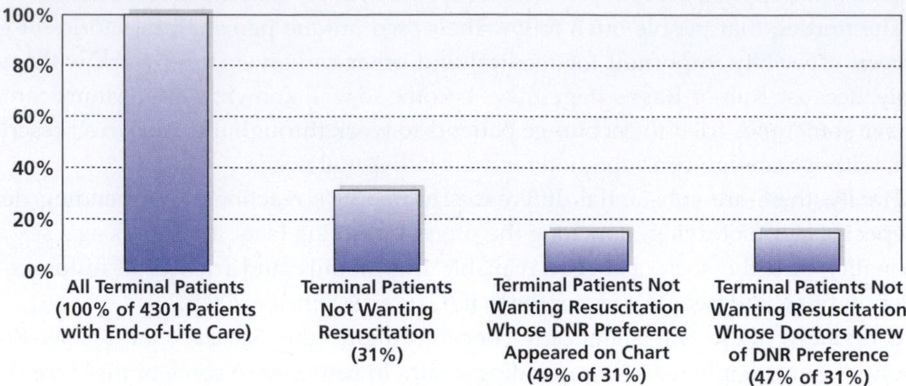

entered on their medical charts. Physicians and other health-care providers may be reluctant to act on DNR requests in part because they are trained to save patients, not to permit them to die, and in part to avoid legal liability issues (Goold, Williams, & Arnold, 2000; McArdle, 2002; Wan et al., 2017).

living will

a legal document designating what medical treatments people want or do not want if they cannot express their wishes

LIVING WILLS. In order to gain more control over decisions regarding the nature of their death, people are increasingly signing living wills. A **living will** is a legal document that designates the medical treatments a person does or does not want if the person cannot express his or her wishes (see Figure 19-3).

Some people designate a specific person, called a *health-care proxy*, to act as their representative in making health-care decisions. Health-care proxies are authorized either in living wills or in a legal document known as *durable power of attorney*. Health-care proxies may be authorized to deal with all medical care problems (such as a coma) or only terminal illnesses.

As with DNR orders, living wills are ineffective unless people take steps to make sure their health-care proxies and doctors know their wishes. Although they may be reluctant to do so in advance, people should also have frank conversations clarifying their wishes with the representatives they choose as their health-care proxies.

EUTHANASIA AND ASSISTED SUICIDE. In the 1990s, Dr. Jack Kevorkian became well known for his invention and promotion of a "suicide machine," which allowed patients to push a button that releases anesthesia and a drug that stops the heart. By supplying the machine and the drugs, which patients administered themselves, Kevorkian was participating in a process known as *assisted suicide*, in which a person provides the means for a terminally ill individual to commit suicide. Kevorkian ended up spending 8 years in prison after being convicted of second-degree murder for his participation in an assisted suicide that was shown on the television show *60 Minutes*.

Assisted suicide continues to raise bitter conflict in the United States, and the practice is illegal in most states. Today, seven major jurisdictions (California, Colorado, Montana, Oregon, Vermont, Washington, and Washington, DC) have passed "right to die" laws, and Montana has legal physician-assisted suicide following a court order. In Oregon alone, more than 1,100 people have taken medication to end their own lives (Edwards, 2015; Oregon Death with Dignity Act, 2016).

In many countries, assisted suicide is an accepted practice. For instance, in the Netherlands medical personnel may help end their patients' lives. However, several conditions must be met to make the practice permissible: At least two physicians must determine that the patient is terminally ill, there must be unbearable physical or mental suffering, the patient must give informed consent in writing, and relatives must be informed beforehand (Naik, 2002; Kleespies, 2004; Battin et al., 2007).

Assisted suicide is one form of **euthanasia**, the practice of assisting terminally ill people to die more quickly. Popularly known as "mercy killing," euthanasia can take a range of forms. *Passive euthanasia* involves removing respirators or other medical equipment that may be sustaining a patient's life, allowing the individual to die naturally. This happens when medical staff follow a DNR order, for example. In *voluntary active euthanasia*, caregivers or medical staff act to end a person's life before death would normally occur, perhaps by administering a dose of pain medication that they know will be fatal. Assisted suicide, as we have seen, lies between passive and voluntary active euthanasia. Euthanasia is an emotional and controversial—although surprisingly widespread—practice.

No one knows how widespread euthanasia truly is. However, one survey of nurses in intensive care units found that 20 percent had deliberately hastened a patient's death at least once, and other experts assert that euthanasia is far from rare (Asch, 1996).

Euthanasia is highly controversial, in part because it centers on decisions about who should control life. Does the right belong solely to an individual, a person's physicians, his or her dependents, the government, or some deity? Because, at least in the United States, we assume that we all have the absolute right to create lives by bringing children into the world, some people argue that we should also have the absolute right to end our lives (Allen et al., 2006; Goldney, 2012; Monteverde et al., 2017).

In contrast, many opponents of euthanasia argue that the practice is morally wrong. In their view, prematurely ending someone's life, no matter how willing that person may be, is the equivalent of murder. Others point out that physicians are often inaccurate in predicting how long a person's life will last. For example, in some cases, patients have lived for years after being given no more than a 50 percent chance of living for 6 more months (Bishop, 2006; Peel & Harding, 2015; also see Figure 19-4).

Another argument against euthanasia focuses on the emotional state of the patient. Even if patients ask or sometimes beg health-care providers to help them die, they may be suffering from a form of deep depression. In such cases, patients may be treated with antidepressant drugs that can alleviate the depression. Once the depression lifts, patients may change their minds about their earlier wish for death.

The debate over euthanasia is likely to continue. It is a highly personal issue, yet one that society increasingly must face as the world's elderly population increases (Becvar, 2000; Gostin, 2006; McLachlan, 2008).

euthanasia
the practice of assisting people who are terminally ill to die more quickly

Figure 19-3 A Living Will

What steps can people take to make sure the wishes they write into their living wills are carried out?

I,______________________________,
being of sound mind, make this statement as a directive to be followed if I become permanently unable to participate in decisions regarding my medical care. These instructions reflect my firm and settled commitment to decline medical treatment under the circumstances indicated below:

I direct my attending physician to withhold or withdraw treatment that merely prolongs my dying, if I should be in **an incurable or irreversible mental or physical condition** with no reasonable expectation of recovery, including but not limited to: (a) a **terminal condition**; (b) a **permanently unconscious condition**; or (c) a **minimally conscious condition in which I am permanently unable to make decisions or express my wishes**.

I direct that treatment be limited to measures to keep me comfortable and to relieve pain, including any pain that might occur by withholding or withdrawing treatment.
While I understand that I am not legally required to be specific about future treatments, **if I am in the condition(s) described above I feel especially strongly about the following treatments**:

I do not want cardiac resuscitation.
I do not want mechanical respiration.
I do not want tube feeding.
I do not want antibiotics.

However, I **do want** maximum pain relief, even if it may hasten my death.

Other directions (insert personal instructions):

These directions express my legal right to refuse treatment under federal and state law. I intend my instructions to be carried out, unless I have revoked them in a new writing or by clearly indicating that I have changed my mind.

Signed:______________________________ Date:____________

Address:______________________________

- -

Statement by Witnesses
I declare that the person who signed this document appears to be at least eighteen (18) years of age, of sound mind, and under no constraint or undue influence. The person who signed this document appeared to do so willingly and free from duress. He or she signed (or asked another to sign for him or her) this document in my presence.

Witness:______________________________

Address:______________________________

- -

Witness:______________________________

Address:______________________________

- -

Figure 19-4 How Long Do "Terminal" Patients Really Live?

Physicians' estimates of how long dying patients have to live are not always accurate. This figure shows a summary of studies and their findings. Bars to the left indicate underestimates of how long patients will live compared to how long they actually did; bars to the right indicate overestimates. Clearly, most physicians overestimated the length of time patients would live.

(**Source:** White et al., 2016.)

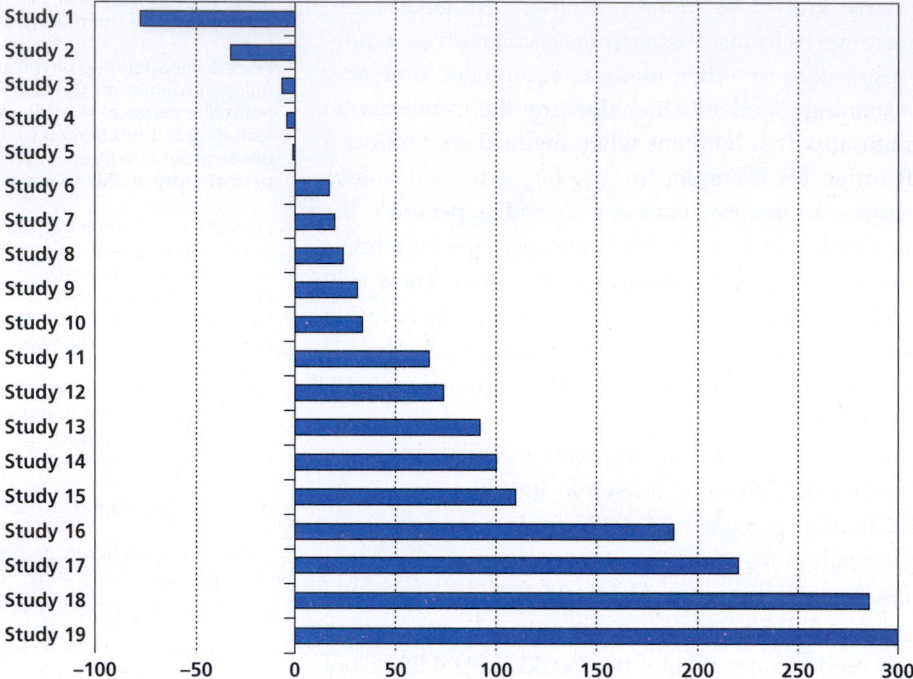

Caring for the Terminally Ill: The Place of Death

LO 19.7 Compare and contrast the advantages of hospice and home care for the end of life.

About half the people in the United States who die do so in hospitals. It need not be that way. There are several reasons why hospitals are among the least desirable locales in which to face death. Hospitals are typically impersonal, with staff rotating throughout the day. Because visiting hours are limited, people frequently die alone, without the comfort of loved ones at their bedside.

Furthermore, hospitals are designed to make people better, not to deal with the dying, and it is extraordinarily expensive to provide custodial care for dying people. Consequently, hospitals typically don't have the resources needed to deal adequately with the emotional requirements of terminally ill patients and their families.

home care
an alternative to hospitalization in which dying people stay in their homes and receive treatment from their families and visiting medical staff

Because of the limitations of traditional hospitals in dealing with the dying, there are now several alternatives to hospitalization. In **home care**, dying people stay in their homes and receive treatment from their families and visiting medical staff. Many dying patients prefer home care because they can spend their final days in a familiar environment, with people they love and a lifetime accumulation of treasures around them.

Although the dying may prefer home care, it can be quite difficult for family members. Furnishing final care can offer family members a good deal of emotional solace because they are giving something precious to people they love. But it is extraordinarily draining, both physically and emotionally, to be on call 24 hours a day. Furthermore, because most relatives are not trained in nursing, they may provide less than optimal medical care. Many people decide they just aren't equipped to care for a dying family member at home (Perreault, Fothergill-Bourbonnais, & Fiset, 2004).

For these families, another alternative to hospitalization that is becoming increasingly prevalent is hospice care. **Hospice care** is care for the dying provided in places devoted to those who are terminally ill. In the Middle Ages, hospices were facilities that provided comfort and hospitality to travelers. Drawing on that concept, today's hospices are designed to provide a warm, supportive environment for the dying. They do not focus on extending people's lives but rather on making their final days pleasant and meaningful. Typically, people who go to hospices are removed from treatments that are painful, and no extraordinary or invasive means are employed to make their lives longer. The emphasis is on making patients' lives as full as possible, not on squeezing out every possible moment of life at any cost (Corr, 2007; York et al., 2012; Prochaska et al., 2017).

hospice care
care provided for the dying in places devoted to those who are terminally ill

Although the research is far from conclusive, hospice patients appear to be more satisfied with the care they receive than those who receive treatment in more traditional settings. Hospice care, then, provides a clear alternative to traditional hospitalization for the terminally ill (Seymour et al., 2007; Rhodes et al., 2008; Clark, 2015).

Module 19.2 Review

LO 19.5 Describe ways in which people face the prospect of their own death.

Elisabeth Kübler-Ross has identified five steps toward dying: denial, anger, bargaining, depression, and acceptance. The stage nature of her theory has been criticized as too inflexible, and other theorists have suggested alternatives.

LO 19.6 Describe ways in which people exercise control over the death decision.

Issues surrounding dying are highly controversial, including the degree of measures that physicians should apply to keep dying patients alive and who should make the decisions about those measures. Living wills are a way for people to take some control over the decision. Assisted suicide and, more generally, euthanasia are highly controversial and are illegal in most of the United States, although many people believe they should be legalized if they are regulated.

LO 19.7 Compare and contrast the advantages of hospice and home care for the end of life.

Although most people in the United States die in hospitals, increasing numbers are choosing home care or hospice care for their final days.

Journal Writing Prompt

Applying Lifespan Development: Do you think assisted suicide should be permissible? What about other forms of euthanasia? Why or why not?

Grief and Bereavement

No one ever told me that grief felt so like fear. I am not afraid, but the sensation is like being afraid. The same fluttering in the stomach, the same restlessness, the yawning. I keep on swallowing.

At other times it feels like being mildly drunk, or concussed. There is a sort of invisible blanket between the world and me. I find it hard to take in what anyone says. Or perhaps, hard to want to take it in. It is so uninteresting. (Lewis, 1985, p. 394)

For something that is a universal experience, most of us are surprisingly ill prepared for the grief that follows the death of a loved one. Particularly in Western societies, where life expectancy is long and mortality rates are lower than at any time in history, people are apt to view death as an atypical event rather than an expected part of life. This attitude makes grief all the more difficult to bear, particularly when we compare the present day with historical eras in which people lived shorter lives and the death rate was considerably higher. The first step in grieving, for most survivors in Western countries, is some sort of funeral (Nolen-Hoeksema & Larson, 1999; Bryant, 2003; Kleinman, 2012).

Mourning and Funerals: Final Rites

LO 19.8 Describe how survivors react to and cope with death.

Death is a big business in the United States. The average funeral and burial costs nearly $7,000. The purchase of an ornate, polished coffin; transportation to and from the cemetery in a limousine; and preparation of the body for preservation and viewing are among the services that people typically purchase in planning a funeral (Sheridan, 2013; Beard & Burger, 2017).

In part, the relatively grandiose nature of funerals is due to the vulnerability of those planning the funeral, who are typically close survivors of the deceased. Wishing to demonstrate love and affection, the survivors are susceptible to suggestions to "provide the best" for the deceased (Culver, 2003; Varga, 2014).

But it is not only the pressure of enterprising salespersons that leads many people to spend thousands of dollars on a funeral. In large measure, the nature of funerals, like that of weddings, is determined by social norms and customs. Because an individual's death represents an important transition not only for loved ones but also for an entire community, the rites associated with death take on an added importance. In a sense, then, a funeral is not only a public acknowledgment that an individual has died but is also a recognition of everyone's ultimate mortality and an acceptance of the cycle of life.

In Western societies, funeral rituals follow a typical pattern, despite some surface variations. Prior to the funeral, the body is prepared in some way and is dressed in special clothing. Funerals usually include the celebration of a religious rite, the delivery of a eulogy, a procession of some sort, and some formal period, such as the wake for Irish Catholics and shiva for Jews, in which relatives and friends visit the mourning family and pay their respects. Military funerals typically include the firing of weapons and a flag draped over the coffin.

CULTURAL DIFFERENCES IN GRIEVING. Non-Western cultures include funeral rituals of quite different sorts. For instance, in some societies mourners shave their heads as a sign of grief, while in others they allow the hair to grow and men stop shaving for a period of time. In other cultures, mourners may be hired to wail and grieve. Sometimes noisy celebrations take place at funerals, while in other cultures silence is the norm. Even the nature of emotional displays, such as the amount and timing of crying, are determined culturally (Rosenblatt, 2001).

For example, mourners in Balinese funerals in Indonesia attempt to show little emotion because they believe they must be calm in order for the gods to hear their prayers. In contrast, mourners at African American funerals are encouraged to show their grief, and the funeral rituals are meant to allow attendees to display their feelings. Widows in Egypt are considered abnormal if they don't weep unconsolably, and Chinese mourners sometimes hire professional wailers (Collins & Doolittle, 2006; Walter, 2012; Carteret, 2017).

Historically, some cultures have developed funeral rites that strike us as extreme. For example, in *suttee*, a traditional Hindu practice in India that is now illegal, a widow was expected to throw herself into the fire that consumed her husband's body. In ancient China, servants were sometimes buried (alive) with their masters' bodies.

Ultimately, no matter what the particular ritual, all funerals basically serve the same underlying function: They mark the endpoint for the life of the person who has died—and provide a formal forum for the feelings of the survivors, a place where they can come together and share their grief and comfort one another.

Bereavement and Grief: Adjusting to the Death of a Loved One

bereavement
acknowledgment of the objective fact that one has experienced a death

LO 19.9 Describe ways in which people experience grief and the functions it serves.

After the death of a loved one, a painful period of adjustment follows, involving bereavement and grief. **Bereavement** is acknowledgment of the objective fact that one has experienced a death, whereas **grief** is the emotional response to one's loss. Everyone's grief is different, but there are certain similarities in the ways people in Western societies adjust to the loss.

grief
the emotional response to one's loss

Survivors' first stage of grief typically entails shock, numbness, disbelief, or outright denial. People may avoid the reality of the situation, trying to carry on with the usual routines of their lives, although the pain may break through, causing anguish, fear, and deep sorrow and distress. If the pain is too severe, however, the person may cycle back to numbness. In some ways, such a psychological state may be beneficial, since it permits the survivor to make funeral arrangements and carry out other psychologically difficult tasks. Typically, people pass through this stage in a few days or weeks, although in some cases it lasts longer.

In the next phase, people begin to confront the death and realize the extent of their loss. They fully experience their grief, and they begin to acknowledge the reality that the separation from the dead person will be permanent. In so doing, mourners may suffer deep unhappiness or even depression, a normal feeling in this situation and not one necessarily requiring treatment. They may yearn for the dead individual. Emotions can range from impatient to lethargic. However, they also begin to view their past relationship with the deceased realistically, good and bad. In so doing, they begin to free themselves from some of the bonds that tied them to their loved ones (Norton & Gino, 2014; Rosenblatt, 2015).

Finally, people who have lost a loved one reach the accommodation stage. They begin to pick up the pieces of their lives and to construct new identities. For instance, rather than seeing herself as someone's widowed spouse, a woman whose husband has died may come to regard herself as a single person. Still, there are moments when intense feelings of grief occur.

Ultimately, most people are able to emerge from the grieving process and live new lives, independent from the person who has died. They form new relationships, and some even find that coping with the death has helped them to grow as individuals. They become more self-reliant and more appreciative of life.

It is important to keep in mind that not everyone passes through the stages of grief in the same manner and in the same order. People display vast individual differences, partly due to their personalities, the nature of the relationship with the deceased, and the opportunities that are available to them for continuing their lives after the loss. In fact, most bereaved people are quite resilient, experiencing strong positive emotion, such as joy, even soon after the death of a loved one. According to psychologist George Bonanno, who has studied bereavement extensively, humans are prepared in an evolutionary sense to move on after the death of someone close. He rejects the notion that there are fixed stages of mourning and argues that most people move on with their lives quite effectively (Bonanno, 2009; Mancini & Bonanno, 2012; Kosminsky, 2017).

DIFFERENTIATING UNHEALTHY GRIEF FROM NORMAL GRIEF. Although ideas abound about what separates normal grief from unhealthy grief, careful research has shown that many of the assumptions that both laypersons and clinicians hold are wrong. There is no particular timetable for grieving, particularly the common notion that grieving should be complete a year after a spouse has died. For some people (but not all), grieving may take considerably longer than a year. And some individuals experience *complicated grief* (or sometimes *prolonged grief disorder*), a type of mourning that continues unceasingly for months and years (as we discussed in the previous chapter). An estimated 15 percent of those who are bereaved suffer from complicated grief (Schumer, 2009; Zisook & Shear, 2009; Maercker, Neimeyer & Simiola, 2017).

Research also contradicts the common assumption that depression following the death of a loved one is widespread. In fact, only 15 to 30 percent of people show relatively deep depression following the loss of a loved one (Bonanno, Wortman, & Lehman, 2002; Hensley, 2006).

From a *social worker's* perspective

Why do you think the risk of death is so high for people who have recently lost a spouse? Why might remarriage lower the risk?

Similarly, it is often assumed that people who show little initial distress over a death are simply not facing up to reality, and that as a consequence they are likely to have problems later. This is not the case. In fact, those who show the most intense distress immediately after a death are the most apt to have adjustment difficulties and health problems later on (Boerner et al., 2005; also see the *From Research to Practice* box).

From Research to Practice

Moving On: Surviving the Loss of a Longtime Spouse

As you may well imagine, the death of a spouse is almost always a traumatic experience that is usually followed by intense grief and anguish. In the case of older couples who had been married for a very long time, losing a spouse can mean losing a lifelong companion and typically a partner's primary and sometimes sole source of emotional support. Intuition may therefore suggest that the period of grieving such a loss would be particularly prolonged for a surviving spouse who had enjoyed a close and happy marriage.

But a growing body of research suggests otherwise: It seems in fact that people who had a successful marriage are better able to work through their mourning of a lost spouse and get on with the rest of their lives than those with less successful marriages. In fact, research now suggests that around half of those who report having satisfying marriages are able to get past their grief within 6 months of the death of their spouses (Carr, Nesse, & Wortman, 2005; Carr, 2015; Carr, 2016).

One explanation for these findings is that people who enjoy close and happy marriages tend to have strong interpersonal skills on which to rely during their time of loss. They may be better equipped to call upon friends, family, and even a professional counselor if necessary to assist them through their grieving period. One way that others help the surviving spouse is by providing a diversion to keep him or her from dwelling on the loss and also by encouraging him or her to replace the void with new interests and activities. Strong interpersonal skills may also facilitate a positive approach to dating new people when the time is right (Carr, Nesse, & Wortman, 2005; Stitch, 2006; Carr, 2015).

Another reason for the resiliency of surviving spouses of close marriages is the knowledge that they and their departed partner had culminated what they set out to achieve: a successful and satisfying relationship. Surviving partners of strained marriages might feel more sadness over never having achieved a desired level of closeness, or they might regret not having an opportunity to resolve lingering conflicts, or they might feel guilty about not working harder to make their marriage better when they had the chance.

However, surviving spouses who enjoyed a close marriage are more likely to have settled lingering issues and to have talked through what would happen after either of them died; they therefore are more likely to feel secure in knowing what their departed would have wanted for them in widowhood. Finally, spouses who have a close and secure relationship may simply have a better opportunity to say their final goodbyes as one of the partners' health fails (Mancini, Sinan, & Bonanno, 2015).

Of course, having a secure marriage is no guarantee that life as a widow or widower will be lacking in pain. Even very resilient survivors grieve deeply in the immediate months following the death of their spouses. And indeed, it's possible to be too close to one's spouse, making the loss more difficult; men in particular may be hit hard by the loss of a wife who was their only emotional confidant. But in many cases, the final gift of a close and loving spouse is the security to move on with one's life within a reasonable time after his or her death (Boerner, et al., 2005; Maccallum, Malgaroli, & Bonanno, 2017).

Shared Writing Prompt

Do you think that these same findings would apply in the case of losing a spouse earlier in life? Why or why not? What other factors besides interpersonal closeness might affect the duration of grief after losing a longtime spouse?

THE CONSEQUENCES OF GRIEF AND BEREAVEMENT. In a sense, death is catching, at least in terms of survivors' mortality. Widowed people are particularly at risk of death. Some studies find that the risk of death is as much as seven times higher than normal in the first year after the death of a spouse. At particular risk are men and younger women who have been widowed. Remarriage seems to lower the risk of death for survivors. This is particularly true for men who have lost their wives, although the reasons are not clear (Aiken, 2000; Elwert & Christakis, 2008).

Bereavement is more likely to produce depression or other negative consequences if the person who has lost a loved one is already insecure, anxious, or fearful and therefore is less able to cope effectively. Furthermore, people whose relationships were marked by ambivalence before death are more apt to suffer poor post-death outcomes than those who were secure in their relationships. Those who were highly dependent on the person who died, and who therefore feel more vulnerable without them, are apt to suffer more after the death, as are those who spend a great deal of time reflecting on a loved one's death and their feelings of grief.

Bereaved people who lack social support from family, friends, or a connection to some other group, religious or otherwise, are more likely to experience feelings of loneliness, and therefore are more at risk. Finally, people who are unable to make sense of the death or find meaning in it (such as a new appreciation of life) show less overall adjustment (Nolen-Hoeksema & Davis, 2002; Torges, Stewart, & Nolen-Hoeksema, 2008).

The suddenness of a loved one's death also appears to affect the course of grieving. People who unexpectedly lose their loved ones are less able to cope than those who were able to anticipate the death. For instance, in one study, people who experienced a sudden death still had not fully recovered 4 years later. In part, this may be because sudden, unanticipated deaths are often the result of violence, which occurs more frequently among younger individuals (Burton, Haley, & Small, 2006; De Leo et al., 2014). (Also see the *Development in Your Life* feature.)

Development in Your Life

Helping a Child Cope with Grief

Because of their limited understanding of death, younger children need special help in coping with grief. Among the strategies that can help are the following:

- Be honest. Don't say that a dead person is "sleeping" or "on a long trip." Use age-appropriate language to tell children the truth. Gently, but clearly, point out the irreversibility and the final and universal nature of death.
- Encourage expressions of grief. Don't tell children not to cry or show their feelings. Instead, tell them that it is understandable to feel terrible and that they may always miss the deceased. Encourage them to draw a picture, write a letter, or express their feelings in some other way. At the same time, assure them that they will always have good memories of the person who has died.
- Reassure children that they are not to blame for the death. Children sometimes attribute a loved one's death to their own behavior—if they had not misbehaved, they mistakenly reason, the person would not have died.
- Understand that children's grief may surface in unanticipated ways. Children may show little or no grief at the time of the death, but later they may become upset for no apparent reason or revert to behaviors such as sucking their thumb. Death can be overwhelming for a child, so try to be consistently loving and supportive.
- Talk to children about funerals, wakes, and other rituals associated with death, and what they should expect. You might give them a role to play, such as reading a poem, if they are old enough.

Module 19.3 Review

LO 19.8 Describe how survivors react to and cope with death.

Bereavement refers to the loss of a loved one; grief refers to the emotional response to that loss. Funeral rites play a significant role in helping people acknowledge the death of a loved one, recognize their own mortality, and proceed with their lives.

LO 19.9 Describe ways in which people experience grief and the functions it serves.

For many people, grief passes through denial, sorrow, and accommodation stages. Children need special help coping with grief.

Journal Writing Prompt

Applying Lifespan Development: Why do so many people in U.S. society feel reluctant to think and talk about death?

Epilogue

This chapter and the final part of the book focus on late adulthood and the end of life. Genuine physical and cognitive declines finally become the norm, but people can continue to lead healthy, engaged lives throughout most of the period—in defiance of stereotypes that characterize them as decrepit and doddering.

As in other periods of the life span, continuity and change are both evident in late adulthood. For example, we noticed that individual differences in cognitive performance, even as they show declines, reflect individual differences that were present in earlier years. We saw that lifestyle choices made earlier, such as participation in exercise, contribute to health and longevity later in life.

Social and personality development can continue throughout late adulthood. We saw that although most people show similar personality traits to those of their earlier years, late adulthood also affords a unique perspective on the more turbulent years that have gone before. People defy stereotypes of late adulthood in the varied ways they live and the rich relationships they sustain in this period.

We ended the book with a consideration of the inevitable end of life. Even here, as we considered death and its meaning at various stages in the life span and across cultures, we saw that there are challenges to be faced and satisfaction to be drawn from a graceful departure from life whether in a hospital, hospice, or palliative or home care setting.

In sum, the story of the entire life span is one of fresh challenges and opportunities as we continuously undergo and adjust to physical and cognitive changes and learn to relate to new social situations. Development persists virtually to the point of death, and with preparation, we can appreciate and learn from all parts of the life span.

Before you leave the book, return to the chapter prologue, about Jackson LeRoi, the 71-year-old who refused treatment for his terminal cancer. Based on your understanding of death and dying, answer the following questions.

1. To what extent do you think LeRoi went through the stages described by Kübler-Ross?
2. How might LeRoi have reacted differently to his impending death if he were a young man in his early 20s?
3. How might LeRoi's celebratory attitude toward the ending of his life have affected the bereavement process for his family?
4. How might LeRoi's final days have been different if he had elected to receive cancer treatment in the hospital? How might they have been different if he had required hospice care?

Looking Back

LO 19.1 Review the difficulties in defining death.

The precise point of death is difficult to define. Functional death refers to the absence of heartbeat and respiration, from which people can be resuscitated, while brain death refers to the absence of electrical activity in the brain, which is irreversible.

LO 19.2 Describe what death means at different stages of the life span.

The death of an infant or a young child is among the most devastating experiences for parents, largely because it seems unnatural and entirely incomprehensible. Adolescents have an unrealistic sense of invulnerability that makes them susceptible to accidental death. Denial often makes it impossible for terminally ill adolescents to accept the seriousness of their condition. For young adults, death is virtually unthinkable. Young adults who are terminally ill can be difficult patients because of their strong sense of the injustice of their fate. In middle adulthood, disease becomes the leading cause of death, and awareness of the reality of death can lead to a substantial fear of death. People in late adulthood begin to prepare for death. Older people generally prefer to know if death is near, and the main issue they have to deal with is whether their lives continue to have value.

LO 19.3 Describe how dying is affected by culture.

Responses to death are in part determined by culture. Death may be regarded as a release from the pains of the world, the beginning of a pleasurable afterlife, a punishment or judgment, or simply the end to life.

LO 19.4 Summarize how we can prepare for death.

Death education can help people learn about death and consider their own mortality realistically.

LO 19.5 Describe ways in which people face the prospect of their own death.

Elisabeth Kübler-Ross suggests that people pass through five basic stages on their way to death: denial, anger, bargaining, depression, and acceptance. The stage nature of her theory has been criticized, and other theorists have suggested alternatives.

LO 19.6 Describe ways in which people exercise control over the death decision.

A living will is a means of asserting control over decisions surrounding one's death through specification of desired medical treatments in life-threatening situations and designation of a health-care proxy to enforce one's wishes. Assisted suicide, a form of euthanasia, is illegal in most of the United States.

LO 19.7 Compare and contrast the advantages of hospice and home care for the end of life.

Although most deaths in the United States occur in hospitals, an increasing number of terminal patients are opting for either home care or hospice care.

LO 19.8 Describe how survivors react to and cope with death.

Funeral rituals serve a dual function: acknowledging the death of a loved one and recognizing and anticipating the mortality of all who participate.

LO 19.9 Describe ways in which people experience grief and the functions it serves.

The death of a loved one brings a period of adjustment involving bereavement and grief. Grief may proceed through stages of shock and denial, the beginning of acceptance, and accommodation. One consequence of bereavement is an increase in the risk of death for the survivor. Children need particular help in dealing with death, including honesty, encouragement of expressions of grief, reassurance that the death was not caused by the child's behavior, and understanding that the child's grief may be delayed and indirect.

Key Terms and Concepts

functional death 612
brain death 612
sudden infant death syndrome (SIDS) 613
thanatologists 617
living will 622
euthanasia 623
home care 624
hospice care 625
bereavement 626
grief 627

Summary 8
Late Adulthood and the End of Life

Blend Images/Shutterstock

ARTHUR WINSTON AND BEN TUFTY have chosen two distinct ways to live out their late adulthood. While Arthur loves his job and can't conceive of retiring, Ben couldn't wait to retire and now enjoys his leisure to the fullest. What the two retirees have in common is their commitment to maintaining their physical health, intellectual activity, and key relationships—even if they have chosen radically different ways to do these things. By paying attention to their needs in all three spheres, Arthur and Ben have remained optimistic and cheerful. Clearly, each looks forward to every day he spends in the world.

WHAT WOULD YOU DO?

■ If you were asked to do an oral history project involving Arthur and Ben, how complete and accurate would you expect their recollections to be? Would they be more reliable about the 1950s or the 1990s? Which man do you think you would enjoy talking to more?

What's your response?

Sinisa Bobic/ Shutterstock

WHAT WOULD A RETIREMENT COUNSELOR DO?

■ What advice would you give a person who wants to stay on the job forever, the way Arthur has done? What advice would you give someone like Ben, who wants to retire early? What characteristics would you look for in these individuals that would help you give the right advice?

What's your response?

IMAGEMORE Co., Ltd./Getty Images

Physical Development

Echo/Getty Images

- Though both are chronologically among the "oldest old," Arthur and Ben are "young old" in their functional ages.
- Both defy ageist stereotypes in their health and attitudes.
- Arthur and Ben have made healthy lifestyle choices—exercising, eating right, and avoiding bad habits—and both appear to have avoided Alzheimer's and most of the other physical and psychological disorders associated with old age. But they are increasingly aware that the end of life is approaching.

Cognitive Development

santypan/Shutterstock

- Both Arthur and Ben are apparently rich in crystallized intelligence—their store of information, skills, and strategies.
- They demonstrate plasticity by using stimulation, practice, and motivation to maintain their mental abilities.
- Both men may have slight memory problems, such as a decline in episodic or autobiographical memory.

Social and Personality Development

ASTIER/BSIP/Getty Images

- Arthur and Ben are navigating Erikson's ego-integrity-versus-despair stage, but they seem to have chosen different answers to Peck's developmental task of redefinition of self versus preoccupation with work role.
- The two appear to be coping with aging differently, according to Neugarten's personality categories.
- Both seem to have acquired wisdom with age, knowing who they are and how to deal with others.
- In playing low-pressure games, Ben might be engaging in compensation for slowed reaction time or less-than-perfect recall.
- Both men have chosen to continue living at home, although they are concerned as many of their friends, close to their own age, have died.

WHAT WOULD A HEALTH CARE PROVIDER DO?

- Why do you think Arthur and Ben are in such good mental health? What strategies has Arthur used that Ben may not have? What strategies has Ben used that Arthur may not have? What strategies do they share?

What's your response?

Rubberball/Mark Andersen/Getty Images

WHAT WOULD AN EDUCATOR DO?

- Would you recommend cognitive training for either Arthur or Ben? What about academic courses via Road Scholar or online? Why or why not?

What's your response?

Imtmphoto/Shutterstock

References

AAP Council on Communications and the Media. (2016). Media and young minds. *Pediatrics, 138*(5).

AARP (American Association of Retired Persons). (1990). *A profile of older Americans*. Washington, DC: Author.

AARP (American Association of Retired Persons). (1999). Modern Maturity Sexuality Study. Retrieved April 30, 2018 from https://www.aarp.org/relationships/love-sex/info-1999/aresearch-import-726.html

AARP (American Association of Retired Persons). (2005). *A profile of older Americans*. Washington, DC: Author.

Abdo, C., Afif-Abdo, J., Otani, F., & Machado, A. (2008). Sexual satisfaction among patients with erectile dysfunction treated with counseling, sildenafil, or both. *Journal of Sexual Medicine, 5*, 1720–1726.

Abrutyn, S., & Mueller, A. S. (2014). Are suicidal behaviors contagious in adolescence? Using longitudinal data to examine suicide suggestion. *American Sociological Review, 79*, 211–227.

Acierno, R., et al. (2010). Prevalence and correlates of emotional, physical, sexual, and financial abuse and potential neglect in the United States: The National Elder Mistreatment Study. *American Journal of Public Health, 100*, 292–297.

Ackerman, B. P., & Izard, C. E. (2004). Emotion cognition in children and adolescents: Introduction to the special issue. *Journal of Experimental Child Psychology, 89* [Special issue: Emotional cognition in children], 271–275.

Acocella, J. (2003, August 18 & 25). Little people. *New Yorker*, pp. 138–143.

ACOG. (2002). *Guidelines for perinatal care*. Elk Grove, IN: Author.

Adams, C., & Labouvie-Vief, G. (1986, November 20). Modes of knowing and language processing. Symposium on developmental dimensions of adult adaptations. Perspectives in mind, self, and emotion. Paper presented at the meeting of the Gerontological Association of America, Chicago.

Adams, G. R., Montemayor, R., & Gullotta, T. P. (Eds.). (1996). *Psychosocial development during adolescence*. Thousand Oaks, CA: Sage Publications.

Adams, K. B. (2004). Changing investment in activ-ities and interests in elders' lives: Theory and measurement. *International Journal of Aging and Human Development, 58*, 87–108.

Addati, L., Cassirer, N., & Gilchrist, K. (2014, May 13). *Maternity and paternity at work: Law and practice across the world*. Geneva, Switzerland: International Labour Organization.

Adebayo, B. (2008). Gender gaps in college enrollment and degree attainment: An exploratory analysis. *College Student Journal, 42*, 232–237.

Adelmann, P. K., Antonucci, T. C., & Crohan, S. E. (1990). A causal analysis of employment and health in midlife women. *Women and Health, 16*, 5–20.

ADL. (2017). Myths and facts about immigrants and immigration. Accessed online, 11-29-17; https://www.adl.org/education/resources/fact-sheets/myths-and-facts-about-immigrants-and-immigration.

Administration on Aging. (2003). *A profile of older Americans: 2003*. Washington, DC: U.S. Department of Health and Human Services.

Administration on Aging. (2006). *Profiles of older Americans 2005: Research report*. Washington, DC: U.S. Department of Health and Human Resources.

Adolph, K. E., Kretch, K. S., & LoBue, V. (2014). Fear of heights in infants? *Current Directions in Psychological Science, 23*, 60–66.

Agrawal, A., & Lynskey, M. (2008). Are there genetic influences on addiction? Evidence from family, adoption and twin studies. *Addiction, 103*, 1069–1081. http://search.ebscohost.com, doi:10.1111/j.1360-0443.2008.02213.x

Aguirre, G. K. (2006). Interpretation of clinical functional neuroimaging studies. In M. D'Esposisto (Ed.), Functional MRI: *Applications in clinical neurology and psychiatry*. Boca Raton, FL: Informa Healthcare.

Ahn, W., Gelman, S., & Amsterlaw, J. (2000). Causal status effect in children's categorization. *Cognition, 76*, B35–B43.

Aiken, L. R. (2000). *Dying, death, and bereavement* (4th ed.). Mahwah, NJ: Lawrence Erlbaum.

Ainsworth, M. D. S., Blehar, M. C., Waters, E., & Wall, S. (1978). *Patterns of attachment: A psychological study of the strange situation*. Hillsdale, NJ: Lawrence Erlbaum.

Aitken, R. J. (1995, July 7). The complexities of conception. *Science, 269*, 39–40.

Akyil, Y., Prouty, A., Blanchard, A., & Lyness, K. (2016). Experiences of families transmitting values in a rapidly changing society: Implications for family therapists. *Family Process, 55*, 368–381.

Alberts, A., Elkind, D., & Ginsberg, S. (2007). The personal fable and risk-taking in early adolescence. *Journal of Youth and Adolescence, 36*, 71–76.

Albrecht, G. L. (2005). *Encyclopedia of disability* (General ed.). Thousand Oaks, CA: Sage Publications.

Alderfer, C. (2003). The science and nonscience of psychologists' responses to The Bell Curve. *Professional Psychology: Research & Practice, 34*, 287–293.

Aldwin, C., & Gilmer, D. (2004). *Health, illness, and optimal aging: Biological and psychosocial perspectives*. Thousand Oaks, CA: Sage Publications.

Aldwin, C. M., & Igarashi, H. (2015). Successful, optimal, and resilient aging: A psychosocial perspective. In P. A. Lichtenberg, B. T. Mast, B. D. Carpenter, J. Loebach Wetherell (Eds.), *APA handbook of clinical geropsychology*, Vol. 1: History and status of the field and perspectives on aging. Washington, DC: American Psychological Association.

Alexander, B., Turnbull, D., & Cyna, A. (2009). The effect of pregnancy on hypnotizability. *American Journal of Clinical Hypnosis, 52*, 13–22.

Alexander, G. M., & Hines, M. (2002). Sex differences in response to children's toys in nonhuman primates. *Evolution and Human Behavior, 23*, 467–479.

Alexander, G., Wilcox, T., & Woods, R. (2009). Sex differences in infants' visual interest in toys. *Archives of Sexual Behavior, 38*, 427–433.

Alexandersen, P., Karsdal, M. A., & Christiansen, C. (2009). Long-term prevention with hormone-replacement therapy after the menopause: Which women should be targeted? *Womens Health (London, England), 5*, 637–647.

Alfred, M. V., & Chlup, D. T. (2010). Making the invisible, visible: Race matters in human resource development. *Advances in Developing Human Resources, 12*, 332–351.

Alhusen, J. L., Hayat, M. J., & Gross, D. (2013). A longitudinal study of maternal attachment and infant developmental outcomes. *Archives of Women's Mental Health, 16*, 521–529.

Alisky, J. M. (2007). The coming problem of HIV-associated Alzheimer's disease. *Medical Hypotheses, 12*, 47–55.

Allam, M. D., Marlier, L., & Schall, B. (2006). Learning at the breast: Preference formation for an artificial scent and its attraction against the odor of maternal milk. *Infant Behavior & Development, 29*, 308–321.

Allan, N. P., Joye, S. W., & Lonigan, C. J. (2017). Does gender moderate the relations between externalizing behavior and key emergent literacy abilities? Evidence from a longitudinal study. *Journal of Attention Disorders, 21*, 600–609.

Allen, B. (2008). An analysis of the impact of diverse forms of childhood psychological maltreatment on emotional adjustment in early adulthood. *Child Maltreatment, 13*, 307–312.

Allen, J., Chavez, S., DeSimone, S., Howard, D., Johnson, K., LaPierre, L., et al. (2006, June). Americans' attitudes toward euthanasia and physician-assisted suicide, 1936–2002. *Journal of Sociology & Social Welfare, 33*, 5–23.

Allen, M., & Bissell, M. (2004). Safety and stability for foster children: The policy context. *The Future of Children, 14*, 49–74.

Allison, B., & Schultz, J. (2001). Interpersonal identity formation during early adolescence. *Adolescence, 36*, 509–523.

Al-Namlah, A. S., Meins, E., & Fernyhough, C. (2012). Self-regulatory private speech relates to children's recall and organization of autobiographical memories. *Early Childhood Research Quarterly*. Accessed online, 7-18-12; http://www.sciencedirect.com/science/article/pii/S0885200612000300.

Al-Owidha, A., Green, K., & Kroger, J. (2009). On the question of an identity status category order: Rasch model step and scale statistics used to identify category order. *International Journal of Behavioral Development, 33*, 88–96.

Alshaarawy, O., & Anthony, J. C. (2014). Month-wise estimates of tobacco smoking during pregnancy for the United States, 2002–2009. *Maternal and Child Health Journal*. Accessed online, 3-14-15; http://www.ncbi.nlm.nih.gov/pubmed/25112459.

Alstad, Z., Sanders, E., Abbott, R. D., Barnett, A. L., Henderson, S. E., Connelly, V., & Berninger, V. W. (2015). Modes of alphabet letter production during middle childhood and adolescence: Interrelationships with each other and other writing skills. *Journal of Writing Research*, 6, 199-231.

Altermatt, E. R., & Broady, E. F. (2009). Coping with achievement-related failure: An examination of conversations between friends. *Merrill-Palmer Quarterly, 55*, 454–487.

Altholz, S., & Golensky, M. (2004). Counseling, support, and advocacy for clients who stutter. *Health & Social Work, 29*, 197–205.

Álvarez, M. J., Fernández, D., Gómez-Salgado, J., Rodríguez-González, D., Rosón, M., & Lapeña, S. (2017). The effects of massage therapy in hospitalized preterm neonates: A systematic review. *International Journal of Nursing Studies, 69*, 119–136.

Alwin, D. F. (2012). Integrating varieties of life course concepts. *Journals of Gerontology: Series B: Psychological Sciences and Social Sciences, 67B*, 206–220.

Alzheimer's Association. (2004, May 28). *Standard prescriptions for Alzheimer's*. Accessed online; http://www.alz.org/AboutAD/Treatment/Standard.asp.

Alzheimer's Association. (2017). 2017 *Alzheimer's disease facts and figures*. Accessed online, 12-11-17; https://www.alz.org/facts/overview.asp#prevalence.

Amato, P. R., & Afifi, T. D. (2006). Feeling caught between parents: Adult children's relations with parents and subjective well-being. *Journal of Marriage and Family, 68*, 222–235.

Amato, P., & Booth, A. (1997). *A generation at risk*. Cambridge, MA: Harvard University Press.

American Academy of Pediatrics. (2014). *Caring for Your Baby and Young Child*. (5th ed.). NY: Bantam

American Academy of Pediatrics. (2000). Clinical practice guideline: Diagnosis and evaluation of the child with attention-deficit/hyperactivity disorder. *Pediatrics*. Accessed online, 2-2-18; http://www.pediatrics.org/cgi/content/full/105/5/1158.

American Academy of Pediatrics. (2004, June 3). *Sports programs*. Accessed online, http://www.medem.com/medlb/article_detaillb_for_printer.cfm?article.

American Academy of Pediatrics. (2005). Breastfeeding and the use of human milk: Policy statement. *Pediatrics, 115*, 496–506.

American Academy of Pediatrics. (2012, March 5). *Discipline and your child*. Ac-cessed online, 7-23-12; http://www.healthychildren.org/english/family-life/family-dynamics/communication-discipline/pages/disciplining-your-child.aspx?nfstatus=401&nftoken=00000000-0000-0000-0000-000000000000&nfstatusdescription=ERROR%3a+No+local+token.

American Academy of Pediatrics. (2013). Prevalence and reasons for introducing infants early to solid foods: Variations by milk feeding type. *Pediatrics, 131*. Ac-cessed online, 6-25-14; http://pediatrics.aappublications.org/content/131/4/e1108.

American Academy of Pediatrics. (2014). *Caring for Your Baby and Young Child*. (5th ed.). NY: Ban-tam.

American Academy of Pediatrics (2016, October 21). *American Academy of Pediatrics announces new recommendations for children's media use*. Accessed online, 3-3-17; https://www.aap.org/en-us/about-the-aap/aap-press-room/pages/american-academy-of-pediatrics-announces-new-recommendations-for-childrens-media-use.aspx.

American Academy of Pediatrics Healthychildren.org. (2015). *Choosing a child care center*. Accessed online, 10-31-17; https://www.healthychildren.org/English/family-life/work-play/Pages/Choosing-a-Childcare-Center.aspx.

American Association of Community Colleges. (2015). *2015 fact sheet*. Washington, DC: American Association of Community Colleges.

American Association of Neurological Surgeons. (2012). Shaken baby syndrome. Accessed online, 7-4-12; http://www.aans.org/Patient%20Information/Conditions%20and%20Treatments/Shaken%20Baby%20Syndrome.aspx.

American Association on Intellectual and Developmental Disabilities. (2012). Definition of intellectual disability. Accessed online, 7-23-12; www.aamr.org.

American Cancer Society. (2017). American Cancer Society guidelines for the early detection of cancer. Accessed online, 11-28-17; https://www.cancer.org/healthy/find-cancer-early/cancer-screening-guidelines/american-cancer-society-guidelines-for-the-early-detection-of-cancer.html.

American College of Medical Genetics. (2006*). Genetics in Medicine, 8*(5), Supplement.

American Heart Association. (2010). *Heart facts*. Dallas, TX: Author.

American Psychological Association. (2017). Ethical Principles of Psychologists and Code of Conduct. Accessed online May 1, 2018 http://www.apa.org/ethics/code/

Amitai, Y., Haringman, M., Meiraz, H., Baram, N., & Leventhal, A. (2004). Increased awareness, knowledge and utilization of preconceptional folic acid in Israel following a national campaign. *Preventive Medicine: An International Journal Devoted to Practice and Theory, 39*, 731–737.

Ammerman, R. T., & Patz, R. J. (1996). Determinants of child abuse potential: Contribution of parent and child factors. *Journal of Clinical Child Psychology, 25*, 300–307.

Amsterlaw, J., & Wellman, H. (2006). Theories of mind in transition: A microgenetic study of the development of false belief understanding. *Journal of Cognition and Development, 7*, 139–172.

Anand, K. J. S., & Hickey, P. R. (1992). Halothane-morphine compared with high-dose sufentanil for anesthesia and post-operative analgesia in neonatal cardiac surgery. *New England Journal of Medicine, 326*(1), 1–9.

Anders, T. F., & Taylor, T. (1994). Babies and their sleep environment. *Children's Environments, 11*, 123–134.

Anderson, J. (2016, March 2). The idea that Mozart makes your baby smarter is one of parenting's most persistent myths. Accessed online, 10-30-17; https://qz.com/628331/the-idea-that-mozart-makes-babies-smarter-is-one-of-parentings-most-bizarre-myths/.

Anderson, M., & Perrin, A. (2017, May 17.) *Tech adoption climbs among older adults*. Washington, DC: Pew Research Center.

Andreotti, C., Garrard, P., Venkatraman, S. L., & Compas, B. E. (2014). Stress-related changes in attentional bias to social threat in young adults: Psychobiological associations with the early family environment. *Cognitive Therapy and Research, 39*(3), 332–342. Accessed online, 3-23-15; http://link.springer.com/article/10.1007/s10608-014-9659-z#page-1.

Andrew, M., McCanlies, E., Burchfiel, C., Charles, L., Hartley, T., Fekedulegn, D., et al. (2008). Hardiness and psychological distress in a cohort of police officers. *International Journal of Emergency Mental Health, 10*, 137–148.

Andrews, B., d'Avossa, G., & Sapir, A. (2017). Aging changes 3D perception: Evidence for hemispheric rebalancing of lateralized processes. *Neuropsychologia, 99*, 121–127.

Andrews, G., Halford, G., & Bunch, K. (2003). Theory of mind and relational complexity. *Child Development, 74*, 1476–1499.

Andruski, J. E., Casielles, E., & Nathan, G. (2014). Is bilingual babbling language-specific? Some evidence from a case study of Spanish–English dual acquisition. *Bilingualism: Language and Cognition, 17*, 660–672.

Ansaldo, A. I., Arguin, M., & Roch Locours, A. (2002). The contribution of the right cerebral hemisphere to the recovery from aphasia: A single longitudinal case study. *Brain and Language, 82*, 206–222.

Ansberry, C. (1997, November 14). Women of Troy: For ladies on a hill, friendships are a balm in the passages of life. *Wall Street Journal*, pp. A1, A6.

Antonucci, T. C. (2001). Social relations: An examination of social networks, social support, and sense of control. In J. E. Birren & K. W. Schaie (Eds.), *Handbook of the psychology of aging* (5th ed.). San Diego: Academic Press.

Antshel, K., & Antshel, K. (2002). Integrating culture as a means of improving treatment adherence in the Latino population. *Psychology, Health & Medicine, 7*, 435–449.

Anyan, F., & Hjemdal, O. (2016). Adolescent stress and symptoms of anxiety and depression: Resilience explains and differentiates the relationships. *Journal of Affective Disorders, 203*, 213–220.

Anzman-Frasca, S., Liu, S., Gates, K. M., Paul, I. M., Rovine, M. J., & Birch, L. L. (2013). Infants' transitions out of a fussing/crying state are modifiable and are related to weight status. *Infancy, 18*, 662–686.

Aoyagi, K., Santos, C. E., & Updegraff, K. A. (2017). Longitudinal associations between gender and ethnic-racial identity felt pressure from family and peers and self-esteem among African American and Latino/a youth. *Journal of Youth and Adolescence*. Accessed online, 11-29-17; https://www.ncbi.nlm.nih.gov/pubmed/28986744.

APA Reproductive Choice Working Group. (2000). *Reproductive choice and abortion: A resource packet*. Washington, DC: American Psychological Association.

Apfelbaum, E. P., Pauker, K., Sommers, S. R., & Ambady, N. (2010). In blind pursuit of racial equality?. *Psychological Science, 21*(11), 1587-1592. doi:10.1177/0956797610384741

Apperly, I., & Robinson, E. (2002). Five-year-olds' handling of reference and description in the domains of language and mental representation. *Journal of Experimental Child Psychology, 83*, 53–75.

Arai, J., Li, S., Hartley, D., and Feig, L. (2009). Transgenerational rescue of a genetic defect in long-term potentiation and memory formation by juvenile enrichment. *Journal of Neuroscience, 29*, 1496–1502.

Archer, J. (2009). The nature of human aggression. *International Journal of Law and Psychiatry, 32*, 202–208.

Archimi, A., & Kuntsche, E. (2014). Do offenders and victims drink for different reasons? Testing mediation of drinking motives in the link between bullying subgroups and alcohol use in adolescence. *Addictive Behaviors, 39*, 713–716.

Ariès, P. (1962). *Centuries of childhood*. New York: Knopf.

Armstrong, J., Hutchinson, I., Laing, D., & Jinks, A. (2006). Facial electromyography: Responses of children to odor and taste stimuli. *Chemical Senses, 32*, 611–621.

Armstrong, P., Rounds, J., & Hubert, L. (2008). Re-conceptualizing the past: Historical data in vocational interest research. *Jounal of Vocational Behavior, 72*, 284–297.

Arnett, J. J. (2000). Emerging adulthood: A theory of development from the late teens through the twenties. *American Psychologist, 55*, 469–480.

Arnett, J. J. (2006). *Emerging adulthood: The winding road from the late teens through the twenties*. New York: Oxford University Press.

Arnett, J. J. (2011). Emerging adulthood(s): The cultural psychology of a new life stage. In L. Jensen & L. Jensen (Eds.), *Bridging cultural and developmental approaches to psychology: New syntheses in theory, research, and policy*. New York: Oxford University Press.

Arnett, J. J. (2014a). *Emerging adulthood: The winding road from the late teens through the twenties* (2nd ed.). New York: Oxford University Press.

Arnett, J. J. (2014b). Presidential address: The emer-gence of emerging adulthood: A personal history. *Emerging Adulthood, 2*, 155–162.

Arnett, J. J. (2015). Identity development from adolescence to emerging adulthood: What we know and (especially) don't know. In K. C. McLean, & M. Syed (Eds.), *The Oxford handbook of identity development*. New York: Oxford University Press.

Arnett, J. J. (2016). *The Oxford handbook of emerging adulthood*. New York: Oxford University Press.

Arnon, I., & Ramscar, M. (2012). Granularity and the acquisition of grammatical gender: How order-of-acquisition affects what gets learned. *Cognition, 122*, 292–305.

Arnsten, A., Berridge, C., & McCracken, J. (2009). The neurobiological basis of attention-deficit/hyperactivity disorder. *Primary Psychiatry, 16*, 47–54.

Aronson, J. D. (2007). Brain imaging, culpability and the juvenile death penalty. *Psychology, Public Policy, and Law, 13*, 115–142.

Aronson, M., & Bialostok, S. (2016). 'Do some wondering': Children and their self-understanding selves in early elementary classrooms. *Symbolic Interaction, 39*, 229–251.

Arseneault, L., Moffitt, T. E., & Caspi, A. (2003). Strong genetic effects on cross-situational antisocial behavior among 5-year-old children according to mothers, teachers, examiner-observers, and twins' self-reports. *Journal of Child Psychology and Psychiatry and Allied Disciplines, 44*, 832–848.

Arts, J. A. R., Gijselaers, W. H., & Boshuizen, H. P. A. (2006). Understanding managerial problem-solving, knowledge use and information processing: Investigating stages from school to the workplace. *Contemporary Educational Psychology, 31*, 387–410.

Asadi, S., Amiri, S., & Molavi, H. (2014). Development of post-formal thinking from adolescence through adulthood. *Journal of Iranian Psychologists, 10*, 161–174.

Asbury, K., & Plomin, R. (2014). *G is for genes: the impact of genetics on education and achievement*. New York: Wiley-Blackwell.

Asch, D. A. (1996, May 23). The role of critical care nurses in euthanasia and assisted suicide. *New England Journal of Medicine, 334*, 1374–1379.

Asendorpf, J. (2002). Self-awareness, other awareness, and secondary representation. In A. Meltzoff & W. Prinz (Eds.), *The imitative mind: Development, evolution, and brain bases*. New York: Cambridge University Press.

Asher, S. R., & Rose, A. J. (1997). Promoting children's social-emotional adjustment with peers. In P. Salovey & D. Sluyter (Eds.), *Emotional development and emotional intelligence: Educational implications*. New York: Basic Books.

Astin, A., Korn, W., & Berg, E. (1989). *The American freshman: National norms for fall, 1989*. Los Angeles: University of California, American Council on Education.

Atchley, R. (2003). Why most people cope well with retirement. In J. Ronch & J. Goldfield (Eds.), *Mental wellness in aging: Strengths-based approaches*. Baltimore, MD: Health Professions Press.

Atchley, R. C. (1982). Retirement: Leaving the world of work. *Annals of the American Academy of Political and Social Science, 464*, 120–131.

Atchley, R. C. (2000). *Social forces and aging* (9th ed.). Belmont, CA: Wadsworth Thomson Learning.

Athanasiu, L., Giddaluru, S., Fernandes, C., Christoforou, A., Reinvang, I., Lundervold, A. J., & … Le Hellard, S. (2017). A genetic association study of CSMD1 and CSMD2 with cognitive function. *Brain, Behavior, and Immunity, 61*, 209–216.

Athanasopoulou, E., & Fox, J. E. (2014). Effects of kangaroo mother care on maternal mood and interaction patterns between parents and their preterm, low birth weight infants: A systematic review. *Infant Mental Health Journal, 35*, 245–262.

Atkins, D. C., & Furrow, J. (2008, November). *Infidelity is on the rise: But for whom and why?* Paper presented at the annual meeting of the Association for Behavioral and Cognitive Therapies, Orlando, FL.

Atkins, S. M., Bunting, M. F., Bolger, D. J., & Dougherty, M. R. (2012). Training the adolescent brain: Neural plasticity and the acquisition of cognitive abilities. In V. F. Reyna, S. B. Chapman, M. R. Dougherty, & J. Confrey (Eds.), *The adolescent brain: Learning, reasoning, and decision making*. Washington, DC: American Psychological Association.

Auestad, N., Scott, D. T., Janowsky, J. S., Jacobsen, C., Carroll, R. E., Montalto, M. B., et al. (2003). Visual cognitive and language assessments at 39 months: A follow-up study of children fed formulas containing long-chain polyunsaturated fatty acids to 1 year of age. *Pediatrics, 112*, e177–e183.

Augustyn, M. (2003). "G" is for growing. Thirty years of research on children and Sesame Street. *Journal of Developmental and Behavioral Pediatrics, 24*, 451.

Aujoulat, I., Luminet, O., & Deccache, A. (2007). The perspective of patients on their experience of powerlessness. *Qualitative Health Research, 17*, 772–785.

Austin, J. (2016). 2020 vision: Genetic counselors as acknowledged leaders in integrating genetics and genomics into healthcare. *Journal of Genetic Counseling, 25*, 1–5.

Avinun, R., Israel, S., Shalev, I., Grtsenko, I., Bornstein, G., Ebstein, R. P., & Knafo, A. (2011). AVPR1A variant associated with preschoolers' lower altruistic behavior. *PLoS One, 6*, Accessed online, 7-5-12; http://www.sproutonline.com/kindnesscounts/dr-nancy-eisenberg/eight-tips-for-developing-caring-kids.

Avlund, K., Lund, R., & Holstein, B. (2004). Social relations as determinant of onset of disability in aging. *Archives of Gerontology & Geriatrics, 38*, 85–99.

Axelson, H. W., Winkler, T., Flygt, J., Djupsjö, A., Hånell, A., & Marklund, N. (2013). Plasticity of the contralateral motor cortex following focal traumatic brain injury in the rat. *Restorative Neurology and Neuroscience, 31*, 73–85.

Axia, G., Bonichini, S., & Benini, F. (1995). Pain in infancy: Individual differences. *Perceptual and Motor Skills, 81*, 142.

Ayalon, L., & Koren, C. (2015). Marriage, second couplehood, divorce, and singlehood in old age. In P. A. Lichtenberg, B. T. Mast, B. D. Carpenter, & J. Loebach Wetherell (Eds.), *APA handbook of clinical geropsychology, Vol. 2: Assessment, treatment, and issues of later life*. Washington, DC: American Psychological Association.

Ayalon, L., & Tesch-Römer, C. (2017). Taking a closer look at ageism: Self- and other-directed ageist attitudes and discrimination. *European Journal of Ageing, 14*, 1–4.

Aydt, H., & Corsaro, W. (2003). Differences in children's construction of gender across culture: An interpretive approach. *American Behavioral Scientist, 46*, 1306–1325.

Aylward, G. P., & Verhulst, S. J. (2000). Predictive utility of the Bayley Infant Neurodevelopmental Screener (BINS) risk status classifications: Clinical interpretation and application. *Developmental Medicine & Child Neurology, 42*, 25–31.

Ayoub, N. C. (2005, February 25). A pleasing birth: Midwives and maternity care in the Netherlands. *The Chronicle of Higher Education*, p. 9.

Ayres, M. M., & Leaper, C. (2013). Adolescent girls' experiences of discrimination: An examination of coping strategies, social support, and self-esteem. *Journal of Adolescent Research, 28*, 479–508.

Azlan, H. A., Overton, P. G., Simpson, J., & Powell, P. A. (2017). Differential disgust responding in people with cancer and implications for psychological wellbeing. *Psychology & Health, 32*, 19–37.

Aznar, A., & Tenenbaum, H. R. (2016). Parent–child positive touch: Gender, age, and task differences. *Journal of Nonverbal Behavior, 40*, 317–333.

Babitz, E. (2016). *Slow days, fast company: The world, the flesh, and L.A.* New York: NYRB Classics.

Bacchus, L., Mezey, G., & Bewley, S. (2006). A qualitative exploration of the nature of domestic violence in pregnancy. *Violence Against Women, 12*, 588–604.

Badenhorst, W., Riches, S., Turton, P., & Hughes, P. (2006). The psychological effects of stillbirth and neonatal death on fathers: Systematic review. *Journal of Psychosomatic Obstetrics & Gynecology, 27*, 245–256.

Baer, J. S., Sampson, P. D., & Barr, H. M. (2003). A 21-year longitudinal analysis of the effects of prenatal alcohol exposure on young adult drinking. *Archives of General Psychiatry, 60*, 377–385.

Bagci, S. C., Kumashiro, M., Smith, P. K., Blumberg, H., & Rutland, A. (2014). Cross-ethnic friendships: Are they really rare? Evidence from secondary schools around London. *International Journal of Intercultural Relations, 41*, 125–137.

Bahenko, O., Kovalchuk, I., & Metz, G. S. (2015). Stress-induced perinatal and transgenerational epigenetic programming of brain development and mental health. *Neuroscience and Biobehavioral Reviews, 48*, 70–91.

Bahrick, L. E., Todd, J. T., Castellanos, I., & Sorondo, B. M. (2016). Enhanced attention to speaking faces versus other event types emerges gradually across infancy. *Developmental Psychology, 52*, 1705–1720.

Bai, L. (2005). Children at play: A childhood beyond the Confucian shadow. *Childhood: A Global Journal of Child Research, 12*, 9–32.

Bailey-Davis, L., Poulsen, M. N., Hirsch, A. G., Pollak, J., Glass, T. A., & Schwartz, B. S. (2017). Home food rules in relation to youth eating behaviors, body mass index, waist circumference, and percent body fat. *Journal of Adolescent Health, 60*, 270–276.

Baillargeon, R. (2008). Innate ideas revisited: For a principle of persistence in infants' physical reasoning. *Perspectives on Psychological Science, 3*, 2–13.

Baillargeon, R., & DeJong, G. F. (2017). Explanation-based learning in infancy. *Psychonomic Bulletin & Review*. Accessed online, 10-29-17; https://www.ncbi.nlm.nih.gov/pubmed/28698990.

Baillargeon, R., Scott, R. M., He, Z., Sloane, S., Setoh, P., Jin, K., & … Bian, L. (2015). Psychological and sociomoral reasoning in infancy. In M. Mikulincer, P. R. Shaver, E. Borgida, & J. A. Bargh (Eds.), *APA handbook of personality and social psychology, Volume 1: Attitudes and social cognition*. Washington, DC: American Psychological Association.

Bainbridge, K. E., & Wallhagen, M. I. (2014). Hearing loss in an aging American population: Extent, impact, and management. *Annual Review of Public Health, 35*, 139–152.

Baker, J., Maes, H., Lissner, L., Aggen, S., Lichtenstein, P., & Kendler, K. (2009). Genetic risk factors for disordered eating in adolescent males and females. *Journal of Abnormal Psychology, 118*, 576–586.

Baker, L. R., McNulty, J. K., & VanderDrift, L. E. (2017). Expectations for future relationship satisfaction: Unique sources and critical implications for commitment. *Journal of Experimental Psychology: General, 146*, 700–721.

Baker, M. (2007, December). Elder mistreatment: Risk, vulnerability, and early mortality. *Journal of the American Psychiatric Nurses Association, 12*, 313–321.

Baker, P., & Sussman, D. (2012, May 15). Obama's switch on same-sex marriage stirs skepticism. *New York Times*, p. A17.

Baker, T., Brandon, T., & Chassin, L. (2004). Motivational influences on cigarette smoking. *Annual Review of Psychology, 55*, 463–491.

Bakoyiannis, I., Gkioka, E., Pergialiotis, V., Mastroleon, I., Prodromidou, A., Vlachos, G. D., & Perrea, D. (2014). Fetal alcohol spectrum disorders and cognitive functions of young children. *Reviews in the Neurosciences, 25*, 631–639.

Balakrishnan, V., & Claiborne, L. (2012). Vygotsky from ZPD to ZCD in moral education: Reshaping Western theory and practices in local context. *Journal of Moral Education, 41*, 225–243.

Ball, H. L., & Volpe, L. E. (2013). Sudden Infant Death Syndrome (SIDS) risk reduction and infant sleep location—Moving the discussion forward. *Social Science & Medicine, 79*, 84–91.

Ball, M., & Orford, J. (2002). Meaningful patterns of activity amongst the long-term inner city unemployed: A qualitative study. *Journal of Community & Applied Social Psychology, 12*, 377–396.

Ballesteros-Meseguer, C., Carrillo-García, C., Meseguer-de-Pedro, M., Canteras-Jordana, M., & Martínez-Roche, M. E. (2016). Episiotomy and its relationship to various clinical variables that influence its performance. *Revista Latino-Americana de Enfermagem, 24*, 22–27

Baltes, M. M. (1996). *The many faces of dependency in old age*. New York: Cambridge University Press.

Baltes, P. B. (2003). On the incomplete architecture of human ontogeny: Selection, optimization and compensation as foundation of developmental theory. In U. M. Staudinger & U. Lindenberger (Eds.), *Understanding human development: Dialogues with lifespan psychology*. Dordrecht, Netherlands: Kluwer Academic Publishers.

Baltes, P. B., & Baltes, M. M. (1990). Psychological perspectives on successful aging: The model of selective optimization with compensation. In P. B. Baltes & M. M. Baltes (Eds.), *Successful aging: Perspectives from the behavioral sciences*. Cambridge, UK: Cambridge University Press.

Baltes, P. B., & Schaie, K. W. (1974, March). The myth of the twilight years. *Psychology Today*, pp. 35–38.

Baltes, P. B, & Smith, J. (2008). The fascination of wisdom: Its nature, ontogeny, and function. *Perspectives on Psychological Science, 3*, 56–64.

Baltes, P. B., & Staudinger, U. M. (2000). Wisdom: A metaheuristic (pragmatic) to orchestrate mind and virtue toward excellence. *American Psychologist, 55*, 122–136.

Bandura, A. (1977). *Social learning theory*. Englewood Cliffs, NJ: Prentice Hall.

Bandura, A. (1986). *Social foundations of thought and action*. Englewood Cliffs, NJ: Prentice Hall.

Bandura, A. (1991). Social cognitive theory of self-regulation. *Organizational Behavior and Human Decision Processes, 50*, [Special issue: Theories of cognitive self-regulation], 248–287.

Bandura, A. (1994). Social cognitive theory of mass communication. In J. Bryant & D. Zillmann (Eds.), *Media effects: Advances in theory and research*. LEA's communication series. Hillsdale, NJ: Lawrence Erlbaum.

Bandura, A. (2002). Social cognitive theory in cultural context. *Applied Psychology: An International Review, 51*, [Special issue], 269–290.

Bandura, A., Grusec, J. E., & Menlove, F. L. (1967). Vicarious extinction of avoidance behavior. *Journal of Personality and Social Psychology, 5*, 16–23.

Bandura, A., Ross, D., & Ross, S. (1963). Vicarious extinction of avoidance behavior. *Journal of Personality and Social Psychology, 67*, 601–607.

Baptista, T., Aldana, E., Angeles, F., & Beaulieu, S. (2008). Evolution theory: An overview of its applications in psychiatry. *Psychopathology, 41*, 17–27.

Barbaro, N., Boutwell, B. B., Barnes, J. C., & Shackelford, T. K. (2017). Rethinking the transmission gap: What behavioral genetics and evolutionary psychology mean for attachment theory: A comment on Verhage et al. (2016). *Psychological Bulletin, 143*, 107–113.

Barber, A. D., Srinivasan, P., Joel, S. E., Caffo, B. S., Pekar, J. J., & Mostofsky, S. H. (2012). Motor "dexterity"?: Evidence that left hemisphere lateralization of motor circuit connectivity is associated with better motor performance in children. *Cerebral Cortex, 22*, 51–59.

Barber, S., & Gertler, P. (2009). Empowering women to obtain high quality care: Evidence from an evaluation of Mexico's conditional cash transfer programme. *Health Policy and Planning, 24*, 18–25.

Barboza, G., Schiamberg, L., Oehmke, J., Korzeniewski, S., Post, L., & Heraux, C. (2009). Individual characteristics and the multiple contexts of adolescent bullying: An ecological perspective. *Journal of Youth and Adolescence, 38*, 101–121.

Barelds, D. H., Dijkstra, P., Groothof, H. K., & Pastoor, C. D. (2017). The dark triad and three types of jealousy: Its relations among heterosexuals and homosexuals involved in a romantic relationship. *Personality and Individual Differences, 116*, 6–10.

Barlett, C., Chamberlin, K., & Witkower, Z. (2017). Predicting cyberbullying perpetration in emerging adults: A theoretical test of the Barlett Gentile Cyberbullying Model. *Aggressive Behavior, 43*, 147–154.

Barlett, C. P., & Chamberlin, K. (2017). Examining cyberbullying across the lifespan. *Computers in Human Behavior, 71*, 444–449.

Barnes, J. C., & Boutwell, B. B. (2012). On the relationship of past to future involvement in crime and delinquency: A behavior genetic analysis. *Journal of Criminal Justice, 40*, 94–102.

Barnett, R. C., & Hyde, J. S. (2001). Women, men, work, and family. *American Psychologist, 56*, 781–796.

Barr, R., Muentener, P., Garcia, A., Fujimoto, M., & Chávez, V. (2007). The effect of repetition on imitation from television during infancy. *Developmental Psychobiology, 49*, 196–207.

Barrett, D. E., & Frank, D. A. (1987). *The effects of undernutrition on children's behavior*. New York: Gordon & Breach.

Barrett, D. E., & Radke-Yarrow, M. R. (1985). Ef-fects of nutritional supplementation on children's responses to novel, frustrating, and competitive situations. *American Journal of Clinical Nutrition, 42*, 102–120.

Barrouillet, P. (2015). Theories of cognitive devel-opment: From Piaget to today. *Developmental Review, 38*, 1–12.

Barrouillet, P., & Gaillard, V. (2011). *Cognitive development and working memory: A dialogue between neo-Piagetian theories and cognitive approaches*. New York: Psychology Press.

Barry, L. M., Hudley, C., Kelly, M., & Cho, S. (2009). Differences in self-reported disclosure of college experiences by first-generation college student status. *Adolescence, 44*, 55–68.

Barsade, S. G., & O'Neill, O. A. (2014). What's love got to do with it? A longitudinal study of the culture of companionate love and employee and client outcomes in a long-term care setting. *Administrative Science Quarterly, 59*, 551–598.

Bartlett, C. P., Prot, S., Anderson, C. A., & Gentile, D. A. (2017). An empirical examination of the strength differential hypothesis in cyberbullying behavior. *Psychology of Violence, 7*, 22–32.

Bartlett, K., Kelley, E., Purdy, J., & Stein, M. T. (2017). Auditory processing disorder: What does it mean and what can be done? *Journal of Developmental and Behavioral Pediatrics, 38*, 349–351.

Bass, S., Shields, M. K., & Behrman, R. E. (2004). Children, families, and foster care: Analysis and recommendations. *The Future of Children, 14*, 5–30.

Bates, J. E., Marvinney, D., Kelly, T., Dodge, K. A., Bennett, D. S., & Pettit, G. S. (1994). Child-care history and kindergarten adjustment. *Developmental Psychology, 30*, 690–700.

Battin, M., van der Heide, A., Ganzini, L., van der Wal, G., & Onwuteaka-Philipsen, B. (2007). Legal physician-assisted dying in Oregon and the Netherlands: Evidence concerning the impact on patients in "vulnerable" groups. *Journal of Medical Ethics, 33*, 591–597.

Bauer, P. J. (2007). Recall in infancy: A neurodevelopmental account. *Current Directions in Psychological Science, 16*, 142–146.

Baulac, S., Lu, H., Strahle, J., Yang, T., Goldberg, M., Shen, J., et al. (2009). Increased DJ-1 expression under oxidative stress and in Alzheimer's disease brains. *Molecular Neurodegeneration, 4*, 27–37.

Bauld, R., & Brown, R. (2009). Stress, psychological distress, psychosocial factors, menopause symptoms and physical health in women. *Maturitas, 62*, 160–165.

Baum, A. (1994). Behavioral, biological, and environmental interactions in disease processes. In S. Blumenthal, K. Matthews, & S. Weiss (Eds.), *New research frontiers in behavioral medicine: Proceedings of the National Conference*. Washington, DC: NIH Publications.

Baumrind, D. (1980). New directions in socialization research. *Psychological Bulletin, 35*, 639–652.

Baumrind, D. (2005). Patterns of parental authority. *New Directions in Child Adolescent Development, 108*, 61–69.

Bayley, N. 2005. *Bayley Scales of Infant Development* [BSID-III], 3rd ed. San Antonio, TX: The Psychological Corporation.

Bayley, N., & Oden, M. (1955). The maintenance of intellectual ability in gifted adults. *Journal of Gerontology, 10*, 91–107.

Beale, C. R. (1994). *Boys and girls: The development of gender roles*. New York: McGraw-Hill.

Beale, E. A., Baile, W. F., & Aaron, J. (2005). Silence is not golden: Communicating with children dying from cancer. *Journal of Clinical Oncology, 23*, 3629–3631.

Beals, K., Impett, E., & Peplau, L. (2002). Lesbians in love: Why some relationships endure and others end. *Journal of Lesbian Studies, 6*, 53–63.

Beard, V. R., & Burger, W. C. (2017). Change and innovation in the funeral industry: A typology of motivations. Omega: *Journal of Death and Dying, 75*, 47–68.

Bearman, P., & Bruckner, H. (2004). *Study on teenage virginity pledge*. Paper presented at meeting of the National STD Prevention Conference, Philadelphia, PA.

Beck, M. (2012, June 5). Hormone use benefits may trump risks; age matters. *Wall Street Journal*, pp. D1, D2.

Becker, B., & Luthar, S. (2007, March). Peer-perceived admiration and social preference: Contextual correlates of positive peer regard among suburban and urban adolescents. *Journal of Research on Adolescence, 17*, 117–144.

Becker, G., Beyene, Y., & Newsom, E. (2003). Creating continuity through mutual assistance: Intergenerational reciprocity in four ethnic groups. *Journals of Gerontology: Series B: Psychological Sciences & Social Sci-ences, 58B*, S151–S159.

Beckman, M. (2004, July 30). Neuroscience: Crime, culpability, and the adolescent brain. *Science, 305*, 596–599.

Becvar, D. S. (2000). Euthanasia decisions. In F. W. Kaslow et al. (Eds.), *Handbook of couple and family forensics: A sourcebook for mental health and legal professionals*. New York: Wiley.

Beets, M., Flay, B., Vuchinich, S., Li, K., Acock, A., & Snyder, F. (2009). Longitudinal patterns of binge drinking among first-year college students with a history of tobacco use. *Drug and Alcohol Dependence, 103*, 1–8.

Begeer, S., Bernstein, D. M., van Wijhe, J., Schleeren, A. M., & Koot, H. (2012). A continuous false belief task reveals egocentric biases in children and adolescents with autism spectrum disorders. *Autism, 16*, 357–366.

Begley, S. (1995, July 10). Deliver, then depart. *Newsweek*, p. 62.

Behm, I., Kabir, Z., Connolly, G. N., & Alpert, H. R. (2012). Increasing prevalence of smoke-free homes and decreasing rates of sudden infant death syndrome in the United States: An ecological association study. *Tobacco Control: An International Journal, 21*, 6–11.

Beilby, J. M., Byrnes, M. L., & Young, K. N. (2012). The experiences of living with a sibling who stutters: A preliminary study. *Journal of Fluency Disorders, 37*, 135–148.

Beisert, M., Zmyj, N., Liepelt, R., Jung, F., Prinz, W., & Daum, M. M. (2012). Rethinking 'rational imitation' in 14-month-old infants: A perceptual distraction approach. Plos ONE, 7(3), Accessed online, 7-9-12; http://www.plosone.org/article/info%3Adoi%2F10.1371%2Fjournal.pone.0032563.

Beitel, M., Bogus, S., Hutz, A., Green, D., Cecero, J. J., & Barry, D. T. (2014). Stillness and motion: An empirical investigation of mindfulness and self-actualization. *Person-Centered and Experiential Psychotherapies, 13*, 187–202.

Belcher, J. R. (2003). Stepparenting: Creating and recreating families in America today. *Journal of Nervous & Mental Disease, 191*, 837–838.

Belkin, L. (1999, July 25). Getting the girl. *New York Times Magazine*, pp. 26–35.

Belkin, L. (2004, September 12). The lessons of Classroom 506: What happens when a boy with cerebral palsy goes to kindergarten like all the other kids. *New York Times Magazine*, pp. 41–49.

Bell, H., Pellis, S., & Kolb, B. (2009). Juvenile peer play experience and the development of the orbitofrontal and medial prefrontal cortices. *Behavioural Brain Research, 207*, 7–13.

Bell, I. P. (1989). The double standard: Age. In J. Freeman (Ed.), *Women: A feminist perspective* (4th ed.). Mountain View, CA: Mayfield.

Bell, M. (2012). A psychobiological perspective on working memory performance at 8 months of age. *Child Development, 83*, 251–265.

Bell, S. M., & Ainsworth, M. D. S. (1972). Infant crying and maternal responsiveness. *Child Development, 43*, 1171–1190.

Bell, T., & Roman, E. (2012). Opinions about child corporal punishment and influencing factors. *Journal of Interpersonal Violence, 27*, 2208–2229.

Bellezza, F. S. (2000). Mnemonic devices. In A. E. Kazdin (Ed.), *Encyclopedia of psychology* (vol. 5). Washington, DC: American Psychological Association.

Bellezza, F. S., Six, L. S., & Phillips, D. S. (1992). A mnemonic for remembering long strings of digits. *Bulletin of the Psychonomic Society, 30*, 271–274.

Belluck, P. (2000, October 18). New advice for parents: Saying "that's great!" may not be. *New York Times*, p. A14.

Belsky, J. (2006). Early child care and early child development: Major findings from the NICHD Study of Early Child Care. European *Journal of Developmental Psychology, 3*, 95–110.

Belsky, J. (2009). Classroom composition, childcare history and social development: Are childcare effects disappearing or spreading? *Social Development, 18*, 230–238.

Belsky, J., Vandell, D. L., Burchinal, M., Clarke-Stewart, A. K., McCartney, K., & Owen, M. T. (2007). Are there long-term effects of early child care? *Child Development, 78*, 188–193.

Beltz, A. M., Corley, R. P., Bricker, J. B., Wadsworth, S. J., & Berenbaum, S. A. (2014). Modeling pubertal timing and tempo and examining links to behavior problems. *Developmental Psychology, 50*, 2715–2726.

Bem, S. (1987). Gender schema theory and its implications for child development: Raising gender-aschematic children in a gender-schematic society. In M. R. Walsh (Ed.), *The psychology of women: Ongoing debates*. New Haven, CT: Yale University Press.

Benedict, H. (1979). Early lexical development: Comprehension and production. *Journal of Child Language, 6*, 183–200.

Benelli, B., Belacchi, C., Gini, G., & Lucangeli, D. (2006, February). "To define means to say what you know about things": The development of definitional skills as metalinguistic acquisition. *Journal of Child Language, 33*, 71–97.

Benenson, J. F., & Apostoleris, N. H. (1993, March). *Gender differences in group interaction in early childhood*. Paper presented at the biennial meeting of the Society for Research in Child Development, New Orleans, LA.

Bengtson, V. L., Acock, A. C., Allen, K. R., & Dil-worth-Anderson, P. (Eds.). (2004). *Sourcebook of family theory and research*. Thousand Oaks, CA: Sage Publications.

Benjet, C., & Kazdin, A. E. (2003). Spanking children: The controversies, findings and new directions. *Clinical Psychology Review, 23*, 197–224.

Benjuya, N., Melzer, I., & Kaplanski, J. (2004). Aging-induced shifts from a reliance on sensory input to muscle cocontraction during balanced standing. *Journal of Gerontology: Series A: Biological Sciences and Medical Sciences, 59*, 166–171.

Bennani, L., Allali, F., Rostom, S., Hmamouchi, I., Khazzani, H., El Mansouri, L., et al. (2009). Relationship between historical height loss and vertebral fractures in postmenopausal women. *Clinical Rheumatology, 28*, 1283–1289.

Benner, A. D., & Wang, Y. (2017). Racial/ethnic discrimination and adolescents' well-being: The role of cross-ethnic friendships and friends' experiences of discrimination. *Child Development, 88*, 493–504.

Bennett, J. (2008, September 15). It's not just white girls. *Newsweek*, p. 96.

Benoit, A., Lacourse, E., & Claes, M. (2014). Pubertal timing and depressive symptoms in late adolescence: The moderating role of individual, peer, and parental factors. *Development and Psychopathology, 25*, 455–471.

Benson, E. (2003, March). Goo, gaa, grr? *Monitor on Psychology*, pp. 50–51.

Benson, H. (1993). The relaxation response. In D. Goleman & J. Guerin (Eds.), *Mind–body medicine: How to use your mind for better health*. Yonkers, NY: Consumer Reports Publications.

Benton, S. A., Robertson, J. M., Tseng, W.-C., Newton, F. B., & Benton, S. L. (2003). Changes in counseling center client problems across 13 years. *Professional Psychology: Research and Practice, 34*, 66–72.

Bentz, W. E. (2015). Hospital stay for healthy newborn infants. *Pediatrics*. Accessed online 10-25-17; www.pediatrics.org/cgi/doi/10.1542/peds.2015-0699.

Berenson, P. (2005). *Understand and treat alcoholism*. New York: Basic Books.

Bergelson, E., & Swingley, D. (2013). The acquisition of abstract words by young infants. *Cognition, 127*(3), 391–397.

Bergen, D., Davis, D. R., & Abbitt, J. T. (2016). *Technology play and brain development: Infancy to adolescence and future implications*. New York: Routledge/Taylor & Francis Group.

Bergen, H., Martin, G., & Richardson, A. (2003). Sexual abuse and suicidal behavior: A model constructed from a large community sample of adolescents. *Journal of the American Academy of Child & Adolescent Psychiatry, 42*, 1301–1309.

Berger, L. (2000, April 11). What children do when home and alone. *New York Times*, p. F8.

Berger, L. M., Hill, J., & Waldfogel, J. (2005). Maternity leave, early maternal employment and child health and development in the US. *Economic Journal, 115*(501), F29–F47.

Berger, S. E., Chin, B., Basra, S., & Kim, H. (2015). Step by step: A microgenetic study of the development of strategy choice in infancy. *British Journal of Developmental Psychology, 33*, 106–122.

Bergman, A., Blom, I., & Polyak, D. (2012). Attachment and separation–individuation: Two ways of looking at the mother/infant relationship. In S. Akhtar (Ed.), *The mother and her child: Clinical aspects of attachment, separation, and loss*. Lanham, MD: Jason Aronson.

Bergman, A., Blom, I., Polyak, D., & Mayers, L. (2015). Attachment and separation–individuation: Two ways of looking at the mother–infant relationship. *International Forum of Psychoanalysis, 24*, 16–21.

Bergmann, R. L., Bergman, K. E., & Dudenhausen, J. W. (2008). Undernutrition and growth restriction in pregnancy. *Nestle Nutritional Workshop Series; Pediatrics Program, 61*, 103–121.

Bergsma, A., & Ardelt, M. (2012). Self-reported wisdom and happiness: An empirical investigation. *Journal of Happiness Studies, 13*, 481–499.

Bergström, M. (2017). 'I could've had a better life': Reflective life reviews told by late-middle-aged and older women and men with ongoing long-term alcohol problems. *NAT Nordisk Alkohol & Narkotikatidskrift, 34*, 6–17.

Bergstrom, M. J., & Holmes, M. E. (2000). Lay theories of successful aging after the death of a spouse: A network text analysis of bereavement advice. *Health Communication, 12*, 377–406.

Berkman, R. (Ed.). (2006). *Handbook of social work in health and aging*. New York: Oxford University Press.

Berko, J. (1958). The child's learning of English morphology. *Word, 14*, 150–177.

Berlin, L., Cassidy, J., & Appleyard, K. (2008). The influence of early attachments on other relationships. In *Handbook of attachment: Theory, research, and clinical applications* (2nd ed., pp. 333–347). New York: Guilford Press.

Bernal, M. E. (1994, August). *Ethnic identity of Mexican–American children*. Address at the annual meeting of the American Psychological Association, Los Angeles, CA.

Bernard, D. (2012, February 17). Why older workers are better workers. *U.S. News & World Report, Money*, p. 21.

Bernard, J. (1982). *The future of marriage*. New Haven, CT: Yale University Press.

Berndt, T. J. (1999). Friends' influence on students' adjustment to school. *Educational Psychologist, 34*, 15–28.

Berndt, T. J. (2002). Friendship quality and social development. *Current Directions in Psychological Science, 11*, 7–10.

Bernier, A., & Meins, E. (2008). A threshold approach to understanding the origins of attachment disorganization. *Developmental Psychology, 44*, 969–982.

Berninger, V. W., Abbott, R. D., Jones, J., et al. (2006). Early development of language by hand: Composing, reading, listening, and speaking connections; three letter-writing modes; and fast mapping in spelling. *Developmental Neuropsychology, 29*, 61–92.

Bernstein, E. (2010, April 20). Honey, do you have to… *Wall Street Journal*, pp. D1, D3.

Bernstein, N. (2004, March 7). Behind fall in pregnancy, a new teenage culture of restraint. *New York Times*, pp. 1, 20.

Berry, G. L. (2003). Developing children and multicultural attitudes: The systemic psychosocial influences of television portrayals in a multimedia society. *Cultural Diversity and Ethnic Minority Psychology, 9*, 360–366.

Berscheid, E. (1985). Interpersonal attraction. In G. Lindzey & E. Aronson (Eds.), *Handbook of social psychology* (3rd ed.). New York: Random House.

Berscheid, E., & Walster, E. (1974). Physical attractiveness. In G. Lindzey & E. Aronson (Eds.), *Handbook of social psychology* (3rd ed.). New York: Random House.

Berteletti, I., & Booth, J. R. (2016). Finger representation and finger-based strategies in the acquisition of number meaning and arithmetic. In D. B. Berch, D. C. Geary, & K. Mann Koepke (Eds.), *Development of mathematical cognition: Neural substrates and genetic influences*. San Diego, CA: Elsevier Academic Press.

Berteletti, I., & Booth, J. R. (2015). Perceiving fingers in single-digit arithmetic problems. *Frontiers in Psychology, 6*. 88–97.

Bertin, E., & Striano, T. (2006, April). The still-face response in newborn, 1.5-, and 3-month-old infants. *Infant Behavior & Development, 29*, 294–297.

Besag, V. E. (2006). *Understanding girls' friendships, fights and feuds: A practical approach to girls' bullying*. Maidenhead, Berkshire: Open University Press/McGraw-Hill Education.

Besharov, D. J., & West, A. (2002). African American marriage patterns. In A. Thernstrom & S. Thernstrom (Eds.), *Beyond the color line: New perspectives on race and ethnicity in America*. Stanford, CA: Hoover Institution Press.

Bešić, E., Paleczek, L., Krammer, M., & Gasteiger-Klicpera, B. (2017). Inclusive practices at the teacher and class level: The experts' view. *European Journal of Special Needs Education, 32*, 329–345.

Best, P., Manktelow, R., & Taylor, B. (2014). Online communication, social media and adolescent wellbeing: A systematic narrative review. *Children and Youth Services Review, 41*, 27–36.

Bhagat, N., Laskar, A., & Sharma, N. (2012). Women's perception about sex selection in an urban slum in Delhi. *Journal of Reproductive and Infant Psychology, 30*, 92–104.

Bhargava, P. (2014). 'I have a family, therefore I am': Children's understanding of self and others. In N. Chaudhary, S. Anandalakshmy, & J. Valsiner (Eds.), *Cultural realities of being: Abstract ideas within everyday lives*. New York: Routledge/Taylor & Francis Group.

Bibace, R. (2013). Challenges in Piaget's legacy. *Integrative Psychological & Behavioral Science, 47*, 167–175.

Biblarz, T. J., & Stacey, J. (2010). How does the gender of parents matter? *Journal of Marriage and Family, 72*, 3–22.

Biddle, B. J. (2001). *Social class, poverty, and education*. London: Falmer Press.

Biedenharn, B. J., & Normoyle, J. B. (1991). Elderly community residents' reactions to the nursing home: An analysis of nursing home-related beliefs. *Gerontologist, 31*, 107–115.

Bienvenu, C., & Ramsey, C. J. (2006). The culture of socioeconomic disadvantage: Practical approaches to counseling. In C. C. Lee (Ed.), *Multicultural issues in counseling: New approaches to diversity* (3rd ed.). Alexandria, VA: American Counseling Association.

Bierman, K. L. (2004). *Peer rejection: Developmental processes and intervention strategies*. New York: Guilford Press.

Bierman, K., Torres, M., Domitrovich, C., Welsh, J., & Gest, S. (2009). Behavioral and cognitive readiness for school: Cross-domain associations for children attending Head Start. *Social Development, 18*, 305–323.

Bigelow, A. E., & Power, M. (2012). The effect of mother–infant skin-to-skin contact on infants' response to the Still Face Task from newborn to three months of age. *Infant Behavior & Development, 35*, 240–251.

Bijeljac-Babic, R., Bertoncini, J., & Mehler, J. (1993). How do 4-day-old infants categorize multisyllabic utterances? *Developmental Psychology, 29*, 711–721.

Bionna, R. (2006). *Coping with stress in a changing world*. New York: McGraw-Hill.

Biro, F., Striegel-Moore, R., Franko, D., Padgett, J., & Bean, J. (2006, October). Self-esteem in adolescent females. *Journal of Adolescent Health, 39*, 501–507.

Biro, S., Alink, L. A., van IJzendoorn, M. H., & Bakermans-Kranenburg, M. J. (2014). Infants' monitoring of social interactions: The effect of emotional cues. *Emotion, 14*, 263–271.

Bischof-Köhler, D. (2012). Empathy and self-recognition in phylogenetic and ontogenetic perspective. *Emotion Review, 4*, 40–48.

Bishop, D., Meyer, B., Schmidt, T., & Gray, B. (2009). Differential investment behavior between grandparents and grandchildren: The role of paternity uncertainty. *Evolutionary Psychology, 7*, 66–77.

Bishop, D. V. M., & Leonard, L. B. (Eds.). (2001). *Speech and language impairments in children: Causes, characteristics, intervention and outcome*. Philadelphia, PA: Psychology Press.

Bishop, J. (2006, April). Euthanasia, efficiency, and the historical distinction between killing a patient and allowing a patient to die. *Journal of Medical Ethics, 32*, 220–224.

Bjorklund, D. F. (1997b). The role of immaturity in human development. *Psychological Bulletin, 122*, 153–169.

Bjorklund, D. F., & Ellis, B. (2005). Evolutionary psychology and child development: An emerging synthesis. In B. J. Ellis (Ed.), *Origins of the social mind: Evolutionary psychology and child development*. New York: Guilford Press.

Black, K. (2002). Associations between adolescent–mother and adolescent–best friend interactions. *Adolescence, 37*, 235–253.

Blackburn, E., & Epel, E. (2017). *The telomere effect*. New York: Grand Central Publishing.

Blair, P., Sidebotham, P., Berry, P., Evans, M., & Fleming, P. (2006). Major epidemiological changes in sudden infant death syndrome: A 20-year population-based study in the UK. *Lancet, 367*, 314–319.

Blake, G., Velikonja, D., Pepper, V., Jilderda, I., & Georgiou, G. (2008). Evaluating an in-school injury prevention programme's effect on children's helmet wearing habits. *Brain Injury, 22*, 501–507.

Blake, J., & de Boysson-Bardies, B. (1992). Patterns in babbling: A cross-linguistic study. *Journal of Child Language, 19*, 51–74.

Blakemore, J. (2003). Children's beliefs about violating gender norms: Boys shouldn't look like girls, and girls shouldn't act like boys. *Sex Roles, 48*, 411–419.

Blakemore, S. (2012). Imaging brain development: The adolescent brain. *Neuroimage, 61*, 397–406.

Blass, E. M., & Camp, C. A. (2015). The ontogeny of face recognition: Eye contact and sweet taste induce face preference in 9- and 12-week-old human infants. *Developmental Psychology, 37*, 762–774.

Bleidorn, W., Kandler, C., & Caspi, A. (2014). The behavioral genetics of personality development in adulthood—Classic, contemporary, and future trends. *European Journal of Personality, 28*, 244–255.

Blewitt, P., Rump, K., Shealy, S., & Cook, S. (2009). Shared book reading: When and how questions affect young children's word learning. *Journal of Educational Psychology, 101*, 294–304.

Blom, E. H., Ho, T. C., Connolly, C. G., LeWinn, K. Z., Sacchet, M. D., Tymofiyeva, O., & … Yang, T. T. (2016). The neuroscience and context of adolescent depression. *Acta Paediatrica, 105*, 358–365.

Blomqvist, Y. T., Nyqvist, K. H., Rubertsson, C., & Funkquist, E. (2017). Parents need support to find ways to optimise their own sleep without seeing their preterm infant's sleeping patterns as a problem. *Acta Paediatrica, 106*, 223–228.

Bloom, C., & Lamkin, D. (2006). The Olympian struggle to remember the cranial nerves: Mnemonics and student success. *Teaching of Psychology, 33*, 128–129.

Blount, B. G. (1982). Culture and the language of socialization: Parental speech. In D. A. Wagner & H. W. Stevenson (Eds.), *Cultural perspectives on child development*. San Francisco: Freeman.

Bluebond-Langner, M. (2000). *In the shadow of illness*. Princeton, NJ: Princeton University Press.

Blum, D. (2002). *Love at Goon Park: Harry Harlow and the science of affection*. New York: Perseus Publishing.

Blumberg, M., Coleman, C., Gerth, A., & McMurray, B. (2013). Spatiotemporal structure of REM sleep twitching reveals developmental origins of motor syner-gies. *Current Biology, 232*, 100–109.

Blumberg, M. S., Gall, A. J., & Todd, W. D. (2014). The development of sleep–wake rhythms and the search for elemental circuits in the infant brain. *Behavioral Neuroscience, 128*, 250–263.

Blumenshine, P. M., Egerter, S. A., Libet, M. L., & Braveman, P. A. (2011). Father's education: An independent marker of risk for preterm birth. *Maternal and Child Health Journal, 15*, 60–67.

Blumenthal, S. (2000). Developmental aspects of violence and the institutional response. *Criminal Behavior & Mental Health, 10*, 185–198.

Boatella-Costa, E., Costas-Moragas, C., Botet-Mussons, F., Fornieles-Deu, A., & De Cáceres-Zurita, M. (2007). Behavioral gender differences in the neonatal period according to the Brazelton scale. *Early Human De-velopment, 83*, 91–97.

Bober, S., Humphry, R., & Carswell, H. (2001). Toddlers' persistence in the emerging occupations of functional play and self-feeding. *American Journal of Occupational Therapy, 55*, 369–376.

Bode, M. M., D'Eugenio, D. B., Mettelman, B. B., & Gross, S. J. (2014). Predictive validity of the Bayley, third edition at 2 years for intelligence quotient at 4 years in preterm infants. *Journal of Developmental and Behavioral Pediatrics, 35*, 570–575.

Bodell, L. P., Joiner, T. E., & Ialongo, N. S. (2012). Longitudinal association between childhood impulsivity and bulimic symptoms in African American adolescent girls. *Journal of Consulting and Clinical Psychology, 80*, 313–316.

Bodner, E., Bergman, Y. S., & Cohen-Fridel, S. (2012). Different dimensions of ageist attitudes among men and women: A multigenerational perspective. *International Psychogeriatrics, 24*(6), 895–901. doi:10.1017/S1041610211002936.

Boehm, K. E., & Campbell, N. B. (1995). Suicide: A review of calls to an adolescent peer listening phone service. *Child Psychiatry & Human Development, 26*, 61–66.

Boerner, K., Wortman, C. B., & Bonanno, G. A. (2005). Resilient or at risk? A 4-year study of older adults who initially showed high or low distress following conjugal loss. *Journals of Gerontology: Series B, Psychological Sciences and Social Sciences, 60*, P67–P73.

Bogle, K. A. (2008). "Hooking up": What educators need to know. *The Chronicle of Higher Education*, p. A32.

Boissicat, N., Pansu, P., Bouffard, T., & Cottin, F. (2012). Relation between perceived scholastic competence and social comparison mechanisms among elementary school children. *Social Psychology Of Education, 15*(4), 603-614. doi:10.1007/s11218-012-9189-z

Boivin, M., Perusse, D., Dionne, G., Saysset, V., Zoccolilo, M., Tarabulsy, G. M., et al. (2005). The genetic-environmental etiology of parents' perceptions and self-assessed behaviors toward their 5-month-old infants in a large twin and singleton sample. *Journal of Child Psychology and Psychiatry, 46*, 612–630.

Bojanowska, A., & Zalewska, A. M. (2015). Lay understanding of happiness and the experience of well-being: Are some conceptions of happiness more beneficial than others? *Journal of Happiness Studies*. Accessed online, 3-23-15; http://download.springer.com/static/pdf/57/art%253A10.1007%252Fs10902-015-9620-1.pdf?auth66=1427131881_bf7fda3652936c4179ca90e4db529c3f&ext=.pdf.

Bolhuis, J. J., Tattersal, I., Chomsky, N., & Berwick, R. C. (2014). How could language have evolved? *PLoS Biology, 12*, 88–95.

Bonanno, G. A. (2009). *The other side of sadness*. New York: Basic Books.

Bonanno, G. A., Wortman, C. B., Lehman, D. R., Tweed, R. G., Haring, M., Sonnega, J., et al. (2002). Resilience to loss and chronic grief: A prospective study from preloss to 18-months postloss. *Journal of Personality and Social Psychology, 83*, 1150–1164.

Bonavita, S., & Tedeschi, G. (2017). Neural structure, connectivity, and cognition changes associated to physical exercise. In R. R. Watson (Ed.), *Physical activity and the aging brain: Effects of exercise on neurological function*. San Diego, CA: Elsevier Academic Press.

Boneva, B., Quinn, A., Kraut, R., Kiesler, S., & Shklovski, I. (2006). Teenage communication in the instant messaging era. In R. Kraut & M. Brynin (Eds.), *Computers, phones, and the Internet: Domesticating information technology*. New York: Oxford University Press.

Bonifacci, P., Storti, M., Tobia, V., & Suardi, A. (2016). Specific learning disorders: A look inside children's and parents' psychological well-being and relationships. *Journal of Learning Disabilities, 49*, 532–545.

Bonke, B., Tibben, A., Lindhout, D., Clarke, A. J., & Stijnen, T. (2005). Genetic risk estimation by healthcare professionals. *Medical Journal of Autism, 182*, 116–118.

Bonnicksen, A. (2007). Oversight of assisted reproductive technologies: The last twenty years. *Reprogenetics: Law, policy, and ethical issues*. Baltimore, MD: Johns Hopkins University Press.

Bookheimer, S. Y., Strojwas, M. H., Cohen, M. S., Saunders, A. M., Pericak-Vance, M. A., Mazziotta, J. C., & Small, G. W. (2000). Patterns of brain activation in people at risk for Alzheimer's disease. *The New England Journal Of Medicine, 343*(7), 450-456. doi:10.1056/NEJM200008173430701

Bookstein, F. L., Sampson, P. D., Streissguth, A. P., & Barr, H. M. (1996). Exploiting redundant measurement of dose and developmental outcome: New methods from the behavioral teratology of alcohol. *Developmental Psychology, 32*, 404–415.

Booth, C., Kelly, J., & Spieker, S. (2003). Toddlers' attachment security to child-care providers: The Safe and Secure Scale. *Early Education & Development, 14*, 83–100.

Bor, W., & Bor, W. (2004). Prevention and treatment of childhood and adolescent aggression and antisocial behavior: A selective review. *Australian & New Zealand Journal of Psychiatry, 38*, 373–380.

Borden, M. E. (1998). *Smart start: The parents' complete guide to preschool education*. New York: Facts on File.

Bornstein, M. H. (2000). Infant into conversant: Lan-guage and nonlanguage processes in developing early communication. In N. Budwig, I. C. Uzgiris, & J. V. Wertsch (Eds.), *Communication: An arena of development* (pp. 109–129). Stamford, CT: Amblex.

Bornstein, M. H., Cote, L., & Maital, S. (2004). Cross-linguistic analysis of vocabulary in young children: Spanish, Dutch, French, Hebrew, Italian, Korean, and American English. *Child Development, 75*, 1115–1139.

Bornstein, M. H., & Lamb, M. E. (Eds.). (2005). *Developmental science*. Mahwah, NJ: Lawrence Erlbaum.

Bornstein, M. H., Putnick, D. L., Suwalsky, T. D., & Gini, M. (2006). Maternal chronological age, prenatal and perinatal history, social support, and parenting of infants. *Child Development, 77*, 875–892.

Bornstein, M. H., Suwalsky, J. D., & Breakstone, D. A. (2012). Emotional relationships between mothers and infants: Knowns, unknowns, and unknown unknowns. *Development and Psychopathology, 24*, 113–123.

Bornstein, M. H., Tamis-LeMonda, C. S., Hahn, C., & Haynes, O. M. (2008). Maternal responsiveness to young children at three ages: Longitudinal analysis of a multidimensional, modular, and specific parenting construct. *Developmental Psychology, 44*, 867–874.

Borse, N. N., Gilchrist, J., Dellinger, A. M., Rudd, R. A., Ballesteros, M. F., & Sleet, D. A. (2008). *CDC childhood injury report: Patterns of unintentional injuries among 0–19 Year Olds in the United States, 2000–2006*. Atlanta, GA: Centers for Disease Control and Prevention, National Center for Injury Prevention and Control.

Bos, A. F. (2013). Bayley-II or Bayley-III: What do the scores tell us? *Developmental Medicine & Child Neurology, 55*, 978–979.

Bos, C. S., & Vaughn, S. S. (2005). *Strategies for teaching students with learning and behavior problems* (6th ed.). Boston: Allyn & Bacon.

Bos, H. W., Knox, J. R., van Rijn-van Gelderen, L., & Gartrell, N. K. (2016). Same-sex and different-sex parent households and child health outcomes: Findings from the National Survey of Children's Health. *Journal of Developmental and Behavioral Pediatrics, 37*, 179–187.

Bosacki, S. L. (2014). Brief report: The role of psychological language in children's theory of mind and self-concept development. *Psychology of Language and Communication, 18*, 41–52.

Bosco, F. M., Angeleri, R., Colle, L., Sacco, K., & Bara, B. G. (2013). Communicative abilities in children: An assessment through different phenomena and expressive means. *Journal of Child Language, 40*, 741–778.

Boseley, S. (2008, February 7). Tobacco could kill 1 billion people over course of century, says UN. *The Guardian*, p. B3.

Bostwick, J. M. (2006). Do SSRIs cause suicide in children? The evidence is underwhelming. *Journal of Clinical Psychology, 62*, 235–241.

Bouchard, T. J., Jr. (1997, September/October). Whenever the twain shall meet. *The Sciences*, pp. 52–57.

Bouchard, T. J., Jr. (2004). Genetic influence on human psychological traits: A survey. *Current Directions in Psychological Science, 13*, 148–153.

Bouchard, T. J., Jr., Lykken, D. T., McGue, M., Segal, N. L., & Tellegen, A. (1990, October 12). Sources of human psychological differences: The Minnesota Study of twins reared apart. *Science, 250*, 223–228.

Bourne, V., & Todd, B. (2004). When left means right: An explanation of the left cradling bias in terms of right hemisphere specializations. *Developmental Science, 7*, 19–24.

Bowen, F. (2013). Asthma education and health outcomes of children aged 8 to 12 years. *Clinical Nursing Research, 22*, 172–185.

Bowen, G. L., & Jensen, T. M. (2017). Late-life divorce and postdivorce adult subjective well-being. *Journal of Family Issues, 38*, 1363–1388.

Bower, J. E., Greendale, G., Crosswell, A. D., Garet, D., Sternlieb, B., Ganz, P. A., & … Cole, S. W. (2014). Yoga reduces inflammatory signaling in fatigued breast cancer survivors: A randomized controlled trial. *Psychoneuroendocrinology, 43*, 20–29.

Bower, T. G. R. (1977). *A primer of infant development*. San Francisco: Freeman.

Bowlby, J. (1951). Maternal care and mental health. *Bulletin of the World Health Organization, 3*, 355–534.

Bowlby, R. (2007). Babies and toddlers in non-parental daycare can avoid stress and anxiety if they develop a lasting secondary attachment bond with one carer who is consistently accessible to them. *Attachment & Human Development, 9*, [Special issue: The Life and Work of John Bowlby: A Tribute to his Centenary], 307–319.

Boyatzis, C. J. (2013). The nature and functions of religion and spirituality in children. In K. I. Pargament, J. J. Exline, & J. W. Jones (Eds.), *APA handbook of psychology, religion, and spirituality (Vol 1): Context, theory, and research*. Washington, DC: American Psychological Association.

Boyse, K., & Fitzgerald, K. (2010). Toilet training. Accessed online, 6.23.15; http://www.med.umich.edu/yourchild/topics/toilet.htm.

Bracey, J., Bamaca, M., & Umana-Taylor, A. (2004). Examining ethnic identity and self-esteem among biracial and monoracial adolescents. *Journal of Youth & Adolescence, 33*, 123–132.

Bracken, B., & Brown, E. (2006, June). Behavioral identification and assessment of gifted and talented students. *Journal of Psychoeducational Assessment, 24*, 112–122.

Bracken, B., & Lamprecht, M. (2003). Positive self-concept: An equal opportunity construct. *School Psychology Quarterly, 18*, 103–121.

Braden, B. B., Dassel, K. B., Bimonte-Nelson, H. A., O'Rourke, H. P., Connor, D. J., Moorhous, S., & … Baxter, L. C. (2017). Sex and post-menopause hormone therapy effects on hippocampal volume and verbal memory. *Aging, Neuropsychology, and Cognition, 24*, 227–246.

Bradley, R., & Corwyn, R. (2008). Infant temperament, parenting, and externalizing behavior in first grade: A test of the differential susceptibility hypothesis. *Journal of Child Psychology and Psychiatry, 49*, 124–131. http://search.ebscohost.com.

Bradshaw, M., & Ellison, C. (2008). Do genetic factors influence religious life? Findings from a behavior genetic analysis of twin siblings. *Journal for the Scientific Study of Religion, 47*, 529–544. http://search.ebscohost.com, doi:10.1111/j.1468-5906.2008.00425.x.

Brady, S. A. (2011). Efficacy of phonics teaching for reading outcomes: Indications from post-NRP research. In S. A. Brady, D. Braze, & C. A. Fowler (Eds.), *Explaining individual differences in reading: Theory and evidence*. New York: Psychology Press.

Brainerd, C. (2003). Jean Piaget, learning research, and American education. In B. Zimmerman (Ed.), *Educational psychology: A century of contributions*. Mahwah, NJ: Lawrence Erlbaum.

Brandmaier, A. M., Ram, N., Wagner, G. G., & Gerstorf, D. (2017). Terminal decline in well-being: The role of multi-indicator constellations of physical health and psychosocial correlates. *Developmental Psychology, 53*, 996–1012.

Brandone, A. C., Cimpian, A., Leslie, S., & Gelman, S. A. (2012). Do lions have manes? For children, generics are about kinds rather than quantities. *Child Development, 83*, 423–433.

Branum, A. (2006). Teen maternal age and very preterm birth of twins. *Maternal & Child Health Journal, 10*, 229–233.

Brandes, D. W. (2010). The role of glatiramer acetate in the early treatment of multiple sclerosis. *Neuropsychiatric Disease And Treatment, 6*.

Braun, K. L., Pietsch, J. H., & Blanchette, P. L. (Eds.). (2000). *Cultural issues in end-of-life decision making*. Thousand Oaks, CA: Sage Publications.

Braun, S. I., Kim, Y., Jetton, A. E., Kang, M., & Morgan, D. W. (2017). Sedentary behavior, physical activity, and bone health in postmenopausal women. *Journal of Aging and Physical Activity, 25*, 173–181.

Braun, S. S., & Davidson, A. J. (2016). Gender (non)conformity in middle childhood: A mixed methods approach to understanding gender-typed behavior, friendship, and peer preference. *Sex Roles*. Accessed online, 8-9-17; https://link.springer.com/article/10.1007/s11199-016-0693-z.

Braungart-Rieker, J. M., Zentall, S., Lickenbrock, D. M., Ekas, N. V., Oshio, T., & Planalp, E. (2015). Attachment in the making: Mother and father sensitivity and infants' responses during the still-face paradigm. *Journal of Experimental Child Psychology, 125*, 63–84.

Bray, G. A. (2008). Is new hope on the horizon for obesity? *The Lancet, 372*, 1859–1860.

Brazelton, T. B. (1990). Saving the bathwater. *Child Development, 61*, 1661–1671.

Brazelton, T. B. (1997). *Toilet training your child*. New York: Consumer Visions.

Brazelton, T. B., Christophersen, E. R., Frauman, A. C., Gorski, P. A., Poole, J. M., Stadtler, A. C., & Wright, C. L. (1999). Instruction, timeliness, and medical influences affecting toilet training. *Pediatrics, 103*, 1353–1358.

Brazelton, T. B., & Sparrow, J. D. (2003). *Discipline: The Brazelton way*. New York: Perseus.

Bredesen, D. (2009). Neurodegeneration in Alzheimer's disease: Caspases and synaptic element interdependence. *Molecular Neurodegeneration, 4*, 52–59.

Breheny, M., & Stephens, C. (2003). Healthy living and keeping busy: A discourse analysis of mid-aged women's attributions for menopausal experience. *Journal of Language & Social Psychology, 22*, 169–189.

Bremner, G., & Fogel, A. (Eds.). (2004). *Blackwell handbook of infant development*. Malden, MA: Blackwell Publishers.

Bremner, J. G., Slater, A. M., & Johnson, S. P. (2015). Perception of object persistence: The origins of object permanence in infancy. *Child Development Perspectives, 9*, 7–13.

Bridges, J. S. (1993). Pink or blue: Gender-stereotypic perceptions of infants as conveyed by birth congratulations cards. *Psychology of Women Quarterly, 17*, 193–205.

Briley, D. A., & Tucker-Drob, E. M. (2017). Comparing the developmental genetics of cognition and personality over the life span. *Journal of Personality, 85*, 51–64.

Brinkman, B. G., Rabenstein, K. L., Rosén, L. A., & Zimmerman, T. S. (2014). Children's gender identity development: The dynamic negotiation process between conformity and authenticity. *Youth & Society, 46*, 835–852.

Brito, N., & Barr, R. (2014). Flexible memory retrieval in bilingual 6-month-old infants. *Developmental Psychobiology, 56*, 1156–1163.

Brock, J., Jarrold, C., Farran, E. K., Laws, G., & Riby, D. M. (2007). Do children with Williams syndrome really have good vocabulary knowledge? Methods for comparing cognitive and linguistic abilities in developmental disorders. *Clinical Linguistics & Phonetics, 21*, 673–688.

Brod, M., Alolga, S. L., Beck, J. F., Wilkinson, L., Højbjerre, L., & Rasmussen, M. H. (2017). Understanding burden of illness for child growth hormone deficiency. *Quality of Life Research: An International Journal of Quality of Life Aspects of Treatment, Care & Rehabilitation, 26*, 1673–1686.

Brody, N. (1993). Intelligence and the behavioral genetics of personality. In R. Plomin & G. E. McClearn (Eds.), *Nature, nurture, and psychology*. Washington, DC: American Psychological Association.

Broesch, T. L., & Bryant, G. A. (2015). Prosody in infant-directed speech is similar across Western and traditional cultures. *Journal of Cognition and Development, 16*, 31–43.

Bromberger, J. T., & Matthews, K. A. (1994). Employment status and depressive symptoms in middle-aged women: A longitudinal investigation. *American Journal of Public Health, 84*, 202–206.

Brooks-Gunn, J., Klebanov, P. K., & Duncan, G. J. (1996). Ethnic differences in children's intelligence test scores: Role of economic deprivation, home environment, and maternal characteristics. *Child Development, 67*, 396–408.

Brotanek, J., Gosz, J., Weitzman, M., & Flores, G. (2007). Iron deficiency in early childhood in the United States: Risk factors and racial/ethnic disparities. *Pediatrics, 120*, 568–575.

Brouwer, R. M., van Soelen, I. C., Swagerman, S. C., Schnack, H. G., Ehli, E. A., Kahn, R. S., & … Boomsma, D. I. (2014). Genetic associations between intelligence and cortical thickness emerge at the start of pu-berty. *Human Brain Mapping, 35*, 3760–3773.

Brown, P. (2008). Lead Screening. US Department of Health and Human Services Memorandum. Accessed online May 1, 2018 from https://eclkc.ohs.acf.hhs.gov/sites/default/files/docs/policy-im/acf-im-hs-08-07.pdf

Brown, B. B. (2004). Adolescents' relationships with peers. In R. M. Lerner & L. Steinberg (Eds.), *Handbook of Adolescent Psychology, 2nd edition* (pp. 363-394). New York: Wiley.

Brown, B. B., & Klute, C. (2003). Friendships, cliques, and crowds. In G. R. Adams & M. D. Berzonsky (Eds.), *Blackwell handbook of adolescence* (pp. 330–348). Malden, MA: Blackwell Publishing.

Brown, D. L., Jewell, J. D., Stevens, A. L., Crawford, J. D., & Thompson, R. (2012). Suicidal risk in adolescent residential treatment: Being female is more important than a depression diagnosis. *Journal of Child and Family Studies, 21*, 359–367.

Brown, E. L., & Bull, R. (2007). Can task modifications influence children's performance on false belief tasks? *European Journal of Developmental Psychology, 4*, 273–292.

Brown, J. D. (1998). *The self*. New York: McGraw-Hill.

Brown, S., & Lin, I. (2012, March). *The gray divorce revolution: Rising divorce among middle-aged and older adults*, 1990–2009. National Center for Family & Marriage Research, Bowling Green State University. Working Paper Series WP-12-04.

Brown, W. M., Hines, M., & Fane, B. A. (2002). Masculinized finger length patterns in human males and females with congenital adrenal hyperplasia. *Hormones and Behavior, 42*, 380–386.

Browne, K. (2006, March). Evolved sex differences and occupational segregation. *Journal of Organizational Behavior, 27*, 143–162.

Brownell, C. A. (2016). Prosocial behavior in infancy: The role of socialization. *Child Development Perspectives, 10*, 222–227.

Brownell, C. A., Ramani, G. B., & Zerwas, S. (2006). Becoming a social partner with peers: Cooperation and social understanding in one- and two-year-olds. *Child Development, 77*, 803–821.

Brucker, E., & Leppel, K. (2013). Retirement plans: Planners and nonplanners. *Educational Gerontology, 39*(1), 1–11.

Bryant, C. D. (Ed.). (2003). *Handbook of death and dying*. Thousand Oaks, CA: Sage Publications.

Bryant, J., & Bryant, J. (2003). Effects of entertainment televisual media on children. In E. Palmer & B. Young (Eds.), *The faces of televisual media: Teaching, violence, selling to children*. Mahwah, NJ: Lawrence Erlbaum.

Bucci, D., & Stanton, M. (2017). The ontogeny of learning and memory. *Neurobiology of Learning and Memory, 143*, 88–97.

Buchanan, C. M., Eccles, J. S., & Becker, J. B. (1992). Are adolescents the victims of raging hormones? Evidence for activational effects of hormones on moods and behavior at adolescence. *Psychological Bulletin, 111*, 62–107.

Buchmann, C., & DiPrete, T. (2006, August). The growing female advantage in college completion: The role of family background and academic achievement. *American Sociological Review, 7*, 515–541.

Buckley, J., Letukas, L., & Wildavsky, B. (2018). *Measuring success: Testing, grades, and the future of college admissions*. Baltimore, MD: Johns Hopkins University Press.

Budd, K. (1999). The facts of life: Everything you wanted to know about sex (after 50). *Modern Maturity, 42*, 78.

Bull, M., & Durbin, D. (2008). Rear-facing car safety seats: Getting the message right. *Pediatrics, 121*, 619–620.

Bullinger, A. (1997). Sensorimotor function and its evolution. In J. Guimon (Ed.), *The body in psychotherapy* (pp. 25–29). Basil, Switzerland: Karger.

Bumpass, L., Sweet, J., & Martin, T. (1990). Changing patterns of remarriage. *Journal of Marriage and the Family, 52*, 747–756.

Bumpus, M. F., Crouter, A. C., & McHale, S. M. (2001). Parental autonomy granting during adolescence: Exploring gender differences in context. *Developmental Psychology, 37*, 163–173.

Buon, M., Habib, M., & Frey, D. (2017). Moral development: Conflicts and compromises. In J. A. Sommerville & J. Decety (Eds.), *Social cognition: Development across the life span*. New York: Routledge/Taylor & Francis Group.

Burakevych, N., Mckinlay, C. D., Alsweiler, J. M., Wouldes, T. A., & Harding, J. E. (2017). Bayley-III motor scale and neurological examination at 2 years do not predict motor skills at 4.5 years. *Developmental Medicine & Child Neurology, 59*, 216–223.

Burbach, J., & van der Zwaag, B. (2009). Contact in the genetics of autism and schizophrenia. *Trends in Neurosciences, 32*, 69–72. http://search.ebscohost.com, doi:10.1016/j.tins.2008.11.002

Bureau of Labor Statistics. (2012, March 1). Labor force statistics from the Current Population Survey. Accessed online, 7-10-12; http://www.bls.gov/cps/cpsaat37.htm.

Bureau of Labor Statistics, U.S. Department of Labor. (2017, March 8). Women's median earnings 82 percent of men's in 2016. *Economics Daily*. Accessed online, 11-28-17; https://www.bls.gov/opub/ted/2017/womens-median-earnings-82-percent-of-mens-in-2016.htm.

Burgess, K. B., & Rubin, K. H. (2000). Middle child-hood: Social and emotional development. In A. E. Kazdin (Ed.), *Encyclopedia of psychology* (Vol. 5). Washington, DC: American Psychological Association.

Burgess, R. L., & Huston, T. L. (Eds.). (1979). *Social exchanges in developing relationships*. New York: Academic Press.

Burkle, C. M., Sharp, R. R., & Wijdicks, E. F. (2014). Why brain death is considered death and why there should be no confusion. *Neurology, 83*, 1464–1469.

Burnett-Wolle, S., & Godbey, G. (2007). Refining research on older adults' leisure: Implications of selection, optimization, and compensation and socioemotional selectivity theories. *Journal of Leisure Research, 39*, 498–513.

Burnham, M., Goodlin-Jones, B., & Gaylor, E. (2002). Nighttime sleep–wake patterns and self-soothing from birth to one year of age: A longitudinal intervention study. *Journal of Child Psychology & Psychiatry & Allied Disciplines, 43*, 713–725.

Burton, A., Haley, W., & Small, B. (2006, May). Bereavement after caregiving or unexpected death: Effects on elderly spouses. *Aging & Mental Health, 10*, 319–326.

Burton, L., Henninger, D., Hafetz, J., & Cofer, J. (2009). Aggression, gender-typical childhood play, and a prenatal hormonal index. *Social Behavior and Personality, 37*, 105–116.

Bushman, B. J., Gollwitzer, M., & Cruz, C. (2014). There is broad consensus: Media researchers agree that violent media increase aggression in children, and pediatricians and parents concur. *Psychology of Popular Media Culture*. Accessed online, 3-20-15; http://psycnet.apa.org/psycinfo/2014-41977-001/.

Busick, D., Brooks, J., Pernecky, S., Dawson, R., & Petzoldt, J. (2008). Parent food purchases as a measure of exposure and preschool-aged children's willingness to identify and taste fruit and vegetables. *Appetite, 51*, 468–473.

Buss, A. H. (2012). *Pathways to individuality: Evolution and development of personality traits*. Washington, DC: American Psychological Association.

Buss, D., & Shackelford, T. (2008). Attractive women want it all: Good genes, economic investment, parenting proclivities, and emotional commitment. *Evolutionary Psychology, 6*, 134–146.

Buss, D. M. (2003). The dangerous passion: Why jealousy is as necessary as love and sex: Book review. *Archives of Sexual Behavior, 32*, 79–80.

Buss, D. M. (2004). *Evolutionary psychology: The new science of the mind* (2nd ed.). Boston: Allyn & Bacon.

Buss, D. M., et al. (1990). International preferences in selecting mates: A study of 37 cultures. *Journal of Cross-Cultural Psychology, 21*, 5–47.

Buss, K. A., & Kiel, E. J. (2004). Comparison of sadness, anger, and fear facial expressions when toddlers look at their mothers. *Child Development, 75*, 1761–1773.

Bussey, K. (1992). Lying and truthfulness: Children's definition, standards, and evaluative reactions. *Child Development, 63*, 1236–1250.

Butler, R. J., Wilson, B. L., & Johnson, W. G. (2012). A modified measure of health care disparities applied to birth weight disparities and subsequent mortality. *Health Economics, 21*, 113–126.

Butterworth, G. (1994). Infant intelligence. In J. Khalfa (Ed.), What is intelligence? *The Darwin College lecture series* (pp. 49–71). Cambridge, England: Cambridge University Press.

Butzer, B., & Campbell, L. (2008). Adult attachment, sexual satisfaction, and relationship satisfaction: A study of married couples. *Personal Relationships, 15*, 141–154.

Byrd, D., Katcher, M., Peppard, P., Durkin, M., & Remington, P. (2007). Infant mortality: Explaining black/white disparities in Wisconsin. *Maternal and Child Health Journal, 11*, 319–326.

Byrd-Craven, J., Auer, B. J., Granger, D. A., & Massey, A. R. (2012). The father–daughter dance: The rela-tionship between father–daughter relationship quality and daughters' stress response. *Journal of Family Psychology, 26*, 87–94.

Byrne, A. (2000). Singular identities: Managing stigma, resisting voices. *Women's Studies Review, 7*, 13–24.

Byun, S., & Park, H. (2012). The academic success of East Asian American youth: The role of shadow education. *Sociology of Education, 85*, 40–60.

Cabera, N. J. (2013). Positive development of minority children. *SRCD Social Policy Report, 27*, 1–22.

Cacciatore, J., & Bushfield, S. (2007). Stillbirth: The mother's experience and implications for improving care. *Journal of Social Work in End-of-Life & Palliative Care, 3*, 59–79.

Cain, V., Johannes, C., & Avis, N. (2003). Sexual functioning and practices in a multi-ethnic study of midlife women: Baseline results from SWAN. *Journal of Sex Research, 40*, 266–276.

Caino, S., Kelmansky, D., Lejarraga, H., & Adamo, P. (2004). Short-term growth at adolescence in healthy girls. *Annals of Human Biology, 31*, 182–195.

Cale, L., & Harris, J. (2013). 'Every child (of every size) matters' in physical education! Physical education's role in childhood obesity. *Sport, Education and Society, 18*, 433–452.

Calhoun, F., & Warren, K. (2007). Fetal alcohol syndrome: Historical perspectives. *Neuroscience & Biobehavioral Reviews, 31*, 168–171.

Callaghan, B. L., Li, S., & Richardson, R. (2014). The elusive engram: What can infantile amnesia tell us about memory? *Trends in Neurosciences, 37*, 47–53.

Callister, L. C., Khalaf, I., Semenic, S., Kartchner, R., Vehvilainen-Julkunen, K. (2003). The pain of childbirth: Perceptions of culturally diverse women. *Pain Management Nursing, 4*, 145–154.

Calvert, S. L., Kotler, J. A., Zehnder, S., & Shockey, E. (2003). Gender stereotyping in children's reports about educational and informational television programs. *Media Psychology, 5*, 139–162.

Calzada, E. J., Huang, K., Anicama, C., Fernandez, Y., & Brotman, L. (2012). Test of a cultural framework of parenting with Latino families of young children. *Cultural Diversity and Ethnic Minority Psychology, 18*, 285–296.

Camarota, S. A., & Zeigler, K. (2015, April 21). *Immigrant population to hit highest percentage ever in 8 years*. Washington, DC: Center for Immigration Studies.

Cameron, P. (2003). Domestic violence among homosexual partners. *Psychological Reports, 93*, 410–416.

Cami, J., & Farré, M. (2003). Drug addiction. *New England Journal of Medicine, 349*, 975–986.

Campbell, A., Shirley, L., & Candy, J. (2004). A longitudinal study of gender-related cognition and behavior. *Developmental Science, 7*, 1–9.

Campbell, F., Ramey, C., & Pungello, E. (2002). Early childhood education: Young adult outcomes from the Abecedarian Project. *Applied Developmental Science, 6*, 42–57.

Campbell, O. M. R., Cegolon, L., Macleod, D., Benova, L. (2016). Length of stay after childbirth in 92 countries and associated factors in 30 low- and middle-income countries: Compilation of reported data and a cross-sectional analysis from nationally representative surveys. *PLOS Medicine* 13, 88–96.

Campos, J. J., Langer, A., & Krowitz, A. (1970). Car-diac responses on the visual cliff in prelocomotor human infants. *Science, 170*, 196–197.

Camras, L., Oster, H., Bakeman, R., Meng, Z., Ujiie, T., & Campos, J. (2007). Do infants show distinct negative facial expressions for fear and anger? Emotional expression in 11-month-old European American, Chinese, and Japanese Infants. *Infancy, 11*, 131–155.

Canals, J., Fernandez-Ballart, J., & Esparo, G. (2003). Evolution of neonatal behavior assessment scale scores in the first month of life. *Infant Behavior & Development, 26*, 227–237.

Canham, S. L., Mahmood, A., Stott, S., Sixsmith, J., & O'Rourke, N. (2014).'Til divorce do us part: Marriage dissolution in later life. *Journal of Divorce & Remarriage, 55*, 591–612.

Cantin, V., Lavallière, M., Simoneau, M., & Teasdale, N. (2009). Mental workload when driving in a simulator: Effects of age and driving complexity. *Accident Analysis and Prevention, 41*, 763–771.

Caplan, L. J., & Barr, R. A. (1989). On the relationship between category intensions and extensions in children. *Journal of Experimental Child Psychology, 47*, 413–429.

Cappeliez, P., Guindon, M., & Robitaille, A. (2008). Functions of reminiscence and emotional regulation among older adults. *Journal of Aging Studies, 22*, 266–272.

Caputi, M., Lecce, S., Pagnin, A., & Banerjee, R. (2012). Longitudinal effects of theory of mind on later peer relations: The role of prosocial behavior. *Developmental Psychology, 48*, 257–270.

Carbone, I., Lazzarotto, T., Ianni, M., Porcellini, E., Forti, P., Masliah, E., & … Licastro, F. (2014). Herpes virus in Alzheimer's disease: Relation to progression of the disease. *Neurobiology of Aging, 35*, 122–129.

Cardman, M. (2004). Rising GPAs, course loads a mystery to researchers. *Education Daily, 37*, 1–3.

Carey, B. (2012, March 29). Diagnoses of autism on the rise, report says. *New York Times*, p.A20.

Carleton, R. N., Duranceau, S., Freeston, M. H., Boelen, P. A., McCabe, R. E., & Antony, M. M. (2014). 'But it might be a heart attack': Intolerance of uncertainty and panic disorder symptoms. *Journal of Anxiety Disorders, 28*, 463–470.

Carmel, S. (2017). The will-to-live scale: Development, validation, and significance for elderly people. *Aging & Mental Health, 21*, 289–296.

Carmichael, O., Mungas, D., Beckett, L., Harvey, D., Farias, S., Reed, B., et al. (2012). MRI predictors of cognitive change in a diverse and carefully characterized elderly population. *Neurobiology of Aging, 33*, 83–95.

Carmody, K., Haskett, M. E., Loehman, J., & Rose, R. A. (2014). Physically abused children's adjustment at the transition to school: Child, parent, and family factors. *Journal of Child and Family Studies*. Accessed online, 2-13-14; http://link.springer.com/article/10.1007%2Fs10826-014-9906-7#page-1.

Carnegie Task Force on Meeting the Needs of Young Children. (1994). *Starting points: Meeting the needs of our youngest children*. New York: Carnegie Corporation.

Carnell, S., Benson, L., Pryor, K., & Driggin, E. (2013). Appetitive traits from infancy to adolescence: Using behavioral and neural measures to investigate obesity risk. *Physiology & Behavior*. Accessed online 2-11-14; https://www.sciencedirect.com/science/article/pii/S0031938413000449?via%3Dihub.

Carney, R. N., & Levin, J. R. (2003). Promoting higher-order learning benefits by building lower-order mnemonic connections. *Applied Cognitive Psychology, 17*, 563–575.

Caron, A. (2009). Comprehension of the representational mind in infancy. *Developmental Review, 29*, 69–95.

Carpendale, J. I. M. (2000). Kohlberg and Piaget on stages and moral reasoning. *Developmental Review, 20*, 181–205.

Carr, D. (2015). Spousal/intimate partner loss and bereavement. In G. Christ, C. Messner, & L. Behar (Eds.), *Handbook of oncology social work: Psychosocial care for people with cancer*. New York: Oxford University Press.

Carr, D. (2016). Is death 'the great equalizer'? The social stratification of death quality in the United States. *Annals of the American Academy of Political and Social Science, 663*, 331–354.

Carr, P. B., & Steele, C. M. (2009). Stereotype threat and inflexible perseverance in problem solving. *Journal of Experimental Social Psychology, 45*, 853–859.

Carr, D., Nesse, R. M., & Wortman, C. B. (2005). *Spousal Berevement in Late Life*. New York: Springer.

Carrere, S., Buehlman, K. T., Gottman, J. M., Coan, J. A., & Ruckstuhl, L. (2000). Predicting marital stability and divorce in newlywed couples. *Journal of Family Psychology, 14*, 42–58.

Carrns, A. (2016, August 12.) Multigenerational households: The benefits, and perils. *New York Times*. Accessed online, 11-8-17; https://www.nytimes.com/2016/08/12/your-money/multigenerational-households-financial-advice.html?_r=0.

Carroll, L. (2000, February 1). Is memory loss inevitable? Maybe not. *New York Times*, pp. D1, D7.

Carson, A., Chabot, C., Greyson, D., Shannon, K., Duff, P., & Shoveller, J. (2016). A narrative analysis of the birth stories of early-age mothers. *Sociology of Health & Illness*. Accessed online, 3-3-17; http://onlinelibrary.wiley.com/doi/10.1111/1467-9566.12518/abstract.

Carson, R. G. (2005). Neural pathways mediating bilateral interactions between the upper limbs. *Brain Research Review, 49*, 641–662.

Carteret, M. (2017). *Cultural aspects of death and dying*. Accessed online, 10-23-17; http://www.dimensionsofculture.com/2010/11/cultural-aspects-of-death-and-dying/.

Carton, A., & Aiello, J. (2009). Control and anticipation of social interruptions: Reduced stress and improved task performance. *Journal of Applied Social Psychology, 39*, 169–185.

Carver, C., & Scheier, M. (2002). Coping processes and adjustment to chronic illness. In A. Christensen & M. Antoni (Eds.), *Chronic physical disorders: Behavioral medicine's perspective* (pp. 47–68). Malden, MA: Blackwell Publishers.

Casalin, S., Luyten, P., Vliegen, N., & Meurs, P. (2012). The structure and stability of temperament from infancy to toddlerhood: A one-year prospective study. *Infant Behavior & Development, 35*, 94–108.

Casasanto, D., & Henetz, T. (2012). Handedness shapes children's abstract concepts. *Cognitive Science, 36*, 359–372.

Cascalho, M., Ogle, B. M., & Platt, J. L. (2006). The future of organ transplantation. *Annals of Transplantation, 11*, 44–47.

Case, R. (1999). Conceptual development. In M. Bennett (Ed.), *Developmental psychology: Achievements and prospects*. Philadelphia, PA: Psychology Press.

Case, R., Demetriou, A., & Platsidou, M. (2001). Integrating concepts and tests of intelligence from the differential and developmental traditions. *Intelligence, 29*, 307–336.

Caselli, M., Rinaldi, P., Stefanini, S., & Volterra, V. (2012). Early action and gesture "vocabulary" and its relation with word comprehension and production. *Child Development, 83*, 526–542.

Caserta, M. T., O'Connor, T. G., Wyman, P. A., Wang, H., Moynihan, J., Cross, W., et al. (2008). The associations between psychosocial stress and the frequency of illness, and innate and adaptive immune function in children. *Brain, Behavior and Immunity, 22*, 933–940.

Casey, B. J., Jones, R. M., & Somerville, L. H. (2011). Braking and accelerating of the adolescent brain. *Journal of Research on Adolescence, 21*, 21–33.

Caspi, A. (2000). The child is father of the man: Personality continuities from childhood to adulthood. *Journal of Personality and Social Psychology, 78*, 158–172.

Casselman, B. (2014). Race gap narrows in college enrollment, but not in graduation. *FiveThirtyEight Economics*. Accessed online, 8-5-15; http://fivethirtyeight.com/features/race-gap-narrows-in-college-enrollment-but-not-in-graduation/.

Cassidy, J., & Berlin, L. J. (1994). The inse-cure/ambivalent pattern of attachment: Theory and research. *Child Development, 65*, 971–991.

Cassileth, B. R. (2014). Psychiatric benefits of integrative therapies in patients with cancer. *International Review of Psychiatry, 26*, 114–127.

Castel, A., & Craik, F. (2003). The effects of aging and divided attention on memory for item and associative information. *Psychology & Aging, 18*, 873–885.

Castelao, C., & Kröner-Herwig, B. (2013). Different trajectories of depressive symptoms in children and adolescents: Predictors and differences in girls and boys. *Journal of Youth and Adolescence, 42*, 1169–1182.

Catalini, M. (2017, March 11). Forget cribs. A cardboard box may be the safest place for your baby to sleep. *Boston Globe*. Accessed online, 3-14-17; https://www.bostonglobe.com/lifestyle/2017/03/11/forget-cribs-carboard-box-may-safest-placefor-your-baby-sleep/wwEakqRSAHh10ZZturXBHL/story.html.

Catalyst. (2015). Women's earnings and income. *Catalyst*. Accessed online, 8-5-15; http://www.catalyst.org/knowledge/womens-earnings-and-income.

Cath, S., & Shopper, M. (2001). *Stepparenting: Creating and recreating families in America today*. Hillsdale, NJ: Analytic Press.

Cattell, R. B. (1987). *Intelligence: Its structure, growth, and action*. Amsterdam: North-Holland.

Cauce, A. (2008). Parenting, culture, and context: Reflections on excavating culture. *Applied Developmental Science, 12*, 227–229. http://search.ebscohost.com, doi:10.1080/10888690802388177.

Cauce, A., & Domenech-Rodriguez, M. (2002). Latino families: Myths and realities. In J. M. Contreras, J. K. A. Kerns, & A. M. Neal-Barnett (Eds.), *Latino children and families in the United States*. Westport, CT: Praeger.

Cavallini, A., Fazzi, E., & Viviani, V. (2002). Visual acuity in the first two years of life in healthy term newborns: An experience with the Teller Acuity Cards. *Functional Neurology: New Trends in Adaptive & Behavioral Disorders, 17*, 87–92.

CDC (Centers for Disease Control and Prevention). (2010, December). *Vital and Health Statistics. Series 10*, Number 247.

CDC. (2015). *Current cigarette smoking among U.S. adults aged 18 and older*. Atlanta, GA: Centers for Disease Control. Accessed online, 6-30-15; http://www.cdc.gov/tobacco/campaign/tips/resources/data/cigarette-smoking-in-united-states.html.

CDC. (2016). *National vital statistics report*. Hyattsville, MD: Centers for Disease Control and Prevention.

Ceci, S. J., & Williams, W. M. (2010). Sex differences in mathintensive fields. *Current Directions in Psychological Science, 42*, 1–5.

Centers for Disease Control. (2003). *Incidence-surveillance, epidemiology, and end results program, 1973–2000*. Atlanta, GA: Centers for Disease Control.

Centers for Disease Control and Prevention. (2016). *10 leading causes of death by age group, United States—2015*. Washington, DC: National Vital Statistics System, National Center for Health Statistics.

Centers for Disease Control and Prevention. (2017). Pregnancy. Accessed online, 10/25/17; https://www.cdc.gov/pregnancy/during.html.

Centers for Disease Control and Prevention (2017a). Preventing abusive head trauma. Accessed online, 10-27-17; https://www.cdc.gov/violenceprevention/childmaltreatment/Abusive-Head-Trauma.html.

Chaffin, M. (2006). The changing focus of child maltreatment research and practice within psychology. *Journal of Social Issues, 62*, 663–684.

Chaker, A. M. (2003, September 23). *Putting toddlers in a nursing home*. Wall Street Journal, p. D1.

Chakraborty, R., & De, S. (2014). Body image and its relation with the concept of physical self among adolescents and young adults. *Psychological Studies, 59*, 419–426.

Chall, J. (1992). The new reading debates: Evidence from science, art, and ideology. *Teachers College Record, 94*, 315–328.

Chall, J. S. (1979). The great debate: Ten years later, with a modest proposal for reading stages. In L. B. Resnick & P. A. Weaver (Eds.), *Theory and practice of early reading*. Hillsdale, NJ: Lawrence Erlbaum.

Chamberlain, P., Price, J., Reid, J., Landsverk, J., Fisher, P., & Stoolmiller, M. (2006, April). *Who disrupts from placement in foster and kinship care? Child Abuse & Neglect, 30*, 409–424.

Chan, D. W. (1997). Self-concept and global self-worth among Chinese adolescents in Hong Kong. *Personality & Individual Differences, 22*, 511–520.

Chan, S., & Chan, K. (2013). Adolescents' susceptibility to peer pressure: Relations to parent–adolescent relationship and adolescents' emotional autonomy from parents. *Youth & Society, 45*, 286–302.

Chandra, A., Mosher, W. D., Copen, C., & Sionean, C. (2011). Sexual behavior, sexual attraction, and sexual identity in the United States: Data from the 2006–2008 National Survey of Family Growth. *National health statistics reports; no 36*. Hyattsville, MD: National Center for Health Statistics.

Channell, M. M., Thurman, A. J., Kover, S. T., & Abbeduto, L. (2014). Patterns of change in nonverbal cognition in adolescents with Down syndrome. *Research in Developmental Disabilities, 35*, 2933–2941.

Chao, R. K. (1994). Beyond parental control and authoritarian parenting style: Understanding Chinese parenting through the cultural notion of training. *Child Development, 65*, 1111–1119.

Chaplin, T., Gillham, J., & Seligman, M. (2009). Gender, anxiety, and depressive symptoms: A longitudinal study of early adolescents. *Journal of Early Adolescence, 29*, 307–327.

Chapman, R. (2016). A case study of gendered play in preschools: How early childhood educators' perceptions of gender influence children's play. *Early Child Development and Care, 186*, 1271–1284.

Chapple, H. S., Bouton, B. L., Chow, A. M., Gilbert, K. R., Kosminsky, P., Moore, J., & Whiting, P. P. (2017). The body of knowledge in thanatology: An outline. *Death Studies, 41*, 118–125.

Chapuis-de-Andrade, S., de Araujo, R. M., & Lara, D. R. (2017). Association of weight control behaviors with body mass index and weight-based self-evaluation. *Revista Brasileira De Psiquiatria, 39*, 237–243.

Charles, S., & Carstensen, L. (2010). Social and emotional aging. *Annual Review of Psychology, 61*, 383–409.

Charles, S. T., & Carstensen, L. L. (2014). Emotion regulation and aging. In J. J. Gross (Ed.), *Handbook of emotion regulation*. (2nd ed.) New York: Guilford Press.

Charness, N., & Boot, W. R. (2009). Aging and information technology use: Potential and barriers. *Current Directions in Psychological Science, 18*, 253–258.

Chassin, L., Macy, J., Seo, D., Presson, C., & Sherman, S. (2009). The association between membership in the sandwich generation and health behaviors: A longitudinal study. *Journal of Applied Developmental Psychology, 31*, 38–46.

Chasteen, A. L., Bhattacharyya, S., Horhota, M., Tam, R., & Hasher, L. (2005). How feelings of stereotype threat influence older adults' memory performance. *Experimental Aging Research, 31*, 235–260.

Chaudhary, N., & Sharma, N. (2012). India. In J. Arnett (Ed.), *Adolescent psychology around the world*. New York: Psychology Press.

Cheah, C., Leung, C., Tahseen, M., & Schultz, D. (2009). Authoritative parenting among immigrant Chinese mothers of preschoolers. *Journal of Family Psychology, 23*, 311–320.

Chen, D., Yang, X., & Aagard, S. D. (2012). The empty nest syndrome: Ways to enhance quality of life. *Educational Gerontology, 38*, 520–529.

Chen, J., Lin, H., Hsiao, Y. (2016). When the first baby arrives: Parental involvement and marital satisfaction among new parents. *Chinese Journal of Guidance and Counseling, 47*, 91–112.

Chen, J. J., Chen, T., & Zhen, X. X. (2012). Parenting styles and practices among Chinese immigrant mothers with young children. *Early Child Development and Care, 182*, 1–21.

Chen, J. J., Sun, P., & Yu, Z. (2017). A comparative study on parenting of preschool children between the Chinese in China and Chinese immigrants in the United States. *Journal of Family Issues, 38*, 1262–1287.

Chen, J., & Gardner, H. (2005). Assessment based on multiple-intelligences theory. In D. P. Flanagan & P. L. Harrison (Eds.), *Contemporary intellectual assessment: Theories, tests, and issues*. New York: Guilford Press.

Chen, X., Hastings, P. D., Rubin, K. H., Chen, H., Cen, G., & Stewart, S. L. (1998). Child-rearing attitudes and behavioral inhibition in Chinese and Canadian toddlers: A cross-cultural study. *Developmental Psychology, 34*, 677–686.

Cheng, J. T., Tracy, J. L., Ho, S., & Henrich, J. (2016). Listen, follow me: Dynamic vocal signals of dominance predict emergent social rank in humans. *Journal of Experimental Psychology: General, 145*, 536–547.

Cherney, I. (2003). Young children's spontaneous utterances of mental terms and the accuracy of their memory behaviors: A different methodological approach. *Infant & Child Development, 12*, 89–105.

Cherney, I., Kelly-Vance, L., & Glover, K. (2003). The effects of stereotyped toys and gender on play assessment in children aged 18–47 months. *Educational Psychology, 23*, 95–105.

Chetty, R., Stepner, M., Cutler, D., et al. (2016). The association between income and life expectancy in the United States, 2001–2014. JAMA: *Journal of the American Medical Association [serial online], 315*, 1750–1766.

Cheung, A. H., Emslie, G. J., & Mayes, T. L. (2006). The use of antidepressants to treat depression in children and adolescents. *Canadian Medical Association Journal, 174*, 193–200.

Cheung, W., Maio, G. R., Rees, K. J., Kamble, S., & Mane, S. (2016). Cultural differences in values as self-guides. *Personality and Social Psychology Bulletin, 42*, 769–781.

Chien, S., Bronson-Castain, K., Palmer, J., & Teller, D. (2006). Lightness constancy in 4-month-old infants. *Vision Research, 46*, 2139–2148.

Childers, J. (2009). Early verb learners: Creative or not? *Monographs of the Society for Research in Child Development, 74*, 133–139. http://search.ebscohost.com, doi:10.1111/j.1540-5834.2009.00524.x.

ChildStats.gov. (2017). America's children: Key national indicators of well-being, 2017. Accessed online, 11-8-17; https://www.childstats.gov/americaschildren/family1.asp#f1.

Child Welfare Information Gateway. (2013). *Leaving your child home alone*. Washington, DC: Children's Bureau.

Child Welfare Information Gateway. (2017). *Foster care statistics 2015*. Washington, DC: Department of Health and Human Services, Children's Bureau.

Chiodo, L. M., Bailey, B. A., Sokol, R. J., Janisse, J., Delaney-Black, V., & -Hannigan, J. H. (2012). Recognized spontaneous abortion in mid-pregnancy and patterns of pregnancy alcohol use. *Alcohol, 46*, 261–267.

Chisolm, T., Willott, J., & Lister, J. (2003). The aging auditory system: Anatomic and physiologic changes and implications for rehabilitation. *International Journal of Audiology, 42*, 2S3–2S10.

Chiu, M. M., & McBride-Chang, C. (2006). Gender, context, and reading: A comparison of students in 43 countries. *Scientific Studies of Reading, 10*, 331–362.

Cho, S. B., Aliev, F., Clark, S. L., Adkins, A. E., Edenberg, H. J., Bucholz, K. K., & ... Dick, D. M. (2017). Using patterns of genetic association to elucidate shared genetic etiologies across psychiatric disorders. *Behavior Genetics, 47*, 405–415.

Choi, C. Q. (2017). Countries with most twins identified. *LiveScience*. Accessed online, 10-24-17; https://www.livescience.com/16469-twins-countries-twinning-rates.html.

Chonchaiya, W., Tardif, T., Mai, X., Xu, L., Li, M., Kaciroti, N., & ... Lozoff, B. (2013). Developmental trends in auditory processing can provide early predictions of language acquisition in young infants. *Developmental Science, 16*, 159–172.

Chow, T. S., & Wan, H. Y. (2017). Is there any 'Facebook depression'? Exploring the moderating roles of neuroticism, Facebook social comparison and envy. *Personality and Individual Differences, 119*, 277–282.

Choy, C. M., Yeung, Q. S., Briton-Jones, C. M., Cheung, C. K., Lam, C. W., & Haines, C. J. (2002). Relationship between semen parameters and mercury concentrations in blood and in seminal fluid from subfertile males in Hong Kong. *Fertility and Sterility, 78*, 426–428.

Christakis, D., & Zimmerman, F. (2007). Violent television viewing during preschool is associated with antisocial behavior during school age. *Pediatrics, 120*, 993–999.

Christiaens, W., Verhaeghe, M., & Bracke, P. (2010). Pain acceptance and personal control in pain relief in two maternity care models: a cross-national comparison of Belgium and the Netherlands. *BMC Health Services, 10*, 268–273.

Christiansen, D. M. (2017). Posttraumatic stress disorder in parents following infant death: A systematic review. *Clinical Psychology Review, 51*, 60–74.

Christodoulou, J., Lac, A., & Moore, D. S. (2017). Babies and math: A meta-analysis of infants' simple arithmetic competence. *Developmental Psychology, 53*, 1405–1417.

Chung, S. A., Wei, A. Q., Connor, D. E., Webb, G. C., Molloy, T., Pajic, M., & Diwan, A. D. (2007). Nucleus pulposus cellular longevity by telomerase gene therapy. *Spine, 15*, 1188–1196.

Cicchetti, D. (1996). Child maltreatment: Implications for developmental theory and research. *Human Development, 39*, 18–39.

Cicchetti, D., & Cohen, D. J. (2006). *Developmental psychopathology, vol. 1: Theory and method* (2nd ed.). Hoboken, NJ: Wiley.

Cina, V., & Fellmann, F. (2006). Implications of predictive testing in neurodegenerative disorders. *Schweizer Archiv für Neurologie und Psychiatrie, 157*, 359–365.

CIRE (Cooperative Institutional Research Program of the American Council on Education). (1990). *The American freshman: National norms for fall 1990*. Los Angeles: American Council on Education.

Clark, D. (2015). Hospice care of the dying. In J. M. Stillion & T. Attig (Eds.), *Death, dying, and bereavement: Contemporary perspectives, institutions, and practices*. New York: Springer Publishing Co.

Clark, K. B., & Clark, M. P. (1947). Racial identification and preference in Negro children. In T. M. Newcomb & E. L. Hartley (Eds.), *Readings in social psychology*. New York: Holt, Rinehart & Winston.

Clark, R. (1998). *Expertise*. Silver Spring, MD: International Society for Performance Improvement.

Clarke, A. R., Barry, R. J., McCarthy, R., Selikowitz, M., & Johnstone, S. J. (2008). Effects of imipramine hydrochloride on the EEG of children with attention-deficit/hyperactivity disorder who are non-responsive to stimulants. *International Journal of Psychophysiology, 68*, 186–192.

Clarke-Stewart, K., & Allhusen, V. (2002). Nonparen-tal caregiving. In M. Bornstein (Ed.), *Handbook of parenting: Vol. 3: Being and becoming a parent* (2nd ed.). Mahwah, NJ: Lawrence Erlbaum Associates.

Clauss-Ehlers, C. (2008). Sociocultural factors, resilience, and coping: Support for a culturally sensitive measure of resilience. *Journal of Applied Developmental Psychology, 29*, 197–212.

Clearfield, M., & Nelson, N. (2006, January). Sex differences in mothers' speech and play behavior with 6-, 9-, and 14-month-old infants. *Sex Roles, 54*, 127–137.

Cline, K. D., & Edwards, C. P. (2017). Parent–child book-reading styles, emotional quality, and changes in early head start children's cognitive scores. *Early Education and Development, 28*, 41–58.

Close, F. T., Suther, S., Foster, A., El-Amin, S., & Battle, A. M. (2013). Community perceptions of black infant mortality: A qualitative inquiry. *Journal of Health Care for the Poor and Underserved, 24*, 1089–1101.

Closson, L. (2009). Status and gender differences in early adolescents' descriptions of popularity. *Social Development, 18*, 412–426.

Cnattingius, S., Berendes, H., & Forman, M. (1993). Do delayed childbearers face increased risks of adverse pregnancy outcomes after the first birth? *Obstetrics and Gynecology, 81*, 512–516.

Coall, D. A., & Hertwig, R. (2011). Grandparental investment: A relic of the past or a resource for the future? *Current Directions in Psychological Science, 20*, 93–98.

Coates, S. W. (2016). Can babies remember trauma? Symbolic forms of representation in traumatized infants. *Journal of the American Psychoanalytic Association, 64*, 751–776.

Cobbe, E. (2003, September 25). France ups heat toll. *CBS Evening News*.

Cockrill, K., & Gould, H. (2012). Letter to the editor: Response to "What women want from abortion counseling in the United States: A qualitative study of abortion patients in 2008." *Social Work in Health Care, 51*, 191–194.

Coelho, V. A., Marchante, M., & Jimerson, S. R. (2016). Promoting a positive middle school transition: A randomized-controlled treatment study examining self-concept and self-esteem. *Journal of Youth and Adolescence*. Accessed online, 6-13-16; http://www.ncbi.nlm.nih.gov/pubmed/27230119.

Cogan, L. W., Josberger, R. E., Gesten, F. C., & Roohan, P. J. (2012). Can prenatal care impact future well-child visits? The experience of a low income population in New York state Medicaid managed care. *Maternal and Child Health Journal, 16*, 92–99.

Cohen, D. (2013). *How the child's mind develops* (2nd ed.). New York: Routledge/Taylor & Francis Group.

Cohen, J. (1999, March 19). Nurture helps mold able minds. *Science, 283,* 1832–1833.

Cohen, L. B., & Cashon, C. H. (2003). Infant perception and cognition. In R. M. Lerner & M. A. Easterbrooks (Eds.), *Handbook of psychology: Developmental psychology,* Vol. 6. New York: Wiley.

Cohen, R. A., Mather, N., Schneider, D. A., & White, J. M. (2016). A comparison of schools: Teacher knowledge of explicit code-based reading instruction. *Reading and Writing.* Accessed online, 3-16-17; http://link.springer.com/article/10.1007/s11145-016-9694-0.

Cohen-Zion, M., Shabi, A., Levy, S., Glasner, L., & Wiener, A. (2016). Effects of partial sleep deprivation on information processing speed in adolescence. *Journal of the International Neuropsychological Society, 22,* 388–398.

Cohrs, J., Abele, A., & Dette, D. (2006, July). Integrating situational and dispositional determinants of job satisfaction: Findings from three samples of professionals. *Journal of Psychology: Interdisciplinary and Applied, 140,* 363–395.

Cokley, K. (2003). What do we know about the motivation of African American students? Challenging the "anti-intellectual" myth. *Harvard Educational Review, 73,* 524–558.

Colarusso, C., & Nemiroff, R. (1981). *Adult development: A new dimension in psychodynamic theory and practice (critical issues in psychiatry).* New York: Springer.

Colby, A., & Damon, W. (1987). Listening to a different voice: A review of Gilligan's in a different voice. In M. R. Walsh (Ed.), *The psychology of women.* New Haven, CT: Yale University Press.

Colby, A., & Kohlberg, L. (1987). *The measurement of moral judgment* (Vols. 1–2). New York: Cambridge University Press.

Colby, S. L. & Ortman, J. M. (2014). Projections of the size and composition of the U.S. population: 2014 to 2060. *Current Population Reports, P25-1143.* Washington, DC: U.S. Census Bureau.

Cole, C. F., Arafat, C., & Tidhar, C. (2003). The educational impact of Rechov Sumsum/Shara'a Simsim: A Sesame Street television series to promote respect and understanding among children living in Israel, the West Bank and Gaza. *International Journal of Behavioral Development, 27,* 409–422.

Cole, M. (1992). *Culture in development.* In M. H. Bornstein & M. E. Lamb (Eds.), Developmental psychology: An advanced textbook (3rd ed.). Hillsdale, NJ: Lawrence Erlbaum.

Cole, P., Dennis, T., Smith-Simon, K., & Cohen, L. (2009). Preschoolers' emotion regulation strategy understanding: Relations with emotion socialization and child self-regulation. *Social Development, 18,* 324–352.

Cole, S. A. (2005). Infants in foster care: Relational and environmental factors affecting attachment. *Journal of Reproductive & Infant Psychology, 23,* 43–61.

Coleman, H., Chan, C., Ferris, F., & Chew, E. (2008). Age-related macular degeneration. *The Lancet, 372,* 1835–1845.

Coleman, J. (2014). *Why won't my teenager talk to me?* New York: Routledge/Francis Taylor Group.

Coleman, M., Ganong, L., & Weaver, S. (2001). Relationship maintenance and enhancement in remarried families. In J. Harvey & A. Wenzel (Eds.), *Close romantic relationships: Maintenance and enhancement.* Mahwah, NJ: Lawrence Erlbaum.

Coleman, P. (2005, July). Editorial: Uses of reminiscence: Functions and benefits. *Aging & Mental Health, 9,* 291–294.

College Board. (2005). *2001 College bound seniors are the largest, most diverse group in history.* New York: College Board.

Collins, J. (2012). Growing up bicultural in the United States: The case of Japanese-Americans. In R. Josselson & M. Harway (Eds.), *Navigating multiple identities: Race, gender, culture, nationality, and roles.* New York: Oxford University Press.

Collins, W. (2003). More than myth: The developmental significance of romantic relationships during adolescence. *Journal of Research on Adolescence, 13,* 1–24.

Collins, W., & Andrew, L. (2004). Changing relation-ships, changing youth: Interpersonal contexts of adolescent development. *Journal of Early Adolescence, 24,* 55–62.

Collins, W. A., Gleason, T., & Sesma, A. (1997). Internalization, autonomy, and relationships: Development during adolescence. In J. E. Grusec & L. Kuczynski (Eds.), *Parenting and children's internalization of values: A handbook of contemporary theory* (pp. 78–99). New York: Wiley.

Collins, W., & Doolittle, A. (2006, December). Personal reflections of funeral rituals and spirituality in a Kentucky African American family. *Death Studies, 30,* 957–969.

Collishaw, S., Pickles, A., Messer, J., Rutter, M., Shearer, C., & Maughan, B. (2007). Resilience to adult psychopathology following childhood maltreatment: Evidence from a community sample. *Child Abuse & Neglect, 31,* 211–229.

Colom, R., Lluis-Font, J. M., & Andrés-Pueyo, A. (2005). The generational intelligence gains are caused by decreasing variance in the lower half of the distribution: Supporting evidence for the nutrition hypothesis. *Intelligence, 33,* 83–91.

Colpin, H., & Soenen, S. (2004). Bonding through an adoptive mother's eyes. *Midwifery Today with International Midwife, 70,* 30–31.

Coltrane, S., & Adams, M. (1997). Children and gender. In T. Arendell (Ed.), *Contemporary parenting: Challenges and issues.* Understanding families (Vol. 9). Thousand Oaks, CA: Sage Publications.

Commons, M. L., Galaz-Fontes, J. F., & Morse, S. J. (2006). Leadership, cross-cultural contact, socio-economic status, and formal operational reasoning about moral dilemmas among Mexican non-literate adults and high school students. *Journal of Moral Education, 35,* 247–267.

Compton, R., & Weissman, D. (2002). Hemispheric asymmetries in global-local perception: Effects of individual differences in neuroticism. *Laterality, 7,* 333–350.

Comunian, A. L., & Gielen, U. P. (2000). Sociomoral reflection and prosocial and antisocial behavior: Two Italian studies. *Psychological Reports, 87,* 161–175.

Condly, S. (2006, May). Resilience in children: A review of literature with implications for education. *Urban Education, 41,* 211–236.

Condon, J., Corkindale, C., Boyce, P., & Gamble, E. (2013). A longitudinal study of father-to-infant attachment: Antecedents and correlates. *Journal of Reproductive and Infant Psychology, 31,* 15–30.

Condry, J., & Condry, S. (1976). Sex differences: A study of the eye of the beholder. *Child Development, 47,* 812–819.

Conel, J. L. (1930/1963). *Postnatal development of the human cortex* (Vols. 1–6). Cambridge, MA: Harvard University Press.

Congressional Budget Office. (2013). *A description of the immigrant population: 2013 update.* Washington, DC: Congressional Budget Office.

Conn, V. S. (2003). Integrative review of physical activity intervention research with aging adults. *Journal of the American Geriatrics Society, 51,* 1159–1168.

Connell-Carrick, K. (2006). Early child care and early child development: Major findings of the NICHD study of early child care. *Child Welfare Journal, 85,* 819–836.

Conner, K., & Goldston, D. (2007, March). Rates of suicide among males increase steadily from age 11 to 21: Developmental framework and outline for prevention. *Aggression and Violent Behavior, 12(2),* 193–207.

Connor, R. (1992). *Cracking the over-50 job market.* New York: Penguin Books.

Consedine, N., Magai, C., & King, A. (2004). Deconstructing positive affect in later life: A differential functionalist analysis of joy and interest. *International Journal of Aging & Human Development, 58,* 49–68.

Cook, E., Buehler, C., & Henson, R. (2009). Parents and peers as social influences to deter antisocial behavior. *Journal of Youth and Adolescence, 38,* 1240–1252.

Coon, K. D., Myers, A. J., Craig, D. W., Webster, J. A., Pearson, J. V., Lince, D. H., et al. (2007). A high-density whole-genome association study reveals that APOE is the major susceptibility gene for sporadic late-onset Alzheimer's disease. *Journal of Clinical Psychiatry, 68,* 613–618.

Corballis, P. (2003). Visuospatial processing and the right-hemisphere interpreter. *Brain & Cognition, 53,* 171–176.

Corbetta, D., Friedman, D. R., & Bell, M. A. (2014). Brain reorganization as a function of walking experience in 12-month-old infants: Implications for the development of manual laterality. *Frontiers in Psychology.* Accessed online, 3-18-15; http://www.ncbi.nlm.nih.gov/pubmed/24711801.

Corbetta, D., & Snapp-Childs, W. (2009). Seeing and touching: The role of sensory-motor experience on the development of infant reaching. *Infant Behavior & Development, 32,* 44–58.

Corcoran, J., & Pillai, V. (2007, January). Effectiveness of secondary pregnancy prevention programs: A meta-analysis. *Research on Social Work Practice, 17,* 5–18.

Cordes, S., & Brannon, E. (2009). Crossing the divide: Infants discriminate small from large numerosities. *Developmental Psychology, 45,* 1583–1594.

Cordón, I. M., Pipe, M., Sayfan, L., Melinder, A., & Goodman, G. S. (2004). Memory for traumatic experiences in early childhood. *Developmental Review, 24,* 101–132.

Cordova, J. V. (2014). *The marriage checkup practitioner's guide: Promoting lifelong relationship health.* Washington, DC: American Psychological Association.

Cornish, K., Turk, J., & Hagerman, R. (2008). The fragile X continuum: New advances and perspectives. *Journal of Intellectual Disability Research, 52,* 469–482.

Corr, C. (2007). Hospice: Achievements, legacies, and challenges. *Omega: Journal of Death and Dying, 56,* 111–120.

Corr, C. A. (2015). *Death education at the college and university level in North America.* In J. M. Stillion, & T. Attig (Eds.), Death, dying, and bereavement: Contemporary perspectives, institutions, and practices. New York: Springer Publishing Co.

Corr, C. A. (2015). The death system according to Robert Kastenbaum. *Omega: Journal of Death and Dying, 70,* 13–25.

Corr, C., Nabe, C., & Corr, D. (2006). *Death & dying, life & living. Belmont,* CA: Thomson Wadsworth.

Corrow, S., Granrud, C. E., Mathison, J., & Yonas, A. (2012). Infants and adults use line junction information to perceive 3D shape. *Journal of Vision, 12.*

Corry, M. While, A., Neenan, K., & Smith, V. (2014). A systematic review of intervention for caregivers of people with chronic conditions. Accessed online, 1-1-2015; http://onlinelibrary.wiley.com/doi/10.1111/jan.12523/abstract?deniedAccessCustomisedMessage=&userIsAuthenticated=false.

Costa, L. V., & Veloso, A. I. (2016). Factors influencing the adoption of video games in late adulthood: A survey of older adult gamers. *International Journal of Technology and Human Interaction (IJTHI), 12,* 35–50.

Costa, P. T., Busch, C. M., Zonderman, A. B., & McCrae, R. R. (1986). Correlations of MMPI factor scales with measures of the five factor model of personality. *Journal of Personality Assessment, 50,* 640–650.

Costa, P. T., & McCrae, R. R. (1997). Longitudinal stability of adult personality. In R. Hogan, J. A. Johnson, & S. R. Briggs (Eds.), *Handbook of personality psychology* (pp. 269–290). San Diego, CA: Academic Press.

Costa-Martins, J. M., Pereira, M., Martins, H., Moura-Ramos, M., Coelho, R., & Tavares, J. (2014). The role of maternal attachment in the experience of labor pain: A prospective study. *Psychosomatic Medicine, 76,* 221–228.

Costello, E., Compton, S., & Keeler, G. (2003). Relationships between poverty and psychopathology: A natural experiment. *JAMA: Journal of the American Medical Association, 290,* 2023–2029.

Costello, E., Sung, M., Worthman, C., & Angold, A. (2007, April). Pubertal maturation and the development of alcohol use and abuse. *Drug and Alcohol Dependence, 88,* S50–S59.

Cotrufo, P., Cella, S., Cremato, F., & Labella, A. G. (2007). Eating disorder attitude and abnormal behaviours in a sample of 11–13-year-old school children: The role of pubertal body transformation. *Eating Weight Disorders, 12*, 154–160.

Couperus, J., & Nelson, C. (2006). Early brain development and plasticity. *Blackwell handbook of early childhood development*. New York: Blackwell Publishing.

Courtney, E., Gamboz, J., & Johnson, J. (2008). Problematic eating behaviors in adolescents with low self-esteem and elevated depressive symptoms. *Eating Behaviors, 9*, 408–414.

Couzin, J. (2002, June 21). Quirks of fetal environment felt decades later. *Science, 296*, 2167–2169.

Cowan, C. P., & Cowan, P. A. (1992). *When partners become parents*. New York: Wiley.

Cox, C., Kotch, J., & Everson, M. (2003). A longitudinal study of modifying influences in the relationship between domestic violence and child maltreatment. *Journal of Family Violence, 18*, 5–17.

Cox, R., Skouteris, H., Rutherford, L., & Fuller-Tyszkiewicz, M. (2012). The association between television viewing and preschool child body mass index: A systematic review of English papers published from 1995 to 2010. *Journal Of Children And Media, 6(2)*, 198-220. doi:10.1080/17482798.2011.587145

Cox, C., & Miner, J. (2014). Grandchildren raised by grandparents: Comparing the experiences of African-American and Tanzanian grandchildren. *Journal of Intergenerational Relationships, 12*, 9–24.

Coyne, S. M. (2016). Effects of viewing relational aggression on television on aggressive behavior in adolescents: A three-year longitudinal study. *Developmental Psychology, 52*, 284–295.

Craik, F., & Salthouse, T. A. (Eds.). (1999). *The handbook of aging and cognition* (2nd ed.). Mahwah, NJ: Erlbaum.

Cramer, E. M., Song, H., & Drent, A. M. (2016). Social comparison on Facebook: Motivation, affective consequences, self-esteem, and Facebook fatigue. *Computers in Human Behavior, 64*, 739–746.

Cramer, M., Chen, L., Roberts, S., & Clute, D. (2007). Evaluating the social and economic impact of community-based prenatal care. *Public Health Nursing, 24*, 329–336.

Crampton, A., & Hall, J. (2017). Unpacking socio-economic risks for reading and academic self-concept in primary school: Differential effects and the role of the preschool home learning environment. *British Journal of Educational Psychology, 87*, 365–382.

Cratty, B. (1979). *Perceptual and motor development in infants and children* (2nd ed.). Englewood Cliffs, NJ: Prentice Hall.

Cratty, B. (1986). *Perceptual and motor development in infants and children* (3rd ed.). Englewood Cliffs, NJ: Prentice Hall.

Crawford, D., Houts, R., & Huston, T. (2002). Compatibility, leisure, and satisfaction in marital relationships. *Journal of Marriage & Family, 64*, 433–449.

Crawford, M., & Unger, R. (2004). *Women and gender: A feminist psychology* (4th ed.). New York: McGraw-Hill.

Credé, M., & Niehorster, S. (2012). Adjustment to college as measured by the Student Adaptation to College Questionnaire: A quantitative review of its structure and relationships with correlates and consequences. *Educational Psychology Review, 24*, 133–165.

Crews, D., Gillette, R., Scarpino, S. V., Manikkam, M., Savenkova, M. I., & Skinner, M. K. (2012). Epigenetic transgenerational inheritance of altered stress responses. *PNAS Proceedings of the National Academy of Sciences of the United States of America, 109*, 9143–9148.

Crisp, A., Gowers, S., Joughin, N., McClelland, L., Rooney, B., Nielsen, S., et al. (2006, May). Anorexia nervosa in males: Similarities and differences to anorexia nervosa in females. *European Eating Disorders Review, 14*, 163–167.

Crocetti, E. (2017). Identity formation in adolescence: The dynamic of forming and consolidating identity commitments. *Child Development Perspectives*. Accessed online, 3-22-17; http://onlinelibrary.wiley.com/doi/10.1111/cdep.12226/abstract.

Crockenberg, S., & Leerkes, E. (2003). Infant negative emotionality, caregiving, and family relationships. In A. Crouter & A. Booth (Eds.), *Children's influence on family dynamics: The neglected side of family relationships* (pp. 57–78). Mahwah, NJ: Lawrence Erlbaum.

Crosland, K., & Dunlap, G. (2012). Effective strategies for the inclusion of children with autism in general education classrooms. *Behavior Modification, 36*, 251–269.

Crosnoe, R., & Elder, G. H., Jr. (2002). Successful adaptation in the later years: A life course approach to aging. *Social Psychology Quarterly, 65*, 309–328.

Cross, T., Cassady, J., Dixon, F., & Adams, C. (2008). The psychology of gifted adolescents as measured by the MMPI-A. *Gifted Child Quarterly, 52*, 326–339.

Crowley, B., Hayslip, B., & Hobdy, J. (2003). Psychological hardiness and adjustment to life events in adulthood. *Journal of Adult Development, 10*, 237–248.

Crowley, J. (2018). *Gray divorce*. Berkeley: University of California Press.

Crowley, K., Callaman, M. A., Tenenbaum, H. R., & Allen, E. (2001). Parents explain more often to boys than to girls during shared scientific thinking. *Psychological Science, 12*, 258–261.

Crowther, M., & Rodriguez, R. (2003). A stress and coping model of custodial grandparenting among African Americans. In B. Hayslip & J. Patrick (Eds.), *Working with custodial grandparents*. New York: Springer Publishing.

Crozier, S., Robertson, N., & Dale, M. (2015). The psychological impact of predictive genetic testing for Huntington's disease: A systematic review of the literature. *Journal of Genetic Counseling, 24*, 29–39.

Crupi, R., & Brondolo, E. (2017). Posttraumatic stress disorder post 9/11: A review of the evidence and implications for public health policy. *TPM—Testing, Psychometrics, Methodology in Applied Psychology, 24*, 363–378.

Cservenka, A., & Brumback, T. (2017). The burden of binge and heavy drinking on the brain: Effects on adolescent and young adult neural structure and function. *Frontiers in Psychology, 8*, 188–197.

Cuervo, A. (2008). Calorie restriction and aging: The ultimate "cleansing diet." *Journals of Gerontology: Series A: Biological Sciences and Medical Sciences, 63A*, 547–549.

Cuevas, K., Cannon, E. N., Yoo, K., & Fox, N. A. (2015). The infant EEG mu rhythm: Methodological considerations and best practices. *Developmental Review, 34*, 26–43.

Cullen, C. (2017). Difficult conversations: Children, adolescents, and death. In R. G. Stevenson & G. R. Cox (Eds.), *Children, adolescents and death: Questions and answers*. New York: Routledge/Taylor & Francis Group.

Culver, V. (2003, August 26). Funeral expenses overwhelm survivors: $10,000-plus tab often requires aid. *Denver Post*, p. B2.

Cumming, G. P., Currie, H. D., Moncur, R., & Lee, A. J. (2009). Web-based survey on the effect of menopause on women's libido in a computer-literate population. *Menopause International, 15*, 8–12.

Cummings, E., & Henry, W. E. (1961). *Growing old*. New York: Basic Books.

Cuperman, R., Robinson, R. L., & Ickes, W. (2014). On the malleability of self-image in individuals with a weak sense of self. *Self and Identity, 13*, 1–23.

Curl, M. N., Davies, R., Lothian, S., Pascali-Bonaro, D., Scaer, R. M., & Walsh, A. (2004). Childbirth educators, doulas, nurses, and women respond to the six care practices for normal birth. *Journal of Perinatal Education, 13*, 42–50.

Curtis, R. G., Windsor, T. D., & Soubelet, A. (2015). The relationship between Big-5 personality traits and cognitive ability in older adults—A review. *Aging, Neuropsychology, and Cognition, 22*, 42–71.

Curtis, W. J., & Cicchetti, D. (2003). Moving research on resilience into the 21st century: Theoretical and methodological considerations in examining the biological contributors to resilience. *Development and Psychopathology, 15*, 126–131.

Cushman, F., Sheketoff, R., Wharton, S., & Carey, S. (2013). The development of intent-based moral judgment. *Cognition, 127*, 6–21.

Czerwińska-Jasiewicz, M. (2017). The creation of a concept of one's own life by adolescents as a manifestation of subjectivity and autonomy. *Polish Psychological Bulletin, 48*, 28–37.

D'Lima, G. M., Winsler, A., & Kitsantas, A. (2014). Ethnic and gender differences in first-year college students' goal orientation, self-efficacy, and extrinsic and intrinsic motivation. *Journal of Educational Research, 107*, 341–356.

Dabelko, H., & Zimmerman, J. (2008). Outcomes of adult day services for participants: A conceptual model. *Journal of Applied Gerontology, 27*, 78–92.

Dagher, A., Tannenbaum, B., Hayashi, T., Pruessner, J., & McBride, D. (2009). An acute psychosocial stress enhances the neural response to smoking cues. *Brain Research, 129*, 340–348.

Dagys, N., McGlinchey, E. L., Talbot, L. S., Kaplan, K. A., Dahl, R. E., & Harvey, A. G. (2012). Double trouble? The effects of sleep deprivation and chronotype on adolescent affect. *Journal of Child Psychology and Psychiatry, 53*, 660–667.

Dahl, A., Satlof-Bedrick, E. S., Hammond, S. I., Drummond, J. K., Waugh, W. E., & Brownell, C. A. (2017). Explicit scaffolding increases simple helping in younger infants. *Developmental Psychology, 53*, 407–416.

Dahl, A., Sherlock, B. R., Campos, J. J., & Theunissen, F. E. (2014). Mothers' tone of voice depends on the nature of infants' transgressions. *Emotion, 14*, 651–665.

Dahl, E., & Birkelund, E. (1997). Health inequalities in later life in a social democratic welfare state. *Social Science & Medicine, 44*, 871–881.

Dai, D., Tan, X., Marathe, D., Valtcheva, A., Pruzek, R. M., & Shen, J. (2012). Influences of social and educational environments on creativity during adolescence: Does SES matter? *Creativity Research Journal, 24*, 191–199.

Daley, K. C. (2004). Update on sudden infant death syndrome. *Current Opinion in Pediatrics, 16*, 227–232.

Daley, M. F., & Glanz, J. M. (2011). Straight talk about vaccination. *Scientific American, 305*, 32, 34.

Dalton, T. C., & Bergenn, V. W. (2007). *Early experience, the brain, and consciousness: An historical and interdisciplinary synthesis*. Mahwah, NJ: Lawrence Erlbaum Associates Publishers.

Damon, W. (1983). *Social and personality development*. New York: Norton.

Damon, W., & Hart, D. (1988). *Self-understanding in childhood and adolescence*. New York: Cambridge University Press.

Daniel, S., & Goldston, D. (2009). Interventions for suicidal youth: A review of the literature and developmental considerations. *Suicide and Life-Threatening Behavior, 39*, 252–268.

Daniels, H. (2006, February). The 'social' in post-Vygotskian theory. *Theory & Psychology, 16*, 37–49.

Danish, J., Saleh, A., Andrade, A., & Bryan, B. (2017). Observing complex systems thinking in the zone of proximal development. *Instructional Science, 45*, 5–24.

Dare, W. N., Noronha, C. C., Kusemiju, O. T., & Okanlawon, O. A. (2002). The effect of ethanol on sper-matogenesis and fertility in male SpragueDawley rats pretreated with acetylsalicylic acid. *Nigeria Postgraduate Medical Journal, 9*, 194–198.

Darwin, Z., Green, J., McLeish, J., Willmot, H., & Spiby, H. (2017). Evaluation of trained volunteer doula services for disadvantaged women in five areas in England: Women's experiences. *Health & Social Care in the Community, 25*, 466–477.

Das, A. (2007). Masturbation in the United States. *Journal of Sex & Marital Therapy, 33*, 301–317.

Dasen, P., Inhelder, B., Lavallee, M., & Retschitzki, J. (1978). *Naissance de l'intelligence chez l'enfant Baoule de Cote d'Ivoire*. Berne: Hans Huber.

Dasen, P., Ngini, L., & Lavallee, M. (1979). Cross-cultural training studies of concrete operations. In L. H. Eckenberger, W. J. Lonner, & Y. H. Poortinga (Eds.), *Cross-cultural contributions to psychology*. Amsterdam: Swets & Zeilinger.

Dasen, P. R., & Mishra, R. C. (2000). Rapid social change and the turmoil of adolescence: A cross-cultural perspective. *International Journal of Group Tensions, 29*, 17–49.

Daum, M. M., Prinz, W., & Aschersleben, G. (2011). Perception and production of object-related grasping in 6-month-olds. *Journal of Experimental Child Psychology, 108*, 810–818.

Davenport, B., & Bourgeois, N. (2008). Play, aggression, the preschool child, and the family: A review of literature to guide empirically informed play therapy with aggressive preschool children. *International Journal of Play Therapy, 17*, 2–23.

Davey, M., Eaker, D. G., & Walters, L. H. (2003). Resilience processes in adolescents: Personality profiles, self-worth, and coping. *Journal of Adolescent Research, 18*, 347–362.

Davidson, R. J. (2003). Affective neuroscience: A case for interdisciplinary research. In F. Kessel & P. L. Rosenfield (Eds.), *Expanding the boundaries of health and social science: Case studies in interdisciplinary innovation*. London: Oxford University Press.

Davidson, T. (1977). Wifebeating: A recurring phenomenon throughout history. In M. Roy (Ed.), *Battered women: A psychosociological study of domestic violence*. New York: Van Nostrand Reinhold.

Davies, P. G., Spencer, S. J., & Steele, C. M. (2005). Clearing the Air: Identity Safety Moderates the Effects of Stereotype Threat on Women's Leadership Aspirations. *Journal Of Personality And Social Psychology, 88(2)*, 276-287. doi:10.1037/0022-3514.88.2.276

Davies, K., Tropp, L. R., Aron, A. P., Thomas, F., & Wright, S. C. (2011). Cross-group friendships and intergroup attitudes: A meta-analytic review. *Personality and Social Psychology Review, 15*, 332–351.

Davies, P. T., Harold, G. T., Goeke-Morey, M. C., & Cummings, E. M. (2002). Child emotional security and interparental conflict. *Monographs of the Society for Research in Child Development, 67*.

Davies, S., & Denton, M. (2002). The economic well-being of older women who become divorced or separated in mid- or later life. *Canadian Journal on Aging, 21*, 477–493.

Davis, A. (2003). *Your divorce, your dollars: Financial planning before, during, and after divorce*. Bellingham, WA: Self-Counsel Press.

Davis, A. (2008). Children with Down syndrome: Implications for assessment and intervention in the school. *School Psychology Quarterly, 23*, 271–281.

Davis, C. I., Aronson, J., & Salinas, M. (2006). Shades of Threat: Racial Identity as a Moderator of Stereotype Threat. *Journal Of Black Psychology, 32*(4), 399-417. doi:10.1177/0095798406292464

Davis, B. L., Smith-Bynum, M. A., Saleem, F. T., Francois, T., & Lambert, S. F. (2017). Racial socialization, private regard, and behavior problems in African American youth: Global self-esteem as a mediator. *Journal of Child and Family Studies, 26*, 709–720.

Davis, L. L., Chestnutt, D., Molloy, M., Deshefy-Longhi, T., Shim, B., & Gilliss, C. L. (2014). Adapters, strugglers, and case managers: A typology of spouse caregivers. *Qualitative Health Research, 24*, 1492–1500.

Davis, M., Zautra, A., Younger, J., Motivala, S., Attrep, J., & Irwin, M. (2008). Chronic stress and regulation of cellular markers of inflammation in rheumatoid arthritis: Implications for fatigue. *Brain, Behavior, and Immunity, 22*, 24–32.

Davis, N. L., & Voirin, J. (2016). Reciprocal writing as a creative technique. *Journal of Creativity in Mental Health, 11*, 66–77.

Davis, R. R., & Hofferth, S. L. (2012). The association between inadequate gestational weight gain and infant mortality among U.S. infants born in 2002. *Maternal and Child Health Journal, 16*, 119–124.

Davis, T. S., Saltzburg, S., & Locke, C. R. (2009). Supporting the emotional and psychological well-being of sexual minority youth: Youth ideas for action. *Children and Youth Services Review, 31*, 1030–1041.

Davis-Kean, P. E., & Sandler, H. M. (2001). A meta-analysis of measures of self-esteem for young children: A framework for future measures. *Child Development, 72*, 887–906.

Daxinger L. & Whitelaw E. (2012). Understanding transgenerational epigenetic inheritance via the gametes in mammals. *National Review of Genetics, 13*, 153–162.

de C. Williams, A. C., Morris, J. J., Stevens, K. K., Gessler, S. S., Cella, M. M., & Baxter, J. J. (2013). What influences midwives in estimating labour pain? *European Journal of Pain, 17*, 86–93.

de Dios, A. (2012). United States of America. In J. Arnett (Ed.), *Adolescent psychology around the world*. New York: Psychology Press.

de Frias, C. M., & Whyne, E. (2015). Stress on health-related quality of life in older adults: The protective nature of mindfulness. *Aging & Mental Health, 19*, 201–206.

de Graag, J. A., Cox, R. A., Hasselman, F., Jansen, J., & de Weerth, C. (2012). Functioning within a relationship: Mother–infant synchrony and infant sleep. *Infant Behavior & Development, 35*, 252–263.

De Jesus-Zayas, S. R., Buigas, R., & Denney, R. L. (2012). Evaluation of culturally diverse populations. In D. Faust (Ed.), *Coping with psychiatric and psychological testimony: Based on the original work by Jay Ziskin* (6th ed.). New York: Oxford University Press.

de Lauzon-Guillain, B., Wijndaele, K., Clark, M., Acerini, C. L., Hughes, I. A., Dunger, D. B., & Ong, K. K. (2012). Breastfeeding and infant temperament at age three months. *PLoS ONE, 7*, 182–190.

De Leo, D., Cimitan, A., Dyregrov, K., Grad, O., & Andriessen, K. (2014). *Bereavement after traumatic death: Helping the survivors*. Cambridge, MA: Hogrefe Publishing.

de Oliveira Brito, L. V., Maranhao Neto, G. A., Moraes, H., Emerick, R. S., & Deslandes, A. C. (2014). Relationship between level of independence in activities of daily living and estimated cardiovascular capacity in elder-ly women. *Archives of Gerontology and Geriatrics, 59*, 367–371.

de Onis, M., Garza, C., Onyango, A. W., & Borghi, E. (2007). Comparison of the WHO child growth standards and the CDC 2000 growth charts. *Journal of Nutrition, 137*, 144–148.

de Schipper, E. J., Riksen-Walraven, J. M., & Geurts, S. A. E. (2006). Effects of child–caregiver ratio on the interactions between caregivers and children in child-care centers: An experimental study. *Child Development, 77*, 861–874.

de St. Aubin, E., & McAdams, D. P. (Eds.). (2004). *The generative society: Caring for future generations*. Washington, DC: American Psychological Association.

de Vries, M. W. (1984). Temperament and infant mortality among the Masai of East Africa. *American Journal of Psychiatry, 141*, 1189–1194.

de Vries, R. (1969). Constancy of generic identity in the years 3 to 6. *Monographs of the Society for Research in Child Development, 34* (3, Serial No. 127).

Deal, J. J., & Levenson, A. (2016). *What millennials want from work: How to maximize engagement in today's workforce*. New York: McGraw-Hill Education.

Dean, D. I., O'Muircheartaigh, J., Dirks, H., Waskiewicz, N., Lehman, K., Walker, L., & … Deoni, S. L. (2014). Modeling healthy male white matter and myelin development: 3 through 60 months of age. *Neuroimage, 84*, 742–752.

Deaner, R. O., Balish, S. M., & Lombardo, M. P. (2016). Sex differences in sports interest and motivation: An evolutionary perspective. *Evolutionary Behavioral Sciences, 10*, 73–97.

DeAngelis, T. (2010, March). Menopause, the makeover. *Monitor on Psychology*, pp. 41–43.

Dearing, E., McCartney, K., & Taylor, B. (2009). Does higher quality early child care promote low-income children's math and reading achievement in middle childhood? *Child Development, 80*, 1329–1349.

Deary, I. J. (2012). Intelligence. *Annual Review of Psychology, 63*, 453–482.

Deary, I. J. (2014). The stability of intelligence from childhood to old age. *Current Directions in Psychological Science, 23*, 239–245.

Deater-Deckard, K., & Cahill, K. (2006). Nature and nurture in early childhood. *Blackwell handbook of early childhood development* (pp. 3–21). New York: Blackwell Publishing.

Deb, S., & Adak, M. (2006, July). Corporal punishment of children: Attitude, practice and perception of parents. *Social Science International, 22*, 3–13.

Debast, I., van Alphen, S., Rossi, G., Tummers, J. A., Bolwerk, N., Derksen, J. L., & Rosowsky, E. (2014). Personality traits and personality disorders in late middle and old age: Do they remain stable? A literature review. *Clinical Gerontologist: Journal of Aging and Mental Health, 37*, 253–271.

DeBlois, J. P., & Lefferts, W. K. (2017). Maybe the fountain of youth was actually a treadmill: Role of exercise in reversing microvascular and diastolic dysfunction. *Journal of Physiology, 595*, 5755–5756.

DeCasper, A. J., & Fifer, W. P. (1980). Of human bonding: Newborns prefer their mothers' voices. *Science, 208*, 1174–1176.

DeCasper, A. J., & Prescott, P. (1984). Human newborns' perception of male voices: Preference, discrimination, and reinforcing value. *Developmental Psychobiology, 17*, 481–491.

DeCasper, A. J., & Spence, M. J. (1986). Prenatal maternal speech influences newborns' perception of speech sounds. *Infant Behavior & Development, 9(2)*, 133-150. doi:10.1016/0163-6383(86)90025-1

deCastro, J. (2002). Age-related changes in the social, psychological, and temporal influences on food intake in free-living, healthy, adult humans. *Journals of Gerontology: Series A: Biological Sciences & Medical Sciences, 57A*, M368–M377.

Decety, J., & Jackson, P. L. (2006). A social-neuroscience perspective on empathy. *Current Directions in Psychological Science, 15*, 54–61.

De Conto, C. (2017). Intimité et sexualité en gériatrie. (Intimacy and sexuality in geriatrics.) *NPG Neurologie—Psychiatrie—Gériatrie, 17*, 264–269.

DeFrancisco, B., & Rovee-Collier, C. (2008). The specificity of priming effects over the first year of life. *Developmental Psychobiology, 50*, 486–501.

DeGenova, M. K. (1993). Reflections of the past: New variables affecting life satisfaction in later life. *Educational Gerontology, 19*, 191–201.

Degnen, C. (2007). Minding the gap: The construction of old age and oldness amongst peers. *Journal of Aging Studies, 21*, 69–80.

Dehaene-Lambertz, G. (2017). The human infant brain: A neural architecture able to learn language. *Psychonomic Bulletin & Review, 24*, 48–55.

Dehaene-Lambertz, G., Hertz-Pannier, L., & Dubois, J. (2006). Nature and nurture in language acquisition: Anatomical and functional brain-imaging studies in infants. *Neurosciences, 29*, [Special issue: Nature and nurture in brain development and neurological disorders], 367–373.

Del Giudice, M. (2015). Self-regulation in an evolutionary perspective. In G. E. Gendolla, M. Tops, S. L. Koole, G. E. Gendolla, M. Tops, & S. L. Koole (Eds.), *Handbook of biobehavioral approaches to self-regulation*. New York: Springer Science + Business Media.

DeLamater, J. (2012). Sexual expression in later life: A review and synthesis. *Journal of Sex Research, 49*, 125–141.

Delaney, C. H. (1995). Rites of passage in adolescence. *Adolescence, 30*, 891–897.

DeLisi, M. (2006). Zeroing in on early arrest onset: Results from a population of extreme career criminals. *Journal of Criminal Justice, 34*, 17–26.

Dellmann-Jenkins, M., & Brittain, L. (2003). Young adults' attitudes toward filial responsibility and actual assistance to elderly family members. *Journal of Applied Gerontology, 22*, 214–229.

Delva, J., O'Malley, P., & Johnston, L. (2006, October). Racial/ethnic and socioeconomic status differences in overweight and health-related behaviors among American students: National trends 1986–2003. *Journal of Adolescent Health, 39*, 536–545.

Demaree, H. A., & Everhart, D. E. (2004). Healthy high-hostiles: Reduced parasympathetic activity and decreased sympathovagal flexibility during negative emotional processing. *Personality and Individual Differences, 36*, 457–469.

Demire, M., Jaafar, J., Bilyk, N., & Ariff, M. R. M. (2012). Social skills, friendship and happiness: A cross-cultural investigation. *Journal of Social Psychology, 152*, 379–385.

DeNavas-Walt, C. & Proctor, B. D. (2015). *U.S. Census Bureau, current population reports, P60-252, Income and poverty in the United States: 2014*. Washington, DC: U.S. Government Printing Office.

DeNavas-Walt, C., Proctor, B. D., & Smith, J. C. (2013). *U.S. Census Bureau, Current Population Reports, P60-245, Income, Poverty, and Health Insurance Coverage in the United States: 2012*. Washington, DC: U.S. Government Printing Office.

Denizet-Lewis, B. (2004, May 30). *Friends, friends with benefits and the benefits of the local mall*. New York Times Magazine, pp. 30–35, 54–58.

Dennis, T. A., Cole, P. M., Zahn-Wexler, C., & Mizuta, I. (2002). Self in context: Autonomy and relatedness in Japanese and U.S. mother–preschooler dyads. *Child Development, 73*, 1803–1817.

Dennis, W. (1966). Age and creative productivity. *Journal of Gerontology, 21*, 1–8.

Denny, K., & Zhang, W. (2017). In praise of ambidexterity: How a continuum of handedness predicts social adjustment. *Laterality: Asymmetries of Body, Brain and Cognition, 22*, 181–194.

Dent, C. (1984). Development of discourse rules: Children's use of indexical reference and cohesion. *Developmental Psychology, 20*, 229–234.

de Oliveira, E. A., & Jackson, E. A. (2017). The moderation role of self-perceived maternal empathy in observed mother–child collaborative problem solving. *Infant and Child Development, 26*, 1–13.

Deon, M., Landgraf, S. S., Lamberty, J. F., Moura, D. J., Saffi, J., Wajner, M., & Vargas, C. R. (2015). Protective effect of L-carnitine on Phenylalanine-induced DNA damage. *Metabolic Brain Disease*. Accessed online, 3-14-15; http://www.ncbi.nlm.nih.gov/pubmed/25600689.

DePaolis, R. A., Vihman, M. M., & Nakai, S. (2013). The influence of babbling patterns on the processing of speech. *Infant Behavior & Development, 36*, 642–649.

DeParle, J., & Tavernise, S. (2012, February 17). *Unwed mothers now a majority before age of 30*. New York Times, p. A1.

Department of Labor Women's Bureau. (2017). Occupations by gender share of employment. Accessed online, 11-25-17; https://www.dol.gov/wb/stats/occ_gender_share_em_1020_txt.htm.

DePaulo, B. (2004). *The scientific study of people who are single: An annotated bibliography*. Glendale, CA: Unmarried America.

DePaulo, B. (2006). *Singled out: How singles are stereotyped, stigmatized, and ignored, and still live happily ever after*. New York: St Martin's Press.

De Pauw, S. W., & Mervielde, I. (2011). The role of temperament and personality in problem behaviors of children with ADHD. *Journal of Abnormal Child Psychology: An Official Publication of the International Society for Research in Child and Adolescent Psychopathology, 39*, 277–291.

Der, G., & Deary, I. (2006, March). Age sex differences in reaction time in adulthood: Results from the United Kingdom health and lifestyle survey. *Psychology and Aging, 21*(1), 62–73.

Dereli-İman, E. (2013). Adaptation of social problem solving for children questionnaire in 6 age groups and its relationships with preschool behavior problems. *Kuram Ve Uygulamada Eğitim Bilimleri, 13*, 491–498.

Deruelle, F., Nourry, C., Mucci, P., Bart, F., Grosbois, J. M., Lensel, G. H., & Fabre, C. (2008). Difference in breathing strategies during exercise between trained elderly men and women. *Scandinavian Journal of Medical Science in Sports, 18*, 213–220.

Dervic, K., Friedrich, E., Oquendo, M., Voracek, M., Friedrich, M., & Sonneck, G. (2006, October). Suicide in Austrian children and young adolescents aged 14 and younger. *European Child & Adolescent Psychiatry, 15*, 427–434.

Deshields, T., Tibbs, T., Fan, M. Y., & Taylor, M. (2005, August 12). Differences in patterns of depression after treatment for breast cancer. *Psycho-Oncology*, published online, John Wiley & Sons.

Destounis, S., Hanson, S., Morgan, R., Murphy, P., Somerville, P., Seifert, P., Andolina, V., Aarieno, A., Skolny, M., & Logan-Young, W. (2009). Computer-aided detection of breast carcinoma in standard mammographic projections with digital mammography. *International Journal of Computer Assisted Radiological Surgery, 4*, 331–336.

Deurenberg, P., Deurenberg-Yap, M., Foo, L. F., Schmidt, G., & Wang, J. (2003). Differences in body composition between Singapore Chinese, Beijing Chinese and Dutch children. *European Journal of Clinical Nutrition, 57*, 405–409.

Deurenberg, P., Deurenberg-Yap, M., & Guricci, S. (2002). Asians are different from Caucasians and from each other in their body mass index/body fat percent relationship. *Obesity Review, 3*, 141–146.

Dev, D. A., Speirs, K. E., Williams, N. A., Ramsay, S., McBride, B. A., & Hatton-Bowers, H. (2017). Providers' perspectives on self-regulation impact their use of responsive feeding practices in child care. *Appetite, 118*, 66–74.

DeVader, S. R., Neeley, N. L., Myles, T. D., & Leet, T. L. (2007). Evaluation of gestational weight gain guidelines for women with normal prepregnancy body mass index. *Obstetrics & Gynecology, 110*, 745–751.

Deveny, K. (1994, December 5). Chart of kindergarten awards. *Wall Street Journal*, p. B1.

DeVries, R. (2005). *A pleasing birth*. Philadelphia, PA: Temple University Press

DeWolf, M. (2017, March 1). *12 stats about working women*. Accessed online, 11-25-17; https://blog.dol.gov/2017/03/01/12-stats-about-working-women.

Dey, A. N., & Bloom, B. (2005). Summary health statistics for U.S. children: National Health Interview Survey, 2003. *Vital Health Statistics, 10*(223), 1–78.

Dezutter, J., Waterman, A. S., Schwartz, S. J., Luyckx, K., Beyers, W., Meca, A., Caraway, S. J., et al. (2014). Meaning in life in emerging adulthood: A person-oriented approach. *Journal of Personality 82*, 57–68.

Diambra, L., & Menna-Barreto, L. (2004). Infradian rhythmicity in sleep/wake ratio in developing infants. *Chronobiology International, 21*, 217–227.

Diamond, L. (2003a). Love matters: Romantic relationships among sexual-minority adolescents. In P. Florsheim (Ed.), *Adolescent romantic relations and sexual behavior: Theory, research, and practical implications*. Mahwah, NJ: Lawrence Erlbaum.

Diamond, L. (2003b). Was it a phase? Young women's relinquishment of lesbian/bisexual identities over a 5-year period. *Journal of Personality & Social Psychology, 84*, 352–364.

Diamond, A., & Amso, D. (2008). Contributions of neuroscience to our understanding of cognitive development. Current Directions In *Psychological Science, 17*(2), 136-141. doi:10.1111/j.1467-8721.2008.00563.x

Diamond, L. M., Fagundes, C. P., & Butterworth, M. R. (2010). Intimate relationships across the life span. In M. E. Lamb, A. Freund, & R. M. Lerner (Eds.), *The handbook of life-span development, Vol 2: Social and emotional development*. Hoboken, NJ: John Wiley & Sons Inc.

Diamond, L., & Savin-Williams, R. (2003). The intimate relationships of sexual-minority youths. In G. Adams & M. Berzonsky (Eds.), *Blackwell handbook of adolescence*. Malden, MA: Blackwell Publishers.

Diamond, M. (2013). Transsexuality among twins: Identity concordance, transition, rearing, and orientation. *International Journal of Transgenderism, 14*, 24–38.

Diego, M., Field, T., Hernandez-Reif, M., Vera, Y., Gil, K., & Gonzalez-Garcia, A. (2007). Caffeine use affects pregnancy outcome. *Journal of Child & Adolescent Substance Abuse, 17*, 41–49.

Diego, M. A., Field, T., & Hernandez-Reif, M. (2009). Procedural pain heart rate responses in massaged preterm infants. *Infant Behavior & Development, 32*(2), 226-229. doi:10.1016/j.infbeh.2008.12.001

Diener, M., Isabella, R., Behunin, M., & Wong, M. (2008). Attachment to mothers and fathers during middle childhood: Associations with child gender, grade, and competence. *Social Development, 17*, 84–101.

Dietrich, J. F., Huber, S., Dackermann, T., Moeller, K., & Fischer, U. (2016). Place-value understanding in number line estimation predicts future arithmetic performance. *British Journal of Developmental Psychology, 34*, 502–517.

Dietz, W. H., & Stern, L. (Eds.). (1999). *American Academy of Pediatrics guide to your child's nutrition: Making peace at the table and building healthy eating habits for life*. New York: Villard.

DiGiovanna, A. G. (1994). *Human aging: Biological perspectives*. New York: McGraw-Hill.

Dillaway, H., Byrnes, M., Miller, S., & Rehan, S. (2008). Talking 'among us': How women from different racial-ethnic groups define and discuss menopause. *Health Care for Women International, 29*, 766–781.

Dilworth-Bart, J., & Moore, C. (2006, March). Mercy mercy me: Social injustice and the prevention of environmental pollutant exposures among ethnic minority and poor children. *Child Development, 77*, 247–265.

DiNallo, J. M., Downs, D., & Le Masurier, G. (2012). Objectively assessing treadmill walking during the second and third pregnancy trimesters. *Journal of Physical Activity & Health, 9*, 21–28.

Dinella, L. M., Weisgram, E. S., & Fulcher, M. (2017). Children's gender-typed toy interests: Does propulsion matter? *Archives of Sexual Behavior, 46*, 1295–1305.

Dinero, R., Conger, R., Shaver, P., Widaman, K., & Larsen-Rife, D. (2008). Influence of family of origin and adult romantic partners on romantic attachment security. *Journal of Family Psychology, 22*, 622–632.

Dion, K. L., & Dion, K. K. (1988). Romantic love: Individual and cultural perspectives. In R. J. Sternberg & M. L. Barnes (Eds.), *The psychology of love*. New Haven, CT: Yale University Press.

Dionne, J., & Cadoret, G. (2013). Development of active controlled retrieval during middle childhood. *Developmental Psychobiology, 55*, 443–449.

Diop, A. M. (1989). The place of the elderly in African society. *Impact of Science on Society, 153*, 93–98.

Di Paolo, E. A., Buhrmann, T., & Barandiaran, X. E. (2017). *Sensorimotor life: An enactive proposal*. New York: Oxford University Press.

DiPietro, J. A., Bornstein, M. H., & Costigan, K. A. (2002). What does fetal movement predict about behavior during the first two years of life? *Developmental Psychobiology, 40*, 358–371.

DiPietro, J. A., Costigan, K. A., & Gurewitsch, E. D. (2005). Maternal psychophysiological change during the second half of gestation. *Biological Psychology, 69*, 23–39.

Dittmann, M. (2005). Generational differences at work. *Monitor on Psychology, 36*, 54–55.

Dixon, L., & Browne, K. (2003). The heterogeneity of spouse abuse: A review. *Aggression & Violent Behavior, 8*, 107–130.

Dixon, R., & Cohen, A. (2003). Cognitive development in adulthood. In R. Lerner & M. Easterbrooks (Eds.), *Handbook of psychology: Vol. 6: Developmental psychology*. New York: Wiley.

Dixon, W. E., Jr. (2004). There's a long, long way to go. *PsycCRITIQUES*.

Djurdjinovic, L., & Peters, J. A. (2017). Special issue introduction: Dealing with psychological and social complexity in genetic counseling. *Journal of Genetic Counseling, 26*, 1–4.

Dmitrieva, J., Chen, C., & Greenberg, E. (2004). Family relationships and adolescent psychosocial outcomes: Converging findings from Eastern and Western cultures. *Journal of Research on Adolescence, 14*, 425–447.

Dobele, A. R., Rundle-Thiele, S., & Kopanidis, F. (2014). The cracked glass ceiling: Equal work but unequal status. *Higher Education Research & Development, 33*, 456–468.

Dobson, V. (2000). The developing visual brain. *Perception, 29*, 1501–1503.

Dodge, K. A. (1985). A social information processing model of social competence in children. In M. Perlmutter (Ed.), *Minnesota Symposia on Child Psychology, 18*, 77–126.

Dodge, K. A., Lansford, J. E., & Burks, V. S. (2003). Peer rejection and social information-processing factors in the development of aggressive behavior problems in children. *Child Development, 74*, 374–393.

Dombrovski, A. Y., Siegle, G. J., Szanto, K. K., Clark, L. L., Reynolds, C., & Aizenstein, H. H. (2012). The temptation of suicide: Striatal gray matter, discounting of delayed rewards, and suicide attempts in late-life de-pression. *Psychological Medicine, 42*, 1203–1215.

Dominguez, H. D., Lopez, M. F., & Molina, J. C. (1999). Interactions between perinatal and neonatal associative learning defined by contiguous olfactory and tactile stimulation. *Neurobiology of Learning and Memory, 71*, 272–288.

Donat, D. (2006, October). Reading their way: A balanced approach that increases achievement. *Reading & Writing Quarterly: Overcoming Learning Difficulties, 22*, 305–323.

Dondi, M., Simion, F., & Caltran, G. (1999). Can newborns discriminate between their own cry and the cry of another newborn infant? *Developmental Psychology, 35*, 418–426.

Donini, L., Savina, C., & Cannella, C. (2003). Eating habits and appetite control in the elderly: The anorexia of aging. *International Psychogeriatrics, 15*, 73–87.

Donleavy, G. (2008). No man's land: Exploring the space between Gilligan and Kohlberg. *Journal of Business Ethics, 80*, 807–822.

Donnerstein, E. (2005, January). *Media violence and children: What do we know, what do we do?* Paper presented at the annual National Teaching of Psychology meeting, St. Petersburg Beach, FL.

Dotti Sani, G. M., & Treas, J. (2016). Educational gradients in parents' child-care time across countries, 1965–2012. *Journal of Marriage and Family, 78*, 1083–1096.

Douglass, A., & Klerman, L. (2012). The strengthening families initiative and child care quality improvement: How strengthening families influenced change in child care programs in one state. *Early Education and Development, 23*, 373–392.

Douglass, R., & McGadney-Douglass, B. (2008). The role of grandmothers and older women in the survival of children with kwashiorkor in urban Accra, Ghana. *Research in Human Development, 5*, 26–43.

Doussard-Roosevelt, J. A., Porges, S. W., Scanlon, J. W., Alemi, B., & Scanlon, K. B. (1997). Vagal regulation of heart rate in the prediction of developmental outcome for very low birth weight preterm infants. *Child Development, 68*, 173–186.

Dow, B., & Joosten, M. (2012). Understanding elder abuse: A social rights perspective. *International Psychogeriatrics, 24*, 853–855.

Doyle, P. M., Byrne, C., Smyth, A., & Le Grange, D. (2014). Evidence-based interventions for eating disorders. In C. A. Alfano, & D. C. Beidel (Eds.), *Comprehensive evidence based interventions for children and adolescents*. Hoboken, NJ: John Wiley & Sons Inc.

Doyle, R. (2004a, January). Living together. *Scientific American*, p. 28.

Doyle, R. (2004b, April). By the numbers: A surplus of women. *Scientific American, 290*, 33.

Dozor, A. J., & Amler, R. W. (2013). Children's environmental health. *The Journal Of Pediatrics, 162(1)*, 6-7. doi:10.1016/j.jpeds.2012.10.004

Drane, C. F., Modecki, K. L., & Barber, B. L. (2017). Disentangling development of sensation seeking, risky peer affiliation, and binge drinking in adolescent sport. *Addictive Behaviors, 66*, 60–65.

Draper, T., Holman, T., Grandy, S., & Blake, W. (2008). Individual, demographic, and family correlates of romantic attachments in a group of American young adults. *Psychological Reports, 103*, 857–872.

Dreman, S. (Ed.). (1997). *The family on the threshold of the 21st century*. Mahwah, NJ: Lawrence Erlbaum.

Driscoll, A. K., Russell, S. T., & Crockett, L. J. (2008). Parenting styles and youth well-being across immigrant generations. *Journal of Family Issues, 29*, 185–209.

Driver, J., Tabares, A., & Shapiro, A. (2003). Interactional patterns in marital success and failure: Gottman laboratory studies. In F. Walsh (Ed.), *Normal family processes: Growing diversity and complexity* (3rd ed.). New York: Guilford Press.

Drmanac, R. (2012, June 1). The ultimate genetic test. *Science, 336*, 1110–1112.

Dromi, E. (1987). *Early lexical development*. Cambridge, England: Cambridge University Press.

Dubow, E. F., Huesmann, L. R., Boxer, P., & Smith, C. (2016). Childhood and adolescent risk and protective factors for violence in adulthood. *Journal of Criminal Justice, 45*, 26–31.

Dudding, T. C., Vaizey, C. J., & Kamm, M. A. (2008). Obstetric anal sphincter injury: Incidence, risk factors, and management. *Annals of Surgery, 247*, 224–237.

Duenwald, M. (2003, July 15). After 25 years, new ideas in the prenatal test tube. *New York Times*, p. D5.

Duenwald, M. (2004, May 11). For couples, stress without a promise of success. *New York Times*, p. D3.

Duggan, K. A., & Friedman, H. S. (2014). Lifetime biopsychosocial trajectories of the Terman gifted children: Health, well-being, and longevity. In D. K. Simonton (Ed.), *The Wiley handbook of genius*. New York: Wiley-Blackwell.

Duijts, L, Jaddoe, V. W. V., Hofman, A., & Moll, H. A. (2010, June 21). Prolonged and exclusive breastfeeding reduces the risk of infectious diseases in infancy. *Pediatrics*; doi:10.1542/peds. 2008–3256.

Dumka, L., Gonzales, N., Bonds, D., & Millsap, R. (2009). Academic success of Mexican origin adolescent boys and girls: The role of mothers' and fathers' parenting and cultural orientation. *Sex Roles, 60*, 588–599. http://search.ebscohost.com, doi:10.1007/s11199-008-9518-z

Dumont, C., & Paquette, D. (2013). What about the child's tie to the father? A new insight into fathering, father–child attachment, children's socio-emotional development and the activation relationship theory. *Early Child Development and Care, 183*, 430–446.

Dumont, V., Bulla, J., Bessot, N., Gonidec, J., Zabalia, M., Guillois, B., & Roche-Labarbe, N. (2017). The manual orienting response habituation to repeated tactile stimuli in preterm neonates: Discrimination of stimulus locations and interstimulus intervals. *Developmental Psychobiology, 59*, 590–602.

Duncan, G. J., & Brooks-Gunn, J. (2000). Family poverty, welfare reform, and child development. *Child Development, 71*, 188–196.

Duncan, G. J., Magnuson, K., & Votruba-Drzal, E. (2014). Boosting family income to promote child development. *The Future of Children, 24*, 99–120.

Duncan, G. J., Magnuson, K., & Votruba-Drzal, E. (2017). Moving beyond correlations in assessing the consequences of poverty. *Annual Review of Psychology, 68*, 413–434.

Dundas, E. M., Plaut, D. C., & Behrmann, M. (2013). The joint development of hemispheric lateralization for words and faces. *Journal of Experimental Psychology: General, 142*, 348–358.

Dunford, B. B., Shipp, A. J., Boss, R., Angermeier, I., & Boss, A. D. (2012). Is burnout static or dynamic? A career transition perspective of employee burnout trajectories. *Journal of Applied Psychology, 97*, 637–650.

Dunham, R. M., Kidwell, J. S., & Wilson, S. M. (1986). Rites of passage at adolescence: A ritual process paradigm. *Journal of Adolescent Research, 1*, 139–153.

Dunkel, C. S., Kim, J. K., & Papini, D. R. (2012). The general factor of psychosocial development and its relation to the general factor of personality and life history strategy. *Personality and Individual Differences, 52*, 202–206.

Dunn, M., Thomas, J. O., Swift, W., & Burns, L. (2012). Elite athletes' estimates of the prevalence of illicit drug use: Evidence for the false consensus effect. *Drug and Alcohol Review, 31*, 27–32.

Duplassie, D., & Daniluk, J. C. (2007). Sexuality: Young and middle adulthood. In A. Owens & M. Tupper (Eds.), *Sexual health: Vol. 1, Psychological foundations*. Westport, CT: Praeger.

Dupuis, S. (2009). An ecological examination of older remarried couples. *Journal of Divorce & Remarriage, 50*, 369–387.

Durbin, J. (2003, October 6). Internet sex unzipped. *McCleans*, p. 18.

Duriez, B., Luyckx, K., Soenens, B., & Berzonsky, M. (2012). A process-content approach to adolescent identity formation: Examining longitudinal associations between identity styles and goal pursuits. *Journal of Personality, 80*, 135–161.

Dweck, C. (2002). The development of ability conceptions. In A. Wigfield & J. Eccles (Eds.), *Development of achievement motivation*. San Diego: Academic Press.

Dwyer-Lindgren, L., Bertozzi-Villa, A., Stubbs, R. W., Morozoff, C., et al. (2017). Inequalities in life expectancy among US counties, 1980 to 2014: Temporal trends and key drivers. *JAMA, 177*, 1003–1011.

Dyer, S., & Moneta, G. (2006). Frequency of parallel, associative, and co-operative play in British children of different socioeconomic status. *Social Behavior and Personality, 34*, 587–592.

Dykens, E. M., Roof, E., & Hunt-Hawkins, H. (2016). Cognitive and adaptive advantages of growth hormone treatment in children with Prader-Willi syndrome. *Journal of Child Psychology and Psychiatry*. Accessed online, 3-14-17; http://onlinelibrary.wiley.com/doi/10.1111/jcpp.12601/abstract.

Dyson, A. H. (2003). "Welcome to the jam": Popular culture, school literacy and making of childhoods. *Harvard Educational Review, 73*, 328–361.

Eagly, A. H., & Steffen, V. J. (1986). Gender and aggressive behavior: A meta-analytic review of the social psychological literature. *Psychological Bulletin, 100*, 309–330.

Eagly, A. H., & Wood, W. (2003). The origins of sex differences in human behavior: Evolved dispositions versus social roles. In C. B. Travis (Ed.), *Evolution, gender, and rape* (pp. 265–304). Cambridge, MA: MIT Press.

Eaker, E. D., Sullivan, L. M., Kelly-Hayes, M., D'Agostino, R. B., Sr., & Benjamin, E. J. (2004). Anger and hostility predict the development of atrial fibrillation in men in the Framingham Offspring Study. *Circulation*, 109, 1267–1271.

Earl, R., Burns, N., Nettelbeck, T., & Baghurst, P. (2016). Low-level environmental lead exposure still negatively associated with children's cognitive abilities. *Australian Journal Of Psychology, 68*, 98-106.

Earle, J. R., Perricone, P. J., Davidson, J. K., Moore, N. B., Harris, C. T., & Cotton, S. R. (2007). Premarital sexual attitudes and behavior at a religiously-affiliated university: Two decades of change. *Sexuality & Culture: An Interdisciplinary Quarterly, 11*, 39–61.

Easterbrooks, M., Bartlett, J., Beeghly, M., & Thompson, R. A. (2013). Social and emotional development in infancy. In R. M. Lerner, M. Easterbrooks, J. Mistry, & I. B. Weiner (Eds.), *Handbook of psychology, Vol. 6: Developmental psychology (2nd* ed.). Hoboken, NJ: John Wiley & Sons Inc.

Eastman, Q. (2003, June 20). Crib death exoneration in new gene tests. *Science, 300*, 1858.

Easton, J., Schipper, L., & Shackelford, T. (2007). Morbid jealousy from an evolutionary psychological perspective. *Evolution and Human Behavior, 28*, 399–402.

Eaves, B. J., Feldman, N. H., Griffiths, T. L., & Shafto, P. (2016). Infant-directed speech is consistent with teaching. *Psychological Review, 123*, 758–771.

Eberling, J. L., Wu, C., Tong-Turnbeaugh, R., & Jagust, W. J. (2004). Estrogen- and tamoxifen-associated effects on brain structure and function. *Neuroimage, 21*, 364–371.

Eccles, J., Templeton, J., & Barber, B. (2003). Adolescence and emerging adulthood: The critical passage ways to adulthood. In M. Bornstein & L. Davidson (Eds.*), Well-being: Positive development across the life course.* Mahwah, NJ: Lawrence Erlbaum.

Eckerd, L. (2009). Death and dying course offerings in psychology: A survey of nine Midwestern states. *Death Studies, 33*, 762–770.

Eckerman, C. O., & Oehler, J. M. (1992). Very-low-birthweight newborns and parents as early social partners. In S. L. Friedman & M. D. Sigman (Eds.), *The psychological development of low-birthweight children*. Norwood, NJ: Ablex.

Eckerman, C., & Peterman, K. (2001). Peers and infant social/communicative development. In G. Bremner & A. Fogel (Eds.), *Blackwell handbook of infant development* (pp. 326–350). Malden, MA: Blackwell Publishers.

Edgerley, L., El-Sayed, Y., Druzin, M., Kiernan, M., & Daniels, K. (2007). Use of a community mobile health van to increase early access to prenatal care. *Maternal & Child Health Journal, 11*, 235–239.

Edward, J. (2013). Sibling discord: A force for growth and conflict. *Clinical Social Work Journal, 41*, 77–83.

Edwards, J. (2004). Bilingualism: Contexts, constraints, and identities. *Journal of Language and Social Psychology, 23*, [Special issue: Acting Bilingual and Thinking Bilingual], 135–141.

Edwards, J. G. (2015). Assisted Dying Bill calls for stricter safeguards. *The Lancet, 385*, 686–687

Edwards, L. A., Wagner, J. B., Simon, C. E., & Hyde, D. C. (2016). Functional brain organization for number processing in pre-verbal infants. *Developmental Science, 19*, 757–769.

Ehm, J., Lindberg, S., & Hasselhorn, M. (2013). Reading, writing, and math self-concept in elementary school children: Influence of dimensional comparison processes. *European Journal of Psychology of Education*. Accessed online, 2-18-14; http://link.springer.com/article/10.1007%2Fs10212-013-0198-x#page-1.

Ehrensaft, M., Cohen, P., & Brown, J. (2003). Intergen-erational transmission of partner violence: A 20-year prospective study. *Journal of Consulting & Clinical Psychology, 71*, 741–753.

Ehrensaft, M. K., Knous-Westfall, H. M., Cohen, P., & Chen, H. (2015). How does child abuse history influence parenting of the next generation? *Psychology of Violence, 5*, 16–25.

Eid, M., Riemann, R., Angleitner, A., & Borkenau, P. (2003). Sociability and positive emotionality: Genetic and environmental contributions to the covariation between different facets of extraversion. *Journal of Personality, 71*, 319–346.

Eiden, R., Foote, A., & Schuetze, P. (2007). Maternal cocaine use and caregiving status: Group differences in caregiver and infant risk variables. *Addictive Behaviors, 32*, 465–476.

Eimas, P. D., Sigueland, E. R., Jusczyk, P., & Vigorito, J. (1971). Speech perception in infants. *Science, 171*, 303–306.

Einarson, A., Choi, J., Einarson, T., & Koren, G. (2009). Incidence of major malformations in infants following antidepressant exposure in pregnancy: Results of a large prospective cohort study. *The Canadian Journal of Psychiatry / La Revue Canadienne de Psychiatrie, 54*, 242–246.

Eisbach, A. O. (2004). Children's developing awareness of diversity in people's trains of thought. *Child Development, 75*, 1694–1707.

Eisenberg, N. (2012). *Eight tips to developing caring kids*. Accessed online, 7-15-12; http://www.csee.org/products/87.

Eisenberg, N., Fabes, R. A., Guthrie, I. K., & Reiser, M. (2000). Dispositional emotionality and regulation: Their role in predicting quality of social functioning. *Journal of Personality and Social Psychology, 78*, 136–157.

Eisenberg, N., Spinrad, T. L., & Morris, A. (2014). Empathy-related responding in children. In M. Killen, & J. G. Smetana (Eds.), *Handbook of moral development (2nd ed.)*. New York: Psychology Press.

Eisenberg, N., & Valiente, C. (2002). Parenting and children's prosocial and moral development. In M. Bornstein (Ed.), *Handbook of parenting: Vol. 5: Practical issues in parenting*. Mahwah, NJ: Lawrence Erlbaum.

Eisenberg, N., Valiente, C., & Champion, C. (2004). Empathy-related responding: Moral, social, and socialization correlates. In A. G. Miller (Ed.), *Social psychology of good and evil*. New York: Guilford Press.

Eitel, A., Scheiter, K., Schüler, A., Nyström, M., & Holmqvist, K. (2013). How a picture facilitates the process of learning from text: Evidence for scaffolding. *Learning and Instruction, 28*, 48–63.

Eitel, B. J. (2003). Body image satisfaction, appearance importance, and self-esteem: A comparison of Caucasian and African-American women across the adult lifespan. *Dissertation Abstracts International: Section B: The Sciences & Engineering, 63*, 5511.

Ekinci, B. (2014). The relationships among Sternberg's Triarchic Abilities, Gardner's multiple intelligences, and academic achievement. *Social Behavior and Personality, 42*, 625–633.

El Ayoubi, M., Patkai, J., Bordarier, C., Desfrere, L., Moriette, G., Jarreau, P., & Zeitlin, J. (2016). Impact of fetal growth restriction on neurodevelopmental outcome at 2 years for extremely preterm infants: A single institution study. *Developmental Medicine & Child Neurology, 58*, 1249–1256.

Eley, T., Liang, H., & Plomin, R. (2004). Parental familial vulnerability, family environment, and their interactions as predictors of depressive symptoms in adolescents. *Child & Adolescent Social Work Journal, 21*, 298–306.

Elkind, D. (1996). Inhelder and Piaget on adolescence and adulthood: *A postmodern appraisal. Psychological Science, 7*, 216–220.

Elkind, D. (2007). *The Hurried Child*. Cambridge, MA: DaCapo Press.

Elkins, D. (2009). Why humanistic psychology lost its power and influence in American psychology: Implications for advancing humanistic psychology. *Journal of Humanistic Psychology, 49*, 267–291. http://search.ebscohost.com, doi:10.1177/0022167808323575.

Elliott, K., & Urquiza, A. (2006). Ethnicity, culture, and child maltreatment. *Journal of Social Issues, 62*, 787–809.

Ellis, B. H., MacDonald, H. Z., Lincoln, A. K., & Cabral, H. J. (2008). Mental health of Somali adolescent refugees: The role of trauma, stress, and perceived discrimination. *Journal of Consulting and Clinical Psychology, 76*, 184–193.

Ellis, B. J. (2004). Timing of pubertal maturation in girls: An integrated life history approach. *Psychological Bulletin, 130*, 920–958.

Ellis, L. (2006, July). Gender differences in smiling: An evolutionary neuroandrogenic theory. *Physiology & Behavior, 88*, 303–308.

Elmore, J. G., Jackson, S. L., Abraham, L., Miglioretti, D. L., Carney, P. A., Geller, B. M., Yankaskas, B. C., Kerlikowske, K., Onega, T., Rosenberg, R. D., Sickles, E. A., & Buist, D. S. (2009). Variability in interpretive performance at screening mammography and radiologists' characteristics associated with accuracy. *Radiology, 253*, 641–651.

Elwert, F., & Christakis, N. A. (2008). The effect of widowhood on mortality by the causes of death of both spouses. *American Journal of Public Health, 98*(11), 2092–2098.

Emilson, A., Folkesson, A., & Lindberg, I. M. (2016). Gender beliefs and embedded gendered values in preschool. *International Journal of Early Childhood, 48*, 225–240.

Emslie, C., & Hunt, K. (2008). The weaker sex? Exploring lay understandings of gender differences in life expectancy: *A qualitative study. Social Science & Medicine, 67*, 808–816.

Endo, S. (1992). Infant–infant play from 7 to 12 months of age: An analysis of games in infant–peer triads. *Japanese Journal of Child and Adolescent Psychiatry, 33*, 145–162.

Endrass, T., Schreiber, M., & Kathmann, N. (2012). Speeding up older adults: Age-effects on error processing in speed and accuracy conditions. *Biological Psychology, 89*, 426–432.

Engineer, N., Darwin, L., Nishigandh, D., Ngianga-Bakwin, K., Smith, S. C., & Grammatopoulos, D. K. (2013). Association of glucocorticoid and type 1 corticotropin-releasing hormone receptors gene variants and risk for depression during pregnancy and post-partum. *Journal of Psychiatric Research, 47*, 1166–1173.

England, L. J., Bunnell, R. E., Pechacek, T. F., Tong, V. T., & McAfee, T. A. (2015). Nicotine and the developing human: A neglected element in the electronic cigarette debate. *American Journal Of Preventive Medi-cine, 49*(2), 286-293. doi:10.1016/j.amepre.2015.01.015

England, P., & Li, S. (2006, October). Desegregation stalled: The changing gender composition of college majors, 1971–2002. *Gender & Society, 20*, 657–677.

Engler, J., & Goleman, D. (1992). *The consumer's guide to psychotherapy*. New York: Simon & Schuster.

English, T., & Carstensen, L. L. (2014). Selective narrowing of social networks across adulthood is associated with improved emotional experience in daily life. *International Journal of Behavioral Development, 38*, 195–202.

English, D., Lambert, S. F., & Ialongo, N. S. (2014). Longitudinal associations between experienced racial discrimination and depressive symptoms in African American adolescents. *Developmental Psychology, 50*, 1190–1196.

Englund, K., & Behne, D. (2006). Changes in infant directed speech in the first six months. *Infant and Child Development, 15*(2), 139–160.

Ennett, S. T., & Bauman, K. E. (1996). Adolescent social networks: School, demographic, and longitudinal considerations. *Journal of Adolescent Research, 11*, 194–215.

Enright, E. (2004, July & August). A house divided. AARP Magazine, pp. 54, 57.

Epel, E. (2009). Telomeres in a life-span perspective: A new "psychobiomarker"? *Current Directions in Psychological Science, 18*, 6–10.

Erdley, C. A., & Day, H. J. (2017). Friendship in childhood and adolescence. In M. Hojjat, A. Moyer (Eds.), *The psychology of friendship*. New York: Oxford University Press.

Erikson, E. H. (1963). *Childhood and society*. New York: Norton.

Erickson, J., & Johnson, G. M. (2011). Internet use and psychological wellness during late adulthood. *Canadian Journal on Aging, 30*, 197–209.

Eriksson, L., & Mazerolle, P. (2015). A cycle of violence? Examining family-of-origin violence, attitudes, and intimate partner violence perpetration. *Journal of Interpersonal Violence, 30*, 945–964.

Erwin, P. (1993). *Friendship and peer relations in children*. Chichester, England: Wiley.

Espenschade, A. (1960). Motor development. In W. R. Johnson (Ed.), *Science and medicine of exercise and sports*. New York: Harper & Row.

Estell, D. B., Jones, M. H., Pearl, R., Van Acker, R., Farmer, T. W., & Rodkin, P. C. (2008). Peer groups, popularity, and social preference: Trajectories of social functioning among students with and without learning disabilities. *Journal of Learning Disabilities, 41*, 5–14.

Estévez, E., Emler, N. P., Cava, M. J., & Inglés, C. J. (2014). Psychosocial adjustment in aggressive popular and aggressive rejected adolescents at school. *Psychosocial Intervention, 23*, 57–67.

Etaugh, C. (2018). Midlife transitions. In C. B. Travis, J. W. White, A. Rutherford, W. S. Williams, S. L. Cook, K. F. Wyche (Eds.), *APA handbook of the psychology of women: History, theory, and battlegrounds*. Washington, DC: American Psychological Association.

Ethier, L., Couture, G., & Lacharite, C. (2004). Risk factors associated with the chronicity of high potential for child abuse and neglect. *Journal of Family Violence, 19*, 13–24.

Evans, D. W., Leckman, J. F., Carter, A., Reznick, J. S., Henshaw, D., King, R. A., & Pauls, D. (1997). Ritual, habit, and perfectionism: The prevalence and development of compulsive-like behavior in normal young chil-dren. *Child Development, 68*(1), 58-68. doi:10.2307/1131925

Evans, D.W., & Leckman, J.F. (2006). Origins of obsessive-compulsive disorder: Developmental and evolutionary perspectives. In D.Cicchetti & D.Cohen (Eds) *Developmental Psychopathology*. (2nd edition) NY: Wiley.

Evans, G. W. (2004). The environment of childhood poverty. *American Psychologist, 59*, 77–92.

Evans, R. (2009). A comparison of rural and urban older adults in Iowa on specific markers of successful aging. *Journal of Gerontological Social Work, 52*, 423–438.

Evans, T., Whittingham, K., & Boyd, R. (2012). What helps the mother of a preterm infant become securely attached, responsive and well-adjusted? *Infant Behavior & Development, 35,* 1–11.

Eveleth, P., & Tanner, J. (1976). *Worldwide variation in human growth.* New York: Cambridge University Press.

Evenson, K. R. (2011). Towards an understanding of change in physical activity from pregnancy through postpartum. *Psychology of Sport and Exercise, 12,* 36–45.

Evenson, R. J., & Simon, R. W. (2005). Clarifying the relationship between parenthood and depression. *Journal Of Health And Social Behavior, 46*(4), 341-358. doi:10.1177/002214650504600403

Ezzo, F., & Young, K. (2012). Child Maltreatment Risk Inventory: Pilot data for the Cleveland Child Abuse Potential Scale. *Journal of Family Violence, 27,* 145–155.

Facchini, C., & Rampazi, R. (2009). No longer young, not yet old: Biographical uncertainty in late-adult temporality. *Time & Society, 18,* 351–372.

Fagan, J., & Holland, C. (2007). Racial equality in intelligence: Predictions from a theory of intelligence as processing. *Intelligence, 35,* 319–334.

Fagan, J., & Ployhart, R. E. (2015). The information processing foundations of human capital resources: Leveraging insights from information processing approaches to intelligence. *Human Resource Management Review, 25,* 4–11.

Fagan, M. (2009). Mean length of utterance before words and grammar: Longitudinal trends and developmental implications of infant vocalizations. *Journal of Child Language, 36,* 495–527. http://search.ebscohost.com, doi:10.1017/S0305000908009070.

Falck-Ytter, T., Gredebäck, G., & von Hofsten, C. (2006). Infants predict other people's action goals. *Nature Neuroscience, 9,* 878–879.

Falco, M. (2012, July 3). Since IVF began, 5 million babies born. CNN News. Accessed online, 7-3-12; http://thechart.blogs.cnn.com/2012/07/02/5-million-babies-born-so-far-thanks-to-ivf/.

Falk, D. (2004). Prelinguistic evolution in early hom-inins: Whence motherese? *Behavioral and Brain Sciences, 27,* 491–503.

Fanger, S., Frankel, L., & Hazen, N. (2012). Peer exclusion in preschool children's play: Naturalistic observations in a playground setting. *Merrill-Palmer Quarterly, 58,* 224–254.

Fantz, R. (1963). Pattern vision in newborn infants. *Science, 140,* 296–297.

Farkas, C., & Vallotton, C. (2016). Differences in infant temperament between Chile and the U.S. *Infant Behavior & Development, 44,* 208–218.

Farr, R. H. (2017). Does parental sexual orientation matter? A longitudinal follow-up of adoptive families with school-age children. *Developmental Psychology, 53,* 252–264.

Farrant, B., Fletcher, J., & Maybery, M. (2006, November). Specific language impairment, theory of mind, and visual perspective taking: Evidence for simulation theory and the developmental role of language. *Child Development, 77,* 1842–1853.

Farrar, M., Johnson, B., Tompkins, V., Easters, M., Zilisi-Medus, A., & Benigno, J. (2009). Language and theory of mind in preschool children with specific language impairment. *Journal of Communication Disorders, 42,* 428–441.

Farrell, L., Hollingsworth, B., Propper, C., & Shields, M. A. (2014). The socioeconomic gradient in physical inactivity: Evidence from one million adults in England. *Social Science & Medicine, 123,* 55–63.

Farroni, T., Menon, E., Rigato, S., & Johnson, M. (2007). The perception of facial expressions in newborns. *European Journal of Developmental Psychology, 4,* 2–13.

Farver, J. M., & Frosch, D. L. (1996). L. A. stories: Aggression in preschoolers' spontaneous narratives after the riots of 1992. *Child Development, 67,* 19–32.

Farver, J. M., Kim, Y. K., & Lee-Shin, Y. (1995). Cultural differences in Korean- and Anglo-American preschoolers' social interaction and play behaviors. *Child Development, 66,* 1088–1099.

Farver, J. M., & Lee-Shin, Y. (2000). Acculturation and Korean-American children's social and play behavior. *Social Development, 9,* 316–336.

Farver, J. M., Welles-Nystrom, B., Frosch, D. L., & Wimbarti, S. (1997). Toy stories: Aggression in children's narratives in the United States, Sweden, Germany, and Indonesia. *Journal of Cross-Cultural Psychology, 28,* 393–420.

Farzin, F., Charles, E., & Rivera, S. (2009). Development of multimodal processing in infancy. *Infancy, 14,* 563–578.

Fast, A. A., & Olson, K. R. (2017). Gender devel-opment in transgender preschool children. *Child Development.* Accessed online, 11-10-17; https://www.ncbi.nlm.nih.gov/pubmed/28439873.

Fayers, T., Crowley, T., Jenkins, J. M., & Cahill, D. J. (2003). Medical student awareness of sexual health is poor. *International Journal STD/AIDS, 14,* 386–389.

Fedele, D. A., Tooley, E., Busch, A., McQuaid, E. L., Hammond, S. K., & Borrelli, B. (2016). Comparison of secondhand smoke exposure in minority and nonminority children with asthma. *Health Psychology, 35,* 115–122.

Federal Interagency Forum on Age-Related Statistics. (2000*). Older Americans 2000: Key indicators of well-being.* Hyattsville, MD: Federal Interagency Forum on Age-Related Statistics.

Federal Interagency Forum on Child and Family Statistics. (2003). *America's children:* Key national indicators of well-being, 2003. Federal Interagency Forum on Child and Family Statistics. Washington, DC: U.S. Government Printing Office.

Fedewa, A. L., Black, W. W., & Ahn, S. (2015). Children and adolescents with same-gender parents: A meta-analytic approach in assessing outcomes. *Journal of GLBT Family Studies, 11,* 1–34.

Feeney, B. C., & Collins, N. L. (2003). Motivations for caregiving in adult intimate relationships: Influences on caregiving behavior and relationship functioning. *Personality and Social Psychology Bulletin, 29,* 950–968.

Feigelman, W., Jordan, J., & Gorman, B. (2009). How they died, time since loss, and bereavement outcomes. Omega*: Journal of Death and Dying, 58,* 251–273.

Feinberg, T. E. (2000). The nested hierarchy of consciousness: A neurobiological solution to the problem of mental unity. *Neurocase, 6,* 75–81.

Feldhusen, J. (2003). Precocity and acceleration. *Gifted Education International, 17,* 55–58.

Feldman, R. S. (Ed.). (2018). *The first year of college: Research, theory, and practice on improving the student experience and increasing retention.* New York: Cambridge University Press.

Feldman, R., & Masalha, S. (2007). The role of culture in moderating the links between early ecological risk and young children's adaptation. *Development and Psychopathology, 19,* 1–21.

Feldman, R. S., & Rimé, B. (Eds.). (1991). *Fundamentals of nonverbal behavior.* Cambridge, England: Cambridge University Press.

Feldman, R. S., Tomasian, J., & Coats, E. J. (1999). Adolescents' social competence and nonverbal deception abilities: Adolescents with higher social skills are better liars. *Journal of Nonverbal Behavior, 23,* 237–249.

Feldman, S. S., & Wood, D. N. (1994). Parents' expectations for preadolescent sons' behavioral autonomy: A longitudinal study of correlates and outcomes. *Journal of Research on Adolescence, 4,* 45–70.

Fell, J., & Williams, A. (2008). The effect of aging on skeletal-muscle recovery from exercise: Possible implications for aging athletes. *Journal of Aging and Physical Activity, 16,* 97–115. http://search.ebscohost.com.

Fennell, C., Sartorius, G., Ly, L. P., Turner, L., Liu, P. Y., Conway, A. J., & Handelsman, D. J. (2009). Randomized cross-over clinical trial of injectable vs. implantable depot testosterone for maintenance of testosterone replacement therapy in androgen deficient men. *Clinical Endocrinology, 42,* 88–95.

Fenwick, K. D., & Morrongiello, B. A. (1998). Spatial co-location and infants' learning of auditory visual associations. *Behavior & Development, 21,* 745–759.

Ferguson, C. J. (2013). *Adolescents, crime, and the media: A critical analysis.* New York: Springer Science + Business Media.

Ferguson, C. J., & Donnellan, M. B. (2014). Is the as-sociation between children's baby video viewing and poor language development robust? A reanalysis of Zim-merman, Christakis, and Meltzoff (2007). *Developmental Psychology, 50,* 129–137.

Fergusson, D., Horwood, L., Boden, J., & Jenkin, G. (2007, March). Childhood social disadvantage and smoking in adulthood: Results of a 25-year longitudinal study. *Addiction, 102,* 475–482.

Fergusson, E., Maughan, B., & Golding, J. (2008). Which children receive grandparental care and what effect does it have? *Journal of Child Psychology and Psychiatry, 49,* 161–169.

Fernald, A. (2001). Hearing, listening, and understanding: Auditory development in infancy. In G. Bremner & A. Fogel (Eds.), *Blackwell handbook of infant development.* Malden, MA: Blackwell Publishers.

Fernald, A., & Morikawa, H. (1993). Common themes and cultural variations in Japanese and American mothers' speech to infants. *Child Development, 64,* 637–656.

Fernández, C. (2013). Mindful storytellers: Emerging pragmatics and theory of mind development. *First Language, 33,* 20–46.

Ferri, R., Novelli, L., & Bruni, O. (2017). Sleep structure and scoring from infancy to adolescence. In S. Nevšímalová, O. Bruni (Eds.), *Sleep disorders in children.* Cham, Switzerland: Springer International Publishing.

Feshbach, S., & Tangney, J. (2008). Television view-ing and aggression: Some alternative perspectives. *Perspectives on Psychological Science, 3,* 387–389.

Festinger, L. (1954). A theory of social comparison processes. *Human Relations, 7,* 117–140.

Fiedler, N. L. (2012). Gender (sex) differences in response to prenatal lead exposure. In M. Lewis & L. Kestler (Eds.), *Gender differences in prenatal substance exposure.* Washington, DC: American Psychological Association.

Field, M. J., & Behrman, R. E. (Eds.). (2002). *When children die.* Washington, DC: National Academies Press.

Field, T. (2014*). Touch (2nd* ed.). Cambridge, MA: MIT Press.

Field, T., Diego, M., & Hernandez-Reif, M. (2009). Depressed mothers' infants are less responsive to faces and voices. *Infant Behavior & Development, 32,* 239–244.

Field, T., Greenberg, R., Woodson, R., Cohen, D., & Garcia, R. (1984). Facial expression during Brazelton neonatal assessments. *Infant Mental Health Journal, 5,* 61–71.

Field, T. M. (1982). Individual differences in the expressivity of neonates and young infants. In R. S. Feldman (Ed.), *Development of nonverbal behavior in children.* New York: Springer-Verlag.

Field, T. M., & Millsap, R. E. (1991). Personality in advanced old age: Continuity or change? Journals of Gerontology: Series B: *Psychological Sciences and Social Sciences, 46,* P299–P308.

Field, T., & Walden, T. (1982). Perception and pro-duction of facial expression in infancy and early childhood. In H. Reese & L. Lipsitt (Eds.*), Advances in child development and behavior (Vol. 16).* New York: Academic Press.

Fifer, W. (1987). Neonatal preference for mother's voice. In N. A. Kasnegor, E. M. Blass, & M. A. Hofer (Eds.), Perinatal development: A psychobiological perspective. *Behavioral biology* (pp. 111–124). Orlando, FL: Academic Press.

Figley, C. R. (1973). Child density and the marital relationship. *Journal of Marriage and the Family, 35,* 272–282.

Finer, L. .B. & Philbin, J. M. (2013). Sexual initiation, contraceptive use, and pregnancy among young adolescents. *Pediatrics, 131* (5), 886–891.

Fisch, S. M. (2004). *Children's learning from educational television: Sesame Street and beyond*. Mahwah, NJ: Erlbaum.

Fischer, T. (2007). Parental divorce and children's socio-economic success: *Conditional effects of parental resources prior to divorce, and gender of the child. Sociology, 41,* 475–495.

Fish, J. M. (Ed.). (2001). *Race and intelligence: Separating science from myth*. Mahwah, NJ: Lawrence Erlbaum.

Fisher, C. B. (2004). Informed consent and clinical research involving children and adolescents: Implications of the revised APA Ethics Code and HIPAA. *Journal of Clinical Child & Adolescent Psychology, 33,* 832–839.

Fisher, J. P., Steele, J., Gentil, P., Giessing, J., & Westcott, W. L. (2017). A minimal dose approach to resistance training for the older adult; the prophylactic for aging. *Experimental Gerontology, 99,* 80–86.

Fisher-Thompson, D. (2017). Contributions of look duration and gaze shift patterns to infants' novelty preferences. *Infancy, 22,* 190–222.

Fiske, S. T., & Taylor, S. E. (1991). *Social cognition (2nd* ed.). New York: McGraw-Hill.

Fitzgerald, H. (2006). Cross-cultural research during infancy: Methodological considerations. *Infant Mental Health Journal, 27,* 612–617.

Fitzgerald, P. (2008). A neurotransmitter system theory of sexual orientation. *Journal of Sexual Medicine, 5,* 746–748.

Fitzgerald, D., & White, K. (2002). Linking children's social worlds: Perspective-taking in parent-child and peer contexts. *Social Behavior & Personality, 31,* 509–522.

Fitzpatrick, E. M., Al-Essa, R. S., Whittingham, J., & Fitzpatrick, J. (2017). Characteristics of children with unilateral hearing loss. *International Journal of Audiology, 56,* 819–828.

Fivush, R., Kuebli, J., & Clubb, P. A. (1992). The structure of events and event representations: A developmental analysis. *Child Development, 63,* 188–201.

Flanigan, J. (2005, July 3). Immigrants benefit U.S. economy now as ever. *Los Angeles Times*.

Flavell, J. H. (1996). Piaget's legacy. *Psychological Science, 7,* 200–203.

Fleer, M. (2017). Digital role-play: The changing conditions of children's play in preschool settings. *Mind, Culture, and Activity, 24,* 3–17.

Fleer, M., & González Rey, F. (2017). Beyond pathologizing education: Advancing a cultural historical methodology for the re-positioning of children as successful learners. In M. Fleer, F. González Rey, N. Veresov (Eds.), *Perezhivanie, emotions and subjectivity: Advancing Vygotsky's legacy*. New York: Springer Science + Business Media.

Fleer, M., González Rey, F., & Veresov, N. (2017). *Perezhivanie, emotions and subjectivity: Advancing Vygotsky's legacy.* New York: Springer Science + Business Media.

Fleming, M., Greentree, S., Cocotti-Muller, D., Elias, K., & Morrison, S. (2006, December). Safety in cyberspace: Adolescents' safety and exposure online. *Youth & Society, 38,* 135–154.

Fletcher, A. C., Darling, N. E., Steinberg, L., & Dornbusch, S. M. (1995). The company they keep: Relation of adolescents' adjustment and behavior to their friends' perceptions of authoritative parenting in the social network. *Developmental Psychology, 31,* 300–310.

Fling, B. W., Walsh, C. M., Bangert, A. S., Reuter-Lorenz, P. A., Welsh, R. C., & Seidler, R. D. (2011). Differential callosal contributions to bimanual control in young and older adults. *Journal of Cognitive -Neuroscience, 23,* 2171–2185.

Flom, R., & Bahrick, L. (2007). The development of infant discrimination of affect in multimodal and unimodal stimulation: The role of intersensory redundancy. *Developmental Psychology, 43,* 238–252.

Florsheim, P. (2003). Adolescent romantic and sexual behavior: What we know and where we go from here. In P. *Florsheim (Ed.), Adolescent romantic relations and sexual behavior: Theory, research, and practical implications.* Mahwah, NJ: Lawrence Erlbaum.

Flouri, E. (2005). *Fathering and child outcomes.* New York: Wiley.

Flouri, E., & Midouhas, E. (2017). Environmental adversity and children's early trajectories of problem behavior: The role of harsh parental discipline. *Journal of Family Psychology, 31,* 234–243.

Floyd, R. G. (2005). Information-processing approaches to interpretation of contemporary intellectual assessment instruments. In D. P. Flanagan & P. L. Harrison (Eds.), *Contemporary intellectual assessment: Theories, tests, and issues.* New York: Guilford Press.

Fodaro, L. W. (2017, February 13). Baby in a box? Free bassinets encourage safe sleeping. *New York Times,* A18.

Fok, M. S. M., & Tsang, W. Y. W. (2006). "Development of an instrument measuring Chinese adolescent beliefs and attitudes towards substance use": Response to commentary. *Journal of Clinical Nursing, 15,* 1062–1063.

Folbre, N. (2012, July 2). Price tags for parents. *New York Times*. Accessed online, 7-7-12, Economix. http://economix.blogs.nytimes.com/2012//07/02/price-tags-for-parents.

Folkman, S. (2011). Stress, health, and coping: Synthesis, commentary, and future directions. In S. Folkman (Ed.), *The Oxford handbook of stress, health, and coping.* New York: Oxford University Press.

Forbes. (2014). *The Forbes 2014 retirement guide*. New York: Forbes Magazine.

Ford, J. A. (2007). Alcohol use among college students: A comparison of athletes and nonathletes. *Substance Use & Misuse, 42,* 1367–1377.

Forno, E., and Celedon, J. C. (2009, April). Asthma and ethnic minorities: Socioeconomic status and beyond. *Current Opinion in Allergy and Clinical Immunology, 9* (2), 154–160.

Foroud, A., & Whishaw, I. Q. (2012). The consummatory origins of visually guided reaching in human infants: A dynamic integration of whole-body and upper-limb movements. *Behavioural Brain Research, 231,* 343–355.

Fowers, B. J., & Davidov, B. J. (2006). The virtue of multiculturalism: Personal transformation, character, and openness to the other. *American Psychologist, 61,* 581–594.

Fowler, J. W., & Dell, M. L. (2006). Stages of faith from infancy through adolescence: Reflections on three decades of faith development theory. In E. C. Roehlkepartain, P. E. King, L. Wagener, & P. L. Benson (Eds.), *The handbook of spiritual development in childhood and adolescence*. Thousand Oaks, CA: Sage Publications.

Fowler, R. C. (2017). Reframing the debate about the relationship between learning and development: An effort to resolve dilemmas and reestablish dialogue in a fractured field. *Early Childhood Education Journal, 45,* 155–162.

Fox, M., Cacciatore, J., & Lacasse, J. R. (2014). Child death in the United States: Productivity and the economic burden of parental grief. *Death Studies, 38,* 597–602.

Fraenkel, P. (2003). Contemporary two-parent fami-lies: Navigating work and family challenges. In F. Walsh (Ed.), Normal family processes: *Growing diversity and complexity (3rd* ed.). New York: Guilford Press.

Fraley, R. C., & Spieker, S. J. (2003). Are infant attachment patterns continuously or categorically distributed? A taxometric analysis of Strange Situation behavior. *Developmental Psychology, 39,* 387–404.

Franck, I., & Brownstone, D. (1991). *The parent's desk reference.* New York: Prentice Hall.

Frankenburg, W. K., Dodds, J., Archer, P., Shapiro, H., & Bresnick, B. (1992). The Denver II: A major revision and restandardization of the Denver developmental screening test. *Pediatrics, 89,* 91–97.

Frankenhuis, W. E., Barrett, H., & Johnson, S. P. (2013). Developmental origins of biological motion percep-tion. In K. L. Johnson & M. Shiffrar (Eds.), *People watching: Social, perceptual, and neurophysiological studies of body perception*. New York: Oxford University Press.

Fransson, M., Granqvist, P., Marciszko, C., Hagekull, B., & Bohlin, G. (2016). Is middle childhood attachment related to social functioning in young adulthood? *Scandinavian Journal of Psychology, 57,* 108–116.

Frawley, T. (2008). Gender schema and prejudicial recall: How children misremember, fabricate, and distort gendered picture book information. *Journal of Research in Childhood Education, 22,* 291–303.

Frazier, L. M., Grainger, D. A., Schieve, L. A., & Toner, J. P. (2004). Follicle-stimulating hormone and estradiol levels independently predict the success of assisted reproductive technology treatment. *Fertility and Sterility, 82,* 834–840.

Freedman, A. M., & Ellison, S. (2004, May 6). Testosterone patch for women shows promise. *Wall Street Journal*, pp. A1, B2.

Freedman, D. G. (1979, January). Ethnic differences in babies. *Human Nature*, pp. 15–20.

Freeman, E., Sammel, M., & Liu, L. (2004). Hormones and menopausal status as predictors of depression in women in transition to menopause. *Archives of General Psychiatry, 61,* 62–70.

Freeman, J. M. (2007). Beware: The misuse of technology and the law of unintended consequences. *Neurotherapeutics, 4,* 549–554.

Freud, S. (1920). *A general introduction to psychoanalysis.* New York: Boni & Liveright.

Freud, S. (1922/1959). *Group psychology and the analysis of the ego*. London: Hogarth.

Frewen, A. R., Chew, E., Carter, M., Chunn, J., & Jotanovic, D. (2015). A cross-cultural exploration of parental involvement and child-rearing beliefs in Asian cultures. Early Years: *An International Journal of Research and Development, 35,* 36–49.

Frías, M. T., Shaver, P. R., & Mikulincer, M. (2015). Measures of adult attachment and related constructs. In G. J. Boyle, D. H. Saklofske, & G. Matthews (Eds.*), Measures of personality and social psychological constructs.* San Diego, CA: Elsevier Academic Press.

Friborg, O., Barlaug, D., Martinussen, M., Rosenvinge, J. H., & Hjemdal, O. (2005). Resilience in relation to personality and intelligence. *International Journal of Methods in Psychiatric Research, 14,* 29–42.

Frick, P. J., Cornell, A. H., Bodin, S. D., Dane, H. A., Barry, C. T., & Loney, B. R. (2003). Callous-unemotional traits and developmental pathways to severe conduct problems. *Developmental Psychology, 39,* 246–260.

Fridlund, A. J., Beck, H. P., Goldie, W. D., & Irons, G. (2012). Little Albert: A neurologically impaired child. *History of Psychology*. Accessed online, 7-9-12; http://psycnet.apa.org/psycinfo/2012-01974-001.

Frie, R. (2014). What is cultural psychoanalysis? Psychoanalytic anthropology and the interpersonal tradition. *Contemporary Psychoanalysis, 50,* 371–394.

Friedlander, L. J., Connolly, J. A., Pepler, D. J., & Craig, W. M. (2007). Biological, familial, and peer influences on dating in early adolescence. *Archives of Sexual Behavior, 36,* 821–830.

Friedman, D. E. (2004*). The new economics of preschool.* Washington, DC: Early Childhood Funders' Collaborative/NAEYC.

Friedman, S., Heneghan, A., & Rosenthal, M. (2009). Characteristics of women who do not seek prenatal care and implications for prevention. Journal of Obstetric, Gynecologic, & Neonatal Nursing: *Clinical Scholarship for the Care of Women, Childbearing Families, & Newborns, 38,* 174–181.

Friedrich, J. (2014). Vygotsky's idea of psychological tools. In A. Yasnitsky, R. van der Veer, & M. Ferrari (Eds.), *The Cambridge handbook of cultural-historical psychology.* New York: Cambridge University Press.

Fritz, G., & Rockney, R. (2004). Summary of the practice parameter for the assessment and treatment of children and adolescents with enuresis. Work Group on Quality Issues; *Journal of the American Academy of Child & Adolescent Psychiatry, 43,* 123–125.

Froidevaux, A., Hirschi, A., & Wang, M. (2016). The role of mattering as an overlooked key challenge in retirement planning and adjustment. *Journal of Vocational Behavior, 94,* 57–69.

Frome, P., Alfeld, C., Eccles, J., & Barber, B. (2006, August). Why don't they want a male-dominated job? An investigation of young women who changed their occupational aspirations. *Educational Research and Evaluation, 12,* 359–372.

Fry, C. L. (1985). Culture, behavior, and aging in the comparative perspective. In J. E. Birren & K. W. Schaie (Eds.), *Handbook of the psychology of aging.* New York: Van Nostrand Reinhold.

Fry, P. S., & Debats, D. L. (2010). Psychosocial resources as predictors of resilience and healthy longevity of older widows. In P. S. Fry & C. L. M. Keyes (Eds.), *New frontiers in resilient aging: Life-strengths and well-being in late life* (pp. 185–212). New York: Cambridge University Press.

Fu, X., & Heaton, T. (2008). Racial and educational homogamy: 1980 to 2000. *Sociological Perspectives, 51,* 735–758.

Fu, G., Xu, F., Cameron, C., Heyman, G., & Lee, K. (2007, March). Cross-cultural differences in children's choices, categorizations, and evaluations of truths and lies. *Developmental Psychology, 43*(2), 278–293.

Fugate, W. N., & Mitchell, E. S. (1997). Women's images of midlife: Observations from the Seattle Midlife Women's Health Study. Health Care for *Women International, 18,* 439–453.

Fujisawa, T. X., & Shinohara, K. (2011). Sex differences in the recognition of emotional prosody in late childhood and adolescence. *Journal of Physiological Science, 61,* 429–435.

Fujitsuka, N., Asakawa, A., Morinaga, A., Amitani, M. S., Amitani, H., Katsuura, G., & ... Inui, A. (2016). Increased ghrelin signaling prolongs survival in mouse models of human aging through activation of sirtuin1. *Molecular Psychiatry, 21,* 1613–1623.

Fulcher, M., Sutfin, E. L., & Patterson, C. J. (2008). Individual differences in gender development: Associations with parental sexual orientation, attitudes, and division of labor. *Sex Roles, 58,* 330–341.

Fuligni, A. J. (1997). The academic achievement of adolescents from immigrant families: The roles of family background, attitudes, and behavior. *Child Development, 68,* 351–368.

Fuligni, A. J. (2012). The intersection of aspirations and resources in the development of children from immigrant families. In C. Coll & A. Marks (Eds.), *The immigrant paradox in children and adolescents: Is becoming American a developmental risk?* Washington, DC: American Psychological Association.

Fuligni, A. J., & Fuligni, A. S. (2008). Immigrant families and the educational development of their children. In J. E. Lansford, et al (Eds.), *Immigrant families in contemporary society.* New York: Guilford Press.

Fuligni, A. J., Tseng, V., & Lam, M. (1999). Attitudes toward family obligations among American adolescents with Asian, Latin American, and European backgrounds. *Child Development, 70,* 1030–1044.

Fuligni, A., & Yoshikawa, H. (2003). Socioeconomic resources, parenting, and child development among immigrant families. In M. Bornstein & R. Bradley (Eds.), *Socioeconomic status, parenting, and child development.* Mahwah, NJ: Lawrence Erlbaum.

Fuligni, A., & Zhang, W. (2004). Attitudes toward family obligation among adolescents in contemporary urban and rural China. *Child Development, 75,* 180–192.

Funk, L. (2010). Prioritizing parental autonomy: Adult children's accounts of feeling responsible and supporting aging parents. *Journal of Aging Studies, 24,* 57–64.

Furman, W., & Shaffer, L. (2003). The role of romantic relationships in adolescent development. In P. Florsheim (Ed.), *Adolescent romantic relations and sexual behavior: Theory, research, and practical implications.* Mahwah, NJ: Lawrence Erlbaum.

Furnham, A., & Weir, C. (1996). Lay theories *of child development. Journal of Genetic Psychology, 157,* 211–226.

Furstenberg, F. F., Jr. (1996, June). The future of marriage. *American Demographics,* pp. 34–40.

Fuso, A., Nicolia, V., Ricceri, L., Cavallaro, R. A., Isopi, E., Mangia, F., & Scarpa, S. (2012). S-adenosylmethionine reduces the progress of the Alzheimer-like features induced by B-vitamin deficiency in mice. *Neurobiology of Aging, 33,* e1–e16.

Gagneux, P. (2016). *Assisted reproductive technologies: Evolution of human niche construction?* Paper presented at the annual meeting of the American Association for the Advancement of Science. Washington, DC.

Gaias, L. M., Räikkönen, K., Komsi, N., Gartstein, M. A., Fisher, P. A., & Putnam, S. P. (2012). Cross-cultural temperamental differences in infants, children, and adults in the United States of America and Finland. *Scandinavian Journal of Psychology, 53,* 119–128.

Galambos, N., Leadbeater, B., & Barker, E. (2004). Gender differences in and risk factors for depression in adolescence: A 4-year longitudinal study. *International Journal of Behavioral Development, 28,* 16–25.

Gallagher, J. J. (1994). Teaching and learning: New models. *Annual Review of Psychology, 45,* 171–195.

Galland, B. C., Taylor, B. J., Elder, D. E., & Herbison, P. (2012). Normal sleep patterns in infants and children: A systematic review of observational studies. *Sleep Medicine Reviews, 16,* 213–222.

Gallistel, C. (2007). Commentary on Le Corre & Carey. *Cognition, 105,* 439–445.

Gallup Poll. (2004). How many children? *The Gallup Poll Monthly.*

Galvao, T. F., Silva, M. T., Zimmermann, I. R., Souza, K. M., Martins, S. S., & Pereira, M. G. (2013). Pubertal timing in girls and depression: A systematic review. *Journal of Affective Disorders,* Accessed online, 1-28-14; http://www.ncbi.nlm.nih.gov/pubmed/24274962.

Gamino, L. A., & Ritter, R. R. (2012). Death competence: An ethical imperative. *Death Studies, 36,* 23–40.

Gandhi, P. K., Schwartz, C. E., Reeve, B. B., DeWalt, D. A., Gross, H. E., & Huang, I. (2016). An item-level response shift study on the change of health state with the rating of asthma-specific quality of life: A report from the PROMIS® pediatric asthma study. *Quality of Life Research: An International Journal of Quality of Life Aspects of Treatment, Care & Rehabilitation.* Accessed online, 6-13-16; http://www.ncbi.nlm.nih.gov/pubmed/27061424

Garbarino, J. (2013). The emotionally battered child. In R. D. Krugman & J. E. Korbin (Eds.), *C. Henry Kempe: A 50 year legacy to the field of child abuse and neglect.* New York: Springer Science + Business Media.

Garcia-Moreno, C., Heise, L., Jansen, H. A. F. M., Ellsberg, M., & Watts, C. (2005, November 25). Violence against women. *Science, 310,* 1282–1283.

Garcia-Portilla, M. (2009). Depression and perimenopause: A review. *Actas Españolas de Psiquiatría, 37,* 231–321.

García-Ruiz, M., Rodrigo, M., Hernández-Cabrera, J. A., & Máiquez, M. (2013). Contribution of parents' adult attachment and separation attitudes to parent-adolescent conflict resolution. *Scandinavian Journal of Psychology, 54,* 459–467.

Gardner, H. (2000). *Intelligence reframed: Multiple intelligences for the 21st century.* New York: Basic Books.

Gardner, H. (2006). *Changing minds: The art and science of changing our own and other people's minds.* Cambridge, MA: Harvard Business Press.

Gardner, H., & Moran, S. (2006). The science of multiple intelligences theory: A response to Lynn Waterhouse. *Educational Psychologist, 41,* 227–232.

Gardner, P. (2007). *Parent involvement in the college recruiting process: To what extent?* Collegiate Employment Research Institute, Michigan State University. Research Brief 2–2007.

Garland, E. L., Thielking, P., Thomas, E. A., Coombs, M., White, S., Lombardi, J., & Beck, A. (2017). Linking dispositional mindfulness and positive psychological processes in cancer survivorship: A multivariate path analytic test of the mindfulness-to-meaning theory. *Psycho-Oncology, 26,* 686–692.

Garlick, D. (2003). Integrating brain science research with intelligence research. *Current Directions in Psychological Science, 12,* 185–189.

Gartrell, N., & Bos, H. (2010). US national longitudinal lesbian family study: Psychological adjustment of 17-year-old adolescents. *Pediatrics, 126,* 28–36.

Gartstein, M. A., Prokasky, A., Bell, M. A., Calkins, S., Bridgett, D. J., Braungart-Rieker, J., & ... Seamon, E. (2017). Latent profile and cluster analysis of infant temperament: Comparisons across person-centered approaches. *Developmental Psychology, 53,* 1811–1825.

Gates, G. J. (2013, February). *LGBT parenting in the United States.* Los Angeles: Williams Institute.

Gatz, M. (1997, August). Variations of depression in later life. Paper presented at the annual convention of the American Psychological Association, Chicago.

Gaulden, M. E. (1992). Maternal age effect: The enigma of Down syndrome and other trisomic conditions. *Mutation Research, 296,* 69–88.

Gauthier, S., & Scheltens, P. (2009). Can we do better in developing new drugs for Alzheimer's disease? *Alzheimer's & Dementia, 5,* 489–491.

Gauvain, M. (1998). Cognitive development in social and cultural context. *Current Directions in Psychological Science, 7,* 188–194.

Gavin, T., & Myers, A. (2003). Characteristics, enrollment, attendance, and drop-out patterns of older adults in beginner Tai-Chi and line-dancing programs. *Journal of Aging & Physical Activity, 11,* 123–141.

Gawande, A. (2007, April 30). The way we age now. *New Yorker,* pp. 49–59.

Gazmararian, J. A., Petersen, R., Spitz, A. M., Goodwin, M. M., Saltzman, L. E., & Marks, J. S. (2000). Violence and reproductive health: Current knowledge and future research directions. *Mat Child Health, 4,* 79–84.

Geary, D. C., & Berch, D. B. (2016). *Evolutionary perspectives on child development and education.* Cham, Switzerland: Springer International Publishing.

Gelman, C. R., Tompkins, C. J., & Ihara, E. S. (2014). The complexities of caregiving for minority older adults: Rewards and challenges. In K. E. Whitfield, T. A. Baker, C. M. Abdou, J. L. Angel, L. A. Chadiha, K. Gerst-Emerson, ... R. J. Thorpe (Eds.), *Handbook of minority aging.* New York: Springer Publishing Co.

Gelman, S. A., Taylor, M. G., & Nguyen, S. (2004). Mother–child conversations about gender. *Monographs of the Society for Research in Child Development, 69.*

Genetics Home Reference. (2017). *Your Guide to Understanding Genetic Conditions.* Washington, DC: US National Library of Medicine. Accessed online 10-25-17; https://ghr.nlm.nih.gov/.

Genevro, J. L., & Miller, T. L. (2010). The emotional and economic costs of bereavement in health care settings. *Psychologica Belgica, 50,* 69–88.

Genovese, J. (2006). Piaget, pedagogy, and evolutionary psychology. *Evolutionary Psychology, 4,* 127–137.

Gentilucci, M., & Corballis, M. (2006). From manual gesture to speech: A gradual transition. *Neuroscience & Biobehavioral Reviews, 30,* 949–960.

Gerard, C. M., Harris, K. A., & Thach, B. T. (2002). Spontaneous arousals in supine infants while swaddled and unswaddled during rapid eye movement and quiet sleep. *Pediatrics, 110,* 70.

Gerend, M., Aiken, L., & West, S. (2004). Personality factors in older women's perceived susceptibility to diseases of aging. *Journal of Personality, 72,* 243–270.

Gerressu, M., Mercer, C., Graham, C., Wellings, K., & Johnson, A. (2008). Prevalence of masturbation and associated factors in a British national probability survey. *Archives of Sexual Behavior, 37,* 266–278.

Gerrish, C. J., & Mennella, J. A. (2000). Short-term influence of breastfeeding on the infants' interaction with the environment. *Developmental Psychobiology, 36,* 40–48.

Gershkoff-Stowe, L., & Thelen, E. (2004). U-shaped changes in behavior: A dynamic systems perspective. *Journal of Cognition & Development, 5,* 88–97.

Gershoff, E. T. (2002). Parental corporal punishment and associated child behaviors and experiences: A meta-analytic and theoretical review. *Pychological Bulletin, 128*, 539–579.

Gershoff, E. T., Lansford, J. E., Sexton, H. R., Davis-Kean, P., & Sameroff, A. J. (2012). Longitudinal links between spanking and children's externalizing behaviors in a national sample of White, Black, Hispanic, and Asian American families. *Child Development, 83*(3), 838–843.

Gervain, J., Macagno, F., Cogoi, S., Peña, M., & Mehler, J. (2008). The neonate brain detects speech structure. *PNAS Proceedings of the National Academy of Sciences of the United States of America, 105*, 14222–14227.

Gesell, A. L. (1946). The ontogenesis of infant behavior. In L. Carmichael (Ed.), *Manual of child psychology*. New York: Harper.

Geurts, T., van Tilburg, T. G., & Poortman, A. (2012). The grandparent-grandchild relationship in childhood and adulthood: A matter of continuation? *Personal Relationships, 19*, 267–278.

Gfellner, B. M., & Armstrong, H. D. (2013). Racial-ethnic identity and adjustment in Canadian indigenous adolescents. *Journal of Early Adolescence, 33*, 635–662.

Ghazi, A., Henis-Korenblit, S., & Kenyon, C. (2009). A transcription elongation factor that links signals from the reproductive system to lifespan extension in Caenorhabditis elegans. *PLoS Genetics, 5*, 71–77.

Ghetti, S., & Angelini, L. (2008). The development of recollection and familiarity in childhood and adolescence: Evidence from the dual-process signal detection model. *Child Development, 79*, 339–358.

Ghisletta, P., Kennedy, K., Rodrigue, K., Lindenberger, U., & Raz, N. (2010). Adult age differences and the role of cognitive resources in perceptual-motor skill acquisition: Application of a multilevel negative exponential model. *Journals of Gerontology: Series B: Psychological Sciences and Social Sciences, 65B*, 163–173.

Ghule, M., Balaiah, D., & Joshi, B. (2007). Attitude towards premarital sex among rural college youth in Maharashtra, India. *Sexuality & Culture, 11*, 1–17.

Gibbs, N. (2002, April 15). Making time for a baby. *Time*, pp. 48–54.

Gibson, E. J., & Walk, R. D. (1960). The "visual cliff." *Scientific American, 202*, 64–71.

Gidron, Y., Russ, K., Tissarchondou, H., & Warner, J. (2006, July). The relation between psychological factors and DNA damage: A critical review. *Biological Psychology, 72*, 291–304.

Giedd, J. N. (2012). The digital revolution and adolescent brain evolution. *Journal of Adolescent Health, 51*, 101–105.

Gifford-Smith, M., & Brownell, C. (2003). Childhood peer relationships: Social acceptance, friendships, and peer networks. *Journal of School Psychology, 41*, 235–284.

Gilbert, D. (2006). *Stumbling on happiness*. New York: Knopf.

Gilbert, L. A. (1994). Current perspectives on dual-career families. *Current Directions in Psychological Science, 3*, 101–105.

Gillham, A., Law, A., & Hickey, L. (2010). A psychodynamic perspective. In C. Cupitt (Ed.), *Reaching out: The psychology of assertive outreach*. New York, NY: Routledge/Taylor & Francis Group.

Gillies, R. M. (2014). Developments in cooperative learning: Review of research. *Anales De Psicología, 30*, 792–801.

Gilligan, C. (1982). *In a different voice: Psychological theory and women's development*. Cambridge, MA: Harvard University Press.

Gilligan, C. (1987). Adolescent development reconsidered. In C. E. Irwin (Ed.), *Adolescent social behavior and health*. San Francisco: Jossey-Bass.

Gilligan, C. (2004). Recovering psyche: Reflections on life-history and history. *Annual of Psychoanalysis, 32*, 131–147.

Gilligan, C., Lyons, N. P., & Hammer, T. J. (Eds.). (1990). *Making connections*. Cambridge, MA: Harvard University Press.

Gilmore, C. K., & Spelke, E. S. (2008). Children's understanding of the relationship between addition and subtraction. *Cognition, 107*, 932–945.

Gillmore, M., Gilchrist, L., Lee, J., & Oxford, M. (2006, August). Women who gave birth as unmarried adolescents: Trends in substance use from adolescence to adulthood. *Journal of Adolescent Health, 39*, 237–243.

Ginzberg, E. (1972). Toward a theory of occupational choice: A restatement. *Vocational Guidance Quarterly, 12*, 10–14.

Gitlin, L., Reever, K., Dennis, M., Mathieu, E., & Hauck, W. (2006, October). Enhancing quality of life of families who use adult day services: Short- and long-term effects of the Adult Day Services Plus Program. *Gerontologist, 46*, 630–639.

Gitto, E., Aversa, S., Salpietro, C., Barberi, I., Arrigo, T., Trimarchi, G., & Pellegrino, S. (2012). Pain in neonatal intensive care: Role of melatonin as an analgesic antioxidant. *Journal of Pineal Research: Molecular, Biological, Physiological and Clinical Aspects of Melatonin, 52*, 291–295.

Glaser, D. (2012). Effects of child maltreatment on the developing brain. In M. Garralda & J. Raynaud (Eds.), *Brain, mind, and developmental psychopathology in childhood*. Lanham, MD: Jason Aronson.

Glasgow, K. L., Dornbusch, S. M., Troyer, L., Steinberg, L., & Ritter, P. L. (1997). Parenting styles, adolescents' attributions, and educational outcomes in nine heterogeneous high schools. *Child Development, 68*, 507–529.

Glasson, E. J., Jacques, A., Wong, K., Bourke, J., & Leonard, H. (2016). Improved survival in Down syndrome over the last 60 years and the impact of perinatal factors in recent decades. *Journal of Pediatrics, 169*, 214–220.

Glatt, S., Chayavichitsilp, P., Depp, C., Schork, N., & Jeste, D. (2007). Successful aging: From phenotype to genotype. *Biological Psychiatry, 62*, 282–293.

Glauber, R. (2017). Gender differences in spousal care across the later life course. *Research on Aging, 39*, 934–959.

Gleason, J. B., & Ely, R. (2002). Gender differences in language development. In A. McGillicuddy-De Lisi & R. De Lisi (Eds.), *Biology, society, and behavior: The development of sex differences in cognition* (pp. 127–154). Westport, CT: Ablex Publishing.

Gleason, J. B., Perlmann, R. U., Ely, R., & Evans, D. W. (1994). The babytalk register: Parents' use of diminutives. In J. L. Sokolov & C. E. Snow (Eds.), *Handbook of research in language development using CHILDES*. Mahwah, NJ: Lawrence Erlbaum.

Gleason, M., Iida, M., & Bolger, N. (2003). Daily supportive equity in close relationships. *Personality & Social Psychology Bulletin, 29*, 1036–1045.

Glick, P., & Fiske, S. T. (2012). An ambivalent alliance: Hostile and benevolent sexism as complementary justifications for gender inequality. In J. Dixon & M. Levine (Eds.), *Beyond prejudice: Extending the social psychology of conflict, inequality and social change*. New York: Cambridge University Press.

Glick, P., & Raberg, L. (2018). Benevolent sexism and the status of women. In C. B. Travis, J. W. White, A. Rutherford, W. S. Williams, S. L. Cook, K. F. Wyche (Eds.), *APA handbook of the psychology of women: History, theory, and battlegrounds*. Washington, DC: American Psychological Association.

Gliga, T., Elsabbagh, M., Andravizou, A., & Johnson, M. (2009). Faces attract infants' attention in complex displays. *Infancy, 14*, 550–562.

Glina, S., Cohen, D. J., & Vieira, M. (2014). Diagnosis of erectile dysfunction. *Current Opinion in Psychiatry, 27*, 394–399.

Glynn, L. M., & Sandman, C. A. (2014). Evaluation of the association between placental corticotrophin-releasing hormone and postpartum depressive symptoms. *Psychosomatic Medicine, 76*, 355–362.

Goble, M. M. (2008). Medical and psychological complications of obesity. In H. D. Davies, et al. (Eds.), *Obesity in childhood and adolescence, Vol 1: Medical, biological, and social issues*. Westport, CT: Praeger Publishers/Greenwood Publishing.

Goble, P., Eggum-Wilkens, N. D., Bryce, C. I., Foster, S. A., Hanish, L. D., Martin, C. L., & Fabes, R. A. (2017). The transition from preschool to first grade: A transactional model of development. *Journal of Applied Developmental Psychology, 49*, 55–67.

Goede, I., Branje, S., & Meeus, W. (2009). Developmental changes in adolescents' perceptions of relationships with their parents. *Journal of Youth and Adolescence, 38*, 75–88.

Goetz, A., & Shackelford, T. (2006). Modern application of evolutionary theory to psychology: Key concepts and clarifications. *American Journal of Psychology, 119*, 567–584.

Gogtay, N., Sporn, A., Clasen, L. S., Nugent, T. I., Greenstein, D., Nicolson, R., & … Rapoport, J. L. (2004). Comparison of Progressive Cortical Gray Matter Loss in Childhood-Onset Schizophrenia With That in Childhood-Onset Atypical Psychoses. *Archives Of General Psychiatry, 61*(1), 17-22. doi:10.1001/archpsyc.61.1.17

Goldberg, A. E. (2004). But do we need universal grammar? Comment on Lidz et al. *Cognition, 94*, 77–84.

Goldberg, A. E. (2010) *Gay and lesbian parents and their children: Research on the family life cycle*. Washington, DC: American Psychological Association.

Goldberg, W. A. (2014). *Father time: The social clock and the timing of fatherhood*. New York: Palgrave Macmillan.

Goldfield, G. S. (2012). Making access to TV contingent on physical activity: Effects on liking and relative reinforcing value of TV and physical activity in overweight and obese children. *Journal of Behavioral Medicine, 35*, 1–7.

Goldman, D., & Domschke, K. (2014). Making sense of deep sequencing. *International Journal of Neuropsychopharmacology, 17*, 1717–1725.

Goldney, R. D. (2012). Neither euthanasia nor suicide, but rather assisted death. *Australian and New Zealand Journal of Psychiatry, 46*, 185–187.

Goldscheider, F. K. (1994). Divorce and remarriage: Effects on the elderly population. *Reviews in Clinical Gerontology, 4*, 253–259.

Goldschmidt, L., Richardson, G., Willford, J., & Day, N. (2008). Prenatal marijuana exposure and intelligence test performance at age 6. *Journal of the American Academy of Child & Adolescent Psychiatry, 47*, 254–263.

Goldstein, S., & Brooks, R. B. (2013). *Handbook of resilience in children* (2nd ed.). New York: Springer Science + Business Media.

Golombok, S., Golding, J., Perry, B., Burston, A., Murray, C., Mooney-Somers, J., & Stevens, M. (2003). Children with lesbian parents: A community study. *Developmental Psychology, 39*, 20–33.

Golombok, S., & Tasker, F. (1996). Do parents influence the sexual orientation of their children? Findings from a longitudinal study of lesbian families. *Developmental Psychology, 32*, 3–11.

Gomes, A. I., Barros, L., & Pereira, A. I. (2017). Predictors of parental concerns about child weight in parents of healthy-weight and overweight 2–6 year olds. *Appetite, 108*, 491–497.

Gommans, R., Sandstrom, M. J., Stevens, G. M., ter Bogt, T. M., & Cillessen, A. N. (2017). Popularity, likeability, and peer conformity: Four field experiments. *Journal of Experimental Social Psychology, 73*, 279–289.

Göncü, A., & Gauvain, M. (2012). Sociocultural approaches to educational psychology: Theory, research, and application. In K. R. Harris, S. Graham, T. Urdan, C. B. McCormick, G. M. Sinatra, & J. Sweller (Eds.), *APA educational psychology handbook, Vol 1: Theories, constructs, and critical issues*. Washington, DC: American Psychological Association.

Gondolf, E. W. (1985). Fighting for control: A clinical assessment of men who batter. *Social Casework, 66*, 48–54.

Good, C., Aronson, J., & Harder, J. A. (2008). Problems in the pipeline: Stereotype threat and women's achievement in high-level math courses. *Journal Of Applied Developmental Psychology, 29*(1), 17-28. doi:10.1016/j.appdev.2007.10.004

Goode, E. (1999, January 12). Clash over when, and how, to toilet-train. *New York Times*, pp. A1, A17.

Goode, E. (2004, February 3). Stronger warning is urged on antidepressants for teenagers. *New York Times*, p. A12.

Goodlin-Jones, B. L., Burnham, M. M., & Anders, T. F. (2000). Sleep and sleep disturbances: Regulatory processes in infancy. In A. J. Sameroff, M. Lewis, et al. (Eds.), *Handbook of developmental psychopathology* (2nd ed.). New York: Kluwer Academic/Plenum Publishers.

Goodman, E., Huang, B., Schafer-Kalkhoff, T., & Adler, N. E. (2007). Perceived socioeconomic status: A new type of identity which influences adolescents' self-rated health. *Journal of Adolescent Health: Official Publication of the Society for Adolescent Medicine, 41*, 479–487.

Goodman, J. S., Fields, D. L., & Blum, T. C. (2003). Cracks in the glass ceiling: In what kinds of organizations do women make it to the top? *Group & Organization Management, 28*, 475–501.

Goodman, S., Broth, M., Hall, C., & Stowe, Z. (2008). Treatment of postpartum depression in mothers: Secondary benefits to the infants. *Infant Mental Health Journal, 29*, 492–513.

Goodnight, J. A., Donahue, K. L., Waldman, I. D., et al. (2016). Genetic and environmental contributions to associations between infant fussy temperament and antisocial behavior in childhood and adolescence. *Behavior Genetics, 46*, 680–692.

Goodnough, A., & Atkinson, S. (2016, April 30). A potent side effect to the Flint water crisis: Mental health problems. *New York Times*, p. A16.

Goodwin, M. H. (1990). Tactical uses of stories: Participation frameworks within girls' and boys' disputes. *Discourse Processes, 13*, 33–71.

Goold, J. E., & Meng, M. (2017). Categorical learning revealed in activity pattern of left fusiform cortex. *Human Brain Mapping, 38*, 3648–3658.

Goold, S. D., Williams, B., & Arnold, R. M. (2000). Conflicts regarding decisions to limit treatment: A differential diagnosis. *JAMA: Journal of the American Medical Association, 283*, 909–914.

Goorabi, K., Hoseinabadi, R., & Share, H. (2008). Hearing aid effect on elderly depression in nursing home patients. *Asia Pacific Journal of Speech, Language, and Hearing, 11*, 119–124.

Gopinath, B., Schneider, J., Hickson, L., McMahon, C. M., Burlutsky, G., Leeder, S. R., & Mitchell, P. (2012). Hearing handicap, rather than measured hearing impairment, predicts poorer quality of life over 10 years in older adults. *Maturitas, 72*, 146–151.

Gopnik, A. (2012, January 28). What's wrong with the teenage mind? *Wall Street Journal*, C1–C2.

Gopnik, A. I., O'Grady, S., Lucas, C. G., Griffiths, T. L., Wente, A., et al. (2017). Changes in cognitive flexibility and hypothesis search across human life history from childhood to adolescence to adulthood. *PNAS, 114*, 892–899.

Gorchoff, S., John, O., & Helson, R. (2008). Contextualizing change in marital satisfaction during middle age: An 18-year longitudinal study. *Psychological Science, 19*, 1194–1200.

Gordon, I., Pratt, M., Bergunde, K., Zagoory-Sharon, O., & Feldman, R. (2017). Testosterone, oxytocin, and the development of human parental care. *Hormones and Behavior, 93*, 184–192.

Gordon, I., Voos, A. C., Bennett, R. H., Bolling, D. Z., Pelphrey, K. A., & Kaiser, M. D. (2013). Brain mechanisms for processing affective touch. *Human Brain Mapping, 34*, 914–922.

Gordon, N. (2007). The cerebellum and cognition. *European Journal of Paediatric Neurology, 30*, 214–220.

Gören, J. L. (2008). Antidepressants use in pediatric populations. *Expert Opinions on Drug Safety, 7*, 223–225.

Gorman, A. (2010, January 7). UCLA study says legalizing undocumented immigrants would help the economy. *Los Angeles Times*.

Gormley, W. T., Jr., Gayer, T., Phillips, D., & Dawson, B. (2005). The effects of universal pre-K on cognitive development. *Developmental Psychology, 41*, 872–884.

Gostin, L. (2006, April). Physician-assisted suicide: A legitimate medical practice? *JAMA: Journal of the American Medical Association, 295*, 1941–1943.

Gottfried, A., Gottfried, A., & Bathurst, K. (2002). Maternal and dual-earner employment status and parenting. In M. Bornstein (Ed.), *Handbook of parenting: Vol. 2: Biology and ecology of parenting*. Mahwah, NJ: Lawrence Erlbaum.

Gottlieb, G., & Blair, C. (2004). How early experience matters in intellectual development in the case of poverty. *Preventive Science, 5*, 245–252.

Gould, R. L. (1978). *Transformations: Growth and change in adult life*. New York: Simon & Schuster.

Gould, R. L. (1980). Transformations during adult years. In R. Smelzer and E. Erickson (Eds.), *Themes of love and work in adulthood*. Cambridge, MA: Harvard University Press.

Gould, S. J. (1977). *Ontogeny and phylogeny*. Cambridge, MA: Harvard University Press.

Gow, A., Pattie, A., Whiteman, M., Whalley, L., & Deary, I. (2007). Social support and successful aging: Investigating the relationships between lifetime cognitive change and life satisfaction. *Journal of Individual Differences, 28*, 103–115.

Gowey, M. A., Reiter-Purtill, J., Becnel, J., Peugh, J., Mitchell, J. E., & Zeller, M. H. (2016). Weight-related correlates of psychological dysregulation in adolescent and young adult (AYA) females with severe obesity. *Appetite, 99*, 211–218.

Goyal, M. S., Vlassenko, A. G., Blazey, T. M., Su, Y., Couture, L. E., Durbin, T. J., et al. (2017). Loss of brain aerobic glycolysis in normal human aging. *Cell Metabolism, 26*, 353–360.

Goyette-Ewing, M. (2000). Children's after-school arrangements: A study of self-care and developmental outcomes. *Journal of Prevention & Intervention in the Community, 20*, 55–67.

Grabner, R. H., Neubauer, A., C., & Stern, E. (2006). Superior performance and neural efficiency: The impact of intelligence and expertise. *Brain Research Bulletin, 69*, 422–439.

Graddol, D. (2004, February 27). The future of language. *Science, 303*, 1329–1331.

Grady, D. (2009, November 2). Quandary with mammograms: Get a screening, or just skip it? *New York Times*, p. D1.

Graf Estes, K. (2014). Learning builds on learning: Infants' use of native language sound patterns to learn words. *Journal of Experimental Child Psychology, 126*, 313–327.

Graham, J. E., Christian, L. M., & Kiecolt-Glaser, J. K. (2006). Stress, age, and immune function: Toward a lifespan approach. *Journal of Behavioral Medicine, 29*, 389–402.

Graham, S. (1994). Motivation in African Americans. *Review of Educational Research, 64*, 55–117.

Grall, T. S. (2009). *Custodial mothers and fathers and their child support: 2007*. Washington, DC: U.W. Department of Commerce.

Granat, A., Gadassi, R., Gilboa-Schechtman, E., & Feldman, R. (2017). Maternal depression and anxiety, social synchrony, and infant regulation of negative and positive emotions. *Emotion, 17*, 11–27.

Granek, L., Barrera, M., Scheinemann, K., & Bartels, U. (2015). When a child dies: Pediatric oncologists' follow-up practices with families after the death of their child. *Psycho-Oncology*. Accessed online, 4-2-15; http://www.ncbi.nlm.nih.gov/pubmed/25707675.

Granic, I., Hollenstein, T., & Dishion, T. (2003). Longitudinal analysis of flexibility and reorganization in early adolescence: A dynamic systems study of family interactions. *Developmental Psychology, 39*, 606–617.

Grant, C., Wall, C., Brewster, D., Nicholson, R., Whitehall, J., Super, L., et al. (2007). Policy statement on iron deficiency in pre-school-aged children. *Journal of Paediatrics and Child Health, 43*, 513–521.

Grant, R. J. (2017). *Play-based intervention for autism spectrum disorder and other developmental disabilities*. New York: Routledge/Taylor & Francis Group.

Graves, T. A., Tabri, N., Thompson-Brenner, H., Franko, D. L., Eddy, K. T., Bourion-Bedes, S., & … Thomas, J. J. (2017). A meta-analysis of the relation between therapeutic alliance and treatment outcome in eating disorders. *International Journal of Eating Disorders, 50*, 323–340.

Gray, C., Ferguson, J., Behan, S., Dunbar, C., Dunn, J., & Mitchell, D. (2007, March). Developing young readers through the linguistic phonics approach. *International Journal of Early Years Education, 15*, 15–33.

Gredebäck, G., Eriksson, M., Schmitow, C., Laeng, B., & Stenberg, G. (2012). Individual differences in face processing: Infants' scanning patterns and pupil dilations are influenced by the distribution of parental leave. *Infancy, 17*, 79–101.

Gredler, M. E. (2012). Understanding Vygotsky for the classroom: Is it too late? *Educational Psychology Review, 24*, 113–131.

Gredler, M. E., & Shields, C. C. (2008). *Vygotsky's legacy: A foundation for research and practice*. New York: Guilford Press.

Green, C. S., & Bavelier, D. (2012). Learning, attentional control, and action video games. *Current Biology, 22*, 197–206.

Green, M. H. (1995). Influences of job type, job status, and gender on achievement motivation. *Current Psychology: Developmental, Learning, Personality, Social, 14*, 159–165.

Green, M., DeCourville, N., & Sadava, S. (2012). Positive affect, negative affect, stress, and social support as mediators of the forgiveness-health relationship. *Journal of Social Psychology, 152*, 288–307.

Greenberg, J. (2012). Psychoanalysis in North America after Freud. In G. O. Gabbard, B. E. Litowitz, & P. Williams (Eds.), *Textbook of psychoanalysis* (2nd ed.). Arlington, VA: American Psychiatric Publishing, Inc.

Greenberg, L., Cwikel, J., & Mirsky, J. (2007, January). Cultural correlates of eating attitudes: A comparison between native-born and immigrant university students in Israel. *International Journal of Eating Disorders, 40*, 51–58.

Greene, K., Krcmar, M., Walters, L. H., Rubin, D. L., & Hale, J. L. (2000). Targeting adolescent risk-taking behaviors: The contribution of egocentrism and sensation-seeking. *Journal of Adolescence, 23*, 439–461.

Greene, M. M., Patra, K., Silvestri, J. M., & Nelson, M. N. (2013). Re-evaluating preterm infants with the Bayley-III: Patterns and predictors of change. *Research in Developmental Disabilities, 34*(7), 2107–2117.

Greene, S., Anderson, E., & Hetherington, E. (2003). Risk and resilience after divorce. In F. Walsh (Ed.), *Normal family processes: Growing diversity and complexity*. New York: Guilford Press.

Greenway, C. (2002). The process, pitfalls and benefits of implementing a reciprocal teaching intervention to improve the reading comprehension of a group of year 6 pupils. *Educational Psychology in Practice, 18*, 113–137.

Greer, B. D., Neidert, P. L., & Dozier, C. L. (2016). A component analysis of toilet-training procedures recommended for young children. *Journal of Applied Behavior Analysis, 49*, 69–84.

Gregory, K. (2005). Update on nutrition for preterm and full-term infants. *Journal of Obstetrics and Gynecological Neonatal Nursing, 34*, 98–108.

Grey, I. K., & Yates, T. M. (2014). Preschoolers' narrative representations and childhood adaptation in an ethnoracially diverse sample. *Attachment & Human Development, 16*, 613–632.

Greydanus, D. E., & Pratt, H. D. (2016). Human sexuality. *International Journal of Child and Adolescent Health, 9*, 291–312.

Griffin, L. K., Adams, N., & Little, T. D. (2017). Self-determination theory, identity development, and adolescence. In M. L. Wehmeyer, K. A. Shogren, T. D. Little, & S. J. Lopez (Eds.), *Development of self-determination through the life-course*. New York: Springer Science + Business Media.

Grigorenko, E. (2003). Intraindividual fluctuations in intellectual functioning: Selected links between nutrition and the mind. In R. Sternberg & J. Lautrey (Eds.), *Models of intelligence: International perspectives*. Washington, DC: American Psychological Association.

Grigorenko, E., Jarvin, L., Diffley, R., Goodyear, J., Shanahan, E., & Sternberg, R. (2009). Are SSATS and GPA enough? A theory-based approach to predicting academic success in secondary school. *Journal of Educational Psychology, 101*, 964–981.

Grinkevičiūtė, D., Jankauskaitė, L., Kėvalas, R., & Gurskis, V. (2016). Shaken baby syndrome and consciousness. In G. Leisman, J. Merrick (Eds.), *Considering consciousness clinically*. Hauppauge, NY: Nova Biomedical Books.

Grønhøj, A., & Thøgersen, J. (2012). Action speaks louder than words: The effect of personal attitudes and family norms on adolescents' pro-environmental behaviour. *Journal of Economic Psychology, 33*, 292–302.

Gross, R. T., Spiker, D., & Haynes, C. W. (Eds.). (1997). *Helping low-birthweight, premature babies: The Infant Health and Development Program*. Stanford, CA: Stanford University Press.

Grossmann, K. E., Grossmann, K., Huber, F., & Wartner, U. (1982). German children's behavior towards their mothers at 12 months and their fathers at 18 months in Ainsworth's Strange Situation. *International Journal of Behavioral Development, 4*, 157–181.

Grossmann, T., Striano, T., & Friederici, A. (2006, May). Crossmodal integration of emotional information from face and voice in the infant brain. *Developmental Science, 9*, 309–315.

Grunbaum, J. A., Lowry, R., & Kann, L. (2001). Prevalence of health-related behaviors among alternative high school students as compared with students attending regular high schools. *Journal of Adolescent Health, 29*, 337–343.

Grundy, E., & Henretta, J. (2006, September). Between elderly parents and adult children: A new look at the intergenerational care provided by the "sandwich generation." *Ageing & Society, 26*, 707–722.

Gruttadaro, D., & Croudo, D. (2012). *College students speak: A survey report on mental health*. Arlington, VA: National Alliance on Mental Illness.

Guadalupe, K. L., & Welkley, D. L. (2012). *Diversity in family constellations: Implications for practice*. Chicago: Lyceum Books.

Guasti, M. T. (2002). *Language acquisition: The growth of grammar*. Cambridge, MA: MIT Press.

Guérin, E., Goldfield, G., & Prud'homme, D. (2017). Trajectories of mood and stress and relationships with protective factors during the transition to menopause: Results using latent class growth modeling in a Canadian cohort. *Archives of Women's Mental Health*. Accessed online, 12-4-17; https://www.researchgate.net/publication/318411356_Trajectories_of_mood_and_stress_and_relationships_with_protective_factors_during_the_transition_to_menopause_results_using_latent_class_growth_modeling_in_a_Canadian_cohort.

Guerrero, A., Hishinuma, E., Andrade, N., Nishimura, S., & Cunanan, V. (2006, July). Correlations among socioeconomic and family factors and academic, behavioral, and emotional difficulties in Filipino adolescents in Hawaii. *International Journal of Social Psychiatry, 52*, 343–359.

Guerrero, S., Enesco, I., & Lam, V. (2011). Racial awareness, affect and sorting abilities: A study with preschool children. *Anales De Psicología, 27*, 639–646.

Guerrini, I., Thomson, A., & Gurling, H. (2007). The importance of alcohol misuse, malnutrition and genetic susceptibility on brain growth and plasticity. *Neuroscience & Biobehavioral Reviews, 31*, 212–220.

Guinsburg, R., de Araújo Peres, C., Branco de Almeida, M. F., Xavier Balda, R., Bereguel, R. C., Tonelotto, J., & Kopelman, B. I. (2000). Differences in pain expression between male and female newborn infants. *Pain, 85*, 127–133.

Gump, L. S., Baker, R. C., & Roll, S. (2000). Cultural and gender differences in moral judgment: A study of Mexican Americans and Anglo-Americans. *Hispanic Journal of Behavioral Sciences, 22*, 78–93.

Gupta, R., Pascoe, J., Blanchard, T., Langkamp, D., Duncan, P., Gorski, P., et al. (2009). Child health in child care: A multistate survey of Head Start and non–Head Start child care directors. *Journal of Pediatric Health Care, 23*, 143–149.

Gure, A., Ucanok, Z., & Sayil, M. (2006). The associations among perceived pubertal timing, parental relations and self-perception in Turkish adolescents. *Journal of Youth and Adolescence, 35*, 541–550.

Gurin, P. Y., Dey, E. L., Gurin, G., & Hurtado, S. (2003). How does racial/ethnic diversity promote education? *Western Journal of Black Studies, 27*, 20–29.

Gurin, P., Nagda, B. A., & Lopez, G. E. (2004). The benefits of diversity in education for democratic citizenship. *Journal of Social Issues, 60*(1), 17-34. DOI: 10.1111/j.0022-4537.2004.00097.x

Gutek, G. L. (2003). Maria Montessori: Contributions to educational psychology. In B. J. Zimmerman (Ed.), *Educational psychology: A century of contributions*. Mahwah, NJ: Lawrence Erlbaum.

Gutnick, A. L., Robb, M., Takeuchi, L., & Kotler, J. (2010, March 10). *Always connected: the new digital media habits of young children*. New York: Joan Ganz Cooney Center.

Guttmacher Institute. (2012, February). *Facts on American teens' sexual and reproductive health*. New York: Guttmacher Institute.

Guttmacher Institute. (2017, September.) *Induced abortion worldwide*. New York: Guttmacher Institute.

Guttman, M. (1997, May 16–18). Are you losing your mind? *USA Weekend*, pp. 4–5.

Guttmann, J., & Rosenberg, M. (2003). Emotional intimacy and children's adjustment: A comparison between single-parent divorced and intact families. *Educational Psychology, 23*, 457–472.

Guttmannova, K., Hill, K. G., Bailey, J. A., Hartigan, L. A., Small, C. M., & Hawkins, J. D. (2016). Parental alcohol use, parenting, and child on-time development. *Infant and Child Development*. Accessed online, 10-25-17; http://onlinelibrary.wiley.com/doi/10.1002/icd.2013/abstract.

Guzzetta, A., Fiori, S., Scelfo, D., Conti, E., & Bancale, A. (2013). Reorganization of visual fields after periventricular haemorrhagic infarction: Potentials and limitations. *Developmental Medicine & Child Neurology, 55* (Suppl 4), 23–26.

Guzzo, K. (2009). Marital intentions and the stability of first cohabitations. *Journal of Family Issues, 30*, 179–205.

Haas-Thompson, T., Alston, P., & Holbert, D. (2008). The impact of education and death-related experiences on rehabilitation counselor attitudes toward death and dying. *Journal of Applied Rehabilitation Counseling, 39*, 20–27.

Haber, D. (2006). Life review: Implementation, theory, research, and therapy. *International Journal of Aging & Human Development, 63*, 153–171.

Habersaat, S., Pierrehumbert, B., Forcada-Guex, M., Nessi, J., Ansermet, F., Müller-Nix, C., & Borghini, A. (2014). Early stress exposure and later cortisol regulation: Impact of early intervention on mother–infant relationship in preterm infants. *Psychological trauma: Theory, research, practice, and policy, 6*, 457–464.

Hack, M., Flannery, D. J., Schluchter, M., Cartar, L., Borawski, E., & Klein, N. (2002). Outcomes in young adulthood for very-low-birthweight infants. *New England Journal of Medicine, 346*, 149–157.

Haddock, S., & Rattenborg, K. (2003). Benefits and challenges of dual-earning: Perspectives of successful couples. *American Journal of Family Therapy, 31*, 325–344.

Hadzic, R., Magee, C. A., & Robinson, L. (2013). Parental employment and child behaviors: Do parenting practices underlie these relationships? *International Journal of Behavioral Development, 37*, 332–339.

Haeffel, G., Getchell, M., Koposov, R., Yrigollen, C., DeYoung, C., af Klinteberg, B., et al. (2008). Association between polymorphisms in the dopamine transporter gene and depression: Evidence for a gene-environment interaction in a sample of juvenile detainees. *Psychological Science, 19*, 62–69.

Hagan-Burke, S., Coyne, M. D., Kwok, O., Simmons, D. C., Kim, M., Simmons, L. E., & … McSparran Ruby, M. (2013). The effects and interactions of student, teacher, and setting variables on reading outcomes for kindergarteners receiving supplemental reading intervention. *Journal of Learning Disabilities, 46*, 260–277.

Hagerty, R. G., Butow, P. N., Ellis, P. A., Lobb, E. A., Pendlebury, S., Leighl, N., Goldstein, D., Lo, S. K., & Tattersall, M. H. (2004). Cancer patient preferences for communication of prognosis in the metastatic setting. *Journal of Clinical Oncology, 22*, 1721–1730.

Hahn, E. A., & Lachman, M. E. (2015). Everyday experiences of memory problems and control: The adaptive role of selective optimization with compensation in the context of memory decline. *Aging, Neuropsychology, and Cognition, 22*, 25–41.

Hahn, E., Gottschling, J., & Spinath, F. M. (2012). Short measurements of personality—Validity and reliability of the GSOEP Big Five Inventory (BFI-S). *Journal of Research in Personality, 46*, 355–359.

Haight, B. K. (1991). Psychological illness in aging. In E. M. Baines (Ed.), *Perspectives on gerontological nursing*. Newbury Park, CA: Sage Publications.

Haith, M. H. (1986). Sensory and perceptual processes in early infancy. *Journal of Pediatrics, 109*(1), 158–171.

Haith, M. H. (1991, April). Setting a path for the 90s: Some goals and challenges in infant sensory and perceptual development. Paper presented at the biennial meeting of the Society for Research in Child Development, Seattle, WA.

Hakim, D. (2015, July 1). U.S. Chamber Travels the World, Fighting Curbs on Smoking. *New York Times*, p. A1.

Haleem, M., Barton, K., Borges, G., Crozier, A., & Anderson, A. (2008). Increasing antioxidant intake from fruits and vegetables: Practical strategies for the Scottish population. *Journal of Human Nutrition and Dietetics, 21*, 539–546.

Halgunseth, L. C., Ispa, J. M., & Rudy, D. (2006). Parental control in Latino families: An integrated review of the literature. *Child Development, 77*, 1282–1297.

Halim, M. L, Ruble, D. N., & Tamis-LeMonda, C. S. (2013). Four-year-olds' beliefs about how others regard males and females. *British Journal of Developmental Psychology, 31*, 128–135.

Halim, M. L., Ruble, D. N., Tamis-LeMonda, C. S., Zosuls, K. M., Lurye, L. E., & Greulich, F. K. (2014). Pink frilly dresses and the avoidance of all things "girly": Children's appearance rigidity and cognitive theories of gender development. *Developmental Psychology, 50*, 1091–1101.

Halkier, B. (2013). Review of the case study as research method: A practical handbook and how to do your case study: A guide for students & researchers. *Qualitative Research, 13*(1), 107–110.

Hall, E. G., & Lee, A. M. (1984). Sex differences in motor performance of young children: Fact or fiction? *Sex Roles, 10*, 217–230.

Hall, J. J., Neal, T., & Dean, R. S. (2008). Lateralization of cerebral functions. In A. M. McNeil & D. Wedding (Eds.), *The neuropsychology handbook* (3rd ed.). New York: Springer Publishing.

Hall, R. S., Hoffenkamp, H. N., Tooten, A., Bracken, J., Vingerhoets, A. M., & Bakel, H. A. (2014). Child-rearing history and emotional bonding in parents of preterm and full-term infants. *Journal of Child and Family Studies*. Accessed online, 3-14-15; http://link.springer.com/article/10.1007%2Fs10826-014-99757#page-2.

Hallett, R. E., & Barber, K. (2014). Ethnographic research in a cyber era. *Journal of Contemporary Ethnography, 43*, 306–330.

Halpern, D. F. (2014). It's complicated—in fact, it's complex: Explaining the gender gap in academic achievement in science and mathematics. *Psychological Science in the Public Interest, 15*, 72–74.

Hamer, R., & van Rossum, E. J. (2016). Six languages in education—looking for postformal thinking. *Behavioral Development Bulletin*. Accessed online, 3-21-17; http://psycnet.apa.org/psycinfo/2016-59293-001/.

Hamilton, B. E., Martin, J. A., Osterman, M. J. K., et al. (2015). Births: Final data for 2014. *National Vital Statistics Report. 64*, 1–64.

Hamilton, B. E., Martin, J. A., Ventura, S. J. (2011). *Births: Preliminary data for 2010*. National vital statistics reports; vol 60 no 2. Hyattsville, MD: National Center for Health Statistics.

Hamilton, B. S., & Ventura, S. J. (2012, April). Birth rates for U.S. teenagers reach historic lows for all age and ethnic groups. *NCHS Data Brief, No. 89*. Washington, DC: National Center for Health Statistics.

Hamilton, G. (1998). Positively testing. *Families in Society, 79*, 570–576.

Hamlet, H. S., & Herrick, M. (2014). Career challenges in midlife and beyond. In G. T. Eliason, T. Eliason, J. L. Samide, & J. Patrick (Eds.), *Career development across the lifespan: Counseling for community, schools, higher education, and beyond*. Charlotte, NC: IAP Information Age Publishing.

Hamm, J. V., Brown, B. B., & Heck, D. J. (2005). Bridging the ethnic divide: Student and school characteristics in African American, Asian-descent, Latino, and white adolescents' cross-ethnic friend nominations. *Journal of Research on Adolescence, 15*, 21–46.

Hamon, R. R., & Blieszner, R. (1990). Filial responsibility expectations among adult child–older parent pairs. *Journal of Gerontology, 45*, 110–112.

Hane, A., Feldstein, S., & Dernetz, V. (2003). The relation between coordinated interpersonal timing and maternal sensitivity in four-month-old infants. *Journal of Psycholinguistic Research, 32*, 525–539.

Hansen, C., Konradsen, H., Abrahamsen, B., & Pedersen, B. D. (2014). Women's experiences of their osteoporosis diagnosis at the time of diagnosis and 6 months later: A phenomenological hermeneutic study. *International Journal of Qualitative Studies on Health and Well-Being*. Accessed online, 3-31-15; http://www.ncbi.nlm.nih.gov/pubmed/24559545.

Hanson, D. R., & Gottesman, I. I. (2005). Theories of schizophrenia: A genetic-inflammatory-vascular synthesis. *BMC Medical Genetics, 6*, 7.

Hanson, J. D. (2012). Understanding prenatal health care for American Indian women in a northern plains tribe. *Journal of Transcultural Nursing, 23*, 29–37.

Hanson, R., & Hayslip, B. (2000). Widowhood in later life. In J. Harvey & E. Miller (Eds.), *Loss and trauma: General and close relationship perspectives*. New York: Brunner-Routledge.

Harada, C. N, Natelson Love, M. C., & Triebold, K. (2013). Normal cognitive aging. *Clinical and Geriatric Medicine, 29*, 737–752.

Harden, K., Turkheimer, E., & Loehlin, J. (2007). Genotype by environment interaction in adolescents' cognitive aptitude. *Behavior Genetics, 37*, 273–283.

Hardy, S., & Grogan, S. (2009). Preventing disability through exercise: Investigating older adults' influences and motivations to engage in physical activity. *Journal of Health Psychology, 14*, 1036–1046.

Hare, T. A., Tottenham, N., Galvan, A., & Voss, H. U. (2008). Biological substrates of emotional reactivity and regulation in adolescence during an emotional go-nogo task. *Biological Psychiatry, 63*, 927–934.

Hareli, S., & Hess, U. (2008). When does feedback about success at school hurt? The role of causal attributions. *Social Psychology of Education, 11*, 259–272.

Harlow, H. F., & Zimmerman, R. R. (1959). Affectional responses in the infant monkey. *Science, 130*, 421–432.

Harrell, J. S., Bangdiwala, S. I., Deng, S., Webb, J. P., & Bradley, C. (1998). Smoking initiation in youth: The roles of gender, race, socioeconomics, and developmental status. *Journal of Adolescent Health, 23*, 271–279.

Harrell, Z. A., & Karim, N. M. (2008). Is gender relevant only for problem alcohol behaviors? An examination of correlates of alcohol use among college students. *Addictive Behaviors, 33*, 359–365.

Harris, J., Vernon, P., & Jang, K. (2007). Rated personality and measured intelligence in young twin children. *Personality and Individual Differences, 42*, 75–86.

Harris, M. A., Gruenenfelder-Steiger, A. E., Ferrer, E., Donnellan, M. B., Allemand, M., Fend, H., & … Trzesniewski, K. H. (2015). Do parents foster self-esteem? Testing the prospective impact of parent closeness on adolescent self-esteem. *Child Development*. Accessed online, 3-22-15; http://www.ncbi.nlm.nih.gov/pubmed/25703089.

Harris, M., Prior, J., & Koehoorn, M. (2008). Age at menarche in the Canadian population: Secular trends and relationship to adulthood BMI. *Journal of Adolescent Health, 43*, 548–554.

Harris Poll. (2014, September 14.) Doctors, military officers, firefighters, and scientists seen as among America's most prestigious occupations. Accessed online, 11-28-17; http://www.theharrispoll.com/politics/Doctors__Military_Officers__Firefighters__and_Scientists_Seen_as_Among_America_s_Most_Prestigious_Occupations.html.

Harrison, D. A., & Newman, D. A. (2013). Absence, lateness, turnover, and retirement: Narrow and broad understandings of withdrawal and behavioral engagement. In N. W. Schmitt, S. Highhouse, & I. B. Weiner (Eds.), *Handbook of psychology: Industrial and organizational psychology, Vol. 12*. (2nd ed.) Hoboken, NJ: John Wiley & Sons Inc.

Harrison, K., & Hefner, V. (2006, April). Media exposure, current and future body ideals, and disordered eating among preadolescent girls: A longitudinal panel study. *Journal of Youth and Adolescence, 35*, 153–163.

Harrist, A., & Waugh, R. (2002). Dyadic synchrony: Its structure and function in children's development. *Developmental Review, 22*, 555–592.

Hart, B. (2000). A natural history of early language experience. *Topics in Early Childhood Special Education, 20*, 28–32.

Hart, B. (2004). What toddlers talk about. *First Language, 24*, 91–106.

Hart, B., & Risley, T. R. (1995). *Meaningful differences in the everyday experience of young American children*. Baltimore, MD: Paul Brookes.

Hart, D., Burock, D., & London, B. (2003). Prosocial tendencies, antisocial behavior, and moral development. In A. Slater & G. Bremner (Eds.), *An introduction to developmental psychology*. Malden, MA: Blackwell Publishers.

Hart, S. L., Hoyt, M. A., Diefenbach, M., Anderson, D. R., Kilbourn, K. M., Craft, L. L., Steel, J. L., Cuijpers, P., Mohr, D. C., Berendsen, M., Spring, B., & Stanton, A. L. (2012). Metaanalysis of efficacy of interventions for elevated depressive symptoms in adults diagnosed with cancer. *Journal of the National Cancer Institute, 104*, 990–1004.

Harter, S. (1990). Issues in the assessment of self-concept of children and adolescents. In A. LaGreca (Ed.), *Through the eyes of a child*. Boston: Allyn & Bacon.

Harter, S. (2006). The development of self-esteem. *Self-esteem issues and answers: A sourcebook of current perspectives*. New York: Psychology Press.

Hartley, C. A., & Lee, F. S. (2015). Sensitive periods in affective development: Nonlinear maturation of fear learning. *Neuropsychopharmacology, 40*, 50–60.

Hartman, K. M., Ratner, N. B., & Newman, R. S. (2017). Infant-directed speech (IDS) vowel clarity and child language outcomes. *Journal of Child Language, 44*, 1140–1162.

Hartshorne, J., & Ullman, M. (2006). Why girls say "holded" more than boys. *Developmental Science, 9*, 21–32.

Hartup, W. W., & Stevens, N. (1999). Friendships and adaptation across the life span. *Current Directions in Psychological Science, 8*, 76–79.

Harvey, H. A., & Miller, G. E. (2017). Executive function skills, early mathematics, and vocabulary in head start preschool children. *Early Education and Development, 28*, 290–307.

Harvey, J. H., & Fine, M. A. (2004). *Children of divorce: Stories of loss and growth*. Mahwah, NJ: Lawrence Erlbaum.

Haskett, M., Nears, K., Ward, C., & McPherson, A. (2006, October). Diversity in adjustment of maltreated children: Factors associated with resilient functioning. *Clinical Psychology Review, 26*, 796–812.

Haslam, C., & Lawrence, W. (2004). Health-related behavior and beliefs of pregnant smokers. *Health Psychology, 23*, 486–491.

Haslett, A. (2004, May 31). Love supreme. *New Yorker*, pp. 76–80.

Hastings, P. D., Shane, K. E., Parker, R., & Ladha, F. (2007). Ready to make nice: Parental socialization of young sons' and daughters' prosocial behaviors with peers. *Journal of Genetic Psychology, 68*, 177–200.

Hatfield, E., & Rapson, R. L. (1993). Historical and crosscultural perspectives on passionate love and sexual desire. *Annual Review of Sex Research, 4*, 67–97

Hatton, C. (2002). People with intellectual disabilities from ethnic minority communities in the United States and the United Kingdom. In L. M. Glidden (Ed.), *International review of research in mental retardation (Vol. 25)*. San Diego, CA: Academic Press.

Hatton, C. (2015, December 21). Who will take care of China's elderly people? *BBC News Magazine*. Accessed online, 10-24-17; http://www.bbc.com/news/magazine-35155548.

Haugaard, J. J. (2000). The challenge of defining child sexual abuse. *American Psychologist, 55*, 1036–1039.

Hawkins, A. J., Willoughby, B. J., & Doherty, W. J. (2012). Reasons for divorce and openness to marital reconciliation. *Journal of Divorce & Remarriage, 53*, 453–463.

Hawkins-Rodgers, Y. (2007). Adolescents adjusting to a group home environment: A residential care model of reorganizing attachment behavior and building resiliency. *Children and Youth Services Review, 29*, 1131–1141.

Hayashi, A., & Mazuka, R. (2017). Emergence of Japanese infants' prosodic preferences in infant-directed vocabulary. *Developmental Psychology, 53*, 28–37.

Hayden, T. (1998, September 21). The brave new world of sex selection. *Newsweek*, p. 93.

Hayflick, L. (2007). Biological aging is no longer an unsolved problem. *Annals of the New York Academy of Sciences*, pp. 1–13.

Hayslip, B., Jr., Shore, R. J., & Henderson, C. E. (2000). Perceptions of grandparents' influence in the lives of their grandchildren. In B. Hayslip, Jr., Goldberg, & G. Robin (Eds.), *Grandparents raising grandchildren: Theoretical, empirical, and clinical perspectives*. New York: Springer.

Hayward, M., Crimmins, E., & Saito, Y. (1997). Cause of death and active life expectancy in the older population of the United States. *Journal of Aging and Health*, 122–131.

Hazan, C., & Shaver, P. (1987). Romantic love conceptualized as an attachment process. *Journal of Personality and Social Psychology, 52*, 511–524.

Hazin, A. N., Alves, J. G. B., & Rodrigues Falbo, A. (2007). The myelination process in severely malnourished children: MRI findings. *International Journal of Neuroscience, 117*, 1209–1214.

Healthychildren.org. (2016, October 18.) Teen suicide statistics. Accessed online, 11-13-17; https://www.healthychildren.org/English/health-issues/conditions/emotional-problems/Pages/Teen-Suicide-Statistics.aspx.

Healy, S. J., Murray, L., Cooper, P. J., Hughes, C., & Halligan, S. L. (2015). A longitudinal investigation of maternal influences on the development of child hostile attributions and aggression. *Journal of Clinical Child and Adolescent Psychology, 44*, 80–92.

Heard, E., & Martienssen, R. A. (2014). Transgenerational epigenetic inheritance: Myths and mechanisms. *Cell, 157*, 95–109.

Hedegaard, M., & Fleer, M. (2013). *Play, learning, and children's development: Everyday life in families and transition to school*. New York: Cambridge University Press.

Heimann, M., Strid, K., Smith, L., Tjus, T., Ulvund, S., & Meltzoff, A. (2006). Exploring the relation between memory, gestural communication, and the emergence of language in infancy: A longitudinal study. *Infant and Child Development, 15*, 233–249.

Heinemann, G. D., & Evans, P. L. (1990). Widowhood: Loss, change, and adaptation. In T. H. Brubaker (Ed.), *Family relationships in later life*. Newbury Park, CA: Sage Publications.

Heinrich, C. J. (2014). Parents' employment and children's wellbeing. *Future of Children, 24*, 121–146.

Helms, J. E., Jernigan, M., & Mascher, J. (2005). The meaning of race in psychology and how to change it: A methodological perspective. *American Psychologist, 60*, 27–36.

Helmsen, J., Koglin, U., & Petermann, F. (2012). Emotion regulation and aggressive behavior in preschoolers: The mediating role of social information processing. *Child Psychiatry and Human Development, 43*, 87–101.

Helson, R., & McCabe, L. (1994). The social clock project in middle age. In B. F. Turner, L. E. Troll (Eds.), *Women growing older: Psychological perspectives*. Thousand Oaks, CA: Sage Publications, Inc.

Helson, R., & Srivastava, S. (2001). Three paths of adult development: Conservers, seekers, and achievers. *Journal of Personality and Social Psychology, 80*, 995–1010.

Hendren, S., Humiston, S., & Fiscella, K. (2012). Partnering with safety-net primary care clinics: A model to enhance screening in low-income populations—Principles, challenges, and key lessons. In R. Elk & H. Landrine (Eds.), *Cancer disparities: Causes and evidence-based solutions*. New York: Springer Publishing Co.

Hendrick, C., & Hendrick, S. (2003). Romantic love: Measuring cupid's arrow. In S. Lopez & C. Snyder (Eds.), *Positive psychological assessment: A handbook of models and measures*. Washington, DC: American Psychological Association.

Henry, J., & McNab, W. (2003). Forever young: A health promotion focus on sexuality and aging. *Gerontology & Geriatrics Education, 23*, 57–74.

Henry, R., Miller, R., & Giarrusso, R. (2005). Difficulties, disagreements, and disappointments in late-life marriages. *International Journal of Aging & Human Development, 61*, 243–264.

Hensley, P. (2006, July). Treatment of bereavement-related depression and traumatic grief. *Journal of Affective Disorders, 92*, 117–124.

Hentschel, S., Eid, M., & Kutscher, T. (2017). The influence of major life events and personality traits on the stability of affective well-being. *Journal of Happiness Studies, 18*, 719–741.

Hepach, R., & Westermann, G. (2013). Infants' sensitivity to the congruence of others' emotions and actions. *Journal of Experimental Child Psychology, 115*, 16–29.

Herbenick, D., Reece, M., Schick, V., Sanders, S., Dodge, B., & Fortenberry, J. D. (2010). Sexual behavior in the United States: Results from a national probability sample of men and women ages 14 to 94. *Journal of Sexual Medicine, 7(Suppl. 5)*, 255–265.

Herberman Mash, H. B., Fullerton, C. S., Shear, M. K., & Ursano, R. J. (2014). Complicated grief and depression in young adults: Personality and relationship quality. *Journal of Nervous and Mental Disease, 202*, 539–543.

Herbert, J. S., Eckerman, C. O., Goldstein, R. F., Stanton, M. E. (2004). Contrasts in infant classical eyeblink conditioning as a function of premature birth. *Infancy, 5*, 367–383.

Herdt, G. H. (Ed.). (1998). *Rituals of manhood: Male initiation in Papua New Guinea*. Somerset, NJ: Transaction Books.

Herendeen, L. A., & MacDonald, A. (2014). Planning for healthy homes. In I. L. Rubin, J. Merrick, I. L. Rubin, & J. Merrick (Eds.), *Environmental health: Home, school and community*. Hauppauge, NY: Nova Biomedical Books.

Hermanto, N., Moreno, S., & Bialystok, E. (2012). Linguistic and metalinguistic outcomes of intense immersion education: How bilingual? *International Journal of Bilingual Education and Bilingualism, 15*, 131–145.

Hernandez, D. J., Denton, N. A., McCartney, S. E. (2008). Children in immigrant families: Looking to America's Future. *Social Policy Report, 22*, 3–24.

Hernandez-Reif, M., Field, T., Diego, M., Vera, Y., & Pickens, J. (2006, January). Brief report: Happy faces are habituated more slowly by infants of depressed mothers. *Infant Behavior & Development, 29*, 131–135.

Herpertz-Dahlmann, B. (2015). Adolescent eating disorders: Update on definitions, symptomatology, epidemiology, and comorbidity. *Child and Adolescent Psychiatric Clinics of North America, 24*, 177–196.

Herrnstein, R. J., & Murray, C. (1994). *The Bell Curve: Intelligence and class structure in American life*. New York: Free Press.

Hertenstein, M. J. (2002). Touch: Its communicative functions in infancy. *Human Development, 45*, 70–94.

Hertenstein, M. J., & Campos, J. J. (2004). The retention effects of an adult's emotional displays on infant behavior. *Child Development, 75*, 595–613.

Hertz, R., & Nelson, M. K. (2015). Introduction. *Journal of Family Issues, 36*, 447–460.

Hespos, S. J., & Baillargeon, R. (2008). Young infants' actions reveal their developing knowledge of support variables: Converging evidence for violation-of-expectation findings. *Cognition, 107*, 304–316.

Hespos, S. J., & van Marle, K. (2012). *Everyday Physics: How infants learn about objects and entities in their environment*. Invited manuscript for Wiley Interdisciplinary Reviews, Cognitive Science.

Hess, T., Auman, C., & Colcombe, S. (2003). The impact of stereotype threat on age differences in memory performance. *Journals of Gerontology: Series B: Psychological Sciences & Social Sciences, 58B*, P3–P11.

Hess, T. M., Hinson, J. T., & Hodges, E. A. (2009). Moderators of and mechanisms underlying stereotype threat effects on older adults' memory performance. *Experimental Aging Research, 31*, 153–177.

Hetherington, E. M. (Ed.) (1999). *Coping with divorce, single parenting, and remarriage: A risk and resiliency perspective*. Mahwah, NJ: Lawrence Erlbaum.

Hetherington, E., & Elmore, A. (2003). Risk and resilience in children coping with their parents' divorce and remarriage. In S. Luthar (Ed.), *Resilience and vulnerability: Adaptation in the context of childhood adversities*. New York: Cambridge University Press.

Hetherington, E. M., & Kelly, J. (2002). *For better or worse: Divorce reconsidered*. New York: Norton.

Hetrick, S. E., Parker, A. G., Robinson, J., Hall, N., & Vance, A. (2012). Predicting suicidal risk in a cohort of depressed children and adolescents. *Crisis: Journal of Crisis Intervention and Suicide Prevention, 33*, 13–20.

Heubusch, K. (1997, September). A tough job gets tougher. *American Demographics*, p. 39.

Hewitt, B. (1997, December 15). A day in the life. *People Magazine*, pp. 49–58.

Hewlett, B., & Lamb, M. (2002). Integrating evolution, culture and developmental psychology: Explaining caregiver-infant proximity and responsiveness in central Africa and the USA. In H. Keller & Y. Poortinga (Eds.), *Between culture and biology: Perspectives on ontogenetic development*. New York: Cambridge University Press.

Hewstone, M. (2003). Intergroup contact: Panacea for prejudice? *Psychologist, 16*, 352–355.

Heyman, R., & Slep, A. M. (2002). Do child abuse and interparental violence lead to adulthood family violence? *Journal of Marriage & Family, 64*, 864–870.

Hietala, J., Cannon, T. D., & van Erp, T. G. M. (2003). Regional brain morphology and duration of illness in never-medicated first-episode patients with schizophrenia. *Schizophrenia, 64*, 79–81.

Higgins, D., & McCabe, M. (2003). Maltreatment and family dysfunction in childhood and the subsequent adjustment of children and adults. *Journal of Family Violence, 18*, 107–120.

Higley, E., & Dozier, M. (2009). Nighttime maternal responsiveness and infant attachment at one year. *Attachment & Human Development, 11*, 347–363.

Hill, B. D., Foster, J. D., Elliott, E. M., Shelton, J., McCain, J., & Gouvier, W. (2013). Need for cognition is related to higher general intelligence, fluid intelligence, and crystallized intelligence, but not working memory. *Journal of Research in Personality, 47*, 22–25.

Hill, S., & Flom, R. (2007, February). 18- and 24-month-olds' discrimination of gender-consistent and inconsistent activities. *Infant Behavior & Development, 30*, 168–173.

Hillman, J. (2000). *Clinical perspectives on elderly sexuality*. Dordrecht, Netherlands: Kluwer Academic Publishers.

Hillman, J. (2012). *Sexuality and aging: Clinical perspectives*. New York: Springer Science + Business Media.

Hilton, J., & Anderson, T. (2009). Characteristics of women with children who divorce in midlife compared to those who remain married. *Journal of Divorce & Remarriage, 50*, 309–329.

Himmler, S. M., Himmler, B. T., Pellis, V. C., & Pellis, S. M. (2016). Play, variation in play and the development of socially competent rats. *Behaviour, 153*, 1103–1137.

Hipke, K. N., Wolchik, S. A., & Sandler, I. N. (2010). Divorce, children of. In G. Fink (Ed.), *Stress consequences: Mental, neuropsychological and socioeconomic*. San Diego, CA: Elsevier Academic Press.

Hipple, S. F. (2016, September). Labor force participation: What has happened since the peak? *Monthly Labor Review, Bureau of Labor Statistics*. Accessed online, 11-29-17; https://www.bls.gov/opub/mlr/2016/article/labor-force-participation-what-has-happened-since-the-peak.htm#top.

Hirsch, H. V., & Spinelli, D. N. (1970). Visual experience modifies distribution of horizontally and vertically oriented receptive fields in cats. *Science, 168*, 869–871.

Hirschtritt, M. E., Pagano, M. E., Christian, K. M., McNamara, N. K., Stansbrey, R. J., Lingler, J., & Findling, R. L. (2012). Moderators of fluoxetine treatment response for children and adolescents with comorbid depression and substance use disorders. *Journal of Substance Abuse Treatment, 42*, 366–372.

Hirsch, M., & Morlière, C. (2017). Health psychology: Understanding culture's role in health and illness. In G. J. Rich, U. P. Gielen, H. Takooshian (Eds.), *Internationalizing the teaching of psychology*. Charlotte, NC: IAP Information Age Publishing.

Hirsh-Pasek, K., & Michnick-Golinkoff, R. (1995). *The origins of grammar: Evidence from early language comprehension*. Cambridge, MA: MIT Press.

Hiser, E., & Kobayashi, J. (2003). Hemisphere lateralization differences: A cross-cultural study of Japanese and American students in Japan. *Journal of Asian Pacific Communication, 13*, 197–229.

Hispanic Heritage Foundation. (2015, April 28.) *HHF, MyCollege Options: Survey 3k students*. Accessed online, 11-9-17; http://hispanic heritage.org/hispanic-heritage-foundation-mycollegeoptions-family-online-safety-institute-and-other-partners-announce-findings-of-new-study-titled-taking-the-pulse-of-the-high-school-student-experience/.

Hitlin, S., Brown, J. S., & Elder, G. H., Jr. (2006). Racial self-categorization in adolescence. Multiracial development and social pathways. *Child Development, 77*, 1298–1308.

Hjelmstedt, A., Widström, A., & Collins, A. (2006). Psychological correlates of prenatal attachment in women who conceived after in vitro fertilization and women who conceived naturally. *Birth: Issues in Perinatal Care, 33*, 303–310.

Ho, B., Friedland, J., Rappolt, S., Noh, S. (2003). Caregiving for relatives with Alzheimer's disease: Feelings of ChineseCanadian women. *Journal of Aging Studies, 17*, 301–321.

Hocking, D. R., Kogan, C. S., & Cornish, K. M. (2012). Selective spatial processing deficits in an at-risk subgroup of the fragile X premutation. *Brain and Cognition, 79*, 39–44.

Hoehl, S., Wahl, S., Michel, C., & Striano, T. (2012). Effects of eye gaze cues provided by the caregiver compared to a stranger on infants' object processing. *Developmental Cognitive Neuroscience, 2*, 81–89.

Hoelterk, L. F., Axinn, W. G., & Ghimire, D. J. (2004). Social change, premarital nonfamily experiences, and marital dynamics. *Journal of Marriage & Family, 66*, 1131–1151.

Hoersting, R. C., & Jenkins, S. (2011). No place to call home: Cultural homelessness, self-esteem and cross-cultural identities. *International Journal of Intercultural Relations, 35*, 17–30.

Hoessler, C., & Chasteen, A. L. (2008). Does aging affect the use of shifting standards? *Experimental Aging Research, 34*, 1–12.

Hoeve, M., Blokland, A., Dubas, J., Loeber, R., Gerris, J., & van der Laan, P. (2008). Trajectories of delinquency and parenting styles. *Journal of Abnormal Child Psychology: An Official Publication of the International Society for Research in Child and Adolescent Psychopathology, 36*, 223–235.

Hodgson, J. C., Hirst, R. J., & Hudson, J. M. (2016). Hemispheric speech lateralisation in the developing brain is related to motor praxis ability. *Developmental Cognitive Neuroscience, 22*, 9–17.

Hoff, E. (2012). Interpreting the Early Language Trajectories of Children From Low-SES and Language Minority Homes: Implications for Closing Achievement Gaps. *Developmental Psychology*. Accessed online, 7-22-12; http://www.ncbi.nlm.nih.gov/pubmed/22329382.

Hoff, E., & Core, C. (2013). Input and language development in bilingually developing children. *Seminars in Speech and Language, 34*, 215–226.

Hofferth, S., & Sandberg, J. F. (2001). How American children spend their time. *Journal of Marriage and the Family, 63*, 295–308.

Hoffman, J. (2011, March 27) A girl's nude photo and altered lives. *The New York Times*, A1, A18-A19.

Hoffman, L. (2003). Why high schools don't change: What students and their yearbooks tell us. *High School Journal, 86*, 22–37.

Hofmeier, S. M., Runfola, C. D., Sala, M., Gagne, D. A., Brownley, K. A., & Bulik, C. M. (2017). Body image, aging, and identity in women over 50: The Gender and Body Image (GABI) study. *Journal of Women & Aging, 29*, 3–14.

Hohmann-Marriott, B. (2006, November). Shared beliefs and the union stability of married and cohabiting couples. *Journal of Marriage and Family, 68*, 1015–1028.

Holahan, C., & Chapman, J. (2002). Longitudinal predictors of proactive goals and activity participation at age 80. *Journals of Gerontology: Series B: Psychological Sciences & Social Sciences, 57B*, P418–P425.

Holland, J. L. (1997). *Making vocational choices: A theory of vocational personalities and environments* (3rd ed.). Odessa, FL: Psychological Assessment Resources.

Holland, J. M., Neimeyer, R. A., Boelen, P. A., & Prigerson, H. G. (2009). The underlying structure of grief: A taxometric investigation of prolonged and normal reactions to loss. *Journal of Psychopathology and Behavioral Assessment, 31*, 190–201.

Holland, N. (1994, August). Race dissonance—Implications for African American children. Paper presented at the annual meeting of the American Psychological Association, Los Angeles, CA.

Hollich, G. J., Hirsh-Pasek, K., Golinkoff, R. M., Brand, R. J., Brown, E. C., He, L., Hennon, E., & Rocrot, C. (2000). Breaking the language barrier: An emergentist coalition model of the origins of word learning. *Monographs of the Society for Research in Child Development, 65* (3, Serial No. 262).

Holliday, E., & Gould, T. J. (2016). Nicotine, adolescence, and stress: A review of how stress can modulate the negative consequences of adolescent nicotine abuse. *Neuroscience and Biobehavioral Reviews, 65*, 173–184.

Holly, L. E., Little, M., Pina, A. A., & Caterino, L. C. (2015). Assessment of anxiety symptoms in school children: A cross-sex and ethnic examination. *Journal of Abnormal Child Psychology, 43*, 297–309.

Holmes, E. R., & Holmes, L. D. (1995). *Other cultures, elder years*. Thousand Oaks, CA: Sage Publications.

Holmes, R. M., & Romeo, L. (2013). Gender, play, language, and creativity in preschoolers. *Early Child Development and Care, 183*, 1531–1543.

Holowaka, S., & Petitto, L. A. (2002). Left hemisphere cerebral specialization for babies while babbling. *Science, 287*, 1515.

Homae, F., Watanabe, H., Nakano, T., & Taga, G. (2012). Functional development in the infant brain for auditory pitch processing. *Human Brain Mapping, 33*, 596–608.

Hong, D. S., Hoeft, F., Marzelli, M. J., Lepage, J., Roeltgen, D., Ross, J., & Reiss, A. L. (2014). Influence of the X-chromosome on neuroanatomy: Evidence from Turner and Klinefelter syndromes. *Journal of Neuroscience, 34*, 3509–3516.

Hong, S. B., & Trepanier-Street, M. (2004). Technology: A tool for knowledge construction in a Reggio Emilia inspired teacher education program. *Early Childhood Education Journal, 32*, 87–94.

Hooks, B., & Chen, C. (2008). Vision triggers an experience-dependent sensitive period at the retinogeniculate synapse. *Journal of Neuroscience, 28*, 4807–4817. Accessed online, http://search.ebscohost.com, doi:10.1523/JNEUROSCI.4667-07.2008.

Hopkins, B., & Westra, T. (1989). Maternal expectations of their infants' development: Some cultural differences. *Developmental Medicine and Child Neurology, 31*, 384–390.

Hopkins, B., & Westra, T. (1990). Motor development, maternal expectation, and the role of handling. *Infant Behavior and Development, 13*, 117–122.

Horiuchi, S., Finch, C., & Mesle, F. (2003). Differential patterns of age-related mortality increase in middle age and old age. *Journals of Gerontology: Series A: Biological Sciences & Medical Sciences, 58A*, 495–507.

Horne, R. C. (2017). Sleep disorders in newborns and infants. In S. Nevšímalová & O. Bruni (Eds.), *Sleep disorders in children*. Cham, Switzerland: Springer International Publishing

Hornor, G. (2008). Reactive attachment disorder. *Journal of Pediatric Health Care, 22*, 234–239.

Horwitz, B. N., Luong, G., & Charles, G. T. (2008). Neuroticism and extraversion share genetic and environmental effects with negative and positive mood spillover in a nationally representative sample. *Personality and Individual Differences, 45*, 636–642.

Hosogi, M., Okada, A., Fuji, C., Noguchi, K., & Watanabe, K. (2012). Importance and usefulness of evaluating self-esteem in children. *Biopsychosocial Medicine, 6*, 80–88.

Hotelling, B. A., & Humenick, S. S. (2005). Advancing normal birth: Organizations, goals, and research. *Journal of Perinatal Education, 14*, 40–48.

Hou, Y., Kim, S. Y., & Wang, Y. (2016). Parental acculturative stressors and adolescent adjustment through interparental and parent–child relationships in Chinese American families. *Journal of Youth and Adolescence, 45*, 1466–1481.

House, S. H. (2007). Nurturing the brain nutritionally and emotionally from before conception to late adolescence. *Nutritional Health, 19*, 143–61.

Houts, A. (2003). Behavioral treatment for enuresis. In A. Kazdin (Ed.), *Evidence-based psychotherapies for children and adolescents* (pp. 389–406). New York: Guilford Press.

Houwen, S., Visser, L., van der Putten, A., & Vlaskamp, C. (2016). The interrelationships between motor, cognitive, and language development in children with and without intellectual and developmental disabilities. *Research in Developmental Disabilities, 53*, 5419–5431.

Howard, A. (1992). Work and family crossroads spanning the career. In S. Zedeck (Ed.), *Work, families and organizations*. San Francisco: Jossey-Bass.

Howard, J. S., Stanislaw, H., Green, G., Sparkman, C. R., & Cohen, H. G. (2014). Comparison of behavior analytic and eclectic early interventions for young children with autism after three years. *Research in Developmental Disabilities, 35*, 3326–3344.

Howe, M. J. (1997). *IQ in question: The truth about intelligence*. London, England: Sage Publications.

Howe, M. L., Courage, M. L., & Edison, S. C. (2004). When autobiographical memory begins. In S. Algarabel, A. Pitarque, T. Bajo, S. E. Gathercole, & M. A. Conway (Eds.), *Theories of memory* (Vol. 3). New York: Psychology Press.

Howes, O., & Kapur, S. (2009). The dopamine hypothesis of schizophrenia: Version III—The final common pathway. *Schizophrenia Bulletin, 35*, 549–562.

Howlader N., Noone A. M., Krapcho, M. Miller, D., Bishop, K., Kosary, C. L., Yu, M., Ruhl, J., Tatalovich, Z., Mariotto, A., Lewis, D. R., Chen, H. S., Feuer, E. J., Cronin, K. A. (Eds). *SEER Cancer Statistics Review, 1975-2014*. Bethesda, MD: National Cancer Institute. Accessed online, 11-28-17; https://seer.cancer.gov/csr/1975_2014/.

Hsin, L., & Snow, C. (2017). Social perspective taking: A benefit of bilingualism in academic writing. *Reading and Writing*. Accessed online, 3-16-17; http://link.springer.com/article/10.1007/s11145-016-9718-9.

Hu, Y., Xu, Y., & Tornello, S. L. (2016). Stability of self-reported same-sex and both-sex attraction from adolescence to young adulthood. *Archives of Sexual Behavior, 45*, 651–659.

Huang, A., Subak, L., Thom, D., Van Den Eeden, S., Ragins, A., Kuppermann, M., et al. (2009). Sexual function and aging in racially and ethnically diverse women. *Journal of the American Geriatrics Society, 57*, 1362–1368.

Huang, C. T. (2012). Outcome-based observational learning in human infants. *Journal of Comparative Psychology, 126*, 139–149.

Huang, J. (2004). Death: Cultural traditions. *From on Our Own Terms: Moyers on Dying*. Accessed online, 5-24-04, www.pbs.org.

Hubel, D. H., & Wiesel, T. N. (2004). *Brain and visual perception: The story of a 25-year collaboration*. New York: Oxford University Press.

Hubley, A. M., & Arim, R. G. (2012). Subjective age in early adolescence: Relationships with chronological age, pubertal timing, desired age, and problem behaviors. *Journal of Adolescence, 35*, 357–366.

Hudson, J. A., Sosa, B. B., & Shapiro, L. R. (1997). Scripts and plans: The development of preschool children's event knowledge and event planning. In S. L. Friedman & E. K. Scholnick (Eds.), *The developmental psychology of planning: Why, how and when do we plan*. Mahwah, NJ: Lawrence Erlbaum.

Hueston, W., Geesey, M., & Diaz, V. (2008). Prenatal care initiation among pregnant teens in the United States: An analysis over 25 years. *Journal of Adolescent Health, 42*, 243–248.

Huh, S. Y., Rifas-Shiman, S. L., Zera, C. A., Rich Edwards, J. W., Oken, E., Weiss, S. T., & Gilmann, M. W. (2011). Delivery by caesarean section and risk of obesity in preschool age children: A prospective cohort study. *Archives of Disease in Childhood, 34*, 66–79.

Hui, A., Lau, S., Li, C. S., Tong, T., & Zhang, J. (2006). A cross-societal comparative study of Beijing and Hong Kong children's self-concept. *Social Behavior and Personality, 34*, 511–524.

Huijbregts, S., Tavecchio, L., Leseman, P., & Hoffenaar, P. (2009). Child rearing in a group setting: Beliefs of Dutch, Caribbean Dutch, and Mediterranean Dutch caregivers in center-based child care. *Journal of Cross-Cultural Psychology, 40*, 797–815.

Huizink, A., Mulder, E., & Buitelaar, J. (2004). Prenatal stress and risk for psychopathology: Specific effects or induction of general susceptibility? *Psychological Bulletin, 130*, 115–142.

Hülür, G., Gasimova, F., Robitzsch, A., & Wilhelm, O. (2017). Change in fluid and crystallized intelligence and student achievement: The role of intellectual engagement. *Child Development*. Accessed online 11-16-17; https://www.ncbi.nlm.nih.gov/pubmed/28369877.

Human Genome Project. (2006). Accessed online, http://www.ornl.gov/sci/techresources/Human_Genome/medicine/genetest.shtml.

Humphrey, N., Curran, A., Morris, E., Farrell, P., & Woods, K. (2007, April). Emotional intelligence and education: A critical review. *Educational Psychology, 27*, 235–254.

Humphries, M. L., & Korfmacher, J. (2012). The good, the bad, and the ambivalent: Quality of alliance in a support program for young mothers. *Infant Mental Health Journal, 33*, 22–33.

Hunt, M. (1993). *The story of psychology*. New York: Doubleday.

Hunter, J., & Mallon, G. P. (2000). Lesbian, gay, and bisexual adolescent development: Dancing with your feet tied together. In B. Greene & G. L. Croom (Eds.), *Education, research, and practice in lesbian, gay, bisexual, and transgendered psychology: A resource manual (Vol. 5)*. Thousand Oaks, CA: Sage Publications.

Hunter, S., & Smith, D. (2008). Predictors of children's understandings of death: Age, cognitive ability, death experience and maternal communicative competence. *Omega: Journal of Death and Dying, 57*, 143–162.

Huntsinger, C. S., Jose, P. E., Liaw, F., & Ching, W-D. (1997). Cultural differences in early mathematics learning: A comparison of Euro-American, Chinese-American, and Taiwan–Chinese families. *International Journal of Behavioral Development, 21*, 371–388.

Hust, S., Brown, J., & L'Engle, R. (2008). Gender, media use, and effects. *The handbook of children, media, and development* (pp. 98–120). Malden, MA: Blackwell Publishing.

Huster, R. J., Westerhausen, R. R., & Herrmann, C. S. (2011). Sex differences in cognitive control are associated with midcingulate and callosal morphology. *Brain Structure & Function, 215*, 225–235.

Huston, T. L., Caughlin, J. P., Houts, R. M., & Smith, S. E. (2001). The connubial crucible: Newlywed years as predictors of marital delight, distress, and divorce. *Journal of Personality and Social Psychology, 80*, 237–252.

Hutcheon, J. A., Joseph, K. S., Kinniburgh, B., & Lee, L. (2013). Maternal, care provider, and institutional-level risk factors for early term elective repeat cesarean delivery: A population-based cohort study. *Maternal and Child Health Journal*. Accessed online, 2-8-14; http://www.perinatalservicesbc.ca/NR/rdonlyres/3D43DD9D-2367-4729-AF6D-602B5F3ABABA/0/MaternalCare-ProviderInstit_RiskFactors_2014.pdf.

Hutchinson, D., & Rapee, R. (2007). Do friends share similar body image and eating problems? The role of social networks and peer influences in early adolescence. *Behaviour Research and Therapy, 45*, 1557–1577.

Hutchinson, S., & Wexler, B. (2007, January). Is "raging" good for health? Older women's participation in the Raging Grannies. *Health Care for Women International, 28*, 88–118.

Hutton, P. H. (2004). *Phillippe Ariès and the politics of French cultural history*. Amherst: University of Massachusetts Press.

Huurre, T., Junkkari, H., & Aro, H. (2006, June). Long-term psychosocial effects of parental divorce: A follow-up study from adolescence to adulthood. *European Archives of Psychiatry and Clinical Neuroscience, 256*, 256–263.

Hyde, J. S., & DeLamater, J. D. (2003). *Understanding human sexuality* (8th ed.). New York: McGraw-Hill.

Hyde, J. S., & DeLamater, J. D. (2004). *Understanding human sexuality* (8th ed.). New York: McGraw-Hill.

Hyde, J. S., Mezulis, A., & Abramson, L. (2008). The ABCs of depression: Integrating affective, biological, and cognitive models to explain the emergence of the gender difference in depression. *Psychological Review, 115*, 291–313.

Hynes, S. M., Fish, J., & Manly, T. (2014). Intensive working memory training: A single case experimental design in a patient following hypoxic brain damage. *Brain Injury, 28*, 1766–1775.

Hyssaelae, L., Rautava, P., & Helenius, H. (1995). Fathers' smoking and use of alcohol: The viewpoint of maternity health care clinics and well-baby clinics. *Family Practice, 12*, 22–27.

Iavarone, A., Ziello, A. R., Pastore, F., Fasanaro, A. M., & Poderico, C. (2014). Caregiver burden and coping strategies in caregivers of patients with Alzheimer's disease. *Neuropsychiatric Disease and Treatment, 10*, 37–44.

Ibbotson, P., & Tomasello, M. (2016). Language in a new key. *Scientific American*, pp. 71–75.

Iecovich, E., & Biderman, A. (2012). Attendance in adult day care centers and its relation to loneliness among frail older adults. *International Psychogeriatrics, 24*, 439–448.

Ige, T. J., DeLeon, P., & Nabors, L. (2017). Motivational interviewing in an obesity prevention program for children. *Health Promotion Practice, 18*, 263–274.

Ihle, A., Schnitzspahn, K., Rendell, P. G., Luong, C., & Kliegel, M. (2012). Age benefits in everyday prospective memory: The influence of personal task importance, use of reminders and everyday stress. *Aging, Neuropsychology, and Cognition, 19*, 84–101.

Inagaki, M. (2013). Developmental transformation of narcissistic amae in early, middle, and late adolescents: Relation to ego identity. *Japanese Journal of Educational Psychology, 61*, 56–66.

Ingram, D. K., Young, J., & Mattison, J. A. (2007). Calorie restriction in nonhuman primates: Assessing effects on brain and behavioral aging. *Neuroscience, 14*, 1359–1364.

Inguaggiato, E., Sgandurra, G., & Cioni, G. (2017). Brain plasticity and early development: Implications for early intervention in neurodevelopmental disorders. *Neuropsychiatrie De L'enfance Et De L'adolescence, 65*, 299–306.

Inguglia, C., Ingoglia, S., Liga, F., Lo Coco, A., & Lo Cricchio, M. G. (2014). Autonomy and relatedness in adolescence and emerging adulthood: Relationships with parental support and psychological distress. *Journal of Adult Development*. Accessed online, 3-23-15; http://link.springer.com/article/10.1007%2Fs10804-014-9196-8#page-1.

Inoue, K., Tanii, H., Abe, S., Kaiya, H., Nata, M., & Fukunaga, T. (2006, December). The correlation between rates of unemployment and suicide rates in Japan between 1985 and 2002. *International Medical Journal, 13*, 261–263.

Insel, B. J., & Gould, M. S. (2008). Impact of modeling on adolescent suicidal behavior. *Psychiatric Clinics of North America, 31*, 293–316.

International Human Genome Sequencing Consortium. (2001). Initial sequencing and analysis of the human genome. *Nature, 409*, 860–921.

International Literacy Institute. (2001). Literacy overview. Accessed online; http://www.literacyonline.org/explorer.

Ireland, J. L., & Archer, J. (2004). Association between measures of aggression and bullying among juvenile young offenders. *Aggressive Behavior, 30*, 29–42.

Ironson, G., & Schneiderman, N. (2002). Psychological factors, spirituality/religiousness, and immune function in HIV/AIDS patients. In H. G. Koenig & H. J. Cohen (Eds.), *Link between religion and health: Psychoneuroimmunology and the faith factor*. London: Oxford University Press.

Irwin, M. R. (2015). Why sleep is important for health: A psychoneuroimmunology perspective. *Annual Review of Psychology, 66*, 143–172.

Isaacs, K. L., Barr, W. B., Nelson, P. K., & Devinsky, O. (2006). Degree of handedness and cerebral dominance. *Neurology, 66*, 1855–1858.

Isay, R. A. (1990). *Being homosexual: Gay men and their development*. New York: Avon.

Isherwood, L. M., King, D. S., & Luszcz, M. A. (2017). Widowhood in the fourth age: Support exchange, relationships and social participation. *Ageing & Society, 37*, 188–212.

Ishii-Kuntz, M. (2000). Diversity within Asian-American families. In D. H. Demo, K. R. Allen, & M. A. Fine (Eds.), *Handbook of family diversity*. New York: Oxford.

Ishizuka, B., Kudo, Y., & Tango, T. (2008). Cross-sectional community survey of menopause symptoms among Japanese women. *Maturitas, 61*, 260–267.

Ising, M., Mather, K. A., Zimmermann, P., Brückl, T., Höhne, N., Heck, A., & … Reppermund, S. (2014). Genetic effects on information processing speed are moderated by age—converging results from three samples. *Genes, Brain & Behavior*. Accessed online, 3-31-15; http://onlinelibrary.wiley.com/doi/10.1111/gbb.12132/abstract.

Iveniuk, J., Laumann, E. O., Waite, L. J., McClintock, M. K., & Tiedt, A. (2014). Personality measures in the National Social Life, Health, and Aging Project. *Journals of Gerontology: Series B: Psychological Sciences and Social Sciences, 69*(supp 2), S117–S124.

Izard, C. E., King, K. A., Trentacosta, C. J., Morgan, J. K., Laurenceau, J., Krauthamer-Ewing, E., & Finlon, K. J. (2008). Accelerating the development of emotion competence in Head Start children: Effects on adaptive and maladaptive behavior. *Development and Psychopathology, 20*, 369–397.

Izard, V., Sann, C., Spelke, E., & Streri, A. (2009). Newborn infants perceive abstract numbers. *PNAS Proceedings of the National Academy of Sciences of the United States of America, 106*, 10382–10385.

Jack, F., Simcock, G., & Hayne, H. (2012). Magic memories: Young children's verbal recall after a 6-year delay. *Child Development, 83*, 159–172.

Jackson, M. I. (2015). Early childhood WIC participation, cognitive development and academic achievement. *Social Science & Medicine, 126*, 145–153.

Jackson, S. L. (2018). Introduction and overview of elder abuse. In *Understanding elder abuse: A clinician's guide*. Washington, DC: American Psychological Association.

Jacob, K. S. (2014). DSM-5 and culture: The need to move towards a shared model of care within a more equal patient-physician partnership. *Asian Journal of Psychiatry, 7*, 89–91.

Jacobson, C., Batejan, K., Kleinman, M., & Gould, M. (2013). Reasons for attempting suicide among a community sample of adolescents. *Suicide and Life-Threatening Behavior, 43*, 646–662.

Jager, R., Mieler, W., & Miller, J. (2008). Age-related macular degeneration. *New England Journal of Medicine, 358*, 2606–2617.

Jahagirdar, V. (2014). Hemispheric differences: The bilingual brain. In R. R. Heredia, & J. Altarriba (Eds.), *Foundations of bilingual memory*. New York: Springer Science + Business Media.

Jahoda, G. (1983). European "lag" in the development of an economic concept: A study in Zimbabwe. *British Journal of Developmental Psychology, 1*, 113–120.

Jalonick, M. C. (2011, January 13). New guidelines would make school lunches healthier. *Washington Post*.

James, J., Ellis, B. J., Schlomer, G. L., & Garber, J. (2012). Sex-specific pathways to early puberty, sexual debut, and sexual risk taking: Tests of an integrated evolutionary–developmental model. *Developmental Psychology, 48*, 687–702.

James, K. H. & Engelhardt, L. (2012). The effects of handwriting experience on functional brain development in pre-literate children. *Trends in Neuroscience and Education, 1*, 32–42.

James, W. (1890/1950). *The principles of psychology*. New York: Holt.

Jäncke, L., Mérillat, S., Liem, F., & Hänggi, J. (2015). Brain size, sex, and the aging brain. *Human Brain Mapping, 36*, 150–169.

Janda, L. H., & Klenke-Hamel, K. E. (1980). *Human sexuality*. New York: Van Nostrand.

Jansen, B. J., Hofman, A. D., Straatemeier, M., van Bers, B. W., Raijmakers, M. J., & van der Maas, H. J. (2014). The role of pattern recognition in children's exact enumeration of small numbers. *British Journal of Developmental Psychology, 32*, 178–194.

Jansen, P. W., Mieloo, C. L., Dommisse-van Berkel, A., Verlinden, M., van der Ende, J., Stevens, G., & … Tiemeier, H. (2016). Bullying and victimization among young elementary school children: The role of child ethnicity and ethnic school composition. *Race and Social Problems, 8*, 271–280.

Janusek, L., Cooper, D., & Mathews, H. L. (2012). Stress, immunity, and health outcomes. In V. Rice (Ed.), *Handbook of stress, coping, and health: Implications for nursing research, theory, and practice* (2nd ed.). Thousand Oaks, CA: Sage Publications, Inc.

Jao, R., James, T. & James, K. (2014). Multisensory convergence of visual and haptic object preference across development. *Neuropsychologia [serial online], 56,* 381–392.

Jardri, R., Houfflin-Debarge, V., Delion, P., Pruvo, J., Thomas, P., & Pins, D. (2012). Assessing fetal response to maternal speech using a noninvasive functional brain imaging technique. *International Journal of Developmental Neuroscience, 30,* 159–161.

Jarrold, C., & Hall, D. (2013). The development of rehearsal in verbal short-term memory. *Child Development Perspectives, 7,* 182–186.

Jaswal, V., & Dodson, C. (2009). Metamemory development: Understanding the role of similarity in false memories. *Child Development, 80,* 629–635.

Jay, M. (2012, April 14). The downside of cohabiting before marriage. *New York Times,* p. SR4.

Jenkins, L. N., & Demaray, M. K. (2015). Indirect effects in the peer victimization-academic achievement relation: The role of academic self-concept and gender. *Psychology in the Schools, 52,* 235–247.

Jensen, A. (2003). Do age-group differences on mental tests imitate racial differences? *Intelligence, 31,* 107–121.

Jensen, L. A. (2008). Coming of age in a multicultural world: Globalization and adolescent cultural identity formation. In D. L Browning (Ed.), *Adolescent identities: A collection of readings.* New York: Analytic Press/Taylor & Francis Group.

Jensen, L. A., & Dost-Gözkan, A. (2014). Adolescent–parent relations in Asian Indian and Salvadoran immigrant families: A cultural–developmental analysis of autonomy, authority, conflict, and cohesion. *Journal of Research on Adolescence.* Accessed online, 3-23-15; http://onlinelibrary.wiley.com/doi/10.1111/jora.12116/abstract.

Jesmin, S. S. (2014). Review of Agewise: Fighting the new ageism in America. *Journal of Women & Aging, 26,* 369–371.

Jeynes, W. (2007). The impact of parental remarriage on children: A meta-analysis. *Marriage & Family Review, 40,* 75–102.

Jia, R., Lang, S. N., & Schoppe-Sullivan, S. J. (2016). A developmental examination of the psychometric properties and predictive utility of a revised psychological self-concept measure for preschool-age children. *Psychological Assessment, 28,* 226–238.

Jiang, Y., Granja, M. R., & Koball, H. (2017). *Basic facts about low-income children.* New York: National Center for Children in Poverty.

Ji-liang, S., Li-qing, Z., & Yan, T. (2003). The impact of intergenerational social support and filial expectation on the loneliness of elder parents. *Chinese Journal of Clinical Psychology, 11,* 167–169.

Jimenez, J., & Guzman, R. (2003). The influence of code-oriented versus meaning-oriented approaches to reading instruction on word recognition in the Spanish language. *International Journal of Psychology, 38,* 65–78.

Joe, S., & Marcus, S. (2003). Datapoints: Trends by race and gender in suicide attempts among U.S. adolescents, 1991–2001. *Psychiatric Services, 54,* 454.

Johnson, D. J., Jaeger, E., Randolph, S. M., Cauce, A. M., & Ward, J. (2003). Studying the effects of early child care experiences on the development of children of color in the United States: Toward a more inclusive research agenda. *Child Development, 74*(5), 1227-1244. doi:10.1111/1467-8624.00604

Johnson, A. M., Wadsworth, J., Wellings, K., & Bradshaw, S. (1992). Sexual lifestyles and HIV risk. *Nature, 360,* 410–412.

Johnson, P. J., & Aboud, F. E. (2017). Evaluation of an intervention using cross-race friend storybooks to reduce prejudice among majority race young children. *Early Childhood Research Quarterly, 40,* 110–122.

Johnston, L. D., Delva, J., & O'Malley, P. M. (2007). Soft drink availability, contracts, and revenues in American secondary schools. *American Journal of Preventive Medicine, 33,* S209–SS225.

Johnston, L. D., O'Malley, P. M., Miech, R. A, Bachman, J. G., & Schulenberg, J. E. (2015). *Monitoring the future national survey results on drug use: 1975–2014: Overview, key findings on adolescent drug use.* Ann Arbor: Institute for Social Research, University of Michigan.

Johnston, L. D., O'Malley, P.M., Miech, R. A, Bachman, J. G., & Schulenberg, J. E. (2016). *Monitoring the future national survey results on drug use: 1975-2016: Overview, key findings on adolescent drug use.* Ann Arbor: Institute for Social Research, University of Michigan.

Joireman, J., & Van Lange, P. M. (2015). Ethical guidelines for data collection and analysis: A cornerstone for conducting high-quality research. In *How to publish high-quality research.* Washington, DC: American Psychological Association.

Jokela, M., Pekkarinen, T., Sarvimäki, M., Terviö, M., & Uusitalo, R. (2017). Secular rise in economically valuable personality traits. *PNAS Proceedings of the National Academy of Sciences of the United States of America, 114,* 6527–6532.

Jones, D. E., Carson, K. A., Bleich, S. N., & Cooper, L. A. (2012). Patient trust in physicians and adoption of lifestyle behaviors to control high blood pressure. *Patient Education and Counseling.* Accessed online, 7-22-12; http://www.ncbi.nlm.nih.gov/pubmed/22770676.

Jones, H. E. (2006). Drug addiction during pregnancy: Advances in maternal treatment and understanding child outcomes. *Current Directions in Psychological Science, 15,* 126–132.

Jones, N. A., & Mize, K. D. (2016). Introduction to the special issue: Psychophysiology and psychobiology in emotion development. *Journal of Experimental Child Psychology, 142,* 239–244.

Jones, P. R., Kalwarowsky, S., Braddick, O. J., Atkinson, J., & Nardini, M. (2015). Optimizing the rapid measurement of detection thresholds in infants. *Journal of Vision, 15,* 88–97.

Jones Ross, R. W., Cordazzo, S. D., & Scialfa, C. T. (2014). Predicting on-road driving performance and safety in healthy older adults. *Journal of Safety Research, 51,* 73–80.

Jones, R. M., Vaterlaus, J. M., Jackson, M. A., & Morrill, T. B. (2014). Friendship characteristics, psychosocial development, and adolescent identity formation. *Personal Relationships, 21,* 51–67.

Jones, S. (2007). Imitation in infancy: The development of mimicry. *Psychological Science, 18,* 593–599.

Jongudomkarn, D., & Camfield, L. (2006, September). Exploring the quality of life of people in northeastern and southern Thailand. *Social Indicators Research, 78,* 489–529

Jordan, A. B., & Robinson, T. N. (2008). Children's television viewing, and weight status: Summary and recommendations from an expert panel meeting. *Annals of the American Academy of Political and Social Science, 615,* 119–132.

Jordan, A., Trentacoste, N., Henderson, V., Manganello, J., & Fishbein, M. (2007). Measuring the time teens spend with media: Challenges and opportunities. *Media Psychology, 9,* 19–41.

Jordan-Young, R. M. (2012). Hormones, context, and "brain gender": A review of evidence from congenital adrenal hyperplasia. *Social Science & Medicine, 74,* 1738–1744.

Jorgensen, G. (2006, June). Kohlberg and Gilligan: Duet or duel? *Journal of Moral Education, 35,* 179–196.

Jose, O., & Alfons, V. (2007). Do demographics affect marital satisfaction? *Journal of Sex and Marital Therapy, 33,* 73–85.

Judge, T. A., Ilies, R., & Zhang, Z. (2012). Genetic influences on core self-evaluations, job satisfaction, and work stress: A behavioral genetics mediated model. *Organizational Behavior and Human Decision Processes, 117, 208–220.*

Julvez, J., Guxens, M., Carsin, A., Forns, J., Mendez, M., Turner, M. C., & Sunyer, J. (2014). A cohort study on full breastfeeding and child neuropsychological development: The role of maternal social, psychological, and nutritional factors. *Developmental Medicine & Child Neurology, 56,* 148–156.

Jung, E., & Zhang, Y. (2016). Parental involvement, children's aspirations, and achievement in new immigrant families. *Journal of Educational Research, 109,* 333–350.

Jurimae, T., & Saar, M. (2003). Self-perceived and actual indicators of motor abilities in children and adolescents. *Perception and Motor Skills, 97,* 862–866.

Justice, L. M., Logan, J. R., Lin, T., & Kaderavek, J. N. (2014). Peer effects in early childhood education: Testing the assumptions of special-education inclusion. *Psychological Science, 25,* 1722–1729.

Juvonen, J., Schacter, H. L., Sainio, M., & Salmivalli, C. (2016). Can a school-wide bullying prevention program improve the plight of victims? Evidence for risk × intervention effects. *Journal of Consulting and Clinical Psychology, 84,* 334–344.

Kabir, A. A., Pridjian, G., Steinmann, W. C., Herrera, E. A., & Khan, M. M. (2005). Racial differences in cesareans: An analysis of U.S. 2001 national inpatient sample data. *Obstetrics & Gynecology, 105,* 710–718.

Kacapyr, E. (1997, October). Are we having fun yet? *American Demographics,* pp. 28–30.

Kadam, G. (2014). Psychological health of parents whose children are away from them. *Indian Journal of Community Psychology, 10,* 358–363.

Kaffashi, F., Scher, M. S., Ludington-Hoe, S. M., & Loparo, K. A. (2013). An analysis of the kangaroo care intervention using neonatal EEG complexity: A preliminary study. *Clinical Neurophysiology, 124,* 238–246.

Kagan, J. (2000, October). Adult personality and early experience. *Harvard Mental Health Letter,* pp. 4–5.

Kagan, J. (2003). An unwilling rebel. In R. J. Sternberg (Ed.), *Psychologists defying the crowd: Stories of those who battled the establishment and won.* Washington, DC: American Psychological Association.

Kagan, J. (2008). In defense of qualitative changes in development. *Child Development, 79.*

Kagan, J. (2010). *The temperamental thread: How genes, culture, time, and luck make us who we are.* Washington, DC: Dana Press.

Kagan, J., Arcus, D., & Snidman, N. (1993). The idea of temperament: Where do we go from here? In R. Plomin & G. E. McClearn (Eds.), *Nature, nurture, and psychology.* Washington, DC: American Psychological Association.

Kagan, J., Kearsley, R. B., & Zelazo, P. R. (1978). *Infancy: Its place in human development.* Cambridge, MA: Harvard University Press.

Kagan, J., Snidman, N., Kahn, V., & Towsley, S. (2007). The preservation of two infant temperaments into adolescence. *Monographs of the Society for Research in Child Development, 72,* 1–75.

Kahlbaugh, P., & Huffman, L. (2017). Personality, emotional qualities of leisure, and subjective well-being in the elderly. *International Journal of Aging & Human Development, 85,* 164–184.

Kahn, J. P. (2004). Hostility, coronary risk, and alpha-adrenergic to beta-adrenergic receptor density ratio. *Psychosomatic Medicine, 66,* 289–297.

Kahn, R. L., & Rowe, J. W. (1999). *Successful aging.* New York: Dell.

Kail, R. (2003). Information processing and memory. In M. Bornstein & L. Davidson (Eds.), *Well-being: Positive development across the life course.* Mahwah, NJ: Lawrence Erlbaum Associates.

Kail, R. V. (2004). Cognitive development includes global and domain-specific processes. *Merrill-Palmer Quarterly, 50* [Special issue: 50th anniversary issue: Part II, the maturing of the human development sciences: Appraising past, present, and prospective agendas], 445–455.

Kail, R. V., & Miller, C. A. (2006). Developmental change in processing speed: Domain specificity and stability during childhood and adolescence. *Journal of Cognition and Development, 7*, 119–137.

Kalb, C. (1997, Spring/Summer). The top 10 health worries. *Newsweek Special Issue*, pp. 42–43.

Kalb, C. (2004, January 26). Brave new babies. *Newsweek*, pp. 45–53.

Kalb, C. (2006, February 5). In our blood. *Newsweek*. Accessed online May 2, 2018 from http://www.newsweek.com/our-blood-113321

Kalb, C. (2012, February). Fetal armor. *Scientific American*, p. 73.

Kalsi, M., Heron, G., & Charman, W. (2001). Changes in the static accommodation response with age. *Ophthalmic & Physiological Optics, 21*, 77–84.

Kaltiala-Heino, R., Kosunen, E., & Rimpela, M. (2003). Pubertal timing, sexual behaviour and self-reported depression in middle adolescence. *Journal of Adolescence, 26*, 531–545.

Kamijo, K., Hayashi, Y., Sakai, T., Yahiro, T., Tanaka, K., & Nishihira, Y. (2009). Acute effects of aerobic exercise on cognitive function in older adults. *Journals of Gerontology: Series B: Psychological Sciences and Social Sciences, 64B*, 356–363.

Kaminaga, M. (2007). Pubertal development and depression in adolescent boys and girls. *Japanese Journal of Educational Psychology, 55*, 21–33.

Kan, P., & Kohnert, K. (2009). Fast mapping by bilingual preschool children. *Journal of Child Language, 35*, 495–514.

Kandler, C., Bleidorn, W., & Riemann, R. (2012). Left or right? Sources of political orientation: The roles of genetic factors, cultural transmission, assortative mating, and personality. *Journal of Personality and Social Psychology, 102*, 633–645.

Kaneda, H., Maeshima, K., Goto, N., Kobayakawa, T., Ayabe-Kanamura, S., & Saito, S. (2000). Decline in taste and odor discrimination abilities with age, and relationship between gustation and olfaction. *Chemical Senses, 25*, 331–337.

Kanters, M. A., Bocarro, J. N., Edwards, M. B., Casper, J. M., & Floyd, M. F. (2013). School sport participation under two school sport policies: Comparisons by race/ethnicity, gender, and socioeconomic status. *Annals of Behavioral Medicine, 45*(Suppl 1), S113–S121.

Kantor, J. (2015, June 27). Historic day for gay rights, but a twinge of loss for gay culture. *New York Times*, p. A1.

Kantrowitz, E. J., & Evans, G. W. (2004). The relation between the ratio of children per activity area and off-task behavior and type of play in day care centers. *Environment & Behavior, 36*, 541–557.

Kao, G. (2000). Psychological well-being and educational achievement among immigrant youth. In D. J. Hernandez (Ed.), *Children of immigrants: Health, adjustment, and public assistance*. Washington, DC: National Academy Press.

Kapadia, S. (2008). Adolescent-parent relationships in Indian and Indian immigrant families in the US: Intersections and disparities. *Psychology and Developing Societies, 20*, 257–275.

Kapke, T. L., Gerdes, A. C., & Lawton, K. E. (2017). Global self-worth in Latino youth: The role of acculturation and acculturation risk factors. *Child & Youth Care Forum, 46*, 307–333.

Kaplan, H., & Dove, H. (1987). Infant development among the Ache of Eastern Paraguay. *Developmental Psychology, 23*, 190–198.

Kaplan, R. M., Sallis, J. F., Jr., & Patterson, T. L. (1993). *Health and human behavior: Age-specific breast cancer annual incidence*. New York: McGraw-Hill.

Karatzias, T., Yan, E., & Jowett, S. (2015). Adverse life events and health: A population study in Hong Kong. *Journal of Psychosomatic Research, 78*, 173–177.

Karelitz, T. M., Jarvin, L., & Sternberg, R. J. (2010). The meaning of wisdom and its development throughout life. In W. F. Overton & R. M. Lerner (Eds.), *The handbook of life-span development, Vol 1: Cognition, biology, and methods*. Hoboken, NJ: John Wiley & Sons Inc.

Karlsdottir, S. I., Halldorsdottir, S., & Lundgren, I. (2014). The third paradigm in labour pain preparation and management: The childbearing woman's paradigm. *Scandinavian Journal of Caring Sciences, 28*, 315–327.

Karney, B. R., & Bradbury, T. N. (2005). Contextual influences on marriage. *Current Directions in Psychological Science, 14*, 171–174.

Karniol, R. (2009). Israeli kindergarten children's gender constancy for others' counter-stereotypic toy play and appearance: The role of sibling gender and relative age. *Infant and Child Development, 18*, 73–94.

Karraker, A., DeLamater, J & Schwartz, C. R. (2011). Sexual frequency decline from midlife to later life. *Journals of Gerontology, Series B, Psychological Sciences, 66B*, 502–512.

Kaslow, F. W. (2001). Families and family psychology at the millennium: Intersecting crossroads. *American Psychologist, 56*, 37–44.

Kasser, T., & Sharma, Y. S. (1999). Reproductive freedom, educational equality, and females' preference for resource-acquisition characteristics in mates. *Psychological Science, 10*, 374–377.

Kastenbaum, R. (1985). Dying and death: A life-span approach. In J. E. Birren & K. W. Schaie (Eds.), *Handbook of the psychology of aging*. New York: Van Nostrand Reinhold.

Kastenbaum, R. (2000). *The psychology of death* (3rd ed.). New York: Springer.

Kato, K., & Pedersen, N. L. (2005). Personality and coping: A study of twins reared apart and twins reared together. *Behavior Genetics, 35*, 147–158.

Katsimpardi, L., Litterman, N. K., Schein, P. A., Miller, C. M., Loffredo, F. S., Wojtkiewicz, G. R., & … Rubin, L. L. (2014). Vascular and neurogenic rejuvenation of the aging mouse brain by young systemic factors. *Science, 344*, 630–634.

Katz, S., & Marshall, B. (2003). New sex for old: Lifestyle, consumerism, and the ethics of aging well. *Journal Of Aging Studies, 17*(1), 3-16. doi:10.1016/S0890-4065(02)00086-5

Katz, J. (2017, June 15). Drug deaths in America are rising faster than ever. *New York Times*. Accessed online, 11-9-17; from https://www.nytimes.com/interactive/2017/06/05/upshot/opioid-epidemic-drug-overdose-deaths-are-rising-faster-than-ever.html.

Katz, P. A. (2003). Racists or tolerant multiculturalists? How do they begin? *American Psychologist, 58*, 897–909.

Katzer, C., Fetchenhauer, D., & Belschak, F. (2009). Cyberbullying: Who are the victims? A comparison of victimization in internet chatrooms and victimization in school. *Journal of Media Psychology: Theories, Methods, and Applications, 21*, 25–36.

Kaufman, J. C., Kaufman, A. S., Kaufman-Singer, J., & Kaufman, N. L. (2005). The Kaufman Assessment Battery for Children—Second Edition and the Kaufman Adolescent and Adult Intelligence Test. In D. P. Flanagan & P. L. Harrison (Eds.), *Contemporary intellectual assessment: Theories, tests, and issues*. New York: Guilford Press.

Kaufmann, D., Gesten, E., Santa Lucia, R. C., Salcedo, O., Rendina-Gobioff, G., & Gadd, R. (2000). The relationship between parenting style and children's adjustment: The parents' perspective. *Journal of Child & Family Studies, 9*, 231–245.

Kawakami, K. (2014). The early sociability of toddlers: The origins of teaching. *Infant Behavior & Development, 37*, 174–177.

Kayton, A. (2007). Newborn screening: A literature review. *Neonatal Network, 26*, 85–95.

Kazura, K. (2000). Fathers' qualitative and quantitative involvement: An investigation of attachment, play, and social interactions. *Journal of Men's Studies, 9*, 41–57.

Kearney, M. S., & Levine, P. B. (2015). Early childhood education by MOOC: Lessons from Sesame Street. *NBER Working Paper No. 21229*.

Keating, D. (1990). Adolescent thinking. In S. S. Feldman & G. R. Elliott (Eds.), *At the threshold*. Cambridge, MA: Harvard University Press.

Keating, D. P. (2004). Cognitive and brain development. In R. M. Lerner & L. Steinberg (Eds.), *Handbook of adolescent psychology* (2nd ed.). Hoboken, NJ: John Wiley & Sons.

Kedziora-Kornatowski, K., Szewczyk-Golec, K., Czuczejko, J., van Marke de Lumen, K., Pawluk, H., Motyl, J., Karasek, M., & Kedziora, J. (2007). Effect of melatonin on the oxidative stress in erythrocytes of healthy young and elderly subjects. *Journal of Pineal Research, 42*, 153–158.

Keene, J. R., Prokos, A. H., & Held, B. (2012). Grandfather caregivers: Race and ethnic differences in poverty. *Sociological Inquiry, 82*, 49–77.

Kehl, K. A., & McCarty, K. N. (2012). Readability of hospice materials to prepare families for caregiving at the time of death. *Research in Nursing & Health, 35*, 242–249.

Kelch-Oliver, K. (2008). African American grandparent caregivers: Stresses and implications for counselors. *Family Journal, 16*, 43–50.

Kellehear, A. (2015). Death education as a public health issue. In J. M. Stillion, & T. Attig (Eds.), *Death, dying, and bereavement: Contemporary perspectives, institutions, and practices*. New York: Springer Publishing Co.

Keller, H., Otto, H., Lamm, B., Yovsi, R. D., & Kartner, J. (2008). The timing of verbal/vocal communications between mothers and their infants: A longitudinal cross-cultural comparison. *Infant Behavior & Development, 31*, 217–226.

Keller, H., Voelker, S., & Yovsi, R. D. (2005). Conceptions of parenting in different cultural communities: The case of West African Nso and northern German women. *Social Development, 14*, 158–180.

Keller, H., Yovsi, R., Borke, J., Kärtner, J., Henning, J., & Papaligoura, Z. (2004). Developmental consequences of early parenting experiences: Self-recognition and self-regulation in three cultural communities. *Child Development, 75*, 1745–1760.

Kelley, G., Kelley, K., Hootman, J., & Jones, D. (2009). Exercise and health-related quality of life in older community-dwelling adults: A meta-analysis of randomized controlled trials. *Journal of Applied Gerontology, 28*, 369–394.

Kellman, P., & Arterberry, M. (2006). Infant visual perception. In W. Damon & R. M. Lerner (Eds.), *Handbook of child psychology: Vol. 2, Cognition, perception, and language* (6th ed.). New York: Wiley.

Kellow, J. T., & Jones, B. D. (2008). The effects of stereotypes on the achievement gap: Reexamining the academic performance of African American high school students. *Journal Of Black Psychology, 34*(1), 94-120. doi:10.1177/0095798407310537

Kelloway, E., & Francis, L. (2013). Longitudinal research and data analysis. In R. R. Sinclair, M. Wang, & L. E. Tetrick (Eds.), *Research methods in occupational health psychology: Measurement, design, and data analysis*. New York: Routledge/Taylor & Francis Group.

Kelly, G. (2001). *Sexuality today: A human perspective* (7th ed.). New York: McGraw-Hill.

Kelly-Weeder, S., & Cox, C. (2007). The impact of lifestyle risk factors on female infertility. *Women & Health, 44*, 1–23.

Kemker, D. (2017, January 9). Ameen Abdulrasool. My Hero Stories Scientists. Accessed online, 11-13-17; https://myhero.com/Abdulrasool_06.

Kemper, S. (2012). The interaction of linguistic constraints, working memory, and aging on language production and comprehension. In M. Naveh-Benjamin & N. Ohta (Eds.), *Memory and aging: Current issues and future directions*. New York: Psychology Press.

Kendler, K. S., Aggen, S. H., Gillespie, N., Neale, M. C., Knudsen, G. P., Krueger, R. F., & … Reichborn-Kjennerud, T. (2017). The genetic and environmental sources of resemblance between normative personality and personality disorder traits. *Journal of Personality Disorders, 31*, 193–207.

Kenett, Y. N., Beaty, R. E., Silvia, P. J., Anaki, D., & Faust, M. (2016). Structure and flexibility: Investigating the relation between the structure of the mental lexicon, fluid intelligence, and creative achievement. *Psychology of Aesthetics, Creativity, and the Arts, 10*, 377–388.

Kennedy-Hendricks, A., Barry, C. L., Gollust, S. E., Ensminger, M. E., Chisolm, M. S., & McGinty, E. E. (2017). Social stigma toward persons with prescription opioid use disorder: Associations with public support for punitive and public health–oriented policies. *Psychiatric Services, 68*, 462–469.

Kennell, J. H. (2002). On becoming a family: Bonding and the changing patterns in baby and family behavior. In J. GomesPedro & J. K. Nugent (Eds.), *The infant and family in the twenty-first century*. New York: Brunner-Routledge.

Kenney, S. (2015, June 23). This man hopes his peanut sheller can end world hunger. Accessed online, 12-11-17; https://munchies.vice.com/en_us/article/vvxjmx/this-man-hopes-his-peanut-sheller-can-end-world-hunger.

Kenny, D. T. (2013). *Bringing up baby: The psychoanalytic infant comes of age*. London: Karnac Books.

Kenrick, D. T., Keefe, R. C., Bryna, A., Barr, A., & Brown, S. (1995). Age preferences and mate choice among homosexuals and heterosexuals: A case for modular psychological mechanisms. *Journal of Personality and Social Psychology, 69*, 1166–1172.

Khodarahimi, S., & Fathi, R. (2017). Mate selection, meaning of marriage and positive cognitive constructs on younger and older married individuals. *Contemporary Family Therapy: An International Journal, 39*, 132–139.

Kiang, L., Witkow, M. R., & Thompson, T. L. (2016). Model minority stereotyping, perceived discrimination, and adjustment among adolescents from Asian American backgrounds. *Journal of Youth and Adolescence, 45*, 1366–1379.

Kiecolt-Glaser, J. K. (2009). Psychoneuroimmunology: Psychology's gateway to biomedical future. *Perspectives on Psychological Science, 4* [Special issue: Next big questions in psychology], 367–369.

Kieffer, C. C. (2012). Secure connections, the extended family system, and the socio-cultural construction of attachment theory. In S. Akhtar (Ed.), *The mother and her child: Clinical aspects of attachment, separation, and loss*. Lanham, MD: Jason Aronson.

Killeen, L. A., & Teti, D. M. (2012). Mothers' frontal EEG asymmetry in response to infant emotion states and mother–infant emotional availability, emotional experience, and internalizing symptoms. *Development and Psychopathology, 24*, 9–21.

Kim, B., Chow, S., Bray, B., & Teti, D. M. (2017). Trajectories of mothers' emotional availability: Relations with infant temperament in predicting attachment security. *Attachment & Human Development, 19*, 38–57.

Kim, J-S., & Lee, E-H. (2003). Cultural and noncultural predictors of health outcomes in Korean daughter and daughter-in-law caregivers. *Public Health Nursing, 20*, 111–119.

Kim, E. H., & Lee, E. (2009). Effects of a death education program on life satisfaction and attitude toward death in college students. *Journal of Korean Academic Nursing, 39*, 1–9.

Kim, H. I., & Johnson, S. P. (2013). Do young infants prefer an infant-directed face or a happy face? *International Journal of Behavioral Development, 37*, 125–130.

Kim, H., Sherman, D., & Taylor, S. (2008). Culture and social support. *American Psychologist, 63*, 518–526.

Kim, J., Bushway, S., & Tsao, H. (2016). Identifying classes of explanations for crime drop: Period and cohort effects for New York State. *Journal of Quantitative Criminology, 32*, 357–375.

Kim, J., & Cicchetti, D. (2003). Social self-efficacy and behavior problems in maltreated children. *Journal of Clinical Child & Adolescent Psychology,32*, 106–117.

Kim, J. J., Fung, J., Wu, Q., Fang, C., & Lau, A. S. (2017). Parenting variables associated with growth mindset: An examination of three Chinese-heritage samples. *Asian American Journal of Psychology, 8*, 115–125.

Kim, M. A., & Williams, K. A. (2017). Lead levels in landfill areas and childhood exposure: An integrative review. *Public Health Nursing, 34*, 87–97.

Kim, Y., Choi, J. Y., Lee, K. M., Park, S. K., Ahn, S. H., Noh, D. Y., Hong, Y. C., Kang, D., & Yoo, K. Y. (2007). Dose-dependent protective effect of breast-feeding against breast cancer among never-lactated women in Korea. *European Journal of Cancer Prevention, 16*, 124–129.

Kim, Y. K., Curby, T. W., & Winsler, A. (2014). Child, family, and school characteristics related to English proficiency development among low-income, dual language learners. *Developmental Psychology, 50*, 2600–2613.

Kim-Cohen, J. (2007). Resilience and developmental psychopathology. *Child and Adolescent Psychiatric Clinics of North America, 16*, 271–283.

Kimm, S. Y. (2003). Nature versus nurture in childhood obesity: A familiar old conundrum. *American Journal of Clinical Nutrition, 78*, 1051–1052.

Kimm, S., Glynn, N. W., Kriska, A., Barton, B. A., Kronsberg, S. S., Daniels, S. R., & Liu, K. (2002). Decline in physical activity in black girls and white girls during adolescence. *New England Journal of Medicine, 347*, 709–715.

Kinney, H. C., Randall, L. L., Sleeper, L. A., Willinger, M., Beliveau, R. A., Zec, N., Rava, L. A., Dominici, L., Iyasu, S., Randall, B., Habbe, D., Wilson, H., Mandell, F., McClain, M., & Welty, T. K. (2003). Serotonergic brainstem abnormalities in Northern Plains Indians with the sudden infant death syndrome. *Journal of Neuropathology and Experimental Neurology, 62*, 1178–1191.

Kinney, H., & Thach, B. (2009). Medical progress: The sudden infant death syndrome. *New England Journal of Medicine, 361*, 795–805.

Kinsey, A. C., Pomeroy, W. B., & Martin, C. E. (1948). *Sexual behavior in the human male*. Philadelphia, PA: Saunders.

Kirby, J. (2006, May). From single-parent families to stepfamilies: Is the transition associated with adolescent alcohol initiation? *Journal of Family Issues, 27*, 685–711.

Kirchengast, S., & Hartmann, B. (2003). Impact of maternal age and maternal-somatic characteristics on newborn size. *American Journal of Human Biology, 15*, 220–228.

Kirkwood, T. (2010, September). Why can't we live forever? *Scientific American*, pp. 42–49.

Kirsh, S. J. (2012). *Children, adolescents, and media violence: A critical look at the research* (2nd ed.). Thousand Oaks, CA: Sage Publications, Inc.

Kitamura, C., & Lam, C. (2009). Age-specific preferences for infant-directed affective intent. *Infancy, 14*, 77–100.

Kiuru, N., Nurmi, J., Aunola, K., & Salmela-Aro, K. (2009). Peer group homogeneity in adolescents' school adjustment varies according to peer group type and gender. *International Journal of Behavioral Development, 33*, 65–76.

Kjerulff, K. H., & Brubaker, L. H. (2017). New mothers' feelings of disappointment and failure after cesarean delivery. *Birth: Issues in Perinatal Care*. Accessed online 10-29-17; https://www.ncbi.nlm.nih.gov/pubmed/?term=New+mothers%E2%80%99+feelings+of+disappointment+and+failure+after+cesarean+delivery.+Birth%3A+Issues+In+Perinatal+Care.

Klaming, R., Annese, J., Veltman, D. J., & Comijs, H. C. (2017). Episodic memory function is affected by lifestyle factors: A 14-year follow-up study in an elderly population. *Aging, Neuropsychology, and Cognition, 24*, 528–542.

Kleespies, P. (2004). The wish to die: Assisted suicide and voluntary euthanasia. In P. Kleespies (Ed.), *Life and death decisions: Psychological and ethical considerations in end-of-life care*. Washington, DC: American Psychological Association.

Klein, A. (2017, August 29.) On parenting: When is it safe to start leaving kids home alone? *Washington Post*. Accessed online, 11-20-17; https://www.washingtonpost.com/lifestyle/on-parenting/when-is-it-safe-to-start-leaving-kids-home-alone/2017/08/28/a86390c0-7891-11e7-8839-ec48ec4cae25_story.html?utm_term=.dbd0f2e774a8.

Klein, M. C. (2012). The tyranny of meta-analysis and the misuse of randomized controlled trials in maternity care. *Birth: Issues in Perinatal Care, 39*, 80–82.

Kleinman, A. (2012). Culture, bereavement, and psychiatry. *Lancet, 379*, 608–609.

Klier, C. M., Muzik, M., Dervic, K., Mossaheb, N., Benesch, T., Ulm, B., & Zeller, M. (2007). The role of estrogen and progesterone in depression after birth. *Journal of Psychiatric Research, 41*, 273–279.

Klika, J. B. & Conte, J. R. (2017). *The APSAC handbook on child maltreatment. (4th ed.)* Thousand Oaks, CA: SAGE Publications.

Klimstra, T. A., Luyckx, K., Germeijs, V., Meeus, W. J., & Goossens, L. (2012). Personality traits and educational identity formation in late adolescents: Longitudinal associations and academic progress. *Journal of Youth and Adolescence, 41*, 346–361.

Klingberg, T., & Betteridge, N. (2013). *The learning brain: Memory and brain development in children*. New York: Oxford University Press.

Klitzman, R. L. (2012). *Am I my genes? Confronting fate and family secrets in the age of genetic testing*. New York: Oxford University Press.

Kloep, M., Güney, N., Çok, F., & Simsek, Ö. (2009). Motives for risk-taking in adolescence: A cross-cultural study. *Journal of Adolescence, 32*, 135–151.

Kluger, J. (2010, November 1). Keeping young minds healthy. *Time*, pp. 40–50.

Knafo, A., & Schwartz, S. H. (2003). Parenting and accuracy of perception of parental values by adolescents. *Child Development, 73*, 595–611.

Knaus, W. A., Conners, A. F., Dawson, N. V., Desbiens, N. A., Fulkerson, W. J., Jr., Goldman, L., Lynn, J., & Oye, R. K. (1995, November 22). A controlled trial to improve care for seriously ill hospitalized patients: The study to understand prognoses and preferences for outcomes and risks of treatments (SUPPORT). *JAMA: Journal of the American Medical Association, 273*, 1591–1598.

Knežević, M., & Marinković, K. (2017). Neurodynamic correlates of response inhibition from emerging to mid adulthood. *Cognitive Development, 43*, 106–118.

Knickmeyer, R., & Baron-Cohen, S. (2006, December). Fetal testosterone and sex differences. *Early Human Development, 82*, 755–760.

Knifsend, C. A., & Juvonen, J. (2014). Social identity complexity, cross-ethnic friendships, and intergroup attitudes in urban middle schools. *Child Development, 85*, 709–721.

Knight, Z. G. (2017). A proposed model of psychodynamic psychotherapy linked to Erik Erikson's eight stages of psychosocial development. *Clinical Psychology & Psychotherapy*. Accessed online, 3-2-17; https://www.ncbi.nlm.nih.gov/pubmed/28124459.

Knoll, L. J., Fuhrmann, D., Sakhardande, A. L., Stamp, F., Speekenbrink, M., & Blakemore, S. (2016). A window of opportunity for cognitive training in adolescence. *Psychological Science, 27*, 1620–1631.

Knopp, K. Rhoades, G. K., Allen, E. S., Parsons, A., Ritchie, L. L., Markman, H. J., & Stanley, S. M. (2017). Within and between family associations of marital functioning and child well-being. *Journal of Marriage and Family, 79* (2), 451–461.

Knorth, E. J., Harder, A. T., Zandberg, T., & Kendrick, A. J. (2008). Under one roof: A review and selective meta-analysis on the outcomes of residential child and youth care. *Children and Youth Services Review, 30*, 123–140.

Kochanek, K. D., Arias, E., & Anderson, R. N. (2013). *How did cause of death contribute to racial differences in life expectancy in the United States in 2010?* NCHS data brief, no 125. Hyattsville, MD: National Center for Health Statistics.

Kochanska, G. (1998). Mother–child relationship, child fearfulness, and emerging attachment: A short-term longitudinal study. *Developmental Psychology, 34*, 480–490.

Kochanska, G. (2002). Mutually responsive orientation between mothers and their young children: A context for the early development of conscience. *Current Directions in Psychological Science, 11*, 191–195.

Kochanska, G., & Aksan, N. (2004). Development of mutual responsiveness between parents and their young children. *Child Development, 75*, 1657–1676.

Koenig, L. B., McGue, M., Krueger, R. F., & Bouchard, Jr., T. J. (2005). Genetic and environmental influences on religiousness: Findings for retrospective and current religiousness ratings. *Journal of Personality, 73*, 471–488.

Koenig, M., & Cole, C. (2013). Early word learning. In D. Reisberg (Ed.), *The Oxford handbook of cognitive psychology*. New York: Oxford University Press.

Kogan, S. M., Yu, T., Allen, K. A., & Brody, G. H. (2014). Racial microstressors, racial self-concept, and depressive symptoms among male African Americans during the transition to adulthood. *Journal of Youth and Adolescence*. Accessed online, 3-23-15; http://www.ncbi.nlm.nih.gov/pubmed/25344920.

Koh, S., & Sewell, D. D. (2015). Sexual functions in older adults. *American Journal of Geriatric Psychiatry, 23*, 223–226.

Kohlberg, L. (1966). A cognitive-developmental analysis of children's sex-role concepts and attitudes. In E. E. Maccoby (Ed.), *The development of sex differences*. Stanford, CA: Stanford University Press.

Kohlber, L. (1969). Stage and sequence: The cognitive-developmental approach to socialization. In D. A. Goslin (Ed.), *The handbook of socialization theory and research*. Chicago, IL: Rand McNally.

Kohlberg, L. (1984). *The psychology of moral development: Essays on moral development* (Vol. 2). San Francisco: Harper & Row.

Koike, K. J. (2014). *Everyday audiology: A practical guide for health care professionals* (2nd ed.). San Diego, CA: Plural Publishing.

Koinis-Mitchell, D., Kopel, S. J., Salcedo, L., McCue, C., & McQuaid, E. L. (2014). Asthma indicators and neighborhood and family stressors related to urban living in children. *American Journal of Health Behavior, 38*, 22–30.

Kolata, G. (2004, May 11). The heart's desire. *New York Times*, p. D1.

Kolb, B., & Gibb, R. (2006). Critical periods for functional recovery after cortical injury during development. In S. G. Lomber & J. J. Eggermont (Eds.), *Reprogramming the cerebral cortex: Plasticity following central and peripheral lesions*. New York: Oxford University Press.

Kolling, T., & Knopf, M. (2014). Late life human development: Boosting or buffering universal biological aging. *Geropsych: Journal of Gerontopsychology and Geriatric Psychiatry, 27*, 103–108.

Konigsberg, R. D. (2011, August 2). Chore wars. *Time*, pp. 22–26.

Konrad, K., Firk, C., & Uhlhaas, P. J. (2013). Brain development during adolescence. *Deutsches Przteblatt International, 110*, 425–431.

Koopmans, S., & Kooijman, A. (2006, November). Presbyopia correction and accommodative intraocular lenses. *Gerontechnology, 5*, 222–230.

Kopans, D. B. (2017). The facts about mammography screening: A conversation with your physician. American College of Radiology. Accessed online, 11-28-17; https://www.sbi-online.org/Portals/0/downloads/documents/pdfs/THE%20FACTS%20ABOUT%20MAMMOGRAPHY%20SCREENING-Kopans.pdf.

Koren, C. (2014). Together and apart: A typology of re-partnering in old age. *International Psychogeriatrics, 26*, 1327–1350.

Kornides, M., & Kitsantas, P. (2013). Evaluation of breastfeeding promotion, support, and knowledge of benefits on breastfeeding outcomes. *Journal of Child Health Care, 17*, 264–273.

Korotchikova, I., Stevenson, N. J., Livingstone, V., Ryan, C. A., & Boylan, G. B. (2016). Sleep–wake cycle of the healthy term newborn infant in the immediate postnatal period. *Clinical Neurophysiology, 127*, 2095–2101.

Korte, J., Westerhof, G. J., & Bohlmeijer, E. T. (2012). Mediating processes in an effective life-review intervention. *Psychology and Aging*. Accessed online, 7-24-12; http://psycnet.apa.org/psycinfo/2012-17923-001.

Koska, J., Ksinantova, L., Sebokova, E., Kvetnansky, R., Klimes, I., Chrousos, G., & Pacak, K. (2002). Endocrine regulation of subcutaneous fat metabolism during cold exposure in humans. *Annals of the New York Academy of Science, 967*, 500–505.

Kosminsky, P. (2017). CBT for grief: Clearing cognitive obstacles to healing from loss. *Journal of Rational-Emotive & Cognitive-Behavior Therapy, 35*, 26–37.

Kotre, J., & Hall, E. (1990). *Seasons of life*. Boston: Little, Brown.

Kozulin, A. (2004). Vygotsky's theory in the classroom: Introduction. *European Journal of Psychology of Education, 19*, 3–7.

Krcmar, M., Grela, B., & Lin, K. (2007). Can toddlers learn vocabulary from television? An experimental approach. *Media Psychology, 10*, 41–63.

Kreager, D. A., Molloy, L. E., Moody, J., & Feinberg, M. E. (2016). Friends first? The peer network origins of adolescent dating. *Journal of Research on Adolescence, 26*, 257–269.

Kretch, K. S., & Adolph, K. E. (2013). Cliff or step? Posture-specific learning at the edge of a drop-off. *Child Development, 84*, 226–240.

Kretsch, N., Mendle, J., Cance, J. D., & Harden, K. P. (2016). Peer group similarity in perceptions of pubertal timing. *Journal of Youth and Adolescence, 45*, 1696–1710.

Kringelbach, M. L., Lehtonen, A., Squire, S., Harvey, A. G., Craske, M. G., et al. (2008). A specific and rapid Neural signature for parental instinct. *PLoS ONE*, 3(2), e1664. doi:10.1371/journal.pone.0001664

Krishnan-Sarin, S., et al. (2017). Studying the interactive effects of menthol and nicotine among youth: An examination using E-cigarettes. *Drug and Alcohol Dependency, 180*, 193–199.

Kroger, J. (2006). *Identity development: Adolescence through adulthood*. Thousand Oaks, CA: Sage Publications.

Kronberger, N., & Horwath, I. (2013). The ironic costs of performing well: Grades differentially predict male and female dropout from engineering. *Basic And Applied Social Psychology, 35*(6), 534-546. doi:10.1080/01973533.2013.840629

Kroll, L. R. (2017). Early childhood curriculum development: The role of play in building self-regulatory capacity in young children. *Early Child Development and Care, 187*, 854–868.

Kross, E., & Grossmann, I. (2012). Boosting wisdom: Distance from the self enhances wise reasoning, attitudes, and behavior. *Journal of Experimental Psychology: General, 141*, 43–48.

Krueger, G. (2006, September). Meaning-making in the aftermath of sudden infant death syndrome. *Nursing Inquiry, 13*, 163–171.

Krüger, O., Korsten, P., & Hoffman, J. I. (2017). The rise of behavioral genetics and the transition to behavioral genomics and beyond. In J. Call, G. M. Burghardt, I. M. Pepperberg, C. T. Snowdon, T. Zentall, (Eds.), *APA handbook of comparative psychology: Basic concepts, methods, neural substrate, and behavior*. Washington, DC: American Psychological Association.

Kübler-Ross, E. (1969). *On death and dying*. New York: Macmillan.

Kübler-Ross, E. (1982). *Working it through*. New York: Macmillan.

Kübler-Ross, E. (Ed.). (1975). *Death: The final stage of growth*. Englewood Cliffs, NJ: Prentice Hall.

Kuhl, P. K., Andruski, J. E., Chistovich, I. A., Chistovich, L. A., Kozhevnikova, E. V., Ryskina, V. L., Stolyarova, E. I., Sundberg, U., & Lacerda, F. (1997, August 1). Cross-language analysis of phonetic units in language addressed to infants. *Science, 277*, 684–686.

Kuhn, D. (2008). Formal operations from a twenty-first century perspective. *Human Development, 51*, 48–55.

Kuhn, D., Garcia-Mila, M., Zohar, A., & Andersen, C. (1995). Strategies of knowledge acquisition. With commentary by S. H. White, D. Klahr, & S. M. Carver, and a reply by D. Kuhn. *Monographs of the Society for Research in Child Development, 60*, 122–137.

Kulik, L. (2002). "His" and "Her" marriage: Differences in spousal perceptions of marital life in late adulthood. In S. P. Serge (Ed.), *Advances in psychology research* (Vol. 17). Hauppauge, NY: Nova Science Publishers.

Kulik, L., Walfisch, S., & Liberman, G. (2016). Spousal conflict resolution strategies and marital relations in late adulthood. *Personal Relationships, 23*, 456–474.

Kulkarni, V., Khadilkar, R. J., Srivathsa, M. S., & Inamdar, M. S. (2011). Asrij maintains the stem cell niche and controls differentiation during drosophila lymph gland hematopoiesis. *PLoS ONE, 6*, 22–29.

Kupersmidt, J. B., & Dodge, K. A. (Eds.). (2004). *Children's peer relations: From development to intervention*. Washington, DC: American Psychological Association.

Kurdek, L. (2003). Negative representations of the self/spouse and marital distress. *Personal Relationships, 10*, 511–534.

Kurdek, L. (2006, May). Differences between partners from heterosexual, gay, and lesbian cohabiting couples. *Journal of Marriage and Family, 68*, 509–528.

Kurdek, L. (2007). The allocation of household labor by partners in gay and lesbian couples. *Journal of Family Issues, 28*, 132–148.

Kurdek, L. (2008). Change in relationship quality for partners from lesbian, gay male, and heterosexual couples. *Journal of Family Psychology, 22*, 701–711.

Kurdek, L. A. (1999). The nature and predictors of the trajectory of change in marital quality for husbands and wives over the first 10 years of marriage. *Developmental Psychology, 35*, 1283–1296.

Kurdek, L. A. (2005). What do we know about gay and lesbian couples? *Current Directions in Psychological Science, 14*, 251–258.

Kuron, L. J., Lyons, S. T., Schweitzer, L., & Ng, E. W. (2015). Millennials' work values: Differences across the school to work transition. *Personnel Review, 44*, 991–1009.

Kurtines, W. M., & Gewirtz, J. L. (1987). *Moral development through social interaction*. New York: Wiley.

Kurtz-Costes, B., DeFreitas, S. C., Halle, T. G., & Kinlaw, C. R. (2011). Gender and racial favouritism in Black and White preschool girls. *British Journal Of Developmental Psychology, 29*(2), 270-287. doi:10.1111/j.2044-835X.2010.02018.x

Kurtz-Costes, B., Swinton, A. D., & Skinner, O. D. (2014). Racial and ethnic gaps in the school performance of Latino, African American, and White students. In F. L. Leong, L. Comas-Díaz, G. C. Nagayama Hall, V. C. McLoyd, & J. E. Trimble (Eds.), *APA handbook of multicultural psychology, Vol. 1: Theory and research*. Washington, DC: American Psychological Association.

Kusangi, E., Nakano, S., & Kondo-Ikemura, K. (2014). The development of infant temperament and its relationship with maternal temperament. *Psychologia: An International Journal of Psychological Sciences, 57*, 31–38.

Kwant, P. B., Finocchiaro, T., Forster, F., Reul, H., Rau, G., Morshuis, M., El Banayosi, A., Korfer, R., Schmitz-Rode, T., & Steinseifer, U. (2007). The MiniACcor: Constructive redesign of an implantable total artificial heart, initial laboratory testing and further steps. *International Journal of Artificial Organs, 30*, 345–351.

LaBounty, J., Bosse, L., Savicki, S., King, J., & Eisenstat, S. (2017). Relationship between social cognition and temperament in preschool-aged children. *Infant and Child Development, 26*, 104–118.

Labouvie-Vief, G. (1980). Beyond formal operations: Uses and limits of pure logic in life-span development. *Human Development, 23*, 141–161.

Labouvie-Vief, G. (1986). Modes of knowledge and the organization of development. In M. L. Commons, L. Kohlberg, F. Richards, & J. Sinnott (Eds.), *Beyond formal operations 3: Models and methods in the study of adult and adolescent thought*. New York: Praeger.

Labouvie-Vief, G. (2006). Emerging structures of adult thought. In J. J. Arnett & J. L. Tanner (Eds.), *Emerging adults in America: Coming of age in the 21st century*. Washington, DC: American Psychological Association.

Labouvie-Vief, G. (2009). Cognition and equilibrium regulation in development and aging. *Restorative Neurology and Neuroscience, 27*, 551–565.

Labouvie-Vief, G. (2015). *Integrating emotions and cognition throughout the lifespan*. Cham, Switzerland: Springer International Publishing.

Labouvie-Vief, G., & Diehl, M. (2000). Cognitive complexity and cognitive–affective integration: Related or separate domains of adult development? *Psychology & Aging, 15*, 490–504.

Lacerda, F., von Hofsten, C., & Heimann, M. (2001). *Emerging cognitive abilities in early infancy*. Mahwah, NJ: Lawrence Erlbaum.

Lachapelle, U., Noland, R. B., & Von Hagen, L. (2013). Teaching children about bicycle safety: An evaluation of the New Jersey Bike School program. *Accident Analysis and Prevention, 52*, 237–249.

Lachmann, T., Berti, S., Kujala, T., & Schroger, E. (2005). Diagnostic subgroups of developmental dyslexia have different deficits in neural processing of tones and phonemes. *International Journal of Psychophysiology, 56*, 105–120.

Lackey, C. (2003). Violent family heritage, the transition to adulthood, and later partner violence. *Journal of Family Issues, 24*, 74–98.

LaCoursiere, D., Hirst, K. P., & Barrett-Connor, E. (2012). Depression and pregnancy stressors affect the association between abuse and postpartum depression. *Maternal and Child Health Journal, 16*, 929–935.

Lafay, A., St-Pierre, M., & Macoir, J. (2017). The mental number line in dyscalculia: Impaired number sense or access from symbolic numbers? *Journal of Learning Disabilities, 50*, 672–683.

Laflamme, D., Pomerleau, A., & Malcuit, G. (2002). A comparison of fathers' and mothers' involvement in childcare and stimulation behaviors during free-play with their infants at 9 and 15 months. *Sex Roles, 47*, 507–518.

LaFromboise, T., Coleman, H. L., & Gerton, J. (1993). Psychological impact of biculturalism: Evidence and theory. *Psychological Bulletin, 114*, 395–412.

Laghi, F., Baiocco, R., Di Norcia, A., Cannoni, E., Baumgartner, E., & Bombi, A. S. (2014). Emotion understanding, pictorial representations of friendship and reciprocity in school-aged children. *Cognition and Emotion, 28*, 1338–1346.

Lago, P., Allegro, A., & Heun, N. (2014). Improving newborn pain management: Systematic pain assessment and operators' compliance with potentially better practices. *Journal of Clinical Nursing, 23*, 596–599.

Lagrou, K., Froidecoeur, C., Thomas, M., Massa, G., Beckers, D., Craen, M., de Beaufort, C., Rooman, R., François, I., Heinrichs, C., Lebrethon, M. C., Thiry-Counson, G., Maes, M., & De Schepper, J. (2008). Concerns, expectations and perception regarding stature, physical appearance and psychosocial functioning before and during high-dose growth hormone treatment of short pre-pubertal children born small for gestational age. *Hormone Research, 69*, 334–342.

Lahat, A., Walker, O. L., Lamm, C., Degnan, K. A., Henderson, H. A., & Fox, N. A. (2014). Cognitive conflict links behavioural inhibition and social problem solving during social exclusion in childhood. *Infant and Child Development, 23*, 273–282.

Lahiri, D. K., Maloney, B., Basha, M. R., Ge, Y. W., & Zawia, N. H. (2007). How and when environmental agents and dietary factors affect the course of Alzheimer's disease: The "LEARn" model (latent early-life associated regulation) may explain the triggering of AD. *Current Alzheimer Research, 4*, 219–228.

Laible, D., Panfile, T., & Makariev, D. (2008). The quality and frequency of mother-toddler conflict: Links with attachment and temperament. *Child Development, 79*, 426–443.

Lain, D. (2012). Working past 65 in the UK and the USA: Segregation into "Lopaq" occupations? *Work, Employment and Society, 26*, 78–94.

Lam, V., & Leman, P. (2003). The influence of gender and ethnicity on children's inferences about toy choice. *Social Development, 12*, 269–287.

Lamaze, F. (1970). *Painless childbirth: The Lamaze method*. Chicago: Regnery.

Lambert, C. A. (2016). *Women with controlling partners*. New York: New Harbinger Publications.

Lambiase, A., Aloe, L., Centofanti, M., Parisi, V., Mantelli, F., Colafrancesco, V., et al. (2009). Experimental and clinical evidence of neuroprotection by nerve growth factor eye drops: Implications for glaucoma. *PNAS Proceedings of the National Academy of Sciences of the United States of America, 106*, 13469–13474.

Lambrick, D., Westrupp, N., Kaufmann, S., Stoner, L., & Faulkner, J. (2016). The effectiveness of a high-intensity games intervention on improving indices of health in young children. *Journal of Sports Sciences, 34*, 190–198.

Lamidi, E., & Cruz, J. (2014). *Remarriage rate in the U.S., 2012. (FP-14-10)*. National Center for Family & Marriage Research. Accessed online, 11-29-17; http://www.bgsu. edu/content/dam/ BGSU/college-ofarts-and-sciences/ NCFMR/documents/ FP/FP-14-10-remarriage-rate-2012.pdf.

Lamm, B., & Keller, H. (2007). Understanding cultural models of parenting: The role of intracultural variation and response style. *Journal of Cross-Cultural Psychology, 38*, 50–57.

Lamont, J. A. (1997). Sexuality. In D. E. Stewart & G. E. Robinson (Eds.), *A clinician's guide to menopause. Clinical practice* (pp. 63–75). Washington, DC: Health Press International.

Landau, R. (2008). Sex selection for social purposes in Israel: Quest for the 'perfect child' of a particular gender or centuries old prejudice against women? *Journal of Medical Ethics, 34*, 101–110.

Landrine, H., & Klonoff, E. A. (1994). Cultural diversity in causal attributions for illness: The role of the supernatural. *Journal of Behavior Medicine, 17*, 181–193.

Landy, F., & Conte, J. M. (2004). *Work in the 21st century*. New York: McGraw-Hill.

Lane, K. A., Goh, J. X., & Driver-Linn, E. (2012). Implicit science stereotypes mediate the relationship between gender and academic participation. *Sex Roles, 66*, 220–234.

Langer, E., & Janis, I. (1979). *The psychology of control*. Beverly Hills, CA: Sage Publications.

Langford, P. E. (1995). *Approaches to the development of moral reasoning*. Hillsdale, NJ: Lawrence Erlbaum.

Langfur, S. (2013). The You-I event: On the genesis of self-awareness. *Phenomenology and the Cognitive Sciences, 12*, 769–790.

Langille, D. (2007). Teenage pregnancy: Trends, contributing factors and the physician's role. *Canadian Medical Association Journal, 176*, 1601–1602.

Langrehr, K. J., Thomas, A. J., & Morgan, S. K. (2016). Confirmatory evidence for a multidimensional model of racial-ethnic socialization for transracially adoptive families. *Cultural Diversity and Ethnic Minority Psychology, 22*, 432–439.

Lansford, J. (2009). Parental divorce and children's adjustment. *Perspectives on Psychological Science, 4*, 140–152.

Lansford, J. E., Chang, L., Dodge, K. A., Malone, P. S., Oburu, P., Palmérus, K., Bacchini, D., Pastorelli, C., Bombi, A. S., Zelli, A., Tapanya, S., Chaudhary, N., Deater-Deckard, K., Manke, B., & Quinn, N. (2005). Physical discipline and children's adjustment: Cultural normativeness as a moderator. *Child Development, 76*, 1234–1246.

Lansford, J. E., Malone, P. P., Dodge, K. A., Crozier, J. C., Pettit, G. S., & Bates, J. E. (2006). A 12-year prospective study of patterns of social information processing problems and externalizing behaviors. *Journal of Abnormal Child Psychology: An Official Publication of the International Society for Research in Child and Adolescent Psychopathology, 34*, 715–724.

Lansford, J. E., Yu, T., Pettit, G. S., Bates, J. E., & Dodge, K. A. (2014). Pathways of peer relationships from childhood to young adulthood. *Journal of Applied Developmental Psychology, 35*, 111–117.

Lanza, S. T., Russell, M. A., & Braymiller, J. L. (2017). Emergence of electronic cigarette use in US adolescents and the link to traditional cigarette use. *Addictive Behaviors, 67*, 38–43.

Lapan, C., & Boseovski, J. J. (2017). When peer performance matters: Effects of expertise and traits on children's self-evaluations after social comparison. *Child Development, 88*, 1860–1872.

Lapidot-Lefler, N., & Dolev-Cohen, M. (2014). Comparing cyberbullying and school bullying among school students: Prevalence, gender, and grade level differences. *Social Psychology of Education*. Accessed online, 3-22-15; http://link.springer.com/article/10.1007%2Fs11218-014-9280-8#close.

Largo, R. H., Fischer, J. E., & Rousson, V. (2003). Neuromotor development from kindergarten age to adolescence: Developmental course and variability. *Swedish Medical Weekly, 133*, 193–199.

Larsen, K. E., O'Hara, M. W., & Brewer, K. K. (2001). A prospective study of self-efficacy expectancies and labor pain. *Journal of Reproductive and Infant Psychology, 19*, 203–214.

Larson, D. G. (2014). Taking stock: Past contributions and current thinking on death, dying, and grief. *Death Studies, 38*, 349–352.

Larson, R. W., Richards, M. H., Moneta, G., Holmbeck, G., & Duckett, E. (1996). Changes in adolescents' daily interactions with their families from ages 10 to 18: Disengagement and transformation. *Developmental Psychology, 32*, 744–754.

Laska, M. N., Murray, D. M., Lytle, L. A., & Harnack, L. J. (2012). Longitudinal associations between key dietary behaviors and weight gain over time: Transitions through the adolescent years. *Obesity, 20*, 118–125.

Lassonde, K. A., Surla, C., Buchanan, J. A., & O'Brien, E. J. (2012). Using the contradiction paradigm to assess ageism. *Journal of Aging Studies, 26*(2), 174–181. doi:10.1016/j.jaging.2011.12.002.

Latorre, J. M., Serrano, J. P., Ricarte, J., Bonete, B., Ros, L., & Sitges, E. (2015). Life review based on remembering specific positive events in active aging. *Journal of Aging and Health, 27*, 140–157.

Lau, I., Lee, S., & Chiu, C. (2004). Language, cognition, and reality: Constructing shared meanings through communication. In M. Schaller & C. Crandall (Eds.), *The psychological foundations of culture*. Mahwah, NJ: Lawrence Erlbaum.

Lau, M., Markham, C., Lin, H., Flores, G., & Chacko, M. (2009). Dating and sexual attitudes in Asian-American adolescents. *Journal of Adolescent Research, 24*, 91–113.

Lauer, J. C., & Lauer, R. H. (1999). *How to survive and thrive in an empty nest*. Oakland, CA: New Harbinger Publications.

Laugharne, J., Janca, A., & Widiger, T. (2007). Posttraumatic stress disorder and terrorism: 5 years after 9/11. *Current Opinion in Psychiatry, 20*, 36–41.

Lauter, J. L. (1998). Neuroimaging and the trimodal brain: Applications for developmental communication neuroscience. *Phoniatrica et Logopaedica, 50*, 118–145.

Lavers-Preston, C., & Sonuga-Barke, E. (2003). An intergenerational perspective on parent–child relationships: The reciprocal effects of tri-generational grandparent–parent–child relationships. In R. Gupta & D. Parry-Gupta (Eds.), *Children and parents: Clinical issues for psychologists and psychiatrists*. London: Whurr Publishers, Ltd.

Lavzer, J. I., & Goodson, B. D. (2006). The "quality" of early care and education settings: Definitional and measurement issues. *Evaluation Review, 30*, 556–576.

Law, D. M., Shapka, J. D., Hymel, S., Olson, B. F., & Waterhouse, T. (2012). The changing face of bullying: An empirical comparison between traditional and internet bullying and victimization. *Computers in Human Behavior, 28*, 226–232.

Lawrence, E., Rothman, A., Cobb, R., Rothman, M., & Bradbury, T. (2008). Marital satisfaction across the transition to parenthood. *Journal of Family Psychology, 22*, 41–50.

Lawrence, H. R., Nangle, D. W., Schwartz-Mette, R. A., & Erdley, C. A. (2017). Medication for child and adolescent depression: Questions, answers, clarifications, and caveats. *Practice Innovations, 2*, 39–53.

Lazarus, R. S. (1968). Emotions and adaptations: Conceptual and empirical relations. In W. Arnold (Ed.), *Nebraska symposium on motivation*. Lincoln: University of Nebraska.

Lazarus, R. S., & Folkman, S. (1984). *Stress, appraisal, and coping*. New York: Springer.

Lazarus, R. S., & Folkman, S. (1991). The concept of coping. In A. Monat & R. S. Lazarus (Eds.), *Stress and coping: An anthology* (3rd ed.). New York: Columbia University Press.

Le, H., Oh, I., Shaffer, J., & Schmidt, F. (2010). Implications of methodological advances for the practice of personnel selection: How practitioners benefit from meta-analysis. In *Readings in organizational behavior*. New York: Routledge/Taylor & Francis.

Le Corre, M., & Carey, S. (2007). One, two, three, four, nothing more: An investigation of the conceptual sources of the verbal counting principles. *Cognition, 105*, 395–438.

Leach, P., Barnes, J., Malmberg, L., Sylva, K., & Stein, A. (2008). The quality of different types of child care at 10 and 18 months: A comparison between types and factors related to quality. *Early Child Development and Care, 178*, 177–209.

Leandro-França, C., Murta, S. G., Hershey, D. A., & Martins, L. B. (2016). Evaluation of retirement planning programs: A qualitative analysis of methodologies and efficacy. *Educational Gerontology, 42*, 497–512.

Leaper, C. (2002). Parenting girls and boys. In M. Bornstein (Ed.), *Handbook of parenting: Vol. 1: Children and parenting*. Mahwah, NJ: Lawrence Erlbaum.

Leathers, H. D., & Foster, P. (2004). *The world food problem: Tackling causes of undernutrition in the third world*. Boulder, CO: Lynne Rienner Publishers.

Leathers, S., & Kelley, M. (2000). Unintended pregnancy and depressive symptoms among first-time mothers and fathers. *American Journal of Orthopsychiatry, 70*, 523–531.

Leavitt, L. A., & Goldson, E. (1996). Introduction to special section: Biomedicine and developmental psychology: New areas of common ground. *Developmental Psychology, 32*, 387–389.

Lecce, S., Bianco, F., Demicheli, P., & Cavallini, E. (2014). Training preschoolers on first-order false belief understanding: Transfer on advanced ToM skills and metamemory. *Child Development, 85*, 2404–2418.

Lecce, S., Ceccato, I., Bianco, F., Rosi, A., Bottiroli, S., & Cavallini, E. (2017). Theory of mind and social relationships in older adults: The role of social motivation. *Aging & Mental Health, 21*, 253–258.

Lecours, A. R. (1982). Correlates of developmental behavior in brain maturation. In T. Bever (Ed.), *Regressions in mental development*. Hillsdale, NJ: Lawrence Erlbaum.

Lee, G. Y., & Kisilevsky, B. S. (2014). Fetuses respond to father's voice but prefer mother's voice after birth. *Developmental Psychobiology, 56*, 1–11.

Lee, M. (2008). Caregiver stress and elder abuse among Korean family caregivers of older adults with disabilities. *Journal of Family Violence, 23*, 707–712.

Lee, M., Vernon-Feagans, L., & Vazquez, A. (2003). The influence of family environment and child temperament on work/family role strain for mothers and fathers. *Infant & Child Development, 12*, 421–439.

Lee, P. C. (2017). Maternal behavior. In J. Call, G. M. Burghardt, I. M. Pepperberg, C. T. Snowdon, T. Zentall (Eds.), *APA handbook of comparative psychology: Basic concepts, methods, neural substrate, and behavior*. Washington, DC: American Psychological Association.

Lee, R. M. (2005). Resilience against discrimination: Ethnic identity and other-group orientation as protective factors for Korean Americans. *Journal of Counseling Psychology, 52*, 36–44.

Lee, R., Zhai, F., Brooks-Gunn, J., Han, W., & Waldfogel, J. (2014). Head Start participation and school readiness: Evidence from the early childhood longitudinal study–birth cohort. *Developmental Psychology, 50*, 202–215.

Lee, S., Olszewski-Kubilius, P., & Thomson, D. (2012). Academically gifted students' perceived interpersonal competence and peer relationships. *Gifted Child Quarterly, 56*, 90–104.

Leen-Feldmer, E. W., Reardon, L. E., Hayward, C., & Smith, R. C. (2008). The relation between puberty and adolescent anxiety: Theory and evidence. In M. J. Zvolensky & J. A. Smits (Eds.), *Anxiety in health behaviors and physical illness*. New York: Springer Science + Business Media.

Legerstee, M., Anderson, D., & Schaffer, A. (1998). Five- and eight-month-old infants recognize their faces and voices as familiar and social stimuli. *Child Development, 69*, 37–50.

Legerstee, M., Haley, D. W., & Bornstein, M. H. (2013). *The infant mind: Origins of the social brain*. New York: Guilford Press.

Legerstee, M., & Markova, G. (2008). Variations in 10-month-old infant imitation of people and things. *Infant Behavior & Development, 31*, 81–91.

Lehman, D., Chiu, C., & Schaller, M. (2004). Psychology and culture. *Annual Review of Psychology, 55*, 689–714.

Lehr, U., Seiler, E., & Thomae, H. (2000). Aging in a cross-cultural perspective. In A. L. Comunian, & U. P. Gielen (Eds.), *International perspectives on human development*. Lengerich, Germany: Pabst Science Publishers.

Leis-Newman, E. (2012, June). Miscarriage and loss. *Monitor on Psychology*, 57–59.

Leloux-Opmeer, H., Kuiper, C., Swaab, H., & Scholte, E. (2016). Characteristics of children in foster care, family-style group care, and residential care: A scoping review. *Journal of Child and Family Studies, 25*, 2357–2371.

Lenhart, A. (2010, April 20). *Teens, cell phones, and texting*. Washington, DC: Pew Research Center.

Lenhart, A., Smith, A., & Anderson, M. (2015, October). *Teens, technology and romantic relationships*. Washington, DC: Pew Research Center.

Leonard, J., & Higson, H. (2014). A strategic activity model of enterprise system implementation and use: Scaffolding fluidity. *Journal of Strategic Information Systems, 23*, 62–86.

Lepage, J. F., & Théret, H. (2007). The mirror neuron system: Grasping others' actions from birth? *Developmental Science, 10*, 513–523.

Lerner, J. W. (2002). *Learning disabilities: Theories, diagnosis, and teaching strategies*. Boston: Houghton Mifflin.

Lerner, R. M., Fisher, C. B., & Weinberg, R. A. (2000). Toward a science for and of the people: Promoting civil society through the application of developmental science. *Child Development, 71*, 11–20.

Lerner, R. M., Theokas, C., & Jelicic, H. (2005). Youth as active agents in their own positive development: A developmental systems perspective. In W. Greve, K. Rothermund, & D. Wentura (Eds.), *Adaptive self: Personal continuity and intentional self-development*. Ashland, OH: Hogrefe & Huber.

Lesner, S. (2003). Candidacy and management of assistive listening devices: Special needs of the elderly. *International Journal of Audiology, 42*, 2S68–2S76.

Lester, H., Mead, N., Graham, C., Gask, L., & Reilly, S. (2012). An exploration of the value and mechanisms of befriending for older adults in England. *Ageing & Society, 32*, 307–328.

Lester, P., Paley, B., Saltzman, W., & Klosinski, L. E. (2013). Military service, war, and families: Considerations for child development, prevention and intervention, and public health policy— Part 2. *Clinical Child and Family Psychology Review, 16*, 345–347.

Leung, C., Pe-Pua, R., & Karnilowicz, W. (2006, January). Psychological adaptation and autonomy among adolescents in Australia: A comparison of Anglo-Celtic and three Asian groups. *International Journal of Intercultural Relations, 30*, 99–118.

Levant, R. F., McDermott, R. C., Hewitt, A. A., Alto, K. M., & Harris, K. T. (2016). Confirmatory factor analytic investigation of variance composition, gender invariance, and validity of the Male Role Norms Inventory-Adolescent-revised (MRNI-A-r). *Journal of Counseling Psychology, 63*, 543–556.

LeVay, S., & Valente, S. M. (2003). *Human sexuality*. Sunderland, MA: Sinauer Associates.

Levenson, D. (2012). Genomic testing update: Whole genome sequencing may be worth the money. *Annals of Neurology, 71*, A7–A9.

Levenson, M. R., Aldwin, C. M., & Igarashi, H. (2013). Religious development from adolescence to middle adulthood. In R. F. Paloutzian & C. L. Park (Eds.), *Handbook of the psychology of religion and spirituality* (2nd ed.). New York: Guilford Press.

Levenson, R. W., Carstensen, L. L., & Gottman, J. M. (1993). Long-term marriage: Age, gender, and satisfaction. *Psychology and Aging, 8*, 301–313.

Levy, B. L., & Langer, E. (1994). Aging free from negative stereotypes: Successful memory in China and among the American deaf. *Journal of Personality and Social Psychology, 66*, 989–997.

Levin, R. J. (2007). Sexual activity, health and well-being—the beneficial roles of coitus and masturbation. *Sexual and Relationship Therapy, 22*, 135–148.

Levin, R. J. (2015). Sexuality of the ageing female—The underlying physiology. *Sexual and Relationship Therapy, 30*, 25–36.

Levin, S., Matthews, M., Guimond, S., Sidanius, J., Pratto, F., Kteily, N., & Dover, T. (2012). Assimilation, multiculturalism, and colorblindness: Mediated and moderated relationships between social dominance orientation and prejudice. *Journal of Experimental Social Psychology, 48*, 207–212.

Levine, R. V. (1993, February). Is love a luxury? *American Demographics*, pp. 29–37.

Levine, R. (1994). *Child care and culture*. Cambridge: Cambridge University Press.

Levine, R. (1997a, November). The pace of life in 31 countries. *American Demographics*, pp. 20–29.

Levine, R. (1997b). *A geography of time: The temporal misadventures of a social psychologist, or how every culture keeps time just a little bit differently*. New York: HarperCollins.

Levinson, D. (1992). *The seasons of a woman's life*. New York: Knopf.

Levinson, D. J. (1986). A conception of adult development. *American Psychologist, 41*, 3–13.

Levy, B. (2009). Stereotype embodiment: A psychosocial approach to aging. *Current Directions in Psychological Science, 18*, 332–336.

Levy, B. R. (2003). Mind matters: Cognitive and physical effects of aging self-stereotypes. *Journal of Gerontology: Series B: Psychological Sciences and Social Sciences, 58B*, P203–P211.

Levy, B. R., Slade, M. D., & Kasl, S. V. (2002). Longevity increased by positive self-perceptions of aging. *Journal of Personality and Social Psychology, 83*, 261–270.

Lewis, B., Legato, M., & Fisch, H. (2006). Medical implications of the male biological clock. *JAMA: Journal of the American Medical Association, 296*, 2369–2371.

Lewis, C. S. (1985). A grief observed. In E. S. Shneidman (Ed.), *Death: Current perspectives* (3rd ed.). Palo Alto, CA: Mayfield.

Lewis, J., & Elman, J. (2008). Growth-related neural reorganization and the autism phenotype: A test of the hypothesis that altered brain growth leads to altered connectivity. *Developmental Science, 11*, 135–155.

Lewis, M., & Carmody, D. (2008). Self-representation and brain development. *Developmental Psychology, 44*, 1329–1334.

Lewis, M., & Ramsay, D. (2004). Development of self-recognition, personal pronoun use, and pretend play during the 2nd year. *Child Development, 75*, 1821–1831.

Lewis, R., Freneau, P., & Roberts, C. (1979). Fathers and the postparental transition. *Family Coordinator, 28*, 514–520.

Lewis, V. (2009). Undertreatment of menopausal symptoms and novel options for comprehensive management. *Current Medical Research Opinion, 25*, 2689–2698

Lewkowicz, D. (2002). Heterogeneity and heterochrony in the development of intersensory perception. *Cognitive Brain Research, 14*, 41–63.

Leyens, J. P., Camino, L., Parke, R. D., & Berkowitz, L. (1975). Effects of movie violence on aggression in a field setting as a function of group dominance and cohesion. *Journal of Personality and Social Psychology, 32*, 346–360.

Li, G. R., & Zhu, X. D. (2007). Development of the functionally total artificial heart using an artery pump. *ASAIO Journal, 53*, 288–291.

Li, H., Ji, Y., & Chen, T. (2014). The roles of different sources of social support on emotional well-being among Chinese elderly. *Plos ONE, 9*(3), 88–97.

Li, J., Laursen, T. M., Precht, D. H., Olsen, J., & Mortensen, P. B. (2005). Hospitalization for mental illness among parents after the death of a child. *New England Journal of Medicine, 352*, 1190–1196.

Li, N. P., Bailey, J. M., Kenrick, D. T., & Linsenmeier, J. A. W. (2002). The necessities and luxuries of mate preferences: Testing the tradeoffs. *Journal of Personality and Social Psychology, 82*, 947–955.

Li, Q., Xu, W., & Li, L. (2014). Elderly mental health quality and mental health condition: Mediating effect of social support. *Chinese Journal of Clinical Psychology, 22*, 688–690.

Li, S. (2003). Biocultural orchestration of developmental plasticity across levels: The interplay of biology and culture in shaping the mind and behavior across the life span. *Psychological Bulletin, 129*, 171–194.

Li, S. (2012). Neuromodulation of behavioral and cognitive development across the life span. *Developmental Psychology, 48*, 810–814.

Li, S., Callaghan, B. L., & Richardson, R. (2014). Infantile amnesia: Forgotten but not gone. *Learning & Memory, 21*, 135–139.

Li, T., & Chan, D. K. (2012). How anxious and avoidant attachment affect romantic relationship quality differently: A meta-analytic review. *European Journal of Social Psychology, 42*, 406–419.

Li, X., Allen, P. A., Lien, M., & Yamamoto, N. (2017). Practice makes it better: A psychophysical study of visual perceptual learning and its transfer effects on aging. *Psychology and Aging, 32*, 16–27.

Li, Y., Allen, J., & Casillas, A. (2017). Relating psychological and social factors to academic performance: A longitudinal investigation of high-poverty middle school students. *Journal of Adolescence, 56*, 179–189.

Li, Y., & Wright, M. F. (2013). Adolescents' social status goals: Relationships to social status insecurity, aggression, and prosocial behavior. *Journal of Youth and Adolescence, 43*, 146–160.

Lian, C., Wan Muda, W., Hussin, Z., & Thon, C. (2012). Factors associated with undernutrition among children in a rural district of Kelantan, Malaysia. *Asia-Pacific Journal of Public Health, 24*, 330–342.

Liang, J., & Luo, B. (2012). Toward a discourse shift in social gerontology: From successful aging to harmonious aging. *Journal of Aging Studies, 26*, 327–334.

Libert, S., Zwiener, J., Chu, X., Vanvoorhies, W., Roman, G., & Pletcher, S. D. (2007, February 23). Regulation of Drosophila life span by olfaction and food-derived odors. *Science, 315*, 1133–1137.

Libertus, K., Joh, A. S., & Needham, A. W. (2016). Motor training at 3 months affects object exploration 12 months later. *Developmental Science, 19*, 1058–1066.

Lickliter, R., & Bahrick, L. E. (2000). The development of infant intersensory perception: Advantages of a comparative convergent-operations approach. *Psychological Bulletin, 126*, 260–280.

Light, L. L. (2000). Memory changes in adulthood. In S. H. Qualls, N. Abeles et al. (Eds.), *Psychology and the aging revolution: How we adapt to longer life*. Washington, DC: American Psychological Association.

Lin, C., Chiu, H., & Yeh, C. (2012). Impact of socio-economic backgrounds, experiences of being disciplined in early childhood, and parenting value on parenting styles of preschool children's parents. *Chinese Journal of Guidance and Counseling, 32*, 123–149.

Lin, F., Heffner, K., Mapstone, M., Chen, D., & Porsteisson, A. (2014). Frequency of mentally stimulating activities modifies the relationship between cardiovascular reactivity and executive function in old age. *American Journal of Geriatric Psychiatry, 22*, 1210–1221.

Lin, I., Wang, S., Chu, I., Lu, Y., Lee, C., Lin, T., & Fan, S. (2017). The association of Type D personality with heart rate variability and lipid profiles among patients with coronary artery disease. *International Journal of Behavioral Medicine, 24*, 101–109.

Lin, P. (2016). Risky behaviors: Integrating adolescent egocentrism with the theory of planned behavior. *Review of General Psychology, 20*, 392–398.

Lindau, S., Schumm, L., Laumann, E., Levinson, W., O'Muircheartaigh, C., & Waite, L. (2007). A study of sexuality and health among older adults in the United States. *New England Journal of Medicine, 357*, 762–775.

Lindemann, B. T., & Kadue, D. D. (2003). *Age discrimination in employment law*. Washington, DC: BNA Books.

Lindsey, E., & Colwell, M. (2003). Preschoolers' emotional competence: Links to pretend and physical play. *Child Study Journal, 33*, 39–52.

Lindsey, E. W. (2012). Girls' and boys' play form preferences and gender segregation in early childhood. In S. P. McGeown (Ed.), *Psychology of gender differences*. Hauppauge, NY: Nova Science Publishers.

Lindstrom, H., Fritsch, T., Petot, G., Smyth, K., Chen, C., Debanne, S., et al. (2005, July). The relationships between television viewing in midlife and the development of Alzheimer's disease in a case-control study. *Brain and Cognition, 58*, 157–165.

Linebarger, D. L. (2015). Contextualizing video game play: The moderating effects of cumulative risk and parenting styles on the relations among video game exposure and problem behaviors. *Psychology of Popular Media Culture, 4*, 375–396.

Linebarger, D. L., & Walker, D. (2005). Infants' and toddlers' television viewing and language outcomes. *American Behavioral Scientist, 48*, 624–645.

Linebarger, D. N., Brey, E., Fenstermacher, S., & Barr, R. (2017). What makes preschool educational television educational? A content analysis of literacy, language-promoting, and prosocial preschool programming. In R. Barr, D. N. Linebarger (Eds.), *Media exposure during infancy and early childhood: The effects of content and context on learning and development*. Cham, Switzerland: Springer International Publishing.

Link, B. G., Susser, E. S., Factor-Litvak, P., March, D., Kezios, K. L., Lovasi, G. S., & … Cohn, B. A. (2017). Disparities in self-rated health across generations and through the life course. *Social Science & Medicine, 174*, 17–25.

Lino, M., & Carlson, A. (2009). *Expenditures on Children by Families, 2008*.

Lipina, S. J., & Evers, K. (2017). Neuroscience of childhood poverty: Evidence of impacts and mechanisms as vehicles of dialog with ethics. *Frontiers in Psychology, 8*, 88–97.

Lippman, J. R., & Campbell, S. W. (2014). Damned if you do, damned if you don't…if you're a girl: Relational and normative contexts of adolescent sexting in the United States. *Journal of Children and Media, 8*, 371–386.

Lipsitt, L. P. (1986). Toward understanding the hedonic nature of infancy. In L. P. Lipsitt & J. H. Cantor (Eds.), *Experimental child psychologist: Essays and experiments in honor of Charles C. Spiker* (pp. 97–109). Hillsdale, NJ: Lawrence Erlbaum.

Lipsitt, L. P. (2003). Crib death: A biobehavioral phenomenon? *Current Directions in Psychological Science, 12*, 164–170.

Lipsitt, L. P., & Rovee-Collier, C. (2012). The psychophysics of olfaction in the human newborn: Habituation and cross-adaptation. In G. M. Zucco, R. S. Herz, & B. Schaal (Eds.), *Olfactory cognition: From perception and memory to environmental odours and neuroscience*. Amsterdam, Netherlands: John Benjamins Publishing Company.

Lipsitt, L. R., & Demick, J. (2012). Theory and measurement of resilience: Views from development. In M. Ungar (Ed.), *The social ecology of resilience: A handbook of theory and practice*. New York: Springer Science + Business Media.

Lisabeth, L., & Bushnell, C. (2012). Stroke risk in women: The role of menopause and hormone therapy. *Lancet Neurology, 11*, 82–91.

Little, T., Miyashita, T., & Karasawa, M. (2003). The links among action-control beliefs, intellective skill, and school performance in Japanese, US, and German school children. *International Journal of Behavioral Development, 27*, 41–48.

Litzinger, S., & Gordon, K. (2005, October). Exploring relationships among communication, sexual satisfaction, and marital satisfaction. *Journal of Sex & Marital Therapy, 31*, 409–424.

Liu, D., Wellman, H., Tardif, T., & Sabbagh, M. (2008, March). Theory of mind development in Chinese children: A meta-analysis of false-belief understanding across cultures and languages. *Developmental Psychology, 44*, 523–531.

Liu, N., Chen, Y., Yang, X., & Hu, Y. (2017). Do demographic characteristics make differences? Demographic characteristics as moderators in the associations between only child status and cognitive/non-cognitive outcomes in China. *Frontiers in Psychology, 8*, 221–232.

Liu, N., Liang, Z., Li, Z., Yan, J., & Guo, W. (2012). Chronic stress on IL-2, IL-4, IL-18 content in SD rats. *Chinese Journal of Clinical Psychology, 20*, 35–36.

Lloyd, K. K. (2012). Health-related quality of life and children's happiness with their childcare. *Child: Care, Health and Development, 38*, 244–250.

Lobo, R. A. (2009). The risk of stroke in postmenopausal women receiving hormonal therapy. *Climacteric, 12*(Suppl. 1), 81–85.

Lock, M. (1993). *Encounters with aging: Mythologies of menopause in Japan and North America*. Berkeley: University of California Press.

Loeb, S., Fuller, B., Kagan, S. L., & Carrol, B. (2004). Child care in poor communities: Early learning effects of type, quality and stability. *Child Development, 75*, 47–65.

Loehlin, J. C., Neiderhiser, J. M., & Reiss, D. (2005). Genetic and environmental components of adolescent adjustment and parental behavior: A multivariate analysis. *Child Development, 76*, 1104–1115.

Loessl, B., Valerius, G., Kopasz, M., Hornyak, M., Riemann, D., & Voderholzer, U. (2008). Are adolescents chronically sleepdeprived? An investigation of sleep habits of adolescents in the southwest of Germany. *Child: Care, Health and Development, 34*, 549–556.

Loewen, S. (2006). Exceptional intellectual performance: A neo-Piagetian perspective. *High Ability Studies, 17*, 159–181.

Loftus, E. F. (2003, November). Make-believe memories. *American Psychologist*, pp. 867–873.

Loggins, S., & Andrade, F. D. (2014). Despite an overall decline in U.S. infant mortality rates, the black/white disparity persists: Recent trends and future projections. *Journal of Community Health: The Publication for Health Promotion and Disease Prevention, 39*, 118–123.

Logsdon, R., McCurry, S., Pike, K., & Teri, L. (2009). Making physical activity accessible to older adults with memory loss: A feasibility study. *Gerontologist, 49*(Suppl. 1), S94–S99.

Lohbeck, A., Grube, D., & Moschner, B. (2017). Academic self-concept and causal attributions for success and failure amongst elementary school children. *International Journal of Early Years Education, 25*, 190–203.

Lohbeck, A., Tietjens, M., & Bund, A. (2016). Physical self-concept and physical activity enjoyment in elementary school children. *Early Child Development and Care, 186*, 1792–1801.

Lohman, D. (2005). Reasoning abilities. In *Cognition and intelligence: Identifying the mechanisms of the mind*. New York: Cambridge University Press.

Longo, G. S., Bray, B. C., & Kim-Spoon, J. (2017). Profiles of adolescent religiousness using latent profile analysis: Implications for psychopathology. *British Journal of Developmental Psychology, 35*, 91–105.

Lopez, M. H., & Gonzalez-Barrera, A. (2014, March 6). *Women's college enrolment gains leave men behind*. Washington, DC: Pew Research Center.

López, S. R., & Guarnaccia, P. J. J. (2000). Cultural psychopathology: Uncovering the social world of mental illness. *Annual Review of Psychology, 51*, 571–598.

Lorenz, K. (1957). Companionship in bird life. In C. Scholler (Ed.), *Instinctive behavior*. New York: International Universities Press.

Lorenz, K. (1974). *Civilized man's eight deadly sins*. New York: Harcourt Brace Jovanovich.

Lorenz, K. Z. (1965). *Evolution and the modification of behavior*. Chicago, IL: University of Chicago Press.

Losonczy-Marshall, M. (2008). Gender differences in latency and duration of emotional expression in 7- through 13-month-old infants. *Social Behavior and Personality, 36*, 267–274.

Lothian, J. (2005). *The official Lamaze guide: Giving birth with confidence*. Minnetonka, MN: Meadowbrook Press.

Louca, M., & Short, M. A. (2014). The effect of one night's sleep deprivation on adolescent neurobehavioral performance. *SLEEP, 37*, 1799–1807.

Love, J. M., Tarullo, L. B., Raikes, H., & Chazan-Cohen, R. (2006). Head Start: What Do We Know About Its Effectiveness? What Do We Need to Know?. In K. McCartney, D. Phillips, K. McCartney, D. Phillips (Eds.), *Blackwell handbook of early childhood development* (pp. 550-575). Malden: Blackwell Publishing. doi:10.1002/9780470757703.ch27

Love, A., & Burns, M. S. (2006). "It's a hurricane! It's a hurricane!": Can music facilitate social constructive and sociodramatic play in a preschool classroom? *Journal of Genetic Psychology, 167*, 383–391.

Lovrin, M. (2009). Treatment of major depression in adolescents: Weighing the evidence of risk and benefit in light of black box warnings. *Journal of Child and Adolescent Psychiatric Nursing, 22*, 63–68.

Low, J., & Perner, J. (2012). Implicit and explicit theory of mind: State of the art. *British Journal of Developmental Psychology, 30*, 1–13.

Lowe, M. R., Doshi, S. D., Katterman, S. N., & Feig, E. H. (2013). Dieting and restrained eating as prospective predictors of weight gain. *Frontiers in Psychology, 4*, 577–586.

Lu, L. (2006). The transition to parenthood: Stress, resources, and gender differences in a Chinese society. *Journal of Community Psychology, 34*, 471–488.

Lu, M. C., Prentice, J., Yu, S. M., Inkelas, M., Lange, L. O., & Halfon, N. (2003). Childbirth education classes: Sociodemographic disparities in attendance and the association of attendance with breastfeeding initiation. *Maternal Child Health, 7*, 87–93.

Lu, T., Pan, Y., Lap. S-Y., Li, C., Kohane, I., Chang, J., & Yankner, B. A. (2004, June 9). Gene regulation and DNA damage in the aging human brain. *Nature*, p. 1038.

Lu, X. (2001). Bicultural identity development and Chinese community formation: An ethnographic study of Chinese schools in Chicago. *Howard Journal of Communications, 12*, 203–220.

Lubinski, D. (2004). Introduction to the special section on cognitive abilities: 100 years after Spearman's (1904) "General Intelligence," objectively determined and measured. *Journal of Personality and Social Psychology, 86*, 96–111.

Lubinski, D., & Benbow, C. P. (2006). Study of mathematically precocious youth after 35 years: Uncovering antecedents for the development of math-science expertise. *Perspectives on Psychological Science, 1*, 316–345.

Lucas, R. E. (2005). Time does not heal all wounds: A longitudinal study of reaction and adaptation to divorce. *Psychological Science, 16*, 945–951.

Lucas, S. R., & Berends, M. (2002). Sociodemographic diversity, correlated achievement, and de facto tracking. *Sociology of Education, 75*, 328–349.

Lucassen, A. (2012). Ethical implications of new genetic technologies. *Developmental Medicine & Child Technology, 54*, 196.

Ludden, J. (2012, February 6). Helicopter parents hover in the workplace. *All Things Considered*. National Public Radio.

Ludlow, V., Newhook, L., Newhook, J., Bonia, K., Goodridge, J., & Twells, L. (2012). How formula feeding mothers balance risks and define themselves as "good mothers." *Health, Risk & Society, 14*, 291–306.

Ludwig, M., & Field, T. (2014). Touch in parent-infant mental health: Arousal, regulation, and relationships. In K. Brandt, B. D. Perry, S. Seligman, & E. Tronick (Eds.), *Infant and early childhood mental health: Core concepts and clinical practice*. Arlington, VA: American Psychiatric Publishing.

Lui, P. P., & Rollock, D. (2013). Tiger mother: Popular and psychological scientific perspectives on Asian culture and parenting. *American Journal of Orthopsychiatry, 83*(4), 450–456.

Luke, B., & Brown, M. B. (2008). Maternal morbidity and infant death in twin vs. triplet and quadruplet pregnancies. *American Journal of Obstetrics and Gynecology, 198*, 1–10.

Luke, M. A., Sedikides, C., & Carnelley, K. (2012). Your love lifts me higher! The energizing quality of secure relationships. *Personality and Social Psychology Bulletin, 38*, 721–735.

Luna, B., & Wright, C. (2016). Adolescent brain development: Implications for the juvenile criminal justice system. In K. Heilbrun, D. DeMatteo, N. S. Goldstein (Eds.), *APA handbook of psychology and juvenile justice*. Washington, DC: American Psychological Association.

Lundberg, I., & Reichenberg, M. (2013). Developing reading comprehension among students with mild intellectual disabilities: An intervention study. *Scandinavian Journal of Educational Research, 57*, 89–100.

Lundby, E. (2013). "You can't buy friends, but ...": Children's perception of consumption and friendship. *Young Consumers, 14*, 360–374.

Luo, J., Derringer, J., Briley, D. A., & Roberts, B. W. (2017). Genetic and environmental pathways underlying personality traits and perceived stress: Concurrent and longitudinal twin studies. *European Journal of Personality*. Accessed online 10-27-17; http://onlinelibrary.wiley.com/doi/10.1002/per.2127/abstract.

Luo, L., & Craik, F. (2008). Aging and memory: A cognitive approach. *The Canadian Journal of Psychiatry / La Revue canadienne de psychiatrie, 53*, 346–353.

Luo, L., & Craik, F. (2009). Age differences in recollection: Specificity effects at retrieval. *Journal of Memory and Language, 60*, 421–436.

Luz, R., George, A., Vieux, R., & Spitz, E. (2017). Antenatal determinants of parental attachment and parenting alliance: How do mothers and fathers differ? *Infant Mental Health Journal, 38*, 183–197.

Lyall, S. (2004, February 15). In Europe, lovers now propose: Marry me, a little. *New York Times*, p. D2.

Lye, T. C., Piguet, O., Grayson, D. A., Creasey, H., Ridley, L. J., Bennett, H. P., & Broe, G. A. (2004). Hippocampal size and memory function in the ninth and tenth decades of life: The Sydney Older Persons Study. *Journal of Neurology, Neurosurgery, and Psychiatry, 75*, 548–554.

Lynam, D. R. (1996). Early identification of chronic offenders: Who is the fledgling psychopath? *Psychological Bulletin, 120*, 209–234.

Lynne, S., Graber, J., Nichols, T., Brooks-Gunn, J., & Botvin, G. (2007, February). Links between pubertal timing, peer influences, and externalizing behaviors among urban students followed through middle school. *Journal of Adolescent Health, 40*, 35–44.

Lyon, G. J. (2012). Bring clinical standards to human-genetics research. *Nature, 482*, 300–301.

Lyons, M. J., Bar, J. L., & Kremen, W. S. (2002). Nicotine and familial vulnerability to schizophrenia: A discordant twin study. *Journal of Abnormal Psychology, 111*, 687–693.

Mabbott, D. J., Noseworthy, M., Bouffet, E., Laughlin, S., & Rockel, C. (2006). White matter growth as a mechanism of cognitive development in children. *Neuroimaging, 15*, 936–946.

Maccallum, F., Malgaroli, M., & Bonanno, G. A. (2017). Networks of loss: Relationships among symptoms of prolonged grief following spousal and parental loss. *Journal of Abnormal Psychology, 126*, 652–662.

Macchi Cassia, V., Picozzi, M., Girelli, L., & de Hevia, M. (2012). Increasing magnitude counts more: Asymmetrical processing of ordinality in 4-month-old infants. *Cognition, 124*, 183–193.

Maccoby, E. E., & Lewis, C. C. (2003). Less day care or different day care? *Child Development, 74*, 1069–1075.

Maccoby, E. E., & Martin, J. A. (1983). Socialization in the context of the family: Parent–child interaction. In P. H. Mussen (Ed.) & E. M. Hetherington (Vol. Ed.), *Handbook of child psychology: Vol. 4. Socialization, personality, and social development* (4th ed., pp. 1–101). New York: Wiley.

MacDonald, W. (2003). The impact of job demands and workload stress and fatigue. *Australian Psychologist, 38*, 102–117.

MacDonald, H., Beeghly, M., Grant-Knight, W., Augustyn, M., Woods, R., Cabral, H., et al. (2008). Longitudinal association between infant disorganized attachment and childhood posttraumatic stress symptoms. *Development and Psychopathology, 20*, 493–508.

MacDorman, M. F., Hoyert, D. L., & Mathews, T. J. (2013). Recent declines in infant mortality in the United States, 2005–2011. *NCHS data brief, no 120*. Hyattsville, MD: National Center for Health Statistics.

MacDorman, M. F., Martin, J. A., Mathews, T. J., Hoyert, D. L., & Ventura, S. J. (2005). Explaining the 2001–02 infant mortality increase: Data from the linked birth/infant death data set. *National Vital Statistics Report, 53*, 1–22.

MacDorman, M., Declercq, E., Menacker, F., & Malloy, M. (2008). Neonatal mortality for primary cesarean and vaginal births to low-risk women: Application of an "intention-to-treat" model. *Birth: Issues in Perinatal Care, 35*, 3–8.

MacDorman, M. F., & Matthews, T. J. (2009). Behind international rankings of infant mortality: How the United States compares with Europe. *NCHS Data Brief, # 23*.

Maciejewski, P. K., Zhang, B., Block, S. D., & Prigerson, H. G. (2007). An empirical examination of the stage theory of grief. *JAMA: Journal of the American Medical Association, 297*, 716–723.

Macionis, J. J. (2001). *Sociology*. Upper Saddle River, NJ: Prentice Hall.

MacLean, P. C., Rynes, K. N., Aragón, C., Caprihan, A., Phillips, J. P., & Lowe, J. R. (2014). Mother–infant mutual eye gaze supports emotion regulation in infancy during the Still-Face paradigm. *Infant Behavior & Development, 37*, 512–522.

Madden, M., Lenhart, A., Cortesi, S., Gasser, U., Duggan, M., Smith, A., & Beaton, M. (2013, May 21). *Teens, social media, and privacy*. Washington, DC: Pew Research Center: Internet & Technology.

Maddi, S. R. (2014). Hardiness leads to meaningful growth through what is learned when resolving stressful circumstances. In A. Batthyany, & P. Russo-Netzer (Eds.), *Meaning in positive and existential psychology*. New York: Springer Science + Business Media.

Maddi, S. R., Harvey, R. H., Khoshaba, D. M., Lu, J. L., Persico, M., & Brow, M. (2006). The personality construct of hardiness, III: Relationships with repression, innovativeness, authoritarianism, and performance. *Journal of Personality, 74*, 575–598.

Madigan, S., Plamondon, A., & Jenkins, J. M. (2017). Marital conflict trajectories and associations with children's disruptive behavior. *Journal of Marriage and Family, 79*, 437–450.

Madison, G., Mosing, M. A., Verweij, K. H., Pedersen, N. L., & Ullén, F. (2016). Common genetic influences on intelligence and auditory simple reaction time in a large Swedish sample. *Intelligence, 59*, 157–162.

Madlensky, L., Trepanier, A. M., Cragun, D., Lerner, B., Shannon, K. M., & Zierhut, H. (2017). A rapid systematic review of outcomes studies in genetic counseling. *Journal of Genetic Counseling, 26*, 361–378.

Madsen, P. B., & Green, R. (2012). Gay adolescent males' effective coping with discrimination: A qualitative study. *Journal of LGBT Issues in Counseling, 6*, 139–155.

Maercker, A., Neimeyer, R. A., & Simiola, V. (2017). Depression and complicated grief. In S. N. Gold (Ed.), *APA handbook of trauma psychology: Foundations in knowledge*. Washington, DC: American Psychological Association.

Maes, S. J., De Mol, J., & Buysse, A. (2012). Children's experiences and meaning construction on parental divorce: A focus group study. *Childhood: A Global Journal of Child Research, 19,* 266–279.

Magee, C. A., Gordon, R., & Caputi, P. (2014). Distinct developmental trends in sleep duration during early childhood. *Pediatrics, 133,* e1561–e1567.

Mages, W. K. (2016). Taking inspiration from Reggio Emilia: An analysis of a professional development workshop on fostering authentic art in the early childhood classroom. *Journal of Early Childhood Teacher Education, 37,* 175–185.

Maggi, S., Busetto, L., Noale, M., Limongi, F., & Crepaldi, G. (2015). Obesity: Definition and epidemiology. In A. Lenzi, S. Migliaccio, & L. M. Donini (Eds.), *Multidisciplinary approach to obesity: From assessment to treatment.* Cham, Switzerland: Springer International Publishing.

Mahrer, N. E., & Wolchik, S. A. (2017). Moody child: Depression in the context of parental divorce. In C. A. Galanter, P. S. Jensen (Eds.), *DSM-5® casebook and treatment guide for child mental health.* Arlington, VA: American Psychiatric Publishing, Inc.

Maier-Hein, K. H., Brunner, R., Lutz, K., Henze, R., Parzer, P., Feigl, N., & ... Stieltjes, B. (2014). Disorder-specific white matter alterations in adolescent borderline personality disorder. *Biological Psychiatry, 75,* 81–88.

Maimari, I. (2017). Stress hormones. In S. Wadhwa (Ed.), *Stress in the modern world: Understanding science and society.* Santa Barbara, CA: Greenwood Press/ABC-CLIO.

Majors, K. (2012). Friendships: The power of positive alliance. In S. Roffey (Ed.), *Positive relationships: Evidence based practice across the world.* New York: Springer Science + Business Media.

Makel, M. C., Kell, H. J., Lubinski, D., Putallaz, M., & Benbow, C. P. (2016). When lightning strikes twice: Profoundly gifted, profoundly accomplished. *Psychological Science, 27,* 1004–1018.

Makino, M., Hashizume, M., Tsuboi, K., Yasushi, M., & Dennerstein, L. (2006, September). Comparative study of attitudes to eating between male and female students in the People's Republic of China. *Eating and Weight Disorders, 11,* 111–117.

Malchiodi, C. A. (2012). Humanistic approaches. In C. A. Malchiodi (Ed.), *Handbook of art therapy* (2nd ed.). New York, NY: Guilford Press.

Mallan, K. M., Sullivan, S. E., de Jersey, S. J., & Daniels, L. A. (2016). The relationship between maternal feeding beliefs and practices and perceptions of infant eating behaviours at 4 months. *Appetite, 105,* 1–7.

Maller, S. (2003). Best practices in detecting bias in nonverbal tests. In R. McCallum (Ed.), *Handbook of nonverbal assessment.* New York: Kluwer Academic/Plenum Publishers.

Malone, J. C., Liu, S. R., Vaillant, G. E., Rentz, D. M., & Waldinger, R. J. (2016). Midlife Eriksonian psychosocial development: Setting the stage for late-life cognitive and emotional health. *Developmental Psychology, 52,* 496–508.

Mameli, M. (2007). Reproductive cloning, genetic engineering and the autonomy of the child: The moral agent and the open future. *Journal of Medical Ethics, 33,* 87–93.

Manard, M., Carabin, D., Jaspar, M., & Collette, F. (2014). Age-related decline in cognitive control: The role of fluid intelligence and processing speed. *BMC Neuroscience, 15.* Accessed online, 10-14-15; http://www.biomedcentral.com/1471-2202/15/7.

Mancini, A. D., & Bonanno, G. A. (2012). Differential pathways to resilience after loss and trauma. In R. A. McMackin, E. Newman, J. M. Fogler, & T. M. Keane (Eds.), *Trauma therapy in context: The science and craft of evidence-based practice.* Washington, DC: American Psychological Association.

Mancini, A. D., Sinan, B., & Bonanno, G. A. (2015). Predictors of prolonged grief, resilience, and recovery among bereaved spouses. *Journal of Clinical Psychology, 71,* 1245–1258.

Mancini, J. A., & Blieszner, R. (1991). Aging parents and adult children. In A. Booth (Ed.), *Contemporary families.* Minneapolis, MN: National Council on Family Relations.

Mangiatordi, A. (2012). Inclusion of mobility-impaired children in the one-to-one computing era: A case study. *Mind, Brain, and Education, 6,* 54–62.

Mangweth, B., Hausmann, A., & Walch, T. (2004). Body fat perception in eating-disordered men. *International Journal of Eating Disorders, 35,* 102–108.

Manlove, J., Franzetta, K., McKinney, K., Romano-Papillo, A., & Terry-Humen, E. (2004). *No time to waste: Programs to reduce teen pregnancy among middle school-aged youth.* Washington, DC: National Campaign to Prevent Teen Pregnancy.

Manning, M., & Hoyme, H. (2007). Fetal alcohol spectrum disorders: A practical clinical approach to diagnosis. *Neuroscience & Biobehavioral Reviews, 31,* 230–238.

Manning, R. C., Dickson, J. M., Palmier-Claus, J., Cunliffe, A., & Taylor, P. J. (2017). A systematic review of adult attachment and social anxiety. *Journal of Affective Disorders, 211,* 44–59.

Manstead, A. S. R. (1997). Situations, belongingness, attitudes, and culture: Four lessons learned from social psychology. In C. McGarty, S. A. Haslam et al. (Eds.), *The message of social psychology: Perspectives on mind in society.* Oxford, England: Blackwell Publishers, Inc.

Manzanares, S., Cobo, D., Moreno-Martínez, M., Sánchez-Gila, M., & Pineda, A. (2013). Risk of episiotomy and perineal lacerations recurring after first delivery. *Birth: Issues in Perinatal Care, 40,* 307–311.

Mao, A., Burnham, M. M., Goodlin-Jones, B. L., Gaylor, E. E., & Anders, T. F. (2004). A comparison of the sleep-wake patterns of cosleeping and solitary-sleeping infants. *Child Psychiatry and Human Development, 35,* 95–105.

Marcia, J. E. (1980). Identity in adolescence. In J. Adelson (Ed.), *Handbook of adolescent psychology.* New York: Wiley.

Marcia, J. E. (2007). Theory and measure: The identity status interview. In M. Watzlawik & A. Born (Eds.), *Capturing identity: Quantitative and qualitative methods.* Lanham, MD: University Press of America.

Marcovitch, S., Zelazo, P., & Schmuckler, M. (2003). The effect of the number of A trials on performance on the A-not-B task. *Infancy, 3,* 519–529.

Marcus, A. D. (2004, February 3). The new math on when to have kids. *Wall Street Journal,* pp. D1, D4.

Marin, T., Chen, E., Munch, J., & Miller, G. (2009). Double-exposure to acute stress and chronic family stress is associated with immune changes in children with asthma. *Psychosomatic Medicine, 71,* 378–384.

Marinellie, S. A., & Kneile, L. A. (2012). Acquiring knowledge of derived nominals and derived adjectives in context. *Language, Speech, and Hearing Services in Schools, 43,* 53–65.

Marques, A. H., Bjørke-Monsen, A., Teixeira, A. L., & Silverman, M. N. (2014). Maternal stress, nutrition and physical activity: Impact on immune function, cns development and psychopathology. *Brain Research.* Accessed online, 6-22-15; http://www.ncbi.nlm.nih.gov/pubmed/25451133.

Marschark, M., Spencer, P. E., & Newsom, C. A. (Eds.). (2003). *Oxford handbook of deaf students, language, and education.* London: Oxford University Press.

Marschik, P., Einspieler, C., Strohmeier, A., Plienegger, J., Garzarolli, B., & Prechtl, H. (2008). From the reaching behavior at 5 months of age to hand preference at preschool age. *Developmental Psychobiology, 50,* 512–518.

Marsh, H. W., & Hau, K. T. (2003). Big-fish-little-pond effect on academic self-concept. *American Psychologist, 58,* 364–376.

Marsh, H., Ellis, L., & Craven, R. (2002). How do preschool children feel about themselves? Unraveling measurement and multidimensional self-concept structure. *Developmental Psychology,* 38, 376–393.

Marsh, H., Seaton, M., Trautwein, U., Lüdtke, O., Hau, K., O'Mara, A., et al. (2008). The big-fish-little-pond-effect stands up to critical scrutiny: Implications for theory, methodology, and future research. *Educational Psychology Review, 20,* 319–350.

Martin, A., Onishi, K. H., & Vouloumanos, A. (2012). Understanding the abstract role of speech in communication at 12 months. *Cognition, 123,* 50–60.

Martin, C. L., & Ruble, D. (2004). Children's search for gender cues: Cognitive perspectives on gender development. *Current Directions in Psychological Science, 13,* 67–70.

Martin, C., & Dinella, L. M. (2012). Congruence between gender stereotypes and activity preference in self-identified tomboys and non-tomboys. *Archives of Sexual Behavior, 41,* 599–610.

Martin, C., & Fabes, R. (2001). The stability and consequences of young children's same-sex peer interactions. *Developmental Psychology, 37,* 431–446.

Martin, J. A., Hamilton, B. E., Sutton, P. D., Ventura, S. J., Menacker, F., & Munson, M. L. (2005). Births: Final data for 2003. *National Vital Statistics Reports, 54,* Table J, 21.

Martin, L., McNamara, M., Milot, A., Halle, T., & Hair, E. (2007). The effects of father involvement during pregnancy on receipt of prenatal care and maternal smoking. *Maternal and Child Health Journal, 11,* 595–602.

Martin, P., Martin, D., & Martin, M. (2001). Adolescent premarital sexual activity, cohabitation, and attitudes toward marriage. *Adolescence, 36,* 601–609.

Martin, S., Li, Y., Casanueva, C., Harris-Britt, A., Kupper, L., & Cloutier, S. (2006). Intimate partner violence and women's depression before and during pregnancy. *Violence Against Women, 12,* 221–239.

Martin-Prudent, A., Lartz, M., Borders, C., & Meehan, T. (2016). Early intervention practices for children with hearing loss: Impact of professional development. *Communication Disorders Quarterly, 38,* 13–23.

Martincin, K. M., & Stead, G. B. (2015). Five-factor model and difficulties in career decision making: A meta-analysis. *Journal of Career Assessment, 23,* 3–19.

Martineau, J., Cochin, S., Magne, R., & Barthelemy, C. (2008). Impaired cortical activation in autistic children: Is the mirror neuron system involved? *International Journal of Psychophysiology, 68,* 35–40.

Martinez, G., Copen, C. E., Abma, J. C. (2011). *Teenagers in the United States: Sexual activity, contraceptive use, and childbearing, 2006–2010 National Survey of Family Growth.* National Center for Health Statistics. Vital Health Stat 23(31).

Martinez-Torteya, C., Bogat, G., von Eye, A., & Levendosky, A. (2009). Resilience among children exposed to domestic violence: The role of risk and protective factors. *Child Development, 80,* 562–577.

Marvan, M. L., Rosa, L. C. & Arroyo, L. (2013). Mexican beliefs and attitudes toward menopause and menopausal-related symptoms. *Journal of Psychosomatic Obstetrics & Gynecology 34,* 39–45.

Masapollo, M., Polka, L., & Ménard, L. (2015). When infants talk, infants listen: Pre-babbling infants prefer listening to speech with infant vocal properties. *Developmental Science.* Accessed online, 3-19-15; http://onlinelibrary.wiley.com/doi/10.1111/desc.12298/abstract.

Masataka, N. (1996). Perception of motherese in a signed language by 6-month-old deaf infants. *Developmental Psychology, 32,* 874–879.

Masataka, N. (1998). Perception of motherese in Japanese sign language by 6-month-old hearing infants. *Developmental Psychology, 34,* 241–246.

Masataka, N. (2000). The role of modality and input in the earliest stage of language acquisition: Studies of Japanese sign language. In C. Chamerlain & J. P. Morford (Eds.), *Language acquisition by eye.* Mahwah, NJ: Lawrence Erlbaum.

Masataka, N. (2003). *The onset of language.* Cambridge, England: Cambridge University Press.

Masataka, N. (2006). Preference for consonance over dissonance by hearing newborns of deaf parents and of hearing parents. *Developmental Science, 9,* 46–50.

Mash, C., Bornstein, M. H., & Arterberry, M. E. (2013). Brain dynamics in young infants' recognition of faces: EEG oscillatory activity in response to mother and stranger. *Neuroreport: For Rapid Communication of Neuroscience Research, 24*, 359–363.

Maslow, A. H. (1970). *Motivation and personality* (2nd ed.). New York: Harper & Row.

Master, S., Amodio, D., Stanton, A., Yee, C., Hilmert, C., & Taylor, S. (2009). Neurobiological correlates of coping through emotional approach. *Brain, Behavior, and Immunity, 23*, 27–35.

Mather, M., Jacobsen, L. A., & Pollard, K. M. (2016). Aging in the United States. *Population Bulletin, 70*, 2.

Mathews, G., Fane, B., Conway, G., Brook, C., & Hines, M. (2009). Personality and congenital adrenal hyperplasia: Possible effects of prenatal androgen exposure. *Hormones and Behavior, 55*, 285–291.

Matias, M., Ferreira, T., Vieira, J., Cadima, J., Leal, T., & Mena Matos, P. (2017). Workplace family support, parental satisfaction, and work–family conflict: Individual and crossover effects among dual-earner couples. *Applied Psychology: An International Review, 66*, 628–652.

Matlin, M. (2003). From menarche to menopause: Misconceptions about women's reproductive lives. *Psychology Science, 45*, 106–122.

Matlung, S. E., Bilo, R. A. C., Kubat, B., & van Rijn, R. R. (2011). Multicysticencephalomalacia as an end-stage finding in abusive head trauma. *Forensic Scientific Medicine and Pathology, 7*, 355–363.

Maton, K. I., Schellenbach, C. J., Leadbeater, B. J., & Solarz, A. L. (Eds.). (2004). *Investing in children, youth, families and communities*. Washington, DC: American Psychological Association.

Matsumoto, D., & Yoo, S. H. (2006). Toward a new generation of cross-cultural research. *Perspectives on Psychological Science, 1*, 234–250.

Mattes, E., McCarthy, S., Gong, G., van Eekelen, J. M., Dunstan, J., Foster, J., & Prescott, S. L. (2009). Maternal mood scores in mid-pregnancy are related to aspects of neonatal immune function. *Brain, Behavior, And Immunity, 23*(3), 380-388.

Matthes, J., Prieler, M., & Adam, K. (2016). Gender-role portrayals in television advertising across the globe. *Sex Roles*. Accessed online 5-27-16; http://link.springer.com/article/10.1007/s11199-016-0617-y.

Matthews, K. A., Wing, R. R., Kuller, L. H., Meilahn, E. N., & Owens, J. F. (2000). Menopause as a turning point in midlife. In S. B. Manuck, R. Jennings, et al. (Eds.), *Behavior, health, and aging*. Mahwah, NJ: Lawrence Erlbaum.

Mattson, M. (2003). Will caloric restriction and folate protect against AD and PD? *Neurology, 60*, 690–695.

Mattson, S., Calarco, K., & Lang, A. (2006). Focused and shifting attention in children with heavy prenatal alcohol exposure. *Neuropsychology, 20*, 361–369.

Mauas, V., Kopala-Sibley, D. C., & Zuroff, D. C. (2014). Depressive symptoms in the transition to menopause: The roles of irritability, personality vulnerability, and self-regulation. *Archives of Women's Mental Health, 17*, 279–289.

Mausbach, B. T., Roepke, S. K., Chattillion, E. A., Harmell, A. L., Moore, R., Romero-Moreno, R., & Grant, I. (2012). Multiple mediators of the relations between caregiving stress and depressive symptoms. *Aging & Mental Health, 16*, 27–38.

Maxmen, A. (2012, February). Harnessing the wisdom of the ages. *Monitor on Psychology*, pp. 50–53.

Maxwell, K., Callahan, J. L., Ruggero, C. J., & Janis, B. (2016). Breaking the cycle: Association of attending therapy following childhood abuse and subsequent perpetration of violence. *Journal of Family Violence, 31*, 251–258.

Mayer, J. D., Salovey, P., & Caruso, D. R. (2000). Emotional intelligence as zeitgeist, as personality, and as a mental ability. In R. Bar-On & J. D. A. Parker (Eds.), *The handbook of emotional intelligence: Theory, development, assessment, and application at home, school, and in the workplace*. San Francisco, CA: Jossey-Bass.

Mayer, J., Salovey, P., & Caruso, D. (2008). Emotional intelligence: New ability or eclectic traits? *American Psychologist, 63*, 503–517.

Mayes, L., Snyder, P., Langlois, E., & Hunter, N. (2007). Visuospatial working memory in school-aged children exposed in utero to cocaine. *Child Neuropsychology, 13*, 205–218.

Maynard, A. (2008). What we thought we knew and how we came to know it: Four decades of cross-cultural research from a Piagetian point of view. *Human Development, 51*, 56–65.

Mayseless, O. (1996). Attachment patterns and their outcomes. *Human Development, 39*, 206–223.

Mazoyer, B., Houdé, O., Joliot, M., Mellet, E., & Tzourio-Mazoyer, N. (2009). Regional cerebral blood flow increases during wakeful rest following cognitive training. *Brain Research Bulletin, 80*, 133–138. Accessed online, http://search.ebscohost.com, doi:10.1016/j.brainresbull.2009.06.021.

McArdle, E. F. (2002). New York's Do-Not-Resuscitate law: Groundbreaking protection of patient autonomy or a physician's right to make medical futility determinations? *DePaul Journal of Health Care Law, 8*, 55–82.

McCarthy, B., & Pierpaoli, C. (2015). Sexual challenges with aging: Integrating the GES approach in an elderly couple. *Journal of Sex & Marital Therapy, 41*, 72–82.

McClain, M. R., Hokanson, J. S., Grazel, R., Braun, K. N., Garg, L. F., Morris, M. R., & … Sontag, M. K. (2017). Critical congenital heart disease newborn screening implementation: Lessons learned. *Maternal and Child Health Journal*. Accessed online, 10-27-17; https://www.ncbi.nlm.nih.gov/pubmed/28092064.

McClain, S., & Cokley, K. (2017). Academic disidentification in black college students: The role of teacher trust and gender. *Cultural Diversity and Ethnic Minority Psychology, 23*, 125–133.

McClelland, D. C. (1993). Intelligence is not the best predictor of job performance. *Current Directions in Psychological Research, 2*, 5–8.

McConnell, V. (2012, February 16). Great granny to the rescue! *Mail Online*. Accessed online, 7-13-12; http://www.dailymail.co.uk/femail/article-2101720/As-live-work-longer-great-grandparents-filling-childcare-gap.html.

McCowan, L. M. E., Dekker, G. A., Chan, E., Stewart, A., Chappell, L. C., Hunger, M., Moss-Morris, R., & North, R. A. (2009, June 27). Spontaneous preterm birth and small for gestational age infants in women who stop smoking early in pregnancy: Prospective cohort study. *BMJ: British Medical Journal, 338* (7710), 2009.

McCrae, R., & Costa, P. (2003). *Personality in adulthood: A five-factor theory perspective* (2nd ed.). New York: Guilford Press.

McCrink, K., & Wynn, K. (2009). Operational momentum in large-number addition and subtraction by 9-month-olds. *Journal of Experimental Child Psychology, 103*, 400–408.

McCue, R. E., & Balasubramaniam, M. (2017). *Rational suicide in the elderly: Clinical, ethical, and sociocultural aspects*. Cham, Switzerland: Springer International Publishing.

McCullough, M. E., Tsang, J., & Brion, S. (2003). Personality traits in adolescence as predictors of religiousness in early maturity: Findings from the terman longitudinal study. *Personality & Social Psychology Bulletin, 29*, 980–991.

McDonnell, C. G., Valentino, K., Comas, M., & Nuttall, A. K. (2016). Mother–child reminiscing at risk: Maternal attachment, elaboration, and child autobiographical memory specificity. *Journal of Experimental Child Psychology, 143*, 65–84.

McDonnell, L. M. (2004). *Politics, persuasion, and educational testing*. Cambridge, MA: Harvard University Press.

McDonough, L. (2002). Basic-level nouns: First learned but misunderstood. *Journal of Child Language, 29*, 357–377.

McElhaney, K., Antonishak, J., & Allen, J. (2008). "They like me, they like me not": Popularity and adolescents' perceptions of acceptance predicting social functioning over time. *Child Development, 79*, 720–731.

McElwain, N., & Booth-LaForce, C. (2006, June). Maternal sensitivity to infant distress and nondistress as predictors of infant–mother attachment security. *Journal of Family Psychology, 20*, 247–255.

McFadden, J. R., & Rawson Swan, K. T. (2012). Women during midlife: Is it transition or crisis? *Family and Consumer Sciences Research Journal, 40*, 313–325.

McFarland-Piazza, L., Hazen, N., Jacobvitz, D., & Boyd-Soisson, E. (2012). The development of father–child attachment: Associations between adult attachment representations, recollections of childhood experiences and caregiving. *Early Child Development and Care, 182*, 701–721.

McGill, R. J., & Spurgin, A. R. (2016). Assessing the incremental value of KABC-II Luria model scores in predicting achievement: What do they tell us beyond the MPI? *Psychology in the Schools, 53*, 677–689.

McGillion, M., Herbert, J. S., Pine, J., Vihman, M., dePaolis, R., Keren-Portnoy, T., & Matthews, D. (2017). What paves the way to conventional language? The predictive value of babble, pointing, and socioeconomic status. *Child Development, 88*, 156–166.

McGinnis, E. (2012). *Skillstreaming in early childhood: A guide for teaching prosocial skills* (3rd ed.). Champaign, IL: Research Press.

McGlothlin, H., Killen, M. (2005). Children's perceptions of intergroup and intragroup similarity and the role of social experience. *Journal of Applied Developmental Psychology, 26*, 680–698.

McGonigle-Chalmers, M., Slater, H., & Smith, A. (2014). Rethinking private speech in preschoolers: The effects of social presence. *Developmental Psychology, 50*, 829–836.

McGue, M., Bouchard, T. J., Jr., Iacono, W., & Lykken, D. T. (1993). Behavioral genetics of cognitive ability: A life-span perspective. In R. Plornin & G. E. McClearn (Eds.), *Nature, nurture, and psychology*. Washington, DC: American Psychological Association.

McGuffin, P., Riley, B., & Plomin, R. (2001, February 16). Toward behavioral genomics. *Science, 291*, 1232–1233.

McGuinness, D. (1972). Hearing: Individual differences in perceiving. *Perception, 1*, 465–473.

McGuire, S., & Shanahan, L. (2010). Sibling experiences in diverse family contexts. *Child Development Perspectives, 4*, 72–79.

McHale, J. P., & Rotman, T. (2007). Is seeing believing? Expectant parents' outlooks on coparenting and later coparenting solidarity. *Infant Behavior & Development, 30*, 63–81.

McHale, S. M., Updegraff, K. A., Shanahna, L., Crouter, A. C., & Killoren, S. E. (2005). Gender, culture, and family dynamics: Diffferential treatment of siblings in Mexican American families. *Journal of Marriage and the Family, 67*, 1259–1274.

McHale, S. M., Updegraff, K. A., & Whiteman, S. D. (2012). Sibling relationships and influences in childhood and adolescence. *Journal of Marriage and Family, 74*, 913–930.

McLachlan, H. (2008). The ethics of killing and letting die: Active and passive euthanasia. *Journal of Medical Ethics, 34*, 636–638.

McLean, K. C., & Syed, M. (2015). *The Oxford handbook of identity development*. New York: Oxford University Press.

McLoyd, V. C. (2006). The legacy of Child Development's 1990 Special Issue on Minority Children: An editorial retrospective. *Child Development, 77*, 1142–1148.

McLoyd, V. C., Cauce, A. M., Takeuchi, D., & Wilson, L. (2000). Marital processes and parental socialization in families of color: A decade review of research. *Journal of Marriage and Family, 62*, 1070–1093.

McMurray, B., Aslin, R. N., & Toscano, J. C. (2009). Statistical learning of phonetic categories: Insights from a computational approach. *Developmental Science, 12*, 369–378.

McNulty, J. K., & Karney, B. R. (2004). Positive expectations in the early years of marriage: Should couples expect the best or brace for the worst? *Journal of Personality and Social Psychology, 86,* 729–743.

McQuade, J., Achufusi, A., Shoulberg, E., & Murray-Close, D. (2014). Biased self-perceptions of social competence and engagement in physical and relational aggression: The moderating role of peer status and sex. *Aggressive Behavior [serial online], 40,* 512–525.

McQuade, J. D., Breaux, R. P., Gómez, A. F., Zakarian, R. J., & Weatherly, J. (2016). Biased self-perceived social competence and engagement in subtypes of aggression: Examination of peer rejection, social dominance goals, and sex of the child as moderators. *Aggressive Behavior*. Accessed online, 6-13-16; http://onlinelibrary.wiley.com/doi/10.1002/ab.21645/abstract.

McQueeny, T., Schweinsburg, B. C., Schweinsburg, A. D., Jacobus, J., Bava, S., Frank, L. R., & Tapert, S. F. (2009). Altered white matter integrity in adolescent binge drinkers. *Alcoholism: Clinical and Experimental Research, 33,* 1278–1285.

McVittie, C., McKinlay, A., & Widdicombe, S. (2003). Committed to (un)equal opportunities? "New ageism" and the older worker. *British Journal of Social Psychology, 42,* 595–612.

McWhirter, L., Young, V., & Majury, Y. (1983). Belfast children's awareness of violent death. *British Journal of Psychology, 22,* 81–92.

Mead, M. (1942). *Environment and education, a symposium held in connection with the fiftieth anniversary celebration of the University of Chicago*. Chicago: University of Chicago.

Meade, C., Kershaw, T., & Ickovics, J. (2008). The intergenerational cycle of teenage motherhood: An ecological approach. *Health Psychology, 27,* 419–429.

Meador, K. J., Boyd, A., & Loring, D. W. (2017). Relationship of reaction time to perception of a stimulus and volitionally delayed response. *Cognitive and Behavioral Neurology, 30,* 57–61.

Mealey, L. (2000). *Sex differences: Developmental and evolutionary strategies*. Orlando, FL: Academic Press.

Medeiros, R., Prediger, R. D., Passos, G. F., Pandolfo, P., Duarte, F. S., Franco, J. L., Dafre, A. L., Di Giunta, G., Figueiredo, C. P., Takahashi, R. N., Campos, M. M., & Calixto, J. B. (2007). Connecting TNF-alpha signaling pathways to iNOS expression in a mouse model of Alzheimer's disease: Relevance for the behavioral and synaptic deficits induced by amyloid beta protein. *Journal of Neuroscience, 16,* 5394–5404.

Medina, A., Lederhos, C., & Lillis, T. (2009). Sleep disruption and decline in marital satisfaction across the transition to parenthood. *Families, Systems, & Health, 27,* 153–160.

Meece, J. L., & Kurtz-Costes, B. (2001). Introduction: The schooling of ethnic minority children and youth. *Educational Psychologist, 36,* 1–7.

Meeks, T., & Jeste, D. (2009). Neurobiology of wisdom: A literature overview. *Archives of General Psychiatry, 66,* 355–365.

Mehlenbeck, R. S., Farmer, A. S., & Ward, W. L. (2014). Obesity in children and adolescents. In L. Grossman & S. Walfish (Eds.), *Translating psychological research into practice*. New York: Springer Publishing Co.

Mehta, C. M., & Strough, J. (2009). Sex segregation in friendships and normative contexts across the life span. *Developmental Review, 29,* 201–220.

Meijer, A. M., & van den Wittenboer, G. L. H. (2007). Contribution of infants' sleep and crying to marital relationship of first-time parent couples in the first year after childbirth. *Journal of Family Psychology, 21,* 49–57.

Meinzen-Derr, J., Wiley, S., Grether, S., Phillips, J., Choo, D., Hibner, J., & Barnard, H. (2014). Functional communication of children who are deaf or hard-of-hearing. *Journal of Developmental and Behavioral Pediatrics, 35,* 197–206.

Meister, H., & von Wedel, H. (2003). Demands on hearing aid features—special signal processing for elderly users? *International Journal of Audiology, 42,* 2S58–2S62.

Meland, A., Ishimatsu, K., Pensgaard, A. M., Wagstaff, A., Fonne, V., Garde, A. H., & Harris, A. (2015). Impact of mindfulness training on physiological measures of stress and objective measures of attention control in a military helicopter unit. *International Journal of Aviation Psychology, 25,* 191–208.

Meldrum, R. C., Miller, H. V., & Flexon, J. L. (2013). Susceptibility to peer influence, self control, and delinquency. *Sociological Inquiry, 83,* 106–129.

Meltzoff, A. (2002). Elements of a developmental theory of imitation. In A. Meltzoff & W. Prinz (Eds.), *The imitative mind: Development, evolution, and brain bases* (pp. 19–41). New York: Cambridge University Press.

Meltzoff, A. N., & Moore, M. (2002). Imitation, memory, and the representation of persons. *Infant Behavior & Development, 25,* 39–61.

Meltzoff, A. N., & Moore, M. K. (1977). Imitation of facial and manual gestures by human neonates. *Science, 198,* 75–78.

Meltzoff, A. N., Waismeyer, A., & Gopnik, A. (2012). Learning about causes from people: Observational causal learning in 24-month-old infants. *Developmental Psychology*. Accessed online, 7-18-12; http://www.alisongopnik.com/Papers_Alison/Observational%20Causal%20Learning.pdf.

Melzer, D., Hurst, A., & Frayling, T. (2007). Genetic variation and human aging: Progress and prospects. *Journals of Gerontology: Series A: Biological Sciences and Medical Sciences, 62,* 301–307. Accessed online, http://search.ebscohost.com.

Ménard, C., Pfau, M. L., Hodes, G. E., & Russo, S. J. (2017). Immune and neuroendocrine mechanisms of stress vulnerability and resilience. *Neuropsychopharmacology, 42,* 62–80.

Mendle, J., Turkheimer, E., & Emery, R. E. (2007). Detrimental psychological outcomes associated with early pubertal timing in adolescent girls. *Developmental Review, 27,* 151–171.

Mendonça, B., Sargent, B., & Fetters, L. (2016). Cross-cultural validity of standardized motor development screening and assessment tools: A systematic review. *Developmental Medicine & Child Neurology, 58,* 1213–1222.

Mendoza, C. (2006, September). Inside today's classrooms: Teacher voices on No Child Left Behind and the education of gifted children. *Roeper Review, 29,* 28–31.

Mendoza, M. M., Dmitrieva, J., Perreira, K. M., Hurwich-Reiss, E., & Watamura, S. E. (2017). The effects of economic and sociocultural stressors on the well-being of children of Latino immigrants living in poverty. *Cultural Diversity and Ethnic Minority Psychology, 23,* 15–26.

Mensah, F. K., Bayer, J. K., Wake, M., Carlin, J. B., Allen, N. B., & Patton, G. C. (2013). Early puberty and childhood social and behavioral adjustment. *Journal of Adolescent Health, 53,* 118–124.

Menzel, J. (2008). Depression in the elderly after traumatic brain injury: A systematic review. *Brain Injury, 22,* 375–380.

Mercado, E. (2009). Cognitive plasticity and cortical modules. *Current Directions in Psychological Science, 18,* 153–158.

Mercer, J. R. (1973). *Labeling the mentally retarded*. Berkeley: University of California Press.

Merikangas, K. R., Nakamura, E. F. & Kessler, R. C. (2009). Epidemiology of mental disorders in children and adolescents. *Dialogues Clinical Neuroscience, 11,* 7–20

Merrow, J. (2012, January 11). In education, back to basics. *Huffington Post*. Accessed online, 11-7-17; https://www.huffingtonpost.com/john-merrow/in-education-back-to-basi_b_1199924.html.

Merlo, L., Bowman, M., & Barnett, D. (2007). Parental nurturance promotes reading acquisition in low socioeconomic status children. *Early Education and Development, 18,* 51–69.

Merrill, D. M. (1997). *Caring for elderly parents: Juggling work, family, and caregiving in middle and working class families*. Wesport, CT: Auburn House/Greenwood Publishing Group.

Merritt, A., LaQuea, R., Cromwell, R., & Ferguson, C. J. (2016). Media managing mood: A look at the possible effects of violent media on affect. *Child & Youth Care Forum, 45,* 241–258.

Mervis, J. (2011). A passion for early education. *Science, 333,* 957–958.

Mervis, J. (2011a, 19 August). Past successes shape effort to expand early intervention. *Science, 333,* 952–956.

Mervis, J. (2011b, 19 August). Giving children a head start is possible—but it's not easy. *Science, 333,* 956–957.

Merwin, S. M., Smith, V. C., Kushner, M., Lemay, E. J., & Dougherty, L. R. (2017). Parent-child adrenocortical concordance in early childhood: The moderating role of parental depression and child temperament. *Biological Psychology, 124,* 100–110.

Mesinas, M., & Perez, W. (2016). Cultural involvement, indigenous identity, and language: An exploratory study of Zapotec adolescents and their parents. *Hispanic Journal of Behavioral Sciences, 38,* 482–506.

Mesman, J., van Ijzendoorn, M., Behrens, K., Carbonell, O. A., Cárcamo, R., Cohen-Paraira, I., & … Zreik, G. (2016). Is the ideal mother a sensitive mother? Beliefs about early childhood parenting in mothers across the globe. *International Journal of Behavioral Development, 40,* 385–397.

Messinger, D. S., Mattson, W. I., Mahoor, M. H., & Cohn, J. F. (2012). The eyes have it: Making positive expressions more positive and negative expressions more negative. *Emotion, 12,* 430–436.

MetLife Mature Market Institute. (2009). *The MetLife market survey of nursing home & home care costs 2008*. Westport, CT: MetLife Mature Market Institute.

Meyer, M., Wolf, D., & Himes, C. (2006, March). Declining eligibility for Social Security spouse and widow benefits in the United States? *Research on Aging, 28,* 240–260.

Meyers, J. (2015, October 2). Which countries have the most deaths from heart disease? Accessed online, 11-28-17; https://www.weforum.org/agenda/2015/10/which-countries-have-the-most-deaths-from-heartdisease/.

Mezuk, B., Prescott, M., Tardiff, K., Vlahov, D., & Galea, S. (2008). Suicide in older adults in long-term care: 1990 to 2005. *Journal of the American Geriatrics Society, 56,* 2107–2111.

Miao, X., & Wang, W. (2003). A century of Chinese developmental psychology. *International Journal of Psychology, 38,* 258–273.

Michael, R. T., Gagnon, J. H., Laumann, E. O., & Kolata, G. (1994). *Sex in America: A definitive survey*. Boston: Little, Brown.

Michael, Y. L., Carlson, N. E., Chlebowski, R. T., Aickin, M., Weihs, K. L., Ockene, J. K., & … Ritenbaugh, C. (2009). Influence of stressors on breast cancer incidence in the Women's Health Initiative. *Health Psychology,* 28, 137–146.

Michaels, M. (2006). Factors that contribute to stepfamily success: A qualitative analysis. *Journal of Divorce & Remarriage, 44,* 53–66.

Miche, M., Elsässer, V. C., Schilling, O. K., & Wahl, H. (2014). Attitude toward own aging in midlife and early old age over a 12-year period: Examination of measurement equivalence and developmental trajectories. *Psychology and Aging, 29,* 588–600.

Mickelson, K. D., Biehle, S., Chong, A., & Gordon, A. E. (2017). Perceived stigma of postpartum depression in first-time parents: A dual-pathway model. *Sex Roles, 76,* 306–318.

Miesnik, S., & Reale, B. (2007). A review of issues surrounding medically elective cesarean delivery. *Journal of Obstetric, Gynecologic, & Neonatal Nursing: Clinical Scholarship for the Care of Women, Childbearing Families, & Newborns, 36,* 605–615.

Mikkola, T. M., Portegijs, E., Rantakokko, M., Gagné, J., Rantanen, T., & Viljanen, A. (2015). Association of self-reported hearing difficulty to objective and perceived participation outside the home in older community-dwelling adults. *Journal of Aging and Health, 27,* 103–122.

Mikulincer, M., & Shaver, P. (2009). An attachment and behavioral systems perspective on social support. *Journal of Social and Personal Relationships, 26,* 7–19.

Mikulincer, M., Shaver, P. R., Simpson, J. A., & Dovidio, J. F. (2015). *APA handbook of personality and social psychology, Volume 3: Interpersonal relations*. Washington, DC: American Psychological Association.

Mikulovic, J., Marcellini, A., Compte, R., et al. (2011). Prevalence of overweight in adolescents with intellectual deficiency. Differences in socio-educative context, physical activity, and dietary habits. *Appetite, 56*, 403–407.

Miles, R., Cowan, F., Glover, V., Stevenson, J., & Modi, N. (2006). A controlled trial of skin-to-skin contact in extremely preterm infants. *Early Human Development*, 2(7), 447–455.

Millei, Z., & Gallagher, J. (2012). Opening spaces for dialogue and re-envisioning children's bathroom in a preschool: Practitioner research with children on a sensitive and neglected area of concern. *International Journal of Early Childhood, 44*, 9–29.

Miller, A. J., Sassler, S., & Kus-Appough. (2011). The specter of divorce: Views from working- and middle-class cohabitors. *Family Relations, 60, 602–616.*

Miller, B. G., Kors, S., & Macfie, J. (2017). No differences? Meta-analytic comparisons of psychological adjustment in children of gay fathers and heterosexual parents. *Psychology of Sexual Orientation and Gender Diversity, 4*, 14–22.

Miller, E. M. (1998). Evidence from opposite-sex twins for the effects of prenatal sex hormones. In L. Ellis & L. Ebertz (Eds.), *Males, females, and behavior: Toward biological understanding*. Westport, CT: Praeger Publishers/Greenwood Publishing Group.

Miller, S. A. (2012). *Theory of mind: Beyond the preschool years*. New York: Psychology Press.

Miller, D. P., & Brooks-Gunn, J. (2015). Obesity. In T. P. Gullotta, R. W. Plant, & M. A. Evans (Eds.), *Handbook of adolescent behavioral problems: Evidence-based approaches to prevention and treatment* (2nd ed.). New York: Springer Science + Business Media.

Miller, J. L., & Eimas, P. D. (1995). Speech perception: From signal to word. *Annual Review of Psychology, 46*, 467–492.

Miltenberger, R. G. (2016). *Behavior modification: Principles and procedures* (6th ed.) Boston: Cengage Learning.

Minai, U., Gustafson, K., Fiorentino, R., Jongman, A., & Sereno, J. (2017, July 5). Fetal rhythm-based language discrimination: A biomagnetometry study. *Neuroreport, 28* (10), 561–564.

Mireault, G. C., Crockenberg, S. C., Sparrow, J. E., Pettinato, C. A., Woodard, K. C., & Malzac, K. (2014). Social looking, social referencing and humor perception in 6- and-12-month-old infants. *Infant Behavior & Development, 37*, 536–545.

Mishna, F., Saini, M., & Solomon, S. (2009). Ongoing and online: Children and youth's perceptions of cyber bullying. *Children and Youth Services Review, 31*, 1222–1228.

Misri, S. (2007). Suffering in silence: The burden of perinatal depression. *Canadian Journal of Psychiatry / La Revue canadienne de psychiatrie, 52*, 477–478.

Missana, M., Altvater-Mackensen, N., & Grossmann, T. (2017). Neural correlates of infants' sensitivity to vocal expressions of peers. *Developmental Cognitive Neuroscience, 26*, 39–44.

Mistry, J., & Saraswathi, T. (2003). The cultural context of child development. In R. Lerner & M. Easterbrooks (Eds.), *Handbook of psychology: Developmental psychology* (Vol. 6, pp. 267–291). New York: Wiley.

Missana, M., Altvater-Mackensen, N., & Grossmann, T. (2017). Neural correlates of infants' sensitivity to vocal expressions of peers. *Developmental Cognitive Neuroscience, 26*, 39–44.

Mitchell, E. (2009). What is the mechanism of SIDS? Clues from epidemiology. *Developmental Psychobiology, 51*, 215–222.

Mitchell, K., Wolak, J., & Finkelhor, D. (2007, February). Trends in youth reports of sexual solicitations, harassment and unwanted exposure to pornography on the Internet. *Journal of Adolescent Health, 40*, 116–126.

Mitchell, K. J., & Porteous, D. J. (2011). Rethinking the genetic architecture of schizophrenia. *Psychological Medicine, 41*, 19–32.

Mitchell, K. J., Ybarra, M. L., & Korchmaros, J. D. (2014). Sexual harassment among adolescents of different sexual orientations and gender identities. *Child Abuse & Neglect, 38*, 280–295.

Mittal, V., Ellman, L., & Cannon, T. (2008). Gene-environment interaction and covariation in schizophrenia: The role of obstetric complications. *Schizophrenia Bulletin, 34*, 1083–1094. Accessed online, http://search.ebscohost.com, doi:10.1093/schbul/sbn080.

Miyasaki, J. M., Rheaume, C., Gulya, L., Ellenstein, A., Schwarz, H. B., Vidic, T. R., & Busis, N. A. (2017). Qualitative study of burnout, career satisfaction, and well-being among US neurologists in 2016. *Neurology, 89*, 1730–1738.

Mizuno, K., & Ueda, A. (2004). Antenatal olfactory learning influences infant feeding. *Early Human Development, 76*, 83–90.

MMWR. (2008, August 1). Trends in HIV- and STD-related risk behaviors among high school students—United States, 1991–2007. *Morbidity and Mortality Weekly Report, 57*, 817–822.

Mohajeri, M., & Leuba, G. (2009). Prevention of age-associated dementia. *Brain Research Bulletin, 80*, 315–325.

Mok, A., & Morris, M. W. (2012). Managing two cultural identities: The malleability of bicultural identity integration as a function of induced global or local processing. *Personality and Social Psychology Bulletin, 38*, 233–246.

Moldin, S. O., & Gottesman, I. I. (1997). Genes, experience, and chance in schizophrenia—positioning for the 21st century. *Schizophrenia Bulletin, 23*, 547–561.

Mølgaard-Nielsen, D., Pasternak, B., & Hviid, A. (2013). Use of oral fluconazole during pregnancy and the risk of birth defects. *New England Journal of Medicine, 369*, 830–839.

Molina, J. C., Spear, N. E., Spear, L. P., Mennella, J. A., & Lewis, M. J. (2007). The International Society for Developmental Psychobiology 39th annual meeting symposium: Alcohol and development: Beyond fetal alcohol syndrome. *Developmental Psychobiology, 49*, 227–242.

Monahan, C. I., Beeber, L. S., & Harden, B. (2012). Finding family strengths in the midst of adversity: Using risk and resilience models to promote mental health. In S. Summers & R. Chazan-Cohen (Eds.), *Understanding early childhood mental health: A practical guide for professionals*. Baltimore: Paul H Brookes Publishing.

Monahan, K., Steinberg, L., & Cauffman, E. (2009). Affiliation with antisocial peers, susceptibility to peer influence, and antisocial behavior during the transition to adulthood. *Developmental Psychology, 45*, 1520–1530.

Monastra, V. (2008). The etiology of ADHD: A neurological perspective. *Unlocking the potential of patients with ADHD: A model for clinical practice*. Washington, DC: American Psychological Association.

Monsour, M. (2002). *Women and men as friends: Relationships across the life span in the 21st century*. Mahwah, NJ: Lawrence Erlbaum Associates Publishers.

Montague, D., & Walker-Andrews, A. (2002). Mothers, fathers, and infants: The role of person familiarity and parental involvement in infants' perception of emotion expressions. *Child Development, 73*, 1339–1352.

Montepare, J. M., Kempler, D., & McLaughlin-Volpe, T. (2014). The voice of wisdom: New insights on social impressions of aging voices. *Journal of Language and Social Psychology, 33*, 241–259.

Monteverde, S., Terkamo-Moisio, A., Kvist, T., Kangasniemi, M., Laitila, T., Ryynänen, O., & Pietilä, A. (2017). Nurses' attitudes towards euthanasia in conflict with professional ethical guidelines. *Nursing Ethics, 24*, 70–86.

Moon, C. (2002). Learning in early infancy. *Advances in Neonatal Care, 2*, 81–83.

Moon, R. Y. (2016). Task force on sudden infant death syndrome. *Pediatrics, 138*, 105–111.

Moore, K. L. (1974). *Before we are born: Basic embryology and birth defects*. Philadelphia, PA: Saunders.

Moore, K. L., & Persaud, T. V. N. (2003). *Before we were born* (6th ed.). Philadelphia, PA: Saunders.

Moore, M. C. & de Costa, C. M. (2006). *Pregnancy and parenting after thirty-five: Midlife, new life*. Baltimore, MD: Johns Hopkins University Press.

Moore, R. L., & Wei, L. (2012). Modern love in China. In M. A. Paludi (Ed.), *The psychology of love (Vols. 1–4)*. Santa Barbara, CA: Praeger/ABC-CLIO.

Moore, S., & Rosenthal, D. (2017). *Grandparenting: Contemporary perspectives*. New York: Routledge/Taylor & Francis Group.

Morales, J. R., & Guerra, N. F. (2006). Effects of multiple context and cumulative stress on urban children's adjustment in elementary school. *Child Development, 77*, 907–923.

Morfei, M. Z., Hooker, K., Carpenter, J., Blakeley, E., & Mix, C. (2004). Agentic and communal generative behavior in four areas of adult life: Implications for psychological well-being. *Journal of Adult Development, 11*, 55–58.

Morita, J., Miwa, K., Kitasaka, T., Mori, K., Suenaga, Y., Iwano, S., et al. (2008). Interactions of perceptual and conceptual processing: Expertise in medical image diagnosis. *International Journal of Human-Computer Studies, 66*, 370–390.

Morley, J. E. (2012). Sarcopenia in the elderly. *Family Practice, 29*(Suppl. 1), I44–I48. doi:10.1093/fampra/cmr063.

Morris, P., & Fritz, C. (2006, October). How to improve your memory. *Psychologist, 19*, 608–611.

Morrison, K. M., Shin, S., Tarnopolsky, M., & Taylor, V. H. (2015). Association of depression & health related quality of life with body composition in children and youth with obesity. *Journal of Affective Disorders, 172*, 18–23.

Morrongiello, B., Corbett, M., & Bellissimo, A. (2008). "Do as I say, not as I do": Family influences on children's safety and risk behaviors. *Health Psychology, 27*, 498–503.

Morrongiello, B., Corbett, M., McCourt, M., & Johnston, N. (2006, July). Understanding unintentional injury-risk in young children I. The nature and scope of caregiver supervision of children at home. *Journal of Pediatric Psychology, 31*, 529–539.

Morrongiello, B. A., Klemencic, N., & Corbett, M. (2008). Interactions between child behavior patterns and parent supervision: Implications for children's risk of unintentional injury. *Child Development, 79*(3), 627-638. doi:10.1111/j.1467-8624.2008.01147.x

Morrongiello, B., Zdzieborski, D., Sandomierski, M., & Lasenby-Lessard, J. (2009). Video messaging: What works to persuade mothers to supervise young children more closely in order to reduce injury risk? *Social Science & Medicine, 68*, 1030–1037.

Moser, S., Luxenberger, W., & Freidl, W. (2017). The influence of social support and coping on quality of life among elderly with age-related hearing loss. *American Journal of Audiology, 26*, 170–179.

Motschnig, R., & Nykl, L. (2003). Toward a cognitiveemotional model of Rogers's person-centered approach. *Journal of Humanistic Psychology, 43*, 8–45.

Mõttus, R., Kandler, C., Bleidorn, W., Riemann, R., & McCrae, R. R. (2017). Personality traits below facets: The consensual validity, longitudinal stability, heritability, and utility of personality nuances. *Journal of Personality and Social Psychology, 112*, 474–490.

Moyle, J., Fox, A., Arthur, M., Bynevelt, M., & Burnett, J. (2007). Meta-analysis of neuropsychological symptoms of adolescents and adults with PKU. *Neuropsychology Review, 17*, 9–101.

Mpofu, E., Bracken, B. A., van de Vijver, F. R., & Saklofske, D. H. (2017). Teaching about intelligence, concept formation, and emotional intelligence. In G. J. Rich, U. P. Gielen, H. Takooshian (Eds.), *Internationalizing the teaching of psychology*. Charlotte, NC: IAP Information Age Publishing.

Mrazek, A. J., Harada, T., & Chiao, J. Y. (2015). Cultural neuroscience of identity development. In K. C. McLean, & M. Syed (Eds.), *The Oxford handbook of identity development*. New York: Oxford University Press.

Mrug, S., Elliott, M. N., Davies, S., Tortolero, S. R., Cuccaro, P., & Schuster, M. A. (2014). Early puberty, negative peer influence, and problem behaviors in adolescent girls. *Pediatrics, 133*, 7–14.

Mu, Z., & Xie, Y. (2014). Marital age homogamy in China: A reversal of trend in the reform era? *Social Science Research, 44*, 141–157

Mueller, M., Wilhelm, B., & Elder, G. (2002). Variations in grandparenting. *Research on Aging, 24*, 360–388.

Muenchow, S., & Marsland, K. W. (2007). Beyond baby steps: Promoting the growth and development of U.S. child-care policy. In L. J. Aber, et al. (Eds.). *Child development and social policy: Knowledge for action*. Washington, DC: American Psychological Association.

Mugai, W. J. J. (2016). *Psychology of spousal abuse in marriage: Help for victims*. New York: Lap Lambert Academic Publishing.

Muhonen, H., Rasku-Puttonen, H., Pakarinen, E., Poikkeus, A., & Lerkkanen, M. (2016). Scaffolding through dialogic teaching in early school classrooms. *Teaching and Teacher Education, 55*, 143–154.

Muiños, M., & Ballesteros, S. (2014). Peripheral vision and perceptual asymmetries in young and older martial arts athletes and non-athletes. *Attention, Perception, & Psychophysics*, 76, 2465–2476.

Müller, D., Ziegelmann, J. P., Simonson, J., Tesch-Römer, C., & Huxhold, O. (2014). Volunteering and subjective well-being in later adulthood: Is self-efficacy the key? *International Journal of Developmental Science, 8*, 125–135.

Muller, R. T. (2013). Not just a phase: Depression in preschoolers. Recognizing the signs and reducing the risk. *Psychology Today*. Accessed online, 2-27-14; http://www.psychologytoday.com/blog/talking-about-trauma/201306/not-just-phase-depression-in-preschoolers.

Müller, U., Liebermann-Finestone, D. P., Carpendale, J. M., Hammond, S. I., & Bibok, M. B. (2012). Knowing minds, controlling actions: The developmental relations between theory of mind and executive function from 2 to 4 years of age. *Journal of Experimental Child Psychology, 111*, 331–348.

Müller, U., Ten Eycke, K., & Baker, L. (2015). Piaget's theory of intelligence. In S. Goldstein, D. Princiotta, & J. A. Naglieri (Eds.), *Handbook of intelligence: Evolutionary theory, historical perspective, and current concepts*. New York: Springer Science + Business Media.

Mumme, D., & Fernald, A. (2003). The infant as onlooker: Learning from emotional reactions observed in a television scenario. *Child Development, 74*, 221–237.

Mundy, B., & Wofsy, M. (2017). Diverse couple and family forms and universal family processes. In S. Kelly (Ed.), *Diversity in couple and family therapy: Ethnicities, sexualities, and socioeconomics*. Santa Barbara, CA: Praeger/ABC-CLIO.

Munniksma, A., Scheepers, P., Stark, T. H., & Tolsma, J. (2017). The impact of adolescents' classroom and neighborhood ethnic diversity on same- and cross-ethnic friendships within classrooms. *Journal of Research on Adolescence, 27*, 20–33.

Munro, B. A., Weyandt, L. L., Marraccini, M. E., & Oster, D. R. (2017). The relationship between nonmedical use of prescription stimulants, executive functioning and academic outcomes. *Addictive Behaviors, 65*, 250–257.

Munro, C., Randall, L. & Lawrie, S. M. (2017). An integrative bio-psycho-social theory of anorexia nervosa. *Clinical Psychology and Psychotherapy, 24*, 1–24.

Munsey, C. (2012, February). Anti-bullying efforts ramp up. *Monitor on Psychology*, pp. 54–57.

Munzar, P., Cami, J., & Farré, M. (2003). Mechanisms of drug addiction. *New England Journal of Medicine, 349*, 2365–2365.

Muramoto, Y., Yamaguchi, S., & Kim, U. (2009). Perception of achievement attribution in individual and group contexts: Comparative analysis of Japanese, Korean, and Asian-American results. *Asian Journal Of Social Psychology, 12*(3), 199-210. doi:10.1111/j.1467-839X.2009.01285.x

Murasko, J. E. (2015). Overweight/obesity and human capital formation from infancy to adolescence: Evidence from two large US cohorts. *Journal of Biosocial Science, 47*, 220–237.

Muratore, A. M., & Earl, J. K. (2015). Improving retirement outcomes: The role of resources, pre-retirement planning and transition characteristics. *Ageing & Society, 35*, 2100–2140.

Murdock, K. W., Zilioli, S., Ziauddin, K., Heijnen, C. J., & Fagundes, C. P. (2017). Attachment and telomere length: More evidence for psychobiological connections between close relationships, health, and aging. *Journal of Behavioral Medicine*. Accessed online, 12-12-17; https://www.ncbi.nlm.nih.gov/pubmed/29067540.

Murguia, A., Peterson, R. A., & Zea, M. C. (1997, August). Cultural health beliefs. Paper presented at the annual meeting of the American Psychological Association, Toronto, Canada.

Murphy, C. (2008). The chemical senses and nutrition in older adults. *Journal Of Nutrition For The Elderly, 27*(3-4), 247-265. doi:10.1080/01639360802261862

Murphy, B., & Eisenberg, N. (2002). An integrative examination of peer conflict: Children's reported goals, emotions, and behaviors. *Social Development, 11*, 534–557.

Murphy, F. A., Lipp, A., & Powles, D. L. (2012, March 14). Follow-up for improving psychological well being for women after a miscarriage. *Cochrane Database System Reviews*.

Murphy, M. (2009). Language and literacy in individuals with Turner syndrome. *Topics in Language Disorders, 29*, 187–194. Accessed online, http://search.ebscohost.com.

Murphy, S., Johnson, L., & Wu, L. (2003). Bereaved parents' outcomes 4 to 60 months after their children's death by accident, suicide, or homicide: A comparative study demonstrating differences. *Death Studies, 27*, 39–61.

Murray, L., Cooper, P., Creswell, C., Schofield, E., & Sack, C. (2007, January). The effects of maternal social phobia on mother–infant interactions and infant social responsiveness. *Journal of Child Psychology and Psychiatry, 48*, 45–52.

Murray, L., de Rosnay, M., Pearson, J., Bergeron, C., Schofield, E., Royal-Lawson, M., et al. (2008). Intergenerational transmission of social anxiety: The role of social referencing processes in infancy. *Child Development, 79*, 1049–1064.

Murray, S., Bellavia, G., & Rose, P. (2003). Once hurt, twice hurtful: How perceived regard regulates daily marital interactions. *Journal of Personality & Social Psychology, 84*, 126–147.

Murray, T., & Lewis, V. (2014). Gender-role conflict and men's body satisfaction: The moderating role of age. *Psychology of Men & Masculinity, 15*, 40–48.

Murray-Close, D., Ostrov, J., & Crick, N. (2007, December). A short-term longitudinal study of growth of relational aggression during middle childhood: Associations with gender, friendship intimacy, and internalizing problems. *Development and Psychopathology, 19*, 187–203.

Musacchia, G., Ortiz-Mantilla, S., Choudhury, N., Realpe-Bonilla, T., Roesler, C., & Benasich, A. A. (2017). Active auditory experience in infancy promotes brain plasticity in Theta and Gamma oscillations. *Developmental Cognitive Neuroscience, 26*, 9–19.

Mustanski, B., Kuper, L., & Greene, G. J. (2014). Development of sexual orientation and identity. In D. L. Tolman, L. M. Diamond, J. A. Bauermeister, W. H. George, J. G. Pfaus, & L. M. Ward (Eds.), *APA handbook of sexuality and psychology, Vol. 1: Person-based approaches*. Washington, DC: American Psychological Association.

Musu-Gillette, L., Robinson, J., McFarland, J., KewalRamani, A., Zhang, A., and Wilkinson-Flicker, S. (2016). *Status and trends in the education of racial and ethnic groups 2016 (NCES 2016-007)*. Washington, DC: U.S. Department of Education, National Center for Education Statistics.

Mychasiuk, R., & Metz, G. S. (2016). Epigenetic and gene expression changes in the adolescent brain: What have we learned from animal models? *Neuroscience and Biobehavioral Reviews, 70*, 189–197.

Myers, D. (2000). *A quiet world: Living with hearing loss*. New Haven, CT: Yale University Press.

Myers, R. H. (2004). Huntington's disease genetics. *NeuroRx, 1*, 255–262.

Myklebust, B. M., & Gottlieb, G. L. (1993). Development of the stretch reflex in the newborn: Reciprocal excitation and reflex irradation. *Child Development, 64*, 1036–1045.

Myrtek, M. (2007). *Type A behavior and hostility as independent risk factors for coronary heart disease*. Washington, DC: American Psychological Association.

Nagahashi, S. (2013). Meaning making by preschool children during pretend play and construction of play space. *Japanese Journal of Developmental Psychology, 24*, 88–98.

Nagy, E. (2006). From imitation to conversation: The first dialogues with human neonates. *Infant and Child Development, 15*, 223–232.

Nagy, E., Pal, A., & Orvos, H. (2014). Learning to imitate individual finger movements by the human neonate. *Developmental Science, 17*, 841–857.

Nagy, M. (1948). The child's theories concerning death. *Journal of Genetic Psychology, 73*, 3–27.

Naik, G. (2002, November 22). The grim mission of a Swiss group: Visitor's suicides. *Wall Street Journal*, pp. A1, A6.

Nanda, S., & Konnur, N. (2006, October). Adolescent drug & alcohol use in the 21st century. *Psychiatric Annals, 36*, 706–712.

Nangle, D. W., & Erdley, C. A. (Eds.). (2001). *The role of friendship in psychological adjustment*. San Francisco: Jossey-Bass.

Nappi, R., & Polatti, F. (2009). The use of estrogen therapy in women's sexual functioning. *Journal of Sexual Medicine, 6*, 603–616.

Narang, S., & Clarke, J. (2014). Abusive head trauma: Past, present, and future. *Journal of Child Neurology, 29*, 1747–1756.

Nash, A., Pine, K., & Messer, D. (2009). Television alcohol advertising: Do children really mean what they say? *British Journal of Developmental Psychology, 27*, 85–104.

Nassif, A., & Gunter, B. (2008). Gender representation in television advertisements in Britain and Saudi Arabia. *Sex Roles, 58*, 752–760.

Nation, M., & Heflinger, C. (2006). Risk factors for serious alcohol and drug use: The role of psychosocial variables in predicting the frequency of substance use among adolescents. *American Journal of Drug and Alcohol Abuse, 32*, 415–433.

National Association for Sport and Physical Education. (2006). *Shape of the nation: Status of physical education in the USA*. Reston, VA: Author.

National Association for the Education of Young Children. (2005). Position statements of the NAEYC. Accessed online, http://www.naeyc.org/about/positions.asp#where.

National Cancer Institute. (2012, November 6.) NIH study finds leisure-time physical activity increases life expectancy as much as 4.5 years. Accessed online, 1-18-18; https://www.cancer.gov/news-events/press-releases/2012/PhysicalActivityLifeExpectancy.

National Center for Education Statistics. (2002). *Dropout rates in the United States: 2000*. Washington, DC: NCES.

National Center for Education Statistics. (2003). *Dropout rates in the United States: 2003*. Washington, DC: NCES.

National Center for Health Statistics. (2015). *Leading causes of deaths among adolescents 15–19 years of age*. Atlanta, GA: Centers for Disease Control. Accessed online, 8-14-15; http://www.cdc.gov/nchs/fastats/adolescent-health.htm.

National Center for Health Statistics. (2017, November 25.) National marriage and divorce trends. Accessed online, 11-25-17; https://www.cdc.gov/nchs/nvss/marriage_divorce_tables.htm.

National Center for Injury Prevention and Control. (2016). *Youth violence facts at a glance 2016*. Washington, DC: Centers for Disease Control and Prevention.

National Clearinghouse on Child Abuse and Neglect Information. (2004). *Child maltreatment 2002: Summary of key findings/National Clearinghouse on Child Abuse and Neglect Information*. Washington, DC: Author.

National Council on Aging. (2015). USA15 national fact sheet. Accessed online, 12-11-17; https://www.ncoa.org/resources/usa15-national-fact-sheet-pdf/.

National Health and Nutrition Examination Survey. (2014). *Prevalence of overweight, obesity, and extreme obesity among adults: United States, 1960–1962 Through 2011–2012*.

National Health Interview Survey. (2015). *Health status of children*. Accessed online, 11-1-17; https://ftp.cdc.gov/pub/Health_Statistics/NCHS/NHIS/SHS/2015_SHS_Table_C-5.pdf.

National Institute of Aging. (2004, May 31). Sexuality in later life. In S. I. S. Rattan, P. Kristensen, & B. F. C. Clark (Eds.), *Understanding and modulating aging*. Malden, MA: Blackwell Publishing on behalf of the New York Academy of Sciences. Accessed online, http://www.niapublications.org/engagepages/sexuality.asp.

National Safety Council. (2013). *Accident facts: 2013 edition*. Chicago: National Safety Council.

National Science Foundation (NSF), Division of Science Resources Statistics. (2002). *Women, minorities, and persons with disabilities in science and engineering: 2002*. Arlington, VA: National Science Foundation.

National Vital Statistics System, National Center for Health Statistics, CDC. (2015). Leading causes of death by age group, United States. Accessed online, 1-18-18; https://www.cdc.gov/injury/wisqars/pdf/leading_causes_of_death_by_age_group_2014-a.pdf.

Navarro, M. (2006, May 25). Families add 3rd generation to households. *New York Times*, pp. A1, A22.

Nazzi, T., & Bertoncini, J. (2003). Before and after the vocabulary spurt: Two modes of word acquisition? *Developmental Science, 6*, 136–142.

NCB (National Children's Bureau) Now. (2011, February 8.) *ABA's anti-bullying tools for schools*. London: England.

NCD Risk Factor Collaboration. (2017). Worldwide trends in body mass index, underweight, overweight, and obesity from 1975 to 2016: a pooled analysis of 2416 population-based measurement studies in 128·9 million children, adolescents, and adults. doi: http://dx.doi.org/10.1016/S0140-6736(17)32129-3.

Needleman, H. L., Riess, J. A., Tobin, M. J., Biesecker, G. E., & Greenhouse, J. B. (1996, February 7). Bone lead levels and delinquent behavior. *JAMA: Journal of the American Medical Association, 2755*, 363–369.

Negy, C., Shreve, T., & Jensen, B. (2003). Ethnic identity, self-esteem, and ethnocentrism: A study of social identity versus multicultural theory of development. *Cultural Diversity & Ethnic Minority Psychology, 9*, 333–344.

Neisser, U. (2004). Memory development: New questions and old. *Developmental Review, 24*, 154–158.

Nelis, D., Quoidbach, J., Mikolajczak, M., & Hansenne, M. (2009). Increasing emotional intelligence: (How) is it possible? *Personality and Individual Differences, 47*, 36–41.

Nelson, C. A., & Bosquet, M. (2000). Neurobiology of fetal and infant development: Implications for infant mental health. In C. H. Zeanah, Jr. (Ed.), *Handbook of infant mental health* (2nd ed.). New York: Guilford Press.

Nelson, D. A., Hart, C. H., Yang, C., Olsen, J. A., & Jin, S. (2006). Aversive parenting in China: Associations with child physical and relational aggression. *Child Development, 77*, 554–572.

Nelson, E. L., Campbell, J. M., & Michel, G. F. (2013). Early handedness in infancy predicts language ability in toddlers. *Developmental Psychology*. Accessed online, 2-13-14; http://www.ncbi.nlm.nih.gov/pubmed/23855258.

Nelson, K. (1996). *Language in cognitive development: Emergence of the mediated mind*. New York: Cambridge University Press.

Nelson, K., & Fivush, R. (2004). The emergence of autobiographical memory: A social cultural developmental theory. *Psychological Review, 111*, 486–511.

Nelson, L., Badger, S., & Wu, B. (2004). The influence of culture in emerging adulthood: Perspectives of Chinese college students. *International Journal of Behavioral Development, 28*, 26–36.

Nelson, P., Adamson, L., & Bakeman, R. (2008). Toddlers' joint engagement experience facilitates preschoolers' acquisition of theory of mind. *Developmental Science, 11*, 847–853.

Nelson, T. (2004). *Ageism: Stereotyping and prejudice against older persons*. Cambridge, MA: MIT Press.

Nesheim, S., Henderson, S., Lindsay, M., Zuberi, J., Grimes, V., Buehler, J., Lindegren, M. L., & Bulterys, M. (2004). *Prenatal HIV testing and antiretroviral prophylaxis at an urban hospital—Atlanta, Georgia, 1997–2000*. Atlanta, GA: Centers for Disease Control.

Nestler, E. J. (2016). Transgenerational epigenetic contributions to stress responses: Fact or fiction? *Plos Biology, 14*, 22–26.

Nestler, E. J. (2011). Hidden Switches in the Mind. *Scientific American, 305*(6), 76–83.

Neugarten, B. L. (1972). Personality and the aging process. *Gerontologist, 12*, 9–15.

Neugarten, B. L. (1977). Personality and aging. In J. E. Birren & K. W. Schaie (Eds.), *Handbook for the psychology of aging*. New York: Van Nostrand Reinhold.

Newland, L. A. (2014). Supportive family contexts: Promoting child well-being and resilience. *Early Child Development and Care, 184*(9–10), 1336–1346. doi:10.1080/03004430.2013.875543.

Newport, F., & Wilke, J. (2013, October 28). Economy would benefit if marriage rate increases in U.S. *Gallup*. Accessed online, 8-8-15; http://www.gallup.com/poll/165599/economy-benefit-marriage-rate-increases.aspx.

Newston, R. L., & Keith, P. M. (1997). Single women later in life. In J. M. Coyle (Ed.), *Handbook on women and aging* (pp. 385–399). Westport, CT: Greenwood Press.

Newton, K., Reed, S., LaCroix, A., Grothaus, L., Ehrlich, K., & Guiltinan, J. (2006). Treatment of vasomotor symptoms of menopause with black cohosh, multibotanicals, soy, hormone therapy, or placebo. *Annals of Internal Medicine, 145*, 869–879.

Nagda, B. (R.) A., Gurin, P., & Johnson, S. M. (2005). Living, *Improving the first year of college: Research and practice* (pp. 73-108). Mahwah, NJ, US: Lawrence Erlbaum Associates Publishers.

Ng, W., & Nicholas, H. (2010). A progressive pedagogy for online learning with high-ability secondary school students: A case study. *Gifted Child Quarterly, 54*, 239–251.

NICHD Early Child Care Research Network. (2001). Child-care and family predictors of preschool attachment and stability from infancy. *Development Psychology, 37*, 847–862.

NICHD Early Child Care Research Network. (2001b). Child-care and family predictors of preschool attachment and stability from infancy. *Development Psychology, 37*, 847–862.

NICHD Early Child Care Research Network. (2003a). Does quality of child care affect child outcomes at age 4 1/2? *Developmental Psychology, 39*, 451–469.

NICHD Early Child Care Research Network. (2003b). Families matter—even for kids in child care. *Journal of Developmental and Behavioral Pediatrics, 24*, 58–62.

NICHD Early Child Care Research Network. (2005). *Child care and child development: Results from the NICHD study of early child care and youth development*. New York: Guilford Press.

NICHD Early Child Care Research Network. (2006a). *Child care and child development: Results from the NICHD study of early child care and youth development*. New York: Guilford Press.

Nicholson, J. M., D'Esposito, F., Lucas, N., & Westrupp, E. M. (2014). Raising children in single-parent families. In A. Abela, J. Walker (Eds.), *Contemporary issues in family studies: Global perspectives on partnerships, parenting and support in a changing world*. New York: Wiley-Blackwell.

Nicholson, L. M., & Browning, C. R. (2012). Racial and ethnic disparities in obesity during the transition to adulthood: The contingent and nonlinear impact of neighborhood disadvantage. *Journal of Youth and Adolescence, 41*, 53–66.

Nicklas, T. A., Goh, E. T., Goodell, L. S., Acuff, D. S., Reiher, R., Buday, R., & Ottenbacher, A. (2011). Impact of commercials on food preferences of low-income, minority preschoolers. *Journal Of Nutrition Education And Behavior, 43*(1), 35-41. doi:10.1016/j.jneb.2009.11.007

Niederhofer, H. (2004). A longitudinal study: Some preliminary results of association of prenatal maternal stress and fetal movements, temperament factors in early childhood and behavior at age 2 years. *Psychological Reports, 95*, 767–770.

Nieto, S. (2005). Public education in the twentieth century and beyond: High hopes, broken promises, and an uncertain future. *Harvard Educational Review, 75*, 43–65.

Nihart, M. A. (1993). Growth and development of the brain. *Journal of Child and Adolescent Psychiatric and Mental Health Nursing, 6*, 39–40.

Nikčević, A. V., & Nicolaides, K. H. (2014). Search for meaning, finding meaning and adjustment in women following miscarriage: A longitudinal study. *Psychology & Health, 29*, 50–63.

Nikolas, M., Klump, K. L., & Burt, S. (2012). Youth appraisals of inter-parental conflict and genetic and environmental contributions to attention-deficit hyperactivity disorder: Examination of GxE effects in a twin sample. *Journal of Abnormal Child Psychology, 40*, 543–554.

Nilsson, L. (2003). Memory function in normal aging. *Acta Neurologica Scandinavica, 107*, 7–13.

Nisbett, R. (1994, October 31). Blue genes. *New Republic, 211*, 15.

Nisbett, R. (2008). *Intelligence and how to get it: Why schools and cultures count*. New York: WW Norton.

Nisbett, R. E., Aronson, J., Blair, C., Dickens, W., Flynn, J., Halpern, D. F., & Turkheimer, E. (2012). Intelligence: New findings and theoretical developments. *American Psychologist, 67*, 130–159.

Nishi, D. (2008, December 23) Segueing from a life of rock 'n' roll into therapy. *Wall Street Journal*. Accessed online, 11-29-17; https://www.wsj.com/articles/SB122998382930027825.

Njoroge, W. M., Elenbaas, L. M., Myaing, M. T., Garrison, M. M., & Christakis, D. A. (2016). What are young children watching? Disparities in concordant TV viewing. *Howard Journal of Communications, 27*, 203–217.

Noakes, M. A., Rinaldi, C. M. (2006). Age and gender differences in peer conflict, *Journal of Youth and Adolescence, 35*, 881–891.

Noble, Y., & Boyd, R. (2012). Neonatal assessments for the preterm infant up to 4 months corrected age: A systematic review. *Developmental Medicine & Child Neurology, 54*, 129–139.

Nobre, R. G., de Azevedo, D. V., de Almeida, P. C., de Almeida, N. S., & de Lucena Feitosa, F. E. (2017). Weight-gain velocity in newborn infants managed with the kangaroo method and associated variables. *Maternal and Child Health Journal, 21*, 128–135.

Nockels, R., & Oakeshott, P. (1999). Awareness among young women of sexually transmitted chlamydia infection. *Family Practice, 16*, 94.

Nolen-Hoeksema, S., & Davis, C. (2002). Positive responses to loss: Perceiving benefits and growth. In C. Snyder & S. Lopez (Eds.), *Handbook of positive psychology*. London: Oxford University Press.

Nolen-Hoeksema, S., & Larson, J. (1999). *Coping with loss*. Mahwah, NJ: Lawrence Erlbaum.

Noonan, C. W., & Ward, T. J. (2007). Environmental tobacco smoke, woodstove heating and risk of asthma symptoms. *Journal of Asthma, 44*, 735–738.

Noonan, D. (2003, September 22). When safety is the name of the game. *Newsweek*, pp. 64–66.

Noone, J., Stephens, C., & Alpass, F. (2009). Preretirement planning and well-being in later life: A prospective study. *Research on Aging, 31*, 295–317.

Nordenmark, M., & Stattin, M. (2009). Psychosocial wellbeing and reasons for retirement in Sweden. *Ageing & Society, 29*, 413–430.

Nordin, S., Razani, L., & Markison, S. (2003). Age-associated increases in intensity discrimination for taste. *Experimental Aging Research, 29*, 371–381.

Norman, R. M. G., Malla, A. K. (2001). Family history of schizophrenia and the relationship of stress to symptoms: Preliminary findings. *Australian & New Zealand Journal of Psychiatry, 35*, 217–223.

Norona, J. C., Roberson, P. E., & Welsh, D. P. (2017). 'I learned things that make me happy, things that bring me down': Lessons from romantic relationships in adolescence and emerging adulthood. *Journal of Adolescent Research, 32*, 155–182.

Norton, A., & D'Ambrosio, B. (2008). ZPC and ZPD: Zones of teaching and learning. *Journal for Research in Mathematics Education, 39*, 220–246.

Norton, M. I., & Gino, F. (2014). Rituals alleviate grieving for loved ones, lovers, and lotteries. *Journal of Experimental Psychology: General, 143*, 266–272.

Nosarti, C., Reichenberg, A., Murray, R. M., Cnattingius, S., Lambe, M. P., Yin, L., Maccabe, J., Rifkin, L., & Hultman, C. M. (2012). Preterm birth and psychiatric disorders in young adult life preterm birth and psychiatric disorders. *Archives of General Psychiatry, 155*, 610–617.

Notaro, P., Gelman, S., & Zimmerman, M. (2002). Biases in reasoning about the consequences of psychogenic bodily reactions: Domain boundaries in cognitive development. *Merrill-Palmer Quarterly, 48*, 427–449.

Nugent, J. K., Lester, B. M., & Brazelton, T. B. (Eds.). (1989). *The cultural context of infancy, Vol. 1: Biology, culture, and infant development*. Norwood, NJ: Ablex.

Nursing Home Data Compendium. (2013). *Nursing Home Data Compendium, 2013*. Woodlawn, MD: Centers for Medicare and Medicaid Services.

Nyaradi, A., Li, J., Hickling, S., Foster, J., & Oddy, W. H. (2013). The role of nutrition in children's neurocognitive development, from pregnancy through childhood. *Frontiers in Human Neuroscience*. Accessed online, 2-18-14; http://www.ncbi.nlm.nih.gov/pubmed/23532379.

Nygaard, E., Slinning, K., Moe, V., & Walhovd, K. B. (2017). Cognitive function of youths born to mothers with opioid and poly-substance abuse problems during pregnancy. *Child Neuropsychology, 23*, 159–187.

Nypaver, C. F., & Shambley-Ebron, D. (2016). Using community-based participatory research to investigate meaningful prenatal care among African American women. *Journal of Transcultural Nursing, 27*, 558–566.

O'Connor, M., & Whaley, S. (2006). Health care provider advice and risk factors associated with alcohol consumption following pregnancy recognition. *Journal of Studies on Alcohol, 67*, 22–31.

O'Connor, T. M., Cerin, E., Hughes, S. O., et al. (2013). What Hispanic parents do to encourage and discourage 3–5-year-old children to be active: A qualitative study using nominal group technique. *The International Journal of Behavioral Nutrition and Physical Activity, 10*, 88–97.

O'Doherty, K. (2014). Review of Telling genes: The story of genetic counseling in America. *Journal of the History of the Behavioral Sciences, 50*, 115–117.

O'Grady, W., & Aitchison, J. (2005). *How children learn language*. New York: Cambridge University Press.

O'Leary, S. G. (1995). Parental discipline mistakes. *Current Directions in Psychological Science, 4*, 11–13.

O'Neil, J. M., & Denke, R. (2016). An empirical review of gender role conflict research: New conceptual models and research paradigms. In Y. J. Wong & S. R. Wester (Eds.), *APA handbook of men and masculinities*. Washington, DC: American Psychological Association.

O'Reilly, J., & Peterson, C. C. (2015). Maltreatment and advanced theory of mind development in school-aged children. *Journal of Family Violence, 30*, 93–102.

Oberlander, S. E., Black, M., & Starr, R. H. (2007). African American adolescent mothers and grandmothers: A multigenerational approach to parenting. *American Journal of Community Psychology, 39*, 37–46.

Ockerman, E. (2017, August 15). Pregnant women addicted to opioids face tough choices. *Washington Post*. Accessed online, 10-25-17; https://www.washingtonpost.com/national/pregnant-women-addicted-to-opioids-face-tough-choices-fear-treatment-can-lead-to-separation-and-harm/2017/08/13/8844e51a-6d78-11e7-b9e2-2056e768a7e5_story.html?utm_term=.8e1a5948eb1d.

Ocorr, K., Reeves, N. L., Wessells, R. J., Fink, M., Chen, H. S., Akasaka, T., Yasuda, S., Metzger, J. M., Giles, W., Posakony, J. W., & Bodmer, R. (2007). KCNQ potassium channel mutations cause cardiac arrhythmias in Drosophila that mimic the effects of aging. *Proceedings of the National Academy of Sciences, 104*, 3943–3948.

OECD (Organization for Economic Cooperation and Development). (2001). *Education at a glance: OECD indicators, 2001*. Paris: Author.

OECD. (2014). *PISA 2012 results in focus: What 15-year-olds know and what they can do with what they know*. Paris: Organization for Economic Co-operation and Development (OECD).

Office of Adolescent Health. (2016, February.) *Teens' social media use: How they connect and what it means for health*. U.S. Department of Health & Human Services. Accessed online, 11-9-17; https://www.hhs.gov/ash/oah/news/e-updates/february-2016-teens-social-media-use/index.html.

Office of Head Start. (2015). *History of Head Start*. Accessed online, 4-6-15; http://www.acf.hhs.gov/programs/ohs/about/history-of-head-start.

Ogbu, J. (1992). Understanding cultural diversity and learning. *Educational Researcher, 21*, 5–14.

Ogbu, J. U. (1988). Black education: A cultural-ecological perspective. In H. P. McAdoo (Ed.), *Black families*. Beverly Hills, CA: Sage Publications.

Ogden, C. L., Carroll, M. D., Fryar, C. D., & Flegal, K .M. (2015). Prevalence of obesity among adults and youth: United States, 2011–2014. *NCHS data brief, no 219*. Hyattsville, MD: National Center for Health Statistics.

Ogden, C. L., Kuczmarski, R. J., Flegal, K. M., Mei, Z., Guo, S., Wei, R., … & Johnson, C. L. (2002). Centers for Disease Control and Prevention 2000 growth charts for the United States: Improvements to the 1977 National Center for Health Statistics Version. *Pediatrics, 109*, 45–60.

Ogolsky, B. G., Dennison, R. P., & Monk, J. K. (2014). The role of couple discrepancies in cognitive and behavioral egalitarianism in marital quality. *Sex Roles, 70*, 329–342.

Ohta, H., & Ohgi, S. (2013). Review of 'The Neonatal Behavioral Assessment Scale.' *Brain & Development, 35*, 79–80.

Okie, S. (2005). *Winning the war against childhood obesity*. Washington, DC: Joseph Henry Publications.

Okumura, Y., Kasai, T., & Murohashi, H. (2015). Attention that covers letters is necessary for the left-lateralization of an early print-tuned ERP in Japanese hiragana. *Neuropsychologia, 69*, 22–30.

Olivardia, R., & Pope, H. (2002). Body image disturbance in childhood and adolescence. In D. Castle & K. Phillips (Eds.), *Disorders of body image*. Petersfield, England: Wrightson Biomedical Publishing.

Oliveira, E. T., de Menezes, T. N., & de Olinda, R. A. (2017). High blood pressure and self-reported systemic hypertension in elderly enrolled in the family health strategy program. *Journal of Aging and Health, 29*, 708–728.

Oliver, B., & Plomin, R. (2007). Twins' Early Development Study (TEDS): A multivariate, longitudinal genetic investigation of language, cognition and behavior problems from childhood through adolescence. *Twin Research and Human Genetics, 10*, 96–105.

Olness, K. (2003). Effects on brain development leading to cognitive impairement: A worldwide epidemic. *Journal of Developmental & Behavioral Pediatrics, 24*, 120–130.

Olson, E. (2006, April 27). You're in labor, and getting sleeeepy. *New York Times*, p. C2.

Olsen, S. (2009, October 30). Will the digital divide close by itself? *New York Times*. Accessed online, 11-23-09; http://bits.blogs.nytimes.com/2009/10/30/will-the-digital-divide-close-by-itself.

Olszewski-Kubilius, P., & Thomson, D. (2013). Gifted education programs and procedures. In W. M. Reynolds, G. E. Miller, & I. B. Weiner (Eds.), *Handbook of psychology, Vol. 7: Educational psychology* (2nd ed.). Hoboken, NJ: John Wiley & Sons Inc.

Oostermeijer, M., Boonen, A. H., & Jolles, J. (2014). The relation between children's constructive play activities, spatial ability, and mathematical word problem-solving performance: A mediation analysis in sixth-grade students. *Frontiers in Psychology, 5*. Accessed online, 3-20-15; http://journal.frontiersin.org/article/10.3389/fpsyg.2014.00782/abstract.

Opendak, M., Gould, E., Sullivan, R. (2017). Early life adversity during the infant sensitive period for attachment: Programming of behavioral neurobiology of threat processing and social behavior. *Developmental Cognitive Neuroscience, 25*, 145–159.

Orbuch, T. (2009). *Five simple steps to take your marriage from good to great*. Oakland, CA: Oakland Press.

Orbuch, T. L., House, J. S., Mero, R. P., & Webster, P. S. (1996). Marital quality over the life course. *Social Psychology Quarterly, 59*, 162–171.

Oregon Death with Dignity Act. (2016). Oregon Death with Dignity Act: Annual Report for 2016. Portland, OR: Death with Dignity National Center.

Oretti, R. G., Harris, B., & Lazarus, J. H. (2003). Is there an association between life events, postnatal depression and thyroid dysfunction in thyroid antibody positive women? *International Journal of Social Psychiatry, 49*, 70–76.

Ormont, L. R. (2001). Developing emotional insulation (1994). In L. B. Fugeri (Ed.), *The technique of group treatment: The collected papers of Louis R. Ormont*. Madison, CT: Psychosocial Press.

Ornaghi, V., Pepe, A., & Grazzani, I. (2016). False-belief understanding and language ability mediate the relationship between emotion comprehension and prosocial orientation in preschoolers. *Frontiers in Psychology, 7*, 212–222.

Orth, U. (2017). The family environment in early childhood has a long-term effect on self-esteem: A longitudinal study from birth to age 27 years. *Journal of Personality and Social Psychology*. Accessed online, 3-17-17; https://www.ncbi.nlm.nih.gov/pubmed/28182449.

Ortiz, S. O., & Dynda, A. M. (2005). Use of intelligence tests with culturally and linguistically diverse populations. In D. P. Flanagan & P. L. Harrison (Eds.), *Contemporary intellectual assessment: Theories, tests, and issues*. New York: Guilford Press.

Osborne, J. W. (2012). Psychological effects of the transition to retirement. *Canadian Journal of Counselling and Psychotherapy, 46*, 45–58.

Osofsky, J. (2003). Prevalence of children's exposure to domestic violence and child maltreatment: Implications for prevention and intervention. *Clinical Child & Family Psychology Review, 6*, 161–170.

Osterman, M. J. K. & Martin, J. A. (2011). Epidural and spinal anesthesia use during labor: 27-state reporting area, 2008. *National vital statistics reports; Vol. 59 No 5*. Hyattsville, MD: National Center for Health Statistics.

Ostrov, J., Gentile, D., & Crick, N. (2006, November). Media exposure, aggression and prosocial behavior during early childhood: A longitudinal study. *Social Development, 15*, 612–627.

Otsuka, Y., Hill, H. H., Kanazawa, S., Yamaguchi, M. K., & Spehar, B. (2012). Perception of Mooney faces by young infants: The role of local feature visibility, contrast polarity, and motion. *Journal of Experimental Child Psychology, 111*, 164–179.

Otsuka, Y., Ichikawa, H., Kanazawa, S., Yamaguchi, M. K., & Spehar, B. (2014). Temporal dynamics of spatial frequency processing in infants. *Journal of Experimental Psychology: Human Perception and Performance, 40*, 995–1008.

Ott, C., Sanders, S., & Kelber, S. (2007). Grief and personal growth experience of spouses and adult-child caregivers of individuals with Alzheimer's disease and related dementias. *Gerontologist, 47*, 798–809.

Ouwehand, C., de Ridder, D. T., & Bensing, J. M. (2007). A review of successful aging models: Proposing proactive coping as an important additional strategy. *Clinical Psychology Review, 43*, 101–116.

Owsley, C., Stalvey, B., & Phillips, J. (2003). The efficacy of an educational intervention in promoting self-regulation among high-risk older drivers. *Accident Analysis & Prevention, 35*, 393–400.

Oxford, M., Gilchrist, L., Gillmore, M., & Lohr, M. (2006, July). Predicting variation in the life course of adolescent mothers as they enter adulthood. *Journal of Adolescent Health, 39*, 20–26.

Oyserman, D., Kemmelmeier, M., Fryberg, S., Brosh, H., & Hart-Johnson, T. (2003). Racial ethnic self-schemas. *Social Psychology Quarterly, 66*, 333–347.

Ozawa, M., & Yoon, H. (2003). Economic impact of marital disruption on children. *Children & Youth Services Review, 25*, 611–632.

Ozawa, M., Kanda, K., Hirata, M., Kusakawa, I., & Suzuki, C. (2011). Influence of repeated painful procedures on prefrontal cortical pain responses in newborns. *Acta Paediatrica, 100*, 198–203.

Ozimek, P., & Bierhoff, H. (2016). Facebook use depending on age: The influence of social comparisons. *Computers in Human Behavior, 61*, 271–279.

Ozmen, C. B., Brelsford, G. M., & Danieu, C. R. (2017). Political affiliation, spirituality, and religiosity: Links to emerging adults' life satisfaction and optimism. *Journal of Religion and Health*. Accessed online, 12-3-17; https://www.ncbi.nlm.nih.gov/pubmed/28803368.

Pacala, J. T., & Yueh, B. (2012). Hearing deficits in the older patient: "I didn't notice anything." *JAMA: Journal of the American Medical Association, 307*(11), 1185–1194. doi:10.1001/jama.2012.305.

Pachter, L. M., & Weller, S. C. (1993). Acculturation and compliance with medical therapy. *Journal of Development and Behavior Pediatrics, 14*, 163–168.

Pajkrt, E., Weisz, B., Firth, H. V., & Chitty, L. S. (2004). Fetal cardiac anomalies and genetic syndromes. *Prenatal Diagnosis, 24*, 1104–1115.

Pajulo, M., Helenius, H., & Mayes, L. (2006, May). Prenatal views of baby and parenthood: Association with sociodemographic and pregnancy factors. *Infant Mental Health Journal, 27*, 229–250.

Palanca-Maresca, I., Ruiz-Antorán, B., Centeno-Soto, G. A., Forti-Buratti, M. A., Siles, A., Usano, A., & Avendaño-Solá, C. (2017). Prevalence and risk factors of prolonged corrected QT interval among children and adolescents treated with antipsychotic medications: A long-term follow-up in a real-world population. *Journal of Clinical Psychopharmacology, 37*, 78–83.

Palermo, L., Geberhiwot, T., MacDonald, A., Limback, E., Hall, S. K., & Romani, C. (2017). Cognitive outcomes in early-treated adults with phenylketonuria (PKU): A comprehensive picture across domains. *Neuropsychology, 31*, 255-267.

Palfai, T., Halperin, S., & Hoyer, W. (2003). Age inequalities in recognition memory: Effects of stimulus presentation time and list repetitions. *Aging, Neuropsychology, & Cognition, 10*, 134–140.

Palmore, E. B. (1988). *The facts on aging quiz*. New York: Springer.

Palmore, E. B. (1992). Knowledge about aging: What we know and need to know. *Gerontologist, 32*, 149–150.

Palmore, E. B. (2017). Auto-gerontology: A personal odyssey. *Journal of Applied Gerontology, 36*, 1295–1305.

Paludi, M. A. (2012). *The psychology of love (Vols. 1–4)*. Santa Barbara, CA: Praeger/ABC-CLIO.

Palusci, V. J., & Ondersma, S. J. (2012). Services and recurrence after psychological maltreatment confirmed by child protective services. *Child Maltreatment, 17*, 153–163.

Paolella, F. (2013). La pedagogia di Loris Malaguzzi. Per una storia del Reggio Emiliaapproach. *Rivista Sperimentale Di Freniatria: La Rivista Della Salute Mentale, 137*, 95–112.

Papousek, H., & Papousek, M. (1991). Innate and cultural guidance of infants' integrative competencies: China, the United States, and Germany. In M. H. Borstein (Ed.), *Cultural approaches to parenting*. Hillsdale, NJ: Lawrence Erlbaum.

Pappano, L. (1994, November 27). The new old generation. *Boston Globe Magazine*, pp. 18–38.

Paquette, D., Carbonneau, R., & Dubeau, D. (2003). Prevalence of father–child rough-and-tumble play and physical aggression in preschool children. *European Journal of Psychology of Education, 18*, 171–189.

Parisi, J. M., Gross, A. L., Marsiske, M., Willis, S. L., & Rebok, G. W. (2017). Control beliefs and cognition over a 10-year period: Findings from the ACTIVE trial. *Psychology and Aging, 32*, 69–75.

Park, A. (2008, June 23). Living large. *Time*, pp. 90–92.

Park, C. L., Riley, K. E., & Snyder, L. B. (2012). Meaning making coping, making sense, and post-traumatic growth following the 9/11 terrorist attacks. *Journal of Positive Psychology, 7*, 198–207.

Park, J. E., Lee, J., Suh, G., Kim, B., & Cho, M. J. (2014). Mortality rates and predictors in community-dwelling elderly individuals with cognitive impairment: An eight-year follow-up after initial assessment. *International Psychogeriatrics, 26*, 1295–1304.

Park, K. A., Lay, K., & Ramsay, L. (1993). Individual differences and developmental changes in preschoolers' friendships. *Developmental Psychology, 29*, 264–270.

Parke, R. D. (2004). Development in the family. *Annual Review of Psychology, 55*, 365–399.

Parke, R. D. (2007). Fathers, families, and the future: A plethora of plausible predictions. In G. W. Ladd (Ed.), *Appraising the human developmental sciences: Essays in honor of Merrill-Palmer Quarterly*. Detroit, MI: Wayne State University Press.

Parke, R., Simpkins, S., & McDowell, D. (2002). Relative contributions of families and peers to children's social development. In P. Smith & C. Hart (Eds.), *Blackwell handbook of childhood social development*. Malden, MA: Blackwell Publishers.

Parker, K. (2012). *The boomerang generation*. Washington, DC: Pew Research Center.

Parker, S. T. (2005). Piaget's legacy in cognitive constructivism, niche construction, and phenotype development and evolution. In S. T. Parker & J. Langer (Eds.), *Biology and knowledge revisited: From neurogenesis to psychogenesis*. Mahwah, NJ: Lawrence Erlbaum.

Parks, C., Sanna, L., & Posey, D. (2003). Retrospection in social dilemmas: How thinking about the past affects future cooperation. *Journal of Personality & Social Psychology, 84*, 988–996.

Parks, S. J., & Yoo, H. C. (2016). Does endorsement of the model minority myth relate to anti-Asian sentiments among white college students? The role of a color-blind racial attitude. *Asian American Journal of Psychology, 7*, 287–294.

Parsons, A., & Howe, N. (2013). 'This is Spiderman's mask.' 'No, it's Green Goblin's': Shared meanings during boys' pretend play with superhero and generic toys. *Journal of Research in Childhood Education, 27*, 190–207.

Parsons, C. E., Young, K. S., Elmholdt, E. J., Stein, A., & Kringelbach, M. L. (2017). Interpreting infant emotional expressions: Parenthood has differential effects on men and women. *The Quarterly Journal of Experimental Psychology, 70*, 554–564.

Parten, M. B. (1932). Social participation among preschool children. *Journal of Abnormal and Social Psychology, 27*, 243–269.

Pascalis, O., de Haan, M., & Nelson, C. A. (2002). Is face processing species-specific during the first year of life? *Science, 296*, 1321–1323.

Pascarella, E. T., Martin, G. L., Hanson, J. M., Trolian, T. L., Gillig, B., & Blaich, C. (2014). Effects of diversity experiences on critical thinking skills over 4 years of college. *Journal of College Student Development, 55*, 86–92.

Paterno, M. T., McElroy, K., & Regan, M. (2016). Electronic fetal monitoring and cesarean birth: A scoping review. *Birth: Issues in Perinatal Care, 43*, 277–284.

Pathman, T., Larkina, M., Burch, M. M., & Bauer, P. J. (2013). Young children's memory for the times of personal past events. *Journal of Cognition and Development, 14*, 120–140.

Patterson, C. (2009). Children of lesbian and gay parents: Psychology, law, and policy. *American Psychologist*, (64), 727–736.

Patterson, C. J. (2007). In K. J. Bieschke, R. M. Perez, & K. A. DeBord (Eds.), *Handbook of counseling and psychotherapy with lesbian, gay, bisexual, and transgender clients* (2nd ed.). Washington, DC: American Psychological Association.

Patterson, C. J. (2013). Children of lesbian and gay parents: Psychology, law, and policy. *Psychology of Sexual Orientation and Gender Diversity, 1*(S), 27–34.

Paul, K., & Moser, K. (2009). Unemployment impairs mental health: Meta-analyses. *Journal of Vocational Behavior, 74*, 264–282.

Paulus, M. (2014). How and why do infants imitate? An ideomotor approach to social and imitative learning in infancy (and beyond). *Psychonomic Bulletin & Review, 21*, 1139–1156.

Paulus, M. (2016). Friendship trumps neediness: The impact of social relations and others' wealth on preschool children's sharing. *Journal of Experimental Child Psychology, 146*, 106–120.

Paulus, M., & Moore, C. (2014). The development of recipient-dependent sharing behavior and sharing expectations in preschool children. *Developmental Psychology, 50*, 914–921.

Pavlov, I. P. (1927). *Conditioned reflexes*. London: Oxford University Press.

Pawluski, J. L., Lonstein, J. S., & Fleming, A. S. (2017). The neurobiology of postpartum anxiety and depression. *Trends in Neurosciences, 40*(2), 106–120.

Payá-González, B., López-Gil, J., Noval-Aldaco, E., & Ruiz-Torres, M. (2015). Gender and first psychotic episodes in adolescence. In M. Sáenz-Herrero & M. Sáenz-Herrero (Eds.), *Psychopathology in women: Incorporating gender perspective into descriptive psychopathology*. Cham, Switzerland: Springer International Publishing.

Peach, H. D., & Gaultney, J. F. (2013). Sleep, impulse control, and sensation-seeking predict delinquent behavior in adolescents, emerging adults, and adults. *Journal of Adolescent Health, 53, 293–299.*

Pearson, J., & Wilkinson, L. (2013). Adolescent sexual experiences. In A. K. Baumle (Ed.), *International handbook on the demography of sexuality*. New York: Springer Science + Business Media.

Pearson, R. M., Lightman, S. L., & Evans, J. J. (2011). The impact of breastfeeding on mothers' attentional sensitivity towards infant distress. *Infant Behavior & Development, 34*, 200–205.

Peck, S. (2003). Measuring sensitivity moment-by-moment: A microanalytic look at the transmission of attachment. *Attachment & Human Development, 5*, 38–63.

Peck, R. C. (1968). Psychological developments in the second half of life. In B. L. Neugarten (Ed.), *Middle age and aging*. Chicago: University of Chicago Press.

Pedersen, S., Vitaro, F., Barker, E. D., & Borge, A. I. H. (2007). The timing of middle-childhood peer rejection and friendship: Linking early behavior to early-adolescent adjustment. *Child Development, 78*, 1037–1051.

Pedersen, S., Yagensky, A., Smith, O., Yagenska, O., Shpak, V., & Denollet, J. (2009). Preliminary evidence for the cross-cultural utility of the type D personality construct in the Ukraine. *International Journal of Behavioral Medicine, 16*, 108–115.

Pederson, D. R., Bailey, H. N., Tarabulsy, G. M., Bento, S., & Moran, G. (2014). Understanding sensitivity: Lessons learned from the legacy of Mary Ainsworth. *Attachment & Human Development, 16*, 261–270.

Peel, E., & Harding, R. (2015). A right to "dying well" with dementia? Capacity, "choice" and relationality. *Feminism & Psychology, 25*, 137–142.

Peisah, C., Latif, E., Wilhelm, K., & Williams, B. (2009). Secrets to psychological success: Why older doctors might have lower psychological distress and burnout than younger doctors. *Aging & Mental Health, 13*, 300–307.

Pejovic, J., & Molnar, M. (2017). The development of spontaneous sound-shape matching in monolingual and bilingual infants during the first year. *Developmental Psychology, 53*, 581–586.

Pelaez, M., Virues-Ortega, J., & Gewirtz, J. L. (2012). Acquisition of social referencing via discrimination training in infants. *Journal of Applied Behavior Analysis, 45*, 23–36.

Pelham, W. J., Fabiano, G. A., Waxmonsky, J. G., Greiner, A. R., Gnagy, E. M., Pelham, W. I., & … Murphy, S. A. (2016). Treatment sequencing for childhood ADHD: A multiple-randomization study of adaptive medication and behavioral interventions. *Journal of Clinical Child and Adolescent Psychology, 45*, 396–415.

Pellis, S. M., & Burghardt, G. M. (2017). Play and exploration. In J. Call, G. M. Burghardt, I. M. Pepperberg, C. T. Snowdon, & T. Zentall (Eds.), *APA handbook of comparative psychology: Basic concepts, methods, neural substrate, and behavior*. Washington, DC: American Psychological Association.

Pellis, S. M., & Pellis, V. C. (2007). Rough-and-tumble play and the development of the social brain. *Current Directions in Psychological Science, 16*, 95–98.

Peltonen, L., & McKusick, V. A. (2001, February 16). Dissecting the human disease in the postgenomic era. *Science, 291*, 1224–1229.

Peltzer, K., & Pengpid, S. (2006). Sexuality of 16- to 17-year-old South Africans in the context of HIV/AIDS. *Social Behavior and Personality, 34*, 239–256.

Pelzer, B., Schaffrath, S., & Vernaleken, I. (2014). Coping with unemployment: The impact of unemployment on mental health, personality, and social interaction skills. *Work: Journal of Prevention, Assessment & Rehabilitation, 48*, 289–295.

Penido, A., de Souza Rezende, G., Abreu, R., de Oliveira, A., Guidine, P., Pereira, G., & Moraes, M. (2012). Malnutrition during central nervous system growth and development impairs permanently the subcortical auditory pathway. *Nutritional Neuroscience, 15*, 31–36.

Penningroth, S., & Scott, W. D. (2012). Age-related differences in goals: Testing predictions form selection, optimization, and compensation theory and socioemotional selectivity theory. *International Journal of Aging & Human Development, 74*, 87–111.

Pennisi, E. (2000, May 19). And the gene number is …? *Science, 288*, 1146–1147.

Penuel, W. R., Bates, L., Gallagher, L. P., Pasnik, S., Llorente, C., Townsend, E., & Vander-Borght, M. (2012). Supplementing literacy instruction with a media-rich intervention: Results of a randomized controlled trial. *Early Childhood Research Quarterly, 27*, 115–127.

Peralta, O., Salsa, A., del Rosario Maita, M., & Mareovich, F. (2013). Scaffolding young children's understanding of symbolic objects. *Early Years: An International Journal of Research and Development, 33*, 266–274.

Pereira, A. C., Huddleston, D. E., Brickman, A. M., Sosunov, A. A., Hen, R., McKhann, G. M., Sloan, R., Gage, F. H., Brown, T. R., & Small, S. A. (2007). An in vivo correlate of exercise-induced neurogenesis in the adult dentate gyrus. *Proceedings of the National Academy of Sciences, 104*, 5638–5643.

Perelli-Harris, B., & Styrc, M. (2017). Mental well-being differences in cohabitation and marriage: The role of childhood selection. *Journal of Marriage and Family*. Accessed online, 12-3-17; http://onlinelibrary.wiley.com/doi/10.1111/jomf.12431/full.

Perez-Brena, N. J., Updegraff, K. A., & Umaña-Taylor, A. J. (2012). Father- and mother-adolescent decision-making in Mexican-origin families. *Journal of Youth and Adolescence, 41*, 460–473.

Perlmann, R. Y., & Gleason, J. B. (1990, July). Patterns of prohibition in mothers' speech to children. Paper presented at the Fifth International Congress for the Study of Child Language, Budapest, Hungary.

Perone, S., & Simmering, V. R. (2017). Applications of dynamic systems theory to cognition and development: New frontiers. In J. B. Benson (Ed.), *Advances in child development and behavior*. San Diego, CA: Elsevier Academic Press.

Perreault, A., Fothergill-Bourbonnais, F., & Fiset, V. (2004). The experience of family members caring for a dying loved one. *International Journal of Palliative Nursing, 10*, 133–143.

Perreira, K. M., & Ornelas, I. J. (2011, Spring). The physical and psychological well-being of immigrant children. *Future of Children, 21*, 195–218.

Perrine, N. E., & Aloise-Young, P. A. (2004). The role of self-monitoring in adolescents' susceptibility to passive peer pressure. *Personality & Individual Differences, 37*, 1701–1716.

Perry, W. G. (1981). Cognitive and ethical growth: The making of meaning. In A. W. Chickering and Associates (Eds.), *The Modern American College*. San Francisco: Jossey-Bass.

Persson, G. E. B. (2005). Developmental perspectives on prosocial and aggressive motives in preschoolers' peer interactions. *International Journal of Behavioral Development, 29*, 80–91.

Persson, A., & Musher-Eizenman, D. R. (2003). The impact of a prejudice-prevention television program on young children's ideas about race. *Early Childhood Research Quarterly, 18*, 530–546.

Petanjek, Z., Judas, M., Kostovic, I., & Uylings, H. B. M. (2008). Lifespan alterations of basal dendritic trees of pyramidal neurons in the human prefrontal cortex: A layer-specific pattern. *Cerebral Cortex, 18*, 915–929.

Peter, C. J., Fischer, L. K., Kundakovic, M., Garg, P., Jakovcevski, M., Dincer, A., & … Akbarian, S. (2016). DNA methylation signatures of early childhood malnutrition associated with impairments in attention and cognition. *Biological Psychiatry, 80*, 765–774.

Peters, E., Hess, T. M., Vastfjall, D., & Auman, C. (2007). Adult age differences in dual information processes: Implications for the role of affective and deliberative processes in older adults' decision making. *Perspectives on Psychological Science, 2*, 1–23.

Peters, S. J., Matthews, M. S., McBee, M. T., & McCoach, D. B. (2014). *Beyond gifted education: Designing and implementing advanced academic programs*. Waco, TX: Prufrock Press.

Petersen, A. (2000). A longitudinal investigation of adolescents' changing perceptions of pubertal timing. *Developmental Psychology*, 36, 37–43.

Peterson, A. C. (1988, September). Those gangly years. *Psychology Today*, pp. 28–34.

Peterson, C. (2014). Theory of mind understanding and empathic behavior in children with autism spectrum disorders. *International Journal of Developmental Neuroscience, 39*, 16–21.

Peterson, L. (1994). Child injury and abuse-neglect: Common etiologies, challenges, and courses toward prevention. *Current Directions in Psychological Science, 3*, 116–120.

Peterson, C., & Park, N. (2007). Explanatory style and emotion regulation. In J. J. Gross (Ed.), *Handbook of emotion regulation*. New York: Guilford Press.

Peterson, C., Wang, Q., & Hou, Y. (2009). "When I was little": Childhood recollections in Chinese and European Canadian grade school children. *Child Development, 80*, 506–518.

Peterson, D. M., Marcia, J. E., & Carependale, J. I. (2004). Identity: Does thinking make it so? In C. Lightfood, C. Lalonde, & M. Chandler (Eds.), *Changing conceptions of psychological life*. Mahwah, NJ: Lawrence Erlbaum.

Peterson, M., & Wilson, J. F. (2004). Work stress in America. *International Journal of Stress Management, 11*, 91–113.

Peterson, R. A., & Brown, S. P. (2005). On the use of beta coefficients in meta-analysis. *Journal of Applied Psychology, 90*, 175–181.

Petit, G., & Dodge, K. A. (2003). Violent children: Bridging development, intervention, and public policy. *Developmental Psychology*, [Special Issue: Violent Children], *39*, 187–188.

Petkoska, J., & Earl, J. (2009). Understanding the influence of demographic and psychological variables on retirement planning. *Psychology and Aging, 24*, 245–251.

Petrican, R., Moscovitch, M., & Grady, C. (2014). Proficiency in positive vs. negative emotion identification and subjective well-being among long term married elderly couples. *Frontiers in Psychology, 5*, 121–129.

Petrou, S. (2006). Preterm birth—What are the relevant economic issues? *Early Human Development, 82*(2), 75–76.

Pettit, G. S., Bates, J. E., & Dodge, K. A. (1997). Supportive parenting, ecological context, and children's adjustment: A 7-year longitudinal study. *Child Development, 68*, 908–923.

Pew Research Center. (2009, June 29). *Growing old in America: Expectations vs. reality*. Washington, DC: Pew Research Center.

Pew Research Center. (2014, November 14). *Four-in-ten couples are saying "I do" again*. Washington, DC: Pew Research Center. Accessed online, 7-23-15; http://www.pewsocialtrends.org/2014/11/14/four-in-ten-couples-are-saying-i-do-again/.

Phelan, P., Yu, H. C., & Davidson, A. L. (1994). Navigating the psychosocial pressures of adolescence: The voices and experiences of high school youth. *American Educational Research Journal, 31*, 415–447.

Philippot, P., & Feldman, R. S. (Eds.). (2005). *The regulation of emotion*. Mahwah, NJ: Lawrence Erlbaum.

Phillips, D., Gormley, W., & Anderson, S. (2016). The effects of Tulsa's CAP Head Start program on middle-school academic outcomes and progress. *Developmental Psychology, 52*, 1247–1261.

Phillips, M. L. (2011, April). The mind at midlife. *Monitor on Psychology*, pp. 39–41.

Phillipson, S. (2006, October). Cultural variability in parent and child achievement attributions: A study from Hong Kong. *Educational Psychology, 26*, 625–642.

Phillips-Silver, J., & Trainor, L. J. (2005, June 3). Feeling the beat: Movement influences infant rhythm perception. *Science, 308*, 1430.

Phinney, J. S. (2005). Ethnic identity in late modern times: A response to Rattansi and Phoenix. *Identity, 5*, 187–194.

Phinney, J. S. (2008). Ethnic identity exploration in emerging adulthood. In D. L. Browning (Ed.), *Adolescent identities: A collection of readings*. New York: Analytic Press/Taylor & Francis Group.

Phinney, J. S., Ferguson, D. L., & Tate, J. D. (1997). Intergroup attitudes among ethnic minority adolescents: A causal model. *Child Development, 68*, 955–969.

Phung, J. N., Milojevich, H. M., & Lukowski, A. F. (2014). Adult language use and infant comprehension of English: Associations with encoding and generalization across cues at 20 months. *Infant Behavior & Development, 37*, 465–479.

Piaget, J. (1954). *The construction of reality in the child*. New York, NY, US: Basic Books.

Piaget, J. (1932). *The moral judgment of the child*. New York: Harcourt, Brace & World.

Piaget, J. (1952). *The origins of intelligence in children*. New York: International Universities Press.

Piaget, J. (1962). *Play, dreams and imitation in childhood*. New York: Norton.

Piaget, J. (1983). Piaget's theory. In W. Kessen (Ed.), P. H. Mussen (Series Ed.), *Handbook of child psychology: Vol 1. History, theory, and methods* (pp. 103–128). New York: Wiley.

Piaget, J., & Inhelder, B. (1958). *The growth of logical thinking from childhood to adolescence* (A. Parsons & S. Seagrin, Trans.). New York: Basic Books.

Piaget, J., Inhelder, B., & Szeminska, A. (1960). *The child's conception of geometry*. New York: Basic Books. (Original work published 1948).

Pianata, R. C., Barnett, W. S., Burchinal, M., & Thornburg, K. R. (2009, August). The effects of preschool education: What we know, how public policy is or is not aligned with the evidence base, and what we need to know. *Psychological Science in the Public Interest, 10*, 49–88.

Picard, A. (2008, February 14). Health study: Tobacco will soon claim one million lives a year. *The Globe and Mail*, p. A15.

Pickles, A., Hill, J., Breen, G., Quinn, J., Abbott, K., Jones, H., & Sharp, H. (2013). Evidence for interplay between genes and parenting on infant temperament in the first year of life: Monoamine oxidase a polymorphism moderates effects of maternal sensitivity on infant anger proneness. *Journal of Child Psychology and Psychiatry, 54*, 1308–1317.

Piekarski, D. J., Johnson, C. M., Boivin, J. R., et al. (2017). Does puberty mark a transition in sensitive periods for plasticity in the associative neocortex? *Brain Research, 1654(Part B)*, 123–144.

Pine, K. J., Wilson, P., & Nash, A. S. (2007). The relationship between television advertising, children's viewing and their requests to Father Christmas. *Journal of Developmental & Behavioral Pediatrics, 28*, 456–461.

Ping, R., & Goldin-Meadow, S. (2008). Hands in the air: Using ungrounded iconic gestures to teach children conservation of quantity. *Developmental Psychology, 44*, 1277–1287.

Pinker, S. (1994). *The language instinct*. New York: William Morrow.

Pinquart, M. M. (2013). Body image of children and adolescents with chronic illness: A meta-analytic comparison with healthy peers. *Body Image, 10*, 141–148.

Piper, W. E., Ogrodniczuk, J. S., Joyce, A. S., & Weidman, R. (2009). Follow-up outcome in short-term group therapy for complicated grief. *Group Dynamics: Theory, Research, and Practice, 13*, 46–58.

Pisinger, C., & Døssing, M. (2014). A Systematic Review Of Health Effects Of Electronic Cigarettes. *Preventative Medicine, 69*, 248-260.

Pittman, L. D., & Boswell, M. K. (2007). The role of grandmothers in the lives of preschoolers growing up in urban poverty. *Applied Developmental Science, 11*, 20–42.

Pitts, D. G. (1982). The effects of aging upon selected visual functions. In R. Sekuler, D. Kline, & K. Dismukes (Eds.), *Aging and human visual function*. New York: Alan R. Liss.

Planalp, E. M., Van Hulle, C., Lemery-Chalfant, K., & Goldsmith, H. H. (2016). Genetic and environmental contributions to the development of positive affect in infancy. Accessed online, 10-31-17; https://www.ncbi.nlm.nih.gov/pubmed/27797564.

Plante, E., Schmithorst, V., Holland, S., & Byars, A. (2006). Sex differences in the activation of language cortex during childhood. *Neuropsychologia, 44*, 1210–1221.

Platt, I., Green, H. J., Jayasinghe, R., & Morrissey, S. A. (2014). Understanding adherence in patients with coronary heart disease: Illness representations and readiness to engage in healthy behaviours. *Australian Psychologist, 49*, 127–137.

Plomin, R. (2005). Finding genes in child psychology and psychiatry: When are we going to be there? *Journal of Child Psychology and Psychiatry, 46*, 1030–1038.

Plomin, R. (2016). Bringing genetics into the mainstream of psychology. In R. J. Sternberg, S. T. Fiske, D. J. Foss, (Eds.) *Scientists making a difference: One hundred eminent behavioral and brain scientists talk about their most important contributions*. New York: Cambridge University Press.

Plomin, R., DeFries, J. C., Knopik, V. S., & Neiderhiser, J. M. (2016). Top 10 replicated findings from behavioral genetics. *Perspectives on Psychological Science, 11*, 3–23.

Plosker, G., & Keam, S. (2006). Bimatoprost: A pharmacoeconomic review of its use in open-angle glaucoma and ocular hypertension. *PharmacoEconomics, 24*, 297–314.

Plummer, A. R., & Beckman, M. E. (2015). Framing a socio-indexical basis for the emergence and cultural transmission of phonological systems. *Journal of Phonetics, 53*, 66–78.

Poidvin, A., Touzé, E., Ecosse, E., Landier, F., Béjot, Y., Giroud, M., & … Coste, J. (2014). Growth hormone treatment for childhood short stature and risk of stroke in early adulthood. *Neurology, 83*, 780–786.

Polivka, B. (2006, January). Needs assessment and intervention strategies to reduce lead-poisoning risk among low-income Ohio toddlers. *Public Health Nursing, 23*, 52–58.

Polkinghorne, D. E. (2005). Language and meaning: Data collection in qualitative research. *Journal of Counseling Psychology, 52* [Special issue: Knowledge in context: Qualitative methods in counseling psychology research], 137–145.

Pölkki, T., Korhonen, A., Axelin, A., Saarela, T., & Laukkala, H. (2014). Development and preliminary validation of the Neonatal Infant Acute Pain Assessment Scale (NIAPAS). *International Journal of Nursing Studies, 51*, 1585–1594.

Pollack, W., Shuster, T., & Trelease, J. (2001). *Real boys' voices*. New York: Penguin.

Pollak, S., Holt, L., & Wismer Fries, A. (2004). Hemispheric asymmetries in children's perception of nonlinguistic human affective sounds. *Developmental Science, 7*, 10–18.

Pomares, C. G., Schirrer, J., & Abadie, V. (2002). Analysis of the olfactory capacity of healthy children before language acquisition. *Journal of Developmental Behavior and Pediatrics, 23*, 203–207.

Pompili, M., Masocco, M., Vichi, M., Lester, D., Innamorati, M., Tatarelli, R., et al. (2009). Suicide among Italian adolescents: 1970–2002. *European Child & Adolescent Psychiatry, 18*, 525–533.

Ponton, L. E. (2001). *The sex lives of teenagers: Revealing the secret world of adolescent boys and girls*. New York: Penguin Putnam.

Poorthuis, A. G., Thomaes, S., Aken, M. G., Denissen, J. A., & de Castro, B. O. (2014). Dashed hopes, dashed selves? A sociometer perspective on self-esteem change across the transition to secondary school. *Social Development, 23*, 770–783.

Population Council Report. (2009). *Divorce rates around the world*. New York: Population Council.

Porac, C. (2016). *Laterality: Exploring the enigma of left-handedness*. San Diego, CA: Elsevier Academic Press.

Porges, S. W., Lipsitt, & Lewis, P. (1993). Neonatal responsivity to gustatory stimulation: The gustatory-vagal hypothesis. *Infant Behavior & Development, 16*, 487–494.

Posada, G., & Trumbell, J. M. (2017). Universality and cultural specificity in child-mother attachment relationships: In search of answers. In S. Gojman-de-Millan, C. Herreman, L. A. Sroufe (Eds.), *Attachment across clinical and cultural perspectives: A relational psychoanalytic approach*. New York: Routledge/Taylor & Francis Group.

Posid, T., & Cordes, S. (2015). The small-large divide: A case of incompatible numerical representations in infancy. In D. C. Geary, D. B. Berch, & K. M. Koepke (Eds.), *Evolutionary origins and early development of number processing*. San Diego: Elsevier Academic Press.

Posso, M., Puig, T. Carles, M., Rue, M., Canelo-Aybar, C. & Bonfill, X. (2017). Effectiveness and cost-effectiveness of double reading in digital mammography screening: A systematic review and meta-analysis. *European Journal of Radiology, 96*, 40–49.

Posthuma, D., & de Geus, E. (2006, August). Progress in the molecular-genetic study of intelligence. *Current Directions in Psychological Science, 15*, 151–155.

Pote, K. (2017). Menopause around the world. Accessed online, 11-28-17; https://womeninbalance.org/2014/09/17/menopause-around-the-world/.

Poulin-Dubois, D., Serbin, L., & Eichstedt, J. (2002). Men don't put on make-up: Toddlers' knowledge of the gender stereotyping of household activities. *Social Development, 11*, 166–181.

Poulton, R., & Caspi, A. (2005). Commentary: How does socioeconomic disadvantage during childhood damage health in adulthood? Testing psychosocial pathways. *International Journal of Epidemiology, 23*, 51–55.

Pow, A. M., & Cashwell, C. S. (2017). Posttraumatic stress disorder and emotion-focused coping among disaster mental health counselors. *Journal of Counseling & Development, 95*, 322–331.

Powell, R. (2004, June 19). Colleges construct housing for elderly: Retiree students move to campus. *Washington Post*, p. F13.

Powdthavee, N. (2009). Think having children will make you happy? *The Psychologist, 22*(4), 308-310.

Powdthavee, N. (2008). Putting a price tag on friends, relatives, and neighbours: Using surveys of life satisfaction to value social relationships. *The Journal Of Socio-Economics, 37*(4), 1459-1480. doi:10.1016/j.socec.2007.04.004

Pozzi-Monzo, M. (2012). Ritalin for whom? Revisited: Further thinking on ADHD. *Journal of Child Psychotherapy, 38*, 49–60.

Prasad, V., Brogan, E., Mulvaney, C., Grainge, M., Stanton, W., & Sayal, K. (2013). How effective are drug treatments for children with ADHD at improving on-task behaviour and academic achievement in the school classroom? A systematic review and meta-analysis. *European Child & Adolescent Psychiatry, 22*, 203–216.

Prater, L. (2002). African American families: Equal partners in general and special education. In F. Obiakor & A. Ford (Eds.), *Creating successful learning environments for African American learners with exceptionalities*. Thousand Oaks, CA: Corwin Press.

Preciado, P., Snijders, T. B., Burk, W. J., Stattin, H., & Kerr, M. (2012). Does proximity matter? Distance dependence of adolescent friendships. *Social Networks, 34*, 18–31.

Preckel, F., Niepel, C., Schneider, M., & Brunner, M. (2013). Self-concept in adolescence: A longitudinal study on reciprocal effects of self-perceptions in academic and social domains. *Journal of Adolescence, 36*, 1165–1175.

Prentice, A., Schoenmakers, I., Laskey, M. A., de Bono, S., Ginty, F., & Goldberg, G. R. (2006). Nutrition and bone growth and development. *Proceedings of the Nutritional Society, 65*, 348–360.

Presseau, C., Contractor, A. A., Reddy, M. K., & Shea, M. T. (2017). Childhood maltreatment and post-deployment psychological distress: The indirect role of emotional numbing. *Psychological Trauma: Theory, Research, Practice, and Policy*. Accessed online, 11-13-17; https://www.ncbi.nlm.nih.gov/pubmed/2898131.

Pressley, M., & Schneider, W. (1997). *Introduction to memory development during childhood and adolescence*. Mahwah, NJ: Lawrence Erlbaum.

Price, C. S., Thompson, W. W., Goodson, B., Weintraub, E. S., Croen, L. A., Hinrichsen, V. L., & DeStefano, F. (2010). Prenatal and infant exposure to thimerosal from vaccines and immunoglobulins and risk of autism. *Pediatrics, 126*, 656–664.

Price, R., & Gottesman, I. (1991). Body fat in identical twins reared apart: Roles for genes and environment. *Behavior Genetics, 21*, 1–7.

Priddis, L., & Howieson, N. (2009). The vicissitudes of mother-infant relationships between birth and six years. *Early Child Development and Care, 179*, 43–53.

Prieler, M., Kohlbacher, F., Hagiwara, S., & Arima, A. (2011). Gender representation of older people in Japanese television advertisements. *Sex Roles, 64*, 405–415.

Prigerson, H. (2003). Costs to society of family caregiving for patients with end-stage Alzheimer's disease. *New England Journal of Medicine, 349*, 1891–1892.

PRIMEDIA/Roper. (1999). *Roper National Youth Survey*. Storrs, CT: Roper Center for Public Opinion Research.

Prince, C. B., Young, M. B., Sappenfield, W., & Parrish, J. W. (2016). Investigating the decline of fetal and infant mortality rates in Alaska during 2010 and 2011. *Maternal and Child Health Journal*. Accessed online 10-27-17; http://www.ncbi.nlm.nih.gov/pubmed/26754348.

Prince, M. (2000, November 13). How technology has changed the way we have babies. *Wall Street Journal*, pp. R4, R13.

Prince-Embury, S., & Saklofske, D. H. (2014). *Resilience interventions for youth in diverse populations*. New York: Springer Science + Business Media.

Prochaska, M. T., Putman, M. S., Tak, H. J., Yoon, J. D., & Curlin, F. A. (2017). US physicians overwhelmingly endorse hospice as the better option for most patients at the end of life. *American Journal of Hospice & Palliative Medicine, 34*, 556–558.

Proctor, C., Barnett, J., & Muilenburg, J. (2012). Investigating race, gender, and access to cigarettes in an adolescent population. *American Journal of Health Behavior, 36*, 513–521.

Prohaska, V. (2012). Strategies for encouraging ethical student behavior. In R. Landrum & M. A. McCarthy (Eds.), *Teaching ethically: Challenges and opportunities*. Washington, DC: American Psychological Association.

Proper, K., Cerin, E., & Owen, N. (2006, April). Neighborhood and individual socio-economic variations in the contribution of occupational physical activity to total physical activity. *Journal of Physical Activity & Health, 3*, 179–190.

Propper, C., & Moore, G. (2006, December). The influence of parenting on infant emotionality: A multi-level psychobiological perspective. *Developmental Review, 26*, 427–460.

Proulx, M., & Poulin, F. (2013). Stability and change in kindergartners' friendships: Examination of links with social functioning. *Social Development, 22*, 111–125.

Pruchno, R., & Rosenbaum, J. (2003). Social relationships in adulthood and old age. In R. Lerner & M. Easterbrooks (Eds.), *Handbook of psychology, Vol. 6: Developmental psychology*. New York: Wiley.

Puchalski, M., & Hummel, P. (2002). The reality of neonatal pain. *Advances in Neonatal Care, 2*, 245–247.

Puckering, C., Connolly, B., Werner, C., et al. (2011). Rebuilding relationships: A pilot study of the effectiveness of the Mellow Parenting Programme for children with reactive attachment disorder. *Clinical Child Psychology and Psychiatry, 16*, 73–87.

Pun, A., Birch, S. A., & Baron, A. S. (2017). Foundations of reasoning about social dominance. *Child Development Perspectives*. Accessed online, 11-17-17; http://onlinelibrary.wiley.com/doi/10.1111/cdep.12235/full.

Pundir, A., Hameed, L., Dikshit, P. C., Kumar, P., Mohan, S., Radotra, B., & Iyengar, S. (2012). Expression of medium and heavy chain neurofilaments in the developing human auditory cortex. *Brain Structure & Function, 217*, 303–321.

Puntambekar, S., & Hübscher, R. (2005). Tools for scaffolding students in a complex learning environment: What have we gained and what have we missed? *Educational Psychologist, 40*, 1–12.

Purcell, K., Heaps, A., Buchanan, J., & Friedrich, L. (2013, February 28). *How teachers are using technology at home and in their classrooms*. Washington, DC: Pew Research Center.

Purswell, K. E., & Dillman Taylor, D. (2013). Creative use of sibling play therapy: An example of a blended family. *Journal of Creativity in Mental Health, 8*, 162–174.

Puterman, E., Prather, A. A., Epel, E. S., Loharuka, S., Adler, N. E., Laraia, B., & Tomiyama, A. J. (2016). Exercise mitigates cumulative associations between stress and BMI in girls age 10 to 19. *Health Psychology, 35*, 191–194.

Putney, N. M., & Bengtson, V. L. (2001). Families, intergenerational relationships and kinkeeping in midlife. In M. E. Lachman (Ed.), *Handbook of midlife development*. Hoboken, NJ: Wiley.

Putsch, R.W., III, and Joyce, M. (2017). *Clinical methods: The history, physical, and laboratory examinations. (3rd ed.)*. Accessed online, 9-24-17; https://www.ncbi.nlm.nih.gov/books/NBK340/.

Qian, Z., Zhang, D., & Wang, L. (2013). Is aggressive trait responsible for violence? Priming effects of aggressive words and violent movies. *Psychology, 4*, 96–100.

Qiu, Z., Liu, C., Gao, Z., He, J., Liu, X., Wei, Q., & Chen, J. (2016). The inulin-type oligosaccharides extract from morinda officinalis, a traditional Chinese herb, ameliorated behavioral deficits in an animal model of post-traumatic stress disorder. *Metabolic Brain Disease, 31*, 1143–1149.

Quinn, P. (2008). In defense of core competencies, quantitative change, and continuity. *Child Development, 79*, 1633–1638.

Quinn, P., Uttley, L., Lee, K., Gibson, A., Smith, M., Slater, A., et al. (2008). Infant preference for female faces occurs for same- but not other-race faces. *Journal of Neuropsychology, 2*, 15–26.

Quintana, S. M. (2007). Racial and ethnic identity: Developmental perspectives and research. *Journal of Counseling Psychology, 54*, 259–270.

Quintana, S. M., Aboud, F. E., Chao, R. K., Contreras-Grau, J., Cross, Jr, W. E., Hudley, C., Hughes, D., Liben, L. S., Nelson-Le Gall, S., & Vietze, D. L. (2006). Race, ethnicity, and culture in child development: Contemporary research and future directions. *Child Development, 77*, 1129–1141.

Quintana, S. M., McKown, C., Cross, W. E., & Cross, T. B. (2008). In S. M. Quintana & C. McKown (Eds.), *Handbook of race, racism, and the developing child*. Hoboken, NJ: John Wiley & Sons Inc.

Ra, J. S., & Cho, Y. H. (2017). Depression moderates the relationship between body image and health-related quality of life in adolescent girls. *Journal of Child and Family Studies, 26*, 1799–1807.

Raag, T. (2003). Racism, gender identities and young children: Social relations in a multi-ethnic, inner-city primary school. *Archives of Sexual Behavior, 32*, 392–393.

Rabin, R. (2006, June 13). Breast-feed or else. *New York Times*, p. D1.

Raboteg-Saric, Z., & Sakic, M. (2013). Relations of parenting styles and friendship quality to self-esteem, life satisfaction and happiness in adolescents. *Applied Research in Quality of Life*, Accessed online, 1-25-14; http://link.springer.com/article/10.1007%2Fs11482-013-9268-0.

Raeburn, P. (2004, October 1). Too immature for the death penalty? *New York Times Magazine*, pp. 26–29.

Rafalski, J. C., Noone, J. H., O'Loughlin, K., & de Andrade, A. L. (2017). Assessing the process of retirement: A cross-cultural review of available measures. *Journal of Cross-Cultural Gerontology, 32*, 255–279.

Rahko, J. S., Vuontela, V. A., Carlson, S., Nikkinen, J., Hurtig, T. M., Kuusikko-Gauffin, S., & … Kiviniemi, V. J. (2016). Attention and working memory in adolescents with autism spectrum disorder: A functional MRI study. *Child Psychiatry and Human Development, 47*, 503–517.

Rai, R., Mitchell, P., Kadar, T., & Mackenzie, L. (2014). Adolescent egocentrism and the illusion of transparency: Are adolescents as egocentric as we might think? *Current Psychology: A Journal for Diverse Perspectives on Diverse Psychological Issues*. Accessed online, 3-22-15; http://link.springer.com/article/10.1007%2Fs12144-014-9293-7#page-1.

Rai, R., Mitchell, P., Kadar, T., & Mackenzie, L. (2016). Adolescent egocentrism and the illusion of transparency: Are adolescents as egocentric as we might think? *Current Psychology: A Journal for Diverse Perspectives on Diverse Psychological Issues, 35*, 285–294.

Raikes, H. H., Roggman, L. A., Peterson, C. A., Brooks-Gunn, J., Chazan-Cohen, R., Zhang, X., & Schiffman, R. F. (2014). Theories of change and outcomes in home-based Early Head Start programs. *Early Childhood Research Quarterly, 29*, 574–585.

Rajhans, P., Jessen, S., Missana, M., & Grossmann, T. (2016). Putting the face in context: Body expressions impact facial emotion processing in human infants. *Developmental Cognitive Neuroscience, 19*, 115–121.

Rakison, D., & Oakes, L. (2003). *Early category and concept development: Making sense of the blooming, buzzing confusion*. London: Oxford University Press.

Rakison, D. H., & Krogh, L. (2012). Does causal action facilitate causal perception in infants younger than 6 months of age? *Developmental Science, 15*, 43–53.

Rakoczy, H., Harder-Kasten, A., & Sturm, L. (2012). The decline of theory of mind in old age is (partly) mediated by developmental changes in domain-general abilities. *British Journal of Psychology, 103*, 58–72.

Rakoczy, H., Wandt, R., Thomas, S., Nowak, J., & Kunzmann, U. (2017). Theory of mind and wisdom: The development of different forms of perspective-taking in late adulthood. *British Journal of Psychology*. Accessed online, 12-14-17; https://www.ncbi.nlm.nih.gov/pubmed/28266717

Raman, L., & Winer, G. (2002). Children's and adults' understanding of illness: Evidence in support of a coexistence model. *Genetic, Social, & General Psychology Monographs, 128*, 325–355.

Ramasubramanian, S. (2017). Mindfulness, stress coping and everyday resilience among emerging youth in a university setting: A mixed methods approach. *International Journal of Adolescence and Youth, 22*, 308–321.

Ramaswamy, V., & Bergin, C. (2009). Do reinforcement and induction increase prosocial behavior? Results of a teacher-based intervention in preschools. *Journal of Research in Childhood Education, 23*, 527–538.

Rancourt, D., Conway, C. C., Burk, W. J., & Prinstein, M. J. (2012). Gender composition of preadolescents' friendship groups moderates peer socialization of body change behaviors. *Health Psychology*, Accessed online, 7-21-12; http://www.ncbi.nlm.nih.gov/pubmed/22545975.

Randall, W. L. (2012). Positive aging through reading our lives: On the poetics of growing old. *Psychological Studies, 57*, 172–178.

Ranganath, C., Minzenberg, M., & Ragland, J. (2008). The cognitive neuroscience of memory function and dysfunction in schizophrenia. *Biological Psychiatry, 64*, 18–25. Accessed online, http://search.ebscohost.com, doi:10.1016/j.biopsych.2008.04.011.

Rankin, B. (2004). The importance of intentional socialization among children in small groups: A conversation with Loris Malaguzzi. *Early Childhood Education Journal, 32*, 81–85.

Rantanen, J., Kinnunen, U., Pulkkinen, L., & Kokko, K. (2012). Developmental trajectories of work–family conflict for Finnish workers in midlife. *Journal of Occupational Health Psychology, 17*, 290–303.

Ransjö-Arvidson, A. B., Matthiesen, A. S., Lilja, G., Nissen, E., Widström, A. M., & Unväs-Moberg. (2001). Maternal analgesia during labor disturbs newborn behavior: Effects on breastfeeding, temperature, and crying. *Birth, 28*, 5–12.

Rao, V. (1997). Wife-beating in rural South India: A qualitative and econometric analysis. *Social Science & Medicine, 44*, 1169–1180.

Ratanachu-Ek, S. (2003). Effects of multivitamin and folic acid supplementation in malnourished children. *Journal of the Medical Association of Thailand, 4*, 86–91.

Rattan, S. I. S., Kristensen, P., & Clark, B. F. C. (Eds.). (2006). *Understanding and modulating aging*. Malden, MA: Blackwell Publishing on behalf of the New York Academy of Sciences.

Ray, E., & Heyes, C. (2011). Imitation in infancy: The wealth of the stimulus. *Developmental Science, 14*, 92–105.

Ray, L., Bryan, A., MacKillop, J., McGeary, J., Hesterberg, K., & Hutchison, K. (2009). The dopamine D receptor (4) gene exon III polymorphism, problematic alcohol use and novelty seeking: Direct and mediated genetic effects. *Addiction Biology, 14*, 238–244. Accessed online; http://search.ebscohost.com, doi:10.1111/j.1369-1600.2008.00120.x.

Rayner, K., Foorman, B. R., Perfetti, C. A., Pesetsky, D., & Seidenberg, M. S. (2002, March). How should reading be taught? *Scientific American*, pp. 85–91.

Razani, J., Murcia, G., Tabares, J., & Wong, J. (2007). The effects of culture on WASI test performance in ethnically diverse individuals. *Clinical Neuropsychologist, 21*, 776–788.

Rebok, G. W., Ball, K., Guey, L. T., Jones, R. N., Kim, H., King, J. W., & … Willis, S. L. (2014). Ten-year effects of the advanced cognitive training for independent and vital elderly cognitive training trial on cognition and everyday functioning in older adults. *Journal of the American Geriatrics Society, 62*, 16–24.

Rebok, G. W., Langbaum, J. S., Jones, R. N., Gross, A. L., Parisi, J. M., Spira, A. P., & … Brandt, J. (2013). Memory training in the ACTIVE study: How much is needed and who benefits? *Journal of Aging and Health, 25*, 21S–42S.

Reddy, V. (1999). Prelinguistic communication. In M. Barrett (Ed.), *The development of language* (pp. 25–50). Philadelphia, PA: Psychology Press.

Reed, A. E., & Carstensen, L. L. (2012). The theory behind the age-related positivity effect. *Frontiers in Psychology*. Accessed online, 12-14-17; https://www.ncbi.nlm.nih.gov/pmc/articles/PMC3459016/.

Reed, R. K. (2005). *Birthing fathers: The transformation of men in American rites of birth*. New Brunswick, NJ: Rutgers University Press.

Reese, E., & Cox, A. (1999). Quality of adult book reading affects children's emergent literacy. *Developmental Psychology, 35*, 20–28.

Reese, E., & Newcombe, R. (2007). Training mothers in elaborative reminiscing enhances children's autobiographical memory and narrative. *Child Development, 78*, 1153–1170.

Reeves, M. L., & Fernandez, B. S. (2017). Evidence-based interventions for comprehensive school crises. In L. A. Theodore (Ed.), *Handbook of evidence-based interventions for children and adolescents*. New York: Springer Publishing Co.

Reich, S. M. (2017). Connecting offline social competence to online peer interactions. *Psychology of Popular Media Culture, 6*, 291–310.

Reichert, F., Menezes, A., Wells, J., Dumith, C., & Hallal, P. (2009). Physical activity as a predictor of adolescent body fatness: A systematic review. *Sports Medicine, 39*, 279–294.

Reifman, A. (2000). Revisiting *The Bell Curve*. *Psycoloquy*, 11.

Reijntjes, A., Vermande, M., Thomaes, S., Goossens, F., Olthof, T., Aleva, L., & Meulen, M. (2015). Narcissism, bullying, and social dominance in youth: A longitudinal analysis. *Journal of Abnormal Child Psychology*. Accessed online, 3-22-15; http://www.ncbi.nlm.nih.gov/pubmed/25640909.

Reiner, W. G., & Gearhart, J. P. (2004). Discordant sexual identity in some genetic males with cloacal exstrophy assigned to female sex at birth. *New England Journal of Medicine, 350*, 333–341.

Reio, T. J., & Ortega, C. L. (2016). Cyberbullying and its emotional consequences: What we know and what we can do. In S. Y. Tettegah & D. L. Espelage (Eds.), *Emotions, technology, and behaviors*. San Diego, CA: Elsevier Academic Press.

Reis, S., & Renzulli, J. (2004). Current research on the social and emotional development of gifted and talented students: Good news and future possibilities. *Psychology in the Schools, 41*, 119–130.

Reissland, N., & Cohen, D. (2012). *The development of emotional intelligence: A case study*. New York: Routledge/Taylor & Francis Group.

Reissland, N., & Shepherd, J. (2006, March). The effect of maternal depressed mood on infant emotional reaction in a surprise-eliciting situation. *Infant Mental Health Journal, 27*, 173–187.

Rembis, M. (2009). (Re)defining disability in the "genetic age": Behavioral genetics, "new" eugenics and the future of impairment. *Disability & Society, 24*, 585–597. Accessed online; http://search.ebscohost.com, doi:10.1080/09687590903010941.

Renner, L., & Slack, K. (2006, June). Intimate partner violence and child maltreatment: Understanding intra- and intergenerational connections. *Child Abuse & Neglect, 30*, 599–617.

Rentmeester, S. T., Pringle, J., & Hogue, C. R. (2017). An evaluation of the addition of critical congenital heart defect screening in Georgia newborn screening procedures. *Maternal and Child Health Journal*. Accessed online 10-29-17; https://www.ncbi.nlm.nih.gov/pubmed/28730329.

Rentner, T. L., Dixon, L., & Lengel, L. (2012). Critiquing fetal alcohol syndrome health communication campaigns targeted to American Indians. *Journal of Health Communication, 17*, 6–21.

Reschly, D. J. (1996). Identification and assessment of students with disabilities. *Future of Children, 6*, 40–53.

Resing, W. M., Bakker, M., Pronk, C. E., & Elliott, J. G. (2017). Progression paths in children's problem solving: The influence of dynamic testing, initial variability, and working memory. *Journal of Experimental Child Psychology, 153*, 83–109.

Resnick, M. D., Bearman, P. S., Blum, R. W., Bauman, K. E., Harris, M. R., Jones, L., Tabor, J., Beuhring, T., Sieving, R., Shew, M., Ireland, M., Bearinger, L. H., & Udry, J. R. (1997). Protecting adolescents from harm: Findings from the National Longitudinal Study on Adolescent Health. *JAMA: Journal of the American Medical Association, 278*, 823–832.

Rethorst, C., Wipfli, B., & Landers, D. (2009). The antidepressive effects of exercise: A meta-analysis of randomized trials. *Sports Medicine, 39*, 491–511.

Reuter, E., Voelcker-Rehage, C., Vieluf, S., & Godde, B. (2012). Touch perception throughout working life: Effects of age and expertise. *Experimental Brain Research, 216*, 287–297.

Reuter, E., Voelcker-Rehage, C., Vieluf, S., & Godde, B. (2014). Effects of age and expertise on tactile learning in humans. *European Journal of Neuroscience, 40*, 2589–2599.

Reuters Health eLine. (2002, June 26). Baby's injuring points to danger of kids imitating television. *Reuters Health eLine*.

Reyna, V. F., & Farley, F. (2006). Risk and rationality in adolescent decision making. *Psychological Science in the Public Interest, 7*, 1–44.

Reynolds, A. J., Temple, J. A., Ou, S. R., Arteaga, I. A., & White, B. A. (2011). School based early childhood education and age 28 well-being: Effects by timing, dosage, and subgroups. *Science, 333*, 360–364.

Reynolds, C. I. (2016). Telomere attrition: A window into common mental disorders and cellular aging. *American Journal of Psychiatry, 173*, 556–558.

Rhoades, G., Stanley, S., & Markman, H. (2006, December). Pre-engagement cohabitation and gender asymmetry in marital commitment. *Journal of Family Psychology, 20*, 553–560.

Rhoades, G., Stanley, S., & Markman, H. (2009). The preengagement cohabitation effect: A replication and extension of previous findings. *Journal of Family Psychology, 23*, 107–111.

Rhodes, R., Mitchell, S., Miller, S., Connor, S., & Teno, J. (2008). Bereaved family members' evaluation of hospice care: What factors influence overall satisfaction with services? *Journal of Pain and Symptom Management, 35*, 365–371.

Rice, F. P. (1999). *Intimate relationships, marriages, & families* (4th ed.). Mountain View, CA: Mayfield.

Rice, T. M., McGill, J., & Adler-Baeder, F. (2017). Relationship education for youth in high school: Preliminary evidence from a non-controlled study on dating behavior and parent–adolescent relationships. *Child & Youth Care Forum, 46*, 51–68.

Rice, W. S., Goldfarb, S. S., Brisendine, A. E., Burrows, S., & Wingate, M. S. (2017). Disparities in infant mortality by race among Hispanic and non-Hispanic infants. *Maternal and Child Health Journal*. Accessed online 10-29-17; https://www.ncbi.nlm.nih.gov/pubmed/28197819.

Richards, M. H., Crowe, P. A., Larson, R., & Swarr, A. (1998). Developmental patterns and gender differences in the experience of peer companionship during adolescence. *Child Development, 69*, 154–163.

Richardson, G., Goldschmidt, L., & Willford, J. (2009). Continued effects of prenatal cocaine use: Preschool development. *Neurotoxicology and Teratology, 31*, 325–333.

Richardson, H., Walker, A., & Horne, R. (2009). Maternal smoking impairs arousal patterns in sleeping infants. *Sleep: Journal of Sleep and Sleep Disorders Research, 32*, 515–521.

Richardson, K. A., Hester, A. K., & McLemore, G. L. (2016). Prenatal cannabis exposure—The 'first hit' to the endocannabinoid system. *Neurotoxicology and Teratology, 58*, 5–14.

Richtel, M. (2010, November 21). Growing up digital, wired for distraction. *New York Times*, pp. A1, A20.

Rick, S., & Douglas, D. (2007). Neurobiologlcal effects of childhood abuse. *Journal of Psychosocial Nursing & Mental Health Services, 45*, 47–54.

Riebe, D., Burbank, P., & Garber, C. (2002). Setting the stage for active older adults. In P. Burbank & D. Riebe (Eds.), *Promoting exercise and behavior change in older adults: Interventions with the transtheoretical mode*. New York: Springer Publishing Co.

Rinaldi, C. (2002). Social conflict abilities of children identified as sociable, aggressive, and isolated: Developmental implications for children at-risk for impaired peer relations. *Developmental Disabilities Bulletin, 30*, 77–94.

Rippon, I., & Steptoe, A. (2014). Feeling old vs being old: Associations between self-perceived age and mortality. *JAMA, 175*, 307–309.

Ritzen, E. M. (2003). Early puberty: What is normal and when is treatment indicated? *Hormone Research, 60*, Supplement, 31–34.

Rizzoli, R., Abraham, C., & Brandi, M. (2014). Nutrition and bone health: Turning knowledge and beliefs into healthy behaviour. *Current Medical Research and Opinion, 30*, 131–141.

Robb, M., Richert, R., & Wartella, E. (2009). Just a talking book? Word learning from watching baby videos. *British Journal of Developmental Psychology, 27*, 27–45. Accessed online; http://search.ebscohost.com, doi:10.1348/026151008X320156.

Robbins, W. W. (1990, December 10). Sparing the child: How to intervene when you suspect abuse. *New York Magazine*, pp. 42–53.

Robbins, R. (2016, September 6). The Federal Trade Commission will be sending out rebates to thousands of Lumosity customers misled by company ads. *Scientific American*. Accessed online, 12-11-17; https://www.scientificamerican.com/article/u-s-cracking-down-on-brain-training-games/.

Roberts, S. (2006, October 15). To Be Married Means To Be Outnumbered. *New York Times*. Accessed May 2, 2018 from https://www.nytimes.com/2006/10/15/us/15census.html

Roberts, B., Helson, R., & Klohnen, E. (2002). Personality development and growth in women across 30 years: Three perspectives. *Journal of Personality, 70*, 79–102.

Roberts, B. W., Walton, K. E., & Viechtbauer, W. (2006). Patterns of mean-level change in personality traits across the life course: A meta-analysis of longitudinal studies. *Psychological Bulletin, 132*, 1–25.

Roberts, R., Roberts, C., & Duong, H. (2009). Sleepless in adolescence: Prospective data on sleep deprivation, health and functioning. *Journal of Adolescence, 32*, 1045–1057.

Roberts, R. D., & Lipnevich, A. A. (2012). From general intelligence to multiple intelligences: Meanings, models, and measures. In K. R. Harris, S. Graham, T. Urdan, S. Graham, J. M. Royer, & M. Zeidner (Eds.), *APA educational psychology handbook, Vol 2: Individual differences and cultural and contextual factors*. Washington, DC: American Psychological Association.

Roberts, R. E., Roberts, C. R., & Xing, Y. (2011). Restricted sleep among adolescents: Prevalence, incidence, persistence, and associated factors. *Behavioral Sleep Medicine, 9*, 18–30.

Roberts, S. (2007, January 16). 51% of women are now living without spouse. *New York Times*, p. A1.

Roberts, S. (2009, November 24). Economy is forcing young adults back home in big numbers, survey finds. *New York Times*, p. A16.

Roberts, S. (2013, September 22). Divorce after 50 grows more common. *New York Times*, p. ST26.

Robins, R. W., & Trzesniewski, K. H. (2005). Self-esteem development across the lifespan. *Current Directions in Psychological Science, 14*, 158–162.

Robinson, A., & Stark, D. R. (2005). *Advocates in action*. Washington, DC: National Association for the Education of Young Children.

Robinson, A. J., & Pascalis, O. (2005). Development of flexible visual recognition memory in human infants. *Developmental Science, 7*, 527–533.

Robinson, G. (2002). Cross-cultural perspectives on menopause. In A. Hunter & C. Forden (Eds.), *Readings in the psychology of gender: Exploring our differences and commonalities*. Needham Heights, MA: Allyn & Bacon.

Robinson, G. E. (2004, April 16). Beyond nature and nurture. *Science, 304*, 397–399.

Robinson, J. P., & Godbey, G. (1997). *Time for life: The surprising ways Americans use their time*. College Park: Pennsylvania State University Press.

Robinson, O. C., Demetre, J. D., & Litman, J. A. (2017). Adult life stage and crisis as predictors of curiosity and authenticity: Testing inferences from Erikson's lifespan theory. *International Journal of Behavioral Development, 41*, 426–431.

Rocha, N. F., de Campos, A. C., dos Santos Silva, F. P., & Tudella, E. (2013). Adaptive actions of young infants in the task of reaching for objects. *Developmental Psychobiology, 55*, 275–282.

Rocha-Ferreira, E., & Hristova, M. (2016). Plasticity in the neonatal brain following hypoxic-ischaemic injury. *Neural Plasticity*. Accessed online 10-29-17; https://www.hindawi.com/journals/np/2016/4901014/.

Rochat, P. (2004). Emerging co-awareness. In G. Bremner & A. Slater (Eds.), *Theories of infant development*. Malden, MA: Blackwell Publishers.

Rochat, P., Broesch, T., & Jayne, K. (2012). Social awareness and early self-recognition. *Consciousness and Cognition: An International Journal*, Accessed online, 7-18-12; http://www.sciencedirect.com/science/article/pii/S1053810012001225.

Roche, T. (2000, November 13). The crisis of foster care. *Time*, pp. 74–82.

Rocheleau, M. (2016, March 28). On campus, women outnumber men more than ever. *Boston Globe*. Accessed online, 11-16-17; https://www.bostonglobe.com/metro/2016/03/28/look-how-women-outnumber-men-college-campuses-nationwide/YROqwfCPSlKPtSMAzpWloK/story.html#comments.

Rodgers, K. A., & Summers, J. J. (2008). African American students at predominantly white institutions: A motivational and self-systems approach to understanding retention. *Educational Psychology Review, 20*, 171–190.

Rodkey, E. N., & Riddell, R. P. (2013). The infancy of infant pain research: The experimental origins of infant pain denial. *Journal of Pain, 14*, 338–350.

Rodkin, P. C., & Ryan, A. M. (2012). Child and adolescent peer relations in educational context. In K. R. Harris, S. Graham, T. Urdan, S. Graham, J. M. Royer, & M. Zeidner (Eds.), *APA educational psychology handbook, Vol 2: Individual differences and cultural and contextual factors*. Washington, DC: American Psychological Association.

Rodnitzky, R. L. (2012). Upcoming treatments in Parkinson's disease, including gene therapy. *Parkinsonism & Related Disorders, 18* (Suppl. 1), S37–S40.

Roecke, C., & Cherry, K. (2002). Death at the end of the 20th century: Individual processes and developmental tasks in old age. *International Journal of Aging & Human Development, 54*, 315–333.

Roehrig, M., Masheb, R., White, M., & Grilo, C. (2009). Dieting frequency in obese patients with binge eating disorder: Behavioral and metabolic correlates. *Obesity, 17*, 689–697.

Roelofs, J., Meesters, C., Ter Huurne, M., Bamelis, L., & Muris, P. (2006, June). On the links between attachment style, parental rearing behaviors, and internalizing and externalizing problems in non-clinical children. *Journal of Child and Family Studies, 15*, 331–344.

Roffwarg, H. P., Muzio, J. N., & Dement, W. C. (1966). Ontogenic development of the human sleep–dream cycle. *Science, 152*, 604–619.

Rogan, J. (2007). How much curriculum change is appropriate? Defining a zone of feasible innovation. *Science Education, 91*, 439–460.

Rogers, C. R. (1971). A theory of personality. In S. Maddi (Ed.), *Perspectives on personality*. Boston: Little, Brown.

Rogers, S. L., & Blissett, J. (2017). Breastfeeding duration and its relation to weight gain, eating behaviours and positive maternal feeding practices in infancy. *Appetite, 108*, 399–406.

Roggeveen, A. B., Prime, D. J., & Ward, L. M. (2007). Lateralized readiness potentials reveal motor slowing in the aging brain. *Journals of Gerontology: Series B: Psychological Science and Social Science, 62*, P78–P84.

Rohleder, N. (2012). Acute and chronic stress induced changes in sensitivity of peripheral inflammatory pathways to the signals of multiple stress systems–2011 Curt Richter award winner. *Psychoneuroendocrinology, 37*, 307–316.

Roksa, J., Trolian, T. L., Pascarella, E. T., Kilgo, C. A., Blaich, C., & Wise, K. S. (2017). Racial inequality in critical thinking skills: The role of academic and diversity experiences. *Research in Higher Education, 58*, 119–140.

Rollins, B., & Cannon, K. (1974). Marital Satisfaction over the Family Life Cycle: A Reevaluation. *Journal of Marriage and Family, 36*(2), 271-282. doi:10.2307/351153

Rolls, E. (2000). Memory systems in the brain. *Annual Review of Psychology, 51*, 599–630.

Rom, S. A., Miller, L., & Peluso, J. (2009). Playing the game: Psychological factors in surviving cancer. *International Journal of Emergency Mental Health, 11*, 25–35.

Romero, S. T., Coulson, C. C., & Galvin, S. L. (2012). Cesarean delivery on maternal request: A western North Carolina perspective. *Maternal and Child Health Journal, 16*, 725–734.

Ron, P. (2006). Care giving offspring to aging parents: How it affects their marital relations, parenthood, and mental health. *Illness, Crisis, & Loss, 14*, 1–21.

Ron, P. (2014). Attitudes towards filial responsibility in a traditional vs modern culture: A comparison between three generations of Arabs in the Israeli society. *Gerontechnology, 13*, 31–38.

Roopnarine, J. (1992). Father–child play in India. In K. MacDonald (Ed.), *Parent–child play*. Albany: State University of New York Press.

Rosburg, T., Weigl, M., & Sörös, P. (2014). Habituation in the absence of a response decrease? *Clinical Neurophysiology, 125*, 210–211.

Rose, A. J., & Asher, S. R. (1999). Children's goals and strategies in response to conflicts within a friendship. *Developmental Psychology, 35*, 69–79.

Rose, C. A., Richman, D. M., Fettig, K., Hayner, A., Slavin, C., & Preast, J. L. (2016). Peer reactions to early childhood aggression in a preschool setting: Defenders, encouragers, or neutral bystander. *Developmental Neurorehabilitation, 19*, 246–254.

Rose, R. J., Viken, R. J., Dick, D. M., Bates, J. E., Pulkkinen, L., & Kaprio, J. (2003). It does take a village: Nonfamilial environments and children's behavior. *Psychological Science, 14*, 273–278.

Rose, S. (2008, January 21). Drugging unruly children is a method of social control. *Nature, 451*, 521.

Rose, S., Feldman, J., & Jankowski, J. (2009). Information processing in toddlers: Continuity from infancy and persistence of preterm deficits. *Intelligence, 37*, 311–320.

Rose, S. A., Feldman, J. F., Jankowski, J. J., & Van Rossem, R. (2012). Information processing from infancy to 11 years: Continuities and prediction of IQ. *Intelligence, 40*, 445–457.

Rose, S. A., Feldman, J. F., & Jankowski, J. J. (2015). Pathways from toddler information processing to adolescent lexical proficiency. *Child Development, 86*, 1935–1947.

Rosenberg, T. (2013). The power of talking to your baby. The New York Times Opinionator Blog. Accessed online, 2-27-14; http://opinionator.blogs.nytimes.com/2013/04/10/the-powerof-talking-to-your-baby/?_php=true&_type=blogs&_r=0.

Rosenblatt, P. C. (2001). A social constructionist perspective on cultural differences in grief. In M. S. Stroebe, R. O. Hansson, W. Stroebe, & H. Schut (Eds.), *Handbook of bereavement research: Consequences, coping, and care*. Washington, DC: American Psychological Association Press.

Rosenblatt, P. C. (2015). Death and bereavement in later adulthood: Cultural beliefs, behaviors, and emotions. In L.A. Jensen (Ed.), *The Oxford handbook of human development and culture: An interdisciplinary perspective* (pp. 697–709). New York: Oxford University Press.

Rosenman, R. H. (1990). Type A behavior pattern: A personal overview. *Journal of Social Behavior and Personality, 5*, 1–24.

Ross, C. E., Microwsky, J., & Goldsteen, K. (1991). The impact of the family on health. In A. Booth (Ed.), *Contemporary families*. Minneapolis, MN: National Council on Family Relations.

Ross, J., Yilmaz, M., Dale, R., Cassidy, R., Yildirim, I., & Zeedyk, M. S. (2017). Cultural differences in self-recognition: The early development of autonomous and related selves? *Developmental Science, 20*, 27–33.

Ross, K. R., Storfer-Isser, A., Hart, M. A., Kibler, A. V., Rueschman, M., Rosen, C. L., & Redline, S. (2012). Sleepdisordered breathing is associated with asthma severity in children. *Journal of Pediatrics, 160*, 736–742.

Rossi, A. (2014). The art and science of child rearing. *Psyccritiques, 59*, 102–114.

Rossi, S., Telkemeyer, S., Wartenburger, I., & Obrig, H. (2012). Shedding light on words and sentences: Near-infrared spectroscopy in language research. *Brain and Language, 121*, 152–163.

Rössler, W., Hengartner, M. P., Ajdacic-Gross, V., & Angst, J. (2015). Predictors of burnout: Results from a prospective community study. *European Archives of Psychiatry and Clinical Neuroscience, 265*, 19–25.

Rossman, I. (1977). Anatomic and body composition changes with aging. In C. E. Finch & L. Hayflick (Eds.), *Handbook of the biology of aging*. New York: Van Nostrand Reinhold

Rossouw, J. E., Prentice, R. L., Manson, J. E., Wu, L., Barad, D., Barnabei, V. M., Ko, M., La-Croix, A. Z., Margolis, K. L., & Stefanick, M. L. (2007). Postmenopausal hormone therapy and risk of cardiovascular disease by age and years since menopause. *JAMA: Journal of the American Medical Association, 297*, 1465–1477.

Rote, W. M., Smetana, J. G., Campione-Barr, N., Villalobos, M., & Tasopoulos-Chan, M. (2012). Associations between observed mother–adolescent interactions and adolescent information management. *Journal of Research on Adolescence, 22*, 206–214.

Rothbart, M. (2007). Temperament, development, and personality. *Current Directions in Psychological Science, 16*, 207–212.

Rothbaum, F., Rosen, K., & Ujiie, T. (2002). Family systems theory, attachment theory and culture. *Family Process, 41,* 328–350.

Rothbaum, F., Weisz, J., Pott, M., Miyake, K., & Morelli, G. (2000). Attachment and culture: Security in the United States and Japan. *American Psychologist, 55,* 1093–1104.

Rotigel, J. V. (2003). Understanding the young gifted child: Guidelines for parents, families, and educators. *Early Childhood Education Journal, 30,* 209–214.

Roth, M. S. (2016). Psychoanalysis and history. *Psychoanalytic Psychology, 33*(Suppl 1), S19–S33.

Rothenberger, A., & Rothenberger, L. G. (2013). Psychopharmacological treatment in children: Always keeping an eye on adherence and ethics. *European Child & Adolescent Psychiatry, 22,* 453–455.

Rousseau, P. V., Matton, F., Lecuyer, R., & Lahaye, W. (2017). The Moro reaction: More than a reflex, a ritualized behavior of nonverbal communication. *Infant Behavior & Development, 46,* 169–177.

Roussotte, F. F., Gutman, B. A., Madsen, S. K., Colby, J. B., & Thompson, P. M. (2014). Combined effects of Alzheimer risk variants in the CLU and ApoE genes on ventricular expansion patterns in the elderly. *Journal of Neuroscience, 34,* 6537–6545.

Rovee-Collier, C. (1993). The capacity for long-term memory in infancy. *Current Directions in Psychological Science, 2,* 130–135.

Rovee-Collier, C., & Cuevas, K. (2009). The development of infant memory. In M. L. Courage, N. Cowan, (Eds.), *The development of memory in infancy and childhood,* 2nd ed. (pp. 11–41). New York: Psychology Press.

Rowe, J. W., & Kahn, R. L. (1998). *Successful aging*. New York: Pantheon.

Rowe, J. W., & Kahn, R. L. (1999). *Successful aging*. New York: Pantheon.

Rowe-Finkbeiner, K., Martin, R., Abrams, B., Zuccaro, A., & Dardari, Y. (2016). Why paid family and medical leave matters for the future of America's families, businesses and economy. *Maternal and Child Health Journal, 20*(Suppl 1), 8–12.

Rowley, S., Burchinal, M., Roberts, J., & Zeisel, S. (2008). Racial identity, social context, and race-related social cognition in African Americans during middle childhood. *Developmental Psychology, 44,* 1537–1546.

Roy, A. L., & Raver, C. C. (2014). Are all risks equal? Early experiences of poverty-related risk and children's functioning. *Journal of Family Psychology, 28,* 391–400.

Rubin, D., & Greenberg, D. (2003). The role of narrative in recollection: A view from cognitive psychology and neuropsychology. In G. Fireman & T. McVay (Eds.), *Narrative and consciousness: Literature, psychology, and the brain*. London: Oxford University Press.

Rubin, D. C. (1986). *Autobiographical memory*. Cambridge, England: Cambridge University Press.

Rubin, D. C. (2000). Autobiographical memory and aging. In C. D. Park, N. Schwarz et al. (Eds.), *Cognitive aging: A primer*. Philadelphia, PA: Psychology Press/Taylor & Francis.

Rubin, K. H., & Chung, O. B. (Eds.). (2006). *Parenting beliefs, behaviors, and parent-child relations: A cross-cultural perspective*. New York: Psychology Press.

Ruble, D. N., Taylor, L. J., Cyphers, L., Greulich, F. K., Lurye, L. E., & Shrout, P. E. (2007). The role of gender constancy in early gender development. *Child Development, 78,* 1121–1136.

Ruda, M. A., Ling, Q-D., Hohmann, A. G., Peng, Y. B., & Tachibana, T. (2000, July 28). Altered nociceptive neuronal circuits after neonatal peripheral inflammation. *Science, 289,* 628–630.

Rudd, L. C., Cain, D. W., & Saxon, T. F. (2008). Does improving joint attention in low-quality child-care enhance language development? *Early Child Development and Care, 178,* 315–338.

Rudman, L. A., & Fetterolf, J. C. (2014). How accurate are metaperceptions of sexism? Evidence for the illusion of antagonism between hostile and benevolent sexism. *Group Processes & Intergroup Relations, 17,* 275–285.

Ruff, H. A. (1989). The infant's use of visual and haptic information in the perception and recognition of objects. *Canadian Journal of Psychology, 43,* 302–319.

Ruffman, T. (2014). To belief or not belief: Children's theory of mind. *Developmental Review, 34,* 265–293.

Ruffman, T., Lorimer, B., & Scarf, D. (2017). Do infants really experience emotional contagion? *Child Development Perspectives*. Accessed online, 11-13-17; http://onlinelibrary.wiley.com/doi/10.1111/cdep.12244/full.

Rupp, D., Vodanovich, S., & Credé, M. (2006, June). Age bias in the workplace: The impact of ageism and causal attributions. *Journal of Applied Social Psychology, 36,* 1337–1364.

Russ, S. W. (2014). Pretend play and creativity: An overview. In *Pretend play in childhood: Foundation of adult creativity*. Washington, DC: American Psychological Association.

Russell, J. (2017). 'Everything has to die one day.' Children's explorations of the meanings of death in human-animal-nature relationships. *Environmental Education Research, 23*(1), 75–90.

Russell, S., & Consolacion, T. (2003). Adolescent romance and emotional health in the United States: Beyond binaries. *Journal of Clinical Child & Adolescent Psychology, 32,* 499–508.

Rust, J., Golombok, S., Hines, M., Johnston, K., & Golding, J., ALSPAC Study Team. (2000). The role of brothers and sisters in the gender development of preschool children. *Journal of Experimental Child Psychology, 77,* 292–303.

Rutter, M. (2003). Commentary: Causal processes leading to antisocial behavior. *Developmental Psychology, 39,* 372–378.

Rutter, M. (2006). *Genes and behavior: Nature-nurture interplay explained*. New York: Blackwell Publishing.

Ruzek, E., Burchinal, M., Farkas, G., & Duncan, G. J. (2014). The quality of toddler child care and cognitive skills at 24 months: Propensity score analysis results from the ECLS-B. *Early Childhood Research Quarterly, 29,* 12–21.

Ryan, B. P. (2001). *Programmed therapy for stuttering in children and adults (2nd ed.)*. Springfield, IL: Charles C. Thomas.

Ryding, E. L., Lukasse, M., Van Parys, A., Wangel, A., Karro, H., Kristjansdottir, H., & … Schei, B. (2015). Fear of childbirth and risk of cesarean delivery: A cohort study in six European countries. *Birth: Issues in Perinatal Care, 42,* 48–55.

Saad, L. (2011, June 30). *Americans' preference for smaller families edges higher*. Princeton, NJ: Gallup Poll.

Saarento, S., Boulton, A. J., & Salmivalli, C. (2015). Reducing bullying and victimization: Student and classroom level mechanisms of change. *Journal of Abnormal Child Psychology, 43,* 61–76.

Sabbagh, M. A., Bowman, L. C., Evraire, L. E., & Ito, J. B. (2009). Neurodevelopmental correlates of theory of mind in preschool children. *Child Development, 80*(4), 1147-1162. doi:10.1111/j.1467-8624.2009.01322.x

Sacks, M. H. (1993). Exercise for stress control. In D. Goleman & J. Gurin (Eds.), *Mind–body medicine*. Yonkers, NY: Consumer Reports Books.

Sadker, D., Zittleman, K., Earley, P., McCormick, T., Strawn, C., & Preston, J. A. (2007). The treatment of gender equity in teacher education. In S. S. Klein, B. Richardson, D. A. Grayson, L. H. Fox, C. Kramarae, D. S. Pollard, … C. A. Dwyer (Eds.), *Handbook for achieving gender equity through education, 2nd ed*. Mahwah, NJ: Lawrence Erlbaum Associates Publishers.

Sadker, M., & Sadker, D. (1994). *Failing at fairness: How America's schools cheat girls*. New York: Scribner's.

Safar, K., & Moulson, M. C. (2017). Recognizing facial expressions of emotion in infancy: A replication and extension. *Developmental Psychobiology, 59,* 507–514.

Saiegh-Haddad, E. (2007). Linguistic constraints on children's ability to isolate phonemes in Arabic. *Applied Psycholinguistics, 28,* 607–625.

Salihu, H. M., August, E. M., de la Cruz, C., Mogos, M. F., Weldeselasse, H., & Alio, A. P. (2013). Infant mortality and the risk of small size for gestational age in the subsequent pregnancy: A retrospective cohort study. *Maternal and Child Health Journal, 17,* 1044–1051.

Salley, B., Miller, A., & Bell, M. (2013). Associations between temperament and social responsiveness in young children. *Infant and Child Development, 22,* 270–288.

Sallis, J., & Glanz, K. (2006, March). The role of built environments in physical activity, eating, and obesity in childhood. *Future of Children, 16,* 89–108.

Salovey, P., & Pizarro, D. (2003). The value of emotional intelligence. In R. Sternberg & J. Lautrey (Eds.), *Models of intelligence: International perspectives*. Washington, DC: American Psychological Association.

Salthouse, T. (2009). When does age-related cognitive decline begin? *Neurobiology of Aging, 30,* 507–514.

Salthouse, T. (2012). Consequences of age-related cognitive declines. *Annual Review of Psychology, 63,* 201–226.

Salthouse, T. A. (1994). The aging of working memory. *Neuropsychology, 8,* 535–543.

Salthouse, T. A. (2006). Mental exercise and mental aging: Evaluating the validity of the "Use it or lose it" hypothesis. *Perspectives on Psychological Science, 1,* 68–87.

Salthouse, T. A. (2016). Continuity of cognitive change across adulthood. *Psychonomic Bulletin & Review, 23,* 932–939.

Salthouse, T. A. (2017). Why is cognitive change more negative with increased age? *Neuropsychology*. Accessed online, 12-11-17; http://psycnet.apa.org/record/2017-43357-001.

Salthouse, T. A., Atkinson, T. M., & Berish, D. E. (2003). Executive functioning as a potential mediator of age-related cognitive decline in normal adults. *Journal of Experimental Psychology: General, 132,* 566–594.

Salthouse, T., Pink, J., & Tucker-Drob, E. (2008). Contextual analysis of fluid intelligence. *Intelligence, 36,* 464–486.

Samet, J. H., De Marini, D. M., & Malling, H. V. (2004, May 14). Do airborne particles induce heritable mutations? *Science, 304,* 971.

Sammons, M. (2009). Writing a wrong: Factors influencing the overprescription of antidepressants to youth. *Professional Psychology: Research and Practice, 40,* 327–329.

Sanchez, Y. M., Lambert, S. F., & Ialongo, N. S. (2012). Life events and depressive symptoms in African American adolescents: Do ecological domains and timing of life events matter? *Journal of Youth and Adolescence, 41,* 438–448.

Sánchez-Castañeda, C., Squitieri, F., Di Paola, M., Dayan, M., Petrollini, M., & Sabatini, U. (2015). The role of iron in gray matter degeneration in Huntington's disease: A magnetic resonance imaging study. *Human Brain Mapping, 36,* 50–66.

Sanchez-Garrido, M. A., & Tena-Sempere, M. (2013). Metabolic control of puberty: Roles of leptin and kisspeptins. *Hormones and Behavior, 64,* 187–194.

Sandall, J. (2014). The 30th international confederation of midwives triennial congress: Improving women's health globally. *Birth: Issues in Perinatal Care, 41,* 303–305.

Sanders, S., Ott, C., Kelber, S., & Noonan, P. (2008). The experience of high levels of grief in caregivers of persons with Alzheimer's disease and related dementia. *Death Studies, 32,* 495–523.

Sandis, E. (2000). The aging and their families: A cross-national review. In A. L. Comunian & U. P. Gielen (Eds.), *International perspectives on human development*. Lengerich, Germany: Pabst Science Publishers.

Sandoval, J., Frisby, C. L., Geisinger, K. F., Scheuneman, J. D., & Grenier, J. R. (Eds.). (1998). *Test interpretation and diversity: Achieving equity in assessment*. Washington, DC: APA Books.

Sandoval, J., Scott, A., & Padilla, I. (2009). Crisis counseling: An overview. *Psychology in the Schools, 46,* 246–256.

Sang, B., Miao, X., & Deng, C. (2002). The development of gifted and nongifted young children in metamemory knowledge. *Psychological Science (China), 25*, 406–409, 424.

Sangree, W. H. (1989). Age and power: Life-course trajectories and age structuring of power relations in East and West Africa. In D. I. Kertzer & K. W. Schaie (Eds.), *Age structuring in comparative perspective*. Hillsdale, NJ: Lawrence Erlbaum.

Santos, M., Richards, C., & Bleckley, M. (2007). Comorbidity between depression and disordered eating in adolescents. *Eating Behaviors, 8*, 440–449.

Santos, R. X., Correia, S. C., Cardoso, S., Carvalho, C., Santos, M. S., & Moreira, P. I. (2011). Effects of rapamycin and TOR on aging and memory: Implications for Alzheimer's disease. *Journal of Neurochemistry, 117*, 927–936.

Santtila, P., Sandnabba, N., Harlaar, N., Varjonen, M., Alanko, K., & von der Pahlen, B. (2008, January). Potential for homosexual response is prevalent and genetic. *Biological Psychology, 77*(1), 102–105.

Sapolsky, R. (2005, December). Sick of poverty. *Scientific American*, pp. 93–99.

Sapyla, J. J., & March, J. S. (2012). Integrating medical and psychological therapies in child mental health: An evidence-based medicine approach. In M. Garralda, & J. Raynaud (Eds.), *Brain, mind, and developmental psychopathology in childhood*. Lanham, MD: Jason Aronson.

Sargent-Cox, K. A., Anstey, K. J., & Luszcz, M. A. (2012). The relationship between change in self-perceptions of aging and physical functioning in older adults. *Psychology and Aging*. doi:10.1037/a0027578.

SART. (2012, July 3). 2009 Clinic summary report. *Society for Reproductive Medicine*. Accessed online, 7-14-11.

Sasisekaran, J. (2014). Exploring the link between stuttering and phonology: A review and implications for treatment. *Seminars in Speech and Language, 35*, 95–113.

Sato, Y., Fukasawa, T., Hayakawa, M., Yatsuya, H., Hatakeyama, M., Ogawa, A., et al. (2007). A new method of blood sampling reduces pain for newborn infants: A prospective, randomized controlled clinical trial. *Early Human Development, 83*, 389–394.

Saul, S. (2009). The gift of life, and its price. *New York Times*, pp. A1, A26–27.

Saunders, J., Davis, L., & Williams, T. (2004). Gender differences in self-perceptions and academic outcomes: A study of African American high school students. *Journal of Youth & Adolescence, 33*, 81–90.

Savage-Rumbaugh, E. S., Murphy, J., Sevcik, R. A., Brakke, K. E., Williams, S. L., & Rumbaugh, D. M. (1993). Language and comprehension in ape and child. *Monographs of the Society for Research in Child Development, 58* (3–4, Serial No. 233).

Savina, E. (2014). Does play promote self-regulation in children? *Early Child Development and Care, 184*, 1692–1705.

Savin-Williams, R. C. (2003). Are adolescent same-sex romantic relationships on our radar screen?. In P. Florsheim, P. Florsheim (Eds.), *Adolescent romantic relations and sexual behavior: Theory, research, and practical implications* (pp. 325-336). Mahwah, NJ, US: Lawrence Erlbaum Associates Publishers.

Sawatzky, J., & Naimark, B. (2002). Physical activity and cardiovascular health in aging women: A health-promotion perspective. *Journal of Aging & Physical Activity, 10*, 396–412.

Sawicka, M. (2016). Searching for a narrative of loss. Interactional ordering of ambiguous grief. *Symbolic Interaction*. Accessed online, 10-24-17; http://onlinelibrary.wiley.com/doi/10.1002/symb.270/full.

Sawyer, J. (2017). I think I can: Preschoolers' private speech and motivation in playful versus non-playful contexts. *Early Childhood Research Quarterly, 38*, 84–96.

Sawyer, R. (2012). *Explaining creativity: The science of human innovation* (2nd ed.). New York: Oxford University Press.

Sax, L., & Kautz, K. J. (2003). Who first suggests the diagnosis of attention-deficit/hyperactivity disorder? *Annals of Family Medicine, 1*, 171–174.

Sayal, K., Heron, J., Maughan, B., Rowe, R., & Ramchandani, P. (2014). Infant temperament and childhood psychiatric disorder: Longitudinal study. *Child: Care, Health and Development, 40*, 292–297.

Scarborough, P., Nnoaham, K. E., Clarke, D., Capewell, S., & Rayner, M. (2012). Modelling the impact of a healthy diet on cardiovascular disease and cancer mortality. *Journal of Epidemiology and Community Health, 66*, 420–426.

Scarr, S. (1993). Biological and cultural diversity: The legacy of Darwin for development. *Child Development, 64*, 1333–1353.

Scarr, S. (1998). American child care today. *American Psychologist, 53*, 95–108.

Scarr, S., & Carter-Saltzman, L. (1982). Genetics and intelligence. In R. J. Sternberg (Ed.), *Handbook of human intelligence* (pp. 792–896). Cambridge, England: Cambridge University Press.

Schaan, V. K., & Vögele, C. (2016). Resilience and rejection sensitivity mediate long-term outcomes of parental divorce. *European Child & Adolescent Psychiatry, 25*, 1267–1269.

Schachner, A., & Hannon, E. E. (2011). Infant-directed speech drives social preferences in 5-month-old infants. *Developmental Psychology, 47*(1), 19–25.

Schachner, D., Shaver, P., & Gillath, O. (2008). Attachment style and long-term singlehood. *Personal Relationships, 15*, 479–491.

Schachter, E. P. (2005). Erikson meets the postmodern: Can classic identity theory rise to the challenge? *Identity, 5*, 137–160.

Schafer, D. P., & Stevens, B. (2013). Phagocytic glial cells: Sculpting synaptic circuits in the developing nervous system. *Current Opinion in Neurobiology, 23*, 1034–1040.

Schaefer, M. K., & Salafia, E. B. (2014). The connection of teasing by parents, siblings, and peers with girls' body dissatisfaction and boys' drive for muscularity: The role of social comparison as a mediator. *Eating Behaviors, 15*, 599–608.

Schaeffer, C., Petras, H., & Ialongo, N. (2003). Modeling growth in boys' aggressive behavior across elementary school: Links to later criminal involvement, conduct disorder, and antisocial personality disorder. *Developmental Psychology, 39*, 1020–1035.

Schaie, K. W. (1977–1978). Toward a stage of adult theory of adult cognitive development. *Journal of Aging and Human Development, 8*, 129–138.

Schaie, K. W. (1993). The Seattle longitudinal studies of adult intelligence. *Current Directions in Psychological Science, 2*, 171–175.

Schaie, K. W. (1994). The course of adult intellectual development. *American Psychologist, 49*, 304–313.

Schaie, K. W. (2016). The longitudinal study of adult cognitive development. In R. J. Sternberg, S. T. Fiske, D. J. Foss (Eds.), *Scientists making a difference: One hundred eminent behavioral and brain scientists talk about their most important contributions*. New York: Cambridge University Press.

Schaie, K. W., & Willis, S. L. (1993). Age difference patterns of psychometric intelligence in adulthood: Generalizability within and across ability domains. *Psychology and Aging, 8*, 44–55.

Schaie, K. W., & Willis, S. L. (2011). *Handbook of the psychology of aging*. (7th ed.) San Diego, CA: Elsevier Academic Press.

Schaie, K. W., & Zanjani, F. A. K. (2006). Intellectual development across adulthood. In C. Hoare (Ed.), *Handbook of adult development and learning*. New York: Oxford University Press.

Schaller, M., & Crandall, C. S. (Eds.). (2004). *The psychological foundations of culture*. Mahwah, NJ: Lawrence Erlbaum.

Scharf, M. (2014). Children's social competence within close friendship: The role of self-perception and attachment orientations. *School Psychology International, 35*, 206–220.

Scharoun, S. M., & Bryden, P. J. (2014). Hand preference, performance abilities, and hand selection in children. *Frontiers in Psychology*. Accessed online, 3-20-15; http://www.ncbi.nlm.nih.gov/pmc/articles/PMC3927078/.

Scharrer, E., Kim, D., Lin, K., & Liu, Z. (2006). Working hard or hardly working? Gender, humor, and the performance of domestic chores in television commercials. *Mass Communication and Society, 9*, 215–238.

Schechter, D., & Willheim, E. (2009). Disturbances of attachment and parental psychopathology in early childhood. *Child and Adolescent Psychiatric Clinics of North America, 18*, 665–686.

Schecklmann, M., Pfannstiel, C., Fallgatter, A. J., Warnke, A., Gerlach, M., & Romanos, M. (2012). Olfaction in child and adolescent anorexia nervosa. *Journal of Neural Transmission, 119*, 721–728.

Schecter, T., Finkelstein, Y., & Koren, G. (2005). Pregnant "DES daughters" and their offspring. *Canadian Family Physician, 51*, 493–494.

Scheibner, G., & Leathem, J. (2012). Memory control beliefs and everyday forgetfulness in adulthood: The effects of selection, optimization, and compensation strategies. *Aging, Neuropsychology, and Cognition, 19*, 362–379.

Schemo, D. J. (2001, December 5). U.S. students prove middling on 32-nation test. *New York Times*, p. A21.

Schemo, D. J. (2003, November 13). Students' scores rise in math, not in reading. *New York Times*, p. A2.

Schemo, D. J. (2004, March 2). Schools, facing tight budgets, leave gifted programs behind. *New York Times*, pp. A1, A18.

Scherer, M. (2004). Contrasting inclusive with exclusive education. In M. Scherer (Ed.), *Connecting to learn: Educational and assistive technology for people with disabilities*. Washington, DC: American Psychological Association.

Scherf, K. S., Sweeney, J. A., & Luna, B. (2006). Brain basis of developmental change in visuospatial working memory. *Journal of Cognitive Neuroscience, 18*, 1045–1058.

Schieman, S., McBrier, D. B., & van Gundy, K. (2003). Home-to-work conflict, work qualities, and emotional distress. *Sociological Forum, 18*, 137–164.

Schiffer, A., Pedersen, S., Broers, H., Widdershoven, J., & Denollet, J. (2008). Type-D personality but not depression predicts severity of anxiety in heart failure patients at 1-year follow-up. *Journal of Affective Disorders, 106*, 73–81.

Schiller, J. S., & Bernadel, L. (2004). Summary health statistics for the U.S. population: National Health Interview Survey, 2002. *Vital Health Statistics, 10*, 1–110.

Schlossberg, N. K. (2004). *Retire smart, retire happy: Finding your true path in life*. Washington, DC: American Psychological Association.

Schlossberg, N. K. (2017). *Too young to be old: Love, learn, work, and play as you age*. Washington, DC: American Psychological Association.

Schlosser, F., Zinni, D., & Armstrong-Stassen, M. (2012). Intention to unretire: HR and the boomerang effect. *Career Development International, 17*, 149–167.

Schmalz, D., & Kerstetter, D. (2006). Girlie girls and manly men: Chidren's stigma consciousness of gender in sports and physical activities. *Journal of Leisure Research, 38*, 536–557.

Schmidt, D., Seehagen, S., Hirschfeld, G., Vocks, S., Schneider, S., & Teismann, T. (2016). Repetitive negative thinking and impaired mother–infant bonding: A longitudinal study. *Cognitive Therapy and Research, 14*, 88–97.

Schmiedek, F. (2017). Development of cognition and intelligence. In J. Specht, J. Specht (Eds.), *Personality development across the lifespan*. San Diego, CA: Elsevier Academic Press.

Schmitow, C., & Stenberg, G. (2013). Social referencing in 10-month-old infants. *European Journal of Developmental Psychology, 10*, 533–545.

Schnitzer, P. G. (2006). Prevention of unintentional childhood injuries. *American Family Physician, 74*, 1864–1869.

Schoenfeld, E. A., Loving, T. J., Pope, M. T., Huston, T. L., & Štulhofer, A. (2017). Does sex really matter? Examining the connections between spouses' nonsexual behaviors, sexual frequency, sexual satisfaction, and marital satisfaction. *Archives of Sexual Behavior, 46*, 489–501.

Schoklitsch, A., & Baumann, U. (2012). Generativity and aging: A promising future research topic? *Journal of Aging Studies, 26*, 262–272.

Schonert-Reichl, K. A., Smith, V., Zaidman-Zait, A., & Hertzman, C. (2012). Promoting children's prosocial behaviors in school: Impact of the 'Roots of Empathy' program on the social and emotional competence of school-aged children. *School Mental Health, 4*, 1–21.

Schoppe-Sullivan, S., Diener, M., Mangelsdorf, S., Brown, G., McHale, J., & Frosch, C. (2006, July). Attachment and sensitivity in family context: The roles of parent and infant gender. *Infant and Child Development, 15*, 367–385.

Schoppe-Sullivan, S., Mangelsdorf, S., Brown, G., & Sokolowski, M. (2007, February). Goodness-of-fit in family context: Infant temperament, marital quality, and early coparenting behavior. *Infant Behavior & Development, 30*, 82–96.

Schore, A. (2003). *Affect regulation and the repair of the self*. New York: Norton.

Schuetze, P., Eiden, R., & Coles, C. (2007). Prenatal cocaine and other substance exposure: Effects on infant autonomic regulation at 7 months of age. *Developmental Psychobiology, 49*, 276–289.

Schulz, K., Rudolph, A., Tscharaktschiew, N., & Rudolph, U. (2013). Daniel has fallen into a muddy puddle—Schadenfreude or sympathy? *British Journal of Developmental Psychology, 31*, 363–378.

Schultz, A. H. (1969). *The life of primates*. New York: Universe.

Schumer, F. (2009, September 29). After a death, the pain that doesn't go away. *New York Times*, p. D1.

Schutt, R. K. (2001). *Investigating the social world: The process and practice of research*. Thousand Oaks, CA: Sage Publications.

Schvey, N. A., Eddy, K. T., & Tanofsky-Kraff, M. (2016). Diagnosis of feeding and eating disorders in children and adolescents. In B. T. Walsh, E. Attia, D. R. Glasofer, R. Sysko (Eds.), *Handbook of assessment and treatment of eating disorders*. Arlington, VA: American Psychiatric Publishing, Inc.

Schwartz, C. E., & Rauch, S. L. (2004). Temperament and its implications for neuroimaging of anxiety disorders. *CNS Spectrums, 9*, 284–291.

Schwartz, I. M. (1999). Sexual activity prior to coital interaction: A comparison between males and females. *Archives of Sexual Behavior, 28*, 63–69.

Schwarz, A. (2012, June 12). Risky Rise of the Good-Grade Pill. *New York Times*. Acessed May 2, 2018 from https://www.nytimes.com/2012/06/10/education/seeking-academic-edge-teenagers-abuse-stimulants.html

Schwarz, J. M., & Bilbo, S. D. (2014). Microglia and neurodevelopment: Programming of cognition throughout the lifespan. In A. W. Kusnecov, & H. Anisman (Eds.), *The Wiley-Blackwell handbook of psychoneuroimmunology*. New York: Wiley-Blackwell.

Schwartz, P., Maynard, A., & Uzelac, S. (2008). Adolescent egocentrism: A contemporary view. *Adolescence, 43*, 441–448.

Schwarz, T. F., Huang, L., Medina, D., Valencia, A., Lin, T., Behre, U., & Descamps, D. (2012). Four-year follow-up of the immunogenicity and safety of the HPV-16/18 AS04-adjuvanted vaccine when administered to adolescent girls aged 10–14 years. *Journal of Adolescent Health, 50*, 187–194.

Schwenkhagen, A. (2007). Hormonal changes in menopause and implications on sexual health. *Journal of Sexual Medicine, 4*, Supplement, 220–226.

Sciaraffa, M. A., Zeanah, P. D., & Zeanah, C. H. (2017). Understanding and promoting resilience in the context of adverse childhood experiences. *Early Childhood Education Journal*. Accessed online, 11-13-17; https://link.springer.com/article/10.1007/s10643-017-0869-3.

Scott, J. C., & Henderson, A. E. (2013). Language matters: Thirteen-month-olds understand that the language a speaker uses constrains conventionality. *Developmental Psychology, 49*, 2102–2111.

Scott, K. M., McLaughlin, K. A., Smith, D. A., & Ellis, P. M. (2012). Childhood maltreatment and DSM-IV adult mental disorders: Comparison of prospective and retrospective findings. *British Journal of Psychiatry, 104*, 188–199.

Scott, R. M., & Baillargeon, R. (2013). Do infants really expect others to act efficiently? A critical test of the rationality principle. *Psychological Science, 24*, 466–474.

Scrimsher, S., & Tudge, J. (2003). The teaching/learning relationship in the first years of school: Some revolutionary implications of Vygotsky's theory. *Early Education and Development, 14* [Special issue], 293–312.

Seaton, S. E., King, S., Manktelow, B. N., Draper, E. S., & Field, D. J. (2012). Babies born at the threshold of viability: Changes in survival and workload over 20 years. *Archives of Disable Children and Neonatal Education, 9*, 22–35.

Sedgh, G., Singh, S., Shah, I. H., Ahman, E., Henshaw, S. K., & Kankole, A. (2012). Induced abortion: Incidence and trends worldwide from 1995 to 2008. *Lancet, 379*, 625–632.

Sedikides, C., Gaertner, L., & Toguchi, Y. (2003). Pancultural self-enhancement. *Journal of Personality and Social Psychology, 84*, 60–79.

Seedat, S. (2014). Controversies in the use of antidepressants in children and adolescents: A decade since the storm and where do we stand now? *Journal of Child and Adolescent Mental Health, 26*, iii–v.

SEER. (2014), *Cancer Statistics Review, 1975–2011*, National Cancer Institute. Bethesda, MD. Accessed online, http://seer.cancer.gov/csr/1975_2011/, based on November 2013 SEER data submission, posted to the SEER website, April 2014.

Segal, J., & Segal, Z. (1992, September). No more couch potatoes. *Parents*, p. 235.

Segal, N. L. (2000). Virtual twins: New findings on withinfamily environmental influences on intelligence. *Journal of Educational Psychology, 92*, 188–194.

Segal, N. L., Cortez, F. A., Zettel-Watson, L., Cherry, B. J., Mechanic, M., Munson, J. E., & … Reed, B. (2015). Genetic and experiential influences on behavior: Twins reunited at seventy-eight years. *Personality and Individual Differences, 73*, 110–117.

Segall, M. H., Dasen, P. R., Berry, J. W., & Poortinga, Y. H. (1990). *Human behavior in global perspective*. Boston: Allyn & Bacon.

Segalowitz, S. J., & Rapin, I. (Eds.). (2003). *Child neuropsychology, Part I*. Amsterdam, Netherlands: Elsevier Science.

Seibert, A., & Kerns, K. (2009). Attachment figures in middle childhood. *International Journal of Behavioral Development, 33*, 347–355.

Seidman, S. (2003). The aging male: Androgens, erectile dysfunction, and depression. *Journal of Clinical Psychiatry, 64*, 31–37.

Selfhout, M., Denissen, J., Branje, S., & Meeus, W. (2009). In the eye of the beholder: Perceived, actual, and peer-rated similarity in personality, communication, and friendship intensity during the acquaintanceship process. *Journal of Personality and Social Psychology, 96*, 1152–1165.

Seligman, M. E. P. (2007). Coaching and positive psychology. *Australian Psychologist, 42*, 266–267.

Sella, F., Berteletti, I., Lucangeli, D., & Zorzi, M. (2017). Preschool children use space, rather than counting, to infer the numerical magnitude of digits: Evidence for a spatial mapping principle. *Cognition, 158*, 56–67.

Semerci, Ç. (2006). The opinions of medicine faculty students regarding cheating in relation to Kohlberg's moral development concept. *Social Behavior and Personality, 34*, 41–50.

Sengoelge, M., Hasselberg, M., Ormandy, D., & Laflamme, L. (2014). Housing, income inequality and child injury mortality in Europe: A cross-sectional study. *Child: Care, Health and Development, 40*(2), 283–291.

Senín-Calderón, C., Rodríguez-Testal, J. F., Perona-Garcelán, S., & Perpiñá, C. (2017). Body image and adolescence: A behavioral impairment model. *Psychiatry Research, 248*, 121–126.

Senju, A., Southgate, V., Snape, C., Leonard, M., & Csibra, G. (2011). Do 18 month olds really attribute mental states to others? A critical test. *Science, 331*, 477–480.

Senna, I., Addabbo, M., Bolognini, N., Longhi, E., Macchi Cassia, V., & Turati, C. (2017). Infants' visual recognition of pincer grip emerges between 9 and 12 months of age. *Infancy, 22*, 389–402.

Sepehri, A., & Guliani, H. (2017). Regional gradients in institutional cesarean delivery rates: Evidence from five countries in Asia. *Birth: Issues in Perinatal Care, 44*, 11–20.

Sephton, S. E., Dhabhar, F. S., Keuroghlian, A. S., Giese-Davis, J., McEwen, B. S., Ionan, A. C., & Spiegel, D. (2009). Depression, cortisol, and suppressed cell-mediated immunity in metastatic breast cancer. *Brain Behavioral Immunology, 23*, 1148–1155.

Serbin, L., Poulin-Dubois, D., & Colburne, K. (2001). Gender stereotyping in infancy: Visual preferences for and knowledge of gender-stereotyped toys in the second year. *International Journal of Behavioral Development, 25*, 7–15.

Serrat, R., Villar, F., Pratt, M. W., & Stukas, A. A. (2017). On the quality of adjustment to retirement: The longitudinal role of personality traits and generativity. *Journal of Personality*. Accessed online, 12-12-17; https://www.ncbi.nlm.nih.gov/pubmed/28509366.

Serretti, A., Calati, R., Ferrari, B., & De Ronchi, D. (2007). Personality and genetics. *Current Psychiatry Reviews, 3*, 147–159.

Servin, A., Nordenström, A., Larsson, A., & Bohlin, G. (2003). Prenatal adrogens and gender-typed behavior: A study of girls with mild and severe forms of congenital adrenal hyperplasia. *Developmental Psychology, 39*, 440–450.

Setoh, P., Lee, K. J., Zhang, L., Qian, M. K., Quinn, P. C., Heyman, G. D., & Lee, K. (2017). Racial categorization predicts implicit racial bias in preschool children. *Child Development*. Accessed online, 11-13-17; https://www.ncbi.nlm.nih.gov/pubmed/28605007.

Settersten, R. (2002). Social sources of meaning in later life. In R. Weiss & S. Bass (Eds.), *Challenges of the third age: Meaning and purpose in later life*. London: Oxford University Press.

Seyfarth, R. M., & Cheney, D. L. (2013). The evolution of concepts about agents. In M. R. Banaji, S. A. Gelman (Eds.), *Navigating the social world: What infants, children, and other species can teach us*. New York: Oxford University Press.

Seymour, J., Payne, S., Chapman, A., & Holloway, M. (2007). Hospice or home? Expectations of end-of-life care among white and Chinese older people in the UK. *Sociology of Health & Illness, 29*, 872–890.

Shafto, C. L., Conway, C. M., Field, S. L., & Houston, D. M. (2012). Visual sequence learning in infancy: Domain-general and domain-specific associations with language. *Infancy, 17*, 247–271.

Shah, R., Chauhan, N., Gupta, A. K., & Sen, M. S. (2016). Adolescent-parent conflict in the age of social media: Case reports from India. *Asian Journal of Psychiatry, 23*, 24–26.

Shangguan, F., & Shi, J. (2009). Puberty timing and fluid intelligence: A study of correlations between testosterone and intelligence in 8- to 12-year-old Chinese boys. *Psychoneuroendocrinology, 34*, 983–988.

Shapiro, A. F., Gottman, J. M., & Carrère, S. (2000). The baby and the marriage: Identifying factors that buffer against decline in marital satisfaction after the first baby arrives. *Journal of Family Psychology, 14*, 124–130.

Shapiro, L., & Solity, J. (2008). Delivering phonological and phonics training within whole-class teaching. *British Journal of Educational Psychology, 78*, 597–620.

Shapiro, L. R., & Solity, J. (2016). Differing effects of two synthetic phonics programmes on early reading development. *British Journal of Educational Psychology, 86*, 182–203.

Sharf, R. S. (1992). *Applying career development theory to counseling*. Pacific Grove, CA: Brooks/Cole.

Sharkins, K. A., Leger, S. E., & Ernest, J. M. (2016). Examining effects of poverty, maternal depression, and children's self-regulation abilities on the development of language and cognition in early childhood: An early head start perspective. *Early Childhood Education Journal*. Accessed online, 3-12-17; http://link.springer.com/article/10.1007/s10643-016-0787-9.

Sharma, M. (2008). Twenty-first century pink or blue: How sex selection technology facilitates gendercide and what we can do about it. *Family Court Review, 46*, 198–215.

Shatz, M. (1994). *A toddler's life: Becoming a person*. New York, NY, US: Oxford University Press.

Shaughnessy, E., Suldo, S., Hardesty, R., & Shaffer, E. (2006, December). School functioning and psychological well-being of international baccalaureate and general education students: A preliminary examination. *Journal of Secondary Gifted Education, 17*, 76–89.

Shavelson, R., Hubner, J. J., & Stanton, J. C. (1976). Self-concept: Validation of construct interpretations. *Review of Educational Research, 46*, 407–441.

Shaver, P. R., Hazan, C., & Bradshaw, D. (1988). Love as attachment: The integration of three behavioral systems. In R. J. Sternberg & M. L. Barnes (Eds.), *The psychology of love* (pp. 68–99). New Haven, CT: Yale University Press.

Shaver, P. R., Mikulincer, M., Sahdra, B. K., & Gross, J. T. (2017). Attachment security as a foundation for kindness toward self and others. In K. W. Brown, M. R. Leary (Eds.), *The Oxford handbook of hypo-egoic phenomena*. New York: Oxford University Press.

Shaw, M. L. (2003). Creativity and whole language. In J. Houtz (Ed.), *The educational psychology of creativity*. Cresskill, NJ: Hampton Press.

Shaw, P., Eckstrand, K., Sharp, W., Blumenthal, J., Lerch, J. P., Greenstein, D., Classen, L., Evans, A., Giedd, J., & Rapoport, J. L. (2007). Attention-deficit/hyperactivity disorder is characterized by a delay in cortical maturation. *Proceedings of the National Academy of Sciences, 104*, 19649–19654.

Shaywitz, B. A., Shaywitz, S. E., Blachman, B. A., Pugh, K. R., Fulbright, R. K., Skudlarski, P., Mencl, W. E., Constable, R. T., Holahan, J. M., Marchione, K. E., Fletccher, J. M., Lyon, G. R., & Gore, J. C. (2004). Development of left occipitotemporal systems for skilled reading in children after a phonologically-based intervention. *Biological Psychiatry, 55*, 926–933.

Shea, J. (2006, September). Cross-cultural comparison of women's midlife symptom-reporting: A China study. *Culture, Medicine and Psychiatry, 30*, 331–362.

Shea, K. M., Wilcox, A. J., & Little, R. E. (1998). Postterm delivery: A challenge for epidemiologic research. *Epidemiology, 9*, 199–204.

Sheese, B., Voelker, P., Posner, M., & Rothbart, M. (2009). Genetic variation influences on the early development of reactive emotions and their regulation by attention. *Cognitive Neuropsychiatry, 14*, 332–355.

Shelby, R., Crespin, T., Wells-Di Gregorio, S., Lamdan, R., Siegel, J., & Taylor, K. (2008). Optimism, social support, and adjustment in African American women with breast cancer. *Journal of Behavioral Medicine, 31*, 433–444.

Sheldon, K. M., Joiner, T. E., Jr., & Pettit, J. W. (2003). Reconciling humanistic ideals and scientific clinical practice. *Clinical Psychology, 10*, 302–315.

Sheldon, S., & Wilkinson, S. (2004). Should selecting saviour siblings be banned? *Journal of Medical Ethics, 30*, 533–537.

Shellenbarger, S. (2003, January 9). Yes, that weird day-care center could scar your child, researchers say. *Wall Street Journal*, p. D1.

Shelton, A. L., Cornish, K., Clough, M., Gajamange, S., Kolbe, S., & Fielding, J. (2017). Disassociation between brain activation and executive function in Fragile X premutation females. *Human Brain Mapping, 38*, 1056–1067.

Shen, Y., Hu, H., Taylor, B., Kan, H., & Xu, X. (2016). Early menarche and gestational diabetes mellitus at first live birth. *Maternal and Child Health Journal, 21*, 593–598.

Shenhav, S., Campos, B., & Goldberg, W. A. (2017). Dating out is intercultural: Experience and perceived parent disapproval by ethnicity and immigrant generation. *Journal of Social and Personal Relationships, 34*, 397–422.

Sheridan, C., & Radmacher, S. (2003). Significance of psychosocial factors to health and disease. In L. Schein & H. Bernard (Eds.), *Psychosocial treatment for medical conditions: Principles and techniques*. New York: Brunner-Routledge.

Sheridan, T. (2013, April 11). 10 facts funeral directors won't tell you. Fox Business. Accessed online; http://www.foxbusiness.com/personal-finance/2013/04/11/10-facts-funeral-directors-may-not-tell/.

Shernoff, D., & Schmidt, J. (2008). Further evidence of an engagement-achievement paradox among U.S. high school students. *Journal of Youth and Adolescence, 37*, 564–580.

Sherry, A., Tomlinson, J. M., Loe, M., Johnston, K., & Feeney, B. C. (2017). Apprehensive about retirement: Women, life transitions, and relationships. *Journal of Women & Aging, 29*, 173–184.

Sheskin, M., Bloom, P., & Wynn, K. (2014). Anti-equality: Social comparison in young children. *Cognition, 130*, 152–156.

Shi, L. (2003). Facilitating constructive parent–child play: Family therapy with young children. *Journal of Family Psychotherapy, 14*, 19–31.

Shi, X., & Lu, X. (2007). Bilingual and bicultural development of Chinese American adolescents and young adults: A comparative study. *Howard Journal of Communications, 18*, 313–333.

Shimizu, M., & Pelham, B. (2004). The unconscious cost of good fortune: Implicit and explicit self-esteem, positive life events, and health. *Health Psychology, 23*, 101–105.

Shneidman, E. (2007). Criteria for a good death. *Suicide and life-threatening behavior, 37*, 245–247.

Shiner, R., Masten, A., & Roberts, J. (2003). Childhood personality foreshadows adult personality and life outcomes two decades later. *Journal of Personality, 71*, 1145–1170.

Shoemark, H. (2014). The fundamental interaction of singing. *Nordic Journal of Music Therapy, 23*, 2–4.

Shor, R. (2006, May). Physical punishment as perceived by parents in Russia: Implications for professionals involved in the care of children. *Early Child Development and Care, 176*, 429–439.

Shutts, K 2015, Young children's preferences: Gender, race, and social status. *Child Development Perspectives, 9*, 262–266.

Shweder, R. A. (2003). *Why do men barbecue? Recipes for cultural psychology*. Cambridge, MA: Harvard University Press.

Shweder, R. A. (Ed.). (1998). *Welcome to middle age! (And other cultural fictions)*. New York: University of Chicago Press.

Sieber, J. E. (2000). Planning research: Basic ethical decision-making. In B. D. Sales & S. Folkman (Eds.), *Ethics in research with human participants*. Washington, DC: American Psychological Association.

Siegal, M. (1997). *Knowing children: Experiments in conversation and cognition* (2nd ed.). Hove, England: Psychology Press/Lawrence Erlbaum (UK), Taylor & Francis.

Siegel, S., Dittrich, R., & Vollmann, J. (2008). Ethical opinions and personal attitudes of young adults conceived by in vitro fertilisation. *Journal of Medical Ethics, 34*, 236–240.

Siegler, R. S. (1994). Cognitive variability: A key to understanding cognitive development. *Current Directions in Psychological Science, 3*, 1–5.

Siegler, R. S. (1998). *Children's thinking* (3rd ed.). Upper Saddle River, NJ: Prentice Hall.

Siegler, R. S. (2012). From theory to application and back: Following in the giant footsteps of David Klahr. In J. Shrager & S. Carver (Eds.), *The journey from child to scientist: Integrating cognitive development and the education sciences*. Washington, DC: American Psychological Association.

Siegler, R. S. (2016). Continuity and change in the field of cognitive development and in the perspectives of one cognitive developmentalist. *Child Development Perspectives, 10*, 128–133.

Siegler, R. S., & Ellis, S. (1996). Piaget on childhood. *Psychological Science, 7*, 211–215.

Siegler, R. S., & Lortie-Forgues, H. (2014). An integrative theory of numerical development. *Child Development Perspectives, 8*, 144–150.

Siegler, R. S., & Richards, D. (1982). The development of intelligence. In R. Sternberg (Ed.), *Handbook of human intelligence*. London: Cambridge University Press.

Sierra, F. (2006, June). Is (your cellular response to) stress killing you? *Journals of Gerontology: Series A: Biological Sciences and Medical Sciences, 61*, 557–561.

Signorella, M., & Frieze, I. (2008). Interrelations of gender schemas in children and adolescents: Attitudes, preferences, and self-perceptions. *Social Behavior and Personality, 36*, 941–954.

Silton, N. R., & Ferris, A. (2017). I want to know what love is: The ingredients of liking, attraction, dating, and successful marital relationships. In N. R. Silton (Ed.), *Family dynamics and romantic relationships in a changing society*. Hershey, PA: Information Science Reference/IGI Global.

Silventoinen, K., Iacono, W. G., Krueger, R., & McGue, M. (2012). Genetic and environmental contributions to the association between anthropometric measures and IQ: A study of Minnesota twins at age 11 and 17. *Behavior Genetics, 42*, 393–401.

Silverthorn, P., & Frick, P. J. (1999). Developmental pathways to antisocial behavior: The delayed-onset pathway in girls. *Developmental & Psychopathology, 11*, 101–126.

Sim, Z. L., & Xu, F. (2017). Infants preferentially approach and explore the unexpected. *British Journal of Developmental Psychology, 35*, 596–608.

Simcock, G., & Hayne, H. (2002). Breaking the barrier? Children fail to translate their preverbal memories into language. *Psychological Science, 13*, 225–231.

Simkin, P. (2014). Preventing primary cesareans: Implications for laboring women, their partners, nurses, educators, and doulas. *Birth: Issues in Perinatal Care, 41*, 220–222.

Simmons, S. W., Cyna, A. M., Dennis, A. T., & Hughes, D. (2007). Combined spinal-epidural versus epidural analgesia in labour. *Cochrane Database and Systematic Review, 18*, CD003401.

Simon, R. W. (2008). The joys of parenthood, reconsidered. *Contexts, 7*, 40–45.

Simon, R. W. (2014). Twenty years of the sociology of mental health: The continued significance of gender and marital status for emotional well-being. In R.J. Johnson, R. J. Turner, and B. G. Link (Eds.), *Sociology of mental health: Selected topics from forty years, 1970s–2010s*. New York: Springer.

Simonton, D. K. (1997). Creative productivity: A predictive and explanatory model of career trajectories and landmarks. *Psychological Review, 104*, 66–89.

Simonton, D. K. (2009). Varieties of (scientific) creativity: A hierarchical model of domain-specific disposition, development, and achievement. *Perspectives on Psychological Science, 4*, 441–452.

Simonton, D. K. (2017). Creative productivity across the life span. In J. A. Plucker (Ed.), *Creativity and innovation: Theory, research, and practice*. Waco, TX: Prufrock Press.

Simpson, E. (2017, March 3). America's 1st test-tube baby, a Norfolk native, set to meet world's 1st test-tube baby. *Virginian-Pilot*.

Simpson, J. A. (1990). Influence of attachment styles on romantic relationships. *Journal of Personality & Social Psychology, 59*, 971–980.

Simpson, J., Collins, W., Tran, S., & Haydon, K. (2007, February). Attachment and the experience and expression of emotions in romantic relationships: A developmental perspective. *Journal of Personality and Social Psychology, 92*, 355–367.

Simson, S., Thompson, E., & Wilson, L. B. (2001). Who is teaching lifelong learners? A study of peer educators in Institutes for Learning in Retirement. *Gerontology & Geriatrics Education, 22*, 31–43.

Simson, S. P., Wilson, L. B., & Harlow-Rosentraub, K. (2006). Civic engagement and lifelong learning institutes: Current status and future directions. In L. Wilson & S. P. Simson (Eds.), *Civic engagement and the baby boomer generation: Research, policy, and practice perspectives*. New York: Haworth Press.

Sinclair, D. A., & Guarente, L. (2006). Unlocking the secrets of longevity genes. *Scientific American, 294*, 48–51, 54–57.

Singer, D. G., & Singer, J. L. (Eds.). (2000). *Handbook of children and the media*. Thousand Oaks, CA: Sage Publications.

Singh, K., & Srivastava, S. K. (2014). Loneliness and quality of life among elderly people. *Journal of Psychosocial Research, 9*, 11–18.

Singh, S., & Darroch, J. E. (2000). Adolescent pregnancy and childbearing: Levels and trends in developed countries. *Canadian Journal of Human Sexuality, 9*, 67–72.

Sinnott, J. D. (1998a). Career paths and creative lives: A theoretical perspective on late-life potential. In C. Adams-Price (Ed.), *Creativity and successful aging: Theoretical and empirical approaches*. New York: Springer.

Sinnott, J. D. (2009). Cognitive development as the dance of adaptive transformation: Neo-Piagetian perspectives on adult cognitive development. In C. M. Smith & N. DeFrates-Densch (Eds.), *Handbook of research on adult learning and development*. New York: Routledge/Taylor & Francis Group.

Sinnott, J., Tobin, E., Chrzanowska, E., & Hilton, S. (2017). The relationship between attachment style and postformal thought. *Journal of Adult Development*. Accessed online, 11-30-17; https://link.springer.com/article/10.1007/s10804-017-9262-0.

Skinner, B. F. (1957). *Verbal behavior*. New York: Appleton-Century-Crofts.

Skinner, B. F. (1975). The steep and thorny road to a science of behavior. *American Psychologist, 30*, 42–49.

Skinner, J. D., Ziegler, P., Pac, S., & Devaney, B. (2004). Meal and snack patterns of infants and toddlers. *Journal of the American Dietary Association, 104*, S65–S70.

Skinner, M. (2010). Metabolic disorders: Fathers' nutritional legacy. *Nature, 467*, 922–923.

Skledar, M., Nikolac, M., Dodig-Curkovic, K., Curkovic, M., Borovecki, F., & Pivac, N. (2012). Association between brain-derived neurotrophic factor Val66Met and obesity in children and adolescents. *Progress in Neuro-Psychopharmacology & Biological Psychiatry, 36*, 136–140.

Skoog, T., & Özdemir, S. B. (2016). Explaining why early-maturing girls are more exposed to sexual harassment in early adolescence. *Journal of Early Adolescence, 36*, 490–509.

Skowronski, J., Walker, W., & Betz, A. (2003). Ordering our world: An examination of time in autobiographical memory. *Memory, 11*, 247–260.

Skrzypek, K., Maciejewska-Sobczak, B., & Stadnicka-Dmitriew, Z. (2014). *Siblings: Envy and rivalry, coexistence and concern*. London: Karnac Books.

Slaughter, V., & Peterson, C. C. (2012). How conversational input shapes theory of mind development in infancy and early childhood. In M. Siegal, & L. Surian (Eds.), *Access to language and cognitive development*. New York: Oxford University Press.

Slavin, R. E. (2013). Cooperative learning and achievement: Theory and research. In W. M. Reynolds, G. E. Miller, & I. B. Weiner (Eds.), *Handbook of psychology, Vol. 7: Educational psychology* (2nd ed.). Hoboken, NJ: John Wiley & Sons Inc.

Sleath, B., Sayner, R., Vitko, M., Carpenter, D. M., Blalock, S. J., Muir, K. W., & … Robin, A. L. (2017). Glaucoma patient-provider communication about vision quality of life. *Patient Education and Counseling, 100*, 703–709.

Sliwinski, M., Buschke, H., Kuslansky, G., & Senior, G. (1994). Proportional slowing and addition speed in old and young adults. *Psychology and Aging, 9*, 72–80.

Sloane, S., Baillargeon, R., & Premack, D. (2012). Do infants have a sense of fairness? *Psychological Science, 23*, 196–207.

Slugocki, C., & Trainor, L. J. (2014). Cortical indices of sound localization mature monotonically in early infancy. *European Journal of Neuroscience, 40*, 3608–3619.

Slusser, E., Ditta, A., & Sarnecka, B. (2013). Connecting numbers to discrete quantification: A step in the child's construction of integer concepts. *Cognition, 129*, 31–41.

Smedley, A., & Smedley, B. D. (2005). Race as biology is fiction, racism as a social problem is real: Anthropological and historical perspectives on the social construction of race. *American Psychologist, 60*, 16–26.

Smedley, B. D., & Syme, S. L. (Eds.). (2000). *Promoting health: Intervention strategies from social and behavioral research*. Washington, DC: National Academy of Sciences.

Smetana, J. G. (1995). Parenting styles and conceptions of parental authority during adolescence. *Child Development, 66*, 299–316.

Smetana, J. G. (2005). Adolescent–parent conflict: Resistance and subversion as developmental process. In L. Nucci (Ed.), *Conflict, contradiction, and contrarian elements in moral development and education*. Mahwah, NJ: Lawrence Erlbaum.

Smetana, J. G. (2006). Social-cognitive domain theory: Consistencies and variations in children's moral and social judgments. In M. Killen, & J. G. Smetana (Eds.), *Handbook of moral development*. Mahwah, NJ: Lawrence Erlbaum Associates.

Smetana, J., Daddis, C., & Chuang, S. (2003). "Clean your room!" A longitudinal investigation of adolescent–parent conflict and conflict resolution in middle-class African American families. *Journal of Adolescent Research, 18*, 631–650.

Smiley, P. A., Tan, S. J., Goldstein, A., & Sweda, J. (2016). Mother emotion, child temperament, and young children's helpless responses to failure. *Social Development, 25*, 285–303.

Smith, C., & Hung, L. (2012). The influence of Eastern philosophy on elder care by Chinese Americans: Attitudes toward long-term care. *Journal of Transcultural Nursing, 23*, 100–105.

Smith, C. G., & Weiss, A. (2017). Evolutionary aspects of personality development: Evidence from nonhuman animals. In J. Specht (Ed.), *Personality development across the lifespan*. San Diego, CA: Elsevier Academic Press.

Smith, B. L. (2012) The Case Against Spanking. *American Psychological Association, 43*(4). Accessed May 2, 2018 from http://www.apa.org/monitor/2012/04/spanking.aspx

Smith, N. A., & Trainor, L. J. (2008). Infant-directed speech is modulated by infant feedback. *Infancy, 13*, 410–420.

Smith, P. K., & Drew, L. M. (2002). Grandparenthood. In M. Bornstein (Ed.), *Handbook of parenting*. Mahwah, NJ: Lawrence Erlbaum.

Smith, R. J., Bale, J. F., Jr., & White, K. R. (2005, March 2). Sensorineural hearing loss in children. *Lancet, 365*, 879–890.

Smith, S., Quandt, S., Arcury, T., Wetmore, L., Bell, R., & Vitolins, M. (2006, January). Aging and eating in the rural, southern United States: Beliefs about salt and its effect on health. *Social Science & Medicine, 62*, 189–198.

Smith-Nielsen, J., Tharner, A., Krogh, M. T., & Væver, M. S. (2016). Effects of maternal postpartum depression in a well-resourced sample: Early concurrent and long-term effects on infant cognitive, language, and motor development. *Scandinavian Journal of Psychology, 57*, 571–583.

Smith-Nielsen, J., Tharner, A., Steele, H., Cordes, K., Mehlhase, H., & Vaever, M. S. (2016). Postpartum depression and infant-mother attachment security at one year: The impact of co-morbid maternal personality disorders. *Infant Behavior & Development, 44*, 148–158.

Smutny, J. F., Walker, S. Y., & Macksroth, E. A. (2007). *Acceleration for gifted learners, k-5*. Thousand Oaks, CA: Corwin Press.

Smuts, A. B., & Hagen, J. W. (1985). History of the family and of child development: Introduction to Part 1. *Monographs of the Society for Research in Child Development, 50* (4–5, Serial No. 211).

Snarey, J. R. (1995). In a communitarian voice: The sociological expansion of Kohlbergian theory, research, and practice. In W. M. Kurtines & J. L. Gerwirtz (Eds.), *Moral development: An introduction*. Boston: Allyn & Bacon.

Sneed, J. R., Whitbourne, S. K., Schwartz, S. J., & Huang, S. (2012). The relationship between identity, intimacy, and midlife well-being: Findings from the Rochester Adult Longitudinal Study. *Psychology and Aging, 27*, 318–323.

Snowdon, C. T., & Burghardt, G. M. (2017). Studying animal behavior: Integration of field and laboratory approaches. In J. Call, G. M. Burghardt, I. M. Pepperberg, C. T. Snowdon, T. Zentall, J. Call, T. Zentall (Eds.), *APA handbook of comparative psychology: Basic concepts, methods, neural substrate, and behavior*. Washington, DC: American Psychological Association.

Society for Personality and Social Psychology. (2017). *A reflection on the legacy of Ravenna M. Helson's work*. Accessed online, 11-22-17; http://www.spsp.org/news-center/announcements/2017-convention-legacy-ravenna-m-helson.

Soderstrom, M. (2007). Beyond babytalk: Re-evaluating the nature and content of speech input to preverbal infants. *Developmental Review, 27*, 501–532.

Soderstrom, M., Blossom, M., Foygel, R., & Morgan, J. (2008). Acoustical cues and grammatical units in speech to two preverbal infants. *Journal of Child Language, 35*, 869–902.

Soderstrom, M., Reimchen, M., Sauter, D., & Morgan, J. L. (2017). Do infants discriminate non-linguistic vocal expressions of positive emotions? *Cognition and Emotion, 31*, 298–311.

Solomon, W., Richards, M., Huppert, F. A., Brayne, C., & Morgan, K. (1998). Divorce, current marital status and well-being in an elderly population. *International Journal of Law, Policy and the Family, 12*, 323–344.

Somerset, W., Newport, D., Ragan, K., & Stowe, Z. (2006). Depressive disorders in women: From menarche to beyond the menopause. In L. M. Keyes & S. H. Goodman (Eds.), *Women and depression: A handbook for the social, behavioral, and biomedical sciences*. New York: Cambridge University Press.

Sonne, J. L. (2012). Psychological assessment measures. In *PsycEssentials: A pocket resource for mental health practitioners*. Washington, DC: American Psychological Association.

Sonnen, J., Larson, E., Gray, S., Wilson, A., Kohama, S., Crane, P., et al. (2009). Free radical damage to cerebral cortex in Alzheimer's disease, microvascular brain injury, and smoking. *Annals of Neurology, 65*, 226–229.

Sonnentag, S. (2012). Psychological detachment from work during leisure time: The benefits of mentally disengaging from work. *Current Directions in Psychological Science, 21*, 114–118.

Sontag, S. (1979). The double standard of aging. In J. H. Williams (Ed.), *Psychology of women: Selected readings*. New York: Norton.

Sorkhabi, N., & Middaugh, E. (2014). How variations in parents' use of confrontive and coercive control relate to variations in parent–adolescent conflict, adolescent disclosure, and parental knowledge: Adolescents' perspective. *Journal of Child and Family Studies, 23*, 1227–1241.

Sosinsky, L., & Kim, S. (2013). A profile approach to child care quality, quantity, and type of setting: Parent selection of infant child care arrangements. *Applied Developmental Science, 17*, 39–56.

Sousa, D. L. (2005). *How the brain learns to read*. Thousand Oaks, CA: Corwin Press.

Soussignan, R., Schaal, B., Marlier, L., & Jiang, T. (1997). Facial and autonomic responses to biological and artificial olfactory stimuli in human neonates: Re-examining early hedonic discrimination of odors. *Physiology and Behavior, 62*, 745–758.

South, A. (2013). Perceptions of romantic relationships in adult children of divorce. *Journal of Divorce & Remarriage, 54*, 126–141.

South, S. C., Reichborn-Kjennerud, T., Eaton, N. R., & Krueger, R. F. (2015). Genetics of personality. In M. Mikulincer, P. R. Shaver, M. L. Cooper, & R. J. Larsen (Eds.), *APA handbook of personality and social psychology, Volume 4: Personality processes and individual differences*. Washington, DC: American Psychological Association.

Sowell, E. R., Peterson, B. S., Thompson, P. M., Welcome, S. E., Henkenius, A. L., & Toga, A. W. (2003). Mapping cortical change across the human life span. *Nature Neuroscience, 6*, 309–315.

Sowell, E. R., Thompson, P. M., Tessner, K. D., & Toga, A. W. (2001). Mapping continued brain growth and gray matter density reduction in dorsal frontal cortex: Inverse relationships during postadolescent brain maturation. *Journal of Neuroscience, 21*, 8819–8829.

Sparrow, J. (2016). Culture, community, and context in child development: Implications for family programs and policies. In D. Narvaez, J. M. Braungart-Rieker, L. E. Miller-Graff, L. T. Gettler, P. D. Hastings, D. Narvaez, … P. D. Hastings (Eds.), *Contexts for young child flourishing: Evolution, family, and society*. New York: Oxford University Press.

Spear, C. F., Strickland-Cohen, M. K., Romer, N., & Albin, R. W. (2013). An examination of social validity within single-case research with students with emotional and behavioral disorders. *Remedial and Special Education, 34*, 357–370.

Spear, P. D. (1993). Neural bases of visual deficits during aging. *Vision Research, 33*, 2589–2609.

Spearman, C. (1927). *The abilities of man*. London: Macmillan.

Spessato, B., Gabbard, C., Valentini, N., & Rudisill, M. (2013). Gender differences in Brazilian children's fundamental movement skill performance. *Early Child Development and Care, 183*, 916–923.

Spiegel, D. (2011). Mind matters in cancer survival. *Journal of the American Medical Association (JAMA), 305*, 502–503.

Spiegel, D., & Giese-Davis, J. (2003). Depression and cancer: Mechanisms and disease progression. *Biological Psychiatry, 54*, 269–282.

Spinazzola, J., Hodgdon, H., Liang, L., Ford, J. D., Layne, C. M., Pynoos, R., & … Kisiel, C. (2014). Unseen wounds: The contribution of psychological maltreatment to child and adolescent mental health and risk outcomes. *Psychological Trauma: Theory, Research, Practice, and Policy, 6*(Suppl. 1), S18–S28.

Spinelli, L. (2015, September 14.) Fighting for every child. *Northern Virginia*. Accessed online, 10-24-17; https://www.northernvirginiamag.com/family/family-features/2015/09/14/fighting-for-every-child/.

Spinrad, T. L., & Stifler, C. A. (2006). Toddlers' empathy-related responding to distress: Predictions from negative emotionality and maternal behavior in infancy. *Infancy, 10*, 97–121.

Spörer, N., Brunstein, J., & Kieschke, U. (2009). Improving students' reading comprehension skills: Effects of strategy instruction and reciprocal teaching. *Learning and Instruction, 19*, 272–286.

Spraggins, R. E. (2003). *Women and men in the United States: March 2002*. Washington, DC: U.S. Department of Commerce.

Sprecher, S., Brooks, J. E., & Avogo, W. (2013). Self-esteem among young adults: Differences and similarities based on gender, race, and cohort (1990–2012). *Sex Roles, 69*, 264–275.

Sprecher, S., Sullivan, Q., & Hatfield, E. (1994). Mate selection preferences: Gender differences examined in a national sample. *Journal of Personality and Social Psychology, 66*, 1074–1080.

Sprenger, M. (2007). *Memory 101 for educators*. Thousand Oaks, CA: Corwin Press.

Spring, L. (2015). Older women and sexuality—Are we still just talking lube? *Sexual and Relationship Therapy, 30*, 4–9.

Squeglia, L. M., Sorg, S. F. Schweinsburg, A., Dager, W., Reagan, R., & Tapert, S. F. (2012). Binge drinking differentially affects adolescent male and female brain morphometry. *Psychopharmacology, 220*, 529–539.

Squire, L. R., & Knowlton, B. J. (1995). Memory, hippocampus, and brain systems. In M. S. Gazzaniga, *Cognitive neurosciences*. Cambridge, MA: The MIT Press.

Star Tribune. (2016, August 27). Richard J. Thomas. *Star Tribune* (Minneapolis, MN). Accessed online, 12-12-17; http://www.startribune.com/obituaries/detail/153095/?fullname=richard-j-thomas.

Starr, A., Libertus, M. E., & Brannon, E. M. (2013). Number sense in infancy predicts mathematical abilities in childhood. *PNAS Proceedings of the National Academy of Sciences of the United States of America, 110*, 18116–18120.

Staudinger, U. (2008). A psychology of wisdom: History and recent developments. *Research in Human Development, 5*, 107–120.

Staudinger, U. M., & Baltes, P. B. (1996). Interactive minds: A facilitative setting for wisdom-related performance? *Journal of Personality and Social Psychology, 71*, 746–762.

Staudinger, U. M., & Leipold, B. (2003). The assessment of wisdom-related performance. In C. R. Snyder (Ed.), *Positive psychological assessment: A handbook of models and measures*. Washington, DC: American Psychological Association.

Staunton, H. (2005). Mammalian sleep. *Naturwissenschaften, 35*, 15.

Stearns, E., & Glennie, E. J. (2006). When and why dropouts leave high school. *Youth & Society, 38*, 29–57.

Stecker, M., Wolfe, J., & Stevenson, M. (2013). Neurophysiologic responses of peripheral nerve to repeated episodes of anoxia. *Clinical Neurophysiology, 124*, 792–800.

Stedman, L. C. (1997). International achievement differences: An assessment of a new perspective. *Educational Researcher, 26*, 4–15.

Steel, A., Adams, J., Sibbritt, D., Broom, A., Frawley, J., & Gallois, C. (2014). The influence of complementary and alternative medicine use in pregnancy on labor pain management choices: Results from a nationally representative sample of 1,835 women. *Journal of Alternative and Complementary Medicine, 20*, 87–97.

Steers, R. M., & Porter, L. W. (1991). *Motivation and work behavior* (5th ed.). New York: McGraw-Hill.

Stefanopoulou, E., & Grunfeld, E. A. (2017). Mind–body interventions for vasomotor symptoms in healthy menopausal women and breast cancer survivors: A systematic review. *Journal of Psychosomatic Obstetrics & Gynecology, 38*, 210–225.

Stein, D., Latzer, Y., & Merick, J. (2009). Eating disorders: From etiology to treatment. *International Journal of Child and Adolescent Health, 2*, 139–151.

Stein, J. H., & Reiser, L. W. (1994). A study of white middle-class adolescent boys' responses to "semenarche" (the first ejaculation). *Journal of Youth and Adolescence, 23*, 373–384.

Stein, Z., Susser, M., Saenger, G., & Marolla, F. (1975). *Famine and human development: The Dutch hunger winter of 1944–1945*. New York: Oxford University Press.

Steinberg, L. (2014). *Age of opportunity: Lessons from the new science of adolescence*. Boston, MA: Houghton Mifflin Harcourt.

Steinberg, L., Dornbusch, S., & Brown, B. B. (1992). Ethnic differences in adolescent achievement: An ecological perspective. *American Psychologist, 47*, 723–729.

Steinberg, L., & Silverberg, S. (1986). The vicissitudes of autonomy in early adolescence. *Child Development, 57*, 841–851.

Steinberg, L. D., & Scott, S. S. (2003). Less guilty by reason of adolescence: Developmental immaturity, diminished responsibility, and the juvenile death penalty. *American Psychologist, 58*, 1009–1018.

Steiner, A. M., & Fletcher, P. C. (2017). Sandwich generation caregiving: A complex and dynamic role. *Journal of Adult Development, 24*, 133–143.

Steiner, J. E. (1979). Human facial expressions in response to taste and smell stimulation. *Advances in Child Development and Behavior, 13*, 257.

Steiner, L. M., Durand, S., Groves, D., & Rozzell, C. (2015). Effect of infidelity, initiator status, and spiritual well-being on men's divorce adjustment. *Journal of Divorce & Remarriage, 56*, 95–108.

Stephany, C., Frantz, M. G., & McGee, A. W. (2016). Multiple roles for nogo receptor 1 in visual system plasticity. *Neuroscientist, 22*, 653–666.

Stepler, R. (2016, February 18). *Living arrangements of older Americans by gender*. Washington, DC: Pew Research Center, Social & Demographic Trends. Accessed online, 12-12-17; http://www.pewsocialtrends.org/2016/02/18/2-living-arrangements-of-older-americans-by-gender/.

Stepler, R. (2016, April 21). World's centenarian population projected to grow eightfold by 2015. *Factank*. Washington, DC: Pew Research Center. Accessed online, 12-11-17; http://www.pewresearch.org/fact-tank/2016/04/21/worlds-centenarian-population-projected-to-grow-eightfold-by-2050/.

Stepler, R. (2017, March 9). Led by baby boomers, divorce rates climb for America's 50+ population. *Facttank News in the Numbers*. Pew Research Center. Accessed online, 11-29-17; http://www.pewresearch.org/fact-tank/2017/03/09/led-by-baby-boomers-divorce-rates-climb-for-americas-50-population/.

Steri, A. O., & Spelke, E. S. (1988). Haptic perception of objects in infancy. *Cognitive Psychology, 20*, 1–23.

Sternberg, J. (2005). The triarchic theory of successful intelligence. In D. P. Flanagan & P. L. Harrison (Eds.), *Contemporary intellectual assessment: Theories, tests, and issues*. New York: Guilford Press.

Sternberg, R. (2003a). A broad view of intelligence: The theory of successful intelligence. *Consulting Psychology Journal: Practice & Research, 55*, 139–154.

Sternberg, R. (2003b). Our research program validating the triarchic theory of successful intelligence: Reply to Gottfredson. *Intelligence, 31*, 399–413.

Sternberg, R. J. (1985). *Beyond IQ: A triarchic theory of human intelligence*. New York: Cambridge University Press.

Sternberg, R. J. (1986). Triangular theory of love. *Psychological Review, 93*, 119–135

Sternberg, R. J. (1988). Triangulating love. In R. J. Sternberg & M. J. Barnes (Eds.), *The psychology of love*. New Haven, CT: Yale University Press.

Sternberg, R. J. (1990). *Metaphors of mind: Conceptions of the nature of intelligence*. Cambridge, England: Cambridge University Press.

Sternberg, R. J. (1991). Theory-based testing of intellectual abilities: Rationale for the Sternberg triarchic abilities test. In H. A. H. Rowe (Ed.), *Intelligence: Reconceptualization and measurement*. Hillsdale, NJ: Lawrence Erlbaum.

Sternberg, R. J. (2006). Intelligence. In K. Pawlik, & G. d'Ydewalle (Eds.), *Psychological concepts: An international historical perspective*. Hove, England: Psychology Press/Taylor & Francis.

Sternberg, R. J. (2008). Schools should nurture wisdom. In B. Z. Presseisen (Ed.), *Teaching for intelligence* (2nd ed.). Thousand Oaks, CA: Corwin Press, 2008.

Sternberg, R. J. (2015). Successful intelligence: A model for testing intelligence beyond IQ tests. *European Journal of Education and Psychology, 8*, 76–84.

Sternberg, R. J. (2016). A triangular theory of creativity. *Psychology of Aesthetics, Creativity, and the Arts*. Accessed online, 3-16-17; http://psycnet.apa.org/index.cfm?fa=buy.optionToBuy&id=2016-60691-001.

Sternberg, R. J., Conway, B. E., Ketron, J. L., & Bernstein, M. (1981). Peoples' conceptions of intelligence. *Journal of Personality and Social Psychology, 41*, 37–55.

Sternberg, R. J., & Grigorenko, E. L. (Eds.). (2002). *The general factor of intelligence: How general is it?* Mahwah, NJ: Lawrence Lawrence Erlbaum.

Sternberg, R. J., Kaufman, J. C., & Pretz, J. E. (2002). *The creativity conundrum: A propulsion model of creative contributions*. Philadelphia, PA: Psychology Press.

Sternberg, R. J., Wagner, R. K., Williams, W. M., & Horvath, J. A. (1997). Testing common sense. In D. Russ-Eft, H. Preskill, & C. Sleezer (Eds.), *Human resource development review: Research and implications* (pp. 102–132). Thousand Oaks, CA: Sage Publications.

Stevens, J., Cai, J., Evenson, K. R., & Thomas, R. (2002). Fitness and fatness as predictors of mortality from all causes and from cardiovascular disease in men and women in the lipid research clinics study. *American Journal of Epidemiology, 156*, 832–841.

Stevens, N., Martina, C., & Westerhof, G. (2006, August). Meeting the need to belong: Predicting effects of a friendship enrichment program for older women. *Gerontologist, 46*, 495–502.

Stevens, W., Hasher, L., Chiew, K., & Grady, C. (2008). A neural mechanism underlying memory failure in older adults. *Journal of Neuroscience, 28*, 12820–12824.

Stevenson, C. E., Heiser, W. J., & Resing, W. M. (2016). Dynamic testing: Assessing cognitive potential of children with culturally diverse backgrounds. *Learning and Individual Differences, 47*, 27–36.

Stevenson, H. W., Chen, C., & Lee, S. Y. (1992). A comparison of the parent–child relationship in Japan and the United States. In L. L. Roopnarine & D. B. Carter (Eds.), *Parent-child socialization in diverse cultures.* Norwood, NJ: Ablex.

Stevenson, H. W., Lee, S., & Mu, X. (2000). Successful achievement in mathematics: China and the United States. In C. F. M. van Lieshout & P. G. Heymans (Eds.), *Developing talent across the life span.* Philadelphia, PA: Psychology Press.

Stevenson, H. W., & Lee, S. Y. (1990). Contexts of achievement: A study of American, Chinese, and Japanese children. *Monographs of the Society for Research in Child Development, 55*, 1–123.

Stevenson, M., Henderson, T., & Baugh, E. (2007, February). Vital defenses: Social support appraisals of black grandmothers parenting grandchildren. *Journal of Family Issues, 28*, 182–211.

Stewart, A. J., Copeland, A. P., Chester, N. L., Mallery, J. E., & Barenbaum, N. B. (1997). *Separating together: How divorce transforms families.* New York: Guilford Press.

Stewart, A. J., & Vandewater, E. A. (1999). "If I had it to do over again…": Midlife review, midcourse corrections, and women's well-being in midlife. *Journal of Personality and Social Psychology, 76*, 270–283.

Stewart, M., Scherer, J., & Lehman, M. (2003). Perceived effects of high frequency hearing loss in a farming population. *Journal of the American Academy of Audiology, 14*, 100–108.

Stice, E. (2003). Puberty and body image. In C. Hayward (Ed.), *Gender differences at puberty.* New York: Cambridge University Press.

Stiles, J. (2012). The effects of injury to dynamic neural networks in the mature and developing brain. *Developmental Psychobiology, 54*, 343–349.

Stipp, S. (2012, January). A new path to longevity. *Scientific American*, pp. 33–39.

Stockdale, M. S., & Crosby, F. J. (2004). *Psychology and management of workplace diversity.* Malden, MA: Blackwell Publishers.

Stolberg, S. G. (1998, April 3). Rise in smoking by young blacks erodes a success story in health. *New York Times*, p. A1.

Stopa, L., Denton, R., Wingfield, M., & Taylor, K. (2013). The fear of others: A qualitative analysis of interpersonal threat in social phobia and paranoia. *Behavioural and Cognitive Psychotherapy, 41*, 188–209.

Storey, K., Slaby, R., Adler, M., Minotti, J., & Katz, R. (2008). *Eyes on bullying… What can you do?* Boston: Education Development Center.

Storfer, M. (1990). *Intelligence and giftedness: The contributions of heredity and early environment.* San Francisco: Jossey-Bass.

Story, M., Nanney, M., & Schwartz, M. (2009). Schools and obesity prevention: Creating school environments and policies to promote healthy eating and physical activity. *Milbank Quarterly, 87*, 71–100.

Strachan, E., Duncan, G., Horn, E., & Turkheimer, E. (2017). Neighborhood deprivation and depression in adult twins: Genetics and gene×environment interaction. *Psychological Medicine, 47*, 627–638.

Strasburger, V. (2009). Media and children: What needs to happen now? *JAMA: Journal of the American Medical Association, 301*, 2265–2266.

Strassberg, D. S., Cann, D., & Velarde, V. (2017). Sexting by high school students. *Archives of Sexual Behavior.* Accessed online 8-9-17; https://www.ncbi.nlm.nih.gov/pubmed/28050742.

Straus, M. A., & McCord, J. (1998). Do physically punished children become violent adults? In S. Nolen-Hoeksema (Ed.), *Clashing views on abnormal psychology: A Taking Sides custom reader* (pp. 130–155). Guilford, CT: Dushkin/McGraw-Hill.

Strauss, J. R. (2011). Contextual influences on women's health concerns and attitudes toward menopause. *Health & Social Work, 36*, 121–127.

Streissguth, A. (2007). Offspring effects of prenatal alcohol exposure from birth to 25 years: The Seattle Prospective Longitudinal Study. *Journal of Clinical Psychology in Medical Settings, 14*, 81–101.

Strelau, J. (1998). *Temperament: A psychological perspective.* New York: Plenum Publishers.

Striano, T., & Vaish, A. (2006, November). Seven- to 9-month-old infants use facial expressions to interpret others' actions. *British Journal of Developmental Psychology, 24*, 753–760.

Stright, A., Gallagher, K., & Kelley, K. (2008). Infant temperament moderates relations between maternal parenting in early childhood and children's adjustment in first grade. *Child Development, 79*(1), 186–200. Accessed online; http://search.ebscohost.com, doi:10.1111/j.1467-8624.2007.01119.x.

Strobel, A., Dreisbach, G., Müller, J., Goschke, T., Brocke, B., & Lesch, K. (2007, December). Genetic variation of serotonin function and cognitive control. *Journal of Cognitive Neuroscience, 19*, 1923–1931.

Stroebe, M., Schut, H., Boerner, K. (2017). Cautioning health-care professionals: Bereaved persons are misguided through the stages of grief. *Omega—Journal of Death and Dying, 74*, 455–473.

Strohl, M., Bednar, C., & Longley, C. (2012). Residents' perceptions of food and nutrition services at assisted living facilities. *Family and Consumer Sciences Research Journal, 40*, 241–254.

Stroope, S., McFarland, M. J., & Uecker, J. E. (2015). Marital characteristics and the sexual relationships of U.S. older adults: An analysis of national social life, health, and aging project data. *Archives of Sexual Behavior, 44*, 233–247.

Struempler, B. J., Parmer, S. M., Mastropietro, L. M., Arsiwalla, D., & Bubb, R. R. (2014). Changes in fruit and vegetable consumption of third-grade students in body quest: Food of the warrior, a 17-class childhood obesity prevention program. *Journal of Nutrition Education and Behavior, 46*, 286–292.

Stupica, B., Sherman, L. J., & Cassidy, J. (2011). Newborn irritability moderates the association between infant attachment security and toddler exploration and sociability. *Child Development, 82*(5), 1381–1389.

Stutzer, A., & Frey, B. (2006, April). Does marriage make people happy, or do happy people get married? *Journal of Socio-Economics, 35*, 326–347.

Suarez-Orozco, C., Suarez-Orozco, M., & Todorova, I. (2008). *Learning a new land: Immigrant students in American society.* Cambridge, MA: Belknap Press/Harvard University Press.

Subotnik, R. (2006). Longitudinal studies: Answering our most important questions of prediction and effectiveness. *Journal for the Education of the Gifted, 29*, 379–383.

Sudharsanan, N., Behrman, J. R., & Kohler, H. (2016). Limited common origins of multiple adult health-related behaviors: Evidence from U.S. twins. *Social Science & Medicine, 171*, 67–83.

Sudia-Robinson, T. (2011, March 14). Ethical implications of newborn screening, life-limiting conditions, and palliative care. *MCN, American Journal of Maternal Child Nursing.* Accessed 4-3-11; http://journals.lww.com/mcnjournal/Abstract/publishahead/Ethical_Implications_of_Newborn_Screening,.99982.aspx.

Sugarman, S. (1988). *Piaget's construction of the child's reality.* Cambridge, England: Cambridge University Press.

Suinn, R. M. (2001). The terrible twos—Anger and anxiety: Hazardous to your health. *American Psychologist, 56*, 27–36.

Suitor, J. J., Minyard, S. A., & Carter, R. S. (2001). "Did you see what I saw?" Gender differences in perceptions of avenues to prestige among adolescents. *Sociological Inquiry, 71*, 437–454.

Summers, J., Schallert, D., & Ritter, P. (2003). The role of social comparison in students' perceptions of ability: An enriched view of academic motivation in middle school students. *Contemporary Educational Psychology, 28*, 510–523.

Sumner, E., Connelly, V., & Barnett, A. L. (2014). The influence of spelling ability on handwriting production: Children with and without dyslexia. *Journal of Experimental Psychology: Learning, Memory, and Cognition, 40*, 1441–1447.

Sumner, R., Burrow, A. L., & Hill, P. L. (2015). Identity and purpose as predictors of subjective well-being in emerging adulthood. *Emerging Adulthood, 3*, 46–54.

Sun, A., Lam, C, & Wong, D. A. (2012). Expanded newborn screening for inborn errors of metabolism. *Advances in Pediatrics, 59*, 209–245.

Sun, B. H., Wu, C. W., & Kalunian, K. C. (2007). New developments in osteoarthritis. *Rheumatoid Disease Clinics of North America, 33*, 135–148.

Sun, Y., Liu, Y., Yan, S., Hu, J., Xu, G., Liu, J., & Tao, F. (2016). Longitudinal pattern of early maturation on morning cortisol and depressive symptoms: Sex-specific effects. *Psychoneuroendocrinology, 71*, 58–63.

Sun, Y., Mensah, F. K., Azzopardi, P., Patton, G. C., & Wake, M. (2017). Childhood social disadvantage and pubertal timing: A national birth cohort from Australia. *Pediatrics, 139*, 1–10.

Super, C. M. (1976). Environmental effects on motor development: A case of African infant precocity. *Developmental Medicine and Child Neurology, 18*, 561–576.

Super, C. M., & Harkness, S. (1982). The infant's niche in rural Kenya and metropolitan America. In L. Adler (Ed.), *Issues in cross-cultural research.* New York: Academic Press.

Supple, A., Ghazarian, S., Peterson, G., & Bush, K. (2009). Assessing the cross-cultural validity of a parental autonomy granting measure: Comparing adolescents in the United States, China, Mexico, and India. *Journal of Cross-Cultural Psychology, 40*, 816–833.

Sutherland, R., Pipe, M., & Schick, K. (2003). Knowing in advance: The impact of prior event information on memory and event knowledge. *Journal of Experimental Child Psychology, 84*, 244–263.

Sutipan, P., Intarakamhang, U., & Macaskill, A. (2017). The impact of positive psychological interventions on well-being in healthy elderly people. *Journal of Happiness Studies, 18*, 269–291.

Swaim, R., Barner, J., & Brown, C. (2008). The relationship of calcium intake and exercise to osteoporosis health beliefs in postmenopausal women. *Research in Social & Administrative Pharmacy, 4*, 153–163.

Swain, J. E., Lorberbaum, J. P., Kose, S., & Strathearn, L. (2007). Brain basis of early parent-*infant* interactions: Psychology, physiology, and in vivo functional neuroimaging studies. *Journal of Child Psychology and Psychiatry, 48*, 262–287.

Swanson, L. A., Leonard, L. B., & Gandour, J. (1992). Vowel duration in mothers' speech to young children. *Journal of Speech and Hearing Research, 35*, 617–625.

Swenson, P. F., & Ebell, M. H. (2016, May 1). Introducing a one-page adult preventative health care schedule: USPSTF recommendation at a glance. *American Family Physician, 93*, 738–740.

Swiatek, M. (2002). Social coping among gifted elementary school students. *Journal for the Education of the Gifted, 26*, 65–86.

Swift, H. J., Abrams, D., Lamont, R. A., & Drury, L. (2017). The risks of ageism model: How ageism and negative attitudes toward age can be a barrier to active aging. *Social Issues and Policy Review, 11*, 195–231.

Swingler, M. M., Sweet, M. A., & Carver, L. J. (2007). Relations between mother-child interaction and the neural correlates of face processing in 6-month-olds. *Infancy, 11*, 63–86.

Swingley, D. (2017). The infant's developmental path in phonological acquisition. *British Journal of Psychology, 108*, 28–30.

Swingley, D., & Humphrey, C. (2017). Quantitative linguistic predictors of infants' learning of specific English words. *Child Development*. Accessed online, 10-29-17; https://www.ncbi.nlm.nih.gov/pubmed/28146333.

Szaflarski, J. P., Rajagopal, A., Altaye, M., Byars, A. W., Jacola, L., Schmithorst, V. J., & Holland, S. K. (2012). Left-handedness and language lateralization in children. *Brain Research, 1433*, 85–97. Accessed online, 7-18-12; http://www.ncbi.nlm.nih.gov/pubmed/22177775.

Szczygieł, D., & Mikolajczak, M. (2017). Why are people high in emotional intelligence happier? They make the most of their positive emotions. *Personality and Individual Differences, 117*, 177–181.

Taddio, A., Shah, V., & Gilbert-MacLeod, C. (2002). Conditioning and hyperalgesia in newborns exposed to repeated heel lances. *JAMA: Journal of the American Medical Association, 288*, 857–861.

Tadic, I., Stevanovic, D., Tasic, L., & Stupar, N. (2012). Development of a shorter version of the osteoporosis knowledge assessment tool. *Women & Health, 52*(1), 18–31. doi:10.1080/03630242.2011.635246.

Tajfel, H., & Turner, J. C. (2004). The social identity theory of intergroup behavior. In J. T. Jost & J. Sidanius (Eds.). *Political psychology: Key readings*. New York: Psychology Press.

Takahashi, K. (1986). Examining the Strange Situation procedure with Japanese mothers and 12-month-old infants. *Developmental Psychology, 22*, 265–270.

Takala, M. (2006, November). The effects of reciprocal teaching on reading comprehension in mainstream and special (SLI) education. *Scandinavian Journal of Educational Research, 50*, 559–576.

Tamis-LeMonda, C. S., & Cabrera, N. (2002). *Handbook of father involvement: Multidisciplinary perspectives*. Mahwah, NJ: Lawrence Erlbaum.

Tamis-LeMonda, C. S., Song, L., Leavell, A., Kahana-Kalman, R., & Yoshikawa, H. (2012). Ethnic differences in mother–infant language and gestural communications are associated with specific skills in infants. *Developmental Science, 15*, 384–397.

Tamnes, C. K., Herting, M. M., Goddings, A., Meuwese, R., Blakemore, S., Dahl, R. E., & … Mills, K. L. (2017). Development of the cerebral cortex across adolescence: A multisample study of inter-related longitudinal changes in cortical volume, surface area, and thickness. *Journal of Neuroscience, 37*, 3402–3412.

Tandon, P. S., Zhou, C., Lozano, P., & Christakis, D. A. (2011). Preschoolers' total daily screen time at home and by type of child care. *The Journal of Pediatrics, 158*(2), 297-300. doi:10.1016/j.jpeds.2010.08.005

Tang, C., Curran, M., & Arroyo, A. (2014). Cohabitors' reasons for living together, satisfaction with sacrifices, and relationship quality. *Marriage & Family Review, 50*, 598–620.

Tang, C., Wu, M., Liu, J., Lin, H., & Hsu, C. (2006). Delayed parenthood and the risk of cesarean delivery—Is paternal age an independent risk factor? *Birth: Issues in Perinatal Care, 33*, 18–26.

Tang, Z., & Orwin, R. (2009). Marijuana initiation among American youth and its risks as dynamic processes: Prospective findings from a national longitudinal study. *Substance Use & Misuse, 44*, 195–211.

Tangri, S., Thomas, V., & Mednick, M. (2003). Predictors of satisfaction among college-educated African American women in midlife. *Journal of Adult Development, 10*, 113–125.

Tanner, E., & Finn-Stevenson, M. (2002). Nutrition and brain development: Social policy implications. *American Journal of Orthopsychiatry, 72*, 182–193.

Tanner, J. (1972). Sequence, tempo, and individual variation in growth and development of boys and girls aged twelve to sixteen. In J. Kagan & R. Coles (Eds.), *Twelve to sixteen: Early adolescence*. New York: Norton.

Tanner, J. M. (1978). *Education and physical growth* (2nd ed.). New York: International Universities Press.

Tappan, M. (2006, March). Moral functioning as mediated action. *Journal of Moral Education, 35*, 1–18.

Tardif, T. (1996). Nouns are not always learned before verbs: Evidence from Mandarin speakers' early vocabularies. *Developmental Psychology, 32*, 492–504.

Tardif, T., Fletcher, P., Liang, W., Zhang, Z., Kaciroti, N., & Marchman, V. A. (2008). Baby's first 10 words. *Developmental Psychology, 44*, 929–938.

Tardif, T., Gelman, S. A., Fu, X., & Zhu, L. (2012). Acquisition of generic noun phrases in Chinese: Learning about lions without an '-s.' *Journal of Child Language, 39*, 130–161.

Tardif, T., Wellman, H. M., & Cheung, K. M. (2004). False belief understanding in Cantonese-speaking children. *Journal of Child Language, 31*, 779–800.

Tattersall, M., Cordeaux, Y., Charnock-Jones, D., & Smith, G. S. (2012). Expression of gastrin-releasing peptide is increased by prolonged stretch of human myometrium, and antagonists of its receptor inhibit contractility. *Journal of Physiology, 590*, 2081–2093.

Tatum, B. (2007). *Can we talk about race? And other conversations in an era of school resegregation*. Boston: Beacon Press.

Taumoepeau, M., & Ruffman, T. (2008). Stepping stones to others' minds: Maternal talk relates to child mental state language and emotion understanding at 15, 24, and 33 months. *Child Development, 79*(2), 284-302. doi:10.1111/j.1467-8624.2007.01126.x

Tauriac, J., & Scruggs, N. (2006, January). Elder abuse among African Americans. *Educational Gerontology, 32*, 37–48.

Taveras, E. M., et al. (2009). Weight status in the first 6 months of life and obesity at 3 years of age. *Pediatrics, 4*, 201–114.

Tavernise, S. (2013, September 6). Rise is seen in students who use e-cigarettes. *New York Times*, p. A11.

Tavernise, S. (2014). Obesity rate for young children plummets 43% in a decade. *New York Times*, p 1.

Tavernise, S. (2016, May 9). Black Americans narrow the gap in life spans. *New York Times*, p. A1.

Taylor, D. M. (2002). *The quest for identity: From minority groups to Generation Xers*. Westport, CT: Praeger Publishers/Greenwood Publishing.

Taylor, G., Liu, H., & Herbert, J. S. (2016). The role of verbal labels on flexible memory retrieval at 12 months of age. *Infant Behavior & Development, 45(Part A)*, 11–17.

Taylor, H. G., Klein, N., Minich, N. M., & Hack, M. (2000). Middle-school-age outcomes in children with very low birthweight. *Child Development, 71*, 1495–1511.

Taylor, P., Fry, R., & Oates, R. (2014). *The rising cost of not going to college*. Washington, DC: Pew Research Center.

Taylor, R. L., & Rosenbach, W. E. (Eds.). (2005). *Military leadership: In pursuit of excellence* (5th ed.). Boulder, CO: Westview Press.

Taylor, S. E. (1991). *Health psychology* (2nd ed.). New York: McGraw-Hill.

Taylor, S. (2015). *Health psychology* (9th ed.). New York: McGraw-Hill.

Taylor, S. E. (2009). Publishing in scientific journals: We're not just talking to ourselves anymore. *Perspectives on Psychological Science, 4*, 38–39.

Taylor, S., & Stanton, A. (2007). Coping resources, coping processes, and mental health. *Annual Review of Clinical Psychology, 33*, 77–401.

Taylor, W. D. (2014). Depression in the elderly. *New England Journal of Medicine, 371*, 1228–1235.

Tazopoulou, E., Miljkovitch, R., Truelle, J., Schnitzler, A., Onillon, M., Zucco, T., & … Montreuil, M. (2016). Rehabilitation following cerebral anoxia: An assessment of 27 patients. *Brain Injury, 30*, 95–103.

Tefft, B.C. (2012, November). *Motor vehicle crashes, injuries, and deaths in relation to driver age: United States, 1995–2010*. Washington, DC: AAA Foundation for Traffic Safety.

Teitelman, J., Hartman, G., Moossa, J., Uhl, K., & Vizzier, E. (2017). Assessing wellness outcomes for participants in adult day services: Options for activity professionals. *Activities, Adaptation & Aging, 41*, 258–267.

Tellegen, A., Lykken, D. T., Bouchard, T. J., Jr., Wilcox, K. J., Segal, N. L., & Rich, S. (1988). Personality similarity in twins reared apart and together. *Journal of Personality and Social Psychology, 54*, 1031–1039.

Tenenbaum, H. R., & Leaper, C. (1998). Gender effects on Mexican-descent parents' questions and scaffolding during toy play: A sequential analysis. *First Language, 18*, 129–147.

Tenenbaum, H., & Leaper, C. (2003). Parent-child conversations about science: The socialization of gender inequities? *Developmental Psychology, 39*, 34–47.

Teoli, D. A., Zullig, K. J., & Hendryx, M. S. (2015). Maternal fair/poor self-rated health and adverse infant birth outcomes. *Health Care for Women International, 36*, 108–120.

Terracciano, A., McCrae, R., & Costa, P. (2009). Intra-individual change in personality stability and age. *Journal of Research in Personality, 27*, 88–97.

Terzidou, V. (2007). Preterm labour. Biochemical and endocrinological preparation for parturition. *Best Practices of Research in Clinical Obstetrics and Gynecology, 21*, 729–756.

Teutsch, C. (2003). Patient–doctor communication. *Medical Clinics of North America, 87*, 1115–1147.

Thapar, A., & Cooper, M. (2016). Attention deficit hyperactivity disorder. *Lancet, 387*, 1240–1250.

Tharp, R. G. (1989). Psychocultural variables and constants: Effects on teaching and learning in schools: Special issue: Children and their development: Knowledge base, research agenda, and social policy application. *American Psychologist, 44*, 349–359.

Thelen, E., & Bates, E. (2003). Connectionism and dynamic systems: Are they really different? *Developmental Science, 6*, 378–391.

Thelen, E., & Smith, L. (2006). *Dynamic systems theories. Handbook of child psychology. Vol. 1, Theoretical models of human development* (6th ed.). New York: Wiley.

Theodosiou-Zipiti, G., & Lamprianou, I. (2016). Linguistic and cultural effects on the attainment of ethnic minority students: Some methodological considerations. *British Journal of Sociology of Education, 37*, 1229–1250.

Thibodeau, R. B., Gilpin, A. T., Brown, M. M., & Meyer, B. A. (2016). The effects of fantastical pretend-play on the development of executive functions: An intervention study. *Journal of Experimental Child Psychology, 145*, 120–138.

Thielsch, C., Andor, T., & Ehring, T. (2015). Metacognitions, intolerance of uncertainty and worry: An investigation in adolescents. *Personality and Individual Differences, 74*, 94–98.

Thijs, J., & Verkuyten, M. (2013). Multiculturalism in the classroom: Ethnic attitudes and classmates' beliefs. *International Journal of Intercultural Relations, 37*, 176–187.

Thivel, D., Isacco, L., Rousset, S., Boirie, Y., Morio, B., & Duché, P. (2011). Intensive exercise: A remedy for childhood obesity? *Physiology & Behavior, 102*(2), 132–136.

Thoermer, C., Woodward, A., Sodian, B., Perst, H., & Kristen, S. (2013). To get the grasp: Seven-month-olds encode and selectively reproduce goal-directed grasping. *Journal of Experimental Child Psychology, 116*, 499–509.

Thomaes, S., Brummelman, E., & Sedikides, C. (2017). Why most children think well of themselves. *Child Development, 88*, 1873-1884.

Thoman, E. B., & Whitney, M. P. (1990). Sleep states of infants monitored in the home: Individual differences, developmental trends, and origins of diurnal cyclicity. *Infant Behavior and Development, 12*, 59–75.

Thomas, A., & Chess, S. (1980). *The dynamics of psychological development*. New York: Brunner-Mazel.

Thomas, A., Chess, S., & Birch, H. G. (1968). *Temperament and behavior disorders in children*. New York: New York University Press.

Thomas, P., & Fenech, M. (2007). A review of genome mutation and Alzheimer's disease. *Mutagenesis, 22*, 15–33.

Thomas, R. M. (2001). *Recent human development theories*. Thousand Oaks, CA: Sage Publications.

Thomas, S. G. (2012, March 3). The gray divorces. *Wall Street Journal*, pp. C1, C2.

Thomas, T. L., Strickland, O., Diclemente, R., & Higgins, M. (2013). An opportunity for cancer prevention during preadolescence and adolescence: Stopping human papillomavirus (HPV)-related cancer through HPV vaccination. *Journal of Adolescent Health, 52*(5, Suppl), S60–S68.

Thompson, C., & Prottas, D. (2006, January). Relationships among organizational family support, job autonomy, perceived control, and employee well-being. *Journal of Occupational Health Psychology, 11*, 100–118.

Thompson, R., Briggs-King, E. C., & LaTouche-Howard, S. A. (2012). Psychology of African American children: Strengths and challenges. In E. C. Chang & C. A. Downey (Eds.), *Handbook of race and development in mental health*. New York: Springer Science + Business Media.

Thoms, K. M., Kuschel, C., & Emmert, S. (2007). Lessons learned from DNA repair defective syndromes. *Experimental Dermatology, 16*, 532–544.

Thomson, M., & Sharma, V. (2017). Therapeutics of postpartum depression. *Expert Review of Neurotherapeutics, 17*, 495–507.

Thöni A, Mussner K, & Ploner, F. (2010). Water birthing: Retrospective review of 2625 water births. Contamination of birth pool water and risk of microbial cross-infection. *Minerva Ginecologia, 62*, 203–211.

Thordstein, M., Löfgren, N., Flisberg, A., Lindecrantz, K., & Kjellmer, I. (2006). Sex differences in electrocortical activity in human neonates. *Neuroreport: For Rapid Communication of Neuroscience Research, 17*, 1165–1168.

Thornberry, T. P., & Krohn, M. D. (1997). Peers, drug use, and delinquency. In D. M. Stoff, J. Breiling, & J. D. Maser (Eds.), *Handbook of antisocial behavior*. New York: Wiley.

Thornton, J. (2004). Life-span learning: A developmental perspective. *International Journal of Aging & Human Development, 57*, 55–76.

Thorpe, A. M., Pearson, J. F., Schluter, P. J., Spittlehouse, J. K., & Joyce, P. R. (2014). Attitudes to aging in midlife are related to health conditions and mood. *International Psychogeriatrics, 26*, 2061–2071.

Thorsen, C., Gustafsson, J., & Cliffordson, C. (2014). The influence of fluid and crystallized intelligence on the development of knowledge and skills. *British Journal of Educational Psychology, 84*, 556–570.

Thorson, J. A., Powell, F., Abdel-Khalek, A. M., & Beshai, J. A. (1997). Constructions of religiosity and death anxiety in two cultures: The United States and Kuwait. *Journal of Psychology and Theology, 25*, 374–383.

Thorvaldsson, V., Hofer, S., Berg, S., Skoog, I., Sacuiu, S., & Johansson, B. (2008). Onset of terminal decline in cognitive abilities in individuals without dementia. *Neurology, 71*, 882–887.

Tian, L., Yu, T., & Huebner, E. S. (2017). Achievement goal orientations and adolescents' subjective well-being in school: The mediating roles of academic social comparison directions. *Frontiers in Psychology, 8*, 27–37.

Tibben, A. (2007). Predictive testing for Huntington's disease. *Brain Research Bulletin, 72*, 165–171. Accessed online; http://search.ebscohost.com, doi:10.1016/j.brainresbull.2006.10.023.

Tiesler, C. T., & Heinrich, J. (2014). Prenatal nicotine exposure and child behavioural problems. *European Child & Adolescent Psychiatry, 23*, 913–929.

Time. (1980, September 8). People section.

Timmermans, S., & Buchbinder, M. (2012). Expanded newborn screening: Articulating the ontology of diseases with bridging work in the clinic. *Sociology of Health & Illness, 34*, 208–220.

Tine, M. (2014). Working memory differences between children living in rural and urban poverty. *Journal of Cognition and Development, 15*(4), 599–613.

Tinsley, B., Lees, N., & Sumartojo, E. (2004). Child and adolescent HIV risk: Familial and cultural perspectives. *Journal of Family Psychology, 18*, 208–224.

Tissaw, M. (2007). Making sense of neonatal imitation. *Theory & Psychology, 17*, 217–242.

Toga, A. W., & Thompson, P. M. (2003). Temporal dynamics of brain anatomy. *Annual Review of Biomedical Engineering, 5*, 119–145.

Tomasello, M. (2011). Human culture in evolutionary perspective. In M. J. Gelfand, C. Chiu, & Y. Hong (Eds.), *Advances in culture and psychology* (Vol. 1). New York: Oxford University Press.

Tomblin, J. B., Hammer, C. S., & Zhang, X. (1998). The association of prenatal tobacco use and SLI. *International Journal of Language and Communication Disorders, 33*, 357–368.

Tomlinson-Keasey, C. (1985). *Child development: Psychological, sociological, and biological factors*. Homewood, IL: Dorsey.

Tongsong, T., Iamthongin, A., Wanapirak, C., Piyamongkol, W., Sirichotiyakul, S., Boonyanurak, P., Tatiyapornkul, T., & Neelasri, C. (2005). Accuracy of fetal heart-rate variability interpretation by obstetricians using the criteria of the National Institute of Child Health and Human Development compared with computer-aided interpretation. *Journal of Obstetric and Gynaecological Research, 31*, 68–71.

Tooley, U. A., Makhoul, Z., & Fisher, P. A. (2016). Nutritional status of foster children in the U.S.: Implications for cognitive and behavioral development. *Children and Youth Services Review, 70*, 369–374.

Toomey, R., B., Ryan, C. D., Rafael, M., Card, N. A., & Russell, S. T. (2010). Gender-nonconforming lesbian, gay, bisexual, and transgender youth: School victimization and young adult psychosocial adjustment. *Developmental Psychology, 46*, 1580–1589.

Tooten, A., Hall, R. A., Hoffenkamp, H. N., Braeken, J., Vingerhoets, A. J., & van Bakel, H. J. (2014). Maternal and paternal infant representations: A comparison between parents of term and preterm infants. *Infant Behavior & Development, 37*, 366–379.

Toporek, R. L., Kwan, K., & Wlliams, R. A. (2012). Ethics and social justice in counseling psychology. In N. A. Fouad, J. A. Carter, & L. M. Subich (Eds.), *APA handbook of counseling psychology, vol. 1: Theories, research, and methods*. APA handbooks in psychology. Washington, DC: American Psychological Association.

Torges, C., Stewart, A., & Nolen-Hoeksema, S. (2008). Regret resolution, aging, and adapting to loss. *Psychology and Aging, 23*, 169–180.

Torvaldsen, S., Roberts, C. L, Simpson, J. M., Thompson, J. F., & Ellwood, D. A. (2006). Intrapartum epidural analgesia and breastfeeding: A prospective cohort study. *International Breastfeeding Journal, 24*, 1–24.

Tracy, M., Zimmerman, F., Galea, S., McCauley, E., & Vander Stoep, A. (2008). What explains the relation between family poverty and childhood depressive symptoms? *Journal of Psychiatric Research, 42*, 1163–1175.

Trainor, L. J. (2012). Predictive information processing is a fundamental learning mechanism present in early development: Evidence from infants. *International Journal of Psychophysiology, 83*, 256–258.

Trainor, L., & Desjardins, R. (2002). Pitch characteristics of infant-directed speech affect infants' ability to discriminate vowels. *Psychonomic Bulletin & Review, 9*, 335–340.

Trapnell, P. D., & Paulhus, D. L. (2012). Agentic and communal values: Their scope and measurement. *Journal of Personality Assessment, 94*, 39–52.

Traywick, L., & Schoenberg, N. (2008). Determinants of exercise among older female heart attack survivors. *Journal of Applied Gerontology, 27*, 52–77.

Treas, J., & Bengston, V. L. (1987). The family in later years. In M. B. Sussman & S. K. Steinmetz (Eds.), *Handbook of marriage and the family*. New York: Plenum.

Treat-Jacobson, D., Bronäs, U. G., & Salisbury, D. (2014). Exercise. In R. Lindquist, M. Snyder, M. F. Tracy, R. Lindquist, M. Snyder, & M. F. Tracy (Eds.), *Complementary and alternative therapies in nursing* (7th ed.). New York: Springer Publishing Co.

Trehub, S. E. (2003). The developmental origins of musicality. *Nature Neuroscience, 6*, 669–673.

Trehub, S. E., & Hannon, E. (2009). Conventional rhythms enhance infants' and adults' perception of musical patterns. *Cortex, 45*, 110–118.

Tremblay, A., & Chaput, J. (2012). Obesity: The allostatic load of weight loss dieting. *Physiology & Behavior, 106*, 16–21.

Tremblay, R. E. (2001). The development of physical aggression during childhood and the prediction of later dangerousness. In G. F. Pinard & L. Pagani (Eds.), *Clinical assessment of dangerousness: Empirical contributions*. New York: Cambridge University Press.

Triche, E. W., & Hossain, N. (2007). Environmental factors implicated in the causation of adverse pregnancy outcome. *Seminars in Perinatology, 31*, 240–242.

Tronick, E. Z. (1995). Touch in mother–infant interactions. In T. M. Field (Ed.), *Touch in early development*. Hillsdale, NJ: Lawrence Erlbaum.

Tronick, E. Z. (2003). Emotions and emotional communication in infants. In J. Raphael-Leff (Ed.), *Parent–infant psychodynamics: Wild things, mirrors and ghosts* (pp. 35–53). London: Whurr Publishers.

Tropp, L. (2003). The psychological impact of prejudice: Implications for intergroup contact. *Group Processes & Intergroup Relations, 6*, 131–149.

Tropp, L., & Wright, S. (2003). Evaluations and perceptions of self, ingroup, and outgroup: Comparisons between Mexican-American and European-American children. *Self & Identity, 2*, 203–221.

Truman, J. L., & Morgan, R. E. (2014). *Nonfatal domestic violence, 2003–2012*. Washington, DC: U.S. Department of Justice.

Trzesniewski, K. H., Donnellan, M. B., & Robins, R. W. (2003). Stability of self-esteem across the life span. *Journal of Personality and Social Psychology, 84*, 205–220.

Tsantefski, M., Humphreys, C., & Jackson, A. C. (2014). Infant risk and safety in the context of maternal substance use. *Children and Youth Services Review, 47*, 10–17.

Tsapelas, I., Aron, A., & Orbuch, T. (2009). Marital boredom now predicts less satisfaction 9 years later. *Psychological Science, 20*, 543–545.

Tsunoda, T. (1985). *The Japanese brain: Uniqueness and universality*. Tokyo: Taishukan.

Tucker, J. S., Martínez, J. F., Ellickson, P. L., & Edelen, M. O. (2008). Temporal associations of cigarette smoking with social influences, academic performance, and delinquency: a four-wave longitudinal study from ages 13–23. *Psychology of Addictive Behaviors, 22*, 1–11.

Tucker-Drob, E. M., & Briley, D. A. (2014). Continuity of genetic and environmental influences on cognition across the life span: A meta-analysis of longitudinal twin and adoption studies. *Psychological Bulletin, 140*, 949–979.

Tucker-Drob, E. M., & Harden, K. (2012). Intellectual interest mediates gene × socioeconomic status interaction on adolescent academic achievement. *Child Development, 83*, 743–757.

Tudge, J., & Scrimsher, S. (2003). Lev S. Vygotsky on education: A cultural-historical, interpersonal, and individual approach to development. In B. Zimmerman (Ed.), *Educational psychology: A century of contributions*. Mahwah, NJ: Lawrence Erlbaum.

Tuggle, F. J., Kerpelman, J. L., & Pittman, J. F. (2014). Parental support, psychological control, and early adolescents' relationships with friends and dating partners. *Family Relations: An Interdisciplinary Journal of Applied Family Studies, 63*, 496–512.

Tulving, E., & Thompson, D. M. (1973). Encoding specificity and retrieval processes in episodic memory. *Psychological Review, 80*, 352–373.

Turati, C. (2008). Newborns' memory processes: A study on the effects of retroactive interference and repetition priming. *Infancy, 13*, 557–569.

Turkheimer, E., Beam, C. R., Sundet, J. M., & Tambs, K. (2017). Interaction between parental education and twin correlations for cognitive ability in a Norwegian conscript sample. *Behavior Genetics, 47*, 507–515.

Turney, K., & Kao, G. (2009). Barriers to school involvement: Are immigrant parents disadvantaged? *Journal of Educational Research, 102*, 257–271.

Turriff, A., Macnamara, E., Levy, H. P., & Biesecker, B. (2016). The impact of living with Klinefelter syndrome: A qualitative exploration of adolescents and adults. *Journal of Genetic Counseling*. Accessed online, 10-25-17; https://www.ncbi.nlm.nih.gov/pubmed/27832510.

Turton, P., Evans, C., & Hughes, P. (2009). Long-term psychosocial sequelae of stillbirth: Phase II of a nested case-control cohort study. *Archives of Women's Mental Health, 12*, 35–41.

Twardosz, S., & Lutzker, J. (2009). Child maltreatment and the developing brain: A review of neuroscience perspectives. *Aggression and Violent Behavior, 15*, 59–68.

Twenge, J. M., & Campbell, W. K. (2001). Age and birth cohort differences in self-esteem: A cross-temporal meta-analysis. *Personality and Social Psychology Review, 5*, 321–344.

Twenge, J. M., Gentile, B., & Campbell, W. K. (2015). Birth cohort differences in personality. In M. Mikulincer, P. R. Shaver, M. L. Cooper, & R. J. Larsen (Eds.), *APA handbook of personality and social psychology, Volume 4: Personality processes and individual differences* (pp. 535–551). Washington, DC: American Psychological Association.

Twomey, J. (2006). Issues in genetic testing of children. *MCN: American Journal of Maternal/Child Nursing, 31*, 156–163.

Tyler, S., Corvin, J., McNab, P., Fishleder, S., Blunt, H., & VandeWeerd, C. (2014). "You can't get a side of willpower": Nutritional supports and barriers in the Villages, Florida. *Journal of Nutrition in Gerontology and Geriatrics, 33*, 108–125.

Tyre, P., & McGinn, D. (2003, May 12). She works, he doesn't. *Newsweek*, pp. 45–52.

Tyre, P., & Scelfo, J. (2003, September 22). Helping kids get fit. *Newsweek*, pp. 60–62.

U.S. Bureau of the Census. (2001). *Living arrangements of children*. Washington, DC: Author.

U.S. Bureau of the Census. (2003). *Population reports*. Washington, DC: U.S. Government Printing Office.

U.S. Bureau of the Census. (2010). *Statistical abstract of the United States* (130th ed.). Washington, DC: U.S. Government Printing Office.

U.S. Bureau of the Census. (2011). *Current population survey and annual social and economic supplements*. Washington, DC: U.S. Bureau of the Census.

U.S. Bureau of the Census. (2012). *Current population survey and annual social and economic supplements*. Washington, DC: U.S. Bureau of the Census.

U.S. Bureau of Labor Statistics. (2010, July). *Highlights of women's earnings in 2009*. Washington: U.S. Department of Labor.

U.S. Bureau of Labor Statistics. (2012). *Current population survey*. Washington, DC: U.S. Bureau of Labor Statistics.

U.S. Bureau of Labor Statistics. (2014). *Highlights of women's earnings in 2013*. Washington, DC: U.S. Bureau of Labor Statistics.

U.S. Census Bureau. (2011). *Overview of race and Hispanic origin: 2010–2010 Census briefs*. Washington, DC: U.S. Department of Commerce.

U.S. Census Bureau, Current Population Reports. (2013). *Income, poverty, and health insurance coverage in the United States: 2012*, Washington, DC: U.S. Government Printing Office.

U.S. Department of Education. (2005). *2003–2004 National Postsecondary Student Aid Study (NPSAS:04)*, unpublished tabulations. Washington, DC: U.S. Department of Education.

U.S. Department of Education. (2012). *National Center for Education Statistics; Pew Research Center tabulations of the March 2012 current population survey*. Washington, DC: National Center for Education Statistics.

U.S. Department of Education. (2015). *The condition of education, 2014*. Washington, DC: U.S. Department of Education.

U.S. Department of Health and Human Services, Administration on Children Youth and Families. (2007). *Child maltreatment 2005*. Washington, DC: U.S. Government Printing Office.

U.S. Department of Health and Human Services, National Institutes of Health, Eunice Kennedy Shriver Institute of Child Health and Human Development, 2017. Accessed online 10-26-17; https://www.nichd.nih.gov/health/topics/preterm/conditioninfo/Pages/who_risk.aspx.

U.S. Preventive Services Task Force. (2017) Screening for obesity in children and adolescents: U.S. Preventive Services Task Force recommendation statement. *JAMA: Journal of the American Medical Association, 317*, 2417–2426.

Uchikoshi, Y. (2006). Early reading in bilingual kindergartners: Can educational television help? *Scientific Studies of Reading, 10*, 89–120.

Ugarte, A. U., López-Peña, P., Vangeneberg, C. S., Royo, J. T., Ugarte, M. A., Compains, M. Z., & … González-Pinto, A. (2017). Psychoeducational preventive treatment for women at risk of postpartum depression: Study protocol for a randomized controlled trial, PROGEA. *BMC Psychiatry, 17*, 88–97.

Umaña-Taylor, A. J., Quintana, S. M., Lee, R. M., Cross, W. E., Rivas-Drake, D., Schwartz, S. J., … Seaton, E. (2014). Ethnic and racial identity during adolescence and into young adulthood: An integrated conceptualization. *Child Development, 85*, 21–39.

UNAIDS & World Health Organization. (2009). *Cases of AIDS around the world*. New York: United Nations.

UNAIDS. (2011). *2011 World AIDS day*. New York: United Nations

Underwood, M. (2005). Introduction to the special section: Deception and observation. *Ethics & Behavior, 15*, 233–234.

Unger, R., & Crawford, M. (1992). *Women and gender: A feminist psychology* (2nd ed.). New York: McGraw-Hill.

Unger, R., & Crawford, M. (2003). *Women and gender: A feminist psychology*. New York: McGraw-Hill.

UNICEF, WHO. (2016). *World Bank joint child malnutrition set*. Geneva, Switzerland: UNICEF.

United Nations Statistics Division. (2012). Statistical Annex Table 2.A Health—*United Nations* Statistics Division Accessed online, 7-18-12; unstats.un.org/unsd/demographic/products/…%20pdf/Table2A.pdf.

United Nations World Food Programme. (2013). *The 2013 annual performance report*. Rome: World Food Programme.

United Nations World Population Prospects. (2006). Accessed online, 7-12-12; http://www.un.org/esa/population/publications/wpp2006/WPP2006_Highlights_rev.pdf.

United Nations, Department of Economic and Social Affairs, Population Division. (2013). *World population ageing 2013. ST/ESA/SER.A/348*. New York: United Nations.

UNODC. (2013). *Global study on homicide 2013 (United Nations publication, Sales No. 14.IV.1)* New York: United Nations.

Updegraff, K. A., McHale, S. M., Whiteman, S. D., Thayer, S. M., & Crouter, A. C. (2006). The nature and correlates of Mexican-American adolescents' time with parents and peers. *Child Development, 77*, 1470–1486.

Uphold-Carrier, H., & Utz, R. (2012). Parental divorce among young and adult children: A long-term quantitative analysis of mental health and family solidarity. *Journal of Divorce & Remarriage, 53*, 247–266. doi:10.1080/10502556.2012.663272.

Urberg, K., Luo, Q., & Pilgrim, C. (2003). A two-stage model of peer influence in adolescent substance use: Individual and relationship-specific differences in susceptibility to influence. *Addictive Behaviors, 28*, 1243–1256.

Urso, A. (2007). The reality of neonatal pain and the resulting effects. *Journal of Neonatal Nursing, 13*, 236–238.

USA Weekend. (1997, August 22–24). Fears among adults, p. 5.

Uttal, D. H., Meadow, N. G., Tipton, E., Hand, L. L., Alden, A. R., Warren, C., & Newcombe, N. S. (2013). The malleability of spatial skills: A meta-analysis of training studies. *Psychological Bulletin, 139*, 352–402.

Vacha-Haase, T., Hill, R. D., & Bermingham, D. W. (2012). Aging theory and research. In N. A. Fouad, J. A. Carter, & L. M. Subich (Eds.), *APA handbook of counseling psychology, vol. 1: Theories, research, and methods*. Washington, DC: American Psychological Association.

Vaillant, G. E. (1977). *Adaptation to life*. Boston: Little, Brown.

Vaillant, G. E., & Vaillant, C. O. (1981). Natural history of male psychological health, X: Work as a predictor of positive mental health. *American Journal of Psychiatry, 138*, 1433–1440.

Vaillant, G. E., & Vaillant, C. O. (1990). Natural history of male psychological health, XII: A 45-year study of predictors of successful aging. *American Journal of Psychiatry, 147(1)*, 31–37.

Vaish, V. (2014). Whole language versus code-based skills and interactional patterns in Singapore's early literacy program. *Cambridge Journal of Education, 44*, 199–215.

Vaish, A., & Striano, T. (2004). Is visual reference necessary? Contributions of facial versus vocal cues in 12-month-olds' social referencing behavior. *Developmental Science, 7*, 261–269.

Valenti, C. (2006). Infant vision guidance: Fundamental vision development in infancy. *Optometry and Vision Development, 37*, 147–155.

Valentino, K., Nuttall, A. K., Comas, M., McDonnell, C. G., Piper, B., Thomas, T. E., & Fanuele, S. (2014). Mother–child reminiscing and autobiographical memory specific among preschool-age children. *Developmental Psychology, 50*, 1197–1207.

Valeri, B. O., Gaspardo, C. M., Martinez, F. E., & Linhares, M. M. (2014). Pain reactivity in preterm neonates: Examining the sex differences. *European Journal of Pain, 18*, 1431–1439.

Vallejo-Sánchez, B., & Pérez-García, A. M. (2015). The role of personality and coping in adjustment disorder. *Clinical Psychologist*. Accessed online, 3-23-15; http://onlinelibrary.wiley.com/doi/10.1111/cp.12064/abstract.

Valles, N., & Knutson, J. (2008). Contingent responses of mothers and peers to indirect and direct aggression in preschool and school-aged children. *Aggressive Behavior, 34*, 497–510.

Van Balen, F. (2005). The choice for sons or daughters. *Journal of Psychosomatic Obstetrics & Gynecology, 26*, 229–320.

Vandenberghe-Descamps, M., Labouré, H., Septier, C., Feron, G., & Sulmont-Rossé, C. (2017). Oral comfort: A new concept to understand elderly people's expectations in terms of food sensory characteristics. *Food Quality and Preference*. Accessed online, 12-12-17; http://www.sciencedirect.com/science/article/pii/S095032931730188X.

van der Mark, I., van Ijzendoorn, M., & Bakermans-Kranenburg, M. (2002). Development of empathy in girls during the second year of life: Associations with parenting, attachment, and temperament. *Social Development, 11*, 451–468.

van der Veer, R., & Yasnitsky, A. (2016). Vygotsky the published: Who wrote Vygotsky and what Vygotsky actually wrote. In A. Yasnitsky & R. van der Veer (Eds.), *Revisionist revolution in Vygotsky studies*. New York: Routledge/Taylor & Francis Group.

van den Berg, Y. M., Deutz, M. F., Smeekens, S., & Cillessen, A. N. (2017). Developmental pathways to preference and popularity in middle childhood. *Child Development, 88*, 1629–1641

van den Herik, J. C. (2017). Linguistic know-how and the orders of language. *Language Sciences, 61*, 17–27.

van Ditzhuijzen, J., ten Have, M., de Graaf, R. van Nijnatten, C. H. C. J., & Vollebergh, W. A. M. (2013). Psychiatric history of women who have had an abortion. *Journal of Psychiatric Research, 47*, 1737–1743.

van Haren, N. M., Rijsdijk, F., Schnack, H. G., Picchioni, M. M., Toulopoulou, T., Weisbrod, M., & Kahn, R. S. (2012). The genetic and environmental determinants of the association between brain abnormalities and schizophrenia: The schizophrenia twins and relatives consortium. *Biological Psychiatry, 71*, 915–921.

van Kleeck, A., & Stahl, S. (2003). *On reading books to children: Parents and teachers*. Mahwah, NJ: Lawrence Erlbaum.

Van Manen, S., & Pietromonaco, P. (1993). *Acquaintance and consistency influence memory from interpersonal information*. Unpublished manuscript, University of Massachusetts, Amherst.

van Marle, K., & Wynn, K. (2009). Infants' auditory enumeration: Evidence for analog magnitudes in the small number range. *Cognition, 111*, 302–316.

van Marle, K., & Wynn, K. (2011). Tracking and quantifying objects and non-cohesive substances. *Developmental Science, 15*, 302–316.

Van Neste, J., Hayden, A., Lorch, E. P., & Milich, R. (2015). Inference generation and story comprehension among children with ADHD. *Journal of Abnormal Child Psychology, 43*, 259–270.

van Oosten, J. F., & Vandenbosch, L. (2017). Sexy online self-presentation on social network sites and the willingness to engage in sexting: A comparison of gender and age. *Journal of Adolescence, 54*, 42–50.

van Reenen, S. L., & van Rensburg, E. (2013). The influence of an unplanned Caesarean section on initial mother-infant bonding: Mothers' subjective experiences. *Journal of Psychology in Africa, 23*, 269–274.

Vandell, D. L. (2000). Parents, peer groups, and other socializing influences. *Developmental Psychology, 36*, 699–710.

Vandell, D. L. (2004). Early child care: The known and the unknown. *Merrill-Palmer Quarterly, 50* [Special issue: The maturing of human developmental sciences: Appraising past, present, and prospective agendas], 387–414.

Vandell, D. L., Burchinal, M. R., Belsky, J., Owen, M. T., Friedman, S. L., Clarke-Stewart, A., McCartney, K., & Weinraub, M. (2005). Early child care and children's development in the primary grades: Follow-up results from the NICHD Study of Early Child Care. Paper presented at the biennial meeting of the Society for Research in Child Development, Atlanta, GA.

Vandell, D. L., Shumow, L., & Posner, J. (2005). After-school programs for low-income children: Differences in program quality. In J. L. Mahoney, R. W. Larson, & J. S. Ecccles, *Organized activities as contexts of development: Extracurricular activities, after-school and community programs*. Mahwah, NJ: Lawrence Erlbaum.

Vandello, J., & Cohen, D. (2003). Male honor and female fidelity: Implicit cultural scripts that perpetuate domestic violence. *Journal of Personality & Social Psychology, 84*, 997–1010.

Vanden Abeele, M., Campbell, S. W., Eggermont, S., & Roe, K. (2014). Sexting, mobile porn use, and peer group dynamics: Boys' and girls' self-perceived popularity, need for popularity, and perceived peer pressure. *Media Psychology, 17*, 6–33.

Varga, M. A. (2014). Why funerals matter: Death rituals across cultures. *Death Studies, 38*, 546–547.

Vartanian, L. R. (2000). Revisiting the imaginary audience and personal fable constructs of adolescent egocentrism: A conceptual review. *Adolescence, 35*, 639–646.

Vauclair, C., Hanke, K., Huang, L., & Abrams, D. (2017). Are Asian cultures really less ageist than Western ones? It depends on the questions asked. *International Journal of Psychology, 52*, 136–144.

Vedantam, S. (2006, December 20). Short mental workouts may slow decline of aging minds, study finds. *Washington Post*, p. A1.

Venker, C. E., Kover, S. T., & Weismer, S. E. (2016). Brief report: Fast mapping predicts differences in concurrent and later language abilities among children with ASD. *Journal of Autism and Developmental Disorders, 46*, 1118–1123.

Veras, R. P., & Mattos, L. C. (2007). Audiology and aging: Literature review and current horizons. *Revista Brasileira de Otorrinolaringologia (English Edition), 73*, 122–128.

Veraksa, N., Shiyan, O., Shiyan, I., Pramling, N., & Pramling-Samuelsson, I. (2016). Communication between teacher and child in early child education: Vygotskian theory and educational practice. *Infancia Y Aprendizaje / Journal for the Study of Education and Development, 39*, 221–243.

Verkuyten, M. (2003). Positive and negative self-esteem among ethnic minority early adolescents: Social and cultural sources and threats. *Journal of Youth & Adolescence, 32*, 267–277.

Verkuyten, M. (2008). Life satisfaction among ethnic minorities: The role of discrimination and group identification. *Social Indicators Research, 89*(3), 391–404.

Vermandel, A., Weyler, J., De Wachter, S., & Wyndaele, J. (2008). Toilet training of healthy young toddlers: A randomized trial between a daytime wetting alarm and timed potty training. *Journal of Developmental & Behavioral Pediatrics, 29*, 191–196.

Verschueren, K., Doumen, S., & Buyse, E. (2012). Relationships with mother, teacher, and peers: Unique and joint effects on young children's self-concept. *Attachment & Human Development, 14*, 233–248.

Verschueren, M., Rassart, J., Claes, L., Moons, P., & Luyckx, K. (2017). Identity statuses throughout adolescence and emerging adulthood: A large-scale study into gender, age, and contextual differences. *Psychologica Belgica, 57*, 32–42.

Veselka, L., Just, C., Jang, K. L., Johnson, A. M., & Vernon, P. A. (2012). The General Factor of Personality: A critical test. *Personality and Individual Differences, 52*, 261–264.

Vidaver, R. M. et al. (2000). Women subjects in NIH-funded clinical research literature: Lack of progress in both representation and analysis by sex. *Journal of Women's Health, Gender-Based Medicine, 9*, 495–504.

Villarosa, L. (2003, December 23). More teenagers say no to sex, and experts are sure why. *New York Times*, p. D6.

Vincent, J. A., Phillipson, C. R., & Downs, M. (2006). *The futures of old age*. Thousand Oaks, CA: Sage Publications.

Vink, D., Aartsen, M., Comijs, H., Heymans, M., Penninx, B., Stek, M., et al. (2009). Onset of anxiety and depression in the aging population: Comparison of risk factors in a 9-year prospective study. *American Journal of Geriatric Psychiatry, 17*, 642–652.

Vinukonda, G., Dohare, P., Arshad, A., Zia, M. T., Panda, S., Korumilli, R., & … Ballabh, P. (2016). Hyaluronidase and hyaluronan oligosaccharides promote neurological recovery after intraventricular hemorrhage. *Journal of Neuroscience, 36*, 872–889.

Visconti, K., Kochenderfer-Ladd, B., & Clifford, C. A. (2013). Children's attributions for peer victimization: A social comparison approach. *Journal of Applied Developmental Psychology, 34*, 277–287.

Vivanti, G., Paynter, J., Duncan, E., Fothergill, H., Dissanayake, C., & Rogers, S. J. (2014). Effectiveness and feasibility of the Early Start Denver Model implemented in a group-based community childcare setting. *Journal of Autism and Developmental Disorders, 44*, 3140–3153.

Vogel, M., Monesson, A., & Scott, L. S. (2012). Building biases in infancy: The influence of race on face and voice emotion matching. *Developmental Science, 15*(3), 359-372. doi:10.1111/j.1467-7687.2012.01138.x

Volker, S. (2007). Infants' vocal engagement oriented towards mother versus stranger at 3 months and avoidant attachment behavior at 12 months. *International Journal of Behavioral Development, 31*, 88–95.

von Hofsten, C., & Rosander, K. (2015). On the development of the mirror neuron system. In P. F. Ferrari, G. Rizzolatti (Eds.), *New frontiers in mirror neurons research*. New York: Oxford University Press.

Voss, P., Wolff, J. K., & Rothermund, K. (2017). Relations between views on ageing and perceived age discrimination: A domain-specific perspective. *European Journal of Ageing, 14*, 5–15.

Votruba-Drzal, E., Coley, R. L., & Chase-Lansdale, L. (2004). Child care and low-income children's development: Direct and moderated effects. *Child Development, 75*, 396–312.

Vreeswijk, C. M., Maas, A. M., Rijk, C. M., & van Bakel, H. A. (2013). Fathers' experiences during pregnancy: Paternal prenatal attachment and representations of the fetus. *Psychology of Men & Masculinity*. Accessed online 10-25-17; http://psycnet.apa.org/psycinfo/2013-27681-001/.

Vue, W., Wolff, C., & Goto, K. (2011). Hmong food helps us remember who we are: Perspectives of food culture and health among Hmong women with young children. *Journal of Nutrition Education and Behavior, 43*, 199–204.

Vyas, S. (2004). Exploring bicultural identities of Asian high school students through the analytic window of a literature club. *Journal of Adolescent & Adult Literacy, 48*, 12–18.

Vygotsky, L. S. (1926/1997). *Educational psychology*. Delray Beach, FL: St. Lucie Press.

Waber, D. P., Bryce, C. P., Fitzmaurice, G. M., Zichlin, M. L., McGaughy, J., Girard, J. M., & Galler, J. R. (2014). Neuropsychological outcomes at midlife following moderate to severe malnutrition in infancy. *Neuropsychology, 28*, 530–540.

Wada, A., Kunii, Y., Ikemoto, K., Yang, Q., Hino, M., Matsumoto, J., & Niwa, S. (2012). Increased ratio of calcineurin immunoreactive neurons in the caudate nucleus of patients with schizophrenia. *Progress in Neuro-Psychopharmacology & Biological Psychiatry, 37*, 8–14.

Wade, T. D. (2008). Shared temperament risk factors for anorexia nervosa: A twin study. *Psychosomatic Medicine, 70*, 239–244.

Wade, T. D., & Watson, H. J. (2012). Psychotherapies in eating disorders. In J. Alexander, J. Treasure (Eds.), *A collaborative approach to eating disorders*. New York: Routledge/Taylor & Francis Group.

Wagner, R. K., & Sternberg, R. J. (1985). Alternate conceptions of intelligence and their implications for education. *Review of Educational Research, 54*, 179–223.

Wahlin, T. (2007). To know or not to know: A review of behaviour and suicidal ideation in preclinical Huntington's disease. *Patient Education and Counseling, 65*, 279–287.

Wainright, J. L., & Patterson, C. J. (2008). Peer relations among adolescents with female same-sex parents. *Developmental Psychology, 44*, 117–126.

Wainright, J. L., Russell, S. T., & Patterson, C. J. (2004). Psychosocial adjustment, school outcomes, and romantic relationships of adolescents with same-sex parents. *Child Development, 75*, 1886–1898.

Waismeyer, A., & Meltzoff, A. N. (2017). Learning to make things happen: Infants' observational learning of social and physical causal events. *Journal of Experimental Child Psychology, 162*, 58–71.

Wałaszewska, E. (2011). Broadening and narrowing in lexical development: How relevance theory can account for children's overextensions and underextensions. *Journal of Pragmatics, 43*, 314–326.

Walder, D. J., Faraone, S. V., Glatt, S. J., Tsuang, M. T., & Seidman, L. J. (2014). Genetic liability, prenatal health, stress and family environment: Risk factors in the Harvard Adolescent Family High Risk for Schizophrenia Study. *Schizophrenia Research, 157*, 142–148.

Waldrop, D. P., & Kirkendall, A. M. (2009). Comfort measures: A qualitative study of nursing home-based end-of-life care. *Journal of Palliative Medicine, 12*, 718–724.

Walker, J., Anstey, K., & Lord, S. (2006, May). Psychological distress and visual functioning in relation to vision-related disability in older individuals with cataracts. *British Journal of Health Psychology, 11*, 303–317.

Walker, L. (1984). *The battered woman syndrome*. New York: Springer.

Walker, L. E. (1989). Psychology and violence against women. *American Psychologist, 44*, 695–702.

Walker, W. A., & Humphries, C. (2005). *The Harvard Medical School guide to healthy eating during pregnancy*. New York: McGraw-Hill.

Walker, W. A., & Humphries, C. (2007, September 17). Starting the good life in the womb. *Newsweek*, pp. 56–57.

Walle, E. A., Reschke, P. J., & Knothe, J. M. (2017). Social referencing: Defining and delineating a basic process of emotion. *Emotion Review, 9*, 245–252.

Walpole, S. C., et al. (2012, June 18). The weight of nations: an estimation of adult human biomass. *BMC Public Health 2012*. Accessed online, 7-12-12; http://www.biomedcentral.com/1471-2458/12/439/abstract.

Walter, A. (1997). The evolutionary psychology of mate selection in Morocco: A multivariate analysis. *Human Nature, 8*, 113–137.

Walter, T. (2012). Why different countries manage death differently: A comparative analysis of modern urban societies. *British Journal of Sociology, 63*, 123–145.

Walters, A., & Rye, D. (2009). Review of the relationship of restless legs syndrome and periodic limb movements in sleep to hypertension, heart disease, and stroke. *Sleep: Journal of Sleep and Sleep Disorders Research, 32*, 589–597.

Walters, E., & Gardner, H. (1986). The theory of multiple intelligences: Some issues and answers. In R. J. Sternberg & R. K. Wagner (Eds.), *Practical intelligence*. New York: Cambridge University Press.

Wan, B. A., Jiang, C., Agarwal, A., Lam, M., Chow, E., & Henry, B. (2017). Impact of 'do-not-resuscitate' orders on mortality and quality of care. In B. Henry, A. Agarwal, E. Chow, & J. Merrick (Eds.), *Palliative care: Psychosocial and ethical considerations*. Hauppauge, NY: Nova Biomedical Books.

Wang, C., Tsai, C., Tseng, P., Yang, A. C., Lo, M., Peng, C., & … Liang, W. (2014). The association of physical activity to neural adaptability during visuo-spatial processing in healthy elderly adults: A multiscale entropy analysis. *Brain and Cognition, 92*, 73–83.

Wang, H. H., Varelas, P. N., Henderson, G. V., Wijdicks, E. M., & Greer, D. M. (2017). Improving uniformity in brain death determination policies over time. *Neurology, 88*, 562–568.

Wang, H. J., Zhang, H., Zhang, W. W., Pan, Y. P., & Ma, J. (2008). Association of the common genetic variant upstream of INSIG2 gene with obesity related phenotypes in Chinese children and adolescents. *Biomedical and Environmental Sciences, 21*, 528–536.

Wang, M. (2007). Profiling retirees in the retirement transition and adjustment process: Examining the longitudinal change patterns of retirees' psychological well-being. *Journal of Applied Psychology, 92*, 455–474.

Wang, Q. (2004). The emergence of cultural self-constructs: Autobiographical memory and self-description in European American and Chinese children. *Developmental Psychology, 40*, 3–15.

Wang, Q. (2006). Culture and the development of self-knowledge. *Current Directions in Psychological Science, 15*, 182–187.

Wang, Q. (2008). Emotion knowledge and autobiographical memory across the preschool years: A cross-cultural longitudinal investigation. *Cognition, 108*, 117–135.

Wang, Q., Pomerantz, E., & Chen, H. (2007). The role of parents' control in early adolescents' psychological functioning: A longitudinal investigation in the United States and China. *Child Development, 78*, 1592–1610.

Wang, Y., Douglass, S., & Yip, T. (2017). Longitudinal relations between ethnic/racial identity process and content: Exploration, commitment, and salience among diverse adolescents. *Developmental Psychology, 53*, 2154–2169.

Wang, Z., Deater-Deckard, K., Cutting, L., Thompson, L. A., & Petrill, S. A. (2012). Working memory and parent-rated components of attention in middle childhood: A behavioral genetic study. *Behavior Genetics, 42*, 199–208.

Wang, Z., Devine, R. T., Wong, K. K., & Hughes, C. (2016). Theory of mind and executive function during middle childhood across cultures. *Journal of Experimental Child Psychology, 149*, 6–22.

Wang/Pew Research Center. (2012). *The rise of intermarriage: Rates characteristics vary by race and gender*. Washington, DC: Pew Research Center.

Wannamethee, S. G., Shaper, A. G., Walker, M., & Ebrahim, S. (1998). Lifestyle and 15-year survival free of heart attack, stroke, and diabetes in middle-aged British men. *Archives of Internal Medicine, 158*, 2433–2440.

Wardle, J., Guthrie, C., & Sanderson, S. (2001). Food and activity preferences in children of lean and obese parents. *International Journal of Obesity & Related Metabolic Disorders, 25*, 971–977.

Warford, M. K. (2011). The zone of proximal teacher development. *Teaching and Teacher Education, 27*, 252–258.

Warne, R. T., & Liu, J. K. (2017). Income differences among grade skippers and non-grade skippers across genders in the Terman sample, 1936–1976. *Learning and Instruction, 47*, 1–12.

Warshak, R. A. (2000). Remarriage as a trigger of parental alienation syndrome. *American Journal of Family Therapy, 28*, 229–241.

Wasserman, J. D., & Tulsky, D. S. (2005). The history of intelligence assessment. In D. P. Flanagan & P. L. Harrison (Eds.), *Contemporary intellectual assessment: Theories, tests, and issues*. New York: Guilford Press.

Waterhouse, J. M., & DeCoursey, P. J. (2004). Human circadian organization. In J. C. Dunlap & J. J. Loros (Eds.), *Chronobiology: Biological timekeeping*. Sunderland, MA: Sinauer Associates.

Waterland, R. A., & Jirtle, R. L. (2004). Early nutrition, epigenetic changes at transposons and imprinted genes, and enhanced susceptibility to adult chronic diseases. *Nutrition*, 63–68.

Waters, L., & Moore, K. (2002). Predicting self-esteem during unemployment: The effect of gender financial deprivation, alternate roles and social support. *Journal of Employment Counseling, 39*, 171–189.

Waters, S. F., West, T. V., Karnilowicz, H. R., & Mendes, W. B. (2017). Affect contagion between mothers and infants: Examining valence and touch. *Journal of Experimental Psychology: General, 146*, 1043–1051.

Watling, D., & Bourne, V. J. (2007). Linking children's neuropsychological processing of emotion with their knowledge of emotion expression regulation. *Laterality: Asymmetries of Body, Brain and Cognition, 12*, 381–396.

Watson, J. B. (1925). *Behaviorism*. New York: Norton.

Watson, J. B., & Rayner, R. (1920). Conditioned, emotional reactions. *Journal of Experimental Psychology, 3*, 1–14.

Weaver, J. M., & Schofield, T. J. (2015). Mediation and moderation of divorce effects on children's behavior problems. *Journal of Family Psychology, 29*, 39–48.

Webb, E. A., O'Reilly, M. A., Clayden, J. D., Seunarine, K. K., Chong, W. K., Dale, N., & Dattani, M. T. (2012). Effect of growth hormone deficiency on brain structure, motor function and cognition. *Brain: A Journal of Neurology, 135*.

Wechsler, D. (1975). Intelligence defined and undefined. *American Psychologist, 30*, 135–139.

Wechsler, H., Issac, R., Grodstein, L., & Sellers, M. (2000). *College binge drinking in the 1990s: A continuing problem: Results of the Harvard School of Public Health 1999 college health alcohol study*. Cambridge, MA: Harvard University.

Wechsler, H., Lee, J. E., Kuo, M., Seibring, M., Nelson, T. F., & Lee, H. (2002). Trends in college binge drinking during a period of increased prevention efforts: Findings from 4 Harvard School of Public Health college alcohol study surveys, 1993–2001.

Wechsler, H., Nelson, T. F., Lee, J. E., Seibring, M., Lewis, C., & Keeling, R. P. (2003). Perception and reality: A national evaluation of social norms marketing interventions to reduce college students' heavy alcohol use. *Journal of Studies on Alcohol, 64*, 484–494.

Wehmeyer, M. L., & Lee, S. (2017). Individualized education programs to promote access to the general education curriculum for students with intellectual disability. In M. L. Wehmeyer & K. A. Shogren (Eds.), *Handbook of research-based practices for educating students with intellectual disability*. New York: Routledge/Taylor & Francis Group.

Wehmeyer, M. L., & Shogren, K. A. (2017). *Handbook of research-based practices for educating students with intellectual disability*. New York: Routledge/Taylor & Francis Group.

Weiner, B. (2007). Examining emotional diversity in the classroom: An attribution theorist considers the moral emotions. In P. A. Schutz, & R. Pekrun (Eds.), *Emotion in education*. San Diego: Elsevier Academic Press.

Weiner, B. A., & Zinner, L. (2015). Attitudes toward straight, gay male, and transsexual parenting. *Journal of Homosexuality, 62*, 327–339.

Wiener, R. L., Gervais, S. J., Brnjic, E., & Nuss, G. D. (2014). Dehumanization of older people: The evaluation of hostile work environments. *Psychology, Public Policy, and Law, 20*, 384–397.

Weinstock, H., Berman, S., & Cates, W., Jr. (2004). Sexually transmitted diseases among American youth: Incidence and prevalence estimates, 2000. *Perspectives on Sexual and Reproductive Health, 36*, 182–191.

Weiss, R. (2003, September 2). Genes' sway over IQ may vary with class. *Washington Post*, p. A1.

Weiss, M. R., Ebbeck, V., & Horn. T. S. (1997). Children's self-perceptions and sources of physical competence information: A cluster analysis. *Journal of Sport & Exercise Psychology, 19*, 52–70.

Weiss, R., & Raz, I. (2006, July). Focus on childhood fitness, not just fatness. *Lancet, 368*, 261–262.

Weissman, A. S., Chu, B. C., Reddy, L. A., & Mohlman, J. (2012). Attention mechanisms in children with anxiety disorders and in children with attention deficit hyperactivity disorder: Implications for research and practice. *Journal of Clinical Child and Adolescent Psychology, 41*, 117–126.

Weisz, A., & Black, B. (2002). Gender and moral reasoning: African American youth respond to dating dilemmas. *Journal of Human Behavior in the Social Environment, 5*, 35–52.

Welch, M. G. (2016). Calming cycle theory: The role of visceral/autonomic learning in early mother and infant/child behaviour and development. *Acta Paediatrica, 105*, 1266–1274.

Wellings, K., Collumbien, M., Slaymaker, E., Singh, S., Hodges, Z., Patel, D., & Bajos, N. (2006). Sexual behaviour in context: A global perspective. *Lancet, 368*, 1706–1738.

Wellman, H. M. (2012). Theory of mind: Better methods, clearer findings, more development. *European Journal of Developmental Psychology, 9*, 313–330.

Wellman, H., Fang, F., Liu, D., Zhu, L., & Liu, G. (2006, December). Scaling of theory-of-mind understandings in Chinese children. *Psychological Science, 17*, 1075–1081.

Wellman, H., Lopez-Duran, S., LaBounty, J., & Hamilton, B. (2008). Infant attention to intentional action predicts preschool theory of mind. *Developmental Psychology, 44*, 618–623.

Wells, B., Peppe, S., & Goulandris, N. (2004). Intonation development from five to thirteen. *Journal of Child Language, 31*, 749–778.

Wells, R., Lohman, D., & Marron, M. (2009). What factors are associated with grade acceleration? An analysis and comparison of two U.S. databases. *Journal of Advanced Academics, 20*, 248–273.

Welsh, T., Ray, M., Weeks, D., Dewey, D., & Elliott, D. (2009). Does Joe influence Fred's action? Not if Fred has autism spectrum disorder. *Brain Research, 1248*, 141–148.

Wentzell, E. (2017). How did erectile dysfunction become 'natural'? A review of the critical social scientific literature on medical treatment for male sexual dysfunction. *Journal of Sex Research, 54*, 486–506.

Werker, J. F., Pons, F., Dietrich, C., Kajikawa, S., Fais, L., & Amano, S. (2007). Infant-directed speech supports phonetic category learning in English and Japanese. *Cognition, 103*, 147–162.

Werner, E. E. (2005). What can we learn about resilience from large-scale longitudinal studies? In S. Goldstein & R. B. Brooks (Eds.), *Handbook of resilience in children*. New York: Kluwer Academic/Plenum Publishers.

Werner, E. E., & Smith, R. S. (2002). Journeys from childhood to midlife: Risk, resilience and recovery. *Journal of Developmental and Behavioral Pediatrics, 23*, 456.

Werner, E., Myers, M., Fifer, W., Cheng, B., Fang, Y., Allen, R., et al. (2007). Prenatal predictors of infant temperament. *Developmental Psychobiology, 49*, 474–484.

Werner, N. E., & Crick, N. R. (2004). Maladaptive peer relationships and the development of relational and physical aggression during middle childhood. *Social Development, 13*, 495–514.

Wertsch, J. (2008). From social interaction to higher psychological processes: A clarification and application of Vygotsky's theory. *Human Development, 51*, 66–79.

West, J. H., Romero, R. A., & Trinidad, D. R. (2007). Adolescent receptivity to tobacco marketing by racial/ethnic groups in California. *American Journal of Preventive Medicine, 33*, 121–123.

West, J. R., & Blake, C. A. (2005). Fetal alcohol syndrome: An assessment of the field. *Experimental Biology and Medicine, 230*, 354–356.

Westerhausen, R., Kreuder, F., Sequeira Sdos, S., Walter, C., Woerner, W., Wittling, R. A., Schweiger, E., & Wittling, W. (2004). Effects of handedness and gender on macro- and microstructure of the corpus callosum and its subregions: A combined high-resolution and diffusion-tensor MRI study. *Brain Research and Cognitive Brain Research, 21*, 418–426.

Westermann, G., Mareschal, D., Johnson, M. H., Sirois, S., Spratling, M. W., & Thomas, M. S. (2007). Neurosconstructivism. *Developmental Science, 10*, 75–83.

Westervelt, A. (2015, April). The medical research gender gap: How excluding women from clinical trials is hurting our health. *The Guardian*. Accessed online, 11-28-17; https://www.theguardian.com/lifeandstyle/2015/apr/30/fda-clinical-trials-gender-gap-epa-nih-institute-of-medicine-cardiovascular-disease.

Wettstein, M., Tauber, B., Kuźma, E., & Wahl, H. (2017). The interplay between personality and cognitive ability across 12 years in middle and late adulthood: Evidence for reciprocal associations. *Psychology and Aging, 32*, 259–277.

Wexler, B. (2006). *Brain and culture: Neurobiology, ideology, and social change*. Cambridge, MA: MIT Press.

Whalen, C. K., Jamner, L. D., Henker, B., Delfino, R. J., & Lozano, J. M. (2002). The ADHD spectrum and everyday life: Experience sampling of adolescent moods, activities, smoking, and drinking. *Child Development, 73*, 209–227.

Whalen, D., Levitt, A., & Goldstein, L. (2007). VOT in the babbling of French- and English-learning infants. *Journal of Phonetics, 35*, 341–352.

Whalen, D. J., Sylvester, C. M., & Luby, J. L. (2017). Depression and anxiety in preschoolers: A review of the past 7 years. *Child and Adolescent Psychiatric Clinics of North America, 26*, 503–522.

Wheeler, S., & Austin, J. (2001). The impact of early pregnancy loss. *American Journal of Maternal/Child Nursing, 26*, 154–159.

Whelan, T., & Lally, C. (2002). Paternal commitment and father's quality of life. *Journal of Family Studies, 8*, 181–196.

Whitbourne, S. K. (2001). *Adult development and aging: Biopsychosocial perspectives*. New York: Wiley.

Whitbourne, S. K. (2007, October). *Crossing over the bridges of adulthood: Multiple pathways through midlife*. Presidential keynote presented at the 4th Biannual Meeting of the Society for the Study of Human Development, Pennsylvania State University, University Park, PA.

Whitbourne, S. K., & Sliwinski, M. J. (2012). *The Wiley-Blackwell handbook of adulthood and aging*. New York: Wiley-Blackwell.

Whitbourne, S. K., & Whitbourne, S. B. (2016). *Adult development and aging: Biopsychosocial perspectives. (6th ed.)* New York: Wiley.

Whitbourne, S., Sneed, J., & Sayer, A. (2009). Psychosocial development from college through midlife: A 34-year sequential study. *Developmental Psychology, 45*, 1328–1340.

White, K. (2007). Hypnobirthing: The Mongan method. *Australian Journal of Clinical Hypnotherapy and Hypnosis, 28*, 12–24.

White, M. G. (2017). *Which professionals are prone to burnout?* Accessed online, 11-29-17; http://stress.lovetoknow.com/Which_Professionals_are_Prone_to_Burnout.

White, N., Reid, F., Harris, A., Harries, P. & Stone, P. (2016). A systematic review of predictions of survival in palliative care: How accurate are clinicians and who are the experts? *PLOS*. Accessed online, 10-24-17; https://doi.org/10.1371/journal.pone.0161407.

Whiting, B. B., & Edwards, C. P. (1988). *Children of different worlds: The formation of social behavior*. Cambridge, MA: Harvard University Press.

Whiting, J., Simmons, L., Havens, J., Smith, D., & Oka, M. (2009). Intergenerational transmission of violence: The influence of self-appraisals, mental disorders and substance abuse. *Journal of Family Violence, 24*, 639–648.

Wickelgren, W. A. (1999). Webs, cell assemblies, and chunking in neural nets: Introduction. *Canadian Journal of Experimental Psychology, 53*, 118–131.

Widaman, K. (2009). Phenylketonuria in children and mothers: Genes, environments, behavior. *Current Directions in Psychological Science, 18*, 48–52.

Widman, L., Nesi, J., Choukas-Bradley, S., & Prinstein, M. J. (2014). Safe sext: Adolescents' use of technology to communicate about sexual health with dating partners. *Journal of Adolescent Health, 54*, 612–614.

Widom, C. S. (2000). Motivation and mechanisms in the "cycle of violence" In D. J. Hansen (Ed.), *Nebraska Symposium on Motivation Vol. 46, 1998: Motivation and child maltreatment* (Current theory and research in motivation series). Lincoln: University of Nebraska Press.

Wielgosz, A. T., & Nolan, R. P. (2000). Biobehavioral factors in the context of ischemic cardiovascular disease. *Journal of Psychosomatic Research, 48*, 339–345.

Wiggins, J. L., Bedoyan, J. K., Carrasco, M., Swartz, J. R., Martin, D. M., & Monk, C. S. (2014). Age-related effect of serotonin transporter genotype on amygdala and prefrontal cortex function in adolescence. *Human Brain Mapping, 35*, 646–658.

Wiggins, M., & Uwaydat, S. (2006, January). Age-related macular degeneration: Options for earlier detection and improved treatment. *Journal of Family Practice, 55*, 22–27.

Wilcox, A., Skjaerven, R., Buekens, P., & Kiely, J. (1995, March 1). Birth weight and perinatal mortality: A comparison of the United States and Norway. *JAMA: Journal of the American Medical Association, 273*, 709–711.

Wilcox, H. C., Conner, K. R., & Caine, E. D. (2004). Association of alcohol and drug use disorders and completed suicide: An empirical review of cohort studies. *Drug & Alcohol Dependence, 76* [Special issue: Drug abuse and suicidal behavior], S11–S19.

Wilcox, T., Woods, R., Chapa, C., & McCurry, S. (2007). Multisensory exploration and object individuation in infancy. *Developmental Psychology, 43*, 479–495.

Wild, B., Heider, D., Maatouk, I., Slaets, J., König, H., Niehoff, D., & … Herzog, W. (2014). Significance and costs of complex biopsychosocial health care needs in elderly people: Results of a population-based study. *Psychosomatic Medicine, 76*, 497–502.

Wildberger, S. (2003, August). So you're having a baby. *Washingtonian*, pp. 85–86, 88–90.

Wiley, T. L., Nondahl, D. M., Cruickshanks, K. J., & Tweed, T. S. (2005). Five-year changes in middle ear function for older adults. *Journal of the American Academy of Audiology, 16*, 129–139.

Wilfond, B., & Ross, L. (2009). From genetics to genomics: Ethics, policy, and parental decision-making. *Journal of Pediatric Psychology, 34*, 639–647. Accessed online; http://search.ebscohost.com, doi:10.1093/jpepsy/jsn075.

Wilhoit, L. F., Scott, D. A., & Simecka, B. A. (2017). Fetal alcohol spectrum disorders: Characteristics, complications, and treatment. *Community Mental Health Journal*. Accessed online, 10-27-17; https://www.ncbi.nlm.nih.gov/pubmed/28168434

Wilkes, S., Chinn, D., Murdoch, A., & Rubin, G. (2009). Epidemiology and management of infertility: A population-based study in UK primary care. *Family Practice, 26*, 269–274.

Wilkinson, C. B., Infantolino, Z. P., & Wacha-Montes, A. (2017). Evidence-based practice as a potential solution to burnout in university counseling center clinicians. *Psychological Services, 14*, 543–548.

Wilkinson, N., Paikan, A., Gredebäck, G., Rea, F., & Metta, G. (2014). Staring us in the face? An embodied theory of innate face preference. *Developmental Science, 17*, 809–825.

Willford, J. A., Richardson, G. A., & Day, N. L. (2012). Sex-specific effects of prenatal marijuana exposure on neurodevelopment and behavior. In M. Lewis & L. Kestler (Eds.), *Gender differences in prenatal substance exposure*. Washington, DC: American Psychological Association.

Williams, J., & Binnie, L. (2002). Children's concept of illness: An intervention to improve knowledge. *British Journal of Health Psychology, 7*, 129–148.

Williams, K., & Dunne-Bryant, A. (2006, December). Divorce and adult psychological well-being: Clarifying the role of gender and child age. *Journal of Marriage and Family, 68*, 1178–1196.

Williams, P., Sheridan, S., & Sandberg, A. (2014). Preschool—An arena for children's learning of social and cognitive knowledge. *Early Years: An International Journal of Research and Development, 34*, 226–240.

Williams, R., Barefoot, J., & Schneiderman, N. (2003). Psychosocial risk factors for cardiovascular disease: More than one culprit at work. *JAMA: Journal of the American Medical Association, 290*, 2190–2192.

Willie, C., & Reddick, R. (2003). *A new look at black families* (5th ed.). Walnut Creek, CA: AltaMira Press.

Willis, S. (1996). Everyday problem solving. In J. E. Birren, K. W. Schaie, R. P. Abeles, M. Gatz, & T. A. Salthouse (Eds.), *Handbook of the psychology of aging* (4th ed.). San Diego: Academic Press.

Willis, S. L. (1985). Educational psychology of the older adult learner. In J. E. Birren & K. W. Schaie (Eds.), *Handbook of the psychology of aging* (2nd ed.). New York: Van Nostrand Reinhold.

Willis, S., Tennstedt, S., Marsiske, M., Ball, K., Elias, J., Koepke, K., Morris, J., Rebok, G., Unverzagt, F., Stoddard, A., & Wright, E. (2006). Long-term effects of cognitive training on everyday functional outcomes in older adults. *JAMA: Journal of the American Medical Association, 296*, 2805–2814.

Wills, T., Sargent, J., Stoolmiller, M., Gibbons, F., & Gerrard, M. (2008). Movie smoking exposure and smoking onset: A longitudinal study of mediation processes in a representative sample of U.S. adolescents. *Psychology of Addictive Behaviors, 22*, 269–277.

Wilson, K. L., Smith, M. L., Rosen, B. L., Pulczinski, J. C., & Ory, M. G. (2017). HPV vaccination status and mandate support for school-aged adolescents among college females: A descriptive study. *Journal of School Nursing, 33*, 232–245.

Wilson, R. S., Boyle, P. A., Yu, L., Segawa, E., Sytsma, J., & Bennett, D. A. (2015). Conscientiousness, dementia related pathology, and trajectories of cognitive aging. *Psychology and Aging, 30*, 74–82.

Wilson, S. L. (2003). Post-institutionalization: The effects of early deprivation on development of Romanian adoptees. *Child & Adolescent Social Work Journal, 20*, 473–483.

Wilsona, C. L., & Simpson, J. A. (2016). Childbirth pain, attachment orientations, and romantic partner support during labor and delivery. *Personal Relationships, 23*, 622–644.

Wines, M. (2006, August 24). Africa adds to miserable ranks for child workers. *New York Times*, p. D1.

Winger, G., & Woods, J. H. (2004). *A handbook on drug and alcohol abuse: The biomedical aspects*. Oxford, England: Oxford University Press.

Wingfield, A., Tun, P. A., & McCoy, S. L. (2005). Hearing loss in older adulthood: What it is and how it interacts with cognitive performance. *Current Directions in Psychological Science, 14*, 144–147.

Wink, P., & Staudinger, U. M. (2015). Wisdom and psychosocial functioning in later life. *Journal of Personality*. Accessed online, 4-1-15; http://onlinelibrary.wiley.com/doi/10.1111/jopy.12160/abstract.

Winkler, I., Haden, G. P., Nemeth, R., Haden, G. P., Winkler, I., & Toeroek, M. (2016). Processing of horizontal sound localization cues in newborn infants. *Ear and Hearing, 36* (5), 550–556.

Winsler, A. (2003). Introduction to special issue: Vygotskian perspectives in early childhood education. *Early Education and Development, 14, [Special Issue]*, 253–269.

Winterich, J. (2003). Sex, menopause, and culture: Sexual orientation and the meaning of menopause for women's sex lives. *Gender & Society, 17*, 627–642.

Winters, K. C., Stinchfield, R. D., & Botzet, A. (2005). Pathways of youth gambling problem severity. *Psychology of Addictive Behaviors, 19*, 104–107.

Winters, S., Martin, C., Murphy, D., & Shokar, N. K. (2017). Breast cancer epidemiology, prevention and screening. *Progress in Molecular Biology and Translational Science, 151*, 1–32.

Wippert, P., & Niemeyer, H. (2014). Types of coping strategies as predictors for the development of psychosomatic disorders after the life event "career termination." In C. Mohiyeddini (Ed.), *Contemporary topics and trends in the psychology of sports*. Hauppauge, NY: Nova Science Publishers.

Wirth, A., Wabitsch, M., & Hauner, H. (2014). The prevention and treatment of obesity. *Deutsches Ärzteblatt International, 111*, 705–713.

Wisborg, K., Kesmodel, U., Bech, B. H., Hedegaard, M., & Henriksen, T. B. (2003). Maternal consumption of coffee during pregnancy and stillbirth and infant death in first year of life: Prospective study. *British Medical Journal, 326*, 420.

Wisdom, J. P., & Agnor, C. (2007). Family heritage and depression guides: Family and peer views influence adolescent attitudes about depression. *Journal of Adolescence, 30*, 333–346.

Wise, L., Adams-Campbell, L., Palmer, J., & Rosenberg, L. (2006, August). Leisure time physical activity in relation to depressive symptoms in the Black Women's Health Study. *Annals of Behavioral Medicine, 32*, 68–76.

Witt, E. A., Donnellan, M., & Trzesniewski, K. H. (2011). Self-esteem, narcissism, and Machiavellianism: Implications for understanding antisocial behavior in adolescents and young adults. In C. T. Barry, P. K. Kerig, K. K. Stellwagen, & T. D. Barry (Eds.), *Narcissism and Machiavellianism in youth: Implications for the development of adaptive and maladaptive behavior*. Washington, DC: American Psychological Association.

Woelfle, J. F., Harz, K., & Roth, C. (2007). Modulation of circulating IGF-I and IGFBP-3 levels by hormonal regulators of energy homeostasis in obese children. *Experimental and Clinical Endocrinology Diabetes, 115*, 17–23.

Wolfe, M. S. (2006, May). Shutting down Alzheimer's. *Scientific American*, pp. 73–79.

Wolfe, W. (2007, February 24). Late life love: Older couples find that love comes when they aren't looking for it and share the stories of their late-in-life romance. *Star Tribune* (Minneapolis, MN), p. 1E.

Wolfson, A. R., & Richards, M. (2011). Young adolescents: Struggles with insufficient sleep. In M. El-Sheikh (Ed.), *Sleep and development: Familial and socio-cultural considerations*. New York: Oxford University Press.

Wolinsky, F., Wyrwich, K., & Babu, A. (2003). Age, aging, and the sense of control among older adults: A longitudinal reconsideration. *Journals of Gerontology: Series B: Psychological Sciences & Social Sciences, 58B*, S212–S220.

Wolkorte, R., Kamphuis, J., & Zijdewind, I. (2014). Increased reaction times and reduced response preparation already starts at middle age. *Frontiers in Aging Neuroscience, 6*, 118–127.

Woodhouse, S. S., Dykas, M. J., & Cassidy, J. (2012). Loneliness and peer relations in adolescence. *Social Development, 21*, 273–293.

Woods, R. (2009). The use of aggression in primary school boys' decisions about inclusion in and exclusion from playground football games. *British Journal of Educational Psychology, 79*, 223–238.

Woodspring, N. (2012). Review of Agewise: Fighting the new ageism in America. *Health: An Interdisciplinary Journal for the Social Study of Health, Illness and Medicine, 16*(3), 343–344. doi:10.1177/1363459311423335.

Woolf, A., & Lesperance, L. (2003, September 22). What should we worry about? *Newsweek*, p. 72.

World Bank. (2003). *Global development finance 2003—Striving for stability in development finance*. Washington, DC: Author.

World Factbook. (2012). *Estimates of infant mortality*. Accessed online; https://www.cia.gov/library/publications/the-world-factbook/rankorder/2091rank.html.

World Factbook. (2016). *Estimates of infant mortality*. Accessed online, 10-27-17; https://www.cia.gov/library/publications/the-world-factbook/fields/2091.html.

World Factbook. (2017). Life expectancy at birth. Accessed online, 12-11-17; https://www.cia.gov/library/publications/the-world-factbook/rankorder/2102rank.html.

World Factbook. (2017). Total fertility rate. Accessed online, 11-22-17; https://www.cia.gov/library/publications/the-world-factbook/fields/2127.html.

World Factbook. (2017). *World Factbook*. Washington, DC: Central Intelligence Agency. Accessed online, 10-27-17; https://www.cia.gov/library/publications/the-world-factbook/rankorder/2091rank.html.

World Food Programme. (2106). *Hunger statistics*. Rome: World Food Programme. Accessed online 10-25-17; https://www.wfp.org/hunger/stats.

Wörmann, V., Holodynski, M., Kärtner, J., & Keller, H. (2014). The emergence of social smiling: The interplay of maternal and infant imitation during the first three months in cross-cultural comparison. *Journal of Cross-Cultural Psychology, 45*, 339–361.

Worrell, F., Szarko, J., & Gabelko, N. (2001). Multi-year persistence of nontraditional students in an academic talent development program. *Journal of Secondary Gifted Education, 12*, 80–89.

Wright, J. C., Huston, A. C., Murphy, K. C., St. Peters, M., Piñon, M., Scantlin, R., & Kotler, J. (2001). The relations of early television viewing to school readiness and vocabulary of children from low-income families: The Early Window Project. *Child Development, 72*, 1347–1366.

Wright, J. C., Huston, A. C., Reitz, A. L., & Piemyat, S. (1994). Young children's perceptions of television reality: Determinants and developmental differences. *Developmental Psychology, 30*, 229–239.

Wright, M., Wintemute, G., & Claire, B. (2008). Gun suicide by young people in California: Descriptive epidemiology and gun ownership. *Journal of Adolescent Health, 43*, 619–622.

Wrosch, C., Bauer, I., & Scheier, M. (2005, December). Regret and quality of life across the adult life span: The influence of disengagement and available future goals. *Psychology and Aging, 20*, 657–670.

Wrzus, C., Zimmermann, J., Mund, M., & Neyer, F. J. (2017). Friendships in young and middle adulthood: Normative patterns and personality differences. In M. Hojjat, A. Moyer (Eds.), *The psychology of friendship*. New York: Oxford University Press.

Wu, P., Hoven, C. W., Okezie, N., Fuller, C. J., & Cohen, P. (2007). Alcohol abuse and depression in children and adolescents. *Journal of Child & Adolescent Substance Abuse, 17*, 51–69.

Wu, P., & Liu, H. (2014). Association between moral reasoning and moral behavior: A systematic review and meta-analysis. *Acta Psychologica Sinica, 46*, 1192–1207.

Wu, T., Treiber, F. A., & Snieder, H. (2013). Genetic influence on blood pressure and underlying hemodynamics measured at rest and during stress. *Psychosomatic Medicine, 75*, 404–412.

Wu, Y., Tsou, K., Hsu, C., Fang, L., Yao, G., & Jeng, S. (2008). Brief report: Taiwanese infants' mental and motor development—6–24 months. *Journal of Pediatric Psychology, 33*, 102–108.

Wu, Z., & Su, Y. (2014). How do preschoolers' sharing behaviors relate to their theory of mind understanding? *Journal of Experimental Child Psychology, 120*, 73–86.

Wupperman, P., Marlatt, G., Cunningham, A., Bowen, S., Berking, M., Mulvihill-Rivera, N., & Easton, C. (2012). Mindfulness and modification therapy for behavioral dysregulation: Results from a pilot study targeting alcohol use and aggression in women. *Journal of Clinical Psychology, 68*, 50–66.

Wyer, R. (2004). The cognitive organization and use of general knowledge. In J. Jost & M. Banaji (Eds.), *Perspectivism in social psychology: The yin and yang of scientific progress*. Washington, DC: American Psychological Association.

Wynn, K. (1995). Infants possess a system of numerical knowledge. *Current Directions in Psychological Science, 4*, 172–177.

Wynn, K. (2000). Findings of addition and subtraction in infants are robust and consistent: Reply to Wakeley, Rivera, and Langer. *Child Development, 71*, 1535–1536.

Wyra, M., Lawson, M. J., & Hungi, N. (2007). The mnemonic keyword method: The effects of bidirectional retrieval training and of ability to image on foreign language vocabulary recall. *Learning and Instruction, 17*, 360–371.

Xiao, H., Kwong, E., Pang, S., & Mok, E. (2012). Perceptions of a life review programme among Chinese patients with advanced cancer. *Journal of Clinical Nursing, 21*, 564–572.

Xiao, N. G., Quinn, P. C., Liu, S., Ge, L., Pascalis, O., & Lee, K. (2017a). Older but not younger infants associate own-race faces with happy music and other-race faces with sad music. *Developmental Science*. Accessed online, 10-31-17; http://onlinelibrary.wiley.com/doi/10.1111/desc.12537/abstract.

Xiao, N. G., Wu, R., Quinn, P. C., Liu, S., Tummeltshammer, K. S., Kirkham, N. Z., & ...: Lee, K. (2017b). Infants rely more on gaze cues from own-race than other-race adults for learning under uncertainty. *Child Development*. Accessed online, 10-31-17; http://onlinelibrary.wiley.com/doi/10.1111/cdev.12798/abstract.

Xiao, R., Qi, X., Patino, A., Fagg, A. H., Kolobe, T. H., Miller, D. P., & Ding, L. (2017). Characterization of infant mu rhythm immediately before crawling: A high-resolution EEG study. *Neuroimage, 146*, 47–57.

Xiaohe, X., & Whyte, M. K. (1990). Love matches and arranged marriages: A Chinese replication. *Journal of Marriage and the Family, 52*, 709–722.

Xie, R., Gaudet, L., Krewski, D., Graham, I. D., Walker, M. C., & Wen, S. W. (2015). Higher cesarean delivery rates are associated with higher infant mortality rates in industrialized countries. *Birth: Issues in Perinatal Care*. Accessed online, 3-14-15; http://onlinelibrary.wiley.com/doi/10.1111/birt.12153/pdf.

Xu, C., & LeFevre, J. (2016). Training young children on sequential relations among numbers and spatial decomposition: Differential transfer to number line and mental transformation tasks. *Developmental Psychology, 52*, 854–866.

Xu, J., Harper, J. A., Van Enkevort, E. A., Latimer, K., Kelley, U., & McAdams, C. J. (2017). Neural activations are related to body shape, anxiety, and outcomes in adolescent anorexia nervosa. *Journal of Psychiatric Research, 87*, 1–7.

Xu, J., Saether, L., & Sommerville, J. A. (2016). Experience facilitates the emergence of sharing behavior among 7.5-month-old infants. *Developmental Psychology, 52*, 1732–1743.

Yagmurlu, B., & Sanson, A. (2009). Parenting and temperament as predictors of prosocial behaviour in Australian and Turkish Australian children. *Australian Journal of Psychology, 61*, 77–88.

Yamada, J., Stinson, J., Lamba, J., Dickson, A., McGrath, P., & Stevens, B. (2008). A review of systematic reviews on pain interventions in hospitalized infants. *Pain Research & Management, 13*, 413–420.

Yang, C., Crain, S., Berwick, R. C., Chomsky, N., & Bolhuis, J. J. (2017). The growth of language: Universal grammar, experience, and principles of computation. *Neuroscience and Biobehavioral Reviews*. Accessed online, 10-29-17; http://www.sciencedirect.com/science/article/pii/S0149763416305656.

Yang, C. D. (2006). *The infinite gift: How children learn and unlearn the languages of the world*. New York: Scribner.

Yang, C., & Brown, B. B. (2015). Factors involved in associations between Facebook use and college adjustment: Social competence, perceived usefulness, and use patterns. *Computers in Human Behavior, 46*, 245–253.

Yang, Q., Liu, S., Sullivan, D., & Pan, S. (2016). Interpreting suffering from illness: The role of culture and repressive suffering construal. *Social Science & Medicine, 160*, 67–74.

Yang, R., & Blodgett, B. (2000). Effects of race and adolescent decision-making on status attainment and self-esteem. *Journal of Ethnic & Cultural Diversity in Social Work, 9*, 135–153.

Yang, S., & Rettig, K. D. (2004). Korean-American mothers' experiences in facilitating academic success for their adolescents. *Marriage & Family Review, 36*, 53–74.

Yang, Y. (2008). Social inequalities in happiness in the U.S. 1972–2004: An age-period-cohort analysis. *American Sociological Review, 73*, 204–226.

Yardley, J. (2001, July 2). Child-death case in Texas raises penalty questions. *New York Times*, p. A1.

Yarrow, M. R., Scott, P. M., & Waxler, C. Z. (1973). Learning concern for others. *Developmental Psychology, 8*, 240–260.

Yasnitsky, A., & van der Veer, R. (2016). *Revisionist revolution in Vygotsky studies*. New York: Routledge/Taylor & Francis Group.

Yato, Y., Kawai, M., Negayama, K., Sogon, S., Tomiwa, K., & Yamamoto, H. (2008). Infant responses to maternal still-face at 4 and 9 months. *Infant Behavior & Development, 31*, 570–577.

Ybarra, M. L., & Thompson, R. E. (2017). Predicting the emergence of sexual violence in adolescence. *Prevention Science*. Accessed online, 12-12-17; https://www.ncbi.nlm.nih.gov/pubmed/28685211.

Yell, M. L. (2015). *Law and special education*. (4th ed.) Hoboken, NJ: Pearson.

Yell, M. L., & Drasgow, E. (2010). The continuing influence of the law in special education: Introduction to the special issue. *Exceptionality, 18*, 107–108.

Yildiz, O. (2007). Vascular smooth muscle and endothelial functions in aging. *Annals of the New York Academy of Sciences, 1100*, 353–360.

Yim, I., Glynn, L., Schetter, C., Hobel, C., Chicz-DeMet, A., & Sandman, C. (2009). Risk of postpartum depressive symptoms with elevated corticotropin-releasing hormone in human pregnancy. *Archives of General Psychiatry, 66*, 162–169.

Yinger, J. (Ed.). (2004). *Helping children left behind: State aid and the pursuit of educational equity*. Cambridge, MA: MIT Press.

Yip, T., Sellers, R. M., & Seaton, E. K. (2006). African American racial identity across the lifespan: Identity status, identity content, and depressive symptoms. *Child Development, 77*, 1504–1517.

Yon, Y., Wister, A. V., Mitchell, B., & Gutman, G. (2014). A national comparison of spousal abuse in mid- and old age. *Journal of Elder Abuse & Neglect, 26*, 80–105.

Yonker, J. E., Schnabelrauch, C. A., & DeHaan, L. G. (2012). The relationship between spirituality and religiosity on psychological outcomes in adolescents and emerging adults: A meta-analytic review. *Journal of Adolescence, 35*, 299–314.

Yoon, E., Adams, K., Clawson, A., Chang, H., Surya, S., & Jérémie-Brink, G. (2017). East Asian adolescents' ethnic identity development and cultural integration: A qualitative investigation. *Journal of Counseling Psychology, 64*, 65–79.

York, E. (2008). Gender differences in the college and career aspirations of high school valedictorians. *Journal of Advanced Academics, 19*, 578–600.

York, G. S., Churchman, R., Woodard, B., Wainright, C., & Rau-Foster, M. (2012). Free-text comments: Understanding the value in family member descriptions of hospice caregiver relationships. *American Journal of Hospice & Palliative Medicine, 29*, 98–105.

Yoshinaga-Itano, C. (2003). From screening to early identification and intervention: Discovering predictors to successful outcomes for children with significant hearing loss. *Journal of Deaf Studies & Deaf Education, 8*, 11–30.

Yott, J., & Poulin-Dubois, D. (2016). Are infants' theory-of-mind abilities well integrated? Implicit understanding of intentions, desires, and beliefs. *Journal of Cognition and Development, 17*, 683–698.

You, J-I., & Bellmore, A. (2012). Relational peer victimization and psychosocial adjustment: The mediating role of best friendship qualities. *Personal Relationships, 19*, 340–353.

Young, A. M., Elliston, A., & Ruble, L. A. (2016). Children with autism and vaccinations. In J. Merrick, J. Merrick (Eds.), *Children and childhood: Some international aspects*. Hauppauge, NY: Nova Biomedical Books.

Young, S., Rhee, S., Stallings, M., Corley, R., & Hewitt, J. (2006, July). Genetic and environmental vulnerabilities underlying adolescent substance use and problem use: General or specific? *Behavior Genetics, 36*, 603–615.

Yu, C., Hung, C., Chan, T., Yeh, C., & Lai, C. (2012). Prenatal predictors for father-infant attachment after childbirth. *Journal of Clinical Nursing, 21*, 1577–1583.

Yu, M., & Stiffman, A. (2007). Culture and environment as predictors of alcohol abuse/dependence symptoms in American Indian youths. *Addictive Behaviors, 32*, 2253–2259.

Yuan, A. (2012). Perceived breast development and adolescent girls' psychological well-being. *Sex Roles, 66*, 790–806.

Yuill, N., & Perner, J. (1988). Intentionality and knowledge in children's judgments of actor's responsibility and recipient's emotional reaction. *Developmental Psychology, 24*, 358–365.

Zacchilli, T. L., & Valerio, C. (2011). The knowledge and prevalence of cyber bullying in a college sample. *Journal of Scientific Psychology*.

Zafeiriou, D. I. (2004). Primitive reflexes and postural reactions in the neurodevelopmental examination. *Pediatric Neurology, 31*, 1–8.

Zahn-Waxler, C., Shirtcliff, E., & Marceau, K. (2008). Disorders of childhood and adolescence: Gender and psychopathology. *Annual Review of Clinical Psychology, 4*, 275–303.

Zakrzewski, A. C., Johnson, J. M., & Smith, J. D. (2017). The comparative psychology of metacognition. In J. Call, G. M. Burghardt, I. M. Pepperberg, C. T. Snowdon, T. Zentall (Eds.), *APA handbook of comparative psychology: Perception, learning, and cognition*. Washington, DC: American Psychological Association.

Zalenski, R., & Raspa, R. (2006). Maslow's hierarchy of needs: A framework for achieving human potential in hospice. *Journal of Palliative Medicine, 9*, 1120–1127.

Zalsman, G., Oquendo, M., Greenhill, L., Goldberg, P., Kamali, M., Martin, A., et al. (2006, October). Neurobiology of depression in children and adolescents. *Child and Adolescent Psychiatric Clinics of North America, 15*, 843–868.

Zampi, C., Fagioli, I., & Salzarulo, P. (2002). Time course of EEG background activity level before spontaneous awakening in infants. *Journal of Sleep Research, 11*, 283–287.

Zanardo, S., Nicolussi, F., Favaro, D., Faggian, M., Plebani, F., Marzari, F., & Freato, V. (2001). Effect of postpartum anxiety on the colostral milk beta-endorphin concentrations of breastfeeding mothers. *Journal of Obstetrics and Gynaecology, 21*, 130–134.

Zarbatany, L., Hartmann, D. P., & Rankin, D. B. (1990). The psychological funcitons of preadolescent peer activities. *Child Development, 61*, 1067–1080.

Zauszniewski, J. A., & Martin, M. H. (1999). Developmental task achievement and learned resourcefulness in healthy older adults. *Archives of Psychiatric Nursing, 13*, 41–47.

Zautra, E. K., Zautra, A. J., Gallardo, C. E., & Velasco, L. (2015). Can we learn to treat one another better? A test of a social intelligence curriculum. *Plos ONE, 10*, 88–97.

Zeanah, C. (2009). The importance of early experiences: Clinical, research and policy perspectives. *Journal of Loss and Trauma, 14*, 266–279.

Zebrowitz, L., Luevano, V., Bronstad, P., & Aharon, I. (2009). Neural activation to babyfaced men matches activation to babies. *Social Neuroscience, 4*, 1–10.

Zelazo, P. D., Muller, U., Frye, D., & Marcovitch, S. (2003). The development of executive function in early childhood. *Monographs of the Society for Research in Child Development, 68*, 103–122.

Zelazo, P. R. (1998). McGraw and the development of unaided walking. *Developmental Review, 18*, 449–471.

Zemach, I., Chang, S., & Teller, D. (2007). Infant color vision: Prediction of infants' spontaneous color preferences. *Vision Research, 47*, 1368–1381.

Zhai, F., Raver, C., & Jones, S. M. (2012). Academic performance of subsequent schools and impacts of early interventions: Evidence from a randomized controlled trial in Head Start settings. *Children and Youth Services Review, 34*, 946–954.

Zhang, N., Baker, H. W., Tufts, M., Raymond, R. E., Salihu, H., & Elliott, M. R. (2013). Early childhood lead exposure and academic achievement: Evidence from Detroit public schools, 2008-2010. *American Journal Of Public Health, 103*(3), e72-e77. doi:10.2105/AJPH.2012.301164

Zhang, Y., Bokov, A., Gelfond, J., Soto, V., Ikeno, Y., Hubbard, G., & … Fischer, K. (2014). Rapamycin extends life and health in C57BL/6 mice. *Journals of Gerontology: Series A: Biological Sciences and Medical Sciences, 69A*, 119–130.

Zhe, C., & Siegler, R. S. (2000). Across the great divide: Bridging the gap between understanding of toddlers' and older children's thinking. *Monographs of the Society for Research in Child Development, 65* (2, Serial No. 261).

Zhu, J., & Weiss, L. (2005). The Wechsler Scales. In D. P. Flanagan & P. L. Harrison (Eds.), *Contemporary intellectual assessment: Theories, tests, and issues*. New York: Guilford Press.

Ziegler, M., Danay, E., Heene, M., Asendorpf, J., & Bühner, M. (2012). Openness, fluid intelligence, and crystallized intelligence: Toward an integrative model. *Journal of Research in Personality, 46*, 173–183.

Zimmer-Gembeck, M. J., & Collins, W. A. (2003). Autonomy development during adolescence. In G. R. Adams & M. D. Berzonsky (Eds.), *Blackwell handbook of adolescence*. Malden, MA: Blackwell Publishing.

Zimmer-Gembeck, M. J., & Gallaty, K. J. (2006). Hanging out or hanging in? Young females' socioemotional functioning and the changing motives for dating and romance. In A. Columbus (Ed.), *Advances in psychology research (Vol. 44)*. Hauppauge, NY: Nova Science Publishers.

Zimmerman, F. J., Christakis, D. A., & Meltzoff, A. N. (2007). Associations between media viewing and language development in children under age 2 years. *Journal of Pediatrics, 151*, 364–368.

Zirkel, S., & Cantor, N. (2004). 50 years after *Brown v. Board of Education*: The promise and challenge of multicultural education. *Journal of Social Issues, 60*, 1–15.

Zisook, S., & Shear, K. (2009). Grief and bereavement: What psychiatrists need to know. *World Psychiatry, 8*, 67–74.

Zito, J. M., Safer, D. J., dosReis, S., Gardner, J. F., Boles, M., & Lynch, F. (2000). Trends in prescribing of psychotropic medications to preschoolers. *JAMA: Journal of the American Medical Association, 283*, 1025–1030.

Zolotor, A., Theodore, A., Chang, J., Berkoff, M., & Runyan, D. (2008). Speak softly—and forget the stick: Corporal punishment and child physical abuse. *American Journal of Preventive Medicine, 35*, 364–369.

Zong, N., Nam, S., Eom, J., Ahn, J., Joe, H., & Kim, H. (2015). Aligning ontologies with subsumption and equivalence relations in Linked Data. *Knowledge-Based Systems, 76*, 30–41.

Zosuls, K. M., Field, R. D., Martin, C. L., Andrews, N. Z., & England, D. E. (2014). Gender-based relationship efficacy: Children's self-perceptions in intergroup contexts. *Child Development, 85*, 1663–1676.

Zosuls, K. M., Ruble, D. N., & Tamis-LeMonda, C. S. (2014). Self-socialization of gender in African American, Dominican immigrant, and Mexican immigrant toddlers. *Child Development, 85*, 2202–2217.

Zuccarini, M., Sansavini, A., Iverson, J. M., Savini, S., Guarini, A., Alessandroni, R., & … Aureli, T. (2016). Object engagement and manipulation in extremely preterm and full term infants at 6 months of age. *Research in Developmental Disabilities, 55*, 173–184.

Zucker, J. & Alexander-Tanner, R. (2017, May 11). Well illustrated: Childbirth. *New York Times.* Accessed online, 10-25-17: https://www.nytimes.com/2017/05/11/well/family/well-illustrated-childbirth.html?_r=0.

Zuckerman, G., & Shenfield, S. D. (2007). Child-adult interaction that creates a zone of proximal development. *Journal of Russian & East European Psychology, 45*, 43–69.

Zwelling, E. (2006). A challenging time in the history of Lamaze international: An interview with Francine Nichols. *Journal of Perinatal Education, 15*, 10–17.

Zyphur, M. J., Zhang, Z., Barsky, A. P., & Li, W. (2013). An ACE in the hole: Twin family models for applied behavioral genetics research. *The Leadership Quarterly, 24*, 572–594.

Name Index

D

G

H

I

J

L

M

N

O

P

Q

T

U

V

W

X

Y

Z

Subject Index

D

E

F

G

H

I

N

O

P

Q

R

T

U

V

W

X

Y

Z

	PRENATAL PERIOD (conception to birth)	INFANCY AND TODDLERHOOD (birth to 3 years)
PHYSICAL DEVELOPMENT	*GERMINAL STAGE* (fertilization to 2 weeks): • Cells divide rapidly. • Zygote attaches to uterine wall. *EMBRYONIC STAGE* (2 to 8 weeks): • Major organs and body systems grow. *FETAL STAGE* (8 weeks to birth): • Major organs become differentiated. • Fetus kicks and clinches fist, hears sounds outside the uterus. • Health can be affected by mother's diet, health, age, or substance use. • Reflexes emerge.	• Rapid height and weight gains. • Neurons grow and form interconnections in the brain. Some functions have "critical periods" for normal development. • Infants wiggle, push upward, sit up, crawl, and eventually walk. • Infants reach, grasp, and pick up small objects. • Vision is 20/20 by 6 months, with depth perception and recognition of patterns, faces, shapes, and colors. • Infants hear a wide range of frequencies, localize sound, and make sound distinctions that underlie language development.
COGNITIVE DEVELOPMENT	• Intelligence is partly determined, and some psychological disorders may take root. • Cognitive functions can be affected by tobacco, alcohol, or drug use by mother.	• Infants begin to understand object permanence and "experiment" with the physical world. • Use of representations and symbols begins. • Information-processing speed increases. • Language develops rapidly through prelinguistic communication (babbling), use of single words to stand for whole ideas (holophrases), and telegraphic speech.
SOCIAL/PERSONALITY DEVELOPMENT	• Some personality traits are partly determined genetically (e.g., neuroticism, extroversion). • Drug and alcohol use by mother can lead to irritability, difficulty forming attachments in the child.	• Infants exhibit different temperaments and activity levels. • Facial expressions appear to reflect emotions; facial expressions of others are understood. • Toddlers begin to feel empathy. • A style of attachment to others emerges.
THEORIES & THEORISTS		
Jean Piaget		Sensorimotor stage
Erik Erikson		Trust-versus-mistrust stage (birth–1½ yrs) Autonomy-versus-shame-and-doubt stage (1½–3 yrs)
Sigmund Freud		Oral and anal stages
Lawrence Kohlberg		Premoral period

PRESCHOOL PERIOD (3 to 6 years)	MIDDLE CHILDHOOD (6 to 12 years)
• Height and weight continue to increase rapidly. • The body becomes less rounded and more muscular. • The brain grows larger, neural interconnections continue to develop, and lateralization emerges. • Gross and fine motor skills advance quickly. Children can throw and catch balls, run, use forks and spoons, and tie shoelaces. • Children begin to develop handedness.	• Growth becomes slow and steady. Muscles develop, and "baby fat" is lost. • Gross motor skills (biking, swimming, skating, ball handling) and fine motor skills (writing, typing, fastening buttons) continue to improve.
• Children show egocentric thinking (viewing world from their own perspective) and "centration," a focus on only one aspect of a stimulus. • Memory, attention span, and symbolic thinking improve, and intuitive thought begins. • Language (sentence length, vocabulary, syntax, and grammar) improves rapidly.	• Children apply logical operations to problems. • Understanding of conservation (that changes in shape do not necessarily affect quantity) and transformation (that objects can go through many states without changing) emerge. • Children can "decenter"— take multiple perspectives into account. • Memory encoding, storage, and retrieval improve, and control strategies (metamemory) develop. • Language pragmatics (social conventions) and metalinguistic awareness (self-monitoring) improve.
• Children develop self-concepts, which may be exaggerated. • A sense of gender and racial identity emerges. • Children begin to see peers as individuals and form friendships based on trust and shared interests. • Morality is rule-based and focused on rewards and punishments. • Play becomes more constructive and cooperative, and social skills become important.	• Children refer to psychological traits to define themselves. Sense of self becomes differentiated. • Social comparison is used to understand one's standing and identity. • Self-esteem grows differentiated, and a sense of self-efficacy (an appraisal of what one can and cannot do) develops. • Children approach moral problems intent on maintaining social respect and accepting what society defines as right. • Friendship patterns of boys and girls differ. Boys mostly interact with boys in groups, and girls tend to interact singly or in pairs with other girls.
Preoperational stage	Concrete operational stage
Initiative-versus-guilt stage	Industry-versus-inferiority stage
Phallic stage	Latency period
Preconventional morality level	Conventional morality level

	ADOLESCENCE (12 to 20 years)	YOUNG ADULTHOOD (20 to 40 years)
PHYSICAL DEVELOPMENT	• Girls begin the adolescent growth spurt around age 10, boys around age 12. • Girls reach puberty around age 11 or 12, boys around age 13 or 14. • Primary sexual characteristics develop (affecting the reproductive organs), as do secondary sexual characteristics (pubic and underarm hair in both sexes, breasts in girls, deep voices in boys).	• Physical capabilities peak in the 20's, including strength, senses, coordination, and reaction time. • Growth is mostly complete, although some organs, including the brain, continue to grow. • For many young adults, obesity becomes a threat for the first time, as body fat increases. • Stress can become a significant health threat. • In the mid-30's, disease replaces accidents as the leading cause of death.
COGNITIVE DEVELOPMENT	• Abstract thought prevails. Adolescents use formal logic to consider problems in the abstract. • Relative, not absolute, thinking is typical. • Verbal, mathematical, and spatial skills improve. • Adolescents are able to think hypothetically, divide attention, and monitor thought through metacognition. • Egocentrism develops, with a sense that one is always being observed. Self-consciousness and introspection are typical. • A sense of invulnerability can lead adolescents to ignore danger.	• As world experience increases, thought becomes more flexible and subjective, geared to adept problem solving. • Intelligence is applied to long-term goals involving career, family, and society. • Significant life events of young adulthood may shape cognitive development.
SOCIAL/PERSONALITY DEVELOPMENT	• Self-concept becomes organized and accurate and reflects others' perceptions. Self-esteem grows differentiated. • Defining identity is a key task. Peer relationships provide social comparison and help define acceptable roles. Popularity issues become acute; peer pressure can enforce conformity. • Adolescents' quest for autonomy can bring conflict with parents as family roles are renegotiated. • Sexuality assumes importance in identity formation. Dating begins.	• Forming intimate relationships becomes highly important. Commitment may be partly determined by the attachment style developed in infancy. • Marriage and children bring developmental changes, often stressful. Divorce may result, with new stresses. • Identity is largely defined in terms of work, as young adults consolidate their careers.
THEORIES & THEORISTS		
Jean Piaget	Formal operations stage	
Erik Erikson	Identity-versus-confusion stage	Intimacy-versus-isolation stage
Sigmund Freud	Genital stage	
Lawrence Kohlberg	Postconventional morality level may be reached	

MIDDLE ADULTHOOD (40 to 65 years)	LATE ADULTHOOD (65 years to death)
• Physical changes become evident. Vision declines noticeably, as does hearing, but less obviously. • Height reaches a peak and declines slowly. Osteoporosis speeds this process in women. Weight increases, and strength decreases. • Reaction time slows, but performance of complex tasks is mostly unchanged due to lifelong practice. • Women experience menopause, with unpredictable effects. The male climacteric brings gradual changes in men's reproductive systems.	• Wrinkles and gray or thinning hair are marks of late adulthood. Height declines as backbone disk cartilage thins. Women are especially susceptible to osteoporosis. • The brain shrinks, and the heart pumps less blood through the body. Reactions slow, and the senses become less acute. Cataracts and glaucoma may affect the eyes, and hearing loss is common. • Chronic diseases, especially heart disease, grow more common. Mental disorders, such as depression and Alzheimer's disease, may occur.
• Some loss of cognitive functioning may begin in middle adulthood, but overall cognitive competence holds steady because adults use life experience and effective strategies to compensate. • Slight declines occur in the efficiency of retrieval from long-term memory.	• Cognitive declines are minimal until the 80's. Cognitive abilities can be maintained with training and practice, and learning remains possible throughout the life span. • Short-term memory and memory of specific life episodes may decline, but other types of memory are largely unaffected.
• People in middle adulthood take stock, appraising accomplishments against a "social clock" and developing a consciousness of mortality. • Middle adulthood, despite the supposed "midlife crisis," usually is tranquil and satisfying. Individuals' personality traits are generally stable over time. • While marital satisfaction is usually high, family relationships can present challenges. • The view of one's career shifts from outward ambition to inner satisfaction or, in some cases, dissatisfaction. Career changes are increasingly common.	• Basic personality traits remain stable, but changes are possible. "Life review," a feature of this period, can bring either fulfillment or dissatisfaction. • Retirement is a major event of late adulthood, causing adjustments to self-concept and self-esteem. • A healthy lifestyle and continuing activity in areas of interest can bring satisfaction in late adulthood. • Typical circumstances of late adulthood (reduced income, the aging or death of a spouse, a change in living arrangements) cause stress.
Generativity-versus-stagnation stage	Ego-integrity-versus-despair stage